The Oxford

Colour

Italian
Dictionary

With new word-games
supplement

ITALIAN – ENGLISH
ENGLISH – ITALIAN

ITALIANO – INGLESE
INGLESE – ITALIANO

OXFORD
UNIVERSITY PRESS

OXFORD
UNIVERSITY PRESS

Great Clarendon Street, Oxford OX2 6DP

Oxford University Press is a department of the University of Oxford.
It furthers the University's objective of excellence in research, scholarship,
and education by publishing worldwide in

Oxford New York

Auckland Bangkok Buenos Aires Cape Town Chennai
Dar es Salaam Delhi Hong Kong Istanbul Karachi Kolkata
Kuala Lumpur Madrid Melbourne Mexico City Mumbai Nairobi
São Paulo Shanghai Singapore Taipei Tokyo Toronto

with an associated company in Berlin

Oxford is a registered trade mark of Oxford University Press
in the UK and in certain other countries

Published in the United States
by Oxford University Press Inc., New York

First published as the Oxford Paperback Italian Dictionary, second edition 1997
First two-color edition published 1997
First published in this format with new material added 1999

British Library Cataloguing in Publication Data

Data available

Library of Congress Cataloging in Publication Data

Data available

ISBN 0-19-860250-2

10 9 8 7 6 5

Typeset in Nimrod and Arial
by Lexus Ltd.
Printed in Hong Kong

Contents/Indice

Editors/Redazione

Debora Mazza   Jane Goldie
Donatella Boi   Francesca Logi
Sonia Tinagli-Baxter   Carla Zipoli
Peter Terrell

Copy Editors/Segreteria di redazione

Jacqueline Gregan   Daphne Trotter

Project management by/A cura di

LEXUS

Word games/Giochi enigmistici

Loredana Riu

Preface/Prefazione

This revised edition of the *Oxford Colour Italian Dictionary* is an updated and expanded version of the *Oxford Italian Minidictionary* edited by Joyce Andrews. Colloquial words and phrases figure largely, as do neologisms. Noteworthy additions include terms from special areas such as computing and business that have become a familiar feature of current language. This revised edition also includes word games specifically designed to develop skills in the effective use of the dictionary, and to help improve users' knowledge of Italian vocabulary and usage in a fun and entertaining way.

Questa edizione riveduta, in colore, è il risultato di un lavoro di ampliamento e aggiornamento della precedente edizione curata da Joyce Andrews. Un'attenzione particolare è stata rivolta a vocaboli ed espressioni colloquiali di coniazione recente e a termini relativi a settori specifici, quali l'informatica e il commercio, divenuti ricorrenti nella lingua di tutti i giorni. Questa edizione riveduta contiene inoltre dei giochi enigmistici ideati espressamente per sviluppare l'abilità nell'usare efficacemente il dizionario e per consolidare la conoscenza dell'italiano in modo stimolante e divertente.

Proprietary terms/Marchi registrati

This dictionary includes some words which are, or are asserted to be, proprietary names or trademarks. Their inclusion does not imply that they have acquired for legal purposes a non-proprietary or general significance, nor is any other judgement implied concerning their legal status. In cases where the editor has some evidence that a word is used as proprietary name or trademark this is indicated by the symbol ®, but no judgement concerning the legal status of such words is made or implied thereby.

Questo dizionario include alcune parole che sono o vengono considerate marchi registrati. La loro presenza non implica che abbiano acquisito legalmente un significato generale, né si suggerisce alcun altro giudizio riguardo il loro stato giuridico. Qualora il redattore abbia trovato testimonianza dell'uso di una parola come marchio registrato, quest'ultima è stata contrassegnata dal simbolo ®, ma nessun giudizio riguardo lo stato giuridico di tale parola viene espresso o suggerito in tal modo.

Introduction/Introduzione

In order to give the maximum information about English and Italian in the space available, this new dictionary uses certain space-saving conventions. A swung dash ∼ is used to replace the headword within the entry. Where the headword contains a vertical bar | the swung dash replaces only the part of the headword that comes in front of the | . For example, **efficien|te** *a* efficient. ∼**za** *nf* efficiency (the second bold word reads **efficienza**). Indicators are provided to guide the user to the best translation for a specific sense of a word. Types of indicator are:

field labels (see the list on pp vii–viii), which indicate a general area of usage (commercial, computing etc);

sense indicators, eg: **bore** *n* (*of gun*) calibro *m*; (*person*) seccatore, -trice *mf*;

typical subjects of verbs, eg: **bond** *vt* (*glue*:) attaccare;

typical objects of verbs, placed after the translation of the verb, eg: **boost** *vt* stimolare (*sales*); sollevare (*morale*);

nouns that typically go together with certain adjectives, eg: **rich** *a* ricco; (*food*) pesante.

A solid black circle means that the same word is being translated as a different part of speech, eg: **partition** *n* ... ● *vt* ... Italian stress is shown by a ' placed in front of the stressed syllable in a word. Square brackets are used around parts of an expression which can be omitted without altering the sense.

Allo scopo di fornire il maggior numero possibile di informazioni in inglese e in italiano, questo nuovo dizionario ricorre ad alcune convenzioni per sfruttare al massimo lo spazio disponibile. Un trattino ondulato ∼ è utilizzato al posto del lemma all'interno della voce. Qualora il lemma contenga una barra verticale | , il trattino ondulato sostituisce solo la parte del lemma che precede | . Ad esempio: **dark|en** *vt* oscurare. ∼**ness** *n* buio *m* (la seconda parola in neretto va letta **darkness**). Degli indicatori vengono forniti per indirizzare l'utente verso la traduzione corrispondente al senso voluto di una parola. I tipi di indicatori sono:

etichette semantiche (vedi la lista a pp vii–viii), indicanti l'ambito specifico in cui la parola viene generalmente usata in quel senso (commercio, informatica ecc);

indicatori di significato, es.: **redazione** *nf* (*ufficio*) editorial office; (*di testi*) editing;

soggetti tipici di verbi, es.: **trovarsi** *vr* (*luogo*:) be;

complementi oggetti tipici di verbi, collocati dopo la traduzione dello stesso verbo, es.: **superare** *vt* overtake (*veicolo*); pass (*esame*);

sostantivi che ricorrono tipicamente con certi aggettivi, es.: **solare** *a* (*energia, raggi*) solar; (*crema*) sun.

Un pallino nero indica che la stessa parola viene tradotta come una diversa parte del discorso, es.: **calcolatore** *a* ...● *nm* ... La pronuncia inglese è data usando l'Alfabeto Fonetico Internazionale. Delle parentesi quadre racchiudono parti di espressioni che possono essere omesse senza alterazioni di senso.

Pronunciation of Italian

Vowels:

a   is broad like *a* in *father*: **casa**.
e   has two sounds: closed like *ey* in *they*: **sera**; open like *e* in *egg*: **sette**.
i   is like *ee* in *feet*: **venire**.
o   has two sounds: closed like *o* in *show*: **bocca**; open like *o* in *dog*: **croma**.
u   is like *oo* in *moon*: **luna**.

When two or more vowels come together each vowel is pronounced separately:
buono; **baia**.

Consonants:

b, d, f, l, m, n, p, t, v are pronounced as in English. When these are double they are
sounded distinctly: **bello**.

c   before **a**, **o**, or **u** and before consonants is like *k* in *king*: **cane**.
      before **e** or **i** is like *ch* in *church*: **cena**.
ch   is also like *k* in *king*: **chiesa**.
g   before **a**, **o**, or **u** is hard like *g* in *got*: **gufo**.
      before **e** or **i** is like *j* in *jelly*: **gentile**.
gh   is like *g* in *gun*: **ghiaccio**.
gl   when followed by **a, e, o, u** is like *gl* in *glass*: **gloria**.
gli   is like *lli* in *million*: **figlio**.
gn   is like *ni* in *onion*: **bagno**.
h   is silent.
ng   is like *ng* in *finger* (not *singer*): **ringraziare**.
r   is pronounced distinctly.
s   between two vowels is like *s* in *rose*: **riso**;
      at the beginning of a word it is like *s* in *soap*: **sapone**.
sc   before **e** or **i** is like *sh* in *shell*: **scienza**.
z   sounds like *ts* within a word: **fazione**; like *dz* at the beginning: **zoo**.

The stress is shown by the sign ' printed before the stressed syllable.

Pronuncia inglese

Simboli fonetici
Vocali e dittonghi

i:	*see*	ɔ:	s*aw*	eɪ	p*age*	ɔɪ	j*oin*	ʊ	g*o*t
ɪ	s*i*t	ʊ	p*u*t	əʊ	h*o*me	ɪə	n*ear*	ə	*ago*
e	t*e*n	u:	t*oo*	aɪ	f*i*ve	eə	h*air*	aʊə	fl*our*
æ	h*a*t	ʌ	c*u*p	aɪə	f*ire*	ʊə	p*oor*	ɑ:	*ar*m
ɜ:	f*ur*	aʊ	n*ow*						

Consonanti:

p	*p*en	tʃ	*ch*in	s	*s*o	n	*n*o
b	*b*ad	dʒ	*J*une	z	*z*oo	ŋ	si*ng*
t	*t*ea	f	*f*all	ʃ	*sh*e	l	*l*eg
d	*d*ip	v	*v*oice	ʒ	mea*s*ure	r	*r*ed
k	*c*at	θ	*th*in	h	*h*ow	j	*y*es
g	*g*ot	ð	*th*en	m	*m*an	w	*w*et

Note: ' precede la sillaba accentata. La vocale nasale in parole quali *nuance* è indi-
cata nella trascrizione fonetica come ɒ̃: ṅjuːɒ̃s.

Abbreviations/Abbreviazioni

adjective	*a*	aggettivo
abbreviation	*abbr*	abbreviazione
administration	*Admin*	amministrazione
adverb	*adv*	avverbio
aeronautics	*Aeron*	aeronautica
American	*Am*	americano
anatomy	*Anat*	anatomia
archaeology	*Archaeol*	archeologia
architecture	*Archit*	architettura
astrology	*Astr*	astrologia
attributive	*attrib*	attributo
automobiles	*Auto*	automobile
auxiliary	*aux*	ausiliario
biology	*Biol*	biologia
botany	*Bot*	botanica
British English	*Br*	inglese britannico
chemistry	*Chem*	chimica
commerce	*Comm*	commercio
computers	*Comput*	informatica
conjunction	*conj*	congiunzione
cooking	*Culin*	cucina
definite article	*def art*	articolo determinativo
	ecc	eccetera
electricity	*Electr*	elettricità
et cetera	*etc*	
feminine	*f*	femminile
familiar	*fam*	familiare
figurative	*fig*	figurato
formal	*fml*	formale
geography	*Geog*	geografia
geology	*Geol*	geologia
grammar	*Gram*	grammatica
humorous	*hum*	umoristico
indefinite article	*indef art*	articolo indeterminativo
interjection	*int*	interiezione
interrogative	*inter*	interrogativo
invariable (no plural form)	*inv*	invariabile
law	*Jur*	legge/giuridico
literary	*liter*	letterario
masculine	*m*	maschile
mathematics	*Math*	matematica
mechanics	*Mech*	meccanica
medicine	*Med*	medicina

masculine or feminine	*mf*	maschile o femminile
military	*Mil*	militare
music	*Mus*	musica
noun	*n*	sostantivo
nautical	*Naut*	nautica
pejorative	*pej*	peggiorativo
personal	*pers*	personale
photography	*Phot*	fotografia
physics	*Phys*	fisica
plural	*pl*	plurale
politics	*Pol*	politica
possessive	*poss*	possessivo
past participle	*pp*	participio passato
prefix	*pref*	prefisso
preposition	*prep*	preposizione
present tense	*pres*	presente
pronoun	*pron*	pronome
psychology	*psych*	psicologia
past tense	*pt*	passato
	qcno	qualcuno
	qcsa	qualcosa
proprietary term	®	marchio registrato
rail	*Rail*	ferrovia
reflexive	*refl*	riflessivo
religion	*Relig*	religione
relative pronoun	*rel pron*	pronome relativo
somebody	*sb*	
school	*Sch*	scuola
singular	*sg*	singolare
slang	*sl*	gergo
something	*sth*	
technical	*Techn*	tecnico
telephone	*Teleph*	telefono
theatrical	*Theat*	teatro
television	*TV*	televisione
typography	*Typ*	tipografia
university	*Univ*	università
auxiliary verb	*v aux*	verbo ausiliare
intransitive verb	*vi*	verbo intransitivo
reflexive verb	*vr*	verbo riflessivo
transitive verb	*vt*	verbo transitivo
transitive and intransitive verb	*vt/i*	verbo transitivo e intransitivo
vulgar	*vulg*	volgare
cultural equivalent	≈	equivalenza culturale

Aa

a (ad *before vowel*) *prep* to; (*stato in luogo, tempo, età*) at; (*con mese, città*) in; (*mezzo, modo*) by; **dire qcsa a qcno** tell sb sth; **alle tre** at three o'clock; **a vent'anni** at the age of twenty; **a Natale** at Christmas; **a dicembre** in December; **ero al cinema** I was at the cinema; **vivo a Londra** I live in London; **a due a due** two by two; **a piedi** on *o* by foot; **maglia a maniche lunghe** long-sleeved sweater; **casa a tre piani** house with three floors; **giocare a tennis** play tennis; **50 km all'ora** 50 km an hour; **2 000 lire al chilo** 2,000 lire a kilo; **al mattino/alla sera** in the morning/evening; **a venti chilometri/due ore da qui** twenty kilometres/two hours away

a'bate *nm* abbot

abbacchi'ato *a* downhearted

ab'bacchio *nm* [young] lamb

abbagli'ante *a* dazzling ● *nm* headlight, high beam

abbagli'are *vt* dazzle. **ab'baglio** *nm* blunder; **prendere un ~** make a blunder

abbai'are *vi* bark

abba'ino *nm* dormer window

abbando'na|re *vt* abandon; leave (*luogo*); give up (*piani ecc*). **~rsi** *vr* let oneself go; **~rsi a** give oneself up to (*ricordi ecc*). **~to** *a* abandoned. **abban'dono** *nm* abandoning; *fig* abandon; (*stato*) neglect

abbas'sa|mento *nm* (*di temperatura, acqua, prezzi*) drop

abbas'sar|e *vt* lower; turn down (*radio, TV*); **~e i fari** dip the headlights. **~si** *vr* stoop; (*sole ecc*) sink; *fig* demean oneself

ab'basso *adv* below ● *int* down with

abba'stanza *adv* enough; (*alquanto*) quite

ab'batter|e *vt* demolish; shoot down (*aereo*); put down (*animale*); topple (*regime*); (*fig: demoralizzare*) dishearten. **~si** *vr* (*cadere*) fall; *fig* be discouraged

abbatti'mento *nm* (*morale*) despondency

abbat'tuto *a* despondent, down-in-the-mouth

abba'zia *nf* abbey

abbel'lir|e *vt* embellish. **~si** *vr* adorn oneself

abbeve'ra|re *vt* water. **~'toio** *nm* drinking trough

abbi'ente *a* well-to-do

abbiglia'mento *nm* clothes *pl*; (*industria*) clothing industry, rag trade

abbigli'ar|e *vt* dress. **~si** *vr* dress up

abbina'mento *nm* combining

abbi'nare *vt* combine; match (*colori*)

abbindo'lare *vt* cheat

abbocca'mento *nm* interview; (*conversazione*) talk

abboc'care *vi* bite, (*tubi*) join; *fig* swallow the bait

abboc'cato *a* (*vino*) fairly sweet

abbof'farsi *vr* stuff oneself

abbona'mento *nm* subscription; (*ferroviario ecc*) season-ticket; **fare l'~** take out a subscription

abbo'na|re *vt* make a subscriber. **~rsi** *vr* subscribe (**a** to); take out a season-ticket (**a** for) (*teatro, stadio*). **~to, -a** *nmf* subscriber

abbon'dan|te *a* abundant; (*quantità*) copious; (*nevicata*) heavy; (*vestiario*) roomy. **~te di** abounding in. **~te'mente** *adv* (*mangiare*) copiously. **~za** *nf* abundance

abbon'dare *vi* abound

abbor'da|bile *a* (*persona*) approachable; (*prezzo*) reasonable. **~ggio** *nm* Mil boarding. **~re** *vt* board (*nave*); approach (*persona*); (*fam: attaccar bottone a*) chat up; tackle (*compito ecc*)

abbotto'na|re *vt* button up. **~'tura** *nf* [row of] buttons. **~to** *a fig* tight-lipped

abboz'zare *vt* sketch [out]; **~ un sorriso** give a hint of a smile. **ab'bozzo** *nm* sketch

abbracci'are *vt* embrace; hug, embrace (*persona*); take up (*professione*); *fig* include. **ab'braccio** *nm* hug

abbrevi'a|re *vt* shorten; (*ridurre*) curtail; abbreviate (*parola*). **~zi'one** *nf* abbreviation abbron'zante nm sun-tan lotion

abbron'za|re vt bronze; tan ⟨pelle⟩. ~rsi vr get a tan. ~to a tanned. ~'tura nf [sun-]tan

abbrusto'lire vt toast; roast ⟨caffè ecc⟩

abbruti'mento nm brutalization. abbru'tire vt brutalize. abbru'tirsi vr become brutalized

abbuf'fa|rsi vr fam stuff oneself. ~ta nf blowout

abbuo'nare vt reduce

abbu'ono nm allowance; Sport handicap

abdi'ca|re vi abdicate. ~zi'one nf abdication

aber'rante a aberrant

aberrazi'one nf aberration

a'bete nm fir

abi'etto a despicable

'abil|e a able; ⟨idoneo⟩ fit; ⟨astuto⟩ clever. ~ità nf inv ability; ⟨idoneità⟩ fitness; ⟨astuzia⟩ cleverness. ~'mente adv ably; ⟨con astuzia⟩ cleverly

abili'ta|re vt qualify. ~to a qualified. ~zi'one nf qualification; ⟨titolo⟩ diploma

abis'sale a abysmal. a'bisso nm abyss

abi'tabile a inhabitable

abi'tacolo nm Auto passenger compartment

abi'tante nmf inhabitant

abi'ta|re vi live. ~to a inhabited ● nm built-up area. ~zi'one nf house

'abito nm ⟨da donna⟩ dress; ⟨da uomo⟩ suit. ~ da cerimonia/da sera formal/evening dress

abitu'al|e a usual, habitual. ~'mente adv usually

abitu'are vt accustom. ~si a vr get used to

abitudi'nario, -a a of fixed habits ● nmf person of fixed habits

abi'tudine nf habit; d'~ usually; per ~ out of habit; avere l'~ di fare qcsa be in the habit of doing sth

abnegazi'one nf self-sacrifice

ab'norme a abnormal

abo'li|re vt abolish; repeal ⟨legge⟩. ~zi'one nf abolition; repeal

abomi'nevole a abominable

abo'rigeno, -a a & nmf aboriginal

abor'rire vt abhor

abor'ti|re vi miscarry; ⟨volontariamente⟩ have an abortion; fig fail. ~vo a abortive. a'borto nm miscarriage; ⟨volontario⟩ abortion. ~sta a pro-choice

abras|i'one nf abrasion. abra'sivo a & nm abrasive

abro'ga|re vt repeal. ~zi'one nf repeal

'abside nf apse

abu'lia nf apathy. a'bulico a apathetic

abu's|are vi ~ di abuse; over-indulge in ⟨alcol⟩; ⟨approfittare di⟩ take advantage of; ⟨violentare⟩ rape. ~ivo a illegal

a'buso nm abuse. ~ di confidenza breach of confidence

a.C. abbr ⟨avanti Cristo⟩ BC

'acca nf fam non ho capito un'~ I understood damn all

acca'demi|a nf academy. A~a di Belle Arti Academy of Fine Arts. ~co, -a a academic ● nmf academician

acca'd|ere vi happen; accada quel che accada come what may. ~uto nm event

accalappi'are vt catch; fig allure

accal'carsi vr crowd

accal'da|rsi vr get overheated; fig get excited. ~to a overheated

accalo'rarsi vr get excited

accampa'mento nm camp. accam'pare vt fig put forth. accam'parsi vr camp

accani'mento nm tenacity; ⟨odio⟩ rage

acca'ni|rsi vr persist; ⟨infierire⟩ rage. ~to a persistent; ⟨odio⟩ fierce; fig inveterate

ac'canto adv near; ~ a prep next to

accanto'nare vt set aside; Mil billet

accaparra'mento nm hoarding; Comm cornering

accapar'ra|re vt hoard. ~rsi vr grab; corner ⟨mercato⟩. ~'tore, ~'trice nmf hoarder

accapigli'arsi vr scuffle; ⟨litigare⟩ squabble

accappa'toio nm bathrobe; ⟨per spiaggia⟩ beachrobe

accappo'nare vt fare ~ la pelle a qcno make sb's flesh creep

accarez'zare vt caress, stroke; fig cherish

accartocci'ar|e vt scrunch up. ~si vr curl up

acca'sarsi vr get married

accasci'arsi vr flop down; fig lose heart

accata'stare vt pile up

accatti'vante a beguiling

accatti'varsi vr ~ le simpatie/la stima/l'affetto di qcno gain sb's sympathy/respect/affection

accatto'naggio nm begging. accat'tone, -a nmf beggar

accaval'lar|e *vt* cross ⟨*gambe*⟩. **~si** *vr* pile up; *fig* overlap

acce'cante *a* ⟨*luce*⟩ blinding

acce'care *vt* blind ● *vi* go blind

ac'cedere *vi* **~ a** enter; ⟨*acconsentire*⟩ comply with

accele'ra|re *vi* accelerate ● *vt* speed up, accelerate; **~re il passo** quicken one's pace. **~to** *a* rapid. **~'tore** *nm* accelerator. **~zi'one** *nf* acceleration

ac'cender|e *vt* light; turn on ⟨*luce, TV ecc*⟩; *fig* inflame; **ha da ~e?** have you got a light?. **~si** *vr* catch fire; ⟨*illuminarsi*⟩ light up; *fig* become inflamed

accendi'gas *nm inv* gas lighter; ⟨*su cucina*⟩ automatic ignition

accen'dino *nm* lighter

accendi'sigari *nm* cigar-lighter

accen'nare *vt* indicate; hum ⟨*melodia*⟩ ● *vi* **~ a** beckon to; *fig* hint at; (*far l'atto di*) make as if to; **accenna a piovere** it looks like rain. **ac'cenno** *nm* gesture; ⟨*con il capo*⟩ nod; *fig* hint

accensi'one *nf* lighting; ⟨*di motore*⟩ ignition

accen'ta|re *vt* accent; ⟨*con accento to nico*⟩ stress. **~zi'one** *nf* accentuation. **ac'cento** *nm* accent; ⟨*tonico*⟩ stress

accentra'mento *nm* centralizing

accen'trare *vt* centralize

accentu'a|re *vt* accentuate. **~rsi** *vr* become more noticeable. **~to** *a* marked

accerchia'mento *nm* surrounding

accerchi'are *vt* surround

accerta'mento *nm* check

accer'tare *vt* ascertain; ⟨*controllare*⟩ check; assess ⟨*reddito*⟩

ac'ceso *a* lighted; ⟨*radio, TV ecc*⟩ on; ⟨*colore*⟩ bright

acces'sibile *a* accessible; ⟨*persona*⟩ approachable; ⟨*spesa*⟩ reasonable

ac'cesso *nm* access; ⟨*Med: di rabbia*⟩ fit; **vietato l'~** no entry

acces'sorio *a* accessory; ⟨*secondario*⟩ of secondary importance ● *nm* accessory; **accessori** *pl* ⟨*rifiniture*⟩ fittings

ac'cetta *nf* hatchet

accet'tabile *a* acceptable

accet'tare *vt* accept; ⟨*aderire a*⟩ agree to

accettazi'one *nf* acceptance; ⟨*luogo*⟩ reception. **~** ⟨*bagagli*⟩ check-in. **[banco]** **~** check-in [desk]

ac'cetto *a* agreeable; **essere bene ~** be very welcome

accezi'one *nf* meaning

acchiap'pare *vt* catch

acchito *nm* **di primo ~** at first

acciac'ca|re *vt* crush; *fig* prostrate. **~to, -a** *a* essere **~to** ache all over.

acci'acco *nm* infirmity; ⟨*pl: afflizioni*⟩ aches and pains

acciaie'ria *nf* steelworks

acci'aio *nm* steel; **~ inossidabile** stainless steel

acciden'ta|le *a* accidental. **~l'mente** *adv* accidentally. **~to** *a* ⟨*terreno*⟩ uneven

acci'dente *nm* accident; *Med* stroke; **non capisce/non vede un ~** *fam* he doesn't understand/can't see a damn thing. **acci'denti!** *int* damn!

accigli'a|rsi *vr* frown. **~to** *a* frowning

ac'cingersi *vr* **~ a** be about to

acci'picchia *int* good Lord!

acciuf'fare *vt* catch

acci'uga *nf* anchovy

accla'ma|re *vt* applaud; ⟨*eleggere*⟩ acclaim. **~zi'one** *nf* applause

acclima'tar|e *vt* acclimatize. **~si** *vr* get acclimatized

ac'clu|dere *vt* enclose. **~so** *a* enclosed

accocco'larsi *vr* squat

accogli'en|te *a* welcoming; ⟨*confortevole*⟩ cosy. **~za** *nf* welcome

ac'cogliere *vt* receive; ⟨*conpiacere*⟩ welcome; ⟨*contenere*⟩ hold

accol'larsi *vr* take on ⟨*responsabilità, debiti, doveri*⟩. **accol'lato** *a* highnecked

accoltel'lare *vt* knife

accomia'tar|e *vt* dismiss. **~si** *vr* take one's leave (**da** of)

accomo'dante *a* accommodating

accomo'dar|e *vt* ⟨*riparare*⟩ mend; ⟨*disporre*⟩ arrange. **~si** *vr* make oneself at home; **si accomodi!** come in!; ⟨*si sieda*⟩ take a seat!

accompagna'mento *nm* accompaniment; ⟨*seguito*⟩ retinue

accompa'gna|re *vt* accompany; **~re qcno a casa** see sb home; **~re qcno alla porta** show sb out. **~'tore, ~'trice** *nmf* companion; ⟨*di comitiva*⟩ escort; *Mus* accompanist

accomu'nare *vt* pool

acconci'a|re *vt* arrange. **~'tura** *nf* hair-style; ⟨*ornamento*⟩ head-dress

accondiscen'den|te *a* too obliging. **~za** *nf* excessive desire to please

accondi'scendere *vt* **~ a** condescend; comply with ⟨*desiderio*⟩; ⟨*acconsentire*⟩ consent to

acconsen'tire *vi* consent

acconten'tar|e *vt* satisfy. **~si** *vr* be content (**di** with)

ac'conto *nm* deposit; **in ~** on account; **lasciare un ~** leave a deposit

accop'pare *vt fam* bump off

accoppia'mento *nm* coupling; *(di animali)* mating

accoppi'a|re *vt* couple; mate *(animali)*. **~rsi** *vr* pair off; mate. **~ta** *nf* *(scommessa)* bet placed on two horses for first and second place

acco'rato *a* sorrowful

accorci'ar|e *vt* shorten. **~si** *vr* get shorter

accor'dar|e *vt* concede; match *(colori ecc)*; *Mus* tune. **~si** *vr* agree

ac'cordo *nm* agreement; *Mus* chord; *(armonia)* harmony; **andare d'~** get on well; **d'~!** agreed!; **essere d'~** agree; **prendere accordi con qcno** make arrangements with sb

ac'corgersi *vr* **~ di** notice; *(capire)* realize

accorgi'mento *nm* shrewdness; *(espediente)* device

ac'correre *vi* hasten

accor'tezza *nf* *(previdenza)* forethought

ac'corto *a* shrewd; **mal ~** incautious

accosta'mento *nm* *(di colori)* combination

acco'star|e *vt* draw close to; approach *(persona)*; set ajar *(porta ecc)*. **~si** *vr* **~si a** come near to

accovacci'a|rsi *vr* crouch, squat down. **~to** *a* squatting

accoz'zaglia *nf* jumble; *(di persone)* mob

accoz'zare *vt* **~ colori** mix colours that clash

accredita'mento *nm* credit; **~ tramite bancogiro** Bank Giro Credit

accredi'tare *vt* confirm *(notizia)*; *Comm* credit

ac'cresc|ere *vt* increase. **~ersi** *vr* grow larger. **~i'tivo** *a* augmentative

accucci'arsi *vr* *(cane:)* lie down; *(persona:)* crouch

accu'dire *vi* **~ a** attend to

accumu'la|re *vt* accumulate. **~rsi** *vr* pile up, accumulate. **~tore** *nm* accumulator; *Auto* battery. **~zi'one** *nf* accumulation. **ac'cumulo** *nm* *(di merce)* build-up

accura'tezza *nf* care

accu'rato *a* careful

ac'cusa *nf* accusation; *Jur* charge; **essere in stato di ~** *Jur* have been charged; **la Pubblica A~** *Jur* the public prosecutor

accu'sa|re *vt* accuse; *Jur* charge; complain of *(dolore)*. **~re ricevuta di** *Comm* acknowledge receipt of. **~to, -a** *nmf* accused. **~'tore** *nm Jur* prosecutor

a'cerbo *a* sharp; *(immaturo)* unripe

'acero *nm* maple

a'cerrimo *a* implacable

ace'tone *nm* nail polish remover

a'ceto *nm* vinegar

A.C.I. *abbr* (**Automobile Club d'Italia**) Italian Automobile Association

acidità *nf* acidity. **~ di stomaco** acid stomach

'acido *a* acid; *(persona)* sour ● *nm* acid

a'cidulo *a* slightly sour

'acino *nm* berry; *(chicco)* grape

'acne *nf* acne

'acqua *nf* water; **fare ~** *Naut* leak; **~ in bocca!** *fig* mum's the word!. **~ di Colonia** eau de Cologne. **~ corrente** running water. **~ dolce** fresh water. **~ minerale** mineral water. **~ minerale gassata** fizzy mineral water. **~ naturale** still mineral water. **~ potabile** drinking water. **~ salata** salt water. **~ tonica** tonic water

acqua'forte *nf* etching

ac'quaio *nm* sink

acquama'rina *a* aquamarine

acqua'rello *nm* = **acquerello**

ac'quario *nm* aquarium; *Astr* Aquarius

acqua'santa *nf* holy water

acqua'scooter *nm inv* water-scooter

ac'quatico *a* aquatic

acquat'tarsi *vr* crouch

acqua'vite *nf* brandy

acquaz'zone *nm* downpour

acque'dotto *nm* aqueduct

'acqueo *a* **~ vapore** ~ water vapour

acque'rello *nm* water-colour

acqui'rente *nmf* purchaser

acqui'si|re *vt* acquire. **~to** *a* acquired. **~zi'one** *nf* attainment

acqui'st|are *vt* purchase; *(ottenere)* acquire. **ac'quisto** *nm* purchase; **uscire per ~i** go shopping; **fare ~i** shop

acquo'lina *nf* **far venire l'~ in bocca a qcno** make sb's mouth water

ac'quoso *a* watery

'acre *a* acrid; *(al gusto)* sour; *fig* harsh

a'crilico *nm* acrylic

a'croba|ta *nmf* acrobat. **~'zia** *nf* acrobatics *pl*

a'cronimo *nm* acronym

acu'ir|e *vt* sharpen. **~si** *vr* become more intense

a'culeo *nm* sting; *Bot* prickle

a'cume *nm* acumen

acumi'nato *a* pointed

a'custic|a *nf* acoustics *pl*.**~o** *a* acoustic

acu'tezza *nf* acuteness

acutiz'zarsi *vr* become worse

a'cuto *a* sharp; (*suono*) shrill; (*freddo, odore*) intense; *Gram, Math, Med* acute ● *nm Mus* high note

adagi'ar|e *vt* lay down. **~si** *vr* lie down

a'dagio *adv* slowly ● *nm Mus* adagio; (*proverbio*) adage

adattabilità *nf* adaptability

adatta'mento *nm* adaptation; **avere spirito di ~** be adaptable

adat'ta|re *vt* adapt; (*aggiustare*) fit. **~rsi** *vr* adapt. **~'tore** *nm* adaptor. a'datto *a* suitable (**a** for); (*giusto*) right

addebita'mento *nm* debit. **~ diretto** direct debit

addebi'tare *vt* debit; *fig* ascribe (*colpa*)

ad'debito *nm* charge

addensa'mento *nm* thickening; (*di persone*) gathering

adden'sar|e *vt* thicken. **~si** *vr* thicken; (*affollarsi*) gather

adden'tare *vt* bite

adden'trarsi *vr* penetrate

ad'dentro *adv* deeply;**essere ~ in** be in on

addestra'mento *nm* training

adde'strar|e *vt* train. **~si** *vr* train

ad'detto, -a *a* assigned ● *nmf* employee; (*diplomatico*) attaché; **addetti** *pl* **ai lavori** persons involved in the work. **~ stampa** information officer, press officer

addiaccio *nm*;**dormire all'~** sleep in the open

addi'etro *adv* (*indietro*) back; (*nel passato*) before

ad'dio *adv* & *int* goodbye. **~ al celibato** stag night, stag party

addirit'tura *adv* (*perfino*) even; (*assolutamente*) absolutely; **~!** really!

ad'dirsi *vr* **~ a** suit

addi'tare *vt* point at; (*in mezzo a un gruppo*) point out; *fig* point to

addi'tivo *a* & *nm* additive

addizio'nal|e *a* additional. **~'mente** *adv* additionally

addizio'nare *vt* add [up]. **addizi'one** *nf* addition

addob'bare *vt* decorate. **ad'dobbo** *nm* decoration

addol'cir|e *vt* sweeten; tone down (*colore*); *fig* soften. **~si** *vr* *fig* mellow

addolo'ra|re *vt* grieve. **~rsi** *vr* be upset (**per** by). **~to** *a* pained, distressed

ad'dom|e *nm* abdomen. **~i'nale** *a* abdominal;**[muscoli] addominali** *pl* abdominals

addormen'ta|re *vt* put to sleep. **~rsi** *vr* go to sleep. **~to** *a* asleep; *fig* slow

addos'sar|e *vt*~**e a** (*appoggiare*) lean against; (*attribuire*) lay on. **~si** *vr* (*ammassarsi*) crowd; shoulder (*responsabilità ecc*)

ad'dosso *adv* on; **~ a** *prep* on; (*molto vicino*) right next to;**mettere gli occhi ~ a qcno/qcsa** hanker after sb/sth; **non mettermi le mani ~!** keep your hands off me!; **stare ~ a qcno** *fig* be on sb's back

ad'durre *vt* produce (*prova, documento*); give (*pretesto, esempio*)

adegua'mento *nm* adjustment

adegu'a|re *vt* adjust. **~rsi** *vr* conform. **~to** *a* adequate; (*conforme*) consistent

a'dempi|ere *vt* fulfil. **~'mento** *nm* fulfilment

ade'noidi *nfpl* adenoids

ade'ren|te *a* adhesive; (*vestito*) tight ● *nmf* follower. **~za** *nf* adhesion. **~ze** *npl* connections

ade'rire *vi*~ **a** stick to, adhere to; support (*sciopero, petizione*); agree to (*richiesta*)

adesca'mento *nm Jur* soliciting

ade'scare *vt* bait; *fig* entice

adesi'one *nf* adhesion; *fig* agreement

ade'sivo *a* adhesive● *nm* sticker; *Auto* bumper sticker

a'desso *adv* now; (*poco fa*) just now; (*tra poco*) any moment now; **da ~ in poi** from now on;**per ~** for the moment

adia'cente *a* adjacent; **~ a** next to

adi'bire *vt* **~ a** put to use as

'adipe *nm* adipose tissue

adi'ra|rsi *vr* get irate. **~to** *a* irate

a'dire *vt* resort to; **~ le vie legali** take legal proceedings

'adito *nm*;**dare ~ a** give rise to

adocchi'are *vt* eye; (*con desiderio*) covet

adole'scen|te *a* & *nmf* adolescent. **~za** *nf* adolescence. **~zi'ale** *a* adolescent

adom'brar|e *vt* darken; *fig* veil. **~si** *vr* (*offendersi*) take offence

adope'rar|e *vt* use. **~si** *vr* take trouble

ado'rabile *a* adorable

ado'ra|re *vt* adore. **~zi'one** *nf* adoration

ador'nare *vt* adorn

adot't|are *vt* adopt. **~ivo** *a* adoptive. **adozi'one** *nf* adoption

ad *prep* = **a** (*davanti a vocale*)

adrena'lina *nf* adrenalin

adri'atico *a* Adriatic ● *nm* **l'A~** the Adriatic

adu'la|re *vt* flatter. **~'tore**, **~'trice** *nmf* flatterer. **~zi'one** *nf* flattery

adulte'ra|re *vt* adulterate. **~to** *a* adulterated

adul'terio *nm* adultery. **a'dultero, -a** *a* adulterous ● *nm* adulterer ● *nf* adulteress

a'dulto, -a *a & nmf* adult; (*maturo*) mature

adu'nanza *nf* assembly

adu'na|re *vt* gather. **~ta** *nf Mil* parade

a'dunco *a* hooked

ae'rare *vt* air (*stanza*)

a'ereo *a* aerial; (*dell'aviazione*) air *attrib* ● *nm* aeroplane, plane

ae'robic|a *nf* aerobics. **~o** *a* aerobic

aerodi'namic|a *nf* aerodynamics *sg*. **~o** *a* aerodynamic

aero'nautic|a *nf* aeronautics *sg*; *Mil* Air Force. **~o** *a* aeronautical

aero'plano *nm* aeroplane

aero'porto *nm* airport

aero'scalo *nm* cargo and servicing area

aero'sol *nm inv* aerosol

'afa *nf* sultriness

af'fabil|e *a* affable. **~ità** *nf* affability

affaccen'dar|si *vr* busy oneself (**a** with). **~to** *a* busy

affacci'arsi *vr* show oneself; **~ alla finestra** appear at the window

affa'ma|re *vt* starve [out]. **~to** *a* starving

affan'na|re *vt* leave breathless. **~rsi** *vr* busy oneself; (*agitarsi*) get worked up. **~to** *a* breathless; **dal respiro ~to** wheezy. **af'fanno** *nm* breathlessness; *fig* worry

af'fare *nm* matter; *Comm* transaction, deal; (*occasione*) bargain; **affari** *pl* business; **non sono affari tuoi** *fam* it's none of your business. **affa'rista** *nmf* wheeler-dealer

affasci'nante *a* fascinating; (*persona, sorriso*) bewitching

affasci'nare *vt* bewitch; *fig* charm

affatica'mento *nm* fatigue

affati'car|e *vt* tire; (*sfinire*) exhaust. **~si** *vr* tire oneself out; (*affannarsi*) strive

af'fatto *adv* completely; **non... ~** not...; at all; **niente ~!** not at all!

affer'ma|re *vt* affirm; (*sostenere*) assert. **~rsi** *vr* establish oneself

affermativa'mente *adv* in the affirmative

afferma'tivo *a* affirmative

affermazi'one *nf* assertion; (*successo*) achievement

affer'rar|e *vt* seize; catch (*oggetto*); (*capire*) grasp; **~e al volo** *fig* be quick on the uptake. **~si** *vr* **~si a** grasp at

affet'ta|re *vt* slice; (*ostentare*) affect. **~to** *a* sliced; (*sorriso, maniere*) affected ● *nm* cold meat, sliced meat. **~zi'one** *nf* affectation

affet'tivo *a* affective; **rapporto ~** emotional tie

af'fetto¹ *nm* affection; **con ~** affectionately

af'fetto² *a* **~ da** suffering from

affettuosità *nf inv* (*gesto*) affectionate gesture

affettu'oso *a* affectionate

affezio'na|rsi *vr* **~rsi a** grow fond of. **~to** *a* devoted (**a** to)

affian'car|e *vt* put side by side; *Mil* flank; *fig* support. **~si** *vr* come side by side; *fig* stand together; **~si a qcno** *fig* help sb out

affiata'mento *nm* harmony

affia'ta|rsi *vr* get on well together. **~to** *a* close-knit; **una coppia ~ta** a very close couple

affibbi'are *vt* **~ a qcno** saddle sb with sth; **~ un pugno a qcno** let fly at sb

affi'dabil|e *a* dependable. **~ità** *nf* dependability

affida'mento *nm* (*Jur: dei minori*) custody; **fare ~ su qcno** rely on sb; **non dare ~** not inspire confidence

affi'dar|e *vt* entrust. **~si** *vr* **~si a** rely on

affievo'lirsi *vr* grow weak

af'figgere *vt* affix

affi'lare *vt* sharpen

affili'ar|e *vt* affiliate. **~si** *vr* become affiliated

affi'nare *vt* sharpen; (*perfezionare*) refine

affinché *conj* so that, in order that

af'fin|e *a* similar. **~ità** *nf* affinity

affiora'mento *nm* emergence; *Naut* surfacing

affio'rare *vi* emerge; *fig* come to light

af'fisso *nm* bill; *Gram* affix

affitta'camere *nm inv* landlord ● *nf inv* landlady

affit'tare *vt* (*dare in affitto*) let; (*prendere in affitto*) rent; **'af'fittasi'** 'to let', 'for rent'

af'fitt|o *nm* rent; **contratto d'~o** lease; **dare in ~o** let; **prendere in ~o** rent. **~u'ario , -a** *nmf Jur* lessee

af'fligger|e *vt* torment. **~si** *vr* distress oneself

af'fli|tto *a* distressed; **~tto da** suffering from. **~zi'one** *nf* distress; *fig* affliction

afflosci'arsi *vr* become floppy; (*accasciarsi*) flop down; (*morale:*) decline

afflu'en|te *a* & *nm* tributary. **~za** *nf* flow; (*di gente*) crowd

afflu'ire *vi* flow; *fig* pour in

af'flusso *nm* influx

affo'ga|re *vt/i* drown; (*Culin*) poach; **~re in** *fig* be swamped with. **~to** *a* (*persona*) drowned; (*uova*) poached. **~to al caffè** *nm* ice cream with hot espresso poured over it

affol'la|re *vt*, **~rsi** *vr* crowd. **~to** *a* crowded

affonda'mento *nm* sinking

affon'dare *vt/i* sink

affossa'mento *nm* pothole

affran'ca|re *vt* redeem (*bene*); stamp (*lettera*); free (*schiavo*). **~rsi** *vr* free oneself. **~'tura** *nf* stamping; (*di spedizione*) postage

af'franto *a* prostrated; (*esausto*) worn out

af'fresco *nm* fresco

affret'ta|re *vt* speed up. **~rsi** *vr* hurry. **~ta'mente** *adv* hastily. **~to** *a* hasty

affron'tar|e *vt* face; confront (*il nemico*); meet (*le spese*). **~si** *vr* clash

af'fronto *nm* affront, insult; **fare un ~ a qcno** insult sb

affumi'ca|re *vt* fill with smoke; *Culin* smoke. **~to** *a* (*prosciutto, formaggio*) smoked

affuso'la|re *vt* taper [off]. **~to** *a* tapering

afo'risma *nm* aphorism

a'foso *a* sultry

'Africa *nf* Africa. **afri'cano, -a** *a* & *nmf* African

afrodi'siaco *a* & *nm* aphrodisiac

a'genda *nf* diary

agen'dina *nf* pocket-diary

a'gente *nm* agent; **agenti** *pl* **atmosferici** atmospheric agents. **~ di cambio** stockbroker. **~ di polizia** policeman

agen'zia *nf* agency; (*filiale*) branch office; (*di banca*) branch. **~ di viaggi** travel agency. **~ immobiliare** estate agency

agevo'la|re *vt* facilitate. **~zi'one** *nf* facilitation

a'gevol|e *a* easy; (*strada*) smooth. **~'mente** *adv* easily

agganci'ar|e *vt* hook up; *Rail* couple. **~si** *vr* (*vestito:*) hook up

ag'geggio *nm* gadget

agget'tivo *nm* adjective

agghiacci'ante *a* terrifying

agghiacci'ar|e *vt fig* **~ qcno** make sb's blood run cold. **~si** *vr* freeze

agghin'da|re *vt fam* dress up. **~rsi** *vr fam* doll oneself up. **~to** *a* dressed up

aggiorna'mento *nm* up-date

aggior'na|re *vt* (*rinviare*) postpone; (*mettere a giorno*) bring up to date. **~rsi** *vr* get up to date. **~to** *a* up-to-date; (*versione*) updated

aggi'rar|e *vt* surround; (*fig: ingannare*) trick. **~si** *vr* hang about; **~si su** (*discorso ecc:*) be about; (*approssimarsi*) be around

aggiudi'car|e *vt* award; (*all'asta*) knock down. **~si** *vr* win

aggi'un|gere *vt* add. **~ta** *nf* addition. **~'tivo** *a* supplementary. **~to** *a* added ● *a* & *nm* (*assistente*) assistant

aggiu'star|e *vt* mend; (*sistemare*) settle; (*fam: mettere a posto*) fix. **~si** *vr* adapt; (*mettersi in ordine*) tidy oneself up; (*decidere*) sort things out; (*tempo:*) clear up

agglomera'mento *nm* conglomeration

agglome'rato *nm* built-up area

aggrap'par|e *vt* grasp. **~si** *vr* **~si a** cling to

aggra'vante *Jur nf* aggravation ● *a* aggravating

aggra'var|e *vt* (*peggiorare*) make worse; increase (*pena*); (*appesantire*) weigh down. **~si** *vr* worsen

aggrazi'ato *a* graceful

aggre'dire *vt* attack

aggre'ga|re *vt* add; (*associare a un gruppo ecc*) admit. **~rsi** *vr* **~rsi a** join. **~to** *a* associated ● *nm* aggregate; (*di case*) block

aggressi'one *nf* aggression; *(atto)* attack

aggres's|ivo *a* aggressive. **~ività** *nf* aggressiveness. **~ore** *nm* aggressor

aggrin'zare, aggrin'zire *vt* wrinkle

aggrot'tare *vt* **~ le ciglia/la fronte** frown

aggrovigli'a|re *vt* tangle. **~rsi** *vr* get entangled; *fig* get complicated. **~to** *a* entangled; *fig* confused

agguan'tare *vt* catch

aggu'ato *nm* ambush; *(tranello)* trap; **stare in ~** lie in wait

agguer'rito *a* fierce

agia'tezza *nf* comfort

agi'ato *a* *(persona)* well off; *(vita)* comfortable

a'gibil|e *a* *(palazzo)* fit for human habitation. **~ità** *nf* fitness for human habitation

'agil|e *a* agile. **~ità** *nf* agility

'agio *nm* ease; **mettersi a proprio ~** make oneself at home

a'gire *vi* act; *(comportarsi)* behave; *(funzionare)* work; **~ su** affect

agi'ta|re *vt* shake; wave *(mano)*; *(fig: turbare)* trouble. **~rsi** *vr* toss about; *(essere inquieto)* be restless; *(mare:)* get rough. **~to** *a* restless; *(mare)* rough. **~tore, ~'trice** *nmf* *(persona)* agitator. **~zi'one** *nf* agitation; **mettere in ~zione qcno** make sb worried

'agli = a + **gli**

'aglio *nm* garlic

a'gnello *nm* lamb

agno'lotti *nmpl* ravioli *sg*

a'gnostico, -a *a & nmf* agnostic

'ago *nm* needle

ago'ni|a *nf* agony. **~z'zare** *vi* be on one's deathbed

ago'nistic|a *nf* competition. **~o** *a* competitive

agopun'tura *nf* acupuncture

a'gosto *nm* August

a'grari|a *nf* agriculture. **~o** *a* agricultural ●*nm* landowner

a'gricol|o *a* agricultural. **~'tore** *nm* farmer. **~'tura** *nf* agriculture

agri'foglio *nm* holly

agritu'rismo *nm* farm holidays, agrotourism

'agro *a* sour

agroalimen'tare *a* food *attrib*

agro'dolce *a* bitter-sweet; *Culin* sweet-and-sour; **in ~** sweet and sour

agrono'mia *nf* agronomy

a'grume *nm* citrus fruit; *(pianta)* citrus tree

aguz'zare *vt* sharpen; **~ le orecchie** prick up one's ears; **~ la vista** look hard

aguz'zino *nm* slave-driver; *(carceriere)* jailer

ahimè *int* alas

'ai = **a + i**

'Aia *nf* **L'~** The Hague

'aia *nf* threshing-floor

Aids *nmf* Aids

ai'rone *nm* heron

ai'tante *a* sturdy

aiu'ola *nf* flower-bed

aiu'tante *nmf* assistant ●*nm* Mil adjutant. **~ di campo** aide-de-camp

aiu'tare *vt* help

ai'uto *nm* help, aid; *(assistente)* assistant

aiz'zare *vt* incite; **~ contro** set on

al = **a + il**

'ala *nf* wing; **fare ~** make way

ala'bastro *nm* alabaster

'alacre *a* brisk

a'lano *nm* Great Dane

'alba *nf* dawn

Alba'n|ia *nf* Albania. **a~ese** *a & nmf* Albanian

albeggi'are *vi* dawn

albe'ra|to *a* wooded; *(viale)* tree-lined. **~'tura** *nf* Naut masts *pl*. **albe'rello** *nm* sapling

al'berg|o *nm* hotel. **~o diurno** *hotel where rooms are rented during the daytime.* **~a'tore, ~a'trice** *nmf* hotel-keeper. **~hi'ero** *a* hotel *attrib*

'albero *nm* tree; *Naut* mast; *Mech* shaft. **~ genealogico** family tree. **~ maestro** *Naut* mainmast. **~ di Natale** Christmas tree

albi'cocc|a *nf* apricot. **~o** *nm* apricot-tree

al'bino *nm* albino

'albo *nm* register; *(libro ecc)* album; *(per avvisi)* notice board

'album *nm* album. **~ da disegno** sketch-book

al'bume *nm* albumen

'alce *nm* elk

'alcol *nm* alcohol; *Med* spirit; *(liquori forti)* spirits *pl*; **~' take to drink. **al'colici** *nmpl* alcoholic drinks. **al'colico** *a* alcoholic. **alco'lismo** *nm* alcoholism. **~iz'zato, -a** *a & nmf* alcoholic

alco'test® *nm inv* Breathalyser®

al'cova *nf* alcove

al'cun, al'cuno *a & pron* any; **non ha ~ amico** he hasn't any friends, he has no friends. **alcuni** *pl* some, a few; **~i suoi amici** some of his friends

alea'torio *a* unpredictable

a'letta *nf Mech* fin

alfa'betico *a* alphabetical

alfabetizzazi'one *nf* **~ della popolazione** teaching people to read and write

alfa'beto *nm* alphabet

alfi'ere *nm* (scacchi) bishop

al'fine *adv* eventually, in the end

'alga *nf* seaweed

'algebra *nf* algebra

Alge'ri|a *nf* Algeria. **a~no, -a** *a & nmf* Algerian

ali'ante *nm* glider

'alibi *nm inv* alibi

alie'na|re *vt* alienate. **~rsi** *vr* become estranged; **~rsi le simpatie di qcno** lose sb's good will. **~to, -a** *a* alienated ● *nmf* lunatic

a'lieno, -a *nmf* alien ● *a* **è ~ da invidia** envy is foreign to him

alimen'ta|re *vt* feed; *fig* foment ● *a* food *attrib*; (abitudine) dietary. **~ri** *nmpl* food-stuffs. **~'tore** *nm* power unit. **~zi'one** *nf* feeding

ali'mento *nm* food; **alimenti** *pl* food; *Jur* alimony

a'liquota *nf* share; (di imposta) rate

ali'scafo *nm* hydrofoil

'alito *nm* breath

'alla = **a + la**

allaccia'mento *nm* connection

allacci'ar|e *vt* fasten (cintura); lace up (scarpe); do up (vestito); (collegare) connect; form (amicizia). **~si** *vr* do up, fasten (vestito, cintura)

allaga'mento *nm* flooding

alla'gar|e *vt* flood. **~si** *vr* become flooded

allampa'nato *a* lanky

allarga'mento *nm* (di una strada, delle ricerche) widening

allar'gar|e *vt* widen; open (braccia, gambe); let out (vestito ecc); *fig* extend. **~si** *vr* widen

allar'mante *a* alarming

allar'ma|re *vt* alarm. **~to** *a* panicky

al'larme *nm* alarm; **dare l'~** raise the alarm; **falso ~** *fig* false alarm. **~ aereo** air raid warning

allar'mis|mo *nm* alarmism. **~ta** *nmf* alarmist

allatta'mento *nm* (di animale) suckling; (di neonato) feeding

allat'tare *vt* suckle (animale); feed (neonato)

'alle = **a + le**

alle'a|nza *nf* alliance. **~to, -a** *a* allied ● *nmf* ally

alle'ar|e *vt* unite. **~si** *vr* form an alliance

alle'gare[1] *vt Jur* allege

alle'ga|re[2] *vt* (accludere) enclose; set on edge (denti). **~to** *a* enclosed ● *nm* enclosure; **in ~to** attached, appended. **~zi'one** *nf Jur* allegation

allegge'rir|e *vt* lighten; *fig* alleviate. **~si** *vr* become lighter; (vestirsi leggero) put on lighter clothes

allego'ria *nf* allegory. **alle'gorico** *a* allegorical

allegra'mente *adv* breezily

alle'gria *nf* gaiety

al'legro *a* cheerful; (colore) bright; (brillo) tipsy ● *nm Mus* allegro

alle'luia *int* hallelujah!

allena'mento *nm* training

alle'na|re *vt*, **~rsi** *vr* train. **~'tore, ~'trice** *nmf* trainer, coach

allen'ta|re *vt* loosen; *fig* relax. **~si** *vr* become loose; *Mech* work loose

aller'gia *nf* allergy. **al'lergico** *a* allergic

allerta *nf* o *nm inv* **stare ~** be on the alert

allesti'mento *nm* preparation. **~ scenico** *Theat* set

alle'stire *vt* prepare; stage (spettacolo); *Naut* fit out

allet'tante *a* alluring

allet'tare *vt* entice

alleva'mento *nm* breeding; (processo) bringing up; (luogo) farm; (per piante) nursery; **pollo di ~** battery hen *or* chicken

alle'vare *vt* bring up (bambini); breed (animali); grow (piante)

allevi'are *vt* alleviate; *fig* lighten

alli'bito *a* astounded

allibra'tore *nm* bookmaker

alli'etar|e** *vt* gladden. **~si** *vr* rejoice

alli'evo, -a *nmf* pupil ● *nm Mil* cadet

alli'gatore *nm* alligator

allinea'mento *nm* alignment

alline'ar|e *vt* line up; *Typ* align; *Fin* adjust. **~si** *vr* fall into line

'allo = **a + lo**

al'locco *nm* tawny owl; *fig* dunce

al'lodola *nf* [sky]lark

alloggi'are *vt* (persona:) put up; (casa:) provide accommodation for; *Mil* billet ● *vi* put up, stay; *Mil* be billeted.

al'loggio nm (appartamento) flat; Mil billet

allontana'mento nm removal

allonta'nar|e vt move away; (licenziare) dismiss; avert (pericolo). **~si** vr go away

al'lora adv then; (in quel tempo) at that time; (in tal caso) in that case; **d'~ in poi** from then on; **e ~?** what now?; (e con ciò?) so what?; **fino ~** until then

al'loro nm laurel; Culin bay

'alluce nm big toe

alluci'na|nte a fam incredible; **sostanza ~nte** hallucinogen. **~to, -a** nmf fam space cadet. **~zi'one** nf hallucination

allucino'geno a (sostanza) hallucinatory

al'ludere vi **~ a** allude to

allu'minio nm aluminium

allun'gar|e vt lengthen; stretch [out] (gamba); extend (tavolo); (diluire) dilute; **~e il collo** crane one's neck. **~e le mani su qcno** touch sb up. **~e il passo** quicken one's step. **~si** vr grow longer; (crescere) grow taller; (sdraiarsi) lie down

allusi'one nf allusion

allu'sivo a allusive

alluvio'nale a alluvial

alluvi'one nf flood

al'meno adv at least; **[se] ~ venisse il sole!** if only the sun would come out!

a'logeno nm halogen ● a **lampada alogena** halogen lamp

a'lone nm halo

'Alpi nfpl **le ~** the Alps

alpi'nis|mo nm mountaineering. **~ta** nmf mountaineer

al'pino a Alpine ● nm Mil **gli alpini** the Alpine troops

al'quanto a a certain amount of ● adv rather

alt int stop

alta'lena nf swing; (tavola in bilico) see-saw

altale'nare vi fig vacillate

alta'mente adv highly

al'tare nm altar

alta'rino nm **scoprire gli altarini di qcno** reveal sb's guilty secrets

alte'ra|re vt alter; adulterate (vino); (falsificare) falsify. **~rsi** vr be altered; (cibo:) go bad; (merci:) deteriorate; (arrabbiarsi) get angry. **~to** a (vino) adulterated. **~zi'one** nf alteration; (di vino) adulteration

al'terco nm altercation

alter'nanza nf alternation

alter'na|re vt, **~rsi** vr alternate. **~'tiva** nf alternative. **~'tivo** a alternate. **~to** a alternating. **~'tore** nm Electr alternator

al'tern|o a alternate; **a giorni ~i** every other day

al'tero a haughty

al'tezza nf height; (profondità) depth; (suono) pitch; (di tessuto) width; (titolo) Highness; **essere all'~ di** be on a level with; fig be up to

altezzos|a'mente adv haughtily. **~ità** nf haughtiness

altez'zoso a haughty

al'ticcio a tipsy, merry

altipi'ano nm plateau

alti'tudine nf altitude

'alto a high; (di statura) tall; (profondo) deep; (suono) high-pitched; (tessuto) wide; Geog northern; **a notte alta** in the middle of the night; **avere degli alti e bassi** have some ups and downs; **ad alta fedeltà** high-fidelity; **a voce alta, ad alta voce** in a loud voice; (leggere) aloud; **essere in ~ mare** be on the high seas. **alta finanza** nf high finance. **alta moda** nf high fashion. **alta tensione** nf high voltage ● adv high; **in ~** at the top; (guardare) up; **mani in ~!** hands up!

alto'forno nm blast-furnace

altolà int halt there!

altolo'cato a highly placed

altopar'lante nm loudspeaker

altopi'ano nm plateau

altret'tanto a & pron as much; (pl) as many ● adv likewise; **buona fortuna! grazie, ~** good luck! thank you, the same to you

altri'menti adv otherwise

'altro a other; **un ~, un'altra** another; **l'altr'anno** last year; **domani l'~** the day after tomorrow; **l'ho visto l'~ giorno** I saw him the other day ● pron other [one]; **un ~, un'altra** another [one]; **ne vuoi dell'~?** would you like some more?; **l'un l'~** one another; **nessun ~** nobody else; **gli altri** (la gente) other people ● nm something else; **non fa ~ che lavorare** he does nothing but work; **desidera ~?** (in negozio) anything else?; **più che ~, sono stanco** I'm tired more than anything; **se non ~** at least; **senz'~** certainly; **tra l'~** what's more; **~ che!** and how!

altroi'eri nm **l'~** the day before yesterday

al'tronde *adv* **d'~** on the other hand

al'trove *adv* elsewhere

al'trui *a* other people's ● *nm* other people's belongings *pl*

altru'is|mo *nm* altruism. **~ta** *nmf* altruist

al'tura *nf* high ground; *Naut* deep sea

a'lunno, -a *nmf* pupil

alve'are *nm* hive

al'za|re *vt* lift, raise; (*costruire*) build; *Naut* hoist; **~re le spalle** shrug one's shoulders; **~re i tacchi** *fig* take to one's heels. **~rsi** *vr* rise; (*in piedi*) stand up; (*da letto*) get up; **~rsi in piedi** get to one's feet. **~ta** *nf* lifting; (*aumento*) rise; (*da letto*) getting up; *Archit* elevation. **~to** *a* up

a'mabile *a* lovable; (*vino*) sweet

a'maca *nf* hammock

amalga'mar|e *vt*, **~si** *vr* amalgamate

a'mante *a* **~ di** fond of ● *nm* lover ● *nf* mistress, lover

ama'rena *nf* sour black cherry

ama'retto *nm* macaroon

a'ma|re *vt* love; be fond of, like (*musica, sport ecc*). **~to, -a** *a* loved ● *nmf* beloved

ama'rezza *nf* bitterness; (*dolore*) sorrow

a'maro *a* bitter ● *nm* bitterness; (*liquore*) bitters *pl*

ama'rognolo *a* rather bitter

ama'tore, -'trice *nmf* lover

ambasci'a|ta *nf* embassy; (*messaggio*) message. **~'tore, ~'trice** *nm* ambassador ● *nf* ambassadress

ambe'due *a* & *pron* both

ambien'ta|le *a* environmental. **~'lista** *a* & *nmf* environmentalist

ambien'tar|e *vt* acclimatize; set (*personaggio, film ecc*). **~si** *vr* get acclimatized

ambi'ente *nm* environment; (*stanza*) room; *fig* milieu

ambiguità *nf inv* ambiguity; (*di persona*) shadiness

am'biguo *a* ambiguous; (*persona*) shady

am'bire *vi* **~ a** aspire to

'ambito *nm* sphere

ambiva'len|te *a* ambivalent. **~za** *nf* ambivalence

ambizi'o|ne *nf* ambition. **~so** *a* ambitious

'ambra *nf* amber. **am'brato** *a* amber

ambu'lante *a* wandering; **venditore ~** hawker

ambu'lanza *nf* ambulance

ambula'torio *nm* (*di medico*) surgery; (*di ospedale*) out-patients' [department]

a'meba *nf* amoeba

'amen *int* amen

a'meno *a* pleasant

A'merica *nf* America. **~ del Sud** South America. **ameri'cano, -a** *a* & *nmf* American

ame'tista *nf* amethyst

ami'anto *nm* asbestos

ami'chevole *a* friendly

ami'cizia *nf* friendship; **fare ~ con qcno** make friends with sb; **amicizie** *pl* (*amici*) friends

a'mico, -a *nmf* friend; **~ del cuore** bosom friend

'amido *nm* starch

ammac'ca|re *vt* dent; bruise (*frutto*). **~rsi** *vr* (*metallo:*) get dented; (*frutto:*) bruise. **~to** *a* dented; (*frutto*) bruised. **~'tura** *nf* dent; (*livido*) bruise

ammae'stra|re *vt* (*istruire*) teach; train (*animale*). **~to** *a* trained

ammai'nare *vt* lower (*bandiera*); furl (*vele*)

amma'lo|rsi *vr* fall ill. **~to, -a** *a* ill ● *nmf* sick person; (*paziente*) patient

ammali'are *vt* bewitch

am'manco *nm* deficit

ammanet'tare *vt* handcuff

ammani'cato *a* **essere ~** have connections

amma'raggio *nm* splashdown

amma'rare *vi* put down on the sea; (*nave spaziale:*) splash down

ammas'sar|e *vt* amass. **~si** *vr* crowd together. **am'masso** *nm* mass; (*mucchio*) pile

ammat'tire *vi* go mad

ammaz'zar|e *vt* kill. **~si** *vr* (*suicidarsi*) kill oneself; (*rimanere ucciso*) be killed

am'menda *nf* amends *pl*; (*multa*) fine; **fare ~ di qcsa** make amends for sth

am'messo *pp di* **ammettere** ● *conj* **~ che** supposing that

am'mettere *vt* admit; (*riconoscere*) acknowledge; (*supporre*) suppose

ammic'care *vi* wink

ammini'stra|re *vt* administer; (*gestire*) run. **~'tivo** *a* administrative. **~'tore, ~'trice** *nmf* administrator; (*di azienda*) manager; (*di società*) director. **~tore delegato** managing director. **~zi'one** *nf* administration; **fatti di ordinaria ~zione** routine matters

ammi'ragli|o *nm* admiral. **~'ato** *nm* admiralty

ammi'ra|re *vt* admire. **~to** *a* **restare/**

essere ~to be full of admiration. **~'tore, ~'trice** *nmf* admirer. **~zi'one** *nf* admiration. **ammi'revole** *a* admirable

ammis'sibile *a* admissible

ammissi'one *nf* admission; *(approvazione)* acknowledgement

ammobili'a|re *vt* furnish. **~to** *a* furnished

am'modo *a* proper ● *adv* properly

am'mollo *nm* **in ~** soaking

ammo'niaca *nf* ammonia

ammoni'mento *nm* warning; *(di rimprovero)* admonishment

ammo'ni|re *vt* warn; *(rimproverare)* admonish. **~'tore** *a* admonishing. **~zi'one** *nf Sport* warning

ammon'tare *vi* **~ a** amount to ● *nm* amount

ammonticchi'a|re *vt* heap up

ammorbi'dente *nm (per panni)* softener

ammorbi'dir|e *vt, ~si* *vr* soften

ammorta'mento *nm Comm* amortization

ammor'tare *vt* pay off *(spesa)*; *Comm* amortize *(debito)*

ammortiz'za|re *vt Comm* = **ammortare**; *Mech* damp. **~'tore** *nm* shock-absorber

ammosci'ar|e *vt* make flabby. **~si** *vi* get flabby

ammucchi'a|re *vt, ~rsi* *vr* pile up. **~ta** *nf (sl: orgia)* orgy

ammuf'fi|re *vi* go mouldy. **~to** *a* mouldy

ammuti'mento *nm* mutiny

ammuti'narsi *vr* mutiny

ammuto'lire *vi* be struck dumb

amne'sia *nf* amnesia

amni'stia *nf* amnesty

'amo *nm* hook; *fig* bait

amo'rale *a* amoral

a'more *nm* love; **fare l'~** make love; **per l'amor di Dio/del cielo!** for heaven's sake!; **andare d'~ e d'accordo** get on like a house on fire; **~ proprio** self-respect; **è un ~** *(persona)* he/she is a darling; **per ~ di** for the sake of; **amori** *pl* love affairs. **~'ggi'are** *vi* flirt. **amo'revole** *a* loving

a'morfo *a* shapeless; *(persona)* colourless, grey

amo'roso *a* loving; *(sguardo ecc)* amorous; *(lettera, relazione)* love

ampi'ezza *nf (di esperienza)* breadth; *(di stanza)* spaciousness; *(di gonna)* fullness; *(importanza)* scale

'ampio *a* ample; *(esperienza)* wide; *(stanza)* spacious; *(vestito)* loose; *(gonna)* full; *(pantaloni)* baggy

am'plesso *nm* embrace

amplia'mento *nm (di casa, porto)* enlargement; *(di strada)* widening

ampli'are *vt* broaden *(conoscenze)*

amplifi'ca|re *vt* amplify; *fig* magnify. **~'tore** *nm* amplifier. **~zi'one** *nf* amplification

am'polla *nf* cruet

ampol'loso *a* pompous

ampu'ta|re *vt* amputate. **~zi'one** *nf* amputation

amu'leto *nm* amulet

anabbagli'ante *a Auto* dipped ● *nmpl* **anabbaglianti** dipped headlights

anacro'nis|mo *nm* anachronism. **~tico** *a* **essere ~** be an anachronism

a'nagrafe *nf (ufficio)* registry office; *(registro)* register of births, marriages and deaths

ana'grafico *a* **dati** *nmpl* **anagrafici** personal data

ana'gramma *nm* anagram

anal'colico *a* non-alcoholic ● *nm* soft drink, non-alcoholic drink

a'nale *a* anal

analfa'be|ta *a & nmf* illiterate. **~'tismo** *nm* illiteracy

anal'gesico *nm* painkiller

a'nalisi *nf inv* analysis; *Med* test. **~ grammaticale/del periodo/logica** parsing. **~ del sangue** blood test

ana'li|sta *nmf* analyst. **~tico** *a* analytical. **~z'zare** *vt* analyse; *Med* test

anal'lergico *a* hypoallergenic

analo'gia *nf* analogy. **a'nalogo** *a* analogous

'ananas *nm inv* pineapple

anar'chi|a *nf* anarchy. **a'narchico, -a** *a* anarchic ● *nmf* anarchist. **~smo** *nm* anarchism

A.N.A.S. *nf abbr* **(Azienda Nazionale Autonoma delle Strade)** *national road maintenance authority*

anato'mia *nf* anatomy. **ana'tomico** *a* anatomical; *(sedia)* contoured, ergonomic

'anatra *nf* duck

ana'troccolo *nm* duckling

'anca *nf* hip; *(di animale)* flank

ance'strale *a* ancestral

'anche *conj* also, too; *(persino)* even; **~ se** even if; **~ domani** tomorrow also *o* too, also tomorrow

anchilo'sato *a fig* stiff

an'cora *adv* still, yet; (*di nuovo*) again; (*di più*) some more; ~ **una volta** once more

'anco|ra *nf* anchor; **gettare l'~ra** drop anchor. ~'**raggio** *nm* anchorage. ~'**rare** *vt* anchor

anda'mento *nm* (*del mercato, degli affari*) trend

an'dante *a* (*corrente*) current; (*di poco valore*) cheap ● *nm Mus* andante

an'da|re *vi* go; (*funzionare*) work; ~ **via** (*partire*) leave; ⟨macchia:⟩ come out; ~ [**bene**] (*confarsi*) suit; ⟨taglia:⟩ fit; **ti va bene alle tre?** does three o'clock suit you?; **non mi va di mangiare** I don't feel like eating; ~ **di fretta** be in a hurry; ~ **fiero di** be proud of; ~ **di moda** be in fashion; **va per i 20 anni** he's nearly 20; **ma va'** [là]! come on!; **come va?** how are things?; ~ **a male** go off; ~ **a fuoco** go up in flames; **va spedito** [**entro**] **stamattina** it must be sent this morning; **ne va del mio lavoro** my job is at stake; **come è andata a finire?** how did it turn out?; **cosa vai dicendo?** what are you talking about?. ~**rsene** go away; (*morire*) pass away ● *nm* going; **a lungo ~re** eventually

'andito *nm* passage

an'drone *nm* entrance

a'neddoto *nm* anecdote

ane'lare *vt* ~ **a** long for. **a'nelito** *nm* longing

a'nello *nm* ring; (*di catena*) link

ane'mia *nf* anaemia. **a'nemico** *a* anaemic

a'nemone *nm* anemone

aneste'si|a *nf* anaesthesia; (*sostanza*) anaesthetic. ~'**sta** *nmf* anaesthetist. **ane'stetico** *a & nm* anaesthetic

an'fibi *nmpl* (*stivali*) army boots

an'fibio *nm* (*animale*) amphibian ● *a* amphibious

anfite'atro *nm* amphitheatre

'anfora *nf* amphora

an'fratto *nm* ravine

an'gelico *a* angelic

'angelo *nm* angel. ~ **custode** guardian angel

angli'c|ano *a* Anglican. ~**ismo** *nm* Anglicism

an'glofilo, -a *a & nmf* Anglophile

an'glofono, -a *nmf* English-speaker

anglo'sassone *a & nmf* Anglo-Saxon

ango'la|re *a* angular. ~**zi'one** *nf* angle shot

'angolo *nm* corner; *Math* angle. ~ [**di**] **cottura** kitchenette

ango'loso *a* angular

an'gosci|a *nf* anguish. ~**are** *vt* torment. ~**ato** *a* agonized. ~**oso** *a* (*disperato*) anguished; (*che dà angoscia*) distressing

angu'illa *nf* eel

an'guria *nf* water-melon

an'gusti|a *nf* (*ansia*) anxiety; (*penuria*) poverty. ~**are** *vt* distress. ~**arsi** *vr* be very worried (**per** about)

an'gusto *a* narrow

'anice *nm* anise; *Culin* aniseed; (*liquore*) anisette

ani'dride *nf* ~ **carbonica** carbon dioxide

'anima *nf* soul; **non c'era ~ viva** there was not a soul about; **all'~!** good grief!; **un'~ in pena** a soul in torment. ~ **gemella** soul mate

ani'ma|le *a & nm* animal; ~**li** **domestici** *pl* pets. ~'**lesco** *a* animal

ani'ma|re *vt* give life to; (*ravvivare*) enliven; (*incoraggiare*) encourage. ~**rsi** *vr* come to life; (*accalorarsi*) become animated. ~**to** *a* animate; (*discussione*) animated; (*strada, paese*) lively. ~'**tore**, ~'**trice** *nmf* leading spirit; *Cinema* animator. ~**zi'one** *nf* animation

'animo *nm* (*mente*) mind; (*indole*) disposition; (*cuore*) heart; **perdersi d'~** lose heart; **farsi ~** take heart. ~**sità** *nf* animosity

ani'moso *a* brave; (*ostile*) hostile

'anitra *nf* = **anatra**

annac'qua|re *vt anche fig* water down. ~**to** *a* watered down

annaffi'a|re *vt* water. ~'**toio** *nm* watering-can

an'nali *nmpl* annals

anna'spare *vi* flounder

an'nata *nf* year; (*importo annuale*) annual amount; (*di vino*) vintage

annebbia'mento *nm* fog build-up; *fig* clouding

annebbi'ar|e *vt* cloud (*vista, mente*). ~**si** *vr* become foggy; (*vista, mente*) grow dim

annega'mento *nm* drowning

anne'ga|re *vt/i* drown

anne'rir|e *vt/i* blacken. ~**si** *vr* become black

annessi'one *nf* (*di nazione*) annexation

an'nesso *pp di* **annettere** ● *a* attached; (*Stato*) annexed an'nettere *vt* add; (*accludere*) enclose; annex (*Stato*)

annichi'lire *vt* annihilate

anni'darsi *vr* nest

annienta'mento *nm* annihilation

annien'tar|e *vt* annihilate. ~si *vr* abase oneself

anniver'sario *a & nm* anniversary. ~ di matrimonio wedding anniversary

'anno *nm* year; Buon A~! Happy New Year!; quanti anni ha? how old are you?; Tommaso ha dieci anni Thomas is ten [years old]. ~ bisestile leap year

anno'dar|e *vt* knot; do up (*cintura*); *fig* form. ~si *vr* become knotted

annoi'a|re *vt* bore; (*recare fastidio*) annoy. ~rsi *vr* get bored; (*condizione*) be bored. ~to *a* bored

anno'ta|re *vt* note down; annotate (*testo*). ~zi'one *nf* note

annove'rare *vt* number

annu'a|le *a* annual, yearly. ~rio *nm* year-book

annu'ire *vi* nod; (*acconsentire*) agree

annulla'mento *nm* annulment; (*di appuntamento*) cancellation

annul'lar|e *vt* annul; cancel (*appuntamento*); (*togliere efficacia a*) undo; disallow (*gol*); (*distruggere*) destroy. ~si *vr* cancel each other out

annunci'a|re *vt* announce; (*preannunciare*) foretell. ~'tore, ~'trice *nmf* announcer. ~zi'one *nf* Annunciation

an'nuncio *nm* announcement; (*pubblicitario*) advertisement; (*notizia*) news. annunci *pl* economici classified advertisements

'annuo *a* annual, yearly

annu'sare *vt* sniff

annuvo'lar|e *vt* cloud. ~si *vr* cloud over

'ano *nm* anus

anoma'lia *nf* anomaly

a'nomalo *a* anomalous

anoni'mato *nm* mantenere l'~ remain anonymous

a'nonimo, -a *a* anonymous ●*nmf* (*pittore, scrittore*) anonymous painter/writer

anores'sia *nf* Med anorexia

ano'ressico, -a *nmf* anorexic

anor'mal|e *a* abnormal ●*nmf* deviant, abnormal person. ~ità *nf inv* abnormality

'ansa *nf* handle; (*di fiume*) bend

an'sare *vi* pant

'ansia, ansietà *nf* anxiety; stare/essere in ~ per be anxious about

ansi'oso *a* anxious

antago'nis|mo *nm* antagonism. ~ta *nmf* antagonist

an'tartico *a & nm* Antarctic

antece'dente *a* preceding ●*nm* precedent

ante'fatto *nm* prior event

ante'guerra *a* pre-war ●*nm* pre-war period

an'tenato, -a *nmf* ancestor

an'tenna *nf* Radio, TV aerial; (*di animale*) antenna; Naut yard. ~ parabolica satellite dish

ante'porre *vt* put before

ante'prima *nf* preview; vedere qcsa in ~ have a sneak preview of sth

anteri'ore *a* front *attrib*; (*nel tempo*) previous

antiade'rente *a* (*padella*) nonstick

antia'ereo *a* anti-aircraft *attrib*

antial'lergico *a* hypoallergenic

antia'tomico *a* rifugio ~ fallout shelter

antibi'otico *a & nm* antibiotic

anti'caglia *nf* (*oggetto*) piece of old junk

antica'mente *adv* in ancient times, long ago

anti'camera *nf* ante-room; far ~ be kept waiting

antichità *nf inv* antiquity; (*oggetto*) antique

anti'clone *nm* anticyclone

antici'pa|re *vt* advance; Comm pay in advance; (*prevedere*) anticipate; (*prevenire*) forestall ●*vi* be early. ~ta'mente *adv* in advance. ~zi'one *nf* anticipation; (*notizia*) advance news

an'ticipo *nm* advance; (*caparra*) deposit; in ~ early; (*nel lavoro*) ahead of schedule

an'tico *a* ancient; (*mobile ecc*) antique; (*vecchio*) old; all'antica old-fashioned ●*nmpl* gli antichi the ancients

anticoncezio'nale *a & nm* contraceptive

anticonfor'mis|mo *nm* unconventionality. ~ta *nmf* nonconformist. ~tico *a* unconventional, nonconformist

anticonge'lante *a & nm* anti-freeze

anti'corpo *nm* antibody

anticostituzio'nale *a* unconstitutional

anti'crimine *a inv* (*squadra*) crime *attrib*

antidemo'cratico *a* undemocratic

antidolo'rifico *nm* painkiller

an'tidoto *nm* antidote

anti'droga *a inv* ⟨*campagna*⟩ anti-drugs; ⟨*squadra*⟩ drug *attrib*

antie'stetico *a* ugly

antifa'scismo *nm* anti-fascism

antifa'scista *a* & *nmf* anti-fascist

anti'forfora *a inv* dandruff *attrib*

anti'furto *nm* anti-theft device; ⟨*allarme*⟩ alarm ● *a inv* ⟨*sistema*⟩ anti-theft

anti'gelo *nm* antifreeze; ⟨*parabrezza*⟩ defroster

antigi'enico *a* unhygienic

An'tille *nfpl* **le** ~ the West Indies

an'tilope *nf* antelope

antin'cendio *a inv* **allarme** ~ fire alarm; **porta** ~ fire door

anti'nebbia *nm inv* Auto **[faro]** ~ foglamp, foglight

antinfiamma'torio *a* & *nm* anti-inflammatory

antinucle'are *a* anti-nuclear

antio'rario *a* anti-clockwise

anti'pasto *nm* hors d'oeuvre, starter

antipa'tia *nf* antipathy. **anti'patico** *a* unpleasant

an'tipodi *nmpl* antipodes; **essere agli** ~ *fig* be poles apart

antiquari'ato *nm* antique trade

anti'quario, -a *nmf* antique dealer

anti'quato *a* antiquated

anti'ruggine *nm inv* rust-inhibitor

anti'rughe *a inv* anti-wrinkle *attrib*

anti'scippo *a inv* theft-proof

antise'mita *a* anti-Semitic

anti'settico *a* & *nm* antiseptic

antisoci'ale *a* anti-social

antista'minico *nm* antihistamine

anti'stante a *prep* in front of

anti'tarlo *nm inv* woodworm treatment

antiterro'ristico *a* antiterrorist *attrib*

an'titesi *nf inv* antithesis

antolo'gia *nf* anthology

'antro *nm* cavern

antropolo'gia *nf* anthropology. **antro'pologo, -a** *nmf* anthropologist

anu'lare *nm* ring-finger

'anzi *conj* in fact; ⟨*o meglio*⟩ better still; ⟨*al contrario*⟩ on the contrary

anziani'tà *nf* old age; ⟨*di servizio*⟩ seniority

anzi'ano, -a *a* old, elderly; ⟨*di grado ecc*⟩ senior ● *nmf* elderly person

anziché *conj* rather than

anzi'tempo *adv* prematurely

anzi'tutto *adv* first of all

a'orta *nf* aorta

apar'titico *a* unaligned

apa'tia *nf* apathy. **a'patico** *a* apathetic

'ape *nf* bee; **nido** *nm* **di api** honeycomb

aperi'tivo *nm* aperitif

aperta'mente *adv* openly

a'perto *a* open; **all'aria aperta** in the open air; **all'~** open-air

aper'tura *nf* opening; ⟨*inizio*⟩ beginning; ⟨*ampiezza*⟩ spread; ⟨*di arco*⟩ span; *Pol* overtures *pl*; *Phot* aperture; ~ **mentale** openness

'apice *nm* apex

apicol'tura *nf* beekeeping

ap'nea *nf* **immersione in** ~ free diving

a'polide *a* stateless ● *nmf* stateless person

a'postolo *nm* apostle

apostro'fare *vt* ⟨*mettere un apostrofo a*⟩ write with an apostrophe; reprimand ⟨*persona*⟩

a'postrofo *nm* apostrophe

appaga'mento *nm* fulfilment

appa'ga|re *vt* satisfy. ~**rsi** *vr* ~**rsi di** be satisfied with

appai'are *vt* pair; mate ⟨*animali*⟩

appallotto'lare *vt* roll into a ball

appalta'tore *nm* contractor

ap'palto *nm* contract; **dare in** ~ contract out

appan'naggio *nm* ⟨*in denaro*⟩ annuity; *fig* prerogative

appan'na|re *vt* mist ⟨*vetro*⟩; dim ⟨*vista*⟩. ~**si** *vr* mist over; ⟨*vista*⟩ grow dim

appa'rato *nm* apparatus; ⟨*pompa*⟩ display

apparecchi'a|re *vt* prepare ● *vi* lay the table. ~**tura** *nf* ⟨*impianti*⟩ equipment

appa'recchio *nm* apparatus; ⟨*congegno*⟩ device; ⟨*radio, TV ecc*⟩ set; ⟨*aeroplano*⟩ aircraft. ~ **acustico** hearing aid

appa'ren|te *a* apparent. ~**te'mente** *adv* apparently. ~**za** *nf* appearance; **in** ~**za** apparently

appa'ri|re *vi* appear; ⟨*sembrare*⟩ look. ~'**scente** *a* striking; *pej* gaudy. ~**zi'one** *nf* apparition

apparta'mento *nm* flat, apartment *Am*

appar'ta|rsi *vr* withdraw. ~**to** *a* secluded

appar'tenenza *nf* membership

apparte'nere *vi* belong

appassio'nante *a* ⟨*storia, argomento*⟩ exciting

appassio'na|re *vt* excite; ⟨*commuovere*⟩ move. ~**rsi** *vr* ~**rsi a** become excited by. **~to**a passionate; **~to di**(entusiastico) fond of

appas'sir|evi wither. **~si**vr fade

appel'larsivr **~ a**appeal to

ap'pello nm appeal; (chiamata per nome) rollcall; (esami) exam session; **fare l'~**call the roll

ap'pena adv just; (a fatica) hardly ●conj [non] **~** as soon as, no sooner... than

ap'penderevt hang [up]

appendi'abitinm inv hat-stand

appen'dice nf appendix. **appendi-'cite** nf appendicitis

Appen'nininmpl **gli ~** the Apennines

appesan'tir|e vt weigh down. **~si**vr become heavy

ap'peso pp di **appendere** ●a hanging; (impiccato) hanged

appe'ti|to nm appetite; **aver ~to** be hungry; **buon ~to!** enjoy your meal!. **~'toso**a appetizing;fig tempting

appezza'mento nm plot of land

appia'nar|e vt level; fig smooth over. **~si**vr improve

appiat'tir|e vt flatten. **~si**vr flatten oneself

appic'carevt **~ il fuoco** aset fire to

appicci'car|e vt stick; **~e a** (fig: appioppare) palm off on ●vi be sticky. **~si**vr stick; (cose:) stick together; **~si a qcno**fig stick to sb like glue

appicci'caticcioa sticky;fig clingy

appicci'cosoa sticky;fig clingy

appie'dato a **sono ~** I don't have the car; **sono rimasto ~** I was stranded

appi'enoadv fully

appigli'arsi vr **~ a** get hold of; fig stick to. **ap'piglio** nm fingerhold; (per piedi) foothold; fig pretext

appiop'parevt **~ a**palm off on; (fam: dare) give

appiso'larsivr doze off

applau'dire vt/i applaud. **ap'plauso** nm applause

appli'cabilea applicable

appli'ca|re vt apply; enforce (legge ecc). **~rsi**vr apply oneself. **~'tore** nm applicator. **~zi'one** nf application; (di legge) enforcement

appoggi'are vt lean (a against); (mettere) put; (sostenere) back. **~si**vr **~si a** a lean against; fig rely on. **ap'poggio**nm support

appollai'arsivr fig perch

ap'porrevt affix

appor'tare vt bring; (causare) cause. **ap'porto**nm contribution

apposita'mente adv (specialmente) especially

ap'positoa proper

ap'posta adv on purpose; (espressamente) specially

apposta'mento nm ambush; (caccia) lying in wait

appo'star|evt post (soldati). **~si**vr lie in wait

ap'prend|ere vt understand; (imparare) learn. **~i'mento**nm learning

appren'di|sta nmf apprentice. **~'sta-to**nm apprenticeship

apprensi'one nf apprehension; **essere in ~ per** be anxious about. **appren'sivo**a apprehensive

ap'presso adv & prep (vicino) near; (dietro) behind; **come ~** as follows

appre'star|e vt prepare. **~si** vr get ready

apprez'za|bilea appreciable. **~'men-to**nm appreciation; (giudizio) opinion

apprez'za|re vt appreciate. **~to**a appreciated

ap'proccionm approach

appro'dare vi land; **~ a** afig come to; **non ~ a nulla**come to nothing. **ap'pro-do**nm landing; (luogo) landing-stage

approfit'ta|re vi take advantage (di of), profit (di by). **~'tore**, **~'trice** nmf chancer

approfondi'mentonm deepening; **di ~** (fig: corso) advanced

approfon'di|re vt deepen. **~rsi** vr (divario:) widen. **~to**a (studio, ricerca) in-depth

appropri'a|rsi vr take possession (di of); (essere adatto a) suit. **~to** a appropriate. **~zi'one** nf Jur appropriation. **~zione indebita**Jur embezzlement

approssi'ma|re ~re per eccesso/difetto round up/down. **~rsi** vr draw near. **~tiva'mente** adv approximately. **~'tivo** a approximate. **~zi'one** nf approximation

appro'va|re vt approve of; approve (legge). **~zi'one**nf approval

approvvigiona'mento nm supplying; **approvvigionamenti** pl provisions

approvvigio'nar|evt supply. **~si**vr stock up

appunta'mento nm appointment, date fam; **fissare un ~** make an appointment; **darsi ~**decide to meet

appun'tar|e vt (annotare) take notes; (fissare) fix; (con spillo) pin; (appuntire) sharpen. **~si** *vr* **~si su** *(teoria:)* be based on

appun'ti|re *vt* sharpen. **~to** *a (mento)* pointed

ap'punto[1] *nm* note; *(piccola critica)* niggle

ap'punto[2] *adv* exactly; **per l'~!** exactly!; **stavo ~ dicendo...** I was just saying...

appu'rare *vt* verify

a'pribile *a* that can be opened

apribot'tiglie *nm inv* bottle-opener

a'prile *nm* April; **il primo d'~** April Fools' Day

a'pri|re *vt* open; turn on *(luce, acqua ecc)*; *(con chiave)* unlock; open up *(ferita ecc)*. **~si** *vr* open; *(spaccarsi)* split; *(confidarsi)* confide **(con** in)

apri'scatole *nf inv* tin-opener

aqua'planing *nm* **andare in ~** aquaplane

'aquila *nf* eagle; **non è un'~a!** he is no genius!. **~ 'lino** *a* aquiline

aqui'lone *nm (giocattolo)* kite

ara'besco *nm* arabesque; *hum* scribble

A'rabia Sau'dita *nf* **l'~** Saudi Arabia

'arabo, -a *a* Arab; *(lingua)* Arabic ● *nmf* Arab ● *nm (lingua)* Arabic

a'rachide *nf* peanut

ara'gosta *nf* lobster

a'rancl|a *nf* orange. **~ata** *nf* orangeade. **~o** *nm* orange-tree; *(colore)* orange. **~'one** *a & nm* orange

a'ra|re *vt* plough. **~tro** *nm* plough

ara'tura *nf* ploughing

a'razzo *nm* tapestry

arbi'tra|re *vt* arbitrate in; *Sport* referee. **~ietà** *nf* arbitrariness. **~io** *a* arbitrary

ar'bitrio *nm* will; **è un ~** it's very highhanded

'arbitro *nm* arbiter; *Sport* referee; *(nel baseball)* umpire

ar'busto *nm* shrub

'arca *nf* ark; *(cassa)* chest

ar'ca|ico *a* archaic. **~'ismo** *nm* archaism

ar'cangelo *nm* archangel

ar'cata *nf* arch; *(serie di archi)* arcade

arche|olo'gia *nf* archaeology. **~o'logico** *a* archaeological. **~'ologo, -a** *nmf* archaeologist

ar'chetto *nm Mus* bow

architet'tare *vt fig* devise; **cosa state architettando?** *fig* what are you plotting?

archi'tet|to *nm* architect. **~'tonico** *a* architectural. **~'tura** *nf* architecture

archivi'are *vt* file; *Jur* close

ar'chivio *nm* archives *pl*; *Comput* file

archi'vista *nmf* filing clerk

ar'cigno *a* grim

arci'pelago *nm* archipelago

arci'vescovo *nm* archbishop

'arco *nm* arch; *Math* arc; *(arma, Mus)* bow; **nell'~ di una giornata/due mesi** in the space of a day/two months

arcoba'leno *nm* rainbow

arcu'a|re *vt* bend. **~rsi** *vr* bend. **~to** *a* bent, curved; *(schiena di gatto)* arched

ar'dente *a* burning; *fig* ardent. **~'mente** *adv* ardently

'ardere *vt/i* burn

ar'desia *nf* slate

ar'di|re *vi* dare. **~to** *a* daring; *(coraggioso)* bold; *(sfacciato)* impudent

ar'dore *nm (calore)* heat; *fig* ardour

'arduo *a* arduous; *(ripido)* steep

'area *nf* area. **~ di rigore** *(in calcio)* penalty area. **~ di servizio** service area

a'rena *nf* arena

are'narsi *vr* run aground; *(fig: trattative)* reach deadlock; **mi sono arenato** I'm stuck

'argano *nm* winch

argen'tato *a* silver-plated

argente'ria *nf* silver[ware]

ar'gento *nm* silver

ar'gil|la *nf* clay. **~'loso** *a* *(terreno)* clayey

argi'nare *vt* embank; *fig* hold in check, contain

'argine *nm* embankment; *(diga)* dike

argomen'tare *vi* argue

argo'mento *nm* argument; *(motivo)* reason; *(soggetto)* subject

argu'ire *vt* deduce

ar'gu|to *a* witty. **~'zia** *nf* wit; *(battuta)* witticism

'aria *nf* air; *(aspetto)* appearance; *Mus* tune; **andare all'~** *fig* come to nothing; **avere l'~...** look...; **corrente** *nf* **d'~** draught; **mandare all'~** qcsa *fig* ruin sth

aridità *nf* dryness

'arido *a* arid

arieggi'a|re *vt* air. **~to** *a* airy

ari'ete *nm* ram. **A~** *Astr* Aries

ari'etta *nf (brezza)* breeze

a'ringa *nf* herring

arl'oso *a* *(locale)* light and airy

aristo'cra|tico, -a *a* aristocratic ● *nmf* aristocrat. **~'zia** *nf* aristocracy

arit'metica *nf* arithmetic

arlec'chino *nm* Harlequin; *fig* buffoon

'arma *nf* weapon; **armi** *pl* arms; (*forze armate*) [armed] forces; **chiamare alle armi** call up; **sotto le armi** in the army; **alle prime armi** *fig* inexperienced, fledg[e]ling. **~ da fuoco** firearm. **~ impropria** makeshift weapon. **~ a doppio taglio** *fig* double-edged sword

armadi'etto *nm* locker, cupboard

ar'madio *nm* cupboard; (*guardaroba*) wardrobe

armamen'tario *nm* tools *pl*; *fig* paraphernalia

arma'mento *nm* armament; *Naut* fitting out

ar'ma|re *vt* arm; (*equipaggiare*) fit out; *Archit* reinforce. **~rsi** *vr* arm oneself (**di** with). **~ta** *nf* army; (*flotta*) fleet. **~'tore** *nm* shipowner. **~'tura** *nf* framework; (*impalcatura*) scaffolding; (*di guerriero*) armour

armeggi'are *vi fig* manoeuvre

armi'stizio *nm* armistice

armo'ni|a *nf* harmony. **ar'monica** *nf* **~ [a bocca]** mouth organ. **ar'monico** *a* harmonic. **~'oso** *a* harmonious

armoniz'zare *vt* harmonize ● *vi* match. **~si** *vr* ⟨*colori:*⟩ go together, match

ar'nese *nm* tool; (*oggetto*) thing; (*congegno*) gadget; **male in ~** in bad condition

'arnia *nf* beehive

a'roma *nm* aroma; **aromi** *pl* herbs. **~tera'pia** *nf* aromatherapy

aro'matico *a* aromatic

aromatiz'zare *vt* flavour

'arpa *nf* harp

ar'peggio *nm* arpeggio

ar'pia *nf* harpy

arpi'one *nm* hook; (*pesca*) harpoon

arrabat'tarsi *vr* do all one can

arrabbi'a|rsi *vr* get angry. **~to** *a* angry. **~'tura** *nf* rage; **prendersi un'~tura** fly into a rage

arraf'fare *vt* grab

arrampi'ca|rsi *vr* climb [up]. **~ta** *nf* climb. **~'tore**, **~'trice** *nmf* climber. **~'tore sociale** social climber

arran'care *vi* limp, hobble; *fig* struggle, limp along

arrangia'mento *nm* arrangement

arrangi'a|re *vt* arrange. **~si** *vr* manage; **~si alla meglio** get by; **ar'rangiati!** get on with it!

arra'parsi *vr fam* get randy

arre'care *vt* bring; (*causare*) cause

arreda'mento *nm* interior decoration; (*l'arredare*) furnishing; (*mobili ecc*) furnishings *pl*

arre'da|re *vt* furnish. **~'tore**, **~'trice** *nmf* interior designer. **ar'redo** *nm* furnishings *pl*

ar'rendersi *vr* surrender

arren'devo|le *a* ⟨*persona*⟩ yielding. **~'lezza** *nf* softness

arre'sta|re *vt* arrest; (*fermare*) stop. **~si** *vr* halt. **ar'resto** *nm* stop; *Med, Jur* arrest; **la dichiaro in [stato d']arresto** you are under arrest; **mandato di arresto** warrant. **arresti** *pl* **domiciliari** *Jur* house arrest

arre'tra|re *vt/i* withdraw; pull back ⟨*giocatore*⟩. **~to** *a* ⟨*paese ecc*⟩ backward; ⟨*Mil: posizione*⟩ rear; **numero ~** *nm* (*di rivista*) back number; **del lavoro ~to** a backlog of work ● *nm* (*di stipendio*) back pay

arre'trati *nmpl* arrears

arricchi'mento *nm* enrichment

arric'chi|re *vt* enrich. **~rsi** *vr* get rich. **~to**, **-a** *nmf* nouveau riche

arricci'are *vt* curl; **~ il naso** turn up one's nose

ar'ringa *nf* harangue; *Jur* closing address

arrischi'a|rsi *vr* dare. **~to** *a* risky; (*imprudente*) rash

arri'va|re *vi* arrive; **~re a** (*raggiungere*) reach; (*ridursi*) be reduced to. **~to**, **-a** *a* successful; **ben ~to!** welcome! ● *nmf* successful person

arrive'derci *int* goodbye; **~ a domani** see you tomorrow

arri'vis|mo *nm* social climbing; (*nel lavoro*) careerism. **~ta** *nmf* social climber; (*nel lavoro*) careerist

ar'rivo *nm* arrival; *Sport* finish

arro'gan|te *a* arrogant. **~za** *nf* arrogance

arro'garsi *vr* **~ il diritto di fare qcsa** take it upon oneself to do sth

arrossa'mento *nm* reddening

arros'sa|re *vt* make red, redden ⟨*occhi*⟩. **~si** *vr* go red

arros'sire *vi* blush, go red

arro'stire *vt* roast; toast ⟨*pane*⟩; (*ai ferri*) grill. **ar'rosto** *a & nm* roast

arroto'lare *vt* roll up

arroton'da|re *vt* round; *Math ecc* round off. **~si** *vr* become round; (*persona:*) get plump

arrovel'larsi vr ~ **il cervello** rack one's brains

arroven'ta|re vt make red-hot. **~rsi** vr become red-hot. **~to** a red-hot

arruf'fa|re vt ruffle; fig confuse. **~to** a ⟨capelli⟩ ruffled

arruffianarsi vr ~ **qcno** fig butter sb up

arruggi'ni|re vt rust. **~rsi** vr go rusty; fig ⟨fisicamente⟩ stiffen up; ⟨conoscenze:⟩ go rusty. **~to** a rusty

arruola'mento nm enlistment

arruo'la|re vt/i, **~si** vr enlist

arse'nale nm arsenal; ⟨cantiere⟩ [naval] dockyard

ar'senico nm arsenic

'arso pp di **ardere ● a** burnt; ⟨arido⟩ dry. **ar'sura** nf burning heat; ⟨sete⟩ parching thirst

'arte nf art; ⟨abilità⟩ craftsmanship; **le belle arti** the fine arts. **arti figurative** figurative arts

arte'fa|re vt adulterate ⟨vino⟩; disguise ⟨voce⟩. **~tto** a fake; ⟨vino⟩ adulterated

ar'tefice nmf craftsman; craftswoman; fig author

ar'teria nf artery. ~ **[stradale]** arterial road

arterioscle'rosi nf arteriosclerosis, hardening of the arteries

'artico a & nm Arctic

artico'la|re a articular **● vt** articulate; ⟨suddividere⟩ divide. **~rsi** vr fig **~rsi in** consist of. **~to** a Auto articulated; fig well-constructed. **~zi'one** nf Anat articulation

ar'ticolo nm article. ~ **di fondo** leader

artifici'ale a artificial

arti'fici|o nm artifice; ⟨affettazione⟩ affectation. **~'oso** a artful; ⟨affettato⟩ affected

artigia'na|le a made by hand; hum amateurish. **~'mente** adv with craftsmanship; hum amateurishly

artigi'a'nato nm craftsmanship; ⟨ceto⟩ craftsmen pl. **~'ano, -a** nm craftsman **● nf** craftswoman

artigli'ere nm artilleryman. **~e'ria** nf artillery

ar'tiglio nm claw; fig clutch

ar'tist|a nmf artist. **~ica'mente** adv artistically. **~ico** a artistic

'arto nm limb

ar'trite nf arthritis

ar'trosi nf rheumatism

arzigogo'lato a fantastic, bizarre

ar'zillo a sprightly

a'scella nf armpit

ascen'den|te a ascending **● nm** ⟨antenato⟩ ancestor; ⟨influenza⟩ ascendancy; Astr ascendant

ascensi'one nf ascent; **l'A~** the Ascension

ascen'sore nm lift, elevator Am

a'scesa nf ascent; ⟨al trono⟩ accession; ⟨al potere⟩ rise

a'scesso nm abscess

a'sceta nmf ascetic

'ascia nf axe

asciugabianche'ria nm inv ⟨stenditoio⟩ clothes horse

asciugaca'pelli nm inv hair dryer, hairdrier

asciuga'mano nm towel

asciu'ga|re vt dry. **~si** vr dry oneself; ⟨diventare asciutto⟩ dry up

asci'utto a dry; ⟨magro⟩ wiry; ⟨risposta⟩ curt; **essere all'~** fig be hard up

ascol'ta|re vt listen to **● vi** listen. **~'tore, ~'trice** nmf listener

a'scolto nm listening; **dare ~ a** pay attention to; **mettersi in ~** Radio tune in

asfal'tare vt asphalt

a'sfalto nm asphalt

asfis'si|a nf asphyxia. **~'ante** a ⟨caldo⟩ oppressive; ⟨fig: persona⟩ annoying. **~'are** vt asphyxiate; fig annoy

'Asia nf Asia. **asi'atico, -a** a & nmf Asian

a'silo nm shelter; ⟨d'infanzia⟩ nursery school. ~ **nido** day nursery. ~ **politico** political asylum

asim'metrico a asymmetrical

'asino nm donkey; ⟨fig: persona stupida⟩ ass

'asma nf asthma. **a'smatico** a asthmatic

asoci'ale a asocial

'asola nf buttonhole

a'sparagi nmpl asparagus sg

a'sparago nm asparagus spear

asperità nf inv harshness; ⟨di terreno⟩ roughness

aspet'ta|re vt wait for; ⟨prevedere⟩ expect; **~re un bambino** be expecting [a baby]; **fare ~re qcno** keep sb waiting **● vi** wait. **~rsi** vr expect. **~'tiva** nf expectation

a'spetto¹ nm appearance; ⟨di problema⟩ aspect; **di bell'~** good-looking

a'spetto² nm **sala** nf **d'~** waiting room

aspi'rante a aspiring; ⟨pompa⟩ suction attrib **● nmf** ⟨a un posto⟩ applicant;

(*al trono*) aspirant; **gli aspiranti al titolo** the contenders for the title

aspira'polvere *nm inv* vacuum cleaner

aspi'ra|re *vt* inhale; *Mech* suck in ● *vi* ~**re a** aspire to. ~**tore** *nm* extractor fan. ~**zi'one** *nf* inhalation; *Mech* suction; (*ambizione*) ambition

aspi'rina *nf* aspirin

aspor'tare *vt* take away

aspra'mente *adv* (*duramente*) severely

a'sprezza *nf* (*al gusto*) sourness; (*di clima*) severity; (*di suono*) harshness; (*di odore*) pungency

'aspro *a* (*al gusto*) sour; ‹*clima*› severe; ‹*suono, parole*› harsh; ‹*odore*› pungent; ‹*litigio*› bitter

assag'gi|are *vt* taste. ~**'gini** *nmpl* *Culin* samples. **as'saggio** *nm* tasting; (*piccola quantità*) taste

as'sai *adv* very; (*moltissimo*) very much; (*abbastanza*) enough

assa'li|re *vt* attack. ~**'tore**, ~**'trice** *nmf* assailant

as'salto *nm* attack; **prendere d'**~ storm ‹*città*›; *fig* mob ‹*persona*›; hold up ‹*banca*›

assapo'rare *vt* savour

assassi'nare *vt* murder, assassinate; *fig* murder

assas'sin|io *nm* murder, assassination. ~**o, -a** *a* murderous ●*nm* murderer ●*nf* murderess

'asse *nf* board ●*nm* *Techn* axle; *Math* axis. ~ **da stiro** ironing board

assecon'dare *vt* satisfy; (*favorire*) support

assedi'are *vt* besiege. **as'sedio** *nm* siege

assegna'mento *nm* allotment; **fare** ~ **su** rely on

asse'gna|re *vt* allot; award ‹*premio*›. ~**'tario** *nmf* recipient. ~**zi'one** *nf* (*di alloggio, denaro, borsa di studio*) allocation

as'segno *nm* allowance; (*bancario*) cheque; **contro** ~ cash on delivery. ~ **circolare** bank draft. **assegni** *pl* **familiari** family allowance. ~ **non trasferibile** cheque made out to 'account payee only'

assem'blea *nf* assembly; (*adunanza*) gathering

assembra'mento *nm* gathering

assen'nato *a* sensible

as'senso *nm* assent

assen'tarsi *vr* go away; (*da stanza*) leave the room

as'sen|te *a* absent; (*distratto*) absent-minded ●*nmf* absentee. ~**te'ismo** *nm* absenteeism. ~**te'ista** *nmf* frequent absentee. ~**za** *nf* absence; (*mancanza*) lack

asse'r|ire *vt* assert. ~**'tivo** *a* assertive. ~**zi'one** *nf* assertion

asses'sorato *nm* department

asses'sore *nm* councillor

assesta'mento *nm* settlement

asse'sta|re *vt* arrange; ~**e un colpo** deal a blow. ~**si** *vr* settle oneself

asse'tato *a* parched

as'setto *nm* order; *Naut, Aeron* trim

assicu'ra|re *vt* assure; *Comm* insure; register ‹*posta*›; (*fissare*) secure; (*accertare*) ensure. ~**rsi** *vr* (*con contratto*) insure oneself; (*legarsi*) fasten oneself; ~**rsi che** make sure that. ~**'tivo** *a* insurance *attrib*. ~**'tore**, ~**'trice** *nmf* insurance agent ●*a* insurance *attrib*. ~**zi'one** *nf* assurance; (*contratto*) insurance

assidera'mento *nm* exposure. **asside'rato** *a Med* suffering from exposure; *fam* frozen

assidu|a'mente *adv* assiduously. ~**ità** *nf* assiduity

as'siduo *a* assiduous; ‹*cliente*› regular

assil'lante *a* ‹*persona, pensiero*› nagging

assil'lare *vt* pester

as'sillo *nm* worry

assimi'la|re *vt* assimilate. ~**zi'one** *nf* assimilation

as'sise *nfpl* assizes; **Corte d'A**~ Court of Assize[s]

assi'sten|te *nmf* assistant. ~**te sociale** social worker. ~**te di volo** flight attendant. ~**za** *nf* assistance; (*presenza*) presence. ~**za sociale** social work

assistenzi'a|le *a* welfare *attrib*. ~**'lismo** *nm* welfare

as'sistere *vt* assist; (*curare*) nurse ●*vi* ~ **a** (*essere presente*) be present at; watch ‹*spettacolo ecc*›

'asso *nm* ace; **piantare in** ~ leave in the lurch

associ'a|re *vt* join; (*collegare*) associate. ~**rsi** *vr* join forces; *Comm* enter into partnership. ~**rsi a** join; subscribe to ‹*giornale ecc*›. ~**zi'one** *nf* association

assogget'tar|e *vt* subject. ~**si** *vr* submit

asso'lato *a* sunny

assol'dare *vt* recruit

as'solo nm Mus solo

as'solto pp di **assolvere**

assoluta'mente adv absolutely

assolu'tismo nm absolutism

asso'lu|to a absolute. **~zi'one** nf acquittal; Relig absolution

as'solvere vt perform ⟨compito⟩; Jur acquit; Relig absolve

assomigli'ar|e vi ~**e a** be like, resemble. **~si** vr resemble each other

assom'marsi vr combine; **~ a qcsa** add to sth

asso'nanza nf assonance

asson'nato a drowsy

asso'pirsi vr doze off

assor'bente a & nm absorbent. **~ igienico** sanitary towel

assor'bire vt absorb

assor'da|re vt deafen. **~nte** a deafening

assorti'mento nm assortment

assor'ti|re vt match ⟨colori⟩. **~to** a assorted; ⟨colori, persone⟩ matched

as'sorto a engrossed

assottigli'ar|e vt make thin; ⟨aguzzare⟩ sharpen; ⟨ridurre⟩ reduce. **~si** vr grow thin; ⟨finanze⟩ be whittled away

assue'fa|re vt accustom. **~rsi** vr **~rsi a** get used to. **~tto** a ⟨a caffè, aspirina⟩ immune to the effects; ⟨a droga⟩ addicted. **~zi'one** nf ⟨a caffè, aspirina⟩ immunity to the effects; ⟨a droga⟩ addiction

as'sumere vt assume; take on ⟨impiegato⟩; **~ informazioni** make inquiries

as'sunto pp di **assumere** ● nm task. **assunzi'one** nf ⟨di impiegato⟩ employment

assur'dità nf inv absurdity; **~ pl** nonsense

as'surdo a absurd

'asta nf pole; Mech bar; Comm auction; **a mezz'~** at half-mast

a'stemio a abstemious

aste'n|ersi vr abstain (**da** from). **~si'one** nf abstention

aste'nuto, -a nmf abstainer

aste'risco nm asterisk

astig'ma|tico a astigmatic. **~'tismo** nm astigmatism

asti'nenza nf abstinence; **crisi di ~** cold turkey

'asti|o nm rancour; **avere ~o contro qcno** bear sb a grudge. **~'oso** a resentful

a'stratto a abstract

astrin'gente a & nm astringent

'astro nm star

astrolo'gia nf astrology. **a'strologo, -a** nmf astrologer

astro'nauta nmf astronaut

astro'nave nf spaceship

astro'nomia nf astronomy. **~o'nomico** a astronomical. **a'stronomo** nm astronomer

astrusità nf abstruseness

a'stuccio nm case

a'stu|to a shrewd; ⟨furbo⟩ cunning. **~zia** nf shrewdness; ⟨azione⟩ trick

ate'ismo nm atheism

A'tene nf Athens

'ateo, -a a & nmf atheist

a'tipico a atypical

at'lant|e nm atlas. **~ico** a Atlantic; **l'[Oceano] A~ico** the Atlantic [Ocean]

at'let|a nmf athlete. **~ica** nf athletics sg. **~ica leggera** track and field events. **~ica pesante** weight-lifting, boxing, wrestling, etc. **~ico** a athletic

atmo'sfer|a nf atmosphere. **~ico** a atmospheric

a'tomic|a nf atom bomb. **~o** a atomic

'atomo nm atom

'atrio nm entrance hall

a'troc|e a atrocious; ⟨terribile⟩ dreadful. **~ità** nf inv atrocity

atrofiz'zarsi vr Med, fig atrophy

attaccabot'toni nmf inv [crashing] bore

attacca'brighe nmf inv troublemaker

attacca'mento nm attachment

attacca'panni nm inv [coat-]hanger; ⟨a muro⟩ clothes hook

attac'car|e vt attach; ⟨legare⟩ tie; ⟨appendere⟩ hang; ⟨cucire⟩ sew on; ⟨contagiare⟩ pass on; ⟨assalire⟩ attack; ⟨iniziare⟩ start ● vi stick; ⟨diffondersi⟩ catch on. **~rsi** vr cling; ⟨affezionarsi⟩ become attached; ⟨litigare⟩ quarrel

attacca'ticcio a sticky

at'tacco nm attack; ⟨punto d'unione⟩ junction

attar'darsi vr stay late; ⟨indugiare⟩ linger

attec'chire vi take; ⟨moda ecc:⟩ catch on

attegia'mento nm attitude

atteggi'ar|e vt assume. **~si** vr **~si a** pose as

attem'pato a elderly

at'tender|e vt wait for ● vi **~e a** attend to. **~si** vr expect

atten'dibil|e a reliable. **~ità** nf reliability

atte'nersi vr **~ a** stick to

atten'ta'mente adv attentively

atten'ta|re vi ~re a make an attempt on. ~**to** nm act of violence; (contro politico ecc) assassination attempt. ~'tore, ~'trice nmf (a scopo politico) terrorist

at'tento a attentive; (accurato) careful; ~! look out!; **stare ~** pay attention

attenu'ante nf extenuating circumstance

attenu'a|re vt attenuate; (minimizzare) minimize; subdue (colori ecc); calm (dolore); soften (colpo). ~**rsi** vr diminish. ~**zi'one** nf lessening

attenzi'one nf attention; ~! watch out!

atter'ra|ggio nm landing. ~**re** vt knock down ● vi land

atter'rir|e vt terrorize. ~**si** vr be terrified

at'tes|a nf waiting; (aspettativa) expectation; **in** ~**a di** waiting for. ~**o** pp di **attendere**

atte'sta|re vt state; (certificare) certify. ~**to** nm certificate. ~**zi'one** nf certificate; (dichiarazione) declaration

'**attico** nm attic

at'tiguo a adjacent

attil'lato a (vestito) close-fitting; (elegante) dressed up

'**attimo** nm moment

atti'nente a ~ a pertaining to

at'tingere vt draw; fig obtain

atti'rare vt attract

atti'tudine nf (disposizione) aptitude; (atteggiamento) attitude

atti'v|are vt activate. ~**ismo** nm activism. ~**ista** nmf activist. **attività** nf inv activity; Comm assets pl. ~**o** a active; Comm productive ● nm assets pl

attiz'za|re vt poke; fig stir up. ~**toio** nm poker

'**atto** nm act; (azione) action; Comm, Jur deed; (certificato) certificate; **atti** pl (di società ecc) proceedings; **mettere in** ~ put into effect

at'tonito a astonished

attorcigli'ar|e vt twist. ~**si** vr get twisted

at'tore nm actor

attorni'ar|e vt surround. ~**si** vr ~**si di** surround oneself with

at'torno adv around, about ● prep ~ **a** around, about

attrac'care vt/i dock

attra'ente a attractive

at'tra|rre vt attract. ~**rsi** vr be attracted to each other. ~**t'tiva** nf

charm. ~**zi'one** nf attraction. ~**zioni turistiche** tourist attractions

attraversa'mento nm (di strada) crossing. ~ **pedonale** pedestrian crossing, crosswalk Am

attraver'sare vt cross; (passare) go through

attra'verso prep through; (obliquamente) across

attrez'za|re vt equip; Naut rig. ~**rsi** vr kit oneself out; ~**tura** nf equipment; Naut rigging

at'trezzo nm tool; **attrezzi** pl equipment; Sport appliances pl; Theat props pl

attribu'ir|e vt attribute. ~**si** vr ascribe to oneself; ~**si il merito di** claim credit for

attri'buto nm attribute. ~**zi'one** nf attribution

at'trice nf actress

at'trito nm friction

attu'abile a feasible

attu'al|e a present; (di attualità) topical; (effettivo) actual. ~**ità** nf topicality; (avvenimento) news; **programma di** ~**ità** current affairs programme. ~**iz'zare** vt update. ~'**mente** adv at present

attu'a|re vt carry out. ~**rsi** vr be realized. ~**zi'one** nf carrying out

attu'tire vt deaden; ~ **il colpo** soften the blow

au'dac|e a daring, bold; (insolente) audacious;. ~**ia** nf daring, boldness; (insolenza) audacity

'**audience** nf inv (telespettatori) audience

'**audio** nm audio

audiovi'sivo a audiovisual

audi'torio nm auditorium

audizi'one nf audition; Jur hearing

'**auge** nm height; **essere in** ~ be popular

augu'rare vt wish. ~**si** vr hope. **au'gurio** nm wish; (presagio) omen; **auguri!** all the best!; (a Natale) Happy Christmas!; **tanti auguri** best wishes

'**aula** nf classroom; (università) lecture-hall; (sala) hall. ~ **magna** (in università) great hall. ~ **del tribunale** courtroom

aumen'tare vt/i increase. **au'mento** nm increase; (di stipendio) [pay] rise

au'reola nf halo

au'rora nf dawn

auscul'tare vt Med auscultate

ausili'are a & nmf auxiliary

auspicabile *a* è ~ **che...** it is to be hoped that...

auspi'care *vt* hope for

au'spicio *nm* omen; **auspici** (*pl: protezione*) auspices

austerità *nf* austerity

au'stero *a* austere.

Au'stral|ia *nf* Australia. **a~'ano, -a** *a & nmf* Australian

'Austria *nf* Austria. **au'striaco, -a** *a & nmf* Austrian

autar'chia *nf* autarchy. **au'tarchico** *a* autarchic

autenti'c|are *vt* authenticate. **~ità** *nf* authenticity

au'tentico *a* authentic; (*vero*) true

au'tista *nm* driver

'auto *nf inv* car

'auto+ *pref* self+

autoabbron'zante *nm* self-tan ● *a* self-tanning

autoambu'lanza *nf* ambulance

autoartico'lato *nm* articulated lorry

autobio|gra'fia *nf* autobiography. **~'grafico** *a* autobiographical

auto'botte *nf* tanker

'autobus *nm inv* bus

auto'carro *nm* lorry

autocommiserazi'one *nf* self-pity

autoconcessio'nario *nm* car dealer

auto'critica *nf* self-criticism

autodi'datta *nmf* self-educated person, autodidact

autodi'fesa *nf* self-defence

auto'gol *nm inv* own goal

au'tografo *a & nm* autograph

autolesio'nis|mo *nm fig* selfdestruction. **~tico** *a* self-destructive

auto'linea *nf* bus line

au'toma *nm* robot

automatica'mente *adv* automatically

auto'matico *a* automatic ● *nm* (*bottone*) press-stud; (*fucile*) automatic

automatiz'za|re *vt* automate. **~zi'one** *nf* automation

auto'mezzo *nm* motor vehicle

auto'mobi|le *nf* [motor] car. **~'lismo** *nm* motoring. **~'lista** *nmf* motorist. **~'listico** *a* (*industria*) automobile *attrib*

autonoma'mente *adv* autonomously

autono'mia *nf* autonomy; *Auto* range; (*di laptop, cellulare*) battery life. **au'tonomo** *a* autonomous

au'topsia *nf* autopsy

auto'radio *nf inv* car radio; (*veicolo*) radio car

au'tore, -'trice *nmf* author; (*di pittura*) painter; (*di furto ecc*) perpetrator; **quadro d'~** genuine master

auto'revo|le *a* authoritative; (*che ha influenza*) influential. **~'lezza** *nf* authority

autori'messa *nf* garage

autori|tà *nf inv* authority. **~'tario** *a* autocratic. **~ta'rismo** *nm* authoritarianism

autori'tratto *nm* self-portrait

autoriz'za|re *vt* authorize. **~zi'one** *nf* authorization

auto'scontro *nm inv* bumper car

autoscu'ola *nf* driving school

auto'stop *nm inv* hitch-hiking; **fare l'~** hitch-hike. **~'pista** *nmf* hitch-hiker

auto'strada *nf* motorway

autostra'dale *a* motorway *attrib*

autosuffici'en|te *a* self-sufficient. **~za** *nf* self-sufficiency

autotrasporta|'tore, ~'trice *nmf* haulier, carrier

auto'treno *nm* articulated lorry, roadtrain

autove'icolo *nm* motor vehicle

auto'velox *nm inv* speed camera

autovet'tura *nf* motor vehicle

autun'nale *a* autumn[al]

au'tunno *nm* autumn

aval'lare *vt* endorse, back (*cambiale*); *fig* endorse

a'vallo *nm* endorsement

avam'braccio *nm* forearm

avangu'ardia *nf* vanguard; *fig* avant-garde; **essere all'~** be in the forefront; *Techn* be at the leading edge

a'vanti *adv* (*in avanti*) forward; (*davanti*) in front; (*prima*) before; **~!** (*entrate*) come in!; (*suvvia*) come on!; (*su semaforo*) cross now, walk *Am*; **va' ~!** go ahead!; **andare ~** (*precedere*) go ahead; (*orologio:*) be fast; **● e indietro** backwards and forwards ● *a* (*precedente*) before ● *prep* ~ **a** before; (*in presenza di*) in the presence of

avanti'eri *adv* the day before yesterday

avanza'mento *nm* progress; (*promozione*) promotion

avan'za|re *vi* advance; (*progredire*) progress; (*essere d'avanzo*) be left [over] ● *vt* advance; (*superare*) surpass; (*promuovere*) promote. **~rsi** *vr* advance; (*avvicinarsi*) approach. **~ta** *nf* advance. **~to** *a* advanced; (*nella notte*) late; **in età ~ta** elderly. **a'vanzo** nm remainder; Comm surplus; **avanzi** pl ⟨rovine⟩ remains; ⟨di cibo⟩ left-overs

ava'ri|a nf ⟨di motore⟩ engine failure. **~'ato** a ⟨frutta, verdura⟩ rotten; ⟨carne⟩ tainted

ava'rizia nf avarice. **a'varo, -a** a stingy ● nmf miser

a'vena nf oats pl

a'vere vt have; ⟨ottenere⟩ get; ⟨indossare⟩ wear; ⟨provare⟩ feel; **ho trent'anni** I'm thirty; **ha avuto il posto** he got the job; **~ fame/freddo** be hungry/cold; **ho mal di denti** I've got toothache; **cos'ha a che fare con lui?** what has it got to do with him?; **~ da fare** be busy; **che hai?** what's the matter with you?; **nei hai per molto?** will you be long?; **quanti ne abbiamo oggi?** what date is it today?; **avercela con qcno** have it in for sb ● v aux have; **non l'ho visto** I haven't seen him; **lo hai visto?** have you seen him?; **l'ho visto ieri** I saw him yesterday ● nm **averi** pl wealth sg

avia'tore nm flyer, aviator. **~zi'one** nf aviation; Mil Air Force

avidità nf avidness. **'avido** a avid

avio'getto nm jet

'avo, -a nmf ancestor

avo'cado nm inv avocado

a'vorio nm ivory

Avv. abbr avvocato

avva'lersi vr avail oneself (**of** di)

avvalla'mento nm depression

avvalo'rare vt bear out ⟨tesi⟩; endorse ⟨documento⟩; ⟨accrescere⟩ enhance

avvam'pare vi flare up; ⟨arrossire⟩ blush

avvantaggi'ar|e vt favour. **~si** vr **~si di** benefit from; ⟨approfittare⟩ take advantage of

avve'd|ersi vr ⟨accorgersi⟩ notice; ⟨capire⟩ realize. **~uto** a shrewd

avvelena'mento nm poisoning

avvele'na|re vt poison. **~rsi** vr poison oneself. **~to** a poisoned

avve'nente a attractive

avveni'mento nm event

avve'nire[1] vi happen; ⟨aver luogo⟩ take place

avve'ni|re[2] nm future. **~'ristico** a futuristic

avven'ta|rsi vr fling oneself. **~to** a ⟨decisione⟩ rash

av'vento nm advent; Relig Advent

avven'tore nm regular customer

avven'tu|ra nf adventure; ⟨amorosa⟩ affair; **d'~** ⟨film⟩ adventure attrib.

~'rarsi vr venture. **~ri'ero, -a** nm adventurer ● nf adventuress. **~'roso** a adventurous

avve'ra|bile a ⟨previsione⟩ that may come true. **~rsi** vr come true

av'verbio nm adverb

avver'sar|e vt oppose. **~io, -a** a opposing ● nmf opponent

avversi|'one nf aversion. **~tà** nf inv adversity

av'verso a ⟨sfavorevole⟩ adverse; ⟨contrario⟩ averse

avver'tenza nf ⟨cura⟩ care; ⟨avvertimento⟩ warning; ⟨avviso⟩ notice; ⟨premessa⟩ foreword; **avvertenze** pl ⟨istruzioni⟩ instructions

avverti'mento nm warning

avver'tire vt warn; ⟨informare⟩ inform; ⟨sentire⟩ feel

avvez'zar|e vt accustom. **~si** vr accustom oneself. **av'vezzo** a **avvezzo a** used to

avvia'mento nm starting; Comm goodwill

avvi'a|re vt start. **~rsi** vr set out. **~to** a under way; **bene ~to** thriving

avvicenda'mento nm ⟨in agricoltura⟩ rotation; ⟨nel lavoro⟩ replacement

avvicen'darsi vr take turns, alternate

avvicina'mento nm approach

avvici'nar|e vt bring near; approach ⟨persona⟩. **~si** vr come nearer, approach; **~si a** come nearer to, approach

avvi'lente a demoralizing; ⟨umiliante⟩ humiliating

avvili'mento nm despondency; ⟨degradazione⟩ degradation

avvi'li|re vt dishearten; ⟨degradare⟩ degrade. **~rsi** vr lose heart; ⟨degradarsi⟩ degrade oneself. **~to** a disheartened; ⟨degradato⟩ degraded

avvilup'par|e vt envelop. **~si** vr wrap oneself up; ⟨aggrovigliarsi⟩ get entangled

avvinaz'zato a drunk

avvin'cente a ⟨libro ecc⟩ enthralling. **av'vincere** vt enthral

avvinghi'ar|e vt clutch. **~si** vr cling

av'vio nm start-up; **dare l'~ a qcsa** get sth under way; **prendere l'~** get under way

avvi'sare vt inform; ⟨mettere in guardia⟩ warn

av'viso nm notice; ⟨annuncio⟩ announcement; ⟨avvertimento⟩ warning; ⟨pubblicitario⟩ advertisement; **a mio ~**

25 **avvistare | bagnare**

in my opinion. ~ **di garanzia** *Jur noti-
fication that one is to be the subject of a
legal enquiry*
avvi'stare *vt* catch sight of
avvi'tare *vt* screw in; screw down
‹*coperchio*›
avviz'zire *vi* wither
avvo'ca|to *nm* lawyer; *fig* advocate.
~'**tura** *nf* legal profession
av'volger|e *vt* wrap [up]. ~**si** *vr* wrap
oneself up
avvol'gibile *nm* roller blind
avvol'toio *nm* vulture
aza'lea *nf* azalea
azi'en|da *nf* business, firm. ~ **agrico-
la** farm. ~ **di soggiorno** tourist
bureau. ~'**dale** *a* ‹*politica, dirigente*›
company *attrib*; ‹*giornale*› in-house

aziona'mento *nm* operation
azio'nare *vt* operate
azio'nario *a* share *attrib*
azi'one *nf* action; *Fin* share; **d'~** ‹*romanzo, film*› action[-packed]. **azio'nista** *nmf* shareholder
a'zoto *nm* nitrogen
azzan'nare *vt* seize with its teeth;
sink its teeth into ‹*gamba*›
azzar'd|are *vt* risk. ~**arsi** *vr* dare.
~**ato** *a* risky; ‹*precipitoso*› rash. **az-
'zardo** *nm* hazard; **gioco d'azzardo**
game of chance
azzec'care *vt* hit; ‹*fig: indovinare*›
guess
azzuf'farsi *vr* come to blows
az'zur|ro *a & nm* blue; **il principe ~**
Prince Charming. ~'**rognolo** *a* bluish

Bb

bab'beo *a* foolish ●*nm* idiot
'**babbo** *nm fam* dad, daddy. **B~ Natale**
Father Christmas
bab'buccia *nf* slipper
babbu'ino *nm* baboon
ba'bordo *nm Naut* port side
'**babysitter** *nmf inv* baby-sitter; **fare
la ~** babysit
ba'cato *a* wormeaten
'**bacca** *nf* berry
baccalà *nm inv* dried salted cod
bac'cano *nm* din
bac'cello *nm* pod
bac'chetta *nf* rod; ‹*magica*› wand; ‹*di
direttore d'orchestra*› baton; ‹*di tamburo*› drumstick
ba'checa *nf* showcase; ‹*in ufficio*› notice board. ~ **elettronica** *Comput* bulletin board
bacia'mano *nm* kiss on the hand;
fare il ~ a qcno kiss sb's hand
baci'ar|e *vt* kiss. ~**si** *vr* kiss [each
other]
ba'cillo *nm* bacillus
baci'nella *nf* basin
ba'cino *nm* basin; *Anat* pelvis; ‹*di
porto*› dock; ‹*di minerali*› field
'**bacio** *nm* kiss
'**baco** *nm* worm. ~ **da seta** silkworm

ba'cucco *a* **un vecchio ~** a senile old
man
'**bada** *nf* **tenere qcno a ~** keep sb at
bay
ba'dare *vi* take care (**a** of); ‹*fare attenzione*› look out; **bada ai fatti tuoi!**
mind your own business!
ba'dia *nf* abbey
ba'dile *nm* shovel
'**badminton** *nm* badminton
'**baffi** *nmpl* moustache *sg*; ‹*di animale*›
whiskers; **mi fa un baffo** I don't give a
damn; **ridere sotto i ~** laugh up one's
sleeve
baf'futo *a* moustached
ba'gagli *nmpl* luggage, baggage. ~'**aio**
nm Rail luggage van; *Auto* boot
ba'gaglio *nm* luggage; **un ~** a piece of
luggage. ~ **a mano** hand luggage, hand
baggage
baggia'nata *nf* **non dire
baggianate** don't talk nonsense
bagli'ore *nm* glare; ‹*improvviso*› flash;
‹*fig: di speranza*› glimmer
ba'gnante *nmf* bather
ba'gna|re *vt* wet; ‹*inzuppare*› soak;
‹*immergere*› dip; ‹*innaffiare*› water;
‹*mare, lago:*› wash; ‹*fiume:*› flow
through. ~**rsi** *vr* get wet; ‹*al mare ecc*›
swim, bathe

bagnasci'uga *nm inv* edge of the water, waterline

ba'gnato *a* wet

ba'gnino, -a *nmf* life guard

'**bagno** *nm* bath; (*stanza*) bathroom; (*gabinetto*) toilet; (*in casa*) toilet, bathroom; (*al mare*) swim, bathe; **bagni** *pl* (*stabilimento*) lido; **fare il ~** have a bath; (*nel mare ecc*) [have a] swim *or* bathe; **andare in ~** go to the bathroom *or* toilet; **mettere a ~** soak. **~ turco** Turkish bath

bagnoma'ria *nm* **cuocere a ~** cook in a double saucepan

bagnoschi'uma *nm inv* bubble bath

'**baia** *nf* bay

baio'netta *nf* bayonet

'**baita** *nf* mountain chalet

bala'ustra, balaus'trata *nf* balustrade

balbet't|are *vt/i* stammer; (*bambino:*) babble. **~io** *nm* stammering; babble

bal'buzi|e *nf* stutter. **~'ente** *a* stuttering ● *nmf* stutterer

Bal'can|i *nmpl* Balkans. **b~ico** *a* Balkan

balco'nata *nf* *Theat* balcony, dress circle

balcon'cino *nm* **reggiseno a ~** underwired bra

bal'cone *nm* balcony

baldac'chino *nm* canopy; **letto a ~** four-poster bed

bal'dan|za *nf* boldness. **~'zoso** *a* bold

bal'doria *nf* revelry; **far ~** have a riotous time

Bale'ari *nfpl* **le [isole] ~** the Balearics, the Balearic Islands

ba'lena *nf* whale

bale'nare *vi* lighten; *fig* flash; **mi è balenata un'idea** I've just had an idea

bale'niera *nf* whaler

ba'leno *nm* **in un ~** in a flash

ba'lera *nf* dance hall

'**balia** *nf* wetnurse

ba'lia *nf* **in ~ di** at the mercy of

ba'listico *a* ballistic; **perito ~** ballistics expert

'**balla** *nf* bale; (*fam: frottola*) tall story

bal'labile *a* good for dancing to

bal'la|re *vi* dance. **~ta** *nf* ballad

balla'toio *nm* (*nelle scale*) landing

balle'rino, -a *nmf* dancer; (*classico*) ballet dancer; **ballerina** (*classica*) ballet dancer, ballerina

bal'letto *nm* ballet

bal'lista *nmf fam* bull-shitter

'**ballo** *nm* dance; (*il ballare*) dancing;

---

sala da ~ ballroom; **essere in ~** (*lavoro, vita:*) be committed; **tirare qcno in ~** involve sb

ballonzo'lare *vi* skip about

ballot'taggio *nm* second count (*of votes*)

balne'a|re *a* bathing *attrib.* **stagione ~** swimming season. **stazione ~** seaside resort. **~zi'one** *nf* è **vietata la ~zione** no swimming

ba'lordo *a* foolish; (*stordito*) stunned; **tempo ~** nasty weather

'**balsamo** *nm* balsam; (*per capelli*) conditioner; (*lenimento*) remedy

'**baltico** *a* Baltic. **il [mar] B~** the Baltic [Sea]

balu'ardo *nm* bulwark

'**balza** *nf* crag; (*di abito*) flounce

bal'zano *a* (*idea*) weird

bal'zare *vi* bounce; (*saltare*) jump; **~ in piedi** leap to one's feet. '**balzo** *nm* bounce; (*salto*) jump; **prendere la palla al balzo** seize an opportunity

bam'bagia *nf* cotton wool; **vivere nella ~** *fig* be in clover

bambi'nata *nf* childish thing to do/ say

bam'bi|no, -a *nmf* child; (*appena nato*) baby; **avere un ~no** have a baby. **~'none, -a** *nmf pej* overgrown child

bam'boccio *nm* chubby child; (*sciocco*) simpleton; (*fantoccio*) rag doll

'**bambo|la** *nf* doll. **~'lotto** *nm* male doll

bambù *nm* bamboo

ba'nal|e *a* banal; **~ità** *nf inv* banality; **~iz'zare** *vt* trivialize

ba'nan|a *nf* banana. **~o** *nm* banana-tree

'**banca** *nf* bank. **~ [di] dati** databank

banca'rella *nf* stall

ban'cario, -a *a* banking *attrib*; **trasferimento ~** bank transfer ● *nmf* bank employee

banca'rotta *nf* bankruptcy; **fare ~** go bankrupt

banchet'tare *vi* banquet. **ban'chetto** *nm* banquet

banchi'ere *nm* banker

ban'china *nf* *Naut* quay; (*in stazione*) platform; (*di strada*) path; **~ non transitabile** soft verge

ban'chisa *nf* floe

'**banco** *nm* (*di scuola*) desk; (*di negozio*) counter; (*di officina*) bench; (*di gioco, banca*) bank; (*di mercato*) stall; (*degli imputati*) dock; **sotto ~** under the counter; **medicinale da ~** over the

counter medicines. ~ **informazioni** information desk. ~ **di nebbia** fog bank
bancomat® *nm inv* autobank, cashpoint; *(carta)* bank card, cash card
ban'cone *nm* counter; *(in bar)* bar
banco'nota *nf* banknote, bill *Am*; **banco'note** *pl* paper currency
banda *nf* band; *(di delinquenti)* gang. ~ **d'atterraggio** *Aeron* landing strip. ~ **rumorosa** rumble strip
banderu'ola *nf* weathercock; *Naut* pennant
bandi'e|ra *nf* flag; **cambiare** ~**ra** change sides, switch allegiances. ~**'rina** *nf (nel calcio)* corner flag. ~**'rine** *pl* bunting *sg*
ban'di|re *vt* banish; *(pubblicare)* publish; *fig* dispense with *(formalità, complimenti)*. ~**to** *nm* bandit. ~**'tore** *nm (di aste)* auctioneer
bando *nm* proclamation; ~ **di concorso** job advertisement *(published in an official gazette for a job for which a competitive examination has to be taken)*
bar *nm inv* bar
bara *nf* coffin
ba'rac|ca *nf* hut; *(catapecchia)* hovel; **mandare avanti la** ~**ca** keep the ship afloat. ~**'cato** *nm* person living in a makeshift shelter. ~**'chino** *nm (di gelati, giornali)* kiosk; *Radio* CB radio. ~**'cone** *nm (roulotte)* circus caravan; *(in luna park)* booth. ~**'copoli** *nf inv* shanty town
bara'onda *nf* chaos; **non fare** ~ don't make a mess
ba'rare *vi* cheat
bar'atro *nm* chasm
barat'tare *vt* barter. **ba'ratto** *nm* barter
ba'rattolo *nm* jar; *(di latta)* tin
barba *nf* beard; *(fam: noia)* bore; **farsi la** ~ shave; **è una** ~ *(noia)* it's boring
barbabi'etola *nf* beetroot. ~ **da zucchero** sugar-beet
bar'barico *a* barbaric. **bar'barie** *nf* barbarity. **barbaro** *a* barbarous ●*nm* barbarian
barbecue *nm inv* barbecue
barbi'ere *nm* barber; *(negozio)* barber's
barbi'turico *nm* barbiturate
bar'bone *nm (vagabondo)* vagrant; *(cane)* poodle
bar'boso *a fam* boring
barbu'gliare *vi* mumble
bar'buto *a* bearded

barca *nf* boat; **una** ~ **di** *fig* a lot of. ~ **a motore** motorboat. ~ **da pesca** fishing boat. ~ **a remi** rowing boat, rowboat *Am*. ~ **di salvataggio** lifeboat. ~ **a vela** sailing boat, sailboat *Am*. ~**i'olo** *nm* boatman
barcame'narsi *vr* manage
barcol'lare *vi* stagger
bar'cone *nm* barge; *(di ponte)* pontoon
bar'dar|e *vt* harness. ~**si** *vr hum* dress up
ba'rel|la *nf* stretcher. ~**li'ere** *nm* stretcher-bearer
'Barents: il mare di ~ the Barents Sea
bari'centro *nm* centre of gravity
ba'ri|le *nm* barrel. ~**'lotto** *nm fig* tub of lard
ba'rista *nm* barman ● *nf* barmaid
ba'ritono *nm* baritone
bar'lume *nm* glimmer; **un** ~ **di speranza** a glimmer of hope
barman *nm inv* barman
baro *nm* cardsharper
ba'rocco *a & nm* baroque
ba'rometro *nm* barometer
ba'rone *nm* baron; **i baroni** *fig* the top brass. **baro'nessa** *nf* baroness
barra *nf* bar; *(lineetta)* oblique; *Naut* tiller. ~ **spazio** *Comput* space bar. ~ **strumenti** *Comput* tool bar
bar'rare *vt* block off *(strada)*
barri'ca|re *vt* barricade. ~**ta** *nf* barricade
barri'era *nf* barrier; *(stradale)* roadblock; *Geol* reef. ~ **razziale** colour bar
bar'ri|re *vi* trumpet. ~**to** *nm* trumpeting
barzel'letta *nf* joke; ~ **sporca** *o* **spinta** dirty joke
basa'mento *nm* base
ba'sar|e *vt* base. ~**si** *vr* ~**si su** be based on; **mi baso su ciò che ho visto** I'm going on [the basis of] what I saw
basco, -a *nmf & a* Basque ●*nm (copricapo)* beret
base *nf* basis; *(fondamento)* foundation; *Mil* base; *Pol* rank and file; **a** ~ **di** containing; **in** ~ **a** on the basis of. ~ **dati** database
baseball *nm* baseball
ba'setta *nf* sideburn
basi'lare *a* basic
ba'silica *nf* basilica
ba'silico *nm* basil
ba'sista *nm* grass roots politician; *(di un crimine)* mastermind
basket *nm* basketball

bas'sezza *nf* lowness; *(di statura)* shortness; *(viltà)* vileness

bas'sista *nmf* bassist

'**basso** *a* low; *(di statura)* short; *(acqua)* shallow; *(televisione)* quiet; *(vile)* despicable; **parlare a bassa voce** speak quietly, speak in a low voice; **la bassa Italia** southern Italy ● *nm* lower part; *Mus* bass. **guardare in ~** look down

basso'fondo *nm* (*pl* **bassi'fondi**) shallows *pl*; **bassifondi** *pl* *(quartieri poveri)* slums

bassorili'evo *nm* bas-relief

bas'sotto *nm* dachshund

ba'stardo, -a *a* bastard; *(di animale)* mongrel ● *nmf* bastard; *(animale)* mongrel

ba'stare *vi* be enough; *(durare)* last; **basta!** that's enough!, that'll do!; **basta che** (*purché*) provided that; **basta così** that's enough; **basta così?** is that enough?, will that do?; *(in negozio)* will there be anything else?; **basta andare alla posta** you only have to go to the post office

Basti'an con'trario *nm* contrary old so-and-so

basti'one *nm* bastion

basto'nare *vt* beat

baston'cino *nm* (*da sci*) ski pole. **~ di pesce** fish finger, fish stick *Am*

ba'stone *nm* stick; *(da golf)* club; *(da passeggio)* walking stick

ba'tosta *nf* blow

bat'tagli|a *nf* battle; *(lotta)* fight. **~'are** *vi* battle; *fig* fight

bat'taglio *nm* (*di campana*) clapper; *(di porta)* knocker

battagli'one *nm* battalion

bat'tello *nm* boat; *(motonave)* steamer

bat'tente *nm* (*di porta*) wing; *(di finestra*) shutter; *(battaglio)* knocker

'**batter|e** *vt* beat; *(percorrere)* scour; thresh *(grano)*; break *(record)* ● *vi* (*bussare, urtare*) knock; *(cuore:)* beat; *(ali ecc:)* flap; *Tennis* serve; **~e a macchina** type; **~e gli occhi** blink; **~e le mani** clap [one's hands]; **~e le ore** strike the hours. **~si** *vr* fight

bat'teri *nmpl* bacteria

batte'ria *nf* battery; *Mus* drums *pl*

bat'terio *nm* bacterium. **~'logico** *a* bacteriological

batte'rista *nmf* drummer

bat'tesimo *nm* baptism, christening

battez'zare *vt* baptize, christen

battiba'leno *nm* **in un ~** in a flash

batti'becco *nm* squabble

batticu'ore *nm* palpitation; **mi venne il ~** I was scared

bat'tigia *nf* water's edge

batti'mano *nm* applause

batti'panni *nm inv* carpetbeater

batti'stero *nm* baptistery

batti'strada *nm inv* outrider; *(di pneumatico)* tread; S*port* pacesetter

battitap'peto *nm inv* carpet sweeper

'**battito** *nm* (*del cuore*) [heart]beat; *(alle tempie)* throbbing; *(di orologio)* ticking; *(della pioggia)* beating

bat'tuta *nf* beat; *(colpo)* knock; *(spiritosaggine)* wisecrack; *(osservazione)* remark; *Mus* bar; *Tennis* service; *Theat* cue; *(dattilografia)* stroke

ba'tuffolo *nm* flock

ba'ule *nm* trunk

'**bava** *nf* dribble; *(di cane ecc)* slobber; **aver la ~ alla bocca** foam at the mouth

bava'glino *nm* bib

ba'vaglio *nm* gag

'**bavero** *nm* collar

ba'zar *nm inv* bazaar

baz'zecola *nf* trifle

bazzi'care *vt/i* haunt

be'arsi *vr* delight (**di** in)

beati'tudine *nf* bliss. **be'ato** *a* blissful; *Relig* blessed; **beato te!** lucky you!

beauty-'case *nm inv* toilet bag

bebè *nm inv* baby

bec'caccia *nf* woodcock

bec'ca|re *vt* peck; *fig* catch. **~rsi** *vr* *(litigare)* quarrel. **~ta** *nf* peck

beccheggi'are *vi* pitch

bec'chino *nm* grave-digger

'**bec|co** *nm* beak; *(di caffettiera ecc)* spout. **~'cuccio** *nm* spout

be'fana *nf* Epiphany; *(donna brutta)* old witch

'**beffa** *nf* hoax; **farsi beffe di qcno** mock sb. **bef'fardo** *a* derisory; *(persona)* mocking

bef'far|e *vt* mock. **~si** *vr* **~si di** make fun of

'**bega** *nf* quarrel; **è una bella ~** it's really annoying

be'gonia *nf* begonia

'**beige** *a & nm* beige

be'la|re *vi* bleat. **~to** *nm* bleating

'**belga** *a & nmf* Belgian

'**Belgio** *nm* Belgium

'**bella** *nf* *(in carte, Sport)* decider

bel'lezza *nf* beauty; **che ~!** how lovely!; **chiudere/finire in ~** end on a high note 'belli|co *a* war *attrib.* ~'coso *a* war-like.~ge'rante *a* & *nmf* belligerent

'bello *a* nice; (*di aspetto*) beautiful; (*uomo*) handsome; (*moralmente*) good; **cosa fai di ~ stasera?** what are you up to tonight?;**oggi fa ~** it's a nice day; **una bella cifra** a lot;**un bel piatto di pasta** a big plate of pasta; **nel bel mezzo** right in the middle; **un bel niente** absolutely nothing;**bell'e fatto** over and done with;**bell'amico!** [a] fine friend he is/you are!;**questa è bella!** that's a good one!; **scamparla bella** have a narrow escape ● *nm* (*bellezza*) beauty; (*innamorato*) sweetheart; **sul più ~** at the crucial moment; **il ~ è che...** the funny thing is that...

'belva *nf* wild beast

be'molle *nm Mus* flat

ben *vedi* bene

benché *conj* though, although

'benda *nf* bandage; (*per occhi*) blindfold. ben'dare *vt* bandage; blindfold (*occhi*)

'bene *adv* well; **ben ~** thoroughly; ~! good!; **star ~** (*di salute*) be well; (*vestito, stile:*) suit; (*finanziariamente*) be well off; **non sta ~** (*non è educato*) it's not nice; **sta/va ~!** all right!; **ti sta ~!** [it] serves you right!; **ti auguro ~** I wish you well; **di ~ in meglio** better and better; **fare ~** (*aver ragione*) do the right thing;**fare ~ a** (*cibo:*) be good for; **una persona per ~** a good person; **per ~** (*fare*) properly; **è ben difficile** it's very difficult; **come tu ben sai** as you well know; **lo credo ~!** I can well believe it! ● *nm* good; **per il tuo ~** for your own good. beni *nmpl* (*averi*) property *sg*; **un ~ di famiglia** a family heirloom

bene'detto *a* blessed

bene'di|re *vt* bless. ~zi'one *nf* blessing

benedu'cato *a* well-mannered

benefat|'tore, -'trice *nm* benefactor ● *nf* benefactress

benefi'care *vt* help

benefi'cenza *nf* charity

benefici'ar|e *vi* ~e **di** profit by. ~io, -a *a* & *nmf* beneficiary. bene'ficio *nm* benefit. be'nefico *a* beneficial; (*di beneficenza*) charitable

bene'placito *nm* consent, approval

be'nessere *nm* well-being

bene'stante *a* well-off ● *nmf* well-off person

bene'stare *nm* consent

benevo'lenza *nf* benevolence. be'nevolo *a* benevolent

ben'fatto *a* well-made

'beni *nmpl* property *sg*; *Fin* assets;**~ di consumo** consumer goods

benia'mino *nm* favourite

be'nigno *a* kindly; *Med* benign

beninfor'mato *a* well-informed

benintenzio'nato, -a *a* well-meaning ● *nmf* well-meaning person

benin'teso *adv* needless to say, of course

benpen'sante *a* & *nmf* self-righteous

benser'vito *nm*dare **il ~ a** qcno give sb the sack

ben'sì *conj* but rather

benve'nuto *a* & *nm* welcome

ben'visto *a* **essere ~** go down well (**da** with)

benvo'lere *vt* farsi **~ da** qcno win sb's affection; **prendere** qcno **in ~** take a liking to sb; **essere benvoluto da tutti** to be well-liked by everyone

ben'zina *nf* petrol, gas *Am*; **far ~** get petrol. **~ verde** unleaded petrol. benzi-'naio, -a *nmf* petrol station attendant

'bere *vt* drink; (*assorbire*) absorb; *fig* swallow ● *nm* drinking; (*bevande*) drinks *pl*

berga'motto *nm* bergamot

ber'lina *nf Auto* saloon

Ber'lino *nm* Berlin

ber'muda *nfpl* (*pantaloni*) Bermuda shorts

ber'noccolo *nm* bump; (*disposizione*) flair

ber'retto *nm* beret, cap

bersagli'are *vt fig* bombard. ber-'saglio *nm* target

be'stemmi|a *nf* swear-word; (*maledizione*) oath; (*sproposito*) blasphemy. ~'are *vi* swear

'besti|a *nf* animal; (*persona brutale*) beast; (*persona sciocca*) fool; **andare in ~a** *fam* blow one's top. ~'ale *a* bestial; (*espressione, violenza*) brutal; (*fam: freddo, fame*) terrible. ~a'lità *nf inv* bestiality; *fig* nonsense. ~'ame *nm* livestock

'bettola *nf fig* dive

be'tulla *nf* birch

be'vanda *nf* drink

bevi|'tore, -'trice *nmf* drinker

be'vut|a *nf* drink. ~o *pp di* bere

bi'ada *nf* fodder

bianche'ria *nf* linen. **~ intima** underwear

bi'anco *a* white; (*foglio, pagina*) blank

●*nm* white; **mangiare in** ~ not eat fried or heavy foods; **andare in** ~ *fam* not score; **in** ~ **e nero** ⟨*film, fotografia*⟩ black and white, monochrome; **passare una notte in** ~ have a sleepless night

bian'core *nm* (*bianchezza*) whiteness

bianco'spino *nm* hawthorn

biasci'care *vt* (*mangiare*) eat noisily; (*parlare*) mumble

biasi'mare *vt* blame. **bi'asimo** *nm* blame

'Bibbia *nf* Bible

bibe'ron *nm inv* [baby's] bottle

'bibita *nf* [soft] drink

'biblico *a* biblical

bibliogra'fia *nf* bibliography

biblio'te|ca *nf* library; (*mobile*) bookcase. ~'**cario, -a** *nmf* librarian

bicarbo'nato *nm* bicarbonate. ~ **di sodio** bicarbonate of soda

bicchi'ere *nm* glass

bicchie'rino *nm fam* tipple

bici'cletta *nf* bicycle; **andare in** ~ ride a bicycle

bico'lore *a* two-coloured

bidè *nm inv* bidet

bi'dello, -a *nmf* janitor, [school] caretaker

bido'nata *nf fam* swindle

bi'done *nm* bin; (*fam: truffa*) swindle; **fare un** ~ **a qcno** *fam* stand sb up

bien'nale *a* biennial

bi'ennio *nm* two-year period

bi'etola *nf* beet

bifo'cale *a* bifocal

bi'folco, -a *nmf fig* boor

bifor'c|arsi *vr* fork. ~**azi'one** *nf* fork. ~**uto** *a* forked

biga'mia *nf* bigamy. **'bigamo, -a** *a* bigamous ●*nmf* bigamist

bighello'nare *vi* loaf around. **bighel'lone** *nm* loafer

bigiotte'ria *nf* costume jewellery; (*negozio*) jeweller's

bigliet't|aio *nm* booking clerk; (*sui treni*) ticket-collector. ~**e'ria** *nf* ticket-office; *Theat* box-office

bigli'et|to *nm* ticket; (*lettera breve*) note; (*cartoncino*) card; (*di banca*) banknote. ~**to da visita** business card. ~'**tone** *nm* (*fam: soldi*) big one

bignè *nm inv* cream puff

bigo'dino *nm* roller

bi'gotto *nm* bigot

bi'kini *nm inv* bikini

bi'lanc|ia *nf* scales *pl*; (*di orologio, Comm*) balance. **B**~**a** *Astr* Libra. ~'**are**

vt balance; *fig* weigh. ~**o** *nm* budget; *Comm* balance sheet; **fare il** ~**o** balance the books; *fig* take stock

'bile *nf* bile; *fig* rage

bili'ardo *nm* billiards *sg*

'bilico *nm* equilibrium; **in** ~ in the balance

bi'lingue *a* bilingual

bili'one *nm* billion

bilo'cale *a* two-room

'bimbo, -a *nmf* child

bimen'sile *a* fortnightly

bime'strale *a* bimonthly

bi'nario *nm* track; (*piattaforma*) platform

bi'nocolo *nm* binoculars *pl*

bio'chimica *nf* biochemistry

biodegra'dabile *a* biodegradable

bio'etica *nf* bioethics

bio'fisica *nf* biophysics

biogra'fia *nf* biography. **bio'grafico** *a* biographical. **bi'ografo, -a** *nmf* biographer

biolo'gia *nf* biology. **bio'logico** *a* biological. **bi'ologo, -a** *nmf* biologist

bi'ond|a *nf* blonde. ~**o** *a* blond ●*nm* fair colour; (*uomo*) fair-haired man

bio'sfera *nf* biosphere

bi'ossido *nm* ~ **di carbonio** carbon dioxide

biparti'tismo *nm* two-party system

'birba *nf*, **bir'bante** *nm* rascal, rogue. **bir'bone** *a* wicked

biri'chino, -a *a* naughty ●*nmf* little devil

bi'rillo *nm* skittle

'birr|a *nf* beer; **a tutta** ~**a** *fig* flat out. ~**a chiara** lager. ~**a scura** brown ale. ~**e'ria** *nf* beer-house; (*fabbrica*) brewery

bis *nm inv* encore

bi'saccia *nf* haversack

bi'sbetic|a *nf* shrew. ~**o** *a* bad-tempered

bisbigli'are *vt/i* whisper. **bi'sbiglio** *nm* whisper

'bisca *nf* gambling-house

'biscia *nf* snake

bi'scotto *nm* biscuit

bisessu'ale *a & nmf* bisexual

bise'stile *a* **anno** ~ leap year

bisetti'ma'nale *a* fortnightly

bi'slacco *a* peculiar

bis'nonno, -a *nmf* great-grandfather; great-grandmother

biso'gn|are *vi* ~**a agire subito** we must act at once; ~**a farlo** it is necessary to do it; **non** ~**a venire** you don't

bi'sonte *nm* bison
bi'stecca *nf* steak
bisticci'are *vi* quarrel. bi'sticcio *nm* quarrel; (*gioco di parole*) pun
bistrat'tare *vt* mistreat
'bisturi *nm inv* scalpel
bi'torzolo *nm* lump
'bitter *nm inv* (*bitter*) aperitif
bi'vacco *nm* bivouac
'bivio *nm* crossroads; (*di strada*) fork
bizan'tino *a* Byzantine
'bizza *nf* tantrum; fare le bizze *(bambini:)* play up
biz'zarro *a* bizarre
biz'zeffe *adv* a ~ galore
blan'dire *vt* soothe; (*allettare*) flatter.
'blando *a* mild
bla'sone *nm* coat of arms
blate'rare *vi* blether, blather
'blatta *nf* cockroach
blin'dare *vt* armour-plate. ~to *a* armoured
blitz *nm inv* blitz
bloc'care *vt* block; (*isolare*) cut off; *Mil* blockade; *Comm* freeze. ~si *vr Mech* jam
blocca'sterzo *nm* steering lock
'blocco *nm* block; *Mil* blockade; (*dei fitti*) restriction; (*di carta*) pad; (*unione*) coalition; in ~ *Comm* in bulk. ~ stradale road-block
bloc'notes *nm inv* writing pad
blu *a & nm* blue
blue-'jeans *nmpl* jeans
'bluff *nm inv* (*carte, fig*) bluff. bluf'fare *vi* (*carte, fig*) bluff
'blusa *nf* blouse
'boa *nm* boa [constrictor]; (*sciarpa*) [feather] boa ● *nf Naut* buoy
bo'ato *nm* rumbling
bo'bina *nf* spool; (*di film*) reel; *Electr* coil
'bocca *nf* mouth; a ~ aperta *fig* dumbfounded; in ~ al lupo! break a leg!; fare la respirazione ~ a ~ a qcno give sb mouth to mouth resuscitation *or* the kiss of life
boc'caccia *nf* grimace; far boc-cacce make faces
boc'caglio *nm* nozzle
boc'cale *nm* jug; (*da birra*) tankard
bocca'porto *nm Naut* hatch
boc'cata *nf* (*di fumo*) puff; prendere una ~ d'aria get a breath of fresh air

boc'cetta *nf* small bottle
boccheggi'are *vi* gasp
boc'chino *nm* cigarette holder; (*di pipa, Mus*) mouthpiece
'boccia *nf* (*palla*) bowl; ~e *pl* (*gioco*) bowls *sg*
bocci'are *vt* (*agli esami*) fail; (*respin-gere*) reject; (*alle bocce*) hit; essere ~to fail; (*ripetere*) repeat a year. ~'tura *nf* failure
bocci'olo *nm* bud
boccon'cino *nm* morsel
boc'cone *nm* mouthful; (*piccolo pasto*) snack
boc'coni *adv* face downwards
'boia *nm* executioner
boi'ata *nf fam* rubbish
boicot'tare *vt* boycott
bo'lero *nm* bolero
'bolgia *nf* (*caos*) bedlam
'bolide *nm* meteor; passare come un ~ shoot past [like a rocket]
Bo'livia *nf* Bolivia. b~'ano, -a *a & nmf* Bolivian
'bolla *nf* bubble; (*pustola*) blister
bol'lare *vt* stamp; *fig* brand. ~to *a fig* branded; carta ~ta *paper with stamp showing payment of duty*
bol'lente *a* boiling [hot]
bol'let|ta *nf* bill; essere in ~ta be hard up. ~'tino *nm* bulletin; *Comm* list
bol'lino *nm* coupon
bol'li|re *vt/i* boil. ~to *nm* boiled meat. ~'tore *nm* boiler; (*per l'acqua*) kettle. ~'tura *nf* boiling
'bollo *nm* stamp
bol'lore *nm* boil; (*caldo*) intense heat; *fig* ardour
'bomba *nf* bomb; a prova di ~ bomb-proof
bombarda'mento *nm* shelling; (*con aerei*) bombing; *fig* bombardment. ~ aereo air raid
bombar'd|are *vt* shell; (*con aerei*) bomb; *fig* bombard. ~i'ere *nm* bomber
bom'betta *nf* bowler [hat]
'bombola *nf* cylinder. ~ di gas gas bottle, gas cylinder
bombo'lone *nm* doughnut
bomboni'era *nf* wedding keep-sake
bo'naccia *nf Naut* calm
bonacci'one, -a *nmf* good-natured person● *a* good-natured
bo'nario *a* kindly
bo'nifica *nf* land reclamation. bonifi-'care *vt* reclaim
bo'nifico *nm Comm* discount; (*banca-rio*) [credit] transfer

bontà *nf* goodness; (*gentilezza*) kindness

'**bora** *nf* bora (*cold north-east wind in the upper Adriatic*)

borbot't|are *vi* mumble; (*stomaco:*) rumble. **~io** *nm* mumbling; (*di stomaco*) rumbling

'**borchi|a** *nf* stud. **~'ato** *a* studded

bor'da|re *vt* border. **~'tura** *nf* border

bor'deaux *a inv* (*colore*) claret

bor'dello *nm* brothel; *fig* bedlam; (*disordine*) mess

'**bordo** *nm* border; (*estremità*) edge; **a ~** *Naut, Aeron* on board

bor'gata *nf* hamlet

bor'ghese *a* bourgeois; (*abito*) civilian; **in ~** in civilian dress; (*poliziotto*) in plain clothes

borghe'sia *nf* middle classes *pl*

'**borgo** *nm* village; (*quartiere*) district

'**bori|a** *nf* conceit. **~'oso** *a* conceited

bor'lotto *nm* [**fagiolo**] **~** borlotto bean

boro'talco *nm* talcum powder

bor'raccia *nf* flask

'**bors|a** *nf* bag; (*borsetta*) handbag; (*valori*) Stock Exchange. **~a dell'acqua calda** hot-water bottle. **~a frigo** coolbox. **~a della spesa** shopping bag. **~a di studio** scholarship. **~ai'olo** *nm* pickpocket. **~el'lino** *nm* purse. **~'sista** *nmf Fin* speculator; *Sch* scholarship holder

bor'se|llo *nm* (*portamonete*) purse; (*borsetto*) man's handbag. **~tta** *nf* handbag. **~tto** *nm* man's handbag

bo'scaglia *nf* woodlands *pl*

boscai'olo *nm* woodman; (*guardaboschi*) forester

'**bosco** *nm* wood. **bo'scoso** *a* wooded

'**bossolo** *nm* cartridge case

bo'tanic|a *nf* botany. **~o** *a* botanical ● *nm* botanist

botola *nf* trapdoor

'**botta** *nf* blow; (*rumore*) bang; **fare a botte** come to blows. **~ e risposta** *fig* thrust and counter-thrust

'**botte** *nf* barrel

bot'te|ga *nf* shop; (*di artigiano*) workshop. **~'gaio, -a** *nmf* shopkeeper. **~'ghino** *nm Theatr* box-office; (*del lotto*) lottery-shop

bot'tigli|a *nf* bottle; **in ~a** bottled. **~e'ria** *nf* wine shop

bot'tino *nm* loot; *Mil* booty

'**botto** *nm* bang; **di ~** all of a sudden

bot'tone *nm* button; *Bot* bud

bo'vino *a* bovine; **bovini** *pl* cattle

box *nm inv* (*per cavalli*) loosebox; (*recinto per bambini*) play-pen

'**boxe** *nf* boxing

'**bozza** *nf* draft; *Typ* proof; (*bernoccolo*) bump. **boz'zetto** *nm* sketch

'**bozzolo** *nm* cocoon

brac'care *vt* hunt

brac'cetto *nm* **a ~** arm in arm

bracci'a|le *nm* bracelet; (*fascia*) armband. **~'letto** *nm* bracelet; (*di orologio*) watch-strap

bracci'ante *nm* day labourer

bracci'ata *nf* (*nel nuoto*) stroke

'**bracci|o** *nm* (*pl nf* **braccia**) arm; (*di fiume, pl* **bracci**) arm. **~'olo** *nm* (*di sedia*) arm[rest]; (*da nuoto*) armband

'**bracco** *nm* hound

bracconi'ere *nm* poacher

'**brac|e** *nf* embers *pl*; **alla ~e** chargrilled. **~i'ere** *nm* brazier. **~'ola** *nf* chop

'**brado** *a* **allo stato ~** in the wild

'**brama** *nf* longing. **bra'mare** *vt* long for. **bramo'sia** *nf* yearning

'**branca** *nf* branch

'**branchia** *nf* gill

'**branco** *nm* (*di cani*) pack; (*pej: di persone*) gang

branco'lare *vi* grope

'**branda** *nf* camp-bed

bran'dello *nm* scrap; **a brandelli** in tatters

bran'dire *vt* brandish

'**brano** *nm* piece; (*di libro*) passage

Bra'sil|e *nm* Brazil. **b~i'ano, -a** *a & nmf* Brazilian

bra'vata *nf* bragging

'**bravo** *a* good; (*abile*) clever; (*coraggioso*) brave; **~!** well done!. **bra'vura** *nf* skill

'**breccia** *nf* breach; **sulla ~** *fig* very successful, at the top

bre'saola *nf dried, salted beef sliced thinly and eaten cold*

bre'tella *nf* shoulder-strap; **bretelle** *pl* (*di calzoni*) braces

'**breve** *a* brief, short; **in ~** briefly; **tra ~** shortly

brevet'tare *vt* patent. **bre'vetto** *nm* patent; (*attestato*) licence

brevità *nf* shortness

'**brezza** *nf* breeze

'**bricco** *nm* jug

bric'cone *nm* blackguard; *hum* rascal

'**briciol|a** *nf* crumb; *fig* grain. **~o** *nm* fragment

'**briga** *nf* (*fastidio*) trouble; (*lite*) quarrel; **attaccar ~** pick a quarrel;

prendersi la ~ di fare qcsa go to the trouble of doing sth
brigadi'ere *nm (dei carabinieri)* sergeant
bri'gante *nm* bandit; *hum* rogue
bri'gare *vi* intrigue
bri'gata *nf* brigade; *(gruppo)* group
briga'tista *nmf Pol* member of the Red Brigades
'briglia *nf* rein; **a ~ sciolta** at breakneck speed
bril'lante *a* brilliant; *(scintillante)* sparkling ● *nm* diamond
bril'lare *vi* shine; *(metallo:)* glitter; *(scintillare)* sparkle
'brillo *a* tipsy
'brina *nf* hoar-frost
brin'dare *vi* toast; **~ a qcno** drink a toast to sb
'brindisi *nm inv* toast
bri'tannico *a* British
'brivido *nm* shiver; *(di paura ecc)* shudder; *(di emozione)* thrill
brizzo'lato *a* greying
'brocca *nf* jug
broc'cato *nm* brocade
'broccoli *nmpl* broccoli *sg*
bro'daglia *nf pej* dishwater
'brodo *nm* broth; *(per cucinare)* stock. **~ ristretto** consommé
'broglio *nm* **~ elettorale** gerrymandering
bron'chite *nf* bronchitis
'broncio *nm* sulk; **fare il ~** sulk
bronto'l|are *vi* grumble; *(tuono ecc:)* rumble. **~io** *nm* grumbling; *(di tuono)* rumbling. **~one, -a** *nmf* grumbler
'bronzo *nm* bronze
bros'sura *nf* **edizione in ~** paperback
bru'care *vt (pecora:)* graze
bruciacchi'are *vt* scorch
brucia'pelo *adv* **a ~** point-blank
bruci'a|re *vt* burn; *(scottare)* scald; *(incendiare)* set fire to ● *vi* burn; *(scottare)* scald. **~rsi** *vr* burn oneself. **~to** *a* burnt; *fig* burnt-out. **~tore** *nm* burner. **~'tura** *nf* burn. **bruci'ore** *nm* burning sensation
'bruco *nm* grub
'brufolo *nm* spot
brughi'era *nf* heath
bruli'c|are *vi* swarm. **~hio** *nm* swarming
'brullo *a* bare
'bruma *nf* mist

'bruno *a* brown; *(occhi, capelli)* dark
brusca'mente *adv (di colpo)* suddenly
bru'schetta *nf* toasted bread rubbed with garlic and sprinkled with olive oil
'brusco *a* sharp; *(persona)* brusque, abrupt; *(improvviso)* sudden
bru'sio *nm* buzzing
bru'tal|e *a* brutal. **~ità** *nf inv* brutality. **~iz'zare** *vt* brutalize. **'bruto** *a & nm* brute
brut'tezza *nf* ugliness
'brut|to *a* ugly; *(tempo, tipo, situazione, affare)* nasty; *(cattivo)* bad; **~ta copia** rough copy; **~to tiro** dirty trick. **~'tura** *nf* ugly thing
'buca *nf* hole; *(avvallamento)* hollow. **~ delle lettere** *(a casa)* letter-box
buca'neve *nm inv* snowdrop
bu'car|e *vt* make a hole in; *(pungere)* prick; punch *(biglietti)* ● *vi* have a puncture. **~si** *vr* prick oneself; *(con droga)* shoot up
bu'cato *nm* washing
'buccia *nf* peel, skin
bucherel'lare *vt* riddle
'buco *nm* hole
bu'dello *nm (pl nf* **budella)** bowel
'budget *nm inv* budget
bu'dino *nm* pudding
'bue *nm (pl* **buoi)** ox; **carne di ~** beef
'bufalo *nm* buffalo
bu'fera *nf* storm; *(di neve)* blizzard
buf'fetto *nm* cuff
'buffo *a* funny; *Theat* comic ● *nm* funny thing. **~'nata** *nf (scherzo)* joke. **buf'fone** *nm* buffoon; **fare il buffone** play the fool
bu'gi|a *nf* lie; **~a pietosa** white lie. **~'ardo, -a** *a* lying ● *nmf* liar
bugi'gattolo *nm* cubby-hole
'buio *a* dark ● *nm* darkness; **al ~** in the dark; **~ pesto** pitch dark
'bulbo *nm* bulb; *(dell'occhio)* eyeball
Bulga'ria *nf* Bulgaria. **'bulgaro, -a** *a & nmf* Bulgarian
buli'mia *nf* bulimia. **bu'limico** *a* bulimic
'bullo *nm* bully
bul'lone *nm* bolt
'bunker *nm inv* bunker
buona'fede *nf* good faith
buona'notte *int* good night
buona'sera *int* good evening
buon'giorno *int* good morning; *(di pomeriggio)* good afternoon
buon'grado *di ~* *adv* willingly

buongu·staio, -a *nmf* gourmet. **buon·gusto** *nm* good taste

bu·ono *a* good; ⟨*momento*⟩ right; **dar ~** ⟨*convalidare*⟩ accept; **alla buona** easy-going; ⟨*cena*⟩ informal; **buona notte/sera** good night/evening; **buon compleanno/Natale!** happy birthday/merry Christmas!; **~ senso** common sense; **di buon'ora** early; **una buona volta** once and for all; **buona parte di** the best part of; **tre ore buone** three good hours ● *nm* good; ⟨*in film*⟩ goody; ⟨*tagliando*⟩ voucher; ⟨*titolo*⟩ bond; **con le buone** gently; **~ sconto** money-off coupon ● *nmf* **buono, -a a nulla** dead loss

buontem·pone, -a *nmf* happy-go-lucky person

buonu·more *nm* good temper

buonu·scita *nf* retirement bonus; ⟨*di dirigente*⟩ golden handshake

burat·tino *nm* puppet

'burbero *a* surly; ⟨*nei modi*⟩ rough

bu·rocra|te *nm* bureaucrat. **buro·cra·**

·tico *a* bureaucratic. **~·zia** *nf* bureaucracy

bur·ra|sca *nf* storm. **~·scoso** *a* stormy

'burro *nm* butter

bur·rone *nm* ravine

bu·scar|e *vt*, **~·si** *vr* catch; **~·le** *fam* get a hiding

bus·sare *vt* knock

'bussola *nf* compass; **perdere la ~** lose one's bearings

'busta *nf* envelope; ⟨*astuccio*⟩ case. **~ paga** pay packet. **~·'rella** *nf* bribe. **bu·stina** *nf* ⟨*di tè*⟩ tea bag; ⟨*per medicine*⟩ sachet

'busto *nm* bust; ⟨*indumento*⟩ girdle

but·tar|e *vt* throw; **~·e giù** ⟨*demolire*⟩ knock down; ⟨*inghiottire*⟩ gulp down; ⟨*scritto*⟩ scribble down; *fam* put on ⟨*pasta*⟩; ⟨*scoraggiare*⟩ dishearten; **~·e via** throw away. **~·si** *vr* throw oneself; ⟨*saltare*⟩ jump

butte·rato *a* a pock-marked

buz·zurro *nm fam* yokel

Cc

caba·ret *nm inv* cabaret

ca·bina *nf* Naut, Aeron cabin; ⟨*balneare*⟩ beach hut. **~ elettorale** polling booth. **~ di pilotaggio** cockpit. **~ telefonica** telephone box. **cabi·nato** *nm* cabin cruiser

ca·cao *nm* cocoa

'cacca *nf fam* pooh

'caccia *nf* hunt; ⟨*con fucile*⟩ shooting; ⟨*inseguimento*⟩ chase; ⟨*selvaggina*⟩ game ● *nm inv* Aeron fighter; Naut destroyer

cacciabombardi·ere *nm* fighter-bomber

cacciagi·one *nf* game

cacci·a|re *vt* hunt; ⟨*mandar via*⟩ chase away; ⟨*scacciare*⟩ drive out; ⟨*ficcare*⟩ shove ● *vi* go hunting. **~·rsi** *vr* ⟨*nascondersi*⟩ hide; ⟨*andare a finire*⟩ get to; **~·rsi nei guai** get into trouble; **alla ~·'tora** a Culin chasseur. **~·'tore, ~·'trice** *nmf* hunter. **~·tore di frodo** poacher

caccia·vite *nm inv* screwdriver

ca·chet *nm inv* Med capsule; ⟨*colorante*⟩ colour rinse; ⟨*stile*⟩ cachet

'cachi *nm inv* ⟨*albero, frutta*⟩ persimmon

'cacio *nm* ⟨*formaggio*⟩ cheese

'caco *nm fam* ⟨*frutto*⟩ persimmon

'cactus *nm inv* cactus

ca·da|vere *nm* corpse. **~·'verico** *a fig* deathly pale

ca·dente *a* falling; ⟨*casa*⟩ crumbling

ca·denza *nf* cadence; ⟨*ritmo*⟩ rhythm; Mus cadenza

ca·dere *vi* fall; ⟨*capelli ecc:*⟩ fall out; ⟨*capitombolare*⟩ tumble; ⟨*vestito ecc:*⟩ hang; **far ~** ⟨*di mano*⟩ drop; **~ dal sonno** feel very sleepy; **lasciar ~** drop; **~ dalle nuvole** *fig* be taken aback

ca·detto *nm* cadet

ca·duta *nf* fall; ⟨*di capelli*⟩ loss; *fig* downfall

caffè *nm inv* coffee; ⟨*locale*⟩ café. **~ corretto** espresso coffee with a dash of liqueur. **~ lungo** weak black coffee. **~ macchiato** coffee with a dash of milk.

~ ristretto extra-strong espresso coffee. **~ solubile** instant coffee. **~'ina** nf caffeine. **~'l latte** nm inv white coffee.

caffetti'era nf coffee-pot

cafo'naggine nf boorishness

cafo'nata nf boorishness

ca'fone, -a nmf boor

ca'gare vi fam crap

cagio'nare vt cause

cagio'nevole a delicate

cagli'are vi, **~si** vr curdle

'cagna nf bitch

ca'gnara nf fam din

ca'gnesco a **guardare qcno in ~** scowl at sb

'cala nf creek

cala'brone nm hornet

cala'maio nm inkpot

cala'mari nmpl squid

cala'mita nf magnet

calamità nf inv calamity

ca'la|re vi come down; ⟨vento:⟩ drop; ⟨diminuire⟩ fall; ⟨tramontare⟩ set ● vt ⟨abbassare⟩ lower; ⟨nei lavori a maglia⟩ decrease ● nm ⟨di luna⟩ waning. **~si** vr lower oneself

'calca nf throng

cal'cagno nm heel

cal'care[1] nm limestone

cal'care[2] vt tread; ⟨premere⟩ press [down]; **~ la mano** exaggerate; **~ le orme di qcno** fig follow in sb's footsteps

'calce[1] nf lime

'calce[2] nm **in ~** at the foot of the page

calce'struzzo nm concrete

cal'cetto nm Sport five-a-side [football]

calci'a|re vt kick. **~'tore** nm footballer

cal'cina nf mortar

calci'naccio nm ⟨pezzo di intonaco⟩ flake of plaster

'calcio[1] nm kick; Sport football; ⟨di arma da fuoco⟩ butt; **dare un ~ a** kick. **~ d'angolo** corner [kick]

'calcio[2] nm ⟨chimica⟩ calcium

'calco nm ⟨con carta⟩ tracing; ⟨arte⟩ cast

calco'la|re vt calculate; ⟨considerare⟩ consider. **~'tore** a calculating ● nm calculator; ⟨macchina elettronica⟩ computer

'calcolo nm calculation; Med stone

cal'daia nf boiler

caldar'rosta nf roast chestnut

caldeggi'are vt support

'caldo a warm; ⟨molto caldo⟩ hot ● nm

heat; **avere ~** be warm/hot; **fa ~** it is warm/hot

calen'dario nm calendar

'calibro nm calibre; ⟨strumento⟩ callipers pl; **di grosso ~** ⟨persona⟩ top attrib

'calice nm goblet; Relig chalice

ca'ligine nf fog; ⟨industriale⟩ smog

calli'gra'fia nf handwriting; ⟨cinese⟩ calligraphy

cal'lista nmf chiropodist. **'callo** nm corn; **fare il callo a** become hardened to. **cal'loso** a callous

'calma nf calm. **cal'mante** a calming ● nm sedative. **cal'mare** vt calm [down]; ⟨lenire⟩ soothe. **cal'marsi** vr calm down; ⟨vento:⟩ drop; ⟨dolore:⟩ die down. **calmo** a calm

'calo nm Comm fall; ⟨di volume⟩ shrinkage; ⟨di peso⟩ loss

calorosa'mente adv ⟨cordialmente⟩ warmly

ca'lore nm heat; ⟨moderato⟩ warmth; **in ~** ⟨animale⟩ on heat. **calo'roso** a warm

ca'loria nf calorie

ca'lorico a calorific

calo'rifero nm radiator

calpe'stare vt trample [down]; fig trample on ⟨diritti, sentimenti⟩; **vietato ~ l'erba** keep off the grass

calpe'stio nm ⟨passi⟩ footsteps

ca'lunni|a nf slander. **~'are** vt slander. **~'oso** a slanderous

ca'lura nf heat

cal'vario nm Calvary; fig trial

cal'vizie nf baldness. **'calvo** a bald

'calz|a nf ⟨da donna⟩ stocking; ⟨da uomo⟩ sock. **~a'maglia** nf tights pl; ⟨per danza⟩ leotard

cal'zante a fig fitting

cal'zare vt ⟨indossare⟩ wear; ⟨mettersi⟩ put on ● vi fit

calza'scarpe nm inv shoehorn

calza'tura nf footwear

calzaturi'ficio nm shoe factory

cal'zetta nf **è una mezza ~** fig he's no use

calzet'tone nm knee-length woollen sock. **cal'zino** nm sock

calzo'l|aio nm shoemaker. **~e'ria** nf ⟨negozio⟩ shoe shop

calzon'cini nmpl shorts. **~ da bagno** swimming trunks

cal'zone nm Culin folded pizza with tomato and mozzarella or ricotta inside

cal'zoni nmpl trousers, pants Am

camale'onte nm chameleon

cambi'ale nf bill of exchange

cambia'mento nm change

cambi'ar|e vt/i change; move (casa); (fare cambio di) exchange; ~e rotta Naut alter course. ~si vr change. 'cambio nm change; (Comm, scambio) exchange; Mech gear; dare il cambio a qcno relieve sb; in cambio di in exchange for

'camera nf room; (mobili) [bedroom] suite; Phot camera; C~ Pol, Comm Chamber. ~ ardente funeral parlour. ~ d'aria inner tube. C~ di Commercio Chamber of Commerce. C~ dei Deputati Pol ≈ House of Commons. ~ doppia double room. ~ da letto bedroom. ~ matrimoniale double room. ~ oscura darkroom. ~ singola single room

came'rata¹ nf (dormitorio) dormitory; Mil barrack room

came'ra|ta² nmf (amico) mate; Pol comrade. ~'tismo nm comradeship

cameri'era nf maid; (di ristorante) waitress; (in albergo) chamber-maid; (di bordo) stewardess

cameri'ere nm manservant; (di ristorante) waiter; (di bordo) steward

came'rino nm dressing-room

'camice nm overall. **cami'cetta** nf blouse. **ca'micia** nf shirt; **uovo in camicia** poached egg. **camicia da notte** nightdress

cami'netto nm fireplace

ca'mino nm chimney; (focolare) fireplace

'camion nm inv lorry Br, truck

camion'cino nm van

camio'netta nf jeep

camio'nista nm lorry driver Br, truck driver

cam'mello nm camel; (tessuto) camel-hair ●a inv (colore) camel

cam'meo nm cameo

cammi'na|re vi walk; (auto, orologio:) go. ~ta nf walk; **fare una ~ta** go for a walk. **cam'mino** nm way; **essere in cammino** be on the way; **mettersi in cammino** set out

camo'milla nf camomile; (bevanda) camomile tea

ca'morra nf local mafia

ca'moscio nm chamois; (pelle) suede

cam'pagna nf country; (paesaggio) countryside; Comm, Mil campaign; in ~ in the country. ~ elettorale election campaign. ~ pubblicitaria marketing campaign. **campa'gnolo, -a** a rustic ●nm countryman ●nf countrywoman

cam'pale a field attrib; **giornata ~** fig strenuous day

cam'pa|na nf bell; (di vetro) belljar. ~'nella nf (di tenda) curtain ring. ~'nello nm door-bell; (cicalino) buzzer

campa'nile nm belfry

campani'lismo nm parochialism

campani'lista nmf person with a parochial outlook

cam'panula nf Bot campanula

cam'pare vi live; (a stento) get by

cam'pato a ~ **in aria** unfounded

campeggi'a|re vi camp; (spiccare) stand out. ~'tore, ~'trice nmf camper. **cam'peggio** nm camping; (terreno) campsite

cam'pestre a rural

'camping nm inv campsite

campio'nari|o nm [set of] samples ●a samples; **fiera ~a** trade fair

campio'nato nm championship

campiona'tura nf (di merce) range of samples

campi'on|e nm champion; Comm sample; (esemplare) specimen. ~'essa nf ladies' champion

'campo nm field; (accampamento) camp. ~ da calcio football pitch. ~ di concentramento concentration camp. ~ da golf golf course. ~ da tennis tennis court

campo'santo nm cemetery

camuf'far|e vt disguise. ~si vr disguise oneself

'Cana|da nm Canada. ~'dese a & nmf Canadian

ca'naglia nf scoundrel; (plebaglia) rabble

ca'nal|e nm channel; (artificiale) canal. ~iz'zare vt channel (acque). ~izzazi'one nf channelling; (rete) pipes pl

'canapa nf hemp

cana'rino nm canary

cancel'la|re vt cross out; (con la gomma) rub out; fig wipe out; (annullare) cancel; Comput delete, erase. ~'tura nf erasure. ~zi'one nf cancellation; Comput deletion

cancelle'ria nf chancellery; (articoli per scrivere) stationery

cancelli'ere nm chancellor; (di tribunale) clerk

can'cello nm gate

cance'ro|geno nm carcinogen ●a carcinogenic. ~'so a cancerous

can'crena nf gangrene

'cancro nm cancer. C~ Astr Cancer

candeg'gi|na nf bleach. **~'are** vt bleach. **can'deggio** nm bleaching
can'de|la nf candle; Auto spark plug; **~'labro** nm candelabra. **~li'ere** nm candlestick
cande'lotto nm (di dinamite) stick
candida'mente adv candidly
candi'da|rsi vr stand as a candidate. **~to, -a** nmf candidate. **~'tura** nf Pol candidacy; (per lavoro) application
'**candido** a snow-white; (sincero) candid; (puro) pure
can'dito a candied
can'dore nm whiteness; fig innocence
'**cane** nm dog; (di arma da fuoco) cock; **un tempo da cani** foul weather. **~ da caccia** hunting dog
ca'nestro nm basket
cangi'ante a iridescent; **seta ~** shot silk
can'guro nm kangaroo
ca'nile nm kennel; (di allevamento) kennels pl. **~ municipale** dog pound
ca'nino a & nm canine
'**canna** nf reed; (da zucchero) cane; (di fucile) barrel; (bastone) stick; (di bicicletta) crossbar; (asta) rod; (fam: hascish) joint; **povero in ~** destitute. **~ da pesca** fishing-rod
can'nella nf cinnamon
can'neto nm bed of reeds
can'niba|le nm cannibal. **~'lismo** nm cannibalism
cannocchi'ale nm telescope
canno'nata nf cannon shot; **è una ~** fig it's brilliant
cannon'cino nm (dolce) cream horn
can'none nm cannon; fig ace
can'nuccia nf [drinking] straw; (di pipa) stem
ca'noa nf canoe
'**canone** nm canon; (affitto) rent; **equo ~** fair rents act
ca'noni|co nm canon. **~z'zare** vt canonize. **~zzazi'one** nf canonization
ca'noro a melodious
ca'notta nf (estiva) vest top
canot'taggio nm canoeing; (voga) rowing
canotti'era nf singlet
canotti'ere nm oarsman
ca'notto nm [rubber] dinghy
cano'vaccio nm (trama) plot; (straccio) duster
can'tante nmf singer
can't|are vt/i sing. **~au'tore, ~a'trice** nmf singer-songwriter. **~icchi'are** vt sing softly; (a bocca chiusa) hum

canti'ere nm yard; Naut shipyard; (di edificio) construction site. **~ navale** naval dockyard
canti'lena nf singsong; (ninna-nanna) lullaby
can'tina nf cellar; (osteria) wine shop
'**canto**[1] nm singing; (canzone) song; Relig chant; (poesia) poem
'**canto**[2] nm (angolo) corner; (lato) side; **dal ~ mio** for my part; **d'altro ~** on the other hand
canto'nata nf prendere una **~** fig be sadly mistaken
can'tone nm canton; (angolo) corner
can'tuccio nm nook
canzo'na|re vt tease. **~'torio** a teasing. **~'tura** nf teasing
can'zo|ne nf song. **~'netta** nf fam pop song. **~ni'ere** nm songbook
'**caos** nm chaos. **ca'otico** a chaotic
C.A.P. nm abbr (**Codice di Avviamento Postale**) post code, zip code Am
ca'pac|e a able; (esperto) skilled; (stadio, contenitore) big; **~e di** (disposto a) capable of. **~ità** nf inv ability; (attitudine) skill; (capienza) capacity
capaci'tarsi vr **~ di** (rendersi conto) understand; (accorgersi) realize
ca'panna nf hut
capan'nello nm fare **~ intorno a qcno/qcsa** gather round sb/sth
capan'none nm shed; Aeron hangar
ca'parbio a obstinate
ca'parra nf deposit
capa'tina nf short visit; **fare una ~ in città/da qcno** pop into town/in on sb
ca'pel|lo nm hair; **~li** pl (capigliatura) hair sg. **~'lone** nm hippie. **~'luto** a hairy
capez'zale nm bolster; fig bedside
ca'pezzolo nm nipple
capi'en|te a capacious. **~za** nf capacity
capiglia'tura nf hair
ca'pire vt understand; **~ male** misunderstand; **si capisce!** naturally!; **sì, ho capito** yes, I see
capi'ta|le a Jur capital; (principale) main ● nf (città) capital ● nm Comm capital. **~'lismo** nm capitalism. **~'lista** nmf capitalist. **~'listico** a capitalist
capitane'ria nf **~ di porto** port authorities pl
capi'tano nm captain
capi'tare vi (giungere per caso) come; (accadere) happen
capi'tello nm Archit capital

capito'la|re *vi* capitulate. **~zi'one** *nf* capitulation

ca'pitolo *nm* chapter

capi'tombolo *nm* headlong fall; **fare un ~** tumble down

'**capo** *nm* head; (*chi comanda*) boss *fam*; (*di vestiario*) item; *Geog* cape; (*in tribù*) chief; (*parte estrema*) top; **a ~** (*in detta-to*) new paragraph; **da ~** over again; **in ~ a un mese** within a month; **gira-mento di ~** dizziness; **mal di ~** head-ache; **~ d'abbigliamento** item of clothing. **~ d'accusa** *Jur* charge, count. **~ di bestiame** head of cattle

capo'banda *nm Mus* bandmaster; (*di delinquenti*) ringleader

ca'poccia *nf* (*fam: testa*) nut

capocci'one, -a *nmf fam* brainbox

capo'danno *nm* New Year's Day

capofa'miglia *nm* head of the family

capo'fitto *nm* **a ~** headlong

capo'giro *nm* giddiness

capola'voro *nm* masterpiece

capo'linea *nm* terminus

capo'lino *nm* **fare ~** peep in

capolu'ogo *nm* main town

capo'rale *nm* lance-corporal

capo'squadra *nmf Sport* team cap-tain

capo'stipite *nmf* (*di famiglia*) pro-genitor

capo'tavola *nmf* head of the table

capo'treno *nm* guard

capouf'ficio *nmf* head clerk

capo'verso *nm* first line

capo'vol|gere *vt* overturn; *fig* re-verse. **~gersi** *vr* overturn; (*barca*) capsize; *fig* be reversed. **~to** *pp di* **capovolgere ● a** upside-down

'**cappa** *nf* cloak; (*di camino*) cowl; (*di cucina*) hood

cap'pel|la *nf* chapel. **~'lano** *nm* chap-lain

cap'pello *nm* hat. **~ a cilindro** top hat

'**cappero** *nm* caper

'**cappio** *nm* noose

cap'pone *nm* capon

cap'potto *nm* [over]coat

cappuc'cino *nm* (*frate*) Capuchin; (*bevanda*) white coffee

cap'puccio *nm* hood; (*di penna stilo-grafica*) cap

'**capra** *nf* goat. **ca'pretto** *nm* kid

ca'pricci|o *nm* whim; (*bizzarria*) freak; **fare i capricci** have tantrums. **~'oso** *a* capricious; (*bambino*) naughty

Capri'corno *nm Astr* Capricorn

capri'ola *nf* somersault

capri'olo *nm* roe-deer

'**capro** *nm* [billy-]goat. **~ espiatorio** scapegoat. **ca'prone** *nm* [billy] goat

'**capsula** *nf* capsule; (*di proiettile*) cap; (*di dente*) crown

cap'tare *vt Radio, TV* pick up; catch (*attenzione*)

cara'bina *nf* carbine

carabini'ere *nm* carabiniere; **carabi-ni'eri** *pl* Italian police force (*which is a branch of the army*)

ca'raffa *nf* carafe

Ca'raibi *nmpl* (*zona*) Caribbean *sg*; (*isole*) Caribbean Islands; **il mar dei ~** the Caribbean [Sea]

cara'mella *nf* sweet

cara'mello *nm* caramel

ca'rato *nm* carat

ca'ratte|re *nm* character; (*caratteri-stica*) characteristic; *Typ* type; **di buon ~re** good-natured. **~'ristico, -a** *a* char-acteristic; (*pittoresco*) quaint ● *nf* char-acteristic. **~riz'zare** *vt* characterize

carbon'cino *nm* (*per disegno*) char-coal

car'bone *nm* coal

carboniz'zare *vt* burn to a cinder

carbu'rante *nm* fuel

carbura'tore *nm* carburettor

car'cassa *nf* carcass; *fig* old wreck

carce'ra|rio *a* prison *attrib*. **~to, -a** *nmf* prisoner. **~zi'one** *nf* imprison-ment. **~zione preventiva** preventive detention

'**carcer|e** *nm* prison; (*punizione*) im-prisonment. **~i'ere, -a** *nmf* gaoler

carci'ofo *nm* artichoke

car'diaco *a* cardiac

cardi'nale *a & nm* cardinal

'**cardine** *nm* hinge

cardio|chi'rurgo *nm* heart surgeon. **~lo'gia** *nf* cardiology. **cardi'ologo** *nm* heart specialist. **~'tonico** *nm* heart stimulant

'**cardo** *nm* thistle

ca'rena *nf Naut* bottom

ca'ren|te *a* **~te di** lacking in. **~za** *nf* lack; (*scarsità*) scarcity

care'stia *nf* famine; (*mancanza*) dearth

ca'rezza *nf* caress; **fare una ~** a ca-ress

cari'ar|si *vi* decay. **~to** *a* decayed

'**carica** *nf* office; *Mil, Electr* charge; *fig* drive. **cari'care** *vt* load; *Mil, Electr* charge; wind up (*orologio*). **~'tore** *nm* (*per proiettile*) magazine

carica'tu|ra *nf* caricature. ~'rale *a* grotesque. ~'rista *nmf* caricaturist

'carico *a* loaded (**di** with); *(colore)* strong; *(orologio)* wound [up]; *(batteria)* charged ● *nm* load; *(di nave)* cargo; *(il caricare)* loading; **a ~ di** *Comm* to be charged to; *(persona)* dependent on

'carie *nf* [tooth] decay

ca'rino *a* pretty; *(piacevole)* agreeable

ca'risma *nm* charisma. cari'smatico *a* charismatic

carit|à *nf* charity; **per ~à!** *(come rifiuto)* God forbid!. ~a'tevole *a* charitable

carnagi'one *nf* complexion

car'naio *nm fig* shambles

car'nale *a* carnal; **cugino ~** first cousin

'carne *nf* flesh; *(alimento)* meat; ~ **di manzo/maiale/vitello** beef/pork/veal

car'nefi|ce *nm* executioner. ~'cina *nf* slaughter

carne'va|le *nm* carnival. ~'lesco *a* carnival

car'nivoro *nm* carnivore ● *a* carnivorous

car'noso *a* fleshy

'caro, -a *a* dear; **cari saluti** kind regards ● *nmf fam* darling, dear; **i miei cari** my nearest and dearest

ca'rogna *nf* carcass; *fig* bastard

caro'sello *nm* merry-go-round

ca'rota *nf* carrot

caro'vana *nf* caravan; *(di veicoli)* convoy

caro'vita *nm* high cost of living

'carpa *nf* carp

carpenti'ere *nm* carpenter

car'pire *vt* seize; *(con difficoltà)* extort

car'pone, car'poni *adv* on all fours

car'rabile *a* suitable for vehicles; **passo ~** *vedi* carraio

car'raio *a* **passo** *nm* ~ **entrance to driveway, garage etc where parking is forbidden**

carreggi'ata *nf* roadway; **doppia ~** dual carriageway, divided highway *Am*

carrel'lata *nf* TV pan

car'rello *nm* trolley; *(di macchina da scrivere)* carriage; *Aeron* undercarriage; *Cinema, TV* dolly. ~ **d'atterraggio** *Aeron* landing gear

car'retto *nm* cart

carri'e|ra *nf* career; **di gran ~ra** at full speed; **fare ~ra** get on. ~'rismo *nm* careerism

carri'ola *nf* wheelbarrow

'carro *nm* cart. ~ **armato** tank. ~

attrezzi breakdown vehicle, wrecker *Am*. ~ **funebre** hearse. ~ **merci** truck

car'rozza *nf* carriage; *Rail* car, coach. ~ **cuccette** sleeping car. ~ **ristorante** restaurant car

carroz'zella *nf* *(per bambini)* pram; *(per invalidi)* wheelchair

carrozze'ria *nf* bodywork; *(officina)* bodyshop

carroz'zina *nf* pram; *(pieghevole)* push-chair, stroller *Am*

carroz'zone *nm* *(di circo)* caravan

'carta *nf* paper; *(da gioco)* card; *(statuto)* charter; *Geog* map. ~ **d'argento** ≈ senior citizens' railcard. ~ **assorbente** blotting-paper. ~ **di credito** credit card. ~ **geografica** map. ~ **d'identità** identity card. ~ **igienica** toilet-paper. ~ **di imbarco** boarding card. ~ **da lettere** writing-paper. ~ **da parati** wallpaper. ~ **stagnola** silver paper; *Culin* aluminium foil. ~ **straccia** waste paper. ~ **stradale** road map. ~ **velina** tissue-paper. ~ **verde** *Auto* green card. ~ **vetrata** sandpaper

cartacar'bone *nf* carbon paper

car'taccia *nf* waste paper

carta'modello *nm* pattern

cartamo'neta *nf* paper money

carta'pesta *nf* papier mâché

carta'straccia *nf* waste paper

cartave'trare *vt* sand [down]

car'tel|la *nf* *(per documenti ecc)* briefcase; *(di cartone)* folder; *(di scolaro)* satchel. ~**la clinica** medical record. ~'lina *nf* document wallet, folder

cartel'lino *nm* label; *(dei prezzi)* pricetag; *(di presenza)* time-card; **timbrare il ~** clock in; *(all'uscita)* clock out

car'tel|lo *nm* sign; *(pubblicitario)* poster; *(stradale)* road sign; *(di protesta)* placard; *Comm* cartel. ~'lone *nm* poster; *Theat* bill

carti'era *nf* paper-mill

carti'lagine *nf* cartilage

car'tina *nf* map

car'toccio *nm* paper bag; **al ~** *Culin* baked in foil

carto'|laio, -a *nmf* stationer. ~le'ria *nf* stationer's [shop]. ~libre'ria *nf* stationer's and book shop

carto'lina *nf* postcard. ~ **postale** postcard

carto'mante *nmf* fortune-teller

carton'cino *nm* *(materiale)* card

car'tone *nm* cardboard; *(arte)* cartoon. ~ **animato** [animated] cartoon

car'tuccia *nf* cartridge

'casa *nf* house; *(abitazione propria)* home; *(ditta)* firm; amico di ~ family friend; andare a ~ go home; essere di ~ be like one of the family; fatto in ~ home-made; padrone di ~ *(di pensione ecc)* landlord; *(proprietario)* house owner. ~ di cura nursing home. ~ popolare council house. ~ dello studente hall of residence

ca'sacca *nf* military coat; *(giacca)* jacket

ca'saccio *adv* a ~ at random

casa'ling|a *nf* housewife. ~o *a* domestic; *(fatto in casa)* home-made; *(amante della casa)* home-loving; *(semplice)* homely

ca'scante *a* falling; *(floscio)* flabby

ca'sca|re *vi* fall [down]. ~ta *nf* *(di acqua)* waterfall

ca'schetto *nm* [capelli a] ~ bob

ca'scina *nf* farm building

'casco *nm* crash-helmet; *(asciuga-capelli)* [hair-]drier; ~ di banane bunch of bananas

caseggi'ato *nm* block of flats *Br*, apartment block

casei'ficio *nm* dairy

ca'sella *nf* pigeon-hole. ~ postale post office box; *Comput* mailbox

casel'lante *nmf* *(per treni)* signalman

casel'lario *nm* ~ giudiziario record of convictions; avere il ~ giudiziario vergine have no criminal record

ca'sello [autostra'dale] *nm* [motorway] toll booth

case'reccio *a* home-made

ca'serma *nf* barracks *pl*; *(dei carabinieri)* [police] station

casi'nista *nmf fam* muddler. ca'sino *nm fam* *(bordello)* brothel; *(fig: confusione)* racket; *(disordine)* mess; un casino di loads of

casinò *nm inv* casino

ca'sistica *nf* *(classificazione)* case records *pl*

'caso *nm* chance; *(fatto, circostanza, Med, Gram)* case; a ~ at random; ~ mai if need be; far ~ a pay attention to; non far ~ a take no account of; per ~ by chance. ~ [giudiziario] [legal] case

caso'lare *nm* farmhouse

'caspita *int* good gracious!

'cassa *nf* till; *Comm* cash; *(luogo di pagamento)* cash desk; *(mobile)* chest; *(istituto bancario)* bank. ~ automatica prelievi cash dispenser, automatic teller. ~ da morto coffin. ~ toracica ribcage

cassa'forte *nf* safe

cassa'panca *nf* linen chest

casseru'ola *nf* saucepan

cas'setta *nf* case; *(per registratore)* cassette. ~ delle lettere postbox, letterbox. ~ di sicurezza strong-box

cas'set|to *nm* drawer. ~'tone *nm* chest of drawers

cassi'ere, -a *nmf* cashier; *(di supermercato)* checkout assistant, checkout operator; *(di banca)* teller

'casta *nf* caste

ca'stagn|a *nf* chestnut. casta'gneto *nm* chestnut grove. ~o *nm* chestnut[-tree]

ca'stano *a* chestnut

ca'stello *nm* castle; *(impalcatura)* scaffold

casti'gare *vt* punish

casti'gato *a* *(casto)* chaste

ca'stigo *nm* punishment

castità *nf* chastity. 'casto *a* chaste

ca'storo *nm* beaver

ca'strare *vt* castrate

casu'al|e *a* chance *attrib*. ~'mente *adv* by chance

ca'supola *nf* little house

cata'clisma *nm fig* upheaval

cata'comba *nf* catacomb

cata'fascio *nm* andare a ~ go to rack and ruin

cata'litico *a* marmitta catalitica *Auto* catalytic converter

cataliz'za|re *vt fig* heighten. ~'tore *nm Auto* catalytic converter

catalo'gare *vt* catalogue. ca'talogo *nm* catalogue

catama'rano *nm* *(da diporto)* catamaran

cata'pecchia *nf* hovel; *fam* dump

catapul'tar|e *vt* *(scaraventare fuori)* eject. ~si *vr* *(precipitarsi)* dive

catarifran'gente *nm* reflector

ca'tarro *nm* catarrh

ca'tasta *nf* pile

ca'tasto *nm* land register

ca'tastrofe *nf* catastrophe. cata'strofico *a* catastrophic

cate'chismo *nm* catechism

cate|go'ria *nf* category. ~'gorico *a* categorical

ca'tena *nf* chain. ~ montuosa mountain range. catene *pl* da neve tyre-chains. cate'naccio *nm* bolt

cate|'nella *nf* *(collana)* chain. ~'nina *nf* chain

cate'ratta *nf* cataract

ca'terva *nf* una ~ di heaps of

cati'nell|a *nf* basin; **piovere a ~e** bucket down

ca'tino *nm* basin

ca'torcio *nm fam* old wreck

ca'trame *nm* tar

'cattedra *nf* (*tavolo di insegnante*) desk; (*di università*) chair

catte'drale *nf* cathedral

catti'veria *nf* wickedness; (*azione*) wicked action

cattività *nf* captivity

cat'tivo *a* bad; ‹*bambino*› naughty

cattoli'cesimo *nm* Catholicism

cat'tolico, -a *a & nmf* [Roman] Catholic

cat'tu|ra *nf* capture. **~'rare** *vt* capture

caucciù *nm* rubber

'causa *nf* cause; *Jur* lawsuit; **far ~ a qcno** sue sb. **cau'sare** *vt* cause

'caustico *a* caustic

cauta'mente *adv* cautiously

cau'tela *nf* caution

caute'lar|e *vt* protect. **~si** *vr* take precautions

cateriz'z|are *vt* cauterize. **~azi'one** *nf* cauterization

'cauto *a* cautious

cauzi'one *nf* security; (*per libertà provvisoria*) bail

'cava *nf* quarry; *fig* mine

caval'ca|re *vt* ride; (*stare a cavalcioni*) sit astride. **~ta** *nf* ride; (*corteo*) cavalcade. **~'via** *nm* flyover

cavalci'oni *adv* **a ~** astride

cavali'ere *nm* rider; (*titolo*) knight; (*accompagnatore*) escort; (*al ballo*) partner

cavalle|'resco *a* chivalrous. **~'ria** *nf* chivalry; *Mil* cavalry. **~'rizzo, -a** *nm* horseman ● *nf* horsewoman

caval'letta *nf* grasshopper

caval'letto *nm* trestle; (*di macchina fotografica*) tripod; (*di pittore*) easel

caval'lina *nf* (*ginnastica*) horse

ca'vallo *nm* horse; (*misura di potenza*) horsepower; (*scacchi*) knight; (*dei pantaloni*) crotch; **a ~** on horseback; **andare a ~** go horse-riding. **~ a dondolo** rocking-horse

caval'lone *nm* (*ondata*) roller

caval'luccio ma'rino *nm* sea horse

ca'var|e *vt* take out; (*di dosso*) take off; **~sela** get away with it; **se la cava bene** he's/she's doing all right

cava'tappi *nm inv* corkscrew

ca'ver|na *nf* cave. **~'noso** *a* ‹*voce*› deep

'cavia *nf* guinea-pig

cavi'ale *nm* caviar

ca'viglia *nf* ankle

cavil'lare *vi* quibble. **ca'villo** *nm* quibble

cavità *nf inv* cavity

'cavo *a* hollow ● *nm* cavity; (*di metallo*) cable; *Naut* rope

cavo'lata *nf fam* rubbish

cavo'letto *nm* **~ di Bruxelles** Brussels sprout

cavolfi'ore *nm* cauliflower

'cavolo *nm* cabbage; **~! *fam*** sugar!

caz'zo *int vulg* fuck!

caz'zott|o *nm* punch; **prendere qcno a ~i** beat sb up

cazzu'ola *nf* trowel

c/c *abbr* (**conto corrente**) c/a

CD-Rom *nm inv* CD-Rom

ce *pron pers* (*a noi*) (to) us ● *adv* there; **~ ne sono molti** there are many

'cece *nm* chick-pea

cecità *nf* blindness

ceco, -a *a & nmf* Czech; **la Repubblica Ceca** the Czech Republic

Cecoslo'vacc|hia *nf* Czechoslovakia. **c~o, -a** *a & nmf* Czechoslovak

'cedere *vi* (*arrendersi*) surrender; (*concedere*) yield; (*sprofondare*) subside ● *vt* give up; make over ‹*proprietà ecc*›.

ce'devole *a* ‹*terreno ecc*› soft; *fig* yielding. **cedi'mento** *nm* (*di terreno*) subsidence

'cedola *nf* coupon

'cedro *nm* (*albero*) cedar; (*frutto*) citron

C.E.E. *nf abbr* (**Communità Economica Europea**) E[E]C

'ceffo *nm* (*muso*) snout; (*pej: persona*) mug

cef'fone *nm* slap

ce'lar|e *vt* conceal. **~si** *vr* hide

cele'bra|re *vt* celebrate. **~zi'one** *nf* celebration

'celebr|e *a* famous. **~ità** *nf inv* celebrity

'celere *a* swift

ce'leste *a* (*divino*) heavenly ● *a & nm* (*colore*) sky-blue

celi'bato *nm* celibacy

'celibe *a* single ● *nm* bachelor

'cella *nf* cell

'cellofan *nm inv* cellophane; *Culin* cling film

'cellula *nf* cell. **~ fotoelettrica** electronic eye

cellu'lare *nm* (*telefono*) cellular phone ● *a* **furgone ~** police van; **telefono ~** cellular phone

cellu'lite *nf* cellulite
cellu'loide *a* celluloid
cellu'losa *nf* cellulose
'celt|a *nm* Celt. **~ico** *a* Celtic
cemen'tare *vt* cement. **ce'mento** *nm* cement. **cemento armato** reinforced concrete
'cena *nf* dinner; *(leggera)* supper
ce'nacolo *nm* circle
ce'nare *vi* have dinner
'cenci|o *nm* rag; *(per spolverare)* duster. **~oso** *a* in rags
'cenere *nf* ash; *(di carbone ecc)* cinders
ce'netta *nf* *(cena semplice)* informal dinner
'cenno *nm* sign; *(col capo)* nod; *(con la mano)* wave; *(allusione)* hint; *(breve resoconto)* mention
ce'none *nm* **il ~ di Capodanno/ Natale** special New Year's Eve/Christmas Eve dinner
censi'mento *nm* census
cen's|ore *nm* censor. **~ura** *nf* censorship. **~u'rare** *vt* censor
centelli'nare *vt* sip
cente'n|ario, -a *a* & *nmf* centenarian ● *nm* *(commemorazione)* centenary. **~'nale** *a* centennial
cen'tesimo *a* hundredth ● *nm* *(di dollaro)* cent; **non avere un ~** be penniless
cen'ti|grado *a* centigrade. **~metro** *nm* centimetre
centi'naio *nm* hundred
'cento *a* & *nm* a or one hundred; **per ~** per cent
centome'trista *nmf* Sport one hundred metres runner
cento'mila *nm* *a or* one hundred thousand
cen'trale *a* central ● *nf* *(di società ecc)* head office. **~ atomica** atomic power station. **~ elettrica** power station. **~ nucleare** nuclear power station. **~ telefonica** [telephone] exchange
centra'li|na *nf* Teleph switchboard. **~nista** *nmf* operator
centra'lino *nm* Teleph exchange; *(di albergo ecc)* switchboard
centra'li|smo *nm* centralism. **~z'zare** *vt* centralize
cen'trare *vt* **~ qcsa** hit sth in the centre; *(fissare nel centro)* centre; *fig* hit on the head *(idea)*
centri'fu|ga *nf* spin-drier. **~ [asciugaverdure]** shaker. **~'gare** *vt* Techn centrifuge; *(lavatrice:)* spin
cen'trino *nm* doily

'centro *nm* centre. **~ [città]** city centre. **~ commerciale** shopping centre, mall. **~ sociale** community centre
'ceppo *nm* *(di albero)* stump; *(da ardere)* log; *(fig: gruppo)* stock
'cera *nf* wax; *(aspetto)* look. **~ per il pavimento** floor-polish
ce'ramica *nf* *(arte)* ceramics; *(materia)* pottery; *(oggetto)* piece of pottery
ce'rato *a* *(tela)* waxed
cerbi'atto *nm* fawn
'cerca *nf* **andare in ~ di** look for
cercaper'sone *nm inv* beeper
cer'care *vt* look for ● *vi* **~ di** try to
'cerchi|a *nf* circle. **~'are** *vt* circle *(parola)*. **~'ato** *a* *(occhi)* black-ringed. **~'etto** *nm* *(per capelli)* hairband
'cerchi|o *nm* circle; *(giocattolo)* hoop. **~'one** *nm* alloy wheel
cere'ale *nm* cereal
cere'brale *a* cerebral
'cereo *a* waxen
ce'retta *nf* depilatory wax
ceri'moni|a *nf* ceremony. **~'ale** *nm* ceremonial. **~'oso** *a* ceremonious
ce'rino *nm* [wax] match
cerni'era *nf* hinge; *(di borsa)* clasp. **~ lampo** zip[-fastener], zipper Am
'cernita *nf* selection
'cero *nm* candle
ce'rone *nm* grease-paint
ce'rotto *nm* [sticking] plaster
certa'mente *adv* certainly
cer'tezza *nf* certainty
certifi'ca|re *vt* certify. **~to** *nm* certificate
'certo *a* a certain; *(notizia)* definite; *(indeterminativo)* some; **sono ~ di riuscire** I am certain to succeed; **a una certa età** at a certain age; **certi giorni** some days; **un ~ signor Giardini** a Mr Giardini; **una certa Anna** somebody called Anna; **certa gente** *pej* some people; **ho certi dolori!** I'm in such pain!. **certi** *pron pl* some; *(alcune persone)* some people ● *adv* of course; **sapere per ~** know for certain, know for sure; **di ~** surely; **~ che sì!** of course!
cer'vel|lo *nm* brain. **~lone, -a** *nmf hum* genius. **~lotico** *a* *(macchinoso)* over-elaborate
'cervo *nm* deer
ce'sareo *a* Med Caesarean
cesel'la|re *vt* chisel. **~to** *a* chiselled. **ce'sello** *nm* chisel
ce'soie *nfpl* shears
ce'spugli|o *nm* bush. **~'oso** *a* *(terreno)* bushy

ces'sa|re *vi* stop, cease ● *vt* stop. **~re** *nm* **il fuoco** ceasefire. **~zi'one** *nf* cessation

cessi'one *nf* handover

'cesso *nm sl* (*gabinetto*) bog, john *Am*; (*fig: locale, luogo*) dump

'cesta *nf* [large] basket. **ce'stello** *nm* (*per lavatrice*) drum

cesti'nare *vt* throw away. **ce'stino** *nm* [small] basket; (*per la carta straccia*) waste-paper basket. **'cesto** *nm* basket

'ceto *nm* [social] class

'cetra *nf* lyre

cetrio'lino *nm* gherkin. **cetri'olo** *nm* cucumber

cfr *abbr* (**confronta**) cf.

che *pron rel* (*persona: soggetto*) who; (*persona: oggetto*) that, who, whom *fml*; (*cosa, animale*) that, which; **questa è la casa ~ ho comprato** this is the house [that] I've bought; **il ~ mi sorprende** which surprises me; **dal ~ deduco che...** from which I gather that...; **avere di ~ vivere** have enough to live on; **grazie! – non c'è di! ~** thank you! – don't mention it!; **il giorno ~ ti ho visto** the day I saw you ● *a inter* what; (*esclamativo: con aggettivo*) how; (*con nome*) what a; **~ macchina prendiamo, la tua o la mia?** which car are we taking, yours or mine?; **~ bello!** how nice!; **~ idea!** what an idea!; **~ bella giornata!** what a lovely day! ● *pron inter* what; **a ~ pensi?** what are you thinking about? ● *conj* that; (*con comparazioni*) than; **credo ~ abbia ragione** I think [that] he is right; **era così commosso ~ non riusciva a parlare** he was so moved [that] he couldn't speak; **aspetto ~ telefoni** I'm waiting for him to phone; **è da un po' ~ non lo vedo** it's been a while since I saw him; **mi piace più Roma ~ Milano** I like Rome better than Milan; **~ ti piaccia o no** whether you like it or not; **~ io sappia** as far as I know

checché *pron indef* whatever

chemiotera'pia *nf* chemotherapy

chero'sene *nm* paraffin

cheru'bino *nm* cherub

cheti'chella: alla ~ *adv* silently

'cheto *a* quiet

chi *pron rel* whoever; (*coloro che*) people who; **ho trovato ~ ti può aiutare** I found somebody who can help you; **c'è ~ dice che...** some people say that...; **senti ~ parla!** listen to who's talking! ● *pron inter* (*soggetto*) who; (*oggetto,* con preposizione) who, whom *fml*; (*possessivo*) **di ~** whose; **~ sei?** who are you?; **~ hai incontrato?** who did you meet?; **di ~ sono questi libri?** whose books are these?; **con ~ parli?** who are you talking to?; **a ~ lo dici!** tell me about it!

chi'acchie|ra *nf* chat; (*pettegolezzo*) gossip. **~'rare** *vi* chat; (*far pettegolezzi*) gossip. **~'rato** *a* **essere ~rato** ⟨*persona:*⟩ be the subject of gossip; **~re** *pl* chitchat; **far quattro ~re** have a chat. **~'rone, -a** *a* talkative ● *nmf* chatterer

chia'ma|re *vt* call; (*far venire*) send for; **come ti chiami?** what's your name?; **mi chiamo Roberto** my name is Robert; **~re alle armi** call up. **~rsi** *vr* be called. **~ta** *nf* call; *Mil* call-up

chi'appa *nf fam* cheek

chiara'mente *adv* clearly

chia'rezza *nf* clarity; (*limpidezza*) clearness

chiarifi'ca|re *vt* clarify. **~'tore** *a* clarificatory. **~zi'one** *nf* clarification

chiari'mento *nm* clarification

chia'rir|e *vt* make clear; (*spiegare*) clear up. **~si** *vr* become clear

chi'aro *a* clear; (*luminoso*) bright; (*colore*) light. **chia'rore** *nm* light

chiaroveg'gente *a* clear-sighted ● *nmf* clairvoyant

chi'as|so *nm* din. **~'soso** *a* rowdy

chic *a inv* chic

chicches'sia *pron* anybody

'chicco *nm* grain; (*di caffè*) bean; (*d'uva*) grape

chi'eder|e *vt* ask; (*per avere*) ask for; (*esigere*) demand. **~si** *vr* wonder

chi'esa *nf* church

chi'esto *pp di* **chiedere**

'chiglia *nf* keel

'chilo *nm* kilo

chilo'grammo *nm* kilogram[me]

chilome'traggio *nm Auto* ≈ mileage

chilo'metrico *a* in kilometres

chi'lometro *nm* kilometre

chi'mera *nf fig* illusion

'chimic|a *nf* chemistry. **~o, -a** *a* chemical ● *nmf* chemist

'china *nf* (*declivio*) slope; **inchiostro di ~** Indian ink

chi'nar|e *vt* lower. **~si** *vr* stoop

chincaglie'rie *nfpl* knick-knacks

chinesitera'pia *nf* physiotherapy

chi'nino *nm* quinine

'chino *a* bent

chi'notto *nm* sparkling soft drink

chi'occia *nf* sitting hen

chi'occiola *nf* snail; **scala a ~** spiral staircase

chi'odo *nm* nail; *(idea fissa)* obsession. **~ di garofano** clove

chi'oma *nf* head of hair; *(fogliame)* foliage

chi'osco *nm* kiosk; *(per giornali)* news-stand

chi'ostro *nm* cloister

chiro'man|te *nmf* palmist. **~'zia** *nf* palmistry

chirur'gia *nf* surgery. **chi'rurgico** *a* surgical. **chi'rurgo** *nm* surgeon

chissà *adv* who knows; **~ quando arriverà** I wonder when he will arrive

chi'tar|ra *nf* guitar. **~'rista** *nmf* guitarist

chi'uder|e *vt* shut, close; *(con la chiave)* lock; turn off *(luce, acqua ecc)*; *(per sempre)* close down *(negozio, fabbrica ecc)*; *(recingere)* enclose ●*vi* shut, close. **~si** *vr* shut; *(tempo:)* cloud over; *(ferita:)* heal over; *fig* withdraw into oneself

chi'unque *pron indef* anyone, anybody ●*pron rel* whoever

chi'usa *nf* enclosure; *(di canale)* lock; *(conclusione)* close

chi'u|so *pp di* **chiudere** ●*a* shut; *(tempo)* overcast; *(persona)* reserved. **~'sura** *nf* closing; *(sistema)* lock; *(allacciatura)* fastener. **~sura lampo** zip, zipper *Am*

ci *pron (personale)* us; *(riflessivo)* ourselves; *(reciproco)* each other; *(a ciò, di ciò ecc)* about it; **non ci disturbare** don't disturb us; **aspettateci** wait for us; **ci ha detto tutto** he told us everything; **ce lo manderanno** they'll send it to us; **ci consideriamo...** we consider ourselves...; **ci laviamo le mani** we wash our hands; **ci odiamo** we hate each other; **non ci penso mai** I never think about it; **pensaci!** think about it! ●*adv (qui)* here; *(lì)* there; *(moto per luogo)* through it; **ci siamo** we are here; **ci siete?** are you there?; **ci siamo passati tutti** we all went through it; **c'è** there is; **ce ne sono molti** there are many; **ci vuole pazienza** it takes patience; **non ci vedo/sento** I can't see/hear

cia'bat|ta *nf* slipper. **~'tare** *vi* shuffle

ciabat'tino *nm* cobbler

ci'alda *nf* wafer

cial'trone *nm (mascalzone)* scoundrel

ciam'bella *nf Culin* ring-shaped cake; *(salvagente)* lifebelt; *(gonfiabile)* rubber ring

cianci'are *vi* gossip

cianfru'saglie *nfpl* knick-knacks

cia'notico *a (colorito)* puce

ci'ao *int fam (all' arrivo)* hello!, hi!; *(alla partenza)* bye-bye!, cheerio!

ciar'la|re *vi* chat. **~'tano** *nm* charlatan

cias'cuno *a* each ●*pron* everyone, everybody; *(distributivo)* each [one]; **per ~** each

ci'bar|e *vt* feed. **~ie** *nfpl* provisions. **~si** *vr* eat; **~si di** live on

ciber'netico *a* cybernetic

'cibo *nm* food

ci'cala *nf* cicada

cica'lino *nm* buzzer

cica'tri|ce *nf* scar. **~z'zante** *nm* ointment

cicatriz'zarsi *vr* heal [up]. **cicatrizzazi'one** *nf* healing

'cicca *nf* cigarette end; *(fam: sigaretta)* fag; *(fam: gomma)* [chewing] gum

cic'chetto *nm (bicchierino)* nip; *(rimprovero)* telling-off

'cicci|a *nf fam* fat, flab. **~'one, -a** *nmf fam* fatty, fatso

cice'rone *nm* guide

cicla'mino *nm* cyclamen

ci'clis|mo *nm* cycling. **~ta** *nmf* cyclist

'ciclo *nm* cycle; *(di malattia)* course

ciclomo'tore *nm* moped

ci'clone *nm* cyclone

ci'cogna *nf* stork

ci'coria *nf* chicory

ci'eco, -a *a* blind ●*nm* blind man ●*nf* blind woman

ci'elo *nm* sky; *Relig* heaven; **santo ~!** good heavens!

'cifra *nf* figure; *(somma)* sum; *(monogramma)* monogram; *(codice)* code

ci'fra|re *vt* embroider with a monogram; *(codificare)* code. **~to a** monogrammed; coded

'ciglio *nm (bordo)* edge; *(pl nf* **ciglia:** *delle palpebre)* eyelash

'cigno *nm* swan

cigo'l|are *vt* squeak. **~io** *nm* squeak

'Cile *nm* Chile

ci'lecca *nf* far **~ miss**

ci'leno, -a *a & nmf* Chilean

cili'egi|a *nf* cherry. **~o** *nm* cherry [tree]

cilin'drata *nf* cubic capacity, c.c.; **macchina di alta ~** highpowered car

ci'lindro *nm* cylinder; (*cappello*) top hat

'**cima** *nf* top; (*fig: persona*) genius; **da ~ a fondo** from top to bottom

ci'melio *nm* relic

cimen'tar|e *vt* put to the test. **~si** *vr* (*provare*) try one's hand

'**cimice** *nf* bug; (*puntina*) drawing pin, thumbtack *Am*

cimini'era *nf* chimney; *Naut* funnel

cimi'tero *nm* cemetery

ci'murro *nm* distemper

'**Cina** *nf* China

cin cin! *int* cheers!

cincischi'are *vi* fiddle

'**cine** *nm fam* cinema

cine'asta *nmf* film maker

'**cinema** *nm inv* cinema. **cine'presa** *nf* cine-camera

ci'nese *a & nmf* Chinese

cine'teca *nf* (*raccolta*) film collection

ci'netico *a* kinetic

'**cingere** *vt* (*circondare*) surround

'**cinghia** *nf* strap; (*cintura*) belt

cinghi'ale *nm* wild boar; **pelle di ~** pigskin

cinguet't|are *vi* twitter. **~io** *nm* twittering

'**cinico** *a* cynical

ci'niglia *nf* (*tessuto*) chenille

ci'nismo *nm* cynicism

ci'nofilo *a* (*unità*) dog-loving

cin'quanta *a & nm* fifty. **cinquan'tenne** *a & nmf* fifty-year-old. **cinquan'tesimo** *a* fiftieth. **cinquan'tina** *nf* **una cinquantina** about fifty

'**cinque** *a & nm* five

cinquecen'tesco *a* sixteenth-century

cinque'cento *a* five hundred ● *nm* il **C~** the sixteenth century

cinque'mila *a & nm* five thousand

'**cinta** *nf* (*di pantaloni*) belt; **muro di ~** [boundary] wall. **cin'tare** *vt* enclose

'**cintola** *nf* (*di pantaloni*) belt

cin'tura *nf* belt. **~ di salvataggio** lifebelt. **~ di sicurezza** *Aeron, Auto* seat-belt

cintu'rino *nm* **~ dell'orologio** watchstrap

ciò *pron* this, that; **~ che** what; **~ nondimeno** nevertheless

ci'occa *nf* lock

ciocco'la|ta *nf* chocolate; (*bevanda*) [hot] chocolate. **~'tino** *nm* chocolate.

~to *nm* chocolate. **~to al latte/ fondente** milk/plain chocolate

cioè *adv* that is

ciondo'l|are *vi* dangle. **ci'ondolo** *nm* pendant. **~oni** *adv fig* hanging about

cionono'stante *adv* nonetheless

ci'otola *nf* bowl

ci'ottolo *nm* pebble

ci'polla *nf* onion; (*bulbo*) bulb

ci'presso *nm* cypress

'**cipria** *nf* [face] powder

'**Cipro** *nm* Cyprus. **cipri'ota** *a & nmf* Cypriot

'**circa** *adv & prep* about

'**circo** *nm* circus

circo'la|re *a* circular ● *nf* circular; (*di metropolitana*) circle line ● *vi* circulate. **~'torio** *a Med* circulatory. **~zi'one** *nf* circulation; (*traffico*) traffic

'**circolo** *nm* circle; (*società*) club

circon'ci|dere *vt* circumcise. **~si'one** *nf* circumcision

circon'dar|e *vt* surround. **~io** *nm* (*amministrativo*) administrative district. **~si** *vr* surround oneself with

circonfe'renza *nf* circumference. **~ dei fianchi** hip measurement

circonvallazi'one *nf* ring road

circo'scritto *a* limited

circoscrizi'one *nf* area. **~ elettorale** constituency

circo'spetto *a* wary

circospezi'one *nf* **con ~** warily

circo'stante *a* surrounding

circo'stanza *nf* circumstance; (*occasione*) occasion

circu'ire *vt* (*ingannare*) trick

cir'cuito *nm* circuit

circumnavi'ga|re *vt* circumnavigate. **~zi'one** *nf* circumnavigation

'**ciste** *nf inv* cyst

ci'sterna *nf* cistern; (*serbatoio*) tank

'**cisti** *nf inv* cyst

ci'ta|re *vt* (*riportare brani ecc*) quote; (*come esempio*) cite; *Jur* summons. **~zi'one** *nf* quotation; *Jur* summons *sg*

citofo'nare *vt* buzz. **ci'tofono** *nm* entry phone; (*in ufficio, su aereo ecc*) intercom

ci'trullo *nmf fam* dimwit

città *nf inv* town; (*grande*) city

citta'della *nf* citadel

citta'di|nanza *nf* citizenship; (*popolazione*) citizens *pl*. **~'dino, -a** *nmf* citizen; (*abitante di città*) city dweller

ciucci'are *vt fam* suck. **ci'uccio** *nm fam* dummy

ci'uco *nm* ass

ci'uffo nm tuft

ci'urma nf Naut crew

ci'vet|ta nf owl; (fig: donna) flirt; [auto] ~ta unmarked police car. ~'tare vi flirt. ~te'ria nf coquettishness

'**civico** a civic

ci'vil|e a civil. ~iz'zare vt civilize. ~iz'zato a (paese) civilized. ~izzazi'one nf civilization. ~'mente adv civilly

civiltà nf inv civilization; (cortesia) civility

'**clacson** nm inv horn. **clacso'nare** vi beep the horn, hoot

cla'mo|re nm clamour; **fare ~re** cause a sensation. ~rosa'mente adv (sbagliare) sensationally. ~'roso a noisy; (sbaglio) sensational

clan nm inv clan; fig clique

clandestin|a'mente adv secretly. ~ità nf secrecy

clande'stino a clandestine; **movimento ~** underground movement; **passeggero ~** stowaway

clari'netto nm clarinet

'**classe** nf class. ~ **turistica** tourist class

classi'cis|mo nm classicism. ~ta nmf classicist

'**classico** a classical; (tipico) classic ● nm classic

clas'sifi|ca nf classification; Sport results pl. ~'care vt classify. ~'carsi vr be placed. ~ca'tore nm (cartella) folder. ~cazi'one nf classification

clas'sista nmf class-conscious person

'**clausola** nf clause

claustro|fo'bia nf claustrophobia. ~'fobico a claustrophobic

clau'sura nf Relig enclosed order

clavi'cembalo nm harpsichord

cla'vicola nf collar-bone

cle'men|te a merciful; (tempo) mild. ~za nf mercy

cleri'cale a clerical. '**clero** nm clergy

clic nm Comput click; **fare ~ su** click on

cli'en|te nmf client; (di negozio) customer. ~'tela nf customers pl

'**clima** nm climate. **cli'matico** a climatic; **stazione climatica** health resort

'**clinica** nf clinic. **clinico** a clinical ● nm clinician

clo'aca nf sewer

'**cloro** nm chlorine. ~'formio nm chloroform

clou a inv **momenti ~** highlights

coabi'ta|re vi live together. ~zi'one nf cohabitation

coagu'la|re vt, ~rsi vr coagulate. ~zi'one nf coagulation

coalizi'one nf coalition. ~'zarsi vr unite

co'atto a Jur compulsory

'**cobra** nm inv cobra

coca'ina nf cocaine. **cocai'nomane** nmf cocaine addict

cocci'nella nf ladybird

'**coccio** nm earthenware; (frammento) fragment

cocci|u'taggine nf stubbornness. ~'uto a stubborn

'**cocco** nm coconut palm; fam love; **noce di ~** coconut

cocco'drillo nm crocodile

cocco'lare vt cuddle

co'cente a (sole) burning

'**cocktail** nm inv (ricevimento) cocktail party

co'comero nm watermelon

co'cuzzolo nm top; (di testa, cappello) crown

'**coda** nf tail; (di abito) train; (fila) queue; **fare la ~** queue [up], stand in line Am. ~ **di cavallo** (acconciatura) ponytail. ~ **dell'occhio** corner of one's eye ~ **di paglia** guilty conscience

co'dardo, -a a cowardly ● nmf coward

'**codice** nm code. ~ **di avviamento postale** postal code, zip code Am. ~ **a barre** bar-code. ~ **fiscale** tax code. ~ **della strada** highway code.

codifi'care vt codify

coe'ren|te a consistent. ~za nf consistency

coesi'one nf cohesion

coe'sistere vi coexist

coe'taneo, -a a & nmf contemporary

cofa'netto nm casket. '**cofano** nm (forziere) chest; Auto bonnet, hood Am

'**cogliere** vt pick; (sorprendere) catch; (afferrare) seize; (colpire) hit

co'gnato, -a nmf brother-in-law; sister-in-law

cognizi'one nf knowledge

co'gnome nm surname

'**coi** = **con** + **i**

coinci'denza nf coincidence; (di treno ecc) connection

coin'cidere vi coincide

coinqui'lino nm flatmate

coin'vol|gere vt involve. ~gi'mento nm involvement. ~to a involved

'**coito** nm coitus

col = con + il

colà *adv* there

cola|'brodo *nm inv* strainer; **ridotto a un ~brodo** *fam* full of holes. **~'pasta** *nm inv* colander

co'la|re *vt* strain; (*versare lentamente*) drip ● *vi* (*gocciolare*) drip; (*perdere*) leak; **~re a picco** *Naut* sink. **~ta** *nf* (*di metallo*) casting; (*di lava*) flow

colazi'one *nf* (*del mattino*) breakfast; (*di mezzogiorno*) lunch; **prima ~** breakfast; **far ~** have breakfast/lunch. **~ al sacco** packed lunch

co'lei *pron f* the one

co'lera *nm* cholera

coleste'rolo *nm* cholesterol

colf *nf abbr* (**collaboratrice familiare**) home help

'**colica** *nf* colic

co'lino *nm* [tea] strainer

'**colla** *nf* glue; (*di farina*) paste. **~ di pesce** gelatine

collabo'ra|re *vi* collaborate. **~'tore**, **~'trice** *nmf* collaborator. **~zi'one** *nf* collaboration

col'lana *nf* necklace; (*serie*) series

col'lant *nm* tights *pl*

col'lare *nm* collar

col'lasso *nm* collapse

collau'dare *vt* test. **col'laudo** *nm* test

'**colle** *nm* hill

col'lega *nmf* colleague

collega'mento *nm* connection; *Mil* liaison; *Radio ecc* link. **colle'gar|e** *vt* connect. **~si** *vr TV, Radio* link up

collegi'ale *nmf* boarder ● *a* (*responsabilità, decisione*) collective

col'legio *nm* (*convitto*) boarding-school. **~ elettorale** constituency

'**collera** *nf* anger; **andare in ~** get angry. **col'lerico** *a* irascible

col'letta *nf* collection

collet'tività *nf inv* community. **~'tivo** *a* collective; (*interesse*) general; **biglietto ~tivo** group ticket

col'letto *nm* collar

collezi|o'nare *vt* collect. **~'one** *nf* collection. **~o'nista** *nmf* collector

colli'mare *vi* coincide

col'li|na *nf* hill. **~'noso** *a* (*terreno*) hilly

col'lirio *nm* eyewash

collisi'one *nf* collision

'**collo** *nm* neck; (*pacco*) package; **a ~ alto** high-necked. **~ del piede** instep

colloca'mento *nm* placing; (*impiego*) employment

collo'ca|re *vt* place. **~rsi** *vr* take one's place. **~zi'one** *nf* placing

colloqui'ale *a* (*termine*) colloquial. **col'loquio** *nm* conversation; (*udienza ecc*) interview; (*esame*) oral [exam]

collusi'one *nf* collusion

colluttazi'one *nf* scuffle

col'mare *vt* fill [to the brim]; bridge (*divario*); **~ qcno di gentilezze** overwhelm sb with kindness. '**colmo** *a* full ● *nm* top; *fig* height; **al colmo della disperazione** in the depths of despair; **questo è il colmo!** (*con indignazione*) this is the last straw!; (*con stupore*) I don't believe it!

co'lomb|a *nf* dove. **~o** *nm* pigeon

co'loni|a¹ *nf* colony; **~a [estiva]** (*per bambini*) holiday camp. **~'ale** *a* colonial

co'lonia² *nf* [**acqua di**] = [eau de] Cologne

co'lonico *a* (*terreno, casa*) farm

coloniz'za|re *vt* colonize. **~'tore**, **~'trice** *nmf* colonizer

co'lon|na *nf* column. **~ sonora** sound-track. **~ vertebrale** spine. **~'nato** *nm* colonnade

colon'nello *nm* colonel

co'lono *nm* tenant farmer

colo'rante *nm* colouring

colo'rare *vt* colour; colour in (*disegno*)

co'lore *nm* colour; **a colori** in colour; **di ~** coloured. **colo'rito** *a* coloured; (*viso*) rosy; (*racconto*) colourful ● *nm* complexion

co'loro *pron pl* the ones

colos'sale *a* colossal. **co'losso** *nm* colossus

'**colpa** *nf* fault; (*biasimo*) blame; (*colpevolezza*) guilt; (*peccato*) sin; **dare la ~ a** blame; **essere in ~** be at fault; **per ~ di** because of. **col'pevole** *a* guilty ● *nmf* culprit

col'pire *vt* hit, strike; **~ nel segno** hit the nail on the head

'**colpo** *nm* blow; (*di arma da fuoco*) shot; (*urto*) knock; (*emozione*) shock; *Med, Sport* stroke; (*furto*) raid; **di ~** suddenly; **far ~** make a strong impression; **far venire un ~ a qcno** *fig* give sb a fright; **perdere colpi** (*motore:*) keep missing; **a ~ d'occhio** at a glance; **a ~ sicuro** for certain. **~ d'aria** chill. **~ basso** blow below the belt. **~ di scena** coup de théâtre. **~ di sole** sunstroke; **colpi** *pl* **di sole** (*su capelli*) highlights. **~ di stato** coup [d'état]. **~**

di telefono ring; dare un ~ di telefono a qn give sb a ring. ~ di testa [sudden] impulse. ~ di vento gust of wind

col'poso a omicidio ~ manslaughter

coltel'lata nf stab. col'tello nm knife

colti'va|re vt cultivate. ~'tore, ~'trice nmf farmer. ~zi'one nf farming; (di piante) growing

'colto pp di cogliere ●a cultured

'coltre nf blanket

col'tura nf cultivation

co'lui pron inv m the one

'coma nm inv coma; in ~ in a coma

comanda'mento nm commandment

coman'dante nm commander; Naut, Aeron captain

coman'dare vt command; Mech control ●vi in charge. co'mando nm command; (di macchina) control

co'mare nf (madrina) godmother

combaci'are vi fit together; (testimonianze:) concur

combat'tente a fighting ●nm combatant. ex ~ ex-serviceman

com'bat|tere vt/i fight. ~ti'mento nm fight; Mil battle; fuori ~timento (pugilato) knocked out. ~'tuto a (gara) hard fought

combi'na|re vt/i arrange; (mettere insieme) combine; (fam: fare) do; cosa stai ~ndo? what are you doing?. ~rsi vr combine; (mettersi d'accordo) come to an agreement. ~zi'one nf combination; (caso) coincidence; per ~zione by chance

com'briccola nf gang

combu'sti|bile a combustible ●nm fuel. ~'one nf combustion

com'butta nf gang; in ~ in league

'come adv like; (in qualità di) as; (interrogativo, esclamativo) how; questo vestito è ~ il tuo this dress is like yours; ~ stai? how are you?; ~ va? how are things?; ~ mai? how come?; ~ ? what?; non sa ~ fare he doesn't know what to do; ~ sta bene! how well he looks!; ~ no! that will be right!; ~ tu sai as you know; fa ~ vuoi do as you like; ~ se as if ●conj (non appena) as soon as

co'meta nf comet

'comico, -a a comic[al]; (teatro) comic ●nm funny side ●nmf (attore) comedian, comic actor ●nf (a torte in faccia) slapstick sketch

co'mignolo nm chimney-pot

cominci'are vt/i begin, start; a ~ da oggi from today; per ~ to begin with

comi'tato nm committee

comi'tiva nf party, group

co'mizio nm meeting

com'mando nm inv commando

com'medi|a nf comedy; (opera teatrale) play; fig sham. ~a musicale musical. ~'ante nmf comedian; fig pej phoney. ~'ografo, -a nmf playwright

commemo'ra|re vt commemorate. ~zi'one nf commemoration

commen'sale nmf fellow diner

commen't|are vt comment on; (annotare) annotate. ~ario nm commentary. ~a'tore, ~a'trice nmf commentator. com'mento nm comment

commerci'a|le a commercial; (relazioni, trattative) trade; (attività) business. centro ~le shopping centre. ~'lista nmf business consultant; (contabile) accountant. ~liz'zare vt market. ~lizzazi'one nf marketing

commerci'ante nmf trader, merchant; (negoziante) shopkeeper. ~ all'ingrosso wholesaler

commerci'are vi ~ in deal in

com'mercio nm commerce; (internazionale) trade; (affari) business; in ~ (prodotto) on sale. ~ all'ingrosso wholesale trade. ~ al minuto retail trade

com'messo, -a pp di commettere ●nmf shop assistant. ~ viaggiatore commercial traveller ●nf (ordine) order

comme'stibile a edible. commestibili nmpl groceries

com'mettere vt commit; make (sbaglio)

commi'ato nm leave; prendere ~ da take leave of

commise'rar|e vt commiserate. ~si vr feel sorry for oneself

commissari'ato nm (di polizia) police station

commis's|ario nm ≈ [police] superintendent; (membro di commissione) commissioner; (Sport) steward; Comm commission agent. ~ario d'esame examiner. ~i'one nf (incarico) errand; (comitato ecc) commission; (Comm: di merce) order; ~ioni pl (acquisti) fare ~ioni go shopping. ~ione d'esame board of examiners. C~ione Europea European Commission

commit'tente nmf purchaser

com'mo|sso pp di commuovere ●a moved. ~'vente a moving

commozi'one nf emotion. ~ cerebrale concussion

commu'over|e *vt* touch, move. **~si** *vr* be touched

commu'tare *vt* change; *Jur* commute

comò *nm inv* chest of drawers

comoda'mente *adv* comfortably

como'dino *nm* bedside table

comodità *nf inv* comfort; (*convenienza*) convenience

'**comodo** *a* comfortable; (*conveniente*) convenient; (*spazioso*) roomy; (*facile*) easy; **stia ~!** don't get up!; **far ~** be useful ● *nm* comfort; **fare il proprio ~** do as one pleases

compae'sano, -a *nmf* fellow countryman

com'pagine *nf* (*squadra*) team

compa'gnia *nf* company; (*gruppo*) party; **fare ~ a qcno** keep sb company; **essere di ~** be sociable. **~ aerea** airline

com'pagno, -a *nmf* companion, mate; *Comm, Sport* partner; *Pol* comrade. **~ di scuola** schoolmate

compa'rabile *a* comparable

compa'ra|re *vt* compare. **~'tivo** *a* & *nm* comparative. **~zi'one** *nf* comparison

com'pare *nm* (*padrino*) godfather; (*testimone di matrimonio*) witness

compa'rire *vi* appear; (*spiccare*) stand out; **~ in giudizio** appear in court

com'parso, -a *pp di* **comparire** ● *nf* appearance; *Cinema* extra; *Theat* walk-on

compartecipazi'one *nf* sharing; (*quota*) share

comparti'mento *nm* compartment; (*amministrativo*) department

compas'sato *a* calm and collected

compassi'o|ne *nf* compassion; **aver ~** feel pity for; **far ~** arouse pity. **~'nevole** *a* compassionate

com'passo *nm* [pair of] compasses *pl*

compa'tibil|e *a* (*conciliabile*) compatible; (*scusabile*) excusable. **~ità** *nf* compatibility. **~'mente** *adv* **~mente con i miei impegni** if my commitments allow

compa'tire *vt* pity; (*scusare*) make allowances for

compatri'ota *nmf* compatriot

compat'tezza *nf* (*di materia*) compactness. **com'patto** *a* compact; (*denso*) dense; (*solido*) solid; *fig* united

compene'trare *vt* pervade

compen'sar|e *vt* compensate; (*supplire*) make up for. **~si** *vr* balance each other out

compen'sato *nm* (*legno*) plywood

compensazi'one *nf* compensation

com'penso *nm* compensation; (*retribuzione*) remuneration; **in ~** (*in cambio*) in return; (*d'altra parte*) on the other hand; (*invece*) instead

'**comper|a** *nf* purchase; **far ~e** do some shopping

compe'rare *vt* buy

compe'ten|te *a* competent. **~za** *nf* competence; (*responsabilità*) responsibility

com'petere *vi* compete; **~ a** (*compito:*) be the responsibility of

competi'tività *nf* competitiveness. **~'tivo** *a* (*prezzo, carattere*) competitive. **~'tore,** **~'trice** *nmf* competitor. **~zi'one** *nf* competition

compia'cen|te *a* obliging. **~za** *nf* obligingness

compia'c|ere *vt/i* please. **~ersi** *vr* (*congratularsi*) congratulate. **~ersi di** (*degnarsi*) condescend. **~i'mento** *nm* satisfaction. **~i'uto** *a* (*aria, sorriso*) smug

compi'angere *vt* pity; (*per lutto ecc*) sympathize with. **~to** *a* lamented ● *nm* grief

'**compier|e** *vt* (*concludere*) complete; commit (*delitto*); **~e gli anni** have one's birthday. **~si** *vr* end; (*avverarsi*) come true

compi'la|re *vt* compile; fill in (*modulo*). **~zi'one** *nf* compilation

compi'mento *nm* **portare a ~ qcsa** conclude sth

com'pire *vt* = **compiere**

compi'tare *vt* spell

com'pito[1] *a* polite

'**compito**[2] *nm* task; *Sch* homework

compi'ut|o *a* **avere 30 anni ~i** be over 30

comple'anno *nm* birthday

complemen'tare *a* complementary; (*secondario*) subsidiary

comple'mento *nm* complement; *Mil* draft. **~ oggetto** direct object

comples|sità *nf* complexity. **~siva'mente** *adv* on the whole. **~'sivo** *a* comprehensive; (*totale*) total. **com'plesso** *a* complex; (*difficile*) complicated ● *nm* complex; (*di cantanti ecc*) group; (*di circostanze, fattori*) combination; **in ~so** on the whole

completa'mente *adv* completely

comple'tare *vt* complete

com'pleto *a* complete; (*pieno*) full [up]; **essere al ~** (*teatro:*) be sold out;

la famiglia al ~ the whole family ● *nm* (*vestito*) suit; (*insieme di cose*) set
compli'ca|re *vt* complicate. **~rsi** *vr* become complicated. **~to** complicated. **~zi'one** *nf* complication; **salvo ~zioni** all being well
'complic|e *nmf* accomplice ● *a* ⟨*sguardo*⟩ knowing. **~ità** *nf* complicity
complimen'tar|e *vt* compliment. **~si** *vr*~**si con** congratulate
compli'menti *nmpl* (*ossequi*) regards; (*congratulazioni*) congratulations; **far ~** stand on ceremony
compli'mento *nm* compliment
complot'tare *vi* plot. **com'plotto** *nm* plot
compo'nente *a & nm* component ● *nmf* member
compo'nibile *a* ⟨*cucina*⟩ fitted; ⟨*mobili*⟩ modular
componi'mento *nm* composition; (*letterario*) work
com'por|re *vt* compose; (*ordinare*) put in order; *Typ* set. **~si** *vr*~**si di** be made up of
comporta'mento *nm* behaviour
compor'tar|e *vt* involve; (*consentire*) allow. **~si** *vr* behave
composi'tore, -'trice *nmf* composer; *Typ* compositor. **~zi'one** *nf* composition
com'posta *nf* stewed fruit; (*concime*) compost
compo'stezza *nf* composure
com'posto *pp di* **comporre** ● *a* composed; (*costituito*) comprising; **stai ~!** sit properly! ● *nm* Chem compound
compra|re *vt* buy. **~'tore**, **~'trice** *nmf* buyer
compra'vendita *nf* buying and selling
com'pren|dere *vt* understand; (*includere*) comprise. **~'sibile** *a* understandable. **~sibil'mente** *adv* understandably. **~si'one** *nf* understanding. **~'sivo** *a* understanding; (*che include*) inclusive. **com'preso** *pp di* **comprendere** ● *a* included; **tutto compreso** (*prezzo*) all-in
com'pressa *nf* compress; (*pastiglia*) tablet
compressi'one *nf* compression. **com'presso** *pp di* **comprimere** ● *a* compressed
com'primere *vt* press; (*reprimere*) repress
compro'me|sso *pp di* **compromet-**

tere ● *nm* compromise. **~t'tente** *a* compromising. **~ttere** *vt* compromise
compropri'età *nf* multiple ownership
compro'vare *vt* prove
com'punto *a* contrite
compu'tare *vt* calculate
com'puter *nm* computer. **~iz'zare** *vt* computerize. **~iz'zato** *a* computerized
computiste'ria *nf* book-keeping. **'computo** *nm* calculation
comu'nale *a* municipal
co'mune *a* common; (*condiviso*) mutual; (*ordinario*) ordinary ● *nm* borough, council; (*amministrativo*) commune; **fuori del ~** out of the ordinary. **~'mente** *adv* commonly
comuni'ca|re *vt* communicate; pass on ⟨*malattia*⟩; *Relig* administer Communion to. **~rsi** *vr* receive Communion. **~'tiva** *nf* communicativeness. **~'tivo** *a* communicative. **~to** *nm* communiqué. **~to stampa** press release. **~zi'one** *nf* communication; *Teleph* [phone] call; **avere la ~zione** get through; **dare la ~zione a qcno** put sb through
comuni'one *nf* communion; *Relig* [Holy] Communion
comu'nis|mo *nm* communism. **~ta** *a & nmf* communist
comunità *nf inv* community. **C~ [Economica] Europea** European [Economic] Community
co'munque *conj* however ● *adv* anyhow
con *prep* with; (*mezzo*) by; **~ facilità** easily; **~ mia grande gioia** to my great delight; **è gentile ~ tutti** he is kind to everyone; **col treno** by train; **~ questo tempo** in this weather
co'nato *nm*~**di vomito** retching
'conca *nf* basin; (*valle*) dell
concate'na|re *vt* link together. **~zi'one** *nf* connection
'concavo *a* concave
con'ceder|e *vt* grant; award ⟨*premio*⟩; (*ammettere*) admit. **~si** *vr* allow oneself ⟨*pausa*⟩
concentra'mento *nm* concentration
concen'tra|re *vt*, **~rsi** *vr* concentrate. **~to** *a* concentrated ● *nm*~**to di pomodoro** tomato purée. **~zi'one** *nf* concentration
concepi'mento *nm* conception
conce'pire *vt* conceive ⟨*bambino*⟩; (*capire*) understand; (*figurarsi*) conceive of; devise ⟨*piano ecc*⟩
con'cernere *vt* concern

concer'tar|e *vt Mus* harmonize; *(organizzare)* arrange. **~si** *vr* agree

concer'tista *nmf* concert performer.

con'certo *nm* concert; *(composizione)* concerto

concessio'nario *nm* agent

concessi'one *nf* concession

con'cesso *pp di* **concedere**

con'cetto *nm* concept; *(opinione)* opinion

concezi'one *nf* conception; *(idea)* concept

con'chiglia *nf* [sea] shell

'concia *nf* tanning; *(di tabacco)* curing

conci'a|re *vt* tan; cure *(tabacco)*; **~re qcno per le feste** give sb a good hiding. **~rsi** *vr (sporcarsi)* get dirty; *(vestirsi male)* dress badly. **~to** *a (pelle, cuoio)* tanned

concili'abile *a* compatible

concili'ante *a* conciliatory

concili'a|re *vt* reconcile; settle *(contravvenzione)*; *(favorire)* induce. **~rsi** *vr* go together; *(mettersi d'accordo)* become reconciled; *Jur* settlement

~zi'one *nf* reconciliation; *Jur* settlement

con'cilio *nm Relig* council; *(riunione)* assembly

conci'mare *vt* feed *(pianta)*. **con'cime** *nm* manure; *(chimico)* fertilizer

concisi'one *nf* conciseness. **con'ciso** *a* concise

conci'tato *a* excited

concitta'dino, -a *nmf* fellow citizen

con'clu|dere *vt* conclude; *(finire con successo)* achieve. **~dersi** *vr* come to an end. **~si'one** *nf* conclusion; **in ~sione** *(insomma)* in short. **~'sivo** *a* conclusive. **~so** *pp di* **concludere**

concomi'tanza *nf (di circostanze, fatti)* combination

concor'da|nza *nf* agreement. **~re** *vt* agree; *Gram* make agree. **~to** *nm* agreement; *Jur, Comm* arrangement

con'corde *a* in agreement; *(unanime)* unanimous

concor'ren|te *a* concurrent; *(rivale)* competing ●*nmf Comm, Sport* competitor; *(candidato)* candidate. **~za** *nf* competition. **~zi'ale** *a* competitive

con'cor|rere *vi (contribuire)* concur; *(andare insieme)* go together; *(competere)* compete. **~so** *pp di* **concorrere** ●*nm* competition; **fuori ~so** not in the official competition. **~so di bellezza** beauty contest

concreta'mente *adv* concretely

concre'tare *vt (concludere)* achieve.

~tiz'zare *vt* put into concrete form *(idea, progetto)*

con'creto *a* concrete; **in ~** in concrete terms

concussi'one *nf* extortion

con'danna *nf* sentence; **pronunziare una ~** pass a sentence. **condan'nare** *vt* condemn; *Jur* sentence. **condan'nato, -a** *nmf* convict

conden'sa|re *vt, ~rsi* *vr* condense. **~zi'one** *nf* condensation

condi'mento *nm* seasoning; *(salsa)* dressing. **con'dire** *vt* flavour; dress *(insalata)*

condiscen'den|te *a* indulgent; *pej* condescending. **~za** *nf* indulgence; *pej* condescension

condi'videre *vt* share

condizio'na|le *a & nm* conditional ●*nf Jur* suspended sentence. **~'mento** *nm Psych* conditioning

condizio'na|re *vt* condition. **~to** *a* conditional. **~'tore** *nm* air conditioner

condizi'one *nf* condition; **a ~ che** on condition that

condogli'anze *nfpl* condolences; **fare le ~a** offer condolences to

condomini'ale *a (spese)* common. **condo'minio** *nm* joint ownership; *(edificio)* condominium

condo'nare *vt* remit. **con'dono** *nm* remission

con'dotta *nf* conduct, *(circoscrizione di medico)* district; *(di gara ecc)* management; *(tubazione)* piping

con'dotto *pp di* **condurre** ●*a* **medico ~** district doctor ●*nm* pipe; *Anat* duct

condu'cente *nm* driver

con'du|rre *vt* lead; drive *(veicoli)*; *(accompagnare)* take; conduct *(gas, elettricità ecc)*; *(gestire)* run. **~rsi** *vr* behave. **~'tore, ~'trice** *nmf TV* presenter; *(di veicolo)* driver ●*nm Electr* conductor. **~t'tura** *nf* duct

confabu'lare *vi* have a confab

confa'cente *a* suitable. **con'farsi** *vr* **confarsi a** suit

confederazi'one *nf* confederation

confe'renz|a *nf (discorso)* lecture; *(congresso)* conference. **~a stampa** news conference. **~i'ere, -a** *nmf* lecturer

confe'rire *vt (donare)* give ●*vi* confer

con'ferma *nf* confirmation. **confer'mare** *vt* confirm

confes'sa|re *vt, ~arsi* *vr* confess

~io'nale *a* & *nm* confessional. ~i'one *nf* confession. ~ore *nm* confessor

con'fetto *nm* sugared almond

confet'tura *nf* jam

confezio'na|re *vt* manufacture; make ‹*abiti*›; package ‹*merci*›. ~to *a* ‹*vestiti*› off-the-peg; ‹*gelato*› wrapped

confezi'one *nf* manufacture; (*di abiti*) tailoring; (*di pacchi*) packaging; **confezioni** *pl* clothes. ~ **regalo** gift pack

confic'car|e *vt* thrust. ~si *vr* run into

confi'd|are *vi* ~are in trust ● *vt* confide. ~arsi *vr* ~arsi con confide in. ~ente *a* confident ● *nmf* confidant

confi'denz|a *nf* confidence; (*familiarità*) familiarity; prendersi delle ~e take liberties. ~i'ale *a* confidential; (*rapporto, tono*) familiar

configu'ra|re *vt* Comput configure. ~zi'one *nf* configuration

confi'nante *a* neighbouring

confi'na|re *vi* (*relegare*) confine ● *vi* ~re con border on. ~rsi *vr* withdraw. ~to *a* confined

con'fin|e *nm* border; (*tra terreni*) boundary. ~o *nm* political exile

con'fi|sca *nf* (*di proprietà*) forfeiture. ~'scare *vt* confiscate

con'flitt|o *nm* conflict. ~u'ale *a* adversarial

conflu'enza *nf* confluence; (*di strade*) junction

conflu'ire *vi* ‹*fiumi:*› flow together; ‹*strade:*› meet

con'fonder|e *vt* confuse; (*turbare*) confound; (*imbarazzare*) embarrass. ~si *vr* (*mescolarsi*) mingle; (*turbarsi*) become confused; *vr* (*sbagliarsi*) be mistaken

confor'ma|re *vt,* ~rsi *vr* conform. ~zi'one *nf* conformity (a with); (*del terreno*) composition

con'forme *a* according. ~'mente *adv* accordingly

confor'mi|smo *nm* conformity. ~sta *nmf* conformist. ~tà *nf* (*a norma*) conformity

confor'tante *a* comforting

confor't|are *vt* comfort. ~evole *a* (*comodo*) comfortable. con'forto *nm* comfort

confron'tare *vt* compare

con'fronto *nm* comparison; in ~ a by comparison with; nei tuoi confronti towards you; senza ~ far and away

confusi|o'nario *a* ‹*persona*› muddle-headed. ~'one *nf* confusion; (*baccano*)

racket; (*disordine*) mess; (*imbarazzo*) embarrassment. con'fuso *pp di* confondere ● *a* confused; (*indistinto*) indistinct; (*imbarazzato*) embarrassed

confu'tare *vt* confute

conge'dar|e *vt* dismiss; Mil discharge. ~si *vr* take one's leave

con'gedo *nm* leave; essere in ~ be on leave. ~ malattia sick leave. ~ maternità maternity leave

conge'gnare *vt* devise; (*mettere insieme*) assemble. con'gegno *nm* device

congela'mento *nm* freezing; Med frost-bite

conge'la|re *vt* freeze. ~to *a* ‹*cibo*› deep-frozen. ~'tore *nm* freezer

congeni'ale *a* congenial

con'genito *a* congenital

congestio'na|re *vt* congest. ~to *a* ‹*traffico*› congested; (*viso*) flushed. congesti'one *nf* congestion

conget'tura *nf* conjecture

congi'unger|e *vt* join; combine (*sforzi*). ~si *vr* join

congiunti'vite *nf* conjunctivitis

congiun'tivo *nm* subjunctive

congi'unto *pp di* congiungere ● *a* joined ● *nm* relative

congiun'tu|ra *nf* joint; (*circostanza*) juncture; (*situazione*) situation. ~'rale *a* economic

congiunzi'one *nf* Gram conjunction

congi'u|ra *nf* conspiracy. ~'rare *vi* conspire

conglome'rato *nm* conglomerate; *fig* conglomeration; (*da costruzione*) concrete

congratu'la|rsi *vr* ~rsi con qcno per congratulate sb on. ~zi'oni *nfpl* congratulations

con'grega *nf* band

congre'ga|re *vt,* ~rsi *vr* congregate. ~zi'one *nf* congregation

con'gresso *nm* congress

'congruo *a* proper; (*giusto*) fair

conguagli'are *vt* balance. con-gu'aglio *nm* balance

coni'are *vt* coin

'conico *a* conical

co'nifera *nf* conifer

co'niglio *nm* rabbit

coniu'gale *a* marital; (*vita*) married

coniu'ga|re *vt* conjugate. ~rsi *vr* get married. ~zi'one *nf* conjugation

'coniuge *nmf* spouse

connazio'nale *nmf* compatriot

connessi'one *nf* connection. con-'nesso *pp di* connettere

con'nettere vt connect ● vi think rationally

conni'vente a conniving

conno'ta|re vt connote. **~to** nm distinguishing feature; **~ti** pl description

con'nubio nm fig union

'**cono** nm cone

cono'scen|te nmf acquaintance. **~za** nf knowledge; (persona) acquaintance; (sensi) consciousness; **perdere ~za** lose consciousness; **riprendere ~za** regain consciousness, come to

co'nosc|ere vt know; (essere a conoscenza di) be acquainted with; (fare la conoscenza di) meet. **~i'tore, ~i'trice** nmf connoisseur. **~i'uto** pp di **conoscere** ● a well-known

con'quista nf conquest. **conqui'sta·re** vt conquer; fig win

consa'cra|re vt consecrate; ordain (sacerdote); (dedicare) dedicate. **~rsi** vr devote oneself. **~zi'one** nf consecration

consangu'ineo, -a nmf blood-relation

consa'pevo|le a conscious. **~'lezza** nf consciousness. **~'lmente** adv consciously

'**conscio** a conscious

consecu'tivo a consecutive; (seguente) next

con'segna nf delivery; (merce) consignment; (custodia) care; (di prigioniero) handover; (Mil: ordine) orders pl; (Mil: punizione) confinement; **pagamento alla ~** cash on delivery

conse'gnare vt deliver; (affidare) give in charge; Mil confine to barracks

consegu'en|te a consequent. **~za** nf consequence; **di ~za** (perciò) consequently

consegui'mento nm achievement

consegu'ire vt achieve ● vi follow

con'senso nm consent

consensu'ale a consensus-based

consen'tire vi consent ● vt allow

con'serto a **a braccia conserte** with one's arms folded

con'serva nf preserve; (di frutta) jam; (di agrumi) marmalade. **~ di pomodoro** tomato sauce

conser'var|e vt preserve; (mantenere) keep. **~si** vr keep; **~si in salute** keep well

conserva'tore, -'trice nmf Pol conservative

conserva'torio nm conservatory

conservazi'one nf preservation; **a lunga ~** long-life

conside'ra|re vt consider; (stimare) regard. **~to** a (stimato) esteemed. **~zi'one** nf consideration; (osservazione, riflessione) remark

conside'revole a considerable

consigli'abile a advisable

consigli'are vt advise; (raccomandare) recommend. **~'arsi** vr **~arsi con qcno** ask sb's advice. **~'ere, -a** nmf adviser; (membro di consiglio) councillor

con'siglio nm advice; (ente) council. **~ d'amministrazione** board of directors. **C~ dei Ministri** Cabinet

consi'sten|te a substantial; (spesso) thick; (fig: argomento) valid. **~za** nf consistency; (spessore) thickness

con'sistere vi **~ in** consist of

consoci'ata nf (azienda) associate company

conso'lare[1] vt console; (rallegrare) cheer. **~si** vr console oneself

conso'lare[2] a consular. **~to** nm consulate

consolazi'one nf consolation; (gioia) joy

con'sole nf inv (tastiera) console

'**console** nm consul

consoli'dar|e vt, **~si** vr consolidate

conso'nante nf consonant

'**consono** a consistent

con'sorte nmf consort

con'sorzio nm consortium

con'stare vi **~ di** consist of; (risultare) appear; **a quanto mi consta** as far as I know; **mi consta che** it appears that

consta'tare vt ascertain. **~zi'one** nf observation

consu'e|to a & nm usual. **~tudi'nario** a (diritto) common; (persona) set in one's ways. **~'tudine** nf habit; (usanza) custom

consu'len|te nmf consultant. **~za** nf consultancy

consul'tare vt consult. **~rsi con** consult with. **~zi'one** nf consultation

consul'tivo a consultative. **~orio** nm clinic

consu'ma|re vt (usare) consume; wear out (abito, scarpe); consummate (matrimonio); commit (delitto). **~rsi** vr consume; (abito, scarpe:) wear out; (struggersi) pine

consu'mato a (politico) seasoned; (scarpe, tappeto) worn

consuma'|tore, -'trice nmf consumer. **~zi'one** nf (bibita) drink; (spuntino) snack

consu'mis|mo *nm* consumerism. **~ta** *nmf* consumerist

con'sumo *nm* consumption; (*di abito, scarpe*) wear; (*uso*) use; **generi di ~** consumer goods. **~** [**di carburante**] [fuel] consumption

consun'tivo *nm* [**bilancio**] **~** final statement

conta'balle *nmf fam* storyteller

con'tabil|e *a* book-keeping ●*nmf* accountant. **~ità** *nf* accounting; **tenere la ~ità** keep the accounts

contachi'lometri *nm inv* mileometer, odometer *Am*

conta'dino, -a *nmf* farm-worker; (*medievale*) peasant

contagi'are *vt* infect. **con'tagio** *nm* infection. **~'oso** *a* infectious

conta'gocce *nm inv* dropper

contami'na|re *vt* contaminate. **~zi'one** *nf* contamination

con'tante *nm* cash; **pagare in contanti** pay cash

con'tare *vt/i* count; (*tenere conto di*) take into account; (*proporsi*) intend

conta'scatti *nm inv Teleph* time-unit counter

conta'tore *nm* meter

contat'tare *vt* contact. **con'tatto** *nm* contact

'conte *nm* count

conteggi'are *vt* put on the bill ●*vi* calculate. **con'teggio** *nm* calculation. **conteggio alla rovescia** countdown

con'te|gno *nm* behaviour; (*atteggiamento*) attitude. **~'gnoso** *a* dignified

contem'pla|re *vt* contemplate; (*fissare*) gaze at. **~zi'one** *nf* contemplation

con'tempo *nm* **nel ~** in the meantime

contempo|ranea'mente *adv* at once. **~'raneo, -a** *a* & *nmf* contemporary

conten'dente *nmf* competitor. **con'tendere** *vi* compete; (*litigare*) quarrel ●*vt* contend

conte'n|ere *vt* contain; (*reprimere*) repress. **~ersi** *vr* contain oneself. **~i'tore** *nm* container

conten'tarsi *vr* **~ di** be content with

conten'tezza *nf* joy

conten'tino *nm* placebo

con'tento *a* glad; (*soddisfatto*) contented

conte'nuto *nm* contents *pl*; (*soggetto*) content

contenzi'oso *nm* legal department

con'tes|a *nf* disagreement; *Sport* contest. **~o** *pp di* **contendere** ●*a* contested

con'tessa *nf* countess

conte'sta|re *vt* contest; *Jur* notify. **~'tario** *a* anti-establishment. **~'tore, ~'trice** *nmf* protester. **~zi'one** *nf* (*disputa*) dispute

con'testo *nm* context

con'tiguo *a* adjacent

continen'tale *a* continental. **conti'nente** *nm* continent

conti'nenza *nf* continence

contin'gen|te *nm* contingent; (*quota*) quota. **~za** *nf* contingency

continua'mente *adv* (*senza interruzione*) continuously; (*frequentemente*) continually

continu'are *vt/i* continue; (*riprendere*) resume. **~a'tivo** *a* permanent. **~azi'one** *nf* continuation. **~ità** *nf* continuity

con'tinuo *a* continuous; (*molto frequente*) continual. **corrente ~a** direct current; **di ~o** continually

'conto *nm* calculation; (*in banca, negozio*) account; (*di ristorante ecc*) bill; (*stima*) consideration; **a conti fatti** all things considered; **far ~ di** (*supporre*) suppose; (*proporsi*) intend; **far ~ su** rely on; **in fin dei conti** when all is said and done; **per ~ di** on behalf of; **per ~ mio** (*a mio parere*) in my opinion; (*da solo*) on my own; **starsene per ~ proprio** be on one's own; **rendersi ~ di qcsa** realize sth; **sul ~ di qcno** (*voci, informazioni*) about sb; **tener ~ di qcsa** take sth into account; **tenere da ~ qcsa** look after sth; **fare i conti con qcno** *fig* sort sb out. **~ corrente** current account, checking account *Am*. **~ alla rovescia** countdown

con'torcer|e *vt* twist. **~si** *vr* twist about

contor'nare *vt* surround

con'torno *nm* contour; *Culin* vegetables *pl*

contorsi'one *nf* contortion. **con'torto** *pp di* **contorcere** ●*a* twisted

contrabban'dare *vt* smuggle. **~di'ere, -a** *nmf* smuggler. **contrab'bando** *nm* contraband

contrab'basso *nm* double bass

contraccambi'are *vt* return. **contrac'cambio** *nm* return

contracce|t'tivo *nm* contraceptive. **~zi'one** *nf* contraception

contrac'colpo *nm* rebound; (*di arma da fuoco*) recoil; *fig* repercussion

con'trada *nf (rione)* district
contrad'detto *pp di* **contraddire**
contrad'di|re *vt* contradict. **~t'torio**
a contradictory. **~zi'one** *nf* contradiction
contraddi'stin|guere *vt* differentiate. **~to** *a* distinct
contra'ente *nmf* contracting party
contra'ereo *a* anti-aircraft
contraf'fa|re *vt* disguise; *(imitare)*
imitate; *(falsificare)* forge. **~tto** *a*
forged. **~zi'one** *nf* disguising; *(imitazione)* imitation; *(falsificazione)* forgery
con'tralto *nm* countertenor • *nf* contralto
contrap'peso *nm* counterbalance
contrap'por|re *vt* counter; *(confrontare)* compare. **~si** *vr* contrast; **~si a**
be opposed to
contraria'mente *adv* contrary (**a** to)
contrari|'are *vt* oppose; *(infastidire)*
annoy. **~'arsi** *vr* get annoyed. **~età** *nf
inv* adversity; *(ostacolo)* set-back
con'trario *a* contrary, opposite; *(direzione)* opposite; *(sfavorevole)* unfavourable • *nm* contrary, opposite; **al ~** on
the contrary
con'trarre *vt* contract
contras|se'gnare *vt* mark. **~-
'segno** *nm* mark; **[in] ~segno** *(spedizione)* cash on delivery, COD
contra'stante *a* contrasting
contra'stare *vt* oppose; *(contestare)*
contest • *vi* clash. **con'trasto** *nm* contrast; *(litigio)* dispute
contrattac'care *vt* counter-attack.
contrat'tacco *nm* counter-attack
contrat'ta|re *vt/i* negotiate; *(mercanteggiare)* bargain. **~zi'one** *nf (salariale)* bargaining
contrat'tempo *nm* hitch
con'tratt|o *pp di* **contrarre** • *nm* contract. **~o a termine** fixed-term contract. **~u'ale** *a* contractual
contravve'n|ire *vi* contravene. **~zi'one** *nf* contravention; *(multa)* fine
contrazi'one *nf* contraction; *(di prezzi)* reduction
contribu'ente *nmf* contributor; *(del
fisco)* taxpayer
contribu'ire *vi* contribute. **contri-
'buto** *nm* contribution
'contro *prep* against; **~ di me** against
me • *nm* **il pro e il ~** the pros and cons
pl
contro'battere *vt* counter

controbilanci'are *vt* counterbalance
controcor'rente *a (idee, persona)*
non-conformist • *adv* upriver; *fig* upstream
controffen'siva *nf* counter-offensive
controfi'gura *nf* stand-in
controfir'mare *vt* countersign
controindicazi'one *nf Med* contraindication
control'la|re *vt* control; *(verificare)*
check; *(collaudare)* test. **~rsi** *vr* have
self-control. **~to** *a* controlled
con'trol|lo *nm* control; *(verifica)*
check; *Med* check-up. **~lo delle nascite** birth control. **~'lore** *nm* controller;
(sui treni ecc) [ticket] inspector. **~lore
di volo** air-traffic controller
contro'luce *nf* **in ~** against the light
contro'mano *adv* in the wrong direction
contromi'sura *nf* countermeasure
contropi'ede *nm* **prendere in ~**
catch off guard
controprodu'cente *a* self-defeating
con'trordin|e *nm* counter order; **sal-
vo ~i** unless I/you hear to the contrary
contro'senso *nm* contradiction in
terms
controspio'naggio *nm* counterespionage
contro'vento *adv* against the wind
contro'vers|ia *nf* controversy; *Jur*
dispute. **~o** *a* controversial
contro'voglia *adv* unwillingly
contu'macia *nf* default; **in ~** in one's
absence
contun'dente *a (corpo, arma)* blunt
contur'bante *a* perturbing
contusi'one *nf* bruise
convale'scen|te *a* convalescent.
~za *nf* convalescence; **essere in ~za**
be convalescing
con'vali|da *nf* validation. **~'dare** *vt*
confirm; validate *(atto, biglietto)*
con'vegno *nm* meeting; *(congresso)*
congress
conve'nevol|e *a* suitable; **~i** *pl* pleasantries
conveni'en|te *a* convenient; *(prezzo)*
attractive; *(vantaggioso)* advantageous.
~za *nf* convenience; *(interesse)* advantage; *(di prezzo)* attractiveness
conve'nire *vi (riunirsi)* gather; *(concordare)* agree; *(ammettere)* admit; *(essere opportuno)* be convenient • *vt* agree
on; **ci conviene andare** it is better to

go; **non mi conviene stancarmi** I'd better not tire myself out

con'vento *nm* (*di suore*) convent; (*di frati*) monastery

conve'nuto *a* fixed

convenzio'nale *a* conventional. **~'one** *nf* convention

conver'gen|te *a* converging. **~za** *nf* *fig* confluence

con'vergere *vi* converge

conver'sa|re *vi* converse. **~zi'one** *nf* conversation

conversi'one *nf* conversion

con'verso *pp di* **convergere**

conver'tibile *nf Auto* convertible

conver'ti|re *vt* convert. **~rsi** *vr* be converted. **~to, -a** *nmf* convert

con'vesso *a* convex

convin'cente *a* convincing

con'vin|cere *vt* convince. **~zi'one** *nf* conviction

con'vitto *nm* boarding school

convi'ven|te *nm* common-law husband ● *nf* common-law wife. **~za** *nf* cohabitation. **con'vivere** *vi* live together

convivi'ale *a* convivial

convo'ca|re *vt* convene. **~zi'one** *nf* convening

convogli'are *vt* convey; (*navi:*) convoy. **con'voglio** *nm* convoy; (*ferroviario*) train

convulsi'one *nf* convulsion. **con'vulso** *a* convulsive; (*febbrile*) feverish

coope'ra|re *vi* co-operate. **~'tiva** *nf* co-operative. **~'one** *nf* co-operation

coordina'mento *nm* co-ordination

coordi'na|re *vt* co-ordinate. **~ta** *nf Math* coordinate. **~zi'one** *nf* co-ordination

co'perchio *nm* lid; (*copertura*) cover

co'perta *nf* blanket; (*copertura*) cover; *Naut* deck

coper'tina *nf* cover; (*di libro*) dust-jacket

co'perto *pp di* **coprire** ● *a* covered; (*cielo*) overcast ● *nm* (*a tavola*) place; (*prezzo del coperto*) cover charge; **al ~** under cover

coper'tone *nm* tarpaulin; (*gomma*) tyre

coper'tura *nf* covering; *Comm, Fin* cover

'copia *nf* copy; **bella/brutta ~** fair/rough copy. **~ su carta** hardcopy. **copi'are** *vt* copy

copi'one *nm* script

copi'oso *a* plentiful

'coppa *nf* (*calice*) goblet; (*per gelato ecc*) dish; *Sport* cup. **~ [di] gelato** ice-cream (*served in a dish*)

cop'petta *nf* (*di ceramica, vetro*) bowl; (*di gelato*) small tub

'coppia *nf* couple; (*in carte*) pair

co'prente *a* (*cipria, vernice*) covering

copri'capo *nm* headgear

coprifu'oco *nm* curfew

copri'letto *nm* bedspread

copripiu'mino *nm* duvet cover

co'prir|e *vt* cover; drown (*suono:*); hold (*carica*). **~si** *vr* (*vestirsi*) cover up; *fig* cover oneself; (*cielo:*) become overcast

coque *sf* **alla ~** (*uovo*) soft-boiled

co'raggio *nm* courage; (*sfacciataggine*) nerve; **~o!** come on. **~'oso** *a* courageous

co'rale *a* choral

co'rallo *nm* coral

co'rano *nm* Koran

co'raz|za *nf* armour; (*di animali*) shell. **~'zata** *nf* battleship. **~'zato** *a* (*nave*) armour-clad

corbelle'ria *nf* nonsense; (*sproposito*) blunder

'corda *nf* cord; (*spago, Mus*) string; (*fune*) rope; (*cavo*) cable; **essere giù di ~** be depressed; **dare ~ a** qcno encourage sb. **corde** *pl* **vocali** vocal cords

cor'data *nf* roped party

cordi'al|e *a* cordial ● *nm* (*bevanda*) cordial; **saluti ~i** best wishes. **~ità** *nf* cordiality

cor'doglio *nm* grief; (*lutto*) mourning

cor'done *nm* cord; (*schieramento*) cordon. **~ ombelicale** umbilical cord

core|ogra'fia *nf* choreography. **~'ografo, -a** *nmf* choreographer

cori'andoli *nmpl* confetti *sg*

cori'andolo *nm* (*spezia*) coriander

cori'car|e *vt* put to bed. **~si** *vr* go to bed

co'rista *nmf* choir member

cor'nacchia *nf* crow

corna *vedi* **corno**

corna'musa *nf* bagpipes *pl*

'cornea *nf* cornea

cor'nett|a *nf Mus* cornet; (*del telefono*) receiver. **~o** *nm* (*brioche*) croissant

cor'ni|ce *nf* frame. **~ci'one** *nm* cornice

'corno *nm* (*pl nf* **corna**) horn; **fare le corna a** qcno be unfaithful to sb; **fare le corna** (*per scongiuro*) touch wood. **cor'nuto** *a* horned ● *nm* (*fam: marito tradito*) cuckold; (*insulto*) bastard

'coro *nm* chorus; *Relig* choir

co'rolla *nf* corolla

co'rona nf crown; (di fiori) wreath; (rosario) rosary. ~'mento nm (di impresa) crowning. coro'nare vt crown; ⟨sogno⟩ fulfil

cor'petto nm bodice

'corpo nm body; (Mil, diplomatico) corps inv; a ~ a ~ man to man; andare di ~ move one's bowels. ~ di ballo corps de ballet. ~ insegnante teaching staff. ~ del reato incriminating item

corpo'rale a corporal

corporati'vismo nm corporatism

corpora'tura nf build

corporazi'one nf corporation

cor'poreo a bodily

cor'poso a full-bodied

corpu'lento a stout

cor'puscolo nm corpuscle

corre'dare vt equip

cor'rente nm (per neonato) layette

cor'redo nm (nuziale) trousseau

cor'reggere vt correct; lace ⟨bevanda⟩

corre'lare vt correlate

cor'rente a running; (in vigore) current; (frequente) everyday; ⟨inglese ecc⟩ fluent ● a current; ⟨d'aria⟩ draught; essere al ~ be up to date. ~'mente adv ⟨parlare⟩ fluently

'correre vi run; (affrettarsi) hurry; Sport race; ⟨notizie:⟩ circulate; ~ dietro a vt run after ● vt run; ~ un pericolo run a risk; lascia ~! don't bother!

corre|tta'mente adv correctly. cor'retto pp di correggere ● a correct; ⟨caffè⟩ with a drop of alcohol. ~zi'one nf correction. ~zione di bozze proof-reading

cor'rida nf bullfight

corri'doio nm corridor; Aeron aisle

corri'|dore, -'trice nmf racer; (a piedi) runner

corri'era nf coach, bus

corri'ere nm courier; (posta) mail; (spedizioniere) carrier

corri'mano nm bannister

corrispet'tivo nm amount due

corrispon'den|te a corresponding ● nmf correspondent. ~za nf correspondence; scuola/corsi per ~za correspondence course; vendite per ~za mail-order [shopping]. corri'spondere vi correspond; ⟨stanza:⟩ communicate; corrispondere a (contraccambiare) return

corri'sposto a ⟨amore⟩ reciprocated

corrobo'rare vt strengthen; fig corroborate

cor'roder|e vt, ~si vr corrode

cor'rompere vt corrupt; (con denaro) bribe

corrosi'one nf corrosion. corro'sivo a corrosive

cor'roso pp di corrodere

cor'rotto pp di corrompere ● a corrupt

corrucci'a|rsi vr be vexed. ~to a upset

corru'gare vt wrinkle; ~ la fronte knit one's brows

corruzi'one nf corruption; (con denaro) bribery

'corsa nf running; (rapida) dash; Sport race; (di treno ecc) journey; di ~ at a run; fare una ~ run

cor'sia nf gangway; (di ospedale) ward; Auto lane; (di supermercato) aisle

cor'sivo nm italics pl

'corso pp di correre ● nm course; (strada) main street; Comm circulation; lavori in ~ work in progress; nel ~ di during. ~ d'acqua watercourse

'corte nf [court]yard; (Jur, regale) court; fare la ~ a qcno court sb. ~ d'appello court of appeal

cor'teccia nf bark

corteggia'mento nm courtship

corteggi'a|re vt court. ~'tore nm admirer

cor'teo nm procession

cor'te|se a courteous. ~'sia nf courtesy; per ~sia please

cortigi'ano, -a nmf courtier ● nf courtesan

cor'tile nm courtyard

cor'tina nf curtain; (schermo) screen

'corto a short; per farla corta in short; essere a ~ di be short of. ~ circuito nm short [circuit]

cortome'traggio nm Cinema short

cor'vino a jet-black

'corvo nm raven

'cosa nf thing; (faccenda) matter; inter, rel what; [che] ~ what; nessuna ~ nothing; ogni ~ everything; per prima ~ first of all; tante cose so many things; (augurio) all the best

'cosca nf clan

'coscia nf thigh; Culin leg

cosci'en|te a conscious. ~za nf conscience; (consapevolezza) consciousness

co'scri|tto nm conscript. ~zi'one nf conscription

così adv so; (in questo modo) like this, like that; (perciò) therefore; **le cose stanno ~** that's how things stand; **fermo ~!** hold it; **proprio ~!** exactly!; **basta ~!** that will do!; **ah, è ~?** it's like that, is it?; **~ ~** so-so; **e ~ via** and so on; **per ~ dire** so to speak; **più di ~** any more; **una ~ cara ragazza!** such a nice girl!; **è stato ~ generoso da aiutarti** he was kind enough to help you ● conj (allora) so ● a inv (tale) like that, such; **una ragazza ~** a girl like that, such a girl

cosicché conj and so

cosid'detto a so-called

co'smesi nf cosmetics

co'smetico a & nm cosmetic

'cosmico a cosmic

'cosmo nm cosmos

cosmopo'lita a cosmopolitan

co'spargere vt sprinkle; (disseminare) scatter

co'spetto nm **al ~ di** in the presence of

co'spicuo a conspicuous; (somma ecc) considerable

cospi'ra|re vi conspire. **~'tore, ~'trice** nmf conspirator. **~zi'one** nf conspiracy

'costa nf coast, coastline; Anat rib

costà adv there

co'stan|te a & nf constant. **~za** nf constancy

co'stare vi cost; **quanto costa?** how much is it?

co'stata nf chop

costeggi'are vt (per mare) coast; (per terra) skirt

co'stei pron vedi **costui**

costellazi'one nf constellation

coster'na|to a dismayed. **~zi'one** nf consternation

costi'er|a nf stretch of coast. **~o** a coastal

costi'pa|to a constipated. **~zi'one** nf constipation; (raffreddore) bad cold

costitu'ir|e vt constitute; (formare) form; (nominare) appoint. **~si** vr Jur give oneself up

costituzio'nale a constitutional. **costituzi'one** nf constitution; (fondazione) setting up

'costo nm cost; **ad ogni ~** at all costs; **a nessun ~** on no account

'costola nf rib; (di libro) spine

costo'letta nf cutlet

co'storo pron vedi **costui**

co'stoso a costly

co'stretto pp di **costringere**

co'strin|gere vt compel; (stringere) constrict. **~t'tivo** a coercive. **~zi'one** nf constraint

co'stru|'ire vt build, construct. **~t'tivo** a constructive. **~zi'one** nf building, construction

co'stui, co'stei, pl **co'storo** prons (soggetto) he, she, pl they; (complemento) him, her, pl them

co'stume nm (usanza) custom; (condotta) morals pl; (indumento) costume. **~ da bagno** swim-suit; (da uomo) swimming trunks

co'tenna nf pigskin; (della pancetta) rind

coto'letta nf cutlet

co'tone nm cotton. **~ idrofilo** cotton wool, absorbent cotton Am

'cotta nf (fam: innamoramento) crush

cot'timo nm **lavorare a ~** do piece-work

'cotto pp di **cuocere** ● a done; (infatuato) in love; (sbronzo) drunk; **ben ~** (carne) well done

cotton fi'oc® nm inv cotton bud

cot'tura nf cooking

co'vare vt hatch; sicken for (malattia); harbour (odio) ● vi smoulder

'covo nm den

co'vone nm sheaf

'cozza nf mussel

coz'zare vi **~ contro** bump into.
'cozzo nm fig clash

C.P. abbr (**Casella Postale**) PO Box

'crampo nm cramp

'cranio nm skull

cra'tere nm crater

cra'vatta nf tie; (a farfalla) bow-tie

cre'anza nf politeness; **mala ~** bad manners

cre'a|re vt create; (causare) cause. **~tività** nf creativity. **~tivo** a creative. **~to** nm creation. **~'tore, ~'trice** nmf creator. **~zi'one** nf creation

crea'tura nf creature; (bambino) baby; **povera ~!** poor thing!

cre'den|te nmf believer. **~za** nf belief; Comm credit; (mobile) sideboard. **~zi'ali** nfpl credentials

'creder|e vt believe; (pensare) think ● vi **~e in** believe in; **credo di sì** I think so; **non ti credo** I don't believe you. **~si** vr think oneself to be; **si crede uno scrittore** he flatters himself he is a writer. **cre'dibile** a credible.

credibilità nf credibility

'credi|to nm credit; (stima) esteem;

comprare a ~to buy on credit. **~'tore, ~'trice** *nmf* creditor
'credo *nm inv* credo
credulità *nf* credulity
credu|lo *a* credulous. **~'lone, -a** *nmf* simpleton
crema *nf* cream; (*di uova e latte*) custard. **~ idratante** moisturizer. **~ pasticciera** egg custard. **~ solare** suntan lotion
cre'ma|re *vt* cremate. **~'torio** *nm* crematorium. **~zi'one** *nf* cremation
crème cara'mel *nf* crème caramel
creme'ria *nf* dairy (*also selling ice cream and cakes*)
Crem'lino *nm* Kremlin
'crepa *nf* crack
cre'pac|cio *nm* cleft; (*di ghiacciaio*) crevasse
crepacu'ore *nm* heart-break
crepa'pelle *adv* **a ~** fit to burst; **ridere a ~** split one's sides with laughter
cre'pare *vi* crack; (*fam: morire*) kick the bucket; **~ dal ridere** laugh fit to burst
crepa'tura *nf* crevice
crêpe *nf inv* pancake
crepi'tare *vi* crackle
cre'puscolo *nm* twilight
cre'scendo *nm* crescendo
'cresc|ere *vi* grow; (*aumentare*) increase ● *vt* (*allevare*) bring up; (*aumentare*) raise. **~ita** *nf* growth; (*aumento*) increase. **~i'uto** *pp di* **crescere**
'cresi|ma *nf* confirmation. **~'mare** *vt* confirm
'crespo *a* (*capelli*) frizzy ● *nm* crêpe
'cresta *nf* crest; (*cima*) peak
'creta *nf* clay
'Creta *nf* Crete
cre'tino, -a *a* stupid ● *nmf* idiot
cric *nm* jack
'cricca *nf* gang
cri'ceto *nm* hamster
crimi'nal|e *a & nmf* criminal. **~ità** *nf* crime. **'crimine** *nm* crime
crimi'noso *a* criminal
'crin|e *nm* horsehair. **~i'era** *nf* mane
'cripta *nf* crypt
crisan'temo *nm* chrysanthemum
'crisi *nf inv* crisis; *Med* fit
cristal'lino *nm* crystalline
cristalliz'zar|e *vt*, **~si** *vr* crystallize; (*fig: parola, espressione:*) become part of the language
cri'stallo *nm* crystal
Cristia'nesimo *nm* Christianity

cristi'ano, -a *a & nmf* Christian
'Cristo *nm* Christ; **un povero c~** a poor beggar
cri'terio *nm* criterion; (*buon senso*) [common] sense
'criti|ca *nf* criticism; (*recensione*) review. **criti'care** *vt* criticize. **~co** *a* critical ● *nm* critic. **~cone, -a** *nmf* faultfinder
crivel'lare *vt* riddle (**di** with)
cri'vello *nm* sieve
croc'cante *a* crisp ● *nm* type of crunchy nut biscuit
croc'chetta *nf* croquette
'croce *nf* cross; **a occhio e ~** roughly; **fare testa e ~** spin a coin. **C~ Rossa** Red Cross
croce'via *nm inv* crossroads *sg*
croci'ata *nf* crusade
cro'cicchio *nm* crossroads *sg*
croci'era *nf* cruise; *Archit* crossing
croci'fi|ggere *vt* crucify. **~ssi'one** *nf* crucifixion. **~sso** *pp di* **crocifiggere** ● *a* crucified ● *nm* crucifix
crogio'larsi *vr* bask
crogi[u]'olo *nm* crucible; *fig* melting pot
crol'lare *vi* collapse; (*prezzi:*) slump. **'crollo** *nm* collapse; (*dei prezzi*) slump
cro'mato *a* chromium-plated. **'cromo** *nm* chrome. **cromo'soma** *nm* chromosome
'cronaca *nf* chronicle; (*di giornale*) news; *TV, Radio* commentary; **fatto di ~** news item. **~ nera** crime news
'cronico *a* chronic
cro'nista *nmf* reporter
crono'logico *a* chronological
crono'metraggio *nm* timing
cronome'trare *vt* time
cro'nometro *nm* chronometer
'crosta *nf* crust; (*di formaggio*) rind; (*di ferita*) scab; (*quadro*) daub
cro'staceo *nm* shellfish
cro'stata *nf* tart
cro'stino *nm* croûton
crucci'arsi *vr* worry. **'cruccio** *nm* worry
cruci'ale *a* crucial
cruci'verba *nm inv* crossword [puzzle]
cru'del|e *a* cruel. **~tà** *nf inv* cruelty
'crudo *a* raw; (*rigido*) harsh
cru'ento *a* bloody
cru'miro *nm* blackleg, scab
'crusca *nf* bran
cru'scotto *nm* dashboard
'Cuba *nf* Cuba

cu'betto *nm* ~ di ghiaccio ice cube
'cubico *a* cubic
cubi'tal|e *a* a caratteri ~i in enormous letters
'cubo *nm* cube
cuc'cagna *nf* abundance; (*baldoria*) merry-making; paese della ~ land of plenty
cuc'cetta *nf* (*su un treno*) couchette; *Naut* berth
cucchia'ino *nm* teaspoon
cucchi'a|io *nm* spoon; al ~io (*dolce*) creamy. ~i'ata *nf* spoonful
'cuccia *nf* dog's bed; fa la ~! lie down!
cuccio'lata *nf* litter
'cucciolo *nm* puppy
cu'cina *nf* kitchen; (*il cucinare*) cooking; (*cibo*) food; (*apparecchio*) cooker; far da ~ cook; libro di ~ cook[ery] book. ~ a gas gas cooker
cuci'n|are *vt* cook. ~ino *nm* kitchenette
cu'ci|re *vt* sew; macchina per ~re sewing-machine. ~to *nm* sewing. ~'tura *nf* seam
cucù *nm inv* cuckoo
'cuculo *nm* cuckoo
'cuffia *nf* bonnet; (*da bagno*) bathingcap; (*ricevitore*) headphones *pl*
cu'gino, -a *nmf* cousin
'cui *pron rel* (*persona: con prep*) who, whom *fml*; (*cose, animali: con prep*) which; (*tra articolo e nome*) whose; la persona con ~ ho parlato the person [who] I spoke to; la ditta per ~ lavoro the company I work for, the company for which I work; l'amico il ~ libro è stato pubblicato the friend whose book was published; in ~ (*dove*) where; (*quando*) that; per ~ (*perciò*) so; la città in ~ vivo the city I live in, the city where I live; il giorno in ~ l'ho visto the day [that] I saw him
culi'nari|a *nf* cookery. ~o *a* culinary
'culla *nf* cradle. cul'lare *vt* rock
culmi'na|nte *a* culminating. ~re *vi* culminate. 'culmine *nm* peak
'culo *nm vulg* arse; (*fortuna*) luck
'culto *nm* cult; *Relig* religion; (*adorazione*) worship
cul'tu|ra *nf* culture. ~ra generale general knowledge. ~'rale *a* cultural
cultu'ris|mo *nm* body-building. ~ta *nmf* body builder

cumula'tivo *a* cumulative; biglietto ~ group ticket
'cumulo *nm* pile; (*mucchio*) heap; (*nuvola*) cumulus
'cuneo *nm* wedge
cu'netta *nf* gutter
cu'ocere *vt/i* cook; fire (*ceramica*)
cu'oco, -a *nmf* cook
cu'oio *nm* leather. ~ capelluto scalp
cu'ore *nm* heart; cuori *pl* (*carte*) hearts; nel profondo del ~ in one's heart of hearts; di [buon] ~ (*persona*) kind-hearted; nel ~ della notte in the middle of the night; stare a ~ a qcno be very important to sb
cupi'digia *nf* greed
'cupo *a* gloomy; (*suono*) deep
'cupola *nf* dome
'cura *nf* care; (*amministrazione*) management; *Med* treatment; a ~ di edited by; in ~ under treatment. ~ dimagrante [slimming] diet. cu'rante *a* medico curante GP, doctor
cu'rar|e *vt* take care of; *Med* treat; (*guarire*) cure; edit (*testo*). ~si *vr* take care of oneself; *Med* follow a treatment; ~si di (*badare a*) mind
cu'rato *nm* parish priest
cura'tore, -'trice *nmf* trustee; (*di testo*) editor
'curia *nf* curia
curio's|are *vi* be curious; (*mettere il naso*) pry (in into); (*nei negozi*) look around. ~ità *nf inv* curiosity. curi'oso *a* curious; (*strano*) odd
cur'sore *nm Comput* cursor
'curva *nf* curve; (*stradale*) bend. ~ a gomito U-bend. cur'vare *vt* curve; (*strada:*) bend. cur'varsi *vr* bend. 'curvo *a* curved; (*piegato*) bent
cusci'netto *nm* pad; *Mech* bearing
cu'scino *nm* cushion; (*guanciale*) pillow. ~ d'aria air cushion
'cuspide *nf* spire
cu'stod|e *nm* caretaker. ~e giudiziario official receiver. ~ia *nf* care; *Jur* custody; (*astuccio*) case. ~ia cautelare remand. custo'dire *vt* keep; (*badare*) look after
cu'taneo *a* skin *attrib*
'cute *nf* skin
cu'ticola *nf* cuticle

Dd

da *prep* from; (*con verbo passivo*) by; (*moto a luogo*) to; (*moto per luogo*) through; (*stato in luogo*) at; (*temporale*) since; (*continuativo*) for; (*causale*) with; (*in qualità di*) as; (*con caratteristica*) with; (*come*) like; **da Roma a Milano** from Rome to Milan; **staccare un quadro dalla parete** take a picture off the wall; **i bambini dai 5 ai 10 anni** children between 5 and 10; **vedere qcsa da vicino/lontano** see sth from up close/from a distance; **scritto da** written by; **andare dal panettiere** go to the baker's; **passo da te più tardi** I'll come over to your place later; **passiamo da qui** let's go this way; **un appuntamento dal dentista** an appointment at the dentist's; **il treno passa da Venezia** the train goes through Venice; **dall'anno scorso** since last year; **vivo qui da due anni** I've been living here for two years; **da domani** from tomorrow; **piangere dal dolore** cry with pain; **ho molto da fare** I have a lot to do; **occhiali da sole** sunglasses; **qualcosa da mangiare** something to eat; **un uomo dai capelli scuri** a man with dark hair; **è un oggetto da poco** it's not worth much; **l'ho fatto da solo** I did it by myself; **si è fatto da sé** he is a self-made man; **non è da lui** it's not like him

dac'capo *adv* again; (*dall'inizio*) from the beginning

dacché *conj* since

'dado *nm* dice; Culin stock cube; Techn nut

daf'fare *nm* work

'dagli = **da** + **gli**. **'dai** = **da** + **i**

'dai *int* come on!

'daino *nm* deer; (*pelle*) buckskin

dal = **da** + **il**. **'dalla** = **da** + **la**. **'dalle** = **da** + **le**. **'dallo** = **da** + **lo**

'dalia *nf* dahlia

dal'tonico *a* colour-blind

'dama *nf* lady; (*nei balli*) partner; (*gioco*) draughts *sg*

dami'gella *nf* (*di sposa*) bridesmaid

damigi'ana *nf* demijohn

dam'meno *adv* **non essere ~ (di qcno)** be no less good (than sb)

da'naro *nm* = **denaro**

dana'roso *a* (*fam: ricco*) loaded

da'nese *a* Danish ● *nmf* Dane ● *nm* (*lingua*) Danish

Dani'marca *nf* Denmark

dan'na|re *vt* damn; **far ~re qcno** drive sb mad. **~to** *a* damned. **~zi'one** *nf* damnation

danneggi|a'mento *nm* damage. **~'are** *vt* damage; (*nuocere*) harm

'danno *nm* damage; (*a persona*) harm. **dan'noso** *a* harmful

Da'nubio *nm* Danube

'danza *nf* dance; (*il danzare*) dancing. **dan'zare** *vi* dance

dapper'tutto *adv* everywhere

dap'poco *a* worthless

dap'prima *adv* at first

'dardo *nm* dart

'dar|e *vt* give; sit (*esame*); have (*festa*); **~e qcsa a qcno** give sb sth; **~e da mangiare a qcno** give sb something to eat; **~e il benvenuto a qcno** welcome sb; **~e la buonanotte a qcno** say good night to sb; **~e del tu/del lei a qcno** address sb as "tu"/"lei"; **~e del cretino a qcno** call sb an idiot; **~e qcsa per scontato** take sth for granted; **cosa danno alla TV stasera?** what's on TV tonight? ● *vi* **~e nell'occhio** be conspicuous; **~e alla testa** go to one's head; **~e su** (*finestra, casa*) look on to; **~e sui** *o* **ai nervi a qcno** get on sb's nerves ● *nm Comm* debit. **~si** *vr* (*scambiarsi*) give each other; **~si da fare** get down to it; **si è dato tanto da fare!** he went to so much trouble!; **~si** (*a*) (*cominciare*) take up; **~si al bere** take to drink; **~si per** (*malato, assente*) pretend to be; **~si per vinto** give up; **può ~si** maybe

'darsena *nf* dock

'data *nf* date. **~ di emissione** date of issue. **~ di nascita** date of birth. **~ di scadenza** cut-off date

da'ta|re *vt* date; **a ~re da** as from. **~to** *a* dated

'**dato** *a* given; *(dedito)* addicted; ~ **che** seeing that, given that ●*nm* datum. ~ **di fatto** well-established fact; **dati** *pl* data. **da'tore** *nm* giver. **datore, datrice** *nmf* **di lavoro** employer

'**dattero** *nm* date

dattilogra'f|are *vt* type. ~**ia** *nf* typing. **datti'lografo, -a** *nmf* typist

dattilo'scritto *a (copia)* typewritten

dat'torno *a* **togliersi** ~ clear off

da'vanti *adv* before; *(dirimpetto)* opposite; *(di fronte)* in front ●*a inv* front ●*nm* front; ~ **a** *prep* before, in front of

davan'zale *nm* window sill

da'vanzo *adv* more than enough

dav'vero *adv* really; **per** ~ in earnest; **dici** ~? honestly?

'**dazio** *nm* duty; *(ufficio)* customs *pl*

d.C. *abbr* (**dopo Cristo**) AD

'**dea** *nf* goddess

debel'lare *vt* defeat

debili'ta|nte *a* weakening. ~**re** *vt* weaken. ~**rsi** *vr* become debilitated. ~**zi'one** *nf* debilitation

debita'mente *adv* duly

'**debi|to** *a* due; **a tempo** ~ in due course ●*nm* debt. ~**tore,** ~**'trice** *nmf* debtor

'**debo|le** *a* weak; *(luce)* dim; *(suono)* faint ●*nm* weak point; *(preferenza)* weakness. ~**'lezza** *nf* weakness

debor'dare *vi* overflow

debosci'ato *a* debauched

debut'ta|nte *nm (attore)* actor making his début ●*nf* actress making her début. ~**re** *vi* make one's début. **de'butto** *nm* début

deca'den|te *a* decadent. ~**'tismo** *nm* decadence. ~**za** *nf* decline; *Jur* loss. **deca'dere** *vi* lapse. **decadi'mento** *nm (delle arti)* decline

decaffei'nato *a* decaffeinated ●*nm* decaffeinated coffee, decaf *fam*

decan'tare *vt (lodare)* praise

decapi'ta|re *vt* decapitate; behead *(condannato)*. ~**zi'one** *nf* decapitation; beheading

decappott'abile *a* convertible

de'ce|dere *vi (morire)* die. ~**'duto** *a* deceased

dece'rare *vt* decelerate, slow down

decen'nale *a* ten-yearly. **de'cennio** *nm* decade

de'cen|te *a* decent. ~**te'mente** *adv* decently. ~**za** *nf* decency

decentra'mento *nm* decentralization

de'cesso *nm* death; **atto di** ~ death certificate

de'cider|e *vt* decide; settle *(questione)*. ~**si** *vr* make up one's mind

deci'frare *vt* decipher; *(documenti cifrati)* decode

deci'male *a* decimal

deci'mare *vt* decimate

'**decimo** *a* tenth

de'cina *nf Math* ten; **una** ~ **di** *(circa dieci)* about ten

decisa'mente *adv* definitely, decidedly

decisio'nale *a* decision-making

deci|si'one *nf* decision. ~**'sivo** *a* decisive. **de'ciso** *pp di* **decidere** ●*a* decided

decla'ma|re *vt/i* declaim. ~**'torio** *a (stile)* declamatory

declas'sare *vt* downgrade

decli'na|re *vt* decline; ~**re ogni responsabilità** disclaim all responsibility ●*vi* go down; *(tramontare)* set. ~**zi'one** *nf Gram* declension. **de'clino** *nm* decline; **in declino** *(popolarità:)* on the decline

decodificazi'one *nf* decoding

decol'lare *vi* take off

décolle'té *nm inv* décolleté, low neckline

de'collo *nm* take-off

decolo'ra|nte *nm* bleach. ~**re** *vt* bleach

decolorazi'one *nf* bleaching

decom'po|rre *vt*, ~**rsi** *vr* decompose. ~**sizi'one** *nf* decomposition

deconcen'trarsi *vr* become distracted

deconge'lare *vt* defrost

decongestio'nare *vt Med, fig* relieve congestion in

deco'ra|re *vt* decorate. ~**'tivo** *a* decorative. ~**to** *a (ornato)* decorated. ~**'tore,** ~**'trice** *nmf* decorator. ~**zi'one** *nf* decoration

de'coro *nm* decorum

decorosa'mente *adv* decorously. **decoroso** *a* dignified

decor'renza *nf* ~ **dal...** starting from...

de'correre *vi* pass; **a** ~ **da** with effect from. **de'corso** *pp di* **decorrere** ●*nm* passing; *Med* course

de'crepito *a* decrepit

decre'scente *a* decreasing. **de'crescere** *vi* decrease; *(prezzi:)* go down; *(acque:)* subside

decre'tare *vt* decree. **de'creto** *nm* de-

cree. **decreto legge** *decree which has the force of law*
'**dedalo** *nm* maze
'**dedica** *nf* dedication
dedi'car|e *vt* dedicate. **~si** *vr* dedicate oneself
'**dedi|to** *a* **~** *a* given to; (*assorto*) engrossed in; addicted to (*vizi*). **~zi'one** *nf* dedication
de'dotto *pp di* **dedurre**
dedu'cibile *a* (*tassa*) allowable
de'du|rre *vt* deduce; (*sottrarre*) deduct. **~t'tivo** *a* deductive. **~zi'one** *nf* deduction
defal'care *vt* deduct
defe'rire *vt* Jur remit
defezi|o'nare *vi* (*abbandonare*) defect. **~'one** *nf* defection
defici'en|te *a* (*mancante*) deficient; Med mentally deficient ● *nmf* mental defective; *pej* half-wit. **~za** *nf* deficiency; (*lacuna*) gap; Med mental deficiency
'**defici|t** *nm inv* deficit. **~'tario** *a* (*bilancio*) deficit *attrib*
defi'larsi *vr* (*scomparire*) slip away
défilé *nm inv* fashion show
defi'ni|re *vt* define; (*risolvere*) settle. **~tiva'mente** *adv* for good. **~'tivo** *a* definitive. **~to** *a* definite. **~zi'one** *nf* definition; (*soluzione*) settlement
deflazi'one *nf* deflation
deflet'tore *nm* Auto quarterlight
deflu'ire *vi* (*liquidi*) flow away; (*persone*) stream out
de'flusso *nm* (*di marea*) ebb
defor'mar|e *vt* deform (*arto*); *fig* distort. **~si** *vr* lose its shape
defor'm|ato *a* warped. **~azi'one** *nf* (*di fatti*) distortion; **è una ~azione professionale** put it down to the job. **de'forme** *a* deformed. **~ità** *nf* deformity
defrau'dare *vt* defraud
de'funto, -a *a & nmf* deceased
degene'ra|re *vi* degenerate. **~to** *a* degenerate. **~zi'one** *nf* degeneration.
de'genere *a* degenerate
de'gen|te *a* bedridden ● *nmf* patient. **~za** *nf* confinement
'**degli** =di + **gli**
deglu'tire *vt* swallow
de'gnar|e *vt* **~e** qcno di uno sguardo deign to look at sb. **~si** *vr* deign, condescend
'**degno** *a* worthy; (*meritevole*) deserving
degrada'mento *nm* degradation
degra'dante *a* demeaning

degra'da|re *vt* degrade. **~rsi** *vr* lower oneself; (*città*) fall into a state of disrepair. **~zi'one** *nf* degradation
de'grado *nm* damage; **~ ambientale** environmental damage
degu'sta|re *vt* taste. **~zi'one** *nf* tasting
'**dei** =di + **i.** '**del** =di + **il**
dela'|tore, -'trice *nmf* [police] informer. **~zi'one** *nf* informing
'**delega** *nf* proxy
dele'ga|re *vt* delegate. **~to** *nm* delegate. **~zi'one** *nf* delegation
dele'terio *a* harmful
del'fino *nm* dolphin; (*stile di nuoto*) butterfly [stroke]
de'libera *nf* bylaw
delibe'ra|re *vt/i* deliberate; **~ su/in** rule on/in. **~to** *a* deliberate
delicata'mente *adv* delicately
delica'tezza *nf* delicacy; (*fragilità*) frailty; (*tatto*) tact
deli'cato *a* delicate; (*salute*) frail; (*suono, colore*) soft
delimi'tare *vt* delimit
deline'a|re *vt* outline. **~rsi** *vr* be outlined; *fig* take shape. **~to** *a* defined
delin'quen|te *nmf* delinquent. **~za** *nf* delinquency
deli'rante *a* Med delirious; (*assurdo*) insane
deli'rare *vi* be delirious. **de'lirio** *nm* delirium; *fig* frenzy
de'litto *nm* crime. **~u'oso** *a* criminal
de'lizi|a *nf* delight. **~'are** *vt* delight. **~'oso** *a* delightful; (*cibo*) delicious
'**della** =di + **la.** '**delle** =di + **le.** '**dello** = di + **lo**
'**delta** *nm inv* delta
delta'plano *nm* hang-glider; **fare ~** go hang-gliding
delucidazi'one *nf* clarification
delu'dente *a* disappointing
de'lu|dere *vt* disappoint. **~si'one** *nf* disappointment. **de'luso** *a* disappointed
dema'gogico *a* popularity-seeking, demagogic
demar'ca|re *vt* demarcate. **~zi'one** *nf* demarcation
de'men|te *a* demented. **~za** *nf* dementia. **~zi'ale** *a* (*assurdo*) zany
demilitariz'za|re *vt* demilitarize. **~zi'one** *nf* demilitarization
demistificazi'one *nf* debunking
demo'cratico *a* democratic. **~'zia** *nf* democracy

democristi'ano, -a *a & nmf* Christian Democrat

demogra'fia *nf* demography. **demo-'grafico** *a* demographic

demo'li|re *vt* demolish. **~zi'one** · *nf* demolition

'demone *nm* demon.**de'monio** *nm* demon

demoraliz'zar|e *vt* demoralize. **~si** *vr* become demoralized

de'mordere *vi* give up

demoti'vato *a* demotivated

de'nari *nmpl (nelle carte)* diamonds

de'naro *nm* money

deni'gra|re *vt* denigrate. **~'torio** *a* denigratory

denomi'na|re *vt* name.**~'tore** *nm* denominator. **~zi'one** *nf* denomination; **~zione di origine controllata** mark guaranteeing the quality of a wine

deno'tare *vt* denote

densità *nf inv* density.**'denso** *a* thick, dense

den'ta|le *a* dental.**~rio** *a* dental.**~ta** *nf* bite.**~'tura** *nf* teeth *pl*

'dente *nm* tooth; *(di forchetta)* prong;**al ~** *Culin* just slightly firm. **~ del giudizio** wisdom tooth.**~ di latte** milk tooth. **denti'era** *nf* dentures *pl*, false teeth *pl*

denti'fricio *nm* toothpaste

den'tista *nmf* dentist

'dentro *adv* in, inside; *(in casa)* indoors;**da ~** from within;**qui ~** in here ● *prep* in, inside; *(di tempo)* within, by ● *nm* inside

denuclearizzazi'one *nf* denuclearization

denu'dar|e *vt* bare.**~si** *vr* strip

de'nunci|a, de'nunzia *nf* denunciation; *(alla polizia)* reporting; *(dei redditi)* [income] tax return. **~'are** *vt* denounce; *(accusare)* report

denu'tri|to *a* underfed. **~zi'one** *nf* malnutrition

deodo'rante *a & nm* deodorant

dépendance *nf inv* outbuilding

depe'ri|bile *a* perishable. **~'mento** *nm* wasting away; *(di merci)* deterioration.**~re** *vi* waste away

depi'la|re *vt* depilate. **~rsi** *vr* shave *(gambe)*; pluck *(sopracciglia)*. **~'torio** *nm* depilatory

deplo'rabile *a* deplorable

deplo'r|are *vt* deplore; *(dolersi di)* grieve over. **~evole** *a* deplorable

de'porre *vt* put down; lay down *(armi)*;

lay *(uova)*; *(togliere da una carica)* depose; *(testimoniare)* testify

depor'ta|re *vt* deport.**~to, -a** *nmf* deportee.**~zi'one** *nf* deportation

deposi'tar|e *vt* deposit; *(lasciare in custodia)* leave; *(in magazzino)* store. **~io, -a** *nmf (di segreto)* repository.**~si** *vr* settle

de'posito *nm* deposit; *(luogo)* warehouse; *Mil* depot.**~to bagagli** left-luggage office.**~zi'one** *nf* deposition; *(da una carica)* removal

depra'va|re *vt* deprave. **~to** *a* depraved.**~zi'one** *nf* depravity

depre'ca|bile *a* appalling. **~re** *vt* deprecate

depre'dare *vt* plunder

depressi'one *nf* depression. **de'presso** *pp di* **deprimere** ● *a* depressed

deprez'zar|e *vt* depreciate. **~si** *vr* depreciate

depri'mente *a* depressing

de'primer|e *vt* depress.**~si** *vr* become depressed

depu'ra|re *vt* purify. **~'tore** *nm* purifier

depu'ta|re *vt* delegate. **~to, -a** *nmf* deputy, Member of Parliament

deraglia'mento *nm* derailment

deragli'are *vi* go off the lines;**far ~** derail

'derby *nm inv* Sport local Derby

deregolamentazi'one *nf* deregulation

dere'litto *a* derelict

dere'tano *nm* backside, bottom

de'ri|dere *vt* deride. **~si'one** *nf* derision.**~'sorio** *a* derisory

de'riva *nf* drift;**andare alla ~** drift

deri'va|re *vi*--**re da** *(provenire)* derive from ● *vt* derive; *(sviare)* divert.**~zi'o-ne** *nf* derivation; *(di fiume)* diversion

dermato|lo'gia *nf* dermatology. **~'logico** *a* dermatological. **derma'to-logo, -a** *nmf* dermatologist

'deroga *nf* dispensation. **dero'gare** *vi* **derogare a** depart from

der'rat|a *nf* merchandise. **~e alimen-tari** foodstuffs

deru'bare *vt* rob

descrit'tivo *a* descriptive. **des'critto** *pp di* **descrivere**

des'cri|vere *vt* describe. **~'vibile** *a* describable

de'serto *a* uninhabited ● *nm* desert

deside'rabile *a* desirable

deside'rare *vt* wish; *(volere)* want;

(*intensamente*) long for; (*bramare*) desire; **desidera?** what would you like?, can I help you?;**lasciare a ~** leave a lot to be desired

desi'de|rio *nm* wish; (*brama*) desire; (*intenso*) longing. **~'roso** *a* desirous; (*bramoso*) longing

desi'gnare *vt* designate; (*fissare*) fix

desi'nenza *nf* ending

de'sistere *vi* **~ da** desist from

desktop publishing *nm inv* desktop publishing

deso'lante *a* distressing

deso'la|re *vt* distress. **~to** desolate; (*spiacente*) sorry. **~zi'one** *nf* desolation

'**despota** *nm* despot

de'sta|re *vt* waken; *fig* awaken. **~si** *vr* waken; *fig* awaken

desti'na|re *vt* destine; (*nominare*) appoint; (*assegnare*) assign; (*indirizzare*) address. **~'tario** *nm* (*di lettera, pacco*) addressee. **~zi'one** *nf* destination; *fig* purpose

de'stino *nm* destiny; (*fato*) fate

destitu'ire *vt* dismiss. **~zi'one** *nf* dismissal

'**desto** *a liter* awake

'**destra** *nf* (*parte*) right; (*mano*) right hand;**prendere a ~** turn right

destreggi'ar|e *vi,*~**si** *vr* manoeuvre

de'strezza *nf* dexterity; (*abilità*) skill

'**destro** *a* right; (*abile*) skilful

detei'nato *a* tannin-free

dete'n|ere *vt* hold; (*polizia:*) detain. **~uto, -a** *nmf* prisoner. **~zi'one** *nf* detention

deter'gente *a* a cleaning; (*crema*) cleansing● *nm* detergent; (*per la pelle*) cleanser

deteriora'mento *nm* deterioration

deterio'rar|e *vt* cause to deteriorate. **~si** *vr* deteriorate

determi'nante *a* a decisive

determi'na|re *vt* determine. **~rsi** *vr* **~rsi a** resolve to. **~'tezza** *nf* determination. **~'tivo** *a Gram* definite. **~to** *a* (*risoluto*) determined; (*particolare*) specific. **~zi'one** *nf* determination; (*decisione*) decision

deter'rente *a & nm* deterrent

deter'sivo *nm* detergent.**~ per i piatti** washing-up liquid

dete'stare *vt* detest, hate

deto'nare *vi* detonate

de'tra|rre *vt* deduct (**da** from). **~zi'o-ne** *nf* deduction

detri'mento *nm* detriment;**a ~ di** to the detriment of

de'trito *nm* debris

'**detta** *nf* **a ~ di** according to

dettagli'ante *nmf Comm* retailer

dettagli'a|re *vt* detail. **~ta'mente** *adv* in detail

det'taglio *nm* detail;**al ~** *Comm* retail

det'ta|re *vt* dictate; **~re legge** *fig* lay down the law. **~to** *nm*, **~'tura** *nf* dictation

'**detto** *a* said; (*chiamato*) called; (*soprannominato*) nicknamed; **~ fatto** no sooner said than done ● *nm* saying

detur'pare *vt* disfigure

deva'sta|re *vt* devastate. **~to** *a* devastated. **~zi'one** *nf* devastation; *fig* ravages *pl*

devi'a|re *vi* deviate ● *vt* divert. **~zi'o-ne** *nf* deviation; (*stradale*) diversion

devitaliz'zare *vt* deaden (*dente*)

devo'lu|to *pp di* **devolvere** ● *a* devolved. **~zi'one** *nf* devolution

de'volvere *vt* devolve

de'vo|to *a* devout; (*affezionato*) devoted. **~zi'one** *nf* devotion

di *prep* of; (*partitivo*) some; (*scritto da*) by; (*parlare, pensare ecc*) about; (*con causa, mezzo*) with; (*con provenienza*) from; (*in comparazioni*) than; (*con infinito*) to;**la casa di mio padre/dei miei genitori** my father's house/my parents' house;**compra del pane** buy some bread;**hai del pane?** do you have any bread?; **un film di guerra** a war film; **piangere di dolore** cry with pain; **coperto di neve** covered with snow; **sono di Genova** I'm from Genoa; **uscire di casa** leave one's house;**più alto di te** taller than you;**è ora di partire** it's time to go;**crede di aver ragione** he thinks he's right;**dire di sì** say yes;**di domenica** on Sundays; **di sera** in the evening;**una pausa di un'ora** an hour's break; **un corso di due mesi** a two-month course

dia'bet|e *nm* diabetes. **~ico, -a** *a & nmf* diabetic

dia'bolico *a* diabolical

dia'dema *nm* diadem; (*di donna*) tiara

di'afano *a* diaphanous

dia'framma *nm* diaphragm; (*divisione*) screen

di'agnos|i *nf* diagnosis. **~ti'care** *vt* diagnose

diago'nale *a & nf* diagonal

dia'gramma *nm* diagram

dialet'tale *a* dialect.**dia'letto** *nm* dialect

dialo'gante *a***unità ~** *Comput* interactive terminal

di'alogo *nm* dialogue
dia'mante *nm* diamond
di'ametro *nm* diameter
di'amine *int***che ~...** what on earth...
diaposi'tiva *nf* slide
di'ario *nm* diary
diar'rea *nf* diarrhoea
di'avolo *nm* devil; **va al ~** go to hell!;
che ~ fai? what the hell are you doing?
di'batt|ere *vt* debate. **~ersi** *vr* struggle. **~ito** *nm* debate; (*meno formale*) discussion
dica'stero *nm* office
di'cembre *nm* December
dice'ria *nf* rumour
dichia'ra|re *vt* state; (*ufficialmente*) declare. **~rsi** *vr* **si dichiara innocente** he says he's innocent. **~zi'one** *nf* statement; (*documento, di guerra*) declaration
dician'nove *a & nm* nineteen
dicias'sette *a & nm* seventeen
dici'otto *a & nm* eighteen
dici'tura *nf* wording
didasca'lia *nf* (*di film*) subtitle; (*di illustrazione*) caption
di'dattic|a *nf* didactics *sg*. **~o** *a* didactic; (*televisione*) educational
di'dentro *adv* inside
didi'etro *adv* behind ● *nm* *hum* hindquarters *pl*
di'eci *a & nm* ten
die'cina =**decina**
'diesel *a & nf inv* diesel
di'esis *nm inv* sharp
di'eta *nf* diet; **essere a ~** be on a diet.
die'tetico *a* diet. **die'tista** *nmf* dietician. **die'tologo** *nmf* dietician
di'etro *adv* behind ● *prep* behind;
(*dopo*) after ● *a* back; (*di zampe*) hind
● *nm* back; **le stanze di ~** the back rooms; **le zampe di ~** the hind legs
dietro'front *nm inv* about-turn; *fig* U-turn
di'fatti *adv* in fact
di'fen|dere *vt* defend. **~dersi** *vr* defend oneself. **~'siva** *nf* **stare sulla ~siva** be on the defensive. **~'sivo** *a* defensive. **~'sore** *nm* defender; **avvocato ~sore** defence counsel
di'fes|a *nf* defence; **prendere le ~e di qcno** come to sb's defence. **~o** *pp di* **difendere**
difet't|are *vi* be defective. **~are di** lack. **~ivo** *a* defective
di'fet|to *nm* defect; (*morale*) fault, flaw; (*mancanza*) lack; (*in tessuto, abito*) flaw; **essere in ~to** be at fault; **far ~to** be

lacking. **~'toso** *a* defective; (*abto*) flawed
diffa'ma|re *vt* (*con parole*) slander; (*per iscritto*) libel. **~'torio** *a* slanderous; (*per iscritto*) libellous. **~zi'one** *nf* slander; (*scritta*) libel
diffe'ren|te *a* different. **~za** *nf* difference; **a ~za di** unlike; **non fare ~za** make no distinction (*fra* between).
~zi'ale *a & nm* differential
differenzi'ar|e *vt* differentiate. **~si** *vr* **~si da** differ from
diffe'ri|re *vt* postpone ● *vi* be different.
~ta *nf* **in ~ta** *TV* prerecorded
diffi'cile *a* difficult; (*duro*) hard; (*improbabile*) unlikely ● *nm* difficulty.
~'mente *adv* with difficulty
difficoltà *nf inv* difficulty
dif'fida *nf* warning
diffi'da|re *vi* **~are di** distrust ● *vt* warn. **~ente** *a* mistrustful. **~enza** *nf* mistrust
dif'fond|ere *vt* spread; diffuse (*calore, luce ecc*). **~si** *vr* spread. **diffusi'one** *nf* diffusion; (*di giornale*) circulation
dif'fu|so *pp di* **diffondere** ● *a* common; (*malattia*) widespread; (*luce*) diffuse. **~sore** *nm* (*per asciugacapelli*) diffuser
difi'lato *adv* straight; (*subito*) straightaway
'diga *nf* dam; (*argine*) dike
dige'ribile *a* digestible
dige'ri|re *vt* digest; *fam* stomach.
~sti'one *nf* digestion. **~'stivo** *a* digestive ● *nm* digestive; (*dopo cena*) liqueur
digi'tale *a* digital; (*delle dita*) finger *attrib* ● *nf* (*fiore*) foxglove
digi'tare *vt* key in
digiu'nare *vi* fast
digi'uno *a* **essere ~** have an empty stomach ● *nm* fast; **a ~** on an empty stomach
digni|tà *nf* dignity. **~'tario** *nm* dignitary. **~'toso** *a* dignified
digressi'one *nf* digression
digri'gnare *vi* **~ i denti** grind one's teeth
dila'gare *vi* flood; *fig* spread
dilani'are *vt* tear to pieces
dilapi'dare *vt* squander
dila'ta|re *vt*, **~rsi** *vr* dilate; (*metallo, gas*) expand. **~zi'one** *nf* dilation
dilazio'nabile *a* postponable
dilazio'nare *vt* delay. **~'one** *nf* delay
dilegu'ar|e *vt* disperse. **~si** *vr* disappear
di'lemma *nm* dilemma

dilet'tan|te *nmf* amateur. **~'tistico** *a* amateurish

dilet'tare *vt* delight

di'letto, -a *a* beloved ●*nm* (*piacere*) delight ●*nmf* (*persona*) beloved

dili'gen|te *a* diligent; (*lavoro*) accurate. **~za** *nf* diligence

dilu'ire *vt* dilute

dilun'gar|e *vt* prolong. **~si** *vr* **~si su** dwell on (*argomento*)

diluvi'are *vi* pour [down]. **di'luvio** *nm* downpour; *fig* flood

dima'gran|te *a* slimming, diet. **~i-'mento** *nm* loss of weight. **~ire** *vi* slim

dime'nar|e *vt* wave; wag (*coda*). **~si** *vr* be agitated

dimensi'one *nf* dimension; (*misura*) size

dimenti'canza *nf* forgetfulness; (*svista*) oversight

dimenti'car|e *vt*, **~si** *vr* **~** [**di**] forget. **dimentico** *a* **dimentico di** (*che non ricorda*) forgetful of

di'messo *pp di* **dimettere** ●*a* humble; (*trasandato*) shabby; (*voce*) low

dimestl'chezza *nf* familiarity

di'metter|e *vt* dismiss; (*da ospedale ecc*) discharge. **~si** *vr* resign

dimez'zare *vt* halve

diminu'ire *vt/i* diminish; (*in maglia*) decrease. **~'tivo** *a & nm* diminutive. **~zi'one** *nf* decrease; (*riduzione*) reduction

dimissi'oni *nfpl* resignation *sg*; **dare le ~** resign

di'mo|ra *nf* residence. **~'rare** *vi* reside

dimo'strante *nmf* demonstrator

dimo'stra|re *vt* demonstrate; (*provare*) prove; (*mostrare*) show. **~rsi** *vr* prove [to be]. **~'tivo** *a* demonstrative. **~zi'one** *nf* demonstration; *Math* proof

di'namico, -a *a* dynamic ●*nf* dynamics *sg*. **dina'mismo** *nm* dynamism

dinami'tardo *a* **attentato ~** bomb attack

dina'mite *nf* dynamite

'dinamo *nf inv* dynamo

di'nanzi *adv* in front ●*prep* **~ a** in front of

dina'stia *nf* dynasty

dini'ego *nm* denial

dinocco'lato *a* lanky

dino'sauro *nm* dinosaur

din'torn|i *nmpl* outskirts; **nei ~i di** in the vicinity of. **~o** *adv* around

'dio *nm* (*pl* **'dei**) god; **D~** God

di'ocesi *nf inv* diocese

dipa'nare *vt* wind into a ball; *fig* unravel

diparti'mento *nm* department

dipen'den|te *a* depending ●*nmf* employee. **~za** *nf* dependence; (*edificio*) annexe

di'pender|e *vi* **~ da** depend on; (*provenire*) derive from; **dipende** it depends

di'pinger|e *vt* paint; (*descrivere*) describe. **~si** *vr* (*truccarsi*) make up. **di'pinto** *pp di* **dispingere** ●*a* painted ●*nm* painting

di'plo|ma *nm* diploma. **~'marsi** *vr* graduate

diplo'matico *a* diplomatic ●*nm* diplomat; (*pasticcino*) millefeuille (*with alcohol*)

diplo'mato *nmf* person with school qualification ●*a* qualified

diploma'zia *nf* diplomacy

di'porto *nm* **imbarcazione da ~** pleasure craft

dira'dar|e *vt* thin out; make less frequent (*visite*). **~si** *vr* thin out; (*nebbia:*) clear

dira'ma|re *vt* issue ●*vi*, **~rsi** *vr* branch out; (*diffondersi*) spread. **~zi'o-ne** *nf* (*di strada*) fork

'dire *vt* say; (*raccontare, riferire*) tell; **~ quello che si pensa** speak one's mind; **voler ~** mean; **volevo ben ~!** I wondered!; **~ di sì/no** say yes/no; **si dice che...** rumour has it that...; **come si dice "casa" in inglese?** what's the English for "casa"?; **questo nome mi dice qualcosa** the name rings a bell; **che ne dici di...?** how about...?; **non c'è che ~** there's no disputing that; **e ~ che...** to think that...; **a dir poco/tanto** at least/most ●*vi* **~ bene/male di** speak highly/ill of sb; **dica pure** (*in negozio*) how can I help you?; **dici sul serio?** are you serious?; **per modo di ~** in a manner of speaking

diretta'mente *adv* directly

diret'tissima *nf* **processare per ~** *Jur* try as speedily as possible

diret'tissimo *nm* fast train

diret'tiva *nf* directive

di'retto *pp di* **dirigere** ●*a* direct. **~ a** (*inteso*) meant for. **essere ~ a** be heading for. **in diretta** (*trasmissione*) live ●*nm* (*treno*) through train

diret'tore, -'trice *nmf* manager; manageress, (*di scuola*) headmaster; headmistress. **~tore d'orchestra** conductor

direzi'one *nf* direction; (*di società*)

management; *Sch* headmaster's/head-mistress's office (*primary school*)

diri'gen|te *a* ruling ●*nmf* executive; *Pol* leader. **~za** *nf* management. **~zi'ale** *a* management *attrib*, managerial

di'riger|e *vt* direct; conduct (*orchestra*); run (*impresa*). **~si** *vr* **~si verso** head for

dirim'petto *adv* opposite ●*prep* **~ a** facing

di'ritto¹, dritto *a* straight; (*destro*) right ●*adv* straight; **andare ~** go straight on ●*nm* right side; *Tennis* forehand; **fare un ~** (*a maglia*) knit one

di'ritt|o² *nm* right; *Jur* law. **~i d'autore** royalties

dirit'tura *nf* straight line; *fig* honesty. **~ d'arrivo** *Sport* home straight

diroc'cato *a* tumbledown

dirom'pente *a fig* explosive

dirot'ta|re *vt* reroute (*treno, aereo*); (*illegalmente*) hijack; divert (*traffico*) ●*vi* alter course. **~'tore, ~'trice** *nmf* hijacker

di'rotto *a* (*pioggia*) pouring; (*pianto*) uncontrollable; **piovere a ~** rain heavily

di'rupo *nm* precipice

dis'abile *nmf* disabled person

disabi'tato *a* uninhabited

disabitu'arsi *vr* **~ a** get out of the habit of

disac'cordo *nm* disagreement

disadat'tato, -a *a* maladjusted ●*nmf* misfit

disa'dorno *a* unadorned

disa'gevole *a* (*scomodo*) uncomfortable

disagi'ato *a* poor; (*vita*) hard

di'sagio *nm* discomfort; (*difficoltà*) inconvenience; (*imbarazzo*) embarrassment; **sentirsi a ~** feel uncomfortable; **disagi** *pl* (*privazioni*) hardships

disappro'va|re *vt* disapprove of. **~zi'one** *nf* disapproval

disap'punto *nm* disappointment

disar'mante *a fig* disarming

disar'mare *vt/i* disarm. **di'sarmo** *nm* disarmament

disa'strato, -a *a* devastated ●*nmf* disaster victim

di'sastro *nm* disaster; (*fam: grande confusione*) mess; (*fig: persona*) disaster area. **disa'stroso** *a* disastrous

disat'ten|to *a* inattentive. **~zi'one** *nf* inattention; (*svista*) oversight

disatti'vare *vt* de-activate

disa'vanzo *nm* deficit

disavven'tura *nf* misadventure

dis'brigo *nm* dispatch

dis'capito *nm* **a ~ di** to the detriment of

dis'carica *nf* scrap-yard

discen'den|te *a* descending ●*nmf* descendant. **~za** *nf* descent; (*discendenti*) descendants *pl*

di'scendere *vt/i* descend; (*dal treno*) get off; (*da cavallo*) dismount; (*sbarcare*) land. **~ da** (*trarre origine da*) be a descendant of

di'scepolo, -a *nmf* disciple

di'scernere *vt* discern

di'sces|a *nf* descent; (*pendio*) slope; **~a in picchiata** (*di aereo*) nosedive; **essere in ~a** (*strada:*) go downhill. **~a libera** (*in sci*) downhill race. **disce-'sista** *nmf* (*sciatore*) downhill skier. **~o** *pp di* **discendere**

dis'chetto *nm Comput* diskette

dischi'uder|e *vt* open; (*svelare*) disclose. **~si** *vr* open up

disci'oglier|e *vt, ~si* *vr* dissolve; (*neve:*) thaw; (*fondersi*) melt. **disci'olto** *pp di* **disciogliere**

disci'pli|na *nf* discipline. **~nare** *a* disciplinary ●*vt* discipline. **~'nato** *a* disciplined

'disco *nm* disc; *Comput* disk; *Sport* discus; *Mus* record; **ernia del ~** slipped disc. **~ fisso** *Comput* hard disk. **~ volante** flying saucer

discogra'fia *nf* (*insieme di incisioni*) discography. **disco'grafico** *a* (*industria*) record, recording; **casa disco-grafica** record company, recording company

'discolo *nmf* rascal ●*a* unruly

discol'par|e *vt* clear. **~si** *vr* clear oneself

disco'noscere *vt* disown (*figlio*)

discontinuità *nf* (*nel lavoro*) irregularity. **discon'tinuo** *a* intermittent; (*fig: impegno, rendimento*) uneven

discor'dan|te *a* discordant. **~za** *nf* mismatch

discor'dare *vi* (*opinioni:*) conflict. **dis'corde** *a* clashing. **dis'cordia** *nf* discord; (*dissenso*) dissension

dis'cor|rere *vi* talk (**di** about). **~'sivo** *a* colloquial. **dis'corso** *pp di* **discorre-re** ●*nm* speech; (*conversazione*) talk

dis'costo *a* distant ●*adv* far away; **stare ~** stand apart

disco'te|ca *nf* disco; (*raccolta*) record library. **~'caro** *nmf pej* disco freak

discre'pan|te *a* contradictory. **~za** *nf* discrepancy

dis'cre|to *a* discreet; (*moderato*) moderate; (*abbastanza buono*) fairly good. **~zi'one** *nf* discretion; (*giudizio*) judgement;**a ~ zione di** at the discretion of

discrimi'nante *a* extenuating

discrimi'na|re *vt* discriminate. **~ 'to-rio** *a* (*atteggiamento*) discriminatory. **~zi'one** *nf* discrimination

discussi'one *nf* discussion; (*alterco*) argument. **dis'cusso** *pp di* **discutere**
• *a* controversial

dis'cutere *vt* discuss; (*formale*) debate; (*litigare*) argue;**~ sul prezzo** bargain. **discu'tibile** *a* debatable; (*gusto*) questionable

disde'gnare *vt* disdain. **dis'degno** *nm* disdain

dis'dett|a *nf* retraction; (*sfortuna*) bad luck;**Comm** cancellation. **~o** *pp di* **disdire**

disdi'cevole *a* unbecoming

dis'dire *vt* retract; (*annullare*) cancel

diseduca'tivo *a* boorish, uncouth

dise'gna|re *vt* draw; (*progettare*) design. **~ 'tore**, **~ 'trice** *nmf* designer. **di'segno** *nm* drawing; (*progetto, linea*) design

diser'bante *nm* herbicide, weed-killer
• *a* herbicidal, weed-killing

disere'da|re *vt* disinherit. **~to** *a* dispossessed • *nmf* **i ~ti** the dispossessed

diser'|tare *vt/i* desert; **~tare la scuola** stay away from school. **~ 'tore** *nm* deserter. **~zi'one** *nf* desertion

disfaci'mento *nm* decay

dis'fa|re *vt* undo; strip (*letto*); (*smantellare*) take down; (*annientare*) defeat; **~re le valigie** unpack [one's bags]. **~rsi** *vr* fall to pieces; (*sciogliersi*) melt; **~rsi di** (*liberarsi di*) get rid of; **~rsi in lacrime** dissolve into tears. **~tta** *nf* defeat. **~tto** *a fig* worn out

disfat'tis|mo *nm* defeatism. **~ta** *a* & *nmf* defeatist

disfunzi'one *nf* disorder

dis'gelo *nm* thaw

dis'grazi|a *nf* misfortune; (*incidente*) accident; (*sfavore*) disgrace. **~ata'mente** *adv* unfortunately. **~ato, -a** *a* unfortunate • *nmf* wretch

disgre'gar|e *vt* break up. **~si** *vr* disintegrate

disgu'ldo *nm* **~ postale** mistake in delivery

disgu'st|are *vt* disgust. **~arsi** *vr*

~arsi di be disgusted by. **dis'gusto** *nm* disgust. **~oso** *a* disgusting

disidra'ta|re *vt* dehydrate. **~to** *a* dehydrated

disil'ludere *vt* disenchant. **~si'one** *nf* disenchantment. **~so** *a* disillusioned

disimbal'lare *vt* unpack

disimpa'rare *vt* forget

disimpe'gnar|e *vt* release; (*compiere*) fulfil; redeem (*oggetto dato in pegno*). **~si** *vr* disengage oneself; (*cavarsela*) manage.**disim'pegno** *nm* (*locale*) vestibule

disincan'tato *a* (*disilluso*) disillusioned

disinfe'sta|re *vt* disinfest. **~zi'one** *nf* disinfestation

disinfet'tante *a* & *nm* disinfectant

disinfet'|tare *vt* disinfect. **~zi'one** *nf* disinfection

disinfor'mato *a* uninformed

disini'bito *a* uninhibited

disinne'scare *vt* defuse (*mina*). **disin'nesco** *nm* (*di bomba*) bomb disposal

disinse'rire *vt* disconnect

disinte'gra|re *vt*. **~rsi** *vr* disintegrate. **~zi'one** *nf* disintegration

disinteres'sarsi *vr* **~ di** take no interest in. **disinte'resse** *nm* indifference; (*oggettività*) disinterestedness

disintossi'ca|re *vt* detoxify. **~rsi** *vr* come off drugs. **~zi'one** *nf* giving up alcohol/drugs

disin'volto *a* natural. **disinvol'tura** *nf* confidence

disles'sia *nf* dyslexia. **dis'lessico** *a* dyslexic

disli'vello *nm* difference in height; *fig* inequality

dislo'care *vt Mil* post

dismenor'rea *nf* dysmenorrhoea

dismi'sura *nf* excess;**a ~** excessively

disobbedi'ente *a* disobedient

disobbe'dire *vt* disobey

disoccu'pa|to, -a *a* unemployed
• *nmf* unemployed person. **~zi'one** *nf* unemployment

disonestà *nf* dishonesty. **diso'nesto** *a* dishonest

disono'rare *vt* dishonour. **diso'nore** *nm* dishonour

di'sopra *adv* above • *a* upper • *nm* top

disordi'na|re *vt* disarrange. **~ta'mente** *adv* untidily. **~to** *a* untidy; (*sregolato*) immoderate. **di'sordine** *nm* disorder, untidiness; (*sregolatezza*) debauchery

disorganiz'za|re vt disorganize. **~to** a disorganized. **~zi'one** nf disorganization

disorienta'mento nm disorientation

disorien'ta|re vt disorientate. **~rsi** vr lose one's bearings. **~to** a fig bewildered

di'sotto adv below ● a lower ● nm bottom

dis'paccio nm dispatch

dispa'rato a disparate

'dispari a odd, uneven. **~tà** nf inv disparity

dis'parte adv **in ~** apart; **stare in ~** stand aside

dis'pendi|o nm (spreco) waste. **~'oso** a expensive

dis'pen|sa nf pantry; (distribuzione) distribution; (mobile) cupboard; Jur exemption; Relig dispensation; (pubblicazione periodica) number. **~'sare** vt distribute; (esentare) exonerate

dispe'ra|re vi despair (di of). **~rsi** vr despair. **~ta'mente** (piangere) desperately. **~to** a desperate. **~zi'one** nf despair

dis'per|dere vt, **~dersi** vr scatter, disperse. **~si'one** nf dispersion; (di truppe) dispersal. **~'sivo** a disorganized. **~so** pp di **disperdere** ● a scattered; (smarrito) lost ● nm missing soldier

dis'pet|to nm spite; **a ~to di** in spite of; **fare un ~to a qcno** spite sb. **~'toso** a spiteful

dispia'c|ere nm upset; (rammarico) regret; (dolore) sorrow; (preoccupazione) worry ● vi **mi dispiace** I'm sorry; **non mi dispiace** I don't dislike it; **se non ti dispiace** if you don't mind. **~i'uto** a upset; (dolente) sorry

dispo'nibil|e a available; (gentile) helpful. **~ità** nf availability; (gentilezza) helpfulness

dis'por|re vt arrange ● vi dispose; (stabilire) order; **~re di** have at one's disposal. **~si** vr (in fila) line up

disposi'tivo nm device

disposizi'one nf disposition; (ordine) order; (libera disponibilità) disposal. **dis'posto** pp di **disporre** ● a ready; (incline) disposed; **essere ben disposto verso** be favourably disposed towards

di'spotico a despotic. **dispo'tismo** nm despotism

dispregia'tivo a disparaging

disprez'zare vt despise. **dis'prezzo** nm contempt

'disputa nf dispute

dispu'tar|e vi dispute; (gareggiare) compete. **~si** vr **~si qcsa** contend for sth

dissacra'torio a debunking

dissangua'mento nm loss of blood

dissangu'a|re vt, **~rsi** vr bleed. **~rsi** vr fig become impoverished. **~to** a bloodless; fig impoverished

dissa'pore nm disagreement

dissec'car|e vt, **~si** vr dry up

dissemi'nare vt disseminate; (notizie) spread

dis'senso nm dissent; (disaccordo) disagreement

dissente'ria nf dysentery

dissen'tire vi disagree (da with)

dissertazi'one nf dissertation

disser'vizio nm poor service

disse'sta|re vt upset; Comm damage. **~to** a (strada) uneven. **dis'sesto** nm ruin

disse'tante a thirst-quenching

disse'tare vt **~ qcno** quench sb's thirst

dissi'dente a & nmf dissident

dis'sidio nm disagreement

dis'simile a unlike, dissimilar

dissimu'lare vt conceal; (fingere) dissimulate

dissi'pa|re vt dissipate; (sperperare) squander. **~rsi** vr (nebbia:) clear; (dubbio:) disappear. **~to** a dissipated. **~zi'one** nf squandering

dissoci'ar|e vt, **~si** vr dissociate

disso'dare vt till

dis'solto pp di **dissolvere**

disso'luto a dissolute

dis'solver|e vt, **~si** vr dissolve; (disperdere) dispel

disso'nanza nf dissonance

dissu'a|dere vt dissuade. **~si'one** nf dissuasion. **~'sivo** a dissuasive

distac'car|e vt detach; Sport leave behind. **~si** vr be detached. **di'stacco** nm detachment; (separazione) separation; Sport lead

di'stan|te a far away; (fig: person) detached ● adv far away. **~za** nf distance. **~zi'are** vt space out; Sport outdistance

di'stare vi be distant; **quanto dista?** how far is it?

di'sten|dere vt stretch out (parte del corpo); (spiegare) spread; (deporre) lay. **~dersi** vr stretch; (sdraiarsi) lie down; (rilassarsi) relax. **~si'one** nf stretching; (*rilassamento*) relaxation; *Pol* détente. **~'sivo** *a* relaxing

di'steso, -a *pp di* **distendere ●** *nf* expanse

distil'l|are *vt/i* distil. **~azi'one** *nf* distillation. **~e'ria** *nf* distillery

di'stinguer|e *vt* distinguish. **~si** *vr* distinguish oneself. **distin'guibile** *a* distinguishable

di'stinta *nf Comm* list. **~ di pagamento** receipt. **~ di versamento** paying-in slip

distinta'mente *adv* (*separatamente*) individually, separately; (*chiaramente*) clearly

distin'tivo *a* distinctive ● *nm* badge

di'stin|to, -a *pp di* **distinguere ●** *a* distinct; (*signorile*) distinguished; **~ti saluti** Yours faithfully. **~zi'one** *nf* distinction

di'stogliere *vt* **~ da** (*allontanare*) remove from; (*dissuadere*) dissuade from.

di'stolto *pp di* **distogliere**

di'storcere *vt* twist

distorsi'one *nf Med* sprain; (*alterazione*) distortion

di'stra|rre *vt* distract; (*divertire*) amuse. **~rsi** *vr* get distracted; (*svagarsi*) amuse oneself; **non ti distrarre!** pay attention!. **~rsi** *vr* (*deconcentrarsi*) be distracted. **~tta'mente** *adv* absently. **~tto** *pp di* **distrarre ●** *a* absentminded; (*disattento*) inattentive. **~zi'one** *nf* absent-mindedness; (*errore*) inattention; (*svago*) amusement

di'stretto *nm* district

distribu'ire *vt* distribute; (*disporre*) arrange; deal (*carte*). **~'tore** *nm* distributor; (*di benzina*) petrol pump; (*automatico*) slot-machine. **~zi'one** *nf* distribution

distri'car|e *vt* disentangle; **~si** *vr fig* get out of it

di'stru|ggere *vt* destroy. **~t'tivo** *a* destructive; (*critica*) negative. **~tto** *pp di* **distruggere ●** *a* destroyed; **un uomo ~tto** a broken man. **~zi'one** *nf* destruction

distur'bar|e *vt* disturb; (*sconvolgere*) upset. **~si** *vr* trouble oneself. **di'sturbo** *nm* bother; (*indisposizione*) trouble; *Med* problem; *Radio, TV* interference; **disturbi** *pl Radio, TV* static. **disturbi di stomaco** stomach trouble

disubbidi'en|te *a* disobedient. **~za** *nf* disobedience

disubbi'dire *vi* **~ a** disobey

disugu|agli'anza *nf* disparity. **~'ale** *a* unequal; (*irregolare*) irregular

disu'mano *a* inhuman

di'suso *nm* **cadere in ~** fall into disuse

di'tale *nm* thimble

di'tata *nf* poke; (*impronta*) fingermark

'dito *nm* (*pl* *pl* **dita**) finger; (*di vino, acqua*) finger. **~ del piede** toe

'ditta *nf* firm

dit'tafono *nm* dictaphone

ditta'tor|e *nm* dictator. **~i'ale** *a* dictatorial. **ditta'tura** *nf* dictatorship

dit'tongo *nm* diphthong

di'urno *a* daytime; **spettacolo ~** matinée

'diva *nf* diva

diva'ga|re *vi* digress. **~zi'one** *nf* digression

divam'pare *vi* burst into flames; *fig* spread like wildfire

di'vano *nm* settee, sofa. **~ letto** sofa bed

divari'care *vt* open

di'vario *nm* discrepancy. **un ~ di opinioni** a difference of opinion

dive'n|ire *vi* = **diventare**. **~uto** *pp di* **divenire**

diven'tare *vi* become; (*lentamente*) grow; (*rapidamente*) turn

di'verbio *nm* squabble

diver'gen|te *a* divergent. **~za** *nf* divergence; **~za di opinioni** difference of opinion. **di'vergere** *vi* diverge

diversa'mente *adv* (*altrimenti*) otherwise; (*in modo diverso*) differently

diversifi'car|e *vt* diversify. **~rsi** *vr* differ, be different. **~zi'one** *nf* diversification

diversi'one *nf* diversion. **~sità** *nf inv* difference. **~'sivo** *nm* diversion.

di'verso *a* different; **diversi** *pl* (*parecchi*) several ● *pron* several [people]

diver'tente *a* amusing. **diverti'mento** *nm* amusement

diver'tir|e *vt* amuse. **~si** *vr* enjoy oneself

divi'dendo *nm* dividend

di'vider|e *vt* divide; (*condividere*) share. **~si** *vr* (*separarsi*) separate

divi'eto *nm* prohibition; **~ di sosta** no parking

divinco'larsi *vr* wriggle

divinità *nf inv* divinity. **di'vino** *a* divine

di'visa *nf* uniform; *Comm* currency

divisi'one *nf* division

di'vismo *nm* worship; *(atteggiamento)* superstar mentality

di'vi|so *pp di* **dividere**. **~'sore** *nm* divisor. **~'sorio** *a* dividing; **muro ~sorio** partition wall

'divo, -a *nmf* star

divo'rar|e *vt* devour. **~si** *vr* **~si da** be consumed with

divorzi'a|re *vi* divorce. **~to, -a** *nmf* divorcee. **di'vorzio** *nm* divorce

divul'ga|re *vt* divulge; *(rendere popolare)* popularize. **~rsi** *vr* spread. **~'tivo** *a* popular. **~zi'one** *nf* popularization

dizio'nario *nm* dictionary

dizi'one *nf* diction

do *nm Mus (chiave, nota)* C

'doccia *nf* shower; *(grondaia)* gutter; **fare la ~** have a shower

do'cen|te *a* teaching ● *nmf* teacher; *(di università)* lecturer. **~za** *nf* university teacher's qualification

'docile *a* docile

documen'tar|e *vt* document. **~si** *vr* gather information (**su** about)

documen'tario *a & nm* documentary

documen'ta|to *a* well-documented; *(persona)* well-informed. **~zi'one** *nf* documentation

docu'mento *nm* document

dodi'cesimo *a & nm* twelfth. **'dodici** *a & nm* twelve

do'gan|a *nf* customs *pl; (dazio)* duty. **doga'nale** *a* customs. **~i'ere** *nm* customs officer

'doglie *nfpl* labour pains

'dogma *nm* dogma. **dog'matico** *a* dogmatic. **~'tismo** *nm* dogmatism

'dolce *a* sweet; *(clima)* mild; *(voce, consonante)* soft; *(acqua)* fresh ● *nm (portata)* dessert; *(torta)* cake; **non mangio dolci** I don't eat sweet things. **~'mente** *adv* sweetly. **dol'cezza** *nf* sweetness; *(di clima)* mildness

dolce'vita *a inv (maglione)* rollneck

dolci'ario *a* confectionery

dolci'astro *a* sweetish

dolcifi'cante *nm* sweetener ● *a* sweetening

dolci'umi *nmpl* sweets

do'lente *a* painful; *(spiacente)* sorry

do'le|re *vi* ache, hurt; *(dispiacere)* regret. **~rsi** *vr* regret; *(protestare)* complain; **~rsi di** be sorry for

'dollaro *nm* dollar

'dolo *nm Jur* malice; *(truffa)* fraud

Dolo'miti *nfpl* **le ~** the Dolomites

do'lore *nm* pain; *(morale)* sorrow. **dolo'roso** *a* painful

do'loso *a* malicious

do'manda *nf* question; *(richiesta)* request; *(scritta)* application; *Comm* demand; **fare una ~ (a qcno)** ask (sb) a question. **~ di impiego** job application

doman'dar|e *vt* ask; *(esigere)* demand; **~e qcsa a qcno** ask sb for sth. **~si** *vr* wonder

do'mani *adv* tomorrow; **~ sera** tomorrow evening ● *nm il* **~** the future; **a ~** see you tomorrow

do'ma|re *vt* tame; *fig* control *(emozioni)*. **~'tore** *nm* tamer

domat'tina *adv* tomorrow morning

do'meni|ca *nf* Sunday. **~'cale** *a* Sunday *attrib*

do'mestico, -a *a* domestic ● *nm* servant ● *nf* maid

domicili'are *a* **arresti domiciliari** *Jur* house arrest

domicili'arsi *vr* settle

domi'cilio *nm* domicile; *(abitazione)* home; **recapitiamo a ~** we do home deliveries

domi'na|re *vt* dominate; *(controllare)* control ● *vi* rule over; *(prevalere)* be dominant. **~rsi** *vr* control oneself. **~'tore, ~'trice** *nmf* ruler **~zi'one** *nf* domination

do'minio *nm* control; *Pol* dominion; *(ambito)* field; **di ~ pubblico** common knowledge

don *nm inv (ecclesiastico)* Father

do'na|re *vt* give; donate *(sangue, organo)* ● *vi* **~re a** *(giovare esteticamente)* suit. **~'tore, ~'trice** *nmf* donor. **~zi'one** *nf* donation

dondo'l|are *vt* swing; *(cullare)* rock ● *vi* sway. **~arsi** *vr* swing. **~io** *nm* rocking. **'dondolo** *nm* swing; **cavallo/ sedia a dondolo** rocking-horse/chair

dongio'vanni *nm inv* Romeo

'donna *nf* woman. **~ di servizio** domestic help

don'naccia *nf pej* whore

donnai'olo *nm* philanderer

'donnola *nf* weasel

'dono *nm* gift

'dopo *prep* after; *(a partire da)* since ● *adv* after, afterwards; *(più tardi)* later; *(in seguito)* later on; **~ di me** after me

dopo'barba *nm inv* aftershave

dopo'cena *nm inv* evening

dopodi'ché *adv* after which

dopodo'mani *adv* the day after tomorrow

dopogu'erra *nm inv* post-war period

dopo'pranzo *nm inv* afternoon

dopo'sci *a & nm inv* après-ski

doposcu'ola *nm inv* after-school activities *pl*

dopo-'shampoo *nm inv* conditioner ● *a inv* conditioning

dopo'sole *nm inv* aftersun cream ● *a inv* aftersun

dopo'tutto *adv* after all

doppi'aggio *nm* dubbing

doppia'mente *adv* (*in misura doppia*) doubly

doppi'a|re *vt Naut* double; *Sport* lap; *Cinema* dub. **~'tore**, **~'trice** *nmf* dubber

'doppio *a & adv* double. **~ clic** *Comput* double click. **~ fallo** *nm Tennis* double fault. **~ gioco** *nm* double-dealing. **~ mento** *nm* double chin. **~ senso** *nm* double entendre. **doppi vetri** *nmpl* double glazing ● *nm* double, twice the quantity; *Tennis* doubles *pl*. **~ misto** *nm Tennis* mixed doubles ● *adv* double

doppi'one *nm* duplicate

doppio'petto *a* double-breasted

dop'pista *nmf Tennis* doubles player

do'ra|re *vt* gild; *Culin* brown. **~to** *a* gilt; (*color oro*) golden. **~'tura** *nf* gilding

dormicchi'are *vi* doze

dormigli'one, **-a** *nmf* sleepyhead; *fig* lazy-bones

dor'mi|re *vi* sleep; (*essere addormentato*) be asleep; *fig* be asleep. **~ta** *nf* good sleep. **~'tina** *nf* nap. **~'torio** *nm* dormitory

dormi'veglia *nm* **essere in ~** be half asleep

dor'sale *a* dorsal ● *nf* (*di monte*) ridge

'dorso *nm* back; (*di libro*) spine; (*di monte*) crest; (*nel nuoto*) backstroke

do'saggio *nm* dosage

do'sare *vt* dose; *fig* measure; **~ le parole** weigh one's words

dosa'tore *nm* measuring jug

'dose *nf* dose; **in buona ~** *fig* in good measure. **~ eccessiva** overdose

dossi'er *nm inv* (*raccolta di dati, fascicolo*) file

'dosso *nm* (*dorso*) back; **levarsi di ~ gli abiti** take off one's clothes

do'ta|re *vt* endow; (*di accessori*) equip. **~to** *a* (*persona*) gifted; (*fornito*) equipped. **~zi'one** *nf* (*attrezzatura*) equipment; **in ~zione** at one's disposal

'doto *nf* dowry; (*qualità*) gift

'dotto *a* learned ● *nm* scholar; *Anat* duct

dotto'|rato *nm* doctorate. **dot'tore**, **~'ressa** *nmf* doctor

dot'trina *nf* doctrine

'dove *adv* where; **di ~ sei?** where do you come from; **fin ~?** how far?; **per ~?** which way?

do'vere *vi* (*obbligo*) have to, must; **devo andare** I have to go, I must go; **devo venire anch'io?** do I have to come too?; **avresti dovuto dirmelo** you should have told me, you ought to have told me; **devo sedermi un attimo** I must sit down for a minute, I need to sit down for a minute; **dev'essere successo qualcosa** something must have happened; **come si deve** properly ● *vt* (*essere debitore di, derivare*) owe; **essere dovuto a** be due to ● *nm* duty; **per ~** out of duty. **dove'roso** *a* only right and proper

do'vunque *adv* (*dappertutto*) everywhere; (*in qualsiasi luogo*) anywhere ● *conj* wherever

do'vuto *a* due; (*debito*) proper

doz'zi|na *nf* dozen. **~'nale** *a* cheap

dra'gare *vt* dredge

'drago *nm* dragon

'dramm|a *nm* drama. **dram'matico** *a* dramatic. **~atiz'zare** *vt* dramatize. **~a'turgo** *nm* playwright. **dram'mone** *nm* (*film*) tear-jerker

drappeggi'are *vt* drape. **drap'peggio** *nm* drapery

drap'pello *nm Mil* squad; (*gruppo*) band

'drastico *a* drastic

dre'na|ggio *nm* drainage. **~re** *vt* drain

drib'bla|re *vt* (*in calcio*) dribble. **'dribbling** *nm inv* (*in calcio*) dribble

'dritta *nf* (*mano destra*) right hand; *Naut* starboard; (*informazione*) pointer, tip; **a ~ e a manca** (*dappertutto*) left, right and centre

'dritto *a* = diritto¹ ● *nmf fam* crafty so-and-so

driz'zar|e *vt* straighten; (*rizzare*) prick up. **~si** *vr* straighten [up]; (*alzarsi*) raise

'dro|ga *nf* drug. **~'gare** *vt* drug. **~'garsi** *vr* take drugs. **~'gato**, **-a** *nmf* drug addict

droghe|'ria *nf* grocery. **~i'ere**, **-a** *nmf* grocer

drome'dario *nm* dromedary

'dubbi|o *a* doubtful; (*ambiguo*) dubious ● *nm* doubt, (*sospetto*) suspicion, **met-**

tere in ~o doubt; **essere fuori ~o** be
beyond doubt; **essere in ~o** be doubtful. **~'oso** a doubtful

dubi'ta|re vi doubt; **~re di** doubt;
(diffidare) mistrust; **dubito che venga**
I doubt whether he'll come. **~'tivo** a
(ambiguo) ambiguous

'**duca, du'chessa** nmf duke; duchess

'**due** a & nm two

due'cento a & nm two hundred

du'ello nm duel

due'mila a & nm two thousand

due'pezzi nm inv (bikini) bikini

du'etto nm duo; Mus duet

'**duna** nf dune

'**dunque** conj therefore; (allora) well
[then]

'**duo** nm inv duo; Mus duet

du'omo nm cathedral

'**duplex** nm Teleph party line

dupli'ca|re vt duplicate. **~to** nm du-
plicate. '**duplice** a double; **in duplice**
in duplicate

dura'mente adv (lavorare) hard;
(rimproverare) harshly

du'rante prep during

du'r|are vi last; (cibo:) keep; (resistere)
hold out. **~ata** nf duration. **~a'turo,
~evole** a lasting, enduring

du'rezza nf hardness; (di carne)
toughness; (di voce, padre) harshness

'**duro, -a** a hard; (persona, carne)
tough; (voce) harsh; (pane) stale; **tieni
~!** (resistere) hang in there! ● nmf (persona) tough person, toughie fam

du'rone nm hardened skin

'**duttile** a (materiale) ductile; (carattere) malleable

Ee

e, ed conj and

'**ebano** nm ebony

eb'bene conj well [then]

eb'brezza nf inebriation; (euforia)
elation; **guida in stato di ~** drink-
driving. '**ebbro** a inebriated; **ebbro di
gioia** delirious with joy

ebete a stupid

ebollizi'one nf boiling

e'braico a Hebrew ● nm (lingua) He-
brew. **e'br|eo, -a** a Jewish ● nmf Jew;
Jewess

'**Ebridi** nfpl le ~ the Hebrides

eca'tombe nf fare un'~ wreak havoc

ecc abbr (eccetera) etc

ecce'den|te a (peso, bagaglio) excess.
~za nf excess; (d'avanzo) surplus;
avere qcsa in ~za have an excess of
sth; **bagagli in ~za** excess baggage.
~za di cassa surplus. **ec'cedere** vt
exceed ● vi go too far; **eccedere nel
mangiare** overeat; **eccedere nel bere**
drink to excess

eccel'len|te a excellent. **~za** nf ex-
cellence; (titolo) Excellency; **per ~za**
par excellence. **ec'cellere** vi excel (**in**
at)

eccentricità nf eccentricity. **ec'centrico, -a** a & nmf eccentric

eccessiva'mente adv excessively.
ecces'sivo a excessive

ec'cesso nm excess; **andare agli
eccessi** go to extremes; **all'~** to excess. **~ di velocità** speeding

ec'cetera adv et cetera

ec'cetto prep except; **~ che** (a meno
che) unless. **eccettu'are** vt except

eccezio'nal|e a exceptional. **~'men-
te** adv exceptionally; (contrariamente
alla regola) as an exception

eccezi'one nf exception; Jur objection; **a ~ di** with the exception of

ecci'ta'mento nm excitement. **ecci'tante** a exciting; (sostanza) stimulant ● nm stimulant

ecci'ta|re vt excite. **~rsi** vr get ex-
cited. **~to** a excited

eccitazi'one nf excitement

ecclesi'astico a ecclesiastical ● nm
priest

'**ecco** adv (qui) here; (là) there; **~!** exactly!; **~ fatto** there we are; **~ la tua
borsa** here is your bag; **~ [li] mio
figlio** there is my son; **~mi** here I am; **~
tutto** that is all

ec'come adv & int and how!

echeggi'are vi echo

e'clissi nf inv eclipse

'**eco** *nmf* (*pl m* **echi**) echo

eco'gra'fia *nf* scan

ecolo'gia *nf* ecology. **eco'logico** *a* ecological; ⟨*prodotto*⟩ environmentally friendly

e commerci'ale *nf* ampersand

econo'mia *nf* economy; ⟨*scienza*⟩ economics *sg*; **fare ~ia** economize (**di** on). **eco'nomico** *a* economic; ⟨*a buon prezzo*⟩ cheap. **~ista** *nmf* economist. **~iz'zare** *vt/i* economize; save ⟨*tempo, denaro*⟩. **e'conomo, -a** *a* thrifty ●*nmf* (*di collegio*) bursar

écru *a inv* raw

'**Ecu** *nm inv* ECU, ecu

ec'zema *nm* eczema

ed *conj vedi* **e**

'**edera** *nf* ivy

e'dicola *nf* [newspaper] kiosk

edifi'cabile *a* ⟨*area, terreno*⟩ classified *as suitable for development*

edifi'cante *a* edifying

edifi'care *vt* build; ⟨*indurre al bene*⟩ edify

edi'ficio *nm* building; *fig* structure

e'dile *a* building *attrib*

edi'lizi|a *nf* building trade. **~o** *a* building *attrib*

edi|'tore, -'trice *a* publishing ●*nmf* publisher; ⟨*curatore*⟩ editor. **~to'ria** *nf* publishing. **~tori'ale** *a* publishing ●*nm* (*articolo*) editorial, leader

edizi'one *nf* edition; ⟨*di manifestazione*⟩ performance. **~ ridotta** abridg[e]ment. **~ della sera** (*del telegiornale*) evening news

edu'ca|re *vt* educate; ⟨*allevare*⟩ bring up. **~'tivo** *a* educational. **~to** *a* polite. **~'tore, ~'trice** *nmf* educator. **~zi'one** *nf* education; ⟨*di bambini*⟩ upbringing; ⟨*buone maniere*⟩ [good] manners *pl*. **~zione fisica** physical education

e'felide *nf* freckle

effemi'nato *a* effeminate

efferve'scente *a* effervescent; ⟨*frizzante*⟩ fizzy; ⟨*aspirina*⟩ soluble

effettiva'mente *adv* **è troppo tardi – ~** it's too late – so it is

effet'tivo *a* actual; ⟨*efficace*⟩ effective; ⟨*personale*⟩ permanent; *Mil* regular ●*nm* (*somma totale*) sum total

ef'fett|o *nm* effect; ⟨*impressione*⟩ impression; **in ~i** in fact; **a tutti gli ~i** to all intents and purposes; **~i personali** personal belongings. **~u'are** *vt* effect; carry out ⟨*controllo, sondaggio*⟩. **~u'arsi** *vr* take place

effi'cac|e *a* effective. **~ia** *nf* effectiveness

effici'en|te *a* efficient. **~za** *nf* efficiency

ef'fimero *a* ephemeral

effusi'one *nf* effusion

E'geo *nm* **l'~** the Aegean [Sea]

E'gitto *nm* Egypt. **egizi'ano, -a** *a & nmf* Egyptian

'**egli** *pron* he; **~ stesso** he himself

ego'centrico, -a *a* egocentric ●*nmf* egocentric person

ego'is|mo *nm* selfishness. **~ta** *a* selfish ●*nmf* selfish person. **~tico** *a* selfish

e'gregio *a* distinguished; **E~ Signore** Dear Sir

eguali'tario *a & nm* egalitarian

eiaculazi'one *nf* ejaculation

elabo'ra|re *vt* elaborate; process ⟨*dati*⟩. **~to** *a* elaborate. **~zi'one** *nf* elaboration; ⟨*di dati*⟩ processing. **~zione [di] testi** word processing

elar'gire *vt* lavish

elastici'tà *nf* elasticity. **~z'zato** *a* ⟨*stoffa*⟩ elasticated. **e'lastico** *a* elastic; ⟨*tessuto*⟩ stretch; ⟨*orario, mente*⟩ flexible; ⟨*persona*⟩ easy-going ●*nm* elastic; ⟨*fascia*⟩ rubber band

ele'fante *nm* elephant

ele'gan|te *a* elegant. **~za** *nf* elegance

e'leggere *vt* elect. **eleg'gibile** *a* eligible

elemen'tare *a* elementary; **scuola ~** primary school

ele'mento *nm* element; **elementi** *pl* ⟨*fatti*⟩ data; ⟨*rudimenti*⟩ elements

ele'mosina *nf* charity; **chiedere l'~** beg. **elemosi'nare** *vt/i* beg

elen'care *vt* list

e'lenco *nm* list. **~ abbonati** telephone directory. **~ telefonico** telephone directory

elet'tivo *a* ⟨*carica*⟩ elective. **e'letto, -a** *pp di* **eleggere** ●*a* chosen ●*nmf* (*nominato*) elected member; **per pochi eletti** for the chosen few

eletto'ra|le *a* electoral. **~to** *nm* electorate

elet|'tore, -'trice *nmf* voter

elet'trauto *nm* garage for electrical repairs

elettri'cista *nm* electrician

elettri|ci'tà *nf* electricity. **e'lettrico** *a* electric. **~z'zante** *a* ⟨*notizia, gara*⟩ electrifying. **~z'zare** *vt fig* electrify. **~z'zato** *a fig* electrified

elettrocardio'gramma *nm* electro-cardiogram

e'lettrodo *nm* electrode

elettrodo'mestico *nm* [electrical] household appliance

elet'trone *nm* electron

elet'tronico, -a *a* electronic ●*nf* electronics

ele'va|re *vt* raise; (*promuovere*) promote; (*erigere*) erect; (*fig: migliorare*) better; **~ al quadrato/cubo** square/cube. **~rsi** *vr* rise; (*edificio:*) stand. **~to** *a* high. **~zi'one** *nf* elevation

elezi'one *nf* election

'elica *nf Naut* screw, propeller; *Aeron* propeller; (*del ventilatore*) blade

eli'cottero *nm* helicopter

elimi'na|re *vt* eliminate. **~'toria** *nf Sport* preliminary heat. **~zi'one** *nf* elimination

é'li|te *nf inv* élite. **~'tista** *a* élitist

'ella *pron* she

ellepì *nm inv* LP

el'metto *nm* helmet

elogi'are *vt* praise. **e'logio** *nm* praise; (*discorso, scritto*) eulogy

elo'quen|te *a* eloquent; *fig* tell-tale. **~za** *nf* eloquence

e'lu|dere *vt* elude; evade (*sorveglianza, controllo*). **~'sivo** *a* elusive

el'vetico *a* Swiss

emaci'ato *a* emaciated

E-mail *nf* e-mail

ema'na|re *vt* give off; pass (*legge*) ●*vi* emanate. **~zi'one** *nf* giving off; (*di legge*) enactment

emanci'pa|re *vt* emancipate. **~rsi** *vr* become emancipated. **~to** *a* emancipated. **~zi'one** *nf* emancipation

emargi'na|to *nm* marginalized person. **~zi'one** *nf* marginalization

ema'toma *nm* haematoma

em'bargo *nm* embargo

em'ble|ma *nm* emblem. **~'matico** *a* emblematic

embo'lia *nf* embolism

embrio'nale *a Biol, fig* embryonic. **embri'one** *nm* embryo

emen|da'mento *nm* amendment. **~'dare** *vt* amend

emer'gen|te *a* emergent. **~za** *nf* emergency; **in caso di ~za** in an emergency

e'mergere *vi* emerge; (*sottomarino:*) surface; (*distinguersi*) stand out

e'merito *a* (*professore*) emeritus; **un ~ imbecille** a prize idiot

e'merso *pp di* emergere

e'messo *pp di* emettere

e'mettere *vt* emit; give out (*luce, suono*); let out (*grido*); (*mettere in circolazione*) issue

emi'crania *nf* migraine

emi'gra|re *vi* emigrate. **~to, -a** *nmf* immigrant. **~zi'one** *nf* emigration

emi'nen|te *a* eminent. **~za** *nf* eminence

e'miro *nm* emir

emis'fero *nm* hemisphere

emis'sario *nm* emissary

emissi'one *nf* emission; (*di denaro*) issue; (*trasmissione*) broadcast

emit'tente *a* issuing; (*trasmittente*) broadcasting ●*nf Radio* transmitter

emor'ragia *nf* haemorrhage

emor'roidi *nfpl* piles

emotività *nf* emotional make-up. **emo'tivo** *a* emotional

emozio'nan|te *a* exciting; (*commovente*) moving. **~re** *vt* excite; (*commuovere*) move. **~rsi** *vr* become excited; (*commuoversi*) be moved. **~to** *a* excited; (*commosso*) moved. **emozi'one** *nf* emotion; (*agitazione*) excitement

'empio *a* impious; (*spietato*) pitiless; (*malvagio*) wicked

em'pirico *a* empirical

em'porio *nm* emporium; (*negozio*) general store

emu'la|re *vt* emulate. **~zi'one** *nf* emulation

emulsi'one *nf* emulsion

en'ciclica *nf* encyclical

enciclope'dia *nf* encyclopaedia

encomi'are *vt* commend. **en'comio** *nm* commendation

en'demico *a* endemic

endo've|na *nf* intravenous injection. **~'noso** *a* intravenous; **per via ~nosa** intravenously

E.N.I.T. *nm abbr* (**Ente Nazionale Italiano per il Turismo**) Italian State Tourist Office

e'nergetico *a* (*risorse, crisi*) energy *attrib*; (*alimento*) energy-giving

ener'gia *nf* energy. **e'nergico** *a* energetic; (*efficace*) strong

ener'gumeno *nm* Neanderthal

'enfasi *nf* emphasis

en'fatico *a* emphatic. **~z'zare** *vt* emphasize

e'nigma *nm* enigma. **enig'matico** *a* enigmatic. **enig'mistica** *nf* puzzles *pl*

en'nesimo *a Math* nth; *fam* umpteenth

e'norm|e *a* enormous. **~e'mente** *adv*

massively. **~ità** *nf inv* enormity; (*assurdità*) absurdity

eno'teca *nf* wine-tasting shop

'ente *nm* board; (*società*) company; (*filosofia*) being

entità *nf inv* (*filosofia*) entity; (*gravità*) seriousness; (*dimensione*) extent

entou'rage *nm inv* entourage

en'trambi *a & pron* both

en'trare *vi* go in, enter; **~ re in** go into; (*stare, trovar posto*) fit into; (*arruolarsi*) join; **~rci** (*avere a che fare*) have to do with; **tu che c'entri?** what has it got to do with you? **~ta** *nf* entry, entrance; **~te** *pl Comm* takings; (*reddito*) income *sg*

'entro *prep* (*tempo*) within

entro'terra *nm inv* hinterland

entusias'mante *a* fascinating, exciting

entusias'mar|e *vt* arouse enthusiasm in. **~si** *vr* be enthusiastic (**per** about)

entusi'as|mo *nm* enthusiasm. **~ta** *a* enthusiastic ● *nmf* enthusiast. **~tico** *a* enthusiastic

enume'rare *vt* enumerate. **~zi'one** *nf* enumeration

enunci'a|re *vt* enunciate. **~zi'one** *nf* enunciation

epa'tite *nf* hepatitis

'epico *a* epic

epide'mia *nf* epidemic

epi'dermide *nf* epidermis

Epifa'nia *nf* Epiphany

epi'gramma *nm* epigram

epiles'sia *nf* epilepsy. **epi'lettico, -a** *a & nmf* epileptic

e'pilogo *nm* epilogue

epi'sodi|co *a* episodic; **caso ~co** one-off case. **~o** *nm* episode

e'piteto *nm* epithet

'epoca *nf* age; (*periodo*) period; **a quell'~** in those days; **auto d'~** vintage car

ep'pure *conj* [and] yet

epu'rare *vt* purge

equa'tore *nm* equator. **equatori'ale** *a* equatorial

equazi'one *nf* equation

e'questre *a* equestrian; **circo ~** circus

equi'latero *a* equilateral

equili'bra|re *vt* balance. **~to a** (*persona*) well-balanced. **equi'librio** *nm* balance; (*buon senso*) common sense; (*di bilancia*) equilibrium

equili'brismo *nm* **fare ~** do a balancing act

e'quino *a* horse *attrib*

equi'nozio *nm* equinox

equipaggia'mento *nm* equipment

equipaggi'are *vt* equip; (*di persone*) man

equi'paggio *nm* crew; *Aeron* cabin crew

equipa'rare *vt* make equal

équipe *nf inv* team

equità *nf* equity

equiva'len|te *a & nm* equivalent. **~za** *nf* equivalence

equiva'lere *vi* **~ a** be equivalent to

equivo'care *vi* misunderstand

e'quivoco *a* equivocal; (*sospetto*) suspicious; **un tipo ~** a shady character ● *nm* misunderstanding

'equo *a* fair, just

'era *nf* era

'erba *nf* grass; (*aromatica, medicinale*) herb. **~ cipollina** chives *pl.* **er'baccia** *nf weed.* **er'baceo** *a* herbaceous

erbi'cida *nm* weed-killer

erbo'rist|a *nmf* herbalist. **~e'ria** *nf* herbalist's shop

er'boso *a* grassy

er'culeo *a* (*forza*) herculean

e'red|e *nmf* heir; heiress. **~ità** *nf inv* inheritance; *Biol* heredity. **~i'tare** *vt* inherit. **~itarietà** *nf* heredity. **~i'tario** *a* hereditary

ere'mita *nm* hermit

ere'sia *nf* heresy. **e'retico, -a** *a* heretical ● *nmf* heretic

e're|tto *pp di* **erigere** ● *a* erect. **~zi'one** *nf* erection; (*costruzione*) building

er'gastolo *nm* life sentence; (*luogo*) prison

'erica *nf* heather

e'rigere *vt* erect; (*fig: fondare*) found

eri'tema *nm* (*cutaneo*) inflammation; (*solare*) sunburn

ermel'lino *nm* ermine

ermetica'mente *adv* hermetically. **er'metico** *a* hermetic; (*a tenuta d'aria*) airtight

'ernia *nf* hernia

e'rodere *vi* erode

e'ro|e *nm* hero. **~ico** *a* heroic. **~'ismo** *nm* heroism

ero'ga|re *vt* distribute; (*fornire*) supply. **~zi'one** *nf* supply

ero'ina *nf* heroine; (*droga*) heroin

erosi'one *nf* erosion

e'rotico a erotic. **ero'tismo** nm eroticism

er'rante a wandering. **er'rare** vi wander; (sbagliare) be mistaken

er'rato a (sbagliato) mistaken

'erre r̃~ **moscia** burr

erronea'mente adv mistakenly

er'rore nm error, mistake; (di stampa) misprint; **essere in** ~ be wrong

'erta nf **stare all'**~ be on the alert

eru'di|rsi vr be educated. ~**to** a learned

erut'tare vt (vulcano:) erupt ● vi (ruttare) belch. **eruzi'one** nf eruption; Med rash

esacer'bare vt exacerbate

esage'ra|re vt exaggerate ● vi exaggerate; (nel comportamento) go over the top; ~**re nel mangiare** eat too much. ~**ta'mente** adv excessively. ~**to** a exaggerated; (prezzo) exorbitant ● nm person who goes to extremes. ~**zi'one** nf exaggeration; **è costato un'**~**zione** it cost the earth

esa'lare vt/i exhale

esal'ta|re vt exalt; (entusiasmare) elate. ~**to** a (fanatico) fanatical ● nm fanatic. ~**zi'one** nf exaltation; (in discorso) fervour

e'same nm examination, exam; **dare un** ~ take an exam; **prendere in** ~ examine. ~ **del sangue** blood test. **esami** pl **di maturità** ≈ A-levels

esami'na|re vt examine. ~**tore**, ~**trice** nmf examiner

e'sangue a bloodless

e'sanime a lifeless

esaspe'rante a exasperating

esaspe'ra|re vt exasperate. ~**rsi** vr get exasperated. ~**zi'one** nf exasperation

esat|ta'mente adv exactly. ~**'tezza** nf exactness; (precisione) precision; (di risposta, risultato) accuracy

e'satto pp di **esigere** ● a exact; (risposta, risultato) correct; (orologio) right; **hai l'ora esatta?** do you have the right time?; **sono le due esatte** it's two o'clock exactly

esat'tore nm collector

esau'dire vt grant; fulfil (speranze)

esauri'ente a exhaustive

esau'ri|re vt exhaust. ~**rsi** vr exhaust oneself; (merci ecc:) run out. ~**to** a exhausted; (merci) sold out; (libro) out of print; **fare il tutto** ~**to** (spettacolo:) play to a full house

'esca nf bait

escande'scenz|a nf outburst; **dare in** ~**e** lose one's temper

escla'ma|re vi exclaim. ~**'tivo** a exclamatory. ~**zi'one** nf exclamation

es'clu|dere vt exclude; rule out (possibilità, ipotesi). ~**si'one** nf exclusion. ~**'siva** nf exclusive right, sole right; **in** ~**siva** exclusive. ~**siva'mente** adv exclusively. ~**'sivo** a exclusive. ~**so** pp di **escludere** ● a **non è** ~**so che ci sia** it's not out of the question that he'll be there

escogi'tare vt contrive

escre'mento nm excrement

escursi'one nf excursion; (scorreria) raid; (di temperatura) range

ese'crabile a abominable. ~**re** vt abhor

esecu|'tivo a & nm executive. ~**'tore**, ~**'trice** nmf executor; Mus performer. ~**zi'one** nf execution; Mus performance

esegu'ire vt carry out; Jur execute; Mus perform

e'sempio nm example; **ad** o **per** ~ for example; **dare l'**~ **a** qcno set sb an example; **fare un** ~ give an example. **esem'plare** a exemplary ● nm specimen; (di libro) copy. **esemplifi'care** vt exemplify

esen'tar|e vt exempt. ~**si** vr free oneself. **e'sente** a exempt. **esente da imposta** duty-free. **esente da IVA** VAT-exempt

esen'tasse a duty-free

e'sequie nfpl funeral rites

eser'cente nmf shopkeeper

eserci'ta|re vt exercise; (addestrare) train; (fare uso di) exert; (professione) practise. ~**rsi** vr practise. ~**zi'one** nf exercise; Mil drill

e'sercito nm army

eser'cizio nm exercise; (pratica) practice; Comm financial year; (azienda) business; **essere fuori** ~ be out of practice

esi'bi|re vt show off; produce (documenti). ~**rsi** vr Theat perform; fig show off. ~**zi'one** nf production; Theat performance

esibizio'ni|smo nm showing off. ~**ta** nmf exhibitionist

esi'gen|te a exacting; (pignolo) fastidious. ~**za** nf demand; (bisogno) need. **e'sigere** vt demand; (riscuotere) collect

e'siguo a meagre

esila'rante a exhilarating

'esile a slender; (voce) thin

esili'a|re *vt* exile. **~'rsi** *vr* go into exile. **~to, -a** *a* exiled ● *nmf* exile. **e'silio** *nm* exile

e'simer|e *vt* release. **~si** *vr* **~si da** get out of

esi'sten̄te *a* existing. **~za** *nf* existence. **~zi'ale** *a* existential. **~zia'lismo** *nm* existentialism

e'sistere *vi* exist

esi'tante *a* hesitating; ⟨*voce*⟩ faltering

esi'ta|re *vi* hesitate. **~zi'one** *nf* hesitation

'esito *nm* result; **avere buon ~** be a success

'esodo *nm* exodus

e'sofago *nm* oesophagus

esone'rare *vt* exempt. **e'sonero** *nm* exemption

esorbi'tante *a* exorbitant

esorciz'zare *vt* exorcize

esordi'ente *nmf person making his/ her début.* **e'sordio** *nm* opening; ⟨*di attore*⟩ début. **esor'dire** *vi* début

esor'tare *vt* ⟨*pregare*⟩ beg; ⟨*incitare*⟩ urge

eso'terico *a* esoteric

e'sotico *a* exotic

espa'drillas *nfpl* espadrilles

es'pan|dere *vt* expand. **~dersi** *vr* expand; ⟨*diffondersi*⟩ extend. **~si'one** *nf* expansion. **~'sivo** *a* expansive; ⟨*persona*⟩ friendly

espatri'are *vi* leave one's country. **es'patrio** *nm* expatriation

espedi'ent|e *nm* expedient; **vivere di ~i** live by one's wits

es'pellere *vt* expel

esperi'enza *nf* experience; **parlare per ~za** speak from experience. **~'mento** *nm* experiment

es'perto, -a *a* & *nmf* expert

espi'a|re *vt* atone for. **~'torio** *a* expiatory

espi'rare *vt/i* breathe out

espli'care *vt* carry on

esplicita'mente *adv* explicitly. **es'plicito** *a* explicit

es'plodere *vi* explode ● *vt* fire

esplo'ra|re *vt* explore. **~'tore, ~'trice** *nmf* explorer; **giovane ~tore** boy scout. **~zi'one** *nf* exploration

esplosi'one *nf* explosion. **~'sivo** *a* & *nm* explosive

espo'nente *nm* exponent

es'por|re *vt* expose; display ⟨*merci*⟩; ⟨*spiegare*⟩ expound; exhibit ⟨*quadri ecc*⟩. **~si** *vr* ⟨*compromettersi*⟩ compromise oneself; ⟨*al sole*⟩ expose oneself; ⟨*alle critiche*⟩ lay oneself open

espor'ta|re *vt* export. **~'tore, ~'trice** *nmf* exporter. **~zi'one** *nf* export

esposizi'one *nf* ⟨*mostra*⟩ exhibition; ⟨*in vetrina*⟩ display; ⟨*spiegazione ecc*⟩ exposition; ⟨*posizione, fotografia*⟩ exposure. **es'posto** *pp di* **esporre** ● *a* exposed; **esposto a** ⟨*rivolto*⟩ facing ● *nm* Jur ecc statement

espressa'mente *adv* expressly; **non l'ha detto ~** he didn't put it in so many words

espres|si'one *nf* expression. **~'sivo** *a* expressive

es'presso *pp di* **esprimere** ● *a* express ● *nm* ⟨*lettera*⟩ express letter; ⟨*treno*⟩ express train; ⟨*caffè*⟩ espresso; **per ~** ⟨*spedire*⟩ [by] express [post]

es'primer|e *vt* express. **~si** *vr* express oneself

espropri'a|re *vt* dispossess. **~zi'one** *nf* Jur expropriation. **es'proprio** *nm* expropriation

espulsi'one *nf* expulsion. **es'pulso** *pp di* **espellere**

es'senz|a *nf* essence. **~i'ale** *a* essential ● *nm* important thing. **~ial'mente** *a* essentially

'essere *vi* be; **c'è** there is; **ci sono** there are; **che ora è? – sono le dieci** what time is it? – it's ten o'clock; **chi è? – sono io** who is it? – it's me; **ci sono!** ⟨*ho capito*⟩ I've got it!; **ci siamo!** ⟨*siamo arrivati*⟩ here we are at last!; **è stato detto che** it has been said that; **siamo in due** there are two of us; **questa camicia è da lavare** this shirt is to be washed; **non è da te** it's not like you; **~ di** ⟨*provenire da*⟩ be from; **~ per** ⟨*favorevole*⟩ be in favour of; **se fossi in te,...** if I were you,...; **sarà!** if you say so!; **come sarebbe a dire?** what are you getting at? ● *v aux* have; ⟨*in passivi*⟩ be; **siamo arrivati** we have arrived; **ci sono stato ieri** I was there yesterday; **sono nato a Torino** I was born in Turin; **è riconosciuto come...** he is recognized as... ● *nm* being. **~ umano** human being. **~ vivente** living creature

essic'cato *a* Culin desiccated

'esso, -a *pron* he, she; ⟨*cosa, animale*⟩ it

est *nm* east

'estasi *nf* ecstasy; **andare in ~ per** go into raptures over. **~'are** *vt* enrapture

e'state *nf* summer

e'sten|dere *vt* extend. **~dersi** *vr*

spread; *(allungarsi)* stretch. **~si'one** *nf* extension; *(ampiezza)* expanse; *Mus* range. **~'sivo** *a* extensive

estenu'ante *a* exhausting

estenu'a|re *vt* wear out; deplete *(risorse, casse)*. **~rsi** *vr* wear oneself out

esteri'or|e *a & nm* exterior. **~'mente** *adv* externally; *(di persone)* outwardly

esterna'mente *adv* on the outside

ester'nare *vt* express, show

e'sterno *a* external; **per uso ~** for external use only ● *nm (allievo)* day-boy; *Archit* exterior; *(scala)* outside; *(in film)* location shot

'estero *a* foreign ● *nm* foreign countries *pl*; **all'~** abroad

esterre'fatto *a* horrified

e'steso *pp di* **estendere** ● *a* extensive; *(diffuso)* widespread; **per ~** *(scrivere)* in full

e'stetic|a *nf* aesthetics *sg*. **~a'mente** *adv* aesthetically. **~o, -a** *a* aesthetic; *(chirurgia, chirurgo)* plastic. **este'tista** *nf* beautician

'estimo *nm* estimate

e'stin|guere *vt* extinguish. **~guersi** *vr* die out. **~to, -a** *pp di* **estinguere** ● *nmf* deceased. **~'tore** *nm* [fire] extinguisher. **~zi'one** *nf* extinction; *(di incendio)* putting out

estir'pa|re *vt* uproot; extract *(dente)*; *fig* eradicate *(crimine, malattia)*. **~zi'one** *nf* eradication; *(di dente)* extraction

e'stivo *a* summer

e'stor|cere *vt* extort. **~si'one** *nf* extortion. **~to** *pp di* **estorcere**

estradizi'one *nf* extradition

e'straneo, -a *a* extraneous; *(straniero)* foreign ● *nmf* stranger

estrani'ar|e *vt* estrange. **~si** *vr* become estranged

e'stra|rre *vt* extract; *(sorteggiare)* draw. **~tto** *pp di* **estrarre** ● *nm* extract; *(brano)* excerpt; *(documento)* abstract. **~tto conto** statement [of account], bank statement. **~zi'one** *nf* extraction; *(a sorte)* draw

estrema'mente *adv* extremely

estre'mis|mo *nm* extremism. **~ta** *nmf* extremist

estremità *nf inv* extremity; *(di una corda)* end ● *nfpl Anat* extremities

e'stremo *a* extreme; *(ultimo)* last; **misure estreme** drastic measures; **l'E~ Oriente** the Far East ● *nm (limite)* extreme. **estremi** *pl (di documento)* main points; *(di reato)* essential ele-

ments; **essere agli estremi** be at the end of one's tether

'estro *nm (disposizione artistica)* talent; *(ispirazione)* inspiration; *(capriccio)* whim. **e'stroso** *a* talented; *(capriccioso)* unpredictable

estro'mettere *vt* expel

estro'verso *a* extroverted ● *nm* extrovert

estu'ario *nm* estuary

esube'ran|te *a* exuberant. **~za** *nf* exuberance

'esule *nmf* exile

esul'tante *a* exultant

esul'tare *vi* rejoice

esu'mare *vt* exhume

età *nf inv* age; **raggiungere la maggiore ~** come of age; **un uomo di mezz'~** a middle-aged man

'etere *nm* ether. **e'tereo** *a* ethereal

eterna'mente *adv* eternally

eternità *nf* eternity; **è un'~ che non la vedo** I haven't seen her for ages

e'terno *a* eternal; *(questione, problema)* age-old; **in ~** *fam* for ever

etero'geneo *a* diverse, heterogeneous

eterosessu'ale *nmf* heterosexual

'etic|a *nf* ethics. **~o** *a* ethical

eti'chetta[1] *nf* label; *(con il prezzo)* price-tag

eti'chetta[2] *nf (cerimoniale)* etiquette

etichet'tare *vt* label

eti'lometro *nm* Breathalyzer®

etimolo'gia *nf* etymology

Eti'opia *nf* Ethiopia

'etnico *a* ethnic. **etnolo'gia** *nf* ethnology

e'trusco *a & nmf* Etruscan

'ettaro *nm* hectare

'etto, etto'grammo *nm* hundred grams, ≈ quarter pound

euca'lipto *nm* eucalyptus

eucari'stia *nf* Eucharist

eufe'mismo *nm* euphemism

eufo'ria *nf* elation; *Med* euphoria. **eu'forico** *a* elated; *Med* euphoric

Euro'city *nm* international Intercity

eurodepu'tato *nm* Euro MP, MEP

Eu'ropa *nf* Europe. **euro'peo, -a** *a & nmf* European

euta'nasia *nf* euthanasia

evacu'a|re *vt* evacuate. **~zi'one** *nf* evacuation

e'vadere *vt* evade; *(sbrigare)* deal with ● *vi* **~ da** escape from

evane'scente *a* vanishing

evan'gel|ico *a* evangelical. **evange'-lista** *nm* evangelist. **~o** = **vangelo**
evapo'ra|re *vi* evaporate. **~zi'one** *nf* evaporation
evasi'one *nf* escape; (*fiscale*) evasion; *fig* escapism. **eva'sivo** *a* evasive
e'vaso *pp di* **evadere** ● *nm* fugitive
eva'sore *nm* **~ fiscale** tax evader
eveni'enza *nf* eventuality
e'vento *nm* event
eventu'al|e *a* possible. **~ità** *inf* eventuality
evi'den|te *a* evident; **è ~te che** it is obvious that. **~te'mente** *adv* evidently. **~za** *nf* evidence; **mettere in ~za** emphasize; **mettersi in ~za** make oneself conspicuous
evidenzi'a|re *vt* highlight. **~'tore** *nm*

(*penna*) highlighter
evi'tare *vt* avoid; (*risparmiare*) spare
evo'care *vt* evoke
evo'lu|to *pp di* **evolvere** ● *a* evolved; (*progredito*) progressive; (*civiltà, nazione*) advanced; **una donna evoluta** a modern woman. **~zi'one** *nf* evolution; (*di ginnasta, aereo*) circle
e'volver|e *vt* develop. **~si** *vr* evolve
ev'viva *int* hurray; **~ il Papa!** long live the Pope!; **gridare ~** cheer
ex+ *pref* ex+, former
'extra *a inv* extra; (*qualità*) first-class ● *nm inv* extra
extracomuni'tario *a* non-EC
extraconiu'gale *a* extramarital
extrater'restre *nmf* extra-terrestrial

Ff

fa¹ *nm inv Mus* (*chiave, nota*) F
fa² *adv* ago; **due mesi ~** two months ago
fabbi'sogno *nm* requirements *pl*, needs *pl*
'fabbrica *nf* factory
fabbri'cabile *a* (*area, terreno*) that can be built on
fabbri'cante *nm* manufacturer
fabbri'ca|re *vt* build; (*produrre*) manufacture; (*fig: inventare*) fabricate. **~to** *nm* building. **~zi'one** *nf* manufacturing; (*costruzione*) building
'fabbro *nm* blacksmith
fac'cend|a *nf* matter; **~e** *pl* (*lavori domestici*) housework *sg*. **~i'ere** *nm* wheeler-dealer
fac'chino *nm* porter
'facci|a *nf* face; (*di foglio*) side; **~a a ~a** face to face; **~a tosta** cheek; **voltar ~a** change sides; **di ~a** (*palazzo*) opposite; **alla ~a di** (*fam: a dispetto di*) in spite of. **~'ata** *nf* façade; (*di foglio*) side; (*fig: esteriorità*) outward appearance
fa'ceto *a* facetious; **tra il serio e il ~** half joking
fa'chiro *nm* fakir
'facil|e *a* easy; (*affabile*) easy-going; **essere ~e alle critiche** be quick to criticize; **essere ~e al riso** laugh a lot; **~e a farsi** easy to do; **è ~e che**

piova it's likely to rain. **~ità** *nf inv* ease; (*disposizione*) aptitude; **avere ~ità di parola** express oneself well
facili'ta|re *vt* facilitate. **~zi'one** *nf* facility; **~zioni** *pl* special terms
facil'mente *adv* (*con facilità*) easily; (*probabilmente*) probably
faci'lone *a* slapdash. **~'ria** *nf* slapdash attitude
facino'roso *a* violent
facoltà *nf inv* faculty; (*potere*) power. **~'tivo** *a* optional; **fermata ~tiva** request stop
facol'toso *a* wealthy
fac'simile *nm* facsimile
fac'totum *nmf* man/girl Friday, factotum
'faggio *nm* beech
fagi'ano *nm* pheasant
fagio'lino *nm* French bean
fagi'olo *nm* bean; **a ~** (*arrivare, capitare*) at the right time
fagoci'tare *vt* gobble up (*società*)
fa'gotto *nm* bundle; *Mus* bassoon
'faida *nf* feud
fai da te *nm* do-it-yourself, DIY
fal'cata *nf* stride
'falc|e *nf* scythe. **fal'cetto** *nm* sickle. **~i'are** *vt* cut; *fig* mow down. **~ia'trice** *nf* [lawn-]mower

'**falco** *nm* hawk

fal'**cone** *nm* falcon

'**falda** *nf* stratum; (*di neve*) flake; (*di cappello*) brim; (*pendìo*) slope

fale'**gname** *nm* carpenter. ~'**ria** *nf* carpentry

'**falla** *nf* leak

fal'**lace** *a* deceptive

'**fallico** *a* phallic

fallimen'**tare** *a* disastrous; *Jur* bankruptcy. **falli'mento** *nm* Fin bankruptcy; *fig* failure

fal'**li|re** *vi* Fin go bankrupt; *fig* fail ●*vt* miss (*colpo*). ~**to, -a** *a* unsuccessful; *Fin* bankrupt ●*nmf* failure; *Fin* bankrupt

'**fallo** *nm* fault; (*errore*) mistake; *Sport* foul; (*imperfezione*) flaw; **senza ~** without fail

falò *nm inv* bonfire

fal'**sar|e** *vt* alter; (*falsificare*) falsify. ~**io, -a** *nmf* forger; (*di documenti*) counterfeiter

falsifi'**ca|re** *vt* fake; (*contraffare*) forge. ~**zi'one** *nf* (*di documento*) falsification

falsità **à** *nf* falseness

'**falso** *a* false; (*sbagliato*) wrong; (*opera d'arte ecc*) fake; (*gioielli, oro*) imitation ●*nm* forgery; **giurare il ~** commit perjury

'**fama** *nf* fame; (*reputazione*) reputation

'**fame** *nf* hunger; **aver ~** be hungry; **fare la ~** barely scrape a living. **fa'melico** *a* ravenous

famige'rato *a* infamous

fa'**miglia** *nf* family

famili'**ar|e** *a* family *attrib*; (*ben noto*) familiar; (*senza cerimonie*) informal ●*nmf* relative, relation ~**ità** *nf* familiarity; (*informalità*) informality. ~**iz'zarsi** *vr* familiarize oneself

fa'**moso** *a* famous

fa'**nale** *nm* lamp; *Auto ecc* light. **fanali** *pl* **posteriori** *Auto* rear lights

fa'**natico, -a** *a* fanatical; **essere ~ di calcio/cinema** be a football/cinema fanatic ●*nmf* fanatic. **fana'tismo** *nm* fanaticism

fanci'**ul|la** *nf* young girl. ~'**lezza** *nf* childhood. ~**lo** *nm* young boy

fan'**donia** *nf* lie; **fandonie!** nonsense!

fan'**fara** *nf* fanfare; (*complesso*) brass band

fanfaro'**nata** *nf* brag. **fanfa'rone, -a** *nmf* braggart

fan'**ghiglia** *nf* mud. '**fango** *nm* mud. **fan'goso** *a* muddy

fannul'**lone, -a** *nmf* idler

fannasci'**enza** *nf* science fiction

fanta'**si|a** *nf* fantasy; (*immaginazione*) imagination; (*capriccio*) fancy; (*di tessuto*) pattern. ~'**oso** *a* (*stilista, ragazzo*) imaginative; (*resoconto*) improbable

fan'**tasma** *nm* ghost

fantasti'**c|are** *vi* day-dream. ~**he'ria** *nf* day-dream. **fan'tastico** *a* fantastic; (*racconto*) fantasy

'**fante** *nm* infantryman; (*carte*) jack. ~'**ria** *nf* infantry

fan'**tino** *nm* jockey

fan'**toccio** *nm* puppet

fanto'**matico** *a* (*inafferrabile*) phantom *attrib*

fara'**butto** *nm* trickster

fara'**ona** *nf* (*uccello*) guinea-fowl

far'**ci|re** *vt* stuff; fill (*torta*). ~**to a** stuffed; (*dolce*) filled

far'**dello** *nm* bundle; *fig* burden

'**fare** *vt* do; make (*dolce, letto ecc*); (*recitare la parte di*) play; (*trascorrere*) spend; ~ **una pausa/un sogno** have a break/a dream; ~ **colpo su** impress; ~ **paura** a frighten; ~ **piacere a** please; **farla finita** put an end to it; ~ **l'insegnante** be a teacher; ~ **lo scemo** play the idiot; ~ **una settimana al mare** spend a week at the seaside; **3 più 3 fa 6** 3 and 3 makes 6; **quanto fa? – fanno 10 000 lira** how much is it? – it's 10,000 lire; **far ~ qcsa a qcno** get sb to do sth; (*costringere*) make sb do sth; ~ **vedere** show; **fammi parlare** let me speak; **niente a che ~ con** nothing to do with; **non c'è niente da ~** (*per problema*) there is nothing we/you/etc. can do; **fa caldo/buio** it's warm/dark; **non fa niente** it doesn't matter; **strada facendo** on the way. **farcela** (*riuscire*) manage ●*vi* **fai in modo di venire** try and come; ~ **da** act as; ~ **per** make as if to; ~ **presto** be quick; **non fa per me** it's not for me ●*nm* way; **sul far del giorno** at daybreak. **farsi** *vr* (*diventare*) get; (*sl: drogarsi*) shoot up; **farsi avanti** come forward; **farsi i fatti propri** mind one's own business; **farsi la barba** shave; **farsi la villa** *fam* buy a villa; **farsi il ragazzo** *fam* find a boyfriend; **farsi due risate** have a laugh; **farsi male** hurt oneself; **farsi strada** (*aver successo*) make one's way in the world

fa'**retto** *nm* spot[light]

far'**falla** *nf* butterfly

farfal'lino *nm* (*cravatta*) bow tie
farfugli'are *vt* mutter
fa'rina *nf* flour. **fari'nacei** *nmpl* starchy food *sg*
fa'ringe *nf* pharynx
fari'noso *a* (*neve*) powdery; (*mela*) soft; (*patata*) floury
farma|'ceutico *a* pharmaceutical. **~'cia** *nf* pharmacy; (*negozio*) chemist's [shop]. **~cia di turno** duty chemist. **~'cista** *nmf* chemist. **'farmaco** *nm* drug
'faro *nm* Auto headlight; Aeron beacon; (*costruzione*) lighthouse
'farsa *nf* farce
'fasci|a *nf* band; (*zona*) area; (*ufficiale*) sash; (*benda*) bandage. **~'are** *vt* bandage; cling to (*fianchi*). **~a'tura** *nf* dressing; (*azione*) bandaging
fa'scicolo *nm* file; (*di rivista*) issue; (*libretto*) booklet
'fascino *nm* fascination
'fascio *nm* bundle; (*di fiori*) bunch
fa'scis|mo *nm* fascism. **~ta** *nmf* fascist
'fase *nf* phase
fa'stidi|o *nm* nuisance; (*scomodo*) inconvenience; **dar ~o a qcno** bother sb; **~i** *pl* (*preoccupazioni*) worries; (*disturbi*) troubles. **~'oso** *a* tiresome
'fasto *nm* pomp. **fa'stoso** *a* sumptuous
fa'sullo *a* bogus
'fata *nf* fairy
fa'tale *a* fatal; (*inevitabile*) fated
fata'l|ismo *nm* fatalism. **~ista** *nmf* fatalist. **~ità** *nf* inv fate; (*caso sfortunato*) misfortune. **~'mente** *adv* inevitably
fa'tica *nf* effort; (*lavoro faticoso*) hard work; (*stanchezza*) fatigue; **a ~** with great difficulty; **è ~ sprecata** it's a waste of time; **fare ~ a fare qcsa** find it difficult to do sth; **fare ~ a finire qcsa** struggle to finish sth. **fati'caccia** *nf* pain
fati'ca|re *vi* toil; **~re a** (*stentare*) find it difficult to. **~ta** *nf* effort; (*sfacchinata*) grind. **fati'coso** *a* tiring; (*difficile*) difficult
'fato *nm* fate
fat'taccio *nm* hum foul deed
fat'tezze *nfpl* features
fat'tibile *a* feasible
'fatto *pp di* **fare** ●*a* done, made; **~ a mano/in casa** handmade/home-made ●*nm* fact; (*azione*) action; (*avvenimento*) event; **bada ai fatti tuoi!** mind your own business; **sa il ~ suo** he knows his

business; **di ~** in fact; **in ~ di** as regards
fat'to|re *nm* (*causa*, Math) factor; (*di fattoria*) farm manager. **~'ria** *nf* farm; (*casa*) farmhouse
fatto'rino *nm* messenger [boy]
fattucchi'era *nf* witch
fat'tura *nf* (*stile*) cut; (*lavorazione*) workmanship; Comm invoice
fattu'ra|re *vt* invoice; (*adulterare*) adulterate. **~to** *nm* turnover, sales *pl*. **~zi'one** *nf* invoicing, billing
'fatuo *a* fatuous
'fauna *nf* fauna
fau'tore *nm* supporter
'fava *nf* broad bean
fa'vella *nf* speech
fa'villa *nf* spark
'favo|la *nf* fable; (*fiaba*) story; (*oggetto di pettegolezzi*) laughing-stock; (*meraviglia*) dream. **~'loso** *a* fabulous
fa'vore *nm* favour; **essere a ~ di** be in favour of; **per ~** please; **di ~** (*condizioni, trattamento*) preferential. **~ggia'mento** *nm* Jur aiding and abetting. **~'vole** *a* favourable. **~vol'mente** *adv* favourably
favo'ri|re *vt* favour; (*promuovere*) promote; **vuol ~re?** (*accettare*) will you have some?; (*entrare*) will you come in?. **~to, -a** *a & nmf* favourite
fax *nm inv* fax. **fa'xare** *vt* fax
fazi'one *nf* faction
faziosità *nf* bias. **fazi'oso** *nm* sectarian
fazzolet'tino *nm* **~** [**di carta**] [paper] tissue
fazzo'letto *nm* handkerchief; (*da testa*) headscarf
feb'braio *nm* February
'febbre *nf* fever; **avere la ~** have o run a temperature. **~ da fieno** hay fever. **febbrici'tante** *a* fevered. **feb'brile** *a* feverish
'feccia *nf* dregs *pl*
'fecola *nf* potato flour
fecon'da|re *vt* fertilize. **~'tore** *nm* fertilizer. **~zi'one** *nf* fertilization. **~zione artificiale** artificial insemination. **fe'condo** *a* fertile
'fede *nf* faith; (*fiducia*) trust; (*anello*) wedding-ring; **in buona/mala ~** in good/bad faith; **prestar ~ a** believe; **tener ~ alla parola** keep one's word. **fe'dele** *a* faithful ●*nmf* believer; (*seguace*) follower. **~l'mente** *adv* faithfully. **~ltà** *nf* faithfulness; **alta ~ltà** high fidelity

'**federa** nf pillowcase

fede'ra|le a federal. **~'lismo** nm federalism. **~zi'one** nf federation

fe'dina nf **avere la ~ penale sporca/ pulita** have a/no criminal record

'**fegato** nm liver; fig guts pl

'**felce** nf fern

fe'lic|e a happy; (fortunato) lucky. **~ità** nf happiness

felici'ta|rsi vr **~rsi con** congratulate. **~zi'oni** nfpl congratulations

fe'lino a feline

'**felpa** nf (indumento) sweatshirt

fel'pato a brushed; (passo) stealthy

'**feltro** nm felt; (cappello) felt hat

'**femmin|a** nf female. **femmi'nile** a feminine; (rivista, abbigliamento) women's; (sesso) female ●nm feminine. **~ilità** nf femininity. **femmi'nismo** nm feminism

'**femore** nm femur

'**fend|ere** vt split. **~i'tura** nf split; (nella roccia) crack

feni'cottero nm flamingo

feno'me'nale a phenomenal. **fe'no'meno** nm phenomenon

'**feretro** nm coffin

feri'ale a weekday; **giorno ~** weekday

'**ferie** nfpl holidays; (di università, tribunale ecc) vacation sg; **andare in ~** go on holiday

feri'mento nm wounding

fe'ri|re vt wound; (in incidente) injure; fig hurt. **~rsi** vr injure oneself. **~ta** nf wound. **~to** a wounded ●nm wounded person; Mil casualty

'**ferma** nf Mil period of service

ferma'ca'pelli nm inv hairslide

ferma'carte nm inv paperweight

ferma'cra'vatta nm inv tiepin

fer'maglio nm clasp; (spilla) brooch; (per capelli) hair slide

ferma'mente adv firmly

fer'ma|re vt stop; (fissare) fix; Jur detain ●vi stop. **~rsi** vr stop. **~ta** nf stop. **~ta dell'autobus** bus-stop. **~ta a richiesta** request stop

fermen'ta|re vi ferme. **~zi'one** nf fermentation. **fer'mento** nm ferment; (lievito) yeast

fer'mezza nf firmness

'**fermo** a still; (veicolo) stationary; (stabile) steady; (orologio) not working ●nm Jur detention; Mech catch; **in stato di ~** in custody

fe'roc|e a ferocious; (bestia) wild; (freddo, dolore) unbearable. **~e'mente** adv fiercely, ferociously. **~ia** nf ferocity

fer'raglia nf scrap iron

ferra'gosto nm 15 August (bank holiday in Italy); (periodo) August holidays pl

ferra'menta nfpl ironmongery sg; **negozio di ~** ironmonger's

fer'ra|re vt shoe (cavallo). **~to a ~to in** (preparato in) well up in

'**ferreo** a iron

'**ferro** nm iron; (attrezzo) tool; (di chirurgo) instrument; **bistecca ai ferri** grilled steak; **di ~** (memoria) excellent; (alibi) cast-iron; **salute di ~** iron constitution. **~ battuto** wrought iron. **~ da calza** knitting needle. **~ di cavallo** horseshoe. **~ da stiro** iron

ferro'vecchio nm scrap merchant

ferro'vi|a nf railway. **~'ario** a railway. **~'ere** nm railwayman

fertil|e a fertile. **~ità** nf fertility. **~iz'zante** nm fertilizer

fer'vente a blazing; fig fervent

'**fervere** vi (preparativi:) be well under way

'**fervid|o** a fervent; **~i auguri** best wishes

fer'vore nm fervour

fesse'ria nf nonsense

'**fesso** pp di **fendere** ●a cracked; (fam: sciocco) foolish ●nm (fam: idiota) fool; **far ~ qcno** fam con sb

fes'sura nf crack; (per gettone ecc) slot

'**festa** nf feast; (giorno festivo) holiday; (compleanno) birthday; (ricevimento) party; fig joy; **fare ~ a qcno** welcome sb; **essere in ~** be on holiday; **far ~** celebrate. **~i'olo** a festive

festeggia'mento nm celebration; (manifestazione) festivity

festeggi'are vt celebrate; (accogliere festosamente) give a hearty welcome to

fe'stino nm party

festività nfpl festivities. **fe'stivo** a holiday; (lieto) festive. **festivi** nmpl public holidays

fe'stone nm (nel cucito) scallop, scollop

fe'stoso a merry

fe'tente a evil smelling; fig revolting ●nmf fam bastard

fe'ticcio nm fetish

'**feto** nm foetus

fe'tore nm stench

'**fetta** nf slice; **a fette** sliced. **~ biscottata** slices of crispy toast-like bread

fet'tuccia nf tape; (con nome) name tape

feu'dale a feudal. '**feudo** nm feud

FFSS *abbr* (**Ferrovie dello Stato**) Italian state railways

fi'aba *nf* fairy-tale. **fia'besco** *a* fairy-tale

fi'acc|a *nf* weariness; (*indolenza*) laziness; **battere la ~a** be sluggish. **fiac-'care** *vt* weaken. **~o** *a* weak; (*indolente*) slack; (*stanco*) weary; (*partita*) dull

fi'acco|la *nf* torch. **~lata** *nf* torchlight procession

fi'ala *nf* phial

fi'amma *nf* flame; *Naut* pennant; **in fiamme** aflame. **andare in fiamme** go up in flames. **~ ossidrica** blowtorch

fiam'ma|nte *a* flaming; **nuovo ~nte** brand new. **~ta** *nf* blaze

fiammeggi'are *vi* blaze

fiam'mifero *nm* match

fiam'mingo, -a *a* Flemish ● *nmf* Fleming ● *nm* (*lingua*) Flemish

fiancheggi'are *vt* border; *fig* support

fi'anco *nm* side; (*di persona*) hip; (*di animale*) flank; *Mil* wing; **al mio ~** by my side; **~ a ~** (*lavorare*) side by side

fi'asco *nm* flask; *fig* fiasco; **fare ~** be a fiasco

fia'tare *vi* breathe; (*parlare*) breathe a word

fi'ato *nm* breath; (*vigore*) stamina; **strumenti a ~** wind instruments; **senza ~** breathlessly; **tutto d'un ~** (*bere, leggere*) all in one go

'fibbia *nf* buckle

'fibra *nf* fibre; **fibre** *pl* (*alimentari*) roughage. **~ ottica** optical fibre

ficca'naso *nmf* nosey parker

fic'car|e *vt* thrust; drive (*chiodo ecc*); (*fam: mettere*) shove. **~si** *vr* thrust oneself; (*nascondersi*) hide; **~si nei guai** get oneself into trouble

fiche *nf* (*gettone*) chip

'fico *nm* (*albero*) fig-tree; (*frutto*) fig. **~ d'India** prickly pear

'fico, -a *fam nmf* cool sort ● *a* cool

fidanza'mento *nm* engagement

fidan'zar|si *vr* become engaged. **~to, -a** *nmf* fiancé; fiancée

fi'dar|si *vr* **~rsi di** trust. **~to** *a* trustworthy

'fido *nm* devoted follower; *Comm* credit

fi'duci|a *nf* confidence; **degno di ~a** trustworthy; **di ~a** (*fornitore, banca*) regular, usual; **persona di ~a** reliable person. **~oso** *a* trusting

fi'ele *nm* bile; *fig* bitterness

fie'nile *nm* barn. **fi'eno** *nm* hay

fi'era *nf* fair

fie'rezza *nf* (*dignità*) pride. **fi'ero** *a* proud

fi'evole *a* faint; (*luce*) dim

'fifa *nf fam* jitters; **aver ~** have the jitters. **fi'fone, -a** *nmf fam* chicken

'figli|a *nf* daughter; **~a unica** only child. **~astra** *nf* stepdaughter. **~astro** *nm* stepson. **~o** *nm* son; (*generico*) child. **~o di papà** spoilt brat. **~o unico** only child

figli'occi|a *nf* goddaughter. **~o** *nm* godson

figli'o|la *nf* girl. **~lanza** *nf* offspring. **~lo** *nm* boy

'figo, -a *vedi* **fico, -a**

fi'gura *nf* figure; (*aspetto esteriore*) shape; (*illustrazione*) illustration; **far bella/brutta ~** make a good/bad impression; **mi hai fatto fare una brutta ~** you made me look a fool; **che ~!** how embarrassing!. **figu'raccia** *nf* bad impression

figu'ra|re *vt* represent; (*simboleggiare*) symbolize; (*immaginare*) imagine ● *vi* (*far figura*) cut a fine figure; (*in lista*) appear, figure. **~rsi** *vr* (*immaginarsi*) imagine; **~ti!** imagine that!; **posso? – [ma] ~ti!** may I? – of course!. **~'tivo** *a* figurative

figu'rina *nf* (*da raccolta*) ≈ cigarette card

figu|ri'nista *nmf* dress designer. **~rino** *nm* fashion sketch. **~rone** *nm* **fare un ~rone** make an excellent impression

'fila *nf* line; (*di soldati ecc*) file; (*di oggetti*) row; (*coda*) queue; **di ~** in succession; **fare la ~** queue [up], stand in line *Am*; **in ~ indiana** single file

fila'mento *nm* filament

filantro'pia *nf* philanthropy

fi'lare *vt* spin; *Naut* pay out ● *vi* (*andarsene*) run away; (*liquido:*) trickle; **fila!** scram!; **~ con** (*fam: amoreggiare*) go out with; **~ dritto** toe the line

filar'monica *nf* (*orchestra*) orchestra

fila'strocca *nf* rigmarole; (*per bambini*) nursery rhyme

filate'lia *nf* philately

fi'la|to *a* spun; (*ininterrotto*) running; (*continuato*) uninterrupted; **di ~to** (*subito*) immediately ● *nm* yarn. **~'tura** *nf* spinning; (*filanda*) spinning mill

fil di 'ferro *nm* wire

fi'letto *nm* (*bordo*) border; (*di vite*) thread; *Culin* fillet

fili'ale *a* filial ● *nf Comm* branch

fili'grana nf filigree; (su carta) watermark

film nm inv film. **~ giallo** thriller. **~ a lungo metraggio** feature film

fil'ma|re vt film. **~to** nm short film. **fil'mino** nm cine film

'filo nm thread; (tessile) yarn; (metallico) wire; (di lama) edge; (venatura) grain; (di perle) string; (d'erba) blade; (di luce) ray; **con un ~ di voce** in a whisper; **per ~ e per segno** in detail; **fare il ~ a qcno** fancy sb; **perdere il ~** lose the thread. **~ spinato** barbed wire

'filobus nm inv trolleybus

filodiffusi'one nf rediffusion

fi'lone nm vein; (di pane) long loaf

filoso'fia nf philosophy. **fi'losofo, -a** nmf philosopher

fil'trare vt filter. **'filtro** nm filter

'filza nf string

fin vedi **fine, fino¹**

fi'nal|e a final ● nm end ● nf Sport final. **fina'lista** nmf finalist. **~ità** nf inv finality; (scopo) aim. **~'mente** adv at last; (in ultimo) finally

fi'nanz|a nf finance; **~i'ario** a financial. **~i'ere** nm financier; (guardia di finanza) customs officer. **~ia'mento** nm funding

finanzi'a|re vt fund, finance. **~'tore, ~'trice** nmf backer

finché conj until; (per tutto il tempo che) as long as

'fine a fine; (sottile) thin; (udito, vista) keen; (raffinato) refined ● nf end; **alla ~** in the end; **alla fin ~** after all; **in fin dei conti** when all's said and done; **te lo dico a fin di bene** I'm telling you for your own good; **senza ~** endless ● nm aim. **~ settimana** weekend

fi'nestra nf window. **fine'strella** nf di aiuto Comput help window, help box. **fine'strino** nm Rail, Auto window

fi'nezza nf fineness; (sottigliezza) thinness; (raffinatezza) refinement

'finger|e vt pretend; feign (affetto ecc). **~si** vr pretend to be

fini'menti nmpl finishing touches; (per cavallo) harness sg

fini'mondo nm end of the world; fig pandemonium

fi'ni|re vt/i finish, end; (smettere) stop; (diventare, andare a finire) end up; **~scila!** stop it!. **~to** a finished; (abile) accomplished. **~'tura** nf finish

finlan'dese a Finnish ● nmf Finn ● nm (lingua) Finnish

Fin'landia nf Finland

'fino¹ prep **~** till, until; (spazio) as far as; **~ all'ultimo** to the last; **fin da** (tempo) since; (spazio) from; **fin qui** as far as here; **fin troppo** too much; **~ a che punto** how far

'fino² a fine; (acuto) subtle; (puro) pure

fi'nocchio nm fennel; (fam: omosessuale) poof

fi'nora adv so far, up till now

'finta nf pretence, sham; Sport feint; **far ~ di** pretend to; **far ~ di niente** act as if nothing had happened; **per ~** (per scherzo) for a laugh

'fint|o, -a pp di **fingere** ● a false; (artificiale) artificial; **fare il ~o tonto** act dumb

finzi'one nf pretence

fi'occo nm bow; (di neve) flake; (nappa) tassel; **coi fiocchi** fig excellent. **~ di neve** snowflake

fi'ocina nf harpoon

fi'oco a weak; (luce) dim

fi'onda nf catapult

fio'raio, -a nmf florist

fiorda'liso nm cornflower

fi'ordo nm fiord

fi'ore nm flower; (parte scelta) cream; **fiori** pl (nelle carte) clubs; **a fior d'acqua** on the surface of the water; **fior di** (abbondanza) a lot of; **ha i nervi a fior di pelle** his nerves are on edge; **a fiori** flowery

fioren'tino a Florentine

fio'retto nm (scherma) foil; Relig act of mortification

fio'rire vi flower; (albero:) blossom; fig flourish

fio'rista nmf florist

fiori'tura nf (di albero) blossoming

fi'otto nm scorrere a fiotti pour out; **piove a fiotti** the rain is pouring down

Fi'renze nf Florence

'firma nf signature; (nome) name

fir'ma|re vt sign. **~'tario, -a** nmf signatory. **~to** a (abito, borsa) designer attrib

fisar'monica nf accordion

fi'scale a fiscal

fischi'are vi whistle ● vt whistle; (in segno di disapprovazione) boo

fischiet't|are vt whistle. **~io** nm whistling

fischi'etto nm whistle. **'fischio** nm whistle

'fisco nm treasury; (tasse) taxation; **il ~** the taxman

'fisica nf physics

fisica'mente adv physically

'**fisico, -a** *a* physical ● *nmf* physicist ● *nm* physique

'**fisima** *nf* whim

fisio|lo'gia *nf* physiology. **~'logico** *a* physiological

fisiono'mia *nf* features. face; *(di paesaggio)* appearance

fisiotera'pi|a *nf* physiotherapy. **~sta** *nmf* physiotherapist

fis'sa|re *vt* fix, fasten; *(guardare fissa-mente)* stare at; arrange *(appuntamento, ora)*. **~rsi** *vr (stabilirsi)* settle; *(fissare lo sguardo)* stare; **~rsi su** *(ostinarsi)* set one's mind on; **~rsi di fare qcsa** become obsessed with doing sth. **~to** *nm (persona)* person with an obsession. **~zi'one** *nf* fixation; *(ossessione)* obsession

'**fisso** *a* fixed; **un lavoro ~** a regular job; **senza fissa dimora** of no fixed abode

'**fitta** *nf* sharp pain

fit'tizio *a* fictitious

'**fitto¹** *a* thick; **~ di** full of ● *nm* depth

fitto² *nm (affitto)* rent; **dare a ~** let; **prendere a ~** rent; *(noleggiare)* hire

fiu'mana *nf* swollen river; *fig* stream

fi'ume *nm* river; *fig* stream

fiu'tare *vt* smell. **fi'uto** *nm* [sense of] smell; *fig* nose

'**flaccido** *a* flabby

fla'cone *nm* bottle

fla'gello *nm* scourge

fla'grante *a* flagrant; **in ~** in the act

fla'nella *nf* flannel

'**flash** *nm inv Journ* newsflash

'**flauto** *nm* flute

'**flebile** *a* feeble

'**flemma** *nf* calm; *Med* phlegm. **flem'matico** *a* phlegmatic

fles'sibil|e *a* flexible. **~ità** *nf* flexibility

flessi'one *nf (del busto in avanti)* forward bend

'**flesso** *pp di* **flettere**

flessu'oso *a* supple

'**flettere** *vt* bend

flir'tare *vi* flirt

F.lli *abbr* **(fratelli)** Bros

floppy disk *nm inv* floppy disk

'**flora** *nf* flora

'**florido** *a* flourishing

'**floscio** *a* limp; *(flaccido)* flabby

'**flotta** *nf* fleet. **flot'tiglia** *nf* flotilla

flu'ente *a* fluent

flu'ido *nm* fluid

flu'ire *vi* flow

fluore'scente *a* fluorescent

flu'oro *nm* fluorine

'**flusso** *nm* flow; *Med* flux; *(del mare)* flood[-tide]; **~ e riflusso** ebb and flow

fluttu'ante *a* fluctuating

fluttu'a|re *vi (prezzi, moneta:)* fluctuate. **~zi'one** *nf* fluctuation

fluvi'ale *a* river

fo'bia *nf* phobia

'**foca** *nf* seal

fo'caccia *nf (pane)* flat bread; *(dolce)* ≈ raisin bread

fo'cale *a (distanza, punto)* focal. **foca-liz'zare** *vt* get into focus *(fotografia)*; focus *(attenzione)*; define *(problema)*

'**foce** *nf* mouth

foco'laio *nm Med* focus; *fig* centre

foco'lare *nm* hearth; *(caminetto)* fireplace; *Techn* furnace

fo'coso *a* fiery

'foder|a *nf* lining; *(di libro)* dustjacket; *(di poltrona ecc)* loose cover. **fode'rare** *vt* line; cover *(libro)*. **~o** *nm* sheath

'**foga** *nf* impetuosity

foggi|a *nf* fashion; *(maniera)* manner; *(forma)* shape. **~ are** *vt* mould

fogli|a *nf* leaf; *(di metallo)* foil. **~'ame** *nm* foliage

fogli'etto *nm (pezzetto di carta)* piece of paper

'**foglio** *nm* sheet; *(pagina)* leaf. **~ elet-tronico** *Comput* spreadsheet. **~ rosa** ≈ provisional driving licence

'**fogna** *nf* sewer. **~'tura** *nf* sewerage

fo'lata *nf* gust

fol'clo|re *nm* folklore. **~'ristico** *a* folk; *(bizzarro)* weird

folgo'ra|re *vi (splendere)* shine ● *vt (con un fulmine)* strike. **~zi'one** *nf (da fulmine, elettrica)* electrocution; *(idea)* brainwave

'**folgore** *nf* thunderbolt

'**folla** *nf* crowd

'**folle** *a* mad; **in ~** *Auto* in neutral; **andare in ~** *Auto* coast

folle'mente *adv* madly

fol'lia *nf* madness; **alla ~** *(amare)* to distraction

'**folto** *a* thick

fomen'tare *vt* stir up

fond'ale *nm Theat* backcloth

fonda'men|ta *nfpl* foundations. **~'tale** *a* fundamental. **~to** *nm (di prin-cipio, teoria)* foundation

fon'da|re *vt* establish; base *(ragiona-mento, accusa)*. **~to** *a (ragionamento)* well-founded. **~zi'one** *nf* establishment; **~zioni** *pl (di edificio)* foundations

fon'delli *nmpl* **prendere qcno per i ~** pull sb's leg

fon'dente *a* ⟨cioccolato⟩ dark

'fonder|e *vt/i* melt; ⟨colori:⟩ blend. **~si** *vr* melt; *Comm* merge. **fonde'ria** *nf* foundry

'fondi *nmpl* ⟨denaro⟩ funds; ⟨di caffè⟩ grounds

'fondo *a* deep; **è notte fonda** it's the middle of the night ● *nm* bottom; ⟨fine⟩ end; ⟨sfondo⟩ background; ⟨indole⟩ nature; ⟨somma di denaro⟩ fund; ⟨feccia⟩ dregs *pl*; **andare a ~** ⟨nave:⟩ sink; **da cima a ~** from beginning to end; **in ~** after all; **in ~ in ~** deep down; **fino in ~** right to the end; ⟨capire⟩ thoroughly. **~ d'investimento** investment trust

fondo'tinta *nm* foundation cream

fon'duta *nf* fondue made with cheese, milk and eggs

fo'netic|a *nf* phonetics *sg.* **~o** *a* phonetic

fon'tana *nf* fountain

'fonte *nf* spring; *fig* source ● *nm* font

fo'raggio *nm* forage

fo'rar|e *vt* pierce; punch ⟨biglietto⟩ ● *vi* puncture. **~si** *vr* ⟨gomma, pallone:⟩ go soft

'forbici *nfpl* scissors

forbi'cine *nfpl* ⟨per le unghie⟩ nail scissors

for'bito *a* erudite

'forca *nf* fork; ⟨patibolo⟩ gallows *pl*

for'cella *nf* fork; ⟨per capelli⟩ hairpin

for'chet|ta *nf* fork. **~'tata** *nf* ⟨quantità⟩ forkful

for'cina *nf* hairpin

'forcipe *nm* forceps *pl*

for'cone *nm* pitchfork

fo'resta *nf* forest. **fore'stale** *a* forest *attrib*

foresti'ero, -a *a* foreign ● *nmf* foreigner

for'fait *nm inv* fixed price; **dare ~** ⟨abbandonare⟩ give up

'forfora *nf* dandruff

'forgi|a *nf* forge. **~'are** *vt* forge

'forma *nf* form; ⟨sagoma⟩ shape; *Culin* mould; ⟨da calzolaio⟩ last; **essere in ~** be in good form; **a ~ di** in the shape of; **forme** *pl* ⟨del corpo⟩ figure *sg*; ⟨convenzioni⟩ appearances

formag'gino *nm* processed cheese. **for'maggio** *nm* cheese

for'mal|e *a* formal. **~ità** *nf inv* formality. **~iz'zarsi** *vr* stand on ceremony. **~'mente** *adv* formally

for'ma|re *vt* form. **~rsi** *vr* form;

⟨sviluopparsi⟩ develop. **~to** *nm* size; ⟨di libro⟩ format; **~to tessera** ⟨fotografia⟩ passport-size

format'tare *vt* format

formazi'one *nf* formation; *Sport* line-up. **~ professionale** vocational training

for'mica *nf* ant. **~'caio** *nm* anthill

'formica® *nf* ⟨laminato plastico⟩ Formica®

formico'l|are *vi* ⟨braccio ecc:⟩ tingle; **~are di** be swarming with; **mi ~a la mano** I have pins and needles in my hand. **~io** *nm* swarming; ⟨di braccio ecc⟩ pins and needles *pl*

formi'dabile *a* ⟨tremendo⟩ formidable; ⟨eccezionale⟩ tremendous

for'mina *nf* mould

for'moso *a* shapely

'formula *nf* formula. **formu'lare** *vt* formulate; ⟨esprimere⟩ express

for'nace *nf* furnace; ⟨per laterizi⟩ kiln

for'naio *nm* baker; ⟨negozio⟩ bakery

for'nello *nm* stove; ⟨di pipa⟩ bowl

for'ni|re *vt* supply ⟨di with⟩. **~'tore** *nm* supplier. **~'tura** *nf* supply

'forno *nm* oven; ⟨panetteria⟩ bakery; **al ~** roast. **~ a microonde** microwave [oven]

'foro *nm* hole; ⟨romano⟩ forum; ⟨tribunale⟩ [law] court

'forse *adv* perhaps, maybe; **essere in ~** be in doubt

forsen'nato, -a *a* mad ● *nmf* madman; madwoman

'forte *a* strong; ⟨colore⟩ bright; ⟨suono⟩ loud; ⟨resistente⟩ tough; ⟨spesa⟩ considerable; ⟨dolore⟩ severe; ⟨pioggia⟩ heavy; ⟨a tennis, calcio⟩ good; ⟨fam: simpatico⟩ great; ⟨taglia⟩ large ● *adv* strongly; ⟨parlare⟩ loudly; ⟨velocemente⟩ fast; ⟨piovere⟩ heavily ● *nm* ⟨fortezza⟩ fort; ⟨specialità⟩ strong point

for'tezza *nf* fortress; ⟨forza morale⟩ fortitude

fortifi'care *vt* fortify

for'tino *nm* *Mil* blockhouse

for'tuito *a* fortuitous; **incontro ~** chance encounter

for'tuna *nf* fortune; ⟨successo⟩ success; ⟨buona sorte⟩ luck. **atterraggio di ~** forced landing; **aver ~** be lucky; **buona ~!** good luck!; **di ~** makeshift; **per ~** luckily. **fortu'nato** *a* lucky, fortunate; ⟨impresa⟩ successful. **~ta'mente** *adv* fortunately

fo'runcolo *nm* pimple; ⟨grosso⟩ boil

'forza *nf* strength; ⟨potenza⟩ power;

(*fisica*) force;**di ~** by force;**a ~ di** by
dint of;**con ~** hard;**~! come on!;~ di
volontà** will-power; **~ maggiore** circumstances beyond one's control;**la ~
pubblica** the police; **per ~** against
one's will; (*naturalmente*) of course;
farsi ~ bear up;**mare ~ 8** force 8 gale;
bella ~! *fam* big deal!. **~ di gravità**
[force of] gravity.**le forze armate** the
armed forces

for'za|re *vt* force; (*scassare*) break
open; (*sforzare*) strain. **~to** *a* forced;
(*sorriso*) strained● *nm* convict

forzi'ere *nm* coffer

for'zuto *a* strong

fo'schia *nf* haze

'fosco *a* dark

fo'sfato *nm* phosphate

'fosforo *nm* phosphorus

'fossa *nf* pit; (*tomba*) grave. **~ biologica** cesspool. **fos'sato** *nm* (*di fortificazione*) moat

fos'setta *nf* dimple

'fossile *nm* fossil

'fosso *nm* ditch; *Mil* trench

'foto *nf inv fam* photo. **fare delle ~**
take some photos

foto'cellula *nf* photocell

fotocomposizi'one *nf* filmsetting,
photocomposition

foto'cop|ia *nf* photocopy. **~'are** *vt*
photocopy. **~a'trice** *nf* photocopier

foto'finish *nm inv* photo finish

foto'genico *a* photogenic

fotogra'fare *vt* photograph. **~'fia** *nf*
(*arte*) photography; (*immagine*) photograph; **fare ~fie** take photographs.
foto'grafico *a* photographic; **macchina fotografica** camera. **fo'tografo, -a**
nmf photographer

foto'gramma *nm* frame

fotomo'dello *nm* [photographer's]
model

fotomon'taggio *nm* photomontage

fotoro'manzo *nm* photo story

'fotter|e *vt* (*fam: rubare*) nick; *vulg*
fuck, screw. **~sene** *vr vulg* not give a
fuck

fot'tuto *a* (*fam: maledetto*) bloody

fou'lard *nm inv* scarf

fra *prep* (*in mezzo a due*) between; (*in un
insieme*) among; (*tempo, distanza*) in;
detto ~ noi between you and me; **~ sé
e sé** to oneself; **~ l'altro** what's more;
~ breve soon; **~ quindici giorni** in
two weeks' time; **~ tutti, siamo in
venti** there are twenty of us altogether

fracas'sar|e *vt* smash. **~si** *vr* shatter

fra'casso *nm* din; (*di cose che cadono*)
crash

'fradicio *a* (*bagnato*) soaked; (*guasto*)
rotten;**ubriaco ~** blind drunk

'fragile *a* fragile; *fig* frail.**~ità** *nf* fra-
gility; *fig* frailty

'fragola *nf* strawberry

fra'go|re *nm* uproar; (*di cose rotte*) clat-
ter; (*di tuono*) rumble. **~'roso** *a* up-
roarious; (*tuono*) rumbling; (*suono*)
clanging

fra'gran|te *a* fragrant. **~za** *nf* fra-
grance

frain'ten|dere *vt* misunderstand.
~ndersi *vr* be at cross-purposes. **~so**
pp di fraintendere

frammen'tario *a* fragmentary.**fram-
'mento** *nm* fragment

'frana *nf* landslide; (*fam: persona*)
walking disaster area. **fra'nare** *vi* slide
down

franca'mente *adv* frankly

fran'cese *a* French● *nmf* Frenchman;
Frenchwoman● *nm* (*lingua*) French

fran'chezza *nf* frankness

'Francia *nf* France

'franco[1] *a* frank; *Comm* free; **farla
franca** get away with sth

'franco[2] *nm* (*moneta*) franc

franco'bollo *nm* stamp

fran'gente *nm* (*onda*) breaker; (*scoglio*) reef; (*fig: momento difficile*) crisis;
in quel ~ given the situation

'frangia *nf* fringe

fra'noso *a* subject to landslides

fran'toio *nm* olive-press

frantu'mar|e *vt*, **~si** *vr* shatter. **fran-
'tumi** *nmpl* splinters; **andare in frantumi** be smashed to smithereens

frappé *nm inv* milkshake

frap'por|re *vt* interpose. **~si** *vr* inter-
vene

fra'sario *nm* vocabulary; (*libro*)
phrase book

'frase *nf* sentence; (*espressione*)
phrase. **~ fatta** cliché

'frassino *nm* ash[-tree]

frastagli'a|re *vt* make jagged. **~to** *a*
jagged

frastor'na|re *vt* daze. **~to** *a* dazed

frastu'ono *nm* racket

'frate *nm* friar; (*monaco*) monk

fratel'lanza *nf* brotherhood. **~stro**
nm half-brother

fra'tel|li *nmpl* (*fratello e sorella*)
brother and sister. **~o** *nm* brother

fraterniz'zare *vi* fraternize. **fra'terno** *a* brotherly

frat'taglie *nfpl* (*di pollo ecc*) giblets

frat'tanto *adv* in the meantime

frat'tempo *nm* **nel** ~ meanwhile, in the meantime

frat'tu|ra *nf* fracture. ~'**rare** *vt*, ~'**rarsi** *vr* break

fraudo'lento *a* fraudulent

frazi'one *nf* fraction; (*borgata*) hamlet

'frecci|a *nf* arrow; *Auto* indicator. ~'**ata** *nf* (*osservazione pungente*) cutting remark

fredda'mente *adv* coldly

fred'dare *vt* cool; (*fig: con sguardo, battuta*) cut down; (*uccidere*) kill

fred'dezza *nf* coldness

'freddo *a & nm* cold; **aver** ~ be cold; **fa** ~ it's cold

freddo'loso *a* sensitive to cold, chilly

fred'dura *nf* pun

fre'ga|re *vt* rub; (*fam: truffare*) cheat; (*fam: rubare*) swipe. ~**rsene** *fam* not give a damn; **chi se ne frega!** what the heck!. ~**si** *vr* rub (*occhi*). ~**ta** *nf* rub. ~'**tura** *nf fam* (*truffa*) swindle; (*delusione*) letdown

'fregio *nm* Archit frieze; (*ornamento*) decoration

fre'mente *a* quivering

'frem|ere *vi* quiver. ~**ito** *nm* quiver

fre'na|re *vt* brake; *fig* restrain; hold back (*lacrime, impazienza*) ● *vi* brake. ~**rsi** *vr* check oneself. ~**ta** *nf* **fare una** ~**ta brusca** hit the brakes

frene'sia *nf* frenzy; (*desiderio smodato*) craze. **fre'netico** *a* frenzied

'freno *nm* brake; *fig* check; **togliere il** ~ release the brake; **usare il** ~ apply the brake; **tenere a** ~ restrain. ~ **a mano** handbrake

frequen'tare *vt* frequent; attend (*scuola ecc*); mix with (*persone*)

fre'quen|te *a* frequent; **di** ~**te** frequently. ~**za** *nf* frequency; (*assiduità*) attendance

fre'schezza *nf* freshness; (*di temperatura*) coolness

'fresco *a* fresh; (*temperatura*) cool; **stai** ~! you're for it! ● *nm* coolness; **far** ~ be cool; **mettere/tenere in** ~ put/keep in a cool place

'fretta *nf* hurry, haste; **aver** ~ be in a hurry; **far** ~ **a qcno** hurry sb; **in** ~ **e furia** in a great hurry. **frettolosa'mente** *adv* hurriedly. **fretto'loso** *a* (*persona*) in a hurry; (*lavoro*) rushed, hurried

fri'abile *a* crumbly

'friggere *vt* fry; **vai a farti** ~! get lost! ● *vi* sizzle

friggi'trice *nf* chip pan

frigidità *nf* frigidity. **'frigido** *a* frigid

fri'gnare *vi* whine

'frigo *nm* fridge

frigo'bar *nm inv* minibar

frigo'rifero *a* refrigerating ● *nm* refrigerator

fringu'ello *nm* chaffinch

frit'tata *nf* omelette

frit'tella *nf* fritter; (*fam: macchia d'unto*) grease stain

'fritto *pp di* **friggere** ● *a* fried; **essere** ~ be done for ● *nm* fried food. ~ **misto** mixed fried fish/vegetables. **frit'tura** *nf* (*pietanza*) fried dish

frivo'lezza *nf* frivolity. **'frivolo** *a* frivolous

frizio'nare *vt* rub. **frizi'one** *nf* friction; *Mech* clutch; (*di pelle*) rub

friz'zante *a* fizzy; (*vino*) sparkling; (*aria*) bracing

'frizzo *nm* gibe

fro'dare *vt* defraud

'frode *nf* fraud. ~ **fiscale** tax evasion

'frollo *a* tender; (*selvaggina*) high; (*persona*) spineless; **pasta frolla** short[crust] pastry

'fronda *nf* [leafy] branch; *fig* rebellion. **fron'doso** *a* leafy

fron'tale *a* frontal; (*scontro*) head-on

'fronte *nf* forehead; (*di edificio*) front; **di** ~ opposite; **di** ~ **a** opposite, facing; (*a paragone*) compared with; **far** ~ **a** face ● *nm Mil, Pol* front. ~**ggi'are** *vt* face

fronte'spizio *nm* title page

fronti'era *nf* frontier, border

fron'tone *nm* pediment

'fronzolo *nm* frill

'frotta *nf* swarm; (*di animali*) flock

'frottola *nf* fib; **frottole** *pl* nonsense *sg*

fru'gale *a* frugal

fru'gare *vi* rummage ● *vt* search

frul'la|re *vt* Culin whisk ● *vi* (*ali:*) whirr. ~**to** *nm* ~**to di frutta** fruit drink with milk and crushed ice. ~'**tore** *nm* [electric] mixer. **frul'lino** *nm* whisk

fru'mento *nm* wheat

frusci'are *vi* rustle

fru'scio *nm* rustle; (*radio, giradischi*) background noise; (*di acque*) murmur

'frusta *nf* whip; (*frullino*) whisk

fru'sta|re *vt* whip. ~**ta** *nf* lash. **fru'stino** *nm* riding crop

fru'stra|re *vt* frustrate. ~**to** *a* frustrated. ~**zi'one** *nf* frustration

'frutt|a *nf* fruit; (*portata*) dessert. **frut'tare** *vi* bear fruit ● *vt* yield. **frut'teto** *nm* orchard. ~**i'vendolo, -a** *nmf* greengrocer. **~o** nm anche fig fruit; Fin yield; **~i di bosco** fruits of the forest. **~i di mare** seafood sg. **~oso** a profitable

f.to abbr (**firmato**) signed

fu a (defunto) late; **il ~ signor Rossi** the late Mr Rossi

fuci'la|re vt shoot. **~ta** nf shot

fu'cile nm rifle

fu'cina nf forge

'fucsia nf fuchsia

'fuga nf escape; (perdita) leak; Mus fugue; **darsi alla ~** take to flight

fu'gace a fleeting

fug'gevole a short-lived

fuggi'asco, -a nmf fugitive

fuggi'fuggi nm stampede

fug'gi|re vi flee; (innamorati:) elope; fig fly. **~'tivo, -a** nmf fugitive

'fulcro nm fulcrum

ful'gore nm splendour

fu'liggine nf soot

fulmi'nar|e vt strike by lightning; (con sguardo) look daggers at; (con scarica elettrica) electrocute. **~si** vr burn out. **'fulmine** nm lightning. **ful'mineo** a rapid

'fulvo a tawny

fumai'olo nm funnel; (di casa) chimney

fu'ma|re vt/i smoke; (in ebollizione) steam. **~'tore**, **~'trice** nmf smoker; **non fumatori** non-smoker, non-smoking

fu'metto nm comic strip; **fumetti** pl comics

'fumo nm smoke; (vapore) steam; fig hot air; **andare in ~** vanish. **fu'moso** a (ambiente) smoky; (discorso) vague

fu'nambolo, -a nmf tightrope walker

'fune nf rope; (cavo) cable

'funebre a funeral; (cupa) gloomy

fune'rale nm funeral

fu'nereo a (aria) funereal

fu'nesto a sad

'fungere vi **~ da** act as

'fungo nm mushroom; Bot, Med fungus

funico'lare nf funicular [railway]

funi'via nf cableway

funzio'nal|e a functional. **~ità** nf functionality

funziona'mento nm functioning

funzio'nare vi work, function; **~ da** (fungere da) act as

funzio'nario nm official

funzi'one nf function; (carica) office; Relig service; **entrare in ~** take up office

fu'oco nm fire; (fisica, fotografia) focus; **far ~** fire; **dar ~ a** set fire to; **prendere ~** catch fire. **fuochi pl d'artificio** fireworks. **~ di paglia** nine-days' wonder

fuorché prep except

fu'ori adv out; (all'esterno) outside; (all'aperto) outdoors; **andare di ~** (traboccare) spill over; **essere ~ di sé** be beside oneself; **essere in ~** (sporgere) stick out; **far ~** fam do in; **~ mano** out of the way; **~ moda** old-fashioned; **~ pasto** between meals; **~ pericolo** out of danger; **~ questione** out of the question; **~ uso** out of use ● nm outside

fuori'bordo nm speedboat (with outboard motor)

fuori'classe nmf inv champion

fuorigi'oco nm & adv offside

fuori'legge nmf outlaw

fuori'serie a custom-made ● nf custom-built model

fuori'strada nm off-road vehicle

fuorvi'are vt lead astray ● vi go astray

furbacchi'one nm crafty old devil

turbe'ria nf cunning. **fur'bizia** nf cunning

'furbo a cunning; (intelligente) clever; (astuto) shrewd; **bravo ~!** nice one!; **fare il ~** try to be clever

fu'rente a furious

fur'fante nm scoundrel

furgon'cino nm delivery van. **fur'gone** nm van

'furia nf fury; (fretta) haste; **a ~a di** by dint of. **~'bondo, ~'oso** a furious

fu'rore nm fury; (veemenza) frenzy; **far ~** be all the rage. **~ggi'are** vi be a great success

furtiva'mente adv covertly. **fur'tivo** a furtive

'furto nm theft; (con scasso) burglary

'fusa nfpl **fare le ~** purr

fu'scello nm (di legno) twig; (di paglia) straw; **sei un ~** you're as light as a feather

fu'seaux mpl leggings

fusi'one nf fusion; Comm merger

'fuso pp di **fondere** ● a melted ● nm spindle. **~ orario** time zone

fusoli'era nf fuselage

fu'stagno nm corduroy

fu'stino nm (di detersivo) box

'fusto nm stem; (tronco) trunk; (di metallo) drum; (di legno) barrel

'futile a futile

fu'turo a & nm future

Gg

gab'bare vt cheat. ~si vr ~si di make fun of

'gabbia nf cage; (da imballaggio) crate. ~ **degli imputati** dock. ~ **toracica** rib cage

gabbi'ano nm [sea]gull

gabi'netto nm (di medico) consulting room; Pol cabinet; (toletta) lavatory; (laboratorio) laboratory

'gaffe nf inv blunder

gagli'ardo a vigorous

gai'ezza nf gaiety. **'gaio** a cheerful

'gala nf gala

ga'lante a gallant. ~'ria nf gallantry. **galantu'omo** nm (pl **galantuomini**) gentleman

ga'lassia nf galaxy

gala'teo nm [good] manners pl; (trattato) book of etiquette

gale'otto nm (rematore) galley-slave; (condannato) convict

ga'lera nf (nave) galley; fam prison

'galla nf Bot gall; **a ~** adv afloat; **venire a ~** surface

galleggi'ante a floating ●nm craft; (boa) float

galleggi'are vi float

galle'ria nf (traforo) tunnel; (d'arte) gallery; Theat circle; (arcata) arcade. ~ **d'arte** art gallery

'Galles nm Wales. **gal'lese** a welsh ●nm Welshman; (lingua) Welsh ●nf Welshwoman

gal'letto nm cockerel; **fare il ~** show off

gal'lina nf hen

gal'lismo nm machismo

'gallo nm cock

gal'lone nm stripe; (misura) gallon

galop'pare vi gallop. **ga'loppo** nm gallop; **al galoppo** at a gallop

galvaniz'zare vt galvanize

'gamba nf leg; (di lettera) stem; **a quattro gambe** on all fours; **darsela a gambe** take to one's heels; **essere in ~** (essere forte) be strong; (capace) be smart

gamba'letto nm pop sock

gambe'retto nm shrimp. **'gambero** nm prawn; (di fiume) crayfish

'gambo nm stem; (di pianta) stalk

'gamma nf Mus scale; fig range

ga'nascia nf jaw; **ganasce** pl **del freno** brake shoes

'gancio nm hook

'ganghero nm **uscire dai gangheri** fig get into a temper

'gara nf competition; (di velocità) race; **fare a ~** compete. ~ **d'appalto** call for tenders

ga'rage nm inv garage

ga'ran|te nmf guarantor. ~'**tire** vt guarantee; (rendersi garante) vouch for; (assicurare) assure. ~'**zia** nf guarantee; **in ~zia** under guarantee

gar'ba|re vi like; **non mi garba** I don't like it. ~**to a** courteous

'garbo nm courtesy; (grazia) grace; **con ~** graciously

gareggi'are vi compete

garga'nella nf **a ~** from the bottle

garga'rismo nm gargle; **fare i gargarismi** gargle

ga'rofano nm carnation

gar'rire vi chirp

'garza nf gauze

gar'zone nm boy. ~ **di stalla** stable-boy

gas nm inv gas; **dare ~** Auto accelerate; **a tutto ~** flat out. ~ **lacrimogeno** tear gas. ~ **di scarico** pl exhaust fumes

gas'dotto nm natural gas pipeline

ga'solio nm diesel oil

ga'sometro nm gasometer

gas's|are vt aerate; (uccidere col gas) gas. ~**ato** a gassy. ~**oso, -a** a gassy; (bevanda) fizzy ●nf lemonade

'gastrico a gastric. **ga'strite** nf gastritis

gastro'no'mia nf gastronomy. ~'**nomico** a gastronomic. **ga'stronomo, -a** nmf gourmet

'gatta nf **una ~ da pelare** a headache

gatta'buia nf hum clink

gat'tino, -a nmf kitten

'gatto, -a nmf cat. ~ **delle nevi** snowmobile

gat'toni adv on all fours

ga'vetta nf mess tin; **fare la ~** rise through the ranks

gay a inv gay

'gazza nf magpie

gaz'zarra nf racket

gaz'zella nf gazelle; Auto police car

gaz'zetta nf gazette

gaz'zosa nf clear lemonade

'geco nm gecko

ge'la|re vt/i freeze. **~ta** nf frost

gela't|aio, -a nmf ice-cream seller; (negozio) ice-cream shop. **~e'ria** nf ice-cream parlour. **~i'era** nf ice-cream maker

gela'ti|na nf gelatine; (dolce) jelly. **~na di frutta** fruit jelly. **~'noso** a gelatinous

ge'lato a frozen● nm ice-cream

'gelido a freezing

'gelo nm (freddo intenso) freezing cold; (brina) frost; fig chill

ge'lone nm chilblain

gelosa'mente adv jealously

gelo'sia nf jealousy. **ge'loso** a jealous

'gelso nm mulberry[-tree]

gelso'mino nm jasmine

gemel'laggio nm twinning

ge'mello, -a a & nmf twin; (di polsino) cuff-link; **Gemelli** pl Astr Gemini sg

'gem|ere vi groan; (tubare) coo. **~ito** nm groan

'gemma nf gem; Bot bud

'gene nm gene

genealo'gia nf genealogy

gene'ral|e¹ a general; **spese ~i** overheads

gene'rale² nm Mil general

generalità nf (qualità) generality, general nature; **~** pl (dati personali) particulars

generaliz'za|re vt generalize. **~zi'one** nf generalization. **general'mente** adv generally

gene'ra|re vt give birth to; (causare) breed; Techn generate. **~'tore** nm Techn generator. **~zi'one** nf generation

'genere nm kind; Biol genus; Gram gender; (letterario, artistico) genre; (prodotto) product; **il ~ umano** mankind; **in ~** generally. **generi** pl **alimentari** provisions

generica'mente adv generically. **ge'nerico** a generic; **medico generico** general practitioner

'genero nm son-in-law

generosità nf generosity. **gene'roso** a generous

'genesi nf genesis

ge'netico, -a a genetic ● nf genetics sg

gen'giva nf gum

geni'ale a ingenious; (congeniale) congenial

'genio nm genius; **andare a ~** be to one's taste. **~ civile** civil engineering. **~ [militare]** Engineers

geni'tale a genital. **genitali** nmpl genitals

geni'tore nm parent

gen'naio nm January

'Genova nf Genoa

gen'taglia nf rabble

'gente nf people pl

gen'til|e a kind; **G~e Signore** Dear Sir. **genti'lezza** nf kindness; **per gentilezza** (per favore) please. **~'mente** adv kindly. **~u'omo** (pl **~u'omini**) nm gentleman

genu'ino a genuine; (cibo, prodotto) natural

geogra'fia nf geography. **geo'grafico** a geographical. **ge'ografo** nm geographer

geolo'gia nf geology. **geo'logico** a geological. **ge'ologo, -a** nmf geologist

ge'ometra nmf surveyor

geome'tria nf geometry. **geo'metrico** a geometric[al]

ge'ranio nm geranium

gerar'chia nf hierarchy. **ge'rarchico** a hierarchic[al]

ge'rente nm manager ● nf manageress

'gergo nm slang; (di professione ecc) jargon

geria'tria nf geriatrics sg

Ger'mania nf Germany

'germe nm germ; (fig: principio) seed

germogli'are vi sprout. **ger'moglio** nm sprout

gero'glifico nm hieroglyph

'gesso nm chalk; (Med, scultura) plaster

gestazi'one nf gestation

gestico'lare vi gesticulate

gesti'one nf management

ge'stir|e vi manage. **~si** vr budget one's time and money

'gesto nm gesture; (azione pl nf **gesta**) deed

ge'store nm manager

Gesù nm Jesus. **~ bambino** baby Jesus

gesu'ita nm Jesuit

get'ta|re *vt* throw; (*scagliare*) fling; (*emettere*) spout; *Techn, fig* cast; **~re via** throw away.**~rsi** *vr* throw oneself; **~rsi in** (*fiume:*) flow into. **~ta** *nf* throw; *Techn* casting

get'tito *nm* **~ fiscale** tax revenue

'**getto** *nm* throw; (*di liquidi, gas*) jet;**a ~ continuo** in a continuous stream;**di ~** straight off

getto'nato *a* (*canzone*) popular.**get-'tone** *nm* token; (*per giochi*) counter

ghe'pardo *nm* cheetah

ghettiz'zare *vt* ghettoize.'**ghetto** *nm* ghetto

ghiacci'aio *nm* glacier

ghiacci'a|re *vt/i* freeze.**~to** *a* frozen; (*freddissimo*) ice-cold

ghi'acc|io *nm* ice; *Auto* black ice. **~'olo** *nm* icicle; (*gelato*) ice lolly

ghi'aia *nf* gravel

ghi'anda *nf* acorn

ghi'andola *nf* gland

ghigliot'tina *nf* guillotine

ghi'gnare *vi* sneer.'**ghigno** *nm* sneer

ghi'ot|to *a* greedy, gluttonous; (*appetitoso*) appetizing. **~'tone, -a** *nmf* glutton. **~tone'ria** *nf* (*qualità*) gluttony; (*cibo*) tasty morsel

ghir'landa *nf* (*corona*) wreath; (*di fiori*) garland

'**ghiro** *nm* dormouse;**dormire come un ~** sleep like a log

'**ghisa** *nf* cast iron

già *adv* already; (*un tempo*) formerly; **~!** indeed!;**~ da ieri** since yesterday

gi'acca *nf* jacket. **~ a vento** windcheater

giacché *conj* since

giac'cone *nm* jacket

gia'cere *vi* lie

giaci'mento *nm* deposit. **~ di petrolio** oil deposit

gia'cinto *nm* hyacinth

gi'ada *nf* jade

giaggi'olo *nm* iris

giagu'aro *nm* jaguar

gial'lastro *a* yellowish

gi'allo *a & nm* yellow;[**libro**] **~** thriller

Giap'pone *nm* Japan.**giappo'nese** *a & nmf* Japanese

giardi'n|aggio *nm* gardening. **~i'ere, -a** *nmf* gardener ● *nf Auto* estate car; (*sottaceti*) pickles *pl*

giar'dino *nm* garden. **~ d'infanzia** kindergarten. **~ pensile** roof-garden. **~ zoologico** zoo

giarretti'era *nf* garter

giavel'lotto *nm* javelin

gi'gan|te *a* gigantic ● *nm* giant. **~'tesco** *a* gigantic

gigantogra'fia *nf* blow-up

'**giglio** *nm* lily

gilè *nm inv* waistcoat

gin *nm inv* gin

gineco'lo'gia *nf* gynaecology.**~'logico** *a* gynaecological. **gine'cologo, -a** *nmf* gynaecologist

gi'nepro *nm* juniper

gi'nestra *nf* broom

gingil'larsi *vr* fiddle; (*perder tempo*) potter.**gin'gillo** *nm* plaything; (*ninnolo*) knick-knack

gin'nasio *nm* (*scuola*) ≈ grammar school

gin'nast|a *nmf* gymnast. **~ica** *nf* gymnastics; (*esercizi*) exercises *pl*

ginocchi'ata *nf* **prendere una ~** bang one's knee

gi'nocch|io *nm* (*pl nm***ginocchi** *o nf* **ginocchia**) knee;**in ~o** on one's knees; **mettersi in ~o** kneel down; (*per supplicare*) go down on one's knees;**al ~o** (*gonna*) knee-length. **~'oni** *adv* kneeling

gio'ca|re *vt/i* play; (*giocherellare*) toy; (*d'azzardo*) gamble; (*puntare*) stake; (*ingannare*) trick. **~rsi la carriera** throw one's career away. **~'tore, ~'trice** *nmf* player; (*d'azzardo*) gambler

gio'cattolo *nm* toy

giocherel'l|are *vi* toy; (*nervosamente*) fiddle.**~one** *a* skittish

gi'oco *nm* game; (*di bambini, Techn*) play; (*d'azzardo*) gambling; (*scherzo*) joke; (*insieme di pezzi ecc*) set;**essere in ~** be at stake;**fare il doppio ~ con qcno** double-cross sb

giocoli'ere *nm* juggler

gio'coso *a* playful

gi'ogo *nm* yoke

gi'oia *nf* joy; (*gioiello*) jewel; (*appellativo*) sweetie

gioiell|e'ria *nf* jeweller's [shop]. **~i'ere, -a** *nmf* jeweller; (*negozio*) jeweller's. **gioi'ello** *nm* jewel; **gioielli** *pl* jewellery

gioi'oso *a* joyous

gio'ire *vi***~ per** rejoice at

Gior'dania *nf* Jordan

giorna'laio, -a *nmf* newsagent, newsdealer

gior'nale *nm* [news]paper; (*diario*) journal.**~ di bordo** logbook.**~ radio** news bulletin

giornali'ero a daily ● nm (per sciare) day pass

giorna'lino nm comic

giorna'lis|mo nm journalism. **~ta** nmf journalist

giornal'mente adv daily

gior'nata nf day; **in ~** today; **vivere alla ~** live from day to day

gi'orno nm day; **al ~** per day; **al ~ d'oggi** nowadays; **di ~** by day; **in pieno ~** in broad daylight; **un ~ sì, un ~ no** every other day

gi'ostra nf merry-go-round

giova'mento nm **trarre ~ da** derive benefit from

gi'ova|ne a young; (giovanile) youthful ● nm youth, young man ● nf girl, young woman. **~'nile** a youthful. **~'notto** nm young man

gio'var|e vi **~e a** be a useful to; (far bene) be good for. **~si** vr **~si di** avail oneself of

giovedì nm inv Thursday. **~ grasso** last Thursday before Lent

gioventù nf youth; (i giovani) young people pl

giovi'ale a jovial

giovi'nezza nf youth

gira'dischi nm inv record-player

gi'raffa nf giraffe; Cinema boom

gi'randola nf (fuoco d'artificio) Catherine wheel; (giocattolo) windmill; (banderuola) weathercock

gi'ra|re vt turn; (andare intorno, visitare) go round; Comm endorse; Cinema shoot ● vi turn; ‹aerei, uccelli:› circle; (andare in giro) wander; **far ~re le scatole a qcno** fam drive sb round the twist; **~re al largo** steer clear. **~rsi** vr turn [round]; **mi gira la testa** I feel dizzy. **~ta** nf turn; Comm endorsement; (in macchina ecc) ride; **fare una ~ta** (a piedi) go for a walk; (in macchina) go for a ride

girar'rosto nm spit

gira'sole nm sunflower

gira'volta nf spin; fig U-turn

gi'rello nm (per bambini) babywalker; Culin topside

gi'revole a revolving

gi'rino nm tadpole

'giro nm turn; (circolo) circle; (percorso) round; (viaggio) tour; (passeggiata) short walk; (in macchina) drive; (in bicicletta) ride; (circolazione di denaro) circulation; **nel ~ di un mese** within a month; **prendere in ~ qcno** pull sb's leg; **senza giri di parole** without beat-

ing about the bush; **a ~ di posta** by return mail. **~ d'affari** Comm turnover. **~ [della] manica** armhole. **giri pl al minuto** rpm. **~ turistico** sightseeing tour. **~ vita** waist measurement

giro'collo nm choker; **a ~** crewneck

gi'rone nm round

giron'zolare vi wander about

giro'tondo nm ring-a-ring-o'-roses

girova'gare vi wander about. **gi'rovago** nm wanderer

'gita nf trip; **andare in ~** go on a trip. **~ scolastica** school trip. **gi'tante** nmf tripper

giù adv down; (sotto) below; (dabbasso) downstairs; **a testa in ~** (a capofitto) headlong; **essere ~** be down; (di salute) be run down; **~ di corda** down; **~ di lì, su per ~** more or less; **non andare ~ a qcno** stick in sb's craw

gi'ub|ba nf jacket; Mil tunic. **~'botto** nm bomber jacket, jerkin

giudi'care vt judge; (ritenere) consider

gi'udice nm judge. **~ conciliatore** justice of the peace. **~ di gara** umpire. **~ di linea** linesman

giu'dizi|o nm judge[e]ment; (opinione) opinion; (senno) wisdom; (processo) trial; (sentenza) sentence; **mettere ~o** become wise. **~'oso** a sensible

gi'ugno nm June

giu'menta nf mare

gi'unco nm reed

gi'unger|e vi arrive; **~ a** (riuscire) succeed in ● vt (unire) join

gi'ungla nf jungle

gi'unta nf addition; Mil junta; **per ~** in addition. **~ comunale** district council

gi'unto pp di **giungere** ● nm Mech joint

giun'tura nf joint

giuo'care, giu'oco = **giocare, gioco**

giura'mento nm oath; **prestare ~** take the oath

giu'ra|re vt/i swear. **~to, -a** a sworn ● nmf juror

giu'ria nf jury

giu'ridico a legal

giurisdizi'one nf jurisdiction

giurispru'denza nf jurisprudence

giu'rista nmf jurist

giustifi'ca|re vt justify. **~zi'one** nf justification

giu'stizi|a nf justice. **~'are** vt execute. **~'ere** nm executioner

gi'usto a just, fair; (adatto) right;

(esatto) exact ● nm (uomo retto) just man; (cosa giusta) right ● adv exactly; ~ ora just now

glaci'ale a glacial

gla'diolo nm gladiolus

'glassa nf Culin icing

gli def art mpl (before vowel and s + consonant, gn, ps, z) the; vedi il ● pron (a lui) [to] him; (a esso) [to] it; (a loro) [to] them

glice'rina nf glycerine

'glicine nm wisteria

gli'e|lo, -a pron [to] him/her/them; (forma di cortesia) [to] you; ~ chiedo I'll ask him/her/them/you; glie'l'ho prestato I've lent it to him/her/them/you. ~ne pron (di ciò) [of] it; ~ne ho dato un po' I gave him/her/them/you some

glo'bal|e a global; fig overall. ~'mente adv globally

'globo nm globe. ~ oculare eyeball. ~ terrestre globe

'globulo nm globule; Med corpuscle. ~ rosso red cell, red corpuscle

'glori|a nf glory. ~'arsi vr ~arsi di be proud of. ~'oso a glorious

glos'sario nm glossary

glu'cosio nm glucose

'gluteo nm buttock

'gnomo nm gnome

'gnorri nm fare lo ~ play dumb

'gobb|a nf hump. ~o, -a a hunchbacked ● nmf hunchback

'gocci|a nf drop; (di sudore) bead; è stata l'ultima ~a it was the last straw. ~o'lare vi drip. ~o'lio nm dripping

go'der|e vi (sessualmente) come; ~e di enjoy. ~sela have a good time. ~si vr ~si qcsa enjoy sth

godi'mento nm enjoyment

goffa'mente adv awkwardly. 'goffo a awkward

'gola nf throat; (ingordigia) gluttony; Geog gorge; (di camino) flue; avere mal di ~ have a sore throat; far ~ a qcno tempt sb

golf nm inv jersey; Sport golf

'golfo nm gulf

golosità nf inv greediness; (cibo) tasty morsel. go'loso a greedy

'golpe nm inv coup

gomi'tata nf nudge

'gomito nm elbow; alzare il ~ raise one's elbow

go'mitolo nm ball

'gomma nf rubber; (colla, da mastica-

re) gum; (pneumatico) tyre. ~ da masticare chewing gum

gommapi'uma nf foam rubber

gom'mista nm tyre specialist

gom'mone nm [rubber] dinghy

gom'moso a chewy

'gondol|a nf gondola. ~i'ere nm gondolier

gonfa'lone nm banner

gonfi'abile a inflatable

gonfi'ar|e vi swell ● vt blow up; pump up (pneumatico); (esagerare) exaggerate. ~si vr swell; (acque:) rise. 'gonfio a swollen; (pneumatico) inflated; a gonfie vele splendidly. gonfi'ore nm swelling

gongo'la|nte a overjoyed. ~re vi be overjoyed

'gonna nf skirt. ~ pantalone culottes pl

'gonzo nm simpleton

gorgheggi'are vi warble. gor'gheggio nm warble

'gorgo nm whirlpool

gorgogli'are vi gurgle

go'rilla nm inv gorilla; (guardia del corpo) bodyguard, minder

'gotico a & nm Gothic

gover'nante nf housekeeper

gover'na|re vt govern; (dominare) rule; (dirigere) manage; (curare) look after. ~'tivo a government. ~'tore nm governor

go'verno nm government; (dominio) rule; al ~ in power

gracchi'are vi caw; (fig: persona:) screech

graci'dare vi croak

'gracile a delicate

gra'dasso nm braggart

gradata'mente adv gradually

gradazi'one nf gradation. ~ alcolica alcohol[ic] content

gra'devol|e a agreeable. ~'mente adv pleasantly, agreeably

gradi'mento nm liking; indice di ~ Radio, TV popularity rating; non è di mio ~ it's not to my liking

gradi'nata nf flight of steps; (di stadio) stand; (di teatro) tiers pl

gra'dino nm step

gra'di|re vt like; (desiderare) wish. ~to a pleasant; (bene accetto) welcome

'grado nm degree; (rango) rank; di buon ~ willingly; essere in ~ di fare qcsa be in a position to do sth; (essere capace a) be able to do sth

gradu'ale a gradual

gradu'a|re vt graduate. ~to a graded;

97

(*provvisto di scala graduata*) graduated ● *nm Mil* noncommissioned officer.
~'toria *nf* list. ~zi'one *nf* graduation
'graffa *nf* clip; (*segno grafico*) brace
graf'fetta *nf* staple
graffi'a|re *vt* scratch. ~'tura *nf* scratch
'graffio *nm* scratch
gra'fia *nf* [hand]writing; (*ortografia*) spelling
'grafic|a *nf* graphics; ~a pubblici-'taria commercial art. ~a'mente *adv* in graphics, graphically. ~o *a* graphic ● *nm* graph; (*persona*) graphic designer
gra'migna *nf* weed
gram'mati|ca *nf* grammar. ~'cale *a* grammatical
'grammo *nm* gram[me]
gran *a vedi* grande
'grana *nf* grain; (*formaggio*) parmesan; (*fam: seccatura*) trouble; (*fam: soldi*) readies *pl*
gra'naio *nm* barn
gra'nat|a *nf Mil* grenade; (*frutto*) pomegranate. ~'iere *nm Mil* grenadier
Gran Bre'tagna *nf* Great Britain
'granchio *nm* crab; (*fig: errore*) blunder; prendere un ~ make a blunder
grandango'lare *nm* wide-angle lens
'grande (*a volte* gran) *a* (*ampio*) large; (*grosso*) big; (*alto*) tall; (*largo*) wide; (*fig: senso morale*) great; (*grandioso*) grand; (*adulto*) grown-up; ho una gran fame I'm very hungry; fa un gran caldo it is very hot; in ~ on a large scale; in gran parte to a great extent; non è un gran che it is nothing much; un gran ballo a grand ball ● *nmf* (*persona adulta*) grown-up; (*persona eminente*) great man/woman. ~ggi'are *vi* ~ggiare su tower over; (*darsi arie*) show off
gran'dezza *nf* greatness; (*ampiezza*) largeness; (*larghezza*) width, breadth; (*dimensione*) size; (*fasto*) grandeur; (*prodigalità*) lavishness; a ~ naturale life-size
grandi'nare *vi* hail; grandina it's hailing. 'grandine *nf* hail
grandiosità *nf* grandeur. grandi'oso *a* grand
gran'duca *nm* grand duke
gra'nello *nm* grain; (*di frutta*) pip
gra'nita *nf* crushed ice drink
gra'nito *nm* granite
'grano *nm* grain; (*frumento*) wheat
gran'turco *nm* maize
'granulo *nm* granule
'grappa *nf* grappa; (*morsa*) cramp

'grappolo *nm* bunch. ~ d'uva bunch of grapes
gras'setto *nm* bold [type]
gras'sezza *nf* fatness; (*untuosità*) greasiness
'gras|so *a* fat; (*cibo*) fatty; (*unto*) greasy; (*terreno*) rich; (*grossolano*) coarse ● *nm* fat; (*sostanza*) grease. ~'soccio *a* plump
'grata *nf* grating. gra'tella, gra'ticola *nf Culin* grill
gra'tifica *nf* bonus. ~zi'one *nf* satisfaction
grati'na|re *vt* cook au gratin. ~to *a* au gratin
'gratis *adv* free
grati'tudine *nf* gratitude. 'grato *a* grateful; (*gradito*) pleasant
gratta'capo *nm* trouble
gratta'cielo *nm* skyscraper
grat'tar|e *vt* scratch; (*raschiare*) scrape; (*grattugiare*) grate; (*fam: rubare*) pinch ● *vi* grate. ~si *vr* scratch oneself
grat'tugi|a *nf* grater. ~'are *vt* grate
gratuita'mente *adv* free [of charge].
gra'tuito *a* free [of charge]; (*ingiustificato*) gratuitous
gra'vare *vt* burden ● *vi* ~ su weigh on
'grave *a* (*pesante*) heavy; (*serio*) serious; (*difficile*) hard; (*voce, suono*) low; (*fonetica*) grave; essere ~ (*gravemente ammalato*) be seriously ill. ~'mente *adv* seriously, gravely
gravi'danza *nf* pregnancy. 'gravido *a* pregnant
gravità *nf* seriousness; *Phys* gravity
gravi'tare *vi* gravitate
gra'voso *a* onerous
'grazi|a *nf* grace; (*favore*) favour; *Jur* pardon; entrare nelle ~e di qcno get into sb's good books. ~'are *vt* pardon
'grazie *int* thank you!, thanks!; ~ mille! many thanks!, thanks a lot!
grazi'oso *a* charming; (*carino*) pretty
'Grec|ia *nf* Greece. g~o, -a *a & nmf* Greek
'gregge *nm* flock
'greggio *a* raw ● *nm* (*petrolio*) crude [oil]
grembi'ale, grembi'ule *nm* apron
'grembo *nm* lap; (*utero*) womb; *fig* bosom
gre'mi|re *vt* pack. ~rsi *vr* become crowded (di with). ~to *a* packed
'gretto *a* stingy; (*di vedute ristrette*) narrow-minded
'grezzo *a* = greggio

gri'dare *vi* shout; (*di dolore*) scream; ⟨*animale:*⟩ cry ● *vt* shout

'**grido** *nm* (*pl m* **gridi** *o f* **grida**) shout, cry; ⟨*di animale*⟩ cry; **l'ultimo ~** the latest fashion; **scrittore di ~** celebrated writer

'**grigio** *a & nm* grey

'**griglia** *nf* grill; **alla ~** grilled

gril'letto *nm* trigger

'**grillo** *nm* cricket; (*fig: capriccio*) whim

grimal'dello *nm* picklock

grin'fia *nf fig* clutch

'**grin|ta** *nf* grit. **~'toso** *a* determined

'**grinza** *nf* wrinkle; (*di stoffa*) crease

grip'pare *vi Mech* seize

gris'sino *nm* bread-stick

'**gronda** *nf* eaves *pl*

gron'daia *nf* gutter

gron'dare *vi* pour; (*essere bagnato fradicio*) be dripping

'**groppa** *nf* back

'**groppo** *nm* knot; **avere un ~ alla gola** have a lump in one's throat

gros'sezza *nf* size; (*spessore*) thickness

gros'sista *nmf* wholesaler

'**grosso** *a* big, large; (*spesso*) thick; (*grossolano*) coarse; (*grave*) serious ● *nm* big part; (*massa*) bulk; **farla grossa** do a stupid thing

grossola'nità *nf inv* (*qualità*) coarseness; (*di errore*) grossness; (*azione, parola*) coarse thing. **~'lano** *a* coarse; ⟨*errore*⟩ gross

grosso'modo *adv* roughly

'**grotta** *nf* cave, grotto

grot'tesco *a & nm* grotesque

grovi'era *nmf* Gruyère

gro'viglio *nm* tangle; *fig* muddle

gru *nf inv* (*uccello, edilizia*) crane

'**gruccia** *nf* (*stampella*) crutch; (*per vestito*) hanger

gru'gni|re *vi* grunt. **~to** *nm* grunt

'**grugno** *nm* snout

'**grullo** *a* silly

'**grumo** *nm* clot; (*di farina ecc*) lump. **gru'moso** *a* lumpy

'**gruppo** *nm* group; (*comitiva*) party. **~ sanguigno** blood group

gruvi'era *nmf* Gruyère

gruz'zolo *nm* nest-egg

guada'gnare *vt* earn; gain ⟨*tempo, forza ecc*⟩. **gua'dagno** *nm* gain; (*profitto*) profit; (*entrate*) earnings *pl*

gu'ado *nm* ford; **passare a ~** ford

gua'ina *nf* sheath; (*busto*) girdle

gu'aio *nm* trouble; **che ~!** that's just brilliant!; **essere nei guai** be in a fix;

guai a te se lo tocchi! don't you dare touch it!

gua'ire *vi* yelp. **~to** *nm* yelp

gu'ancia *nf* cheek. **~ale** *nm* pillow

gu'anto *nm* glove. **guantoni** *pl* [**da boxe**] boxing gloves

guarda'coste *nm inv* coastguard

guarda'linee *nm inv Sport* linesman

guar'dar|e *vt* look at; (*osservare*) watch; (*badare a*) look after; (*dare su*) look out on ● *vi* look; (*essere orientato verso*) face. **~si** *vr* look at oneself; **~si da** beware of; (*astenersi*) refrain from

guarda'rob|a *nm inv* wardrobe; (*di locale pubblico*) cloakroom. **~i'ere, -a** *nmf* cloakroom attendant

gu'ardia *nf* guard; (*poliziotto*) policeman; (*vigilanza*) watch; **essere di ~** be on guard; ⟨*medico:*⟩ be on duty; **fare la ~ a** keep guard over; **mettere in ~ qcno** warn sb; **stare in ~** be on one's guard. **~ carceraria** prison warder. **~ del corpo** bodyguard, minder. **~ di finanza** ≈ Fraud Squad. **~ forestale** forest ranger. **~ medica** duty doctor

guardi'ano, -a *nmf* caretaker. **~ notturno** night watchman

guar'dingo *a* cautious

guardi'ola *nf* gatekeeper's lodge

guarigi'one *nf* recovery

gua'rire *vt* cure ● *vi* recover; ⟨*ferita:*⟩ heal [up]

guarnigi'one *nf* garrison

guarni're *vt* trim; *Culin* garnish. **~zi'one** *nf* trimming; *Culin* garnish; *Mech* gasket

guasta'feste *nmf inv* spoilsport

gua'star|e *vt* spoil; (*rovinare*) ruin; break ⟨*meccanismo*⟩. **~si** *vr* spoil; (*andare a male*) go bad; ⟨*tempo:*⟩ change for the worse; ⟨*meccanismo:*⟩ break down. **gu'asto** *a* broken; ⟨*ascensore, telefono*⟩ out of order; ⟨*auto*⟩ broken down; ⟨*cibo, dente*⟩ bad ● *nm* breakdown; (*danno*) damage

guazza'buglio *nm* muddle

guaz'zare *vi* wallow

gu'ercio *a* cross-eyed

gu'err|a *nf* war; (*tecnica bellica*) warfare. **~ fredda** Cold War. **~ mondiale** world war. **~afon'daio** *nm* warmonger. **~eggi'are** *vi* wage war. **guer'resco** *a* (*di guerra*) war; (*bellicoso*) warlike. **~i'ero** *nm* warrior

guer'riglia *nf* guerrilla warfare. **~'ero, -a** *nmf* guerrilla

'**gufo** *nm* owl

'**guglia** *nf* spire

gu'id|a *nf* guide; *(direzione)* guidance; *(comando)* leadership; *Auto* driving; *(tappeto)* runner; **~a a destra/sinistra** right-/left-hand drive. **~a telefonica** telephone directory. **~a turistica** tourist guide. **gui'dare** *vt* guide; *Auto* drive; steer *(nave)*. **~a'tore, ~a'trice** *nmf* driver
guin'zaglio *nm* leash

guiz'zare *vi* dart; *(luce:)* flash. **gu'izzo** *nm* dart; *(di luce)* flash
'guscio *nm* shell
gu'stare *vt* taste ● *vi* like. **'gusto** *nm* taste; *(piacere)* liking; **mangiare di gusto** eat heartily; **prenderci gusto** come to enjoy it, develop a taste for it. **gu'stoso** *a* tasty; *fig* delightful
guttu'rale *a* guttural

Hh

---

habitué *nmf inv* regular [customer]
ham'burger *nm inv* hamburger
'handicap *nm inv* Sport handicap
handicap'pa|re *vt* handicap. **~to, -a** *nmf* disabled person ● *a* disabled
'harem *nm inv* harem
'hascisc *nm* hashish

henné *nm* henna
hi-fi *nm inv* hi-fi
'hippy *a* hippy
'hockey *nm* hockey. **~ su ghiaccio** ice hockey. **~ su prato** hockey
hollywoodi'ano *a* Hollywood *attrib*
ho'tel *nm inv* hotel

Ii

---

i *def art mpl* the; *vedi* **il**
i'ato *nm* hiatus
iber'na|re *vi* hibernate. **~zi'one** *nf* hibernation
i'bisco *nm* hibiscus
'ibrido *a* & *nm* hybrid
'iceberg *nm inv* iceberg
i'cona *nf* icon
Id'dio *nm* God
i'dea *nf* idea; *(opinione)* opinion; *(ideale)* ideal; *(indizio)* inkling; *(piccola quantità)* hint; *(intenzione)* intention; **cambiare ~** change one's mind; **neanche per ~!** not on your life!; **chiarirsi le idee** get one's ideas straight. **~ fissa** obsession
ide'a|le *a* & *nm* ideal. **~'lista** *nmf* idealist. **~liz'zare** *vt* idealize
ide'a|re *vt* conceive. **~'tore, ~'trice** *nmf* originator
'idem *adv* the same
i'dentico *a* identical

identifi'cabile *a* identifiable
identifi'ca|re *vt* identify. **~zi'one** *nf* identification
identi'kit *nm inv* identikit
identità *nf inv* identity
ideolo'gia *nf* ideology. **ideo'logico** *a* ideological
i'dilli|co *a* idyllic. **~o** *nm* idyll
idi'oma *nm* idiom. **idio'matico** *a* idiomatic
idi'ota *a* idiotic ● *nmf* idiot. **idio'zia** *nf* *(cosa stupida)* idiocy
idola'trare *vt* worship
idoleggi'are *vt* idolize. **'idolo** *nm* idol
idoneità *nf* suitability; *Mil* fitness; **esame di ~** qualifying examination. **i'doneo** *a* **idoneo a** suitable for; *Mil* fit for
i'drante *nm* hydrant
idra'ta|re *vt* hydrate; *(cosmetico:)* moisturize. **~nte** *a* *(crema, gel)* moisturizing. **~zi'one** *nf* moisturizing

i'draulico *a* hydraulic ● *nm* plumber

'idrico *a* water *attrib*

idrocar'buro *nm* hydrocarbon

idroe'lettrico *a* hydroelectric

i'drofilo *a* *vedi*cotone

i'drogeno *nm* hydrogen

idromas'saggio *nm* (*sistema*) whirl-pool bath

idrovo'lante *nm* seaplane

i'ella *nf* bad luck; portare ~ be bad luck. iel'lato *a* plagued by bad luck

i'ena *nf* hyena

i'eri *adv* yesterday; ~ l'altro, l'altro ~ the day before yesterday; ~ pomeriggio yesterday afternoon; il giornale di ~ yesterday's paper

ietta'tore, -'trice *nmf* jinx. ~ tura *nf* (*sfortuna*) bad luck

igi'en|e *nf* hygiene. ~ico *a* hygienic. igie'nista *nmf* hygienist

i'gnaro *a* unaware

i'gnobile *a* base; (*non onorevole*) dishonourable

igno'ran|te *a* ignorant ● *nmf* ignoramus. ~za *nf* ignorance

igno'rare *vt* (*non sapere*) be unaware of; (*trascurare*) ignore

i'gnoto *a* unknown

il *def art m* the; il latte fa bene milk is good for you; il signor Magnetti Mr Magnetti; il dottor Piazza Dr Piazza; ha il naso storto he has a bent nose; mettiti il cappello put your hat on; il lunedì on Mondays; il 1986 1986; 5 000 lire il chilo 5,000 lire the *o* a kilo

'ilar|e *a* merry. ~ità *nf* hilarity

illazi'one *nf* inference

illecita'mente *adv* illicitly. il'lecito *a* illicit

ille'gal|e *a* illegal. ~ità *nf* illegality. ~'mente *adv* illegally

illeg'gibile *a* illegible; (*libro*) unreadable

illegittimità *nf* illegitimacy. ille'gittimo *a* illegitimate

il'leso *a* unhurt

illette'rato, -a *a & nmf* illiterate

illi'bato *a* chaste

illimi'tato *a* unlimited

illivi'dire *vt* bruise ● *vi* (*per rabbia*) turn livid

il'logico *a* illogical

il'luder|e *vt* deceive. ~si *vr* deceive oneself

illumi'na|re *vt* light [up]; *fig* enlighten; ~re a giorno floodlight. ~rsi *vr* light up. ~zi'one *nf* lighting; *fig* enlightenment

Illumi'nismo *nm* Enlightenment

illusi'one *nf* illusion; farsi illusioni delude oneself

illusio'nis|mo *nm* conjuring. ~ta *nmf* conjurer

il'lu|so, -a *pp di* illudere ● *a* deluded ● *nmf* day-dreamer. ~'sorio *a* illusory

illu'stra|re *vt* illustrate. ~'tivo *a* illustrative. ~'tore, ~'trice *nmf* illustrator. ~zi'one *nf* illustration

il'lustre *a* distinguished

imbacuc'ca|re *vt*, ~rsi *vr* wrap up. ~to *a* wrapped up

imbal'laggio *nm* packing. ~re *vt* pack; *Auto* race

imbalsa'ma|re *vt* embalm; stuff (*animale*). ~to *a* embalmed; (*animale*) stuffed

imbambo'lato *a* vacant

imbaraz'zante *a* embarrassing

imbaraz'za|re *vt* embarrass; (*ostacolare*) encumber. ~to *a* embarrassed

imba'razzo *nm* embarrassment; (*ostacolo*) hindrance; trarre qcno d'~ help sb out of a difficulty; avere l'~ della scelta be spoilt for choice. ~ di stomaco indigestion

imbarca'dero *nm* landing-stage

imbar'ca|re *vt* embark; (*fam: rimorchiare*) score. ~rsi *vr* embark, go on board. ~zi'one *nf* boat. ~zione di salvataggio lifeboat. im'barco *nm* embarkation, boarding; (*banchina*) landing-stage

imba'stire *vt* tack; *fig* sketch. ~'tura *nf* tacking, basting

im'battersi *vr* ~ in run into

imbat'tibile *a* unbeatable. ~uto *a* unbeaten

imbavagli'are *vt* gag

imbec'cata *nf* *Theat* prompt

imbe'cille *a* stupid ● *nmf* *Med* imbecile

imbel'lire *vt* embellish

im'berbe *a* beardless; *fig* inexperienced

imbestia'li|re *vi*, ~rsi *vr* fly into a rage. ~to *a* enraged

im'bever|e *vt* imbue (di with). ~si *vr* absorb

imbe'vibile *a* undrinkable. ~uto *a* ~uto di (*acqua*) soaked in; (*nozioni*) imbued with

imbian'c|are *vt* whiten ● *vi* turn white. ~hino *nm* house painter

imbizzar'rir|e *vi*, ~si *vr* become restless; (*arrabbiarsi*) become angry

imboc'ca|re *vt* feed; (*entrare*) enter;

fig prompt. ~'**tura** *nf* opening; (*ingresso*) entrance; (*Mus: di strumento*) mouthpiece. im'**bocco** *nm* entrance

imbo'scar|e *vt* hide. ~si *vr Mil* shirk military service

imbo'scata *nf* ambush

imbottigli'a|re *vt* bottle. ~rsi *vr* get snarled up in a traffic jam. ~to a (*vino, acqua*) bottled

imbot'ti|re *vt* stuff; pad (*giacca*; *Culin* fill. ~rsi *vr* ~rsi di (*fig: di pasticche*) stuff oneself with. ~ta *nf* quilt. ~to a (*spalle*) padded; (*cuscino*) stuffed; (*panino*) filled. ~'tura *nf* stuffing; (*di giacca*) padding; *Culin* filling

imbracci'are *vt* shoulder (*fucile*)

imbra'nato a clumsy

imbrat'tar|e *vt* mark. ~si *vr* dirty oneself

imbroc'car|e *vt* hit; ~la giusta *vr* hit the nail on the head

imbrogli'a|re *vt* muddle; (*raggirare*) cheat. ~rsi *vr* get tangled; (*confondersi*) get confused. im'broglio *nm* tangle; (*pasticcio*) mess; (*inganno*) trick. ~'one, -a *nmf* cheat

imbronci'a|re *vi,* ~rsi *vr* sulk. ~to a sulky

imbru'nire *vi* get dark; all'~ at dusk

imbrut'tire *vt* make ugly ● *vi* become ugly

imbu'care *vt* post, mail; (*nel biliardo*) pot

imbur'rare *vt* butter

im'buto *nm* funnel

imi'ta|re *vt* imitate. ~'tore, ~'trice *nmf* imitator, impersonator. ~zi'one *nf* imitation

immaco'lato a immaculate, spotless

immagazzi'nare *vt* store

immagi'na|re *vt* imagine; (*supporre*) suppose; s'immagini! imagine that!. ~rio a imaginary. ~zi'one *nf* imagination. im'magine *nf* image; (*rappresentazione, idea*) picture

imman'cabil|e a unfailing. ~'mente *adv* without fail

im'mane a huge; (*orribile*) terrible

imma'nente a immanent

immangi'abile a inedible

immatrico'la|re *vt* register. ~rsi *vr* (*studente:*) matriculate. ~zi'one *nf* registration; (*di studente*) matriculation

immaturità *nf* immaturity. imma'turo a unripe; (*persona*) immature; (*precoce*) premature

immedesi'ma|rsi *vr* ~rsi in identify oneself with. ~zi'one *nf* identification

immedia|ta'mente *adv* immediately. ~'tezza *nf* immediacy. immedi'ato a immediate

immemo'rabile a immemorial

immens|a'mente *adv* enormously. ~ità *nf* immensity. im'menso a immense

immensu'rabile a immeasurable

im'merger|e *vt* immerse. ~si *vr* plunge; (*sommergibile:*) dive; ~si in immerse oneself in

immeri'ta|to a undeserved. ~evole a undeserving

immersi'one *nf* immersion; (*di sommergibile*) dive. im'merso *pp di* immergere

immi'gra|nte a & *nmf* immigrant. ~re *vi* immigrate. ~to, -a *nmf* immigrant. ~zi'one *nf* immigration

immi'nen|te a imminent. ~za *nf* imminence

immischi'ar|e *vt* involve. ~si *vr* ~si in meddle in

immis'sario *nm* tributary

immissi'one *nf* insertion

im'mobile a motionless

im'mobili *nmpl* real estate. ~'are a società ~are building society, savings and loan *Am*

immobili'tà *nf* immobility. ~z'zare *vt* immobilize; *Comm* tie up

immo'desto a immodest

immo'lare *vt* sacrifice

immondez'zaio *nm* rubbish tip. immon'dizia *nf* filth; (*spazzatura*) rubbish. im'mondo a filthy

immo'ral|e a immoral. ~ità *nf* immorality

immorta'lare *vt* immortalize. immor'tale a immortal

immoti'vato a (*gesto*) unjustified

im'mun|e a exempt; *Med* immune. ~ità *nf* immunity. ~iz'zare *vt* immunize. ~izzazi'one *nf* immunization

immunodefici'enza *nf* immunodeficiency

immuso'ni|rsi *vr* sulk. ~to a sulky

immu'ta|bile a unchangeable. ~to a unchanging

impacchet'tare *vt* wrap up

impacci'a|re *vt* hamper; (*disturbare*) inconvenience; (*imbarazzare*) embarrass. ~to a embarrassed; (*goffo*) awkward. im'paccio *nm* embarrassment; (*ostacolo*) hindrance; (*situazione difficile*) awkward situation

im'pacco *nm* compress

impadro'nirsi vr ~ **di** take possession of; (fig: imparare) master

impa'gabile a priceless

impagli'na|re vt paginate. ~**zi'one** nf pagination

impagli'are vt stuff (animale)

impa'lato a fig stiff

impalca'tura nf scaffolding; fig structure

impalli'dire vi turn pale; (fig: perdere d'importanza) pale into insignificance

impa'nare vt Culin roll in breadcrumbs

impanta'narsi vr get bogged down

impape'rarsi vr. **impappi'narsi** vr falter, stammer

impa'rare vt learn

impareggi'abile a incomparable

imparen'ta|rsi vr ~ **con** become related to. ~**to** a related

'impari a unequal; (dispari) odd

impar'tire vt impart

imparzi'al|e a impartial. ~**ità** nf impartiality

impas'sibile a impassive

impa'sta|re vt Culin knead; blend (colori). ~**tura** nf kneading. **im'pasto** nm Culin dough; (miscuglio) mixture

impastic'carsi vr pop pills

im'patto nm impact

impau'rir|e vt frighten. ~**si** vr become frightened

im'pavido a fearless

impazi'en|te a impatient; ~**te di fare qcsa** eager to do sth. ~'**tirsi** vr lose patience. ~**za** nf impatience

impaz'zata nf **all'~** at breakneck speed

impaz'zire vi go mad; (maionese:) separate; **far ~ qcno** drive sb mad; ~ **per** be crazy about; **da ~** (mal di testa) blinding

impec'cabile a impeccable

impedi'mento nm hindrance; (ostacolo) obstacle

impe'dire vt ~ **di** prevent from; (impacciare) hinder; (ostruire) obstruct; ~ **a qcno di fare qcsa** prevent sb [from] doing sth

impe'gna|re vt (dare in pegno) pawn; (vincolare) bind; (prenotare) reserve; (assorbire) take up. ~**rsi** vr apply oneself; ~**rsi a fare qcsa** commit oneself to doing sth. ~'**tiva** nf referral. ~'**tivo** a binding; (lavoro) demanding. ~**ato** a engaged; Pol committed. **im'pegno** nm engagement; Comm commitment; (zelo) care

impel'lente a pressing

impene'trabile a impenetrable

impen'na|rsi vr (cavallo:) rear; fig bristle. ~**ta** nf (di prezzi) sharp rise; (di cavallo) rearing; (di moto) wheelie

impen'sabile a unthinkable. ~**to** a unexpected

impensie'rir|e vt, ~**si** vr worry

impe'ra|nte a prevailing. ~**re** vi reign; (tendenza:) prevail, hold sway

impera'tivo a & nm imperative

impera'tore, -'trice nm emperor ● nf empress

impercet'tibile a imperceptible

imperdo'nabile a unforgivable

imper'fe|tto a & nm imperfect. ~**zi'one** nf imperfection

imperi'a|le a imperial. ~**lismo** nm imperialism. ~**lista** a imperialist. ~**listico** a imperialistic

imperi'oso a imperious; (impellente) urgent

impe'rizia nf lack of skill

imperme'abile a waterproof ● nm raincoat

imperni'ar|e vt pivot; (fondare) base. ~**si** vr ~**si su** be based on

im'pero nm empire; (potere) rule

imperscru'tabile a inscrutable

imperso'nale a impersonal

imperso'nare vt personify; (interpretare) act [the part of]

imper'territo a undaunted

imperti'nen|te a impertinent. ~**za** nf impertinence

impertur'ba|bile a imperturbable. ~**to** a unperturbed

imperver'sare vi rage

im'pervio a inaccessible

'impet|o nm impetus; (impulso) impulse; (slancio) transport. ~**u'oso** a impetuous; (vento) blustering

impe'tito a stiff

impian'tare vt install; set up (azienda)

impi'anto nm plant; (sistema) system; (operazione) installation. ~ **radio** Auto car stereo system

impia'strare vt plaster; (sporcare) dirty. **impi'astro** nm poultice; (persona noiosa) bore; (pasticcione) cack-handed person

impic'car|e vt hang. ~**si** vr hang oneself

impicci'arsi vr meddle. **im'piccio** nm hindrance; (seccatura) bother. ~**'one, -a** nmf nosey parker

impie'ga|re vt employ; (usare) use; spend (tempo, denaro); Fin invest;

l'autobus ha ~to un'ora it took the bus an hour.**~rsi** vr get [oneself] a job

impiega'tizio a clerical

impie'gato, -a nmf employee. **~ di banca** bank clerk. **impi'ego** nm employment; (posto) job; Fin investment

impieto'sir|e vt move to pity. **~si** vr be moved to pity

impie'trito a petrified

impigli'ar|e vt entangle. **~si** vr get entangled

impigri'rir|e vt make lazy. **~si** vr get lazy

impla'cabile a implacable

impli'ca|re vt implicate; (sottintendere) imply. **~rsi** vr become involved. **~zi'one** nf implication

implicita'mente adv implicitly. **im'plicito** a implicit

implo'ra|re vt implore. **~zi'one** nf entreaty

impolve'ra|re vt cover with dust. **~rsi** vr get covered with dust. **~to** a dusty

imponde'rabile a imponderable; (causa, evento) unpredictable

impo'nen|te a imposing. **~za** nf impressiveness

impo'nibile a taxable● nm taxable income

impopo'lar|e a unpopular. **~ità** nf unpopularity

im'por|re vt impose; (ordinare) order. **~si** vr assert oneself; (aver successo) be successful; **~si di** (prefiggersi) set oneself the task of

impor'tan|te a important ● nm important thing. **~za** nf importance

impor'ta|re vt Comm, Comput import; (comportare) cause ● vi matter; (essere necessario) be necessary. **non ~!** it doesn't matter!;**non me ne ~ niente!** I couldn't care less!. **~ tore**, **~ trice** nmf importer. **~zi'one** nf importation; (merce importata) import

im'porto nm amount

importu'nare vt pester. **impor'tuno** a troublesome; (inopportuno) untimely

imposizi'one nf imposition; (imposta) tax

imposses'sarsi vr**~ di** seize

impos'sibil|e a impossible ● nm**fare l'~e** do absolutely all one can. **~ità** nf impossibility

im'posta¹ nf tax, **~ sul reddito** income tax; **~ sul valore aggiunto** value added tax

im'posta² nf (di finestra) shutter

impo'sta|re vt (progettare) plan; (basare) base; Mus pitch; (imbucare) post, mail; set out (domanda, problema). **~zi'one** nf planning; (di voce) pitching

im'posto pp di **imporre**

impo'store, -a nmf impostor

impo'ten|te a powerless; Med impotent. **~za** nf powerlessness; Med impotence

impove'rir|e vt impoverish. **~si** vr become poor

imprati'cabile a impracticable; (strada) impassable

imprati'chir|e vt train. **~si** vr**~si in** o**a** get practice in

impre'ca|re vi curse. **~zi'one** nf curse

impreci's|abile a indeterminable. **~ato** a indeterminate. **~i'one** nf inaccuracy. **impre'ciso** a inaccurate

impre'gnar|e vt impregnate; (imbevere) soak; fig imbue. **~si** vr become impregnated with

imprendi'tor|e, -'trice nmf entrepreneur. **~i'ale** a entrepreneurial

imprepa'rato a unprepared

im'presa nf undertaking; (gesta) exploit; (azienda) firm

impre'sario nm impresario; (appaltatore) contractor

imprescin'dibile a inescapable

impressio'na|bile a impressionable. **~nte** a impressive; (spaventoso) frightening

impressio'nare vt impress; (spaventare) frighten; expose (foto). **~'o'narsi** vr be affected; (spaventarsi) be frightened. **~'one** nf impression; (sensazione) sensation; (impronta) mark; **far ~one a qcno** upset sb

impressio'nis|mo nm impressionism. **~ta** nmf impressionist

im'presso pp di **imprimere** ● a printed

impre'stare vt lend

impreve'dibile a unforeseeable; (persona) unpredictable

imprevi'dente a improvident

impre'visto a unforeseen ● nm unforeseen event; **salvo imprevisti** all being well

imprigiona'mento nm imprisonment. **~'nare** vt imprison

im'primere vt impress; (stampare) print; (comunicare) impart

impro'babil|e a unlikely, improbable. **~ità** nf improbability

improdut'tivo a unproductive

im'pronta *nf* impression; *fig* mark. ~ **digitale** fingerprint. ~ **del piede** footprint

impro'perio *nm* insult; **improperi** *pl* abuse *sg*

im'proprio *a* improper

improvvisa'mente *adv* suddenly

improvvi'sa|re *vt/i* improvise. ~**rsi** *vr* turn oneself into a. ~**ta** *nf* surprise. ~**to** *a* ⟨*discorso*⟩ unrehearsed. ~**zi'one** *nf* improvisation

improv'viso *a* sudden; **all'~** unexpectedly

impru'den|te *a* imprudent. ~**za** *nf* imprudence

impu'gna|re *vt* grasp; *Jur* contest. ~**tura** *nf* grip; ⟨*manico*⟩ handle

impulsività *nf* impulsiveness. **impul'sivo** *a* impulsive

im'pulso *nm* impulse; **agire d'~** act on impulse

impune'mente *adv* with impunity. **impu'nito** *a* unpunished

impun'tarsi *vr* dig one's heels in

impun'tura *nf* stitching

impurità *nf inv* impurity. **im'puro** *a* impure

impu'tabile *a* attributable (**a** to)

impu'ta|re *vt* attribute; ⟨*accusare*⟩ charge. ~**to**, **-a** *nmf* accused. ~**zi'one** *nf* charge

imputri'dire *vi* rot

in *prep* in; ⟨*moto a luogo*⟩ to; ⟨*su*⟩ on; ⟨*entro*⟩ within; ⟨*mezzo*⟩ by; ⟨*con materiale*⟩ made of; **essere in casa/ ufficio** be at home/at the office; **in mano/tasca** in one's hand/pocket; **andare in Francia/campagna** go to France/the country; **salire in treno** get on the train; **versa la birra nel bicchiere** pour the beer into the glass; **in alto** up there; **in giornata** within the day; **nel 1997** in 1997; **una borsa in pelle** a bag made of leather, a leather bag; **in macchina** ⟨*viaggiare, venire*⟩ by car; **in contanti** [in] cash; **in vacanza** on holiday; **di giorno in giorno** from day to day; **se fossi in te** if I were you; **siamo in sette** there are seven of us

inabbor'dabile *a* unapproachable

i'nabi|le *a* incapable; ⟨*fisicamente*⟩ unfit. ~**ità** *nf* incapacity

inabi'tabile *a* uninhabitable

inacces'sibile *a* inaccessible; ⟨*persona*⟩ unapproachable

inaccet'tabil|e *a* unacceptable. ~**ità** *nf* unacceptability

inacer'bi|re *vt* embitter; exacerbate ⟨*rapporto*⟩. ~**si** *vr* grow bitter

inaci'dir|e *vt* turn sour. ~**si** *vr* go sour; ⟨*persona*:⟩ become embittered

ina'datto *a* unsuitable

inadegu'ato *a* inadequate

inadempi'ente *nmf* defaulter. ~'**mento** *nm* non-fulfilment

inaffer'rabile *a* elusive

ina'la|re *vt* inhale. ~'**tore** *nm* inhaler. ~**zi'one** *nf* inhalation

inalbe'rar|e *vt* hoist. ~**si** *vr* ⟨*cavallo*:⟩ rear [up]; ⟨*adirarsi*⟩ lose one's temper

inalte'ra|bile *a* unchangeable; ⟨*colore*⟩ fast. ~**to** *a* unchanged

inami'da|re *vt* starch. ~**to** *a* starched

inammis'sibile *a* inadmissible

inamovi'bile *a* irremovable

inani'mato *a* inanimate; ⟨*senza vita*⟩ lifeless

inappa'ga|bile *a* unsatisfiable. ~**to** *a* unfulfilled

inappel'labile *a* final

inappe'tenza *nf* lack of appetite

inappli'cabile *a* inapplicable

inappun'tabile *a* faultless

inar'ca|re *vt* arch; raise ⟨*sopracciglia*⟩. ~**si** *vr* ⟨*legno*:⟩ warp; ⟨*ripiano*:⟩ sag; ⟨*linea*:⟩ curve

inari'dir|e *vt* parch; empty of feelings ⟨*persona*⟩. ~**si** *vr* dry up; ⟨*persona*:⟩ become empty of feelings

inarti'co'lato *a* inarticulate

inaspettata'mente *adv* unexpectedly. **inaspet'tato** *a* unexpected

inaspri'mento *nm* ⟨*di carattere*⟩ embitterment; ⟨*di conflitto*⟩ worsening

ina'sprir|e *vt* embitter. ~**si** *vr* become embittered

inattac'cabile *a* unassailable; ⟨*irreprensibile*⟩ irreproachable

inatten'dibile *a* unreliable. **inat'teso** *a* unexpected

inattività *nf* inactivity. **inat'tivo** *a* inactive

inattu'abile *a* impracticable

inau'dito *a* unheard of

inaugu'rale *a* inaugural; **viaggio ~** maiden voyage

inaugu'ra|re *vt* inaugurate; open ⟨*mostra*⟩; unveil ⟨*statua*⟩; christen ⟨*lavastoviglie*⟩. ~**zi'one** *nf* inauguration; ⟨*di mostra*⟩ opening; ⟨*di statua*⟩ unveiling

inavver't|enza *nf* inadvertence. ~**ita'mente** *adv* inadvertently

incagli'ar|e *vi* ground ● *vt* hinder. ~**si** *vr* run aground

incalco'labile *a* incalculable

incal'li|rsi *vr* grow callous; *(abituarsi)* become hardened. ~**to** *a* callous; *(abituato)* hardened

incal'za|nte *a* ‹ritmo› driving; ‹richiesta› urgent. ~**re** *vt* pursue; *fig* press

incame'rare *vt* appropriate

incammi'nare *vt* get going; *(fig: guidare)* set off. ~**si** *vr* set out

incana'lar|e *vt* canalize; *fig* channel. ~**si** *vr* converge on

incande'scen|te *a* incandescent; ‹discussione› burning. ~**za** *nf* incandescence

incan'ta|re *vt* enchant. ~**rsi** *vr* stand spellbound; *(incepparsi)* jam. ~ **tore**, ~**'trice** *nm* enchanter ● *nf* enchantress

incan'tesimo *nm* spell

incan'tevole *a* enchanting

in'canto *nm* spell; *fig* delight; ‹asta› auction; **come per ~** as if by magic

incanu'ti|re *vt* turn white. ~**to** *a* white

inca'pac|e *a* incapable. ~**ità** *nf* incapability

incapo'nirsi *vr* be set

incap'par|e *vi* ~ **in** run into

incappucci'arsi *vr* wrap up

incapricci'arsi *vr* ~ **di** take a fancy to

incapsu'lare *vt* seal; crown ‹dente›

incarce'ra|re *vt* imprison. ~**zi'one** *nf* imprisonment

incari'ca|re *vt* charge. ~**rsi** *vr* take upon oneself; **me ne incarico io** I will see to it. ~**to, -a** *a* in charge ● *nmf* representative. **in'carico** *nm* charge; **per incarico di** on behalf of

incar'na|re *vt* embody. ~**rsi** *vr* become incarnate. ~**zi'one** *nf* incarnation

incarta'mento *nm* documents *pl*.
incar'tare *vt* wrap [in paper]

incasi'nato *a fam* ‹vita› screwed up; ‹stanza› messed up

incas'sa|re *vt* pack; *Mech* embed; box in ‹mobile, frigo›; *(riscuotere)* cash; take ‹colpo›. ~**to** *a* set; ‹fiume› deeply embanked. **in'casso** *nm* collection; *(introito)* takings *pl*

incasto'na|re *vt* set. ~**tura** *nf* setting. ~**to** *a* embedded; ‹anello› inset ‹di with›

inca'strar|e *vt* fit in; *(fam: in situazione)* corner. ~**si** *vr* fit. **in'castro** *nm* joint, **a incastro** ‹pezzi› interlocking

incate'nare *vt* chain

incatra'mare *vt* tar

incat'tivire *vt* turn nasty

in'cauto *a* imprudent

inca'va|re *vt* hollow out. ~**to** *a* hollow. ~**tura** *nf* hollow. **in'cavo** *nm* hollow; *(scanalatura)* groove

incendi'ar|e *vt* set fire to; *fig* inflame. ~**si** *vr* catch fire. ~**io, -a** *a* incendiary; *(fig: discorso)* inflammatory; *(fig: bellezza)* sultry ● *nmf* arsonist. **in'cendio** *nm* fire. **incendio doloso** arson

incene'ri|re *vt* burn to ashes; *(cremare)* cremate. ~**rsi** *vr* be burnt to ashes. ~**'tore** *nm* incinerator

in'censo *nm* incense

incensu'rato *a* blameless; **essere ~** *Jur* have a clean record

incenti'vare *vt* motivate. **incen'tivo** *nm* incentive

incen'trarsi *vr* ~ **su** centre on

incep'par|e *vt* block; *fig* hamper. ~**si** *vr* jam

ince'rata *nf* oilcloth

incerot'tato *a* with a plaster on

incer'tezza *nf* uncertainty. **in'certo** *a* uncertain ● *nm* uncertainty

inces'sante *a* unceasing. ~**'mente** *adv* incessantly

in'cest|o *nm* incest. ~**u'oso** *a* incestuous

in'cetta *nf* buying up; **fare ~ di** stockpile

inchi'esta *nf* investigation

inchi'nar|e *vt*, ~**si** *vr* bow. **in'chino** *nm* bow; *(di donna)* curtsy

inchio'dare *vt* nail; nail down ‹coperchio›; ~ **a letto** ‹malattia:› confine to bed

inchi'ostro *nm* ink

inciam'pare *vi* stumble; ~ **in** *(imbattersi)* run into. **inci'ampo** *nm* hindrance

inciden'tale *a* incidental

inci'den|te *nm* *(episodio)* incident; *(infortunio)* accident. ~**za** *nf* incidence

in'cidere *vt* cut; ‹arte› engrave; ‹registrare› record ● *vi* ~ **su** ‹gravare› weigh upon

in'cinta *a* pregnant

incipi'ente *a* incipient

incipri'ar|e *vt* powder. ~**si** *vr* powder one's face

in'circa *adv* **all'~** more or less

incisi'one *nf* incision; ‹arte› engraving; ‹acquaforte› etching; ‹registrazione› recording

inci'sivo *a* incisive ● *nm* ‹dente› incisor

in'ciso nm per ~ incidentally
incita'mento nm incitement. **inci'tare** vt incite
inci'vil|e a uncivilized; (maleducato) impolite. **~tà** nf barbarism; (maleducazione) rudeness
incli'nabile a reclining
incli'na|re vt tilt ● vi ~**re** a be inclined to. **~rsi** vr list. **~to** a tilted; (terreno) sloping. **~zi'one** nf slope, inclination. **in'cline** a inclined
in'clu|dere vt include; (allegare) enclose. **~si'one** nf inclusion. **~'sivo** a inclusive. **~so** pp di **includere** ● a included; (compreso) inclusive; (allegato) enclosed
incoe'ren|te a (contraddittorio) inconsistent. **~za** nf inconsistency
in'cognit|a nf unknown quantity. **~o** a unknown ● nm **in ~o** incognito
incol'lar|e vt stick; (con colla liquida) glue. **~si** vr stick to; **~si a qcno** stick close to sb
incolle'ri|rsi vr lose one's temper. **~to** a enraged
incol'mabile a (differenza) unbridgeable; (vuoto) unfillable
incolon'nare vt line up
inco'lore a colourless
incol'pare vt blame
in'colto a uncultivated; (persona) uneducated
in'colume a unhurt
incom'ben|te a impending. **~za** nf task
in'combere vi ~ **su** hang over; ~ **a** (spettare) be incumbent on
incominci'are vt/i begin, start
incomo'dar|e vt inconvenience. **~si** vr trouble. **in'comodo** a uncomfortable; (inopportuno) inconvenient ● nm inconvenience
incompa'rabile a incomparable
incompa'tibil|e a incompatible. **~ità** nf incompatibility
incompe'ten|te a incompetent. **~za** nf incompetence
incompi'uto a unfinished
incom'pleto a incomplete
incompren'si|bile a incomprehensible. **~'one** nf lack of understanding; (malinteso) misunderstanding. **incom'preso** a misunderstood
inconce'pibile a inconceivable
inconcili'abile a irreconcilable

inconclu'dente a inconclusive; (persona) ineffectual
incondizio|nata'mente adv unconditionally. **~'nato** a unconditional
inconfes'sabile a unmentionable
inconfon'dibile a unmistakable
inconfu'tabile a irrefutable
incongru'ente a inconsistent
in'congruo a inadequate
inconsa'pevol|e a unaware; (inconscio) unconscious. **~'mente** adv unwittingly
inconscia'mente adv unconsciously. **in'conscio** a & nm Psych unconscious
inconsi'sten|te a insubstantial; (notizia ecc) unfounded. **~za** nf (di ragionamento, prove) flimsiness
inconso'labile a inconsolable
inconsu'eto a unusual
incon'sulto a rash
incontami'nato a uncontaminated
inconte'nibile a irrepressible
inconten'tabile a insatiable; (esigente) hard to please
inconte'stabile a indisputable
inconti'nen|te a incontinent. **~za** nf incontinence
incon'trar|e vt meet; encounter, meet with (difficoltà). **~si** vr meet (con qcno sb)
incon'trario: all'~ adv the other way around; (in modo sbagliato) the wrong way around
in'contro nm meeting; Sport match. ~ **al vertice** summit meeting ● prep ~ **a** towards; **andare ~ a qn** go to meet sb; fig meet sb half way
inconveni'ente nm drawback
incoraggia'mento nm encouragement. **~'ante** a encouraging. **~'are** vt encourage
incornici'a|re vt frame. **~'tura** nf framing
incoro'na|re vt crown. **~zi'one** nf coronation
incorpo'rar|e vt incorporate; (mescolare) blend. **~si** vr blend; (territori:) merge
incorreg'gibile a incorrigible
in'correre vt ~ **in** incur; ~ **nel pericolo di...** run the risk of...
incorrut'tibile a incorruptible
incosci'en|te a unconscious; (irresponsabile) reckless ● nmf irresponsi-

ble person. **~za** *nf* unconsciousness; recklessness

inco'stan|te *a* changeable; *(persona)* fickle. **~za** *nf* changeableness; *(di persona)* fickleness

incostituzio'nale *a* unconstitutional

incre'dibile *a* unbelievable, incredible

incredulità *nf* incredulity. **in'credulo** *a* incredulous

incremen'tare *vt* increase; *(intensificare)* step up. **incre'mento** *nm* increase. **incremento demografico** population growth

incresci'oso *a* regrettable

incre'spar|e *vt* ruffle; wrinkle *(tessuto)*; make frizzy *(capelli)*; **~e la fronte** frown. **~si** *vr (acqua:)* ripple; *(tessuto:)* wrinkle; *(capelli:)* go frizzy

incrimi'na|re *vt* indict; *fig* incriminate. **~zi'one** *nf* indictment

incri'na|re *vt* crack; *fig* affect *(amicizia)*. **~rsi** *vr* crack; *(amicizia:)* be affected. **~'tura** *nf* crack

incroci'a|re *vt* cross ● *vi* Naut, Aeron cruise. **~rsi** *vr* cross. **~'tore** *nm* cruiser

in'crocio *nm* crossing; *(di strade)* crossroads *sg*

incrol'labile *a* indestructible

incro'sta|re *vt* encrust. **~zi'one** *nf* encrustation

incuba'trice *nf* incubator. **~zi'one** *nf* incubation

'incubo *nm* nightmare

in'cudine *nf* anvil

incu'rabile *a* incurable

incu'rante *a* careless

incurio'sir|e *vt* make curious. **~si** *vr* become curious

incursi'one *nf* raid. **~ aerea** air raid

incurva'mento *nm* bending

incur'va|re *vt*, **~rsi** *vr* bend. **~'tura** *nf* bending

in'cusso *pp di* incutere

incusto'dito *a* unguarded

in'cutere *vt* arouse; **~ spavento a** qcno strike fear into sb

'indaco *nm* indigo

indaffa'rato *a* busy

inda'gare *vt/i* investigate

in'dagine *nf* research; *(giudiziaria)* investigation. **~ di mercato** market survey

indebi'tar|e *vt*. **~si** *vr* get into debt

in'debito *a* undue

indeboli'mento *nm* weakening

indebo'lir|e *vt*, **~si** *vr* weaken

inde'cen|te *a* indecent. **~za** *nf* indecency; *(vergogna)* disgrace

indeci'frabile *a* indecipherable

indecisi'one *nf* indecision. **inde'ciso** *a* undecided

inde'fesso *a* tireless

indefi'ni|bile *a* indefinable. **~to** *a* indefinite

indefor'mabile *a* crushproof

in'degno *a* unworthy

inde'lebile *a* indelible

indelica'tezza *nf* indelicacy; *(azione)* tactless act. **indeli'cato** *a* indiscreet; *(grossolano)* indelicate

indemoni'ato *a* possessed

in'denne *a* uninjured; *(da malattia)* unaffected. **~ità** *nf inv* allowance; *(per danni)* compensation. **~ità di trasferta** travel allowance. **~iz'zare** *vt* compensate. **inden'nizzo** *nm* compensation

indero'gabile *a* binding

indescri'vibile *a* indescribable

indeside'ra|bile *a* undesirable. **~to** *a (figlio, ospite)* unwanted

indetermi'na|bile *a* indeterminable. **~'tezza** *nf* vagueness. **~to** *a* indeterminate

'Indi|a *nf* India. **i~'ano, -a** *a & nmf* Indian; **in fila i~ana** in single file

indiavo'lato *a* possessed; *(vivace)* wild

indi'ca|re *vt* show, indicate; *(col dito)* point at; *(far notare)* point out; *(consigliare)* advise. **~'tivo** *a* indicative ● *nm* Gram indicative. **~'tore** *nm* indicator; Techn gauge; *(prontuario)* directory. **~zi'one** *nf* indication; *(istruzione)* direction

'indice *nm* index; *(dito)* forefinger; *(lancetta)* pointer; *(di libro, statistica)* index; *(fig: segno)* sign

indi'cibile *a* inexpressible

indietreggi'are *vi* draw back; Mil retreat

indi'etro *adv* back, behind; **all'~** backwards; **avanti e ~** back and forth; **essere ~** be behind; *(mentalmente)* be backward; *(con pagamenti)* be in arrears; *(di orologio)* be slow; **fare marcia ~** reverse; **rimandare ~** send back; **rimanere ~** be left behind; **torna ~!** come back!

indi'feso *a* undefended; *(inerme)* helpless

indiffe'ren|te *a* indifferent; **mi è ~tè** it is all the same to me. **~za** *nf* indifference in'digeno, -a *a* indigenous ●*nmf* native

indi'gen|te *a* needy. ~za *nf* poverty

indigesti'one *nf* indigestion. indi'gesto *a* indigestible

indi'gna|re *vt* make indignant. ~rsi *vr* be indignant. ~to *a* indignant. ~zi'one *nf* indignation

indimenti'cabile *a* unforgettable

indipen'den|te *a* independent. ~te-'mente *adv* independently; ~temente dal tempo regardless of the weather, whatever the weather. ~za *nf* independence

in'dire *vt* announce

indiretta'mente *adv* indirectly. indi'retto *a* indirect

indiriz'zar|e *vt* address; (*mandare*) send; (*dirigere*) direct. ~si *vr* direct one's steps. indi'rizzo *nm* address; (*direzione*) direction

indisci'pli|na *nf* lack of discipline. ~'nato *a* undisciplined

indi'scre|to *a* indiscreet. ~zi'one *nf* indiscretion

indiscrimi'nata'mente *adv* indiscriminately. ~'nato *a* indiscriminate

indi'scusso *a* unquestioned

indiscu'tibil|e *a* unquestionable. ~'mente *adv* unquestionably

indispen'sabile *a* essential, indispensable

indispet'tir|e *vt* irritate. ~si *vr* get irritated

indi'spo|rre *vt* antagonize. ~sto *pp di* indisporre ●*a* indisposed. ~sizi'one *nf* indisposition

indisso'lubile *a* indissoluble

indissolubil'mente *adv* indissolubly

indistin'guibile *a* indiscernible

indistinta'mente *adv* without exception. indi'stinto *a* indistinct

indistrut'tibile *a* indestructible

indistur'bato *a* undisturbed

in'divia *nf* endive

individu'a|le *a* individual. ~'lista *nmf* individualist. ~'lità *nf* individuality. ~re *vt* individualize; (*localizzare*) locate; (*riconoscere*) single out

indi'viduo *nm* individual

indivi'sibile *a* indivisible. indi'viso *a* undivided

indizi'a|re *vt* throw suspicion on. ~to, -a *a* suspected ●*nmf* suspect. in'dizio *nm* sign; *Jur* circumstantial evidence

'indole *nf* nature

indo'len|te *a* indolent. ~za *nf* indolence

indolenzi'mento *nm* stiffness

indolen'zi|rsi *vr* go stiff. ~to *a* stiff

indo'lore *a* painless

indo'mani *nm* l'~ the following day

Indo'nesia *nf* Indonesia

indo'rare *vt* gild

indos'sa|re *vt* wear; (*mettere addosso*) put on. ~tore, ~'trice *nmf* model

in'dotto *pp di* indurre

indottri'nare *vt* indoctrinate

indovi'n|are *vt* guess; (*predire*) foretell. ~ato *a* successful; (*scelta*) well-chosen. ~ello *nm* riddle. indo'vino, -a *nmf* fortune-teller

indubbia'mente *adv* undoubtedly. in'dubbio *a* undoubted

indugi'ar|e *vi*, ~si *vr* linger. in'dugio *nm* delay

indul'gen|te *a* indulgent. ~za *nf* indulgence

in'dul|gere *vi* ~gere a indulge in. ~to *pp di* indulgere ●*nm* *Jur* pardon

indu'mento *nm* garment; indumenti *pl* clothes

induri'mento *nm* hardening

indu'rir|e *vt*, ~si *vr* harden

in'durre *vt* induce

in'dustri|a *nf* industry. ~'ale *a* industrial ●*nm* industrialist

industrializ'za|re *vt* industrialize. ~to *a* industrialized. ~zi'one *nf* industrialization

industrial'mente *adv* industrially

industri'|arsi *vr* try one's hardest. ~'oso *a* industrious

induzi'one *nf* induction

inebe'tito *a* stunned

inebri'ante *a* intoxicating, exciting

inecce'pibile *a* unexceptionable

i'nedia *nf* starvation

i'nedito *a* unpublished

ineffi'cace *a* ineffective

ineffici'en|te *a* inefficient. ~za *nf* inefficiency

ineguagli'abile *a* incomparable

inegu'ale *a* unequal; (*superficie*) uneven

inelut'tabile *a* inescapable

ine'rente *a* ~ a concerning

i'nerme *a* unarmed; *fig* defenceless

inerpi'carsi *vr* ~ su clamber up; (*pianta:*) climb up

i'ner|te *a* inactive; *Phys* inert. ~zia *nf* inactivity; *Phys* inertia

inesat'tezza *nf* inaccuracy. ine'satto

a inaccurate; (*erroneo*) incorrect; (*non riscosso*) uncollected

inesau'ribile *a* inexhaustible

inesi'sten|te *a* non-existent. **~za** *nf* non-existence

ineso'rabile *a* inexorable

inesperi'enza *nf* inexperience. **ine-'sperto** *a* inexperienced

inespli'cabile *a* inexplicable

ine'sploso *a* unexploded

inespri'mibile *a* inexpressible

inesti'mabile *a* inestimable

inetti'tudine *nf* ineptitude. **i'netto** *a* inept; **inetto a** unsuited to

ine'vaso *a* ⟨*pratiche*⟩ pending; ⟨*corrispondenza*⟩ unanswered

inevi'tabil|e *a* inevitable. **~'mente** *adv* inevitably

i'nezia *nf* trifle

infagot'tar|e *vt* wrap up. **~si** *vr* wrap [oneself] up

infal'libile *a* infallible

infa'ma|re *vt* defame. **~'torio** *a* defamatory

in'fam|e *a* infamous; (*fam: orrendo*) awful, shocking. **~ia** *nf* infamy

infan'garsi *vr* get muddy

infan'tile *a* ⟨*letteratura, abbigliamento*⟩ children's; ⟨*ingenuità*⟩ childlike; *pej* childish

in'fanzia *nf* childhood; ⟨*bambini*⟩ children *pl*; **prima ~** infancy

infar'cire *vt* pepper ⟨*discorso*⟩ ⟨*di* with⟩

infari'na|re *vt* flour; **~re di** sprinkle with. **~'tura** *nf fig* smattering

in'farto *nm* coronary

infasti'dir|e *vt* irritate. **~si** *vr* get irritated

infati'cabile *a* untiring

in'fatti *conj* as a matter of fact; (*veramente*) indeed

infatu'a|rsi *vr* become infatuated ⟨*di* with⟩. **~to** *a* infatuated. **~zi'one** *nf* infatuation

in'fausto *a* ill-omened

infe'condo *a* infertile

infe'del|e *a* unfaithful. **~tà** *nf* unfaithfulness; **~** *pl* affairs

infe'lic|e *a* unhappy; (*inappropriato*) unfortunate; (*cattivo*) bad. **~ità** *nf* unhappiness

infel'tri|rsi *vr* get matted. **~to** *a* matted

inferi'or|e *a* (*più basso*) lower; ⟨*qualità*⟩ inferior ● *nmf* inferior. **~ità** *nf* inferiority

inferme'ria *nf* infirmary; (*di nave*) sick-bay

infermi'er|a *nf* nurse. **~e** *nm* [male] nurse

infermità *nf* sickness. **~ mentale** mental illness. **in'fermo, -a** *a* sick ● *nmf* invalid

infer'nale *a* infernal; (*spaventoso*) hellish

in'ferno *nm* hell; **va all'~!** go to hell!

infero'cirsi *vr* become fierce

inferri'ata *nf* grating

infervo'rar|e *vt* arouse enthusiasm in. **~si** *vr* get excited

infe'stare *vt* infest

infet't|are *vt* infect. **~arsi** *vr* become infected. **~ivo** *a* infectious. **in'fetto** *a* infected. **infezi'one** *nf* infection

infiac'chir|e *vt/i*. **~si** *vr* weaken

infiam'mabile *a* [in]flammable

infiam'ma|re *vt* set on fire; *Med, fig* inflame. **~rsi** *vr* catch fire; *Med* become inflamed. **~zi'one** *nf Med* inflammation

in'fido *a* treacherous

infie'rire *vi* (*imperversare*) rage; **~ su** attack furiously

in'figger|e *vt* drive. **~si** *vr*-**si in** penetrate

infi'lar|e *vt* thread; (*mettere*) insert; (*indossare*) put on. **~si** *vr* slip on ⟨*vestito*⟩; **~si in** (*introdursi*) slip into

infil'tra|rsi *vr* infiltrate. **~zi'one** *nf* infiltration; (*d'acqua*) seepage; (*Med: iniezione*) injection

infil'zare *vt* pierce; (*infilare*) string; (*conficcare*) stick

'infimo *a* lowest

in'fine *adv* finally; (*insomma*) in short

infinità *nf* infinity; **un'~ di** masses of. **~'mente** *adv* infinitely. **infi'nito** *a* infinite; *Gram* infinitive ● *nm* infinite; *Gram* infinitive; *Math* infinity; **all'infinito** endlessly

infinocchi'are *vt fam* hoodwink

infischi'arsi *vr* **~ di** not care about; **me ne infischio** *fam* I couldn't care less

in'fisso *pp di* **infiggere** ● *nm* fixture; (*di porta, finestra*) frame

infit'tir|e *vt/i*. **~si** *vr* thicken

inflazi'one *nf* inflation

infles'sibil|e *a* inflexible. **~ità** *nf* inflexibility

inflessi'one *nf* inflexion

in'fliggere *vt* inflict. **~tto** *pp di* **infliggere**

influen|te a influential. **~za** nf influence; Med influenza

influen'za|bile a (mente, opinione) impressionable. **~re** vt influence. **~to** a (malato) with the flu

influ'ire vi~ **su** influence

in'flusso nm influence

info'carsi vr catch fire; (viso:) go red; (discussione:) become heated

info'gnarsi vr fam get into a mess

infol'tire vt/i thicken

infon'dato a unfounded

in'fondere vt instil

infor'care vt fork up; get on (bici); put on (occhiali)

infor'male a informal

infor'ma|re vt inform. **~rsi** vr inquire (di about). **~'tivo** a informative.

infor'matic|a nf computing, IT. **~o** a computer attrib

infor'ma|tivo a informative. **infor'mato** a informed; **male informa** ill-informed. **~'tore, ~'trice** nmf (di polizia) informer. **~zi'one** nf information (solo sg); **un'~zione** a piece of information

in'forme a shapeless

infor'nare vt put into the oven

infortu'narsi vr have an accident.

infor'tu|nio nm accident. **~nio sul lavoro** industrial accident. **~'nistica** nf study of industrial accidents

infos'sa|rsi vr sink; (guance, occhi:) become hollow. **~to** a sunken, hollow

infradici'ar|e vt drench. **~si** vr get drenched; (diventare marcio) rot

infra'dito nm inv (scarpa) flip-flop

in'frang|ere vt break; (in mille pezzi) shatter. **~ersi** vr break. **~'gibile** a unbreakable

in'franto pp di **infrangere** ● a shattered; (fig: cuore) broken

infra'rosso a infra-red

infrastrut'tura nf infrastructure

infrazi'one nf offence

infredda'tura nf cold

infreddo'li|rsi vr feel cold. **~to** a cold

infruttu'oso a fruitless

infuo'ca|re vt make red-hot. **~to** a burning

infu'ori adv all'**~** outwards; all'**~** di except

infuri'a|re vi rage. **~rsi** vr fly into a rage. **~to** a blustering

infusi'one nf infusion. **in'fuso** pp di **infondere** ● nm infusion

Ing. abbr **ingegnere**

ingabbi'are vt cage; (fig: mettere in prigione) jail

ingaggi'are vt engage; sign up (calciatori ecc); begin (lotta, battaglia). **in'gaggio** nm engagement; (di calciatore) signing [up]

ingan'nar|e vt deceive; (essere infedele a) be unfaithful to. **~si** vr deceive oneself; **se non m'inganno** if I am not mistaken

ingan'nevole a deceptive. **in'ganno** nm deceit; (frode) fraud

ingarbugli'a|re vt entangle; (confondere) confuse. **~rsi** vr get entangled; (confondersi) become confused. **~to** a confused

inge'gnarsi vr do one's best

inge'gnere nm engineer. **ingegne'ria** nf engineering

in'gegno nm brains pl; (genio) genius; (abilità) ingenuity. **~sa'mente** adv ingeniously

ingegnosità nf ingenuity. **inge'gnoso** a ingenious

ingelo'sir|e vt make jealous. **~si** vr become jealous

in'gente a huge

ingenu|a'mente adv artlessly. **~ità** nf ingenuousness. **in'genuo** a ingenuous; (credulone) naïve

inge'renza nf interference

inge'rire vt swallow

inges'sa|re vt put in plaster. **~'tura** nf plaster

Inghil'terra nf England

inghiot'tire vt swallow

in'ghippo nm trick

ingial'li|re vi. **~rsi** vr turn yellow. **~to** a yellowed

ingigan'tir|e vt magnify ● vi. **~si** vr grow to enormous proportions

inginocchi'a|rsi vr kneel [down]. **~to** a kneeling. **~'toio** nm prie-dieu

ingioiel'larsi vr put on one's jewels

ingiù adv down; all'**~** downwards; a **testa ~** head downwards

ingi'un|gere vt order. **~zi'one** nf injunction. **~zione di pagamento** final demand

ingi'uri|a nf insult; (torto) wrong; (danno) damage. **~'are** vt insult; (fare un torto a) wrong. **~'oso** a insulting

ingiusta'mente adv unjustly, unfairly. **ingiu'stizia** nf injustice. **ingi'u-sto** a unjust, unfair

in'glese a English ● nm Englishman; (lingua) English ● nf Englishwoman

ingoi'are vt swallow

ingol'far|e *vt* flood ⟨*motore*⟩. **~si** *vr fig* get involved; ⟨*motore:*⟩ flood

ingom'bra|nte *a* cumbersome. **~re** *vt* clutter up; *fig* cram ⟨*mente*⟩

in'gombro *nm* encumbrance; **essere d'~** be in the way

ingor'digia *nf* greed. **in'gordo** *a* greedy

ingor'gar|e *vt* block. **~si** *vr* be blocked [up]. **in'gorgo** *nm* blockage; ⟨*del traffico*⟩ jam

ingoz'zar|e *vt* gobble up; ⟨*nutrire eccessivamente*⟩ stuff; fatten ⟨*animali*⟩. **~si** *vr* stuff oneself ⟨**di** with⟩

ingra'na|ggio *nm* gear; *fig* mechanism. **~re** *vt* engage ● *vi* be in gear

ingrandi'mento *nm* enlargement

ingran'di|re *vt* enlarge; ⟨*esagerare*⟩ magnify. **~rsi** *vr* become larger; ⟨*aumentare*⟩ increase

ingras'sar|e *vt* fatten up; *Mech* grease ● *vi*, **~si** *vr* put on weight

ingrati'tudine *nf* ingratitude. **in'grato** *a* ungrateful; ⟨*sgradevole*⟩ thankless

ingrazi'arsi *vr* ingratiate oneself with

ingredi'ente *nm* ingredient

in'gresso *nm* entrance; ⟨*accesso*⟩ admittance; ⟨*sala*⟩ hall; **~ gratuito/ libero** admission free; **vietato l'~** no entry; no admittance

ingros'sar|e *vt* make big; ⟨*gonfiare*⟩ swell ● *vi*, **~si** *vr* grow big; ⟨*gonfiare*⟩ swell

in'grosso *adv* **all'~** wholesale; ⟨*pressapoco*⟩ roughly

ingua'ribile *a* incurable

'inguine *nm* groin

ingurgi'tare *vt* gulp down

ini'bi|re *vt* inhibit; ⟨*vietare*⟩ forbid. **~to** *a* inhibited. **~zi'one** *nf* inhibition; ⟨*divieto*⟩ prohibition

iniet'tar|e *vt* inject. **~si** *vr* **~si di sangue** ⟨*occhi:*⟩ become bloodshot. **iniezi'one** *nf* injection

inimi'carsi *vr* make an enemy of. **inimi'cizia** *nf* enmity

inimi'tabile *a* inimitable

ininter'rotta'mente *adv* continuously. **~'rotto** *a* continuous

iniquità *nf* iniquity. **i'niquo** *a* iniquitous

inizi'al|e *a* & *nf* initial. **~'mente** *adv* initially

inizi'are *vt* begin; ⟨*avviare*⟩ open; **~ qcno a qcsa** initiate sb in sth ● *vi* begin

inizia'tiva *nf* initiative; **prendere l'~** take the initiative

inizi'a|to, -a *a* initiated ● *nmf* initiate; **gli ~ti** the initiated. **~'tore, ~'trice** *nmf* initiator. **~zi'one** *nf* initiation

i'nizio *nm* beginning, start; **dare ~ a** start; **avere ~** get under way

innaffi'a|re *vt* water. **~'toio** *nm* watering-can

innal'zar|e *vt* raise; ⟨*erigere*⟩ erect. **~si** *vr* rise

innamo'ra|rsi *vr* fall in love ⟨**di** with⟩. **~ta** *nf* girl-friend. **~to** *a* in love ● *nm* boy-friend

in'nanzi *adv* ⟨*stato in luogo*⟩ in front; ⟨*di tempo*⟩ ahead; ⟨*avanti*⟩ forward; ⟨*prima*⟩ before; **d'ora ~** from now on ● *prep* ⟨*prima*⟩ before; **~ a** in front of. **~'tutto** *adv* first of all; ⟨*soprattutto*⟩ above all

in'nato *a* innate

innatu'rale *a* unnatural

inne'gabile *a* undeniable

innervo'sir|e *vt* make nervous. **~si** *vr* get irritated

inne'scare *vt* prime. **in'nesco** *nm* primer

inne'stare *vt* graft; *Mech* engage, ⟨*inserire*⟩ insert. **in'nesto** *nm* graft; *Mech* clutch; *Electr* connection

inne'vato *a* covered in snow

'inno *nm* hymn. **~ nazionale** national anthem

inno'cen|te *a* innocent **~te'mente** *adv* innocently. **~za** *nf* innocence.

in'nocuo *a* innocuous

inno'va|re *vt* make changes in. **~'tivo** *a* innovative. **~'tore** *a* trail-blazing. **~zi'one** *nf* innovation

innume'revole *a* innumerable

ino'doro *a* odourless

inoffen'sivo *a* harmless

inol'trar|e *vt* forward. **~si** *vr* advance

inol'trato *a* late

i'noltre *adv* besides

inon'da|re *vt* flood. **~zi'one** *nf* flood

inope'roso *a* idle

inoppor'tuno *a* untimely

inorgo'glir|e *vt* make proud. **~si** *vr* become proud

inor'ridire *vt* horrify ● *vi* be horrified

inospi'tale *a* inhospitable

inosser'vato *a* unobserved; ⟨*non rispettato*⟩ disregarded; **passare ~** go unnoticed

inossi'dabile *a* stainless

'inox *a inv* ⟨*acciaio*⟩ stainless

inqua'dra|re *vt* frame; *fig* put in context ⟨*scrittore, problema*⟩. **~rsi** *vr* fit into. **~'tura** *nf* framing

inqualifi'cabile *a* unspeakable

inquie'tar|e *vt* worry. **~si** get worried; *(impazientirsi)* get cross. **inqui'e-to** *a* restless; *(preoccupato)* worried. **inquie'tudine** *nf* anxiety

inqui'lino, -a *nmf* tenant

inquina'mento *nm* pollution

inqui'na|re *vt* pollute. **~to** *a* polluted

inqui'rente *a* Jur *(magistrato)* examining; **commissione ~** commission of enquiry

inqui'si|re *vt/i* investigate. **~to** *a* under investigation. **~'tore**, **~'trice** *a* inquiring ● *nmf* inquisitor. **~zi'one** *nf* inquisition

insabbi'are *vt* shelve

insa'lat|a *nf* salad. **~a belga** endive. **~'i'era** *nf* salad bowl

insa'lubre *a* unhealthy

insa'nabile *a* incurable

insangui'na|re *vt* cover with blood. **~to** *a* bloody

insapo'nare *vt* soap

insa'po|re *a* tasteless. **~'rire** *vt* flavour

insa'puta *nf* **all'~ di** unknown to

insazi'abile *a* insatiable

insce'nare *vt* stage

inscin'dibile *a* inseparable

inse'dia|mento *nm* installation

insedi'ar|e *vt* install. **~si** *vr* install oneself

in'segna *nf* sign; *(bandiera)* flag; *(decorazione)* decoration; *(emblema)* insignia *pl*; *(stemma)* symbol. **~ luminosa** neon sign

insegna'mento *nm* teaching. **inse-'gnante** *a* teaching ● *nmf* teacher

inse'gnare *vt/i* teach; **~ qcsa a qcno** teach sb sth

insegui'mento *nmf* pursuit

insegu'i|re *vt* pursue. **~'tore**, **~'trice** *nmf* pursuer

inselvati'chir|e *vt* make wild ● *vi*, **~si** *vr* grow wild

insemi'na|re *vt* inseminate. **~zi'one** *nf* insemination. **~zione artificiale** artificial insemination

insena'tura *nf* inlet

insen'sato *a* senseless; *(folle)* crazy

insen'sibil|e *a* insensitive; *(braccio ecc)* numb. **~ità** *nf* insensitivity

insepa'rabile *a* inseparable

inseri'mento *nm* insertion

inse'rir|e *vt* insert; place *(annuncio)*; Electr connect. **~si in** *vr* **~si in** get into. **in'serto** *nm* file; *(in un film ecc)* insert

inservi'ente *nmf* attendant

inserzi'o|ne *nf* insertion; *(avviso)* advertisement. **~'nista** *nmf* advertiser

insetti'cida *nm* insecticide

in'setto *nm* insect

insicu'rezza *nf* insecurity. **insi'curo** *a* insecure

in'sidi|a *nf* trick; *(tranello)* snare. **~'are** *vt/i* lay a trap for. **~'oso** *a* insidious

insi'eme *adv* together; *(contemporaneamente)* at the same time ● *prep* **~ a** [together] with ● *nm* whole; *(completo)* outfit; Theat ensemble; Math set; **nell'~** as a whole; **tutto ~** all together; *(bere)* at one go

in'signe *a* renowned

insignifi'cante *a* insignificant

insi'gnire *vt* decorate

insinda'cabile *a* final

insinu'ante *a* insinuating

insinu'a|re *vt* insinuate. **~rsi** *vr* penetrate; **~rsi in** *fig* creep into. **~zi'one** *nf* insinuation

in'sipido *a* insipid

insi'sten|te *a* insistent. **~te'mente** *adv* repeatedly. **~za** *nf* insistence. **in'sistere** *vi* insist; *(perseverare)* persevere

insoddisfa'cente *a* unsatisfactory

insoddi'sfa|tto *a* unsatisfied; *(scontento)* dissatisfied. **~zi'one** *nf* dissatisfaction

insoffe'ren|te *a* intolerant. **~za** *nf* intolerance

insolazi'one *nf* sunstroke

inso'len|te *a* rude, insolent. **~za** *nf* rudeness, insolence; *(commento)* insolent remark

in'solito *a* unusual

inso'lubile *a* insoluble

inso'luto *a* unsolved; *(non pagato)* unpaid

insol'venza *nf* insolvency

in'somma *adv* in short; **~!** well really!; *(così così)* so so

in'sonne *a* sleepless. **~ia** *nf* insomnia

insonno'lito *a* sleepy

insonoriz'zato *a* soundproofed

insoppor'tabile *a* unbearable

insor'genza *nf* onset

in'sorgere *vi* revolt, rise up; *(sorgere)* arise; *(difficoltà)* crop up

insormon'tabile *a* *(ostacolo, difficoltà)* insurmountable

in'sorto *pp di* **insorgere** ● *a* rebellious ● *nm* rebel

insospet'tabile *a* unsuspected

insospet'tir|e *vt* make suspicious ● *vi*, **~si** *vr* become suspicious

insoste'nibile *a* untenable; (*insopportabile*) unbearable

insostitu'ibile *a* irreplaceable

inspe'ra|bile *a* **una sua vittoria è ~bile** there is no hope of him winning. **~to** *a* unhoped-for

inspie'gabile *a* inexplicable

inspi'rare *vt* breathe in

in'stabil|e *a* unstable; (*tempo*) changeable. **~ità** *nf* instability; (*di tempo*) changeability

instal'la|re *vt* install. **~rsi** *vr* settle in. **~zi'one** *nf* installation

instan'cabile *a* untiring

instau'ra|re *vt* found. **~rsi** *vr* become established. **~zi'one** *nf* foundation

instra'dare *vt* direct

insù *adv* **all'~** upwards

insubordinazi'one *nf* insubordination

insuc'cesso *nm* failure

insudici'ar|e *vt* dirty. **~si** *vr* get dirty

insuffici'en|te *a* insufficient; (*inadeguato*) inadequate ● *nf Sch* fail. **~za** *nf* insufficiency; (*inadeguatezza*) inadequacy; *Sch* fail. **~za cardiaca** heart failure. **~za di prove** lack of evidence

insu'lare *a* insular

insu'lina *nf* insulin

in'sulso *a* insipid; (*sciocco*) silly

insul'tare *vt* insult. **in'sulto** *nm* insult

insupe'rabile *a* insuperable; (*eccezionale*) incomparable

insurrezi'one *nf* insurrection

insussi'stente *a* groundless

intac'care *vt* nick; (*corrodere*) corrode; draw on (*un capitale*); (*danneggiare*) damage

intagli'are *vt* carve. **in'taglio** *nm* carving

intan'gibile *a* untouchable

in'tanto *adv* meanwhile; (*per ora*) for the moment; (*avversativo*) but; **~ che** while

intarsi'a|re *vt* inlay. **~to** *a* **~to di** inset with. **in'tarsio** *nm* inlay

inta'sare *vt* clog; block (*traffico*). **~rsi** *vr* get blocked. **~to** *a* blocked

inta'scare *vt* pocket

in'tatto *a* intact

intavo'lare *vt* start

inte'gra|le *a* whole; **edizione ~le** unabridged edition; **pane ~le** wholemeal bread. **~l'mente** *adv* fully. **~nte** *a*

integral. **'integro** *a* complete; (*retto*) upright

inte'gra|re *vt* integrate; (*aggiungere*) supplement. **~rsi** *vr* integrate. **~'tivo** *a* (*corso*) supplementary. **~zi'one** *nf* integration

integrità *nf* integrity

intelaia'tura *nf* framework

intel'letto *nm* intellect

intellettu'al|e *a* & *nmf* intellectual. **~'mente** *adv* intellectually

intelli'gen|te *a* intelligent. **~te'mente** *adv* intelligently. **~za** *nf* intelligence

intelli'gibil|e *a* intelligible. **~'mente** *adv* intelligibly

intempe'ranza *nf* intemperance

intem'perie *nfpl* bad weather

inten'den|te *nm* superintendent. **~za** *nf* **~za di finanza** inland revenue office

in'tender|e *vt* (*comprendere*) understand; (*udire*) hear; (*avere intenzione*) intend; (*significare*) mean. **~sela con** have an understanding with; **~si** *vr* (*capirsi*) understand each other; **~si di** (*essere esperto*) have a good knowledge of

intendi'mento *nm* understanding; (*intenzione*) intention. **~'tore**, **~'trice** *nmf* connoisseur

intene'rir|e *vt* soften; (*commuovere*) touch. **~si** *vr* be touched

intensa'mente *adv* intensely

intensifi'car|e *vt*, **~si** *vr* intensify

intensità *nf inv* intensity. **inten'sivo** *a* intensive. **in'tenso** *a* intense

inten'tare *vt* start up; **~ causa contro qcno** bring *o* institute proceedings against sb

in'tento *a* engrossed (**a** in) ● *nm* purpose

intenzio'nato *a* **essere ~ a fare qcsa** have the intention of doing sth

intenzio'nale *a* intentional. **inten-zi'one** *nf* intention; **senza ~ne** unintentionally; **avere ~ne di fare qcsa** intend to do sth, have the intention of doing sth.

intera'gire *vi* interact

intera'mente *adv* completely, entirely

intera|t'tivo *a* interactive. **~zi'one** *nf* interaction

interca'lare[1] *nm* stock phrase

interca'lare[2] *vt* insert

intercambi'abile *a* interchangeable

interca'pedine *nf* cavity

inter'ce|dere *vi* intercede. **~ssi'one** *nf* intercession

intercet'ta|re *vt* intercept; tap ⟨telefono⟩. **~zi'one** *nf* interception. **~zione telefonica** telephone tapping

inter'city *nm inv* inter-city

intercontinen'tale *a* intercontinental

inter'correre *vi* ⟨tempo:⟩ elapse; ⟨esistere⟩ exist

interco'stale *a* intercostal

inter'detto *pp di* **interdire** ● *a* astonished; ⟨proibito⟩ forbidden; **rimanere ~** be taken aback

inter'di|re *vt* forbid; *Jur* deprive of civil rights. **~zi'one** *nf* prohibition

interessa'mento *nm* interest

interes'sante *a* interesting; **essere in stato ~** be pregnant

interes'sa|re *vt* interest; ⟨riguardare⟩ concern ● *vi* **~re a** matter to. **~rsi** *vr* **~rsi a** take an interest in. **~rsi di** take care of. **~to, -a** *nmf* interested party ● *a* interested; **essere ~to** *pej* have an interest

inte'resse *nm* interest; **fare qcsa per ~** do sth out of self-interest

inter'faccia *nf Comput* interface

interfe'renza *nf* interference

interfe'rire *vi* interfere

interiezi'one *nf* interjection

interi'ora *nfpl* entrails

interi'ore *a* interior

inter'ludio *nm* interlude

intermedi'ario, -a *a & nmf* intermediary

inter'medio *a* in-between

inter'mezzo *nm Theat, Mus* intermezzo

intermi'nabile *a* interminable

intermit'ten|te *a* intermittent; ⟨luce⟩ flashing. **~za** *nf* **luce a ~za** flashing light

interna'mento *nm* internment; ⟨in manicomio⟩ committal

inter'nare *vt* intern; ⟨in manicomio⟩ commit [to a mental institution]

in'terno *a* internal; *Geog* inland; ⟨interiore⟩ inner; ⟨politica⟩ national; **alunno ~** boarder ● *nm* interior; ⟨di condominio⟩ flat; *Teleph* extension; *Cinema* interior shot; **all'~** inside

internazio'nale *a* international

in'tero *a* whole, entire; ⟨intatto⟩ intact; ⟨completo⟩ complete; **per ~** in full

interpel'lare *vt* consult

inter'por|re *vt* place ⟨ostacolo⟩. **~si** *vr* come between

interpre'ta|re *vt* interpret; *Mus* perform. **~zi'one** *nf* interpretation; *Mus* performance. **in'terprete** *nmf* interpreter; *Mus* performer

inter'ra|re *vt* ⟨seppellire⟩ bury; plant ⟨pianta, seme⟩. **~to** *nm* basement

interro'ga|re *vt* question; *Sch* test; examine ⟨studenti⟩. **~tiva'mente** *adv* questioningly. **~'tivo** *a* interrogative; ⟨sguardo⟩ questioning; **punto ~'tivo** question mark ● *nm* question. **~'torio** *a & nm* questioning. **~zi'one** *nf* question; *Sch* oral [test]

inter'romper|e *vt* interrupt; ⟨sospendere⟩ stop; cut off ⟨collegamento⟩. **~si** *vr* break off

interrut'tore *nm* switch

interruzi'one *nf* interruption; **senza ~** non-stop. **~ di gravidanza** termination of pregnancy

interse'|care *vt*, **~'carsi** *vr* intersect. **~zi'one** *nf* intersection

inter'stizio *nm* interstice

interur'ban|a *nf* long-distance call. **~o** *a* inter-city; **telefonata ~a** long-distance call

interval'lare *vt* space out. **inter'vallo** *nm* interval; ⟨spazio⟩ space; *Sch* break. **intervallo pubblicitario** commercial break

interve'nire *vi* intervene; ⟨Med: operare⟩ operate; **~ a** take part in. **inter'vento** *nm* intervention; ⟨presenza⟩ presence; ⟨chirurgico⟩ operation; **pronto intervento** emergency services

inter'vista *nf* interview

intervi'sta|re *vt* interview. **~'tore, ~'trice** *nmf* interviewer

in'tes|a *nf* understanding; **cenno d'~a** acknowledgement. **~o** *pp di* **intendere** ● *a* **resta ~o che...** needless to say,...; **~i!** agreed!; **~o a** meant to; **non darsi per ~o** refuse to understand

inte'sta|re *vt* head; write one's name and address at the top of ⟨lettera⟩; *Comm* register. **~rsi** *vr* **~rsi a fare qcsa** take it into one's head to do sth. **~'tario, -a** *nmf* holder. **~zi'one** *nf* heading; ⟨su carta da lettere⟩ letterhead

intesti'nale *a* intestinal

inte'stino *a* ⟨lotte⟩ internal ● *nm* intestine

intima'mente *adv* ⟨conoscere⟩ intimately

inti'ma|re *vt* order; **~re l'alt a qcno** order sb to stop. **~zi'one** *nf* order

intimida'|torio *a* threatening. **~zi'one** *nf* intimidation

intimi'dire vt intimidate

intimità nf cosiness. **'intimo** a intimate; (interno) innermost; (amico) close ● nm (amico) close friend; (dell'animo) heart

intimo'ri|re vt frighten. **~rsi** vr get frightened. **~to** a frightened

in'tingere vt dip

in'tingolo nm sauce; (pietanza) stew

intiriz'zi|re vt numb. **~rsi** vr grow numb. **~to** a **essere ~to** (dal freddo) be perished

intito'lar|e vt entitle; (dedicare) dedicate. **~si** vr be called

intolle'rabile a intolerable

intona'care vt plaster. **in'tonaco** nm plaster

into'na|re vt start to sing; tune (strumento); (accordare) match. **~rsi** vr match. **~to** a (persona) able to sing in tune; (colore) matching

intonazi'one nf (inflessione) intonation; (ironico) tone

inton'ti|re vt daze; (gas:) make dizzy ● vi be dazed. **~to** a dazed

intop'pare vi **~ in** run into

in'toppo nm obstacle

in'torno adv around ● prep **a** around; (circa) about

intorpi'di|re vt numb. **~rsi** vr become numb. **~to** a torpid

intossi'ca|re vt poison. **~rsi** vr be poisoned. **~zi'one** nf poisoning

intralci'are vt hamper

in'tralcio nm hitch; **essere d'~** be a hindrance (**a** to)

intrallaz'zare vi intrigue. **intral'lazzo** nm racket

intramon'tabile a timeless

intramusco'lare a intramuscular

intransi'gen|te a intransigent, uncompromising. **~za** nf intransigence

intransi'tivo a intransitive

intrappo'lato a **rimanere ~** be trapped

intrapren'den|te a enterprising. **~za** nf initiative

intra'prendere vt undertake

intrat'tabile a very difficult

intratte'n|ere vt entertain. **~ersi** vr linger. **~i'mento** nm entertainment

intrave'dere vt catch a glimpse of; (presagire) foresee

intrecci'ar|e vt interweave, plait (capelli, corda). **~si** vr intertwine; (aggrovigliarsi) become tangled; **~e le mani** clasp one's hands

in'treccio nm (trama) plot

in'trepido a intrepid

intri'cato a tangled

intri'gante a scheming; (affascinante) intriguing

intri'ga|re vt entangle; (incuriosire) intrigue ● vi intrigue, scheme. **~rsi** vr meddle. **in'trigo** nm plot; **intrighi** pl intrigues

in'trinseco a intrinsic

in'triso a **~ di** soaked in

intri'stirsi vr grow sad

intro'durre vt introduce; (inserire) insert; **~rre a** (iniziare a) introduce to. **~rsi** vr get in (**in** to). **~t'tivo** a (pagine, discorso) introductory. **~zi'one** nf introduction

in'troito nm income, revenue; (incasso) takings pl

intro'metter|e vt introduce. **~si** vr interfere; (interporsi) intervene. **intromissi'one** nf intervention

intro'vabile a that can't be found; (prodotto) unobtainable

intro'verso, -a a introverted ● nmf introvert

intrufo'larsi vr sneak in

in'truglio nm concoction

intrusi'one nf intrusion. **in'truso, -a** nmf intruder

intu'ire vt perceive

intui|tiva'mente adv intuitively. **~'tivo** a intuitive. **in'tuito** nm intuition. **~zi'one** nf intuition

inuguagli'anza nf inequality

inu'mano a inhuman

inu'mare vt inter

inumi'dir|e vt dampen; moisten (labbra). **~si** vr become damp

i'nutil|e a useless; (superfluo) unnecessary. **~ità** nf uselessness

inutiliz'za|bile a unusable. **~to** a unused

inutil'mente adv fruitlessly

inva'dente a intrusive

in'vadere vt invade; (affollare) overrun

invali'd|are vt invalidate. **~ità** nf disability; Jur invalidity. **in'valido, -a** a invalid; (handicappato) disabled ● nmf disabled person

in'vano adv in vain

invari'abile a invariable

invari'ato a unchanged

invasi'one nf invasion. **in'vaso** pp di **invadere**. **inva'sore** a invading ● nm invader

invecchia'mento nm (di vino) maturation

invecchi'are vt/i age

in'vece adv instead; (anzi) but; ~ di instead of

inve'ire vi ~ contro inveigh against

inven'd|ibile a unsaleable. ~uto a unsold

inven'tare vt invent

inventari'are vt make an inventory of. inven'tario nm inventory

inven|'tivo, -a a inventive ● nf inventiveness. ~-'tore, ~'trice nmf inventor. ~zi'one nf invention

inver'nale a wintry. in'verno nm winter

invero'simile a improbable

inversa'mente adv inversely; ~ proporzionale in inverse proportion

inversi'one nf inversion; Mech reversal. in'verso a inverse; (opposto) opposite ● nm opposite

inverte'brato a & nm invertebrate

inver'ti|re vt reverse; (capovolgere) turn upside down. ~to, -a nmf homosexual

investi'ga|re vt investigate. ~'tore nm investigator. ~zi'one nf investigation

investi'mento nm investment; (incidente) crash

inve'sti|re vt invest; (urtare) collide with; (travolgere) run over; ~re qcno di invest sb with. ~'tura nf investiture

invet'tiva nf invective

invi|'are vt send. ~to, -a nmf envoy; (di giornale) correspondent

invidi|a nf envy. ~'are vt envy. ~'oso a envious

invigo'rir|e vt invigorate. ~si vr become strong

invin'cibile a invincible

in'vio nm dispatch; Comput enter

invio'labile a inviolable

invipe'ri|rsi vr get nasty. ~to a furious

invi'sibil|e a invisible. ~ità nf invisibility

invi'tante a (piatto, profumo) enticing

invi'ta|re vt invite. ~to, -a nmf guest. in'vito nm invitation

invo'ca|re vt invoke; (implorare) beg. ~zi'one nf invocation

invogli'ar|e vt tempt; (indurre) induce. ~si vr ~si di take a fancy to

involon|taria'mente adv involuntarily. ~'tario a involuntary

invol'tino nm Culin beef olive

in'volto nm parcel; (fagotto) bundle

in'volucro nm wrapping

invulne'rabile a invulnerable

inzacche'rare vt splash with mud

inzup'par|e vt soak; (intingere) dip. ~si vr get soaked

'io pron I; chi è? – [sono] io who is it? – [it's] me; l'ho fatto io [stesso] I did it myself ● nm l'~ the ego

i'odio nm iodine

I'onio nm lo ~ the Ionian [Sea]

i'osa: a ~ adv in abundance

iperat'tivo a hyperactive

ipermer'cato nm hypermarket

iper'metrope a long-sighted

ipersen'sibile a hypersensitive

ipertensi'one nf high blood pressure

ip'no|si nf hypnosis. ~tico a hypnotic. ~'tismo nm hypnotism. ~tiz'zare vt hypnotize

ipoca'lorico a low-calorie

ipocon'driaco, -a a & nmf hypochondriac

ipocri'sia nf hypocrisy. i'pocrita a hypocritical ● nmf hypocrite

ipo'te|ca nf mortgage. ~'care vt mortgage

i'potesi nf inv hypothesis; (caso, eventualità) eventuality. ipo'tetico a hypothetical. ipotiz'zare vt hypothesize

'ippico, -a a horse attrib ● nf riding

ippoca'stano nm horse-chestnut

ip'podromo nm racecourse

ippo'potamo nm hippopotamus

'ira nf anger. ~'scibile a irascible

i'rato a irate

'iride nf Anat iris; (arcobaleno) rainbow

Ir'lan|da nf Ireland. ~da del Nord Northern Ireland. i~'dese a Irish ● nm Irishman; (lingua) Irish ● nf Irishwoman

iro'nia nf irony. i'ronico a ironic[al]

irradi'a|re vt/i radiate. ~zi'one nf radiation

irraggiun'gibile a unattainable

irragio'nevole a unreasonable; (speranza, timore) irrational; (assurdo) absurd

irrazio'nal|e a irrational. ~ità a irrationality. ~'mente adv irrationally

irre'a|le a unreal. ~'listico a unrealistic. ~liz'zabile a unattainable. ~ltà nf unreality

irrecupe'rabile a irrecoverable

irrego'lar|e a irregular. ~ità nf inv irregularity

irremo'vibile a fig adamant

irrepa'rabile a irreparable

irrepe'ribile a not to be found; sarò ~ I won't be contactable

irrepren'sibile a irreproachable

irrepri'mibile a irrepressible

irrequi'eto a restless
irresi'stibile a irresistible
irrespon'sabil|e a irresponsible.
  ~ità nf irresponsibility
irrever'sibile a irreversible
irrevo'cabile a irrevocable
irricono'scibile a unrecognizable
irri'ga|re vt irrigate; ⟨fiume:⟩ flow
  through. **~zi'one** nf irrigation
irrigidi'mento nm stiffening
irrigi'dir|e vt, **~si** vr stiffen
irrile'vante a unimportant
irrimedi'abile a irreparable
irripe'tibile a unrepeatable
irri'sorio a derisive; ⟨differenza,
  particolare, somma⟩ insignificant
irri'ta|bile a irritable. **~nte** a aggra-
  vating
irri'ta|re vt irritate. **~rsi** vr get an-
  noyed. **~to** a irritated; ⟨gola⟩ sore.
  ~zi'one nf irritation
irrobu'stir|e vt fortify. **~si** vr get
  stronger
ir'rompere vi burst (in into)
irro'rare vt sprinkle
irru'ente a impetuous
irruzi'one nf fare **~ in** burst into
i'scritto, -a pp di **iscrivere** ● a registered ● nmf member; **per ~ in** writing
i'scriver|e vt register. **~si** vr **~si a**
  register at, enrol at ⟨scuola⟩; join
  ⟨circolo ecc⟩. **iscrizi'one** nf registration; ⟨epigrafe⟩ inscription
i'sla|mico a Islamic. **~'mismo** nm Is-
  lam
I'slan|da nf Iceland. **i~'dese** a Iceland-
  ic ● nmf Icelander
'isola nf island. **le isole britanniche**
  the British Isles. **~ pedonale** traffic island. **~ spartitraffico** traffic island.
  iso'lano, -a a insular ● nmf islander
iso'lante a insulating ● nm insulator
iso'la|re vt isolate; Mech, Electr insu-
  late; ⟨acusticamente⟩ soundproof. **~to**
  a isolated ● nm ⟨di appartamenti⟩
  block
ispes'sir|e vt, **~si** vr thicken
ispetto'rato nm inspectorate. **ispet-**

'tore nm inspector. **ispezio'nare** vt inspect. **ispezi'one** nf inspection
'ispido a bristly
ispi'ra|re vt inspire; suggest ⟨idea,
  soluzione⟩. **~rsi** vr **~rsi a** be based on.
  ~to a inspired. **~zi'one** nf inspiration;
  ⟨idea⟩ idea
Isra'ele nm Israel. **i~i'ano, -a** a &
  nmf Israeli
is'sare vt hoist
istan'taneo, -a a instantaneous ● nf
  snapshot
i'stante nm instant; **all'~** instantly
i'stanza nf petition
i'sterico a hysterical. **iste'rismo** nm
  hysteria
isti'ga|re vt instigate; **~re qcno al
  male** incite sb to evil. **~'tore, ~'trice**
  nmf instigator. **~zi'one** nf instigation
istin'tiva'mente adv instinctively.
  ~'tivo a instinctive. **i'stinto** nm instinct; **d'istinto** instinctively
istitu'ire vt institute; ⟨fondare⟩ found;
  initiate ⟨manifestazione⟩
isti'tu|to nm institute; ⟨universitario⟩
  department; Sch secondary school. **~to
  di bellezza** beauty salon. **~'tore,
  ~'trice** nmf ⟨insegnante⟩ tutor; ⟨fonda-
  tore⟩ founder
istituzio'nale a institutional. **istitu-
  zi'one** nf institution
'istmo nm isthmus
'istrice nm porcupine
istru'i|re vt instruct; ⟨addestrare⟩
  train; ⟨informare⟩ inform; Jur prepare.
  ~to a educated
istrut't|ivo a instructive. **~ore, ~rice**
  nmf instructor; **giudice ~ore** examining magistrate. **~oria** nf Jur investigation. **istruzi'one** nf education; ⟨indi-
  cazione⟩ instruction
I'tali|a nf Italy. **i~'ano, -a** a & nmf Ital-
  ian
itine'rario nm route, itinerary
itte'rizia nf jaundice
'ittico a fishing attrib
I.V.A. nf abbr (**imposta sul valore
  aggiunto**) VAT

Jj

jack *nm inv* jack
jazz *nm* jazz. **jaz'zista** *nmf* jazz player
jeep *nf inv* jeep
'jolly *nm inv* (*carta da gioco*) joker

Jugo'slav|ia *nf* Yugoslavia. **j~o, -a** *a*
& *nmf* Yugoslav[ian]
ju'niores *nmfpl Sport* juniors

Kk

ka'jal *nm inv* kohl
kara'oke *nm inv* karaoke
ka'rate *nm* karate

kg *abbr* (**chilogrammo**) kg
km *abbr* (**chilometro**) km

Ll

l' *def art mf* (*before vowel*) the; *vedi* **il**
la *def art f* the; *vedi* **il** ●*pron* (*oggetto, riferito a persona*) her; (*riferito a cosa, animale*) it; (*forma di cortesia*) you ●*nm inv Mus* (*chiave, nota*) A
là *adv* there; **di là** (*in quel luogo*) in there; (*da quella parte*) that way; **eccolo là!** there he is!; **farsi più in là** (*far largo*) make way; **là dentro** in there; **là fuori** out there; [**ma**] **va là!** come off it!; **più in là** (*nel tempo*) later on; (*nello spazio*) further on
'labbro *nm* (*pl nf Anat* **labbra**) lip
labi'rinto *nm* labyrinth; (*di sentieri ecc*) maze
labora'torio *nm* laboratory; (*di negozio, officina ecc*) workshop
labori'oso *a* (*operoso*) industrious; (*faticoso*) laborious
labu'rista *a* Labour ●*nmf* member of the Labour Party

'lacca *nf* lacquer; (*per capelli*) hairspray, lacquer. **lac'care** *vt* lacquer
'laccio *nm* noose; (*lazo*) lasso; (*trappola*) snare; (*stringa*) lace
lace'rante *a* (*grido*) earsplitting
lace'ra|re *vt* tear; lacerate (*carne*). **~rsi** *vr* tear. **~zi'one** *nf* laceration. **'lacero** *a* torn; (*cencioso*) ragged
la'conico *a* laconic
'lacri|ma *nf* tear; (*goccia*) drop. **~'mare** *vi* weep. **~'mevole** *a* tear-jerking
lacri'mogeno *a* gas ~ tear gas
lacri'moso *a* tearful
la'cuna *nf* gap. **lacu'noso** *a* (*preparazione, resoconto*) incomplete
la'custre *a* lake *attrib*
lad'dove *conj* whereas
'ladro, -a *nmf* thief; **al** ~! stop thief! **~'cinio** *nm* theft. **la'druncolo** *nm* petty thief
'lager *nm inv* concentration camp

laggiù *adv* down there; (*lontano*) over there

'lagna *nf* (*fam: persona*) moaning Minnie; (*film*) bore

la'gna|nza *nf* complaint. **~rsi** *vr* moan; (*protestare*) complain (**di** about).

la'gnoso *a* (*persona*) moaning

'lago *nm* lake

la'guna *nf* lagoon

'laico, -a *a* lay; (*vita*) secular ● *nm* layman ● *nf* laywoman

'lama *nf* blade ● *nm inv* (*animale*) llama

lambic'carsi *vr* **~ il cervello** rack one's brains

lam'bire *vt* lap

lamé *nm inv* lamé

lamen'tar|e *vt* lament. **~si** *vr* moan. **~si di** (*lagnarsi*) complain about

lamen'te|la *nf* complaint. **~vole** *a* mournful; (*pietoso*) pitiful. **la'mento** *nm* moan

la'metta *nf* ~ [**da barba**] razor blade

lami'era *nf* sheet metal

'lamina *nf* foil. ~ **d'oro** gold leaf

lami'na|re *vt* laminate. **~to a** *a* laminated ● *nm* laminate; (*tessuto*) lamé

'lampa|da *nf* lamp. **~da abbronzante** sunlamp. **~da a pila** torch. **~'dario** *nm* chandelier. **~'dina** *nf* light bulb

lam'pante *a* clear

lampeggi'a|re *vi* flash. **~'tore** *nm* *Auto* indicator

lampi'one *nm* street lamp

'lampo *nm* flash of lightning; (*luce*) flash; **lampi** *pl* lightning *sg*. ~ **di genio** stroke of genius. [**cerniera**] ~ zip [fastener], zipper *Am*

lam'pone *nm* raspberry

'lana *nf* wool; **di** ~ woollen. ~ **d'acciaio** steel wool. ~ **vergine** new wool. ~ **di vetro** glass wool

lan'cetta *nf* pointer; (*di orologio*) hand

'lancia *nf* (*arma*) spear, lance; *Naut* launch

lanci'ar|e *vt* throw; (*da un aereo*) drop; launch (*missile, prodotto*); give (*grido*); **~e uno sguardo** a glance at. **~si** *vr* fling oneself; (*intraprendere*) launch out

lanci'nante *a* piercing

'lancio *nm* throwing; (*da aereo*) drop; (*di missile, prodotto*) launch. ~ **del disco** discus [throwing]. ~ **del giavellotto** javelin [throwing]. ~ **del peso** putting the shot

'landa *nf* heath

'languido *a* languid

lani'ero *a* wool

lani'ficio *nm* woollen mill

lan'terna *nf* lantern; (*faro*) lighthouse

la'nugine *nf* down

lapi'dare *vt* stone; *fig* demolish

lapi'dario *a* (*conciso*) terse

'lapide *nf* tombstone; (*commemorativa*) memorial tablet

'lapis *nm inv* pencil

'lapsus *nm inv* lapse, error

'lardo *nm* lard

larga'mente *adv* (*ampiamente*) widely

lar'ghezza *nf* width, breadth; *fig* liberality. ~ **di vedute** broadmindedness

'largo *a* wide; (*ampio*) broad; (*abito*) loose; (*liberale*) liberal; (*abbondante*) generous; **stare alla larga** keep away; ~ **di manica** generous; **essere ~ di spalle/vedute** be broad-shouldered/minded ● *nm* width; **andare al ~** *Naut* go out to sea; **fare ~** make room; **farsi ~** make one's way; **al ~ di** off the coast of

'larice *nm* larch

la'ringe *nf* larynx. **larin'gite** *nf* laryngitis

'larva *nf* larva; (*persona emaciata*) shadow

la'sagne *nfpl* lasagna *sg*

lasciapas'sare *nm inv* pass

lasci'ar|e *vt* leave; (*rinunciare*) give up; (*rimetterci*) lose; (*smettere di tenere*) let go [of]; (*concedere*) let; **~e di fare qcsa** (*smettere*) stop doing sth; **lascia perdere!** forget it!; **lascialo venire, lascia che venga** let him come. **~si** *vr* (*reciproco*) leave each other, split up; **~si andare** let oneself go

'lascito *nm* legacy

'laser *a & nm inv* [**raggio**] ~ laser [beam]

lassa'tivo *a & nm* laxative

'lasso *nm* ~ **di tempo** period of time

lassù *adv* up there

'lastra *nf* slab; (*di ghiaccio*) sheet; (*di metallo, Phot*) plate; (*radiografia*) X-ray [plate]

lastri'care *vt* pave. **~to, 'lastrico** *nm* pavement; **sul lastrico** on one's beamends

la'tente *a* latent

late'rale *a* side *attrib*; *Med, Techn ecc* lateral; **via** ~ side street

late'rizi *nmpl* bricks

lati'fondo *nm* large estate

la'tino *a & nm* Latin

lati'tante *a* in hiding ● *nmf* fugitive [from justice]

lati'tudine *nf* latitude

lato | leggero

'lato a (ampio) broad; in senso ~ broadly speaking ●nm side; (aspetto) aspect; a ~ di beside; dal ~ mio (punto di vista) for my part; d'altro ~ fig on the other hand
la'tra|re vi bark. ~to nm barking
la'trina nf latrine
'latta nf tin, can
lat'taio nm milkman
lat'tante a breast-fed ●nmf suckling
'latt|e nm milk. ~e acido sour milk. ~e condensato condensed milk. ~e detergente cleansing milk. ~e in polvere powdered milk. ~e scremato skimmed milk. ~eo a milky. ~e'ria nf dairy. ~i'cini nmpl dairy products. ~i'era nf milk jug
lat'tina nf can
lat'tuga nf lettuce
'laure|a nf degree; prendere la ~a graduate. ~'ando, -a nmf final-year student
laure'a|rsi vr graduate. ~to, -a a & nmf graduate
'lauro nm laurel
'lauto a lavish; ~ guadagno handsome profit
'lava nf lava
la'vabile a washable
la'vabo nm wash-basin
la'vaggio nm washing. ~ automatico (per auto) carwash. ~ del cervello brainwashing. ~ a secco dry-cleaning
la'vagna nf slate; Sch blackboard
la'van|da nf wash; Bot lavender; fare una ~da gastrica have one's stomach pumped. ~'daia nf washerwoman. ~de'ria nf laundry. ~deria automatica launderette
lavan'dino nm sink; (hum: persona) bottomless pit
lavapi'atti nmf inv dishwasher
la'var|e vt wash; ~e i piatti wash up. ~si vr wash, have a wash; ~si i denti brush one's teeth; ~si le mani wash one's hands
lava'secco nmf inv dry-cleaner's
lavasto'viglie nf inv dishwasher
la'vata nf wash; darsi una ~ have a wash; ~ di capo fig scolding
lava'tivo, -a nmf idler
lava'trice nf washing-machine
lavo'rante nmf worker
lavo'ra|re vi work ●vt work; knead (pasta ecc); till (la terra); ~re a maglia knit. ~'tivo a working. ~to a (pietra, legno) carved; (cuoio) tooled; (metallo) wrought. ~'tore, ~'trice nmf worker

●a working. ~zi'one nf manufacture; (di terra) working; (artigianale) workmanship; (del terreno) cultivation.
lavo'rio nm intense activity
la'voro nm work; (faticoso, sociale) labour; (impiego) job; Theat play; mettersi al ~ set to work (su on). ~ a maglia knitting. ~ nero moonlighting. ~ straordinario overtime. ~ a tempo pieno full-time job. lavori pl di casa housework. lavori pl in corso roadworks. lavori pl forzati hard labour. lavori pl stradali roadworks
le def art fpl the; vedi il ●pron (oggetto) them; (a lei) her; (forma di cortesia) you
le'al|e a loyal. ~'mente adv loyally. ~tà nf loyalty
'lebbra nf leprosy
'lecca 'lecca nm inv lollipop
leccapi'edi nmf inv pej bootlicker
lec'ca|re vt lick; fig suck up to. ~rsi vr lick; (fig: agghindarsi) doll oneself up; da ~rsi i baffi mouth-watering. ~ta nf lick
leccor'nia nf delicacy
'lecito a lawful; (permesso) permissible
'ledere vt damage; Med injure
'lega nf league; (di metalli) alloy; far ~ con qcno take up with sb
le'gaccio nm string; (delle scarpe) shoelace
le'gal|e a legal ●nm lawyer. ~ità nf legality. ~iz'zare vt authenticate; (rendere legale) legalize. ~'mente adv legally
le'game nm tie; (amoroso) liaison; (connessione) link
lega'mento nm Med ligament
le'gar|e vt tie; tie up (persona); tie together (due cose); (unire, rilegare) bind; alloy (metalli); (connettere) connect; ~sela al dito bear a grudge ●vi (far lega) get on well. ~si vr bind oneself; ~si a qcno become attached to sb
le'gato nm legacy; Relig legate
lega'tura nf tying; (di libro) binding
le'genda nf legend
'legge nf law; (parlamentare) act; a norma di ~ by law
leg'genda nf legend; (didascalia) caption. leggen'dario a legendary
'leggere vt/i read
legge'r|ezza nf lightness; (frivolezza) frivolity; (incostanza) fickleness. ~'mente adv slightly
leg'gero a light; (bevanda) weak; (lieve) slight; (frivolo) frivolous; (incostante) fickle; alla leggera frivolously

leg'gibile a ⟨scrittura⟩ legible; ⟨stile⟩ readable

leg'gio nm lectern; Mus music stand

legife'rare vi legislate

legio'nario nm legionary. **legi'one** nf legion

legisla'tivo a legislative. **~'tore** nm legislator. **~'tura** nf legislature. **~zi'one** nf legislation

legittimità nf legitimacy. **le'gittimo** a legitimate; ⟨giusto⟩ proper; **legittima difesa** self-defence

'legna nf firewood

le'gname nm timber

le'gnata nf blow with a stick

'legno nm wood; **di ~** wooden. **~ compensato** plywood. **le'gnoso** a woody

le'gume nm pod

'lei pron ⟨soggetto⟩ she; ⟨oggetto, con prep⟩ her; ⟨forma di cortesia⟩ you; **lo ha fatto ~ stessa** she did it herself

'lembo nm edge; ⟨di terra⟩ strip

'lemma nm headword

'lena nf vigour

le'nire vt soothe

lenta'mente adv slowly

'lente nf lens. **~ a contatto** contact lens. **~ d'ingrandimento** magnifying glass

len'tezza nf slowness

len'ticchia nf lentil

len'tiggine nf freckle

'lento a slow; ⟨allentato⟩ slack; ⟨abito⟩ loose

'lenza nf fishing-line

len'zuolo nm ⟨pl f lenzuola⟩ nm sheet

le'one nm lion; Astr Leo

leo'pardo nm leopard

'lepre nf hare

'lercio a filthy

'lesbica nf lesbian

lesi'nare vt grudge ● vi be stingy

lesio'nare vt damage. **lesi'one** nf lesion

'leso pp di **ledere** ● a injured

les'sare vt boil

'lessico nm vocabulary

'lesso a boiled ● nm boiled meat

'lesto a quick; ⟨mente⟩ sharp

le'tale a lethal

leta'maio nm dunghill; fig pigsty. **le'tame** nm dung

le'targico a lethargic. **~o** nm lethargy; ⟨di animali⟩ hibernation

le'tizia nf joy

'lettera nf letter; **alla ~** literally; **~ maiuscola** capital letter; **~ minuscola** small letter; **lettere** pl ⟨letteratura⟩

literature sg; Univ Arts; **dottore in lettere** BA, Bachelor of Arts

lette'rale a literal

lette'rario a literary

lette'rato a well-read

lettera'tura nf literature

let'tiga nf stretcher

let'tino nm cot; Med couch

'letto nm bed. **~ a castello** bunkbed. **~ a una piazza** single bed. **~ a due piazze** double bed. **~ matrimoniale** double bed

letto'rato nm ⟨corso⟩ ≈ tutorial

let'tore, -'trice nmf reader; Univ language assistant ● nm Comput disk drive. **~ di CD-ROM** CD-Rom drive

let'tura nf reading

leuce'mia nf leukaemia

'leva nf lever; Mil call-up; **far ~** lever. **~ del cambio** gear lever

le'vante nm East; ⟨vento⟩ east wind

le'va|re vt ⟨alzare⟩ raise; ⟨togliere⟩ take away; ⟨rimuovere⟩ take off; ⟨estrarre⟩ pull out; **~re di mezzo qcsa** get sth out of the way. **~rsi** vr rise; ⟨da letto⟩ get up; **~rsi di mezzo, ~rsi dai piedi** get out of the way. **~ta** nf rising; ⟨di posta⟩ collection

leva'taccia nf **fare una ~** get up at the crack of dawn

leva'toio a **ponte ~** drawbridge

levi'ga|re vt smooth; ⟨con carta vetro⟩ rub down. **~to** a ⟨superficie⟩ polished

levri'ero nm greyhound

lezi'one nf lesson; Univ lecture; ⟨rimprovero⟩ rebuke

lezi'oso a ⟨stile, modi⟩ affected

li pron mpl them

lì adv there, **fin lì** as far as there; **giù di lì** thereabouts; **lì per lì** there and then

'Libano nm Lebanon

'libbra nf ⟨peso⟩ pound

li'beccio nm south-west wind

li'bellula nf dragon-fly

libe'rale a liberal; ⟨generoso⟩ generous ● nmf liberal

libe'ra|re vt free; release ⟨prigioniero⟩; vacate ⟨stanza⟩; ⟨salvare⟩ rescue. **~rsi** vr ⟨stanza:⟩ become vacant; Teleph become free; ⟨da impegno⟩ get rid of it; **~rsi di** get rid of. **~'tore, ~'trice** a liberating ● nmf liberator. **~'torio** a liberating. **~zi'one** nf liberation; **la L~zione** ⟨ricorrenza⟩ Liberation Day

'liber|o a free; ⟨strada⟩ clear. **~o docente** a qualified university lecturer. **~o professionista** self-employed person. **~tà** nf inv freedom; ⟨di pri *gioniero)* release. **~tà provvisoria** *Jur* bail; **~tà** *pl (confidenze)* liberties

'liberty *nm & a inv* Art Nouveau

'Libi|a *nf* Libya. **l~co, -a** *a & nmf* Libyan

li'bidi|ne *nf* lust. **~'noso** *a* lustful. **li'bido** *nf* libido

libra'io *nm* bookseller

libre'ria *nf (negozio)* bookshop; *(mobile)* bookcase; *(biblioteca)* library

li'bretto *nm* booklet; *Mus* libretto. **~ degli assegni** cheque book. **~ di circolazione** logbook. **~ d'istruzioni** instruction booklet. **~ di risparmio** bankbook. **~ universitario** *book held by students which records details of their exam performances*

'libro *nm* book. **~ giallo** thriller. **~ paga** payroll

lice'ale *nmf* secondary-school student ● *a* secondary-school *attrib*

li'cenza *nf* licence; *(permesso)* permission; *Mil* leave; *Sch* school-leaving certificate; **essere in ~** be on leave

licenzia'mento *nm* dismissal

licenzi'a|re *vt* dismiss, sack *fam.* **~rsi** *vr (da un impiego)* resign; *(accomiatarsi)* take one's leave

li'ceo *nm* secondary school, high school. **~ classico** *secondary school with an emphasis on humanities.* **~ scientifico** *secondary school with an emphasis on sciences*

li'chene *nm* lichen

'lido *nm* beach

li'eto *a* glad; *(evento)* happy; **molto ~!** pleased to meet you!

li'eve *a* light; *(debole)* faint; *(trascurabile)* slight

lievi'tare *vi* rise ● *vt* leaven. **li'evito** *nm* yeast. **lievito in polvere** baking powder

'lifting *nm inv* face-lift

'ligio *a* **essere ~ al dovere** have a sense of duty

'lilla *nf Bot* lilac ● *nm (colore)* lilac

'lima *nf* file

limacci'oso *a* slimy

li'mare *vt* file

'limbo *nm* limbo

li'metta *nf* nail-file

limi'ta|re *nm* threshold ● *vt* limit. **~rsi** *vr* **~rsi a fare qcsa** restrict oneself to doing sth; **~rsi in qcsa** cut down on sth. **~'tivo** *a* limiting. **~to** *a* limited. **~zi'one** *nf* limitation

'limite *nm* limit; *(confine)* boundary. **~ di velocità** speed limit

li'mitrofo *a* neighbouring

limo'nata *nf (bibita)* lemonade; *(succo)* lemon juice

li'mone *nm* lemon; *(albero)* lemon tree

'limpido *a* clear; *(occhi)* limpid

'lince *nf* lynx

linci'are *vt* lynch

'lindo *a* neat; *(pulito)* clean

'linea *nf* line; *(di autobus, aereo)* route; *(di metro)* line; *(di abito)* cut; *(di auto, mobile)* design; *(fisico)* figure; **in ~ d'aria** as the crow flies; **è caduta la ~** I've been cut off; **in ~ di massima** as a rule; **a grandi linee** in outline; **mantenere la ~** keep one's figure; **in prima ~** in the front line; **mettersi in ~** line up; **nave di ~** liner; **volo di ~** scheduled flight. **~ d'arrivo** finishing line. **~ continua** unbroken line

linea'menti *nmpl* features

line'are *a* linear; *(discorso)* to the point; *(ragionamento)* consistent

line'etta *nf (tratto lungo)* dash; *(d'unione)* hyphen

lin'gotto *nm* ingot

'lingu|a *nf* tongue; *(linguaggio)* language. **~'accia** *nf (persona)* backbiter. **~'aggio** *nm* language. **~'etta** *nf (di scarpa)* tongue; *(di strumento)* reed; *(di busta)* flap

lingu'ist|a *nmf* linguist. **~ica** *nf* linguistics *sg.* **~ico** *a* linguistic

'lino *nm Bot* flax; *(tessuto)* linen

li'noleum *nm* linoleum

liofiliz'za|re *vt* freeze-dry. **~to** *a* freeze-dried

liposuzi'one *nf* liposuction

lique'far|e *vt,* **~si** *vr* liquefy; *(sciogliersi)* melt

liqui'da|re *vt* liquidate; settle *(conto)*; pay off *(debiti)*; clear *(merce)*; *(fam: uccidere)* get rid of. **~zi'one** *nf* liquidation; *(di conti)* settling; *(di merce)* clearance sale

'liquido *a & nm* liquid

liqui'rizia *nf* liquorice

li'quore *nm* liqueur; **liquori** *pl (bevande alcooliche)* liquors

'lira *nf* lira; *Mus* lyre

'lirico, -a *a* lyrical; *(poesia)* lyric; *(cantante, musica)* opera *attrib* ● *nf* lyric poetry; *Mus* opera

'lisca *nf* fishbone; **avere la ~** *(fam: nel parlare)* have a lisp

lisci'are *vt* smooth; *(accarezzare)* stroke. **'liscio** *a* smooth; *(capelli)* straight; *(liquore)* neat; *(non gassato)* still; **passarla liscia** get away with it '**liso** *a* worn [out]

'**lista** *nf* list; (*striscia*) strip. ~ **di attesa** waiting list; **in ~ di attesa** *Aeron* stand-by. ~ **elettorale** electoral register. ~ **di nozze** wedding list. **li'stare** *vt* edge; *Comput* list

li'stino *nm* list. ~ **prezzi** price list

Lit. *abbr* (**lire italiane**) Italian lire

'**lite** *nf* quarrel; (*baruffa*) row; *Jur* lawsuit

liti'gare *vi* quarrel. **li'tigio** *nm* quarrel. **litigi'oso** *a* quarrelsome

lito'rale *a* coastal ● *nm* coast

'**litro** *nm* litre

li'turgico *a* liturgical

li'vella *nf* level. ~ **a bolla d'aria** spirit level

livel'lar|e *vt* level. ~**si** *vr* level out

li'vello *nm* level; **passaggio a ~** level crossing; **sotto/sul ~ del mare** below/above sea level

'**livido** *a* livid; (*per il freddo*) blue; (*per una botta*) black and blue ● *nm* bruise

Li'vorno *nf* Leghorn

'**lizza** *nf* lists *pl*; **essere in ~ per qcsa** be in the running for sth

lo *def art m* (*before s + consonant, gn, ps, z*) the; *vedi* **il** ● *pron* (*riferito a persona*) him; (*riferito a cosa*) it; **non lo so** I don't know

'**lobo** *nm* lobe

lo'cal|e *a* local ● *nm* (*stanza*) room; (*treno*) local train; ~**i** *pl* (*edifici*) premises. ~**e notturno** night-club. ~**ità** *nf inv* locality

localiz'zare *vt* localize; (*trovare*) locate

lo'canda *nf* inn

locan'dina *nf* bill, poster

loca'|tario, -a *nmf* tenant. ~**'tore, ~'trice** *nm* landlord ● *nf* landlady. ~**zi'one** *nf* tenancy

locomo'|tiva *nf* locomotive. ~**zi'one** *nf* locomotion; **mezzi di ~zione** means of transport

'**loculo** *nm* burial niche

lo'custa *nf* locust

locuzi'one *nf* expression

lo'dare *vt* praise. '**lode** *nf* praise; **laurea con lode** first-class degree

'**loden** *nm inv* (*cappotto*) loden coat

lo'devole *a* praiseworthy

'**lodola** *nf* lark

'**loggia** *nf* loggia; (*massonica*) lodge

loggi'one *nm* gallery, the gods

'**logica** *nf* logic

logica'mente *adv* (*in modo logico*) logically; (*ovviamente*) of course

'**logico** *a* logical

lo'gistica *nf* logistics *sg*

logo'rante *a* (*esperienza*) wearing

logo'ra|re *vt* wear out; (*sciupare*) waste. ~**rsi** *vr* wear out; (*persona:*) wear oneself out. **logo'rio** *nm* wear and tear. **lo'goro** *a* worn-out

lom'baggine *nf* lumbago

Lombar'dia *nf* Lombardy

lom'bata *nf* loin. '**lombo** *nm Anat* loin

lom'brico *nm* earthworm

'**Londra** *nf* London

lon'gevo *a* long-lived

longi'lineo *a* tall and slim

longi'tudine *nf* longitude

lontana'mente *adv* distantly; (*vagamente*) vaguely; **neanche ~** not for a moment

lonta'nanza *nf* distance; (*separazione*) separation; **in ~** in the distance

lon'tano *a* far; (*distante*) distant; (*nel tempo*) far-off, distant; (*parente*) distant; (*vago*) vague; (*assente*) absent; **più ~** further ● *adv* far [away]; **da ~** from a distance; **tenersi ~ da** keep away from

'**lontra** *nf* otter

lo'quace *a* talkative

'**lordo** *a* dirty; (*somma, peso*) gross

'**loro**[1] *pron pl* (*soggetto*) they; (*oggetto*) them; (*forma di cortesia*) you; **sta a ~** it is up to them

'**loro**[2] (**il ~** *m,* **la ~** *f,* **i ~** *mpl,* **le ~** *fpl*) *a* their; (*forma di cortesia*) your; **un ~ amico** a friend of theirs; (*forma di cortesia*) a friend of yours ● *pron* theirs; (*forma di cortesia*) yours; **i ~** their folk

lo'sanga *nf* lozenge; **a losanghe** diamond-shaped

'**losco** *a* suspicious

'**loto** *nm* lotus

'**lott|a** *nf* fight, struggle; (*contrasto*) conflict; *Sport* wrestling. **lot'tare** *vi* fight, struggle; *Sport, fig* wrestle. ~**a'tore** *nm* wrestler

lotte'ria *nf* lottery

'**lotto** *nm* [national] lottery; (*porzione*) lot; (*di terreno*) plot

lozi'one *nf* lotion

lubrifi'ca|nte *a* lubricating ● *nm* lubricant. ~**re** *vt* lubricate

luc'chetto *nm* padlock

lucci'ca|nte *a* sparkling. ~**re** *vi* sparkle. **lucci'chio** *nm* sparkle

'**luccio** *nm* pike

'**lucciola** *nf* glow-worm

'**luce** *nf* light; **far ~ su** shed light on, **dare alla ~** give birth to. ~ **della luna** moonlight. **luci** *pl* **di posizione** sidelights. ~ **del sole** sunlight

lu'cen|te a shining. **~'tezza** nf shine
lucer'nario nm skylight
lu'certola nf lizard
lucida'labbra nm inv lip gloss
luci'da|re vt polish. **~'trice** nf
[floor-]polisher. **'lucido** a shiny; ⟨pavimento, scarpe⟩ polished; ⟨chiaro⟩ clear; ⟨persona, mente⟩ lucid; ⟨occhi⟩ watery ● nm shine. **lucido [da scarpe]** [shoe] polish
lucra'tivo a lucrative. **'lucro** nm lucre
'luglio nm July
'lugubre a gloomy
'lui pron ⟨soggetto⟩ he; ⟨oggetto, con prep⟩ him; **lo ha fatto ~ stesso** he did it himself
lu'maca nf ⟨mollusco⟩ snail; fig slowcoach
'lume nm lamp; ⟨luce⟩ light; **a ~ di candela** by candlelight
luminosità nf brightness. **lumi'noso** a luminous; ⟨stanza, cielo ecc⟩ bright
'luna nf moon; **chiaro di ~** moonlight; **avere la ~ storta** be in a bad mood. **~ di miele** honeymoon
luna park nm inv fairground
lu'nare a lunar
lu'nario nm almanac; **sbarcare il ~** make both ends meet
lu'natico a moody
lunedì nm inv Monday
lu'netta nf half-moon [shape]
lun'gaggine nf slowness
lun'ghezza nf length. **~ d'onda** wavelength
'lungi adv **ero [ben] ~ dall'immaginare che...** I never dreamt for a moment that...

lungimi'rante a far-seeing
'lungo a long; ⟨diluito⟩ weak; ⟨lento⟩ slow; **saperla lunga** be shrewd ● nm length; **di gran lunga** by far; **andare per le lunghe** drag on ● prep ⟨durante⟩ throughout; ⟨per la lunghezza di⟩ along
lungofi'ume nm riverside
lungo'lago nm lakeside
lungo'mare nm sea front
lungome'traggio nm feature film
lu'notto nm rear window
lu'ogo nm place; ⟨punto preciso⟩ spot; ⟨passo d'autore⟩ passage; **aver ~** take place; **dar ~ a** give rise to; **del ~** ⟨usanze⟩ local. **~ comune** platitude. **~ pubblico** public place
luogote'nente nm Mil lieutenant
lu'petto nm Cub [Scout]
'lupo nm wolf
'luppolo nm hop
'lurido a filthy. **luri'dume** nm filth
lu'singa nf flattery
lusin'ga|re vt flatter. **~arsi** vr flatter oneself; ⟨illudersi⟩ fool oneself. **~hi'ero** a flattering
lus'sa|re vt, **~rsi** vr dislocate. **~zi'one** nf dislocation
Lussem'burgo nm Luxembourg
'lusso nm luxury; **di ~** luxury attrib
lussu'oso a luxurious
lussureggi'ante a luxuriant
lus'suria nf lust
lu'strare vt polish
lu'strino nm sequin
'lustro a shiny ● nm sheen; fig prestige; ⟨quinquennio⟩ five-year period
'lutt|o nm mourning; **~o stretto** deep mourning. **~u'oso** a mournful**

Mm

m abbr ⟨**metro**⟩ m
ma conj but; ⟨eppure⟩ yet; **ma!** ⟨dubbio⟩ I don't know; ⟨indignazione⟩ really!; **ma davvero?** really?; **ma sì!** why not!; ⟨certo che sì⟩ of course!
'macabro a macabre
macché int of course not!
macche'roni nmpl macaroni sg
macche'ronico a ⟨italiano⟩ broken
'macchia¹ nf stain; ⟨di diverso colore⟩ spot; ⟨piccola⟩ speck; **senza ~** spotless
'macchia² nf ⟨boscaglia⟩ scrub; **darsi alla ~** take to the woods
macchi'a|re vt, **~rsi** vr stain. **~to** a ⟨caffè⟩ with a dash of milk; **~to di** ⟨sporco⟩ stained with
'macchina nf machine; ⟨motore⟩ engine; ⟨automobile⟩ car. **~ da cucire** sewing machine. **~ da presa** cine cam-

era, movie camera. **~ da scrivere** typewriter

macchinal'mente *adv* mechanically

macchi'nare *vt* plot

macchi'nario *nm* machinery

macchi'netta *nf* (*per i denti*) brace

macchi'nista *nm Rail* engine-driver; *Naut* engineer; *Theat* stagehand

macchi'noso *a* complicated

mace'donia *nf* fruit salad

macel'la|o *nm* butcher. **~re** *vt* slaughter. **macelle'ria** *nf* butcher's [shop]. **ma'cello** *nm* slaughterhouse; *fig* shambles *sg*; **andare al macello** *fig* go to the slaughter; **mandare al macello** *fig* send to his/her death

mace'rar|e *vt* macerate; *fig* distress. **~si** *vr* be consumed

ma'cerie *nfpl* rubble *sg*; (*rottami*) debris *sg*

ma'cigno *nm* boulder

maci'lento *a* emaciated

'macina *nf* millstone

macinacaffè *nm inv* coffee mill

macina'pepe *nm inv* pepper mill

maci'na|re *vt* mill. **~to** *a* ground ● *nm* (*carne*) mince. **maci'nino** *nm* mill; (*hum: macchina*) old banger

maciul'lare *vt* (*stritolare*) crush

macrobiotic|a *nf* negozio di **~a** health-food shop. **~o** *a* macrobiotic

macro'scopico *a* macroscopic

macu'lato *a* spotted

'madido *a* **~ di** moist with

Ma'donna *nf* Our Lady

mador'nale *a* gross

'madre *nf* mother. **~ lingua** *a inv* inglese **~lingua** English native speaker. **~'patria** *nf* native land. **~'perla** *nf* mother-of-pearl

ma'drina *nf* godmother

maestà *nf* majesty

maestosità *nf* majesty. **mae'stoso** *a* majestic

mae'strale *nm* northwest wind

mae'stranza *nf* workers *pl*

mae'stria *nf* mastery

ma'estro, -a *nmf* teacher ● *nm* master; *Mus* maestro. **~ di cerimonie** master of ceremonies ● *a* (*principale*) chief; (*di grande abilità*) skilful

'mafi|a *nf* Mafia. **~oso** *a* of the Mafia ● *nm* member of the Mafia, Mafioso

'maga *nf* sorceress

ma'gagna *nf* fault

ma'gari *adv* (*forse*) maybe ● *int* I wish! ● *conj* (*per esprimere desiderio*) if only; (*anche se*) even if

magazzini'ere *nm* storesman, warehouseman. **magaz'zino** *nm* warehouse; (*emporio*) shop; **grande magazzino** department store

'maggio *nm* May

maggio'lino *nm* May bug

maggio'rana *nf* marjoram

maggio'ranza *nf* majority

maggio'rare *vt* increase

maggior'domo *nm* butler

maggi'ore *a* (*di dimensioni, numero*) bigger, larger; (*superlativo*) biggest, largest; (*di età*) older; (*superlativo*) oldest; (*di importanza, Mus*) major; (*superlativo*) greatest; **la maggior parte** *di* most; **la maggior parte del tempo** most of the time ● *pron* (*di dimensioni*) the bigger, the larger; (*superlativo*) the biggest, the largest; (*di età*) the older; (*superlativo*) the oldest; (*di importanza*) the major; (*superlativo*) the greatest ● *nm Mil* major; *Aeron* squadron leader. **maggio'renne** *a* of age ● *nmf* adult

maggiori'tario *a* (*sistema*) first-past-the-post *attrib*. **~'mente** *adv* [all] the more; (*più di tutto*) most

'Magi *nmpl* **i re ~** the Magi

ma'gia *nf* magic; (*trucco*) magic trick

magica'mente *adv* magically. **'magico** *a* magic

magi'stero *nm* (*insegnamento*) teaching; (*maestria*) skill; **facoltà di ~** arts faculty

magi'strale *a* masterly; **istituto ~e** teachers' training college

magi'stra|to *nm* magistrate. **~'tura** *nf* magistrature. **la ~tura** the Bench

'magli|a *nf* stitch; (*lavoro ai ferri*) knitting; (*tessuto*) jersey; (*di rete*) mesh; (*di catena*) link; (*indumento*) vest; **fare la ~a** knit. **~a diritta** knit. **~a rosa** (*ciclismo*) ≈ yellow jersey. **~a rovescia** purl. **~e'ria** *nf* knitwear. **~'etta** *nf* **~etta [a maniche corte]** tee-shirt. **~'ficio** *nm* knitwear factory. **ma'glina** *nf* (*tessuto*) jersey

magli'one *nm* sweater

'magma *nm* magma

ma'gnanimo *a* magnanimous

ma'gnate *nm* magnate

ma'gnesi|a *nf* magnesia. **~o** *nm* magnesium

ma'gne|te *nm* magnet. **~tico** *a* magnetic. **~'tismo** *nm* magnetism

magne'tofono *nm* tape recorder

magnifi|ca'mente *adv* magnificently. **~'cenza** *nf* magnificence;

(*generosità*) munificence. **ma'gnifico** *a* magnificent; (*generoso*) munificent

ma'gnolia *nf* magnolia

'**mago** *nm* magician

ma'gone *nm* **avere il ~** be down; **mi è venuto il ~** I've got a lump in my throat

'**magr|a** *nf* low water. **ma'grezza** *nf* thinness. **~o** *a* thin; (*carne*) lean; (*scarso*) meagre

'**mai** *adv* never; (*inter, talvolta*) ever; **caso ~** if anything; **caso ~ tornasse** in case he comes back; **come ~?** why?; **cosa ~?** what on earth?; **~ più** never again; **più che ~** more than ever; **quando ~?** whenever?; **quasi ~** hardly ever

mai'ale *nm* pig; (*carne*) pork

mai'olica *nf* majolica

maio'nese *nf* mayonnaise

'**mais** *nm* maize

mai'uscol|a *nf* capital [letter]. **~o** *a* capital

mal *vedi* **male**

'**mala** *nf* **la ~** *sl* the underworld

mala'fede *nf* bad faith

malaf'fare *nm* **gente di ~** shady characters *pl*

mala'lingua *nf* backbiter

mala'mente *adv* (*ridotto*) badly

malan'dato *a* in bad shape; (*di salute*) in poor health

ma'lanimo *nm* ill will

ma'lanno *nm* misfortune; (*malattia*) illness; **prendersi un ~** catch something

mala'pena: a ~ *adv* hardly

ma'laria *nf* malaria

mala'ticcio *a* sickly

ma'la|to, -a *a* ill, sick; (*pianta*) diseased ●*nmf* sick person. **~ di mente** mentally ill person. **malat'tia** *nf* disease, illness; **ho preso due giorni di malattia** I had two days off sick. **malattia venerea** venereal disease

malaugu'rato *a* ill-omened. **malau'gurio** *nm* bad *o* ill omen

mala'vita *nf* underworld

mala'voglia *nf* unwillingness; **di ~** unwillingly

malcapi'tato *a* wretched

malce'lato *a* ill-concealed

mal'concio *a* battered

malcon'tento *nm* discontent

malco'stume *nm* immorality

mal'destro *a* awkward; (*inesperto*) inexperienced

maldi'cen|te *a* slanderous. **~za** *nf* slander

maldi'sposto *a* ill-disposed

'**male** *adv* badly; **funzionare ~** not work properly; **star ~** be ill; **star ~ a qcno** (*vestito ecc:*) not suit sb; **rimanerci ~** be hurt; **non c'è ~!** not bad at all! ●*nm* evil; (*dolore*) pain; (*malattia*) illness; (*danno*) harm. **distinguere il bene dal ~** know right from wrong; **andare a ~** go off; **aver ~ a** have a pain in; **dove hai ~?** where does it hurt?; **far ~ a qcno** (*provocare dolore*) hurt sb; (*cibo:*) be bad for sb; **le cipolle mi fanno ~** onions don't agree with me; **mi fa ~ la schiena** my back is hurting; **mal d'auto** car-sickness. **mal di denti** toothache. **mal di gola** sore throat. **mal di mare** sea-sickness; **avere il mal di mare** be sea-sick. **mal di pancia** stomach ache. **mal di testa** headache

male'detto *a* cursed; (*orribile*) awful

male'di|re *vt* curse. **~zi'one** *nf* curse; **~zione!** damn!

maledu|cata'mente *adv* rudely. **~'cato** *a* ill-mannered. **~cazi'one** *nf* rudeness

male'fatta *nf* misdeed

male'ficio *nm* witchcraft. **ma'lefico** *a* (*azione*) evil; (*nocivo*) harmful

maleodo'rante *a* foul-smelling

ma'lessere *nm* indisposition; *fig* uneasiness

ma'levolo *a* malevolent

malfa'mato *a* of ill repute

mal'fat|to *a* badly done; (*malformato*) ill-shaped. **~'tore** *nm* wrongdoer

mal'fermo *a* unsteady; (*salute*) poor

malfor'ma|to *a* misshapen. **~zi'one** *nf* malformation

malgo'verno *nm* misgovernment

mal'grado *prep* in spite of ●*conj* although

ma'lia *nf* spell

mali'gn|are *vi* malign. **~ità** *nf* malice; *Med* malignancy. **ma'ligno** *a* malicious; (*perfido*) evil; *Med* malignant

malinco'ni|a *nf* melancholy. **~ca'mente** *adv* melancholically. **malin'conico** *a* melancholy

malincu'ore: a ~ *adv* unwillingly, reluctantly

malinfor'mato *a* misinformed

malintenzio'nato, -a *nmf* miscreant

malin'teso *a* mistaken ●*nm* misunderstanding

ma'lizi|a *nf* malice; (*astuzia*) cunning; (*espediente*) trick. **~'oso** *a* malicious; (*birichino*) mischievous

malle'abile *a* malleable

mal'loppo *nm fam* loot

malme'nare vt ill-treat
mal'messo a (vestito male) shabbily dressed; (casa) poorly furnished; (fig: senza soldi) hard up
malnu'tri|to a undernourished. **~zi'one** nf malnutrition
'**malo** a **in ~ modo** badly
ma'locchio nm evil eye
ma'lora nf ruin; **della ~** awful; **andare in ~** go to ruin
ma'lore nm illness; **essere colto da ~** be suddenly taken ill
malri'dotto a (persona) in a sorry state
mal'sano a unhealthy
'**malta** nf mortar
mal'tempo nm bad weather
'**malto** nm malt
maltrat|ta'mento nm ill-treatment. **~'tare** vt ill-treat
malu'more nm bad mood; **di ~** in a bad mood
mal'vagi|o a wicked. **~tà** nf wickedness
malversazi'one nf embezzlement
mal'visto a unpopular (**da** with)
malvi'vente nm criminal
malvolenti'eri adv unwillingly
malvo'lere vt **farsi ~** make oneself unpopular
'**mamma** nf mummy, mum; **~ mia!** good gracious!
mam'mella nf breast
mam'mifero nm mammal
'**mammola** nf violet
ma'nata nf handful; (colpo) slap
'**manca** nf vedi **manco**
manca'mento nm **avere un ~** faint
man'can|te a missing. **~za** nf lack; (assenza) absence; (insufficienza) shortage; (fallo) fault; (imperfezione) defect; **in ~za d'altro** failing all else; **sento la sua ~za** I miss him
man'care vi be lacking; (essere assente) be missing; (venir meno) fail; (morire) pass away; **~ di** be lacking in; **~a** fail to keep (promessa); **mi manca casa** I miss home; **mi manchi** I miss you; **è mancato il tempo** I didn't have [the] time; **mi mancano 1000 lire** I'm 1,000 lire short; **quanto manca alla partenza?** how long before we leave?; **è mancata la corrente** there was a power failure; **sentirsi ~** feel faint. **sentirsi ~ il respiro** be unable to breathe [properly]; **● ~** miss (bersaglio); **è mancato poco che cadesse** he nearly fell
'**manche** nf inv heat

man'chevole a defective
'**mancia** nf tip
manci'ata nf handful
man'cino a left-handed
'**manco, -a** a left **● nf** left hand **● adv** (nemmeno) not even
man'dante nmf (di delitto) instigator
manda'rancio nm clementine
man'dare vt send; (emettere) give off; utter (suono); **~ a chiamare** send for; **~ avanti la casa** run the house; **~ giù** (ingoiare) swallow
manda'rino nm Bot mandarin
man'data nf consignment; (di serratura) turn; **chiudere a doppia ~** double lock
man'dato nm (incarico) mandate; Jur warrant; (di pagamento) money order. **~ di comparizione [in giudizio]** subpoena. **~ di perquisizione** search warrant
man'dibola nf jaw
mando'lino nm mandolin
man'dor|la nf almond; **a ~la** (occhi) almond shaped. **~'lato** nm nut brittle (type of nougat). **~lo** nm almond[-tree]
'**mandria** nf herd
maneg'gevole a easy to handle.
maneggi'are vt handle
ma'neggio nm handling; (intrigo) plot; (scuola di equitazione) riding school
ma'nesco a quick to hit out
ma'netta nf hand lever; **manette** pl handcuffs
man'forte nm **dare ~ a qcno** support sb
manga'nello nm truncheon
manga'nese nm manganese
mange'reccio a edible
mangia'dischi® nm inv type of portable record player
mangia'fumo a inv **candela ~** air-purifying candle
mangia'nastri nm inv cassette player
mangia're vt/i eat; (consumare) eat up; (corrodere) eat away; take (scacchi, carte ecc) **● nm** eating; (cibo) food; (pasto) meal. **~rsi** vr **~rsi le parole** mumble; **~rsi le unghie** bite one's nails
mangi'ata nf big meal; **farsi una bella ~ di...** feast on...
mangia'toia nf manger
man'gime nm fodder
mangi'one, -a nmf fam glutton
mangiucchi'are vt nibble
'**mango** nm mango
ma'nia nf mania. **~ di grandezza** de-

lusions of grandeur. **~co, -a** *a* maniacal ● *nmf* maniac

'manica *nf* sleeve; (*fam: gruppo*) band; **a maniche lunghe** long-sleeved; **essere in maniche di camicia** be in shirt sleeves; **essere di ~ larga** be free with one's money. **~ a vento** wind sock

'Manica *nf* la **~** the [English] Channel

manica'retto *nm* tasty dish

mani'chetta *nf* hose

mani'chino *nm* (*da sarto, vetrina*) dummy

'manico *nm* handle; *Mus* neck

mani'comio *nm* mental home; (*fam: confusione*) tip

mani'cotto *nm* muff; *Mech* sleeve

mani'cure *nf* manicure ● *nmf inv* (*persona*) manicurist

mani'e|ra *nf* manner; **in ~ra che** so that. **~'rato** *a* affected; (*stile*) mannered. **~'rismo** *nm* mannerism

manifat'tura *nf* manufacture; (*fabbrica*) factory

manife'stante *nmf* demonstrator

manife'sta|re *vt* show; (*esprimere*) express ● *vi* demonstrate. **~rsi** *vr* show oneself. **~zi'one** *nf* show; (*espressione*) expression; (*sintomo*) manifestation; (*dimostrazione pubblica*) demonstration

mani'festo *a* evident ● *nm* poster; (*dichiarazione pubblica*) manifesto

ma'niglia *nf* handle; (*sostegno, in autobus ecc*) strap

manipo'la|re *vt* handle; (*massaggiare*) massage; (*alterare*) adulterate; *fig* manipulate. **~'tore, ~'trice** *nmf* manipulator. **~zi'one** *nf* handling; (*massaggio*) massage; (*alterazione*) adulteration; *fig* manipulation

mani'scalco *nm* smith

man'naia *nf* (*scure*) axe; (*da macellaio*) cleaver

man'naro *a* lupo *nm* **~** werewolf

'mano *nf* hand; (*strato di vernice ecc*) coat; **alla ~** informal; **fuori ~** out of the way; **man ~** little by little; **man ~ che** as; **sotto ~** to hand

mano'dopera *nf* labour

ma'nometro *nm* gauge

mano'mettere *vt* tamper with; (*violare*) violate

ma'nopola *nf* (*di apparecchio*) knob; (*guanto*) mitten; (*su pullman*) handle

mano'scritto *a* handwritten ● *nm* manuscript

mano'vale *nm* labourer

mano'vella *nf* handle; *Techn* crank

ma'no|vra *nf* manoeuvre; *Rail* shunt-ing; **fare le ~vre** manoeuvre. **~'vrabile** *a fig* easy to manipulate. **~'vrare** *vt* (*azionare*) operate; *fig* manipulate (*persona*) ● *vi* manoeuvre

manro'vescio *nm* slap

man'sarda *nf* attic

mansi'one *nf* task; (*dovere*) duty

mansu'eto *a* meek; (*animale*) docile

man'tell|a *nf* cape. **~o** *nm* cloak; (*soprabito, di animale*) coat; (*di neve*) mantle

mante'ner|e *vt* (*conservare*) keep; (*in buono stato, sostentare*) maintain. **~si** *vr* **~si in forma** keep fit. **manteni-'mento** *nm* maintenance

'mantice *nm* bellows *pl*; (*di automobile*) hood

'manto *nm* cloak; (*coltre*) mantle

manto'vana *nf* pelmet

manu'al|e *a & nm* manual. **~e d'uso** user manual. **~'mente** *adv* manually

ma'nubrio *nm* handle; (*di bicicletta*) handlebars *pl*; (*per ginnastica*) dumbbell

manu'fatto *a* manufactured

manutenzi'one *nf* maintenance

'manzo *nm* steer; (*carne*) beef

'mappa *nf* map

mappa'mondo *nm* globe

mar *vedi* **mare**

ma'rasma *nm fig* decline

mara'to|na *nf* marathon. **~'neta** *nmf* marathon runner

'marca *nf* mark; *Comm* brand; (*fabbricazione*) make; (*scontrino*) ticket. **~ da bollo** revenue stamp

mar'ca|re *vt* mark; *Sport* score. **~ta-'mente** *adv* markedly. **~to** *a* (*tratto, accento*) strong, marked. **~'tore** *nm* (*nel calcio*) scorer

mar'chese, -a *nm* marquis ● *nf* marchioness

marchi'are *vt* brand

'marchio *nm* brand; (*caratteristica*) mark. **~ di fabbrica** trademark. **~ registrato** registered trademark

'marcia *nf* march; *Auto* gear; *Sport* walk; **mettere in ~** put into gear; **mettersi in ~** start off. **~ funebre** funeral march. **~ indietro** reverse gear; **fare ~ indietro** reverse; *fig* back-pedal. **~ nuziale** wedding march

marciapi'ede *nm* pavement; (*di stazione*) platform

marci'a|re *vi* march; (*funzionare*) go, work. **~'tore, ~'trice** *nmf* walker

'marcio *a* rotten ● *nm* rotten part; *fig* corruption. **mar'cire** *vi* go bad, rot

'marco nm (moneta) mark
'mare nm sea; (luogo di mare) seaside; sul ~ (casa) at the seaside; (città) on the sea; in alto ~ on the high seas; essere in alto ~ fig not know which way to turn. ~ Adriatico Adriatic Sea. mar Ionio Ionian Sea. mar Mediterraneo Mediterranean. mar Tirreno Tyrrhenian Sea

ma'rea nf tide; una ~ di hundreds of; alta/bassa ~ high/low tide

mareggi'ata nf [sea] storm

mare'moto nm tidal wave, seaquake

maresci'allo nm (ufficiale) marshal; (sottufficiale) warrant-officer

marga'rina nf margarine

marghe'rita nf marguerite. mar-gheri'tina nf daisy

margi'nal|e a marginal. ~'mente adv marginally

'margine nm margin; (orlo) brink; (bordo) border. ~ di errore margin of error. ~ di sicurezza safety margin

ma'rina nf navy; (costa) seashore; (quadro) seascape. ~ mercantile merchant navy. ~ militare navy

mari'naio nm sailor

mari'na|re vt marinate; ~re la scuola play truant. ~ta nf marinade. ~to a Culin marinated

ma'rino a sea attrib, marine

mario'netta nf puppet

ma'rito nm husband

ma'rittimo a maritime

mar'maglia nf rabble

marmel'lata nf jam; (di agrumi) marmalade

mar'mitta nf pot; Auto silencer. ~ catalitica catalytic converter

'marmo nm marble

mar'mocchio nm fam brat

mar'mor|eo a marble. ~iz'zato a marbled

mar'motta nf marmot

Ma'rocco nm Morocco

ma'roso nm breaker

mar'rone a brown ● nm brown; (casta-gna) chestnut; marroni pl canditi marrons glacés

mar'sina nf tails pl

mar'supio nm (borsa) bumbag

marte'dì nm inv Tuesday. ~ grasso Shrove Tuesday

martel'lante a (mal di testa) pounding

martel'la|re vt hammer ● vi throb. ~ta nf hammer blow

martel'letto nm (di giudice) gavel

mar'tello nm hammer; (di battente) knocker. ~ pneumatico pneumatic drill

marti'netto nm Mech jack

'martire nmf martyr. mar'tirio nm martyrdom

'martora nf marten

martori'are vt torment

mar'xis|mo nm Marxism. ~ta a & nmf Marxist

marza'pane nm marzipan

marzi'ale a martial

marzi'ano, -a nmf Martian

'marzo nm March

mascal'zone nm rascal

ma'scara nm inv mascara

mascar'pone nm full-fat cream cheese often used for desserts

ma'scella nf jaw

'mascher|a nf mask; (costume) fancy dress; Cinema, Theat usher m, usherette f; (nella commedia dell'arte) stock character. ~a antigas gas mask. ~a di bel-lezza face pack. ~a ad ossigeno oxygen mask. ~a'mento nm masking; Mil camouflage. masche'rare vt mask; fig camouflage. ~arsi vr put on a mask; ~arsi da dress up as. ~ata nf masquerade

maschi'accio nm (ragazza) tomboy

ma'schi|le a masculine; (sesso) male ● nm masculine [gender]. ~'lista a sexist. 'maschio a male; (virile) manly ● nm male; (figlio) son. masco'lino a masculine

ma'scotte nf inv mascot

maso'chis|mo nm masochism. ~ta a & nmf masochist

'massa nf mass; Electr earth, ground Am; comunicazioni di ~ mass media

massa'cra|nte a gruelling. ~re vt massacre. mas'sacro nm massacre; fig mess

massaggi'a|re vt massage. mas'sag-gio nm massage. ~'tore, ~'trice nm masseur ● nf masseuse

mas'saia nf housewife

masse'rizie nfpl household effects

mas'siccio a massive; (oro ecc) solid; (corporatura) heavy ● nm massif

'massim|a nf maxim; (temperatura) maximum. ~o a greatest; (quantità) maximum, greatest ● nm il ~o the maximum; al ~o at [the] most, as a maximum

'masso nm rock

mas'sone *nm* [Free]mason. **~'ria** Freemasonry

ma'stello *nm* wooden box for the grape or olive harvest

masti'care *vt* chew; (borbottare) mumble

'mastice *nm* mastic; (per vetri) putty

ma'stino *nm* mastiff

masto'dontico *a* gigantic

'mastro *nm* master; **libro ~** ledger

mastur'ba|rsi *vr* masturbate. **~zi'one** *nf* masturbation

ma'tassa *nf* skein

mate'matic|a *nf* mathematics, maths. **~o, -a** *a* mathematical ● *nmf* mathematician

materas'sino *nm* **~ gonfiabile** air bed

mate'rasso *nm* mattress. **~ a molle** spring mattress

ma'teria *nf* matter; (materiale) material; (di studio) subject. **~ prima** raw material

materi'a|le *a* material; (grossolano) coarse ● *nm* material. **~'lismo** *nm* materialism. **~'lista** *a* materialistic ● *nmf* materialist. **~liz'zarsi** *vr* materialize. **~l'mente** *adv* physically

mater'nità *nf* motherhood; **ospedale di ~** maternity hospital

ma'terno *a* maternal; **lingua materna** mother tongue

ma'tita *nf* pencil

ma'trice *nf* matrix; (origini) roots *pl*; *Comm* counterfoil

ma'tricola *nf* (registro) register; *Univ* fresher

ma'trigna *nf* stepmother

matrimoni'ale *a* matrimonial; **vita ~** married life. **matri'monio** *nm* marriage; (cerimonia) wedding

ma'trona *nf* matron

'matta *nf* (nelle carte) joker

mattacchi'one, -a *nmf* rascal

matta'toio *nm* slaughterhouse

matte'rello *nm* rolling-pin

mat'ti|na *nf* morning; **la ~na** in the morning. **~'nata** *nf* morning; *Theat* matinée. **~ni'ero** *a* essere **~niero** be an early riser. **~no** *nm* morning

'matto, -a *a* mad, crazy; *Med* insane; (falso) false; (opaco) matt; **~ da legare** barking mad; **avere una voglia matta di ~** be dying for ● *nmf* madman; madwoman

mat'tone *nm* brick; (libro) bore

matto'nella *nf* tile

mattu'tino *a* morning *attrib*

matu'rare *vt* ripen. **maturità** *nf* maturity; *Sch* school-leaving certificate. **ma'turo** *a* mature; (frutto) ripe

ma'tusa *nm* old fogey

mauso'leo *nm* mausoleum

maxi+ *pref* maxi+

'mazza *nf* club; (martello) hammer; (da baseball, cricket) bat. **~ da golf** golf-club. **maz'zata** *nf* blow

maz'zetta *nf* (di banconote) bundle

'mazzo *nm* bunch; (carte da gioco) pack

me *pers pron* me; **me lo ha dato** he gave it to me; **fai come me** do as I do; **è più veloce di me** he is faster than me *o* faster than I am

me'andro *nm* meander

M.E.C. *nm abbr* (Mercato Comune Europeo) EEC

mec'canica *nf* mechanics *sg*

meccanica'mente *adv* mechanically

mec'canico *a* mechanical ● *nm* mechanic. **mecca'nismo** *nm* mechanism

mèche *nfpl* [farsi] **fare le ~** have one's hair streaked

me'dagli|a *nf* medal. **~'one** *nm* medallion; (gioiello) locket

me'desimo *a* same

'medi|a *nf* average; *Sch* average mark; *Math* mean; **essere nella ~a** be in the mid-range. **~'ano** *a* middle ● *nm* (calcio) half-back

medi'ante *prep* by

medi'a|re *vt* act as intermediary in. **~'tore, ~'trice** *nmf* mediator; *Comm* middleman. **~zi'one** *nf* mediation

medica'mento *nm* medicine

medi'ca|re *vt* treat; dress (ferita). **~zi'one** *nf* medication; (di ferita) dressing

medi'cina *nf* medicine. **~ina legale** forensic medicine. **~i'nale** *a* medicinal ● *nm* medicine

'medico *a* medical ● *nm* doctor. **~ generico** general practitioner. **~ legale** forensic scientist. **~ di turno** duty doctor

medie'vale *a* medieval

'medio *a* average; (punto) middle; (statura) medium ● *nm* (dito) middle finger

medi'ocre *a* mediocre; (scadente) poor

medio'evo *nm* Middle Ages *pl*

medi'ta|re *vt* meditate; (progettare) plan; (considerare attentamente) think over ● *vi* meditate. **~zi'one** *nf* meditation

mediter'raneo *a* Mediterranean; **il [mar] M~** the Mediterranean [Sea]

me'dusa *nf* jellyfish

me'gafono *nm* megaphone

megaga'lattico *a fam* gigantic

mega'lomane *nmf* megalomaniac

me'gera *nf* hag

'**meglio** *adv* better; **tanto ~, ~ così** so much the better ● *a* better; *(superlativo)* best ● *nmf* best ● *nf* **avere la ~ su** have the better of; **fare qcsa alla [bell'e] ~** do sth as best one can ● *nm* **fare del proprio ~** do one's best; **fare qcsa il ~ possibile** make an excellent job of sth; **al ~ to** the best of one's ability; **per il ~** for the best

'**mela** *nf* apple. **~ cotogna** quince

mela'grana *nf* pomegranate

mela'nina *nf* melanin

melan'zana *nf* aubergine, eggplant *Am*

me'lassa *nf* molasses *sg*

me'lenso *a* (persona, film) dull

mel'lifluo *a* (parole) honeyed; (voce) sugary

'**melma** *nf* slime. **mel'moso** *a* slimy

melo *nm* apple[-tree]

melo'di|a *nf* melody. **me'lodico** *a* melodic. **~'oso** *a* melodious

melo'dram|ma *nm* melodrama. **~'matico** *a* melodramatic

melo'grano *nm* pomegranate tree

me'lone *nm* melon

mem'brana *nf* membrane

'**membro** *nm* member; (*pl nf* **membra** *Anat*) limb

memo'rabile *a* memorable

'**memore** *a* mindful; (riconoscente) grateful

me'mori|a *nf* memory; (oggetto ricordo) souvenir. **Imparare a ~a** learn by heart. **~a permanente** *Comput* non-volatile memory. **~a tampone** *Comput* buffer. **~a volatile** *Comput* volatile memory; **memorie** *pl* (biografiche) memoirs. **~'ale** *nm* memorial. **~z'zare** *vt* memorize; *Comput* save, store

mena'dito: a ~ *adv* perfectly

me'nare *vt* lead; (fam: picchiare) hit

mendi'ca|nte *nmf* beggar. **~re** *vt/i* beg

menefre'ghista *a* devil-may-care

me'ningi *nfpl* **spremersi le ~** rack one's brains

menin'gite *nf* meningitis

me'nisco *nm* meniscus

'**meno** *adv* less; (superlativo) least; (in operazioni, con temperatura) minus; **far qcsa alla ~ peggio** do sth as best one can; **fare a ~ di qcsa** do without sth;

non posso fare a ~ di ridere I can't help laughing; **~ male!** thank goodness!; **sempre ~** less and less; **venir ~** (svenire) faint; **venir ~ a qcno** (coraggio:) fail sb; **sono le tre ~ un quarto** it's a quarter to three; **che tu venga o ~** whether you're coming or not; **quanto ~** at least ● *a inv* less; (con nomi plurali) fewer ● *nm* least; *Math* minus sign; **il ~ possibile** as little as possible; **per lo ~** at least ● *prep* except [for] ● *conj* **a ~ che** unless

meno'ma|re *vt* (incidente:) maim. **~to** *a* disabled

meno'pausa *nf* menopause

'**mensa** *nf* table; *Mil* mess; *Sch, Univ* refectory

men'sil|e *a* monthly ● *nm* (stipendio) [monthly] salary; (rivista) monthly. **~ità** *nf inv* monthly salary. **~'mente** *adv* monthly

'**mensola** *nf* bracket; (scaffale) shelf

'**menta** *nf* mint. **~ peperita** peppermint

men'tal|e *a* mental. **~ità** *nf inv* mentality

'**mente** *nf* mind; **a ~ fredda** in cold blood; **venire in ~ a qcno** occur to sb; **mi è uscito di ~** it slipped my mind

men'tina *nf* mint

men'tire *vi* lie

'**mento** *nm* chin

'**mentre** *conj* (temporale) while; (invece) whereas

menù *nm inv* menu. **~ fisso** set menu. **~ a tendina** *Comput* pulldown menu

menzio'nare *vt* mention. **menzi'one** *nf* mention

men'zogna *nf* lie

mera'viglia *nf* wonder; **a ~** marvellously; **che ~!** how wonderful!; **con mia grande ~** much to my amazement; **mi fa ~ che...** I am surprised that...

meravigli'ar|e *vt* surprise. **~si** *vr* **~si di** be surprised at

meravigli|osa'mente *adv* marvellously. **~'oso** *a* marvellous

mer'can|te *nm* merchant. **~teggi'are** *vi* trade; (sul prezzo) bargain. **~'tile** *a* mercantile. **~'zia** *nf* merchandise, goods *pl* ● *nm* merchant ship

mer'cato *nm* market; *Fin* market [-place]. **a buon ~** (comprare) cheap[ly]; (articolo) cheap. **~ dei cambi** foreign exchange market. **M~ Comune [Europeo]** [European] Common Market. **~ coperto** covered market. **~ libero** free market. **~ nero** black market

'merce nf goods pl

mercé nf alla ~ di at the mercy of

merce'nario a & nm mercenary

merce'ria nf haberdashery; (negozio) haberdasher's

mercoledì nm inv Wednesday. ~ delle Ceneri Ash Wednesday

mer'curio nm mercury

me'renda nf afternoon snack; far ~ have an afternoon snack

meridi'ana nf sundial

meridi'ano nm a midday ●nm meridian

meridio'nale a southern ●nmf southerner. meridi'one nm south

me'rin|ga nf meringue. ~'gata nf meringue pie

meri'tare vt deserve. meri'tevole a deserving

'meri|to nm merit; (valore) worth; in ~to a as to; per ~to di thanks to. ~'torio a meritorious

mer'letto nm lace

'merlo nm blackbird

mer'luzzo nm cod

'mero a mere

meschine'ria nf meanness. me'schino a wretched; (gretto) mean ●nm wretch

mesco|la'mento nm mixing. ~'lanza nf mixture

mesco'la|re vt mix; shuffle (carte); (confondere) mix up; blend (tè, tabacco ecc). ~rsi vr mix; (immischiarsi) meddle. ~ta nf (a carte) shuffle; Culin stir

'mese nm month

me'setto nm un ~ about a month

'messa¹ nf Mass

'messa² nf (il mettere) putting. ~ in moto Auto starting. ~ in piega (di capelli) set. ~ a punto adjustment. ~ in scena production. ~ a terra earthing, grounding Am

messag'gero nm messenger. mes'saggio nm message

mes'sale nm missal

'messe nf harvest

Mes'sia nm Messiah

messi'cano, -a a & nmf Mexican

'Messico nm Mexico

messin'scena nf staging; fig act

'messo pp di mettere ●nm messenger

mesti'ere nm trade; (lavoro) job; essere del ~ be an expert, know one's trade

'mesto a sad

'mestola nf (di cuoco) ladle

mestru'a|le a menstrual. ~zi'one nf menstruation. ~zi'oni pl period

'meta nf destination; fig aim

metà nf inv half; (centro) middle; a ~ strada half-way; fare a ~ con qcno go halves with sb

metabo'lismo nm metabolism

meta'done nm methadone

meta'fisico a metaphysical

me'tafora nf metaphor. meta'forico a metaphorical

me'talli|co a metallic. ~z'zato a ⟨grigio⟩ metallic

me'tall|o nm metal. ~ur'gia nf metallurgy

metalmec'canico a engineering ●nm engineering worker

meta'morfosi nf metamorphosis

me'tano nm methane. ~'dotto nm methane pipeline

meta'nolo nm methanol

me'teora nf meteor. meteo'rite nm meteorite

meteoro|lo'gia nf meteorology. ~'lo-gico a meteorological

me'ticcio, -a nmf half-caste

metico'loso a meticulous

me'tod|ico a methodical. 'metodo nm method. ~olo'gia nf methodology

me'traggio nm length (in metres)

'metrico, -a a metric; (in poesia) metrical ●nf metrics sg

'metro nm metre; (nastro) tape measure ●nf (fam: metropolitana) tube Br, subway

me'tronomo nm metronome

metro'notte nmf inv night security guard

me'tropoli nf inv metropolis. ~'tana nf subway, underground Br. ~'tano a metropolitan

'metter|e vt put; (indossare) put on; (fam: installare) put in; ~e al mondo bring into the world; ~e da parte set aside; ~e fiducia inspire trust; ~e qcsa in chiaro make sth clear; ~e in mostra display; ~e a posto tidy up; ~e in vendita put up for sale; ~e su set up (casa, azienda); metter su famiglia start a family; ci ho messo un'ora it took me an hour; mettiamo che... let's suppose that... ~si vr (indossare) put on; (diventare) turn out; ~si a start to; ~si con qcno (fam: formare una coppia) start to go out with sb; ~si a letto go to bed; ~si a sedere sit down; ~si in viaggio set out

'mezza nf è la ~ it's half past twelve; sono le quattro e ~ it's half past four

mezza'luna nf half moon; (simbolo

islamico) crescent; (*coltello*) two-handled chopping knife; **a ~** half-moon shaped

mezza'manica *nf* **a ~** (*maglia*) short-sleeved

mez'zano *a* middle

mezza'notte *nf* midnight

mezz'asta: a ~ *adv* at half mast

'mezzo *a* half; **di mezza età** middle-aged; **di mezza età** middle-aged; **~ bicchiere** half a glass; **una mezza idea** a vague idea; **siamo mezzi morti** we're half dead; **sono le quattro e ~** it's half past four. **mezz'ora** *nf* half an hour. **mezza pensione** *nf* half board. **mezza stagione** *nf* **una giacca di mezza stagione** a spring/autumn jacket ● *adv* (*a metà*) half ● *nm* (*metà*) half; (*centro*) middle; (*per raggiungere un fine*) means *sg*; **uno e ~** one and a half; **tre anni e ~** three and a half years; **in ~ a** in the middle of; **il giusto ~** the happy medium; **levare di ~** clear away; **per ~ di** by means of; **a ~ posta** by mail; **via di ~** *fig* halfway house; (*soluzione*) middle way. **mezzi** *pl* (*denaro*) means *pl*. **mezzi pl pubblici** public transport. **mezzi pl di trasporto** [means of] transport.

mezzo'busto: a ~ *a* (*foto, ritratto*) half-length

mezzo'fondo *nm* middle-distance running

mezzogi'orno *nm* midday; (*sud*) South. **il M~** Southern Italy. **~ in punto** high noon

mi *pers pron* me; (*refl*) myself; **mi ha dato un libro** he gave me a book; **mi lavo le mani** I wash my hands; **eccomi** here I am ● *nm Mus* (*chiave, nota*) E

miago'l|are *vi* miaow. **~io** *nm* miaowing

'mica¹ *nf* mica

'mica² *adv fam* (*per caso*) by any chance; **hai ~ visto Paolo?** have you seen Paul, by any chance?; **non è ~ bello** it is not at all nice; **~ male** not bad

'miccia *nf* fuse

micidi'ale *a* deadly

'micio *nm* pussy-cat

'microbo *nm* microbe

micro'cosmo *nm* microcosm

micro'fiche *nf inv* microfiche

micro'film *nm inv* microfilm

mi'crofono *nm* microphone

microorga'nismo *nm* microorganism

microproces'sore *nm* microprocessor

micro'scopi|o *nm* microscope. **~co** *a* microscopic

micro'solco *nm* long-playing record

mi'dollo *nm* (*pl nf* **midolla**, *Anat*) marrow; **fino al ~** through and through. **~ osseo** bone marrow. **~ spinale** spinal cord

'mie, mi'ei *vedi* **mio**

mi'ele *nm* honey

mi'et|ere *vt* reap. **~i'trice** *nf Mech* harvester. **~i'tura** *nf* harvest

migli'aio *nm* (*pl nf* **migliaia**) thousand. **a migliaia** in thousands

'miglio *nm Bot* millet; (*pl nf* **miglia**: *misura*) mile

migliora'mento *nm* improvement

miglio'rare *vt/i* improve

migli'ore *a* better; (*superlativo*) best ● *nmf* **il/la ~** the best

'mignolo *nm* little finger; (*del piede*) little toe

mi'gra|re *vi* migrate. **~zi'one** *nf* migration

'mila *vedi* **mille**

Mi'lano *nf* Milan

miliar'dario, -a *nm* millionaire; (*plurimiliardario*) billionaire ● *nf* millionairess; billionairess. **mili'ardo** *nm* billion

mili'are *a* **pietra ~** *nf* milestone

milio'nario, -a *nm* millionaire ● *nf* millionairess

mili'one *nm* million

milio'nesimo *a* millionth

mili'tante *a & nmf* militant

mili'tare *vi* **~ in** be a member of (*partito ecc*) ● *a* military ● *nm* soldier; **fare il ~** do one's military service. **~ di leva** National Serviceman

'milite *nm* soldier. **mil'izia** *nf* militia

'mille *a & nm* (*pl* **mila**) *a o* one thousand; **due/tre mila** two/three thousand; **~ grazie!** thanks a lot!

mille'foglie *nm inv Culin* vanilla slice

mil'lennio *nm* millennium

millepi'edi *nm inv* centipede

mil'lesimo *a & nm* thousandth

milli'grammo *nm* milligram

mil'limetro *nm* millimetre

'milza *nf* spleen

mi'mare *vt* mimic (*persona*) ● *vi* mime

mi'metico *a* camouflage *attrib*

mimetiz'zar|e *vt* camouflage. **~si** *vr* camouflage oneself

'mim|ica *nf* mime. **~ico** *a* mimic. **~o** *nm* mime

mi'mosa *nf* mimosa

'mina *nf* mine; (*di matita*) lead

mi'naccia *nf* threat

minacci'are *vt* threaten. **~'oso** *a* threatening

mi'nare *vt* mine; *fig* undermine

mina'tor|e *nm* miner. **~io** *a* threatening

mine'ra|le *a & nm* mineral. **~rio** *a* mining *attrib*

mi'nestra *nf* soup. **mine'strone** *nm* vegetable soup; *(fam: insieme confuso)* hotchpotch

mingher'lino *a* skinny

mini+ *pref* mini+

minia'tura *nf* miniature. **miniaturiz-'zato** *a* miniaturized

mini'era *nf* mine

mini'golf *nm* miniature golf

mini'gonna *nf* miniskirt

minima'mente *adv* minimally

mini'market *nm inv* minimarket

minimiz'zare *vt* minimize

'minimo *a* least, slightest; *(il più basso)* lowest; *(salario, quantità ecc)* minimum ● *nm* minimum; **girare al ~** *Auto* idle

mini'stero *nm* ministry; *(governo)* government

mi'nistro *nm* minister. **M~ del Tesoro** Finance Minister, Chancellor of the Exchequer *Br*

mino'ranza *nf* minority *attrib*

mino'rato, -a *a* disabled ● *nmf* disabled person

mi'nore *a* *(gruppo, numero)* smaller; *(superlativo)* smallest; *(distanza)* shorter; *(superlativo)* shortest; *(prezzo)* lower; *(superlativo)* lowest; *(di età)* younger; *(superlativo)* youngest; *(di importanza)* minor; *(superlativo)* least important ● *nmf* younger; *(superlativo)* youngest; *Jur* minor; **il ~ dei mali** the lesser of two evils; **i minori di 14 anni** children under 14. **mino'renne** *a* under age ● *nmf* minor

minori'tario *a* minority *attrib*

minu'etto *nm* minuet

mi'nuscolo, -a *a* tiny ● *nf* small letter

mi'nuta *nf* rough copy

mi'nuto¹ *a* minute; *(persona)* delicate; *(ricerca)* detailed; *(pioggia, neve)* fine; **al ~** *Comm* retail

mi'nuto² *nm (di tempo)* minute; **spaccare il ~** be dead on time

mi'nuzi|a *nf* trifle. **~'oso** *a* detailed; *(persona)* meticulous

'mio (il mio *m*, la mia *f*, i miei *mpl*, le mie *fpl*) *a poss* my; **questa macchina**

è mia this car is mine; **~ padre** my father; **un ~ amico** a friend of mine ● *poss pron* mine; **i miei** *(genitori ecc)* my folks

'miope *a* short-sighted. **mio'pia** *nf* short-sightedness

'mira *nf* aim; *(bersaglio)* target; **prendere la ~** take aim; **prendere di ~ qcno** *fig* have it in for sb

mi'racolo *nm* miracle. **~sa'mente** *adv* miraculously. **miraco'loso** *a* miraculous

mi'raggio *nm* mirage

mi'rar|e *vi* [take] aim. **~si** *vr (guardarsi)* look at oneself

mi'riade *nf* myriad

mi'rino *nm* sight; *Phot* view-finder

mir'tillo *nm* blueberry

mi'santropo, -a *nmf* misanthropist

mi'scela *nf* mixture; *(di caffè, tabacco)* blend. **~'tore** *nm (di acqua)* mixer tap

miscel'lanea *nf* miscellany

'mischia *nf* scuffle; *(nel rugby)* scrum

mischi'ar|e *vt* mix; shuffle *(carte da gioco)*. **~si** *vr* mix; *(immischiarsi)* interfere

misco'noscere *vt* not appreciate

mi'scuglio *nm* mixture; *fig* medley

mise'rabile *a* wretched

misera'mente *adv (finire)* miserably; *(vivere)* in abject poverty

mi'seria *nf* poverty; *(infelicità)* misery; **guadagnare una ~** earn a pittance; **porca ~!** hell!; **miserie** *pl (disgrazie)* misfortunes

miseri'cordi|a *nf* mercy. **~'oso** *a* merciful

'misero *a (miserabile)* wretched; *(povero)* poor; *(scarso)* paltry

mi'sfatto *nm* misdeed

mi'sogino *nm* misogynist

mis'saggio *nm* vision mixer

'missile *nm* missile

missio'nario, -a *nmf* missionary. **missi'one** *nf* mission

misteri|osa'mente *adv* mysteriously. **~'oso** *a* mysterious. **mi'stero** *nm* mystery

'misti|ca *nf* mysticism. **~'cismo** *nm* mysticism. **~co** *a* mystic[al] ● *nm* mystic

mistifi'ca|re *vt* distort *(verità)*. **~zi'one** *nf (della verità)* distortion

'misto *a* mixed; **~ lana/cotone** wool/cotton-mix; **scuola mista** school *o* co-educational school ● *nm* mixture

mi'sura *nf* measure; *(dimensione)* measurement; *(taglia)* size; *(limite)* limit; **su ~** ⟨abiti⟩ made to measure; ⟨mobile⟩ custom-made; **a ~** ⟨andare, calzare⟩ perfectly; **a ~ che** as. **~ di sicurezza** safety measure. **misu'rare** vt measure; try on ⟨indumenti⟩; ⟨limitare⟩ limit. **misu'rarsi** vr **misurarsi con** ⟨gareggiare⟩ compete with. **misu'rato** a measured. **misu'rino** nm measuring spoon

'**mite** a mild; ⟨prezzo⟩ moderate

'**mitico** a mythical

miti'gare vt mitigate. **~si** vr calm down; ⟨clima:⟩ become mild

mitiz'zare vt mythicize

'**mito** nm myth. **~lo'gia** nf mythology. **~'logico** a mythological

mi'tomane nmf compulsive liar

'**mitra** nf Relig mitre ● nm inv Mil machine-gun

mitragli'a|re vt machine-gun; **~re di domande** fire questions at. **~'trice** nf machine-gun

mit'tente nmf sender

mne'monico a mnemonic

mo' nm **a ~ di** by way of ⟨esempio, consolazione⟩

'**mobile**[1] a mobile; ⟨volubile⟩ fickle; ⟨che si può muovere⟩ movable; **beni mobili** personal estate; **squadra ~** flying squad

'**mobi|le**[2] nm piece of furniture; **mobili** pl furniture sg. **mo'bilia** nf furniture. **~li'ficio** nm furniture factory

mo'bilio nm furniture

mobilità nf mobility

mobili'tare vt mobilize. **~zi'one** nf mobilization

mocas'sino nm moccasin

mocci'oso, -a nmf brat

'**moccolo** nm ⟨di candela⟩ candle-end; ⟨moccio⟩ snot

'**moda** nf fashion; **di ~** in fashion; **alla ~** ⟨musica, vestiti⟩ up-to-date; **fuori ~** unfashionable

modalità nf inv formality; **~ d'uso** instruction

mo'della nf model. **model'lare** vt model

model'li|no nm model. **~sta** nmf designer

mo'dello nm model; ⟨stampo⟩ mould; ⟨di carta⟩ pattern; ⟨modulo⟩ form

'**modem** nm inv modem; **mandare per ~** modem, send by modem

mode'ra|re vt moderate; ⟨diminuire⟩ reduce. **~rsi** vr control oneself. **~ta'mente** adv moderately **~to** a moderate. **~'tore, ~'trice** nmf ⟨in tavola rotonda⟩ moderator. **~zi'one** nf moderation

modern|a'mente adv ⟨in modo moderno⟩ in a modern style. **~iz'zare** vt modernize. **mo'derno** a modern

mo'dest|ia nf modesty. **~o** a modest

'**modico** a reasonable

mo'difica nf modification

modifi'ca|re vt modify. **~zi'one** nf modification

mo'dista nf milliner

'**modo** nm way; ⟨garbo⟩ manners pl; ⟨occasione⟩ chance; Gram mood; **ad ogni ~** anyhow; **di ~ che** so that; **fare in ~ di** try to; **in che ~** ⟨inter⟩ how; **in qualche ~** somehow; **in questo ~** like this; **~ di dire** idiom; **per ~ di dire** so to speak

modu'la|re vt modulate. **~zi'one** nf modulation. **~zione di frequenza** frequency modulation. **~'tore** nm **~tore di frequenza** frequency modulator

'**modulo** nm form; ⟨lunare, di comando⟩ module. **~ continuo** continuous paper

'**mogano** nm mahogany

'**mogio** a dejected

'**moglie** nf wife

'**mola** nf millstone; Mech grindstone

mo'lare nm molar

'**mole** nf mass; ⟨dimensione⟩ size

mo'lecola nf molecule

mole'stare vt bother; ⟨più forte⟩ molest. **mo'lestia** nf nuisance. **mo'lesto** a bothersome

'**molla** nf spring; **molle** pl tongs

mol'lare vt let go; ⟨fam: lasciare⟩ leave; fam give ⟨ceffone⟩; Naut cast off ● vi cease; **mollala!** fam stop that!

'**molle** a soft; ⟨bagnato⟩ wet

mol'letta nf ⟨per capelli⟩ hair-grip; ⟨per bucato⟩ clothes-peg; **mollette** pl ⟨per ghiaccio ecc⟩ tongs

mol'lezz|a nf softness; **~e** pl fig luxury

mol'lica nf crumb

mol'lusco nm mollusc

'**molo** nm pier; ⟨banchina⟩ dock

mol'teplic|e a manifold; ⟨numeroso⟩ numerous. **~ità** nf multiplicity

moltipli'ca|re vt, **~rsi** vr multiply. **~'tore** nm multiplier. **~'trice** nf calculating machine. **~zi'one** nf multiplication

molti'tudine nf multitude

'**molto** a a lot of; ⟨con negazione e interrogazione⟩ much, a lot of; ⟨con nomi plurali⟩ many, a lot of; **non ~ tempo** not much time, not a lot of time ● adv very;

(con verbi) a lot; *(con avverbi)* much; ~ **stupido** very stupid; **mangiare** ~ eat a lot; ~ **più veloce** much faster; **non mangiare** ~ not eat a lot, not eat much ● *pron* a lot; *(molto tempo)* a lot of time; *(con negazione e interrogazione)* much, a lot; *(plurale)* many; **non ne ho** ~ I don't have much, I don't have a lot; **non ne ho molti** I don't have many, I don't have a lot; **non ci metterò** ~ I won't be long; **fra non** ~ before long; **molti** *(persone)* a lot of people; **eravamo in molti** there were a lot of us

momentanea'mente *adv* momentarily; **è ~ assente** he's not here at the moment. **momen'taneo** *a* momentary

mo'mento *nm* moment; **a momenti** *(a volte)* sometimes; *(fra un momento)* in a moment; **dal ~ che** since; **per il ~** for the time being; **da un ~ all'altro** *(cambiare idea ecc)* from one moment to the next; *(aspettare qcno ecc)* at any moment

'monac|a *nf* nun. **~o** *nm* monk

'Monaco *nm* Monaco ● *nf (di Baviera)* Munich

mo'narc|a *nm* monarch. **monar'chia** *nf* monarchy. **~hico, -a** *a* monarchic ● *nmf* monarchist

mona'stero *nm (di monaci)* monastery; *(di monache)* convent. **mo'nastico** *a* monastic

monche'rino *nm* stump

'monco *a* maimed; *(fig: troncato)* truncated; **~ di un braccio** one-armed

mon'dano *a* worldly; **vita mondana** social life

mondi'ale *a* world *attrib*; **di fama ~** world-famous

'mondo *nm* world; **il bel ~** fashionable society; **un ~** *(molto)* a lot

mondovisi'one *nf* **in ~** transmitted worldwide

mo'nello, -a *nmf* urchin

mo'neta *nf* coin; *(denaro)* money; *(denaro spicciolo)* [small] change. **~ estera** foreign currency. **~ legale** legal tender. **~ unica** single currency. **mone-'tario** *a* monetary

mongolfi'era *nf* hot air balloon

mo'nile *nm* jewel

'monito *nm* warning

moni'tore *nm* monitor

mo'nocolo *nm* monocle

monoco'lore *a Pol* one-party

mono'dose *a inv* individually packaged

monogra'fia *nf* monograph

mono'gramma *nm* monogram

mono'kini *nm inv* monokini

mono'lingue *a* monolingual

monolo'cale *nm* studio flat, studio apartment *Am*

mo'nologo *nm* monologue

mono'pattino *nm* [child's] scooter

mono'poli|o *nm* monopoly. **~o di stato** state monopoly. **~z'zare** *vt* monopolize

mono'sci *nm inv* monoski

monosil'labico *a* monosyllabic. **mono'sillabo** *nm* monosyllable

monoto'nia *nf* monotony. **mo'notono** *a* monotonous

mono'uso *a* disposable

monou'tente *a inv* single-user *attrib*

monsi'gnore *nm* monsignor

mon'sone *nm* monsoon

monta'carichi *nm inv* hoist

mon'taggio *nm Mech* assembly; *Cinema* editing; **catena di ~** production line

mon'ta|gna *nf* mountain; *(zona)* mountains *pl*; **montagne** *pl* **russe** big dipper. **~'gnoso** *a* mountainous. **~'naro, -a** *nmf* highlander. **~no** *a* mountain *attrib*

mon'tante *nm (di finestra, porta)* upright

mon'ta|re *vt/i* mount; get on *(veicolo)*; *(aumentare)* rise; *Mech* assemble; frame *(quadro)*; *Culin* whip; edit *(film)*; *(a cavallo)* ride; *fig* blow up; **~rsi la testa** get big-headed. **~to, -a** *nmf* poser. **~'tura** *nf Mech* assembling; *(di occhiali)* frame; *(di gioiello)* mounting; *fig* exaggeration

'monte *nm anche fig* mountain; **a ~** upstream; **andare a ~** be ruined; **mandare a ~ qcsa** ruin sth. **~ di pietà** pawnshop

monte'premi *nm inv* jackpot

mont'gomery *nm inv* duffle coat

mon'tone *nm* ram; **carne di ~** mutton

montu'oso *a* mountainous

monumen'tale *a* monumental. **monu'mento** *nm* monument

mo'quette *nf (tappeto)* fitted carpet

'mora *nf (del gelso)* mulberry; *(del rovo)* blackberry

mo'ral|e *a* moral ● *nf* morals *pl*; *(di storia)* moral ● *nm* morale. **mora'lista** *nmf* moralist. **~ità** *nf* morality; *(condotta)* morals *pl*. **~iz'zare** *vt/i* moralize. **~'mente** *adv* morally

morbi'dezza *nf* softness

'morbido *a* soft

mor'billo *nm* measles *sg*

'**morbo** nm disease. **~sità** nf (qualità) morbidity

mor'**boso** a morbid

mor'**dace** a cutting

mor'**dente** a biting. **mordere** vt bite; (corrodere) bite into. **mordicchi'are** vt gnaw

mor'**fina** nf morphine. **morfi'nomane** nmf morphine addict

mori'**bondo** a dying; (istituzione) moribund

morige'**rato** a moderate

mo'**rire** vi die; fig die out; **fa un freddo da ~** it's freezing cold, it's perishing; **~ di noia** be bored to death; **c'era da ~ dal ridere** it was hilariously funny

mor'**mone** nmf Mormon

mormo'**r|are** vt/i murmur; (brontolare) mutter. **~io** nm murmuring; (lamentela) grumbling

'**moro** a dark ●nm Moor

mo'**roso** a in arrears

'**morsa** nf vice; fig grip

'**morse** a **alfabeto ~** Morse code

mor'**setto** nm clamp

morsi'**care** vt bite. '**morso** nm bite; (di cibo, briglia) bit; **i morsi della fame** hunger pangs

morta'**della** nf mortadella (type of salted pork)

mor'**taio** nm mortar

mor'**tal|e** a mortal; (simile a morte) deadly; **di una noia ~e** deadly. **~ità** nf mortality. **~'mente** adv (ferito) fatally; (offeso) mortally

morta'**retto** nm firecracker

'**morte** nf death

mortifi'**cante** a mortifying

mortifi'**ca|re** vt mortify. **~rsi** vr be mortified. **~to** a mortified. **~zi'one** nf mortification

'**morto, -a** pp di **morire** ●a dead; **~ di freddo** frozen to death; **stanco ~** dead tired ●nm dead man ●nf dead woman

mor'**torio** nm funeral

mo'**saico** nm mosaic

'**Mosca** nf Moscow

'**mosca** nf fly; (barba) goatee. **~ cieca** blindman's buff

mo'**scato** a muscat; **noce moscata** nutmeg ●nm muscatel

mosce'**rino** nm midge; (fam: persona) midget

mo'**schea** nf mosque

moschi'**cida** a fly attrib

'**moscio** a limp; **avere l'erre moscia** not be able to say one's r's properly

mo'**scone** nm bluebottle; (barca) pedalo

'**moss|a** nf movement; (passo) move. **~o** pp di **muovere** ●a (mare) rough; (capelli) wavy; (fotografia) blurred

mo'**starda** nf mustard

'**mostra** nf show; (d'arte) exhibition; **far ~ di** pretend; **in ~** on show; **mettersi in ~** make oneself conspicuous

mo'**stra|re** vt show; (indicare) point out; (spiegare) explain. **~rsi** vr show oneself; (apparire) appear

'**mostro** nm monster; (fig: persona) genius; **~ sacro** fig sacred cow

mostru'osa'**mente** adv tremendously. **~'oso** a monstrous; (incredibile) enormous

mo'**tel** nm inv motel

moti'**va|re** vt cause; Jur justify. **~to a** (persona) motivated. **~zi'one** nf motivation; (giustificazione) justification

mo'**tivo** nm reason; (movente) motive; (in musica, letteratura) theme; (disegno) motif

'**moto** nm motion; (esercizio) exercise; (gesto) movement; (sommossa) rising ●nf inv (motocicletta) motor bike; **mettere in ~** start (motore)

moto'**carro** nm three-wheeler

motoci'**cl|etta** nf motor cycle. **~ismo** nm motorcycling. **~ista** nmf motor-cyclist

moto'**cros|s** nm motocross. **~'sista** nmf scrambler

moto'**lancia** nf motor launch

moto'**nave** nf motor vessel

mo'**tore** a motor ●nm motor, engine. **moto'retta** nf motor scooter. **moto'rino** nm moped. **motorino d'avviamento** starter

motoriz'**za|to** a Mil motorized. **~zi'one** nf (ufficio) vehicle licensing office

moto'**scafo** nm motorboat

motove'**detta** nf patrol vessel

'**motto** nm motto; (facezia) witticism; (massima) saying

mountain bike nf inv mountain bike

mouse nm inv Comput mouse

mo'**vente** nm motive

movimen'**ta|re** vt enliven. **~to** a lively. **movi'mento** nm movement; **essere sempre in movimento** be always on the go

mozi'**one** nf motion

mozzafi'**ato** a inv nail-biting

moz'**zare** vt cut off; dock (coda); **~ il fiato a qcno** take sb's breath away

mozza'rella *nf* mozzarella, *mild, white cheese*

mozzi'cone *nm* (*di sigaretta*) stub

'**mozzo** *nm Mech* hub; *Naut* ship's boy ● *a* (*coda*) truncated; (*testa*) severed

'**mucca** *nf* cow. **morbo della ~ pazza** mad cow disease

'**mucchio** *nm* heap, pile; **un ~ di** *fig* lots of

'**muco** *nm* mucus

'**muffa** *nf* mould; **fare la ~** go mouldy. **muf'fire** *vi* go mouldy

muf'fole *nfpl* mittens

mug'gi|re *vi* (*mucca:*) moo, low; (*toro:*) bellow. **~to** *nm* moo; bellow; (*azione*) mooing; bellowing

mu'ghetto *nm* lily of the valley

mugo'lare *vi* whine; (*persona:*) moan. **mugo'lio** *nm* whining

mugu'gnare *vt fam* mumble

mulatti'era *nf* mule track

mu'latto, -a *nmf* mulatto

muli'nello *nm* (*d'acqua*) whirl-pool; (*di vento*) eddy; (*giocattolo*) windmill

mu'lino *nm* mill. **~ a vento** windmill

'**mulo** *nm* mule

'**multa** *nf* fine. **mul'tare** *vt* fine

multico'lore *a* multicoloured

multi'lingue *a* multilingual

multi'media *mpl* multimedia

multimedi'ale *a* multimedia *attrib*

multimiliar'dario, -a *nmf* multi-millionaire

multinazio'nale *nf* multinational

'**multiplo** *a & nm* multiple

multiproprietà *nf inv* time-share

multi'uso *a* (*utensile*) all-purpose

'**mummia** *nf* mummy

'**mungere** *vt* milk

mungi'tura *nf* milking

munici'pal|e *a* municipal. **~ità** *nf inv* town council. **muni'cipio** *nm* town hall

mu'nifico *a* munificent

mu'nire *vt* fortify; **~ di** (*provvedere*) supply with

munizi'oni *nfpl* ammunition *sg*

'**munto** *pp di* **mungere**

mu'over|e *vt* move; (*suscitare*) arouse.

~si *vr* move; **muoviti!** hurry up!, come on!

'**mura** *nfpl* (*cinta di città*) walls

mu'raglia *nf* wall

mu'rale *a* mural; (*pittura*) wall *attrib*

mur'a|re *vt* wall up. **~'tore** *nm* bricklayer; (*con pietre*) mason; (*operaio edile*) builder. **~'tura** *nf* (*di pietra*) masonry, stonework; (*di mattoni*) brickwork

mu'rena *nf* moray eel

'**muro** *nm* wall; (*di nebbia*) bank; **a ~** (*armadio*) built-in. **~ portante** load-bearing wall. **~ del suono** sound barrier

'**muschio** *nm Bot* moss

musco'la|re *a* muscular. **~'tura** *nf* muscles *pl*. '**muscolo** *nm* muscle

mu'seo *nm* museum

museru'ola *nf* muzzle

'**musi|ca** *nf* music. **~cal** *nm inv* musical. **~'cale** *a* musical. **~'cista** *nmf* musician.

'**muso** *nm* muzzle; (*pej: di persona*) mug; (*di aeroplano*) nose; **fare il ~** sulk. **mu'sone, -a** *nmf* sulker

'**mussola** *nf* muslin

musul'mano, -a *nmf* Moslem

'**muta** *nf* (*cambio*) change; (*di penne*) moult; (*di cani*) pack; (*per immersione subacquea*) wetsuit

muta'mento *nm* change

mu'tan|de *nfpl* pants; (*da donna*) knickers. **~'doni** *nmpl* (*da uomo*) long johns; (*da donna*) bloomers

mu'tare *vt* change

mu'tevole *a* changeable

muti'la|re *vt* mutilate. **~to, -a** *nmf* disabled person. **~to di guerra** disabled ex-serviceman. **~zi'one** *nf* mutilation

mu'tismo *nm* dumbness; *fig* obstinate silence

'**muto** *a* dumb; (*silenzioso*) silent; (*fonetica*) mute

'**mutu|a** *nf* [**cassa** *nf*] **~** sickness benefit fund. **~'ato, -a** *nmf* ≈ NHS patient

mutuo' *a* mutual

mutuo² *nm* loan; (*per la casa*) mortgage; **fare un ~** take out a mortgage. **~ ipotecario** mortgage

Nn

'nacchera nf castanet

'nafta nf naphtha; (per motori) diesel oil

'naia nf cobra; (sl: servizio militare) national service

'nailon nm nylon

'nanna nf (sl: infantile) byebyes; **andare a ~** go byebyes; **fare la ~** sleep

'nano, -a a & nmf dwarf

napole'tano, -a a & nmf Neapolitan

'Napoli nf Naples

'nappa nf tassel; (pelle) soft leather

narci'sis|mo nm narcissism. **~ta** a & nmf narcissist

nar'ciso nm narcissus

nar'cotico a & nm narcotic

na'rice nf nostril

nar'ra|re vt tell. **~tivo, -a** a narrative ● nf fiction. **~tore, ~trice** nmf narrator. **~zi'one** nf narration; (racconto) story

na'sale a nasal

'nasc|ere vi (venire al mondo) be born; (germogliare) sprout; (sorgere) rise; **~ere da** fig arise from. **~ita** nf birth. **~i'turo** nm unborn child

na'sconder|e vt hide. **~si** vr hide

nascon'diglio nm hiding-place. **~no** nm hide-and-seek. **na'scosto** pp di **nascondere** ● a hidden; **di nascosto** secretly

na'sello nm (pesce) hake

'naso nm nose

'nastro nm ribbon; (di registratore ecc) tape. **~ adesivo** adhesive tape. **~ isolante** insulating tape. **~ trasportatore** conveyor belt

na'tal|e a (paese) of one's birth. **N~e** nm Christmas; **~i** pl parentage. **~ità** nf [number of] births. **nata'lizio** a (del Natale) Christmas attrib; (di nascita) of one's birth

na'tante a floating ● nm craft

'natica nf buttock

na'tio a native

Natività nf Nativity. **na'tivo, -a** a & nmf native

'nato pp di **nascere** ● a born; **uno**

scrittore ~ a born writer; **nata Rossi** née Rossi

NATO nf Nato, NATO

na'tura nf nature; **pagare in ~** pay in kind. **~ morta** still life

natu'ra|le a natural; **al ~le** (alimento) plain, natural; **~le!** naturally, of course. **~'lezza** nf naturalness. **~liz'zare** vt naturalize. **~l'mente** adv (ovviamente) naturally, of course

natu'rista nmf naturalist

naufra'gare vi be wrecked; (persona:) be shipwrecked. **nau'fragio** nm shipwreck; fig wreck. **'naufrago, -a** nmf survivor

'nause|a nf nausea; **avere la ~a** feel sick. **~a'bondo** a nauseating. **~'ante** a nauseating. **~'are** vt nauseate

'nautic|a nf navigation. **~o** a nautical

na'vale a naval

na'vata nf (centrale) nave; (laterale) aisle

'nave nf ship. **~ cisterna** tanker. **~ da guerra** warship. **~ spaziale** spaceship

na'vetta nf shuttle

navicella nf **~ spaziale** nose cone

navi'gabile a navigable

navi'ga|re vi sail; **~re in Internet** surf the Net. **~'tore, ~'trice** mf navigator. **~zi'one** nf navigation

na'viglio nm fleet; (canale) canal

nazio'na|le a national ● nf Sport national team. **~'lismo** nm nationalism. **~'lista** nmf nationalist **~lità** nf inv nationality. **~liz'zare** vt nationalize. **nazi'one** nf nation

na'zista a nmf Nazi

N.B. abbr (nota bene) N.B.

ne pers pron (di lui) about him; (di lei) about her; (di loro) about them; (di ciò) about it; (da ciò) from that; (di un insieme) of it; (di un gruppo) of them; **non ne conosco nessuno** I don't know any of them; **ne ho** I have some; **non ne ho più** I don't have any left ● adv from there; **ne vengo ora** I've just come from there; **me ne vado** I'm off

né conj né... né..., neither... nor...; **non**

ne ho il tempo né la voglia I don't have either the time or the inclination; **né tu né io vogliamo andare** neither you nor I want to go; **né l'uno né l'altro** neither [of them/us]

ne'anche adv (neppure) not even; (senza neppure) without even ●conj (e neppure) neither... nor; **non parlo inglese, e lui ~** I don't speak English, neither does he o and he doesn't either

'nebbi|a nf mist; (in città, su strada) fog. **~'oso** a misty; foggy

necessaria'mente adv necessarily. **neces'sario** a necessary

necessità nf inv necessity; (bisogno) need

necessi'tare vi ~ **di** need; (essere necessario) be necessary

necro'logio nm obituary

ne'cropoli nf inv necropolis

ne'fando a wicked

ne'fasto a ill-omened

ne'ga|re vt deny; (rifiutare) refuse; **essere ~to per qcsa** be no good at sth. **~'tivo, -a** a negative ●nf negative. **~zi'one** nf negation; (diniego) denial; Gram negative

ne'gletto a neglected

'negli = in + gli

negli'gen|te a negligent. **~za** nf negligence

negozi'abile a negotiable

negozi'ante nmf dealer; (bottegaio) shopkeeper

negozi'a|re vt negotiate ●vi ~**re in** trade in. **~ti** nmpl negotiations

ne'gozio nm shop

'negro, -a a Negro, black ●nmf Negro, black; (scrittore) ghost writer

'nei = in + i. nel = in + il. nella = in + la. 'nelle = in + le. 'nello = in + lo

'nembo nm nimbus

ne'mico, -a a hostile ●nmf enemy

nem'meno conj not even

'nenia nf dirge; (per bambini) lullaby; (piagnucolio) wail

'neo nm mole; (applicato) beauty spot

'neo+ pref neo+

neofa'scismo nm neofascism

neo'litico a Neolithic

neolo'gismo nm neologism

'neon nm neon

neo'nato, -a a newborn ●nmf newborn baby

neozelan'dese a New Zealand ●nmf New Zealander

nep'pure conj not even

'nerb|o nm (forza) strength; fig backbone. **~o'ruto** a brawny

ne'retto nm Typ bold [type]

'nero a black; (fam: arrabbiato) fuming ●nm black; **mettere ~ su bianco** put in writing

nerva'tura nf nerves pl; Bot veining; (di libro) band

'nervo nm nerve; Bot vein; **avere i nervi** be bad-tempered; **dare ai nervi a qcno** get on sb's nerves. **~'sismo** nm nerviness

ner'voso a nervous; (irritabile) bad-tempered; **avere il ~** be irritable; **esaurimento ~** nervous breakdown

'nespol|a nf medlar. **~o** nm medlar[-tree]

'nesso nm link

nes'suno a no, not... any; (qualche) any; **non ho nessun problema** I don't have any problems, I have no problems; **non lo trovo da nessuna parte** I can't find it anywhere; **in nessun modo** on no account; **nessuna notizia?** any news? ●pron nobody, no one, not... anybody, not... anyone; (qualcuno) anybody, anyone; **hai delle domande? – nessuna** do you have any questions? – none; **~ di voi** none of you; **~ dei due** (di voi due) neither of you; **non ho visto ~ dei tuoi amici** I haven't seen any of your friends; **c'è ~?** is anybody there?

'nettare¹ nm nectar

net'tare² vt clean

net'tezza nf cleanliness. **~ urbana** cleansing department

'netto a clean; (chiaro) clear; Comm net; **di ~** just like that

nettur'bino nm dustman

neu'tral|e a & nm neutral. **~ità** nf neutrality. **~iz'zare** vt neutralize. **'neutro** a neutral; Gram neuter ●nm Gram neuter

neu'trone nm neutron

'neve nf snow

nevi'care vi snow; **~ca** it is snowing. **~'cata** nf snowfall. **ne'vischio** nm sleet. **ne'voso** a snowy

nevral'gia nf neuralgia. **ne'vralgico** a neuralgic

ne'vro|si nf inv neurosis. **~tico** a neurotic

'nibbio nm kite

'nicchia nf niche

nicchi'are vi shilly-shally

'nichel nm nickel

nichi'lista a & nmf nihilist

nico'tina nf nicotine

nidi'ata nf brood. **'nido** nm nest; (giardino d'infanzia) crèche

ni'ente pron nothing, not... anything; (qualcosa) anything; **non ho fatto ~ di male** I didn't do anything wrong, I did nothing wrong; **grazie! – di ~!** thank you! – don't mention it!; **non serve a ~** it is no use; **vuoi ~?** do you want anything?; **da ~** (poco importante) minor; (di poco valore) worthless ● a inv fam **non ho ~ fame** I'm not the slightest bit hungry ● adv **non fa ~** (non importa) it doesn't matter; **per ~** at all; (litigare) over nothing; **~ affatto!** no way! ● nm **un bel ~** absolutely nothing

nientedi'meno, niente'meno adv **~ che** no less than ● int fancy that!

'ninfa nf nymph

nin'fea nf water-lily

ninna'nanna nf lullaby

'ninnolo nm plaything; (fronzolo) knick-knack

ni'pote nm (di zii) nephew; (di nonni) grandson, grandchild ● nf (di zii) niece; (di nonni) granddaughter, grandchild

nisba pron (sl: niente) zilch

'nitido a neat; (chiaro) clear

ni'trato nm nitrate

ni'tri|re vi neigh. **~to** nm (di cavallo) neigh

n° abbr (**numero**) No

no adv no; (con congiunzione) not; **dire di no** say no; **credo di no** I don't think so; **perché no?** why not?; **io no** not me; **ha detto così, no?** he said so, didn't he?; **fa freddo, no?** it's cold, isn't it?

'nobil|e a noble ● nm noble, nobleman ● nf noble, noblewoman. **~i'are** a noble. **~tà** nf nobility

'nocca nf knuckle

nocci'ol|a nf hazel-nut. **~o** nm (albero) hazel

'nocciolo nm stone; fig heart

'noce nf walnut ● nm (albero, legno) walnut. **~ moscata** nutmeg. **~'pesca** nf nectarine

no'civo a harmful

'nodo nm knot; fig lump; Comput node; **fare il ~ della cravatta** do up one's tie. **~ alla gola** lump in the throat. **no'doso** a knotty. **'nodulo** nm nodule

'noi pers pron (soggetto) we; (oggetto, con prep) us; **chi è? – siamo ~** who is it? – it's us

'noia nf boredom; (fastidio) bother; (persona) bore; **dar ~** annoy

noi'altri pers pron we

noi'oso a boring; (fastidioso) tiresome

noleggi'are vt hire; (dare a noleggio) hire out; charter (nave, aereo). **no'leggio** nm hire; (di nave, aereo) charter. **'nolo** nm hire; Naut freight; **a nolo** for hire

'nomade a nomadic ● nmf nomad

'nome nm name; Gram noun; **a ~ di** in the name of; **di ~** by name; **farsi un ~** make a name for oneself. **~ di famiglia** surname. **~ da ragazza** maiden name. **no'mea** nf reputation

nomencla'tura nf nomenclature

no'mignolo nm nickname

'nomina nf appointment. **nomi'nale** a nominal; Gram noun attrib

nomi'na|re vt name; (menzionare) mention; (eleggere) appoint. **~'tivo** a nominative; Comm registered ● nm nominative; (nome) name

non adv not; **~ ti amo** I do not o don't love you; **~ c'è di che** not at all

nonché conj (tanto meno) let alone; (e anche) as well as

noncu'ran|te a nonchalant; (negligente) indifferent. **~za** nf nonchalance, (negligenza) indifference

nondi'meno conj nevertheless

'nonna nf grandmother, grandma fam

'nonno nm grandfather, grandpa fam; **nonni** pl grandparents

non'nulla nm inv trifle

'nono a & nm ninth

nono'stante prep in spite of ● conj although

nontiscordardimé nm inv forget-me-not

nonvio'lento a nonviolent

nord nm north; **del ~** northern

nor'd-est nm northeast; **a ~** northeasterly

'nordico a northern

nordocciden'tale a northwestern

nordorien'tale a northeastern

nor'd-ovest nm northwest; **a ~** northwesterly

'norma nf rule; (istruzione) instruction; **a ~ di legge** according to law; **è buona ~** it's advisable

nor'mal|e a normal. **~ità** nf normality. **~iz'zare** vt normalize. **~'mente** adv normally

norve'gese a & nmf Norwegian. **Nor'vegia** nf Norway

nossi'gnore adv no way

nostal'gia nf (di casa, patria) homesickness; (del passato) nostalgia; **aver ~ be homesick; aver ~ di qcno** miss sb.

no'stalgico, -a *a* nostalgic ● *nmf* reactionary

no'strano *a* local; (*fatto in casa*) homemade

'nostro (il nostro *m*, la nostra *f*, i nostri *mpl*, le nostre *fpl*) *poss a* our; quella macchina è nostra that car is ours; ~ padre our father; un ~ amico a friend of ours ● *poss pron* ours

'nota *nf* (*segno*) sign; (*comunicazione, commento, Mus*) note; (*conto*) bill; (*lista*) list; degno di ~ noteworthy; prendere ~ take note. note *pl* caratteristiche distinguishing marks

no'tabile *a & nm* notable

no'taio *nm* notary

no'ta|re *vt* (*segnare*) mark; (*annotare*) note down; (*osservare*) notice; far ~re qcsa point sth out; farsi ~re get oneself noticed. ~zi|one *nf* marking; (*annotazione*) notation

'notes *nm inv* notepad

no'tevole *a* (*degno di nota*) remarkable; (*grande*) considerable

no'tifica *nf* notification. notifi'care *vt* notify; *Comm* advise. ~zi|one *nf* notification

no'tizi|a *nf* una ~a a piece of news, some news; (*informazione*) a piece of information, some information; le ~e the news *sg*. ~'ario *nm* news *sg*

'noto *a* [well-]known; rendere ~ (*far sapere*) announce

notorietà *nf* fame; raggiungere la ~ become famous. no'torio *a* well-known; *pej* notorious

not'tambulo *nm* night-bird

not'tata *nf* night; far ~ stay up all night

'notte *nf* night; di ~ at night; ~ bianca sleepless night; peggio che andar di ~ worse than ever. ~'tempo *adv* at night

not'turno *a* nocturnal; (*servizio ecc*) night

no'vanta *a & nm* ninety

novan't|enne *a & nmf* ninety-year-old. ~'esimo *a* ninetieth. ~ina *nf* about ninety. 'nove *a & nm* nine. nove'cento *a & nm* nine hundred. il N~cento the twentieth century

no'vella *nf* short story

novel'lino, -a *a* inexperienced ● *nmf* novice, beginner. no'vello *a* new

no'vembre *nm* November

novità *nf inv* novelty; (*notizie*) news *sg*; l'ultima ~ (*moda*) the latest fashion

novizi'ato *nm Relig* novitiate; (*tirocinio*) apprenticeship

nozi'one *nf* notion; nozioni *pl* rudiments

'nozze *nfpl* marriage *sg*; (*cerimonia*) wedding *sg*. ~ d'argento silver wedding [anniversary]. ~ d'oro golden wedding [anniversary]

'nub|e *nf* cloud. ~e tossica toxic cloud. ~i'fragio *nm* cloudburst

'nubile *a* unmarried ● *nf* unmarried woman

'nuca *nf* nape

nucle'are *a* nuclear

'nucleo *nm* nucleus; (*unità*) unit

nu'di|smo *nm* nudism. ~sta *nmf* nudist. ~tà *nf inv* nudity, nakedness

'nudo *a* naked; (*spoglio*) bare; a occhio ~ to the naked eye

'nugolo *nm* large number

'nulla *pron* = niente; da ~ worthless

nulla'osta *nm inv* permit

nullate'nente *nm* i nullatenenti the have-nots

nullità *nf inv* (*persona*) nonentity

'nullo *a Jur* null and void

nume'ra|bile *a* countable. ~le *a & nm* numeral

nume'ra|re *vt* number. ~zi|one *nf* numbering. nu'merico *a* numerical

'numero *nm* number; (*romano, arabo*) numeral; (*di scarpe ecc*) size; dare i numeri be off one's head. ~ cardinale cardinal [number]. ~ decimale decimal. ~ ordinale ordinal [number]. ~ di telefono phone number. nume'roso *a* numerous

'nunzio *nm* nuncio

nu'ocere *vi* ~ a harm

nu'ora *nf* daughter-in-law

nuo'ta|re *vi* swim; *fig* wallow; ~re nell'oro be stinking rich, be rolling in it. nu'oto *nm* swimming. ~'tore, ~'trice *nmf* swimmer

nu'ov|a *nf* (*notizia*) news *sg*. ~a'mente *adv* again. ~o *a* new; di ~o again; rimettere a ~o give a new lease of life to

nutri'ente *a* nourishing. ~'mento *nm* nourishment

nu'tri|re *vt* nourish; harbour (*sentimenti*). ~rsi eat; ~rsi di *fig* live on. ~'tivo *a* nourishing. ~zi'one *nf* nutrition

'nuvola *nf* cloud. nuvo'loso *a* cloudy

nuzi'ale *a* nuptial; (*vestito, anello ecc*) wedding *attrib*

Oo

O abbr (**ovest**) W

o conj or; **~ l'uno ~ l'altro** one or the other, either

'**oasi** nf inv oasis

obbedi'ente ecc = **ubbidiente** ecc

obbli'ga|re vt force, oblige. **~rsi** vr **~rsi a** undertake to. **~to a** obliged. **~'torio** a compulsory; **~zi'one** nf obligation; Comm bond. '**obbligo** nm obligation; (dovere) duty; **avere obblighi verso** be under an obligation to; **d'obbligo** obligatory

obbligatoria'mente adv fare qcsa **~** be obliged to do sth; **bisogna ~ farlo** you absolutely have to do it

ob'bro|brio nm disgrace. **~'brioso** a disgraceful

obe'lisco nm obelisk

obe'rare vt overburden

obesità nf obesity. **o'beso** a obese

obiet'tare vt/i object; **~ su** object to

obietti|va'mente adv objectively. **~vità** nf objectivity. **obiet'tivo** a objective ● nm objective; (scopo) object

obiet'tore nm objector. **~ttore di coscienza** conscientious objector. **~zi'one** nf objection

obi'torio nm mortuary

o'blio nm oblivion

o'bliquo a oblique; fig underhand

oblite'rare vt obliterate

oblò nm inv porthole

'**oboe** nm oboe

obso'leto a obsolete

'**oca** nf (pl **oche**) goose; (donna) silly girl

occasio'nal|e a occasional. **~'mente** adv occasionally

occasi'one nf occasion; (buon affare) bargain; (motivo) cause; (opportunità) chance; **d'~** secondhand

occhi'aia nf eye socket; **occhiaie** pl shadows under the eyes

occhi'ali nmpl glasses, spectacles. **~ da sole** sunglasses. **~ da vista** glasses, spectacles

occhi'ata nf look; **dare un'~** a have a look at

occhieggi'are vt ogle ● vi (far capolino) peep

occhi'ello nm buttonhole; (asola) eyelet

'**occhio** nm eye; **~!** watch out!; **a quattr'occhi** in private; **tenere d'~ qcno** keep an eye on sb; **a ~ [e croce]** roughly; **chiudere un'~** turn a blind eye; **dare nell'~** attract attention; **pagare** o **spendere un ~ [della testa]** pay an arm and a leg; **saltare agli occhi** be blindingly obvious. **~ nero** (pesto) black eye. **~ di pernice** (callo) corn. **~'lino** nm **fare l'~lino a qcno** wink at sb

occiden'tale a western ● nmf westerner. **occi'dente** nm west

oc'clu|dere vt obstruct. **~si'one** nf occlusion

occor'ren|te a necessary ● nm the necessary. **~za** nf need; **all'~za** if need be

oc'correre vi be necessary

occulta'mento nm **~ di prove** concealment of evidence

occul't|are vt hide. **~ismo** nm occult. **oc'culto** a hidden; (magico) occult

occu'pante nmf occupier; (abusivo) squatter

occu'pa|re vt occupy; spend (tempo); take up (spazio); (dar lavoro a) employ. **~rsi** vr occupy oneself; (trovare lavoro) find a job; **~rsi di** (badare) look after. **~to** a engaged; (persona) busy; (posto) taken. **~zi'one** nf occupation; **trovarsi un'~zione** (interesse) find oneself something to do

o'ceano nm ocean. **~ Atlantico** Atlantic [Ocean]. **~ Pacifico** Pacific [Ocean]

'**ocra** nf ochre

ocu'lare a ocular; (testimone, bagno) eye attrib

ocu'latezza nf care. **ocu'lato** a (scelta) wise

ocu'lista nmf optician; (per malattie) ophthalmologist

od conj or

'**ode** nf ode

odi'are vt hate

odi'erno *a* of today; (*attuale*) present

'**odi|o** *nm* hatred; **avere in ~o** hate. **~'oso** *a* hateful

odo'ra|re *vt* smell; (*profumare*) perfume ● *vi* **~re di** smell of. **~to** *nm* sense of smell. **o'dore** *nm* smell; (*profumo*) scent; **c'è odore di...** there's a smell of...; **sentire odore di** smell; **odori** *pl Culin* herbs. **odo'roso** *a* fragrant

of'fender|e *vt* offend; (*ferire*) injure. **~si** *vr* take offence

offen'siv|a *nf Mil* offensive. **~o** *a* offensive

offe'rente *nmf* offerer; (*in aste*) bidder

of'fert|a *nf* offer; (*donazione*) donation; *Comm* supply; (*nelle aste*) bid; **in ~a speciale** on special offer. **~o** *pp di* **offrire**

of'fes|a *nf* offence. **~o** *pp di* **offendere** ● *a* offended

offi'ciare *vt* officiate

offi'cina *nf* workshop; **~ [meccanica]** garage

of'frire *vt* offer. **~si** *vr* offer oneself; (*occasione:*) present itself; **~si di fare qcsa** offer to do sth

offu'scar|e *vt* darken; *fig* dull (*memoria, bellezza*); blur (*vista*). **~si** *vr* darken; (*fig: memoria, bellezza:*) fade away; (*vista:*) become blurred

of'talmico *a* ophthalmic

oggettività *nf* objectivity. **ogget'tivo** *a* objective

og'getto *nm* object; (*argomento*) subject; **oggetti** *pl* **smarriti** lost property, lost and found *Am*

'**oggi** *adv & nm* today; (*al giorno d'oggi*) nowadays; **da ~ in poi** from today on; **~ a otto** a week today; **dall'~ al domani** overnight; **il giornale di ~** today's paper; **al giorno d'~** these days, nowadays. **~gi'orno** *adv* nowadays

'**ogni** *a inv* every; (*qualsiasi*) any; **~ tre giorni** every three days; **ad ~ costo** at any cost; **ad ~ modo** anyway; **~ cosa** everything; **~ tanto** now and then; **~ volta che** every time, whenever

o'gnuno *pron* everyone, everybody; **~ di voi** each of you

ohimè *int* oh dear!

'**ola** *nf inv* Mexican wave

O'lan|da *nf* Holland. **o~'dese** *a* Dutch ● *nm* Dutchman; (*lingua*) Dutch ● *nf* Dutchwoman

ole'andro *nm* oleander

ole'at|o *a* oiled; **carta ~a** grease-proof paper

oleo'dotto *nm* oil pipeline. **ole'oso** *a* oily

ol'fatto *nm* sense of smell

oli'are *vt* oil

oli'era *nf* cruet

olim'piadi *nfpl* Olympic Games. **o'limpico** *a* Olympic. **olim'pionico** *a* (*primato, squadra*) Olympic

'**olio** *nm* oil; **sott'~** in oil; **colori a ~** oils; **quadro a ~** oil painting. **~ di mais** corn oil. **~ d'oliva** olive oil. **~ di semi** vegetable oil. **~ solare** sun-tan oil

o'**liv|a** *nf* olive. **oli'vastro** *a* olive. **oli'veto** *nm* olive grove. **~o** *nm* olive tree

'**olmo** *nm* elm

olo'gramma *nm* hologram

oltraggi'are *vt* offend. **ol'traggio** *nm* offence

ol'tranza *nf* **ad ~** to the bitter end

'**oltre** *adv* (*di luogo*) further; (*di tempo*) longer ● *prep* (*di luogo*) over; (*di tempo*) later than; (*più di*) more than; (*in aggiunta*) besides; **~ a** (*eccetto*) except, apart from; **per ~ due settimane** for more than two weeks; **una settimana e ~** a week and more. **~'mare** *adv* overseas. **~'modo** *adv* extremely

oltrepas'sare *vt* go beyond; (*eccedere*) exceed

o'**maggio** *nm* homage; (*dono*) gift; **in ~ con** free with; **omaggi** *pl* (*saluti*) respects

ombeli'cale *a* umbilical; **cordone ~** umbilical cord. **ombe'lico** *nm* navel

'**ombr|a** *nf* (*zona*) shade; (*immagine oscura*) shadow; **all'~a** in the shade. **~eggi'are** *vt* shade

om'brello *nm* umbrella. **ombrel'lone** *nm* beach umbrella

om'bretto *nm* eye-shadow

om'broso *a* shady; (*cavallo*) skittish

ome'lette *nf inv* omelette

ome'lia *nf Relig* sermon

omeopa'tia *nf* homoeopathy. **omeo'patico** *a* homoeopathic ● *nm* homoeopath

omertà *nf* conspiracy of silence

o'**messo** *pp di* **omettere**

o'**mettere** *vt* omit

omi'cid|a *a* murderous ● *nmf* murderer. **~io** *nm* murder. **~io colposo** manslaughter

omissi'one *nf* omission

omogeneiz'zato *a* homogenized. **omo'geneo** *a* homogeneous

omolo'gare *vt* approve

o'monimo, -a *nmf* namesake ● *nm* (*parola*) homonym

omosessu'al|e *a* & *nmf* homosexual. ~ità *nf* homosexuality

On. *abbr* (onorevole) M.P.

'oncia *nf* ounce

'onda *nf* wave; andare in ~ *Radio* go on the air. a ondate in waves. onde *pl* corte short wave. onde *pl* lunghe long wave. onde *pl* medie medium wave. on'data *nf* wave

'onde *conj* so that ● *pron* whereby

ondeggi'are *vi* wave; (*barca:*) roll

ondula'torio *a* undulating. ~zi'one *nf* undulation; (*di capelli*) wave

'oner|e *nm* burden. ~'oso *a* onerous

onestà *nf* honesty; (*rettitudine*) integrity. o'nesto *a* honest; (*giusto*) just

'onice *nf* onyx

onnipo'tente *a* omnipotent

onnipre'sente *a* ubiquitous; *Rel* omnipresent

ono'mastico *nm* name-day

ono'ra|bile *a* honourable. ~re *vt* (*fare onore a*) be a credit to; honour (*promessa*). ~rio *a* honorary ● *nm* fee. ~rsi *vr* ~rsi di be proud of

o'nore *nm* honour; in ~ di (*festa, ricevimento*) in honour of; fare ~ a do justice to (*pranzo*); farsi ~ in excel in; fare gli onori di casa do the honours

ono'revole *a* honourable ● *nmf* Member of Parliament

onorifi'cenza *nf* honour; (*decorazione*) decoration. ono'rifico *a* honorary

'onta *nf* shame

O.N.U. *nf abbr* (Organizzazione delle Nazioni Unite) UN

o'paco *a* opaque; (*colori ecc*) dull; (*fotografia, rossetto*) matt

o'pale *nf* opal

'opera *nf* (*lavoro*) work; (*azione*) deed; *Mus* opera; (*teatro*) opera house; (*ente*) institution; mettere in ~ put into effect; mettersi all'~ get to work; opere *pl* pubbliche public works. ~ d'arte work of art. ~ lirica opera

ope'raio, -a *a* working ● *nmf* worker; ~ specializzato skilled worker

ope'ra|re *vt Med* operate on; farsi ~re have an operation ● *vi* operate; (*agire*) work. ~'tivo, ~'torio *a* operating *atti ib.* ~'tore, ~'trice *nmf* operator; *TV* cameraman. ~tore turistico tour operator. ~zi'one *nf* operation; *Comm* transaction

ope'retta *nf* operetta

ope'roso *a* industrious

opini'one *nf* opinion; rimanere della propria ~ still feel the same way. ~ pubblica public opinion, vox pop

'oppio *nm* opium

oppo'nente *a* opposing ● *nmf* opponent

op'por|re *vt* oppose; (*obiettare*) object; ~re resistenza offer resistance. ~si *vr* ~si a oppose

opportu'ni|smo *nm* expediency. ~sta *nmf* opportunist. ~tà *nf inv* opportunity; (*l'essere opportuno*) timeliness. oppor'tuno *a* opportune; (*adeguato*) appropriate; ritenere opportuno fare qcsa think it appropriate to do sth; il momento opportuno the right moment

opposi'tore *nm* opposer. ~zi'one *nf* opposition; d'~zione (*giornale, partito*) opposition

op'posto *pp di* opporre ● *a* opposite; (*opinioni*) opposing ● *nm* opposite; all'~ on the contrary

oppres|si'one *nf* oppression. ~'sivo *a* oppressive. op'presso *pp di* opprimere ● *a* oppressed. ~'sore *nm* oppressor

oppri'mente *a* oppressive. op'prime|re *vt* oppress; (*gravare*) weigh down

op'pure *conj* otherwise, or [else]; lunedì ~ martedì Monday or Tuesday

op'tare *vi* ~ per opt for

opu'scolo *nm* booklet; (*pubblicitario*) brochure

opzio'nale *a* optional. opzi'one *nf* option

'ora¹ *nf* time; (*unità*) hour; di buon'~ early; che ~ è?, che ore sono? what time is it?; mezz'~ half an hour; a ore (*lavorare, pagare*) by the hour; 50 km all'~ 50 km an hour; a un'~ di macchina one hour by car; non vedo l'~ di vederti I can't wait to see you; fare le ore piccole stay up until the small hours. ~ d'arrivo arrival time. l'~ esatta *Teleph* speaking clock. ~ legale daylight saving time. ~ di punta, ore *pl* di punta peak time; (*per il traffico*) rush hour

'ora² *adv* now; (*tra poco*) presently; ~ come ~ just now, at the moment; d'~ in poi from now on; per ~ for the time being, for now; è ~ di finirla! that's enough now! ● *conj* (*dunque*) now [then]; ~ che ci penso,... now that I come to think about it,...

o'racolo nm oracle

'orafo nm goldsmith

o'rale a & nm oral; per via ~ by mouth

ora'mai adv = ormai

o'rario a ⟨tariffa⟩ hourly; ⟨segnale⟩ time attrib; ⟨velocità⟩ per hour ● nm time; ⟨tabella dell'orario⟩ timetable, schedule Am; essere in ~ be on time; in senso ~ clockwise. ~ di chiusura closing time. ~ flessibile flexitime. ~ di sportello banking hours. ~ d'ufficio business hours. ~ di visita Med consulting hours

o'rata nf gilthead

ora'tore, -'trice nmf speaker

ora'torio, -a a oratorical ● nm Mus oratorio ● nmf oratory. orazi'one nf Relig prayer

'orbita nf orbit; Anat [eye-]socket

or'chestra nf orchestra; ⟨parte del teatro⟩ pit

orche'stra|le a orchestral ● nmf member of an/the orchestra. ~re vt orchestrate

orchi'dea nf orchid

'orco nm ogre

'orda nf horde

or'digno nm device; ⟨arnese⟩ tool. ~ esplosivo explosive device

ordi'nale a & nm ordinal

ordina'mento nm order; ⟨leggi⟩ rules pl.

ordi'nanza nf ⟨del sindaco⟩ bylaw; d'~ ⟨soldato⟩ on duty

ordi'nare vt ⟨sistemare⟩ arrange; ⟨comandare⟩ order; ⟨prescrivere⟩ prescribe; Relig ordain

ordi'nario a ordinary; ⟨grossolano⟩ common; ⟨professore⟩ with a permanent position; di ordinaria amministrazione routine ● nm ordinary; Univ professor

ordi'nato a ⟨in ordine⟩ tidy

ordinazi'one nf order; fare un'~ place an order

'ordine nm order; ⟨di avvocati, medici⟩ association; mettere in ~ put in order; tidy up ⟨appartamento ecc⟩; di prim'~ first-class; di terz'~e ⟨film, albergo⟩ third- rate; di ~ pratico/economico ⟨problema⟩ of a practical/economic nature; fino a nuovo ~ until further notice; parola d'~ password. ~ del giorno agenda. ordini sacri pl Holy Orders

or'dire vt ⟨tramare⟩ plot

orec'chino nm ear-ring

o'recchi|o nm ⟨pl nf orecchie⟩ ear; avere ~o have a good ear; mi è giunto all'~o che... I've heard that...; parlare all'~o a qcno whisper in sb's ear; suonare a ~o play by ear; ~'oni pl Med mumps sg

o'refice nm jeweller. ~'ria nf ⟨arte⟩ goldsmith's art; ⟨negozio⟩ goldsmith's [shop]

'orfano, -a a orphan ● nmf orphan. ~'trofio nm orphanage

orga'netto nm barrel-organ; ⟨a bocca⟩ mouth-organ; ⟨fisarmonica⟩ accordion

or'ganico a organic ● nm personnel

orga'nismo nm organism; ⟨corpo umano⟩ body

orga'nista nmf organist

organiz'za|re vt organize. ~rsi vr get organized. ~'tore, ~'trice nmf organizer. ~zi'one nf organization

'organo nm organ

or'gasmo nm orgasm; fig agitation

'orgia nf orgy

or'gogli|o nm pride. ~'oso a proud

orien'tale a eastern; ⟨cinese ecc⟩ oriental

orienta'mento nm orientation; perdere l'~ lose one's bearings; senso dell'~ sense of direction

orien'ta|re vt orientate. ~rsi vr find one's bearings; ⟨tendere⟩ tend

ori'ente nm east. l'Estremo O~ the Far East. il Medio O~ the Middle East

o'rigano nm oregano

origi'na|le a original; ⟨eccentrico⟩ odd ● nm original. ~'lità nf originality. ~re vt/i originate. ~rio a ⟨nativo⟩ native

o'rigine nf origin; in ~ originally; aver ~ da originate from; dare ~ a give rise to

origli'are vi eavesdrop

o'rina nf urine. ori'nale nm chamberpot. ori'nare vi urinate

ori'undo a native

orizzon'tale a horizontal

orizzon'tare vt = orientare oriz'zonte nm horizon

or'la|re vt hem. ~'tura nf hem. 'orlo nm edge; ⟨di vestito ecc⟩ hem

'orma nf track; ⟨di piede⟩ footprint; ⟨impronta⟩ mark

or'mai adv by now; ⟨passato⟩ by then; ⟨quasi⟩ almost

ormeggi'are vt moor. or'meggio nm mooring

ormo'nale a hormonal. or'mone nm hormone

ornamen'tale a ornamental. orna'mento nm ornament

or'na|re *vt* decorate. ~rsi *vr* deck oneself. ~to *a ‹stile›* ornate

ornitolo'gia *nf* ornithology

'oro *nm* gold; d'~ gold; *fig* golden; una persona d'~ a wonderful person

orologi'aio, -a *nmf* clockmaker, watchmaker

oro'logio *nm (portatile)* watch; *(da tavolo, muro ecc)* clock. ~ a pendolo grandfather clock. ~ da polso wristwatch. ~ a sveglia alarm clock

o'roscopo *nm* horoscope

or'rendo *a* awful, dreadful

or'ribile *a* horrible

orripi'lante *a* horrifying

or'rore *nm* horror; avere qcsa in ~ hate sth

orsacchi'otto *nm* teddy bear

'orso *nm* bear; *(persona scontrosa)* hermit. ~ bianco polar bear

or'taggio *nm* vegetable

or'tensia *nf* hydrangea

or'tica *nf* nettle. orti'caria *nf* nettle-rash

orticol'tura *nf* horticulture. 'orto *nm* vegetable plot

orto'dosso *a* orthodox

ortogo'nale *a* perpendicular

orto|gra'fia *nf* spelling. ~'grafico *a* spelling *attrib*

orto'lano *nm* market gardener; *(negozio)* greengrocer's

orto|pe'dia *nf* orthopaedics *sg.* ~'pedico *a* orthopaedic ● *nm* orthopaedist

orzai'olo *nm* sty

or'zata *nf* barley-water

osan'nato *a* praised to the skies

o'sare *vt/i* dare; *(avere audacia)* be daring

oscenità *nf inv* obscenity. o'sceno *a* obscene

oscil'la|re *vi* swing; *(prezzi ecc:)* fluctuate; *Tech* oscillate; *(fig: essere indeciso)* vacillate. ~zi'one *nf* swinging; *(di prezzi)* fluctuation; *Tech* oscillation

oscura'mento *nm* darkening; *(di vista, mente)* dimming; *(totale)* black-out

oscu'r|are *vt* darken; *fig* obscure. ~arsi *vr* get dark. ~ità *nf* darkness. o'scuro *a* dark; *(triste)* gloomy; *(incomprensibile)* obscure

ospe'dale *nm* hospital. ~i'ero *a* hospital *attrib*

ospi'ta|le *a* hospitable. ~lità *nf* hospitality. ~re *vt* give hospitality to. 'ospite *nm (chi ospita)* host; *(chi viene ospitato)* guest ● *nf* hostess; guest

o'spizio *nm (per vecchi)* [old people's] home

ossa'tura *nf* bone structure; *(di romanzo)* structure, framework. 'osseo *a* bone *attrib*

ossequi'are *vt* pay one's respects to. os'sequio *nm* homage; ossequi *pl* respects. ~'oso *a* obsequious

osser'vante *a ‹cattolico›* practising. ~za *nf* observance

osser'va|re *vt* observe; *(notare)* notice; keep *‹ordine, silenzio›*. ~'tore, ~'trice *nmf* observer. ~'torio *nm Astr* observatory; *Mil* observation post. ~zi'one *nf* observation; *(rimprovero)* reproach

ossessio'na|nte *a* haunting; *‹persona›* nagging. ~re *vt* obsess; *(infastidire)* nag. ossessi'one *nf* obsession; *(assillo)* pain in the neck. osses'sivo *a* obsessive. os'sesso *a* obsessed

os'sia *conj* that is

ossi'dabile *a* liable to tarnish

ossi'dar|e *vt*, ~si *vr* oxidize

'ossido *nm* oxide. ~ di carbonio carbon monoxide

os'sidrico *a* fiamma ossidrica blow-lamp

ossige'nar|e *vt* oxygenate; *(decolorare)* bleach; *fig* put back on its feet *‹azienda›*. ~si *vr* ~si i capelli dye one's hair blonde. os'sigeno *nm* oxygen

'osso *nm (Anat: pl nf ossa)* bone; *(di frutto)* stone

osso'buco *nm* marrowbone

os'suto *a* bony

ostaco'lare *vt* hinder, obstruct. o'stacolo *nm* obstacle; *Sport* hurdle

o'staggio *nm* hostage; prendere in ~ take hostage

o'stello *nm* ~ della gioventù youth hostel

osten'ta|re *vt* show off; ~re indifferenza pretend to be indifferent. ~zi'one *nf* ostentation

oste'ria *nf* inn

o'stetrico, -a *a* obstetric ● *nmf* obstetrician

'ostia *nf* host; *(cialda)* wafer

'ostico *a* tough

o'sti|le *a* hostile. ~ità *nf inv* hostility

osti'na|rsi *vr* persist (a in). ~to *a* obstinate. ~zi'one *nf* obstinacy

ostra'cismo *nm* ostracism

'ostrica *nf* oyster

ostro'goto *nm* parlare ~ talk double Dutch

ostru'i|re vt obstruct. **~zi'one** nf obstruction

otorinolaringoi'atra nmf ear, nose and throat specialist

ottago'nale a octagonal. **ot'tagono** nm octagon

ot'tan|ta a & nm eighty. **~'tenne** a & nmf eighty-year-old. **~'tesimo** a eightieth. **~'tina** nf about eighty

ot'tav|a nf octave. **~o** a eighth

otte'nere vt obtain; (più comune) get; (conseguire) achieve

'ottico, -a a optic[al] ● nmf optician ● nf (scienza) optics sg; (di lenti ecc) optics pl

otti'ma|le a optimum. **~'mente** adv very well

otti'mis|mo nm optimism. **~ta** nmf optimist. **~tico** a optimistic

'ottimo a very good ● nm optimum

'otto a & nm eight

ot'tobre nm October

otto'cento a & nm eight hundred; **l'O~** the nineteenth century

ot'tone nm brass

ottuage'nario, -a a & nmf octoge-

narian

ottu'ra|re vt block; fill (dente). **~rsi** vr clog. **~'tore** nm Phot shutter. **~zi'one** nf stopping; (di dente) filling

ot'tuso pp di ottundere ● a obtuse

o'vaia nf ovary

o'vale a & nm oval

o'vat|ta nf cotton wool. **~'tato** a (suono, passi) muffled

ovazi'one nf ovation

over'dose nf inv overdose

'ovest nm west

o'vi|le nm sheep-fold. **~no** a sheep attrib

ovo'via nf two-seater cable car

ovulazi'one nf ovulation

o'vunque adv = dovunque

ov'vero conj or; (cioè) that is

ovvia'mente adv obviously

ovvi'are vi **~ a qcsa** counter sth. **'ovvio** a obvious

ozi'are vi laze around. **'ozio** nm idleness; **stare in ozio** idle about. **ozi'oso** a idle; (questione) pointless

o'zono nm ozone; **buco nell'~** hole in the ozone layer

Pp

pa'ca|re vt quieten. **~to** a quiet

pac'chetto nm packet; (postale) parcel, package; (di sigarette) pack, packet. **~ software** software package

'pacchia nf (fam: situazione) bed of roses

pacchia'nata nf **è una ~** it's so garish. **pacchi'ano** a garish

'pacco nm parcel; (involto) bundle. **~ regalo** gift-wrapped package

paccot'tiglia nf (roba scadente) junk, rubbish

'pace nf peace; **darsi ~** forget it; **fare ~ con qcno** make it up with sb; **lasciare in ~ qcno** leave sb in peace

pachi'derma nm (animale) pachyderm

pachi'stano, -a nmf & a Pakistani

pacifi'ca|re vt reconcile; (mettere pace) pacify. **~zi'one** nf reconciliation

pa'cifico a pacific; (calmo) peaceful; **il P~** the Pacific

paci'fis|mo nm pacifism. **~ta** nmf pacifist

pacioc'cone, -a nmf fam chubbychops

pa'dano a pianura nf padana Po Valley

pa'del|la nf frying-pan; (per malati) bedpan. **~lata** nf **una ~lata di** a frying-panful of

padigli'one nm pavilion

'padre nm father; **~i** pl (antenati) forefathers. **pa'drino** nm godfather. **~e'nostro** nm **il ~enostro** the Lord's Prayer. **~e'terno** nm God Almighty

padro'nanza nf mastery. **~ di sé** self-control

pa'drone, -a nmf master; mistress; (datore di lavoro) boss; (proprietario) owner. **~ggi'are** vt master

pae'sag|gio nm scenery; (pittura) landscape. **~'gista** nmf landscape architect

pae'sano, -a *a* country ● *nmf* villager

pa'ese *nm* (*nazione*) country; (*territorio*) land; (*villaggio*) village; **il Bel P~** Italy; **va' a quel ~!** get lost!; **Paesi** *pl* **Bassi** Netherlands

paf'futo *a* plump

'paga *nf* pay, wages *pl*

pa'gabile *a* payable

pa'gaia *nf* paddle

paga'mento *nm* payment; **a ~** (*parcheggio*) which you have to pay to use. **~ anticipato** *Comm* advance payment. **~ alla consegna** cash on delivery, COD

paga'nesimo *nm* paganism

pa'gano, -a *a & nmf* pagan

pa'gare *vt/i* pay; **~ da bere a qcno** buy sb a drink; **te la faccio ~** you'll pay for this

pa'gella *nf* [school] report

'pagina *nf* page. **Pagine** *pl* **Gialle** Yellow Pages. **~ web** *Comput* web page

'paglia *nf* straw

pagliac'cetto *nm* (*per bambini*) rompers *pl*

pagliac'ciata *nf* farce

pagli'accio *nm* clown

pagli'aio *nm* haystack

paglie'riccio *nm* straw mattress

pagli'etta *nf* (*cappello*) boater; (*per pentole*) steel wool

pagli'uzza *nf* wisp of straw; (*di metallo*) particle

pa'gnotta *nf* [round] loaf

pa'goda *nf* pagoda

pail'lette *nf inv* sequin

'paio *nm* (*pl inv* **paia**) pair; **un ~** (*circa due*) a couple; **un ~ di** (*scarpe, forbici*) a pair of

'Pakistan *nm* Pakistan

'pala *nf* shovel; (*di remo, elica*) blade; (*di ruota*) paddle

pala'fitta *nf* pile-dwelling

pala'sport *nm inv* indoor sports arena

pa'late *nfpl* **a ~** (*fare soldi*) hand over fist

pa'lato *nm* palate

palaz'zetto *nm* **~ dello sport** indoor sports arena

palaz'zina *nf* villa

pa'lazzo *nm* palace; (*edificio*) building. **~ delle esposizioni** exhibition centre. **~ di giustizia** law courts *pl*, courthouse. **~ dello sport** indoor sports arena

'palco *nm* (*pedana*) platform; *Theat* box. **~['scenico]** *nm* stage

pale'sar|e *vt* disclose. **~si** *vr* reveal oneself. **pa'lese** *a* evident

Pale'sti|na *nf* Palestine. **p~'nese** *nmf* Palestinian

pa'lestra *nf* gymnasium, gym; (*ginnastica*) gymnastics *pl*

pa'letta *nf* spade; (*per focolare*) shovel. **~ [della spazzatura]** dustpan

pa'letto *nm* peg

'palio *nm* (*premio*) prize. **il P~** horserace held at Siena

paliz'zata *nf* fence

'palla *nf* ball; (*proiettile*) bullet; (*fam: bugia*) porkie; **che palle!** *vulg* this is a pain in the arse!. **~ di neve** snowball. **~ al piede** *fig* millstone round one's neck

pallaca'nestro *nf* basketball

palla'mano *nf* handball

pallanu'oto *nf* water polo

palla'volo *nf* volley-ball

palleggi'are *vi* (*calcio*) practise ball control; *Tennis* knock up

pallia'tivo *nm* palliative

'pallido *a* pale; **non ne ho la più pallida idea** I don't have the faintest idea

pal'lina *nf* (*di vetro*) marble

pal'lino *nm* **avere il ~ del calcio** be crazy about football

pallon'cino *nm* balloon; (*lanterna*) Chinese lantern; (*fam: etilometro*) Breathalyzer®

pal'lone *nm* ball; (*calcio*) football; (*aerostato*) balloon

pal'lore *nm* pallor

pal'loso *a sl* boring

pal'lottola *nf* pellet; (*proiettile*) bullet

'palm|a *nf Bot* palm. **~o** *nm Anat* palm; (*misura*) hand's-breadth; **restare con un ~o di naso** feel disappointed

'palo *nm* pole; (*di sostegno*) stake; (*in calcio*) goalpost; **fare il ~** (*ladro:*) keep a lookout. **~ della luce** lamppost

palom'baro *nm* diver

pal'pare *vt* feel

'palpebra *nf* eyelid

palpi'ta|re *vi* throb; (*fremere*) quiver. **~zi'one** *nf* palpitation. **'palpito** *nm* throb; (*del cuore*) beat

pa'lude *nf* marsh, swamp

palu'doso *a* marshy

pa'lustre *a* marshy; (*piante, uccelli*) marsh *attrib*

pam'pino *nm* vine leaf

pana'cea *nf* panacea

'panca *nf* bench; (*in chiesa*) pew

pancar'rè *nm* sliced bread

pan'cetta *nf Culin* bacon; (*di una certa età*) paunch

pan'chetto *nm* [foot]stool

pan'china *nf* garden seat; (*in calcio*) bench

'**pancia** *nf* belly, tummy *fam*; **mal di ~** stomach-ache; **metter su ~** develop a paunch; **a ~ in giù** lying face down.

panci'era *nf* corset

panci'olle: stare in ~ lounge about

panci'one *nm* (*persona*) pot belly

panci'otto *nm* waistcoat

pande'monio *nm* pandemonium

pan'doro *nm* kind of sponge cake eaten at Christmas

'**pane** *nm* bread; (*pagnotta*) loaf; (*di burro*) block. **~ a cassetta** sliced bread. **pan grattato** breadcrumbs *pl*. **~ di segale** rye bread. **pan di Spagna** sponge cake. **~ tostato** toast

panett|e'ria *nf* bakery; (*negozio*) baker's [shop]. **~i'ere, -a** *nmf* baker

panet'tone *nf* dome-shaped cake with sultanas and candied fruit eaten at Christmas

'**panfilo** *nm* yacht

pan'forte *nm* nougat-like spicy delicacy from Siena

'**panico** *nm* panic; **lasciarsi prendere dal ~** panic

pani'ere *nm* basket; (*cesta*) hamper

pani'ficio *nm* bakery; (*negozio*) baker's [shop]

pani'naro *nm sl* ≈ preppie

pa'nino *nm* [bread] roll. **~ imbottito** filled roll. **~ al prosciutto** ham roll. **~teca** *nf* sandwich bar

'**panna** *nf* cream. **~ da cucina** [single] cream. **~ montata** whipped cream

'**panne** *nf Mech* **in ~** broken down; **restare in ~** break down

pan'nello *nm* panel. **~ solare** solar panel

'**panno** *nm* cloth; **panni** *pl* (*abiti*) clothes; **mettersi nei panni di qcno** *fig* put oneself in sb's shoes

pan'nocchia *nf* (*di granoturco*) cob

panno'lino *nm* (*per bambini*) nappy; (*da donna*) sanitary towel

pano'ram|a *nm* panorama; *fig* overview. **~ico** *a* panoramic

pantacol'lant *nmpl* leggings

pantalon'cini *nmpl* **~ [corti]** shorts

panta'loni *nmpl* trousers, pants *Am*

pan'tano *nm* bog

pan'tera *nf* panther; (*auto della polizia*) high-speed police car

pan'tofo|la *nf* slipper. **~'laio, -a** *nmf fig* stay-at-home

pan'zana *nf* fib

pao'nazzo *a* purple

'**papa** *nm* Pope

papà *nm inv* dad[dy]

pa'pale *a* papal

papa'lina *nf* skull-cap

papa'razzo *nm* paparazzo

pa'pato *nm* papacy

pa'pavero *nm* poppy

'**paper|a** *nf* (*errore*) slip of the tongue. **~o** *nm* gosling

papil'lon *nm inv* bow tie

pa'piro *nm* papyrus

'**pappa** *nf* (*per bambini*) pap

pappa'gallo *nm* parrot

pappa'molle *nmf* wimp

'**para** *nf* **suole** *nfpl* **di ~** crêpe soles

pa'rabola *nf* parable; (*curva*) parabola

para'bolico *a* parabolic

para'brezza *nm inv* windscreen, windshield *Am*

paracadu'tar|e *vt* parachute. **~si** *vr* parachute

paraca'du|te *nm inv* parachute. **~'tismo** *nm* parachuting. **~'tista** *nmf* parachutist

para'carro *nm* roadside post

paradi'siaco *a* heavenly

para'diso *nm* paradise. **~ terrestre** Eden, earthly paradise

parados'sale *a* paradoxical. **para-'dosso** *nm* paradox

para'fango *nm* mudguard

paraf'fina *nf* paraffin

parafra'sare *vt* paraphrase

para'fulmine *nm* lightning-conductor

pa'raggi *nmpl* neighbourhood *sg*

parago'na|bile *a* comparable (**a** to). **~re** *vt* compare. **para'gone** *nm* comparison; **a paragone di** in comparison with

pa'ragrafo *nm* paragraph

pa'ral|isi *nf inv* paralysis. **~'litico, -a** *a & nmf* paralytic. **~liz'zare** *vt* paralyse. **~liz'zato** *a* (*dalla paura*) transfixed

paral'lel|a *nf* parallel line. **~a'mente** *adv* in parallel. **~o** *a & nm* parallel; **~e** *pl* parallel bars. **~o'gramma** *nm* parallelogram

para'lume *nm* lampshade

para'medico *nm* paramedic

pa'rametro *nm* parameter

para'noi|a *nf* paranoia. **~co, -a** *a & nmf* paranoid

paranor'male *a* (*fenomeno, facoltà*) paranormal

para'occhi *nmpl* blinkers. **parao'recchie** *nm* earmuffs

para'petto *nm* parapet

para'piglia *nm* turmoil

para'plegico, -a *a & nmf* paraplegic

pa'rar|e *vt* (*addobbare*) adorn; (*riparare*) shield; save (*tiro, pallone*); ward off, parry (*schiaffo, pugno*) ●*vi* (*mirare*) lead up to. **~si** *vr* (*abbigliarsi*) dress up; (*da pioggia, pugni*) protect oneself; **~si dinanzi a qcno** appear in front of sb

para'sole *nm inv* parasol

paras'sita *a* parasitic ●*nm* parasite

parasta'tale *a* a government-controlled

pa'rata *nf* parade; (*in calcio*) save; (*in scherma, pugilato*) parry

para'urti *nm inv Auto* bumper, fender *Am*

para'vento *nm* screen

par'cella *nf* bill

parcheggi'a|re *vt* park. **par'cheggio** *nm* parking; (*posteggio*) carpark, parking lot *Am.* **~'tore, ~'trice** *nmf* parking attendant. **~tore abusivo** *person who illegally earns money by looking after parked cars*

par'chimetro *nm* parking-meter

'parco¹ *a* sparing; (*moderato*) moderate

'parco² *nm* park. **~ di divertimenti** fun-fair. **~ giochi** playground. **~ naturale** wildlife park. **~ nazionale** national park. **~ regionale** [regional] wildlife park

pa'recchi *a* a good many ●*pron* several

pa'recchio *a* quite a lot of ●*pron* quite a lot ●*adv* rather; (*parecchio tempo*) quite a time

pareggi'are *vt* level; (*eguagliare*) equal; *Comm* balance ●*vi* draw

pa'reggio *nm Comm* balance; *Sport* draw

paren'tado *nm* relatives *pl*; (*vincolo di sangue*) relationship

pa'rente *nmf* relative. **~ stretto** close relation

paren'tela *nf* relatives *pl*; (*vincolo di sangue*) relationship

pa'rentesi *nf inv* parenthesis; (*segno grafico*) bracket; (*fig: pausa*) break. **~ pl graffe** curly brackets. **~ quadre** square brackets. **~ tonde** round brackets

pa'reo *nm* (*copricostume*) sarong; **a ~** (*gonna*) wrap-around

pa'rere¹ *nm* opinion; **a mio ~** in my opinion

pa'rere² *vi* seem; (*pensare*) think; **che te ne pare?** what do you think of it?; **pare di sì** it seems so

pa'rete *nf* wall; (*in alpinismo*) face. **~ divisoria** partition wall

'pari *a inv* equal; (*numero*) even; **andare di ~ passo** keep pace; **essere ~** be even o quits; **arrivare ~** draw; **~** (*copiare, ripetere*) word for word; **fare ~ o dispari** ≈ toss a coin ●*nmf inv* equal, peer; **ragazza alla ~** au pair [girl]; **mettersi in ~ con qcsa** catch up with sth ●*nm* (*titolo nobiliare*) peer

Pa'rigi *nf* Paris

pa'riglia *nf* pair

pari'tà *nf* equality; *Tennis* deuce. **~'tario** *a* parity *attrib*

parlamen'tare *a* parliamentary ●*nmf* Member of Parliament ●*vi* discuss. **parla'mento** *nm* Parliament. **il Parlamento europeo** the European Parliament

parlan'tina *nf* **avere la ~** be a chatterbox

par'la|re *vt/i* speak, talk; (*confessare*) talk; **~ bene/male di qcno** speak well/ill of somebody; **non parliamone più** let's forget about it; **non se ne parla nemmeno!** don't even mention it!. **~to** *a* (*lingua*) spoken. **~'torio** *nm* parlour; (*in prigione*) visiting room

parlot'tare *vi* mutter. **parlot'tio** *nm* muttering

parmigi'ano *nm* Parmesan

paro'dia *nf* parody

pa'rola *nf* word; (*facoltà*) speech; **è una ~!** it is easier said than done!; **parole** *pl* (*di canzone*) words, lyrics; **rivolgere la ~ a** address; **dare a qcno la propria ~** give sb one's word; **in parole povere** crudely speaking. **parole** *pl* **incrociate** crossword [puzzle] *sg*. **~ d'onore** word of honour. **~ d'ordine** password. **paro'laccia** *nf* swear-word

par'quet *nm inv* (*pavimento*) parquet flooring

par'rocchi|a *nf* parish. **~'ale** *a* parish *attrib*. **~'ano, -a** *nmf* parishioner. **'parroco** *nm* parish priest

par'rucca *nf* wig

parrucchi'ere, -a *nmf* hairdresser

parruc'chino *nm* toupée, hairpiece

parsi'moni|a *nf* thrift. **~'oso** *a* thrifty

'parso *pp di* **parere**

'parte *nf* part; (*lato*) side; (*partito*) party; (*porzione*) share; **a ~** apart from; **in ~** in part; **la maggior ~ di** the majority of; **d'altra ~** on the other hand; **da ~** aside; (*in disparte*) to one side; **farsi da ~** stand aside; **da ~ di** from;

(*per conto di*) on behalf of; **è gentile da ~ tua** it is kind of you; **fare una brutta ~ a qcno** behave badly towards sb; **da che ~ è...?** whereabouts is...?; **da una ~...**, **dall'altra...** on the one hand..., on the other hand...; **dall'altra ~ di** on the other side of; **da nessuna ~** nowhere; **da tutte le parti** (*essere*) everywhere; **da questa ~** (*in questa direzione*) this way; **da un anno a questa ~** for about a year now; **essere dalla ~ di qcno** be on sb's side; **prendere le parti di qcno** take sb's side; **essere ~ in causa** be involved; **fare ~ di** (*appartenere a*) be a member of; **rendere ~ a** take part in. **~ civile** plaintiff

parteci'pante *nmf* participant

parteci'pa|re *vi* **~ re a** participate in, take part in; (*condividere*) share in. **~zi'one** *nf* participation; (*annuncio*) announcement; *Fin* shareholding; (*presenza*) presence. **par'tecipe** *a* participating

parteggi'are *vi* **~ per** side with

par'tenza *nf* departure; *Sport* start; **in ~ per** leaving for

parti'cella *nf* particle

parti'cipio *nm* participle

particolar|e *a* particular; (*privato*) private ●*nm* detail, particular; **fin nei minimi ~i** down to the smallest detail. **~eggi'ato** *a* detailed. **~ità** *nf inv* particularity; (*dettaglio*) detail

partigi'ano, -a *a & nmf* partisan

par'tire *vi* leave; (*aver inizio*) start; **a ~ da** [beginning] from

par'tita *nf* game; (*incontro*) match; *Comm* lot; (*contabilità*) entry. **~ di calcio** football match. **~ a carte** game of cards

par'tito *nm* party; (*scelta*) choice; (*occasione di matrimonio*) match; **per ~ preso** out of sheer pig-headedness

'parto *nm* childbirth; **un ~ facile** an easy birth *o* labour; **dolori** *pl* **del ~** labour pains. **~ cesareo** Caesarian section. **~rire** *vt* give birth to

par'venza *nf* appearance

parzi'al|e *a* partial. **~ità** *nf* partiality. **~'mente** *adv* (*non completamente*) partially; **~mente scremato** semi-skimmed

pasco'lare *vt* graze. **'pascolo** *nm* pasture

'Pasqua *nf* Easter. **pa'squale** *a* Easter *attrib*

'passa: e ~ *adv* (*e oltre*) plus

pas'sabile *a* passable

pas'saggio *nm* passage; (*traversata*) crossing; *Sport* pass; (*su veicolo*) lift; **essere di ~** be passing through. **~ a livello** level crossing, grade crossing *Am.* **~ pedonale** pedestrian crossing

passamon'tagna *nm inv* balaclava

pas'sante *nmf* passer-by ●*nm* (*di cintura*) loop ●*a Tennis* passing

passa'porto *nm* passport

pas'sa|re *vi* pass; (*attraversare*) pass through; (*far visita*) call; (*andare*) go; (*essere approvato*) be passed; **~re alla storia** go down in history; **mi è ~to di mente** it slipped my mind; **~re per un genio/idiota** be taken for a genius/an idiot; **farsi ~re per qcno** pass oneself off as sb ●*vt* (*far scorrere*) pass over; (*sopportare*) go through; (*al telefono*) put through; *Culin* strain; **~re di moda** go out of fashion; **le passo il signor Rossi** I'll put you through to Mr Rossi; **~rsela bene** be well off; **come te la passi?** how are you doing?. **~ta** *nf* (*di vernice*) coat; (*spolverata*) dusting; (*occhiata*) look

passa'tempo *nm* pastime

pas'sato *a* past; **l'anno ~** last year; **sono le tre passate** it's past *o* after three o'clock ●*nm* past; *Culin* purée; *Gram* past tense. **~ prossimo** *Gram* present perfect. **~ remoto** *Gram* [simple] past. **~ di verdure** cream of vegetable soup

passaver'dure *nm inv* food mill

passeg'gero, -a *a* passing ●*nmf* passenger

passeggi'a|re *vi* walk, stroll. **~ta** *nf* walk, stroll; (*luogo*) public walk; (*in bicicletta*) ride; **fare una ~ta** go for a walk

passeg'gino *nm* pushchair, stroller *Am*

pas'seggio *nm* walk; (*luogo*) promenade; **andare a ~** go for a walk; **scarpe da ~** walking shoes

passe-partout *nm inv* master-key

passe'rella *nf* gangway; *Aeron* boarding bridge; (*per sfilate*) catwalk

'passero *nm* sparrow. **passe'rotto** *nm* (*passero*) sparrow

pas'sibile *a* **~ di** liable to

passio'nale *a* passionate. **passi'one** *nf* passion

pas'sivo *a* passive ●*nm* passive; *Comm* liabilities *pl*; **in ~** (*bilancio*) loss-making

'passo *nm* step; (*orma*) footprint; (*andatura*) pace; (*brano*) passage; (*valico*) pass; **a due passi da qui** a stone's throw away; **a ~ d'uomo** at walking pace; **di buon ~** at a spanking pace; **fare due passi** go for a stroll; **di pari ~** *fig* hand in hand. **~ carrabile, ~ carraio** driveway

'pasta *nf* (*impasto per pane ecc*) dough; (*per dolci, pasticcino*) pastry; (*pastasciutta*) pasta; (*massa molle*) paste; *fig* nature. **~ frolla** shortcrust pastry

pastasci'utta *nf* pasta

pa'stella *nf* batter

pa'stello *nm* pastel

pa'sticca *nf* pastille; (*fam: pastiglia*) pill

pasticce'ria *nf* cake shop, patisserie; (*pasticcini*) pastries *pl*; (*arte*) confectionery

pasticci'are *vi* make a mess ● *vt* make a mess of

pasticci'ere, -a *nmf* confectioner

pastic'cino *nm* little cake

pa'sticcio *nm Culin* pie; (*lavoro disordinato*) mess; **mettersi nei pasticci** get into trouble. **~'one, -a** *nmf* bungler ● *a* bungling

pasti'ficio *nm* pasta factory

pa'stiglia *nf Med* pill, tablet; (*di menta*) sweet. **~ dei freni** brake pad

'pasto *nm* meal

pasto'rale *a* pastoral. **pa'store** *nm* shepherd; *Relig* pastor. **pastore tedesco** German shepherd, Alsatian

pastoriz'za|re *vt* pasteurize. **~to a** pasteurized. **~zi'one** *nf* pasteurization

pa'stoso *a* doughy; *fig* mellow

pa'stura *nf* pasture; (*per pesci*) bait

pa'tacca *nf* (*macchia*) stain; (*fig: oggetto senza valore*) piece of junk

pa'tata *nf* potato. **patate** *pl* **fritte** chips *Br*, French fries. **pata'tine** *nfpl* [potato] crisps, chips *Am*

pata'trac *nm inv* (*crollo*) crash

pâté *nm inv* pâté

pa'tella *nf* limpet

pa'tema *nm* anxiety

pa'tente *nf* licence. **~ di guida** driving licence, driver's license *Am*

pater'na|le *nf* scolding. **~'lista** *nm* paternalist

paternità *nf* paternity. **pa'terno** *a* paternal; (*affetto ecc*) fatherly

pa'tetico *a* pathetic. **'pathos** *nm* pathos

pa'tibolo *nm* gallows *sg*

'patina *nf* patina; (*sulla lingua*) coating

pa'ti|re *vt/i* suffer. **~to, -a** *a* suffering

● *nmf* fanatic. **~to della musica** music lover

patolo'gia *nf* pathology. **pato'logico** *a* pathological

'patria *nf* native land

patri'arca *nm* patriarch

pa'trigno *nm* stepfather

patrimoni'ale *a* property *attrib*. **patri'monio** *nm* estate

patri'o|ta *nmf* patriot. **~tico** *a* patriotic. **~'tismo** *nm* patriotism

pa'trizio, -a *a* & *nmf* patrician

patro|ci'nare *vt* support. **~'cinio** *nm* support

patro'nato *nm* patronage. **pa'trono** *nm Relig* patron saint; *Jur* counsel

'patta¹ *nf* (*di tasca*) flap

'patta² *nf* (*pareggio*) draw

patteggi'a|mento *nm* bargaining. **~'are** *vt/i* negotiate

patti'naggio *nm* skating. **~ su ghiaccio** ice skating. **~ a rotelle** roller skating

patti'na|re *vi* skate; (*auto:*) skid. **~'tore, ~'trice** *nmf* skater. **pattino** *nm* skate; *Aeron* skid. **pattino da ghiaccio** iceskate. **pattino a rotelle** roller-skate

'patto *nm* deal; *Pol* pact; **a ~ che** on condition that

pat'tuglia *nf* patrol. **~ stradale** ≈ patrol car; police motorbike, highway patrol *Am*

pattu'ire *vt* negotiate

pattumi'era *nf* dustbin, trashcan *Am*

pa'ura *nf* fear; (*spavento*) fright; **aver ~** be afraid; **mettere ~ a** frighten. **pau'roso** *a* (*che fa paura*) frightening; (*che ha paura*) fearful; (*fam: enorme*) awesome

'pausa *nf* pause; (*nel lavoro*) break; **fare una ~** pause; (*nel lavoro*) have a break

pavimen'ta|re *vt* pave (*strada*). **~zi'one** *nf* (*operazione*) paving. **pavi'mento** *nm* floor

pa'vone *nm* peacock. **~ggi'arsi** *vr* strut

pazien'tare *vi* be patient

pazi'ente *a* & *nmf* patient. **~'mente** *adv* patiently. **pazi'enza** *nf* patience; **pazienza!** never mind!

'pazza *nf* madwoman. **~'mente** *adv* madly

paz'z|esco *a* foolish; (*esagerato*) crazy. **~ia** *nf* madness; (*azione*) (*act of*) folly. **'pazzo** *a* mad; *fig* crazy ● *nm* madman; **essere pazzo di/per** be crazy about; **pazzo di gioia** mad with joy; **da pazzi**

fam crackpot; **darsi alla pazza gioia** live it up. **paz'zoide** *a* whacky

'**pecca** *nf* fault; **senza** ~ flawless. **peccami'noso** *a* sinful

pec'ca|re *vi* sin; ~**re di** be guilty of ⟨*ingratitudine*⟩. ~**to** *nm* sin; ~**to che...** it's a pity that...; [**che**] ~**to!** [what a] pity!. ~'**tore**, ~'**trice** sinner

'**pece** *nf* pitch

'**peco|ra** *nf* sheep. ~**ra nera** black sheep. ~'**raio** *nm* shepherd. ~'**rella** *nf* cielo a ~**relle** sky full of fluffy white clouds. ~'**rino** *nm* ⟨*formaggio*⟩ sheep's milk cheese

peculi'are *a* ~ **di** peculiar to. ~**ità** *nf inv* peculiarity

pe'daggio *nm* toll

pedago'gia *nf* pedagogy. peda'gogico *a* pedagogical

peda'la|re *vi* pedal. pe'dale *nm* pedal. pedalò *nm inv* pedalo

pe'dana *nf* footrest; *Sport* springboard

pe'dante *a* pedantic. ~'ria *nf* pedantry. pedan'tesco *a* pedantic

pe'data *nf* ⟨*in calcio*⟩ kick; ⟨*impronta*⟩ footprint

pede'rasta *nm* pederast

pe'destre *a* pedestrian

pedi'atra *nmf* paediatrician. pedia'tria *nf* paediatrics *sg*

pedi'cure *nmf inv* chiropodist, podiatrist *Am* ● *nm* ⟨*cura dei piedi*⟩ pedicure

pedi'gree *nm inv* pedigree

pe'dina *nf* ⟨*alla dama*⟩ piece; *fig* pawn. ~'mento *nm* shadowing. pedi'nare *vt* shadow

pe'dofilo, -a *nmf* paedophile

pedo'nale *a* pedestrian. pe'done, -a *nmf* pedestrian

peeling *nm inv* exfoliation treatment

'peggio *adv* worse; ~ **per te!** too bad!; ~ **di così** any worse; **la persona** ~ **vestita** the worst dressed person ● *a* worse; **niente di** ~ nothing worse ● *nm* **il** ~ **è che...** the worst of it is that...; **pensare al** ~ think the worst ● *nf* **alla** ~ at worst; **avere la** ~ get the worst of it; **alla meno** ~ as best I can

peggiora'mento *nm* worsening

peggio'ra|re *vt* make worse, worsen ● *vi* get worse, worsen. ~'tivo *a* pejorative

peggi'ore *a* worse; ⟨*superlativo*⟩ worst; **nella** ~ **delle ipotesi** if the worst comes to the worst ● *nmf* **il/la** ~ the worst

'pegno *nm* pledge; ⟨*nei giochi di società*⟩ forfeit; *fig* token

pelan'drone *nm* slob

pe'la|re *vt* ⟨*spennare*⟩ pluck; ⟨*spellare*⟩ skin; ⟨*sbucciare*⟩ peel; ⟨*fam: spillare denaro*⟩ fleece. ~**rsi** *vr fam* lose one's hair. ~**to** *a* bald. ~**ti** *nmpl* ⟨*pomodori*⟩ peeled tomatoes

pel'lame *nm* skins *pl*

'pelle *nf* skin; ⟨*cuoio*⟩ leather; ⟨*buccia*⟩ peel; **avere la** ~ **d'oca** have goose-flesh

pellegri'naggio *nm* pilgrimage. pelle'grino, -a *nmf* pilgrim

pelle'rossa *nmf* Red Indian, Redskin

pelle'ria *nf* leather goods *pl*

pelli'cano *nm* pelican

pellicce'ria *nf* furrier's [shop]. pel'liccia *nf* fur; ⟨*indumento*⟩ fur coat. ~i'aio, -a *nmf* furrier

pel'licola *nf* *Phot, Cinema* film. ~ [**trasparente**] cling film

'pelo *nm* hair; ⟨*di animale*⟩ coat; ⟨*di lana*⟩ pile; **per un** ~ by the skin of one's teeth; **cavarsela per un** ~ have a narrow escape. pe'loso *a* hairy

'peltro *nm* pewter

pe'luche *nm inv* giocattolo di ~ soft toy

pe'luria *nf* down

'pelvico *a* pelvic

'pena *nf* ⟨*punizione*⟩ punishment; ⟨*sofferenza*⟩ pain; ⟨*dispiacere*⟩ sorrow; ⟨*disturbo*⟩ trouble; **a mala** ~ hardly; **mi fa** ~ I pity him; **vale la** ~ **andare** it is worth [while] going. ~ **di morte** death sentence

pe'na|le *a* criminal; **diritto** *nm* ~**e** criminal law. ~**ità** *nf inv* penalty

penaliz'za|re *vt* penalize. ~**zi'one** *nf* ⟨*penalità*⟩ penalty

pe'nare *vi* suffer; ⟨*faticare*⟩ find it difficult

pen'daglio *nm* pendant

pen'dant *nm inv* fare ~ [**con**] match

pen'den|te *a* hanging; *Comm* outstanding ● *nm* ⟨*ciondolo*⟩ pendant; ~**ti** *pl* drop earrings. ~**za** *nf* slope; *Comm* outstanding account

'pendere *vi* hang; ⟨*superficie:*⟩ slope; ⟨*essere inclinato*⟩ lean

pen'dio *nm* slope; **in** ~ sloping

pendo'la|re *a* pendulum ● *nmf* commuter. ~**ino** *nm* ⟨*treno*⟩ special, first class only, fast train

'pendolo *nm* pendulum

'pene *nm* penis

pene'trante *a* penetrating; ⟨*freddo*⟩ biting

pene'tra|re *vt/i* penetrate; ⟨*trafiggere*⟩ pierce ● *vt* ⟨*odore:*⟩ get into ● *vi* ⟨*entrare furtivamente*) steal in. ~**zi'one** *nf* penetration

penicil'lina *nf* penicillin

pe'nisola *nf* peninsula

peni'ten|te *a & nmf* penitent. ~**za** *nf* penitence; (*punizione*) penance; (*in gioco*) forfeit. ~**zi'ario** *nm* penitentiary

'penna *nf* (*da scrivere*) pen; (*di uccello*) feather. ~ **a feltro** felt-tip[ped pen]. ~ **a sfera** ball-point [pen]. ~ **stilografica** fountain-pen

pen'nacchio *nm* plume

penna'rello *nm* felt-tip[ped pen]

pennel'la|re *vt* paint. ~**ta** *nf* brushstroke. **pen'nello** *nm* brush; **a pennello** (*a perfezione*) perfectly

pen'nino *nm* nib

pen'none *nm* (*di bandiera*) flagpole

pen'nuto *a* feathered

pe'nombra *nf* half-light

pe'noso *a* (*fam: pessimo*) painful

pen'sa|re *vi* think; **penso di si** I think so; ~**re a** think of; remember to (*chiudere il gas ecc*); **pensa ai fatti tuoi!** mind your own business!; **ci penso io** I'll take care of it; ~**re di fare qcsa** think of doing sth; ~**re tra sé e sé** think to oneself ● *vt* think. ~**ta** *nf* idea

pensi'e|ro *nm* thought; (*mente*) mind; (*preoccupazione*) worry; **stare in** ~**ro per** be anxious about. ~**roso** *a* pensive

'pensi|le *a* hanging; **giardino** ~**le** roof-garden ● *nm* (*mobile*) wall unit. ~**lina** *nf* (*di fermata d'autobus*) bus shelter

pensio'nante *nmf* boarder; (*ospite pagante*) lodger

pensio'nato, -a *nmf* pensioner ● *nm* (*per anziani*) [old folks'] home; (*per studenti*) hostel. **pensi'one** *nf* pension; (*albergo*) boarding-house; (*vitto e alloggio*) board and lodging; **andare in pensione** retire; **mezza pensione** half board. **pensione completa** full board

pen'soso *a* pensive

pen'tagono *nm* pentagon

Pente'coste *nf* Whitsun

penti'mento *nm* repentance

pen'ti|rsi *vr* ~**rsi di** repent of; (*rammaricarsi*) regret. ~**'tismo** *nm* turning informant. ~**to** *nm* Mafioso turned informant

'pentola *nf* saucepan; (*contenuto*) potful. ~ **a pressione** pressure cooker

pe'nultimo *a* last but one

pe'nuria *nf* shortage

penzo'l|are *vi* dangle. ~**oni** *adv* dangling

pe'pa|re *vt* pepper. ~**to** *a* peppery

'pepe *nm* pepper; **grano di** ~ peppercorn. ~ **in grani** whole peppercorns. ~ **macinato** ground pepper

pepero'n|ata *nf* peppers cooked in olive oil with onion, tomato and garlic. ~**'cino** *nm* chilli pepper. **pepe'rone** *nm* pepper. **peperone verde** green pepper

pe'pita *nf* nugget

per *prep* for; (*attraverso*) through; (*stato in luogo*) in, on; (*distributivo*) per; (*mezzo, entro*) by; (*causa*) with; (*in qualità di*) as; ~ **strada** on the street; ~ **la fine del mese** by the end of the month; **in fila** ~ **due** in double file; **l'ho sentito** ~ **telefono** I spoke to him on the phone; ~ **iscritto** in writing; ~ **caso** by chance; **ho aspettato** ~ **ore** I've been waiting for hours; ~ **tempo** in time; ~ **sempre** forever; ~ **scherzo** as a joke; **gridare** ~ **il dolore** scream with pain; **vendere** ~ **10 milioni** sell for 10 million; **uno** ~ **volta** one at a time; **uno** ~ **uno** one by one; **venti** ~ **cento** twenty per cent; ~ **fare qcsa** [in order] to do sth; **stare** ~ be about to; **è troppo bello** ~ **essere vero** it's too good to be true

'pera *nf* pear; **farsi una** ~ (*sl: di eroina*) shoot up

perbe'nis|mo *nm* prissiness. ~**ta** *a inv* prissy

per'cento *adv* per cent. **percentu'ale** *nf* percentage

perce'pibile *a* perceivable; (*somma*) payable

perce'pire *vt* perceive; (*riscuotere*) cash

perce|t'tibile *a* perceptible. ~**zi'one** *nf* perception

perché *conj* (*in interrogazioni*) why; (*per il fatto che*) because; (*affinché*) so that; ~ **non vieni?** why don't you come?; **dimmi** ~ tell me why; ~ **no/si!** because!; **la ragione** ~ **l'ho fatto** the reason [that] I did it, the reason why I did it; **è troppo difficile** ~ **lo possa capire** it's too difficult for me to understand ● *nm inv* reason [why]; **senza un** ~ without any reason

perciò *conj* so

per'correre *vt* cover (*distanza*); (*viaggiare*) travel. **per'corso** *pp di* **percorrere** ● *nm* (*tragitto*) course, route; (*distanza*) distance; (*viaggio*) journey

per'coss|a *nf* blow. ~**o** *pp di* **percuotere percu'otere** *vt* strike

percussi'one *nf* percussion; **strumenti a** ~**ne** percussion instruments. ~**'nista** *nmf* percussionist

per'dente *nmf* loser

'**perder|e** *vt* lose; (*sprecare*) waste; (*non prendere*) miss; ⟨*fig: vizio:*⟩ ruin; **~e tempo** waste time. ● *vi* lose; ⟨*recipiente:*⟩ leak; **lascia ~e!** forget it!. **~si** *vr* get lost; (*reciproco*) lose touch

perdifi'ato: a ~ *adv* ⟨*gridare*⟩ at the top of one's voice

perdigi'orno *nmf inv* idler

'**perdita** *nf* loss; (*spreco*) waste; (*falla*) leak; **a ~ d'occhio** as far as the eye can see. **~ di tempo** waste of time. **perdi'tempo** *nm* waste of time

perdo'nare *vt* forgive; (*scusare*) excuse. **per'dono** *nm* forgiveness; *Jur* pardon

perdu'rare *vi* last; (*perseverare*) persist

perduta'mente *adv* hopelessly. **per'duto** *pp di* **perdere** ● *a* lost; (*rovinato*) ruined

pe'renne *a* everlasting; *Bot* perennial; **nevi perenni** perpetual snow. **~'mente** *adv* perpetually

peren'torio *a* peremptory

per'fetto *a* perfect ● *nm Gram* perfect [tense]

perfezio'nar|e *vt* perfect; (*migliorare*) improve. **~si** *vr* improve oneself; (*specializzarsi*) specialize

perfezi'o|ne *nf* perfection; **alla ~ne** to perfection. **~'nismo** *nm* perfectionism. **~'nista** *nmf* perfectionist

per'fidia *nf* wickedness; (*atto*) wicked act. '**perfido** *a* treacherous; (*malvagio*) perverse

per'fino *adv* even

perfo'ra|re *vt* pierce; punch ⟨*schede*⟩; *Mech* drill. **~'tore, ~'trice** *nmf* punchcard operator ● *nm* perforator. **~zi'one** *nf* perforation; (*di schede*) punching

per'formance *nf inv* performance

perga'mena *nf* parchment

perico'lante *a* precarious; ⟨*azienda*⟩ shaky

pe'rico|lo *nm* danger; (*rischio*) risk; **mettere in ~lo** endanger. **~lo pubbli-co** danger to society. **~loso** *a* dangerous

perife'ria *nf* periphery; (*di città*) outskirts *pl*; *fig* fringes *pl*

peri'feric|a *nf* peripheral; (*strada*) ring road. **~o** *a* ⟨*quartiere*⟩ outlying

pe'rifrasi *nf inv* circumlocution

pe'rimetro *nm* perimeter

peri'odico *nm* periodical ● *a* periodical; ⟨*vento, mal di testa, Math*⟩ recurring. **pe'riodo** *nm* period; *Gram* sentence. **periodo di prova** trial period

peripe'zie *nfpl* misadventures

pe'rire *vi* perish

peri'scopio *nm* periscope

pe'rito, -a *a* skilled ● *nmf* expert

perito'nite *nf* peritonitis

pe'rizia *nf* skill; (*valutazione*) survey

'**perla** *nf* pearl. **per'lina** *nf* bead

perlo'meno *adv* at least

perlu'stra|re *vt* patrol. **~zi'one** *nf* patrol; **andare in ~zione** go on patrol

perma'loso *a* touchy

perma'ne|nte *a* permanent ● *nf* perm; **farsi** [**fare**] **la ~nte** have a perm. **~nza** *nf* permanence; (*soggiorno*) stay; **in ~nza** permanently. **~re** *vi* remain

perme'are *vt* permeate

per'messo *pp di* **permettere** ● *nm* permission; (*autorizzazione*) permit; *Mil* leave; [**è**] **~?** (*posso entrare?*) may I come in?; (*posso passare?*) excuse me. **~ di lavoro** work permit

per'mettere *vt* allow, permit; **potersi ~ qcsa** (*finanziariamente*) be able to afford sth; **come si permette?** how dare you?. **permis'sivo** *a* permissive

permutazi'one *nf* exchange; *Math* permutation

per'nacchia *nf* ⟨*sl: con la bocca*⟩ raspberry *sl*

per'nic|e *nf* partridge. **~i'oso** *a* pernicious

'**perno** *nm* pivot

pernot'tare *vi* stay overnight

'**pero** *nm* pear-tree

però *conj* but; (*tuttavia*) however

pero'rare *vt* plead

perpendico'lare *a & nf* perpendicular

perpe'trare *vt* perpetrate

perpetu'are *vt* perpetuate. **per'petuo** *a* perpetual

perplessità *nf inv* perplexity; (*dubbio*) doubt. **per'plesso** *a* perplexed

perqui'si|re *vt* search. **~zi'one** *nf* search. **~zione domiciliare** search of the premises

persecu'|tore, -'trice *nmf* persecutor. **~zi'one** *nf* persecution

perse'gu'ire *vt* pursue

persegui'tare *vt* persecute

perseve'ra|nte *a* persevering. **~nza** *nf* perseverance. **~re** *vi* persevere

persi'ano, -a *a* Persian ● *nf* (*di finestra*) shutter. '**persico** *a* Persian

per'sino *adv* = **perfino**

persi'sten|te *a* persistent. **~za** *nf* persistence. **per'sistere** *vi* persist

'perso *pp di* perdere ● *a* lost; a tempo ~ in one's spare time

per'sona *nf* person; (*un tale*) somebody; di ~, in ~ in person, personally; per ~ per person, a head; per interposta ~ through an intermediary; perso ne *pl* people

perso'naggio *nm* (*persona di riguardo*) personality; *Theat ecc* character

perso'nal|e *a* personal ● *nm* staff. ~e di terra ground crew. ~ità *nf inv* personality. ~iz'zare *vt* customize (*auto ecc*); personalize (*penna ecc*)

personifi'ca|re *vt* personify. ~zi'one *nf* personification

perspi'cac|e *a* shrewd. ~ia *nf* shrewdness

persua'dere *vt* convince; impress (*critici*); ~dere qcno a fare qcsa persuade sb to do sth. ~si'one *nf* persuasion. ~'sivo *a* persuasive. persu'aso *pp di* persuadere

per'tanto *conj* therefore

'pertica *nf* pole

perti'nente *a* relevant

per'tosse *nf* whooping cough

pertur'ba|re *vt* perturb. ~rsi *vr* be perturbed. ~zi'one *nf* disturbance. ~zione atmosferica atmospheric disturbance

per'va|dere *vt* pervade. ~so *pp di* pervadere

perve'nire *vi* reach; far ~ qcsa a qcno send sth to sb

pervers|i'one *nf* perversion. ~ità *nf* perversity. per'verso *a* perverse

perver'ti|re *vt* pervert. ~to *a* perverted ● *nm* pervert

per'vinca *nm* (*colore*) blue with a touch of purple

p. es. *abbr* (per esempio) e.g.

pesa *nf* weighing; (*bilancia*) weighing machine; (*per veicoli*) weighbridge

pe'sante *a* heavy; (*stomaco*) overfull ● *adv* (*vestirsi*) warmly. ~'mente *adv* (*cadere*) heavily. pesan'tezza *nf* heaviness

pe'sar|e *vt/i* weigh; ~e su *fig* lie heavy on; ~e le parole weigh one's words. ~si *vr* weigh oneself

'pesca[1] *nf* (*frutto*) peach

'pesca[2] *nf* fishing; andare a ~ go fishing. ~ subacquea underwater fishing. pe'scare *vt* (*andare a pesca di*) fish for; (*prendere*) catch; (*fig: trovare*) fish out. ~'tore *nm* fisherman

'pesce *nm* fish. ~ d'aprile! April Fool!. ~ grosso *fig* big fish. ~ piccolo *fig* small fry. ~ rosso goldfish. ~ spada swordfish. Pesci *Astr* Pisces

pesce'cane *nm* shark

pesche'reccio *nm* fishing boat

pesche'ria *nf* fishmonger's [shop]. ~hi'era *nf* fish-pond. ~i'vendolo *nm* fishmonger

'pesco *nm* peach-tree

'peso *nm* weight; essere di ~ per qcno be a burden to sb; di poco ~ (*senza importanza*) not very important; non dare ~ a qcsa not attach any importance to sth

pessi'mis|mo *nm* pessimism. ~ta *nmf* pessimist ● *a* pessimistic. 'pessimo *a* very bad

pe'staggio *nm* beating-up. pe'stare *vt* tread on; (*schiacciare*) crush; (*picchiare*) beat; crush (*aglio, prezzemolo*)

'peste *nf* plague; (*persona*) pest

pe'stello *nm* pestle

pesti'cida *nm* pesticide. pe'stifero *a* (*fastidioso*) pestilential

pesti'len|za *nf* pestilence; (*fetore*) stench. ~zi'ale *a* (*odore aria*) noxious

'pesto *a* ground; occhio ~ ~ black eye ● *nm* basil and garlic sauce

'petalo *nm* petal

pe'tardo *nm* banger

petizi'one *nf* petition; fare una ~ draw up a petition

petro'li|era *nf* [oil] tanker. ~'lifero *a* oil-bearing. pe'trolio *nm* oil

pettego'lare *vi* gossip. ~'lezzo *nm* piece of gossip; far ~'lezzi gossip

pet'tegolo, -a *a* gossipy ● *nmf* gossip

petti'na|re *vt* comb. ~rsi *vr* comb one's hair. ~'tura *nf* combing; (*acconciatura*) hair-style. 'pettine *nm* comb

'petting *nm* petting

petti'nino *nm* (*fermaglio*) comb

petti'rosso *nm* robin [redbreast]

'petto *nm* chest; (*seno*) breast; a doppio ~ double-breasted

petto'rale *a* (*in gare sportive*) number.. ~'rina *nf* (*di salopette*) bib. ~'ruto *a* (*donna*) full-breasted; (*uomo*) broad-chested

petu'lante *a* impertinent

'pezza *nf* cloth; (*toppa*) patch; (*rotolo di tessuto*) roll

pez'zente *nmf* tramp; (*avaro*) miser

'pezzo *nm* piece; (*parte*) part; un bel ~ d'uomo a fine figure of a man; un ~ (*di tempo*) some time; (*di spazio*) a long way; al ~ (*costare*) each; essere a pezzi (*stanco*) be shattered; fare a pezzi tear to shreds. ~ grosso bigwig

pia'cente a attractive
pia'ce|re nm pleasure; (favore) favour; **a ~re** as much as one likes; **per ~re** please!; **~re [di conoscerla]!** pleased to meet you!; **con ~re** with pleasure ● vi **la Scozia mi piace** I like Scotland; **mi piacciono i dolci** I like sweets; **faccio come mi pare e piace** I do as I please; **ti piace?** do you like it?; **lo spettacolo è piaciuto** the show was a success. **~vole** a pleasant
piaci'mento nm **a ~** as much as you like
pia'dina nf unleavened focaccia bread
pi'aga nf sore; fig scourge; (fig: persona noiosa) pain; (fig: ricordo doloroso) wound
piagni'steo nm whining
piagnuco'lare vi whimper
pi'alla nf plane. **pial'lare** vt plane
pi'ana nf (pianura) plane. **pianeggi'ante** a level
piane'rottolo nm landing
pia'neta nm planet
pi'angere vi cry; (disperatamente) weep ● vt (lamentare) lament; (per un lutto) mourn
pianifi'ca|re vt plan. **~zi'one** nf planning
pia'nista nmf Mus pianist
pi'ano a flat; (a livello) flush; (regolare) smooth; (facile) easy ● adv slowly; (con cautela) gently; **andarci ~** go carefully ● nm plain; (di edificio) floor; (livello) plane; (progetto) plan; Mus piano; **di primo ~** first-rate; **primo ~** Phot close-up; **in primo ~** in the foreground. **~ regolatore** town plan. **~ di studi** syllabus
piano'forte nm piano. **~ a coda** grand piano
piano'terra nm inv ground floor, first floor Am
pi'anta nf plant; (del piede) sole; (disegno) plan; **di sana ~** (totalmente) entirely; **in ~ stabile** permanently. **~ stradale** road map. **~gi'one** nf plantation
piantagrane nmf fam **è un/una ~** he's/she's bolshie
pian'tar|e vt plant; (conficcare) drive; (fam: abbandonare) dump; **piantala!** fam stop it!. **~si** vr plant oneself; (fam: lasciarsi) leave each other
pianter'reno nm ground floor, first floor Am
pi'anto pp di **piangere** ● nm crying; (disperato) weeping; (lacrime) tears pl

pian|to'nare vt guard. **~'tone** nm guard
pia'nura nf plain
p'iastra nf plate; (lastra) slab; Culin griddle. **~ elettronica** circuit board. **~ madre** Comput motherboard
pia'strella nf tile
pia'strina nf Mil identity disc; Med platelet; Comput chip
piatta'forma nf platform. **~ di lancio** launch pad
piat'tino nm saucer
pi'atto a flat ● nm plate; (da portata, vivanda) dish; (portata) course; (parte piatta) flat; (di giradischi) turntable; **piatti** pl Mus cymbals; **lavare i piatti** do the dishes, do the washing-up. **~ fondo** soup plate. **~ piano** [ordinary] plate
pi'azza nf square; Comm market; **letto a una ~** single bed; **letto a due piazze** double bed; **far ~ pulita** make a clean sweep. **~'forte** nf stronghold.
piaz'zale nm large square. **~'mento** nm (in classifica) placing
piaz'za|re vt place. **~rsi** vr Sport be placed; **~rsi secondo** come second. **~to a** (cavallo) placed; **ben ~to** (robusto) well built
piaz'zista nm salesman
piaz'zuola nf **~ di sosta** pull-in
pic'cante a hot; (pungente) sharp; (salace) spicy
pic'carsi vr (risentirsi) take offence; **~ di** (vantarsi di) claim to
'picche nfpl (in carte) spades
picchet'tare vt stake; ⟨scioperanti:⟩ picket. **pic'chetto** nm picket
picchi'a|re vt beat, hit ● vi (bussare) knock; Aeron nosedive; **~re in testa** ⟨motore:⟩ knock. **~ta** nf beating; Aeron nosedive; **scendere in ~ta** nosedive
picchiet'tare vt tap; (punteggiare) spot
picchiet'tio nm tapping
'picchio nm woodpecker
pic'cino a tiny; (gretto) mean; (di poca importanza) petty ● nm little one, child
picci'one nm pigeon
'picco nm peak; **a ~** vertically; **colare a ~** sink
'piccolo, -a a small, little; (di età) young; (di statura) short; (gretto) petty ● nmf child, little one; **da ~** as a child
pic'co|ne nm pickaxe. **~zza** nf ice axe
pic'nic nm inv picnic
pi'docchio nm louse
piè nm inv **a ~ di pagina** at the foot of the page; **saltare a ~ pari** skip

pi'ede *nm* foot; **a piedi** on foot; **andare a piedi** walk; **a piedi nudi** barefoot; **~ libero** free; **in piedi** standing; **alzarsi in piedi** stand up; **in punta di piedi** on tiptoe; **ai piedi di** ⟨*montagna*⟩ at the foot of; **prendere ~** *fig* gain ground; ⟨*moda:*⟩ catch on; **mettere in piedi** ⟨*allestire*⟩ set up; **togliti dai piedi!** get out of the way!. **~ di porco** ⟨*strumento*⟩ jemmy

pie'dino *nm* **fare ~ a** qcno *fam* play footsie with sb

piedi'stallo *nm* pedestal

pi'ega *nf* ⟨*piegatura*⟩ fold; ⟨*di gonna*⟩ pleat; ⟨*di pantaloni*⟩ crease; ⟨*grinza*⟩ wrinkle; ⟨*andamento*⟩ turn; **non fare una ~** ⟨*ragionamento:*⟩ be flawless

pie'ga|re *vt* fold; ⟨*flettere*⟩ bend ● *vi* bend. **~rsi** *vr* bend. **~rsi a** *fig* yield to. **~'tura** *nf* folding

pieghet'ta|re *vt* pleat. **~to** *a* pleated. **pie'ghevole** *a* pliable; ⟨*tavolo*⟩ folding ● *nm* leaflet

piemon'tese *a* Piedmontese

pi'en|a *nf* ⟨*di fiume*⟩ flood; ⟨*folla*⟩ crowd. **~o a** full; ⟨*massiccio*⟩ solid; **in ~a estate** in the middle of summer; **a ~i voti** ⟨*diplomarsi*⟩ with A-grades, with first class honours ● *nm* ⟨*colmo*⟩ height; ⟨*carico*⟩ full load; **in ~o** ⟨*completamente*⟩ fully; **fare il ~o** ⟨*di benzina*⟩ fill up

pie'none *nm* **c'era il ~** the place was packed

pietà *nf* pity; ⟨*misericordia*⟩ mercy; **senza ~** ⟨*persona*⟩ pitiless; ⟨*spietatamente*⟩ pitilessly; **avere ~ di** qcno take pity on sb; **far ~** ⟨*far pena*⟩ be pitiful

pie'tanza *nf* dish

pie'toso *a* pitiful, merciful; ⟨*fam: pessimo*⟩ terrible

pi'etr|a *nf* stone. **~a dura** semi-precious stone. **~a preziosa** precious stone. **~a dello scandalo** cause of the scandal. **pie'trame** *nm* stones *pl*. **~ifi'care** *vt* petrify. **pie'trina** *nf* ⟨*di accendino*⟩ flint. **pie'troso** *a* stony

'piffero *nm* fife

pigi'ama *nm* pyjamas *pl*

'pigia 'pigia *nm inv* crowd, crush. **pigi'are** *vt* press

pigi'one *nf* rent; **dare a ~** let, rent out; **prendere a ~** rent

pigli'are *vt* ⟨*fam: afferrare*⟩ catch. **'piglio** *nm* air

pig'mento *nm* pigment

pig'meo, -a *a* & *nmf* pygmy

'pigna *nf* cone

pi'gnolo *a* pedantic

pigo'lare *vi* chirp. **pigo'lio** *nm* chirping

pi'grizia *nf* laziness. **'pigro** *a* lazy; ⟨*intelletto*⟩ slow

'pila *nf* pile; *Electr* battery; ⟨*fam: lampadina tascabile*⟩ torch; ⟨*vasca*⟩ basin; **a pile** battery operated, battery powered

pi'lastro *nm* pillar

'pillola *nf* pill; **prendere la ~** be on the pill

pi'lone *nm* pylon; ⟨*di ponte*⟩ pier

pi'lota *nmf* pilot ● *nm* *Auto* driver. **pilo'tare** *vt* pilot; drive ⟨*auto*⟩

pinaco'teca *nf* art gallery

'Pinco Pallino *nm* so-and-so

pi'neta *nf* pine-wood

ping-'pong *nm* table tennis, ping-pong *fam*

pingu|e *a* fat. **~'edine** *nf* fatness

pingu'ino *nm* penguin; ⟨*gelato*⟩ choc ice on a stick

'pinna *nf* fin; ⟨*per nuotare*⟩ flipper

'pino *nm* pine[-tree]. **pi'nolo** *nm* pine kernel. **~ marittimo** cluster pine

'pinta *nf* pint

'pinza *nf* pliers *pl*; *Med* forceps *pl*

pin'za|re *vt* ⟨*con pinzatrice*⟩ staple. **~'trice** *nf* stapler

pin'zette *nfpl* tweezers *pl*

pinzi'monio *nm* sauce for crudités

'pio *a* pious; ⟨*benefico*⟩ charitable

pi'oggia *nf* rain; ⟨*fig: di pietre, insulti*⟩ hail, shower; **sotto la ~** in the rain. **~ acida** acid rain

pi'olo *nm* ⟨*di scala*⟩ rung

piom'ba|re *vi* fall heavily; **~re su** fall upon ● *vt* fill ⟨*dente*⟩. **~'tura** *nf* ⟨*di dente*⟩ filling. **piom'bino** *nm* ⟨*sigillo*⟩ [lead] seal; ⟨*da pesca*⟩ sinker; ⟨*in gonne*⟩ weight

pi'ombo *nm* lead; ⟨*sigillo*⟩ [lead] seal; **a ~ plumb; senza ~** ⟨*benzina*⟩ lead-free

pioni'ere, -a *nmf* pioneer

pi'oppo *nm* poplar

pio'vano *a* **acqua piovana** rainwater

pi'ov|ere *vi* rain; **~e** it's raining; **~iggi'nare** *vi* drizzle. **pio'voso** *a* rainy

'pipa *nf* pipe

pipì *nf* **fare [la] ~** pee, piddle; **andare a fare [la] ~** go for a pee

pipi'strello *nm* bat

pi'ramide *nf* pyramid

pi'ranha *nm inv* piranha

pi'rat|a *nm* pirate. **~a della strada** road-hog ● *a inv* pirate. **~e'ria** *nf* piracy

piro'etta *nf* pirouette

pi'rofila *nf* ⟨*tegame*⟩ oven-proof dish. **~o** *a* heat-resistant

pi'romane *nmf* pyromaniac

pi'roscafo nm steamer. ~ **di linea** liner

pisci'are vi vulg piss

pi'scina nf swimming pool. ~ **coperta** indoor swimming pool. ~ **scoperta** outdoor swimming pool

pi'sello nm pea; (fam: pene) willie

piso'lino nm nap; **fare un** ~ have a nap

'pista nf track; Aeron runway; (orma) footprint; (sci) slope, piste. ~ **d'atterraggio** airstrip. ~ **da ballo** dance floor. ~ **ciclabile** cycle track

pi'stacchio nm pistachio

pi'stola nf pistol; (per spruzzare) spray-gun. ~ **a spruzzo** paint spray

pi'stone nm piston

pi'tone nm python

pit'to|re, **-'trice** nmf painter. ~**'resco** a picturesque. **pit'torico** a pictorial

pit'tu|ra nf painting. ~**'rare** vt paint

più adv more; (superlativo) most; Math plus; ~ **importante** more important; **il** ~ **importante** the most important; ~ **caro** dearer; **il** ~ **caro** the dearest; **di** ~ more; **una coperta in** ~ an extra blanket; **non ho** ~ **soldi** I don't have any more money; **non vive** ~ **a Milano** he no longer lives in Milan, he doesn't live in Milan any longer; ~ **o meno** more or less; **il** ~ **lentamente possibile** as slow as possible; **per di** ~ what's more; **mai** ~! never again!; ~ **di** more than; **sempre** ~ more and more ● a more; (superlativo) most; ~ **tempo** more time; **la classe con** ~ **alunni** the class with most pupils; ~ **volte** several times ● nm most; Math plus sign; **il** ~ **è fatto** the worst is over; **parlare del** ~ **e del meno** make small talk; **i** ~ the majority

piuccheper'fetto nm pluperfect

pi'uma nf feather. **piu'maggio** nm plumage. **piu'mino** nm (di cigni) down; (copriletto) eiderdown; (per cipria) powder-puff; (per spolverare) feather duster; (giacca) down jacket. **piu'mone®** nm duvet, continental quilt

piut'tosto adv rather; (invece) instead

pi'vello nm fam greenhorn

'pizza nf pizza; Cinema reel.

pizzai'ola nf slices of beef in tomato sauce, oregano and anchovies

pizze'ria nf pizza restaurant, pizzeria

pizzi'c|are vt pinch; (pungere) sting; (di sapore) taste sharp; (fam: sorprendere) catch; Mus pluck ● vi scratch; (cibo:) be spicy **'pizzico** nm, ~**otto** nm pinch

'pizzo nm lace; (di montagna) peak

pla'ca|re vt placate; assuage (fame, dolore). ~**si** vr calm down

'placca nf plate; (commemorativa, dentale) plaque; Med patch

plac'ca|re vt plate. ~**to a** ~**to d'argento** silver-plated. ~**to d'oro** gold-plated. ~**tura** nf plating

pla'centa nf placenta

'placido a placid

plagi'are vt plagiarize; pressure (persona). **'plagio** nm plagiarism

plaid nm inv tartan rug

pla'nare vi glide

'plancia nf Naut bridge; (passerella) gangplank

plane'tario a planetary ● nm planetarium

pla'smare vt mould

'plastic|a nf (arte) plastic art; Med plastic surgery; (materia) plastic. ~**o a** plastic ● nm plastic model

'platano nm plane[-tree]

pla'tea nf stalls pl; (pubblico) audience

'platino nm platinum

pla'tonico a platonic

plau'sibil|e a plausible. ~**ità** nf plausibility

ple'baglia nf pej mob

pleni'lunio nm full moon

'plettro nm plectrum

pleu'rite nf pleurisy

'plico nm packet; **in** ~ **a parte** under separate cover

plissé a inv plissé; (gonna) accordeon-pleated

plo'tone nm platoon; (di ciclisti) group. ~ **d'esecuzione** firing-squad

'plumbeo a leaden

plu'ral|e a & nm plural; **al** ~**e in** the plural. ~**ità** nf (maggioranza) majority

pluridiscipli'nare a multi-disciplinary

plurien'nale a ~ **esperienza** many years' experience

pluripar'titico a Pol multi-party

plu'tonio nm plutonium

pluvi'ale a rain attrib

pneu'matico a pneumatic ● nm tyre

pneu'monia nf pneumonia

po' vedi poco

po'chette nf inv clutch bag

po'chino nm **un** ~ a little bit

'poco a little; (tempo) short; (con nomi plurali) ● pron little; (poco tempo) a short time; (plurale) few ● nm little; **un po'** a little [bit]; **un po' di** a little, some; (con nomi plurali) a few; **a** ~ **a** ~ little by little; **fra ~ soon; per ~** *(a poco prezzo)* cheap; *(quasi)* nearly; **~ fa a little while ago; sono arrivato da ~** I have just arrived; **un bel po'** quite a lot; **un ~ di buono** a shady character ● *adv (con verbi)* not much; *(con avverbi)* not very; **parla ~** he doesn't speak much; **lo conosco ~** I don't know him very well; **~ spesso** not very often

po'dere *nm* farm

pode'roso *a* powerful

'podio *nm* dais; *Mus* podium

po'dis|mo *nm* walking. **~ta** *nmf* walker

po'e|ma *nm* poem. **~'sia** *nf* poetry; *(componimento)* poem. **~ta** *nm* poet. **~'tessa** *nf* poetess. **~'tico** *a* poetic

poggiapi'edi *nm inv* footrest

poggi'a|re *vt* lean; *(posare)* place ● *vi* **~re su** to be based on. **~'testa** *nm inv* head-rest

'poggio *nm* hillock

poggi'olo *nm* balcony

poi *adv (dopo)* then; *(più tardi)* later [on]; *(finalmente)* finally. **d'ora in ~** from now on; **questa ~!** well!

poiché *conj* since

pois *nm inv* **a ~** polka-dot

'poker *nm* poker

po'lacco, -a *a* Polish ● *nmf* Pole ● *nm (lingua)* Polish

po'lar|e *a* polar. **~iz'zare** *vt* polarize

'polca *nf* polka

po'lemi|ca *nf* controversy. **~ca'men-te** *adv* controversially. **~co** *a* controversial. **~z'zare** *vi* engage in controversy

po'lenta *nf* cornmeal porridge

poli'clinico *nm* general hospital

poli'estere *nm* polyester

poliga'mia *nf* polygamy. **po'ligamo** *a* polygamous

polio[mie'lite] *nf* polio[myelitis]

'polipo *nm* polyp

polisti'rolo *nm* polystyrene

poli'tecnico *nm* polytechnic

po'litic|a *nf* politics *sg*; *(linea di condotta)* policy; **fare ~a** be in politics. **~iz'zare** *vt* politicize. **~o, -a** *a* political ● *nmf* politician

poliva'lente *a* catch-all

poli'zi|a *nf* police. **~a giudiziaria ≈** Criminal Investigation Department, CID. **~a stradale** traffic police. **~'esco** *a* police *attrib*; *(romanzo, film)* detective *attrib*. **~'otto** *nm* policeman

po'lizza *nf* policy

pol'la|io *nm* chicken run; *(fam: luogo chiassoso)* mad house. **~me** *nm* poultry.

~'strello *nm* spring chicken. **~stro** *nm* cockerel

'pollice *nm* thumb; *(unità di misura)* inch

'polline *nm* pollen; **allergia al ~** hay fever

polli'vendolo, -a *nmf* poulterer

'pollo *nm* chicken; *(fam: semplicione)* simpleton. **~ arrosto** roast chicken

polmo'nare *a* pulmonary. **pol'mone** *nm* lung. **polmone d'acciaio** iron lung. **~'nite** *nf* pneumonia

'polo *nm* pole; *Sport* polo; *(maglietta)* polo top. **~ nord** North Pole. **~ sud** South Pole

Po'lonia *nf* Poland

'polpa *nf* pulp

pol'paccio *nm* calf

polpa'strello *nm* fingertip

pol'pet|ta *nf* meatball. **~'tone** *nm* meat loaf

'polpo *nm* octopus

pol'poso *a* fleshy

pol'sino *nm* cuff

'polso *nm* pulse; *Anat* wrist; *fig* authority; **avere ~** be strict

pol'tiglia *nf* mush

pol'trire *vi* lie around

pol'tron|a *nf* armchair; *Theat* seat in the stalls. **~e** *a* lazy

'polve|re *nf* dust; *(sostanza polverizzata)* powder; **in ~re** powdered; **sapone in ~re** soap powder. **~re da sparo** gun powder. **~'rina** *nf (medicina)* powder. **~riz'zare** *vt* pulverize; *(nebulizzare)* atomize. **~'rone** *nm* cloud of dust. **~'roso** *a* dusty

po'mata *nf* ointment, cream

po'mello *nm* knob; *(guancia)* cheek

pomeridi'ano *a* afternoon *attrib*; **alle tre pomeridiane** at three in the afternoon, at three p.m. **pome'riggio** *nm* afternoon

'pomice *nf* pumice

'pomo *nm (oggetto)* knob. **~ d'Adamo** Adam's apple

pomo'doro *nm* tomato

'pompa *nf* pump; *(sfarzo)* pomp. **pompe** *pl* **funebri** *(funzione)* funeral. **pom'pare** *vt* pump; *(gonfiare d'aria)* pump up; *(fig: esagerare)* exaggerate; **pompare fuori** pump out

pom'pelmo *nm* grapefruit

pompi'ere *nm* fireman; **i pompieri** the fire brigade

pom'pon *nm inv* pompom

pom'poso *a* pompous

ponde'rare *vt* ponder

po'nente *nm* west

'ponte *nm* bridge; *Naut* deck; *(impalcatura)* scaffolding; **fare il ~** *fig* make a long weekend of it

pon'tefice *nm* pontiff

pontifi'ca|re *vi* pontificate. **~to** *nm* pontificate

ponti'ficio *a* papal

pon'tile *nm* jetty

popò *nf inv fam* pooh

popo'lano *a* of the [common] people

popo'la|re *a* popular; *(comune)* common ● *vt* populate. **~rsi** *vr* get crowded. **~rità** *nf* popularity. **~zi'one** *nf* population. **'popolo** *nm* people. **popo'loso** *a* populous

'poppa *nf Naut* stern; *(mammella)* breast; **a ~** astern

pop'pa|re *vt* suck. **~ta** *nf (pasto)* feed. **~ 'toio** *nm* [feeding-]bottle

popu'lista *nmf* populist

por'cata *nf* load of rubbish; **porcate** *pl (fam: cibo)* junk food

porcel'lana *nf* porcelain, china

porcel'lino *nm* piglet. **~ d'India** guinea-pig

porche'ria *nf* dirt; *(fig: cosa orrenda)* piece of filth; *(fam: robaccia)* rubbish

por'ci|le *nm* pigsty. **~no** *a* pig attrib ● *nm (fungo)* edible mushroom. **'porco** *nm* pig; *(carne)* pork

porco'spino *nm* porcupine

'porgere *vt* give; *(offrire)* offer; **porgo distinti saluti** *(in lettera)* I remain, yours sincerely

porno|gra'fia *nf* pornography. **~'grafico** *a* pornographic

'poro *nm* pore. **po'roso** *a* porous

'porpora *nf* purple

'por|re *vt* put; *(collocare)* place; *(supporre)* suppose; ask *(domanda)*; present *(candidatura)*; **poniamo il caso che...** let us suppose that...; **~re fine** *o* **termine a** put an end to. **~si** *vr* put oneself; **~si a sedere** sit down; **~si in cammino** set out

'porro *nm Bot* leek; *(verruca)* wart

'porta *nf* door; *Sport* goal; *(di città)* gate; *Comput* port. **~ a ~** door-to-door; **mettere alla ~** show sb the door. **~ di servizio** tradesmen's entrance

portaba'gagli *nm inv (facchino)* porter; *(di treno ecc)* luggage rack; *Auto* boot, trunk *Am; (sul tetto di un'auto)* roof rack

portabot'tiglie *nm inv* bottle rack, wine rack

porta'cenere *nm inv* ashtray

portachi'avi *nm inv* keyring

porta'cipria *nm inv* compact

portadocu'menti *nm inv* document wallet

porta'erei *nf inv* aircraft carrier

portafi'nestra *nf* French window

porta'foglio *nm* wallet; *(per documenti)* portfolio; *(ministero)* ministry

portafor'tuna *nm inv* lucky charm ● *a inv* lucky

portagi'oie *nm inv* jewellery box

por'tale *nm* door

portama'tite *nm inv* pencil case

porta'mento *nm* carriage; *(condotta)* behaviour

porta'mina *nm inv* propelling pencil

portamo'nete *nm inv* purse

por'tante *a* bearing attrib

portaom'brelli *nm inv* umbrella stand

porta'pacchi *nm inv* roof rack; *(su bicicletta)* luggage rack

porta'penne *nm inv* pencil case

por'ta|re *vt (verso chi parla)* bring; *(lontano da chi parla)* take; *(sorreggere, Math)* carry; *(condurre)* lead; *(indossare)* wear; *(avere)* bear. **~rsi** *vr (trasferirsi)* move; *(comportarsi)* behave; **~rsi bene/male gli anni** look young/old for one's age

portari'viste *nm inv* magazine rack

porta'sci *nm inv* ski rack

portasiga'rette *nm inv* cigarette-case

porta'spilli *nm inv* pin-cushion

por'ta|ta *nf (di pranzo)* course; *Auto* carrying capacity; *(di arma)* range; *(fig: abilità)* capability; **a ~ta di mano** within reach; **alla ~ta di tutti** accessible to all; *(finanziariamente)* within everybody's reach. **por'tatile** *a & nm* portable. **~to** *a (indumento)* worn; *(dotato)* gifted; **essere ~to per qcsa** have a gift for sth; **essere ~to a** *(tendere a)* be inclined to. **~'tore, ~'trice** *nmf* bearer; **al ~tore** to the bearer. **~tore di handicap** disabled person

portatovagli'olo *nm* napkin ring

portau'ovo *nm inv* egg-cup

porta'voce *nm inv* spokesman ● *nf inv* spokeswoman

por'tento *nm* marvel; *(persona dotata)* prodigy

'portico *nm* portico

porti'er|a *nf* door; *(tendaggio)* door curtain. **~e** *nm* porter, doorman; *Sport* goalkeeper. **~e di notte** night porter

porti'n|aio, -a *nmf* caretaker, concierge. **~e'ria** *nf* concierge's room; (*di ospedale*) porter's lodge

'porto *pp di* porgere ● *nm* harbour; (*complesso*) port; (*vino*) port [wine]; (*spesa di trasporto*) carriage; **andare in ~** succeed. **~ d'armi** gun licence

Porto'g|allo *nm* Portugal. **p~hese** *a & nmf* Portuguese

por'tone *nm* main door

portu'ale *nm* dockworker, docker

porzi'one *nf* portion

'posa *nf* laying; (*riposo*) rest; *Phot* exposure; (*atteggiamento*) pose; **mettersi in ~** pose

po'sa|re *vt* put; (*giù*) put [down] ● *vi* (*poggiare*) rest; (*per un ritratto*) pose. **~rsi** *vr* alight; (*sostare*) rest; *Aeron* land. **~ta** *nf* piece of cutlery; **~te** *pl* cutlery *sg*. **~to** *a* sedate

po'scritto *nm* postscript

posi'tivo *a* positive

posizio'nare *vt* position

posizi'one *nf* position; **farsi una ~** get ahead

posolo'gia *nf* dosage

po'spo|rre *vt* place after; (*posticipare*) postpone. **~sto** *pp di* posporre

posse'd|ere *vt* possess, own. **~i'mento** *nm* possession

posses|'sivo *a* possessive. **pos'sesso** *nm* ownership; (*bene*) possession. **~'sore** *nm* owner

pos'sibil|e *a* possible; **il più presto ~e** as soon as possible ● *nm* fare [**tutto**] **il ~e** do one's best. **~ità** *nf inv* possibility; (*occasione*) chance ● *nfpl* (*mezzi*) means

possi'dente *nmf* land-owner

'posta *nf* post, mail; (*ufficio postale*) post office; (*al gioco*) stake; **spese di ~** postage; **per ~** by post, by mail; **la ~ in gioco è...** *fig* what's at stake is...; **a bella ~** on purpose; **Poste e Telecomunicazioni** *pl* [Italian] Post Office. **~ elettronica** electronic mail, e-mail. **~ elettronica vocale** voice-mail

posta'giro *nm* postal giro

po'stale *a* postal

postazi'one *nf* position

postda'tare *vt* postdate (*assegno*)

posteggi'a|re *vt/i* park. **~'tore, ~'trice** *nmf* parking attendant. **po'steggio** *nm* car-park, parking lot *Am*; (*di taxi*) taxi-rank

'posteri *nmpl* descendants. **~'ore** *a* rear; (*nel tempo*) later ● *nm fam* posterior, behind. **~tà** *nf* posterity

po'sticcio *a* artificial; (*baffi, barba*) false ● *nm* hair-piece

postici'pare *vt* postpone

po'stilla *nf* note; *Jur* rider

po'stino *nm* postman, mailman *Am*

'posto *pp di* porre ● *nm* place; (*spazio*) room; (*impiego*) job; *Mil* post; (*sedile*) seat; **a|fuori ~** in/out of place; **prendere ~** take up room; **sul ~** on-site; **essere a ~** (*casa, libri*) be tidy; **mettere a ~** tidy (*stanza*); **fare ~ a** make room for; **al ~ di** (*invece di*) in place of, instead of. **~ di blocco** checkpoint. **~ di guida** driving seat. **~ di lavoro** workstation. **~ di polizia** police station. **posti** *pl* in **piedi** standing room. **posti** *pl* **a sedere** seating

post-partum *a* post-natal

'postumo *a* posthumous ● *nm* after-effect

po'tabile *a* drinkable; **acqua ~** drinking water

po'tare *vt* prune

po'tassio *nm* potassium

po'ten|te *a* powerful; (*efficace*) potent. **~za** *nf* power; (*efficacia*) potency. **~zi'ale** *a & nm* potential

po'tere *nm* power; **al ~** in power ● *vi* can, be able to; **posso entrare?** can I come in?; (*formale*) may I come in?; **posso fare qualche cosa?** can I do something?; **che tu possa essere felice!** may you be happy!; **non ne posso più** (*sono stanco*) I can't go on; (*sono stufo*) I can't take any more; **può darsi** perhaps; **può darsi che sia vero** perhaps it's true; **potrebbe aver ragione** he could be right, he might be right; **avresti potuto telefonare** you could have phoned, you might have phoned; **spero di poter venire** I hope to be able to come; **senza poter telefonare** without being able to phone

potestà *nf inv* power

'pover|o, -a *a* poor; (*semplice*) plain ● *nm* poor man ● *nf* poor woman; **i ~i** the poor. **~tà** *nf* poverty

'pozza *nf* pool. **poz'zanghera** *nf* puddle

'pozzo *nm* well; (*minerario*) pit. **~ petrolifero** oil-well

PP.TT. *abbr* (**Poste e Telegrafi**) [Italian] Post Office

prag'matico *a* pragmatic

prali'nato *a* (*mandorla, gelato*) praline-coated

pram'matica *nf* **essere di ~** be customary

pran'zare *vi* dine; *(a mezzogiorno)* lunch. **'pranzo** *nm* dinner; *(a mezzogiorno)* lunch. **pranzo di nozze** wedding breakfast

'prassi *nf* standard procedure

prate'ria *nf* grassland

prati|ca *nf* practice; *(esperienza)* experience; *(documentazione)* file; **avere ~ca di qcsa** be familiar with sth; **far ~ca** gain experience; **fare le pratiche per** gather the necessary papers for. **~'cabile** *a* practicable; *(strada)* passable. **~ca'mente** *adv* practically. **~'cante** *nmf* apprentice; *Relig* [regular] church-goer

prati'care *vt* practise; *(frequentare)* associate with; *(fare)* make

praticità *nf* practicality. **'pratico** *a* practical; *(esperto)* experienced; **essere pratico di qcsa** know about sth

'prato *nm* meadow; *(di giardino)* lawn

pre'ambolo *nm* preamble

preannunci'are *vt* give advance notice of

preavvi'sare *vt* forewarn. **preav'viso** *nm* warning

pre'cario *a* precarious

precauzi'one *nf* precaution; *(cautela)* care

prece'den|te *a* previous ● *nm* precedent. **~te'mente** *adv* previously. **~za** *nf* precedence; *(di veicoli)* right of way; **dare la ~za** give way. **pre'cedere** *vt* precede

pre'cetto *nm* precept

precipi'ta|re *vt*~**re le cose** precipitate events; **~re qcno nella disperazione** cast sb into a state of despair ● *vi* fall headlong; *(situazione, eventi:)* come to a head. **~rsi** *vr (gettarsi)* throw oneself; *(affrettarsi)* rush; **~rsi a fare qcsa** rush to do sth. **~zi'one** *nf (fretta)* haste; *(atmosferica)* precipitation. **pre'cipi'toso** *a* hasty; *(avventato)* reckless; *(caduta)* headlong

preci'pizio *nm* precipice; **a ~** headlong

precisa'mente *adv* precisely

preci'sa|re *vt* specify; *(spiegare)* clarify. **~zi'one** *nf* clarification

precisi'one *nf* precision. **pre'ciso** *a* precise; *(ore)* sharp; *(identico)* identical

pre'clu|dere *vt* preclude. **~so** *pp di* **precludere**

pre'coc|e *a* precocious; *(prematuro)* premature. **~ità** *nf* precociousness

precon'cetto *a* preconceived ● *nm* prejudice

pre'correre *vt*~ **i tempi** be ahead of one's time

precur'sore *nm* forerunner, precursor

'preda *nf* prey; *(bottino)* booty; **essere in ~ al panico** be panic-stricken; **in ~ alle fiamme** engulfed in flames. **pre'dare** *vt* plunder. **~'tore** *nm* predator

predeces'sore *nmf* predecessor

pre'del|la *nf* platform. **~'lino** *nm* step

predesti'na|re *vt* predestine. **~to** *a Relig* predestined, preordained

predetermi'nato *a* predetermined, preordained

pre'detto *pp di* **predire**

'predica *nf* sermon; *fig* lecture

predi'ca|re *vt* preach. **~to** *nm* predicate

predi'le|tto, -a *pp di* **prediligere** ● *a* favourite ● *nmf* pet. **~zi'one** *nf* predilection. **predi'ligere** *vt* prefer

pre'dire *vt* foretell

predi'spo|rre *vt* arrange. **~rsi** *vr* **~rsi a** prepare oneself for. **~sizi'one** *nf* predisposition; *(al disegno ecc)* bent (a for). **~sto** *pp di* **predisporre**

predizi'one *nf* prediction

predomi'na|nte *a* predominant. **~re** *vi* predominate. **predo'minio** *nm* predominance

pre'done *nm* robber

prefabbri'cato *a* prefabricated ● *nm* prefabricated building

prefazi'one *nf* preface

prefe'renz|a *nf* preference; **di ~a** preferably. **~i'ale** *a* preferential; **cor-sia ~iale** bus and taxi lane

prefe'ribil|e *a* preferable. **~'mente** *adv* preferably

prefe'ri|re *vt* prefer. **~to, -a** *a & nmf* favourite

pre'fet|to *nm* prefect. **~'tura** *nf* prefecture

pre'figgersi *vr* be determined

pre'fisso *pp di* **prefiggere** ● *nm* prefix; *Teleph* [dialling] code

pre'gare *vt/i* pray; *(supplicare)* beg; **farsi ~** need persuading

pre'gevole *a* valuable

preghi'era *nf* prayer; *(richiesta)* request

pregi'ato *a* esteemed; *(prezioso)* valuable. **'pregio** *nm* esteem; *(valore)* value; *(di persona)* good point; **di pregio** valuable

pregiudi'ca|re *vt* prejudice; *(danneggiare)* harm. **~to** *a* prejudiced ● *nm Jur* previous offender

pregiu'dizio *nm* prejudice; *(danno)* detriment

'**prego** *int* (*non c'è di che*) don't mention it!; *(per favore)* please; **~?** I beg your pardon?

pregu'stare *vt* look forward to

prei'storia *nf* prehistory. **prei'storico** *a* prehistoric

pre'lato *nm* prelate

prela'vaggio *nm* prewash

preleva'mento *nm* withdrawal. **pre-le'vare** *vt* withdraw *(denaro)*; collect *(merci)*; *Med* take. **preli'evo** *nm (di sol-di)* withdrawal. **prelievo di sangue** blood sample

prelimi'nare *a* preliminary ● *nm* **pre-liminari** *pl* preliminaries

pre'ludio *nm* prelude

prema'man *nm inv* maternity dress ● *a* maternity *attrib*

prematrimoni'ale *a* premarital

prema'turo, -a *a* premature ● *nmf* premature baby

premedi'tare *vt* premeditate. **~zi'o-ne** *nf* premeditation

'**premere** *vt* press; *Comput* hit *(tasto)* ● *vi* **~ a** *(importare)* matter to; **mi pre-me sapere** I need to know; **~ su** press on; push *(pulsante)*

pre'messa *nf* introduction

pre'messo *pp di* **premettere. ~sso che** bearing in mind that. **~ttere** *vt* put forward; *(mettere prima)* put before.

premi'are *vt* give a prize to; *(ricom-pensare)* reward. **~zi'one** *nf* prize giving

premi'nente *a* pre-eminent

'**premio** *nm* prize; *(ricompensa)* re-ward; *Comm* premium. **~ di consola-zione** booby prize

premoni'tore *a (sogno, segno)* pre-monitory. **~zi'one** *nf* premonition

premu'nirle *vt* fortify. **~si** *vr* take pro-tective measures; **~si di** provide one-self with; **~si contro** protect oneself against

pre'mura *nf (fretta)* hurry; *(cura)* care. **~'roso** *a* thoughtful

prena'tale *a* antenatal

'**prenderle** *vt* take; *(afferrare)* seize; catch *(treno, malattia, ladro, pesce)*; have *(cibo, bevanda)*; *(far pagare)* charge; *(assumere)* take on; *(ottenere)* get; *(occupare)* take up; **~e informa-zioni** make inquiries; **~e a calci/pu-gni** kick/punch; **che ti prende?** what's got into you?; **quanto prende?** what do you charge?; **~e una persona per**

un'altra mistake one person for some-body else ● *vi (voltare)* turn; *(attecchire)* take root; *(rapprendersi)* set; **~e a de-stra/sinistra** turn right/left; **~e a fare qcsa** start doing sth. **~si** *vr* **~si a pu-gni** come to blows; **~si cura di** take care of *(ammalato)*; **~sela** take it to heart

prendi'sole *nm* sundress

preno'tarle *vt* book, reserve. **~to** *a* booked, reserved **~zi'one** *nf* booking, reservation

'**prensile** *a* prehensile

preoccu'pante *a* alarming

preoccu'parle *vt* worry. **~rsi** *vr* **~rsi** worry *(di* about); **~rsi di fare qcsa** take the trouble to do sth. **~to** *a (ansioso)* worried. **~zi'one** *nf* worry; *(apprensione)* concern

prepa'rarle *vt* prepare. **~rsi** *vr* get ready. **~ tivi** *nmpl* preparations. **~to** *nm (prodotto)* preparation. **~'torio** *a* preparatory. **~zi'one** *nf* preparation

prepensiona'mento *nm* early re-tirement

preponde'ran|te *a* predominant. **~za** *nf* prevalence

pre'porre *vt* place before

preposizi'one *nf* preposition

pre'posto *pp di* **preporre** ● *a* ~ **a** *(addetto a)* in charge of

prepo'ten|te *a* overbearing ● *nmf* bully. **~za** *nf* high-handedness

preroga'tiva *nf* prerogative

'**presa** *nf* taking; *(conquista)* capture; *(stretta)* hold; *(di cemento ecc)* setting; *Electr* socket; *(pizzico)* pinch; **essere alle prese con** be struggling *o* grap-pling with; **a ~ rapida** *(cemento, colla)* quick-setting; **fare ~ su qcno** influ-ence sb. **~ d'aria** air vent. **~ in giro** leg-pull. **~ multipla** adaptor

pre'sagio *nm* omen. **presa'gire** *vt* foretell

presbite *a* long-sighted

presbiteri'ano, -a *a & nmf* Presbyte-rian. **presbi'terio** *nm* presbytery

pre'scelto *a* selected

pre'scindere *vi* **~ da** leave aside; **a ~ da** apart from

presco'lare *a* **in età ~** preschool

pre'scritto *pp di* **prescrivere**

pre'scri|vere *vt* prescribe. **~zi'one** *nf* prescription; *(norma)* rule

preselezi'one *nf* **chiamare qcno in ~** call sb via the operator

presen'tarle *vt* present; *(far conosce-re)* introduce; show *(documento)*; *(inol-trare)* submit. **~rsi** *vr* present oneself;

(*farsi conoscere*) introduce oneself; (*a ufficio*) attend; (*alla polizia ecc*) report; (*come candidato*) stand, run; (*occasione:*) occur; **~rsi bene/male** (*persona:*) make a good/bad impression; (*situazione:*) look good/bad. **~tore**, **~trice** *nmf* presenter; (*di notizie*) announcer. **~zi|one** *nf* presentation; (*per conoscersi*) introduction

pre'sente *a* present; (*attuale*) current; (*questo*) this; **aver ~** remember ● *nm* present; **i presenti** those present ● *nf* **allegato alla ~** (*in lettera*) enclosed

presenti'mento *nm* foreboding

pre'senza *nf* presence; (*aspetto*) appearance; **in ~ di, alla ~ di** in the presence of; **di bella ~** personable. **~ di spirito** presence of mind

presenzi'are *vi* **~ a** attend

pre'sepe *nm*, pre'sepio *nm* crib

preser'va|re *vt* preserve; (*proteggere*) protect (**da** from). **~'tivo** *nm* condom. **~zi'one** *nf* preservation

'preside *nm* headmaster; *Univ* dean ● *nf* headmistress; *Univ* dean

presi'den|te *nm* chairman; *Pol* president ● *nf* chairwoman; *Pol* president. **~ del consiglio [dei ministri]** Prime Minister. **~ della repubblica** President of the Republic. **~za** *nf* presidency; (*di assemblea*) chairmanship. **~zi'ale** *a* presidential

presidi'are *vt* garrison. pre'sidio *nm* garrison

presi'edere *vt* preside over

'preso *pp di* prendere

'pressa *nf Mech* press

pres'sante *a* urgent

pressap'poco *adv* about

pres'sare *vt* press

pressi'one *nf* pressure; **far ~ su** put pressure on. **~ del sangue** blood pressure

'presso *prep* near; (*a casa di*) with; (*negli indirizzi*) care of, c/o; (*lavorare*) for ● *pressi nmpl:* **nei pressi di...** in the neighbourhood *o* vicinity of...

pressoché *adv* almost

pressuriz'za|re *vt* pressurize. **~to** *a* pressurized

prestabi'li|re *vt* arrange in advance. **~to** *a* agreed

prestam'pato *a* printed ● *nm* (*modulo*) form

pre'stante *a* good-looking

pre'star|e *vt* lend; **~e attenzione** pay attention; **~e aiuto** lend a hand; **farsi**

~e borrow (**da** from). **~si** *vr* (*frase:*) lend itself; (*persona:*) offer

prestazi'one *nf* performance; **prestazioni** *pl* (*servizi*) services

prestigia'tore, -'trice *nmf* conjurer

pre'stigi|o *nm* prestige; **gioco di ~o** conjuring trick. **~'oso** *a* prestigious

'prestito *nm* loan; **dare in ~** lend; **prendere in ~** borrow

'presto *adv* soon; (*di buon'ora*) early; (*in fretta*) quickly; **a ~** see you soon; **al più ~** as soon as possible; **~ o tardi** sooner or later; **far ~** be quick

pre'sumere *vt* presume; (*credere*) think

presu'mibile *a* **è ~ che...** presumably,...

pre'sunto *a* (*colpevole*) presumed

presun|tu'oso *a* presumptuous ● *nmf* presumptuous person. **~zi'one** *nf* presumption

presup|po|rre *vt* suppose; (*richiedere*) presuppose. **~sizi'one** *nf* presupposition. **~sto** *nm* essential requirement

'prete *nm* priest

preten'dente *nmf* pretender ● *nm* (*corteggiatore*) suitor

pre'ten|dere *vt* (*sostenere*) claim; (*esigere*) demand ● *vi* **~dere a** claim to; **~dere di** (*esigere*) demand to. **~si'one** *nf* pretension. **~zi'oso** *a* pretentious

pre'tes|a *nf* pretension; (*esigenza*) claim; **senza ~e** unpretentious. **~o** *pp di* **pretendere**

pre'testo *nm* pretext

pre'tore *nm* magistrate

pretta'mente *adv* decidedly

pre'tura *nf* magistrate's court

preva'le|nte *a* prevalent. **~nte'mente** *adv* primarily. **~nza** *nf* prevalence. **~re** *vi* prevail

pre'valso *pp di* prevalere

preve'dere *vt* foresee; forecast (*tempo*); (*legge ecc:*) provide for

preve'nire *vt* precede; (*evitare*) prevent; (*avvertire*) forewarn

preven|ti'vare *vt* estimate; (*aspettarsi*) budget for. **~'tivo** *a* preventive ● *nm Comm* estimate

preve'n|uto *a* forewarned; (*mal disposto*) prejudiced. **~zi'one** *nf* prevention; (*preconcetto*) prejudice

previ'den|te *a* provident. **~za** *nf* foresight. **~za sociale** social security, welfare *Am*. **~zi'ale** *a* provident

'previo *a* **~ pagamento** on payment

previsi'one *nf* forecast; **in ~ di** in anticipation of

pre'visto *pp di* **prevedere** ● *a* foreseen ● *nm* **più/meno/prima del ~** more/less/earlier than expected

prezi'oso *a* precious

prez'zemolo *nm* parsley

'prezzo *nm* price. ~ **di fabbrica** factory price. ~ **all'ingrosso** wholesale price. [a] **metà ~** half price

prigi'on|e *nf* prison; (*pena*) imprisonment. **prigio'nia** *nf* imprisonment. ~**i'ero, -a** *a* imprisoned ● *nmf* prisoner

'prima *adv* before; (*più presto*) earlier; (*in primo luogo*) first; **~, finiamo questo** let's finish this first; **puoi venire ~?** (*di giorni*) can't you come any sooner?; (*di ore*) can't you come any earlier?; **~ o poi** sooner or later; **quanto ~** as soon as possible ● *prep* **~ di** before; **~ d'ora** before now ● *conj* **~ che** before ● *nf* first class; *Theat* first night; *Auto* first [gear]

pri'mario *a* primary; (*principale*) principal

pri'mat|e *nm* primate. ~**o** *nm* supremacy; *Sport* record

prima've|ra *nf* spring. ~**rile** *a* spring *attrib*

primeggi'are *vi* excel

primi'tivo *a* primitive; (*originario*) original

pri'mizie *nfpl* early produce *sg*

'primo *a* first; (*fondamentale*) principal; (*precedente di due*) former; (*iniziale*) early; (*migliore*) best ● *nm* first; **primi** *pl* (*i primi giorni*) the beginning; **in un ~ tempo** at first. **prima copia** master copy

primo'genito, -a *a & nmf* first-born

primordi'ale *a* primordial

'primula *nf* primrose

princi'pale *a* main ● *nm* head, boss *fam*

princi'pato *nm* principality. 'princi-pe *nm* prince. **principe ereditario** crown prince. ~**pesco** *a* princely. ~**pessa** *nf* princess

principi'ante *nmf* beginner

prin'cipio *nm* beginning; (*concetto*) principle; (*causa*) cause; **per ~** on principle

pri'ore *nm* prior

priori'tà *nf inv* priority. ~**'tario** *a* having priority

'prisma *nm* prism

pri'va|re *vt* deprive. ~**rsi** *vr* deprive oneself

privatizzazi'one *nf* privatization.

pri'vato, -a *a* private ● *nmf* private citizen

privazi'one *nf* deprivation

privilegi'are *vt* privilege; (*considerare più importante*) favour. **privi'legio** *nm* privilege

'privo *a* ~ **di** devoid of; (*mancante*) lacking in

pro *prep* for ● *nm* advantage; **a che ~?** what's the point?; **il ~ e il contro** the pros and cons

pro'babil|e *a* probable. ~**ità** *nf inv* probability. ~**'mente** *adv* probably

pro'ble|ma *nm* problem. ~**'matico** *a* problematic

pro'boscide *nf* trunk

procacci'ar|e *vt, ~si vr* obtain

pro'cace *a* (*ragazza*) provocative

pro'ced|ere *vi* proceed; (*iniziare*) start; ~**ere contro** *Jur* start legal proceedings against. ~**i'mento** *nm* process; *Jur* proceedings *pl*. **proce'dura** *nf* procedure

proces'sare *vt Jur* try

processi'one *nf* procession

pro'cesso *nm* process; *Jur* trial

proces'sore *nm Comput* processor

processu'ale *a* trial

pro'cinto *nm* **essere in ~ di** be about to

pro'clama *nm* proclamation

procla'ma|re *vt* proclaim. ~**zi'one** *nf* proclamation

procrasti'nare *vt liter* postpone

procreazi'one *nf* procreation

pro'cura *nf* power of attorney; **per ~** by proxy

procu'ra|re *vt/i* procure; (*causare*) cause; (*cercare*) try. ~**'tore** *nm* attorney. **P~tore Generale** Attorney General. ~**tore legale** lawyer. ~**tore della repubblica** public prosecutor

'prode *a* brave. **pro'dezza** *nf* bravery

prodi'gar|e *vt* lavish. ~**si** *vr* do one's best

pro'digi|o *nm* prodigy. ~**oso** *a* prodigious

pro'dotto *pp di* **produrre** ● *nm* product. **prodotti agricoli** farm produce *sg*. ~ **derivato** by-product. ~ **interno lordo** gross domestic product. ~ **nazionale lordo** gross national product

pro'du|rre *vt* produce. ~**rsi** *vr* (*attore:*) play; (*accadere*) happen. ~**ttività** *nf* productivity. ~**t'tivo** *a* productive. ~**t'tore**, ~**t'trice** *nmf* producer. ~**zi'one** *nf* production

profa'na|re vt desecrate. **~zi'one** nf desecration. **pro'fano** a profane

profe'rire vt utter

Prof.essa abbr (**Professoressa**) Prof.

profes'sare vt profess; practise (professione)

professio'nale a professional

professi'o|ne nf profession; **libera ~ne** profession. **~'nismo** nm professionalism. **~'nista** nmf professional

profes'sor|e, -'essa nmf Sch teacher; Univ lecturer; (titolare di cattedra) professor

pro'fe|ta nm prophet. **~tico** a prophetic. **~tiz'zare** vt prophesy. **~'zia** nf prophecy

pro'ficuo a profitable

profi'lar|e vt outline; (ornare) border; Aeron streamline. **~si** vr stand out

profi'lattico a prophylactic ● nm condom

pro'filo nm profile; (breve studio) outline; **di ~** in profile

profit'tare vi **~ di** (avvantaggiarsi) profit by; (approfittare) take advantage of. **pro'fitto** nm profit; (vantaggio) advantage

profonda'mente adv deeply, profoundly. **~'ità** nf inv depth

pro'fondo a deep; fig profound; (cultura) great

'**profugo, -a** nmf refugee

profu'mar|e vt perfume. **~si** vr put on perfume

profumata'mente adv **pagare ~** pay through the nose

profu'mato a (fiore) fragrant; (fazzoletto ecc) scented

profume'ria nf perfumery. **pro'fumo** nm perfume, scent

profusi'one nf profusion; **a ~** in profusion. **pro'fuso** pp di **profondere** ● a profuse

proget'tare vt plan. **~'tista** nmf designer. **pro'getto** nm plan; (di lavoro importante) project. **progetto di legge** bill

prog'nosi nf inv prognosis; **in ~ riservata** on the danger list

pro'gramma nm programme; Comput program. **~ scolastico** syllabus

program'ma|re vt programme; Comput program. **~'tore, ~'trice** nmf [computer] programmer. **~zi'one** nf programming

progre'dire vi [make] progress

progres'sione nf progression. **~'sivo** a progressive. **pro'gresso** nm progress

proi'bi|re vt forbid. **~'tivo** a prohibitive. **~to** a forbidden. **~zi'one** nf prohibition

proiet'tare vt project; show (film). **~t'tore** nm projector; Auto headlight

proi'ettile nm bullet

proiezi'one nf projection

'prole nf offspring. **proletari'ato** nm proletariat. **prole'tario** a & nm proletarian

prolife'rare vi proliferate. **pro'lifico** a prolific

pro'lisso a verbose, prolix

'**prologo** nm prologue

pro'lunga nf Electr extension

prolun'gar|e vt prolong; (allungare) lengthen; extend (contratto, scadenza). **~si** vr continue; **~si su** (dilungarsi) dwell upon

prome'moria nm memo; (per se stessi) reminder, note; (formale) memorandum

pro'me|ssa nf promise. **~sso** pp di **promettere. ~ttere** vt/i promise

promet'tente a promising

promi'nente a prominent

promiscuità nf promiscuity. **pro'miscuo** a promiscuous

promon'torio nm promontory

pro'mo|sso pp di **promuovere** ● a Sch who has gone up a year; Univ who has passed an exam. **~'tore, ~'trice** nmf promoter

promozio'nale a promotional. **promozi'one** nf promotion

promul'gare vt promulgate

promu'overe vt promote; Sch move up a class

proni'pote nm (di bisnonno) greatgrandson; (di prozio) great-nephew ● nf (di bisnonno) greatgranddaughter; (di prozio) great-niece

pro'nome nm pronoun

pronosti'care vt forecast, predict. **pro'nostico** nm forecast

pron'tezza nf readiness; (rapidità) quickness

'**pronto** a ready; (rapido) quick; **~!** Teleph hallo!; **tenersi ~** be ready (**per** for); **pronti, via!** (in gare) ready! steady! go!. **~ soccorso** first aid; (in ospedale) accident and emergency

prontu'ario nm handbook

pro'nuncia nf pronunciation

pronunci'a|re vt pronounce; (dire) utter; deliver (discorso). **~rsi** vr (su un *argomento*) give one's opinion. **~to** *a* pronounced; (*prominente*) prominent

pro'nunzia ecc = **pronuncia** ecc

propa'ganda *nf* propaganda

propa'ga|re *vt* propagate. **~rsi** *vr* spread. **~zi'one** *nf* propagation

prope'deutico *a* introductory

pro'pen|dere *vi* **~dere per** be in favour of. **~si'one** *nf* inclination, propensity. **~so** *pp di* **propendere ● a essere ~so a fare qcsa** be inclined to do sth

propi'nare *vt* administer

pro'pizio *a* favourable

proponi'mento *nm* resolution

pro'por|re *vt* propose; (*suggerire*) suggest. **~si** *vr* set oneself (*obiettivo, meta*); **~si di** intend to

proporzio'na|le *a* proportional. **~re** *vt* proportion. **~to** *a* proportioned. **proporzi'one** *nf* proportion

pro'posito *nm* purpose; **a ~** by the way; **a ~ di** with regard to; **di ~** (*apposta*) on purpose; **capitare a ~, giungere a ~** come at just the right time

proposizi'one *nf* clause; (*frase*) sentence

pro'post|a *nf* proposal. **~o** *pp di* **proporre**

proprietà *nf inv* property; (*diritto*) ownership; (*correttezza*) propriety. **~ immobiliare** property. **~ privata** private property. **proprie'taria** *nf* owner; (*di casa affittata*) landlady. **proprie'tario** *nm* owner; (*di casa affittata*) landlord

'proprio *a* one's [own]; (*caratteristico*) typical; (*appropriato*) proper **● adv** just; (*veramente*) really; **non ~** not really, not exactly; (*affatto*) not... at all **● pron** one's own **● nm** one's [own]; **lavorare in ~** be one's own boss; **mettersi in ~** set up on one's own

propul'si|one *nf* propulsion. **~'sore** *nm* propeller

'proroga *nf* extension

proro'ga|bile *a* extendable. **~re** *vt* extend

pro'rompere *vi* burst out

'prosa *nf* prose. **pro'saico** *a* prosaic

pro'scio'gliere *vt* release; *Jur* acquit. **~lto** *pp di* **prosciogliere**

prosciu'gar|e *vt* dry up; (*bonificare*) reclaim. **~si** *vr* dry up

prosci'utto *nm* ham. **~ cotto** cooked ham. **~ crudo** type of dry-cured ham, Parma ham

pro'scri|tto, -a *pp di* **proscrivere ● nmf** exile

prosecuzi'one *nf* continuation

prosegui'mento *nm* continuation; **buon ~!** (*viaggio*) have a good journey!; (*festa*) enjoy the rest of the party!

prosegu'ire *vt* continue **● vi** go on, continue

prospe'r|are *vi* prosper. **~ità** *nf* prosperity. **'prospero** *a* prosperous; (*favorevole*) favourable. **~oso** *a* flourishing; (*ragazza*) buxom

prospet'tar|e *vt* show. **~si** *vr* seem

prospet'tiva *nf* perspective; (*panorama*) view; *fig* prospect. **pro'spetto** *nm* (*vista*) view; (*facciata*) façade; (*tabella*) table

prospici'ente *a* facing

prossima'mente *adv* soon

prossimità *nf* proximity

'prossimo, -a *a* near; (*seguente*) next; (*molto vicino*) close; **l'anno ~** next year **● nmf** neighbour

prosti'tu|ta *nf* prostitute. **~zi'one** *nf* prostitution

pro'stra|re *vt* prostrate. **~rsi** *vr* prostrate oneself. **~to** *a* prostrate

protago'nista *nmf* protagonist

pro'teggere *vt* protect; (*favorire*) favour

prote'ina *nf* protein

pro'tender|e *vt* stretch out. **~si** *vr* (*in avanti*) lean out. **pro'teso** *pp di* **protendere**

pro'te|sta *nf* protest; (*dichiarazione*) protestation. **~'stante** *a* & *nmf* Protestant. **~'stare** *vt/i* protest

protet'tivo *a* protective. **~tto** *pp di* **proteggere**. **~t'tore, ~t'trice** *nmf* protector; (*sostenitore*) patron **● nm** (*di prostituta*) pimp. **~zi'one** *nf* protection

protocol'lare *a* (*visita*) protocol **● vt** register

proto'collo *nm* protocol; (*registro*) register; **carta ~** official stamped paper

pro'totipo *nm* prototype

pro'tra|rre *vt* protract; (*differire*) postpone. **~rsi** *vr* go on, continue. **~tto** *pp di* **protrarre**

protube'ran|te *a* protuberant. **~za** *nf* protuberance

'prova *nf* test; (*dimostrazione*) proof; (*tentativo*) try; (*di abito*) fitting; *Sport* heat; *Theat* rehearsal; (*bozza*) proof; **fino a ~ contraria** until I'm told otherwise; **in ~** (*assumere*) for a trial period;

mettere alla ~ put to the test. **~ generale** dress rehearsal

pro'var|e *vt* test; *(dimostrare)* prove; *(tentare)* try; try on *(abiti ecc)*; *(sentire)* feel; *Theat* rehearse. **~si** *vr* try

proveni'enza *nf* origin. **prove'nire** *vi* **provenire da** come from

pro'vento *nm* proceeds *pl*

prove'nuto *pp di* **provenire**

pro'verbio *nm* proverb

pro'vetta *nf* test-tube; **bambino in ~** test-tube baby

pro'vetto *a* skilled

pro'vinci|a *nf* province; *(strada)* B road, secondary road. **~'ale** *a* provincial; **strada ~ale** B road, secondary road

pro'vino *nm* specimen; *Cinema* screen test

provo'ca|nte *a* provocative. **~re** *vt* provoke; *(causare)* cause. **~ 'tore**, **~ 'tri-ce** *nmf* trouble-maker. **~ 'torio** *a* provocative. **~ 'zi'one** *nf* provocation

provve'd|ere *vi* **~ere a** provide for. **~ 'imento** *nm* measure; *(previdenza)* precaution

provvi'denz|a *nf* providence. **~ 'i'ale** *a* providential

provvigi'one *nf Comm* commission

provvi'sorio *a* provisional

prov'vista *nf* supply

pro'zio, -a *nm* great-uncle ● *nf* great-aunt

'prua *nf* prow

pru'den|te *a* prudent. **~za** *nf* prudence; **per ~za** as a precaution

'prudere *vi* itch

prugn|a *nf* plum. **~a secca** prune. **~o** *nm* plum[-tree]

pruri'gi'noso *a* itchy. **pru'rito** *nm* itch

pseu'donimo *nm* pseudonym

psica'na|lisi *nf* psychoanalysis. **~'lista** *nmf* psychoanalyst. **~liz'zare** *vt* psychoanalyse

'psiche *nf* psyche

psichi'a|tra *nmf* psychiatrist. **~'tria** *nf* psychiatry. **~trico** *a* psychiatric

'psichico *a* mental

psico'lo'gia *nf* psychology. **~'logico** *a* psychological. **psi'cologo, -a** *nmf* psychologist

psico'patico, -a *a* psychopathic ● *nmf* psychopath

PT *abbr (Posta e Telecomunicazioni)* PO

pubbli'ca|re *vt* publish. **~zi'one** *nf* publication. **~zioni** *pl (di matrimonio)* banns

pubbli'cista *nmf Journ* correspondent

pubblicità *nf inv* publicity, advertising; *(annuncio)* advertisement, advert; **fare ~ a qcsa** advertise sth; **piccola ~** small advertisements. **pubblici'tario** *a* advertising

'pubblico *a* public; **scuola pubblica** state school ● *nm* public; *(spettatori)* audience; **grande ~** general public. **Pubblica Sicurezza** Police. **~ uffi-ciale** civil servant

'pube *nm* pubis

pubertà *nf* puberty

pu'dico *a* modest. **pu'dore** *nm* modesty

pue'rile *a* children's; *pej* childish

pugi'lato *nm* boxing. **'pugile** *nm* boxer

pugna'la|re *vt* stab. **~ta** *nf* stab. **pu'gnale** *nm* dagger

'pugno *nm* fist; *(colpo)* punch; *(manciata)* fistful; *(fig: numero limitato)* handful; **dare un ~ a** a punch

'pulce *nf* flea; *(microfono)* bug

pul'cino *nm* chick; *(nel calcio)* junior

pu'ledra *nf* filly

pu'ledro *nm* colt

pu'li|re *vt* clean. **~re a secco** dry-clean. **~to** *a* clean. **~'tura** *nf* cleaning. **~'zia** *nf (il pulire)* cleaning; *(l'essere pulito)* cleanliness; **~zie** *pl* housework; **fare le ~zie** do the cleaning

'pullman *nm inv* bus, coach; *(urbano)* bus

pul'mino *nm* minibus

'pulpito *nm* pulpit

pul'sante *nm* button; *Electr* [push-]button. **~ di accensione** on/off switch

pul'sa|re *vi* pulsate. **~zi'one** *nf* pulsation

pul'viscolo *nm* dust

'puma *nm inv* puma

pun'gente *a* prickly; *(insetto)* stinging; *(odore ecc)* sharp

'punger|e *vt* prick; *(insetto:)* sting. **~si un dito** prick one's finger

pungigli'one *nm* sting

pu'ni|re *vt* punish. **~'tivo** *a* punitive. **~zi'one** *nf* punishment; *Sport* free kick

'punta *nf* point; *(estremità)* tip; *(di monte)* peak; *(un po')* pinch; *Sport* forward; **doppie punte** *(di capelli)* split ends

pun'tare *vt* point; *(spingere con forza)* push; *(scommettere)* bet; *(fam: appunta-re)* fasten ● *vi* **~ su** *fig* rely on; **~ verso** *(dirigersi)* head for; **~ a** aspire to

punta'spilli *nm inv* pincushion

pun'tata *nf (di una storia)* instalment;

(*televisiva*) episode; (*al gioco*) stake, bet; (*breve visita*) flying visit; **a puntate** serialized, in instalments; **fare una ~ a/ in** pop over to (*luogo*)
punteggia'tura *nf* punctuation
pun'teggio *nm* score
puntel'lare *vt* prop. **pun'tello** *nm* prop
pun'tiglio *nm* spite; (*ostinazione*) obstinacy. **~'oso** *a* punctilious, pernickety *pej*
pun'tin|a *nf* (*da disegno*) drawing pin, thumb tack *Am*; (*di giradischi*) stylus. **~o** *nm* dot; **a ~o** perfectly; (*cotto*) to a T
'punto *nm* point; (*in cucito, Med*) stitch; (*in punteggiatura*) full stop; **in che ~?** where, exactly?; **di ~ in bianco** all of a sudden; **due punti** colon; **in ~** sharp; **mettere a ~** put right; *fig* fine tune; tune up (*motore*); **essere sul ~ di fare qcsa** be about to do sth, be on the point of doing sth. **punti** *pl* **cardinali** points of the compass. **~ debole** blind spot. **~ esclamativo** exclamation mark. **~ interrogativo** question mark. **~ nero** *Med* blackhead. **~ di riferimento** landmark; (*per la qualità*) benchmark. **~ di vendita** point of sale. **~ e virgola** semicolon. **~ di vista** point of view
puntu'al|e *a* punctual. **~ità** *nf* punctuality. **~'mente** *adv* punctually, on time
pun'tura *nf* (*di insetto*) sting; (*di ago ecc*) prick; *Med* puncture; (*iniezione*) injection; (*fitta*) stabbing pain

punzecchi'are *vt* prick; *fig* tease
'pupa *nf* doll. **pu'pazzo** *nm* puppet. **pupazzo di neve** snowman
pup'illa *nf Anat* pupil
pu'pillo, -a *nmf* (*di professore*) favourite
purché *conj* provided
'pure *adv* too, also; (*concessivo*) **fate ~!** please do! ● *conj* (*tuttavia*) yet; (*anche se*) even if; **pur di** just to
purè *nm inv* purée. **~ di patate** mashed potatoes, creamed potatoes
pu'rezza *nf* purity
'purga *nf* purge. **pur'gante** *nm* laxative. **pur'gare** *vt* purge
purga'torio *nm* purgatory
purifi'care *vt* purify
puri'tano, -a *a & nmf* Puritan
'puro *a* pure; (*vino ecc*) undiluted; **per ~ caso** by sheer chance, purely by chance
puro'sangue *a & nm* thoroughbred
pur'troppo *adv* unfortunately
pus *nm* pus. **'pustola** *nf* pimple
puti'ferio *nm* uproar
putre'far|e *vi*, **~si** *vr* putrefy
'putrido *a* putrid
put'tana *nf vulg* whore
'puzza *nf* = **puzzo**
puz'zare *vi* stink; **~ di bruciato** *fig* smell fishy
'puzzo *nm* stink, bad smell. **~la** *nf* polecat. **~'lente** *a* stinking
p.zza *abbr* (**piazza**) Sq.

Qq

---

qua *adv* here; **da un anno in ~** for the last year; **da quando in ~?** since when?; **di ~** this way; **di ~ di** on this side of; **~ dentro** in here; **~ sotto** under here; **~ vicino** near here; **~ e là** here and there
qua'derno *nm* exercise book; (*per appunti*) notebook
quadrango'lare *a* (*forma*) quadrangular. **qua'drangolo** *nm* quadrangle
qua'drante *nm* quadrant; (*di orologio*) dial
qua'dra|re *vt* square; (*contabilità*) balance ● *vi* fit in. **~to** *a* square;

(*equilibrato*) levelheaded ● *nm* square; (*pugilato*) ring; **al ~to** squared
quadret'tato *a* squared; (*carta*) graph *attrib*. **qua'dretto** *nm* square; (*piccolo quadro*) small picture; **a quadretti** (*tessuto*) check
quadricro'mia *nf* four-colour printing
quadrien'nale *a* (*che dura quattro anni*) four-year
quadri'foglio *nm* four-leaf clover
quadri'latero *nm* quadrilateral
quadri'mestre *nm* (*periodo*) four-month period

'**quadro** *nm* picture, painting; (*quadro*) square; (*fig: scena*) sight; (*tabella*) table; *Theat* scene; *Comm* executive **quadri** *pl* (*carte*) diamonds; **a quadri** ‹*tessuto, giacca, motivo*› check. **quadri** *pl* **direttivi** senior management

qua'drupede *nm* quadruped

quaggiù *adv* down here

'**quaglia** *nf* quail

'**qualche** *a* (*alcuni*) a few, some; (*un certo*) some; (*in interrogazioni*) any; **ho ~ problema** I have a few problems, I have some problems; **~ tempo fa** some time ago; **hai ~ libro italiano?** have you any Italian books?; **posso prendere ~ libro?** can I take some books?; **in ~ modo** somehow; **in ~ posto** somewhere; **~ volta** sometimes; **~ cosa = qualcosa**

qual'cos‖**a** *pron* something; (*in interrogazioni*) anything; **~'altro** something else; **vuoi ~'altro?** would you like anything else?; **~a di strano** something strange; **vuoi ~a da mangiare?** would you like something to eat?

qual'cuno *pron* someone, somebody; (*in interrogazioni*) anyone, anybody; (*alcuni*) some; (*in interrogazioni*) any; **c'è ~?** is anybody in?; **qualcun altro** someone else, somebody else; **c'è qualcun altro che aspetta** is anybody else waiting?; **ho letto ~ dei suoi libri** I've read some of his books; **conosci ~ dei suoi amici?** do you know any of his friends?

'**quale** *a* which; (*indeterminato*) what; (*come*) as, like; **~ macchina è la tua?** which car is yours?; **~ motivo avrà di parlare così?** what reason would he have to speak like that?; **~ onore!** what an honour!; **città quali Venezia** towns like Venice; **~ che sia la tua opinione** whatever you may think ● *pron inter* which [one]; **~ preferisci?** which [one] do you prefer? ● *pron rel* **il/la ~** (*persona*) who; (*animale, cosa*) that, which; (*oggetto: con prep*) whom; (*animale, cosa*) which; **ho incontrato tua madre, la ~ mi ha detto...** I met your mother, who told me...; **l'ufficio nel ~ lavoro** the office in which I work; **l'uomo con il ~ parlavo** the man to whom I was speaking ● *adv* (*come*) as

qua'lifica *nf* qualification; (*titolo*) title

qualifi'ca‖**re** *vt* qualify; (*definire*) define. **~rsi** *vr* be placed. **~'tivo** *a* qualifying. **~to** *a* ‹*operaio*› semiskilled. **~zi'one** *nf* qualification

qualità *nf inv* quality; (*specie*) kind; **in ~ di** in one's capacity as. **~tiva'mente** *adv* qualitatively. **~'tivo** *a* qualitative

qua'lora *conj* in case

qual'siasi, qua'lunque *a* any; (*non importa quale*) whatever; (*ordinario*) ordinary; **dammi una penna ~** give me any pen [whatsoever]; **farei ~ cosa** I would do anything; **~ cosa io faccia** whatever I do; **~ persona** anyone; **in ~ caso** in any case; **uno ~** any one, whichever; **l'uomo qualunque** the man in the street; **vivo in una casa ~** I live in an ordinary house

qualunqu'ismo *nm* lack of political views

'**quando** *conj* & *adv* when; **da ~ ti ho visto** since I saw you; **da ~ esci con lui?** how long have you been going out with him?; **da ~ in qua?** since when?; **~... ~...** sometimes... sometimes...

quantifi'care *vt* quantify

quantità *nf inv* quantity; **una ~ di** (*gran numero*) a great deal of. **~tiva'mente** *adv* quantitatively. **~'tivo** *nm* amount ● *a* quantitative

'**quanto** *a inter* how much; (*con nomi plurali*) how many; (*in esclamazioni*) what a lot of; (*tempo*) how long; **quanti anni hai?** how old are you? ● *a rel* as much... as; (*tempo*) as long as; (*con nomi plurali*) as many... as; **prendi ~ denaro ti serve** take as much money as you need; **prendi quanti libri vuoi** take as many books as you like ● *pron inter* how much; (*quanto tempo*) how long; (*plurale*) how many; **quanti ne abbiamo oggi?** what date is it today? ● *pron rel* as much as; (*quanto tempo*) as long as; (*plurale*) as many as; **prendine ~/quanti ne vuoi** take as much/as many as you like; **stai ~ vuoi** stay as long as you like; **questo è ~** that's it ● *adv inter* how much; (*quanto tempo*) how long; **~ sei alto?** how tall are you?; **~ hai aspettato?** how long did you wait for?; **~ costa?** how much is it?; **~ mi dispiace!** I'm so sorry!; **~ è bello!** how nice! ● *adv rel* as much as; **lavoro ~ posso** I work as much as I can; **è tanto intelligente ~ bello** he's as intelligent as he's good-looking; **in ~** (*in qualità di*) as; (*poiché*) since; **in ~ a me** as far as I'm concerned; **per ~** however; **per ~ ne sappia** as far as I know; **per ~ mi riguarda** as far as I'm concerned; **per ~ mi sia simpatico** much as I like him; ~ **a** as for; ~ **prima** (*al più presto*) as soon as possible

quan'tunque *conj* although

qua'ranta *a & nm* forty

quaran'tena *nf* quarantine

quaran'tennje *a* forty-year-old. ~**io** *nm* period of forty years

quaran't|esimo *a* fortieth. ~**ina** *nf* una ~**ina** about forty

qua'resima *nf* Lent

quar'tetto *nm* quartet

quar'tiere *nm* district; *Mil* quarters *pl.* ~ **generale** headquarters

quarto *a* fourth ● *nm* fourth; (*quarta parte*) quarter; **le sette e un** ~ **a** quarter past seven. **quarti** *pl* **di finale** quarterfinals. ~ **d'ora** quarter of an hour. **quar'tultimo, -a** *nmf* fourth from the end, fourth last

'quarzo *nm* quartz

'quasi *adv* almost, nearly; ~ **mai** hardly ever ● *conj* (*come se*) as if; ~ **sto a casa** I'm tempted to stay home

quas'sù *adv* up here

'quatto *a* crouching; (*silenzioso*) silent; **starsene** ~ ~ keep very quiet

quat'tordici *a & nm* fourteen

quat'trini *nmpl* money *sg*, dosh *sg fam*

'quattro *a & nm* four; **dirne** ~ **a qcno** give sb a piece of one's mind; **farsi in** ~ (**per qcno/per fare qcsa**) go to a lot of trouble (for sb/to do sth); **in** ~ **e quattr'otto** in a flash. ~ **per** ~ *nm inv* *Auto* four-wheel drive [vehicle]

quat'trocchi: a ~ *adv* in private

quattro'cento *a & nm* four hundred; **il Q~** the fifteenth century

quattro'mila *a & nm* four thousand

'quello *a* that (*pl* those); **quell'albero** that tree; **quegli alberi** those trees; **quel cane** that dog; **quei cani** those dogs ● *pron* that [one] (*pl* those [ones]); ~ **lì** that one over there; ~ **che** the one that; (*ciò che*) what; **quelli che** the ones that, those that; ~ **a destra** the one on the right

'quercia *nf* oak

que'rela *nf* [legal] action

quere'lare *vt* bring an action against

que'sito *nm* question

questio'nario *nm* questionnaire

quest'ione *nf* question; (*faccenda*)

matter; (*litigio*) quarrel; **in** ~ in doubt; **è fuori** ~ it's out of the question; **è** ~ **di vita o di morte** it's a matter of life and death

'quest|o *a* this (*pl* these) ● *pron* this [one] (*pl* these [ones]); ~**o qui**, ~**o qua** this one here; ~**o è quello che è detto** that's what he said; **per** ~**o** for this *or* that reason. **quest'oggi** today

que'store *nm* chief of police

que'stura *nf* police headquarters

qui *adv* here; **da** ~ **in poi** from now on; **fin** ~ (*di tempo*) up till now, until now; ~ **dentro** in here; ~ **sotto** under here; ~ **vicino** *adv* near here ● *nm* ~ **pro quo** misunderstanding

quie'scienza *nf* **trattamento di** ~ retirement package

quie'tanza *nf* receipt

quie'tar|e *vt* calm. ~**si** *vr* quieten down

qui'et|e *nf* quiet; **disturbo della** ~**e pubblica** breach of the peace. ~**o** *a* quiet

'quindi *adv* then ● *conj* therefore

'quindi|ci *a & nm* fifteen. ~**cina** *nf* una ~**cina** about fifteen; una ~**cina di giorni** a fortnight *Br*, two weeks

quinquen'nale *a* (*che dura cinque anni*) five-year. **quin'quennio** *nm* [period of] five years

quin'tale *nm* a hundred kilograms

'quinte *nfpl* *Theat* wings

quin'tetto *nm* quintet

'quinto *a* fifth

quin'tuplo *a* quintuple

qui'squiglia *nf* **perdersi in quisquiglie** get bogged down in details

'quota *nf* quota; (*rata*) instalment; (*altitudine*) height; *Aeron* altitude, height; (*ippica*) odds *pl*; **perdere** ~ lose altitude; **prendere** ~ gain altitude. ~ **di iscrizione** entry fee

quo'ta|re *vt Comm* quote. ~**to** *a* quoted; **essere** ~**to in Borsa** be quoted on the Stock Exchange. ~**zi'one** *nf* quotation

quotidi|ana'mente *adv* daily. ~'**ano** *a* daily; (*ordinario*) everyday ● *nm* daily [paper]

quozi'ente *nm* quotient. ~ **d'intelligenza** intelligence quotient, IQ

Rr

ra'barbaro nm rhubarb

'rabbia nf rage; (ira) anger; Med rabies sg; che ~! what a nuisance!; mi fa ~ it makes me angry

rab'bino nm rabbi

rabbiosa'mente adv furiously. rabbi'oso a hot-tempered; Med rabid; (violento) violent

rabbo'nir|e vt pacify. ~si vr calm down

rabbrivi'dire vi shudder; (di freddo) shiver

rabbui'arsi vr become dark

raccapez'zar|e vt put together. ~si vr see one's way ahead

raccapricci'ante a horrifying

raccatta'palle nm inv ball boy ● nf inv ball girl

raccat'tare vt pick up

rac'chetta nf racket. ~ da ping pong table-tennis bat. ~ da sci ski stick, ski pole. ~ da tennis tennis racket

'racchio a fam ugly

racchi'udere vt contain

rac'cogli|ere vt pick; (da terra) pick up; (mietere) harvest; (collezionare) collect; (radunare) gather; win (voti ecc); (dare asilo a) take in. ~ersi vr gather; (concentrarsi) collect one's thoughts. ~'mento nm concentration. ~'tore, ~'trice nmf collector ● nm (cartella) ring-binder

rac'colto, -a pp di raccogliere ● a (rannicchiato) hunched; (intimo) cosy; (concentrato) engrossed ● nm (mietitura) harvest ● nf collection; (di scritti) compilation; (del grano ecc) harvesting; (adunata) gathering

raccoman'dabile a recommendable; poco ~ (persona) shady

raccoman'da|re vt recommend; (affidare) entrust. ~rsi vr (implorare) beg. ~ta nf registered letter; ~ta con ricevuta di ritorno recorded delivery. ~-espresso nf guaranteed next-day delivery of recorded items. ~zi'one nf recommendation

raccon'tare vt tell. rac'conto nm story

raccorci'are vt shorten

raccor'dare vt join. rac'cordo nm connection; (stradale) feeder. raccordo anulare ring road. raccordo ferroviario siding

ra'chitico a rickety; (poco sviluppato) stunted

racimo'lare vt scrape together

racket nm inv racket

'radar nm radar

raddol'cir|e vt sweeten; fig soften. ~si vr become milder; (carattere:) mellow

raddoppi'are vt double. rad'doppio nm doubling

raddriz'zare vt straighten

'rader|e vt shave; graze (muro); ~e al suolo raze [to the ground]. ~si vr shave

radi'are vt strike off; ~ dall'albo strike off

radia'tore nm radiator. ~zi'one nf radiation

'radica nf briar

radi'cale a radical ● nm Gram root; Pol radical

ra'dicchio nm chicory

ra'dice nf root; mettere [le] radici fig put down roots. ~ quadrata square root

'radio nf inv radio; via ~ by radio. ~ a transistor transistor radio ● nm Chem radium.

radioama'tore, -'trice nmf [radio] ham

radioascolta'tore, -'trice nmf listener

radioat|tività nf radioactivity. ~'tivo a radioactive

radio'cro|naca nf radio commentary; fare la ~naca di commentate on. ~'nista nmf radio reporter

radiodiffusi'one nf broadcasting

radiogra|'fare vt X-ray. ~'fia nf X-ray [photograph]; (radiologia) radiography; fare una ~fia (paziente:) have an X-ray; (dottore:) take an X-ray

radio'fonico a radio attrib

radio'lina nf transistor

radi'ologo, -a nmf radiologist

radi'oso a radiant

radio'sveglia *nf* radio alarm

radio'taxi *nm inv* radio taxi

radiote'lefono *nm* radio-telephone; (*privato*) cordless [phone]

radiotelevi'sivo *a* broadcasting *attrib*

'**rado** *a* sparse; (*non frequente*) rare; **di ~** seldom

radu'nar|e *vt*, **~si** *vr* gather [together]. **ra'duno** *nm* meeting; *Sport* rally

ra'dura *nf* clearing

'**rafano** *nm* horseradish

raffazzo'nato *a* (*discorso, lavoro*) botched

raf'fermo *a* stale

'**raffica** *nf* gust; (*di armi da fuoco*) burst; (*di domande*) barrage

raffigu'ra|re *vt* represent. **~zi'one** *nf* representation

raffi'na|re *vt* refine. **~ta'mente** *adv* elegantly. **~'tezza** *nf* refinement. **~to** *a* refined. **raffine'ria** *nf* refinery

rafforza|'mento *nm* reinforcement; (*di muscolatura*) strengthening. **~re** *vt* reinforce. **~'tivo** *nm Gram* intensifier

raffredda'mento *nm* (*processo*) cooling

raffred'd|are *vt* cool. **~arsi** *vr* get cold; (*prendere un raffreddore*) catch a cold. **~ore** *nm* cold. **~ore da fieno** hay fever

raf'fronto *nm* comparison

'**rafia** *nf* raffia

Rag. *abbr* **ragioniere**

ra'gaz|za *nf* girl; (*fidanzata*) girlfriend. **~za alla pari** au pair [girl]. **~'zata** *nf* prank. **~zo** *nm* boy; (*fidanzato*) boyfriend; **da ~zo** (*da giovane*) as a boy

ragge'lar|e *vt fig* freeze. **~si** *vr fig* turn to ice

raggi'ante *a* radiant; **~ di successo** flushed with success

raggi'era *nf* **a ~** with a pattern like spokes radiating from a centre

'**raggio** *nm* ray; *Math* radius; (*di ruota*) spoke; **~ d'azione** range. **~ laser** laser beam

raggi'rare *vt* trick. **rag'giro** *nm* trick

raggi'un|gere *vt* reach; (*conseguire*) achieve. **~'gibile** *a* (*luogo*) within reach

raggomito'lar|e *vt* wind. **~si** *vr* curl up

raggranel'lare *vt* scrape together

raggrin'zir|e *vt*, **~si** *vr* wrinkle

raggrup|pa'mento *nm* (*gruppo*) group; (*azione*) grouping. **~'pare** *vt* group together

ragguagli'are *vt* compare; (*informare*) inform. **raggu'aglio** *nm* comparison; (*informazione*) information

ragguar'devole *a* considerable

'**ragia** *nf* resin; **acqua** *nf* **~** turpentine

ragiona'mento *nm* reasoning; (*discussione*) discussion. **ragio'nare** *vi* reason; (*discutere*) discuss

ragi'one *nf* reason; (*ciò che è giusto*) right; **a ~ o a torto** rightly or wrongly; **aver ~** be right; **perdere la ~** go out of one's mind; **a ragion veduta** after due consideration

ragione'ria *nf* accountancy

ragio'nevol|e *a* reasonable. **~'mente** *adv* reasonably

ragioni'ere, -a *nmf* accountant

ragli'are *vi* bray

ragna'tela *nf* cobweb. '**ragno** *nm* spider

ragù *nm inv* meat sauce

RAI *nf abbr* (**Radio Audizioni Italiane**) *Italian public broadcasting company*

ralle'gra|re *vt* gladden. **~rsi** *vr* rejoice; **~rsi con qcno** congratulate sb. **~'menti** *nmpl* congratulations

rallenta'mento *nm* slowing down

rallen'ta|re *vt/i* slow down; (*allentare*) slacken. **~rsi** *vr* slow down. **~'tore** *nm* (*su strada*) speed bump; **al ~tore** in slow motion

raman'zina *nf* reprimand

ra'marro *nm* type of lizard

ra'mato *a* (*capelli*) copper[-coloured]

'**rame** *nm* copper

ramifi'ca|re *vi*, **~rsi** *vr* branch out; (*strada:*) branch. **~zi'one** *nf* ramification

rammari'carsi *vr* **~ di** regret; (*lamentarsi*) complain (**di** about). **ram'marico** *nm* regret

rammen'dare *vt* darn. **ram'mendo** *nm* darning

rammen'tar|e *vt* remember; **~e qcsa a qcno** (*richiamare alla memoria*) remind sb of sth. **~si** *vr* remember

rammol'li|re *vt* soften. **~rsi** *vr* go soft. **~to, -a** *nmf* wimp

'**ramo** *nm* branch. **~'scello** *nm* twig

'**rampa** *nf* (*di scale*) flight. **~ d'accesso** slip road. **~ di lancio** launch[ing] pad

ram'pante *a* **giovane ~** yuppie

rampi'cante *a* climbing ● *nm Bot* creeper

ram'pollo nm hum brat; (discendente) descendant

ram'pone nm harpoon; (per scarpe) crampon

'rana nf frog; (nel nuoto) breaststroke; **uomo ~** frogman

'rancido a rancid

ran'core nm resentment

ran'dagio a stray

'rango nm rank

rannicchi'arsi vr huddle up

rannuvola'mento nm clouding over. **rannuvo'larsi** vr cloud over

ra'nocchio nm frog

ranto'lare vi wheeze. **'rantolo** nm wheeze; (di moribondo) death-rattle

'rapa nf turnip

ra'pace a rapacious; (uccello) predatory

ra'pare vt crop

'rapida nf rapids pl. ~'**mente** adv rapidly

rapidità nf speed

'rapido a swift ● nm (treno) express [train]

rapi'mento nm (crimine) kidnapping

ra'pina nf robbery; **~ a mano armata** armed robbery. **~ in banca** bank robbery. **rapi'nare** vt rob. ~'**tore** nm robber

ra'pire vt abduct; (a scopo di riscatto) kidnap; (estasiare) ravish. ~'**tore**, ~'**trice** nmf kidnapper

rappacifi'ca|re vt pacify. ~**rsi** vr be reconciled, make it up. ~**zi'one** nf reconciliation

rappor'tare vt reproduce (disegno); (confrontare) compare

rap'porto nm report; (connessione) relation; (legame) relationship; Math, Techn ratio; **rapporti** pl relationship; **essere in buoni rapporti** be on good terms. **~ di amicizia** friendship. **~ di lavoro** working relationship. **rapporti** pl **sessuali** sexual intercourse

rap'prendersi vr set; (latte:) curdle

rappre'saglia nf reprisal

rappresen'tan|te nmf representative. **~te di classe** class representative. **~te di commercio** sales representative, [sales] rep fam. ~**za** nf delegation; Comm agency; **spese** nf/pl **di ~za** entertainment expenses; **di ~za** (appartamento ecc) company

rappresen'ta|re vt represent; Theat perform. **~'tivo** a representative. ~**zi'one** nf representation; (spettacolo) performance

rap'preso pp di **rapprendersi**

rapso'dia nf rhapsody

'raptus nm inv fit of madness

rara'mente adv rarely, seldom

rare'fa|re vt, ~**rsi** vr rarefy. ~**tto** a rarefied

rarità nf inv rarity. **'raro** a rare

ra'sar|e vt shave; trim (siepe ecc). ~**si** vr shave

raschia'mento nm Med curettage

raschi'are vt scrape; (togliere) scrape off

rasen'tare vt go close to. **ra'sente** prep very close to

'raso pp di **radere** ● a smooth; (colmo) full to the brim; (barba) close-cropped; **~ terra** close to the ground; **un cucchiaio ~** a level spoonful ● nm satin

ra'soio nm razor

ras'segna nf review; (mostra) exhibition; (musicale, cinematografica) festival; **passare in ~** review; Mil inspect

rasse'gna|re vt present. ~**rsi** vr resign oneself. ~**to a** (persona, aria, tono) resigned. ~**zi'one** nf resignation

rassere'nar|e vt clear; fig cheer up. ~**si** vr become clear; fig cheer up

rasset'tare vt tidy up; (riparare) mend

rassicu'ra|nte a (persona, parole, presenza) reassuring. ~**re** vt reassure. ~**zi'one** nf reassurance

rasso'dare vt harden; fig strengthen

rassomigli'a|nza nf resemblance. ~**re** vi ~**re a** resemble

rastrella'mento nm (di fieno) raking; (perlustrazione) combing. **rastrel'lare** vt rake; (perlustrare) comb

rastrelli'era nf rack; (per biciclette) bicycle rack; (scolapiatti) [plate] rack. **ra'strello** nm rake

'rata nf instalment; **pagare a rate** pay by instalments; **comprare qcsa a rate** buy sth on hire purchase, buy sth on the installment plan Am. **rate'ale** a by instalments; **pagamento rateale** payment by instalments

rate'are, rateiz'zare vt divide into instalments

ra'tifica nf Jur ratification

ratifi'care vt Jur ratify

'ratto nm abduction; (roditore) rat

rattop'pare vt patch. **rat'toppo** nm patch

rattrap'pir|e vt make stiff. ~**si** vr become stiff

rattri'star|e vt sadden. **~si** vr become sad

rau'cedine nf hoarseness. **'rauco** a hoarse

rava'nello nm radish

ravi'oli nmpl ravioli sg

ravve'dersi vr mend one's ways

ravvicina'mento nm (tra persone) reconciliation; Pol rapprochement

ravvici'nar|e vt bring closer; (riconciliare) reconcile. **~si** vr be reconciled

ravvi'sare vt recognize

ravvi'var|e vt revive; fig brighten up. **~si** vr revive

'rayon nm rayon

razio'cinio nm rational thought; (buon senso) common sense

razio'nal|e a rational. **~ità** nf (raziocinio) rationality; (di ambiente) functional nature. **~iz'zare** vt rationalize (programmi, metodi, spazio). **~'mente** adv (con raziocinio) rationally

razio'nare vt ration. **razi'one** nf ration

'razza nf race; (di cani ecc) breed; (genere) kind; **che ~ di idiota!** fam what an idiot!

raz'zia nf raid

razzi'ale a racial

raz'zis|mo nm racism. **~ta** a & nmf racist

'razzo nm rocket. **~ da segnalazione** flare

razzo'lare vi (polli:) scratch about

re nm inv king; Mus (chiave, nota) D

rea'gire vi react

re'ale a real; (di re) royal

rea'lis|mo nm realism. **~ta** nmf realist; (fautore del re) royalist

realistica'mente adv realistically. **rea'listico** a realistic

realiz'zabile a (programma) feasible

realiz'zar|e vt (attuare) carry out, realize; Comm make; score (gol, canestro); (rendersi conto di) realize. **~rsi** vr come true; (nel lavoro ecc) fulfil oneself. **~zi'one** nf realization; (di sogno, persona) fulfilment. **~zione scenica** production

rea'lizzo nm (vendita) proceeds pl; (riscossione) yield

real'mente adv really

real'tà nf inv reality. **~ virtuale** virtual reality

re'ato nm crime, criminal offence

reat'tivo a reactive

reat'tore nm reactor; Aeron jet [aircraft]

reazio'nario, -a a & nmf reactionary

reazi'one nf reaction. **~ a catena** chain reaction

'rebus nm inv rebus; (enigma) puzzle

recapi'tare vt deliver. **re'capito** nm address; (consegna) delivery. **recapito a domicilio** home delivery. **recapito telefonico** contact telephone number

re'car|e vt bear; (produrre) cause. **~si** vr go

re'cedere vi recede; fig give up

recensi'one nf review

recen'sire vt review. **~ore** nm reviewer

re'cente a recent; **di ~** recently. **~'mente** adv recently

recessi'one nf recession

reces'sivo a Biol recessive. **re'cesso** nm recess

re'cidere vt cut off

reci'divo, -a a Med recurrent ● nmf repeat offender

recin'|tare vt close off. **re'cinto** nm enclosure; (per animali) pen; (per bambini) play-pen. **~zi'one** nf (muro) wall; (rete) wire fence; (cancellata) railings pl

recipi'ente nm container

re'ciproco a reciprocal

re'ciso pp di recidere

'recita nf performance. **reci'tare** vt recite; Theat act; play (ruolo). **~zi'one** nf recitation; Theat acting

recla'mare vi protest ● vt claim

ré'clame nf inv advertising; (avviso pubblicitario) advertisement

re'clamo nm complaint; **ufficio reclami** complaints department

recli'na|bile a reclining; **sedile ~bile** reclining seat. **~re** vt tilt (sedile); lean (capo)

reclusi'one nf imprisonment. **re'cluso, -a** a secluded ● nmf prisoner

'recluta nf recruit

recluta'mento nm recruitment. **~'tare** vt recruit

'record nm inv record ● a inv (cifra) record attrib

recrimi'na|re vi recriminate. **~zi'one** nf recrimination

recupe'rare vt recover. **re'cupero** nm recovery; **corso di recupero** additional classes; **minuti di recupero** Sport injury time

redargu'ire vt rebuke

re'datto pp di redigere

redat'tore, **-'trice** *nmf* editor; *(di testo)* writer.**redazi'one** *nf (ufficio)* editorial office; *(di testi)* editing

reddi'tizio *a* profitable

'reddito *nm* income. **~ imponibile** taxable income

re'den|to *pp di* redimere **~'tore** *nm* redeemer. **~zi'one** *nf* redemption

re'digere *vt* write; draw up *(documento)*

re'dimer|e *vt* redeem. **~si** *vr* redeem oneself

'redini *nfpl* reins

'reduce **a~ da** back from● *nmf* survivor

refe'rendum *nm inv* referendum

refe'renza *nf* reference

refet'torio *nm* refectory

refrat'tario *a* refractory;**essere ~ a** have no aptitude for

refrige'ra|re *vt* refrigerate. **~zi'one** *nf* refrigeration

refur'tiva *nf* stolen goods *pl*

rega'lare *vt* give

re'gale *a* regal

re'galo *nm* present, gift

re'gata *nf* regatta

reg'gen|te *nmf* regent. **~za** *nf* regency

'regger|e *vt (sorreggere)* bear; *(tenere in mano)* hold; *(dirigere)* run; *(governare)* govern; *Gram* take ● *vi (resistere)* hold out; *(durare)* last; *fig* stand.**~si** *vr* stand

'reggia *nf* royal palace

reggi'calze *nm inv* suspender belt

reggi'mento *nm* regiment; *(fig: molte persone)* army

reggi'petto, reggi'seno *nm* bra

re'gia *nf Cinema* direction; *Theat* production

re'gime *nm* regime; *(dieta)* diet; *Mech* speed. **~ militare** military regime

re'gina *nf* queen

'regio *a* royal

regio'na|le *a* regional. **~'lismo** *nm (parola)* regionalism

regi'one *nf* region

re'gista *nmf Cinema* director; *Theat, TV* producer

regi'stra|re *vt* register; *Comm* enter; *(incidere su nastro)* tape, record; *(su disco)* record. **~'tore** *nm* recorder; *(magnetofono)* tape-recorder. **~tore di cassa** cash register. **~zi'one** *nf* registration; *Comm* entry; *(di programma)* recording

re'gistro *nm* register; *(ufficio)* registry. **~ di cassa** ledger

re'gnare *vi* reign

'regno *nm* kingdom; *(sovranità)* reign. **R~ Unito** United Kingdom

'regola *nf* rule; **essere in ~** be in order; *‹persona:›* have one's papers in order.**rego'labile** *a ‹meccanismo›* adjustable. **~'mento** *nm* regulation; *Comm* settlement. **~mento di conti** settling of scores

rego'lar|e *a* regular ● *vt* regulate; *(ridurre, moderare)* limit; *(sistemare)* settle. **~si** *vr (agire)* act; *(moderarsi)* control oneself. **~ità** *nf inv* regularity. **~iz'zare** *vt* settle *(debito)*

rego'la|ta *nf* **darsi una ~ta** pull oneself together. **~'tore, ~'trice** *a* **piano ~tore** urban development plan

'regolo *nm* ruler

regre'dire *vi Biol, Psych* regress

regres|si'one *nf* regression. **~'sivo** *a* regressive.**re'gresso** *nm* decline

reinseri'mento *nm (di persona)* reintegration

reinser'irsi *vr (in ambiente)* reintegrate

reinte'grare *vt* restore

relativa'mente *adv* relatively;**~ a** as regards. **relatività** *nf* relativity. **rela'tivo** *a* relative

rela'tore, **-'trice** *nmf (in una conferenza)* speaker

re'lax *nm* relaxation

relazi'one *nf* relation[ship]; *(rapporto amoroso)* [love] affair; *(resoconto)* report;**pubbliche relazioni** *pl* public relations

rele'gare *vt* relegate

religi'o|ne *nf* religion. **~so, -a** *a* religious● *nm* monk ● *nf* nun

re'liqui|a *nf* relic. **~'ario** *nm* reliquary

re'litto *nm* wreck

re'ma|re *vi* row. **~'tore, ~'trice** *nmf* rower

remini'scenza *nf* reminiscence

remissi'one *nf* remission; *(sottomissione)* submissiveness.**remis'sivo** *a* submissive

'remo *nm* oar

'remora *nf* **senza remore** without hesitation

re'moto *a* remote

remune'ra|re *vt* remunerate. **~'tivo** *a* remunerative. **~zi'one** *nf* remuneration

'render|e *vt (restituire)* return;

(*esprimere*) render; (*fruttare*) yield; (*far diventare*) make. **~si** *vr* become; **~si conto di** qcsa realize sth; **~si utile** make oneself useful

rendi'conto *nm* report

rendi'mento *nm* rendering; (*produzione*) yield

'rendita *nf* income; (*dello Stato*) revenue; **vivere di ~** *fig* rest on one's laurels

'rene *nm* kidney. **~ artificiale** kidney machine

'reni *nfpl* (*schiena*) back

reni'tente *a* **essere ~ a** (*consigli di* qcno) be unwilling to accept

'renna *nf* reindeer (*pl inv*); (*pelle*) buckskin

'Reno *nm* Rhine

'reo, -a *a* guilty ● *nmf* offender

re'parto *nm* department; *Mil* unit

repel'lente *a* repulsive

repen'taglio *nm* **mettere a ~** risk

repen'tino *a* sudden

reper'ibile *a* available; **non è ~** (*perduto*) it's not to be found

repe'rire *vt* trace (*fondi*)

re'perto *nm* **~ archeologico** find

reper'torio *nm* repertory; (*elenco*) index; **immagini** *pl* **di ~** archive footage

'replica *nf* reply; (*obiezione*) objection; (*copia*) replica; *Theat* repeat performance. **repli'care** *vt* reply; *Theat* repeat

repor'tage *nm inv* report

repres'si|one *nf* repression. **~'sivo** *a* repressive. **re'presso** *pp di* **reprimere**

re'primere *vt* repress

re'pubbli|ca *nf* republic. **~'cano, -a** *a* & *nmf* republican

repu'tare *vt* consider

reputazi'one *nf* reputation

requi'si|re *vt* requisition. **~to** *nm* requirement

requisi'toria *nf* (*arringa*) closing speech

requisizi'one *nf* requisition

'resa *nf* surrender; *Comm* rendering. **~ dei conti** rendering of accounts

'residence *nm inv* residential hotel

resi'den|te *a* & *nmf* resident. **~za** *nf* residence; (*soggiorno*) stay. **~zi'ale** *a* residential; **zona ~ziale** residential district

re'siduo *a* residual ● *nm* remainder

'resina *nf* resin

resi'sten|te *a* resistant, **~te all'acqua** water-resistant. **~za** *nf* resistance; (*fisica*) stamina; *Electr* resistor; **la R~za** the Resistance

re'sistere *vi* **~ [a]** resist; (*a colpi, scosse*) stand up to; **~ alla pioggia/al vento** be rain-/wind-resistant

'reso *pp di* **rendere**

reso'conto *nm* report

respin'gente *nm* *Rail* buffer

re'spin|gere *vt* repel; (*rifiutare*) reject; (*bocciare*) fail. **~to** *pp di* **respingere**

respi'ra|re *vt/i* breathe. **~tore** *nm* respirator. **~'tore** [**a tubo**] snorkel **~'torio** *a* respiratory. **~zi'one** *nf* breathing; *Med* respiration. **~zione bocca a bocca** mouth-to-mouth rescuscitation, kiss of life. **re'spiro** *nm* breath; (*il respirare*) breathing; *fig* respite

respon'sabile *a* responsible (**di** for); *Jur* liable ● *nm* person responsible; **~ della produzione** production manager. **~ità** *nf inv* responsibility; *Jur* liability. **~ità civile** *Jur* civil liability. **~iz'zare** *vt* give responsibility to (*dipendente*)

re'sponso *nm* response

'ressa *nf* crowd

re'stante *a* remaining ● *nm* remainder

re'stare *vi* = **rimanere**

restau'ra|re *vt* restore. **~'tore, ~'trice** *nmf* restorer. **~zi'one** *nf* restoration. **re'stauro** *nm* (*riparazione*) repair

re'stio *a* restive; **~ a** reluctant to

restitu'ire *vt* return; (*reintegrare*) restore. **~zi'one** *nf* return; *Jur* restitution

'resto *nm* remainder; (*saldo*) balance; (*denaro*) change; **resti** *pl* (*avanzi*) remains; **del ~** besides

re'string|ere *vt* contract; take in (*vestiti*); (*limitare*) restrict; shrink (*stoffa*). **~si** *vr* contract; (*farsi più vicini*) close up; (*stoffa:*) shrink. **restrin-gi'mento** *nm* (*di tessuto*) shrinkage

restrit'tivo *a* (*legge, clausola*) restrictive. **~zi'one** *nf* restriction

resurrezi'one *nf* resurrection

resusci'tare *vt/i* revive

re'tata *nf* round-up

'rete *nf* net; (*sistema*) network; (*televisiva*) channel; (*in calcio, hockey*) goal; *fig* trap; (*per la spesa*) string bag. **~ locale** *Comput* local [area] network, LAN. **~ stradale** road network. **~ televisiva** television channel

reti'cen|te *a* reticent. **~za** *nf* reticence

retico'lato *nm* grid; (*rete metallica*) wire netting. **re'ticolo** *nm* network 'retina nf retina

re'tina nf (per capelli) hair net

re'torico, -a a rhetorical; domanda
retorica rhetorical question ● nf
rhetoric

retribu'ire vt remunerate. ~zi'one nf
remuneration

'retro adv behind; vedi ~ see over ● nm
inv back. ~ di copertina outside back
cover

retroat'tivo a retroactive

retro'ce|dere vi retreat ● vt Mil de-
mote; Sport relegate. ~ssi'one nf Sport
relegation

retroda'tare vt backdate

re'trogrado a retrograde; fig old-fashioned; Pol reactionary

retrogu'ardia nf Mil rearguard

retro'marcia nf reverse [gear]

retro'scena nm inv Theat backstage;
fig background details pl

retrospet'tivo a retrospective

retro'stante ail palazzo ~ the building behind

retrovi'sore nm rear-view mirror

'retta¹ nf Math straight line; (di
collegio, pensionato) fee

'retta² nf dar ~ a qcno take sb's advice

rettango'lare a rectangular.
ret'tangolo a right-angled ● nm rectangle

ret'tifi|ca nf rectification. ~'care vt
rectify

'rettile nm reptile

retti'lineo a rectilinear; (retto) upright ● nm Sport back straight

retti'tudine nf rectitude

'retto pp di reggere ● a straight; fig
upright; (giusto) correct; angolo ~
right angle

ret'tore nm Relig rector; Univ chancellor

reu'matico a rheumatic

reuma'tismi nmpl rheumatism

reve'rendo a reverend

rever'sibile a reversible

revisio'nare vt revise; Comm audit;
Auto overhaul. revisi'one nf revision;
Comm audit; Auto overhaul. revi'sore
nm (di conti) auditor; (di bozze) proof-
reader; (di traduzioni) revisor

re'vival nm inv revival

'revoca nf repeal. revo'care vt repeal

riabili'ta|re vt rehabilitate. ~zi'one
nf rehabilitation

riabitu'ar|e vt reaccustom. ~si vr
reaccustom oneself

riac'cender|e vt rekindle (fuoco). ~si
vr (luce:) come back on

riacqui'stare vt buy back; regain
(libertà, prestigio); recover (vista, udito)

riaggancia're vt replace (ricevitore);
~ la cornetta hang up● vi hang up

riallac'ciare vt refasten; reconnect
(corrente); renew (amicizia)

rial'zare vt raise ● vi rise. ri'alzo nm
rise

riani'mar|e vt Med resuscitate; (ridare
forza a) revive; (ridare coraggio a) cheer
up. ~si vr regain consciousness;
(riprendere forza) revive; (riprendere
coraggio) cheer up

riaper'tura nf reopening

ria'prir|e vt, ~si vr reopen

ri'armo nm rearmament

rias'sumere vt (ricapitolare) resume

riassun'tivo a summarizing.
rias'sunto pp di riassumere ● nm
summary

ria'ver|e vt get back; regain (salute,
vista). ~si vr recover

riavvicina'mento nm (tra persone)
reconciliation

riavvici'nar|e vt reconcile (paesi,
persone). ~si vr (riconciliarsi) be recon-
ciled, make it up

riba'dire vt (confermare) reaffirm

ri'balta nf flap; Theat footlights pl; fig
limelight

ribal'tabile a tip-up

ribal'tar|e vt/i, ~si vr tip over; Naut
capsize

ribas'sare vt lower ● vi fall. ri'basso
nm fall; (sconto) discount

ri'battere vt (a macchina) retype;
(contrabattere) deny ● vi answer back

ribel'l|arsi vr rebel. ri'belle a rebel-
lious ● nmf rebel. ~'ione nf rebellion

'ribes nm inv (rosso) redcurrant; (nero)
blackcurrant

ribol'lire vi (fermentare) ferment; fig
seethe

ri'brezzo nm disgust; far ~ a disgust

rica'dere vi fall back; (nel peccato ecc)
lapse; (pendere) hang [down]; ~ su
(riversarsi) fall on. rica'duta nf relapse

rical'care vt trace

rical'citrante a recalcitrant

rica'ma|re vt embroider. ~to a em-
broidered

ri'cambi nmpl spare parts

ricambi'are vt return; reciprocate
(sentimento); ~ qcsa a qcno repay sb
for sth. ri'cambio nm replacement; Biol

metabolism; **pezzo di ricambio** spare [part]

ri'camo nm embroidery

ricapito'la|re vt sum up. **~zi|one** nf summary, recap fam

ri'carica nf (di sveglia) rewinding

ricari'care vt reload (macchina fotografica, fucile, camion); recharge (batteria); Comput reboot

ricat'ta|re vt blackmail. **~'tore, ~'trice** nmf blackmailer. **ri'catto** nm blackmail

rica'va|re vt get; (ottenere) obtain; (dedurre) draw. **~to** nm proceeds pl. **ri'cavo** nm proceeds pl

'ricca nf rich woman. **~'mente** adv lavishly

ric'chezza nf wealth; fig richness; **ricchezze** pl riches

'riccio a curl ● nm curl; (animale) hedgehog. **~ di mare** sea-urchin. **~lo** nm curl. **~'luto** a curly. **ricci'uto** a (barba) curly

'ricco a rich ● nm rich man

ri'cerca nf search; (indagine) investigation; (scientifica) research; Sch project

ricer'ca|re vt search for; (fare ricerche su) research. **~ta** nf wanted woman. **~'tezza** nf refinement. **~to** a sought-after; (raffinato) refined; (affettato) affected ● nm (polizia) wanted man

ricetrasmit'tente nf transceiver

ri'cetta nf Med prescription; Culin recipe

ricet'tacolo nm receptacle

ricet'tario nm (di cucina) recipe book

ricetta'|tore, -'trice nmf fence, receiver of stolen goods. **~zi|one** nf receiving [stolen goods]

rice'vente a (apparecchio, stazione) receiving ● nmf receiver

ri'cev|ere vt receive; (dare il benvenuto) welcome; (di albergo) accommodate. **~i'mento** nm receiving; (accoglienza) welcome; (trattenimento) reception

ricevi'tor|e nm receiver. **~'ia** nf **~ia del lotto** agency authorized to sell lottery tickets

rice'vuta nf receipt. **~ fiscale** tax receipt

ricezi'one nf Radio, TV reception

richia'mare vt (al telefono) call back; (far tornare) recall; (rimproverare) rebuke; (attirare) draw; **~ alla mente** call to mind. **richi'amo** nm recall; (attrazione) call

richi'edere vt ask for; (di nuovo) ask again for; **~ a qcno di fare qcsa** ask o request sb to do sth. **richi'esta** nf request; Comm demand

ri'chiuder|e vt shut again, close again. **~si** vr (ferita:) heal

rici'claggio nm recycling

rici'clar|e vt recycle. **~si** vr retrain; (cambiare lavoro) change one's line of work

'ricino nm **olio di ~** castor oil

ricognizi'one nf Mil reconnaissance

ri'colmo a full

ricominci'are vt/i start again

ricompa'rire vi reappear

ricom'pen|sa nf reward. **~'sare** vt reward

ricom'por|re vt (riscrivere) rewrite; (ricostruire) reform; Typ reset. **~si** vr regain one's composure

riconcili'a|re vt reconcile. **~rsi** vr be reconciled. **~zi|one** nf reconciliation

ricono'scen|te a grateful. **~za** nf gratitude

ricono'sc|ere vt (riscrivere) recognize; (ammettere) acknowledge. **~i'mento** nm recognition; (ammissione) acknowledgement; (per la polizia) identification. **~i'uto** a recognized

riconqui'stare vt Mil retake, reconquer

riconside'rare vt rethink

rico'prire vt recover; (rivestire) coat; (di insulti) shower (di with); hold (carica)

ricor'dar|e vt remember; (richiamare alla memoria) recall; (far ricordare) remind; (rassomigliare) look like. **~si [di]** remember. **ri'cordo** nm memory; (oggetto) memento; (di viaggio) souvenir; **ricordi** pl (memorie) memoirs

ricor'ren|te a recurrent. **~za** nf recurrence; (anniversario) anniversary

ri'correre vi recur; (accadere) occur; (data:) fall; **~ a** have recourse to; (rivolgersi a) turn to. **ri'corso** pp di **ricorrere** ● nm recourse; Jur appeal

ricostitu'ente nm tonic

ricostitu'ire vt re-establish

ricostru'|ire vt reconstruct. **~zi|one** nf reconstruction

ricove'ra|re vt give shelter to; **~re in ospedale** admit to hospital, hospitalize. **~to, -a** nmf hospital patient. **ri'covero** nm shelter; (ospizio) home

ricre'a|re vt re-create; (ristorare) restore. **~rsi** vr amuse oneself. **~ tivo** a recreational. **~zi'one** *nf* recreation; *Sch* break

ri'credersi *vr* change one's mind

ricupe'rare *vt* recover; rehabilitate ⟨tossicodipendente⟩; **~ il tempo perduto** make up for lost time. **ri'cupero** *nm* recovery; (di tossicodipendente) rehabilitation; (salvataggio) rescue; [**minuti** *nmpl* **di**] **ricupero** injury time

ri'curvo *a* bent

ridacchi'are *vi* giggle

ri'dare *vt* give back, return

ri'dente *a* (piacevole) pleasant

'ridere *vi* laugh; **~ di** (deridere) laugh at

ri'detto *pp di* **ridire**

ridicoliz'zare *vt* ridicule. **ri'dicolo** *a* ridiculous

ridimensio'nare *vt* reshape; *fig* see in the right perspective

ri'dire *vt* repeat; (criticare) find fault with; **trova sempre da ~** he's always finding fault

ridon'dante *a* redundant

ri'dotto *pp di* **ridurre** ● *nm Theat* foyer ● *a* reduced

ri'du|rre *vt* reduce. **~rsi** *vr* diminish. **~rsi** *a* be reduced to. **~t'tivo** *a* reductive. **~zi'one** *nf* reduction; (per cinema, teatro) adaptation

rieducazi'one *nf* (di malato) rehabilitation

riem'pi|re *vt* fill [up]; fill in ⟨moduli ecc⟩. **~rsi** *vr* fill [up]. **~'tivo** *a* filling ● *nm* filler

rien'tranza *nf* recess

rien'trare *vi* go/come back in; (tornare) return; (piegare indentro) recede; **~ in** (far parte) fall within. **ri'entro** *nm* return; (di astronave) re-entry

riepilo'gare *vt* recapitulate. **rie'pilogo** *nm* roundup

riesami'nare *vt* reappraise

ri'essere *vi* **ci risiamo!** here we go again!

riesu'mare *vt* exhume

rievo'ca|re *vt* (commemorare) commemorate. **~zi'one** *nf* (commemorazione) commemoration

rifaci'mento *nm* remake

ri'fa|re *vt* do again; (creare) make again; (riparare) repair; (imitare) imitate; make ⟨letto⟩. **~rsi** *vr* (rimettersi) recover; (vendicarsi) get even; **~rsi una vita/carriera** make a new life/career for oneself; **~rsi il trucco** touch up

one's makeup; **~rsi di** make up for. **~tto** *pp di* **rifare**

riferi'mento *nm* reference

rife'ri|re *vt* report; **~e a** attribute to ● *vi* make a report. **~si** *vr* **~si a** refer to

rifi'lare *vt* (tagliare a filo) trim; (fam: affibbiare) saddle

rifi'ni|re *vt* finish off. **~'tura** *nf* finish

rifio'rire *vi* blossom again; *fig* flourish again

rifiu'tare *vt* refuse. **rifi'uto** *nm* refusal; **rifiuti** *pl* (immondizie) rubbish. **rifiuti** *pl* **urbani** urban waste

riflessi'one *nf* reflection; (osservazione) remark. **rifles'sivo** *a* thoughtful; *Gram* reflexive

ri'flesso *pp di* **riflettere** ● *nm* (luce) reflection; *Med* reflex; **per ~** indirectly

ri'flett|ere *vt* reflect ● *vi* think. **~si** *vr* be reflected

riflet'tore *nm* reflector; (proiettore) searchlight

ri'flusso *nm* ebb

rifocil'la|re *vt* restore. **~si** *vr liter, hum* take some refreshment

ri'fondere *vt* (rimborsare) refund

ri'forma *nf* reform; *Relig* reformation; *Mil* exemption on medical grounds

rifor'ma|re *vt* reform; (migliorare) reform; *Mil* declare unfit for military service. **~to** *a* ⟨chiesa⟩ Reformed. **~'tore**, **~'trice** *nmf* reformer. **~'torio** *nm* reformatory. **rifor'mista** *a* reformist

riforni'mento *nm* supply; (scorta) stock; (di combustibile) refuelling; **stazione** *nf* **di ~** petrol station

rifor'ni|re *vt* **~e di** provide with. **~si** *vr* restock, stock up (**di** with)

ri'fra|ngere *vt* refract. **~tto** *pp di* **rifrangere**. **~zi'one** *nf* refraction

rifug'gire *vi* **~ da** *fig* shun

rifugi'a|rsi *vr* take refuge. **~to, -a** *nmf* refugee

ri'fugio *nm* shelter; (nascondiglio) hideaway

'riga *nf* line; (fila) row; (striscia) stripe; (scriminatura) parting; (regolo) rule; **a righe** ⟨stoffa⟩ striped; ⟨quaderno⟩ ruled; **mettersi in ~** line up

ri'gagnolo *nm* rivulet

ri'gare *vt* rule ⟨foglio⟩ ● *vi* **~ dritto** behave well

rigatti'ere *nm* junk dealer

rigene'rare *vt* regenerate

riget'tare *vt* (gettare indietro) throw back; (respingere) reject; (vomitare) throw up. **ri'getto** *nm* rejection

ri'ghello nm ruler

rigid|a'mente adv rigidly. **~ità** nf rigidity; (di clima) severity; (severità) strictness. **'rigido** a rigid; (freddo) severe; (severo) strict

rigi'rar|e vt turn again; (ripercorrere) go round; fig twist (argomentazione) ● vi walk about. **~si** vr turn round; (nel letto) turn over. **ri'giro** nm (imbroglio) trick

'rigo nm line; Mus staff

ri'gogli|o nm bloom. **~'oso** a luxuriant

ri'gonfio a swollen

ri'gore nm rigours pl; **a ~** strictly speaking; **calcio di ~** penalty [kick]; **area di ~** penalty area; **essere di ~** be compulsory

rigo|rosa'mente adv (giudicare) severely. **~'roso** a (severo) strict; (scrupoloso) rigorous.

riguada'gnare vt regain (quota, velocità)

riguar'dar|e vt look at again; (considerare) regard; (concernere) concern; **per quanto riguarda** with regard to. **~si** vr take care of oneself. **rigu'ardo** nm care; (considerazione) consideration; **nei riguardi di** towards; **riguardo a** with regard to

ri'gurgito nm regurgitation

rilanci'are vt throw back (palla); (di nuovo) throw again; increase (offerta); revive (moda); relaunch (prodotto) ● vi (a carte) raise the stakes

rilasci'ar|e vt (concedere) grant; (liberare) release; issue (documento). **~si** vr relax. **ri'lascio** nm release; (di documento) issue

rilassa'mento nm (relax) relaxation

rilas'sar|e vt, **~rsi** vr relax. **~to** a (ambiente) relaxed

rile'gar|e vt bind (libro). **~to** a bound. **~'tura** nf binding

ri'leggere vt reread

ri'lento: a ~ adv slowly

rileva'mento nm survey; Comm buyout

rile'vante a considerable

rile'var|e vt (trarre) get; (mettere in evidenza) point out; (notare) notice; (topografia) survey; Comm take over; Mil relieve. **~zi'one** nf (statistica) survey

rili'evo nm relief; Geog elevation; (topografia) survey, (importanza) importance; (osservazione) remark; **mettere in ~** qcsa point sth out

rilut'tan|te a reluctant. **~za** nf reluctance

'rima nf rhyme; **far ~ con** qcsa rhyme with sth

riman'dare vt (posporre) postpone; (mandare indietro) send back; (mandare di nuovo) send again; (far ridare un esame) make resit an examination. **ri'mando** nm return; (in un libro) cross-reference

rima'nen|te a remaining ● nm remainder. **~za** nf remainder; **~ze** pl remnants

rima'nere vi stay, remain; (essere d'avanzo) be left; (venirsi a trovare) be; (restare stupito) be astonished; (restare d'accordo) agree

rimar'chevole a remarkable

ri'mare vt/i rhyme

rimargi'nar|e vt, **~si** vr heal

ri'masto pp di rimanere

rima'sugli nmpl (di cibo) leftovers

rimbal'zare vi rebound; (proiettile:) ricochet; **far ~** bounce. **rim'balzo** nm rebound; (di proiettile) ricochet

rimbam'bi|re vi be in one's dotage ● vt stun. **~to** a in one's dotage

rimboc'care vt turn up; roll up (maniche); tuck in (coperte)

rimbom'bare vi resound

rimbor'sare vt reimburse, repay. **rim'borso** nm reimbursement, repayment. **rimborso spese** reimbursement of expenses

rimedi'are vi **~ a** remedy; make up for (errore); (procurare) scrape up. **ri'medio** nm remedy

rimesco'lare vt mix [up]; shuffle (carte); (rivangare) rake up

ri'messa nf (locale per veicoli) garage; (per aerei) hangar; (per autobus) depot; (di denaro) remittance; (di merci) consignment

ri'messo pp di rimettere

ri'metter|e vt (a posto) put back; (restituire) return; (affidare) entrust; (perdonare) remit; (rimandare) put off; (vomitare) bring up; **~ci** (fam: perdere) lose [out]. **~si** vr (ristabilirsi) recover; (tempo:) clear up; **~si a** start again

'rimmel® nm inv mascara

rimoder'nare vt modernize

rimon'tare vt (risalire) go up; Mech reassemble ● vi remount; **~ a** (risalire) go back to

rimorchi'ar|e vt tow; fam pick up (ragazza). **~'tore** nm tug[boat]. **ri'morchio** nm tow; (veicolo) trailer

ri'morso nm remorse

rimo'stranza nf complaint

rimozi'one nf removal; (da un incarico) dismissal. **~ forzata** illegally parked vehicles removed at owner's expense

rim'pasto nm Pol reshuffle

rimpatri'are vt/i repatriate. **rim'patrio** nm repatriation

rim'pian|gere vt regret. **~to** pp di **rimpiangere ●** nm regret

rimpiat'tino nm hide-and-seek

rimpiaz'zare vt replace

rimpiccio'lire vi become smaller

rimpinz'are vt **~e di** stuff with. **~si** vr stuff oneself

rimprove'rare vt reproach; **~ qcsa a qcno** reproach sb for sth. **rim'provero** nm reproach

rimugi'nare vt rummage; fig **~ su** brood over

rimune'ra|re vt remunerate. **~'tivo** a remunerative. **~zi'one** nf remuneration

ri'muovere vt remove

ri'nascere vi be reborn, be born again

rinascimen'tale a Renaissance. **Rinasci'mento** nm Renaissance

ri'nascita nf rebirth

rincal'zare vt (sostenere) support; (rimboccare) tuck in. **rin'calzo** nm support; **rincalzi** pl Mil reserves

rincantucci'arsi vr hide oneself away in a corner

rinca'rare vt increase the price of **●** vi become more expensive. **rin'caro** nm price increase

rinca'sare vi return home

rinchi'uder|e vt shut up. **~si** vr shut oneself up

rin'correre vt run after

rin'cors|a nf run-up. **~o** pp di **rincorrere**

rin'cresc|ere vi **mi rincresce di non...** I'm sorry o I regret that I can't...; **se non ti ~e** if you don't mind. **~i'mento** nm regret. **~i'uto** pp di **rincrescere**

rincreti'nire vi be stupid

rincu'lare vi (arma:) recoil; (cavallo:) shy. **rin'culo** nm recoil

rincuo'rar|e vt encourage. **~si** vr take heart

rinfacci'are vt **~ qcsa a qcno** throw sth in sb's face

rinfor'zar|e vt strengthen; (rendere più saldo) reinforce. **~si** vr become

stronger. **rin'forzo** nm reinforcement; fig support

rinfran'care vt reassure

rinfre'scante a cooling

rinfre'scar|e vt cool; (rinnovare) freshen up **●** vi get cooler. **~si** vr freshen [oneself] up. **rin'fresco** nm light refreshment; (ricevimento) party

rin'fusa nf **alla ~** at random

ringhi'are vi snarl

ringhi'era nf railing; (di scala) banisters pl

ringiova'nire vt rejuvenate (pelle, persona); (vestito:) make look younger **●** vi become young again; (sembrare) look young again

ringrazi|a'mento nm thanks pl. **~'are** vt thank

rinne'ga|re vt disown. **~to, -a** nmf renegade

rinnova'mento nm renewal; (di edifici) renovation

rinno'var|e vt renew; renovate (edifici). **~si** vr be renewed; (ripetersi) recur, happen again. **rin'novo** nm renewal

rinoce'ronte nm rhinoceros

rino'mato a renowned

rinsal'dare vt consolidate

rinsa'vire vi come to one's senses

rinsec'chi|re vi shrivel up. **~to** a shrivelled up

rinta'narsi vr hide oneself away; (animale:) retreat into its den

rintoc'care vi (campana:) toll; (orologio:) strike. **rin'tocco** nm toll; (di orologio) stroke

rinton'ti|re vt anche fig stun. **~to** a (stordito) dazed

rintracci'are vt trace

rintro'nare vt stun **●** vi boom

ri'nuncia nf renunciation

rinunci'a|re vi **~re a** renounce, give up. **~'tario** a defeatist

ri'nunzia, rinunzi'are = **rinuncia, rinunciare**

rinveni'mento nm (di reperti) discovery; (di refurtiva) recovery. **rinve'nire** vt find **●** vi (riprendere i sensi) come round; (ridiventare fresco) revive

rinvi'are vt put off; (mandare indietro) return; (in libro) refer; **~ a giudizio** indict

rin'vio nm Sport goal kick; (in libro) cross-reference; (di appuntamento) postponement; (di merce) return

rio'nale a local. **ri'one** nm district

riordi'nare vt tidy [up]; (ordinare di

nuovo) reorder; (*riorganizzare*) reorganize

riorganiz'zare *vt* reorganize

ripa'gare *vt* repay

ripa'ra|re *vt* (*proteggere*) shelter, protect; (*aggiustare*) repair; (*porre rimedio*) remedy ● *vi* ~ **re a** make up for. ~**rsi** *vr* take shelter. ~**to a** ⟨*luogo*⟩ sheltered. ~**zi'one** *nf* repair; *fig* reparation. **ri'paro** *nm* shelter; (*rimedio*) remedy

ripar'ti|re *vt* (*dividere*) divide ● *vi* leave again. ~**zi'one** *nf* division

ripas'sa|re *vt* recross; (*rivedere*) revise ● *vi* pass again. ~**ta** *nf* (*di vernice*) second coat. **ri'passo** *nm* (*di lezione*) revision

ripensa'mento *nm* second thoughts *pl*

ripen'sare *vi* (*cambiare idea*) change one's mind; ~ **a** think of; **ripensaci!** think again!

riper'correre *vt* (*con la memoria*) go back over

riper'cosso *pp di* **ripercuotere**

ripercu'oter|e *vt* strike again. ~**si** *vr* ⟨*suono:*⟩ reverberate; ~**si su** (*fig: avere conseguenze*) impact on. **ripercussi'one** *nf* repercussion

ripe'scare *vt* fish out ⟨*oggetti*⟩

ripe'tente *nmf* student repeating a year

ri'pet|ere *vt* repeat. ~**ersi** *vr* (*evento:*) recur. ~**izi'one** *nf* repetition; (*di lezione*) revision; (*lezione privata*) private lesson. ~**uta'mente** *adv* repeatedly

ri'piano *nm* (*di scaffale*) shelf; (*terreno pianeggiante*) terrace

ri'picc|a *nf* **fare qcsa per** ~ **a** do sth out of spite. ~**o** *nm* spite

'ripido *a* steep

ripie'gar|e *vt* refold; (*abbassare*) lower ● *vi* (*indietreggiare*) retreat. ~**si** *vr* bend; ⟨*sedie:*⟩ fold. **ripi'ego** *nm* expedient; (*via d'uscita*) way out

ripi'eno *a* full; *Culin* stuffed ● *nm* filling; *Culin* stuffing

ripopo'lar|e *vt* repopulate. ~**si** *vr* be repopulated

ri'porre *vt* put back; (*mettere da parte*) put away; (*collocare*) place; repeat ⟨*domanda*⟩

ripor'tar|e *vt* (*restituire*) bring/take back; (*riferire*) report; (*subire*) suffer; *Math* carry; win ⟨*vittoria*⟩; transfer ⟨*disegno*⟩ ~**si** *vr* go back; (*riferirsi*) refer. **ri'porto** *nm* **cane da riporto** gun dog

ripo'sante *a* ⟨*colore*⟩ restful, soothing

ripo'sa|re *vi* rest ● *vt* put back. ~**rsi** *vr* rest. ~**to a** ⟨*mente*⟩ fresh. **ri'poso** *nm* rest; **andare a riposo** retire; **riposo!** *Mil* at ease!; **giorno di riposo** day off

ripo'stiglio *nm* cupboard

ri'posto *pp di* **riporre**

ri'prender|e *vt* take again; (*prendere indietro*) take back; (*riconquistare*) recapture; (*ricuperare*) recover; (*ricominciare*) resume; (*rimproverare*) reprimand; take in ⟨*cucitura*⟩; *Cinema* shoot. ~**si** *vr* recover; (*correggersi*) correct oneself

ri'presa *nf* resumption; (*ricupero*) recovery; *Theat* revival; *Cinema* shot; *Auto* acceleration; *Mus* repeat. ~ **aerea** bird's-eye view

ripresen'tar|e *vt* resubmit ⟨*domanda, certificato*⟩. ~**si** *vr* (*a ufficio*) go/come back again; (*come candidato*) stand *o* run again; (*occasione:*) arise again

ri'preso *pp di* **riprendere**

ripristi'nare *vt* restore

ripro'dotto *pp di* **riprodurre**

ripro'du|rre *vt*, ~**rsi** *vr* reproduce. ~**t'tivo** *a* reproductive. ~**zi'one** *nf* reproduction

ripro'mettersi *vr* (*intendere*) intend

ri'prova *nf* confirmation

ripudi'are *vt* repudiate

ripu'gnan|te *a* repugnant. ~**za** *nf* disgust. **ripu'gnare** *vi* **ripugnare a** disgust

ripu'li|re *vt* clean [up]; *fig* polish. ~**ta** *nf* **darsi una** ~**ta** have a wash and brushup

ripuls|i'one *nf* repulsion. ~**'ivo** *a* repulsive

ri'quadro *nm* square; (*pannello*) panel

ri'sacca *nf* undertow

ri'saia *nf* rice field, paddy field

risa'lire *vt* go back up ● *vi* ~ **a** (*nel tempo*) go back to; (*essere datato a*) date back to, go back to

risal'tare *vi* (*emergere*) stand out. **ri'salto** *nm* prominence; (*rilievo*) relief

risa'nare *vt* heal; (*bonificare*) reclaim

risa'puto *a* well-known

risarci'mento *nm* compensation. **risar'cire** *vt* indemnify

ri'sata *nf* laugh

riscalda'mento *nm* heating. ~ **autonomo** central heating (*for one apartment*)

riscal'dar|e *vt* heat; warm ⟨*persona*⟩. ~**si** *vr* warm up

riscat'tar|e *vt* ransom. ~**si** *vr* redeem

oneself. **ri'scatto** *nm* ransom; *(morale)* redemption

rischia'rar|e *vt* light up; brighten *(colore)*. **~si** *vr* light up; *(cielo:)* clear up

rischi'are *vt* risk ●*vi* run the risk. **'rischio** *nm* risk. **~oso** *a* risky

risciac'quare *vt* rinse. **risci'acquo** *nm* rinse

riscon'trare *vt (confrontare)* compare; *(verificare)* check; *(rilevare)* find. **ri'scontro** *nm* comparison; check; *(Comm: risposta)* reply

ri'scossa *nf* revolt; *(riconquista)* recovery

riscossi'one *nf* collection

ri'scosso *pp di* **riscuotere**

riscu'oter|e *vt* shake; *(percepire)* draw; *(ottenere)* gain; cash *(assegno)*. **~si** *vr* rouse oneself

risen'ti|re *vt* hear again; *(provare)* feel ●*vi* **~re di** feel the effect of. **~rsi** *vr (offendersi)* take offence. **~to** *a* resentful

ri'serbo *nm* reserve; **mantenere il ~** remain tight-lipped

ri'serva *nf* reserve; *(di caccia, pesca)* preserve; *Sport* substitute, reserve. **~ di caccia** game reserve. **~ indiana** Indian reservation. **~ naturale** wildlife reserve

riser'va|re *vt* reserve; *(prenotare)* book; *(per occasione)* keep. **~rsi** *vr (ripromettersi)* plan for oneself *(cambiamento)*. **~'tezza** *nf* reserve. **~to** *a* reserved

ri'siede|re *vi* **~** a reside in

'riso[1] *pp di* **ridere** ●*nm (pl nf* **risa)** laughter; *(singolo)* laugh. **~'lino** *nm* giggle

'riso[2] *nm (cereale)* rice

ri'solto *pp di* **risolvere**

risolu'|tezza *nf* determination. **riso'luto** *a* resolute, determined. **~zi'one** *nf* resolution

ri'solver|e *vt* resolve; *Math* solve. **~si** *vr (decidersi)* decide; **~si in** turn into

riso'na|nza *nf* resonance; **aver ~nza** *fig* arouse great interest. **~re** *vi* resound; *(rimbombare)* echo

ri'sorgere *vi* rise again

risorgi'mento *nm* revival; *(storico)* Risorgimento

ri'sorsa *nf* resource; *(espediente)* resort

ri'sorto *pp di* **risorgere**

ri'sotto *nm* risotto

ri'sparmi *nmpl (soldi)* savings

risparmi'a|re *vt* save; *(salvare)* spare. **~'tore, ~'trice** *nmf* saver **ri'sparmio** *nm* saving

rispecchi'are *vt* reflect

rispet'tabil|e *a* respectable. **~ità** *nf* respectability

rispet'tare *vt* respect; **farsi ~** command respect

rispet'tivo *a* respective

ri'spetto *nm* respect; **~ a** as regards; *(in paragone a)* compared to

rispet'tosa'mente *adv* respectfully. **~'toso** *a* respectful

risplen'dente *a* shining. **ri'splendere** *vi* shine

rispon'den|te *a* **~te a** in keeping with. **~za** *nf* correspondence

ri'spondere *vi* answer; *(rimbeccare)* answer back; *(obbedire)* respond; **~ a** reply to; **~ di** *(rendersi responsabile)* answer for

ri'spost|a *nf* answer, reply; *(reazione)* response. **~o** *pp di* **rispondere**

'rissa *nf* brawl. **ris'soso** *a* pugnacious

ristabi'lir|e *vt* re-establish. **~si** *vr (in salute)* recover

rista'gnare *vi* stagnate; *(sangue:)* coagulate. **ri'stagno** *nm* stagnation

ri'stampa *nf* reprint; *(azione)* reprinting. **ristam'pare** *vt* reprint

risto'rante *nm* restaurant

risto'ra|re *vt* refresh. **~rsi** *vr liter* take some refreshment; *(riposarsi)* take a rest. **~tore, ~'trice** *nmf (proprietario di ristorante)* restaurateur; *(fornitore)* caterer ●*a* refreshing. **ri'storo** *nm* refreshment; *(sollievo)* relief

ristret'tezza *nf* narrowness; *(povertà)* poverty; **vivere in ristrettezze** live in straitened circumstances

ri'stretto *pp di* **restringere** ●*a* narrow; *(condensato)* condensed; *(limitato)* restricted; **di idee ristrette** narrowminded

ristruttu'rare *vt* restructure, reorganize *(ditta)*; refurbish *(casa)*

risucchi'are *vt* suck in. **ri'succhio** *nm* whirlpool; *(di corrente)* undertow

risul'ta|re *vi* result; *(riuscire)* turn out. **~to** *nm* result

risuo'nare *vi (grida, parola:)* echo; *Phys* resonate

risurrezi'one *nf* resurrection

risusci'tare *vt* resuscitate; *fig* revive ●*vi* return to life

risvegli'ar|e *vt* reawaken *(interesse)*. **~si** *vr* wake up; *(natura:)* awake; *(desiderio:)* be aroused. **ri'sveglio** *nm* waking up; *(dell'interesse)* revival; *(del desiderio)* arousal ri'svolto nm (di giacca) lapel; (di pantaloni) turn-up, cuff Am; (di manica) cuff; (di tasca) flap; (di libro) inside flap

ritagli'are vt cut out. ri'taglio nm cutting; (di stoffa) scrap

ritar'da|re vi be late; (orologio:) be slow ● vt delay; slow down (progresso); (differire) postpone. ~'tario, -a nmf late-comer. ~to a Psych retarded

ri'tardo nm delay; essere in ~ be late; (volo:) be delayed

ri'tegno nm reserve

rite'ne|re vt retain; deduct (somma); (credere) believe. ~uta nf (sul salario) deduction

riti'ra|re vt throw back (palla); (prelevare) withdraw; (riscuotere) draw; collect (pacco). ~rsi vr withdraw; (stoffa:) shrink; (da attività) retire; (marea:) recede. ~ta nf retreat; (WC) toilet. ri'tiro nm withdrawal; Relig retreat; (da attività) retirement. ritiro bagagli baggage reclaim

'ritmo nm rhythm

'rito nm rite; di ~ customary

ritoc'care vt (correggere) touch up. ri'tocco nm retouch

ritor'nare vi return; (andare/venire indietro) go/come back; (ricorrere) recur; (ridiventare) become again

ritor'nello nm refrain

ri'torno nm return

ritorsi'one nf retaliation

ri'trarre vt (ritirare) withdraw; (distogliere) turn away; (rappresentare) portray

ritrat'ta|re vt deal with again; retract (dichiarazione). ~zi'one nf withdrawal, retraction

ritrat'tista nmf portrait painter. ri'tratto pp di ritrarre ● nm portrait

ritro'sia nf shyness. ri'troso a backward; (timido) shy; a ritroso backwards; ritroso a reluctant to

ritrova'mento nm (azione) finding

ritro'va|re vt find [again]; regain (salute). ~rsi vr meet; (di nuovo) meet again; (capitare) find oneself; (raccapezzarsi) see one's way. ~to nm discovery. ri'trovo nm meeting-place; (notturno) night-club

'ritto a upright; (diritto) straight

ritu'ale a & nm ritual

riunifi'ca|re vt reunify. ~rsi vr be reunited. ~zi'one nf reunification

riuni'one nf meeting; (fra amici) reunion

riu'nir|e vt (unire) join together; (radunare) gather. ~si vr be reunited; (adunarsi) meet

riusc'i|re vi (aver successo) succeed; (in matematica ecc) be good (in at); (aver esito) turn out; le è riuscito simpatico she found him likeable. ~ta nf (esito) result; (successo) success

'riva nf (di mare, lago) shore; (di fiume) bank

ri'val|e nmf rival. ~ità nf inv rivalry

rivalutazi'one nf revaluation

rivan'gare vt dig up again

rive'dere vt see again; revise (lezione); (verificare) check

rive'la|re vt reveal. ~rsi vr (dimostrarsi) turn out. ~'tore a revealing ● nm Techn detector. ~zi'one nf revelation

ri'vendere vt resell

rivendi'ca|re vt claim. ~zi'one nf claim

ri'vendi|ta nf (negozio) shop. ~'tore, ~'trice nmf retailer. ~tore autorizzato authorized dealer

ri'verbero nm reverberation; (bagliore) glare

rive'renza nf reverence; (inchino) curtsy; (di uomo) bow

rive'rire vt respect; (ossequiare) pay one's respects to

river'sar|e vt pour. ~si vr (fiume:) flow

river'sibile a reversible

rivesti'mento nm covering

rive'sti|re vt (rifornire di abiti) clothe; (ricoprire) cover; (internamente) line; hold (carica). ~rsi vr get dressed again; (per una festa) dress up

rivi'era nf coast; la ~ ligure the Italian Riviera

ri'vincita nf Sport return match; (vendetta) revenge

rivis'suto pp di rivivere

ri'vista nf review; (pubblicazione) magazine; Theat revue; passare in ~ review

ri'vivere vi come to life again; (riprendere le forze) revive ● vt relive

ri'volg|ere vt turn; (indirizzare) address; ~e da (distogliere) turn away from. ~si vr turn round; ~si a (indirizzarsi) turn to

ri'volta nf revolt

rivol'tante a disgusting

rivol'tar|e vt turn [over]; (mettendo l'interno verso l'esterno) turn inside out; (sconvolgere) upset. ~si vr (ribellarsi) revolt

rivol'tella nf revolver

188

ri'volto pp di rivolgere

rivoluzio'nar|e vt revolutionize. ~io, -a a a & nmf revolutionary. rivoluzi'one nf revolution; (fig: disordine) chaos

riz'zar|e vt raise; (innalzare) erect; prick up ‹orecchie›. ~si vr stand up; ‹capelli:› stand on end; ‹orecchie:› prick up

'roba nf stuff; (personale) belongings pl, stuff; (faccenda) thing; (sl: droga) drugs pl;~ da matti! absolute madness!. ~ da mangiare food, things to eat

ro'baccia nf rubbish

ro'bot nm inv robot. ~iz'zato a robotic

robu'stezza nf sturdiness, robustness; (forza) strength. ro'busto a sturdy, robust; (forte) strong

'rocca nf fortress. ~'forte nf stronghold

roc'chetto nm reel

'roccia nf rock

ro'da|ggio nm running in. ~re vt run in

'roder|e vt gnaw; (corrodere) corrode. ~si vr~si da (logorarsi) be consumed with.rodi'tore nm rodent

rodo'dendro nm rhododendron

'rogna nf scabies sg; fig nuisance

ro'gnone nm Culin kidney

'rogo nm (supplizio) stake; (per cadaveri) pyre

'Roma nf Rome

Roma'nia nf Romania

ro'manico a Romanesque

ro'mano, -a a & nmf Roman

romanti'cismo nm romanticism. ro'mantico a romantic

roman'za nf romance. ~'zato a romanticized. ~'zesco a fictional; (stravagante) wild, unrealistic. ~zi'ere nm novelist

ro'manzo a Romance ● nm novel. ~ d'appendice serial story. ~ giallo thriller

'rombo nm rumble; Math rhombus; (pesce) turbot

'romper|e vt break; break off ‹relazione›; non ~e [le scatole]! (fam: seccare) don't be a pain [in the neck]!. ~si vr break; ~si una gamba break one's leg

rompi'capo nm nuisance; (indovinello) puzzle

rompi'collo nm daredevil; a ~ at breakneck speed

rompighi'accio nm ice-breaker

rompi'scatole nmf inv fam pain

'ronda nf rounds pl

ron'della nf washer

'rondine nf swallow

ron'done nm swift

ron'fare vi (russare) snore

ron'zare vi buzz; ~ attorno a qcno fig hang about sb

ron'zino nm jade

ron'zio nm buzz

'rosa nf rose. ~ dei venti wind rose ● a & nm (colore) pink. ro'saio nm rosebush

ro'sario nm rosary

ro'sato a rosy ● nm (vino) rosé

'roseo a pink

ro'seto nm rose garden

rosicchi'are vt nibble; (rodere) gnaw

rosma'rino nm rosemary

'roso pp di rodere

roso'lare vt brown

roso'lia nf German measles

ro'sone nm rosette; (apertura) rose-window

'rospo nm toad

ros'setto nm (per labbra) lipstick

'rosso a & nm red; passare con il ~ jump a red light. ~ d'uovo [egg] yolk. ros'sore nm redness; (della pelle) flush

rosticce'ria nf shop selling cooked meat and other prepared food

ro'tabile a strada ~ carriageway

ro'taia nf rail; (solco) rut

ro'ta|re vt/i rotate. ~zi'one nf rotation

rote'are vt/i roll

ro'tella nf small wheel; (di mobile) castor

roto'lar|e vt/i roll. ~si vr roll [about]. 'rotolo nm roll; andare a rotoli go to rack and ruin

rotondità nf (qualità) roundness; ~ pl (curve femminili) curves. ro'tondo, -a a round ● nf (spiazzo) terrace

ro'tore nm rotor

'rotta[1] nf Naut, Aeron course; far ~ per make course for; fuori ~ off course

'rotta[2] nf a ~ di collo at breakneck speed; essere in ~ con be on bad terms with

rot'tame nm scrap; fig wreck

'rotto pp di rompere ● a broken; (stracciato) torn

rot'tura nf break; che ~ di scatole! fam what a pain!

'rotula nf kneecap

rou'lette nf inv roulette

rou'lotte nf inv caravan, trailer Am

rou'tine nf inv routine; di ~ ‹operazioni, controlli› routine

ro'vente a scorching

'rovere nm (legno) oak

rovesci'ar|e vt (buttare a terra) knock over; (sottosopra) turn upside down; (rivoltare) turn inside out; spill (liquido); overthrow (governo); reverse (situazione). **~si** vr (capovolgersi) overturn; (riversarsi) pour. **ro'vescio** a (contrario) reverse; **alla rovescia** (capovolto) upside down; (con l'interno all'esterno) inside out ● nm reverse; (nella maglia) purl; (di pioggia) downpour; Tennis backhand

ro'vina nf ruin; (crollo) collapse

rovi'na|re vt ruin; (guastare) spoil ● vi crash. **~rsi** vr be ruined. **~to** a (oggetto) ruined. **rovi'noso** a ruinous

rovi'stare vt ransack

'rovo nm bramble

'rozzo a rough

R.R. abbr (ricevuta di ritorno) return receipt for registered mail

'ruba nf andare a **~** sell like hot cakes

ru'bare vt steal

rubi'netto nm tap, faucet Am

ru'bino nm ruby

ru'brica nf (in giornale) column; (in programma televisivo) TV report; (quaderno con indice) address book. **~ telefonica** telephone and address book

'rude a rough

'rudere nm ruin

rudimen'tale a rudimentary. **rudi'menti** nmpl rudiments

ruffi'an|a nf procuress. **~o** nm pimp; (adulatore) bootlicker

'ruga nf wrinkle

'ruggine nf rust; **fare la ~** go rusty

rug'gi|re vi roar. **~to** nm roar

rugi'ada nf dew

ru'goso a wrinkled

rul'lare vi roll; Aeron taxi

rul'lino nm film

rul'lio nm rolling; Aeron taxiing

'rullo nm roll; Techn roller

rum nm inv rum

ru'meno, -a a & nmf Romanian

rumi'nare vt ruminate

ru'mor|e nm noise; fig rumour. **~eggi'are** vi rumble. **rumo'roso** a noisy; (sonoro) loud

ru'olo nm roll; Theat role; **di ~** on the staff

ru'ota nf wheel; **andare a ~ libera** free-wheel. **~ di scorta** spare wheel

'rupe nf cliff

ru'rale a rural

ru'scello nm stream

'ruspa nf bulldozer

rus'sare vi snore

'Russ|ia nf Russia. **r~o, -a** a & nmf Russian; (lingua) Russian

'rustico a rural; (carattere) rough

rut'tare vi belch. **'rutto** nm belch

'ruvido a coarse

ruzzo'l|are vi tumble down. **~one** nm tumble; **cadere ruzzoloni** tumble down

Ss

'sabato nm Saturday

'sabbi|a nf sand. **~e** pl **mobili** quicksand. **~oso** a sandy

sabo'ta|ggio nm sabotage. **~re** vt sabotage. **~tore, ~trice** nmf saboteur

'sacca nf bag. **~ da viaggio** travelling-bag

sacca'rina nf saccharin

sac'cente a pretentious ● nmf knowall

saccheggi'a|re vt sack; hum raid (frigo). **~tore, ~trice** nmf plunderer. **sac'cheggio** nm sack

sac'chetto nm bag

'sacco nm sack; Anat sac; **mettere nel ~** fig swindle; **un ~** (moltissimo) a lot; **un ~ di** (gran quantità) lots of. **~ a pelo** sleeping-bag

sacer'do|te nm priest. **~zio** nm priesthood

sacra'mento nm sacrament

sacrifi'ca|re vt sacrifice. **~rsi** vr sacrifice oneself. **~to** a (non valorizzato) wasted. **sacri'ficio** nm sacrifice

sacri'legio nm sacrilege. **sa'crilego** a sacrilegious

'sacro a sacred ● nm Anat sacrum

sacro'santo a sacrosanct

'**sadico, -a** *a* sadistic ●*nmf* sadist. **sa'dismo** *nm* sadism

sa'etta *nf* arrow

sa'fari *nm inv* safari

'**saga** *nf* saga

sa'gace *a* shrewd

sag'gezza *nf* wisdom

saggi'are *vt* test

'**saggio**[1] *nm* (*scritto*) essay; (*prova*) proof; (*di metallo*) assay; (*campione*) sample; (*esempio*) example

'**saggio**[2] *a* wise ●*nm* (*persona*) sage

sag'gistica *nf* non-fiction

Sagit'tario *nm Astr* Sagittarius

'**sagoma** *nf* shape; (*profilo*) outline; **che ~!** *fam* what a character!. **sa-go'mato** *a* shaped

'**sagra** *nf* festival

sagre|'stano *nm* sacristan. **~'stia** *nf* sacristy

'**sala** *nf* hall; (*stanza*) room; (*salotto*) living room. **~ d'attesa** waiting room. **~ da ballo** ballroom. **~ d'imbarco** departure lounge. **~ macchine** engine room. **~ operatoria** operating theatre *Br*, operating room *Am*. **~ parto** delivery room. **~ da pranzo** dining room

sa'lame *nm* salami

sala'moia *nf* brine

sa'lare *vt* salt

sa'lario *nm* wages *pl*

sa'lasso *nm* **essere un ~** *fig* cost a fortune

sala'tini *nmpl* savouries (*eaten with aperitifs*)

sa'lato *a* salty; (*costoso*) dear

sal'ciccia *nf* = **salsiccia**

sal'dar|e *vt* weld; set (*osso*); pay off (*debito*); settle (*conto*); **~e a stagno** solder. **~si** *vr* (*Med: osso:*) knit

salda'trice *nf* welder; (*a stagno*) soldering iron

salda'tura *nf* weld; (*azione*) welding; (*di osso*) knitting

'**saldo** *a* firm; (*resistente*) strong ●*nm* (*di conto*) settlement; (*svendita*) sale; *Comm* balance

'**sale** *nm* salt; **restare di ~** be struck dumb [with astonishment]. **~ fine** table salt. **~ grosso** cooking salt. **sali** *pl* **da tabacchi** tobacconist's shop

'**salice** *nm* willow. **~ piangente** weeping willow

sali'ente *a* outstanding; **i punti salienti di un discorso** the main points of a speech

sali'era *nf* salt-cellar

---

sa'lina *nf* salt-works *sg*

sa'li|re *vi* go/come up; (*levarsi*) rise; (*su treno ecc*) get on; (*in macchina*) get in ●*vt* go/come up (*scale*). **~ta** *nf* climb; (*aumento*) rise; **in ~ta** uphill

sa'liva *nf* saliva

'**salma** *nf* corpse

'**salmo** *nm* psalm

sal'mone *nm* & *a inv* salmon

sa'lone *nm* hall; (*salotto*) living room; (*di parrucchiere*) salon. **~ di bellezza** beauty parlour

salo'pette *nf inv* dungarees *pl*

salot'tino *nm* bower

sa'lotto *nm* drawing room; (*soggiorno*) sitting room; (*mobili*) [three-piece] suite; **fare ~** chat

sal'pare *vt/i* sail; **~ l'ancora** weigh anchor

'**salsa** *nf* sauce. **~ di pomodoro** tomato sauce

sal'sedine *nf* saltiness

sal'siccia *nf* sausage

salsi'era *nf* sauce-boat

sal'ta|re *vi* jump; (*venir via*) come off; (*balzare*) leap; (*esplodere*) blow up; **~r fuori** spring from nowhere; (*oggetto cercato:*) turn up; **è ~to fuori che...** it emerged that...; **~re fuori con...** come out with...; **~re in aria** blow up; **~re in mente** spring to mind ●*vt* jump [over]; skip (*pasti, lezioni*); *Culin* sauté. **~to a** *Culin* sautéed

saltel'lare *vi* hop; (*di gioia*) skip

saltim'banco *nm* acrobat

'**salto** *nm* jump; (*balzo*) leap; (*dislivello*) drop; (*fig: omissione, lacuna*) gap; **fare un ~ da** (*visitare*) drop in on; **in un ~** *fig* in a jiffy. **~ in alto** high jump. **~ con l'asta** pole-vault. **~ in lungo** long jump. **~ pagina** *Comput* page down

saltuaria'mente *adv* occasionally. **saltu'ario** *a* desultory; **lavoro saltuario** casual work

sa'lubre *a* healthy

salume'ria *nf* ≈ delicatessen. **sa'lumi** *nmpl* cold cuts

salu'tare *vt* greet; (*congedandosi*) say goodbye; (*portare i saluti a*) give one's regards to; *Mil* salute ●*a* healthy

sa'lute *nf* health; **~!** (*dopo uno starnuto*) bless you!; (*a un brindisi*) cheers!

sa'luto *nm* greeting; (*di addio*) goodbye; *Mil* salute; **saluti** *pl* (*ossequi*) regards

'**salva** *nf* salvo; **sparare a salve** fire blanks

salvada'naio *nm* money box
salva'gente *nm* lifebelt; (*a giubbotto*) life-jacket; (*ciambella*) rubber ring; (*spartitraffico*) traffic island
salvaguar'dare *vt* safeguard. **salvagu'ardia** *nf* safeguard
sal'var|e *vt* save; (*proteggere*) protect. **~si** *vr* save oneself
salva'slip *nm inv* panty-liner
salva'taggio *nm* rescue; *Naut* salvage; *Comput* saving; **battello di ~taggio** lifeboat. **~'tore**, **~'trice** *nmf* saviour
sal'vezza *nf* safety; *Relig* salvation
'salvia *nf* sage
salvi'etta *nf* serviette
'salvo *a* safe ● *prep* except [for] ● *conj* **~ che** (*a meno che*) unless; (*eccetto che*) except that
samari'tano, -a *a & nmf* Samaritan
sam'buco *nm* elder
san *nm* **S~ Francesco** Saint Francis
sa'nare *vt* heal
sana'torio *nm* sanatorium
san'cire *vt* sanction
san'dalo *nm* sandal; *Bot* sandalwood
'sangu|e *nm* blood; **al ~e** (*carne*) rare; **farsi cattivo ~e per** worry about; **occhi iniettati di ~e** bloodshot eyes. **~e freddo** composure; **a ~e freddo** in cold blood. **~'igno** *a* blood
sangui'naccio *nm* *Culin* black pudding
sangui'nante *a* bleeding
sangui'nar|e *vi* bleed. **~io** *a* bloodthirsty
sangui'noso *a* bloody
sangui'suga *nf* leech
sani'tà *nf* soundness, (*salute*) health. **~ mentale** sanity, mental health
sani'tario *a* sanitary; **Servizio S~** National Health Service
'sano *a* sound; (*salutare*) healthy; **~ di mente** sane; **~ come un pesce** as fit as a fiddle
San Sil'vestro *nm* New Year's Eve
santifi'care *vt* sanctify
'santo *a* holy; (*con nome proprio*) saint ● *nm* saint. **san'tone** *nm* guru. **santu'ario** *nm* sanctuary
sanzi'one *nf* sanction
sa'pere *vt* know; (*essere capace di*) be able to; (*venire a sapere*) hear; **saperla lunga** know a thing or two ● *vi* **~ di** know about; (*aver sapore di*) taste of; (*aver odore di*) smell of; **saperci fare** have the know-how ● *nm* knowledge

sapi'en|te *a* wise; (*esperto*) expert ● *nm* (*uomo colto*) sage. **~za** *nf* wisdom
sa'pone *nm* soap. **~ da bucato** washing soap. **sapo'netta** *nf* bar of soap
sa'pore *nm* taste. **sapori'ta'mente** *adv* (*dormire*) soundly. **sapo'rito** *a* tasty
sapu'tello, -a *a & nm sl* know-all, know-it-all *Am*
saraci'nesca *nf* roller shutter
sar'cas|mo *nm* sarcasm. **~tico** *a* sarcastic
Sar'degna *nf* Sardinia
sar'dina *nf* sardine
'sardo, -a *a & nmf* Sardinian
sar'donico *a* sardonic
'sarto, -a *nm* tailor ● *nf* dressmaker. **~'ria** *nf* tailor's; dressmaker's; (*arte*) couture
sas'sata *nf* blow with a stone; **prendere a sassate** stone. **'sasso** *nm* stone; (*ciottolo*) pebble
sassofo'nista *nmf* saxophonist. **sas'sofono** *nm* saxophone
sas'soso *a* stony
'Satana *nm* Satan. **sa'tanico** *a* satanic
sa'tellite *a inv & nm* satellite
sati'nato *a* glossy
'satira *nf* satire. **sa'tirico** *a* satirical
satu'ra|re *vt* saturate. **~zi'one** *nf* saturation. **'saturo** *a* saturated; (*pieno*) full
'sauna *nf* sauna
savoi'ardo *nm* (*biscotto*) sponge finger
sazi'ar|e *vt* satiate. **~si** *vr* **~si di** *fig* grow tired of
sazietà *nf* **mangiare a ~** eat one's fill. **'sazio** *a* satiated
sbaciucchi'ar|e *vt* smother with kisses. **~si** *vr* kiss and cuddle
sbada'ta|ggine *nf* carelessness; **è stata una ~ggine** it was careless. **~'mente** *adv* carelessly. **sba'dato** *a* careless
sbadigli'are *vi* yawn. **sba'diglio** *nm* yawn
sba'fa|re *vt* sponge. **~ta** *nf sl* nosh
'sbafo *nm* sponging; **a ~** (*gratis*) without paying
sbagli'ar|e *vi* make a mistake; (*aver torto*) be wrong ● *vt* make a mistake in; **~e strada** go the wrong way; **~e numero** get the number wrong; *Teleph* dial a wrong number. **~si** *vr* make a mistake. **'sbaglio** *nm* mistake; **per sbaglio** by mistake
sbal'l|are *vt* unpack; *fam* screw up (*conti*) ● *vi fam* go crazy. **~ato** *a* (*squilibrato*) unbalanced. **'sballo** *nm*

fam scream; (*per droga*) trip; **da sballo** *sl* terrific

sballot'tare *vt* toss about

sbalor'di|re *vt* stun ● *vi* be stunned. **~'tivo** *a* amazing. **~to** *a* stunned

sbal'zare *vt* throw; (*da una carica*) dismiss ● *vi* bounce; (*saltare*) leap. **'sbalzo** *nm* bounce; (*sussulto*) jolt; (*di temperatura*) sudden change; **a sbalzi** in spurts; **a sbalzo** (*lavoro a rilievo*) embossed

sban'care *vt* bankrupt; **~ il banco** break the bank

sbanda'mento *nm* Auto skid; Naut list; *fig* going off the rails

sban'da|re *vi* Auto skid; Naut list. **~rsi** *vr* (*disperdersi*) disperse. **~ta** *nf* skid; Naut list; **prendere una ~ta per** get a crush on sb. **~to, -a** *a* mixed-up ● *nmf* mixed-up person

sbandie'rare *vt* wave; *fig* display

sbarac'care *vt/i* clear up

sbaragli'are *vt* rout. **sba'raglio** *nm* rout; **mettere allo sbaraglio** rout

sbaraz'zar|e *vt* clear. **~si** *vr* **~si di** get rid of

sbaraz'zino, -a *a* mischievous ● *nmf* scamp

sbar'bar|e *vt*, **~si** *vr* shave

sbar'care *vt/i* disembark; **~ il lunario** make ends meet. **'sbarco** *nm* landing; (*di merci*) unloading

'sbarra *nf* bar; (*di passaggio a livello*) barrier. **~'mento** *nm* barricade. **sbar'rare** *vt* bar; (*ostruire*) block; cross (*assegno*); (*spalancare*) open wide

sbatacchi'are *vt/i* *sl* bang, slam

'sbatter|e *vt* bang; slam, bang (*porta*); (*urtare*) knock; Culin beat; flap (*ali*); shake (*tappeto*) ● *vi* bang; (*porta:*) slam, bang. **~si** *vr sl* rush around; **~sene di qcsa** not give a damn about sth. **sbat'tuto** *a* tossed; Culin beaten; *fig* run down

sba'va|re *vi* dribble; (*colore:*) smear. **~'tura** *nf* smear; **senza ~ture** *fig* faultless

sbelli'carsi *vr* **~ dalle risa** split one's sides [with laughter]

'sberla *nf* slap

sbia'di|re *vt/i*, **~rsi** *vr* fade. **~to** *a* faded; *fig* colourless

sbian'car|e *vt/i*, **~si** *vr* whiten

sbi'eco *a* slanting; **di ~** on the slant; (*guardare*) sidelong; **guardare qcno di ~** look askance at sb; **tagliare di ~** cut on the bias

sbigot'ti|re *vt* dismay ● *vi*, **~rsi** *vr* be dismayed. **~to** *a* dismayed

sbilanci'ar|e *vt* unbalance ● *vi* (*perdere l'equilibrio*) overbalance. **~si** *vr* lose one's balance

sbirci'a|re *vt* cast sidelong glances at. **~ta** *nf* furtive glance. **~'tina** *nf* **dare una ~tina** a sneak a glance at

sbizzar'rirsi *vr* satisfy one's whims

sbloc'care *vt* unblock; Mech release; decontrol (*prezzi*)

sboc'care *vi* **~ in** (*fiume:*) flow into; (*strada:*) lead to; (*folla:*) pour into

sboc'cato *a* foul-mouthed

sbocci'are *vi* blossom

'sbocco *nm* flowing; (*foce*) mouth; Comm outlet

sbolo'gnare *vt fam* get rid of

'sbornia *nf* **prendere una ~** get drunk

sbor'sare *vt* pay out

sbot'tare *vi* burst out

sbotto'nar|e *vt* unbutton. **~si** *vr* (*fam: confidarsi*) open up; **~si la camicia** unbutton one's shirt

sbra'carsi *vr* put on something more comfortable; **~ dalle risate** *fam* kill oneself laughing

sbracci'a|rsi *vr* wave one's arms. **~to** *a* bare-armed; (*abito*) sleeveless

sbrai'tare *vi* bawl

sbra'nare *vt* tear to pieces

sbricio'lar|e *vt*, **~si** *vr* crumble

sbri'ga|re *vt* expedite; (*occuparsi di*) attend to. **~rsi** *vr* be quick. **~'tivo** *a* quick

sbrindel'la|re *vt* tear to shreds. **~to** *a* in rags

sbrodo'l|are *vt* stain. **~one** *nm* messy eater, dribbler

'sbronz|a *nf* **prendersi una ~a** get tight. **sbron'zarsi** *vr* get tight. **~o** *a* (*ubriaco*) tight

sbruffo'nata *nf* boast. **sbruf'fone, -a** *nmf* boaster

sbu'care *vi* come out

sbucci'ar|e *vt* peel; shell (*piselli*). **~si** *vr* graze oneself

sbuf'fare *vi* snort; (*per impazienza*) fume. **'sbuffo** *nm* puff

'scabbia *nf* scabies *sg*

sca'broso *a* rough; *fig* difficult; (*scena*) indecent

scacci'are *vt* chase away

'scacc|o *nm* check; **~hi** *pl* (*gioco*) chess; (*pezzi*) chessmen; **dare ~o matto** checkmate; **a ~hi** (*tessuto*) checked. **~hi'era** *nf* chess-board

sca'dente *a* shoddy

sca'de|nza *nf* (*di contratto*) expiry; Comm maturity; (*di progetto*) deadline; **a breve/lunga ~nza** short-/long-term.

~re *vi* expire; *⟨valore:⟩* decline; *⟨debito:⟩* be due. **sca'duto** *a ⟨biglietto⟩* out-of-date

sca'fandro *nm* diving suit; *(di astronauta)* spacesuit

scaf'fale *nm* shelf; *(libreria)* bookshelf

'scafo *nm* hull

scagion'are *vt* exonerate

'scaglia *nf* scale; *(di sapone)* flake; *(scheggia)* chip

scagli'ar|e *vt* fling. **~si** *vr* fling oneself; **~si contro** *fig* rail against

scagli'o'nare *vt* space out. **~'one** *nm* group; **a ~oni** in groups. **~one di reddito** tax bracket

'scala *nf* staircase; *(portatile)* ladder; *(Mus, misura, fig)* scale; **scale** *pl* stairs. **~ mobile** escalator; *(dei salari)* cost of living index

sca'la|re *vt* climb; layer *(capelli)*; *(detrarre)* deduct. **~ta** *nf* climb; *(dell'Everest ecc)* ascent; **fare delle ~te** go climbing. **~'tore**, **~'trice** *nmf* climber

scalca'gnato *a* down at heel

scalci'are *vi* kick

scalci'nato *a* shabby

scalda'bagno *nm* water heater

scalda'muscoli *nm inv* leg-warmer

scal'dar|e *vt* heat. **~si** *vr* warm up; *(eccitarsi)* get excited

scal'fi|re *vt* scratch. **~t'tura** *nf* scratch

scali'nata *nf* flight of steps. **sca'lino** *nm* step; *(di scala a pioli)* rung

scalma'narsi *vr* get worked up

'scalo *nm* slipway; *Aeron, Naut* port of call; **fare ~ a** call at; *Aeron* land at

sca'lo|gna *nf* bad luck. **~'gnato** *a* unlucky

scalop'pina *nf* escalope

scal'pello *nm* chisel

scalpi'tare *vi* paw the ground; *fig* champ at the bit

'scalpo *nm* scalp

scal'pore *nm* noise; **far ~** *fig* cause a sensation

scal'trezza *nf* shrewdness. **scal'trir-si** *vr* get shrewder. **'scaltro** *a* shrewd

scal'zare *vt* bare the roots of *(albero)*; *fig* undermine; *(da una carica)* oust

'scalzo *a & adv* barefoot

scambi|'are *vt* exchange; **~are qcno per qualcun altro** mistake sb for somebody else. **~'evole** *a* reciprocal

'scambio *nm* exchange; *Comm* trade; **libero ~** free trade

scamosci'ato *a* suede

scampa'gnata *nf* trip to the country

scampa'nato *a ⟨gonna⟩* flared

scampanel'lata *nf* [loud] ring

scam'pare *vt* save; *(evitare)* escape; **scamparla bella** have a lucky escape. **'scampo** *nm* escape

'scampolo *nm* remnant

scanala'tura *nf* groove

scandagli'are *vt* sound

scanda'listico *a* sensational

scandal|iz'zare *vt* scandalize. **~iz'zarsi** *vr* be scandalized

'scanda|lo *nm* scandal. **~'loso** *a ⟨somma ecc⟩* scandalous; *⟨fortuna⟩* outrageous

Scandi'navia *nf* Scandinavia. **scan'dinavo, -a** *a & nmf* Scandinavian

scan'dire *vt* scan *⟨verso⟩*; pronounce clearly *⟨parole⟩*

scan'nare *vt* slaughter

scanneriz'zare *vt Comput* scan

scansafa'tiche *nmf inv* lazybones *sg*

scan'sar|e *vt* shift; *(evitare)* avoid. **~si** *vr* get out of the way

scansi'one *nf Comput* scanning

'scanso *nm* **a ~ di** in order to avoid; **a ~ di equivoci** to avoid any misunderstanding

scanti'nato *nm* basement

scanto'nare *vi* turn the corner; *(svignarsela)* sneak off

scanzo'nato *a* easy-going

scapacci'one *nm* smack

scape'strato *a* dissolute

'scapito *nm* loss; **a ~ di** to the detriment of

'scapola *nf* shoulder-blade

'scapolo *nm* bachelor

scappa'mento *nm Auto* exhaust

scap'pare *vi* escape; *(andarsene)* dash [off]; *(sfuggire)* slip; **mi ~ da ridere!** I want to burst out laughing; **mi ~ la pipì** I'm bursting, I need a pee. **~ta** *nf* short visit. **~'tella** *nf* escapade; *(infedeltà)* fling. **~'toia** *nf* way out

scappel'lotto *nm* cuff

scara'bocchio *nm* scribble

scara'faggio *nm* cockroach

scara'mantico *a ⟨gesto⟩* to ward off the evil eye

scara'muccia *nf* skirmish

scarabocchi'are *vt* scribble

scaraven'tare *vt* hurl

scarce'rare *vt* release [from prison]

scardi'nare *vt* unhinge

'scarica *nf* discharge; *(di arma da fuoco)* volley; *fig* shower

scari'ca|re vt discharge; unload ⟨arma, merci⟩; fig unburden. **~rsi** vr ⟨fiume:⟩ flow; ⟨orologio, batteria:⟩ run down; fig unwind. **~'tore** nm loader; (di porto) docker. **'scarico** a unloaded; (vuoto) empty; ⟨orologio⟩ run-down; ⟨batteria⟩ flat; fig untroubled ● nm unloading; (di rifiuti) dumping; (di acqua) draining; (di sostanze inquinanti) discharge; (luogo) [rubbish] dump; Auto exhaust; (idraulico) drain; (tubo) waste pipe

scarlat'tina nf scarlet fever

scar'latto a scarlet

'scarno a thin; (fig: stile) bare

sca'ro|gna nf fam bad luck. **~'gnato** a fam unlucky

'scarpa nf shoe; (fam: persona) dead loss. **scarpe** pl **da ginnastica** trainers, gym shoes

scar'pata nf slope; (burrone) escarpment

scarpi'nare vi hike

scar'pone nm boot. **scarponi** pl **da sci** ski boot. **scarponi** pl **da trekking** walking boots

scarroz'zare vt/i drive around

scarseggi'are vi be scarce; **~ di** (mancare) be short of

scar'sezza nf scarcity, shortage. **scarsità** nf shortage. **'scarso** a scarce; (manchevole) short

scarta'mento nm Rail gauge. **~ ridotto** narrow gauge

scar'tare vt discard; unwrap ⟨pacco⟩; (respingere) reject ● vi (deviare) swerve. **'scarto** nm scrap; (in carte) discard; (deviazione) swerve; (distacco) gap

scar'toffie nfpl bumf, bumph

scas'sare vt break. **~to** a fam clapped out

scassi'nare vt force open

scassina'tore, -'trice nmf burglar. **'scasso** nm (furto) house-breaking

scate'na|re vt fig stir up. **~rsi** vr break out; (fig: temporale:) break; (fam: infiammarsi) get excited. **~to** a crazy

'scatola nf box; (di latta) can, tin Br; **in ~** ⟨cibo⟩ canned, tinned Br; **rompere le scatole a qcno** fam get on sb's nerves

scat'tare vi go off; (balzare) spring up; (adirarsi) lose one's temper; take ⟨foto⟩. **'scatto** nm (balzo) spring; (d'ira) outburst; (di telefono) unit; (dispositivo) release; **a scatti** jerkily; **di scatto** suddenly

scatu'rire vi spring

scaval'care vt jump over ⟨muretto⟩; climb over ⟨muro⟩; (fig: superare) overtake

sca'vare vt dig ⟨buca⟩; dig up ⟨tesoro⟩; excavate ⟨città sepolta⟩. **'scavo** nm excavation

scazzot'tata nf fam punch-up

'scegliere vt choose, select

scelle'rato a wicked

'scelt|a nf choice; (di articoli) range; **...a ~a** (in menù) choice of...; **prendere uno a ~a** take your choice o pick; **di prima ~a** top-grade, choice. **~o** pp di **scegliere** ● a select; (merce ecc) choice

sce'mare vt/i diminish

sce'menza nf silliness; (azione) silly thing to do/say. **'scemo** a silly

'scempio nm havoc; (fig: di paesaggio) ruination; **fare ~ di** play havoc with

'scena nf scene; (palcoscenico) stage; **entrare in ~** go/come on; fig enter the scene; **fare ~** put on an act; **fare una ~** make a scene; **andare in ~** Theat be staged, be put on. **sce'nario** nm scenery

sce'nata nf row, scene

'scendere vi go/come down; (da treno, autobus) get off; (da macchina) get out; ⟨strada:⟩ slope; ⟨notte, prezzi:⟩ fall ● vt go/come down ⟨scale⟩

sceneggi'a|re vt dramatize. **~to** nm television serial. **~tura** nf screenplay

'scenico a scenic

scervel'la|rsi vr rack one's brains. **~to** a brainless

'sceso pp di **scendere**

scetti'cismo nm scepticism. **'scettico, -a** a sceptical ● nmf sceptic

'scettro nm sceptre

'scheda nf card. **~ elettorale** ballot-paper. **~ di espansione** Comput expansion card. **~ perforata** punch card. **~ telefonica** phonecard. **sche'dare** vt file. **sche'dario** nm file; (mobile) filing cabinet

sche'dina nf pools coupon; **giocare la ~** do the pools

scheggi'a nf fragment; (di legno) splinter. **~'arsi** vr chip; ⟨legno:⟩ splinter

'scheletro nm skeleton

'schema nm diagram; (abbozzo) outline. **sche'matico** a schematic. **~tiz'zare** vt schematize

'scherma nf fencing

scher'mirsi vr protect oneself

'schermo nm screen; **grande ~** big screen

scher'nire vt mock. **'scherno** nm mockery

scher'zare vi joke; (giocare) play

'scherzo nm joke; (trucco) trick; (effetto) play; Mus scherzo; **fare uno ~ a qcno** play a joke on sb; **per ~** for fun; **stare allo ~** take a joke. **scher'zoso** a playful

schiaccia'noci nm inv nutcrackers pl

schiacci'ante a damning

schiacci'are vt crush; Sport smash; press (pulsante); crack (noce); **~ un pisolino** grab forty winks

schiaffeggi'are vt slap. **schi'affo** nm slap; **dare uno schiaffo a** slap

schiamaz'zare vi make a racket; (galline:) cackle

schian'tar|e vt break. **~si** vr crash ● vi **schianto dalla fatica** I'm wiped out. **'schianto** nm crash; fam knock-out; (divertente) scream

schia'rir|e vt clear; (sbiadire) fade ● vi, **~si** vr brighten up; **~si la gola** clear one's throat

schiavitù nf slavery. **schi'avo, -a** nmf slave

schi'ena nf back; **mal di ~** backache. **schie'nale** nm (di sedia) back

schi'er|a nf Mil rank; (moltitudine) crowd. **~a'mento** nm lining up

schie'rar|e vt draw up. **~si** vr draw up; **~si con** (parteggiare) side with

schiet'tezza nf frankness. **schi'etto** a frank; (puro) pure

schi'fezza nf **una ~** rubbish. **schifil'toso** a fussy. **'schifo** nm disgust; **mi fa schifo** it makes me sick. **schi'foso** a disgusting; (di cattiva qualità) rubbishy

schioc'care vt crack; snap (dita). **schi'occo** nm (di frusta) crack; (di bacio) smack; (di dita, lingua) click

schi'oppo nm **ad un tiro di ~** a stone's throw away

schi'uder|e vt, **~si** vr open

schi'u|ma nf foam; (di sapone) lather; (feccia) scum. **~ma da barba** shaving foam. **~'mare** vt skim ● vi foam

schi'uso pp di **schiudere**

schi'vare vt avoid. **'schivo** a bashful

schizo'frenico a schizophrenic

schiz'zare vt squirt; (inzaccherare) splash; (abbozzare) sketch ● vi spurt; **~ via** scurry away

schiz'zato, -a a & nmf sl loony

schizzi'noso a squeamish

'schizzo nm squirt; (di fango) splash; (abbozzo) sketch

sci nm inv ski; (sport) skiing. **~ d'acqua** water-skiing

'scia nf wake; (di fumo ecc) trail

sci'abola nf sabre

sciabor'dare vt/i lap

scia'callo nm jackal; fig profiteer

sciac'quar|e vt rinse. **~si** vr rinse oneself. **sci'acquo** nm mouthwash

scia'gu|ra nf disaster. **~'rato** a unfortunate; (scellerato) wicked

scialac'quare vt squander

scia'lare vi spend money like water

sci'albo a pale; fig dull

sci'alle nm shawl

scia'luppa nf dinghy. **~ di salva-taggio** lifeboat

sci'ame nm swarm

sci'ampo nm shampoo

scian'cato a lame

sci'are vi ski

sci'arpa nf scarf

sci'atica nf Med sciatica

scia'tore, -'trice nmf skier

sci'atto a slovenly; (stile) careless. **sciat'tone, -a** nmf slovenly person

scienti'fico a scientific

sci'enz|a nf science; (sapere) knowledge. **~i'ato, -a** nmf scientist

'scimmia nf monkey. **~ot'tare** vt ape

scimpanzé nm inv chimpanzee, chimp

scimu'nito a idiotic

'scinder|e vt, **~si** vr split

scin'tilla nf spark. **scintil'lante** a sparkling. **scintil'lare** vi sparkle

scioc'ca|nte a shocking. **~re** vt shock

scioc'chezza nf foolishness; (assurdità) nonsense. **sci'occo** a foolish

sci'oglier|e vt untie; undo, untie (nodo); (liberare) release; (liquefare) melt; dissolve (contratto, qcsa nell'acqua); loosen up (muscoli). **~si** vr release oneself; (liquefarsi) melt; (contratto:) be dissolved; (pastiglia:) dissolve

sciogli'lingua nm inv tongue-twister

scio'lina nf wax

sciol'tezza nf agility; (disinvoltura) ease

sci'olto pp di **sciogliere** ● a loose; (agile) agile; (disinvolto) easy; **versi sciolti** blank verse

sciope'ra|nte nmf striker. **~re** vi go on strike, strike. **sci'opero** nm strike. **sciopero a singhiozzo** on-off strike

scion'nare vt/fig show off

sci'pito a insipid

scip'pa|re vt fam snatch. **~tore, ~'trice** nmf bag snatcher. **'scippo** nm bag-snatching

sci'rocco nm sirocco

scirop'pato a ⟨frutta⟩ in syrup. **sci'roppo** nm syrup

'scisma nm schism

scissi'one nf division

'scisso pp di **scindere**

sciu'par|e vt spoil; ⟨sperperare⟩ waste. **~si** vr get spoiled; ⟨deperire⟩ wear oneself out. **sciu'pio** nm waste

scivo'l|are vi slide; ⟨involontariamente⟩ slip. **'scivolo** nm slide; Techn chute. **~oso** a slippery

scle'rosi nf sclerosis

scoc'care vt shoot ● vi ⟨scintilla:⟩ shoot out; ⟨ora:⟩ strike

scocci'a|re vt ⟨dare noia a⟩ bother. **~rsi** vr be bothered. **~to** a fam narked. **~'tore, ~'trice** nmf bore. **~'tura** nf nuisance

sco'della nf bowl

scodinzo'lare vi wag its tail

scogli'era nf cliff; ⟨a fior d'acqua⟩ reef. **'scoglio** nm rock; ⟨fig: ostacolo⟩ stumbling block

scoi'attolo nm squirrel

scola|'pasta nm inv colander. **~pi'atti** nm inv dish drainer

sco'lara nf schoolgirl

sco'lare vt drain; strain ⟨pasta, verdura⟩ ● vi drip

sco'la|ro nm schoolboy. **~'resca** nf pupils pl. **~stico** a school attrib

scoli'osi nf curvature of the spine

scol'la|re vt cut away the neck of ⟨abito⟩; ⟨staccare⟩ unstick. **~to** a ⟨abito⟩ low-necked. **~'tura** nf neckline

'scolo nm drainage

scolo'ri|re vt, **~rsi** vr fade. **~to** a faded

scol'pire vt carve; ⟨imprimere⟩ engrave

scombi'nare vt upset

scombusso'lare vt muddle up

scom'mess|a nf bet. **~o** pp di **scommettere scom'mettere** vt bet

scomo'dar|e vt, **~si** vr trouble. **scomodità** nf discomfort. **'scomodo** a uncomfortable ● nm **essere di sco-modo a qcno** be a trouble to sb

scompa'rire vi disappear; ⟨morire⟩ pass on. **scom'parsa** nf disappearance; ⟨morte⟩ passing, death. **scom'parso, -a** pp di **scomparire** ● nmf departed

scomparti'mento nm compartment. **scom'parto** nf compartment

scom'penso nm imbalance

scompigli'are vt disarrange. **scom'piglio** nm confusion

scom'po|rre vt take to pieces; ⟨fig:

turbare⟩ upset. **~rsi** vr get flustered, lose one's composure. **~sto** pp di **scomporre** ● a ⟨sguaiato⟩ unseemly; ⟨disordinato⟩ untidy

sco'muni|ca nf excommunication. **~'care** vt excommunicate

sconcer'ta|re vt disconcert; ⟨rendere perplesso⟩ bewilder. **~to** a disconcerted; bewildered

scon'cezza nf obscenity. **'sconcio** a ⟨osceno⟩ dirty ● nm **è uno sconcio che...** it's a disgrace that...

sconclusio'nato a incoherent

scon'dito a unseasoned; ⟨insalata⟩ with no dressing

sconfes'sare vt disown

scon'figgere vt defeat

sconfi'na|re vi cross the border; ⟨in proprietà privata⟩ trespass. **~to** a unlimited

scon'fitt|a nf defeat. **~o** pp di **sconfiggere**

scon'forto nm dejection

sconge'lare vt thaw out ⟨cibo⟩, defrost

scongiu'rare vt beseech; ⟨evitare⟩ avert. **~'uro** nm **fare gli scongiuri** ≈ touch wood, knock on wood Am

scon'nesso pp di **sconnettere** ● a fig incoherent. **scon'nettere** vt disconnect

sconosci'uto, -a a unknown ● nmf stranger

sconquas'sare vt smash; ⟨sconvolgere⟩ upset

sconside'rato a inconsiderate

sconsigli'a|bile a not advisable. **~re** vt advise against

sconso'lato a disconsolate

scon'ta|re vt discount; ⟨dedurre⟩ deduct; ⟨pagare⟩ pay off; serve ⟨pena⟩. **~to** a discount; ⟨ovvio⟩ expected; **~to del 10%** with 10% discount; **dare qcsa per ~to** take sth for granted

scon'tento a displeased ● nm discontent

'sconto nm discount; **fare uno ~** give a discount

scon'trarsi vr clash; ⟨urtare⟩ collide

scon'trino nm ticket; ⟨di cassa⟩ receipt

'scontro nm clash; ⟨urto⟩ collision

scon'troso a unsociable

sconveni'ente a unprofitable; ⟨scorretto⟩ unseemly

sconvol'gente a mind-blowing

scon'vol|gere vt upset; ⟨mettere in disordine⟩ disarrange. **~gi'mento** nm upheaval. **~to** pp di **sconvolgere** ● a distraught '**scopa** nf broom. **sco'pare** vt sweep; vulg shag, screw

scoperchi'are vt take the lid off (pentola); take the roof off (casa)

sco'pert|a nf discovery. **~o** pp di **scoprire** ● a uncovered; (senza riparo) exposed; (conto) overdrawn; (spoglio) bare

'**scopo** nm aim; **allo ~ di** in order to

scoppi'are vi burst; fig break out. **scoppiet'tare** vi crackle. '**scoppio** nm burst; (di guerra) outbreak; (esplosione) explosion

sco'prire vt discover; (togliere la copertura a) uncover

scoraggi'ante a discouraging

scoraggi'a|re vt discourage. **~rsi** vr lose heart

scor'butico a peevish

scorcia'toia nf short cut

'**scorcio** nm (di epoca) end; (di cielo) patch; (in arte) foreshortening; **di** ⟨vedere⟩ from an angle. **~ panoramico** panoramic view

scor'da|re vt, **~rsi** vr forget. **~to** a Mus out of tune

sco'reggi|a nf fam fart. **~'are** vi fam fart

'**scorgere** vt make out; (notare) notice

scoria nf waste; (di metallo, carbone) slag; **scorie** pl radioattive radioactive waste

scor'nato a fig hangdog. '**scorno** nm humiliation

scorpacci'ata nf bellyful; **fare una ~ di** stuff oneself with

scorpi'one nm scorpion; Astr Scorpio

scorraz'zare vi run about

'**scorrere** vt (dare un'occhiata) glance through ● vi run; (scivolare) slide; (fluire) flow; Comput scroll. **scor'revole** a porta **scorrevole** sliding door

scorre'ria nf raid

scorret'tezza nf (mancanza di educazione) bad manners pl. **scor'retto** a incorrect; (sconveniente) improper

scorri'banda nf raid; fig excursion

'**scors|a** nf glance. **~o** pp di **scorrere** ● a last

scor'soio a nodo **~** noose

'**scort|a** nf escort; (provvista) supply. **~'tare** vt escort

scor'te|se a discourteous. **~'sia** nf discourtesy

scorti'ca|re vt skin. **~'tura** nf graze

'**scorto** pp di **scorgere**

'**scorza** nf peel; (crosta) crust; (corteccia) bark

'**sco'sceso** a steep

'**scossa** nf shake; Electr, fig shock; **prendere la ~** get an electric shock. **~ elettrica** electric shock. **~ sismica** earth tremor

'**scosso** pp di **scuotere** ● a shaken; (sconvolto) upset

sco'stante a off-putting

sco'sta|re vt push away. **~rsi** vr stand aside

scostu'mato a dissolute; (maleducato) ill-mannered

scot'tante a (argomento) dangerous

scot'ta|re vt scald ● vi burn; (bevanda:) be too hot; (sole, pentola:) be very hot. **~rsi** vr burn oneself; (al sole) get sunburnt; fig get one's fingers burnt. **~'tura** nf burn; (da liquido) scald; **~'tura solare** sunburn; fig painful experience

'**scotto** a overcooked

sco'vare vt (scoprire) discover

'**Scoz|ia** nf Scotland. **s~'zese** a Scottish ● nmf Scot

scredi'tare vt discredit

scre'mare vt skim

screpo'la|re vt, **~rsi** vr crack. **~to** a (labbra) chapped. **~'tura** nf crack

screzi'ato a speckled

screzio nm disagreement

scribac|chi'are vt scribble. **~'chino, -a** nmf scribbler; (impiegato) penpusher

scricchio'l|are vi creak. **~io** nm creaking

'**scricciolo** nm wren

'**scrigno** nm casket

scrimina'tura nf parting

'**scrit|ta** nf writing; (su muro) graffiti. **~to** pp di **scrivere** ● a written ● nm writing; (lettera) letter. **~'toio** nm writing-desk. **~'tore**, **~'trice** nmf writer. **~'tura** nf writing; Relig scripture

scrittu'rare vt engage

scriva'nia nf desk

'**scrivere** vt write; (descrivere) write about; **~ a macchina** type

scroc|c'are vt **~are a** sponge off. '**scrocco** nm fam a **scrocco** fam without paying; **vivere a scrocco** sponge off other people. **~one, -a** nmf sponger

'**scrofa** nf sow

scrol'lar|e vt shake; **~e le spalle** shrug one's shoulders. **~si** vr shake oneself; **~si qcsa di dosso** shake sth off

scrosci'are vi roar; (pioggia:) pelt

down. 'scroscio nm roar; (di pioggia) pelting; uno scroscio di applausi thunderous applause

scro'star|e vt scrape. ~si vr peel off

'scrupo|lo nm scruple; (diligenza) care; senza scrupoli unscrupulous, without scruples. ~'loso a scrupulous

scru'ta|re vt scan; (indagare) search. ~'tore nm (alle elezioni) returning officer

scruti'nare vt scrutinize. scru'tinio nm (di voti alle elezioni) poll; Sch assessment of progress

scu'cire vt unstitch; scuci i soldi! fam cough up [the money]!

scude'ria nf stable

scu'detto nm Sport championship shield

'scudo nm shield

sculacci'|are vt spank. ~'ata nf spanking. ~'one nm spanking

sculet'tare vi wiggle one's hips

scul'to|re, -'trice nm sculptor ● nf sculptress. ~'tura nf sculpture

scu'ola nf school. ~ elementare primary school. ~ guida driving school. ~ materna day nursery. ~ media secondary school. ~ media [inferiore] secondary school (10-13). ~ [media] superiore secondary school (13-18). ~ dell'obbligo compulsory education

scu'oter|e vt shake. ~si vr (destarsi) rouse oneself; ~si di dosso shake off

'scure nf axe

scu'reggia nf fam fart. scureggi'are vi fam fart

scu'rire vt/i darken

'scuro a dark ● nm darkness; (imposta) shutter

scur'rile a scurrilous

'scusa nf excuse; (giustificazione) apology; chiedere ~ apologize; chiedo ~! I'm sorry!

scu'sar|e vt excuse. ~si vr ~si apologize (di for); [mi] scusi! excuse me!; (chiedendo perdono) [I'm] sorry!

sdebi'tarsi vr (disobbligarsi) repay a kindness

sde'gna|re vt despise. ~rsi vr get angry. ~to a indignant. 'sdegno nm disdain. sde'gnoso a disdainful

sden'tato a toothless

sdolci'nato a sentimental, schmaltzy

sdoppi'are vt halve

sdrai'arsi vr lie down. 'sdraio nm [sedia a] sdraio deckchair

sdrammatiz'zare vi provide some comic relief

sdruccio'l|are vi slither. ~evole a slippery

se conj if; (interrogativo) whether, if; se mai (caso mai) if need be; se mai telefonasse,... should he call,..., if he calls,...; se no otherwise, or else; se non altro at least, if nothing else; se pure (sebbene) even though; (anche se) even if; non so se sia vero I don't know whether it's true, I don't know if it's true; come se as if; se lo avessi saputo prima! if only I had known before!; e se andassimo fuori a cena? how about going out for dinner? ● nm inv if

sé pron oneself; (lui) himself; (lei) herself; (esso, essa) itself; (loro) themselves; l'ha fatto da sé he did it himself; ha preso i soldi con sé he took the money with him; si sono tenuti le notizie per sé they kept the news to themselves

seb'bene conj although

'secca nf shallows pl; in ~ (nave) aground

sec'cante a annoying

sec'ca|re vt dry; (importunare) annoy ● vi dry up. ~rsi vr dry up; (irritarsi) get annoyed; (annoiarsi) get bored. ~'tore, ~'trice nmf nuisance. ~'tura nf bother

secchi'ello nm pail

'secchio nm bucket. ~ della spazzatura rubbish bin, trash can Am

'secco, -a a dry; (disseccato) dried; (magro) thin; (brusco) curt; (preciso) sharp; restare a ~ be left penniless; restarci ~ (fam: morire di colpo) be killed on the spot ● nm (siccità) drought; lavare a ~ dry-clean

secessi'one nf secession

seco'lare a age-old; (laico) secular. 'secolo nm century; (epoca) age; è un secolo che non lo vedo fam I haven't seen him for ages o yonks

se'cond|a nf Sch, Rail second class; Auto second [gear]. ~o a second ● nm second; (secondo piatto) main course ● prep according to; ~o me in my opinion

secondo'genito, -a a & nm secondborn

secrezi'one nf secretion

'sedano nm celery

seda'tivo a & nm sedative

'sede nf seat; (centro) centre; Relig see; Comm head office. ~ sociale registered office

seden'tario a sedentary

se'der|e vi sit. **~si** vr sit down ● nm (deretano) bottom

'sedia nf chair. **~ a dondolo** rocking chair. **~ a rotelle** wheelchair

sedi'cente a self-styled

'sedici a & nm sixteen

se'dile nm seat

sedizi'o|ne nf sedition. **~so** a seditious

se'dotto pp di **sedurre**

sedu'cente a seductive; (allettante) enticing

se'durre vt seduce

se'duta nf session; (di posa) sitting. **~ stante** adv here and now

seduzi'one nf seduction

'sega nf saw; vulg wank

'segala nf rye

se'gare vt saw

sega'tura nf sawdust

'seggio nm seat. **~ elettorale** polling station

seg'gio|la nf chair. **~'lino** nm seat; (da bambino) child's seat. **~'lone** nm (per bambini) high chair

seggio'via nf chair lift

seghe'ria nf sawmill

se'ghetto nm hacksaw

seg'mento nm segment

segna'lar|e vt signal; (annunciare) announce; (indicare) point out. **~si** vr distinguish oneself

se'gna|le nm signal; (stradale) sign. **~le acustico** beep. **~le orario** time signal. **~'letica** nf signals pl. **~'letica stradale** road signs pl

segna'libro nm bookmark

se'gnar|e vt mark; (prendere nota) note; (indicare) indicate; Sport score. **~si** vr cross oneself. **'segno** nm sign; (traccia, limite) mark; (bersaglio) target; **far segno** (col capo) nod; (con la mano) beckon. **segno zodiacale** birth sign

segre'gar|e vt segregate. **~zi'one** nf segregation

segretari'ato nm secretariat

segre'tario, -a nmf secretary. **~ comunale** town clerk

segrete'ria nf (ufficio) [administrative] office; (segretariato) secretariat. **~ telefonica** answering machine, answerphone

segre'tezza nf secrecy

se'greto a & nm secret; **in ~** in secret

segu'ace nmf follower

segu'ente a following, next

se'gugio nm bloodhound

segu'ire vt/i follow; (continuare) continue

segui'tare vt/i continue

'seguito nm retinue; (sequela) series; (continuazione) continuation; **di ~** in succession; **in ~** later on; **in ~ a** following; **al ~** in his/her wake; (a causa di) owing to; **fare ~ a** Comm follow up

sei a & nm six. **sei'cento** a & nm six hundred; **il Seicento** the seventeenth century. **sei'mila** a & nm six thousand

sel'ciato nm paving

selet'tivo a selective. **selezio'nare** vt select. **selezi'one** nf selection

'sella nf saddle. **sel'lare** vt saddle

seltz nm soda water

'selva nf forest

selvag'gina nf game

sel'vaggio, -a a wild; (primitivo) savage ● nmf savage

sel'vatico a wild

se'maforo nm traffic lights pl

se'mantica nf semantics sg

sem'brare vi seem; (assomigliare) look like; **che te ne sembra?** what do you think?, **mi sembra che...** I think...

'seme nm seed; (di mela) pip; (di carte) suit; (sperma) semen

se'mestre nm half-year

semi'cerchio nm semicircle

semifi'nale nf semifinal

semi'freddo nm ice cream and sponge dessert

'semina nf sowing

semi'nare vt sow; fam shake off (inseguitori)

semi'nario nm seminar; Relig seminary

se'mitico a Semitic

sem'mai conj in case ● adv **e lui, ~, che...** if anyone, it's him who...

'semola nf bran. **semo'lino** nm semolina

'sempli|ce a simple; **in parole semplici** in plain words. **~'cemente** adv simply. **~ci'otto, -a** nmf simpleton. **~'cistico** a simplistic. **~'cità** nf simplicity. **~fi'care** vt simplify

'sempre adv always; (ancora) still; **per ~** for ever

sempre'verde a & nm evergreen

se'nape nf mustard

se'nato nm senate. **sena'tore** nm senator

se'nil|e a senile. **~ità** nf senility

'senno nm sense

'**seno** *nm* (*petto*) breast; *Math* sine; **in ~ a** in the bosom of
sen'sato *a* sensible
sensazi|o'nale *a* sensational. **~'one** *nf* sensation
sen'sibil|e *a* sensitive; (*percepibile*) perceptible; (*notevole*) considerable. **~ità** *nf* sensitivity. **~iz'zare** *vt* make more aware (**a** of)
sensi'tivo, -a *a* a sensory ● *nmf* sensitive person; (*medium*) medium
'**senso** *nm* sense; (*significato*) meaning; (*direzione*) direction; **far ~ a** qcno make sb shudder; **non ha ~** it doesn't make sense; **senza ~** meaningless; **perdere i sensi** lose consciousness. **~ dell'umorismo** sense of humour. **~ unico** (*strada*) one-way; **~ vietato** no entry
sensu'al|e *a* sensual. **~ità** *nf* sensuality
sen'tenz|a *nf* sentence; (*massima*) saying. **~i'are** *vi Jur* pass judgment
senti'ero *nm* path
sentimen'tale *a* sentimental. **senti'mento** *nm* feeling
senti'nella *nf* sentry
sen'ti|re *vt* feel; (*udire*) hear; (*ascoltare*) listen to; (*gustare*) taste; (*odorare*) smell ● *vi* feel; (*udire*) hear; **~re caldo/freddo** feel hot/cold. **~rsi** *vr* feel; **~rsi di fare qcsa** feel like doing sth; **~rsi bene** feel well; **~rsi poco bene** feel unwell; **~rsela di fare qcsa** feel up to doing sth. **~to** *a* (*sincero*) sincere; **per ~to dire** by hearsay
sen'tore *nm* inkling
'**senza** *prep* without; **~ correre** without running; **~altro** certainly; **~ ombrello** without an umbrella
senza'tetto *nm inv* **i ~** the homeless
sepa'ra|re *vt* separate. **~rsi** *vr* separate; (*amici:*) part; **~rsi da** be separated from. **~ta'mente** *adv* separately. **~zi'one** *nf* separation
se'pol|cro *nm* sepulchre. **~to** *pp di* **seppellire ~'tura** *nf* burial
seppel'lire *vt* bury
'**seppia** *nf* cuttle fish; **nero di ~** sepia
sep'pure *conj* even if
se'quenza *nf* sequence
seque'strare *vt* (*rapire*) kidnap; *Jur* impound; (*confiscare*) confiscate. **se'questro** *nm Jur* impounding; (*di persona*) kidnap[ping]
'**sera** *nf* evening; **di ~** in the evening. **se'rale** *a* evening. **se'rata** *nf* evening; (*ricevimento*) party

ser'bare *vt* keep; harbour (*odio*); cherish (*speranza*)
serba'toio *nm* tank. **~ d'acqua** water tank; (*per una città*) reservoir
'**serbo, -a** *a* & *nmf* Serbian ● *nm* (*lingua*) Serbian; **mettere in ~** put aside
sere'nata *nf* serenade
serenità *nf* serenity. **se'reno** *a* serene; (*cielo*) clear
ser'gente *nm* sergeant
seria'mente *adv* seriously
'**serie** *nf inv* series; (*complesso*) set; *Sport* division; **fuori ~** custom-built; **produzione in ~** mass production; **di ~ B** second-rate
serietà *nf* seriousness. '**serio** *a* serious; (*degno di fiducia*) reliable; **sul serio** seriously; (*davvero*) really
ser'mone *nm* sermon
'**serpe** *nf liter* viper. **~ggi'are** *vi* meander; (*diffondersi*) spread
ser'pente *nm* snake. **~ a sonagli** rattlesnake
'**serra** *nf* greenhouse; **effetto ~** greenhouse effect
ser'randa *nf* shutter
ser'ra|re *vt* shut; (*stringere*) tighten; (*incalzare*) press on. **~'tura** *nf* lock
ser'vir|e *vt* serve; (*al ristorante*) wait on ● *vi* serve; (*essere utile*) be of use; **non serve** it's no good. **~si** *vr* (*di cibo*) help oneself; **~si da** buy from; **~si di** use
servitù *nf inv* servitude; (*personale di servizio*) servants *pl*
servizi'evole *a* obliging
ser'vizio *nm* service; (*da caffè ecc*) set; (*di cronaca, sportivo*) report; **servizi** *pl* bathroom; **essere di ~** be on duty; **fare ~** (*autobus ecc:*) run; **fuori ~** (*bus*) not in service; (*ascensore*) out of order; **~ compreso** service charge included. **~ in camera** room service. **~ civile** civilian duties done instead of national service. **~ militare** military service. **~ pubblico** utility company. **~ al tavolo** waiter service
'**servo, -a** *nmf* servant
servo'sterzo *nm* power steering
ses'san|ta *a* & *nm* sixty. **~'tina** *nf* **una ~tina** about sixty
sessi'one *nf* session
'**sesso** *nm* sex
sessu'al|e *a* sexual. **~ità** *nf* sexuality
'**sesto¹** *a* sixth
'**sesto²** *nm* (*ordine*) order
'**seta** *nf* silk
setacci'are *vt* sieve. **se'taccio** *nm* sieve

'**sete** *nf* thirst; **avere ~** be thirsty
'**setola** *nf* bristle
'**setta** *nf* sect
set'tan|ta *a & nm* seventy. **~'tina** *nf una* **~tina** about seventy
'**sette** *a & nm* seven. **~'cento** *a & nm* seven hundred; **il S~cento** the eighteenth century
set'tembre *nm* September
settentri|o'nale *a* northern ●*nmf* northerner. **~'one** *nm* north
setti'ma|na *nf* week. **~'nale** *a & nm* weekly
'**settimo** *a* seventh
set'tore *nm* sector
severità *nf* severity. **se'vero** *a* severe; *(rigoroso)* strict
se'vizi|a *nf* torture; **se'vizie** *pl* torture *sg*. **~'are** *vt* torture
sezio'nare *vt* divide; *Med* dissect. **sezi'one** *nf* section; *(reparto)* department; *Med* dissection
sfaccen'dato *a* idle
sfacchi'na|re *vi* toil. **~ta** *nf* drudgery
sfacci|a'taggine *nf* cheek, insolence. **~'ato** *a* cheeky, fresh *Am*
sfa'celo *nm* ruin; **in ~** in ruins
sfal'darsi *vr* flake off
sfa'ma|re *vt* feed. **~si** *vr* satisfy one's hunger, eat one's fill
'**sfar|zo** *nm* pomp. **~'zoso** *a* sumptuous
sfa'sato *a fam* confused; *(motore)* which needs tuning
sfasci|a|re *vt* unbandage; *(fracassare)* smash. **~rsi** *vr* fall to pieces. **~to** *a* beat-up
sfa'tare *vt* explode
sfati'cato *a* lazy
sfavil'la|nte *a* sparkling. **~re** *vi* sparkle
sfavo'revole *a* unfavourable
sfavo'rire *vt* disadvantage, put at a disadvantage
'**sfer|a** *nf* sphere. **~ico** *a* spherical
sfer'rare *vt* unshoe *(cavallo)*; *(scagliare)* land
sfer'zare *vt* whip
sfian'carsi *vr* wear oneself out
sfi'bra|re *vt* exhaust. **~to** *a* exhausted
'**sfida** *nf* challenge. **sfi'dare** *vt* challenge
sfi'duci|a *nf* mistrust. **~'ato** *a* discouraged
'**sfiga** *nf vulg* bloody bad luck
sfigu'rare *vt* disfigure ●*vi (far cattiva figura)* look out of place
sfilacci'ar|e *vt*, **~si** *vr* fray

sfi'la|re *vt* unthread; *(togliere di dosso)* take off ●*vi (truppe:)* march past; *(in parata)* parade. **~rsi** *vr* come unthreaded; *(collant:)* ladder; take off *(pantaloni)*. **~ta** *nf* parade; *(sfilza)* series. **~ta di moda** fashion show
'**sfilza** *nf (di errori, domande)* string
'**sfinge** *nf* sphinx
sfi'nito *a* worn out
sfio'rare *vt* skim; touch on *(argomento)*
sfio'rire *vi* wither; *(bellezza:)* fade
sfitto *a* vacant
'**sfizio** *nm* whim, fancy; **togliersi uno ~** satisfy a whim
sfo'cato *a* out of focus
sfoci'are *vi* **~ in** flow into
sfode'ra|re *vt* draw *(pistola, spada)*. **~to** *a* unlined
sfo'gar|e *vt* vent. **~si** *vr* give vent to one's feelings
sfoggi'are *vt/i* show off. '**sfoggio** *nm* show, display; **fare sfoggio di** show off
'**sfoglia** *nf* sheet of pastry; **pasta ~** puff pastry
sfogli'are *vt* leaf through
'**sfogo** *nm* outlet; *fig* outburst; *Med* rash; **dare ~ a** give vent to
sfolgo'ra|nte *a* blazing. **~re** *vi* blaze
sfol'lare *vt* clear ● *vi Mil* be evacuated
sfol'tire *vt* thin [out]
sfon'dare *vt* break down ● *vi (aver successo)* make a name for oneself
'**sfondo** *nm* background
sfor'ma|re *vt* pull out of shape *(tasche)*. **~rsi** *vr* lose its shape; *(persona:)* lose one's figure. **~to** *nm Culin* flan
sfor'nito *a* **~ di** *(negozio)* out of
sfor'tuna *nf* bad luck. **~ta'mente** *adv* unfortunately. **sfortu'nato** *a* unlucky
sfor'zar|e *vt* force. **~si** *vr* try hard. '**sforzo** *nm* effort; *(tensione)* strain
'**sfottere** *vt sl* tease
sfracel'larsi *vr* smash
sfrat'tare *vt* evict. '**sfratto** *nm* eviction
sfrecci'are *vi* flash past
sfregi'a|re *vt* slash. **~to** *a* scarred
'**sfregio** *nm* slash
sfre'na|rsi *vr* run wild. **~to** *a* wild
sfron'tato *a* shameless
sfrutta'mento *nm* exploitation. **sfrut'tare** *vt* exploit
sfug'gente *a* elusive; *(mento)* receding
sfug'gi|re *vi* escape; **~re a** escape [from]; **mi sfugge** it escapes me; **mi è**

sfuggito di mano I lost hold of it ● *vt* avoid. **~ta** *nf* **di ~ta** in passing

sfu'ma|re *vi* (*svanire*) vanish; (*colore:*) shade off ● *vt* soften (*colore*). **~'tura** *nf* shade

sfuri'ata *nf* outburst [of anger]

sga'bello *nm* stool

sgabuz'zino *nm* cupboard

sgam'bato *a* (*costume da bagno*) high-cut

sgambet'tare *vi* kick one's legs; (*camminare*) trot. **sgam'betto** *nm* **fare lo sgambetto a qcno** trip sb up

sganasci'arsi *vr* **~ dalle risa** roar with laughter

sganci'ar|e *vt* unhook; *Rail* uncouple; drop (*bombe*); *fam* cough up (*denaro*). **~si** *vr* become unhooked; *fig* get away

sganghe'rato *a* ramshackle

sgar'bato *a* rude. **'sgarbo** *nm* discourtesy; **fare uno sgarbo** be rude

sgargi'ante *a* garish

sgar'rare *vi* be wrong; (*da regola*) stray from the straight and narrow. **'sgarro** *nm* mistake, slip

sgattaio'lare *vi* sneak away; **~ via** decamp

sghignaz'zare *vi* laugh scornfully, sneer

sgob'b|are *vi* slog; (*fam: studente:*) swot. **~one, -a** *nmf* slogger; (*fam: studente*) swot

sgoccio'lare *vi* drip

sgo'larsi *vr* shout oneself hoarse

sgomb[e]'rare *vt* clear [out]. **'sgombero** *a* clear ● *nm* (*trasloco*) removal; (*pesce*) mackerel

sgomen'tar|e *vt* dismay. **~si** *vr* be dismayed. **sgo'mento** *nm* dismay

sgomi'nare *vt* defeat

sgom'mata *nf* screech of tyres

sgonfi'ar|e *vt* deflate. **~si** *vr* go down. **'sgonfio** *a* flat

'sgorbio *nm* scrawl; (*fig: vista sgradevole*) sight

sgor'gare *vi* gush [out] ● *vt* flush out, unblock (*lavandino*)

sgoz'zare *vt* **~ qcno** cut sb's throat

sgra'd|evole *a* disagreeable. **~ito** *a* unwelcome

sgrammati'cato *a* ungrammatical

sgra'nare *vt* shell (*piselli*); open wide (*occhi*)

sgran'chir|e *vt*, **~si** *vr* stretch

sgranocchi'are *vt* munch

sgras'sare *vt* remove the grease from

sgrazi'ato *a* ungainly

sgreto'lar|e *vt*, **~si** *vr* crumble

sgri'da|re *vt* scold. **~ta** *nf* scolding

sgros'sare *vt* rough-hew (*marmo*); *fig* polish

sguai'ato *a* coarse

sgual'cire *vt* crumple

sgual'drina *nf* slut

sgu'ardo *nm* look; (*breve*) glance

'sguattero, -a *nmf* skivvy

sguaz'zare *vi* splash; (*nel fango*) wallow

sguinzagli'are *vt* unleash

sgusci'are *vt* shell ● *vi* (*sfuggire*) slip away; **~ fuori** slip out

shake'rare *vt* shake

si *pron* (*riflessivo*) oneself; (*lui*) himself; (*lei*) herself; (*esso, essa*) itself; (*loro*) themselves; (*reciproco*) each other; (*tra più di due*) one another; (*impersonale*) you, one; **lavarsi** wash [oneself]; **si è lavata** she washed [herself]; **lavarsi le mani** wash one's hands; **si è lavata le mani** she washed her hands; **si è mangiato un pollo intero** he ate an entire chicken by himself; **incontrarsi** meet each other; **la gente si aiuta a vicenda** people help one another; **non si sa mai** you never know, one never knows; **queste cose si dimenticano facilmente** these things are easily forgotten ● *nm* (*chiave, nota*) B

si *adv* yes

'sia¹ *vedi* **essere**

'sia² *conj* **~...~...** (*entrambi*) both... and...; (*o l'uno o l'altro*) either...or... **~ che venga, ~ che non venga** whether he comes or not; **scegli ~ questo ~ quello** choose either this one or that one; **voglio ~ questo che quello** I want both this one and that one

sia'mese *a* Siamese

sibi'lare *vi* hiss. **'sibilo** *nm* hiss

si'cario *nm* hired killer

sicché *conj* (*perciò*) so [that]; (*allora*) then

siccità *nf* drought

sic'come *conj* as

Si'cili|a *nf* Sicily. **s~'ano, -a** *a* & *nmf* Sicilian

si'cura *nf* safety catch; (*di portiera*) child-proof lock. **~'mente** *adv* definitely

sicu'rezza *nf* (*certezza*) certainty; (*salvezza*) safety; **uscita di ~** emergency exit

si'curo *a* (*non pericoloso*) safe; (*certo*) sure; (*saldo*) steady; *Comm* sound ● *adv* certainly ● *nm* safety; **al ~** safe; **andare sul ~** play [it] safe; **di ~** defi-

203

nitely; **di ~, sarà arrivato** he must
have arrived

siderur'gia *nf* iron and steel industry.
side'rurgico *a* iron and steel *attrib*

'sidro *nm* cider

si'epe *nf* hedge

si'ero *nm* serum

sieroposi'tivo, -a *a* HIV positive
● *nmf* person who is HIV positive

si'esta *nf* afternoon nap, siesta

si'fone *nm* siphon

Sig. *abbr* (**signore**) Mr

Sig.a *abbr* (**signora**) Mrs, Ms

siga'retta *nf* cigarette; **pantaloni a
~** drainpipes

'sigaro *nm* cigar

Sigg. *abbr* (**signori**) Messrs

sigil'lare *vt* seal. **si'gillo** *nm* seal

'sigla *nf* initials *pl*. **~ musicale** signature tune. **si'glare** *vt* initial

Sig.na *abbr* (**signorina**) Miss, Ms

signifi'care *vt* mean. **~'tivo** *a* signifi-
cant. **~to** *nm* meaning

si'gnora *nf* lady; (*davanti a nome proprio*) Mrs; (*non sposata*) Miss; (*in lettere
ufficiali*) Dear Madam; **il signor Venè e
~** Mr and Mrs Venè

si'gnore *nm* gentleman; *Relig* lord;
(*davanti a nome proprio*) Mr; (*in lettere
ufficiali*) Dear Sir. **signo'rile** *a* gentle-
manly; (*di lusso*) luxury

signo'rina *nf* young lady; (*seguito da
nome proprio*) Miss

silenzia'tore *nm* silencer

si'lenzio *nm* silence. **~'oso** *a* silent

silhou'ette *nf* silhouette, outline

si'licio *nm* **piastrina di ~** silicon chip

sili'cone *nm* silicone

'sillaba *nf* syllable

silu'rare *vt* torpedo. **si'luro** *nm* torpedo

simboleggi'are *vt* symbolize

sim'bolico *a* symbolic[al]

'simbolo *nm* symbol

similarità *nf inv* similarity

'simile *a* similar; (*tale*) such; **~e a** like
● *nm* (*il prossimo*) fellow man.
~'mente *adv* similarly. **~'pelle** *nf*
Leatherette®

simme'tria *nf* symmetry. **sim'metrico** *a* symmetric[al]

simpa'tia *nf* liking;
(*compenetrazione*) sympathy; **prendere
qcno in ~a** take a liking to sb.
sim'patico *a* nice. **~iz'zante** *nmf* well-
wisher. **~iz'zare** *vi* **~izzare con** take a
liking to; **~izzare per qcsa/qcno** lean
towards sth/sb

sim'posio *nm* symposium

simu'lare *vt* simulate; feign (*amicizia,
interesse*). **~zi'one** *nf* simulation

simul'tanela *nf* **in ~a** simultane-
ously. **~o** *a* simultaneous

sina'goga *nf* synagogue

sincerità *nf* sincerity. **sin'cero** *a* sincere

'sincope *nf* syncopation; *Med* fainting
fit

sincron'ia *nf* synchronization; **in ~**
with synchronized timing

sincroniz'zalre *vt* synchronize.
~zi'one *nf* synchronization

sinda'callea *nf* [trade] union, [labor] union *Am*. **~'lista** *nmf* trade unionist,
labor union member *Am*. **~re** *vt* inspect. **~to** *nm* [trade] union, [labor] union *Am*; (*associazione*) syndicate

'sindaco *nm* mayor

'sindrome *nf* syndrome

sinfo'nia *nf* symphony. **sin'fonico** *a*
symphonic

singhi'oz'zare *vi* (*di pianto*) sob.
~'ozzo *nm* hiccup; (*di pianto*) sob;
avere il ~ozzo have the hiccups

singo'larle *a* singular ● *nm* singular.
~'mente *adv* individually; (*stranamente*) peculiarly

'singolo *a* single ● *nm* individual; *Tennis* singles *pl*

si'nistra *nf* left; **a ~** on the left; **girare
a ~** turn to the left; **con la guida a ~**
(*auto*) with left-hand drive

sini'strato *a* injured

si'nistro, -a *a* left[-hand]; (*avverso*)
sinister ● *nm* accident ● *nf* left [hand];
Pol left [wing]

'sino *prep* = **fino**[1]

si'nonimo *a* synonymous ● *nm* synonym

sin'tassi *nf* syntax. **~ttico** *a*
syntactic[al]

'sintesi *nf* synthesis; (*riassunto*) summary

sin'tetico *a* synthetic; (*conciso*) summary. **~z'zare** *vt* summarize

sintetizza'tore *nm* synthesizer

sinto'matico *a* symptomatic. **'sintomo** *nm* symptom

sinto'nia *nf* tuning; **in ~** on the same
wavelength

sinu'oso *a* (*strada*) winding

sinu'site *nf* sinusitis

si'pario *nm* curtain

si'rena *nf* siren

'Sirila *nf* Syria. **s~'ano, -a** *a & nmf*
Syrian

si'ringa *nf* syringe

'sismico a seismic

si'stema nm system. **S~ Monetario Europeo** European Monetary System. **~ operativo** Comput operating system

siste'ma|re vt (mettere) put; tidy up (casa, camera); (risolvere) sort out; (procurare lavoro a) fix up with a job; (trovare alloggio a) find accommodation for; (sposare) marry off; (fam: punire) sort out. **~rsi** vr settle down; (trovare un lavoro) find a job; (trovare alloggio) find accommodation; (sposarsi) marry. **~tico** a systematic. **~zi'one** nf arrangement; (di questione) settlement; (lavoro) job; (alloggio) accommodation; (matrimonio) marriage

'sito nm site. **~ web** Comput web site

situ'are vt place

situazi'one nf situation

ski-'lift nm ski tow

slacci'are vt unfasten

slanci'a|rsi vr hurl oneself. **~to** a slender. **'slancio** nm impetus; (impulso) impulse

sla'vato a (carnagione, capelli) fair

'slavo a Slav[onic]

sle'al|e a disloyal. **~tà** nf disloyalty

sle'gare vt untie

'slitta nf sledge, sleigh. **~'mento** nm (di macchina) skid; (fig: di riunione) postponement

slit'ta|re vi Auto skid; (riunione:) be put off. **~ta** nf skid

slit'tino nm toboggan

'slogan nm inv slogan

slo'ga|re vt dislocate. **~rsi** vr **~rsi una caviglia** sprain one's ankle. **~'tura** nf dislocation

sloggi'are vt dislodge ● vi move out

Slo'vacchia nf Slovakia

Slo'venia nf Slovenia

smacchi'a|re vt clean. **~'tore** nm stain remover

'smacco nm humiliating defeat

smagli'ante a dazzling

smagli'a|rsi vr (calza:) ladder Br, run. **~'tura** nf ladder Br, run

smalizi'ato a cunning

smal'ta|re vt enamel; glaze (ceramica); varnish (unghie). **~to** a enamelled

smalti'mento nm disposal; (di merce) selling off. **~ rifiuti** waste disposal; (di grassi) burning off

smal'tire vt burn off; (merce) sell off; fig get through (corrispondenza); **~ la sbornia** sober up

'smalto nm enamel; (di ceramica) glaze; (per le unghie) nail varnish

'smani|a nf fidgets pl; (desiderio) longing. **~'are** vi have the fidgets; **~are per** long for. **~'oso** a restless

smantella'mento nm dismantling. **~'lare** vt dismantle

smarri'mento nm loss; (psicologico) bewilderment

smar'ri|re vt lose; (temporaneamente) mislay. **~rsi** vr get lost; (turbarsi) be bewildered

smasche'rar|e vt unmask. **~si** vr (tradirsi) give oneself away

SME nm abbr (**Sistema Monetario Europeo**) EMS

smemo'rato, -a a forgetful ● nmf scatterbrain

smen'ti|re vt deny. **~ta** nf denial

sme'raldo nm & a emerald

smerci'are vt sell off

smerigli'ato a emery; **vetro ~** frosted glass. **sme'riglio** nm emery

'smesso pp di smettere ● a (abiti) cast-off

'smett|ere vt stop; stop wearing (abiti); **~ila!** stop it!

smidol'lato a spineless

sminu'ir|e vt diminish. **~si** vr fig belittle oneself

sminuz'zare vt crumble; (fig: analizzare) analyse in detail

smista'mento nm clearing; (postale) sorting. **smi'stare** vt sort; Mil post

smisu'rato a boundless; (esorbitante) excessive

smobili'ta|re vt demobilize. **~zi'one** nf demobilization

smo'dato a immoderate

smog nm smog

smoking nm inv dinner jacket, tuxedo Am

smon'tabile a jointed

smon'tar|e vt take to pieces; (scoraggiare) dishearten ● vi (da veicolo) get off; (da cavallo) dismount; (dal servizio) go off duty. **~si** vr lose heart

'smorfi|a nf grimace; (moina) simper; **fare ~e** make faces. **~'oso** a affected

'smorto a pale; (colore) dull

smor'zare vt dim (luce); tone down (colori); deaden (suoni); quench (sete)

'smosso pp di smuovere

smotta'mento nm landslide

'smunto a emaciated

smu'over|e vt shift; (commuovere) move. **~si** vr move; (commuoversi) be moved

smus'sar|e vt round off; (fig: attenuare) tone down. **~si** vr go blunt

205

snatu'rato *a* inhuman
snel'lir|e *vt* slim down. **~si** *vr* slim [down]. **'snello** *a* slim
sner'vante *a* enervating
sner'va|re *vt* enervate. **~rsi** *vr* get exhausted
sni'dare *vt* drive out
snif'fare *vt* snort
snob'bare *vt* snub. **sno'bismo** *nm* snobbery
snoccio'lare *vt* stone; *fig* blurt out
sno'da|re *vt* untie; (*sciogliere*) loosen. **~rsi** *vr* come untied; (*strada:*) wind. **~to a** (*persona*) double-jointed; (*dita*) flexible
so'ave *a* gentle
sobbal'zare *vi* jerk; (*trasalire*) start. **sob'balzo** *nm* jerk; (*trasalimento*) start
sobbar'carsi *vr* **~ a** undertake
sob'borgo *nm* suburb
sobil'lare *vt* stir up
'sobrio *a* sober
socchi'u|dere *vt* half-close. **~so** *pp di* **socchiudere** ● *a* (*occhi*) half-closed; (*porta*) ajar
soc'combere *vi* succumb
soc'cor|rere *vt* assist. **~so** *pp di* **soccorrere** ● *nm* assistance; **soccorsi** *pl* rescuers; (*dopo disastro*) relief workers. **~so stradale** breakdown service
socialdemo'cra|tico, -a *a* Social Democratic ● *nmf* Social Democrat. **~'zia** *nf* Social Democracy
soci'ale *a* social
socia'li|smo *nm* Socialism. **~sta** *a & nmf* Socialist. **~z'zare** *vi* socialize
società *nf inv* society; *Comm* company. **~ per azioni** plc. **~ a responsabilità limitata** limited liability company
soci'evole *a* sociable
'socio, -a *nmf* member; *Comm* partner
sociolo'gia *nf* sociology. **socio'logico** *a* sociological
'soda *nf* soda
soddisfa'cente *a* satisfactory
soddi'sfa|re *vt/i* satisfy; meet (*richiesta*); make amends for (*offesa*). **~tto** *pp di* **soddisfare** ● *a* satisfied. **~zi'one** *nf* satisfaction
'sodo *a* hard; *fig* firm; (*uovo*) hard-boiled ● *adv* hard; **dormire ~** sleep soundly; **~ nm venire al ~** get to the point
sofà *nm inv* sofa
suffe'ren|te *a* (*malato*) ill. **~za** *nf* suffering
soffer'marsi *vr* pause; **~ su** dwell on

sof'ferto *pp di* **soffrire**
soffi'a|re *vt* blow; reveal (*segreto*); (*rubare*) pinch *fam* ● *vi* blow. **~ta** *nf fig sl* tip-off
'soffice *a* soft
'soffio *nm* puff; *Med* murmur
sof'fitt|a *nf* attic. **~o** *nm* ceiling
soffoca'mento *nm* suffocation
soffo'ca|nte *a* suffocating. **~re** *vt/i* suffocate; (*con cibo*) choke; *fig* stifle
sof'friggere *vt* fry lightly
sof'frire *vt/i* suffer; (*sopportare*) bear; **~ di** suffer from
sof'fritto *pp di* **soffriggere**
sof'fuso *a* (*luce*) soft
sofisti'ca|re *vt* (*adulterare*) adulterate ● *vi* (*sottilizzare*) quibble. **~to** *a* sophisticated
sogget|tiva'mente *adv* subjectively. **~'tivo** *a* subjective
sog'getto *nm* subject ● *a* subject; **essere ~ a** be subject to
soggezi'one *nf* subjection; (*rispetto*) awe
sogghi'gnare *vi* sneer. **sog'ghigno** *nm* sneer
soggio'gare *vt* subdue
soggior'nare *vi* stay. **soggi'orno** *nm* stay; (*stanza*) living room
soggi'ungere *vt* add
'soglia *nf* threshold
'sogliola *nf* sole
so'gna|re *vt/i* dream; **~re a occhi aperti** daydream. **~'tore**, **~'trice** *nmf* dreamer. **'sogno** *nm* dream; **fare un sogno** have a dream; **neanche per sogno!** not at all!
'soia *nf* soya
sol *nm Mus* (*chiave, nota*) G
so'laio *nm* attic
sola'mente *adv* only
so'lar|e *a* (*energia, raggi*) solar; (*crema*) sun *attrib.* **~ium** *nm inv* solarium
sol'care *vt* plough. **'solco** *nm* furrow; (*di ruota*) track; (*di nave*) wake; (*di disco*) groove
sol'dato *nm* soldier
'soldo *nm* **non ha un ~** he hasn't got a penny to his name; **senza un ~** penniless; **soldi** *pl* (*denaro*) money *sg*
'sole *nm* sun; (*luce del sole*) sun[light]; **al ~** in the sun; **prendere il ~** sunbathe
soleggi'ato *a* sunny
so'lenn|e *a* solemn. **~ità** *nf* solemnity
so'lere *vi* be in the habit of; **come si suol dire** as they say
sol'fato *nm* sulphate

soli'dal|e a in agreement. **~rietà** nf solidarity
solidifi'car|e vt/i, **~si** vr solidify
solidità nf solidity; (di colori) fastness. **'solido** a solid; (robusto) sturdy; (colore) fast ●nm solid
soli'loquio nm soliloquy
so'lista a solo ●nmf soloist
solita'mente adv usually
soli'tario a solitary; (isolato) lonely ●nm (brillante) solitaire; (gioco di carte) patience, solitaire
'solito a usual; **essere ~ fare qcsa** be in the habit of doing sth ●nm usual; **di ~** usually
soli'tudine nf solitude
solleci'ta|re vt speed up; urge (persona). **~zi'one** nf (richiesta) request; (preghiera) entreaty
sol'leci|to a prompt ●nm reminder. **~tudine** nf promptness; (interessamento) concern
solle'one nm noonday sun; (periodo) dog days of summer
solleti'care vt tickle. **sol'letico** nm tickling; **fare il solletico a qcno** tickle sb; **soffrire il solletico** be ticklish
solleva'mento nm **~ pesi** weightlifting
solle'var|e vt lift; (elevare) raise; (confortare) comfort. **~si** vr rise; (riaversi) recover
solli'evo nm relief
'solo, -a a alone; (isolato) lonely; (unico) only; Mus solo; **da ~** by myself/yourself/himself etc ●nmf **il ~**, **la sola** the only one ●nm Mus solo ●adv only
sol'stizio nm solstice
sol'tanto adv only
so'lubile a soluble; (caffè) instant
soluzi'one nf solution; Comm payment; **in unica ~** Comm as a lump sum
sol'vente a & nm solvent; **~ per unghie** nail polish remover
'soma nf bestia da **~** beast of burden
so'maro nm ass; Sch dunce
so'matico a somatic
somigli'an|te a similar. **~za** nf resemblance
somigli'ar|e vi **~e a** resemble. **~si** vr be alike
'somma nf sum; Math addition
som'mare vt add; (totalizzare) add up
som'mario a & nm summary
som'mato a **tutto ~** all things considered
sommeli'er nm inv wine waiter

som'mer|gere vt submerge. **~'gibile** nm submarine. **~so** pp di **sommergere**
som'messo a soft
sommini'stra|re vt administer. **~zi'one** nf administration
sommità nf inv summit
'sommo a highest; fig supreme ●nm summit
som'mossa nf rising
sommozza'tore nm frogman
so'naglio nm bell
so'nata nf sonata; fig fam beating
'sonda nf Mech drill; (spaziale, Med) probe. **son'daggio** nm drilling; (spaziale, Med) probe; (indagine) survey. **sondaggio d'opinioni** opinion poll. **son'dare** vt sound; (investigare) probe
so'netto nm sonnet
sonnambu'lismo nm sleepwalking. **son'nambulo, -a** nmf sleepwalker
sonnecchi'are vi doze
son'nifero nm sleeping-pill
'sonno nm sleep; **aver ~** be sleepy. **~'lenza** nf sleepiness
so'noro a resonant; (rumoroso) loud; (onde, scheda) sound attrib
sontu'oso a sumptuous
sopo'rifero a soporific
sop'palco nm platform
soppe'rire vi **~ a qcsa** provide for sth
soppe'sare vt weigh up (situazione)
soppi'atto: di ~ adv furtively
soppor'tare vt support; (tollerare) stand; bear (dolore)
soppressi'one nf removal; (di legge) abolition; (di diritti, pubblicazione) suppression; (annullamento) cancellation.
sop'presso pp di **sopprimere**
sop'primere vt get rid of; abolish (legge); suppress (diritti, pubblicazione); (annullare) cancel
'sopra adv on top; (più in alto) higher [up]; (al piano superiore) upstairs; (in testo) above; **mettilo lì ~** put it up there; **di ~** upstairs; **dormirci ~** fig sleep on it; **pensarci ~** think about it; **vedi ~** see above ●prep **~** [**a**] on; (senza contatto, oltre) over; (riguardo a) about; **è ~ al tavolo, è ~ il tavolo** it's on the table; **il quadro è appeso ~ al camino** the picture is hanging over the fireplace; **il ponte passa ~ all'autostrada** the bridge crosses over the motorway; **è caduto ~ il tetto** it fell on the roof; **l'uno ~ l'altro** one on top of the other; (senza contatto) one above the other; **abita ~ di me** he lives

upstairs from me; **i bambini ~ i dieci anni** children over ten; **20° ~ lo zero** 20° above zero; **~ il livello del mare** above sea level; **rifletti ~ quello che è successo** think about what happened; **non ha nessuno ~ di sé** he has nobody above him; **al di ~ di** over ● *nm* **il [di] ~** the top

so'prabito *nm* overcoat

soprac'ciglio *nm* (*pl nf* **sopracciglia**) eyebrow

sopracco'per|ta *nf* (*di letto*) bedspread; (*di libro*) [dust-]jacket. **~'tina** *nf* book jacket

soprad'detto *a* above-mentioned

sopraele'vata *nf* elevated railway

sopraf'fa|re *vt* overwhelm. **~tto** *pp di* **sopraffare ~zi'one** *nf* abuse of power

sopraf'fino *a* excellent; (*gusto, udito*) highly refined

sopraggi'ungere *vi* (*persona:*) turn up; (*accadere*) happen

soprallu'ogo *nm* inspection

sopram'mobile *nm* ornament

soprannatu'rale *a & nm* supernatural

sopran'nom|e *nm* nickname. **~i'nare** *vt* nickname

so'prano *nmf* soprano

soprappensi'ero *adv* lost in thought

sopras'salto *nm* **di ~** with a start

sopras'sedere *vi* **~ a** postpone

soprat'tutto *adv* above all

sopravvalu'tare *vt* overvalue

sopravve'nire *vi* turn up; (*accadere*) happen. **~'vento** *nm fig* upper hand

sopravvi|s'suto *pp di* **sopravvivere ~'venza** *nf* survival. **soprav'vivere** *vi* survive; **sopravvivere a** outlive (*persona*)

soprinten'den|te *nmf* supervisor; (*di museo ecc*) keeper. **~za** *nf* supervision; (*ente*) board

so'pruso *nm* abuse of power

soq'quadro *nm* **mettere a ~** turn upside down

sor'betto *nm* sorbet

sor'bire *vt* sip; *fig* put up with

'sordido *a* sordid; (*avaro*) stingy

sor'dina *nf* mute; **in ~** *fig* on the quiet

sordità *nf* deafness. **'sordo, -a** *a* deaf; (*rumore, dolore*) dull ● *nmf* deaf person. **sordo'muto, -a** *a* deaf-and-dumb ● *nmf* deaf mute

so'rel|la *nf* sister. **~'lastra** *nf* stepsister

sor'gente *nf* spring; (*fonte*) source

'sorgere *vi* rise; *fig* arise

sormon'tare *vt* surmount

sorni'one *a* sly

sorpas'sa|re *vt* surpass; (*eccedere*) exceed; overtake, pass *Am* (*veicolo*). **~to** *a* old-fashioned. **sor'passo** *nm* overtaking, passing *Am*

sorpren'dente *a* surprising; (*straordinario*) remarkable

sor'prendere *vt* surprise; (*cogliere in flagrante*) catch

sor'pre|sa *nf* surprise; **di ~a** by surprise. **~o** *pp di* **sorprendere**

sor're|ggere *vt* support; (*tenere*) hold up. **~ggersi** *vr* support oneself. **~tto** *pp di* **sorreggere**

sorri'dente *a* smiling

sor'ri|dere *vi* smile. **~so** *pp di* **sorridere** ● *nm* smile

sorseggi'are *vt* sip. **'sorso** *nm* sip; (*piccola quantità*) drop

'sorta *nf* sort; **di ~** whatever; **ogni ~ di** all sorts of

'sorte *nf* fate; (*caso imprevisto*) chance; **tirare a ~** draw lots. **~ggi'are** *vt* draw lots for. **sor'teggio** *nm* draw

sorti'legio *nm* witchcraft

sor'ti|re *vi* come out. **~ta** *nf Mil* sortie; (*battuta*) witticism

'sorto *pp di* **sorgere**

sorvegli'an|te *nmf* keeper; (*controllore*) overseer. **~za** *nf* watch; *Mil ecc* surveillance

sorvegli'are *vt* watch over; (*controllare*) oversee; (*polizia:*) watch, keep under surveillance

sorvo'lare *vt* fly over; *fig* skip

'sosia *nm inv* double

so'spen|dere *vt* hang; (*interrompere*) stop; (*privare di una carica*) suspend. **~si'one** *nf* suspension. **~'sorio** *nm Sport* jockstrap

so'speso *pp di* **sospendere** ● *a* (*impiegato, alunno*) suspended; **~ a** hanging from; **~ a un filo** *fig* hanging by a thread ● *nm* **in ~** pending; (*emozionato*) in suspense

sospet'tare *vt* suspect. **so'spetto** *a* suspicious ● *nm* suspicion; (*persona*) suspect. **~'toso** *a* suspicious

so'spin|gere *vt* drive. **~to** *pp di* **sospingere**

sospi'rare *vi* sigh ● *vt* long for. **so'spiro** *nm* sigh

'sosta *nf* stop; (*pausa*) pause; **senza ~** non-stop; **"divieto di ~"** "no parking"

sostan'tivo *nm* noun

so'stanz|a *nf* substance; **~e** *pl*

(*patrimonio*) property *sg*; **in ~a** to sum up. **~i'oso** *a* substantial; ⟨*cibo*⟩ nourishing
so'stare *vi* stop; (*fare una pausa*) pause
so'stegno *nm* support
soste'ner|e *vt* support; (*sopportare*) bear; (*resistere*) withstand; (*affermare*) maintain; (*nutrire*) sustain; sit ⟨*esame*⟩; **~e le spese** meet the costs. **~si** *vr* support oneself
sosteni'tore, -'trice *nmf* supporter
sosten'tamento *nm* maintenance
soste'nuto *a* ⟨*stile*⟩ formal; ⟨*prezzi, velocità*⟩ high
sostitu'ir|e *vt* substitute (**a** for), replace (**con** with). **~si** *vr* **~si a** replace
sosti'tu|to, -a *nmf* replacement, stand-in ● *nm* (*surrogato*) substitute. **~zi'one** *nf* substitution
sotta'ceto *a* pickled; **sottaceti** *pl* pickles
sot'tana *nf* petticoat; (*di prete*) cassock
sotter'fugio *nm* subterfuge; **di ~** secretly
sotter'raneo *a* underground ● *nm* cellar
sotter'rare *vt* bury
sottigli'ezza *nf* slimness; *fig* subtlety
sot'til|e *a* thin; ⟨*udito, odorato*⟩ keen; ⟨*osservazione, distinzione*⟩ subtle. **~iz-'zare** *vi* split hairs
sottin'te|ndere *vt* imply. **~so** *pp di* **sottintendere** ● *nm* allusion; **senza ~si** openly ● *a* implied
'**sotto** *adv* below; (*più in basso*) lower [down]; (*al di sotto*) underneath; (*al piano di sotto*) downstairs; **è li ~** it's underneath; **~ ~** deep down; (*di nascosto*) on the quiet; **di ~** downstairs; **mettersi ~** *fig* get down to it; **mettere ~** (*fam: investire*) knock down; **fatti ~!** *fam* get stuck in! ● *prep* ~ [**a**] under; (*al di sotto di*) under[neath]; **abita ~ di me** he lives downstairs from me; **i bambini ~ i dieci anni** children under ten; **20° ~ zero** 20° below zero; **~ il livello del mare** below sea level; **~ la pioggia** in the rain; **~ Elisabetta I** under Elizabeth I; **~ sedazione** under sedation; **~ condizione che...** on condition that...; **~ giuramento** under oath; **~ sorveglianza** under surveillance; **~ Natale/gli esami** around Christmas/exam time; **andare ~ i 50 all'ora** do less than 50km an hour ● *nm* **il [di] ~** the bottom
sotto'banco *adv* under the counter

sottobicchi'ere *nm* coaster
sotto'bosco *nm* undergrowth
sotto'braccio *adv* arm in arm
sotto'fondo *nm* background
sottoline'are *vt* underline; *fig* stress
sot'tolio *adv* in oil
sotto'mano *adv* within reach
sottoma'rino *a* & *nm* submarine
sotto'messo *pp di* **sottomettere** ● *a* (*remissivo*) submissive
sotto'metter|e *vt* submit; subdue ⟨*popolo*⟩. **~si** *vr* submit. **sottomissi'one** *nf* submission
sottopa'gare *vt* underpay
sottopas'saggio *nm* underpass; (*pedonale*) subway
sotto'por|re *vt* submit; (*costringere*) subject. **~si** *vr* submit oneself; **~si a** undergo. **sotto'posto** *pp di* **sottoporre**
sotto'scala *nm* cupboard under the stairs
sotto'scritto *pp di* **sottoscrivere** ● *nm* undersigned
sotto'scri|vere *vt* sign; (*approvare*) sanction, subscribe to. **~zi'one** *nf* (*petizione*) petition; (*approvazione*) sanction; (*raccolta di denaro*) appeal
sottosegre'tario *nm* undersecretary
sotto'sopra *adv* upside down
sotto'stante *a* **la strada ~** the road below
sottosu'olo *nm* subsoil
sottosvi'lup|pato *a* underdeveloped. **~luppo** *nm* underdevelopment
sotto'terra *adv* underground
sotto'titolo *nm* subtitle
sottovalu'tare *vt* underestimate
sotto'veste *nf* slip
sotto'voce *adv* in a low voice
sottovu'oto *a* vacuum-packed
sot'tra|rre *vt* remove; embezzle ⟨*fondi*⟩; *Math* subtract. **~rsi** *vr* **~rsi a** escape from; avoid ⟨*responsabilità*⟩. **~tto** *pp di* **sottrarre**. **~zi'one** *nf* removal; (*di fondi*) embezzlement; *Math* subtraction
sottuffici'ale *nm* non-commissioned officer; *Naut* petty officer
sou'brette *nf inv* showgirl
so'vietico, -a *a* & *nmf* Soviet
sovraccari'care *vt* overload. **sovrac'carico** *a* overloaded (**di** with) ● *nm* overload
sovraffati'carsi *vr* overexert oneself
sovrannatu'rale *a* & *nm* = **soprannaturale**
so'vrano, -a *a* sovereign; *fig* supreme ● *nmf* sovereign

sovrap'por|re *vt* superimpose. **~si** *vr* overlap. **sovrapposizi'one** *nf* superimposition

sovra'stare *vt* dominate; *(fig: pericolo)* hang over

sovrinten'den|te, ~za = **soprintendente, soprintendenza**

sovru'mano *a* superhuman

sovvenzi'one *nf* subsidy

sovver'sivo *a* subversive

'sozzo *a* filthy

S.p.A. *abbr (società per azioni)* plc

spac'ca|re *vt* split; chop *(legna)*. **~rsi** *vr* split. **~ tura** *nf* split

spacci'a|re *vt* deal in, push *(droga)*; **~re qcsa per qcsa** pass sth off as sth; **essere ~to** be done for, be a goner. **~rsi** *vr* **~rsi per** pass oneself off as. **~ 'tore, ~ 'trice** *nmf (di droga)* pusher; *(di denaro falso)* distributor of forged bank notes. **'spaccio** *nm (di droga)* dealer, pusher; *(negozio)* shop

'spacco *nm* split

spac'cone, -a *nmf* boaster

'spada *nf* sword. **~c'cino** *nm* swordsman

spadroneggi'are *vi* act the boss

spae'sato *a* disorientated

spa'ghetti *nmpl* spaghetti *sg*

spa'ghetto *nm (fam: spavento)* fright

'Spagna *nf* Spain

spa'gnolo, -a *a* Spanish ● *nmf* Spaniard ● *nm (lingua)* Spanish

'spago *nm* string; **dare a ~ a qcno** encourage sb

spai'ato *a* odd

spalan'ca|re *vt*, **~rsi** *vr* open wide. **~to** *a* wide open

spa'lare *vt* shovel

'spall|a *nf* shoulder; *(di comico)* straight man; **~e** *pl (schiena)* back; **alle ~e di qcno** *(ridere)* behind sb's back. **~eggi'are** *vt* back up

spal'letta *nf* parapet

spalli'era *nf* back; *(di letto)* headboard; *(ginnastica)* wall bars *pl*

spal'lina *nf* strap; *(imbottitura)* shoulder pad

spal'mare *vt* spread

'spander|e *vt* spread; *(versare)* spill. **~si** *vr* spread

spappo'lare *vt* crush

spa'ra|re *vt/i* shoot; **~rle grosse** talk big. **~ta** *nf fam* tall story. **~'toria** *nf* shooting

sparecchi'are *vt* clear

spa'reggio *nm* Comm deficit; *Sport* play-off

'sparg|ere *vt* scatter; *(diffondere)* spread; shed *(lacrime, sangue)*. **~ersi** *vr* spread. **~i'mento** *nm* scattering; *(di lacrime, sangue)* shedding; **~i'mento di sangue** bloodshed

spa'ri|re *vi* disappear; **~sci!** get lost!. **~zi'one** *nf* disappearance

spar'lare *vi* **~ di** run down

'sparo *nm* shot

sparpagli'a|re *vt*, **~si** *vr* scatter

'sparso *pp di* **spargere** ● *a* scattered; *(sciolto)* loose

spar'tire *vt* share out; *(separare)* separate

sparti'traffico *nm inv* traffic island; *(di autostrada)* central reservation, median strip *Am*

spartizi'one *nf* division

spa'ruto *a* gaunt; *(gruppo)* small; *(peli, capelli)* sparse

sparvi'ero *nm* sparrow-hawk

spasi'ma|nte *nm hum* admirer. **~re** *vi* suffer agonies

'spasimo *nm* spasm

spa'smodico *a* spasmodic

spas'sar|si *vr* amuse oneself; **~sela** have a good time

spassio'nato *a (osservatore)* dispassionate, impartial

'spasso *nm* fun; **essere uno ~** be hilarious; **andare a ~** go for a walk. **spas'soso** *a* hilarious

'spatola *nf* spatula

spau'racchio *nm* scarecrow; *fig* bugbear. **spau'rire** *vt* frighten

spa'valdo *a* defiant

spaventa'passeri *nm inv* scarecrow

spaven'tar|e *vt* frighten, scare. **~si** *vr* be frightened, be scared. **spa'vento** *nm* fright. **spaven'toso** *a* frightening; *(fam: enorme)* incredible

spazi'ale *a* spatial; *(cosmico)* space *attrib*

spazi'are *vt* space out ● *vi* range

spazien'tirsi *vr* lose [one's] patience

'spazi|o *nm* space. **~'oso** *a* spacious

spazza'camino *nm* chimney sweep

spaz'z|are *vt* sweep; **~are via** sweep away; *(fam: mangiare)* devour. **~a'tura** *nf (immondizia)* rubbish. **~ino** *nm* road sweeper; *(netturbino)* dustman

'spazzo|la *nf* brush; *(di tergicristallo)* blade. **~ lare** *vt* brush. **~ 'lino** *nm* small brush. **~lino da denti** toothbrush. **~ 'lone** *nm* scrubbing brush

specchi'arsi *vr* look at oneself in a/ the mirror; *(riflettersi)* be mirrored; **~ in qcno** model oneself on sb

specchi'etto nm ~ retrovisore driving mirror, rearview mirror

'specchio nm mirror

speci'ale a special ● nm TV special [programme]. ~'lista nmf specialist. ~lità nf inv speciality, specialty Am

specializ'za|re vt, ~rsi vr specialize. ~to a (operaio) skilled

special'mente adv especially

'specie nf inv (scientifico) species; (tipo) kind; **fare** ~ **a** surprise

specifi'care vt specify. **spe'cifico** a specific

specu'lare¹ vi speculate; ~ **su** (indagare) speculate on; Fin speculate in

specu'lare² a mirror attrib

specula'tore, -'trice nmf speculator. ~zi'one nf speculation

spe'di|re vt send. ~to pp di spedire ● a quick; (parlata) fluent. ~zi'one nf (di lettere ecc) dispatch; Comm consignment; (scientifica) expedition

'spegner|e vt put out; turn off (gas, luce); switch off (motore); slake (sete). ~si vr go out; (morire) pass away

spelacchi'ato a (tappeto) threadbare; (cane) mangy

spe'lar|e vt skin (coniglio). ~si vr (cane) moult

speleolo'gia nf potholing, speleology

spel'lar|e vt skin; fig fleece. ~si vr peel off

spe'lonca nf cave; fig dingy hole

spendacci'one, -a nmf spendthrift

'spendere vt spend; ~ **fiato** waste one's breath

spen'nare vt pluck; fam fleece (cliente)

spennel'lare vt brush

spensie|ra'tezza nf lightheartedness. ~'rato a carefree

'spento pp di spegnere ● a off; (gas) out; (smorto) dull

spe'ranza nf hope; **pieno di** ~ hopeful; **senza** ~ hopeless

spe'rare vt hope for; (aspettarsi) expect ● vi ~ **in** trust in; **spero di sì** I hope so

'sper|dersi vr get lost. ~'duto a lost; (isolato) secluded

spergi'uro, -a nmf perjurer ● nm perjury

sperico'lato a swashbuckling

sperimen'ta|le a experimental. ~re vt experiment with; test (resistenza, capacità, teoria). ~zi'one nf experimentation

'sperma nm sperm

spe'rone nm spur

sperpe'rare vt squander. **'sperpero** nm waste

'spes|a nf expense; (acquisto) purchase; **andare a far** ~**e** go shopping; **fare la** ~**a** do the shopping; **fare le** ~**e di** pay for. ~**e** pl **bancarie** bank charges. ~**e a carico del destinatario** carriage forward. ~**e di spedizione** shipping costs. **spe'sato** a all-expenses-paid. ~o pp di spendere

'spesso¹ a thick

'spesso² adv often

'spes'sore nm thickness; (fig: consistenza) substance

spet'tabile a (Comm abbr **Spett.**) S~ **ditta Rossi** Messrs Rossi

spettaco'lare a spectacular. **spet'tacolo** nm spectacle; (rappresentazione) show. ~'loso a spectacular

spet'tare vi ~ **a** be up to; (diritto:) be due to

spetta'tore, -'trice nmf spectator; **spettatori** pl (di cinema ecc) audience sg

spettego'lare vi gossip

spetti'nar|e vt ~**e qcno** ruffle sb's hair. ~**si** vr ruffle one's hair

spet'trale a ghostly. **'spettro** nm ghost; Phys spectrum

'spezie nfpl spices

spez'zar|e vt, ~**si** vr break

spezza'tino nm stew

spez'zato nm coordinated jacket and trousers

spezzet'tare vt break into small pieces

'spia nf spy; (della polizia) informer; (di porta) peep-hole; **fare la** ~ sneak. ~ [**luminosa**] light. ~ **dell'olio** oil [warning] light

spiacci'care vt squash

spia'ce|nte a sorry. ~**vole** a unpleasant

spi'aggia nf beach

spia'nare vt level; (rendere liscio) smooth; roll out (pasta); raze to the ground (edificio)

spi'ano nm **a tutto** ~ flat out

spian'tato a fig penniless

spi'are vt spy on; wait for (occasione ecc)

spiattel'lare vt blurt out; shove (oggetto)

spiaz'zare vt wrong-foot

spi'azzo nm (radura) clearing

spic'ca|re vt ~**re un salto** jump; ~**re il volo** take flight ● vi stand out. ~**to** a marked '**spicchio** nm (di agrumi) segment; (di aglio) clove

spicci'a|rsi vr hurry up. ~'**tivo** a speedy

'**spicciolo** a (comune) banal; ⟨denaro, 10 000 lire⟩ in change. **spiccioli** pl change sg

'**spicco** nm relief; **fare** ~ stand out

'**spider** nmf inv open-top sports car

spie'dino nm kebab. **spi'edo** nm spit; **allo spiedo** on a spit, spit-roasted

spie'ga|re vt explain; open out ⟨cartina⟩; unfurl ⟨vele⟩. ~**rsi** vr explain oneself; ⟨vele, bandiere:⟩ unfurl. ~**zi'one** nf explanation

spiegaz'zato a crumpled

spie'tato a ruthless

spiffe'rare vi blurt out ● vi ⟨vento:⟩ whistle. '**spiffero** nm (corrente d'aria) draught

'**spiga** nf spike; Bot ear

spigli'ato a self-possessed

spigolo nm edge; (angolo) corner

'**spilla** nf (gioiello) brooch. ~ **da balia** safety pin. ~ **di sicurezza** safety pin

spil'lare vt tap

'**spillo** nm pin. ~ **di sicurezza** safety pin; (in arma) safety catch

spi'lorcio a stingy

spilun'gone, -a nmf beanpole

'**spina** nf thorn; (di pesce) bone; Electr plug. ~ **dorsale** spine

spi'naci nmpl spinach sg

spi'nale a spinal

spi'nato a ⟨filo⟩ barbed; ⟨pianta⟩ thorny

spi'nello nm fam joint

'**spinger|e** vt push; fig drive. ~**si** vr (andare) proceed

spi'noso a thorny

'**spint|a** nf push; (violenta) thrust; fig spur. ~**o** pp di spingere

spio'naggio nm espionage, spying

spio'vente a ⟨tetto⟩ sloping

spi'overe vi liter stop raining; (ricadere) fall; (scorrere) flow down

'**spira** nf coil

spi'raglio nm small opening; (soffio d'aria) breath of air; (raggio di luce) gleam of light

spi'rale a spiral ● nf spiral; (negli orologi) hairspring; (anticoncezionale) coil

spi'rare vi (soffiare) blow; (morire) pass away

spiri't|ato a possessed; (espressione) wild. ~**ismo** nm spiritualism. '**spirito** nm spirit; (arguzia) wit; (intelletto)

mind; **fare dello spirito** be witty; **sotto spirito** ≈ in brandy. ~**o'saggine** nf witticism. **spiri'toso** a witty

spiritu'ale a spiritual

splen'dente a shining

'**splen|dere** vi shine. ~**dido** a splendid. ~'**dore** nm splendour

spode'stare vt dispossess; depose ⟨re⟩

'**spoglia** nf (di animale) skin; **spoglie** pl (salma) mortal remains; (bottino) spoils

spogli'a|re vt strip; (svestire) undress; (fare lo spoglio di) go through. ~'**rello** nm strip-tease. ~**rsi** vr strip, undress. ~'**toio** nm dressing room; Sport changing room; (guardaroba) cloakroom, checkroom Am. '**spoglio** a undressed; (albero, muro) bare ● nm (scrutinio) perusal

'**spola** nf shuttle; **fare la** ~ shuttle

spol'pare vt take the flesh off; fig fleece

spolve'rare vt dust; fam devour ⟨cibo⟩

'**sponda** nf (di mare, lago) shore; (di fiume) bank; (bordo) edge

sponsoriz'zare vt sponsor

spon'taneo a spontaneous

spopol'are vt depopulate ● vi (avere successo) draw the crowds. ~**si** vr become depopulated

sporadica'mente adv sporadically. **spo'radico** a sporadic

sporcacci'one, -a nmf dirty pig

spor'c|are vt dirty; (macchiare) soil. ~**arsi** vr get dirty. ~**izia** nf dirt. '**sporco** a dirty; **avere la coscienza sporca** have a guilty conscience ● nm dirt

spor'gen|te a jutting. ~**za** nf projection

'**sporger|e** vt stretch out; ~**e querela contro** take legal action against ● vi jut out. ~**si** vr lean out

sport nm inv sport

'**sporta** nf shopping basket

spor'tello nm door; (di banca ecc) window. ~ **automatico** cash dispenser

spor'tivo, -a a sports attrib; ⟨persona⟩ sporty ● nm sportsman ● nf sportswoman

'**sporto** pp di sporgere

'**sposa** nf bride. ~'**lizio** nm wedding

spo'sa|re vt marry; fig espouse. ~**rsi** vr get married; ⟨vino:⟩ go (**con** with). ~**to** a married. '**sposo** nm bridegroom; **sposi** pl [novelli] newlyweds

spossa'tezza nf exhaustion. **spos'sato** a exhausted, worn out

spo'sta|re vt move; (differire) post-

pone; (*cambiare*) change. **~rsi** *vr* move.
~to, -a *a* ill-adjusted ●*nmf* (*disadattato*) misfit

'spranga *nf* bar. **spran'gare** *vt* bar

'sprazzo *nm* (*di colore*) splash; (*di luce*) flash; *fig* glimmer

spre'care *vt* waste. **'spreco** *nm* waste

spre'g|evole *a* despicable. **~ia'tivo** *a* pejorative. **'spregio** *nm* contempt

spregiudi'cato *a* unscrupulous

'spremere *vt* squeeze. **~si** *vr* **~si le meningi** rack one's brains

spremia'grumi *nm* lemon squeezer

spre'muta *nf* juice. **~ d'arancia** fresh orange [juice]

sprez'zante *a* contemptuous

sprigio'nare *vt* emit. **~si** *vr* burst out

spriz'zare *vt/i* spurt; be bursting with ⟨*salute, gioia*⟩

sprofon'dar|e *vi* sink; (*crollare*) collapse. **~si** *vr* **~si in** sink into; *fig* be engrossed in

spro'nare *vt* spur on. **'sprone** *nm* spur; (*sartoria*) yoke

sproporzi|o'nato *a* disproportionate. **~'one** *nf* disproportion

**s
sproposi'tato *a* full of blunders; (*enorme*) huge. **spro'posito** *nm* blunder; (*eccesso*) excessive amount; **a sproposito** inopportunely

sprovve'duto *a* unprepared; **~ di** lacking in

sprov'visto *a* **~ di** out of; lacking in ⟨*fantasia, pazienza*⟩; **alla sprovvista** unexpectedly

spruz'za|re *vt* sprinkle; (*vaporizzare*) spray; (*inzaccherare*) spatter. **~'tore** *nm* spray; **'spruzzo** *nm* spray; (*di fango*) splash

spudo|ra'tezza *nf* shamelessness. **~'rato** *a* shameless

'spugna *nf* sponge; (*tessuto*) towelling. **spu'gnoso** *a* spongy

'spuma *nf* foam; (*schiuma*) froth; *Culin* mousse. **spu'mante** *nm* sparkling wine, spumante. **spumeggi'are** *vi* foam

spun'ta|re *vt* (*rompere la punta di*) break the point of; trim ⟨*capelli*⟩; **~rla** *fig* win ●*vi* ⟨*pianta:*⟩ sprout; ⟨*capelli:*⟩ begin to grow; (*sorgere*) rise; (*apparire*) appear. **~rsi** *vr* get blunt. **~ta** *nf* trim

spun'tino *nm* snack

'spunto *nm* cue; *fig* starting point; **dare ~ a** give rise to

spur'gar|e *vt* purge. **~si** *vr* *Med* expectorate

spu'tare *vt/i* spit; **~ sentenze** pass judgment. **'sputo** *nm* spit

'squadra *nf* (*gruppo*) team, squad; (*di polizia ecc*) squad; (*da disegno*) square. **squa'drare** *vt* square; (*guardare*) look up and down

squa'dr|iglia *nf*, **~one** *nm* squadron

squagli'ar|e *vt, ~si* *vr* melt; **~sela** (*fam: svignarsela*) steal out

squali'fi|ca *nf* disqualification. **~'care** *vt* disqualify

'squallido *a* squalid. **squal'lore** *nm* squalor

'squalo *nm* shark

'squama *nf* scale; (*di pelle*) flake

squa'm|are *vt* scale. **~arsi** *vr* ⟨*pelle:*⟩ flake off. **~'moso** *a* scaly; ⟨*pelle*⟩ flaky

squarcia'gola: a ~ *adv* at the top of one's voice

squarci'are *vt* rip. **'squarcio** *nm* rip; (*di ferita, in nave*) gash; (*di cielo*) patch

squar'tare *vt* quarter; dismember ⟨*animale*⟩

squattri'nato *a* penniless

squilib'ra|re *vt* unbalance. **~to, -a** *a* unbalanced ●*nmf* lunatic. **squi'librio** *nm* imbalance

squil'la|nte *a* shrill. **~re** *vi* ⟨*campana:*⟩ peal; ⟨*tromba:*⟩ blare; ⟨*telefono:*⟩ ring. **'squillo** *nm* blare; *Teleph* ring; (*ragazza*) call girl

squi'sito *a* exquisite

squit'tire *vi* ⟨*pappagallo, fig:*⟩ squawk; ⟨*topo:*⟩ squeak

sradi'care *vt* uproot; eradicate ⟨*vizio, male*⟩

sragio'nare *vi* rave

srego|la'tezza *nf* dissipation. **~'lato** *a* inordinate; (*dissoluto*) dissolute

s.r.l. *abbr* (**società a responsabilità limitata**) Ltd

sroto'lare *vt* uncoil

SS *abbr* (**strada statale**) national road

'stabile *a* stable; (*permanente*) lasting; ⟨*saldo*⟩ steady; **compagnia ~** *Theat* repertory company ●*nm* (*edificio*) building

stabili'mento *nm* factory; (*industriale*) plant; (*edificio*) establishment. **~ balneare** lido

stabi'li|re *vt* establish; (*decidere*) decide. **~rsi** *vr* settle. **~tà** *nf* stability

stabiliz'za|re *vt* stabilize. **~rsi** *vr* stabilize. **~'tore** *nm* stabilizer

stac'car|e *vt* detach; pronounce clearly ⟨*parole*⟩; (*separare*) separate; turn off ⟨*corrente*⟩; **~e gli occhi da** take one's eyes off ●*vi* (*fam: finire di lavorare*) knock off. **~si** *vr* come off;

~si da break away from ⟨*partito*, *famiglia*⟩

staccio'nata *nf* fence

'stacco *nm* gap

'stadio *nm* stadium

staf'fa *nf* stirrup

staf'fetta *nf* dispatch rider

stagio'nale *a* seasonal

stagio'na|re *vt* season ⟨*legno*⟩; mature ⟨*formaggio*⟩. **~to a** ⟨*legno*⟩ seasoned; ⟨*formaggio*⟩ matured

stagi'one *nf* season; **alta/bassa ~** high/low season

stagli'arsi *vr* stand out

sta'gna|nte *a* stagnant. **~re** *vt* ⟨*saldare*⟩ solder; ⟨*chiudere ermeticamente*⟩ seal ● *vi* ⟨*acqua:*⟩ stagnate. **'stagno** *a* ⟨*a tenuta d'acqua*⟩ watertight ● *nm* ⟨*acqua ferma*⟩ pond; ⟨*metallo*⟩ tin

sta'gnola *nf* tinfoil

stalag'mite *nf* stalagmite

stalat'tite *nf* stalactite

stall|a *nf* stable; ⟨*per buoi*⟩ cowshed. **~i'ere** *nm* groom

stal'lone *nm* stallion

sta'mani, stamat'tina *adv* this morning

stam'becco *nm* ibex

stam'berga *nf* hovel

'stampa *nf* *Typ* printing; ⟨*giornali*, *giornalisti*⟩ press; ⟨*riproduzione*⟩ print

stam'pa|nte *nf* printer. **~nte ad aghi** dot matrix printer. **~nte laser** laser printer. **~re** *vt* print. **~tello** *nm* block letters *pl*

stam'pella *nf* crutch

'stampo *nm* mould; **di vecchio ~** ⟨*persona*⟩ of the old school

sta'nare *vt* drive out

stan'ca|re *vt* tire; ⟨*annoiare*⟩ bore. **~si** *vr* get tired

stan'chezza *nf* tiredness. **'stanco** *a* tired; **stanco di** ⟨*stufo*⟩ fed up with. **stanco morto** dead tired, knackered *fam*

'standard *a* & *nm inv* standard. **~iz'zare** *vt* standardize

'stan|ga *nf* bar; ⟨*persona*⟩ beanpole. **~'gata** *nf fig* blow; ⟨*fam: nel calcio*⟩ big kick; **prendere una ~gata** ⟨*fam: agli esami, economica*⟩ come a cropper. **stan'ghetta** *nf* ⟨*di occhiali*⟩ leg

sta'notte *nf* tonight; ⟨*la notte scorsa*⟩ last night

'stante *prep* on account of; **a sé ~** separate

stan'tio *a* stale

stan'tuffo *nm* piston

'stanza *nf* room; ⟨*metrica*⟩ stanza

stanzi'are *vt* allocate

stap'pare *vt* uncork

'stare *vi* ⟨*rimanere*⟩ stay; ⟨*abitare*⟩ live; ⟨*con gerundio*⟩ be; **sto solo cinque minuti** I'll stay only five minutes; **sto in piazza Peyron** I live in Peyron Square; **sta dormendo** he's sleeping; **~ a** ⟨*attenersi*⟩ keep to; ⟨*spettare*⟩ be up to; **~ bene** ⟨*economicamente*⟩ be well off; ⟨*di salute*⟩ be well; ⟨*addirsi*⟩ suit; **~ dietro a** ⟨*seguire*⟩ follow; ⟨*sorvegliare*⟩ keep an eye on; ⟨*corteggiare*⟩ run after; **~ in piedi** stand; **~ per** be about to; **ben ti sta!** it serves you right!; **come stai/ sta?** how are you?; **lasciar ~** leave alone; **starci** ⟨*essere contenuto*⟩ go into; ⟨*essere d'accordo*⟩ agree; **il 3 nel 12 ci sta 4 volte** 3 into 12 goes 4; **non sa ~ agli scherzi** he can't take a joke; **~ su** ⟨*con la schiena*⟩ sit up straight; **~ sulle proprie** keep oneself to oneself. **starsene** *vr* ⟨*rimanere*⟩ stay

starnu'tire *vi* sneeze. **star'nuto** *nm* sneeze

sta'sera *adv* this evening, tonight

sta'tale *a* state *attrib* ● *nmf* state employee ● *nf* ⟨*strada*⟩ main road, trunk road

'statico *a* static

sta'tista *nm* statesman

sta'tistic|a *nf* statistics *sg*. **~o a** statistical

'stato *pp di* **essere, stare** ● *nm* state; ⟨*posizione sociale*⟩ position; *Jur* status. **~ d'animo** frame of mind. **~ civile** marital status. **S~ Maggiore** *Mil* General Staff. **Stati** *pl* **Uniti [d'America]** United States [of America]

'statua *nf* statue

statuni'tense *a* United States *attrib*, US *attrib* ● *nmf* citizen of the United States, US citizen

sta'tura *nf* height; **di alta ~** tall; **di bassa ~** short

sta'tuto *nm* statute

stazio'nario *a* stationary

stazi'one *nf* station; ⟨*città*⟩ resort. **~ balneare** seaside resort. **~ ferroviaria** railway station *Br*, train station. **~ di servizio** petrol station *Br*, service station. **~ termale** spa

'stecca *nf* stick; ⟨*di ombrello*⟩ rib; ⟨*da biliardo*⟩ cue; *Med* splint; ⟨*di sigarette*⟩ carton; ⟨*di reggiseno*⟩ stiffener

stec'cato *nm* fence

stec'chito *a* skinny; ⟨*rigido*⟩ stiff; ⟨*morto*⟩ stone cold dead

'**stella** *nf* star; **salire alle stelle** *(prezzi:)* rise skyhigh. ~ **alpina** edelweiss. ~ **cadente** shooting star. ~ **filante** streamer. ~ **di mare** starfish

stel'la|re *a* star *attrib*; *(grandezza)* stellar. ~**to** *a* starry

'**stelo** *nm* stem; **lampada** *nf* a ~ standard lamp

'**stemma** *nm* coat of arms

stempi'ato *a* bald at the temples

sten'dardo *nm* standard

'**stender|e** *vt* spread out; *(appendere)* hang out; *(distendere)* stretch [out]; *(scrivere)* write down. ~**si** *vr* stretch out

stendibianche'ria *nm* *inv*, **stendi'toio** *nm* clothes horse

stenodatti|logra'fia *nf* shorthand typing. ~'**lografo, -a** *nmf* shorthand typist

stenogra'f|are *vt* take down in shorthand. ~**ia** *nf* shorthand

sten'ta|re *vi* ~**re a** find it hard to. ~**to** *a* laboured. **'stento** *nm (fatica)* effort; **a stento** with difficulty; **stenti** *pl* hardships, privations

'**sterco** *nm* dung

stereo['fonico] *a* stereo[phonic]

stereoti'pato *a* stereotyped; *(sorriso)* insincere. **stere'otipo** *nm* stereotype

'**steril|e** *a* sterile; *(terreno)* barren. ~**ità** *nf* sterility. ~**iz'zare** *vt* sterilize. ~**izzazi'one** *nf* sterilization

ster'lina *nf* pound; **lira** ~ [pound] sterling

stermi'nare *vt* exterminate

stermi'nato *a* immense

ster'minio *nm* extermination

'**sterno** *nm* breastbone

ster'zare *vi* steer. '**sterzo** *nm* steering

'**steso** *pp di* **stendere**

'**stesso** *a* same; **io** ~ myself; **tu** ~ yourself; **me** ~ myself; **se** ~ himself; **in quel momento** ~ at that very moment; **dalla stessa regina** *(in persona)* by the Queen herself; **tuo fratello** ~ **dice che hai torto** even your brother says you're wrong; **coi miei stessi occhi** with my own eyes ●*pron* **lo** ~ the same one; *(la stessa cosa)* the same; **fa lo** ~ it's all the same; **ci vado lo** ~ I'll go just the same

ste'sura *nf* drawing up; *(documento)* draft

stick *nm* **colla a** ~ glue stick; **deodorante a** ~ stick deodorant

'**stigma** *nm* stigma. ~**te** *nfpl* stigmata

sti'lare *vt* draw up

'**stil|e** *nm* style. ~**e libero** *(nel nuoto)* freestyle, crawl. **sti'lista** *nmf* stylist. ~**iz'zato** *a* stylized

stil'lare *vi* ooze

stilo'grafic|a *nf* fountain pen. ~**o** *a* **penna** ~**a** fountain pen

'**stima** *nf* esteem; *(valutazione)* estimate. **sti'mare** *vt* esteem; *(valutare)* estimate; *(ritenere)* consider

stimo'la|nte *a* stimulating ●*nm* stimulant. ~**re** *vt* stimulate; *(incitare)* incite

'**stimolo** *nm* stimulus; *(fitta)* pang

'**stinco** *nm* shin

'**stinger|e** *vt/i* fade. ~**si** *vr* fade. '**stinto** *pp di* **stingere**

sti'par|e *vt* cram. ~**si** *vr* crowd together

stipendi'ato *a* salaried ●*nm* salaried worker. **sti'pendio** *nm* salary

'**stipite** *nm* doorpost

stipu'la|re *vt* stipulate. ~**zi'one** *nf* stipulation; *(accordo)* agreement

stira'mento *nm* sprain

sti'ra|re *vt* iron; *(distendere)* stretch. ~**rsi** *vr (distendersi)* stretch; pull *(muscolo)*. ~'**tura** *nf* ironing. '**stiro** *nm* **ferro da stiro** iron

'**stirpe** *nf* stock

stiti'chezza *nf* constipation. '**stitico** *a* constipated

'**stiva** *nf Naut* hold

sti'vale *nm* boot. **stivali** *pl* **di gomma** Wellington boots, Wellingtons

'**stizza** *nf* anger

stiz'zi|re *vt* irritate. ~**rsi** *vr* become irritated. ~**to** *a* irritated. **stiz'zoso** *a* peevish

stocca'fisso *nm* stockfish

stoc'cata *nf* stab; *(battuta pungente)* gibe

'**stoffa** *nf* material; *fig* stuff

'**stola** *nf* stole

'**stolto** *a* foolish

stoma'chevole *a* revolting

'**stomaco** *nm* stomach; **mal di** ~ stomach-ache

sto'na|re *vt/i* sing/play out of tune ●*vi (non intonarsi)* clash. ~**to** *a* out of tune; *(discordante)* clashing; *(confuso)* bewildered. ~'**tura** *nf* false note; *(discordanza)* clash

'**stoppia** *nf* stubble

stop'pino *nm* wick

stop'poso *a* tough

'**storcer|e** *vt*, ~**si** *vr* twist

stor'di|re *vt* stun; *(intontire)* daze. ~**rsi** *vr* dull one's senses. ~**to** *a* stunned; *(intontito)* dazed; *(sventato)* heedless

'**storia** *nf* history; (*racconto, bugia*) story; (*pretesto*) excuse; **senza storie!** no fuss!; **fare [delle] storie** make a fuss
'**storico,   -a** *a* historical; (*di importanza storica*) historic ● *nmf* historian
stori'one *nm* sturgeon
'**stormo** *nm* flock
'**storno** *nm* starling
storpi'a|re *vt* cripple; mangle (*parole*). ~'**tura** *nf* deformation. '**storpio, -a** *a* crippled ● *nmf* cripple
'**stort|a** *nf* (*distorsione*) sprain; **prendere una ~a alla caviglia** sprain one's ankle. ~**o** *pp di* **storcere** ● *a* crooked; (*ritorto*) twisted; (*gambe*) bandy; *fig* wrong
sto'viglie *nfpl* crockery *sg*
'**strabico** *a* cross-eyed; **essere** ~ be cross-eyed, have a squint.
strabili'ante *a* astonishing
stra'bismo *nm* squint
straboc'care *vi* overflow
stra'carico *a* overloaded
stracci'a|re *vt* tear; (*fam: vincere*) thrash. ~'**ate** *a* torn; (*persona*) in rags; (*prezzi*) slashed; **a un prezzo ~ato** dirt cheap. '**straccio** *a* torn ● *nm* rag; (*strofinaccio*) cloth ~'**one** *nm* tramp
stra'cotto *a* overdone; (*fam: innamorato*) head over heels ● *nm* stew
'**strada** *nf* road; (*di città*) street; (*fig: cammino*) way; **essere fuori ~** be on the wrong track; **fare ~** lead the way; **farsi ~** make one's way. ~ **maestra** main road. ~ **a senso unico** one-way street. ~ **senza uscita** blind alley. **stra'dale** *a* road *attrib*
strafalci'one *nm* blunder
stra'fare *vi* overdo it, overdo things
stra'foro: di ~ *adv* on the sly
strafot'ten|te *a* arrogant. ~**za** *nf* arrogance
'**strage** *nf* slaughter
stral'cio *nm* (*parte*) extract
stralu'na|re *vt* ~**re gli occhi** open one's eyes wide. ~**to** *a* (*occhi*) staring; (*persona*) distraught
stramaz'zare *vi* fall heavily
strambe'ria *nf* oddity. '**strambo** *a* strange
strampa'lato *a* odd
stra'nezza *nf* strangeness
strango'lare *vt* strangle
strani'ero, -a *a* foreign ● *nmf* foreigner
'**strano** *a* strange
straordi|naria'mente *adv* extraor-

dinarily. ~'**nario** *a* extraordinary; (*notevole*) remarkable; (*edizione*) special; **lavoro ~nario** overtime; **treno ~nario** special train
strapaz'zar|e *vt* ill-treat; scramble (*uova*). ~**si** *vr* tire oneself out. **stra'pazzo** *nm* strain; **da strapazzo** *fig* worthless
strapi'eno *a* overflowing
strapi'ombo *nm* projection; **a ~** sheer
strap'par|e *vt* tear; (*per distruggere*) tear up; pull out (*dente, capelli*); (*sradicare*) pull up; (*estorcere*) wring. ~**si** *vr* get torn; (*allontanarsi*) tear oneself away. '**strappo** *nm* tear; (*strattone*) jerk; (*fam: passaggio*) lift; **fare uno strappo alla regola** make an exception to the rule. ~ **muscolare** muscle strain
strapun'tino *nm* folding seat
strari'pare *vi* flood
strasci'care *vt* trail; shuffle (*piedi*); drawl (*parole*). '**strascico** *nm* train; *fig* after-effect
strass *nm inv* rhinestone
strata'gemma *nm* stratagem
stra'te|gia *nf* strategy. **stra'tegico** *a* strategic
'**strato** *nm* layer; (*di vernice ecc*) coat, layer; (*roccioso, sociale*) stratum. ~'**sfera** *nf* stratosphere. ~'**sferico** *a* stratospheric; *fig* sky-high
stravac'car|si *vr fam* slouch. ~**to** *a* *fam* slouching
strava'gan|te *a* extravagant; (*eccentrico*) eccentric. ~**za** *nf* extravagance; (*eccentricità*) eccentricity
stra'vecchio *a* ancient
strave'dere *vt* ~ **per** worship
stravizi'are *vi* indulge oneself. **stra'vizio** *nm* excess
stra'volg|ere *vt* twist; (*turbare*) upset. ~**i'mento** *nm* twisting. **stra'volto** *a* distraught; (*fam: stanco*) done in
strazi'a|nte *a* heartrending; (*dolore*) agonizing. ~**re** *vt* grate on (*orecchie*); break (*cuore*). '**strazio** *nm* agony; **essere uno strazio** be agony; **che strazio!** *fam* it's awful!
'**strega** *nf* witch. **stre'gare** *vt* bewitch. **stre'gone** *nm* wizard
stregua *nf* **alla ~ di** like
stre'ma|re *vt* exhaust. ~**to** *a* exhausted
'**stremo** *nm* **ridotto allo ~** at the end of one's tether
'**strenuo** *a* strenuous
strepi'tare *vi* make a din. '**strepito**

nm noise. **~'toso** *a* noisy; *fig* resounding

stres'sa|nte *a* ⟨lavoro, situazione⟩ stressful. **~to** *a* stressed [out]

'stretta *nf* grasp; ⟨dolore⟩ pang; **essere alle strette** be in dire straits; **mettere alle strette qcno** have sb's back up against the wall. **~ di mano** handshake

stret'tezza *nf* narrowness; **stret'tezze** *pl* ⟨difficoltà finanziarie⟩ financial difficulties

'stret|to *pp di* **stringere ●** *a* narrow; ⟨serrato⟩ tight; ⟨vicino⟩ close; ⟨dialetto⟩ broad; ⟨rigoroso⟩ strict; **lo ~to necessario** the bare minimum **●** *nm* Geog strait. **~'toia** *nf* bottleneck; ⟨fam: difficoltà⟩ tight spot

stri'a|to *a* striped. **~'tura** *nf* streak

stri'dente *a* strident

'stridere *vi* squeak; *fig* clash. **stri'dore** *nm* screech

'stridulo *a* shrill

strigli'a|re *vt* groom. **~ta** *nf* grooming; *fig* dressing down

stril'lare *vi/t* scream. **'strillo** *nm* scream

strimin'zito *a* skimpy; ⟨magro⟩ skinny

strimpel'lare *vt* strum

'strin|ga *nf* lace; Comput string. **~'gato** *a fig* terse

'string|e|re *vt* press; ⟨serrare⟩ squeeze; ⟨tenere stretto⟩ hold tight; take in ⟨abito⟩; ⟨comprimere⟩ be tight; ⟨restringere⟩ tighten; **~e la mano a** shake hands with **●** *vi* ⟨premere⟩ press. **~si** *vr* ⟨accostarsi⟩ draw close (**a** to); ⟨avvicinarsi⟩ squeeze up

'striscia *nf* strip; ⟨riga⟩ stripe. **strisce** *pl* ⟨pedonali⟩ zebra crossing *sg*

strisci'a|re *vi* crawl; ⟨sfiorare⟩ graze **●** *vt* drag ⟨piedi⟩. **~si** *vr* **~si a** rub against. **'striscio** *nm* graze; Med smear; **colpire di striscio** graze

strisci'one *nm* banner

strito'lare *vt* grind

striz'zare *vt* squeeze; ⟨torcere⟩ wring [out]; **~ l'occhio** wink

'strofa *nf* strophe

strofi'naccio *nm* cloth; ⟨per spolverare⟩ duster. **~ da cucina** tea towel

strofi'nare *vt* rub

strombaz'zare *vt* boast about **●** *vi* hoot

strombaz'zata *nf* ⟨di clacson⟩ hoot

stron'care *vt* cut off; ⟨reprimere⟩ crush; ⟨criticare⟩ tear to shreds

'stronzo *nm vulg* shit

stropicci'are *vt* rub; crumple ⟨vestito⟩

stroz'za|re *vt* strangle. **~'tura** *nf* strangling; ⟨di strada⟩ narrowing

strozzi'naggio *nm* loan-sharking

stroz'zino *nm pej* usurer; ⟨truffatore⟩ shark

strug'gente *a* all-consuming

'struggersi *vr liter* pine [away]

strumen'tale *a* instrumental

strumentaliz'zare *vt* make use of

strumentazi'one *nf* instrumentation

stru'mento *nm* instrument; ⟨arnese⟩ tool. **~ a corda** string instrument. **~ musicale** musical instrument

strusci'are *vt* rub

'strutto *nm* lard

strut'tura *nf* structure. **struttu'rale** *a* structural

struttu'rare *vt* structure

strutturazi'one *nf* structuring

'struzzo *nm* ostrich

stuc'care *vt* stucco

stuc'chevole *a* nauseating

'stucco *nm* stucco

stu'den|te, -'essa *nmf* student; ⟨di scuola⟩ schoolboy; schoolgirl. **~'tesco** *a* student; ⟨di scolaro⟩ school *attrib*

studi'ar|e *vt* study. **~si** *vr* **~si di** try to

'studi|o *nm* studying; ⟨stanza, ricerca⟩ study; ⟨di artista, TV ecc⟩ studio; ⟨di professionista⟩ office. **~'oso, -a** *a* studious **●** *nmf* scholar

'stufa *nf* stove. **~ elettrica** electric fire

stu'fa|re *vt* Culin stew; ⟨dare fastidio⟩ bore. **~rsi** *vr* get bored. **~to** *nm* stew

'stufo *a* bored; **essere ~ di** be fed up with

stu'oia *nf* mat

stupefa'cente *a* amazing **●** *nm* drug

stu'pendo *a* stupendous

stupi'd|aggine *nf* ⟨azione⟩ stupid thing; ⟨cosa da poco⟩ nothing. **~ata** *nf* stupid thing. **~ità** *nf* stupidity. **'stupido** *a* stupid

stu'pir|e *vt* astonish **●** *vi*, **~si** *vr* be astonished. **stu'pore** *nm* amazement

stu'pra|re *vt* rape. **~tore** *nm* rapist. **'stupro** *nm* rape

sturalavan'dini *nm inv* plunger

stu'rare *vt* uncork; unblock ⟨lavandino⟩

stuzzica'denti *nm inv* toothpick

stuzzi'care *vt* prod [at]; pick ⟨denti⟩; poke ⟨fuoco⟩; ⟨molestare⟩ tease; whet ⟨appetito⟩

stuzzi'chino *nm* Culin appetizer

su *prep* on; *(senza contatto)* over; *(riguardo a)* about; *(circa, intorno a)* about, around; **le chiavi sono sul tavolo** the keys are on the table; **il quadro è appeso sul camino** the picture is hanging over the fireplace; **un libro sull'antico Egitto** a book on *o* about Ancient Egypt; **costa sulle 50 000 lire** it costs about 50,000 lire; **decidere sul momento** decide at the time; **su commissione** on commission; **su due piedi** on the spot; **uno su dieci** one out of ten ● *adv (sopra)* up; *(al piano di sopra)* upstairs; *(addosso)* on; **ho su il cappotto** I've got my coat on; **in su** *(guardare)* up; **dalla vita in su** from the waist up; **su!** come on!

su'bacqueo *a* underwater

subaffit'tare *vt* sublet. **subaf'fitto** *nm* sublet

subal'terno *a & nm* subordinate

sub'buglio *nm* turmoil

sub'conscio *a & nm* subconscious

'subdola'mente *adv* deviously. **'subdolo** *a* devious, underhand

suben'trare *vi (circostanze:)* come up; **~ a** take the place of

su'bire *vt* undergo; *(patire)* suffer

subis'sare *vt fig* **~ di** overwhelm with

'subito *adv* at once; **~ dopo** straight after

su'blime *a* sublime

subodo'rare *vt* suspect

subordi'nato, -a *a & nmf* subordinate

subur'bano *a* suburban

suc'ceder|e *vi (accadere)* happen; **~e a** succeed; *(venire dopo)* follow; **~e al trono** succeed to the throne. **~si** *vr* happen one after the other

successi'one *nf* succession; **in ~** in succession

succes|siva'mente *adv* subsequently. **~'sivo** *a* successive

suc'ces|so *pp di* **succedere** ● *nm* success; *(esito)* outcome; *(disco ecc)* hit. **~'sone** *nm* huge success

succes'sore *nm* successor

succhi'are *vt* suck [up]

suc'cinto *a (conciso)* concise; *(abito)* scanty

'succo *nm* juice; *fig* essence; **~ di frutta** fruit juice. **suc'coso** *a* juicy

'succube *nm* **essere ~ di qcno** be totally dominated by sb

succu'lento *a* succulent

succur'sale *nf* branch [office]

sud *nm* south; **del ~** southern

su'da|re *vi* sweat, perspire; *(faticare)* sweat blood; **~re freddo** be in a cold sweat. **~ta** *nf anche fig* sweat. **~'ticcio** *a* sweaty. **~to** *a* sweaty; *(vittoria)* hard-won; *(pane)* hard-earned

sud'detto *a* above-mentioned

'suddito, -a *nmf* subject

suddi'vi|dere *vt* subdivide. **~si'one** *nf* subdivision

su'd-est *nm* southeast

'sudici|o *a* dirty, filthy. **~'ume** *nm* dirt, filth

sudorazi'one *nf* perspiring. **su'dore** *nm* sweat, perspiration; *fig* sweat

su'd-ovest *nm* southwest

suffici'en|te *a* sufficient; *(presuntuoso)* conceited ● *nm* bare essentials *pl*; *Sch* pass mark. **~za** *nf* sufficiency; *(presunzione)* conceit; *Sch* pass; **a ~za** enough

suf'fisso *nm* suffix

suf'fragio *nm (voto)* vote. **~ universale** universal suffrage

suggeri'mento *nm* suggestion

sugge'ri|re *vt* suggest; *Theat* prompt. **~tore, ~trice** *nmf Theat* prompter

suggestiona'bile *a* suggestible

suggestio'na|re *vt* influence. **~to** *a* influenced. **suggesti'one** *nf* influence

sugges'tivo *a* suggestive; *(musica ecc)* evocative

'sughero *nm* cork

'sugli = su + gli

'sugo *nm (di frutta)* juice; *(di carne)* gravy; *(salsa)* sauce; *(sostanza)* substance

'sui = su + i

sui'cid|a *a* suicidal ● *nmf* suicide. **suici'darsi** *vr* commit suicide. **~io** *nm* suicide

su'ino *a* **carne suina** pork ● *nm* swine

sul = su + il. 'sullo = su + lo. 'sulla = su + la. 'sulle = su + le

sul'ta|na *nf* sultana. **~'nina** *a* **uva ~nina** sultana. **~no** *nm* sultan

'sunto *nm* summary

'suo, -a *poss a* **il ~, i suoi** his; *(di cosa, animale)* its; *(forma di cortesia)* your; **la sua, le sue** her; *(di cosa, animale)* its; *(forma di cortesia)* your; **questa macchina è sua** this car is his/hers; **~ padre** his/her/your father; **un ~ amico** a friend of his/hers/yours ● *poss pron* **il ~, i suoi** his; *(di cosa, animale)* its; *(forma di cortesia)* yours; **la sua, le sue** hers; *(di cosa animale)* its; *(forma di cortesia)* yours; **i suoi** his/her folk

su'ocera *nf* mother-in-law

su'ocero nm father-in-law
su'ola nf sole
su'olo nm ground; (terreno) soil
suo'na|re vt/i Mus play; ring ⟨campanello⟩; sound ⟨allarme, clacson⟩; ⟨orologio:⟩ strike. ~'**tore**, ~'**trice** nmf player. **suone'ria** nf alarm. **su'ono** nm sound
su'ora nf nun; **Suor Maria** Sister Maria
superal'colico nm spirit ● a **bevande superalcoliche** spirits
supera'mento nm (di timidezza) overcoming; (di esame) success (**di** in)
supe'rare vt surpass; (eccedere) exceed; (vincere) overcome; overtake, pass Am ⟨veicolo⟩; pass ⟨esame⟩
su'perb|ia nf haughtiness. ~**o** a haughty; (magnifico) superb
superdo'tato a highly gifted
superfici'al|e a superficial ● nmf superficial person. ~**ità** nf superficiality. **super'ficie** nf surface; (area) area
su'perfluo a superfluous
superi'or|e a superior; (di grado) senior; (più elevato) higher; (sovrastante) upper; (al di sopra) above ● nmf superior. ~**ità** nf superiority
superla'tivo a & nm superlative
supermer'cato nm supermarket
super'sonico a supersonic
su'perstite a surviving ● nmf survivor
superstizi'o|ne nf superstition. ~**so** a superstitious
super'strada nf toll-free motorway
supervi'si|one nf supervision. ~'**sore** nm supervisor
su'pino a supine
suppel'lettili nfpl furnishings
suppergiù adv about
supplemen'tare a additional, supplementary
supple'mento nm supplement; ~ **rapido** express train supplement
sup'plen|te a temporary ● nmf Sch supply teacher. ~**za** nf temporary post
'suppli|ca nf plea; (domanda) petition. ~'**care** vt beg. ~'**chevole** a imploring
sup'plire vt replace ● vi ~ **a** (compensare) make up for
sup'plizio nm torture
sup'porre vt suppose
sup'porto nm support
supposizi'one nf supposition
sup'posta nf suppository
sup'posto pp di **supporre**
suprema'zia nf supremacy. **su'premo** a supreme

sur'fare vi ~ **in Internet** surf the Net
surge'la|re vt deep-freeze. ~**ti** nmpl frozen food sg. ~**to** a frozen
surrea'lis|mo nm surrealism. ~**ta** nmf surrealist
surriscal'dare vt overheat
surro'gato nm substitute
suscet'tibil|e a touchy. ~**ità** nf touchiness
susci'tare vt stir up; arouse ⟨ammirazione ecc⟩
su'sin|a nf plum. ~**o** nm plumtree
su'spense nf suspense
sussegu'ente a subsequent. ~'**irsi** vr follow one after the other
sussidi'ar|e vt subsidize. ~**io** a subsidiary. **sus'sidio** nm subsidy; (aiuto) aid. **sussidio di disoccupazione** unemployment benefit
sussi'ego nm haughtiness
sussi'stenza nf subsistence. **sus'sistere** vi subsist; (essere valido) hold good
sussul'tare vi start. **sus'sulto** nm start
sussur'rare vt whisper. **sus'surro** nm whisper
su'tu|ra nf suture. ~'**rare** vt suture
sva'gar|e vt amuse. ~**si** vr amuse oneself. '**svago** nm relaxation; (divertimento) amusement
svaligi'are vt rob; burgle ⟨casa⟩
svalu'ta|re vt devalue; fig underestimate. ~**rsi** vr lose value. ~**zi'one** nf devaluation
svam'pito a absent-minded
sva'nire vi vanish
svantaggi'ato a at a disadvantage; ⟨bambino, paese⟩ disadvantaged. **svan'taggio** nm disadvantage; **essere in svantaggio** Sport be losing; **in svantaggio di tre punti** three points down. ~'**oso** a disadvantageous
svapo'rare vi evaporate
svari'ato a varied
sva'sato a flared
'**svastica** nf swastika
sve'dese a & nm (lingua) Swedish ● nmf Swede
'**sveglia** nf (orologio) alarm [clock]; ~! get up!; **mettere la** ~ set the alarm [clock]
svegli'ar|e vt wake up; fig awaken. ~**si** vr wake up. '**sveglio** a awake; (di mente) quick-witted
sve'lare vt reveal
svel'tezza nf speed; fig quick-wittedness

svel'tir|e *vt* quicken. **~si** *vr (persona:)* liven up. **'svelto** *a* quick; *(slanciato)* svelte; **alla svelta** quickly

'svend|ere *vt* undersell. **~ita** *nf* [clearance] sale

sveni'mento *nm* fainting fit. **sve'nire** *vi* faint

sven'ta|re *vt* foil. **~to** *a* thoughtless ● *nmf* thoughtless person

'sventola *nf* slap; **orecchie** *nfpl* **a ~** protruding ears

svento'lare *vt/i* wave

sven'trare *vt* disembowel; *fig* demolish *(edificio)*

sven'tura *nf* misfortune. **sventu'rato** *a* unfortunate

sve'nuto *pp di* **svenire**

svergo'gnato *a* shameless

sver'nare *vi* winter

sve'stir|e *vt* undress. **~si** *vr* undress, get undressed

'Svezia *nf* Sweden

svezza'mento *nm* weaning. **svez'zare** *vt* wean

svi'ar|e *vt* divert; *(corrompere)* lead astray. **~si** *vr fig* go astray

svico'lare *vi* turn down a side street; *(fig: dalla questione ecc)* evade the issue; *(fig: da una persona)* dodge out of the way

svi'gnarsela *vr* slip away

svi'lire *vt* debase

svilup'par|e *vt*, **~si** *vr* develop. **svi'luppo** *nm* development; **paese in via di sviluppo** developing country

svinco'lar|e *vt* release; clear *(merce)*. **~si** *vr* free oneself. **'svincolo** *nm* clearance; *(di autostrada)* exit

svisce'ra|re *vt* gut; *fig* dissect. **~to** *a (amore)* passionate; *(ossequioso)* obsequious

'svista *nf* oversight

svi'ta|re *vt* unscrew. **~to** *a (fam: matto)* cracked, nutty

'Svizzer|a *nf* Switzerland. **s~o, -a** *a & nmf* Swiss

svogli|a'tezza *nf* half-heartedness. **~'ato** *a* lazy

svolaz'za|nte *a (capelli)* wind-swept. **~re** *vi* flutter

'svolger|e *vt* unwind; unwrap *(pacco)*; *(risolvere)* solve; *(portare a termine)* carry out; *(sviluppare)* develop. **~si** *vr (accadere)* take place. **svolgi'mento** *nm* course; *(sviluppo)* development

'svolta *nf* turning; *fig* turning-point. **svol'tare** *vi* turn

'svolto *pp di* **svolgere**

svuo'tare *vt* empty [out]

tabac'c|aio, -a *nmf* tobacconist. **~he'ria** *nf* tobacconist's *(which also sells stamps, postcards etc)*. **ta'bacco** *nm* tobacco

ta'bel|la *nf* table; *(lista)* list. **~la dei prezzi** price list. **~'lina** *nf Math* multiplication table. **~'lone** *nm* wall chart. **~lone del canestro** backboard

taber'nacolo *nm* tabernacle

tabù *a & nm inv* taboo

tabu'lato *nm Comput* [data] printout

'tacca *nf* notch; **di mezza ~** *(attore, giornalista)* second-rate

tac'cagno *a fam* stingy

tac'cheggio *nm* shoplifting

tac'chetto *nm Sport* stud

tac'chino *nm* turkey

tacci'are *vt* **~ qcno di qcsa** accuse sb of sth

'tacco *nm* heel; **alzare i tacchi** take to one's heels; **scarpe senza ~** flat shoes. **tacchi** *pl* **a spillo** stiletto heels

tac'cuino *nm* notebook

ta'cere *vi* be silent ● *vt* say nothing about; **mettere a ~ qcsa** *(scandalo)* hush sth up; **mettere a ~ qcno** silence sb

ta'chimetro *nm* speedometer

'tacito *a* silent; *(inespresso)* tacit. **taci'turno** *a* taciturn

ta'fano *nm* horsefly

taffe'ruglio *nm* scuffle

'taglia *nf (riscatto)* ransom; *(ricompensa)* reward; *(statura)* height; *(misura)* size. **~ unica** one size

taglia'carte *nm inv* paperknife

taglia'erba *nm inv* lawn-mower

tagliafu'oco *a inv* **porta ~** fire door; **striscia ~** fire break

tagli'ando *nm* coupon; **fare il ~** ≈ put one's car in for its MOT

tagli'ar|e *vt* cut; (*attraversare*) cut across; (*interrompere*) cut off; (*togliere*) cut out; carve ‹*carne*›; mow ‹*erba*›; **farsi ~ e i capelli** have a haircut ●*vi* cut. **~si** *vr* cut oneself; **~si i capelli** have a haircut

taglia'telle *nfpl* tagliatelle *sg*, thin, flat strips of egg pasta

taglieggi'are *vt* extort money from

tagli'e|nte *a* sharp ●*nm* cutting edge. **~re** *nm* chopping board

'taglio *nm* cut; (*il tagliare*) cutting; (*di stoffa*) length; (*parte tagliente*) edge; **a doppio ~** double-edged. **~ cesareo** Caesarean section

tagli'ola *nf* trap

tagli'one *nm* **legge del ~** an eye for an eye and a tooth for a tooth

tagliuz'zare *vt* cut into small pieces

tail'leur *nm inv* [lady's] suit

talassotera'pia *nf* thalassotherapy

'talco *nm* talcum powder

'tale *a* such a; (*con nomi plurali*) such; **c'è un ~ disordine** there is such a mess; **non accetto tali scuse** I won't accept such excuses; **il rumore era ~ che non si sentiva nulla** there was so much noise you couldn't hear yourself think; **il ~ giorno** on such and such a day; **quel tal signore** that gentleman; **~ quale** just like ●*pron* **un ~** someone; **quel ~** that man; **il tal dei tali** such and such a person

ta'lento *nm* talent

tali'smano *nm* talisman

tallo'nare *vt* be hot on the heels of

tallon'cino *nm* coupon

tal'lone *nm* heel

tal'mente *adv* so

ta'lora *adv* = **talvolta**

'talpa *nf* mole

tal'volta *adv* sometimes

tamburel'lare *vi* (*con le dita*) drum; ‹*pioggia:*› beat, drum. **tambu'rello** *nm* tambourine. **tambu'rino** *nm* drummer.

tam'buro *nm* drum

Ta'migi *nm* Thames

tampona'mento *nm* Auto collision; (*di ferita*) dressing; (*di falla*) plugging. **~ a catena** pile-up. **tampo'nare** *vt* (*urtare*) crash into; (*otturare*) plug.

tam'pone *nm* swab; (*per timbri*) pad;

(*per mestruazioni*) tampon; (*per treni, Comput*) buffer

'tana *nf* den

'tanfo *nm* stench

'tanga *nm inv* tanga

tan'gen|te *a* tangent ●*nf* tangent; (*somma*) bribe. **~'topoli** *nf* widespread corruption in Italy in the early 90s. **~zi'ale** *nf* orbital road

tan'gibile *a* tangible

'tango *nm* tango

tan'tino: un ~ *adv* a little [bit]

'tanto *a* [so] much; (*con nomi plurali*) [so] many, [such] a lot of; **~ tempo** [such] a long time; **non ha tanta pazienza** he doesn't have much patience; **~ tempo quanto ti serve** as much time as you need; **non è ~ intelligente quanto suo padre** he's not as intelligent as his father; **tanti amici quanti parenti** as many friends as relatives ●*pron* much; (*plurale*) many; (*tanto tempo*) a long time; **è un uomo come tanti** he's just an ordinary man; **tanti**(*molte persone*) many people; **non ci vuole così ~** it doesn't take that long; **~ quanto** as much as; **tanti quanti** as many as ●*conj* (*comunque*) anyway, in any case ●*adv* (*così*) so; (*con verbi*) so much; **~ debole** so weak; **è ~ ingenuo da crederle** he's naive enough to believe her; **di ~ in ~** every now and then; **~ l'uno come l'altro** both; **~ quanto**as much as; **tre volte ~** three times as much; **una volta ~**once in a while; **~ meglio così!**so much the better!; **tant'è** so much so; **~ per cambiare**for a change

'tappa *nf* stop; (*parte di viaggio*) stage

tappa'buchi *nm inv* stopgap

tap'par|e *vt* plug; cork ‹*bottiglia*›; **~e la bocca a qcno** shut sb up. **~si**vr **~si gli occhi** cover one's eyes; **~si il naso** hold one's nose; **~si le orecchie** put one's fingers in one's ears

tappa'rella *nf fam* roller blind

tappe'tino *nm* mat; *Comput* mouse mat. **~ antiscivolo**safety bathmat

tap'peto *nm* carpet; (*piccolo*) rug; **andare al ~** (*pugilato:*) hit the canvas; **mandare qcno al ~**knock sb down

tappez'z|are *vt* paper ‹*pareti*›; (*rivestire*) cover. **~e'ria** *nf* tapestry; (*di carta*) wallpaper; (*arte*) upholstery. **~'ere** *nm* upholsterer; (*imbianchino*) decorator

'tappo *nm* plug; (*di sughero*) cork; (*di*

metallo, per penna) top; (*fam: persona piccola*) dwarf. **~ di sughero** cork
'tara *nf* (*difetto*) flaw; (*ereditaria*) hereditary defect; (*peso*) tare
ta'rantola *nf* tarantula
ta'ra|re *vt* calibrate (*strumento*). **~to** *a Comm* discounted; *Techn* calibrated; *Med* with a hereditary defect; *fam* crazy
tarchi'ato *a* stocky
tar'dare *vi* be late ● *vt* delay
'tard|i *adv* late; **al più ~i** at the latest; **più ~i** later [on]; **sul ~i** late in the day; **far ~i** (*essere in ritardo*) be late; (*con gli amici*) stay up late; **a più ~i** see you later. **tar'divo** *a* late; (*bambino*) retarded. **~o** *a* slow; (*tempo*) late
'targ|a *nf* plate; *Auto* numberplate. **~a di circolazione** numberplate. **tar'gato** *a* **un'auto targata** ... a car with the registration number.... **~'hetta** *nf* (*su porta*) nameplate; (*sulla valigia*) name tag
ta'rif|fa *nf* rate, tariff. **~'fario** *nm* price list
tar'larsi *vr* get wormeaten. **'tarlo** *nm* woodworm
'tarma *nf* moth. **tar'marsi** *vr* get motheaten
ta'rocco *nm* tarot; **ta'rocchi** *pl* tarot
tartagli'are *vi* stutter
'tartaro *a & nm* tartar
tarta'ruga *nf* tortoise; (*di mare*) turtle; (*per pettine ecc*) tortoiseshell
tartas'sare *vt* (*angariare*) harass
tar'tina *nf* canapé
tar'tufo *nm* truffle
'tasca *nf* pocket; (*in borsa*) compartment; **da ~** pocket *attrib*; **avere le tasche piene di qcsa** *fam* have had a bellyful of sth. **~ da pasticciere** icing bag
ta'scabile *a* pocket *attrib* ● *nm* paperback
tasca'pane *nm inv* haversack
ta'schino *nm* breast pocket
'tassa *nf* tax; (*discrizione ecc*) fee; (*doganale*) duty. **~ di circolazione** road tax. **~ d'iscrizione** registration fee
tas'sametro *nm* taximeter
tas'sare *vt* tax
tassa|tiva'mente *adv* without question. **~'tivo** *a* peremptory
tassazi'one *nf* taxation
tas'sello *nm* wedge; (*di stoffa*) gusset
tassi *nm inv* taxi. **tas'sista** *nmf* taxi driver
'tasso¹ *nm* *Bot* yew; (*animale*) badger

'tasso² *nm* *Comm* rate. **~ di cambio** exchange rate. **~ di interesse** interest rate
ta'stare *vt* feel; (*sondare*) sound; **~ il terreno** *fig* test the water *or* ground, feel one's way
tasti'e|ra *nf* keyboard. **~'rista** *nmf* keyboarder
'tasto *nm* key; (*tatto*) touch. **~ delicato** *fig* touchy subject. **~ funzione** *Comput* function key. **~ tabulatore** tab key
ta'stoni: **a ~** *adv* gropingly
'tattica *nf* tactics *pl*
'tattico *a* tactical
'tatto *nm* (*senso*) touch; (*accortezza*) tact; **aver ~** be tactful
tatu'a|ggio *nm* tattoo. **~re** *vt* tattoo
'tavola *nf* table; (*illustrazione*) plate; (*asse*) plank. **~ calda** snackbar
tavo'lato *nm* boarding; (*pavimento*) wood floor
tavo'letta *nf* bar; (*medicinale*) tablet; **andare a ~** *Auto* drive flat out
tavo'lino *nm* small table
'tavolo *nm* table. **~ operatorio** *Med* operating table
tavo'lozza *nf* palette
'tazza *nf* cup; (*del water*) bowl. **~ da caffè/tè** coffee-cup/teacup
taz'zina *nf* **~ da caffè** espresso coffee cup
T.C.I. *abbr* (**Touring Club Italiano**) Italian Touring Club
te *pers pron* you; **te l'ho dato** I gave it to you
tè *nm inv* tea
tea'trale *a* theatrical
te'atro *nm* theatre. **~ all'aperto** open-air theatre. **~ di posa** *Cinema* set. **~ tenda** marquee for theatre performances
'tecnico, -a *a* technical ● *nmf* technician ● *nf* technique
tec'nigrafo *nm* drawing board
tecno|lo'gia *nf* technology. **~'logico** *a* technological
te'desco, -a *a & nmf* German
'tedi|o *nm* tedium. **~'oso** *a* tedious
'teglia *nf* baking tin
'tegola *nf* tile; *fig* blow
tei'era *nf* teapot
tek *nm* teak
'tela *nf* cloth; (*per quadri, vele*) canvas; *Theat* curtain. **~ cerata** oilcloth. **~ di lino** linen
te'laio *nm* (*di bicicletta, finestra*) frame; *Auto* chassis; (*per tessere*) loom

tele'camera *nf* television camera

teleco|man'dato *a* remote-control-led, remote control *attrib*.~'**mando** *nm* remote control

Telecom Italia *nf* Italian State telephone company

telecomunicazi'oni *nfpl* telecommunications

tele'cro|naca *nf* [television] commentary. ~**naca diretta** live [television] coverage. ~**naca registrata** recording. ~'**nista** *nmf* television commentator

tele'ferica *nf* cableway

telefo'na|re *vt/i* [tele]phone, ring. ~**ta** *nf* call. ~**ta interurbana** long-distance call

telefonica'mente *adv* by [tele]phone

tele'fonico *a* [tele]phone *attrib*.

telefo'nino *nm* mobile [phone]

telefo'nista *nmf* operator

te'lefono *nm* [tele]phone. ~ **senza filo** cordless [phone]. ~ **a gettoni** pay phone, coin-box. ~ **interno** internal telephone. ~ **a schede** cardphone

telegior'nale *nm* television news *sg*

telegra'fare *vt* telegraph. **tele'grafico** *a* telegraphic; *(risposta)* monosyllabic; **sii telegrafico** keep it brief

tele'gramma *nm* telegram

tele'matica *nf* data communications, telematics

teleno'vela *nf* soap opera

teleobiet'tivo *nm* telephoto lens

telepa'tia *nf* telepathy

telero'manzo *nm* television serial

tele'schermo *nm* television screen

tele'scopio *nm* telescope

teleselezi'one *nf* subscriber trunk dialling, STD; **chiamare in ~** dial direct

telespetta'tore, -'trice *nmf* viewer

tele'text® *nm* Teletext®

tele'video *nm* videophone

televisi'one *nf* television; **guardare la ~** watch television

televi'sivo *a* television *attrib*; **operatore ~** television cameraman; **apparecchio ~** television set

televi'sore *nm* television [set]

'tema *nm* theme; *Sch* essay. **te'matica** *nf* main theme

teme'rario *a* reckless

te'mere *vt* be afraid of, fear ● *vi* be afraid, fear

tem'paccio *nm* filthy weather

temperama'tite *nm inv* pencil-sharpener

tempera'mento *nm* temperament

tempe'ra|re *vt* temper; sharpen *(matita)*. ~**to** *a* temperate. ~**tura** *nf* temperature. ~**tura ambiente** room temperature

tempe'rino *nm* penknife

tem'pesta *nf* storm. ~ **di neve** snowstorm. ~ **di sabbia** sandstorm

tempe|stiva'mente *adv* quickly. ~'**stivo** *a* timely. ~'**stoso** *a* stormy

'tempia *nf Anat* temple

'tempio *nm Relig* temple

tem'pismo *nm* timing

'tempo *nm* time; *(atmosferico)* weather; *Mus* tempo; *Gram* tense; *(di film)* part; *(di partita)* half; **a suo ~** in due course; **~ fa** some time ago; **un ~** once; **ha fatto il suo ~** it's superannuated. **~ reale** real time. **~ supplementare** *Sport* extra time, overtime *Am*. ~'**rale** *a* temporal ● *nm* [thunder]storm. ~**ranea'mente** *adv* temporarily. ~'**raneo** *a* temporary. ~**reggi'are** *vi* play for time

tem'prare *vt* temper

te'nac|e *a* tenacious. ~**ia** *nf* tenacity

te'naglia *nf* pincers *pl*

'tenda *nf* curtain; *(per campeggio)* tent; *(tendone)* awning. **~ a ossigeno** oxygen tent

ten'denz|a *nf* tendency. ~**ial'mente** *adv* by nature. ~**i'oso** *a* tendentious

'tendere *vt (allargare)* stretch [out]; *(tirare)* tighten; *(porgere)* hold out; *fig* lay *(trappola)* ● *vi* **~** a aim at; *(essere portato a)* tend to

'tendine *nm* tendon

ten'do|ne *nm* awning; *(di circo)* tent. ~**poli** *nf inv* tent city

'tenebre *nfpl* darkness. **tene'broso** *a* gloomy

te'nente *nm* lieutenant

tenera'mente *adv* tenderly

te'ner|e *vt* hold; *(mantenere)* keep; *(gestire)* run; *(prendere)* take; *(seguire)* follow; *(considerare)* consider ● *vi* hold; ~**ci a**, ~**e a** be keen on; ~**e per** support *(squadra)*. ~**si** *vr* hold on **(a** to); *(in una condizione)* keep oneself; *(seguire)* stick to; ~**si indietro** stand back

te'ne|rezza *nf* tenderness. '**tenero** *a* tender

'tenia *nf* tapeworm

'tennis *nm* tennis. **~ da tavolo** table tennis. **ten'nista** *nmf* tennis player

te'nore *nm* standard; *Mus* tenor; **a ~ di**

legge by law. **~ di vita** standard of living

tensi'one nf tension; *Electr* voltage; **alta ~** high voltage

ten'tacolo nm tentacle

ten'ta|re vt attempt; (*sperimentare*) try; (*indurre in tentazione*) tempt. **~'tivo** nm attempt. **~zi'one** nf temptation

tenten|na'mento nm wavering. **~'nare** vi waver

'**tenue** a fine; (*debole*) weak; (*esiguo*) small; (*leggero*) slight

te'nuta nf (*capacità*) capacity; (*Sport: resistenza*) stamina; (*possedimento*) estate; (*divisa*) uniform; (*abbigliamento*) clothes pl; **a ~ d'aria** airtight. **~ di strada** road holding

teolo'gia nf theology. **teo'logico** a theological. **te'ologo** nm theologian

teo'rema nm theorem

teo'ria nf theory

teorica'mente adv theoretically. **te'orico** a theoretical

te'pore nm warmth

'**teppa** nf mob. **tep'pismo** nm hooliganism. **tep'pista** nm hooligan

tera'peutico a therapeutic. **tera'pia** nf therapy

tergicri'stallo nm windscreen wiper, windshield wiper *Am*

tergilu'notto nm rear windscreen wiper

tergiver'sare vi hesitate

'**tergo** nm **a ~** behind; **segue a ~** please turn over, PTO

ter'male a thermal; **stazione ~** spa. '**terme** nfpl thermal baths

'**termico** a thermal

termi'na|le a & nm terminal; **malato ~le** terminally ill person. **~re** vt/i finish, end. '**termine** nm (*limite*) limit; (*fine*) end; (*condizione, espressione*) term

terminolo'gia nf terminology

termite nf termite

termoco'perta nf electric blanket

ter'mometro nm thermometer

'**termos** nm inv thermos®

termosi'fone nm radiator; (*sistema*) central heating

ter'mostato nm thermostat

'**terra** nf earth; (*regione*) land; (*terreno*) ground; (*argilla*) clay; (*cosmetico*) dark face powder (*which gives the impression of a tan*); **a ~** (*sulla costa*) ashore; (*installazioni*) onshore; **per ~** on the ground; **sotto ~** underground. **~'cot-**

ta nf terracotta; **vasellame di ~cotta** earthenware. **~'ferma** nf dry land. **~pi'eno** nm embankment

ter'razz|a nf, **~o** nm balcony

terremo'tato, -a a (*zona*) affected by an earthquake ● nmf earthquake victim. **terre'moto** nm earthquake

ter'reno a earthly ● nm ground; (*suolo*) soil; (*proprietà terriera*) land; **perdere/guadagnare ~** lose/gain ground. **~ di gioco** playing field

ter'restre a terrestrial; **esercito ~** land forces pl

ter'ribi|le a terrible. **~'mente** adv terribly

ter'riccio nm potting compost

terrifi'cante a terrifying

territori'ale a territorial. **terri'torio** nm territory

ter'rore nm terror

terro'ris|mo nm terrorism. **~ta** nmf terrorist

terroriz'zare vt terrorize

'**terso** a clear

ter'zetto nm trio

terzi'ario a tertiary

'**terzo** a third; **di terz'ordine** (*locale, servizio*) third-rate; **fare il ~ grado a qn** give sb the third degree; **la terza età** the third age ● nm third; **terzi** pl Jur third party sg. **ter'zultimo, -a** a & nmf third from last

'**tesa** nf brim

'**teschio** nm skull

'**tesi** nf inv thesis

'**teso** pp di **tendere** ● a taut; fig tense

tesore'ria nf treasury. **~i'ere** nm treasurer

te'soro nm treasure; (*tesoreria*) treasury

'**tessera** nf card; (*abbonamento all'autobus*) season ticket

tessere vt weave; hatch (*complotto*)

tesse'rino nm travel card

'**tessile** a textile. **tessili** nmpl textiles; (*operai*) textile workers

tessi'tore, -'trice nmf weaver. **~'tura** nf weaving

tes'suto nm fabric; *Anat* tissue

'**testa** nf head; (*cervello*) brain; **essere in ~ a** be ahead of; **in ~** *Sport* in the lead; **~ o croce?** heads or tails?; **fare ~ o croce** have a toss-up to decide

'**testa-'coda** nm inv **fare un ~** spin right round

testa'mento nm will; **T~** *Relig* Testament

testar'daggine *nf* stubbornness. **te'stardo** *a* stubborn

te'stata *nf* head; (*intestazione*) heading; (*colpo*) butt

'teste *nmf* witness

te'sticolo *nm* testicle

testi'mone *nmf* witness. ~ **oculare** eye witness

testi'monial *nmf inv* celebrity who promotes a brand of cosmetics

testimoni|'anza *nf* testimony; **falsa** ~**anza** *Jur* perjury. ~'**are** *vt* testify to ● *vi* testify, give evidence

'testo *nm* text; **far** ~ be an authority

te'stone, -a *nmf* blockhead

testu'ale *a* textual

'tetano *nm* tetanus

'tetro *a* gloomy

tetta'rella *nf* teat

'tetto *nm* roof. ~ **apribile** (*di auto*) sunshine roof. **tet'toia** *nf* roofing. **tet'tuccio** *nm* **tettuccio apribile** sunroof

'Tevere *nm* Tiber

ti *pers pron* you; (*riflessivo*) yourself; **ti ha dato un libro** he gave you a book; **lavati le mani** wash your hands; **eccoti!** here you are!; **sbrigati!** hurry up!

ti'ara *nf* tiara

tic *nm inv* tic

ticchet't|are *vi* tick. ~**io** *nm* ticking

'ticchio *nm* tic; (*ghiribizzo*) whim

'ticket *nm inv* (*per farmaco, esame*) amount paid by National Health patients

tiepida'mente *adv* halfheartedly. **ti'epido** *a anche fig* lukewarm

ti'fare *vi* ~ **per** shout for. **'tifo** *nm Med* typhus; **fare il tifo per** *fig* be a fan of

tifoi'dea *nf* typhoid

ti'fone *nm* typhoon

ti'foso, -a *nmf* fan

'tiglio *nm* lime

ti'grato *a* **gatto** ~ tabby [cat]

'tigre *nf* tiger

'tilde *nmf* tilde

tim'ballo *nm Culin* pie

tim'brare *vt* stamp; ~ **il cartellino** clock in/out

'timbro *nm* stamp; (*di voce*) tone

timida'mente *adv* timidly, shyly. **timi'dezza** *nf* timidity, shyness. **'timido** *a* timid, shy

'timo *nm* thyme

ti'mon|e *nm* rudder. ~**i'ere** *nm* helmsman

ti'more *nm* fear; (*soggezione*) awe. **timo'roso** *a* timorous

'timpano *nm* eardrum; *Mus* kettledrum

ti'nello *nm* dining room

'tinger|e *vt* dye; (*macchiare*) stain. ~**si** *vi* (*viso, cielo:*) be tinged (**di** with); ~**si i capelli** have one's hair dyed; (*da solo*) dye one's hair

'tino *nm*, **ti'nozza** *nf* tub

'tint|a *nf* dye; (*colore*) colour; **in** ~**a unita** plain. ~**a'rella** *nf fam* suntan

tintin'nare *vi* tinkle

'tinto *pp di* **tingere**. ~'**ria** *nf* (*negozio*) cleaner's. **tin'tura** *nf* dyeing; (*colorante*) dye.

'tipico *a* typical

'tipo *nm* type; (*fam: individuo*) chap, guy

tipogra'fia *nf* printery; (*arte*) typography. **tipo'grafico** *a* typographic[al]. **ti'pografo** *nm* printer

tip tap *nm* tap dancing

ti'raggio *nm* draught

tiramisù *nm inv* dessert made of coffee-soaked sponge, eggs, Marsala, cream and cocoa powder

tiran|neggi'are *vt* tyrannize. ~'**nia** *nf* tyranny. **ti'ranno, -a** *a* tyrannical ● *nmf* tyrant

tirapi'edi *nm inv pej* hanger-on

ti'rar|e *vt* pull; (*gettare*) throw; kick (*palla*); (*sparare*) fire; (*tracciare*) draw; (*stampare*) print ● *vi* pull; (*vento:*) blow; (*abito:*) be tight; (*sparare*) fire; ~**e avanti** get by; ~**e su** (*crescere*) bring up; (*da terra*) pick up; **tirar su col naso** sniffle. ~**si** *vr* ~**si indietro** *fig* back out, pull out

tiras'segno *nm* target shooting; (*alla fiera*) rifle range

ti'rata *nf* (*strattone*) pull, tug; **in una** ~ in one go

tira'tore *nm* shot. ~ **scelto** marksman

tira'tura *nf* printing; (*di giornali*) circulation; (*di libri*) [print] run

tirchie'ria *nf* meanness. **'tirchio** *a* mean

tiri'tera *nf* spiel

'tiro *nm* (*traino*) draught; (*lancio*) throw; (*sparo*) shot; (*scherzo*) trick. ~ **con l'arco** archery. ~ **alla fune** tug-of-war. ~ **a segno** rifle-range

tiro'cinio *nm* apprenticeship

ti'roide *nf* thyroid

Tir'reno *nm* **il** [**mar**] ~ the Tyrrhenian Sea

ti'sana *nf* herb[al] tea

225

titolare | tortino

tito'lare a regular ● nmf principal; (proprietario) owner; (calcio) regular player

'titolo nm title; (accademico) qualification; Comm security; **a ~ di** as; **a ~ di favore** as a favour. **titoli** pl **di studio** qualifications

titu'ba|nte a hesitant. **~nza** nf hesitation. **~re** vi hesitate

tivù nf inv fam TV, telly

'tizio nm fellow

tiz'zone nm brand

toc'cante a touching

toc'care vt touch; touch on (argomento); (tastare) feel; (riguardare) concern ● vi **~ a** (capitare) happen to; **mi tocca aspettare** I'll have to wait; **tocca a te** it's your turn; (da pagare da bere) it's your round

tocca'sana nm inv cure-all

'tocco nm touch; (di pennello, orologio) stroke; (di pane ecc) chunk ● a fam crazy, touched

'toga nf toga; (accademica, di magistrato) gown

toglier|e vt take off (coperta); take away (bambino da scuola, sete, Math); take out, remove (dente); **~e qcsa di mano a qcno** take sth away from sb; **~e qcno dei guai** get sb out of trouble; **ciò non toglie che...** nevertheless... **~si** vr take off (abito); **~si la vita** take one's [own] life; **togliti dai piedi!** get out of here!

toilette nf inv, **to'letta** nf toilet; (mobile) dressing table

tolle'ra|nte a tolerant. **~nza** nf tolerance. **~re** vt tolerate

'tolto pp di **togliere**

to'maia nf upper

'tomba nf grave, tomb

tom'bino nm manhole cover

tombola nf bingo; (caduta) tumble

'tomo nm tome

'tonaca nf habit

tonalità nf inv Mus tonality

'tondo a round ● nm circle

'tonfo nm thud; (in acqua) splash

'tonico a & nm tonic

tonifi'care vt brace

tonnel'la|ggio nm tonnage. **~ta** nf ton

'tonno nm tuna [fish]

'tono nm tone

ton'sil|la nf tonsil. **~'lite** nf tonsillitis

'tonto a fam thick

top nm inv (indumento) sun-top

to'pazio nm topaz

'topless nm inv **in ~** topless

'topo nm mouse. **~ di biblioteca** fig bookworm

topogra'fia nf topography. **topo'grafico** a topographic[al]

to'ponimo nm place name

'toppa nf (rattoppo) patch; (serratura) keyhole

to'race nm chest. **to'racico** a thoracic; **gabbia toracica** rib cage

'torba nf peat

'torbido a cloudy; fig troubled

'torcer|e vt twist; wring [out] (biancheria). **~si** vr twist

'torchio nm press

'torcia nf torch

torci'collo nm stiff neck

'tordo nm thrush

to'rero nm bullfighter

To'rino nf Turin

tor'menta nf snowstorm

tormen'tare vt torment. **tor'mento** nm torment

torna'conto nm benefit

tor'nado nm tornado

tor'nante nm hairpin bend

tor'nare vi return, go/come back; (ridiventare) become again; (conto:) add up; **~ a sorridere** become happy again

tor'neo nm tournament

'tornio nm lathe

'torno nm **togliersi di ~** get out of the way

'toro nm bull; Astr Taurus

tor'pedin|e nf torpedo. **~i'era** nf torpedo boat

tor'pore nm torpor

'torre nf tower; (scacchi) castle. **~ di controllo** control tower

torrefazi'one nf roasting

tor'ren|te nm torrent, mountain stream; (fig: di lacrime) flood. **~zi'ale** a torrential

tor'retta nf turret

'torrido a torrid

torri'one nm keep

tor'rone nm nougat

'torso nm torso; (di mela, pera) core; **a ~ nudo** bare-chested

'torsolo nm core

'torta nf cake; (crostata) tart

tortel'lini nmpl tortellini, small packets of pasta stuffed with pork, ham, Parmesan and nutmeg

torti'era nf baking tin

tor'tino nm pie

'torto pp di **torcere** ● a twisted ● nm wrong; (colpa) fault; **aver** ~ be wrong; **a** ~ wrongly

tor'tora nf turtle-dove

tortu'oso a winding; (ambiguo) tortuous

tor'tu|ra nf torture. ~'rare vt torture

'torvo a grim

to'sare vt shear

tosa'tura nf shearing

To'scana nf Tuscany

'tosse nf cough

'tossico a toxic ● nm poison. **tossi'comane** nmf drug addict, drug user

tos'sire vi cough

tosta'pane nm inv toaster

to'stare vt toast (pane); roast (caffè)

'tosto adv (subito) soon ● a fam cool

tot a inv **una cifra** ~ such and such a figure ● nm **un** ~ so much

to'tal|e a & nm total. ~ità nf entirety; **la ~ità dei presenti** all those present

totali'tario a totalitarian

totaliz'zare vt total; score (punti)

total'mente adv totally

'totano nm squid

toto'calcio nm ≈ [football] pools pl

tournée nf inv tour

to'vagli|a nf tablecloth. ~'etta nf ~etta **[all'americana]** place mat. ~'olo nm napkin

'tozzo a squat ● nm ~ **di pane** stale piece of bread

tra = **fra**

trabal'la|nte a staggering; (sedia) rickety, wonky. ~re vi stagger; (veicolo:) jolt

tra'biccolo nm fam contraption; (auto) jalopy

traboc'care vi overflow

traboc'chetto nm trap

tracan'nare vt gulp down

'tracci|a nf track; (orma) footstep; (striscia) trail; (residuo) trace; fig sign. ~'are vt trace; sketch out (schema); draw (linea). ~'ato nm (schema) layout

tra'chea nf windpipe

tra'colla nf shoulder-strap; **borsa a** ~ shoulder-bag

tra'collo nm collapse

tradi'mento nm betrayal; Pol treason

tra'di|re vt betray; be unfaithful to (moglie, marito). ~'tore, ~'trice nmf traitor

tradizio'na|le a traditional. ~'lista nmf traditionalist. ~l'mente adv traditionally. **tradizi'one** nf tradition

tra'dotto pp di **tradurre**

tra'du|rre vt translate. ~t'tore, ~'trice nmf translator. ~ttore **elettronico** electronic phrasebook. ~zi'one nf translation

tra'ente nmf Comm drawer

trafe'lato a breathless

traffi'ca|nte nmf dealer. ~nte **di droga** [drug] pusher. ~re vi (affaccendarsi) busy oneself; ~re in pej traffic in. **'traffico** nm traffic; Comm trade

tra'figgere vt stab; (straziare) pierce

tra'fila nf fig rigmarole

trafo'rare vt bore, drill. **tra'foro** nm boring; (galleria) tunnel

trafu'gare vt steal

tra'gedia nf tragedy

traghet'tare vt ferry. **tra'ghetto** nm ferrying; (nave) ferry

tragica'mente adv tragically. **'tragico** a tragic ● nm (autore) tragedian

tra'gitto nm journey; (per mare) crossing

tragu'ardo nm finishing post; (meta) goal

traiet'toria nf trajectory

trai'nare vt drag; (rimorchiare) tow

tralasci'are vt interrupt; (omettere) leave out

'tralcio nm Bot shoot

tra'liccio nm (graticcio) trellis

tram nm inv tram, streetcar Am

'trama nf weft; (di film ecc) plot

traman'dare vt hand down

tra'mare vt weave; (macchinare) plot

tram'busto nm turmoil, hullaballoo

trame'stio nm bustle

tramez'zino nm sandwich

tra'mezzo nm partition

'tramite prep through ● nm link; **fare da** ~ act as go-between

tramon'tana nf north wind

tramon'tare vi set; (declinare) decline. **tra'monto** nm sunset; (declino) decline

tramor'tire vt stun ● vi faint

trampo'lino nm springboard; (per lo sci) ski-jump

'trampolo nm stilt

tramu'tare vt transform

'trancia nf shears pl; (fetta) slice

tra'nello nm trap

trangugi'are vt gulp down, gobble up

'tranne prep except

tranquilla'mente adv peacefully

tranquil'lante nm tranquillizer

tranquilli|tà nf calm; (di spirito) tranquillity. ~z'zare vt reassure.

tran'quillo a quiet; (*pacifico*) peaceful; (*coscienza*) easy

transat'lantico a transatlantic • nm ocean liner

tran'sa|tto pp di **transigere** ~**zi'one** nf Comm transaction

tran'senna nf (*barriera*) barrier

tran'sigere vi reach an agreement; (*cedere*) yield

transi'ta|bile a passable. ~**re** vi pass

transi'tivo a transitive

transi|to nm transit; **diritto di** ~**to** right of way; **"divieto di** ~**to"** "no thoroughfare". ~**torio** a transitory. ~**zi'one** nf transition

tran'tran nm fam routine

tranvi'ere nm tram driver, streetcar driver Am

'trapano nm drill

trapas'sare vt go [right] through • vi (*morire*) pass away

tra'passo nm passage

trape'lare vi (*liquido, fig:*) leak out

tra'pezio nm trapeze; Math trapezium

trapi|an'tare vt transplant. ~'**anto** nm transplant

'trappola nf trap

tra'punta nf quilt

'trarre vt draw; (*ricavare*) obtain; ~ **in inganno** deceive

trasa'lire vi start

trasan'dato a shabby

trasbor'dare vt transfer; Naut tran[s]ship • vi change. **tra'sbordo** nm trans[s]hipment

tra'scendere vt transcend • vi (*eccedere*) go too far

trasci'nar|e vt drag; (*fig: entusiasmo:*) carry away. ~**si** vr drag oneself

tra'scorrere vt spend • vi pass

tra'scri|tto pp di **trascrivere** ~**vere** vt transcribe. ~**zi'one** nf transcription

trascu'ra|bile a negligible. ~**re** vt neglect; (*non tenere conto di*) disregard. ~'**tezza** nf negligence. ~**to** a negligent; (*curato male*) neglected; (*nel vestire*) slovenly

traseco'lato a amazed

trasferi'mento nm transfer; (*trasloco*) move

trasfe'ri|re vt transfer. ~**rsi** vr move

tra'sferta nf transfer; (*indennità*) subsistence allowance; Sport away match; **in** ~ (*impiegato*) on secondment; **giocare in** ~ play away

trasfigu'rare vt transfigure

trasfor'ma|re vt transform; (*in rugby*) convert. ~'**tore** nm transformer.

~**zi'one** nf transformation; (*in rugby*) conversion

trasfor'mista nmf (*artista*) quick-change artist

trasfusi'one nf transfusion

trasgre'dire vt disobey; Jur infringe

trasgredi'trice nf transgressor

trasgres|si'one nf infringement. ~'**sivo** a intended to shock. ~'**sore** nm transgressor

tra'slato a metaphorical

traslo'car|e vt move • vi, ~**si** vr move house. **tra'sloco** nm removal

tra'smesso pp di **trasmettere**

tra'smett|ere vt pass on; TV, Radio broadcast; Techn, Med transmit. ~**i'tore** nm transmitter

trasmis'si|bile a transmissible. ~'**one** nf transmission; TV, Radio programme

trasmit'tente nm transmitter • nf broadcasting station

traso'gna|re vi day-dream. ~**to** a dreamy

traspa'ren|te a transparent. ~**za** nf transparency; **in** ~**za** against the light.

traspa'rire vi show [through]

traspi'ra|re vi perspire; fig transpire. ~**zi'one** nf perspiration

tra'sporre vt transpose

traspor'tare vt transport; **lasciarsi** ~ **da** get carried away by. **tra'sporto** nm transport; (*passione*) passion

trastul'lar|e vt amuse. ~**si** vr amuse oneself

trasu'dare vi ooze with • vi sweat

trasver'sale a transverse

trasvo'la|re vt fly over • vi ~**re su** fig skim over. ~**ta** nf crossing [by air]

'tratta nf (*traffico illegale*) trade; Comm draft

trat'tabile a or nearest offer, o.n.o.

tratta'mento nm treatment. ~ **di riguardo** special treatment

trat'ta|re vt treat; (*commerciare in*) deal in; (*negoziare*) negotiate • vi ~**re di** deal with. ~**rsi** vr **di che si tratta?** what is it about?; **si tratta di…** it's about… ~'**tive** nfpl negotiations. ~**to** nm treaty; (*opera scritta*) treatise

tratteggi'are vt outline; (*descrivere*) sketch

tratte'ner|e vt (*far restare*) keep; hold (*respiro, in questura*); hold back (*lacrime, riso*); (*frenare*) restrain; (*da paga*) withhold; **sono stato trattenuto** (*ritardato*) I was o got held up. ~**si** vr restrain oneself; (*fermarsi*) stay;

~si su (*indugiare*) dwell on. **tratteni'mento** *nm* entertainment; (*ricevimento*) party

tratte'nuta *nf* deduction

trat'tino *nm* dash; (*in parole composte*) hyphen

'tratto *pp di* **trarre** ● *nm* (*di spazio, tempo*) stretch; (*di penna*) stroke; (*linea*) line; (*brano*) passage; **tratti** *pl* (*lineamenti*) features; **a tratti** at intervals; **ad un ~** suddenly

trat'tore *nm* tractor

tratto'ria *nf* restaurant

'trauma *nm* trauma. **trau'matico** *a* traumatic. **~tiz'zare** *vt* traumatize

tra'vaglio *nm* labour; (*angoscia*) anguish

trava'sare *vt* decant

'trave *nf* beam

tra'veggole *nfpl* **avere le ~** be seeing things

tra'versa *nf* crossbar; **è una ~ di Via Roma** it's off Via Roma, it crosses via Roma

traver'sa|re *vt* cross. **~ta** *nf* crossing

traver'sie *nfpl* misfortunes

traver'sina *nf* Rail sleeper

tra'vers|o *a* crosswise ● *adv* **di ~o** crossways; **andare di ~o** (*cibo:*) go down the wrong way; **camminare di ~o** not walk in a straight line; **guardare qcno di ~o** look askance at sb. **~one** *nm* (*in calcio*) cross

travesti'mento *nm* disguise

traves'ti|re *vt* disguise. **~rsi** *vr* disguise oneself. **~to** *a* disguised ● *nm* transvestite

travi'are *vt* lead astray

travi'sare *vt* distort

travol'gente *a* overwhelming

tra'vol|gere *vt* sweep away; (*sopraffare*) overwhelm. **~to** *pp di* **travolgere**

trazi'one *nf* traction. **~ anteriore/posteriore** front-/rear-wheel drive

tre *a & nm* three

trebbi'are *vt* thresh

'treccia *nf* plait, braid

tre'cento *a & nm* three hundred; **il T~** the fourteenth century

tredi'cesima *nf* extra month's salary paid as a Christmas bonus

'tredici *a & nm* thirteen

'tregua *nf* truce; *fig* respite

tre'mare *vi* tremble; (*di freddo*) shiver. **trema'rella** *nf fam* jitters *pl*

tremenda'mente *adv* terribly.

tre'mendo *a* terrible; **ho una fame tremenda** I'm terribly hungry

tremen'tina *nf* turpentine

tre'mila *a & nm* three thousand

'tremito *nm* tremble

tremo'lare *vi* shake; (*luce:*) flicker. **tre'more** *nm* trembling

tre'nino *nm* miniature railway

'treno *nm* train

'tren|ta *a & nm* thirty; **~ta e lode** top marks. **~tatré giri** *nm inv* LP. **~'tenne** *a & nmf* thirty-year-old. **~'tesimo** *a & nm* thirtieth. **~'tina** *nf* **una ~tina di** about thirty

trepi'dare *vi* be anxious. **'trepido** *a* anxious

treppi'ede *nm* tripod

'tresca *nf* intrigue; (*amorosa*) affair

'trespolo *nm* perch

triango'lare *a* triangular. **tri'angolo** *nm* triangle

tri'bale *a* tribal

tribo'la|re *vi* (*soffrire*) suffer; (*fare fatica*) go through all kinds of trials and tribulations. **~zi'one** *nf* tribulation

tribù *nf inv* tribe

tri'buna *nf* tribune; (*per uditori*) gallery; *Sport* stand. **~ coperta** stand

tribu'nale *nm* court

tribu'tare *vt* bestow

tribu'tario *a* tax *attrib*. **tri'buto** *nm* tribute; (*tassa*) tax

tri'checo *nm* walrus

tri'ciclo *nm* tricycle

trico'lore *a* three-coloured ● *nm* (*bandiera*) tricolour

tri'dente *nm* trident

trien'nale *a* (*ogni tre anni*) three-yearly; (*lungo tre anni*) three-year. **tri'ennio** *nm* three-year period

tri'foglio *nm* clover

trifo'lato *a* sliced thinly and cooked with olive oil, parsley and garlic

'triglia *nf* mullet

trigonome'tria *nf* trigonometry

tril'lare *vi* trill

trilo'gia *nf* trilogy

tri'mestre *nm* quarter; *Sch* term

'trina *nf* lace

trin'ce|a *nf* trench. **~'rare** *vt* entrench

trincia'pollo *nm inv* poultry shears *pl*

trinci'are *vt* cut up

Trinità *nf* Trinity

'trio *nm* trio

trion'fa|le *a* triumphal. **~nte** *a* triumphant. **~re** *vi* triumph; **~re su** triumph over. **tri'onfo** *nm* triumph

tripli'care *vt* triple. **'triplice** *a* triple;

in triplice [copia] in triplicate. **'triplo** a treble ● nm **il triplo (di)** three times as much (as)

'trippa nf tripe; ⟨fam: pancia⟩ belly

'triste a sad; ⟨luogo⟩ gloomy. **tri'stezza** nf sadness. **~o** a wicked; ⟨meschino⟩ miserable

trita'carne nm inv mincer. **~ghi'accio** nm inv ice-crusher

tri'tare vt mince. **'trito** a **trito e ritrito** well-worn, trite

'trittico nm triptych

tritu'rare vt chop finely

triumvi'rato nm triumvirate

tri'vella nf drill. **trivel'lare** vt drill

trivi'ale a vulgar

tro'feo nm trophy

'trogolo nm ⟨per maiali⟩ trough

'troia nf sow; vulg bitch; ⟨sessuale⟩ whore

'tromba nf trumpet; Auto horn; ⟨delle scale⟩ well. **~ d'aria** whirlwind

trom'bare vt vulg screw; ⟨fam: in esame⟩ fail

trom'b|etta nm toy trumpet. **~one** nm trombone

trom'bosi nf thrombosis

tron'care vt sever; truncate ⟨parola⟩

'tronco a truncated; **licenziare in ~** fire on the spot ● nm trunk; ⟨di strada⟩ section. **tron'cone** nm stump

troneggi'are vi **~ su** tower over

'trono nm throne

tropi'cale a tropical. **'tropico** nm tropic

'troppo a too much; ⟨con nomi plurali⟩ too many ● pron too much; ⟨plurale⟩ too many; ⟨troppo tempo⟩ too long; **troppi** ⟨troppa gente⟩ too many people ● adv too; ⟨con verbi⟩ too much; **~ stanco** too tired; **ho mangiato ~** I ate too much; **hai fame? – non ~** are you hungry? – not very; **sentirsi di ~** feel unwanted

'trota nf trout

trot'tare vi trot. **trotterel'lare** vi trot along; ⟨bimbo⟩ toddle

'trotto nm trot; **andare al ~** trot

'trottola nf [spinning] top; ⟨movimento⟩ spin

troupe nf inv **~ televisiva** camera crew

tro'va|re vt find; ⟨scoprire⟩ find out; ⟨incontrare⟩ meet; ⟨ritenere⟩ think; **andare a ~re** go and see. **~rsi** vr find oneself ⟨luogo⟩ be; ⟨sentirsi⟩ feel. **~ta** nf bright idea. **~ta pubblicitaria** advertising gimmick

truc'ca|re vt make up; ⟨falsificare⟩ fix

sl. **~rsi** vr make up. **~tore, ~'trice** nmf make-up artist

'trucco nm ⟨cosmetico⟩ make-up; ⟨imbroglio⟩ trick

'truce a fierce; ⟨delitto⟩ appalling

truci'dare vt slay

truci'olo nm shaving

trucu'lento a truculent

'truffa nf fraud. **truf'fare** vt swindle. **~tore, ~'trice** nmf swindler

'truppa nf troops pl; ⟨gruppo⟩ group

tu pers pron you; **sei tu?** is that you?; **l'hai fatto tu?** did you do it yourself?; **a tu per tu** in private; **darsi del tu** use the familiar tu

'tuba nf Mus tuba; ⟨cappello⟩ top hat

tu'bare vi coo

tuba'tura, tubazi'one nf piping

tubazi'oni nfpl piping sg, pipes

tuberco'losi nf tuberculosis

tu'betto nm tube

tu'bino nm ⟨vestito⟩ shift

'tubo nm pipe; Anat canal; **non ho capito un ~** fam I understood zilch. **~ di scappamento** exhaust [pipe]

tubo'lare a tubular

tuf'fa|re vt plunge. **~rsi** vr dive. **~tore, ~'trice** nmf diver

'tuffo nm dive; ⟨bagno⟩ dip; **ho avuto un ~ al cuore** my heart missed a beat. **~ di testa** dive

'tufo nm tufa

tu'gurio nm hovel

tuli'pano nm tulip

'tulle nm tulle

tume'fa|tto a swollen. **~zi'one** nf swelling. **'tumido** a swollen

tu'more nm tumour

tumulazi'one nf burial

tu'mult|o nm turmoil; ⟨sommossa⟩ riot. **~u'oso** a uproarious

'tunica nf tunic

Tuni'sia nf Tunisia

'tunnel nm inv tunnel

'tu|o (il ~ m, la tua f, i ~i mpl, **le tue** fpl) poss a your; **è tua questa macchina?** is this car yours?; **un ~ amico** a friend of yours; **~ padre** your father ● poss pron yours; **i tuoi** your folks

tuo'nare vi thunder. **tu'ono** nm thunder

tu'orlo nm yolk

tu'racciolo nm stopper; ⟨di sughero⟩ cork

tu'rar|e vt stop; cork ⟨bottiglia⟩. **~si** vr become blocked, **~si le orecchie** stick one's fingers in one's ears; **~si il naso** hold one's nose

turba'mento nm disturbance; (sconvolgimento) upsetting. ~ della quiete pubblica breach of the peace
tur'bante nm turban
tur'ba|re vt upset. ~rsi vr get upset. ~to a upset
tur'bina nf turbine
turbi'nare vi whirl. '**turbine** nm whirl. turbine di vento whirlwind
turbo'len|to a turbulent. ~za nf turbulence
turboreat'tore nm turbo-jet
tur'chese a & nmf turquoise
Tur'chia nf Turkey
tur'chino a & nm deep blue
'**turco, -a** a Turkish ● nmf Turk ● nm (lingua) Turkish; fig double Dutch; fumare come un ~ smoke like a chimney; bestemmiare come un ~ swear like a trooper
tu'ris|mo nm tourism. ~ta nmf tourist. ~tico a tourist attrib
'**turno** nm turn; a ~ in turn; di ~ on duty; fare a ~ take turns. ~ di notte night shift
'**turp|e** a base. ~i'loquio nm foul language
'**tuta** nf overalls pl; Sport tracksuit. ~ da ginnastica tracksuit. ~ da lavoro overalls. ~ mimetica camouflage. ~ spaziale spacesuit. ~ subacquea wetsuit
tu'tela nf Jur guardianship; (protezione) protection. **tute'lare** vt protect
tu'tina nf sleepsuit; (da danza) leotard
tu'tore, -'trice nmf guardian
'**tutta** nf mettercela ~ per fare qcsa go flat out for sth
tutta'via conj nevertheless, still
'**tutto** a whole; (con nomi plurali) all; (ogni) every; tutta la classe the whole class, all the class; tutti gli alunni all the pupils; a tutta velocità at full speed; ho aspettato ~ il giorno I waited all day [long]; in ~ il mondo all over the world; noi tutti all of us; era tutta contenta she was delighted; tutti e due both; tutti e tre all three ● pron all; (tutta la gente) everybody; (tutte le cose) everything; (qualunque cosa) anything; l'ho mangiato ~ I ate it all; le ho lavate tutte I washed them all; raccontami ~ tell me everything; lo sanno tutti everybody knows; è capace di ~ he's capable of anything; ~ compreso all in; del ~ quite; in ~ altogether ● adv completely; tutt'a un tratto all at once; tutt'altro not at all; tutt'altro che anything but ● nm whole; tentare il ~ per ~ go for broke. ~'fare a inv & nmf [impiegato] ~ general handyman; donna ~ general maid
tut'tora adv still
tutù nm inv tutu, ballet dress
tv nf inv TV

Uu

ubbidi'en|te a obedient. ~za nf obedience. **ubbi'dire** vi ~ (a) obey
ubi'ca|to a located. ~zi'one nf location
ubria'car|e vt get drunk. ~si vr get drunk; ~si di fig become intoxicated with
ubria'chezza nf drunkenness; in stato di ~ inebriated
ubri'aco, -a a drunk; ~ fradicio dead o blind drunk ● nmf drunk
ubria'cone nm drunkard
uccelli'era nf aviary. **uc'cello** nm bird; (vulg: pene) cock
uc'cider|e vt kill. ~si vr kill oneself
ucci|si'one nf killing. **uc'ciso** pp di **uccidere** ~'sore nm killer
u'dente a i non udenti the hearing impaired
u'dibile a audible
udi'enza nf audience; (colloquio) interview; Jur hearing
u'di|re vt hear. ~'tivo a auditory. ~to nm hearing. ~'tore, ~'trice nmf listener; Sch unregistered student (allowed to sit in on lectures). ~'torio nm audience
'**uffa** int (con impazienza) come on!; (con tono seccato) damn!
uffici'al|e a official ● nm officer;

(*funzionario*) official; **pubblico** ~**e** public official. ~**e giudiziario** clerk of the court. ~**iz'zare** *vt* make official, officialize

uf'ficio *nm* office; (*dovere*) duty. ~ **di collocamento** employment office. ~ **informazioni** information office. ~ **del personale** personnel department. ~**sa'mente** *adv* unofficially. **uffici'oso** *a* unofficial

'**ufo**[1] *nm inv* UFO

'**ufo**[2]: **a** ~ *adv* without paying

uggi'oso *a* boring

uguagli'a|nza *nf* equality. ~**re** *vt* make equal; (*essere uguale*) equal; (*livellare*) level. ~**rsi** *vr* ~**rsi a** compare oneself to

ugu'al|e *a* equal; (*lo stesso*) the same; (*simile*) like. ~'**mente** *adv* equally; (*malgrado tutto*) all the same

'**ulcera** *nf* ulcer

uli'veto *nm* olive grove

ulteri'or|e *a* further. ~'**mente** *adv* further

ultima'mente *adv* lately

ulti'ma|re *vt* complete. ~**tum** *nm inv* ultimatum

ulti'missime *nfpl Journ* stop press, latest news *sg*

'**ultimo** *a* last; (*notizie ecc*) latest; (*più lontano*) farthest; *fig* ultimate ● *nm* last; **fino all'**~ to the last; **per** ~ at the end; **l'**~ **piano** the top floor

ultrà *nmf inv Sport* fanatical supporter

ultramo'derno *a* ultramodern

ultra'rapido *a* extra-fast

ultrasen'sibile *a* ultrasensitive

ultra's|onico *a* ultrasonic. ~**u'ono** *nm* ultrasound

ultrater'reno *a* (*vita*) after death

ultravio'letto *a* ultraviolet

ulu'la|re *vi* howl. ~**to** *nm* howling; **gli** ~**ti** the howls, the howling

umana'mente *adv* (*trattare*) humanely; ~ **impossibile** not humanly possible

uma'nesimo *nm* humanism

umani|tà *nf* humanity. ~'**tario** *a* humanitarian. **u'mano** *a* human; (*benevolo*) humane

umidifica'tore *nm* humidifier

umidità *nf* dampness; (*di clima*) humidity. '**umido** *a* damp; (*clima*) humid; (*mani, occhi*) moist ● *nm* dampness; **in umido** *Culin* stewed

'**umile** *a* humble

umili'a|nte *a* humiliating. ~**re** *vt* humiliate. ~**rsi** *vr* humble oneself.

~**zi'one** *nf* humiliation. **umiltà** *nf* humility. **umil'mente** *adv* humbly

u'more *nm* humour; (*stato d'animo*) mood; **di cattivo/buon** ~ in a bad/good mood

umo'ris|mo *nm* humour. ~**ta** *nmf* humorist. ~'**tico** *a* humorous

un *indef art* a; (*davanti a vocale o h muta*) an; *vedi* **uno**

una *indef art f* a; *vedi* **un**

u'nanim|e *a* unanimous. ~**e'mente** *adv* unanimously. ~**ità** *nf* unanimity; **all'**~**ità** unanimously

unci'nato *a* hooked; (*parentesi*) angle

unci'netto *nm* crochet hook

un'cino *nm* hook

'**undici** *a & nm* eleven

'**unger|e** *vt* grease; (*sporcare*) get greasy; *Relig* anoint; (*blandire*) flatter. ~**si** *vr* (*con olio solare*) oil oneself; ~**si le mani** get one's hands greasy

unghe'rese *a & nmf* Hungarian.

Unghe'ria *nf* Hungary; (*lingua*) Hungarian

'**unghi|a** *nf* nail; (*di animale*) claw. ~'**ata** *nf* (*graffio*) scratch

ungu'ento *nm* ointment

unica'mente *adv* only. '**unico** *a* only; (*singolo*) single; (*incomparabile*) unique

unifi'ca|re *vt* unify. ~**zi'one** *nf* unification

unifor'mar|e *vt* level. ~**si** *vr* conform (**a** to)

uni'form|e *a & nf* uniform. ~**ità** *nf* uniformity

unilate'rale *a* unilateral

uni'one *nf* union; (*armonia*) unity. **U**~ **Europea** European Union. **U**~ **Monetaria Europea** European Monetary Union. ~ **sindacale** trade union, labor union *Am*. **U**~ **Sovietica** Soviet Union

u'ni|re *vt* unite; (*collegare*) join; blend (*colori ecc*). ~**rsi** *vr* unite; (*collegarsi*) join

'**unisex** *a inv* unisex

unità *nf inv* unity; *Math, Mil* unit; *Comput* drive. ~ **di misura** unit of measurement. ~**rio** *a* unitary

u'nito *a* united; (*tinta*) plain

univer'sal|e *a* universal. ~**iz'zare** *vt* universalize. ~'**mente** *adv* universally

università *nf inv* university. ~**rio, -a** *a* university *attrib* ● *nmf* (*insegnante*) university lecturer; (*studente*) undergraduate

uni'verso *nm* universe

uno, -a *indef art* (*before s + consonant*,

gn, ps, z) a ● *pron* one; a ~ a ~ one by one; l'~ e l'altro both [of them]; né l'~ né l'altro neither [of them]; ~ di noi one of us; ~ fa quello che può you do what you can ● a a, one ● *nm (numerale)* one; *(un tale)* some man ● *nf* some woman

'unto *pp di* ungere ● *a* greasy ● *nm* grease. ~u'oso *a* greasy. unzi'one *nf* l'Estrema Unzione Extreme Unction

u'omo *nm (pl* uomini*)* man. ~ d'affari business man. ~ di fiducia right-hand man. ~ di Stato statesman

u'ovo *nm (pl nf* uova*)* egg. ~ in camicia poached egg. ~ alla coque boiled egg. ~ di Pasqua Easter egg. ~ sodo hard-boiled egg. ~ strapazzato scrambled egg

ura'gano *nm* hurricane

u'ranio *nm* uranium

urba'n|esimo *nm* urbanization. ~ista *nmf* town planner. ~istica *nf* town planning. ~istico *a* urban. urba-nizzazi'one *nf* urbanization. ur'bano *a* urban; *(cortese)* urbane

ur'gen|te *a* urgent. ~te'mente *adv* urgently. ~za *nf* urgency; in caso d'~za in an emergency; d'~za *(misura, chiamata)* emergency

'urgere *vi* be urgent

u'rina *nf* urine. uri'nare *vi* urinate

ur'lare *vi* shout, yell; *(cane, vento:)* howl. 'urlo *nm (pl nm* urli, *nf* urla*)* shout; *(di cane, vento)* howling

'urna *nf* urn; *(elettorale)* ballot box; andare alle urne go to the polls

urrà *int* hurrah!

U.R.S.S. *nf abbr (*Unione delle Repubbliche Socialiste Sovietiche*)* USSR

ur'tar|e *vt* knock against; *(scontrarsi)* bump into; *fig* irritate. ~si *vr* collide; *fig* clash

'urto *nm* knock; *(scontro)* crash; *(contrasto)* conflict; *fig* clash; d'~ *(misure, terapia)* shock

usa e getta *a inv (rasoio, siringa)* throw-away, disposable

u'sanza *nf* custom; *(moda)* fashion

u'sa|re *vt* use; *(impiegare)* employ; *(esercitare)* exercise; ~re fare qcsa be in the habit of doing sth ● *vi (essere di moda)* be fashionable; non si usa più it is out of fashion; *(attrezzatura, espressione:)* it's not used any more. ~to *a* used; *(non nuovo)* second-hand

U.S.A. *nmpl* US[A] *sg*

u'scente *a (presidente)* outgoing

usci'ere *nm* usher. 'uscio *nm* door

u'sci|re *vi* come out; *(andare fuori)* go out; *(sfuggire)* get out; *(essere sorteggiato)* come up; *(giornale:)* come out; ~re da Comput exit from, quit; ~re di strada leave the road. ~ta *nf* exit, way out; *(spesa)* outlay; *(di auto-strada)* junction; *(battuta)* witty remark; essere in libera ~ta be off duty. ~ta di servizio back door. ~ta di sicurezza emergency exit

usi'gnolo *nm* nightingale

'uso *nm* use; *(abitudine)* custom; *(usanza)* usage; fuori ~ out of use; per ~ esterno *(medicina)* for external use only

U.S.S.L. *nf abbr (*Unità Socio-Sani-taria Locale*)* local health centre

ustio'na|rsi *vr* burn oneself. ~to, -a *nmf* burns case ● *a* burnt. usti'one *nf* burn

usu'ale *a* usual

usufru'ire *vi* ~ di take advantage of

u'sura *nf* usury. usu'raio *nm* usurer

usur'pare *vt* usurp

u'tensile *nm* tool; Culin utensil; cassetta degli utensili tool box

u'tente *nmf* user. ~ finale end user

u'tenza *nf* use; *(utenti)* users *pl*

ute'rino *a* uterine. 'utero *nm* womb

'util|e *a* useful ● *nm* Comm profit. ~ità *nf* usefulness, utility; Comput utility. ~i'taria *nf* Auto small car. ~i'tario *a* utilitarian

utiliz'za|re *vt* utilize. ~zi'one *nf* utilization. uti'lizzo *nm (utilizzazione)* use

uto'pistico *a* Utopian

'uva *nf* grapes *pl*; chicco d'~ grape. ~ passa raisins *pl*. ~ sultanina currants *pl*

Vv

va'cante *a* vacant

va'canza *nf* holiday; (*posto vacante*) vacancy. essere in ~ be on holiday

'vacca *nf* cow. ~ da latte dairy cow

vacci'nare *vt* vaccinate. ~inazi'one *nf* vaccination. vac'cino *nm* vaccine

vacil'lante *a* tottering; (*oggetto*) wobbly; (*luce*) flickering; *fig* wavering. ~re *vi* totter; (*oggetto:*) wobble; (*luce:*) flicker; *fig* waver

'vacuo *a* (*vano*) vain; *fig* empty ● *nm* vacuum

vagabon'dare *vi* wander. vaga'bondo, -a *a* (*cane*) stray; gente vagabonda tramps *pl* ● *nmf* tramp

va'gare *vi* wander

vagheggi'are *vt* long for

va'gina *nf* vagina. ~ 'nale *a* vaginal

va'gire *vi* whimper. ~to *nm* whimper

'vaglia *nm* *inv* money order. ~ bancario bank draft. ~ postale postal order

vagli'are *vt* sift; *fig* weigh

'vago *a* vague

vagon'cino *nm* (*di funivia*) car

va'gone *nm* (*per passeggeri*) carriage; (*per merci*) wagon. ~ letto sleeper. ~ ristorante restaurant car

vai'olo *nm* smallpox

va'langa *nf* avalanche

va'lente *a* skilful

va'lere *vi* be worth; (*contare*) count; (*regola:*) apply (per to); (*essere valido*) be valid; far ~ i propri diritti assert one's rights; farsi ~ e assert oneself; non vale! that's not fair!; tanto vale che me ne vada I might as well go ● *vt* ~re qcsa a qcno (*procurare*) earn sb sth; ~ne la pena be worth it; vale la pena di vederlo it's worth seeing; ~si di avail oneself of

valeri'ana *nf* valerian

va'levole *a* valid

vali'care *vt* cross. 'valico *nm* pass

vali'dità *nf* validity; con ~ illimitata valid indefinitely

'valido *a* valid; (*efficace*) efficient; (*contributo*) valuable

valige'ria *nf* (*fabbrica*) leather factory; (*negozio*) leather goods shop

va'ligia *nf* suitcase; fare le valigie pack; *fig* pack one's bags. ~ diplomatica diplomatic bag

val'lata *nf* valley. 'valle *nf* valley; a valle downstream

val'letta *nf* TV assistant. ~o *nm* valet; TV assistant

val'lone *nm* (*valle*) deep valley

va'lore *nm* value, worth; (*merito*) merit; (*coraggio*) valour; ~i *pl* Comm securities; di ~e (*oggetto*) valuable; oggetti *nmpl* di ~e valuables; senza ~e worthless. ~iz'zare *vt* (*mettere in valore*) use to advantage; (*aumentare di valore*) increase the value of; (*migliorare l'aspetto di*) enhance

valo'roso *a* courageous

'valso *pp di* valere

va'luta *nf* currency. ~ estera foreign currency

valu'tare *vt* value; weigh up (*situazione*). ~rio *a* (*mercato, norme*) currency. ~zi'one *nf* valuation

'valva *nf* valve. 'valvola *nf* valve; *Electr* fuse

'valzer *nm* *inv* waltz

vam'pata *nf* blaze; (*di calore*) blast; (*al viso*) flush

vam'piro *nm* vampire; *fig* blood-sucker

vana'mente *adv* (*inutilmente*) in vain

van'dalico *a* atto ~lico act of vandalism. ~'lismo *nm* vandalism. 'vandalo *nm* vandal

vaneggi'are *vi* rave

'vanga *nf* spade. van'gare *vt* dig

van'gelo *nm* Gospel; (*fam: verità*) gospel [truth]

vanifi'care *vt* nullify

va'niglia *nf* vanilla. ~ 'ato *a* (*zucchero*) vanilla *attrib*

vanil'lina *nf* vanillin

vanità *nf* vanity. vani'toso *a* vain

'vano *a* vain ● *nm* (*stanza*) room; (*spazio vuoto*) hollow

van'taggio *nm* advantage; *Sport* lead; *Tennis* advantage; trarre ~o da qcsa derive benefit from sth. ~'**oso** a advantageous

van't|are vt praise; (possedere) boast. ~**arsi** vr boast. ~**e'ria** nf boasting. '**vanto** nm boast

'**vanvera** nf **a** ~ at random; **parlare a** ~ talk nonsense

va'por|e nm steam; (di benzina, cascata) vapour; **a** ~**e** steam attrib; **al** ~**e** Culin steamed. ~**e acqueo** steam, water vapour; **battello a** ~**e** steamboat. **vapo'retto** nm ferry. ~**i'era** nf steam engine

vaporiz'za|re vt vaporize. ~**tore** nm spray

vapo'roso a (vestito) filmy; **capelli vaporosi** big hair sg

va'rare vt launch

var'care vt cross. '**varco** nm passage; **aspettare al varco** lie in wait

vari'abil|e a changeable, variable ●nf variable. ~**ità** nf changeableness, variability

vari'a|nte nf variant. ~**re** vt/i vary; ~**re di umore** change one's mood. ~**zi'one** nf variation

va'rice nf varicose vein

vari'cella nf chickenpox

vari'coso a varicose

varie'gato a variegated

varietà nf inv variety ●nm inv variety show

'**vario** a varied; (al pl, parecchi) various; **vari** pl (molti) several; **varie ed eventuali** any other business

vario'pinto a multicoloured

'**varo** nm launch

va'saio nm potter

'**vasca** nf tub; (piscina) pool; (lunghezza) length. ~ **da bagno** bath

va'scello nm vessel

va'schetta nf tub

vase'lina nf Vaseline®

vasel'lame nm china. ~ **d'oro/d'argento** gold/silver plate

'**vaso** nm pot; (da fiori) vase; Anat vessel; (per cibi) jar. ~ **da notte** chamber pot

vas'soio nm tray

vastità nf vastness. '**vasto** a vast; **di vaste vedute** broad-minded

Vati'cano nm Vatican

vattela'pesca adv fam God knows!

ve pers pron you; **ve l'ho dato** I gave it to you

vecchia nf old woman. **vecchi'aia** nf old age. '**vecchio** a old ●nmf old man; **i vecchi** old people

'**vece** nf **in** ~ **di** in place of; **fare le veci di qcno** take sb's place

ve'dente a **i non vedenti** the visually handicapped

ve'der|e vt/i see; **far** ~**e** show; **farsi** ~**e** show one's face; **non vedo l'ora di ...** I can't wait to... ~**si** vr see oneself; (reciproco) see each other

ve'detta nf (luogo) lookout; Naut patrol vessel

'**vedovo, -a** nm widower ●nf widow

ve'duta nf view

vee'mente a vehement

vege'ta|le a & nm vegetable. ~**li'ano** a & nmf vegan. ~**re** vi vegetate. ~**ri'ano, -a** a & nmf vegetarian. ~**zi'one** nf vegetation

'**vegeto** a vedi **vivo**

veg'gente nmf clairvoyant

'**veglia** nf watch; **fare la** ~ keep watch. ~ **funebre** vigil

vegli'|are vi be awake; ~**are su** watch over. ~'**one** nm ~**one di capodanno** New Year's Eve celebration

ve'icolo nm vehicle

'**vela** nf sail; Sport sailing; **far** ~ set sail

ve'la|re vt veil; (fig: nascondere) hide. ~**rsi** vr (vista:) mist over; (voce:) go husky. ~**ta'mente** adv indirectly. ~**to** a veiled; (occhi) misty; (collant) sheer

'**velcro**® nm velcro®

veleggi'are vi sail

ve'leno nm poison. **vele'noso** a poisonous

veli'ero nm sailing ship

ve'lina nf [carta] ~ tissue paper; (copia) carbon copy

ve'lista nm yachtsman ●nf yachtswoman

ve'livolo nm aircraft

vellei'tà nf inv foolish ambition. ~'**tario** a unrealistic

'**vello** nm fleece

vellu'tato a velvety. **vel'luto** nm velvet. **velluto a coste** corduroy

'**velo** nm veil; (di zucchero, cipria) dusting; (tessuto) voile

ve'loc|e a fast. ~**e'mente** adv quickly. **velo'cista** nmf Sport sprinter. ~**ità** nf inv speed; (Auto: marcia) gear. ~**ità di crociera** cruising speed. ~**iz'zare** vt speed up

ve'lodromo nm cycle track

'**vena** nf vein; **essere in** ~ **di** be in the mood for

ve'nale a venal; (persona) mercenary, venal

ve'nato a grainy

235

vena'torio *a* hunting *attrib*
vena'tura *nf* (*di legno*) grain; (*di foglia, marmo*) vein
ven'demmi|a *nf* grape harvest. **~'are** *vt* harvest
'vender|e *vt* sell. **~si** *vr* sell oneself; **vendesi** for sale
ven'detta *nf* revenge
vendi'ca|re *vt* avenge. **~rsi** *vr* get one's revenge. **~'tivo** *a* vindictive
'vendi|ta *nf* sale; **in ~ta** on sale. **~ta all'asta** by auction. **~ta al dettaglio** retailing. **~ta all'ingrosso** wholesaling. **~ta al minuto** retailing. **~ta porta a porta** door-to-door selling. **~'tore, ~'trice** *nmf* seller. **~tore ambulante** hawker, pedlar
vene'ra|bile, ~ndo *a* venerable
vene'rare *vt* revere
venerdì *nm inv* Friday. **V~ Santo** Good Friday
'Venere *nf* Venus. **ve'nereo** *a* venereal
Ve'nezi|a *nf* Venice. **v~'ano, -a** *a* & *nmf* Venetian **~nf** (*persiana*) Venetian blind; *Culin* sweet bun
veni'ale *a* venial
ve'nire *vi* come; (*riuscire*) turn out; (*costare*) cost; (*in passivo*) be; **~ a sapere** learn; **~ in mente** occur; **~ meno** (*svenire*) faint; **~ meno a un contratto** go back on a contract; **~ via** come away; (*staccarsi*) come off; **mi viene da piangere** I feel like crying; **vieni a prendermi** come and pick me up
ven'taglio *nm* fan
ven'tata *nf* gust [of wind]; *fig* breath
ven'te|nne *a* & *nmf* twenty-year-old. **~simo** *a* & *nm* twentieth. **'venti|a** & *nm* twenty
venti'la|re *vt* air. **~'tore** *nm* fan. **~zi'one** *nf* ventilation
ven'tina *nf* **una ~** (*circa venti*) about twenty
ventiquat'tro|re *nf inv* (*valigia*) overnight case
'vento *nm* wind; **farsi ~** fan oneself
ven'tosa *nf* sucker
ven'toso *a* windy
'ventre *nm* stomach. **ven'triloquo** *nm* ventriloquist
ven'tura *nf* fortune; **andare alla ~** trust to luck
ven'turo *a* next
ve'nuta *nf* coming
vera'mente *adv* really
ve'randa *nf* veranda
ver'bal|e *a* verbal ●*nm* (*di riunione*) minutes *pl*. **~'mente** *adv* verbally

'verbo *nm* verb. **~ ausiliare** auxiliary [verb]
'verde *a* green ●*nm* green; (*vegetazione*) greenery; (*semaforo*) green light; **essere al ~** be broke. **~ oliva** olive green. **~ pisello** pea green. **~'rame** *nm* verdigris
ver'detto *nm* verdict
ver'dura *nf* vegetables *pl*; **una ~** a vegetable
'verga *nf* rod
vergi'n|ale *a* virginal. **'vergine** *nf* virgin; *Astr* Virgo ●*a* virgin; (*cassetta*) blank. **~ità** *nf* virginity
ver'gogna *nf* shame; (*timidezza*) shyness
vergo'gn|arsi *vr* feel ashamed; (*essere timido*) feel shy. **~oso** *a* ashamed; (*timido*) shy; (*disonorevole*) shameful
ve'rifica *nf* check. **verifi'cabile** *a* verifiable
verifi'car|e *vt* check. **~si** *vr* come true
ve'rismo *nm* realism
verit|à *nf* truth. **~i'ero** *a* truthful
'verme *nm* worm. **~ solitario** tapeworm
ver'miglio *a* & *nm* vermilion
'vermut *nm inv* vermouth
ver'nacolo *nm* vernacular
ver'nic|e *nf* paint; (*trasparente*) varnish; (*pelle*) patent leather; *fig* veneer; **"vernice fresca"** "wet paint". **~i'are** *vt* paint; (*con vernice trasparente*) varnish. **~ia'tura** *nf* painting; (*strato*) paintwork; *fig* veneer
'vero *a* true; (*autentico*) real; (*perfetto*) perfect; **è ~?** is that so?; **~ e proprio** full-blown; **sei stanca, ~?** you're tired, aren't you? ●*nm* truth; (*realtà*) life
verosimigli'anza *nf* probability. **vero'simile** *a* probable
ver'ruca *nf* wart; (*sotto la pianta del piede*) verruca
versa'mento *nm* (*pagamento*) payment; (*in banca*) deposit
ver'sante *nm* slope
ver'sa|re *vt* pour; (*spargere*) shed; (*rovesciare*) spill; pay (*denaro*). **~rsi** *vr* spill; (*sfociare*) flow
ver'satil|e *a* versatile. **~ità** *nf* versatility
ver'setto *nm* verse
versi'one *nf* version; (*traduzione*) translation; **"~ integrale"** "unabridged version"; **"~ ridotta"** "abridged version"
'verso[1] *nm* verse; (*grido*) cry; (*gesto*) gesture; (*senso*) direction; (*modo*) man-

ner; **fare il ~ a** qcno ape sb; **non c'è ~ di** there is no way of

'**verso**² *prep* towards; (*nei pressi di*) round about; **~ dove?** which way?

'**vertebra** *nf* vertebra

'**vertere** *vi* **~ su** focus on

verti'cal|e *a* vertical; (*in parole crociate*) down ●*nm* vertical ●*nf* handstand. **~'mente** *adv* vertically

'**vertice** *nm* summit; *Math* vertex; **conferenza al ~** summit conference

ver'tigine *nf* dizziness; *Med* vertigo; **vertigini** *pl* giddy spells; **aver le vertigini** feel dizzy

vertigi|nosa'mente *adv* dizzily. **~'noso** *a* dizzy; (*velocità*) breakneck; (*prezzi*) sky-high; (*scollatura*) plunging

ve'scica *nf* bladder; (*sulla pelle*) blister

'**vescovo** *nm* bishop

'**vespa** *nf* wasp

vespasi'ano *nm* urinal

'**vespro** *nm* vespers *pl*

ves'sillo *nm* standard

ve'staglia *nf* dressing gown

'vest|e *nf* dress; (*rivestimento*) covering; **in ~e di** in the capacity of; **in ~e ufficiale** in an official capacity. **~i'ario** *nm* clothing

ve'stibolo *nm* hall

ve'stigio *nm* (*pl nm* **vestigi,** *pl nf* **vestigia**) trace

ve'sti|re *vt* dress. **~rsi** *vr* get dressed. **~ti** *pl* clothes. **~to** *a* dressed ●*nm* (*da uomo*) suit; (*da donna*) dress

vete'rano, -a *a & nmf* veteran

veteri'naria *nf* veterinary science

veteri'nario *a* veterinary ●*nm* veterinary surgeon

'**veto** *nm inv* veto

ve'tra|io *nm* glazier. **~ta** *nf* big window; (*in chiesa*) stained glass window; (*porta*) glass door. **~to** *a* glazed. **vetre'ria** *nf* glass works

ve'tri|na *nf* [shop-]window; (*mobile*) display cabinet. **~'nista** *nmf* window dresser

vetri'olo *nm* vitriol

'**vetro** *nm* glass; (*di finestra, porta*) pane. **~'resina** *nf* fibreglass

'**vetta** *nf* peak

vet'tore *nm* vector

vetto'vaglie *nfpl* provisions

vet'tura *nf* coach; (*ferroviaria*) carriage; *Auto* car. **vettu'rino** *nm* coachman

vezzeggi'a|re *vt* fondle. **~'tivo** *nm* pet name. '**vezzo** *nm* habit; (*attrattiva*)

charm; **vezzi** *pl* (*moine*) affectation *sg*.

vez'zoso *a* charming; *pej* affected

vi *pers pron* you; (*riflessivo*) yourselves; (*reciproco*) each other; (*tra più persone*) one another; **vi ho dato un libro** I gave you a book; **lavatevi le mani** wash your hands; **eccovi** here you are! ●*adv* = **ci**

'**via**¹ *nf* street, road; *fig* way; *Anat* tract; **in ~ di** in the course of; **per ~ di** on account of; **~ ~ che** as; **per ~ aerea** by airmail

'**via**² *adv* away; (*fuori*) out; **andar ~** go away; **e così ~** and so on; **e ~ dicendo** and whatnot ●*int* **~!** go away!; *Sport* go!; (*andiamo*) come on! ●*nm* starting signal

viabilità *nf* road conditions *pl*; (*rete*) road network; (*norme*) road and traffic laws *pl*

via'card *nf inv* motorway card

via'dotto *nm* viaduct

viaggi'a|re *vi* travel. **~tore, ~trice** *nmf* traveller

vi'aggio *nm* journey; (*breve*) trip; **buon ~!** safe journey!, have a good trip!; **fare un ~** go on a journey. **~ di nozze** honeymoon

vi'ale *nm* avenue; (*privato*) drive

via'vai *nm* coming and going

vi'bra|nte *a* vibrant. **~re** *vi* vibrate; (*fremere*) quiver. **~zi'one** *nf* vibration

vi'cario *nm* vicar

'**vice+** *pref* vice+

'**vice** *nmf* deputy. **~diret'tore** *nm* assistant manager

vi'cenda *nf* event; **a ~** (*fra due*) each other; (*a turno*) in turn[s]

vice'versa *adv* vice versa

vici'na|nza *nf* nearness; **~nze** *pl* (*paraggi*) neighbourhood. **~to** *nm* neighbourhood; (*vicini*) neighbours *pl*

vi'cino, -a *a* near; (*accanto*) next ●*adv* near, close. **~ a** *prep* near [to] ●*nmf* neighbour. **~ di casa** nextdoor neighbour

vicissi'tudine *nf* vicissitude

'**vicolo** *nm* alley

'**video** *nm* video. **~'camera** *nf* camcorder. **~cas'setta** *nf* video cassette

videoci'tofono *nm* video entry phone

video'clip *nm inv* video clip

videogi'oco *nm* video game

videoregistra'tore *nm* videorecorder

video'teca *nf* video library

video'tel® *nm* ≈ Videotex®

videotermi'nale *nm* visual display unit, VDU

vidi'mare *vt* authenticate

vie'ta|re *vt* forbid; **sosta ~ta** no parking; **~to fumare** no smoking; **~to ai minori di 18 anni** prohibited to children under the age of 18

vi'gente a in force. **'vigere** vi be in force

vigi'lante a vigilant. **~nza** nf vigilance. **~re** vt keep an eye on ● vi keep watch

'vigile a watchful ● nm = [urbano] policeman. **~ del fuoco** fireman

vi'gilia nf eve

vigliacche'ria nf cowardice. **vi-gli'acco, -a** a cowardly ● nmf coward

'vigna nf, **vi'gneto** nm vineyard

vi'gnetta nf cartoon

vi'gore nm vigour; **entrare in ~** come into force. **vigo'roso** a vigorous

'vile a cowardly; (abietto) vile

'villa nf villa

vil'laggio nm village. **~ turistico** holiday village

vil'lano a rude ● nm boor; (contadino) peasant

villeggi'ante nmf holiday-maker. **~re** vi spend one's holidays. **~'tura** nf holiday[s] [pl], vacation Am

vil'letta nf small detached house. **~ino** nf detached house

viltà nf cowardice

'vimine nm wicker

'vincere vt win; (sconfiggere) beat; (superare) overcome. **~ita** nf win; (somma vinta) winnings pl. **~i'tore, ~i'trice** nmf winner

vinco'lante a binding. **~re** vt bind; Comm tie up. **'vincolo** nm bond

vi'nicolo a wine attrib

vinil'pelle® nm Leatherette®

'vino nm wine. **~ spumante** sparkling wine. **~ da taglio** blending wine. **~ da tavola** table wine

'vinto pp di **vincere**

vi'ola nf Bot violet; Mus viola. **vio'laceo** a purplish; (labbra) blue

vio'lare vt violate. **~zi'one** nf violation. **~zione di domicilio** breaking and entering

violen'tare vt rape

violente'mente adv violently

vio'lento a violent. **~za** nf violence. **~za carnale** rape

vio'letta nf violet

vio'letto a & nm (colore) violet

violi'nista nmf violinist. **vio'lino** nm violin. **violon'cello** nm cello

vi'ottolo nm path

'vipera nf viper

vi'raggio nm Phot toning; Naut, Aeron turn. **~re** vi turn; **~re di bordo** veer

'virgola nf comma. **~ette** nfpl inverted commas

vi'rile a virile; (da uomo) manly. **~ità** nf virility; manliness

virtù nf inv virtue; **in ~ di** (legge) under. **~'ale** a virtual. **~'oso** a virtuous ● nm virtuoso

viru'lento a virulent

'virus nm inv virus

visa'gista nmf beautician

visce'rale a visceral; (odio) deep-seated; (reazione) gut

'viscere nm internal organ ● nfpl guts

'vischio nm mistletoe. **~'oso** a viscous; (appiccicoso) sticky

'viscido a slimy

vi'sconte nm viscount. **~'essa** nf viscountess

vi'scoso a viscous

vi'sibile a visible

visi'bilio nm profusion; **andare in ~** go into ecstasies

visibilità nf visibility

visi'era nf (di elmo) visor; (di berretto) peak

visio'nare vt examine; Cinema screen. **visi'one** nf vision; **prima visione** Cinema first showing

'visita nf visit; (breve) call; Med examination; **fare ~ a a qcno** pay sb a visit. **~a di controllo** Med checkup. **visi'tare** vt visit; (brevemente) call on; Med examine; **~a'tore, ~a'trice** nmf visitor

vi'sivo a visual

'viso nm face

vi'sone nm mink

'vispo a lively

vis'suto pp di **vivere** ● a experienced

'vista nf sight; (veduta) view; **a ~a d'occhio** (crescere) visibly; (estendersi) as far as the eye can see; **in ~a di** in view of; **perdere di ~a qcno** lose sight of sb; fig lose touch with sb. **~o** pp di **vedere** ● nm visa. **vi'stoso** a showy; (notevole) considerable

visu'ale a visual. **~izza'tore** nm Comput display, VDU. **~izzazi'one** nf Comput display

'vita nf life; (durata della vita) lifetime; Anat waist; **a ~** for life; **essere in fin di ~** be at death's door; **essere in ~** be alive

vi'tale a vital. **~ità** nf vitality

vita'lizio a life attrib ● nm [life] annuity

vita'mina nf vitamin. **~iz'zato** a vitamin-enriched

'vite nf Mech screw; Bot vine

vi'tello nm calf; Culin veal; (pelle) calfskin

vi'ticcio nm tendril
viticol't|ore nm wine grower. **~ura** nf wine growing
'vitreo a vitreous; ⟨sguardo⟩ glassy
'vittima nf victim
'vitto nm food; ⟨pasti⟩ board. **~ e alloggio** board and lodging
vit'toria nf victory
vittori'ano a Victorian
vittori'oso a victorious
vi'uzza nf narrow lane
'viva int hurrah!; **~ la Regina!** long live the Queen!
vi'vac|e a vivacious; ⟨mente⟩ lively; ⟨colore⟩ bright. **~ità** nf vivacity; ⟨di mente⟩ liveliness; ⟨di colore⟩ brightness. **~iz'zare** vt liven up
vi'vaio nm nursery; ⟨per pesci⟩ pond; fig breeding ground
viva'mente adv ⟨ringraziare⟩ warmly
vi'vanda nf food; ⟨piatto⟩ dish
vi'vente a living ● nmpl **i viventi** the living
'vivere vi live; **~ di** live on ● vt ⟨passare⟩ go through ● nm life
'viveri nmpl provisions
'vivido a vivid
vivisezi'one nf vivisection
'vivo a alive; ⟨vivente⟩ living; ⟨vivace⟩ lively; ⟨colore⟩ bright; **~ e vegeto** alive and kicking; **farsi ~** keep in touch; ⟨arrivare⟩ come ● nm **colpire qcno sul ~** cut sb to the quick; **dal ~** ⟨trasmissione⟩ live; ⟨disegnare⟩ from life; **i vivi** the living
vizi|'are vt spoil ⟨bambino ecc⟩; ⟨guastare⟩ vitiate. **~'ato** a spoilt; ⟨aria⟩ stale. **'vizio** nm vice; ⟨cattiva abitudine⟩ bad habit; ⟨difetto⟩ flaw. **~'oso** a dissolute; ⟨difettoso⟩ faulty; **circolo ~oso** vicious circle
vocabo'lario nm dictionary; ⟨lessico⟩ vocabulary. **vo'cabolo** nm word
vo'cale a vocal ● nf vowel. **vo'calico** a ⟨corde⟩ vocal; ⟨suono⟩ vowel attrib
vocazi'one nf vocation
'voce nf voice; ⟨diceria⟩ rumour; ⟨di bilancio, dizionario⟩ entry
voci'are vi ⟨spettegolare⟩ gossip ● nm buzz of conversation
vocife'rare vi shout; **si vocifera che...** it is rumoured that...
'vog|a nf rowing; ⟨lena⟩ enthusiasm; ⟨moda⟩ vogue; **essere in ~a** be in fashion. **vo'gare** vi row. **~a'tore** nm oarsman; ⟨attrezzo⟩ rowing machine
'vogli|a nf desire; ⟨volontà⟩ will; ⟨della pelle⟩ birthmark; **aver ~a di fare qcsa**

feel like doing sth. **~'oso** a ⟨occhi, persona⟩ covetous
'voi pers pron you; **siete ~?** is that you?; **l'avete fatto ~?** did you do it yourself?. **~a'ltri** pers pron you
vo'lano nm shuttlecock; Mech flywheel
vo'lante a flying; ⟨foglio⟩ loose ● nm steering-wheel
volan'tino nm leaflet
vo'la|re vi fly. **~ta** nf Sport final sprint; **di ~ta** in a rush
vo'latile a ⟨liquido⟩ volatile ● nm bird
volée nf inv Tennis volley
vo'lente a **~ o nolente** whether you like it or not
volente'roso a willing
volenti'eri adv willingly; **~!** with pleasure!
vo'lere vt want; ⟨chiedere di⟩ ask for; ⟨aver bisogno di⟩ need; **vuole che lo faccia io** he wants me to do it; **fai come vuoi** do as you like; **se tuo padre vuole, ti porto al cinema** if your father agrees, I'll take you to the cinema; **vorrei un caffè** I'd like a coffee; **la leggenda vuole che...** legend has it that...; **la vuoi smettere?** will you stop that!; **senza ~** without meaning to; **voler bene/male a qcno** love/have something against sb; **voler dire** mean; **ci vuole il latte** we need milk; **ci vuole tempo/pazienza** it takes time/patience; **volerne a** have a grudge against; **vuoi...vuoi...** either...or... ● nm will; **voleri** pl wishes
vol'gar|e a vulgar; ⟨popolare⟩ common. **~ità** nf inv vulgarity. **~iz'zare** vt popularize. **~'mente** adv ⟨grossolanamente⟩ vulgarly, coarsely; ⟨comunemente⟩ commonly
'volger|e vt/i turn. **~si** vr turn [round]; **~si a** ⟨dedicarsi⟩ take up
voli'era nf aviary
voli'tivo a strong-minded
'volo nm flight; **al ~** ⟨fare qcsa⟩ quickly; ⟨prendere qcsa⟩ in mid-air; **alzarsi in ~** ⟨uccello:⟩ take off; **in ~** airborne. **~ di linea** scheduled flight. **~ nazionale** domestic flight. **~ a vela** gliding.
volontà nf inv will; ⟨desiderio⟩ wish; **a ~** ⟨mangiare⟩ as much as you like. **~ria'mente** adv voluntarily. **volonta'rio** a voluntary ● nm volunteer
volonte'roso a willing
'volpe nf fox
volt nm inv volt
'volta nf time; ⟨turno⟩ turn; ⟨curva⟩ bend; Archit vault; **4 volte** 4 times 4; **a volte** sometimes; **c'era una ~...** once

upon a time, there was...; **una ~** once; **due volte** twice; **tre/quattro volte** three/four times; **una ~ per tutte** once and for all; **uno per ~** one at a time; **uno alla ~** one at a time; **alla ~ di** in the direction of

volta'faccia nm inv volte-face

vol'taggio nm voltage

vol'ta|re vt/i turn; (rigirare) turn round; (rivoltare) turn over; **~re pagi-na** fig forget the past. **~rsi** vr turn [round]

volta'stomaco nm nausea; fig disgust

volteggi'are vi circle; (ginnastica) vault

'volto pp di **volgere** ● nm face; **mi ha mostrato il suo vero ~** he revealed his true colours

vo'lubile a fickle

vo'lum|e nm volume. **~i'noso** a voluminous

voluta'mente adv deliberately

voluttu|osità nf voluptuousness. **~'oso** a voluptuous

vomi'tare vt vomit. **vomi'tevole** a nauseating. **'vomito** nm vomit.

'vongola nf clam

vo'race a voracious. **~'mente** adv voraciously

vo'ragine nf abyss

'vortice nm whirl; (gorgo) whirlpool; (di vento) whirlwind

'vostro (**il ~** m, **la vostra** f, **i vostri** mpl, **le vostre** fpl) poss a your; **è vostra questa macchina?** is this car yours?; **un ~ amico** a friend of yours; **~ padre** your father ● poss pron yours; **i vostri** your folks

vo'ta|nte nmf voter. **~re** vi vote. **~zi'one** nf voting; Sch marks pl. **'voto** nm vote; Sch mark; Relig vow

vs. abbr Comm (**vostro**) yours

vul'canico a volcanic. **vul'cano** nm volcano

vulne'rabil|e a vulnerable. **~ità** nf vulnerability

vuo'tare vt, **vuo'tarsi** vr empty

vu'oto a empty; (non occupato) vacant; **~ di** (sprovvisto) devoid of ● nm empty space; Phys vacuum; fig void; **assegno a ~** dud cheque; **sotto ~** (prodotto) vacuum-packed; **~ a perdere** no deposit. **~ d'aria** air pocket

WwXxYy

W abbr (**viva**) long live

'wafer nm inv (biscotto) wafer

walkie-'talkie nm inv walkie-talkie

water nm inv toilet, loo fam

watt nm inv watt

wat'tora nm inv Phys watt-hour

WC nm WC

'western a inv cowboy attrib ● nm Cinema western

X, x a raggi nmpl X X-rays; **il giorno X** D-day

xenofo'bia nf xenophobia. **xe'nofo-bo, -a** a xenophobic ● nmf xenophobe

xe'res nm inv sherry

xi'lofono nm xylophone

yacht nm inv yacht

yen nm inv Fin yen

'yeti nm yeti

'yoga nm yoga; (praticante) yogi

'yogurt nm inv yoghurt. **~i'era** nf yoghurt-maker

'yorkshire nm inv (cane) Yorkshire terrier

yo-yo nm inv yoyo®

Zz

zaba[gl]i'one *nm* zabaglione (*dessert made from eggs, wine or marsala and sugar*)

'zacchera *nf* (*schizzo*) splash of mud

zaf'fata *nf* whiff; (*di fumo*) cloud

zaffe'rano *nm* saffron

zaf'firo *nm* sapphire

'zaino *nm* rucksack

'zampa *nf* leg; **a quattro zampe** (*animale*) four-legged; (*carponi*) on all fours. **zampe** *pl*/**di gallina** crow's feet

zampil'la|nte *a* spurting. **~re** *vi* spurt. **zam'pillo** *nm* spurt

zam'pogna *nf* bagpipe. **zampo'gnaro** *nm* piper

'zanna *nf* fang; (*di elefante*) tusk

zan'zar|a *nf* mosquito. **~i'era** *nf* (*velo*) mosquito net; (*su finestra*) insect screen

'zappa *nf* hoe. **zap'pare** *vt* hoe

'zattera *nf* raft

za'vorra *nf* ballast; *fig* dead wood

'zazzera *nf* mop of hair

'zebra *nf* zebra; **zebre** *pl* (*passaggio pedonale*) zebra crossing

'zecca[1] *nf* mint; **nuovo di ~** brand-new

'zecca[2] *nf* (*parassita*) tick

zec'chino *nm* sequin; **oro ~** pure gold

ze'lante *a* zealous. **'zelo** *nm* zeal

'zenit *nm* zenith

'zenzero *nm* ginger

'zeppa *nf* wedge

'zeppo *a* packed full; **pieno ~ di** crammed *o* packed with

zer'bino *nm* doormat

'zero *nm* zero, nought; (*in calcio*) nil; *Tennis* love; **due a ~** (*in partite*) two nil; **ricominciare da ~** *fig* start again from scratch

'zeta *nf* zed, zee *Am*

'zia *nf* aunt

zibel'lino *nm* sable

'zigomo *nm* cheek-bone

zigri'nato *a* (*pelle*) grained; (*metallo*) milled

zig'zag *nm inv* zigzag

zim'bello *nm* decoy; (*oggetto di scherno*) laughing-stock

'zinco *nm* zinc

'zingaro, -a *nmf* gypsy

'zio *nm* uncle

zi'tel|la *nf* spinster; *pej* old maid. **~'lona** *nf pej* old maid

zit'tire *vi* fall silent ● *vt* silence. **'zitto** *a* silent; **sta' zitto!** keep quiet!

ziz'zania *nf* (*discordia*) discord; **seminare ~** cause trouble

'zoccolo *nm* clog; (*di cavallo*) hoof; (*di terra*) clump; (*di parete*) skirting board, baseboard *Am*; (*di colonna*) base

zodia'cale *a* of the zodiac. **zo'diaco** *nm* zodiac

'zolfo *nm* sulphur

'zolla *nf* clod; (*di zucchero*) lump

zol'letta *nf* sugar cube, sugar lump

'zombi *nmf inv fig* zombi

'zona *nf* zone; (*area*) area. **~ di depressione** area of low pressure. **~ disco** area for parking discs only. **~ pedonale** pedestrian precinct. **~ verde** green belt

'zonzo *adv* **andare a ~** stroll about

zoo *nm inv* zoo

zoolo'gia *nf* zoology. **zoo'logico** *a* zoological. **zo'ologo, -a** *nmf* zoologist

zoo sa'fari *nm inv* safari park

zoppi'ca|nte *a* limping; *fig* shaky. **~re** *vi* limp; (*essere debole*) be shaky. **'zoppo, -a** *a* lame ● *nmf* cripple

zoti'cone *nm* boor

zu'ava *nf* **calzoni alla ~** plus-fours

'zucca *nf* marrow; (*fam: testa*) head; (*fam: persona*) thickie

zucche'r|are *vt* sugar. **~i'era** *nf* sugar bowl. **~i'ficio** *nm* sugar refinery. **zucche'rino** *a* sugary ● *nm* sugar lump

'zucchero *nm* sugar. **~ di canna** cane sugar. **~ a velo** icing sugar. **zuc-che'roso** *a fig* honeyed

zuc'chin|a *nf*, **~o** *nm* courgette, zucchini *Am*

zuc'cone *nm* blockhead

'zuffa *nf* scuffle

zufo'lare *vt/i* whistle

zu'mare *vi* zoom

'zuppa *nf* soup. **~ inglese** trifle

zup'petta *nf* **fare ~** [**con**] dunk

zuppi'era *nf* soup tureen

'zuppo *a* soaked

TEST YOURSELF WITH WORD GAMES

This section contains a number of word games which will help you to use your dictionary more effectively and to build up your knowledge of Italian vocabulary and usage in a fun and entertaining way. You will find answers to all puzzles and games at the end of the section.

1 X files

A freak power cut in the office has caused all the computers to go down. When they are re-booted, all the words on the screen have become mysteriously jumbled. Use the English to Italian side of the dictionary to help you decipher these Italian names of everyday office and computer equipment.

ATTAIM

TECHISOTD

DANEGA

TALARCEL

PUMETROC

NANEP

RIBICOF

ATTERISA

2 Crowded suitcase

You are at the airport on your way to visit your Welsh cousins in Patagonia when you are told that your suitcase is overweight. Luckily, you had packed a number of things that you did not need because you had forgotten that it was wintertime in the southern hemisphere. Decide which 5 items to jettison from your luggage.

occhiali da sole   calzettoni   sandali

pigiama   guanti   spazzolino da denti   maglietta

crema solare   maglione   cintura

costume da bagno   cappotto   riviste

pantaloncini   sciarpa

3 What are they like?

Here are two lists of adjectives you can use to describe people's characteristics. Each word in the second column is the opposite of one of the adjectives in the first column. Can you link them?

1.	grande	A.	intelligente
2.	biondo	B.	cattivo
3.	stupido	C.	grasso
4.	nervoso	D.	piccolo
5.	buono	E.	simpatico
6.	alto	F.	bruno
7.	paziente	G.	calmo
8.	antipatico	H.	basso
9.	educato	I.	impaziente
10.	magro	J.	maleducato

Example: 1.D. **grande** è il contrario di **piccolo**

4 Link-up

The Italian nouns on the left-hand side are all made up of two separate words but they have been split apart. Try to link up the two halves of each compound, then do the same for the English compounds in the right-hand columns. Now you can match up the Italian compounds with their English translations.

spaventa	capelli	nut	sport
macina	noci	pencil	gloss
taglia	labbra	pepper	screw
dopo	erba	hair	shave
guasta	matite	key	crackers
schiaccia	barba	spoil	crow
porta	tappi	lawn	sharpener
lucida	feste	after	ring
tempera	pepe	lip	mill
asciuga	chiavi	scare	dryer
cava	passeri	cork	mower

5 Body parts

Can you put the right number in the boxes next to the Italian words in the list?

- ☐ l'alluce
- ☐ la bocca
- ☐ il braccio
- ☐ la caviglia
- ☐ il collo
- ☐ la coscia
- ☐ il dito
- ☐ il fianco
- ☐ la fronte
- ☐ la gamba
- ☐ il ginocchio
- ☐ il gomito
- ☐ la mano
- ☐ il mento
- ☐ il naso
- ☐ l'occhio
- ☐ l'ombelico
- ☐ l'orecchio
- ☐ il piede
- ☐ il polpaccio
- ☐ il polso
- ☐ la spalla
- ☐ la testa
- ☐ lo zigomo

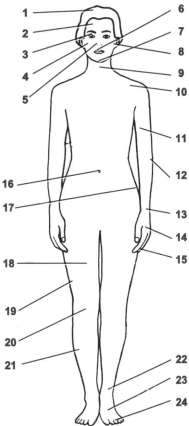

6 Mystery word

To fill in the grid, find the Italian words for all the musical instruments illustrated below. Once you have completed the grid, you'll discover the name of a famous Italian opera singer.

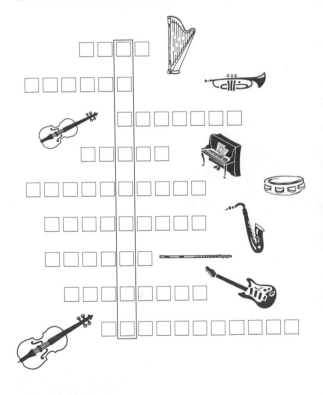

The opera singer is _ _ _ _ _ _ _ _ _

7 The odd one out

In each of the following series, all the words but one are related. Find the odd one out and explain why. If there are words you don't know, use your dictionary to find out what they mean.

example:

- ❏ penna
- ❏ diario
- ❏ libro
- ❏ quaderno
- ☑ spazzola

The odd one out is 'spazzola', because you wouldn't find it in a school-bag.

- ❏ auto
- ❏ aereo
- ❏ motore
- ❏ treno
- ❏ camion

- ❏ nuoto
- ❏ calcio
- ❏ pugilato
- ❏ equitazione
- ❏ ciclismo

- ❏ pentola
- ❏ padella
- ❏ caffettiera
- ❏ portacenere
- ❏ friggitrice

- ❏ correre
- ❏ saltare
- ❏ ballare
- ❏ sognare
- ❏ salire

- ❏ televisore
- ❏ registratore
- ❏ stereo
- ❏ videocassetta
- ❏ giradischi

- ❏ batteria
- ❏ chitarra
- ❏ violino
- ❏ arpa
- ❏ contrabbasso

8 Hidden words — false friends

Hidden in the grid are nine Italian words. First look at the list of false friends below – look up the translation of the Italian words listed, then using your own knowledge and the dictionary, find the translations of the English to search for in the grid.

O	S	E	P	O	G	D	I	C	B
I	S	O	G	L	I	O	L	A	Q
S	U	P	T	C	U	S	T	R	O
C	R	M	S	R	M	A	E	I	V
I	O	U	L	G	E	S	N	N	E
M	F	L	V	A	N	C	U	O	N
M	V	T	O	I	T	Q	T	L	D
I	I	A	T	M	A	R	A	F	I
A	P	S	V	U	B	O	C	H	T
F	D	A	T	I	Z	A	X	E	A

English   Italian

English	Italian		
fine[1]	fine	....	....
sale	sale	....	....
mare	mare	....	....
sole[2]	sole	....	....
estate	estate	....	....
dove	dove	....	....
data	data	....	....
ape	ape	....	....
cute	cute	....	....

9 Curly words

One word is missing in each of the curly lists. Which day, month, capital city and number are missing?
Can you write out the four lists in the right order?

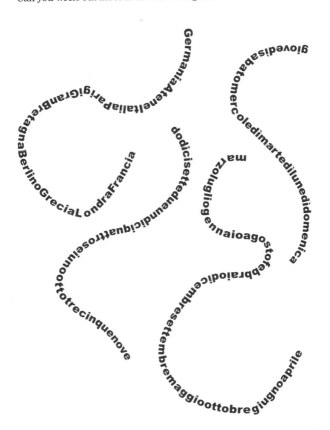

10 Amelia's shooting stars

Amelia is very good at predicting the future, but she is not very good at conjugating Italian verbs in the future tense. Help her to replace all the verbs in brackets with the correct future form.

Leone
23 luglio–22 agosto

(Essere) una settimana fortunata per i Leoni. Lavoro: Un superiore vi (affidare) un compito di grande responsabilità e ciò (potere) creare gelosie tra i colleghi, ma con un po' di diplomazia (risolvere) la situazione. Un viaggio (portare) spese impreviste. Amore: (Fare) incontri piacevoli e interessanti e con Venere che vi protegge nessuno (sapere) resistere al vostro fascino! Gli amici (avere) bisogno del vostro aiuto. Salute: Attenzione allo stress: fate dello sport o prendete una vacanza, (essere) più rilassati e anche l'umore (migliorare).

11 Recipe of the week

The printers have left out some important words in this recipe. Can you supply the missing words from the jumble below?

Ricetta della settimana

Soffriggete una .... piccola e uno spicchio d' .... in 5 cucchiai di ....

Dopo un paio di minuti aggiungete 2 .... sottolio e spappolatele con una ....

Poi, sempre a .... basso, aggiungete il .... sottolio spezzettato e una scatola di .... , ... e ....

Cuocete per una ventina di minuti, poi aggiungete il ....

Nel frattempo lessate 350 grammi di .... in abbondante acqua salata, scolatela al dente e servitela con la .... preparata e, se volete, con ....

prezzemolo   pasta   **acciughe**

cipolla   salsa   parmigiano   **pelati**

sale   **tonno**   olio d'oliva   **pepe**

aglio   **forchetta**   fuoco

12 My life's a mess

Sabrina has a busy schedule but she is a creature of habit and likes to stick to her daily routine. The order of her normal workday has been muddled up in the sentences below. Link up the matching halves of each sentence in the two columns and then try to put the complete sentences in sequence. Be careful, some can link up with more than one from the other column, so you'll have to do them all before you can be sure which go together best.

legge il giornale	per pranzo
torna a casa	come prima cosa
non beve mai caffè	prima delle nove
di solito porta fuori il cane	stanchissima
le piace fare un giro	durante il viaggio di ritorno
legge la corrispondenza	dopo cena
esce a mezzogiorno	durante una riunione
preferisce fare la doccia	di mattina
entra al lavoro	prima di tornare in ufficio
insiste a tenere le riunioni	prima di cena

13 Crossword

Across

1 chicken
4 dog
7 indefinite article (masculine)
8 veil
9 bag
12 ship
13 future of the verb meaning 'to burn' (1st person singular)
15 to tie up
16 one
18 art
19 interrogative pronoun
20 beautiful (feminine)
21 you and me, us
22 beginning of the word meaning 'den'
23 three
24 heart

26 definite article (feminine)
27 age

Down

1 advertising
2 honour
3 fishbone
4 past historic of the verb meaning 'to have dinner' (3rd person singular)
5 wing
6 ninety
10 rust
11 aerobics
14 king
16 to yell
17 first and last letter of the word meaning 'smell'
18 high
25 beginning of the word meaning 'label'

Answers

1

matita	dischetto	agenda	cartella
computer	penna	forbici	tastiera

2

sandali	maglietta	crema solare
costume da bagno	pantaloncini	

3

1. D. *grande* è il contrario di *piccolo*.
2. F. *biondo* è il contrario di *bruno*.
3. A. *stupido* è il contrario di *intelligente*.
4. G. *nervoso* è il contrario di *calmo*.
5. B. *buono* è il contrario di *cattivo*.
6. H. *alto* è il contrario di *basso*.
7. I. *paziente* è il contrario di *impaziente*.
8. E. *antipatico* è il contrario di *simpatico*.
9. J. *educato* è il contrario di *maleducato*.
10. C. *magro* è il contrario di *grasso*.

4

spaventapasseri	=	scarecrow
macinapepe	=	peppermill
tagliaerba	=	lawn-mower
dopobarba	=	aftershave
guastafeste	=	spoilsport
schiaccianoci	=	nutcrackers
portachiavi	=	keyring
lucidalabbra	=	lipgloss
temperamatite	=	pencil sharpener
asciugacapelli	=	hairdryer
cavatappi	=	corkscrew

5

1	la testa	10	la spalla	19	la gamba
2	la fronte	11	il braccio	20	il ginocchio
3	l'occhio	12	il gomito	21	il polpaccio
4	lo zigomo	13	il polso	22	la caviglia
5	il naso	14	la mano	23	il piede
6	la bocca	15	il dito	24	l'alluce
7	il mento	16	l'ombelico		
8	l'orecchio	17	il fianco		
9	il collo	18	la coscia		

6

ARPA   The opera singer's name is **PAVAROTTI**
TROMBA
      VIOLINO
    PIANO
TAMBURELLO
  SASSOFONO
  FLAUTO
    CHITARRA
     VIOLONCELLO

7

motore – because it isn't a vehicle
portacenere – because it isn't used for cooking
videocassetta – because it isn't an electrical device
calcio – because it's the only team game in the list
sognare – because it's the only verb in the list which doesn't describe a
   movement
batteria – because it isn't a stringed instrument

8

end	summer	skin	giumenta	dati
salt	where		sogliola	scimmia
sea	date	multa	tenuta	carino
sun	bee	vendita	colomba	

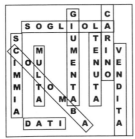

9

venerdì;   domenica, lunedì, martedì, mercoledì, giovedì, venerdì,
               sabato

novembre;   gennaio, febbraio, marzo, aprile, maggio, giugno, luglio,
               agosto, settembre, ottobre, novembre, dicembre

Roma;   Germania/Berlino, Francia/Parigi, Grecia/Atene, Gran
               Bretagna/Londra, Italia/Roma

dieci;   uno, due, tre, quattro, cinque, sei, sette, otto, nove, dieci,
               undici, dodici

10

sarà	affiderà	potrà	risolverete
porterà	farete	saprà	avranno
sarete	migliorerà		

11

Soffriggete una CIPOLLA piccola e uno spicchio d'AGLIO in 5 cucchiai di OLIO D'OLIVA

Dopo un paio di minuti aggiungete 2 ACCIUGHE sottolio e spappolatele con una FORCHETTA.

Poi, sempre a FUOCO basso, aggiungete il TONNO sottolio spezzettato e una scatola di PELATI, SALE e PEPE.

Cuocete per una ventina di minuti, poi aggiungete il PREZZEMOLO.

Nel frattempo lessate 350 grammi di PASTA in abbondante acqua salata, scolatela al dente e servitela con la SALSA preparata e, se volete, con PARMIGIANO.

12

entra al lavoro prima delle nove
legge la corrispondenza come prima cosa
insiste a tenere le riunioni di mattina
non beve mai caffè durante una riunione
esce a mezzogiorno per pranzo
le piace fare un giro prima di tornare in ufficio
legge il giornale durante il viaggio di ritorno
torna a casa stanchissima
preferisce fare la doccia prima di cena
di solito porta fuori il cane dopo cena

13

Aa

A /eɪ/ n Mus la m inv
a /ə/, accentato /eɪ/ (davanti a una vocale **an**) indef art un m, una f; (before s + consonant, gn, ps and z) uno; (before feminine noun starting with a vowel) un'; (each) (a). **I am a lawyer** sono avvocato; **a tiger is a feline** la tigre è un felino; **a knife and fork** un coltello e una forchetta; **a Mr Smith is looking for you** un certo signor Smith ti sta cercando; **£2 a kilo/a head** due sterline al chilo/a testa
aback /ə'bæk/ adv **be taken ~** essere preso in contropiede
abandon /ə'bændən/ vt abbandonare; (give up) rinunciare a ● n abbandono m. **~ed** a abbandonato
abashed /ə'bæʃt/ a imbarazzato
abate /ə'beɪt/ vi calmarsi
abattoir /'æbətwɑː(r)/ n mattatoio m
abbey /'æbɪ/ n abbazia f
abbreviat|e /ə'briːvɪeɪt/ vt abbreviare. **~ion** /-'eɪʃn/ n abbreviazione f
abdicat|e /'æbdɪkeɪt/ vi abdicare. ● vt rinunciare a. **~ion** /-'keɪʃn/ n abdicazione f
abdom|en /'æbdəmən/ n addome m. **~inal** /-'dɒmɪnl/ a addominale
abduct /əb'dʌkt/ vt rapire. **~ion** /-'ʌkʃn/ n rapimento m
aberration /æbə'reɪʃn/ n aberrazione f
abet /ə'bet/ vt (pt/pp **abetted**) **aid and ~** Jur essere complice di
abeyance /ə'beɪəns/ n **in ~** in sospeso; **fall into ~** cadere in disuso
abhor /əb'hɔː(r)/ vt (pt/pp **abhorred**) aborrire. **~rence** /-'hɒrəns/ n orrore m
abid|e /ə'baɪd/ vt (pt/pp **abided**) (tolerate) sopportare ● **abide by** vi rispettare. **~ing** a perpetuo
ability /ə'bɪlətɪ/ n capacità f inv
abject /'æbdʒekt/ a (poverty) degradante; (apology) umile; (coward) abietto
ablaze /ə'bleɪz/ a in fiamme; **be ~ with light** risplendere di luci
able /'eɪbl/ a capace, abile; **be ~ to do sth** poter fare qcsa; **were you ~ to...?**

sei riuscito a...? **~-bodied** a robusto; Mil abile
ably /'eɪblɪ/ adv abilmente
abnormal /æb'nɔːml/ a anormale. **~ity** /-'mælətɪ/ n anormalità f inv. **~ly** adv in modo anormale
aboard /ə'bɔːd/ adv & prep a bordo
aboli|sh /ə'bɒlɪʃ/ vt abolire. **~tion** /æbə'lɪʃn/ n abolizione f
abomina|ble /ə'bɒmɪnəbl/ a abominevole
Aborigine /æbə'rɪdʒənɪ/ n aborigeno, -a mf d'Australia
abort /ə'bɔːt/ vt fare abortire; fig annullare. **~ion** /-ɔːʃn/ n aborto m; **have an ~ion** abortire. **~ive** /-tɪv/ a (attempt) infruttuoso
abound /ə'baʊnd/ vi abbondare; **~ in** abbondare di
about /ə'baʊt/ adv (here and there) [di] qua e [di] là; (approximately) circa; **be ~** (illness, tourists:) essere in giro; **be up and ~** essere alzato; **leave sth lying ~** lasciare in giro qcsa ● prep (concerning) su; (in the region of) intorno a; (here and there in) per; **what is the book/the film ~?** di cosa parla il libro/il film?; **he wants to see you - what ~?** ti vuole vedere - a che proposito?; **talk/know ~** parlare/sapere di; **I know nothing ~** non ne so niente; **~ 5 o'clock** intorno alle 5; **travel ~ the world** viaggiare per il mondo; **be ~ to do sth** stare per fare qcsa; **how ~ going to the cinema?** e se andassimo al cinema?
about: **~-face** n, **~-turn** n dietro front m inv
above /ə'bʌv/ adv & prep sopra; **~ all** soprattutto
above: **~-board** a onesto. **~-mentioned** a suddetto
abrasive /ə'breɪsɪv/ a abrasivo; (remark) caustico ● n abrasivo m
abreast /ə'brest/ adv fianco a fianco; **come ~ of** allinearsi con; **keep ~ of** tenersi al corrente di
abridged /ə'brɪdʒd/ a ridotto
abroad /ə'brɔːd/ adv all'estero

abrupt /ə'brʌpt/ a brusco

abscess /'æbsɪs/ n ascesso m

abscond /əb'skɒnd/ vi fuggire

absence /'æbsəns/ n assenza f; ⟨lack⟩ mancanza f

absent[1] /'æbsənt/ a assente

absent[2] /æb'sent/ vt ~ oneself essere assente

absentee /æbsən'ti:/ n assente mf

absent-minded /æbsənt'maɪndɪd/ a distratto

absolute /'æbsəlu:t/ a assoluto; **an ~ idiot** un perfetto idiota. **~ly** adv assolutamente; ⟨fam: indicating agreement⟩ esattamente

absolution /æbsə'lu:ʃn/ n assoluzione f

absolve /əb'zɒlv/ vt assolvere

absorb /əb'sɔ:b/ vt assorbire; ~ed in assorto in. **~ent** /-ənt/ a assorbente

absorption /əb'sɔ:pʃn/ n assorbimento m; ⟨in activity⟩ concentrazione f

abstain /əb'steɪn/ vi astenersi ⟨from da⟩

abstemious /əb'sti:mɪəs/ a moderato

abstention /əb'stenʃn/ n Pol astensione f

abstinence /'æbstɪnəns/ n astinenza f

abstract /'æbstrækt/ a astratto ● n astratto m; ⟨summary⟩ estratto m

absurd /əb'sɜ:d/ a assurdo. **~ity** n assurdità f inv

abundan|ce /ə'bʌndəns/ n abbondanza f. **~t** a abbondante

abuse[1] /ə'bju:z/ vt ⟨misuse⟩ abusare di; ⟨insult⟩ insultare; ⟨ill-treat⟩ maltrattare

abus|e[2] /ə'bju:s/ n abuso m; ⟨verbal⟩ insulti mpl; ⟨ill-treatment⟩ maltrattamento m. **~ive** /-ɪv/ a offensivo

abut /ə'bʌt/ vi (pt/pp **abutted**) confinare ⟨onto con⟩

abysmal /ə'bɪzml/ a fam pessimo; ⟨ignorance⟩ abissale

abyss /ə'bɪs/ n abisso m

academic /ækə'demɪk/ a teorico; ⟨qualifications, system⟩ scolastico; **be ~** ⟨person:⟩ avere predisposizione allo studio ● n docente mf universitario, -a

academy /ə'kædəmɪ/ n accademia f; ⟨of music⟩ conservatorio m

accede /ək'si:d/ vi ~ **to** accedere a ⟨request⟩; salire a ⟨throne⟩

accelerat|e /ək'seləreɪt/ vt/i accelerare. **~ion** /-'reɪʃn/ n accelerazione f. **~or** n Auto acceleratore m

accent /'æksənt/ n accento m

accentuate /ək'sentjʊeɪt/ vt accentuare

accept /ək'sept/ vt accettare. **~able**

/-əbl/ a accettabile. **~ance** n accettazione f

access /'ækses/ n accesso m. **~ible** /ək'sesɪbl/ a accessibile

accession /ək'seʃn/ n ⟨to throne⟩ ascesa f al trono

accessory /ək'sesərɪ/ n accessorio m; Jur complice mf

accident /'æksɪdənt/ n incidente m; ⟨chance⟩ caso m; **by ~** per caso; ⟨unintentionally⟩ senza volere; **I'm sorry, it was an ~** mi dispiace, non l'ho fatto apposta. **~al** /-'dentl/ a ⟨meeting⟩ casuale; ⟨death⟩ incidentale; ⟨unintentional⟩ involontario. **~ally** adv per caso; ⟨unintentionally⟩ inavvertitamente

acclaim /ə'kleɪm/ n acclamazione f ● vt acclamare ⟨as come⟩

acclimatize /ə'klaɪmətaɪz/ vt **become ~d** acclimatarsi

accolade /'ækəleɪd/ n riconoscimento m

accommodat|e /ə'kɒmədeɪt/ vt ospitare; ⟨oblige⟩ favorire. **~ing** a accomodante. **~ion** /-'deɪʃn/ n ⟨place to stay⟩ sistemazione f

accompan|iment /ə'kʌmpənɪmənt/ n accompagnamento m. **~ist** n Mus accompagnatore, -trice mf

accompany /ə'kʌmpənɪ/ vt (pt/pp **-ied**) accompagnare

accomplice /ə'kʌmplɪs/ n complice mf

accomplish /ə'kʌmplɪʃ/ vt ⟨achieve⟩ concludere; realizzare ⟨aim⟩. **~ed** a dotato; ⟨fact⟩ compiuto. **~ment** n realizzazione f; ⟨achievement⟩ risultato m; ⟨talent⟩ talento m

accord /ə'kɔ:d/ n ⟨treaty⟩ accordo m; **with one ~** tutti d'accordo; **of his own ~** di sua spontanea volontà. **~ance** n **in ~ance with** in conformità di o a

according /ə'kɔ:dɪŋ/ adv ~ **to** secondo. **~ly** adv di conseguenza

accordion /ə'kɔ:dɪən/ n fisarmonica f

accost /ə'kɒst/ vt abbordare

account /ə'kaʊnt/ n conto m; ⟨report⟩ descrizione f; ⟨of eye-witness⟩ resoconto m; **~s** pl Comm conti mpl; **on ~ of** a causa di; **on no ~** per nessun motivo; **on this ~** per questo motivo; **on my ~** per causa mia; **of no ~** di nessuna importanza; **take into ~** tener conto di ● **account for** vi ⟨explain⟩ spiegare; ⟨person:⟩ render conto di; ⟨constitute⟩ costituire. **~ability** n responsabilità f inv. **~able** a responsabile ⟨for di⟩

accountant /ə'kauntənt/ n (book-keeper) contabile mf; (consultant) commercialista mf

accredited /ə'kredıtıd/ a accreditato

accrue /ə'kru:/ vi (interest:) maturare

accumulat|e /ə'kju:mjulеıt/ vt accumulare ● vi accumularsi. **~ion** /-'leıʃn/ n accumulazione f

accura|cy /'ækʊrəsɪ/ n precisione f. **~te** /-rət/ a preciso. **~tely** adv con precisione

accusation /ækjʊ'zeıʃn/ n accusa f

accusative /ə'kju:zətɪv/ a & n ~ [case] Gram accusativo m

accuse /ə'kju:z/ vt accusare; ~ sb of doing sth accusare qcno di fare qcsa. **~d** the **~d** l'accusato m, l'accusata f

accustom /ə'kʌstəm/ vt abituare (to a); **grow** or **get ~ed to** abituarsi a. **~ed** a abituato

ace /eıs/ n Cards asso m; (tennis) ace m inv

ache /eık/ n dolore m ● vi dolere, far male; ~ **all over** essere tutto indolenzito

achieve /ə'tʃi:v/ vt ottenere (success); realizzare (goal, ambition). **~ment** n (feat) successo m

acid /'æsıd/ a acido ● n acido m. **~ity** /ə'sıdətı/ n acidità f. ~ **'rain** n pioggia f acida

acknowledge /ək'nɒlıdʒ/ vt riconoscere; rispondere a (greeting); far cenno di aver notato (sb's presence); ~ **receipt of** accusare ricevuta di. **~ment** n riconoscimento m; **send an ~ment of a letter** confermare il ricevimento di una lettera

acne /'æknı/ n acne f

acorn /'eıkɔ:n/ n ghianda f

acoustic /ə'ku:stık/ a acustico. **~s** npl acustica fsg

acquaint /ə'kweınt/ vt ~ **sb with** mettere qcno al corrente di; **be ~ed with** conoscere (person); essere a conoscenza di (fact). **~ance** n (person) conoscente mf; **make sb's ~ance** fare la conoscenza di qcno

acquiesce /ækwı'es/ vi acconsentire (to, in a). **~nce** n acquiescenza f

acquire /ə'kwaıə(r)/ vt acquisire

acquisit|ion /ækwı'zıʃn/ n acquisizione f. **~ive** /ə'kwızətıv/ a avido

acquit /ə'kwıt/ vt (pt/pp acquitted) assolvere; ~ **oneself well** cavarsela bene. **~tal** n assoluzione f

acre /'eıkə(r)/ n acro m (= 4 047 m²)

acrid /'ækrıd/ a acre

acrimon|ious /ækrı'məunıəs/ a aspro. **~y** /'ækrımənı/ n asprezza f

acrobat /'ækrəbæt/ n acrobata mf. **~ic** /-'bætık/ a acrobatico

across /ə'krɒs/ adv dall'altra parte; (wide) in larghezza; (not lengthwise) attraverso; (in crossword) orizzontale; **come ~ sth** imbattersi in qcsa; **go ~** attraversare ● prep (crosswise) di traverso su; (on the other side of) dall'altra parte di

act /ækt/ n atto m; (in variety show) numero m; **put on an ~** fam fare scena ● vi agire; (behave) comportarsi; Theat recitare; (pretend) fingere; ~ **as** fare da ● vt recitare (role). **~ing** a (deputy) provvisorio ● n Theat recitazione f; (profession) teatro m. **~ing profession** n professione f dell'attore

action /'ækʃn/ n azione f; Mil combattimento m; Jur azione f legale; **out of ~** (machine:) fuori uso; **take ~** agire. ~ **'replay** n replay m inv

activ|e /'æktıv/ a attivo. **~ely** adv attivamente. **~ity** /-'tıvətı/ n attività f inv

act|or /'æktə(r)/ n attore m. **~ress** n attrice f

actual /'æktʃʊəl/ a (real) reale. **~ly** adv in realtà

acumen /'ækjʊmən/ n acume m

acupuncture /'ækjʊ-/ n agopuntura f

acute /ə'kju:t/ a acuto; (shortage, hardship) estremo

ad /æd/ n fam pubblicità f inv; (in paper) inserzione f, annuncio m

AD abbr (Anno Domini) d.C.

adamant /'ædəmənt/ a categorico (that sul fatto che)

adapt /ə'dæpt/ vt adattare (play) ● vi adattarsi. **~ability** /-ə'bılətı/ n adattabilità f. **~able** /-əbl/ a adattabile

adaptation /ædæp'teıʃn/ n Theat adattamento m

adapter, adaptor /ə'dæptə(r)/ n adattatore m; (two-way) presa f multipla

add /æd/ vt aggiungere; Math addizionare ● vi addizionare; ~ **to** (fig: increase) aggravare. **add up** vt addizionare (figures) ● vi addizionare; ~ **up to** ammontare a; **it doesn't ~ up** fig non quadra

adder /'ædə(r)/ n vipera f

addict /'ædıkt/ n tossicodipendente mf, fig fanatico, -a mf

addict|ed /ə'dıktıd/ a assuefatto (to a); **~ed to drugs** tossicodipendente; **he's ~ed to television** è videodipendente. **~ion** /-ıkʃn/ n dipendenza f; (to drugs) tossicodipendenza *f*. **~ive** /-ɪv/ *a* be ~ive dare assuefazione

addition /ə'dɪʃn/ *n Math* addizione *f*; ⟨*thing added*⟩ aggiunta *f*; **in** ~ in aggiunta. **~al** *a* supplementare. **~ally** *adv* in più

additive /'ædɪtɪv/ *n* additivo *m*

address /ə'dres/ *n* indirizzo *m*; ⟨*speech*⟩ discorso *m*; **form of** ~ formula *f* di cortesia ● *vt* indirizzare; ⟨*speak to*⟩ rivolgersi a ⟨*person*⟩; tenere un discorso a ⟨*meeting*⟩. **~ee** /ædre'siː/ *n* destinatario, -a *mf*

adenoids /'ædənɔɪdz/ *npl* adenoidi *fpl*

adept /'ædept/ *a & n* esperto, -a *mf* (at in)

adequate /'ædɪkwət/ *a* adeguato. **~ly** *adv* adeguatamente

adhere /əd'hɪə(r)/ *vi* aderire; ~ to attenersi a ⟨*principles, rules*⟩

adhesive /əd'hiːsɪv/ *a* adesivo ● *n* adesivo *m*

adjacent /ə'dʒeɪsənt/ *a* adiacente

adjective /'ædʒɪktɪv/ *n* aggettivo *m*

adjoin /ə'dʒɔɪn/ *vt* essere adiacente a. **~ing** *a* adiacente

adjourn /ə'dʒɜːn/ *vt/i* aggiornare ⟨*until a*⟩. **~ment** *n* aggiornamento *m*

adjudicate /ə'dʒuːdɪkeɪt/ *vi* decidere; ⟨*in competition*⟩ giudicare

adjust /ə'dʒʌst/ *vt* modificare; regolare ⟨*focus, sound etc*⟩ ● *vi* adattarsi. **~able** /-əbl/ *a* regolabile. **~ment** *n* adattamento *m*; *Techn* regolamento *m*

ad lib /æd'lɪb/ *a* improvvisato ● *adv* a piacere ● *vi* (*pt/pp* **ad libbed**) *fam* improvvisare

administer /əd'mɪnɪstə(r)/ *vt* amministrare; somministrare ⟨*medicine*⟩

administrat|ion /ədmɪnɪ'streɪʃn/ *n* amministrazione *f*; *Pol* governo *m*. **~or** /əd'mɪnɪstreɪtə(r)/ *n* amministratore, -trice *mf*

admirable /'ædmərəbl/ *a* ammirevole

admiral /'ædmərəl/ *n* ammiraglio *m*

admiration /ædmə'reɪʃn/ *n* ammirazione *f*

admire /əd'maɪə(r)/ *vt* ammirare. **~r** *n* ammiratore, -trice *mf*

admissible /əd'mɪsəbl/ *a* ammissibile

admission /əd'mɪʃn/ *n* ammissione *f*; ⟨*to hospital*⟩ ricovero *m*; ⟨*entry*⟩ ingresso *m*

admit /əd'mɪt/ *vt* (*pt/pp* **admitted**) ⟨*let in*⟩ far entrare; ⟨*to hospital*⟩ ricoverare; ⟨*acknowledge*⟩ ammettere ● *vi* ~ to sth ammettere qcsa. **~tance** *n* ammissione

f; **'no ~tance'** 'vietato l'ingresso'. **~tedly** *adv* bisogna riconoscerlo

admonish /əd'mɒnɪʃ/ *vt* ammonire

ado /ə'duː/ *n* without more ~ senza ulteriori indugi

adolescen|ce /ædə'lesns/ *n* adolescenza *f*. **~t** *a & n* adolescente *mf*

adopt /ə'dɒpt/ *vt* adottare; *Pol* scegliere ⟨*candidate*⟩. **~ion** /-ɒpʃn/ *n* adozione *f*. **~ive** /-ɪv/ *a* adottivo

ador|able /ə'dɔːrəbl/ *a* adorabile. **~ation** /ædə'reɪʃn/ *n* adorazione *f*

adore /ə'dɔː(r)/ *vt* adorare

adrenalin /ə'drenəlɪn/ *n* adrenalina *f*

Adriatic /eɪdrɪ'ætɪk/ *a* & **the** ~ [**Sea**] il mare Adriatico, l'Adriatico

adrift /ə'drɪft/ *a* alla deriva; **be** ~ andare alla deriva; **come** ~ staccarsi

adroit /ə'drɔɪt/ *a* abile

adulation /ædjʊ'leɪʃn/ *n* adulazione *f*

adult /'ædʌlt/ *n* adulto, -a *mf*

adulterate /ə'dʌltəreɪt/ *vt* adulterare ⟨*wine*⟩

adultery /ə'dʌltərɪ/ *n* adulterio *m*

advance /əd'vɑːns/ *n* avanzamento *m*; *Mil* avanzata *f*; ⟨*payment*⟩ anticipo *m*; **in** ~ in anticipo ● *vi* avanzare; ⟨*make progress*⟩ fare progressi ● *vt* avanzare ⟨*theory*⟩; promuovere ⟨*cause*⟩; anticipare ⟨*money*⟩. **~ booking** *n* prenotazione *f* [in anticipo]. **~d** *a* avanzato. **~ment** *n* promozione *f*

advantage /əd'vɑːntɪdʒ/ *n* vantaggio *m*; **take** ~ **of** approfittare di. **~ous** /ædvən'teɪdʒəs/ *a* vantaggioso

advent /'ædvent/ *n* avvento *m*

adventur|e /əd'ventʃə(r)/ *n* avventura *f*. **~ous** /-rəs/ *a* avventuroso

adverb /'ædvɜːb/ *n* avverbio *m*

adversary /'ædvəsərɪ/ *n* avversario, -a *mf*

advers|e /'ædvɜːs/ *a* avverso. **~ity** /əd'vɜːsətɪ/ *n* avversità *f*

advert /'ædvɜːt/ *n fam* = **advertisement**

advertise /'ædvətaɪz/ *vt* reclamizzare; mettere un annuncio per ⟨*job, flat*⟩ ● *vi* fare pubblicità; ⟨*for job, flat*⟩ mettere un annuncio

advertisement /əd'vɜːtɪsmənt/ *n* pubblicità *f inv*; ⟨*in paper*⟩ inserzione *f*, annuncio *m*

advertis|er /'ædvətaɪzə(r)/ *n* ⟨*in newspaper*⟩ inserzionista *mf*. **~ing** *n* pubblicità *f* ● *attrib* pubblicitario

advice /əd'vaɪs/ *n* consigli *mpl*; **piece of** ~ consiglio *m*

advisable /əd'vaɪzəbl/ *a* consigliabile

advis|e /əd'vaɪz/ vt consigliare; (*inform*) avvisare; **~e sb to do sth** consigliare a qcno di fare qcsa; **~e sb against sth** sconsigliare qcsa a qcno. **~er** n consulente mf. **~ory** a consultivo

advocate[1] /'ædvəkət/ n (*supporter*) fautore, -trice mf

advocate[2] /'ædvəkeɪt/ vt propugnare

aerial /'eərɪəl/ a aereo ● n antenna f

aerobics /eə'rəʊbɪks/ n aerobica fsg

aero|drome /'eərədrəʊm/ n aerodromo m. **~plane** n aeroplano m

aerosol /'eərəsɒl/ n bomboletta f spray

aesthetic /iːs'θetɪk/ a estetico

afar /ə'fɑː(r)/ adv **from ~** da lontano

affable /'æfəbl/ a affabile

affair /ə'feə(r)/ n affare m; (*scandal*) caso m; (*sexual*) relazione f

affect /ə'fekt/ vt influire su; (*emotionally*) colpire; (*concern*) riguardare. **~ation** /æfek'teɪʃn/ n affettazione f. **~ed** a affettato

affection /ə'fekʃn/ n affetto m. **~ate** /-ət/ a affettuoso

affiliated /ə'fɪlɪeɪtɪd/ a affiliato

affinity /ə'fɪnətɪ/ n affinità f inv

affirm /ə'fɜːm/ vt affermare; Jur dichiarare solennemente

affirmative /ə'fɜːmətɪv/ a affermativo ● n **in the ~** affermativamente

afflict /ə'flɪkt/ vt affliggere. **~ion** /-ɪkʃn/ n afflizione f

affluen|ce /'æfluəns/ n agiatezza f. **~t** a agiato

afford /ə'fɔːd/ vt **be able to ~ sth** potersi permettere qcsa. **~able** /-əbl/ a abbordabile

affray /ə'freɪ/ n rissa f

affront /ə'frʌnt/ n affronto m

afield /ə'fiːld/ adv **further ~** più lontano

afloat /ə'fləʊt/ a a galla

afoot /ə'fʊt/ a **there's something ~** si sta preparando qualcosa

aforesaid /ə'fɔːsed/ a Jur suddetto

afraid /ə'freɪd/ a **be ~** aver paura; **I'm ~ not** purtroppo no; **I'm ~ so** temo di sì; **I'm ~ I can't help you** mi dispiace, ma non posso esserle d'aiuto

afresh /ə'freʃ/ adv da capo

Africa /'æfrɪkə/ n Africa f. **~n** a & n africano, -a mf

after /'ɑːftə(r)/ adv dopo; **the day ~** il giorno dopo; **be ~** cercare ● prep dopo; **~ all** dopotutto; **the day ~ tomorrow** dopodomani ● conj dopo che

after: ~-effect n conseguenza f. **~math** /-mɑːθ/ n conseguenze fpl; **the**

~math of war il dopoguerra; **in the ~math of** nel periodo successivo a. **~'noon** n pomeriggio m; **good ~noon!** buon giorno! **~-sales service** n servizio m assistenza clienti. **~shave** n [lozione f] dopobarba m inv. **~thought** n added as an **~thought** aggiunto in un secondo momento; **~wards** adv in seguito

again /ə'geɪn/ adv di nuovo; [then] **~** (*besides*) inoltre; (*on the other hand*) d'altra parte; **~ and ~** continuamente

against /ə'geɪnst/ prep contro

age /eɪdʒ/ n età f inv; (*era*) era f; **~s** fam secoli; **what ~ are you?** quanti anni hai?; **be under ~** non avere l'età richiesta; **he's two years of ~** ha due anni ● vt/i (*pres p* **ageing**) invecchiare

aged[1] /eɪdʒd/ a **~ two** di due anni

aged[2] /'eɪdʒɪd/ a anziano ● npl **the ~** gli anziani

ageless /'eɪdʒlɪs/ a senza età

agency /'eɪdʒənsɪ/ n agenzia f; **have the ~ for** essere un concessionario di

agenda /ə'dʒendə/ n ordine m del giorno; **on the ~** all'ordine del giorno; fig in programma

agent /'eɪdʒənt/ n agente mf

aggravat|e /'ægrəveɪt/ vt aggravare; (*annoy*) esasperare. **~ion** /-'veɪʃn/ n aggravamento m; (*annoyance*) esasperazione f

aggregate /'ægrɪgət/ a totale ● n totale m; **on ~** nel complesso

aggress|ion /ə'greʃn/ n aggressione f. **~ive** /-sɪv/ a aggressivo. **~iveness** n aggressività f. **~or** n aggressore m

aggro /'ægrəʊ/ n fam aggressività f; (*problems*) grane fpl

aghast /ə'gɑːst/ a inorridito

agil|e /'ædʒaɪl/ a agile. **~ity** /ə'dʒɪlətɪ/ n agilità f

agitat|e /'ædʒɪteɪt/ vt mettere in agitazione; (*shake*) agitare ● vi fig **~e for** creare delle agitazioni per. **~ed** a agitato. **~ion** /-'teɪʃn/ n agitazione f. **~or** n agitatore, -trice mf

agnostic /æg'nɒstɪk/ a agnostico, -a mf

ago /ə'gəʊ/ adv fa; **a long time/a month ~** molto tempo/un mese fa

agog /ə'gɒg/ a eccitato

agonize /'ægənaɪz/ vi angosciarsi (**over** per). **~ing** a angosciante

agony /'ægənɪ/ n agonia f; (*mental*) angoscia f; **be in ~** avere dei dolori atroci

agree /ə'griː/ vt accordarsi su; **~ to do sth** accettare di fare qcsa; **~ that** essere d'accordo [sul fatto] che ● *vi* essere d'accordo; ⟨*figures:*⟩ concordare; ⟨*reach agreement*⟩ mettersi d'accordo; ⟨*get on*⟩ andare d'accordo; ⟨*consent*⟩ acconsentire (**to** a); **it doesn't ~ with me** mi fa male; **~ with sth** ⟨*approve of*⟩ approvare qcsa

agreeable /əˈgriːəbl/ *a* gradevole; ⟨*willing*⟩ d'accordo

agreed /əˈgriːd/ *a* convenuto

agreement /əˈgriːmənt/ *n* accordo *m*; **in ~** d'accordo

agricultur|al /ægrɪˈkʌltʃərəl/ *a* agricolo. **~e** /ˈægrɪkʌltʃə(r)/ *n* agricoltura *f*

aground /əˈgraʊnd/ *adv* **run ~** ⟨*ship:*⟩ arenarsi

ahead /əˈhed/ *adv* avanti; **be ~ of** essere davanti rispetto a; **draw ~** passare davanti (**of** a); **get ~** ⟨*in life*⟩ riuscire; **go ~!** fai pure!; **look ~** pensare all'avvenire; **plan ~** fare progetti per l'avvenire

aid /eɪd/ *n* aiuto *m*; **in ~ of** a favore di ● *vt* aiutare

aide /eɪd/ *n* assistente *mf*

Aids /eɪdz/ *n* AIDS *m*

ail|ing /ˈeɪlɪŋ/ *a* malato. **~ment** *n* disturbo *m*

aim /eɪm/ *n* mira *f*; *fig* scopo *m*; **take ~** prendere la mira ● *vt* puntare ⟨*gun*⟩ (**at** contro) ● *vi* mirare; **~ to do sth** aspirare a fare qcsa. **~less** *a*, **~lessly** *adv* senza scopo

air /eə(r)/ *n* aria *f*; **be on the ~** ⟨*programme:*⟩ essere in onda; **put on ~s** darsi delle arie; **by ~** in aereo; ⟨*airmail*⟩ per via aerea ● *vt* arieggiare; far conoscere ⟨*views*⟩

air: **~-bed** *n* materassino *m* [gonfiabile]. **~-conditioned** *a* con aria condizionata. **~-conditioning** *n* aria *f* condizionata. **~craft** *n* aereo *m*. **~craft carrier** *n* portaerei *f inv*. **~fare** *n* tariffa *f* aerea. **~field** *n* campo *m* d'aviazione. **~ force** *n* aviazione *f*. **~ freshener** *n* deodorante *m* per l'ambiente. **~gun** *n* fucile *m* pneumatico. **~ hostess** *n* hostess *f inv*. **~ letter** *n* aerogramma *m*. **~line** *n* compagnia *f* aerea. **~lock** *n* bolla *f* d'aria. **~mail** *n* posta *f* aerea. **~plane** *n Am* aereo *m*. **~ pocket** *n* vuoto *m* d'aria. **~port** *n* aeroporto *m*. **~-raid** *n* incursione *f* aerea. **~-raid shelter** *n* rifugio *m* antiaereo. **~ship** *n* dirigibile *m*. **~tight** *a* ermetico. **~ traffic** *n* traffico *m* aereo. **~-traffic controller** *n* controllore *m* di volo. **~worthy** *a* idoneo al volo

airy /ˈeərɪ/ *a* (**-ier, -iest**) arieggiato; ⟨*manner*⟩ noncurante

aisle /aɪl/ *n* corridoio *m*; ⟨*in supermarket*⟩ corsia *f*; ⟨*in church*⟩ navata *f*

ajar /əˈdʒɑː(r)/ *a* socchiuso

akin /əˈkɪn/ *a* **~ to** simile a

alacrity /əˈlækrətɪ/ *n* alacrità *f inv*

alarm /əˈlɑːm/ *n* allarme *m*; **set the ~** ⟨*of alarm clock*⟩ mettere la sveglia ● *vt* allarmare. **~ clock** *n* sveglia *f*

alas /əˈlæs/ *int* ahimè

album /ˈælbəm/ *n* album *m inv*

alcohol /ˈælkəhɒl/ *n* alcol *m*. **~ic** /-ˈhɒlɪk/ *a* alcolico ● *n* alcolizzato, -a *mf*. **~ism** *n* alcolismo *m*

alcove /ˈælkəʊv/ *n* alcova *f*

alert /əˈlɜːt/ *a* sveglio; ⟨*watchful*⟩ vigile ● *n* segnale *m* d'allarme; **be on the ~** stare allerta ● *vt* allertare

algae /ˈældʒiː/ *npl* alghe *fpl*

algebra /ˈældʒɪbrə/ *n* algebra *f*

Algeria /ælˈdʒɪərɪə/ *n* Algeria *f*. **~n** *a* & *n* algerino, -a *mf*

alias /ˈeɪlɪəs/ *n* pseudonimo *m* ● *adv* alias

alibi /ˈælɪbaɪ/ *n* alibi *m inv*

alien /ˈeɪlɪən/ *a* straniero; *fig* estraneo ● *n* straniero, -a *mf*; ⟨*from space*⟩ alieno, -a *mf*

alienat|e /ˈeɪlɪəneɪt/ *vt* alienare. **~ion** /-ˈneɪʃn/ *n* alienazione *f*

alight[1] /əˈlaɪt/ *vi* scendere; ⟨*bird:*⟩ posarsi

alight[2] *a* **be ~** essere in fiamme; **set ~** dar fuoco a

align /əˈlaɪn/ *vt* allineare. **~ment** *n* allineamento *m*; **out of ~ment** non allineato

alike /əˈlaɪk/ *a* simile; **be ~** rassomigliarsi ● *adv* in modo simile; **look ~** rassomigliarsi; **summer and winter ~** sia d'estate che d'inverno

alimony /ˈælɪmənɪ/ *n* alimenti *mpl*

alive /əˈlaɪv/ *a* vivo; **~ with** brulicante di; **~ to** sensibile a

alkali /ˈælkəlaɪ/ *n* alcali *m*

all /ɔːl/ *a* tutto; **~ the children, ~ children** tutti i bambini; **~ day** tutto il giorno; **he refused ~ help** ha rifiutato qualsiasi aiuto; **for ~ that** ⟨*nevertheless*⟩ ciononostante; **in ~ sincerity** in tutta sincerità; **be ~ for** essere favorevole a ● *pron* tutto; **~ of you/them** tutti voi/loro; **~ of it** tutto; **~ of the town** tutta la città; **in ~** in tutto; **~ in ~** tutto sommato; **most of ~** più di ogni altra cosa; **once and for ~** una volta per tutte ● *adv* completamente; ~ **but** quasi; ~ **at once** (*at the same time*) tutto in una volta; ~ **at once**, ~ **of a sudden** all'improvviso; ~ **too soon** troppo presto; ~ **the same** (*nevertheless*) ciononostante; ~ **the better** meglio ancora; **she's not** ~ **that good an actress** non è poi così brava come attrice; ~ **in** in tutto; *fam* esausto; **thirty/three** ~ (*in sport*) trenta/tre pari; ~ **over** (*finished*) tutto finito; (*everywhere*) dappertutto; **it's** ~ **right** (*I don't mind*) non fa niente; **I'm** ~ **right** (*not hurt*) non ho niente; ~ **right!** va bene!

allay /ə'leɪ/ *vt* placare (*suspicions, anger*)

allegation /ælɪ'geɪʃn/ *n* accusa *f*

allege /ə'ledʒ/ *vt* dichiarare. ~**d** *a* presunto. ~**dly** /-ɪdlɪ/ *adv* a quanto si dice

allegiance /ə'liːdʒəns/ *n* fedeltà *f*

allegoric|al /ælɪ'gorɪkl/ *a* allegorico. ~**y** /'ælɪɡərɪ/ *n* allegoria *f*

allerg|ic /ə'lɜːdʒɪk/ *a* allergico. ~**y** /'ælədʒɪ/ *n* allergia *f*

alleviate /ə'liːvɪeɪt/ *vt* alleviare

alley /'ælɪ/ *n* vicolo *m*; (*for bowling*) corsia *f*

alliance /ə'laɪəns/ *n* alleanza *f*

allied /'ælaɪd/ *a* alleato; (*fig: related*) connesso (**to** a)

alligator /'ælɪɡeɪtə(r)/ *n* alligatore *m*

allocat|e /'æləkeɪt/ *vt* assegnare; distribuire (*resources*). ~**ion** /-'keɪʃn/ *n* assegnazione *f*; (*of resources*) distribuzione *f*

allot /ə'lɒt/ *vt* (*pt/pp* **allotted**) distribuire. ~**ment** *n* distribuzione *f*; (*share*) parte *f*; (*land*) piccolo lotto *m* di terreno

allow /ə'laʊ/ *vt* permettere; (*grant*) accordare; (*reckon on*) contare; (*agree*) ammettere; ~ **for** tener conto di; ~ **sb to do sth** permettere a qcno di fare qcsa; **you are not** ~**ed to...** è vietato...

allowance /ə'laʊəns/ *n* sussidio *m*; (*Am: pocket money*) paghetta *f*; (*for petrol etc*) indennità *f* *inv*; (*of luggage, duty free*) limite *m*; **make** ~**s for** essere indulgente verso (*sb*); tener conto di (*sth*)

alloy /'ælɔɪ/ *n* lega *f*

allude /ə'luːd/ *vi* alludere

allusion /ə'luːʒn/ *n* allusione *f*

ally¹ /'ælaɪ/ *n* alleato, -a *mf*

ally² /ə'laɪ/ *vt* (*pt/pp* **-ied**) alleare; ~ **oneself with** allearsi con

almighty /ɔːl'maɪtɪ/ *a* (*fam: big*) mega *inv* ● *n* **the A-~** l'Onnipotente *m*

almond /'ɑːmənd/ *n* mandorla *f*; (*tree*) mandorlo *m*

almost /'ɔːlməʊst/ *adv* quasi

alone /ə'ləʊn/ *a* solo; **leave me** ~! lasciami in pace!; **let** ~ (*not to mention*) figurarsi ● *adv* da solo

along /ə'lɒŋ/ *prep* lungo ● *adv* ~ **with** assieme a; **all** ~ tutto il tempo; **come** ~! (*hurry up*) vieni qui!; **I'll be** ~ **in a minute** arrivo tra un attimo; **move** ~ spostarsi; **move** ~! circolare!

along'side *adv* lungo bordo ● *prep* lungo; **work** ~ **sb** lavorare fianco a fianco con qcno

aloof /ə'luːf/ *a* distante

aloud /ə'laʊd/ *adv* ad alta voce

alphabet /'ælfəbet/ *n* alfabeto *m*. ~**ical** /-'betɪkl/ *a* alfabetico

alpine /'ælpaɪn/ *a* alpino

Alps /ælps/ *npl* Alpi *fpl*

already /ɔːl'redɪ/ *adv* già

Alsatian /æl'seɪʃn/ *n* (*dog*) pastore *m* tedesco

also /'ɔːlsəʊ/ *adv* anche; ~, **I need...** [e] inoltre, ho bisogno di...

altar /'ɔːltə(r)/ *n* altare *m*

alter /'ɔːltə(r)/ *vt* cambiare; aggiustare (*clothes*) ● *vi* cambiare. ~**ation** /-'reɪʃn/ *n* modifica *f*

alternate¹ /'ɔːltəneɪt/ *vi* alternarsi ● *vt* alternare

alternate² /ɔːl'tɜːnət/ *a* alterno; **on** ~ **days** a giorni alterni

'**alternating current** *n* corrente *f* alternata

alternative /ɔːl'tɜːnətɪv/ *a* alternativo ● *n* alternativa *f*. ~**ly** *adv* alternativamente

although /ɔːl'ðəʊ/ *conj* benché, sebbene

altitude /'æltɪtjuːd/ *n* altitudine *f*

altogether /ɔːltə'geðə(r)/ *adv* (*in all*) in tutto; (*completely*) completamente; **I'm not** ~ **sure** non sono del tutto sicuro

altruistic /æltrʊ'ɪstɪk/ *a* altruistico

aluminium /æljʊ'mɪnɪəm/ *n*, *Am* **aluminum** /ə'luːmɪnəm/ *n* alluminio *m*

always /'ɔːlweɪz/ *adv* sempre

am /æm/ *see* **be**

a.m. *abbr* (**ante meridiem**) del mattino

amalgamate /ə'mælɡəmeɪt/ *vt* fondere ● *vi* fondersi

amass /ə'mæs/ *vt* accumulare

amateur /'æmətə(r)/ *n* non professionista *mf*; *pej* dilettante *mf* ● *attrib* dilet-

tante; **~ dramatics** filodrammatica *f.*
~ish *a* dilettantesco

amaze /əˈmeɪz/ *vt* stupire. **~d** *a* stupito. **~ment** *n* stupore *m*

amazing /əˈmeɪzɪŋ/ *a* incredibile

ambassador /æmˈbæsədə(r)/ *n* ambasciatore, -trice *mf*

amber /ˈæmbə(r)/ *n* ambra *f* ● *a* (*colour*) ambra *inv*

ambidextrous /æmbɪˈdekstrəs/ *a* ambidestro

ambience /ˈæmbɪəns/ *n* atmosfera *f*

ambigu|ity /æmbɪˈgjuːəti/ *n* ambiguità *f inv*. **~ous** /-ˈbɪɡjʊəs/ *a* ambiguo

ambiti|on /æmˈbɪʃn/ *n* ambizione *f*; (*aim*) aspirazione *f*. **~ous** /-ʃəs/ *a* ambizioso

ambivalent /æmˈbɪvələnt/ *a* ambivalente

amble /ˈæmbl/ *vi* camminare senza fretta

ambulance /ˈæmbjʊləns/ *n* ambulanza *f*

ambush /ˈæmbʊʃ/ *n* imboscata *f* ● *vt* tendere un'imboscata a

amenable /əˈmiːnəbl/ *a* conciliante; **~ to** sensibile a

amend /əˈmend/ *vt* modificare. **~ment** *n* modifica *f*. **~s** *npl* **make ~s** fare ammenda (**for** di, per)

amenities /əˈmiːnətɪz/ *npl* comodità *fpl*

America /əˈmerɪkə/ *n* America *f*. **~n** *a & n* americano, -a *mf*

amiable /ˈeɪmɪəbl/ *a* amabile

amicable /ˈæmɪkəbl/ *a* amichevole

amiss /əˈmɪs/ *a* **there's something ~** c'è qualcosa che non va ● *adv* **take sth ~** prendersela [a male]; **it won't come ~** non sarebbe sgradito

ammonia /əˈməʊnɪə/ *n* ammoniaca *f*

ammunition /æmjʊˈnɪʃn/ *n* munizioni *fpl*

amnesia /æmˈniːzɪə/ *n* amnesia *f*

amnesty /ˈæmnəstɪ/ *n* amnistia *f*

among[st] /əˈmʌŋ[st]/ *prep* tra, fra

amoral /eɪˈmɒrəl/ *a* amorale

amorous /ˈæmərəs/ *a* amoroso

amount /əˈmaʊnt/ *n* quantità *f inv*; (*sum of money*) importo *m* ● *vi* **~ to** ammontare a; *fig* equivalere a

amp /æmp/ *n* ampère *m inv*

amphibi|an /æmˈfɪbɪən/ *n* anfibio *m*. **~ous** /-ɪəs/ *a* anfibio

amphitheatre /ˈæmfɪ-/ *n* anfiteatro *m*

ample /ˈæmpl/ *a* (*large*) grande; (*proportions*) ampio; (*enough*) largamente sufficiente

amplif|ier /ˈæmplɪfaɪə(r)/ *n* amplificatore *m*. **~y** /-faɪ/ *vt* (*pt/pp*-**ied**) amplificare (*sound*)

amputat|e /ˈæmpjʊteɪt/ *vt* amputare. **~ion** /-ˈteɪʃn/ *n* amputazione *f*

amuse /əˈmjuːz/ *vt* divertire. **~ment** *n* divertimento *m*. **~ment arcade** *n* sala *f* giochi

amusing /əˈmjuːzɪŋ/ *a* divertente

an /ən/, *accentato* /æn/ *see* **a**

anaem|ia /əˈniːmɪə/ *n* anemia *f*. **~ic** *a* anemico

anaesthetic /ænəsˈθetɪk/ *n* anestesia *f*

anaesthetist /əˈniːsθətɪst/ *n* anestesista *mf*

analog[ue] /ˈænəlɒɡ/ *a* analogico

analogy /əˈnælədʒɪ/ *n* analogia *f*

analyse /ˈænəlaɪz/ *vt* analizzare

analysis /əˈnæləsɪs/ *n* analisi *f inv*

analyst /ˈænəlɪst/ *n* analista *mf*

analytical /ænəˈlɪtɪkl/ *a* analitico

anarch|ist /ˈænəkɪst/ *n* anarchico, -a *mf*. **~y** *n* anarchia *f*

anatom|ical /ænəˈtɒmɪkl/ *a* anatomico. **~ically** *adv* anatomicamente. **~y** /əˈnætəmɪ/ *n* anatomia *f*

ancest|or /ˈænsestə(r)/ *n* antenato, -a *mf*. **~ry** *n* antenati *mpl*

anchor /ˈæŋkə(r)/ *n* ancora *f* ● *vi* gettar l'ancora ● *vt* ancorare

anchovy /ˈæntʃəvɪ/ *n* acciuga *f*

ancient /ˈeɪnʃənt/ *a* antico; *fam* vecchio

ancillary /ænˈsɪlərɪ/ *a* ausiliario

and /ənd/, *accentato* /ænd/ *conj* e; **two ~ two** due più due; **six hundred ~ two** seicentodue; **more ~ more** sempre più; **nice ~ warm** bello caldo; **try ~ come** cerca di venire; **go ~ get** vai a prendere

anecdote /ˈænɪkdəʊt/ *n* aneddoto *m*

anew /əˈnjuː/ *adv* di nuovo

angel /ˈeɪndʒl/ *n* angelo *m*. **~ic** /ænˈdʒelɪk/ *a* angelico

anger /ˈæŋɡə(r)/ *n* rabbia *f* ● *vt* far arrabbiare

angle[1] /ˈæŋɡl/ *n* angolo *m*; *fig* angolazione *f*; **at an ~** storto

angle[2] *vi* pescare con la lenza; **~ for** *fig* cercare di ottenere. **~r** *n* pescatore, -trice *mf*

Anglican /ˈæŋɡlɪkən/ *a & n* anglicano, -a *mf*

Anglo-Saxon /æŋɡləʊˈsæksn/ *a & n* anglo-sassone *mf*

angr|y /ˈæŋɡrɪ/ *a* (-**ier, -iest**) arrabbiato; **get ~y** arrabbiarsi; **~y with** *or* **at sb** arrabbiato con qcno; **~y at** *or*

about sth arrabbiato per qcsa. **~ily** *adv* rabbiosamente

anguish /'æŋgwɪʃ/ *n* angoscia *f*

angular /'æŋgjʊlə(r)/ *a* angolare

animal /'ænɪml/ *a & n* animale *m*

animate¹ /'ænɪmət/ *a* animato

animate² /'ænɪmeɪt/ *vt* animare. **~ed** *a* animato; ⟨person⟩ vivace. **~ion** /-'meɪʃn/ *n* animazione *f*

animosity /ænɪ'mɒsətɪ/ *n* animosità *f* *inv*

ankle /'æŋkl/ *n* caviglia *f*

annex /ə'neks/ *vt* annettere

annex[e] /'æneks/ *n* annesso *m*

annihilat|e /ə'naɪəleɪt/ *vt* annientare. **~ion** /-'leɪʃn/ *n* annientamento *m*

anniversary /ænɪ'vɜːsərɪ/ *n* anniversario *m*

announce /ə'naʊns/ *vt* annunciare. **~ment** *n* annuncio *m*. **~r** *n* annunciatore, -trice *mf*

annoy /ə'nɔɪ/ *vt* dare fastidio a; **get ~ed** essere infastidito. **~ance** *n* seccatura *f*; (*anger*) irritazione *f*. **~ing** *a* fastidioso

annual /'ænjʊəl/ *a* annuale; (*income*) annuo ● *n Bot* pianta *f* annua; (*children's book*) almanacco *m*

annuity /ə'njuːətɪ/ *n* annualità *f* *inv*

annul /ə'nʌl/ *vt* (*pt/pp* **annulled**) annullare

anomaly /ə'nɒmǝlɪ/ *n* anomalia *f*

anonymous /ə'nɒnɪməs/ *a* anonimo

anorak /'ænəræk/ *n* giacca *f* a vento

anorex|ia /ænə'reksɪə/ *n* anoressia *f*. **~ic** *a* anoressico

another /ə'nʌðə(r)/ *a & pron*; **~ [one]** un altro, un'altra; **in ~ way** diversamente; **one ~** l'un l'altro

answer /'ɑːnsə(r)/ *n* risposta *f*; (*solution*) soluzione *f* ● *vt* rispondere a ⟨person, question, letter⟩; esaudire ⟨prayer⟩; **~ the door** aprire la porta; **~ the telephone** rispondere al telefono ● *vi* rispondere; **~ back** ribattere; **~ for** rispondere di. **~able** /-əbl/ *a* responsabile; **be ~able to sb** rispondere a qcno. **~ing machine** *n Teleph* segreteria *f* telefonica

ant /ænt/ *n* formica *f*

antagonis|m /æn'tægənɪzm/ *n* antagonismo *m*. **~tic** /-'nɪstɪk/ *a* antagonistico

antagonize /æn'tægənaɪz/ *vt* provocare l'ostilità di

Antarctic /æn'tɑːktɪk/ *n* Antartico *m* ● *a* antartico

antenatal /æntɪ'neɪtl/ *a* prenatale

antenna /æn'tenə/ *n* antenna *f*

anthem /'ænθəm/ *n* inno *m*

anthology /æn'θɒlədʒɪ/ *n* antologia *f*

anthropology /ænθrə'pɒlədʒɪ/ *n* antropologia *f*

anti-'aircraft /æntɪ-/ *a* antiaereo

antibiotic /æntɪbaɪ'ɒtɪk/ *n* antibiotico *m*

'antibody *n* anticorpo *m*

anticipat|e /æn'tɪsɪpeɪt/ *vt* prevedere; (*forestall*) anticipare. **~ion** /-'peɪʃn/ *n* anticipo *m*; (*excitement*) attesa *f*

anti'climax *n* delusione *f*

anti'clockwise *a & adv* in senso antiorario

antics /'æntɪks/ *npl* gesti *mpl* buffi

anti'cyclone *n* anticiclone *m*

antidote /'æntɪdəʊt/ *n* antidoto *m*

'antifreeze *n* antigelo *m*

antipathy /æn'tɪpəθɪ/ *n* antipatia *f*

antiquated /'æntɪkweɪtɪd/ *a* antiquato

antique /æn'tiːk/ *a* antico ● *n* antichità *f* *inv*. **~ dealer** *n* antiquario, -a *mf*

antiquity /æn'tɪkwətɪ/ *n* antichità *f*

anti-Semitic /æntɪsɪ'mɪtɪk/ *a* antisemita

anti'septic *a & n* antisettico *m*

anti'social *a* ⟨behaviour⟩ antisociale; ⟨person⟩ asociale

anti'virus program *n Comput* programma *m* di antivirus

antlers /'æntləz/ *npl* corna *fpl*

anus /'eɪnəs/ *n* ano *m*

anxiety /æŋ'zaɪətɪ/ *n* ansia *f*

anxious /'æŋkʃəs/ *a* ansioso. **~ly** *adv* con ansia

any /'enɪ/ *a* (*no matter which*) qualsiasi, qualunque; **have we ~ wine/ biscuits?** abbiamo del vino/dei biscotti?; **have we ~ jam/apples?** abbiamo della marmellata/delle mele?; **~ colour/number you like** qualsiasi colore/numero ti piaccia; **we don't have ~ wine/biscuits** non abbiamo vino/biscotti; **I don't have ~ reason to lie** non ho nessun motivo per mentire; **for ~ reason** per qualsiasi ragione ● *pron* (*some*) ne; (*no matter which*) uno qualsiasi; **I don't want ~ [of it]** non ne voglio [nessuno]; **there aren't ~** non ce ne sono; **have we ~?** ne abbiamo?; **have you read ~ of her books?** hai letto qualcuno dei suoi libri? ● *adv* **I can't go ~ quicker** non posso andare più in fretta; **is it ~ better?** va un po' meglio?; **would you like ~ more?** ne vuoi ancora?; **I can't eat ~ more** non posso mangiare più niente '**anybody** *pron* chiunque; (*after negative*) nessuno; **I haven't seen ~** non ho visto nessuno

'**anyhow** *adv* ad ogni modo, comunque; (*badly*) non importa come

'**anyone** *pron* = **anybody**

'**anything** *pron* qualche cosa, qualcosa; (*no matter what*) qualsiasi cosa; (*after negative*) niente; **take/ buy ~ you like** prendi/compra quello che vuoi; **I don't remember ~** non mi ricordo niente; **he's ~ but stupid** è tutto, ma non stupido; **I'll do ~ but that** farò qualsiasi cosa, tranne quello

'**anyway** *adv* ad ogni modo, comunque

'**anywhere** *adv* dovunque; (*after negative*) da nessuna parte; **put it ~** mettilo dove vuoi; **I can't find it ~** non lo trovo da nessuna parte; **~ else** da qualch'altra parte; (*after negative*) da nessun'altra parte; **I don't want to go ~ else** non voglio andare da nessun'altra parte

apart /ə'pɑ:t/ *adv* lontano; **live ~** vivere separati; **100 miles ~** lontani 100 miglia; **~ from** a parte; **you can't tell them ~** non si possono distinguere; **joking ~** scherzi a parte

apartment /ə'pɑ:tmənt/ *n* (*Am: flat*) appartamento m; **in my ~** a casa mia

apathy /'æpəθɪ/ *n* apatia f

ape /eɪp/ *n* scimmia f ● *vt* scimmiottare

aperitif /ə'perəti:f/ *n* aperitivo m

aperture /'æpətʃə(r)/ *n* apertura f

apex /'eɪpeks/ *n* vertice m

apiece /ə'pi:s/ *adv* ciascuno

apologetic /əpɒlə'dʒetɪk/ *a* ⟨air, remark⟩ di scusa; **be ~** essere spiacente

apologize /ə'pɒlədʒaɪz/ *vi* scusarsi (**for** per)

apology /ə'pɒlədʒɪ/ *n* scusa f; fig **an ~ for a dinner** una sottospecie di cena

apostle /ə'pɒsl/ *n* apostolo m

apostrophe /ə'pɒstrəfɪ/ *n* apostrofo m

appal /ə'pɔ:l/ *vt* (*pt/pp* **appalled**) sconvolgere. **~ling** *a* sconvolgente

apparatus /æpə'reɪtəs/ *n* apparato m

apparent /ə'pærənt/ *a* evidente; (*seeming*) apparente. **~ly** *adv* apparentemente

apparition /æpə'rɪʃn/ *n* apparizione f

appeal /ə'pi:l/ *n* appello m; (*attraction*) attrattiva f ● *vi* fare appello; **~ to** (*be attractive to*) attrarre. **~ing** *a* attraente

appear /ə'pɪə(r)/ *vi* apparire; (*seem*) sembrare; ⟨publication⟩ uscire; *Theat* esibirsi. **~ance** *n* apparizione f; (*look*)

aspetto m; **to all ~ances** a giudicare dalle apparenze; **keep up ~ances** salvare le apparenze

appease /ə'pi:z/ *vt* placare

appendicitis /əpendɪ'saɪtɪs/ *n* appendicite f

appendix /ə'pendɪks/ *n* (*pl* **-ices** /-ɪsɪːz/) (*of book*) appendice f; (*pl* **-es**) *Anat* appendice f

appetite /'æpɪtaɪt/ *n* appetito m

appetiz|er /'æpɪtaɪzə(r)/ *n* stuzzichino m. **~ing** *a* appetitoso

applaud /ə'plɔ:d/ *vt/i* applaudire. **~se** *n* applauso m

apple /'æpl/ *n* mela f. **~-tree** *n* melo m

appliance /ə'plaɪəns/ *n* attrezzo m; |**electrical**| **~** elettrodomestico m

applicable /'æplɪkəbl/ *a* **be ~ to** essere valido per; **not ~** (*on form*) non applicabile

applicant /'æplɪkənt/ *n* candidato, -a mf

application /æplɪ'keɪʃn/ *n* applicazione f; (*request*) domanda f; (*for job*) candidatura f. **~ form** *n* modulo m di domanda

applied /ə'plaɪd/ *a* applicato

apply /ə'plaɪ/ *vt* (*pt/pp* **-ied**) applicare; **~ oneself** applicarsi ● *vi* applicarsi; ⟨law⟩ essere applicabile; **~ to** (*ask*) rivolgersi a; **~ for** fare domanda per ⟨job etc⟩

appoint /ə'pɔɪnt/ *vt* nominare; fissare ⟨time⟩. **~ment** *n* appuntamento m; (*to job*) nomina f; (*job*) posto m

appraisal /ə'preɪz(ə)l/ *n* valutazione f

appreciable /ə'pri:ʃəbl/ *a* sensibile

appreciat|e /ə'pri:ʃɪeɪt/ *vt* apprezzare; (*understand*) comprendere ● *vi* (*increase in value*) aumentare di valore. **~ion** /-'eɪʃn/ *n* (*gratitude*) riconoscenza f; (*enjoyment*) apprezzamento m; (*understanding*) comprensione f; (*in value*) aumento m. **~ive** /-ətɪv/ *a* riconoscente

apprehend /æprɪ'hend/ *vt* arrestare

apprehens|ion /æprɪ'henʃn/ *n* arresto m; (*fear*) apprensione f. **~ive** /-sɪv/ *a* apprensivo

apprentice /ə'prentɪs/ *n* apprendista mf. **~ship** *n* apprendistato m

approach /ə'prəʊtʃ/ *n* avvicinamento m; (*to problem*) approccio m; (*access*) accesso m; **make ~es to** fare degli approcci con ● *vi* avvicinarsi ● *vt* avvicinarsi a; (*with request*) rivolgersi a; affrontare ⟨problem⟩. **~able** /-əbl/ *a* accessibile

appropriate[1] /ə'prəʊprɪət/ a appropriato

appropriate[2] /ə'prəʊprɪeɪt/ vt appropriarsi di

approval /ə'pruːvl/ n approvazione f; **on ~** in prova

approve /ə'pruːv/ vt approvare • vi **~e of** approvare ⟨sth⟩; avere una buona opinione di ⟨sb⟩. **~ing** ⟨smile, nod⟩ d'approvazione

approximate /ə'prɒksɪmət/ a approssimativo. **~ly** adv approssimativamente

approximation /əprɒksɪ'meɪʃn/ n approssimazione f

apricot /'eɪprɪkɒt/ n albicocca f

April /'eɪprəl/ n aprile m; **~ Fool's Day** il primo d'aprile

apron /'eɪprən/ n grembiule m

apt /æpt/ a appropriato: **be ~ to do sth** avere tendenza a fare qcsa

aptitude /'æptɪtjuːd/ n disposizione f. **~ test** n test m inv attitudinale

aqualung /'ækwəlʌŋ/ n autorespiratoro m

aquarium /ə'kweərɪəm/ n acquario m

Aquarius /ə'kweərɪəs/ n Astr Acquario m

aquatic /ə'kwætɪk/ a acquatico

Arab /'ærəb/ a & n arabo, -a mf. **~ian** /ə'reɪbɪən/ a arabo

Arabic /'ærəbɪk/ a arabo; **~ numerals** numeri mpl arabici • n arabo m

arable /'ærəbl/ a coltivabile

arbitrary /'ɑːbɪtrəri/ a arbitrario

arbitrat|e /'ɑːbɪtreɪt/ vi arbitrare. **~ion** /-'treɪʃn/ n arbitraggio m

arc /ɑːk/ n arco m

arcade /ɑː'keɪd/ n portico m; ⟨shops⟩ galleria f

arch /ɑːtʃ/ n arco m; ⟨of foot⟩ dorso m del piede

archaeological /ɑːkɪə'lɒdʒɪkl/ a archeologico

archaeolog|ist /ɑːkɪ'ɒlədʒɪst/ n archeologo, -a mf. **~y** n archeologia f

archaic /ɑː'keɪɪk/ a arcaico

arch'bishop /ɑːtʃ-/ n arcivescovo m

arch-'enemy n acerrimo nemico m

architect /'ɑːkɪtekt/ n architetto m. **~ural** /ɑːkɪ'tektʃərəl/ a architettonico

architecture /'ɑːkɪtektʃə(r)/ n architettura f

archives /'ɑːkaɪvz/ npl archivi mpl

archiving /'ɑːkaɪvɪŋ/ n Comput archiviazione f

archway /'ɑːtʃweɪ/ n arco m

Arctic /'ɑːktɪk/ a artico • n **the ~** l'Artico

ardent /'ɑːdənt/ a ardente

arduous /'ɑːdjʊəs/ a arduo

are /ɑː(r)/ see **be**

area /'eərɪə/ n area f; ⟨region⟩ zona f; ⟨fig: field⟩ campo m. **~ code** n prefisso m [telefonico]

arena /ə'riːnə/ n arena f

aren't /ɑːnt/ = **are not** see **be**

Argentina /ɑːdʒən'tiːnə/ n Argentina f

Argentinian /-'tɪnɪən/ a & n argentino, -a mf

argue /'ɑːgjuː/ vi litigare (**about** su); ⟨debate⟩ dibattere; **don't ~!** non discutere! • vt ⟨debate⟩ dibattere; ⟨reason⟩ **~ that** sostenere che

argument /'ɑːgjʊmənt/ n argomento m; ⟨reasoning⟩ ragionamento m; **have an ~** litigare. **~ative** /-'mentətɪv/ a polemico

aria /'ɑːrɪə/ n aria f

arid /'ærɪd/ a arido

Aries /'eəriːz/ n Astr Ariete m

arise /ə'raɪz/ vi (pt **arose**, pp **arisen**) ⟨opportunity, need, problem:⟩ presentarsi; ⟨result⟩ derivare

aristocracy /ærɪ'stɒkrəsi/ n aristocrazia f

aristocrat /'ærɪstəkræt/ n aristocratico, -a mf. **~ic** /-'krætɪk/ a aristocratico

arithmetic /ə'rɪθmətɪk/ n aritmetica f

arm /ɑːm/ n braccio m; ⟨of chair⟩ bracciolo m; **~s** pl ⟨weapons⟩ armi fpl. **~ in ~** a braccetto; **up in ~s** fam furioso (**about** per) • vt armare

armaments /'ɑːməmənts/ npl armamenti mpl

armchair n poltrona f

armed /ɑːmd/ a armato; **~ forces** forze fpl armate; **~ robbery** rapina f a mano armata

armistice /'ɑːmɪstɪs/ n armistizio m

armour /'ɑːmə(r)/ n armatura f. **~ed** ⟨vehicle⟩ blindato

armpit n ascella f

army /'ɑːmi/ n esercito m; **join the ~** arruolarsi

aroma /ə'rəʊmə/ n aroma f. **~tic** /ærə'mætɪk/ a aromatico

arose /ə'rəʊz/ see **arise**

around /ə'raʊnd/ adv intorno; **all ~** tutt'intorno; **I'm not from ~ here** non sono di qui; **he's not ~** non c'è • prep intorno a; in giro per ⟨room, shops, world⟩

arouse /ə'raʊz/ vt svegliare; ⟨sexually⟩ eccitare

arrange /ə'reɪndʒ/ vt sistemare ⟨furniture, books⟩; organizzare ⟨meeting⟩; fissare ⟨date, time⟩; ~ **to do sth** combinare di fare qcsa. **~ment** n ⟨of furniture⟩ sistemazione f; Mus arrangiamento m; ⟨agreement⟩ accordo; ⟨of flowers⟩ composizione f; **make ~ments** prendere disposizioni

arrears /ə'rɪəz/ npl arretrati mpl; **be in ~** essere in arretrato; **paid in ~** pagato a lavoro eseguito

arrest /ə'rest/ n arresto m; **under ~** in stato d'arresto ● vt arrestare

arrival /ə'raɪvl/ n arrivo m; **new ~s** pl nuovi arrivati mpl

arrive /ə'raɪv/ vi arrivare; ~ **at** fig raggiungere

arrogan|ce /'ærəgəns/ n arroganza f. **~t** a arrogante

arrow /'ærəʊ/ n freccia f

arse /ɑːs/ n vulg culo m

arsenic /'ɑːsənɪk/ n arsenico m

arson /'ɑːsn/ n incendio m doloso. **~ist** /-sənɪst/ n incendiario, -a mf

art /ɑːt/ n arte f; **~s and crafts** pl artigianato m; **the A~s** pl l'arte f; **A~s degree** Univ laurea f in Lettere

artery /'ɑːtərɪ/ n arteria f

artful /'ɑːtfl/ a scaltro

'art gallery n galleria f d'arte

arthritis /ɑː'θraɪtɪs/ n artrite f

artichoke /'ɑːtɪtʃəʊk/ n carciofo m

article /'ɑːtɪkl/ n articolo m; ~ **of clothing** capo m d'abbigliamento

articulate¹ /ɑː'tɪkjʊlət/ a ⟨speech⟩ chiaro; **be ~** esprimersi bene

articulate² /ɑː'tɪkjʊleɪt/ vt scandire ⟨words⟩. **~d lorry** n autotreno m

artifice /'ɑːtɪfɪs/ n artificio m

artificial /ɑːtɪ'fɪʃl/ a artificiale. **~ly** adv artificialmente; ⟨smile⟩ artificiosamente

artillery /ɑː'tɪlərɪ/ n artiglieria f

artist /'ɑːtɪst/ n artista mf

artiste /ɑː'tiːst/ n Theat artista mf

artistic /ɑː'tɪstɪk/ a artistico

as /æz/ conj come; ⟨since⟩ siccome; ⟨while⟩ mentre; **as he grew older** diventando vecchio; **as you get to know her** conoscendola meglio; **young as she is** per quanto sia giovane ● prep come; **as a friend** come amico; **as a child** da bambino; **as a foreigner** in quanto straniero; **disguised as** travestito da ● adv **as well as** ⟨also⟩ anche; **as soon as I get home** [non] appena arrivo a casa; **as quick as you** veloce quanto te; **as quick as you can** più

veloce che puoi; **as far as** ⟨distance⟩ fino a; **as far as I'm concerned** per quanto mi riguarda; **as long as** finché; ⟨provided that⟩ purché

asbestos /æz'bestɒs/ n amianto m

ascend /ə'send/ vi salire ● vt salire a ⟨throne⟩

Ascension /ə'senʃn/ n Relig Ascensione f

ascent /ə'sent/ n ascesa f

ascertain /æsə'teɪn/ vt accertare

ascribe /ə'skraɪb/ vt attribuire

ash¹ /æʃ/ n ⟨tree⟩ frassino m

ash² /æʃ/ n cenere f

ashamed /ə'ʃeɪmd/ a **be/feel ~** vergognarsi

ashore /ə'ʃɔː(r)/ adv a terra; **go ~** sbarcare

ash: **~tray** n portacenere m. **A~ 'Wednesday** n mercoledì m inv delle Ceneri

Asia /'eɪʒə/ n Asia f. **~n** a & n asiatico, -a mf. **~tic** /eɪʒɪ'ætɪk/ a asiatico

aside /ə'saɪd/ adv **take sb ~** prendere qcno a parte; **put sth ~** mettere qcsa da parte; ~ **from you** Am a parte te

ask /ɑːsk/ vt fare ⟨question⟩; ⟨invite⟩ invitare; ~ **sb sth** domandare or chiedere qcsa a qcno; ~ **sb to do sth** domandare or chiedere a qcno di fare qcsa ● vi ~ **about sth** informarsi su qcsa; ~ **after** chiedere [notizie] di; ~ **for** chiedere ⟨sth⟩; chiedere di ⟨sb⟩; ~ **for trouble** fam andare in cerca di guai. **ask in** vt ~ **sb in** invitare qcno ad entrare. **ask out** vt ~ **sb out** chiedere a qcno di uscire

askance /ə'skɑːns/ adv **look ~ at sb/sth** guardare qcno/qcsa di traverso

askew /ə'skjuː/ a & adv di traverso

asleep /ə'sliːp/ a **be ~** dormire; **fall ~** addormentarsi

asparagus /ə'spærəgəs/ n asparagi mpl

aspect /'æspekt/ n aspetto m

aspersions /ə'spɜːʃnz/ npl **cast ~ on** diffamare

asphalt /'æsfælt/ n asfalto m

asphyxia /əs'fɪksɪə/ n asfissia f. **~te** /əs'fɪksɪeɪt/ vt asfissiare. **~tion** /-'eɪʃn/ n asfissia f

aspirations /æspə'reɪʃnz/ npl aspirazioni fpl

aspire /ə'spaɪə(r)/ vi ~ **to** aspirare a

ass /æs/ n asino m

assailant /ə'seɪlənt/ n assalitore, -trice mf

assassin /ə'sæsɪn/ n assassino, -a mf.

~**ate** *vt* assassinare. ~**ation** /-'neɪʃn/ *n* assassinio *m*

assault /ə'sɔ:lt/ *n* Mil assalto *m*; Jur aggressione *f* ● *vt* aggredire

assemble /ə'sembl/ *vi* radunarsi ● *vt* radunare; Techn montare

assembly /ə'sembl/ *n* assemblea *f*; Sch assemblea *f* giornaliera di alunni e professori di una scuola; Techn montaggio *m*. ~ **line** *n* catena *f* di montaggio

assent /ə'sent/ *n* assenso *m* ● *vi* acconsentire

assert /ə'sɜ:t/ *vt* asserire; far valere (one's rights); ~ **oneself** farsi valere. ~**ion** /-ʒn/ *n* asserzione *f*. ~**ive** /-tɪv/ *a* be ~ive farsi valere

assess /ə'ses/ *vt* valutare; (for tax purposes) stabilire l'imponibile di. ~**ment** *n* valutazione *f*; (of tax) accertamento *m*

asset /'æset/ *n* (advantage) vantaggio *m*; (person) elemento *m* prezioso. ~**s** *pl* beni *mpl*; (on balance sheet) attivo *msg*

assign /ə'saɪn/ *vt* assegnare. ~**ment** *n* (task) incarico *m*

assimilate /ə'sɪmɪleɪt/ *vt* assimilare, integrare (person)

assist /ə'sɪst/ *vt/i* assistere; ~ **sb to do sth** assistere qcno nel fare qcsa. ~**ance** *n* assistenza *f*. ~**ant** *a* ~**ant manager** vicedirettore, -trice *mf* ● *n* assistente *mf*; (in shop) commesso, -a *mf*

associate¹ /ə'səʊʃɪeɪt/ *vt* associare (with a); be ~**ed with sth** (involved in) essere coinvolto in qcsa ● *vi* ~**e with** frequentare. ~**ion** /-'eɪʃn/ *n* associazione *f*. A~**ion** 'Football *n* [gioco *m* del] calcio *m*

associate² /ə'səʊʃɪət/ *a* associato ● *n* collega *mf*; (member) socio, -a *mf*

assorted /ə'sɔ:tɪd/ *a* assortito. ~**ment** *n* assortimento *m*

assume /ə'sju:m/ *vt* presumere; assumere (control); ~**e office** entrare in carica; ~**ing that you're right,...** ammettendo che tu abbia ragione,...

assumption /ə'sʌmpʃn/ *n* supposizione *f*; **on the ~ that** partendo dal presupposto che; **the A~** Relig l'Assunzione *f*

assurance /ə'ʃʊərəns/ *n* assicurazione *f*; (confidence) sicurezza *f*

assure /ə'ʃʊə(r)/ *vt* assicurare. ~**d** *a* sicuro

asterisk /'æstərɪsk/ *n* asterisco *m*

astern /ə'stɜ:n/ *adv* a poppa

asthma /'æsmə/ *n* asma *f*. ~**tic** /-'mætɪk/ *a* asmatico

astonish /ə'stɒnɪʃ/ *vt* stupire. ~**ing** *a* stupefacente. ~**ment** *n* stupore *m*

astound /ə'staʊnd/ *vt* stupire

astray /ə'streɪ/ *adv* **go ~** smarrirsi; (morally) uscire dalla retta via; **lead ~** traviare

astride /ə'straɪd/ *adv* [a] cavalcioni ● *prep* a cavalcioni di

astrologer /ə'strɒlədʒə(r)/ *n* astrologo, -a *mf*. ~**y** *n* astrologia *f*

astronaut /'æstrənɔ:t/ *n* astronauta *mf*

astronomer /ə'strɒnəmə(r)/ *n* astronomo, -a *mf*. ~**ical** /æstrə'nɒmɪkl/ *a* astronomico. ~**y** *n* astronomia *f*

astute /ə'stju:t/ *a* astuto

asylum /ə'saɪləm/ *n* [political] ~ asilo *m* politico; [lunatic] ~ manicomio *m*

at /ət/, accentato /æt/ *prep* a; **at the station/the market** alla stazione/al mercato; **at the office/the bank** in ufficio/banca; **at the beginning** all'inizio; **at John's** da John; **at the hairdresser's** dal parrucchiere; **at home** a casa; **at work** al lavoro; **at school** a scuola; **at a party/wedding** a una festa/un matrimonio; **at 1 o'clock** all'una; **at 50 km an hour** ai 50 all'ora; **at Christmas/Easter** a Natale/Pasqua; **at times** talvolta; **two at a time** due alla volta; **good at languages** bravo nelle lingue; **at sb's request** su richiesta di qcno; **are you at all worried?** sei preoccupato?

ate /et/ see **eat**

atheist /'eɪθɪɪst/ *n* ateo, -a *mf*

athlete /'æθli:t/ *n* atleta *mf*. ~**ic** /-'letɪk/ *a* atletico. ~**ics** /-'letɪks/ *n* atletica *fsg*

Atlantic /ət'læntɪk/ *a* & *n* **the ~ [Ocean]** l'[Oceano *m*] Atlantico *m*

atlas /'ætləs/ *n* atlante *m*

atmosphere /'ætməsfɪə(r)/ *n* atmosfera *f*. ~**ic** /-'ferɪk/ *a* atmosferico

atom /'ætəm/ *n* atomo *m*. ~ **bomb** *n* bomba *f* atomica

atomic /ə'tɒmɪk/ *a* atomico

atone /ə'təʊn/ *vi* ~ **for** pagare per. ~**ment** *n* espiazione *f*

atrocious /ə'trəʊʃəs/ *a* atroce; (fam: meal, weather) abominevole

atrocity /ə'trɒsəti/ *n* atrocità *f inv*

attach /ə'tætʃ/ *vt* attaccare; attribuire (importance); **be ~ed to** fig essere attaccato a

attaché /ə'tæʃeɪ/ *n* addetto *m*. ~ **case** *n* ventiquattrore *f inv*

attachment /ə'tætʃmənt/ n (affection) attaccamento m; (accessory) accessorio m

attack /ə'tæk/ n attacco m; (physical) aggressione f ●vt attaccare; (physically) aggredire. **~er** n assalitore, -trice mf; (critic) detrattore, -trice mf

attain /ə'teɪn/ vt realizzare (ambition); raggiungere (success, age, goal)

attempt /ə'tempt/ n tentativo m ●vt tentare

attend /ə'tend/ vt essere presente a; (go regularly to) frequentare; (doctor:) avere in cura ●vi essere presente; (pay attention) prestare attenzione. **attend to** vt occuparsi di; (in shop) servire. **~ance** n presenza f. **~ant** n guardiano, -a mf

attention /ə'tenʃn/ n attenzione f. **~!** Mil attenti!; **pay ~** prestare attenzione; **need ~** aver bisogno di attenzioni; (skin, hair, plant:) dover essere curato; (car, tyres:) dover essere riparato; **for the ~ of** all'attenzione di

attentive /ə'tentɪv/ a (pupil, audience) attento

attest /ə'test/ vt/i attestare

attic /'ætɪk/ n soffitta f

attitude /'ætɪtjuːd/ n atteggiamento m

attorney /ə'tɜːnɪ/ n (Am: lawyer) avvocato m; **power of ~** delega f

attract /ə'trækt/ vt attirare. **~ion** /-ækʃn/ n attrazione f; (feature) attrattiva f. **~ive** /-tɪv/ a (person) attraente; (proposal, price) allettante

attribute¹ /'ætrɪbjuːt/ n attributo m

attribute² /ə'trɪbjuːt/ vt attribuire

attrition /ə'trɪʃn/ n **war of ~** guerra f di logoramento

aubergine /'əʊbəʒiːn/ n melanzana f

auburn /'ɔːbən/ a castano ramato

auction /'ɔːkʃn/ n asta f ●vt vendere all'asta. **~eer** /-ʃə'nɪə(r)/ n banditore m

audacious /ɔː'deɪʃəs/ a sfacciato; (daring) audace. **~ty** /-'dæsətɪ/ n sfacciataggine f; (daring) audacia f

audible /'ɔːdəbl/ a udibile

audience /'ɔːdɪəns/ n Theat pubblico m; TV telespettatori mpl; Radio ascoltatori mpl; (meeting) udienza f

audio /'ɔːdɪəʊ/: **~tape** n audiocassetta f. **~ typist** n dattilografo, -a mf (che trascrive registrazioni). **~'visual** a audiovisivo

audit /'ɔːdɪt/ n verifica f del bilancio ●vt verificare

audition /ɔː'dɪʃn/ n audizione f ●vi fare un'audizione

auditor /'ɔːdɪtə(r)/ n revisore m di conti

auditorium /ɔːdɪ'tɔːrɪəm/ n sala f

augment /ɔːg'ment/ vt aumentare

augur /'ɔːgə(r)/ vi **~ well/ill** essere di buon/cattivo augurio

August /'ɔːgəst/ n agosto m

aunt /ɑːnt/ n zia f

au pair /əʊ'peə(r)/ n **~ [girl]** ragazza f alla pari

aura /'ɔːrə/ n aura f

auspices /'ɔːspɪsɪz/ npl **under the ~ of** sotto l'egida di

auspicious /ɔː'spɪʃəs/ a di buon augurio

auster|e /ɒ'stɪə(r)/ a austero. **~ity** /-'terətɪ/ n austerità f

Australia /ɒ'streɪlɪə/ n Australia f. **~n** a & n australiano, -a mf

Austria /'ɒstrɪə/ n Austria f. **~n** a & n austriaco, -a mf

authentic /ɔː'θentɪk/ a autentico. **~ate** vt autenticare. **~ity** /-'tɪsətɪ/ n autenticità f

author /'ɔːθə(r)/ n autore m

authoritarian /ɔːθɒrɪ'teərɪən/ a autoritario

authoritative /ɔː'θɒrɪtətɪv/ a autorevole; (manner) autoritario

authority /ɔː'θɒrətɪ/ n autorità f; (permission) autorizzazione f; **be in ~ over** avere autorità su

authorization /ɔːθəraɪ'zeɪʃn/ n autorizzazione f

authorize /'ɔːθəraɪz/ vt autorizzare

autobi'ography /ɔːtə-/ n autobiografia f

autocratic /ɔːtə'krætɪk/ a autocratico

autograph /'ɔːtəgrɑːf/ n autografo m

automate /'ɔːtəment/ vt automatizzare

automatic /ɔːtə'mætɪk/ a automatico ●n (car) macchina f col cambio automatico; (washing machine) lavatrice f automatica. **~ally** adv automaticamente

automation /ɔːtə'meɪʃn/ n automazione f

automobile /'ɔːtəməbiːl/ n automobile f

autonom|ous /ɔː'tɒnəməs/ a autonomo. **~y** n autonomia f

autopsy /'ɔːtɒpsɪ/ n autopsia f

autumn /'ɔːtəm/ n autunno m. **~al** /-'tʌmnl/ a autunnale

auxiliary /ɔːg'zɪlɪərɪ/ a ausiliario ●n ausiliare m

avail /ə'veɪl/ n **to no ~** invano ●vi **~ oneself of** approfittare di

available /əˈveɪləbl/ a disponibile; ⟨book, record etc⟩ in vendita

avalanche /ˈævəlɑːnʃ/ n valanga f

avarice /ˈævərɪs/ n avidità f

avenge /əˈvendʒ/ vt vendicare

avenue /ˈævənjuː/ n viale m; fig strada f

average /ˈævərɪdʒ/ a medio; ⟨mediocre⟩ mediocre ● n media f; **on ~** in media ● vt ⟨sales, attendance etc⟩ raggiungere una media di. **average out at** vt risultare in media

avers|e /əˈvɜːs/ a **not be ~e to sth** non essere contro qcsa. **~ion** /-ɜːʃn/ n avversione f (**to** per)

avert /əˈvɜːt/ vt evitare ⟨crisis⟩; distogliere ⟨eyes⟩

aviary /ˈeɪvɪərɪ/ n uccelliera f

aviation /eɪvɪˈeɪʃn/ n aviazione f

avid /ˈævɪd/ a avido (**for** di); ⟨reader⟩ appassionato

avocado /ævəˈkɑːdəʊ/ n avocado m

avoid /əˈvɔɪd/ vt evitare. **~able** /-əbl/ a evitabile

await /əˈweɪt/ vt attendere

awake /əˈweɪk/ a sveglio; **wide ~** completamente sveglio ● vi ⟨pt **awoke**, pp **awoken**⟩ svegliarsi

awaken /əˈweɪkn/ vt svegliare. **~ing** n risveglio m

award /əˈwɔːd/ n premio m; ⟨medal⟩ riconoscimento m; ⟨of prize⟩ assegnazione f ● vt assegnare; ⟨hand over⟩ consegnare

aware /əˈweə(r)/ a **be ~ of** ⟨sense⟩ percepire; ⟨know⟩ essere conscio di; **become ~ of** accorgersi di; ⟨learn⟩ venire a sapere di; **be ~ that** rendersi conto che. **~ness** n percezione f; ⟨knowledge⟩ consapevolezza f

awash /əˈwɒʃ/ a inondato (**with** di)

away /əˈweɪ/ adv via; **go/stay ~** andare/stare via; **he's ~ from his desk/the office** non è alla sua scrivania/in ufficio; **far ~** lontano; **four kilometres ~** a quattro chilometri; **play ~** Sport giocare fuori casa. **~ game** n partita f fuori casa

awe /ɔː/ n soggezione f

awful /ˈɔːfl/ a terribile. **~ly** adv /ˈɔːf(ʊ)lɪ/ terribilmente; ⟨pretty⟩ estremamente

awhile /əˈwaɪl/ adv per un po'

awkward /ˈɔːkwəd/ a ⟨movement⟩ goffo; ⟨moment, situation⟩ imbarazzante; ⟨time⟩ scomodo. **~ly** adv ⟨move⟩ goffamente; ⟨say⟩ con imbarazzo

awning /ˈɔːnɪŋ/ n tendone m

awoke(n) /əˈwəʊk(ən)/ see **awake**

awry /əˈraɪ/ adv storto

axe /æks/ n scure f ● vt ⟨pres p **axing**⟩ fare dei tagli a ⟨budget⟩; sopprimere ⟨jobs⟩; annullare ⟨project⟩

axis /ˈæksɪs/ n ⟨pl **axes** /-siːz/⟩ asse m

axle /ˈæksl/ n Techn asse m

ay[e] /aɪ/ adv sì ● n sì m invar

Bb

B /biː/ n Mus si m inv

BA n abbr **Bachelor of Arts**

babble /ˈbæbl/ vi farfugliare; ⟨stream⟩ gorgogliare

baby /ˈbeɪbɪ/ n bambino, -a mf. ⟨fam: darling⟩ tesoro m

baby: **~ carriage** n Am carrozzina f. **~ish** a bambinesco. **~-sit** vi fare da baby-sitter. **~-sitter** n baby-sitter mf

bachelor /ˈbætʃələ(r)/ n scapolo m; **B~ of Arts/Science** laureato, -a mf in lettere/in scienza

back /bæk/ n ⟨of person⟩ schiena f; ⟨of horse, hand⟩ dorso m; ⟨of chair⟩ schienale m; ⟨of house, cheque, page⟩ retro m; ⟨in football⟩ difesa f; **at the ~** in fondo; **in the ~** Auto dietro; **~ to front** ⟨sweater⟩ il davanti di dietro; **at the ~ of beyond** in un posto sperduto ● a posteriore; ⟨taxes, payments⟩ arretrato ● adv indietro; ⟨returned⟩ di ritorno; **turn/move ~** tornare/spostarsi indietro; **put it ~ here/there** rimettilo qui/là; **~ at home** di ritorno a casa; **I'll be ~ in five minutes** torno fra cinque minuti; **I'm just ~** sono appena tornato; **when do you want the book ~?** quando rivuoi il libro?; **pay ~** ripagare ⟨sb⟩; restituire ⟨money⟩; **~ in power** di nuovo al potere ● vt ⟨support⟩ sostenere; ⟨with money⟩

finanziare; puntare su ⟨horse⟩; ⟨cover the back of⟩ rivestire il retro di. ● vi Auto fare retromarcia. **back down** vi battere in ritirata. **back in** vi Auto entrare in retromarcia; ⟨person:⟩ entrare camminando all'indietro. **back out** vi Auto uscire in retromarcia; ⟨person:⟩ uscire camminando all'indietro; fig tirarsi indietro (**of** da). **back up** vt sostenere; confermare ⟨person's alibi⟩; Comput fare una copia di salvataggio di; **be ~ed up** ⟨traffic:⟩ essere congestionato ● vi Auto fare retromarcia

back: **~ache** n mal m di schiena. **~bencher** n parlamentare mf ordinario, -a. **~biting** n maldicenza f. **~bone** n spina f dorsale. **~chat** n risposta f impertinente. **~date** vt retrodatare ⟨cheque⟩; **~dated to** valido a partire da. **~ 'door** n porta f di servizio

backer /'bækə(r)/ n sostenitore, -trice mf; ⟨with money⟩ finanziatore, -trice mf

back: **~ 'fire** vi Auto avere un ritorno di fiamma; ⟨fig: plan⟩ fallire. **~ground** n sfondo m; ⟨environment⟩ ambiente m. **~hand** n ⟨tennis⟩ rovescio m. **~'handed** a ⟨compliment⟩ implicito. **~'hander** n ⟨fam: bribe⟩ bustarella f

backing /'bækɪŋ/ n ⟨support⟩ supporto m; ⟨material⟩ riserva f; Mus accompagnamento m; **~ group** gruppo m d'accompagnamento

back: **~lash** n fig reazione f opposta. **~log** n **~log of work** lavoro m arretrato. **~ 'seat** n sedile m posteriore. **~side** n fam fondoschiena m inv. **~slash** n Typ barra f retroversa. **~stage** a & adv dietro le quinte. **~stroke** n dorso m. **~up** n rinforzi mpl; Comput riserva f. **~up copy** n Comput copia f di riserva

backward /'bækwəd/ a ⟨step⟩ indietro; ⟨child⟩ lento nell'apprendimento; ⟨country⟩ arretrato ● adv **~s** (also Am: **~**) indietro; ⟨fall, walk⟩ all'indietro; **~s and forwards** avanti e indietro

back: **~water** n fig luogo m allo scarto. **~ 'yard** n cortile m

bacon /'beɪkn/ n ≈ pancetta f

bacteria /bæk'tɪərɪə/ npl batteri mpl

bad /bæd/ a ⟨worse, worst⟩ cattivo; ⟨weather, habit, news, accident⟩ brutto; ⟨apple etc⟩ marcio; **the light is ~** non c'è una buona luce; **use ~ language** dire delle parolacce; **feel ~** sentirsi male; ⟨feel guilty⟩ sentirsi in colpa; **have a ~ back** avere dei problemi alla schiena; **smoking is ~ for you** fumare fa male;

go ~ andare a male; **that's just too ~!** pazienza!; **not ~** niente male

bade /bæd/ see **bid**

badge /bædʒ/ n distintivo m

badger /'bædʒə(r)/ n tasso m ● vt tormentare

badly /'bædlɪ/ adv male; ⟨hurt⟩ gravemente; **~ off** povero; **~ behaved** maleducato; **need ~** aver bisogno di

bad-'mannered a maleducato

badminton /'bædmɪntən/ n badminton m

bad-'tempered a irascibile

baffle /'bæfl/ vt confondere

bag /bæg/ n borsa f; ⟨of paper⟩ sacchetto m; **old ~** sl megera f; **~s under the eyes** occhiaie fpl; **~s of** fam un sacco di

baggage /'bægɪdʒ/ n bagagli mpl

baggy /'bægɪ/ a ⟨clothes⟩ ampio

'bagpipes npl cornamusa fsg

Bahamas /bə'hɑːməz/ npl **the ~** le Bahamas

bail /beɪl/ n cauzione f; **on ~** su cauzione ● **bail out** vt Naut aggottare; **~ sb out** Jur pagare la cauzione per qcno ● vi Aeron paracadutarsi

bait /beɪt/ n esca f ● vt innescare; ⟨fig: torment⟩ tormentare

bake /beɪk/ vt cuocere al forno; ⟨make⟩ fare ● vi cuocersi al forno

baker /'beɪkə(r)/ n fornaio, -a mf, panettiere, -a mf; **~'s** ⟨shop⟩ panetteria f. **~y** n panificio m, forno m

baking /'beɪkɪŋ/ n cottura f al forno. **~-powder** n lievito m in polvere. **~-tin** n teglia f

balance /'bæləns/ n equilibrio m; Comm bilancio m; ⟨outstanding sum⟩ saldo m; [**bank**] **~** saldo m; **be** or **hang in the ~** fig essere in sospeso ● vt bilanciare; equilibrare ⟨budget⟩; Comm fare il bilancio di ⟨books⟩ ● vi bilanciarsi; Comm essere in pareggio. **~d** a equilibrato. **~ sheet** n bilancio m [d'esercizio]

balcony /'bælkənɪ/ n balcone m

bald /bɔːld/ a ⟨person⟩ calvo; ⟨tyre⟩ liscio; ⟨statement⟩ nudo e crudo; **go ~** perdere i capelli

bald|ing /'bɔːldɪŋ/ a **be ~ing** stare perdendo i capelli. **~ness** n calvizie f

bale /beɪl/ n balla f

baleful /'beɪlfl/ a malvagio; ⟨sad⟩ triste

balk /bɔːlk/ vt ostacolare ● vi **~ at** ⟨horse:⟩ impennarsi davanti a; fig tirarsi indietro davanti a

Balkans /'bɔːlknz/ npl Balcani mpl

ball¹ /bɔːl/ n palla f; (football) pallone m; (of yarn) gomitolo m; **on the ~** fam sveglio

ball² n (dance) ballo m

ballad /'bæləd/ n ballata f

ballast /'bæləst/ n zavorra f

ball-'bearing n cuscinetto m a sfera

ballerina /bælə'riːnə/ n ballerina f [classica]

ballet /'bæleɪ/ n balletto m; (art form) danza f; **~ dancer** n ballerino, -a mf [classico, -a]

ballistic /bə'lɪstɪk/ a balistico. **~s** n balistica fsg

balloon /bə'luːn/ n pallone m; Aeron mongolfiera f

ballot /'bælət/ n votazione f. **~-box** n urna f. **~-paper** n scheda f di votazione

ball: **~-point** ['pen] n penna f a sfera. **~-room** n sala f da ballo

balm /bɑːm/ n balsamo m

balmy /'bɑːmɪ/ a (-ier, -iest) mite; (fam: crazy) strampalato

Baltic /'bɔːltɪk/ a & n **the ~** [Sea] il [mar] Baltico

bamboo /bæm'buː/ n bambù m inv

bamboozle /bæm'buːzl/ vt (fam: mystify) confondere

ban /bæn/ n proibizione f ● vt (pt/pp banned) proibire; **~ from** espellere da ⟨club⟩; **she was ~ned from driving** le hanno ritirato la patente

banal /bə'nɑːl/ a banale. **~ity** /-'nælətɪ/ n banalità f inv

banana /bə'nɑːnə/ n banana f

band /bænd/ n banda f; (stripe) nastro m; (Mus: pop group) complesso m; (Mus: brass ~) banda f; Mil fanfara f ● **band together** vi riunirsi

bandage /'bændɪdʒ/ n benda f ● vt fasciare ⟨limb⟩

b. & b. abbr bed and breakfast

bandit /'bændɪt/ n bandito m

band: **~stand** n palco m coperto [dell'orchestra]. **~wagon** n **jump on the ~wagon** fig seguire la corrente

bandy¹ /'bændɪ/ vt (pt/pp -ied) scambiarsi ⟨words⟩. **bandy about** vt far circolare

bandy² a (-ier, -iest) **be ~** avere le gambe storte

bang /bæŋ/ n (noise) fragore m; (of gun, firework) scoppio m; (blow) colpo m ● adv **~ in the middle of** fam proprio nel mezzo di; **go ~** ⟨gun:⟩ sparare; ⟨balloon:⟩ esplodere ● int bum! ● vt battere ⟨fist⟩; battere su ⟨table⟩; sbattere

⟨door, head⟩ ● vi scoppiare; ⟨door:⟩ sbattere

banger /'bæŋə(r)/ n (firework) petardo m; (fam: sausage) salsiccia f; **old ~** (fam: car) macinino m

bangle /'bæŋgl/ n braccialetto m

banish /'bænɪʃ/ vt bandire

banisters /'bænɪstəz/ npl ringhiera fsg

bank¹ /bæŋk/ n (of river) sponda f; (slope) scarpata f ● vi Aeron inclinarsi in virata

bank² n banca f ● vt depositare in banca ● vi **~ with** avere un conto [bancario] presso. **bank on** vt contare su

'bank account n conto m in banca

'bank card n carta f assegno

banker /'bæŋkə(r)/ n banchiere m

bank: **~ holiday** n giorno m festivo. **~ing** n bancario m. **~ manager** n direttore, -trice mf di banca. **~note** n banconota f

bankrupt /'bæŋkrʌpt/ a fallito; **go ~** fallire ● n persona f che ha fatto fallimento ● vt far fallire. **~cy** n bancarotta f

banner /'bænə(r)/ n stendardo m; (of demonstrators) striscione m

banns /bænz/ npl Relig pubblicazioni fpl [di matrimonio]

banquet /'bæŋkwɪt/ n banchetto m

banter /'bæntə(r)/ n battute fpl di spirito

baptism /'bæptɪzm/ n battesimo m

Baptist /'bæptɪst/ a & n battista mf

baptize /bæp'taɪz/ vt battezzare

bar /bɑː(r)/ n sbarra f; Jur ordine m degli avvocati; (of chocolate) tavoletta f; (café) bar m inv; (counter) banco m; Mus battuta f; (fig: obstacle) ostacolo m; **~ of soap/gold** saponetta f/lingotto m; **behind ~s** fam dietro le sbarre ● vt (pt/pp barred) sbarrare ⟨way⟩; sprangare ⟨door⟩; escludere ⟨person⟩ ● prep tranne; **~ none** in assoluto

barbarian /bɑː'beərɪən/ n barbaro, -a mf

barbaric /bɑː'bærɪk/ a barbarico. **~ity** n barbarie f inv. **~ous** /'bɑːbərəs/ a barbaro

barbecue /'bɑːbɪkjuː/ n barbecue m inv; (party) grigliata f, barbecue m inv ● vt arrostire sul barbecue

barbed /bɑːbd/ a **~ wire** filo m spinato

barber /'bɑːbə(r)/ n barbiere m

barbiturate /bɑː'bɪtjʊrət/ n barbiturico m

'bar code n codice m a barre

bare /beə(r)/ a nudo; (tree, room) spoglio; ⟨floor⟩ senza moquette ● vt scoprire; mostrare ⟨teeth⟩

bare: ~**back** adv senza sella. ~**faced** a sfacciato. ~**foot** adv scalzo. ~'**headed** a a capo scoperto

barely /'beəlɪ/ adv appena

bargain /'bɑːgɪn/ n ⟨agreement⟩ patto m; ⟨good buy⟩ affare m; **into the** ~ per di più ● vi contrattare; ⟨haggle⟩ trattare. **bargain for** vt ⟨expect⟩ aspettarsi

barge /bɑːdʒ/ n barcone m ● **barge in** vi fam ⟨to room⟩ piombare dentro; ⟨into conversation⟩ interrompere bruscamente. ~ **into** vt piombare dentro a ⟨room⟩; venire addosso a ⟨person⟩

baritone /'bærɪtəʊn/ n baritono m

bark¹ /bɑːk/ n ⟨of tree⟩ corteccia f

bark² /bɑːk/ n abbaiamento m ● vi abbaiare

barley /'bɑːlɪ/ n orzo m

bar: ~**maid** n barista f. ~**man** n barista m

barmy /'bɑːmɪ/ a fam strampalato

barn /bɑːn/ n granaio m

barometer /bə'rɒmɪtə(r)/ n barometro m

baron /'bærn/ n barone m. ~**ess** n baronessa f

baroque /bə'rɒk/ a & n barocco m

barracks /'bærəks/ npl caserma fsg

barrage /'bærɑːʒ/ n Mil sbarramento m; ⟨fig: of criticism⟩ sfilza f

barrel /'bærl/ n barile m, botte f; ⟨of gun⟩ canna f. ~-**organ** n organetto m [a cilindro]

barren /'bærən/ a sterile; ⟨landscape⟩ brullo

barricade /bærɪ'keɪd/ n barricata f ● vt barricare

barrier /'bærɪə(r)/ n barriera f; Rail cancello m; fig ostacolo m

barring /'bɑːrɪŋ/ prep ~ **accidents** tranne imprevisti

barrister /'bærɪstə(r)/ n avvocato m

barrow /'bærəʊ/ n carretto m; ⟨wheel~⟩ carriola f

barter /'bɑːtə(r)/ vi barattare (**for** con)

base /beɪs/ n base f ● a vile ● vt basare; **be** ~**d on** basarsi su

base: ~**ball** n baseball m. ~**less** a infondato. ~**ment** n seminterrato m. ~**ment flat** n appartamento m nel seminterrato

bash /bæʃ/ n colpo m [violento] ● vt colpire [violentemente]; ⟨dent⟩ ammaccare; ~**ed in** ammaccato

bashful /'bæʃfl/ a timido

basic /'beɪsɪk/ a di base; ⟨condition, requirement⟩ basilare; ⟨living conditions⟩ povero; **my Italian is pretty** ~ il mio italiano è abbastanza rudimentale; **the** ~**s** ⟨of language, science⟩ i rudimenti; ⟨essentials⟩ l'essenziale m. ~**ally** adv fondamentalmente

basil /'bæzɪl/ n basilico m

basilica /bə'zɪlɪkə/ n basilica f

basin /'beɪsn/ n bacinella f; ⟨wash-hand ~⟩ lavabo m; ⟨for food⟩ recipiente m; Geog bacino m

basis /'beɪsɪs/ n ⟨pl **-ses** /-siːz/⟩ base f

bask /bɑːsk/ vi crogiolarsi

basket /'bɑːskɪt/ n cestino m. ~**ball** n pallacanestro f

Basle /bɑːl/ n Basilea f

bass /beɪs/ a basso; ~ **voice** voce f di basso ● n basso m

bastard /'bɑːstəd/ n ⟨illegitimate child⟩ bastardo, -a mf; sl figlio m di puttana

bastion /'bæstɪən/ n bastione m

bat¹ /bæt/ n mazza f; ⟨for table tennis⟩ racchetta f; **off one's own** ~ fam tutto da solo ● vt ⟨pt/pp **batted**⟩ battere; **she didn't** ~ **an eyelid** fig non ha battuto ciglio

bat² n Zool pipistrello m

batch /bætʃ/ n gruppo m; ⟨of goods⟩ partita f; ⟨of bread⟩ infornata f

bated /'beɪtɪd/ a **with** ~ **breath** col fiato sospeso

bath /bɑːθ/ n ⟨pl ~**s** /bɑːðz/⟩ bagno m; ⟨tub⟩ vasca f da bagno; ~**s** pl piscina f; **have a** ~ fare un bagno ● vt fare il bagno a

bathe /beɪð/ n bagno m ● vi fare il bagno ● vt lavare ⟨wound⟩. ~**r** n bagnante mf

bathing /'beɪðɪŋ/ n bagni mpl. ~**cap** n cuffia f. ~-**costume** n costume m da bagno

bath: ~-**mat** n tappetino m da bagno. ~**robe** n accappatoio m. ~**room** n bagno m. ~-**towel** n asciugamano m da bagno

baton /'bætn/ n Mus bacchetta f

battalion /bə'tælɪən/ n battaglione m

batter /'bætə(r)/ n Culin pastella f; ~**ed** a ⟨car⟩ malandato; ⟨wife, baby⟩ maltrattato

battery /'bætərɪ/ n batteria f; ⟨of torch, radio⟩ pila f

battle /'bætl/ n battaglia f; fig lotta f ● vi fig lottare

battle: ~**field** n campo m di battaglia. ~**ship** n corazzata f

bawdy /'bɔːdɪ/ a ⟨-**ier**, -**iest**⟩ piccante

bawl /bɔːl/ vt/i urlare

bay¹ /beɪ/ n Geog baia f

bay² n **keep at** ~ tenere a bada

bay³ *n Bot* alloro *m*. **~-leaf** *n* foglia *f* d'alloro

bayonet /'beɪənt/ *n* baionetta *f*

bay 'window *n* bay window *f inv* (*grande finestra sporgente*)

bazaar /bə'zɑ:(r)/ *n* bazar *m inv*

BC *abbr* (**before Christ**) a.C.

be /bi:/ *vi* (*pres* **am, are, is, are;** *pt* **was, were;** *pp* **been**) essere; **he is a teacher** è insegnante, fa l'insegnante; **what do you want to be?** cosa vuoi fare?; **be quiet!** sta' zitto!; **I am cold/hot** ho freddo/caldo; **it's cold/hot, isn't it?** fa freddo/caldo, vero?; **how are you?** come stai?; **I am well** sto bene; **there is** c'è; **there are** ci sono; **I have been to Venice** sono stato a Venezia; **has the postman been?** è passato il postino?; **you're coming too, aren't you?** vieni anche tu, no?; **it's yours, is it?** è tuo, vero?; **was John there? - yes, he was** c'era John? - sì; **John wasn't there - yes he was!** John non c'era - sì che c'era!; **three and three are six** tre più tre fanno sei; **he is five** ha cinque anni; **that will be £10, please** fanno 10 sterline, per favore; **how much is it?** quanto costa?; **that's £5 you owe me** mi devi 5 sterline ● *v aux* **I am coming/reading** sto venendo/leggendo; **I'm staying** (*not leaving*) resto; **I am being taken** sto in giro; **I was thinking of you** stavo pensando a te; **you are not to tell him** non devi dirgielo; **you are to do that immediately** devi farlo subito ● *passive* essere; **I have been robbed** sono stato derubato

beach /bi:tʃ/ *n* spiaggia *f*. **~wear** *n* abbigliamento *m* da spiaggia

bead /bi:d/ *n* perlina *f*

beak /bi:k/ *n* becco *m*

beaker /'bi:kə(r)/ *n* coppa *f*

beam /bi:m/ *n* trave *f*; (*of light*) raggio *m* ● *vi* irradiare; ⟨*person:*⟩ essere raggiante. **~ing** *a* raggiante

bean /bi:n/ *n* fagiolo *m*; (*of coffee*) chicco *m*

bear¹ /beə(r)/ *n* orso *m*

bear² *v* (*pt* **bore,** *pp* **borne**) ● *vt* (*endure*) sopportare; mettere al mondo ⟨*child*⟩; (*carry*) portare; **~ in mind** tenere presente ● *vi* **~ left/right** andare a sinistra/a destra. **bear with** *vt* aver pazienza con. **~able** /-əbl/ *a* sopportabile

beard /bɪəd/ *n* barba *f*. **~ed** *a* barbuto

bearer /'beərə(r)/ *n* portatore, -trice *mf*; (*of passport*) titolare *mf*

bearing /'beərɪŋ/ *n* portamento *m*;

Techn cuscinetto *m* [a sfera]; **have a ~ on** avere attinenza con; **get one's ~s** orientarsi

beast /bi:st/ *n* bestia *f*; (*fam: person*) animale *m*

beat /bi:t/ *n* battito *m*; (*rhythm*) battuta *f*; (*of policeman*) giro *m* d'ispezione ● *v* (*pt* **beat,** *pp* **beaten**) ● *vt* battere; picchiare ⟨*person:*⟩; **~ it!** *fam* darsela a gambe!; **it ~s me why...** *fam* non capisco proprio perché. **beat up** *vt* picchiare

beat|en /'bi:tn/ *a* **off the ~en track** fuori mano. **~ing** *n* bastonata *f*; **get a ~ing** (*with fists*) essere preso a pugni; ⟨*team, player:*⟩ prendere una batosta

beautician /bju:'tɪʃn/ *n* estetista *mf*

beauti|ful /'bju:tɪfl/ *a* bello. **~fully** *adv* splendidamente

beauty /'bju:tɪ/ *n* bellezza *f*. **~ parlour** *n* istituto *m* di bellezza. **~ spot** *n* neo *m*; (*place*) luogo *m* pittoresco

beaver /'bi:və(r)/ *n* castoro *m*

became /bɪ'keɪm/ *see* **become**

because /bɪ'kɒz/ *conj* perché; **~ you didn't tell me, I...** perché non me lo hai detto,... ● *adv* **~ of** a causa di

beck /bek/ *n* **at the ~ and call of** a completa disposizione di

beckon /'bekn/ *vt/i* **[to]** chiamare con un cenno

become /bɪ'kʌm/ *v* (*pt* **became,** *pp* **become**) ● *vt* diventare ● *vi* diventare; **what has ~e of her?** che ne è di lei? **~ing** *a* ⟨*clothes*⟩ bello

bed /bed/ *n* letto *m*; (*of sea, lake*) fondo *m*; (*layer*) strato *m*; (*of flowers*) aiuola *f*; **in ~** a letto; **go to ~** andare a letto; **~ and breakfast** pensione *f* familiare in cui il prezzo della camera comprende la prima colazione. **~clothes** *npl* lenzuola e coperte *fpl*. **~ding** *n* biancheria *f* per il letto, materasso e guanciali

bedlam /'bedləm/ *n* baraonda *f*

bedraggled /bɪ'drægld/ *a* inzaccherato

bed: ~ridden *a* costretto a letto. **~room** *n* camera *f* da letto

'bedside *n* **at his ~** al suo capezzale. **~ lamp** *n* abat-jour *m inv*. **~ table** *n* comodino *m*

bed: ~'sit *n*, **~'sitter** *n*, **~'sitting-room** *n* = camera *f* ammobiliata fornita di cucina. **~spread** *n* copriletto *m*. **~time** *n* l'ora *f* di andare a letto

bee /bi:/ *n* ape *f*

beech /bi:tʃ/ *n* faggio *m*

beef /bi:f/ *n* manzo *m*. **~burger** *n* hamburger *m inv*

bee: ~**hive** *n* alveare *m*. ~**-line** *n* make a ~**line for** *fam* precipitarsi verso

been /biːn/ *see* **be**

beer /bɪə(r)/ *n* birra *f*

beetle /ˈbiːtl/ *n* scarafaggio *m*

beetroot /ˈbiːtruːt/ *n* barbabietola *f*

before /bɪˈfɔː(r)/ *prep* prima di; **the day** ~ **yesterday** ieri l'altro; ~ **long** fra poco ● *adv* prima; **never** ~ **have I seen…** non ho mai visto prima…; ~ **that** prima; ~ **going** prima di andare ● *conj* (*time*) prima che; ~ **you go** prima che tu vada. ~**hand** *adv* in anticipo

befriend /bɪˈfrend/ *vt* trattare da amico

beg /beg/ *v* (*pt/pp* **begged**) ● *vi* mendicare ● *vt* pregare; chiedere (*favour, forgiveness*)

began /bɪˈgæn/ *see* **begin**

beggar /ˈbegə(r)/ *n* mendicante *mf*; **poor** ~**!** povero cristo!

begin /bɪˈgɪn/ *vt/i* (*pt* **began**, *pp* **begun**, *pres p* **beginning**) cominciare. ~**ner** *n* principiante *mf*. ~**ning** *n* principio *m*

begonia /bɪˈgəʊnɪə/ *n* begonia *f*

begrudge /bɪˈgrʌdʒ/ *vt* (*envy*) essere invidioso di; dare malvolentieri (*money*)

begun /bɪˈgʌn/ *see* **begin**

behalf /bɪˈhɑːf/ *n* **on** ~ **of** a nome di; **on my** ~ a nome mio

behave /bɪˈheɪv/ *vi* comportarsi; ~ **[oneself]** comportarsi bene

behaviour /bɪˈheɪvjə(r)/ *n* comportamento *m*; (*of prisoner, soldier*) condotta *f*

behead /bɪˈhed/ *vt* decapitare

behind /bɪˈhaɪnd/ *prep* dietro; **be** ~ **sth** *fig* stare dietro qcsa ● *adv* dietro, indietro; (*late*) in ritardo; **a long way** ~ molto indietro ● *n fam* didietro *m*. ~**hand** *adv* indietro

beholden /bɪˈhəʊldn/ *a* obbligato (**to** verso)

beige /beɪʒ/ *a & n* beige *m inv*

being /ˈbiːɪŋ/ *n* essere *m*; **come into** ~ nascere

belated /bɪˈleɪtɪd/ *a* tardivo

belch /beltʃ/ *vi* ruttare ● *vt* ~ **[out]** eruttare (*smoke*)

belfry /ˈbelfrɪ/ *n* campanile *m*

Belgian /ˈbeldʒən/ *a & n* belga *mf*

Belgium /ˈbeldʒəm/ *n* Belgio *m*

belief /bɪˈliːf/ *n* fede *f*; (*opinion*) convinzione *f*

believable /bɪˈliːvəbl/ *a* credibile

believe /bɪˈliːv/ *vt/i* credere. ~**r** *n* Relig credente *mf*; **be a great** ~**r in** credere fermamente in

belittle /bɪˈlɪtl/ *vt* sminuire (*person, achievements*)

bell /bel/ *n* campana *f*; (*on door*) campanello *m*

belligerent /bɪˈlɪdʒərənt/ *a* belligerante; (*aggressive*) bellicoso

bellow /ˈbeləʊ/ *vi* gridare a squarciagola; (*animal:*) muggire

bellows /ˈbeləʊz/ *npl* (*for fire*) soffietto *msg*

belly /ˈbelɪ/ *n* pancia *f*

belong /bɪˈlɒŋ/ *vi* appartenere (**to** a); (*be member*) essere socio (**to** di). ~**ings** *npl* cose *fpl*

beloved /bɪˈlʌvɪd/ *a & n* amato, -a *mf*

below /bɪˈləʊ/ *prep* sotto; (*with numbers*) al di sotto di ● *adv* sotto, di sotto; *Naut* sotto coperta; **see** ~ guardare qui di seguito

belt /belt/ *n* cintura *f*; (*area*) zona *f*; *Techn* cinghia *f* ● *vi* ~ **along** (*fam: rush*) filare velocemente ● *vt* (*fam: hit*) picchiare

bemused /bɪˈmjuːzd/ *a* confuso

bench /bentʃ/ *n* panchina *f*; (*work*~) piano *m* da lavoro; **the B**~ *Jur* la magistratura

bend /bend/ *n* curva *f*; (*of river*) ansa *f* ● *v* (*pt/pp* **bent**) ● *vt* piegare ● *vi* piegarsi; (*road:*) curvare; ~ **[down]** chinarsi. **bend over** *vi* inchinarsi

beneath /bɪˈniːθ/ *prep* sotto, al di sotto di; **he thinks it's** ~ **him** *fig* pensa che sia sotto al suo livello ● *adv* giù

benediction /benɪˈdɪkʃn/ *n* Relig benedizione *f*

benefactor /ˈbenɪfæktə(r)/ *n* benefattore, -trice *mf*

beneficial /benɪˈfɪʃl/ *a* benefico

beneficiary /benɪˈfɪʃərɪ/ *n* beneficiario, -a *mf*

benefit /ˈbenɪfɪt/ *n* vantaggio *m*; (*allowance*) indennità *f inv* ● *v* (*pt/pp* **-fited**, *pres p* **-fiting**) ● *vt* giovare a ● *vi* trarre vantaggio (**from** da)

benevolen|ce /bɪˈnevələns/ *n* benevolenza *f*. ~**t** *a* benevolo

benign /bɪˈnaɪn/ *a* benevolo; *Med* benigno

bent /bent/ *see* **bend** ● *a* (*person*) ricurvo; (*distorted*) curvato; (*fam: dishonest*) corrotto; **be** ~ **on doing sth** essere ben deciso a fare qcsa ● *n* predisposizione *f*

be|queath /bɪˈkwiːð/ *vt* lasciare in eredità. ~**quest** /-ˈkwest/ *n* lascito *m*

bereave|d /bɪˈriːvd/ *n* **the** ~**d** *pl* i familiari del defunto. ~**ment** *n* lutto *m*

bereft /bɪˈreft/ a ~ **of** privo di
beret /ˈbereɪ/ n berretto m
berry /ˈberɪ/ n bacca f
berserk /bəˈsɜːk/ a **go** ~ diventare una belva
berth /bɜːθ/ n (bed) cuccetta f; (anchorage) ormeggio m ● vi ormeggiare
beseech /bɪˈsiːtʃ/ vt (pt/pp **beseeched** or **besought**) supplicare
beside /bɪˈsaɪd/ prep accanto a; ~ **oneself** fuori di sé
besides /bɪˈsaɪdz/ prep oltre a ● adv inoltre
besiege /bɪˈsiːdʒ/ vt assediare
besought /bɪˈsɔːt/ see **beseech**
best /best/ a migliore; **the ~ part of a year** la maggior parte dell'anno; ~ **before** Comm preferibilmente prima di ● n the ~ il meglio; (person) il/la migliore; **at** ~ tutt'al più; **all the ~!** tanti auguri!; **do one's** ~ fare del proprio meglio; **to the ~ of my knowledge** per quel che ne so; **make the ~ of it** cogliere il lato buono della cosa ● adv meglio, nel modo migliore; **as ~ I could** meglio che potevo ● ~'**man** n testimone m
bestow /bɪˈstəʊ/ vt conferire (**on** a)
best'seller n bestseller m inv
bet /bet/ n scommessa f ● vt/i (pt/pp **bet** or **betted**) scommettere
betray /bɪˈtreɪ/ vt tradire. **~al** n tradimento m
better /ˈbetə(r)/ a migliore, meglio; **get** ~ migliorare; (after illness) rimettersi ● adv meglio; ~ **off** meglio; (wealthier) più ricco; **all the** ~ tanto meglio; **the sooner the** ~ prima è, meglio è; **I've thought** ~ **of it** ci ho ripensato; **you'd** ~ **not** è meglio che non lo faccia ● vt migliorare; ~ **oneself** migliorare le proprie condizioni
'**betting shop** n ricevitoria f (dell'allibratore)
between /bɪˈtwiːn/ prep fra, tra; ~ **you and me** detto fra di noi; ~ **us** (together) tra me e te ● adv [**in**] ~ in mezzo; (time) frattempo
beverage /ˈbevərɪdʒ/ n bevanda f
beware /bɪˈweə(r)/ vi guardarsi (**of** da); ~ **of the dog!** attenti al cane!
bewilder /bɪˈwɪldə(r)/ vt disorientare; **~ed** perplesso. **~ment** n perplessità f
beyond /bɪˈjɒnd/ prep oltre; ~ **reach** irraggiungibile; ~ **doubt** senza alcun dubbio; ~ **belief** da non credere; **it's** ~ **me** fam non riesco proprio a capire ● adv più in là

bias /ˈbaɪəs/ n (preference) preferenza f; pej pregiudizio m ● vt (pt/pp **biased**) (influence) influenzare. **~ed** a parziale
bib /bɪb/ n bavaglino m
Bible /ˈbaɪbl/ n Bibbia f
biblical /ˈbɪblɪkl/ a biblico
bicarbonate /baɪˈkɑːbəneɪt/ n ~ **of soda** bicarbonato m di sodio
biceps /ˈbaɪseps/ n bicipite m
bicker /ˈbɪkə(r)/ vi litigare
bicycle /ˈbaɪsɪkl/ n bicicletta f ● vi andare in bicicletta
bid[1] /bɪd/ n offerta f; (attempt) tentativo m ● vt/i (pt/pp **bid**, pres p **bidding**) offrire; (in cards) dichiarare
bid[2] vt (pt **bade** or **bid**, pp **bidden** or **bid**, pres p **bidding**) liter (command) comandare; ~ **sb welcome** dare il benvenuto a qcno
bidder /ˈbɪdə(r)/ n offerente mf
bide /baɪd/ vt ~ **one's time** aspettare il momento buono
biennial /baɪˈenɪəl/ a biennale
bifocals /baɪˈfəʊklz/ npl occhiali mpl bifocali
big /bɪg/ a (**bigger, biggest**) grande; (brother, sister) più grande, (fam. generous) generoso ● adv **talk** ~ fam spararle grosse
bigam|ist /ˈbɪgəmɪst/ n bigamo, -a mf. **~y** n bigamia f
'**big-head** n fam gasato, -a mf
big-'headed a fam gasato
bigot /ˈbɪgət/ n fanatico, -a mf. **~ed** a di mentalità ristretta
'**bigwig** n fam pezzo m grosso
bike /baɪk/ n fam bici f inv
bikini /bɪˈkiːnɪ/ n bikini m inv
bile /baɪl/ n bile f
bilingual /baɪˈlɪŋgwəl/ a bilingue
bill[1] /bɪl/ n fattura f; (in restaurant etc) conto m; (poster) manifesto m; Pol progetto m di legge; (Am: note) biglietto m di banca ● vt fatturare
bill[2] n (beak) becco m
'**billfold** n Am portafoglio m
billiards /ˈbɪljədz/ n biliardo m
billion /ˈbɪljən/ n (thousand million) miliardo m; (old-fashioned Br: million million) mille miliardi mpl
'**billy-goat** /ˈbɪlɪ-/ n caprone m
bin /bɪn/ n bidone m
bind /baɪnd/ vt (pt/pp **bound**) legare (**to** a); (bandage) fasciare; Jur obbligare. **~ing** a (promise, contract) vincolante ● n (of book) rilegatura f; (on ski) attacco m [di sicurezza]
binge /bɪndʒ/ n fam **have a** ~ fare bal-

doria; (*eat a lot*) abbuffarsi ● *vi* abbuffarsi (**on** di)

binoculars /bɪˈnɒkjʊləz/ *npl* [**pair of**] ~ binocolo *m sg*

bio'chemist /baɪəʊ-/ *n* biochimico, -a *mf*. ~**ry** *n* biochimica *f*

biodegradable /-dɪˈgreɪdəbl/ *a* biodegradabile

biograph|er /baɪˈɒgrəfə(r)/ *n* biografo, -a *mf*. ~**y** *n* biografia *f*

biological /baɪəˈlɒdʒɪkl/ *a* biologico

biolog|ist /baɪˈɒlədʒɪst/ *n* biologo, -a *mf*. ~**y** *n* biologia *f*

birch /bɜːtʃ/ *n* (*tree*) betulla *f*

bird /bɜːd/ *n* uccello *m*; (*fam: girl*) ragazza *f*

Biro® /ˈbaɪrəʊ/ *n* biro *f inv*

birth /bɜːθ/ *n* nascita *f*

birth: ~ **certificate** *n* certificato *m* di nascita. ~-**control** *n* controllo *m* delle nascite. ~**day** *n* compleanno *m*. ~**mark** *n* voglia *f*. ~-**rate** *n* natalità *f*

biscuit /ˈbɪskɪt/ *n* biscotto *m*

bisect /baɪˈsekt/ *vt* dividere in due [parti]

bishop /ˈbɪʃəp/ *n* vescovo *m*; (*in chess*) alfiere *m*

bit¹ /bɪt/ *n* pezzo *m*; (*smaller*) pezzetto *m*; (*for horse*) morso *m*; Comput bit *m inv*; **a ~ of** un pezzo di (*cheese, paper*); un po' di (*time, rain, silence*); ~ **by** ~ poco a poco; **do one's** ~ fare la propria parte

bit² *see* **bite**

bitch /bɪtʃ/ *n* cagna *f*; *sl* stronza *f*. ~**y** *a* velenoso

bit|e /baɪt/ *n* morso *m*; (*insect* ~) puntura *f*; (*mouthful*) boccone *m* ● *vt* (*pt* **bit**, *pp* **bitten**) mordere; (*insect:*) pungere; ~**e one's nails** mangiarsi le unghie ● *vi* mordere; (*insect:*) pungere. ~**ing** *a* (*wind, criticism*) pungente; (*remark*) mordace

bitter /ˈbɪtə(r)/ *a* amaro ● *n* Br birra *f* amara. ~**ly** *adv* amaramente; **it's** ~**ly cold** c'è un freddo pungente. ~**ness** *n* amarezza *f*

bitty /ˈbɪtɪ/ *a* Br *fam* frammentario

bizarre /bɪˈzɑː(r)/ *a* bizzarro

blab /blæb/ *vi* (*pt/pp* **blabbed**) spifferare

black /blæk/ *a* nero; **be** ~ **and blue** essere pieno di lividi ● *n* negro, -a *mf* ● *vt* boicottare (*goods*). **black out** *vt* cancellare ● *vi* (*lose consciousness*) perdere coscienza

black: ~**berry** *n* mora *f*. ~**bird** *n* merlo *m*. ~**board** *n* Sch lavagna *f*. ~**currant** *n* ribes® nero; ~**eye** *n* occhio *m* nero.

~ '**ice** *n* ghiaccio *m* (*sulla strada*). ~**leg** *n* Br crumiro *m*. ~**list** *vt* mettere sulla lista nera. ~**mail** *n* ricatto *m* ● *vt* ricattare. ~**mailer** *n* ricattatore, -trice *mf*. ~ '**market** *n* mercato *m* nero. ~-**out** *n* blackout *m inv*; **have a** ~-**out** Med perdere coscienza. ~**smith** *n* fabbro *m*

bladder /ˈblædə(r)/ *n* Anat vescica *f*

blade /bleɪd/ *n* lama *f*; (*of grass*) filo *m*

blame /bleɪm/ *n* colpa *f* ● *vt* dare la colpa a; ~ **sb for doing sth** dare la colpa a qcno per aver fatto qcsa; **no one is to** ~ non è colpa di nessuno. ~**less** *a* innocente

blanch /blɑːntʃ/ *vi* sbiancare ● *vt* Culin sbollentare

blancmange /bləˈmɒnʒ/ *n* biancomangiare *m inv*

bland /blænd/ *a* (*food*) insipido; (*person*) insulso

blank /blæŋk/ *a* bianco; (*look*) vuoto ● *n* spazio *m* vuoto; (*cartridge*) a salve. ~ '**cheque** *n* assegno *m* in bianco

blanket /ˈblæŋkɪt/ *n* coperta *f*

blank 'verse *n* versi *mpl* sciolti

blare /bleə(r)/ *vi* suonare a tutto volume. **blare out** *vt* far risuonare ● *vi* (*music, radio:*) strillare

blasé /ˈblɑːzeɪ/ *a* vissuto, blasé *inv*

blaspheme /blæsˈfiːm/ *vi* bestemmiare

blasphem|ous /ˈblæsfəməs/ *a* blasfemo. ~**y** *n* bestemmia *f*

blast /blɑːst/ *n* (*gust*) raffica *f*; (*sound*) scoppio *m* ● *vt* (*with explosive*) far saltare ● *int* *sl* maledizione!. ~**ed** *a* *sl* maledetto

blast: ~-**furnace** *n* altoforno *m*. ~-**off** *n* (*of missile*) lancio *m*

blatant /ˈbleɪtənt/ *a* sfacciato

blaze /bleɪz/ *n* incendio *m*; **a** ~ **of colour** un'esplosione *f* di colori ● *vi* ardere

blazer /ˈbleɪzə(r)/ *n* blazer *m inv*

bleach /bliːtʃ/ *n* decolorante *m*; (*for cleaning*) candeggina *f* ● *vt* sbiancare; ossigenare (*hair*)

bleak /bliːk/ *a* desolato; (*fig: prospects, future*) tetro

bleary-eyed /blɪərɪˈaɪd/ *a* **look** ~ avere gli occhi assonnati

bleat /bliːt/ *vi* belare ● *n* belato *m*

bleed /bliːd/ *v* (*pt/pp* **bled**) ● *vi* sanguinare ● *vt* spurgare (*brakes, radiator*)

bleep /bliːp/ *n* bip *m* ● *vi* suonare ● *vt* chiamare (*col cercapersone*) (*doctor*). ~**er** *n* cercapersone *m inv*

blemish /ˈblemɪʃ/ *n* macchia *f*

blend /blend/ n (of tea, coffee, whisky) miscela f; (of colours) insieme m ● vt mescolare ● vi (colours, sounds:) fondersi (with con). ~**er** n Culin frullatore m

bless /bles/ vt benedire. ~**ed** /'blesɪd/ a also sl benedetto. ~**ing** n benedizione f

blew /blu:/ see **blow²**

blight /blaɪt/ n Bot ruggine f ● vt far avvizzire (plants)

blind¹ /blaɪnd/ a cieco; ~ **man/woman** cieco/cieca m; npl **the** ~ i ciechi mpl; ● vt accecare

blind² n [roller] ~ avvolgibile m; [Venetian] ~ veneziana f

blind: ~ **'alley** n vicolo m cieco. ~**fold** a be ~**fold** avere gli occhi bendati ● n benda f ● vt bendare gli occhi a. ~**ly** adv ciecamente. ~**ness** n cecità f

blink /blɪŋk/ vi sbattere le palpebre; (light:) tremolare

blinkered /'blɪŋkəd/ adj fig be ~ avere i paraocchi

blinkers /'blɪŋkəz/ npl paraocchi mpl

bliss /blɪs/ n Rel beatitudine f; (happiness) felicità f. ~**ful** a beato; (happy) meraviglioso

blister /'blɪstə(r)/ n Med vescica f; (in paint) bolla f ● vi (paint:) formare una bolla/delle bolle

blitz /blɪts/ n bombardamento m aereo; **have a** ~ **on sth** fig darci sotto con qcsa

blizzard /'blɪzəd/ n tormenta f

bloated /'bləʊtɪd/ a gonfio

blob /blɒb/ n goccia f

bloc /blɒk/ n Pol blocco m

block /blɒk/ n blocco m; (building) isolato m; (building ~) cubo m (per giochi di costruzione); ~ **of flats** palazzo m ● vt bloccare. **block up** vt bloccare

blockade /blɒ'keɪd/ n blocco m ● vt bloccare

blockage /'blɒkɪdʒ/ n ostruzione f

block: ~**head** n fam testone, -a mf. ~ **'letters** npl stampatello m

bloke /bləʊk/ n fam tizio m

blonde /blɒnd/ a biondo ● n bionda f

blood /blʌd/ n sangue m

blood: ~ **bath** n bagno m di sangue. ~ **count** n esame m emocromocitometrico. ~ **donor** n donatore m di sangue. ~ **group** n gruppo m sanguigno. ~**hound** n segugio m. ~**-poisoning** n setticemia f. ~ **pressure** n pressione f del sangue. ~**shed** n spargimento m di sangue. ~**shot** a iniettato di sangue. ~ **sports** npl sport mpl cruenti. ~**-stained** a macchiato di sangue. ~**stream** n sangue m. ~ **test** n analisi f

del sangue. ~**thirsty** a assetato di sangue. ~ **transfusion** n trasfusione f del sangue

bloody /'blʌdɪ/ a (-ier, -iest) insanguinato; sl maledetto ● adv sl ~ **easy/difficult** facile/difficile da matti. ~**-minded** a scorbutico

bloom /blu:m/ n fiore m; (in ~ (flower:) sbocciato; (tree:) in fiore ● vi fiorire; fig essere in forma smagliante

bloom|er /'blu:mə(r)/ n fam papera f. ~**ing** a fam maledetto. ~**ers** npl mutandoni mpl (da donna)

blossom /'blɒsəm/ n fiori mpl (d'albero); (single one) fiore m ● vi sbocciare

blot /blɒt/ n also fig macchia f ● **blot out** vt (pt/pp **blotted**) fig cancellare

blotch /blɒtʃ/ n macchia f. ~**y** a chiazzato

'blotting-paper n carta f assorbente

blouse /blaʊz/ n camicetta f

blow¹ /bləʊ/ n colpo m

blow² v (pt **blew**, pp **blown**) ● vi (wind:) soffiare; (fuse:) saltare ● vt (fam: squander) sperperare; ~ **one's nose** soffiarsi il naso. **blow away** vt far volar via (papers) ● vi (papers:) volare via. **blow down** vt abbattere ● vi abbattersi al suolo. **blow out** vt (extinguish) spegnere. **blow over** vi (storm:) passare; (fuss, trouble:) dissiparsi. **blow up** vt (inflate) gonfiare; (enlarge) ingrandire (photograph); (by explosion) far esplodere ● vi esplodere

blow: ~**-dry** vt asciugare col fon. ~**lamp** n fiamma f ossidrica

blown /bləʊn/ see **blow²**

'blowtorch n fiamma f ossidrica

blowy /'bləʊɪ/ a ventoso

blue /blu:/ a (pale) celeste; (navy) blu inv; (royal) azzurro; ~ **with cold** livido per il freddo ● n blu m inv; **have the ~s** essere giù [di tono]; **out of the** ~ inaspettatamente

blue: ~**bell** n giacinto m di bosco. ~**berry** n mirtillo m. ~**bottle** n moscone m. ~ **film** n film m inv a luci rosse. ~**print** n fig riferimento m

bluff /blʌf/ n bluff m inv ● vi bluffare

blunder /'blʌndə(r)/ n gaffe f inv ● vi fare una/delle gaffe

blunt /blʌnt/ a spuntato; (person) reciso. ~**ly** adv schiettamente

blur /blɜ:(r)/ n **it's all a** ~ fig è tutto un insieme confuso ● vt (pt/pp **blurred**) rendere confuso. ~**red** a (vision, photo) sfocato

hlurb /blɜ:b/ n soffietto m editoriale

blurt /blɜ:t/ vt ~ **out** spifferare

blush /blʌʃ/ n rossore m ● vi arrossire

blusher /'blʌʃə(r)/ n fard m

bluster /'blʌstə(r)/ n sbruffonata f. ~**y** a ⟨wind⟩ furioso; ⟨day, weather⟩ molto ventoso

boar /bɔ:(r)/ n cinghiale m

board /bɔ:d/ n tavola f; ⟨for notices⟩ tabellone m; ⟨committee⟩ assemblea f; ⟨of directors⟩ consiglio m; **full ~** Br pensione f completa; **half ~** Br mezza pensione f; ~ **and lodging** vitto e alloggio m; **go by the ~** fam andare a monte ● vt Naut, Aeron salire a bordo di ● vi ⟨passengers:⟩ salire a bordo. **board up** vt sbarrare con delle assi. **board with** vt stare a pensione da.

boarder /'bɔ:də(r)/ n pensionante mf; Sch convittore, -trice mf

board: ~**-game** n gioco m da tavolo. ~**ing-house** n pensione f. ~**ing-school** n collegio m

boast /bəʊst/ vi vantarsi (**about** di). ~**ful** a vanaglorioso

boat /bəʊt/ n barca f; ⟨ship⟩ nave f. ~**er** n ⟨hat⟩ paglietta f

bob /bɒb/ n ⟨hairstyle⟩ caschetto m ● vi (pt/pp **bobbed**) (also ~ **up and down**) andare su e giù

'bob-sleigh n bob m inv

bode /bəʊd/ vi ~ **well/ill** essere di buono/cattivo augurio

bodily /'bɒdɪlɪ/ a fisico ● adv ⟨forcibly⟩ fisicamente

body /'bɒdɪ/ n corpo m; ⟨organization⟩ ente m; ⟨amount: of poems etc⟩ quantità f. ~**guard** n guardia f del corpo. ~**work** n Auto carrozzeria f

bog /bɒg/ n palude f ● vt (pt/pp **bogged**) **get ~ged down** impantanarsi

boggle /'bɒgl/ vi **the mind ~s** non posso neanche immaginarlo

bogus /'bəʊgəs/ a falso

boil¹ /bɔɪl/ n Med foruncolo m

boil² n **bring/come to the ~** portare/arrivare ad ebollizione ● vt [far] bollire ● vi bollire; ⟨fig: with anger⟩ ribollire; **the water** or **kettle's ~ing** l'acqua bolle. **boil down to** vt fig ridursi a. **boil over** vi straboccare (bollendo). **boil up** vt far bollire

boiler /'bɔɪlə(r)/ n caldaia f. ~**suit** n tuta f

'boiling point n punto m di ebollizione

boisterous /'bɔɪstərəs/ a chiassoso

bold /bəʊld/ a audace ● n Typ neretto m. ~**ness** n audacia f

bollard /'bɒlɑ:d/ n colonnina m di sbarramento al traffico

bolster /'bəʊlstə(r)/ n cuscino m ⟨e rotondo⟩ ● vt ~ [**up**] sostenere

bolt /bəʊlt/ n ⟨for door⟩ catenaccio m; ⟨for fixing⟩ bullone m ● vt fissare ⟨con i bulloni⟩ (**to** a); chiudere col chiavistello ⟨door⟩; ingurgitare ⟨food⟩ ● vi svignarsela; ⟨horse:⟩ scappar via ● adv ~ **upright** diritto come un fuso

bomb /bɒm/ n bomba f ● vt bombardare

bombard /bɒm'bɑ:d/ vt also fig bombardare

bombastic /bɒm'bæstɪk/ a ampolloso

bomb|er /'bɒmə(r)/ n Aeron bombardiere m; ⟨person⟩ dinamitardo m. ~**er jacket** n giubbotto m, bomber m inv. ~**shell** n ⟨fig: news⟩ bomba f

bond /bɒnd/ n fig legame m; Comm obbligazione f ● vt ⟨glue:⟩ attaccare

bondage /'bɒndɪdʒ/ n schiavitù f

bone /bəʊn/ n osso m; ⟨of fish⟩ spina f ● vt disossare ⟨meat⟩; togliere le spine da ⟨fish⟩. ~**-'dry** a secco

bonfire /'bɒn-/ n falò m inv. ~ **night** festa celebrata la notte del 5 novembre con fuochi d'artificio e falò

bonnet /'bɒnɪt/ n cuffia f; ⟨of car⟩ cofano m

bonus /'bəʊnəs/ n ⟨individual⟩ gratifica f; ⟨production ~⟩ premio m; ⟨life insurance⟩ dividendo m; **a ~** fig qualcosa in più

bony /'bəʊnɪ/ a (**-ier, -iest**) ossuto; ⟨fish⟩ pieno di spine

boo /bu:/ int ⟨to surprise or frighten⟩ bu! ● vt/i fischiare

boob /bu:b/ n ⟨fam: mistake⟩ gaffe f inv; ⟨breast⟩ tetta f ● vi fam fare una gaffe

book /bʊk/ n libro m; ⟨of tickets⟩ blocchetto m; **keep the ~s** Comm tenere la contabilità; **be in sb's bad/good ~s** essere nel libro nero/nelle grazie di qcno ● vt ⟨reserve⟩ prenotare; ⟨for offence⟩ multare ● vi ⟨reserve⟩ prenotare

book: ~**case** n libreria f. ~**-ends** npl reggilibri mpl. ~**ing-office** n biglietteria f. ~**keeping** n contabilità f. ~**let** n opuscolo m. ~**maker** n allibratore m. ~**mark** n segnalibro m. ~**seller** n libraio, -a mf. ~**shop** n libreria f. ~**worm** n topo m di biblioteca

boom /bu:m/ n Comm boom m inv; ⟨upturn⟩ impennata f; ⟨of thunder, gun⟩ rimbombo m ● vi ⟨thunder, gun:⟩ rimbombare; fig prosperare

boon /bu:n/ n benedizione f

boor /bʊə(r)/ n zoticone m. **~ish** a maleducato

boost /bu:st/ n spinta f ● vt stimolare
⟨sales⟩; sollevare ⟨morale⟩; far crescere
⟨hopes⟩. **~er** n Med dose f supplémenta-
re

boot /bu:t/ n stivale m; (up to ankle)
stivaletto m; (football) scarpetta f;
(climbing) scarpone m; Auto portabagagli m inv ● vt Comput inizializzare

booth /bu:ð/ n (Teleph, voting) cabina f;
(at market) bancarella f

'boot-up n Comput boot m inv

booty /'bu:tɪ/ n bottino m

booze /bu:z/ fam n alcolici mpl. **~-up** n
bella bevuta f

border /'bɔ:də(r)/ n bordo m; ⟨frontier⟩
frontiera f; (in garden) bordura f ● vi **~
on** confinare con; fig essere ai confini di
⟨madness⟩. **~line** n linea f di demarcazione; **~line case** caso m dubbio

bore¹ /bɔ:(r)/ see **bear²**

bore² vt Techn forare

bor|e³ n (of gun) calibro m; (person) sec-
catore, -trice mf; (thing) seccatura f ● vt
annoiare. **~edom** n noia f. **be ~ed (to
tears** or **to death)** annoiarsi (da morire). **~ing** a noioso

born /bɔ:n/ ppbe **~** nascere; **I was ~ in
1966** sono nato nel 1966 ● a nato; **a ~
liar/actor** un bugiardo/attore nato

borne /bɔ:n/ see **bear²**

borough /'bʌrə/ n municipalità f inv

borrow /'bɒrəʊ/ vt prendere a prestito
(**from** da); **can I ~ your pen?** mi presti
la tua penna?

bosom /'bʊzm/ n seno m

boss /bɒs/ n direttore, -trice mf ● vt
(also **~ about**) comandare a bacchetta.
~y a autoritario

botanical /bə'tænɪkl/ a botanico

botan|ist /'bɒtənɪst/ n botanico, -a mf.
~y n botanica f

botch /bɒtʃ/ vt fare un pasticcio con

both /bəʊθ/ a & pron tutti e due, entrambi ● adv **~ men and women** entrambi
uomini e donne; **~** [**of**] **the children**
tutti e due i bambini; **they are ~ dead**
sono morti entrambi; **~ of them** tutti e
due

bother /'bɒðə(r)/ n preoccupazione f;
(minor trouble) fastidio m; **it's no ~** non
c'è problema ● int fam che seccatura! ●
vt (annoy) dare fastidio a; (disturb)
disturbare ● vi preoccuparsi (**about** di);
don't ~ lascia perdere

bottle /'hɒtl/ n bottiglia f; (baby's) bibe-

ron m inv ● vt imbottigliare. **bottle up**
vt fig reprimere

bottle: ~ bank n contenitore m per la
raccolta del vetro. **~-neck** n fig ingorgo
m. **~-opener** n apribottiglie m inv

bottom /'bɒtm/ a ultimo; **the ~ shelf**
l'ultimo scaffale in basso ● n (of
container) fondo m; (of river) fondale m;
(of hill) piedi mpl; (buttocks) sedere m;
at the ~ of the page in fondo alla pagina; **get to the ~ of** fig vedere cosa c'è
sotto. **~less** a senza fondo

bough /baʊ/ n ramoscello m

bought /bɔ:t/ see **buy**

boulder /'bəʊldə(r)/ n masso m

bounce /baʊns/ vi rimbalzare; (fam:
cheque:) essere respinto ● vt far rimbalzare (ball)

bouncer /'baʊnsə(r)/ n fam buttafuori
m inv

bound¹ /baʊnd/ n balzo m ● vi balzare

bound² see **bind** ● a **~ for** (ship) diretto
a; **be ~ to do** (likely) dovere fare per forza; (obliged) essere costretto a fare

boundary /'baʊndərɪ/ n limite m

'boundless a illimitato

bounds /baʊndz/ npl fig limiti mpl; **out
of ~** fuori dai limiti

bouquet /bʊ'keɪ/ n mazzo m di fiori; (of
wine) bouquet m

bourgeois /'bʊəʒwɑ:/ a pej borghese

bout /baʊt/ n Med attacco m; Sport incontro m

bow¹ /bəʊ/ n (weapon) arco m; Mus ar-
chetto m; (knot) nodo m

bow² /baʊ/ n inchino m ● vi inchinarsi
● vt piegare (head)

bow³ /baʊ/ n Naut prua f

bowel /'baʊəl/ n intestino m; **~s** pl inte-
stini mpl

bowl¹ /bəʊl/ n (for soup, cereal) scodella
f; (of pipe) fornello m

bowl² n (ball) boccia f ● vt lanciare ● vi
Cricket servire; (in bowls) lanciare.
bowl over vt buttar giù; (fig: leave
speechless) lasciar senza parole

bow-legged /bəʊ'legd/ a dalle gambe
storte

bowler¹ /'bəʊlə(r)/ n Cricket lanciatore
m; Bowls giocatore m di bocce

bowler² n **~** [**hat**] bombetta f

bowling /'bəʊlɪŋ/ n gioco m delle bocce.
~-alley n pista f da bowling

bowls /bəʊlz/ n gioco m delle bocce

bow-'tie /bəʊ-/ n cravatta f a farfalla

box¹ /bɒks/ n scatola f; Theat palco m

box² vi Sport fare il pugile ● vt **~ sb's
ears** dare uno scappaccione a qcno

box|er /'bɒksə(r)/ n pugile m. **~ing** n pugilato m. **B~ing Day** n [giorno m di] Santo Stefano m

box: **~-office** n Theat botteghino m. **~-room** n Br sgabuzzino m

boy /bɔɪ/ n ragazzo m; (younger) bambino m

boycott /'bɔɪkɒt/ n boicottaggio m ● vt boicottare

boy: **~friend** n ragazzo m. **~ish** a da ragazzino

bra /brɑː/ n reggiseno m

brace /breɪs/ n sostegno m; (dental) apparecchio m; **~s** npl bretelle fpl ● vt **~ oneself** fig farsi forza (**for** per affrontare)

bracelet /'breɪslɪt/ n braccialetto m

bracing /'breɪsɪŋ/ a tonificante

bracken /'brækn/ n felce f

bracket /'brækɪt/ n mensola f; (group) categoria f; Typ parentesi f inv ● vt mettere fra parentesi

brag /bræg/ vi (pt/pp **bragged**) vantarsi (**about** di)

braid /breɪd/ n (edging) passamano m

braille /breɪl/ n braille m

brain /breɪn/ n cervello m; **~s** pl fig testa fsg

brain: **~child** n invenzione f personale. **~ dead** a Med celebralmente morto; fig fam senza cervello. **~less** a senza cervello. **~wash** vt fare il lavaggio del cervello a. **~wave** n lampo m di genio

brainy /'breɪnɪ/ a (-ier, -iest) intelligente

braise /breɪz/ vt brasare

brake /breɪk/ n freno m ● vi frenare. **~-light** n stop m inv

bramble /'bræmbl/ n rovo m; (fruit) mora f

bran /bræn/ n crusca f

branch /brɑːntʃ/ n also fig ramo m; Comm succursale f ● vi (road:) biforcarsi. **branch off** vi biforcarsi. **branch out** vi **~ out into** allargare le proprie attività nel ramo di

brand /brænd/ n marca f; (on animal) marchio m ● vt marcare (animal); fig tacciare (**as** di)

brandish /'brændɪʃ/ vt brandire

brand-new a nuovo fiammante

brandy /'brændɪ/ n brandy m inv

brash /bræʃ/ a sfrontato

brass /brɑːs/ n ottone m; **the ~** Mus gli ottoni mpl; **top ~** fam pezzi mpl grossi. **~ band** n banda f (di soli ottoni)

brassiere /'bræzɪə(r)/ n fml, Am reggipetto m

brat /bræt/ n pej marmocchio, -a mf

bravado /brə'vɑːdəʊ/ n bravata f

brave /breɪv/ a coraggioso ● vt affrontare. **~ry** /-ərɪ/ n coraggio m

brawl /brɔːl/ n rissa f ● vi azzuffarsi

brawn /brɔːn/ n Culin soppressata f

brawny /'brɔːnɪ/ a muscoloso

brazen /'breɪzn/ a sfrontato

brazier /'breɪzɪə(r)/ n braciere m

Brazil /brə'zɪl/ n Brasile m. **~ian** a & n brasiliano, -a mf. **~ nut** n noce f del Brasile

breach /briːtʃ/ n (of law) violazione f; (gap) breccia f; (fig: in party) frattura f; **~ of contract** inadempienza f di contratto; **~ of the peace** violazione f della quiete pubblica ● vt recedere (contract)

bread /bred/ n pane m; **a slice of ~ and butter** una fetta di pane imburrato

bread: **~ bin** n cassetta f portapane inv. **~crumbs** npl briciole fpl; Culin pangrattato m. **~line** n **be on the ~line** essere povero in canna

breadth /bredθ/ n larghezza f

bread-winner n quello, -a mf che porta i soldi a casa

break /breɪk/ n rottura f; (interval) intervallo m; (interruption) interruzione f; (fam: chance) opportunità f inv ● v (pt **broke**, pp **broken**) ● vt rompere; (interrupt) interrompere; **~ one's arm** rompersi un braccio ● vi rompersi; (day:) spuntare; (storm:) scoppiare; (news:) diffondersi; (boy's voice:) cambiare. **break away** vi scappare; fig chiudere (**from** con). **break down** vi (machine, car:) guastarsi; (emotionally) cedere (psicologicamente) ● vt sfondare (door); ripartire (figures). **break into** vt introdursi (con la forza) in; forzare (car). **break off** vt rompere (engagement) ● vi (part of whole:) rompersi. **break out** vi (fight, war:) scoppiare. **break up** vt far cessare (fight); disperdere (crowd) ● vi (crowd:) disperdersi; (couple:) separarsi; Sch iniziare le vacanze

break|able /'breɪkəbl/ a fragile. **~age** /-ɪdʒ/ n rottura f. **~down** n (of car, machine) guasto m; Med esaurimento m nervoso; (of figures) analisi f inv. **~er** n (wave) frangente m

breakfast /'brekfəst/ n [prima] colazione f

break: **~through** n scoperta f. **~water** n frangiflutti m inv

breast /brest/ n seno m. **~-feed** vt allattare [al seno]. **~-stroke** n nuoto m a rana

breath /breθ/ n respiro m, fiato m; **out of ~** senza fiato

breathalyse /'breθəlaɪz/ vt sottoporre alla prova [etilica] del palloncino. **~r®** n Br alcoltest m inv

breathe /briːð/ vt/i respirare. **breathe in** vi inspirare ● vt respirare ‹scent, air›. **breathe out** vt/i espirare

breath|er /'briːðə(r)/ n pausa f. **~ing** n respirazione f

breath /breθ/: **~less** a senza fiato. **~-taking** a mozzafiato. **~ test** n prova [etilica] del palloncino

bred /bred/ see **breed**

breed /briːd/ n razza f ● v (pt/pp **bred**) ● vt allevare; ‹give rise to› generare ● vi riprodursi. **~er** n allevatore, -trice mf. **~ing** n allevamento m; fig educazione f

breeze /briːz/ n brezza f. **~y** a ventoso

brew /bruː/ n infuso m ● vt mettere in infusione ‹tea›; produrre ‹beer› ● vi fig ‹trouble:› essere nell'aria. **~er** n birraio m. **~ery** n fabbrica f di birra

bribe /braɪb/ n (money) bustarella f, (large sum of money) tangente f ● vt corrompere. **~ry** /-əri/ n corruzione f

brick /brɪk/ n mattone m. **'~layer** n muratore m ● **brick up** vt murare

bridal /'braɪdl/ a nuziale

bride /braɪd/ n sposa f. **~groom** n sposo m. **~smaid** n damigella f d'onore

bridge¹ /brɪdʒ/ n ponte m; (of nose) setto m nasale; (of spectacles) ponticello m ● vt fig colmare ‹gap›

bridge² n Cards bridge m

bridle /'braɪdl/ n briglia f

brief¹ /briːf/ a breve

brief² n istruzioni fpl; (Jur: case) causa f ● vt dare istruzioni a; Jur affidare la causa a. **~case** n cartella f

briefing /'briːfɪŋ/ n briefing m inv. **~ly** adv brevemente. **~ly,...** in breve,... **~ness** n brevità f

briefs /briːfs/ npl slip m inv

brigad|e /brɪ'geɪd/ n brigata f. **~ier** /-ə'dɪə(r)/ n generale m di brigata

bright /braɪt/ a (metal, idea) brillante; (day, room, future) luminoso; (clever) intelligente. **~ red** rosso m acceso

bright|en /'braɪtn/ v **~en [up]** ● vt ravvivare; rallegrare ‹person› ● vi ‹weather:› schiarirsi; ‹face:› illuminarsi; ‹person:› rallegrarsi. **~ly** adv ‹shine› intensamente; ‹smile› allegramente. **~ness** n luminosità f; (intelligence) intelligenza f

brilliance /'brɪljəns/ n luminosità f; (of person) genialità f

brilliant /'brɪljənt/ a (very good) eccezionale; (very intelligent) brillante; ‹sunshine› splendente

brim /brɪm/ n bordo m; (of hat) tesa f ● **brim over** vi (pt/pp **brimmed**) traboccare

brine /braɪn/ n salamoia f

bring /brɪŋ/ vt (pt/pp **brought**) portare ‹person, object›. **bring about** vt causare. **bring along** vt portare [con sé]. **bring back** vt restituire ‹sth borrowed›; reintrodurre ‹hanging›; fare ritornare in mente ‹memories›. **bring down** vt portare giù; fare cadere ‹government›; fare abbassare ‹price›. **bring off** vt **~ sth off** riuscire a fare qcsa. **bring on** vt (cause) provocare. **bring out** vt (emphasize) mettere in evidenza; pubblicare ‹book›. **bring round** vt portare; (persuade) convincere; far rinvenire ‹unconscious person›. **bring up** vt (vomit) rimettere; allevare ‹children›; tirare fuori ‹question, subject›

brink /brɪŋk/ n orlo m

brisk /brɪsk/ a svelto; ‹person› sbrigativo; ‹trade, business› redditizio; ‹walk› a passo spedito

brist|le /'brɪsl/ n setola f ● vi **~ling with** pieno di. **~ly** a ‹chin› ispido

Brit|ain /'brɪtn/ n Gran Bretagna f. **~ish** a britannico; ‹ambassador› della Gran Bretagna ● npl **the ~ish** il popolo britannico. **~on** n cittadino, -a britannico, -a mf

brittle /'brɪtl/ a fragile

broach /brəʊtʃ/ vt toccare ‹subject›

broad /brɔːd/ a ampio; ‹hint› chiaro; ‹accent› marcato. **two metres ~** largo due metri; **in ~ daylight** in pieno giorno. **~ beans** npl fave fpl

broadcast n trasmissione f ● vt/i (pt/pp **-cast**) trasmettere. **~er** n giornalista mf radiotelevisivo, -a. **~ing** n diffusione f radiotelevisiva; **be in ~ing** lavorare per la televisione/radio

broaden /'brɔːdn/ vt allargare ● vi allargarsi

broadly /'brɔːdlɪ/ adv largamente; **~ [speaking]** generalmente

broad'minded a di larghe vedute

broccoli /'brɒkəlɪ/ n inv broccoli mpl

brochure /'brəʊʃə(r)/ n opuscolo m; (travel ~) dépliant m inv

broke /brəʊk/ see **break** ● a fam al verde

broken /'brəʊkn/ see **break** ● a rotto;

⟨*fig: marriage*⟩ fallito. **~ English** inglese *m* stentato. **~-hearted** *a* affranto

broker /'brəʊkə(r)/ *n* broker *m inv*

brolly /'brɒlɪ/ *n fam* ombrello *m*

bronchitis /brɒŋ'kaɪtɪs/ *n* bronchite *f*

bronze /brɒnz/ *n* bronzo *m* ●*attrib* di bronzo

brooch /brəʊtʃ/ *n* spilla *f*

brood /bruːd/ *n* covata *f*; ⟨*hum: children*⟩ prole *f* ●*vi fig* rimuginare

brook /brʊk/ *n* ruscello *m*

broom /bruːm/ *n* scopa *f*. **~stick** *n* manico *m* di scopa

broth /brɒθ/ *n* brodo *m*

brothel /'brɒθl/ *n* bordello *m*

brother /'brʌðə(r)/ *n* fratello *m*

brother: ~-in-law *n* (*pl* **~s-in-law**) cognato *m*. **~ly** *a* fraterno

brought /brɔːt/ *see* bring

brow /braʊ/ *n* fronte *f*; ⟨*of hill*⟩ cima *f*

'browbeat *vt* (*pt* **-beat**, *pp* **-beaten**) intimidire

brown /braʊn/ *a* marrone; castano ⟨*hair*⟩ ●*n* marrone *m* ●*vt* rosolare ⟨*meat*⟩ ●*vi* ⟨*meat:*⟩ rosolarsi. **~ 'paper** *n* carta *f* da pacchi

Brownie /'braʊnɪ/ *n* coccinella *f* ⟨*negli scout*⟩

browse /braʊz/ *vi* ⟨*read*⟩ leggicchiare; ⟨*in shop*⟩ curiosare

bruise /bruːz/ *n* livido *m*; ⟨*on fruit*⟩ maccatura *f* ●*vt* ammaccare ⟨*fruit*⟩; **~ one's arm** farsi un livido sul braccio. **~d** *a* contuso

brunette /bruː'net/ *n* bruna *f*

brunt /brʌnt/ *n* **bear the ~ of sth** subire maggiormente qcsa

brush /brʌʃ/ *n* spazzola *f*; ⟨*with long handle*⟩ spazzolone *m*; ⟨*for paint*⟩ pennello *m*; ⟨*bushes*⟩ boscaglia *f*; ⟨*fig: conflict*⟩ breve scontro *m* ●*vt* spazzolare ⟨*hair*⟩; lavarsi ⟨*teeth*⟩; scopare ⟨*stairs, floor*⟩. **brush against** *vt* sfiorare. **brush aside** *vt fig* ignorare. **brush off** *vt* spazzolare; ⟨*with hands*⟩ togliere; ignorare ⟨*criticism*⟩. **brush up** *vt/i fig* **~ up [on]** rinfrescare

brusque /brʊsk/ *a* brusco

Brussels /'brʌslz/ *n* Bruxelles *f*. **~ sprouts** *npl* cavoletti *mpl* di Bruxelles

brutal /'bruːtl/ *a* brutale. **~ity** /-'tælɪtɪ/ *n* brutalità *f inv*

brute /bruːt/ *n* bruto *m*. **~ force** *n* forza *f* bruta

BSc *n abbr* **Bachelor of Science**

BSE *n abbr* (**bovine spongiform encephalitis**) encefalite *f* bovina spongiforme

bubble /'bʌbl/ *n* bolla *f*; ⟨*in drink*⟩ bollicina *f*

buck¹ /bʌk/ *n* maschio *m* del cervo; ⟨*rabbit*⟩ maschio *m* del coniglio ●*vi* ⟨*horse:*⟩ saltare a quattro zampe. **buck up** *vi fam* tirarsi su; ⟨*hurry*⟩ sbrigarsi

buck² *n Am fam* dollaro *m*

buck³ *n* **pass the ~** scaricare la responsabilità

bucket /'bʌkɪt/ *n* secchio *m*

buckle /'bʌkl/ *n* fibbia *f* ●*vt* allacciare ●*vi* ⟨*shelf:*⟩ piegarsi; ⟨*wheel:*⟩ storcersi

bud /bʌd/ *n* bocciolo *m*

Buddhis|m /'bʊdɪzm/ *n* buddismo *m*. **~t** *a & n* buddista *mf*

buddy /'bʌdɪ/ *n fam* amico, -a *mf*

budge /bʌdʒ/ *vt* spostare ●*vi* spostarsi

budgerigar /'bʌdʒərɪgaː(r)/ *n* cocorita *f*

budget /'bʌdʒɪt/ *n* bilancio *m*; ⟨*allotted to specific activity*⟩ budget *m inv* ●*vi* (*pt/pp* **budgeted**) prevedere le spese; **~ for sth** includere qcsa nelle spese previste

buff /bʌf/ *a* ⟨*colour*⟩ [color] camoscio ●*n fam* fanatico, -a *mf*

buffalo /'bʌfələʊ/ *n* (*inv or pl* **-es**) bufalo *m*

buffer /'bʌfə(r)/ *n Rail* respingente *m*; **old ~** *fam* vecchio bacucco *m*. **~ zone** *n* zona *f* cuscinetto

buffet¹ /'bʊfeɪ/ *n* buffet *m inv*

buffet² /'bʌfɪt/ *vt* (*pt/pp* **buffeted**) sferzare

buffoon /bə'fuːn/ *n* buffone, -a *mf*

bug /bʌg/ *n* ⟨*insect*⟩ insetto *m*; *Comput* bug *m inv*; ⟨*fam: device*⟩ cimice *f* ●*vt* (*pt/pp* **bugged**) *fam* installare delle microspie in ⟨*room*⟩; mettere sotto controllo ⟨*telephone*⟩; ⟨*fam: annoy*⟩ scocciare

buggy /'bʌgɪ/ *n* [**baby**] **~** passeggino *m*

bugle /'bjuːgl/ *n* tromba *f*

build /bɪld/ *n* ⟨*of person*⟩ corporatura *f* ●*vt/i* (*pt/pp* **built**) costruire. **build on** *vt* aggiungere ⟨*extra storey*⟩; sviluppare ⟨*previous work*⟩. **build up** *vt* **~ up one's strength** rimettersi in forza ●*vi* ⟨*pressure, traffic:*⟩ aumentare; ⟨*excitement, tension:*⟩ crescere

builder /'bɪldə(r)/ *n* ⟨*company*⟩ costruttore *m*; ⟨*worker*⟩ muratore *m*

building /'bɪldɪŋ/ *n* edificio *m*. **~ site** *n* cantiere *m* [di costruzione]. **~ society** *n* istituto *m* di credito immobiliare

'build-up *n* ⟨*of gas etc*⟩ accumulo *m*; *fig* battage *m inv* pubblicitario

built /bɪlt/ *see* build **~-in** *a* ⟨*unit*⟩ a

muro; ⟨*fig: feature*⟩ incorporato. **~-up area** *n Auto* centro *m* abitato

bulb /bʌlb/ *n* bulbo *m*; *Electr* lampadina *f*

bulg|e /bʌldʒ/ *n* rigonfiamento *m* ● *vi* esser gonfio (**with** di); ⟨*stomach, wall:*⟩ sporgere; ⟨*eyes, with surprise:*⟩ uscire dalle orbite. **~ing** *a* gonfio; ⟨*eyes*⟩ sporgente

bulk /bʌlk/ *n* volume *m*; ⟨*greater part*⟩ grosso *m*; **in** ~ in grande quantità; ⟨*loose*⟩ sfuso. **~y** *a* voluminoso

bull /bʊl/ *n* toro *m*

'bulldog *n* bulldog *m inv*

bulldozer /'bʊldəʊzə(r)/ *n* bull-dozer *m inv*

bullet /'bʊlɪt/ *n* pallottola *f*

bulletin /'bʊlɪtɪn/ *n* bollettino *m*. **~ board** *n Comput* bacheca *f* elettronica

'bullet-proof *a* antiproiettile *inv*; ⟨*vehicle*⟩ blindato

bullfight *n* corrida *f*. **~er** *n* torero *m*

bullion /'bʊlɪən/ *n* **gold** ~ oro *m* in lingotti

bullock /'bʊlək/ *n* manzo *m*

bull: **~ring** *n* arena *f*. **~'s-eye** *n* centro *m* del bersaglio; **score a ~'s-eye** fare centro

bully /'bʊlɪ/ *n* prepotente *mf* ● *vt* fare il/la prepotente con. **~ing** *n* prepotenze *fpl*

bum[1] /bʌm/ *n sl* sedere *m*

bum[2] *n Am fam* vagabondo, -a *mf* ● **bum around** *vi fam* vagabondare

bumble-bee /'bʌmbl-/ *n* calabrone *m*

bump /bʌmp/ *n* botta *f*; ⟨*swelling*⟩ bozzo *m*, gonfiore *m*; ⟨*in road*⟩ protuberanza *f* ● *vt* sbattere. **bump into** *vt* sbattere contro; ⟨*meet*⟩ imbattersi in. **bump off** *vt fam* far fuori

bumper /'bʌmpə(r)/ *n Auto* paraurti *m inv* ● *a* abbondante

bumpkin /'bʌmpkɪn/ *n* **country** ~ zoticone, -a *mf*

bumptious /'bʌmpʃəs/ *a* presuntuoso

bumpy /'bʌmpɪ/ *a* ⟨*road*⟩ accidentato; ⟨*flight*⟩ turbolento

bun /bʌn/ *n* focaccia *f* ⟨*dolce*⟩; ⟨*hair*⟩ chignon *m inv*

bunch /bʌntʃ/ *n* ⟨*of flowers, keys*⟩ mazzo *m*; ⟨*of bananas*⟩ casco *m*; ⟨*of people*⟩ gruppo *m*; ~ **of grapes** grappolo *m* d'uva

bundle /'bʌndl/ *n* fascio *m*; ⟨*of money*⟩ mazzetta *f*, **a** ~ **of nerves** *fam* un fascio di nervi ● *vt* ~ [**up**] affastellare

bung /bʌŋ/ *vt fam* ⟨*throw*⟩ buttare. **bung up** *vt* ⟨*block*⟩ otturare

bungalow /'bʌŋgələʊ/ *n* bungalow *m inv*

bungle /'bʌŋgl/ *vt* fare un pasticcio di

bunion /'bʌnjən/ *n Med* callo *m* all'alluce

bunk /bʌŋk/ *n* cuccetta *f*. **~-beds** *npl* letti *mpl* a castello

bunny /'bʌnɪ/ *n fam* coniglietto *m*

buoy /bɔɪ/ *n* boa *f*

buoyan|cy /'bɔɪənsɪ/ *n* galleggiabilità *f*. **~t** *a* ⟨*boat*⟩ galleggiante; ⟨*water*⟩ che aiuta a galleggiare

burden /'bɜːdn/ *n* carico *m* ● *vt* caricare. **~some** /-səm/ *a* gravoso

bureau /'bjʊərəʊ/ *n* (*pl* -**x** /-əʊz/ *or* ~**s**) ⟨*desk*⟩ scrivania *f*; ⟨*office*⟩ ufficio *m*

bureaucracy /bjʊə'rɒkrəsɪ/ *n* burocrazia *f*

bureaucrat /'bjʊərəkræt/ *n* burocrate *mf*. **~ic** /-'krætɪk/ *a* burocratico

burger /'bɜːgə(r)/ *n* hamburger *m inv*

burglar /'bɜːglə(r)/ *n* svaligiatore, -trice *mf*. **~ alarm** *n* antifurto *m inv*

burglar|ize /'bɜːgləraɪz/ *vt Am* svaligiare. **~y** *n* furto *m* con scasso

burgle /'bɜːgl/ *vt* svaligiare

Burgundy /'bɜːgəndɪ/ *n* Borgogna *f*

burial /'berɪəl/ *n* sepoltura *f*. ~ **ground** *n* cimitero *m*

burlesque /bɜː'lesk/ *n* parodia *f*

burly /'bɜːlɪ/ *a* (**-ier**, **-iest**) corpulento

Burm|a /'bɜːmə/ *n* Birmania *f*. **~ese** /-'miːz/ *a* & *n* birmano, -a *mf*

burn /bɜːn/ *n* bruciatura *f* ● *v* (*pt/pp* **burnt** *or* **burned**) ● *vt* bruciare ● *vi* bruciare. **burn down** *vt/i* bruciare. **burn out** *vi fig* esaurirsi. **~er** *n* ⟨*on stove*⟩ bruciatore *m*

burnish /'bɜːnɪʃ/ *vt* lucidare

burnt /bɜːnt/ *see* **burn**

burp /bɜːp/ *n fam* rutto *m* ● *vi fam* ruttare

burrow /'bʌrəʊ/ *n* tana *f* ● *vt* scavare ⟨*hole*⟩

bursar /'bɜːsə(r)/ *n* economo, -a *mf*. **~y** *n* borsa *f* di studio

burst /bɜːst/ *n* ⟨*of gunfire, energy, laughter*⟩ scoppio *m*; ⟨*of speed*⟩ scatto *m* ● *v* (*pt/pp* **burst**) ● *vt* far scoppiare ● *vi* scoppiare; ~ **into tears** scoppiare in lacrime; **she ~ into the room** fece irruzione nella stanza. **burst out** *vi* ~ **out laughing/crying** scoppiare a ridere/piangere

bury /'berɪ/ *vt* (*pt/pp* **-ied**) seppellire; ⟨*hide*⟩ nascondere

bus /bʌs/ *n* autobus *m inv*, pullman *m*

inv; (*long distance*) pullman *m inv*, corriera *f*

bush /buʃ/ *n* cespuglio *m*; (*land*) boscaglia *f*.~**y** *a* (**-ier**, **-iest**) folto

busily /'bɪzɪlɪ/ *adv* con grande impegno

business /'bɪznɪs/ *n* affare *m*; *Comm* affari *mpl*; (*establishment*) attività *f* di commercio;**on** ~ per affari;**he has no** ~ **to** non ha alcun diritto di;**mind one's own** ~ farsi gli affari propri; **that's none of your** ~ non sono affari tuoi. ~**like** *a* efficiente. ~**man** *n* uomo *m* d'affari. ~**woman** *n* donna *f* d'affari

busker /'bʌskə(r)/ *n* suonatore, -trice *mf* ambulante

'bus station *n* stazione *f* degli autobus

'bus-stop *n* fermata *f* d'autobus

bust[1] /bʌst/ *n* busto *m*; (*chest*) petto *m*

bust[2] *a fam* rotto;**go** ~ fallire● *v* (*pt/pp* **busted** *or* **bust**) *fam* ● *vt* far scoppiare ● *vi* scoppiare

bustl|e /'bʌsl/ *n* (*activity*) trambusto *m* ● **bustle about** *vi* affannarsi. ~**ing** *a* animato

'bust-up *n fam* lite *f*

busy /'bɪzɪ/ *a* (**-ier**, **-iest**) occupato; (*day, time*) intenso; (*street*) affollato; (*with traffic*) pieno di traffico;**be** ~ **doing** essere occupato a fare ● *vt* ~ **oneself** darsi da fare

'busybody *n* ficcanaso *mf inv*

but /bʌt/, *atono* /bət/ *conj* ma ● *prep* eccetto, tranne; **nobody** ~ **you** nessuno tranne te; ~ **for** (*without*) se non fosse stato per;**the last** ~ **one** il penultimo; **the next** ~ **one** il secondo● *adv* (*only*) soltanto;**there were** ~ **two** ce n'erano soltanto due

butcher /'butʃə(r)/ *n* macellaio *m*; ~**'s** [**shop**] macelleria *f* ● *vt* macellare; *fig* massacrare

butler /'bʌtlə(r)/ *n* maggiordomo *m*

butt /bʌt/ *n* (*of gun*) calcio *m*; (*of cigarette*) mozzicone *m*; (*for water*) barile *m*; (*fig: target*) bersaglio *m* ● *vt* dare una testata a; (*goat:*) dare una cornata a. **butt in** *vi* interrompere

butter /'bʌtə(r)/ *n* burro *m* ● *vt* imburrare. **butter up** *vt fam* arruffianarsi

butter: ~**cup** *n* ranuncolo *m*.~**fingers** *nsg fam*be a ~**fingers** avere le mani di pasta frolla.~**fly** *n* farfalla *f*

buttocks /'bʌtəks/ *npl* natiche *fpl*

button /'bʌtn/ *n* bottone *m*● *vt*~ [**up**] abbottonare ● *vi* ~ [**up**] abbottonarsi. ~**hole** *n* occhiello *m*, asola *f*

buttress /'bʌtrɪs/ *n* contrafforte *m*

buxom /'bʌksəm/ *a* formosa

buy /baɪ/ *n* **good/bad** ~ buon/cattivo acquisto *m*● *vt* (*pt/pp* **bought**) comprare; ~ **sb a drink** pagare da bere a qcno; **I'll** ~ **this one** (*drink*) questo, lo offro io. ~**er** *n* compratore, -trice *mf*

buzz /bʌz/ *n* ronzio *m*;**give sb a** ~ *fam* (*on phone*) dare un colpo di telefono a qcno; (*excite*) mettere in fermento qcno ● *vi* ronzare ● *vt* ~ **sb** chiamare qcno col cicalino. **buzz off** *vi fam* levarsi di torno

buzzer /'bʌzə(r)/ *n* cicalino *m*

by /baɪ/ *prep* (*near, next to*) vicino a; (*at the latest*) per;**by Mozart** di Mozart;**he was run over by a bus** è stato investito da un autobus;**by oneself** da solo;**by the sea** al mare;**by sea** via mare;**by car/bus** in macchina/autobus;**by day/night** di giorno/notte; **by the hour/metre** a ore/metri;**six metres by four** sei metri per quattro;**he won by six metres** ha vinto di sei metri;**I missed the train by a minute** ho perso il treno per un minuto;**I'll be home by six** sarò a casa per le sei; **by this time next week** a quest'ora tra una settimana;**he rushed by me** mi è passato accanto di corsa● *adv***she'll be here by and by** sarà qui fra poco; **by and large** in complesso

bye[**-bye**] /baɪ['baɪ]/ *int fam* ciao

by: ~**-election** *n* elezione *f straordinaria* indetta per coprire una carica rimasta vacante in Parlamento.~**gone** *a* passato. ~**-law** *n* legge *f* locale. ~**pass** *n* circonvallazione *f*; *Med* by-pass *m inv* ● *vt* evitare. ~**-product** *n* sottoprodotto *m*. ~**stander** *n* spettatore, -trice *mf*. ~**word** *n*be a ~**word for** essere sinonimo di

Cc

cab /kæb/ n taxi m inv; (of lorry, train) cabina f

cabaret /'kæbareɪ/ n cabaret m inv

cabbage /'kæbɪdʒ/ n cavolo m

cabin /'kæbɪn/ n (of plane, ship) cabina f; (hut) capanna f

cabinet /'kæbɪnɪt/ n armadietto m; [display] ~ vetrina f; C~ Pol consiglio m dei ministri. **~-maker** n ebanista m

cable /'keɪbl/ n cavo m. ~ '**railway** n funicolare f. ~ '**television** n televisione f via cavo

cache /kæʃ/ n nascondiglio m; ~ **of arms** deposito m segreto di armi

cackle /'kækl/ vi ridacchiare

cactus /'kæktəs/ n (pl **-ti** /-taɪ/ or **-tuses**) cactus m inv

caddie /'kædɪ/ n portabastoni m inv

caddy /'kædɪ/ n [**tea-**]~ barattolo m del tè

cadet /kə'det/ n cadetto m

cadge /kædʒ/ vt/i fam scroccare

Caesarean /sɪ'zeərɪən/ n parto m cesareo

café /'kæfeɪ/ n caffè m inv

cafeteria /kæfə'tɪərɪə/ n tavola f calda

caffeine /'kæfiːn/ n caffeina f

cage /keɪdʒ/ n gabbia f

cagey /'keɪdʒɪ/ a fam riservato (**about** su)

cajole /kə'dʒəʊl/ vt persuadere con le lusinghe

cake /keɪk/ n torta f; (small) pasticcino m. ~**d** a incrostato (**with** di)

calamity /kə'læmətɪ/ n calamità f inv

calcium /'kælsɪəm/ n calcio m

calcul|ate /'kælkjʊleɪt/ vt calcolare. ~**ing** a fig calcolatore. ~**ion** /-'leɪʃn/ n calcolo m. ~**or** n calcolatrice f

calendar /'kælɪndə(r)/ n calendario m

calf[1] /kɑːf/ n (pl **calves**) vitello m

calf[2] n (pl **calves**) Anat polpaccio m

calibre /'kælɪbə(r)/ n calibro m

call /kɔːl/ n grido m; Teleph telefonata f; (visit) visita f; **be on** ~ (doctor:) essere di guardia ● vt chiamare; indire (strike; **be ~ed** chiamarsi ● vi chiamare; ~ [**in** or **round**] passare. **call back** vt/i richiamare. **call for** vt (ask

for) chiedere; (require) richiedere; (fetch) passare a prendere. **call off** vt richiamare (dog); disdire (meeting); revocare (strike). **call on** vt chiamare; (appeal to) fare un appello a; (visit) visitare. **call out** vt chiamare ad alta voce (names) ● vi chiamare ad alta voce. **call together** vt riunire. **call up** vt Mil chiamare alle armi; Teleph chiamare

call: ~-**box** n cabina f telefonica. ~**er** n visitatore, -trice mf; Teleph persona f che telefona. ~**ing** n vocazione f

callous /'kæləs/ a insensibile

'**call-up** n Mil chiamata f alle armi

calm /kɑːm/ a calmo ● n calma f. **calm down** vt calmare ● vi calmarsi. ~**ly** adv con calma

calorie /'kælərɪ/ n caloria f

calves /kɑːvz/ npl see **calf**[1] & [2]

camber /'kæmbə(r)/ n curvatura f

Cambodia /kæm'bəʊdɪə/ n Cambogia f. ~**n** a & n cambogiano, -a mf

camcorder /'kæmkɔːdə(r)/ n videocamera f

came /keɪm/ see **come**

camel /'kæml/ n cammello m

camera /'kæmərə/ n macchina f fotografica; TV telecamera f. ~**man** n operatore m [televisivo], cameraman m inv

camouflage /'kæməflɑːʒ/ n mimetizzazione f ● vt mimetizzare

camp /kæmp/ n campeggio f; Mil campo m ● vi campeggiare; Mil accamparsi

campaign /kæm'peɪn/ n campagna f ● vi fare una campagna

camp: ~-**bed** n letto m da campo. ~**er** n campeggiatore, -trice mf; Auto camper m inv. ~**ing** n campeggio m. ~**site** n campeggio m

campus /'kæmpəs/ n (pl **-puses**) Univ città f universitaria, campus m inv

can[1] /kæn/ n (for petrol) latta f; (tin) scatola f; ~ **of beer** lattina f di birra ● vt mettere in scatola

can[2] /kæn/, atono /kən/ v aux (pres **can**; pt **could**) (be able to) potere; (know how to) sapere; **I cannot** or **can't go** non posso andare; **he could not** or **couldn't go** non poteva andare; **she** ●

can't swim non sa nuotare;**I ~ smell something burning** sento odor di bruciato

Canad|a /'kænədə/ n Canada m. **~ian** /kə'neɪdɪən/ a & n canadese

canal /kə'næl/ n canale m

Canaries /kə'neərɪz/ npl Canarie fpl

canary /kə'neərɪ/ n canarino m

cancel /'kænsl/ v (pt/pp **cancelled**) ● vt disdire ⟨meeting, newspaper⟩; revocare ⟨contract, order⟩; annullare ⟨reservation, appointment, stamp⟩. **~lation** /-ə'leɪʃn/ n (of meeting, contract) revoca f; (in hotel, restaurant, for flight) cancellazione f

cancer /'kænsə(r)/ n cancro m; **C~** Astr Cancro m. **~ous** /-rəs/ a canceroso

candelabra /kændə'lɑːbrə/ n candelabro m

candid /'kændɪd/ a franco

candidate /'kændɪdət/ n candidato, -a mf

candle /'kændl/ n candela f. **~stick** n portacandele m inv

candour /'kændə(r)/ n franchezza f

candy /'kændɪ/ n Am caramella f; **a [piece of] ~** una caramella. **~floss** /-flɒs/ n zucchero m filato

cane /keɪn/ n ⟨stick⟩ bastone m; Sch bacchetta f ● vt prendere a bacchettate ⟨pupil⟩

canine /'keɪnaɪn/ a canino. **~ tooth** n canino m

canister /'kænɪstə(r)/ n barattolo m (di metallo)

cannabis /'kænəbɪs/ n cannabis f

canned /kænd/ a in scatola; **~ music** fam musica f registrata

cannibal /'kænɪbl/ n cannibale mf. **~ism** n cannibalismo m

cannon /'kænən/ n inv cannone m. **~-ball** n palla f di cannone

cannot /'kænɒt/ see **can²**

canny /'kænɪ/ a astuto

canoe /kə'nuː/ n canoa f ● vi andare in canoa

'can-opener n apriscatole m inv

canopy /'kænəpɪ/ n baldacchino f; (of parachute) calotta f

can't /kɑːnt/ = **cannot** see **can²**

cantankerous /kæn'tæŋkərəs/ a stizzoso

canteen /kæn'tiːn/ n mensa f; **~ of cutlery** servizio m di posate

canter /'kæntə(r)/ vi andare a piccolo galoppo

canvas /'kænvəs/ n tela f; (painting) dipinto m su tela

canvass /'kænvəs/ vi Pol fare propaganda elettorale. **~ing** n sollecitazione f di voti

canyon /'kænjən/ n canyon m inv

cap /kæp/ n berretto m; (nurse's) cuffia f; (top, lid) tappo m ● vt (pt/pp**capped**) (fig: do better than) superare

capability /keɪpə'bɪlətɪ/ n capacità f

capab|le /'keɪpəbl/ a capace; (skilful) abile;**be ~e of doing sth** essere capace di fare qcsa. **~y** adv con abilità

capacity /kə'pæsətɪ/ n capacità f; (function) qualità f;**in my ~ as** in qualità di

cape¹ /keɪp/ n (cloak) cappa f

cape² n Geog capo m

caper¹ /'keɪpə(r)/ vi saltellare ● n fam birichinata f

caper² n Culin cappero m

capital /'kæpɪtl/ n (town) capitale f; (money) capitale m; (letter) lettera f maiuscola. **~ city** n capitale f

capital|ism /'kæpɪtəlɪzm/ n capitalismo m. **~ist** /-ɪst/ a & n capitalista mf. **~ize** /-aɪz/ vi **~ize on** fig trarre vantaggio da. **~ 'letter** n lettera f maiuscola. **~ 'punishment** n pena f capitale

capitulat|e /kə'pɪtjʊleɪt/ vi capitolare. **~ion** /-'leɪʃn/ n capitolazione f

capricious /kə'prɪʃəs/ a capriccioso

Capricorn /'kæprɪkɔːn/ n Astr Capricorno m

capsize /kæp'saɪz/ vi capovolgersi ● vt capovolgere

capsule /'kæpsjʊl/ n capsula f

captain /'kæptɪn/ n capitano m ● vt comandare ⟨team⟩

caption /'kæpʃn/ n intestazione f; (of illustration) didascalia f

captivate /'kæptɪveɪt/ vt incantare

captiv|e /'kæptɪv/ a prigioniero; **hold/take ~e** tenere/fare prigioniero ● n prigioniero, -a mf. **~ity** /-'tɪvətɪ/ n prigionia f; (animals) cattività f

capture /'kæptʃə(r)/ n cattura f ● vt catturare; attirare ⟨attention⟩

car /kɑː(r)/ n macchina f;**by ~** in macchina

carafe /kə'ræf/ n caraffa f

caramel /'kærəmel/ n (sweet) caramella f al mou; Culin caramello m

carat /'kærət/ n carato m

caravan /'kærəvæn/ n roulotte f inv; (horse-drawn) carovana f

carbohydrate /kɑːbə'haɪdreɪt/ n carboidrato m

carbon /'kɑːbən/ n carbonio m

carbon: ~ copy n copia f in carta carbone; (*fig: person*) ritratto *m*. ~ di'oxide *n* anidride *f* carbonica. ~ paper *n* carta *f* carbone

carburettor /ˈkɑːbjʊˈretə(r)/ *n* carburatore *m*

carcass /ˈkɑːkəs/ *n* carcassa *f*

card /kɑːd/ *n* (*for birthday, Christmas etc*) biglietto *m* di auguri; (*playing* ~) carta *f* [da gioco]; (*membership* ~) tessera *f*; (*business* ~) biglietto *m* da visita; (*credit* ~) carta *f* di credito; *Comput* scheda *f*

'**cardboard** *n* cartone *m*. ~ '**box** *n* scatola *f* di cartone; (*large*) scatolone *m*

'**card-game** *n* gioco *m* di carte

cardiac /ˈkɑːdɪæk/ *a* cardiaco

cardigan /ˈkɑːdɪgən/ *n* cardigan *m inv*

cardinal /ˈkɑːdɪnl/ *a* cardinale; ~ **number** numero *m* cardinale ● *n Relig* cardinale *m*

card 'index *n* schedario *m*

care /keə(r)/ *n* cura *f*; (*caution*) attenzione *f*; (*worry*) preoccupazione *f*; ~ **of** (*on letter abbr* **c/o**) presso; **take** ~ (*be cautious*) fare attenzione; **bye, take** ~ ciao, stammi bene; **take** ~ **of** occuparsi di; **be taken into** ~ essere preso in custodia da un ente assistenziale ● *vi* ~ **about** interessarsi di; ~ **for** (*feel affection for*) volere bene a; (*look after*) aver cura di; **I don't** ~ **for chocolate** non mi piace il cioccolato; **I don't** ~ non me ne importa; **who** ~**s?** chi se ne frega?

career /kəˈrɪə(r)/ *n* carriera *f*; (*profession*) professione *f* ● *vi* andare a tutta velocità

care: ~**free** *a* spensierato. ~**ful** *a* attento; (*driver*) prudente. ~**fully** *adv* con attenzione. ~**less** *a* irresponsabile; (*in work*) trascurato; (*work*) fatto con poca cura; (*driver*) distratto. ~**lessly** *adv* negligentemente. ~**lessness** *n* trascuratezza *f*. ~**r** *n* persona *f* che accudisce a un anziano o a un malato

caress /kəˈres/ *n* carezza *f* ● *vt* accarezzare

'**caretaker** *n* custode *mf*; (*in school*) bidello *m*

'**car ferry** *n* traghetto *m* (*per il trasporto di auto*)

cargo /ˈkɑːgəʊ/ *n* (*pl* -**es**) carico *m*

Caribbean /kærɪˈbiːən/ *n* **the** ~ (*sea*) il Mar dei Caraibi ● *a* caraibico

caricature /ˈkærɪkətjʊə(r)/ *n* caricatura *f*

caring /ˈkeərɪŋ/ *a* (*parent*) premuroso;

(*attitude*) altruista; **the** ~ **professions** le attività assistenziali

carnage /ˈkɑːnɪdʒ/ *n* carneficina *f*

carnal /ˈkɑːnl/ *a* carnale

carnation /kɑːˈneɪʃn/ *n* garofano *m*

carnival /ˈkɑːnɪvl/ *n* carnevale *m*

carnivorous /kɑːˈnɪvərəs/ *a* carnivoro

carol /ˈkærəl/ *n* [**Christmas**] ~ canzone *f* natalizia

carp[1] /kɑːp/ *n inv* carpa *f*

carp[2] *vi* ~ **at** trovare da ridire su

'**car park** *n* parcheggio *m*

carpenter /ˈkɑːpɪntə(r)/ *n* falegname *m*. ~**ry** *n* falegnameria *f*

carpet /ˈkɑːpɪt/ *n* tappeto *m*; (*wall-to-wall*) moquette *f inv* ● *vt* mettere la moquette in (*room*)

'**car phone** *n* telefono *m* in macchina

carriage /ˈkærɪdʒ/ *n* carrozza *f*; (*of goods*) trasporto *m*; (*cost*) spese *fpl* di trasporto; (*bearing*) portamento *m*; ~**way** *n* strada *f* carrozzabile; **north-bound** ~**way** carreggiata *f* nord

carrier /ˈkærɪə(r)/ *n* (*company*) impresa *f* di trasporti; *Aeron* compagnia *f* di trasporto aereo; (*of disease*) portatore *m*. ~ [**bag**] *n* borsa *f* [per la spesa]

carrot /ˈkærət/ *n* carota *f*

carry /ˈkæri/ *v* (*pt/pp* -**ied**) ● *vt* portare; (*transport*) trasportare; **get carried away** *fam* lasciarsi prender la mano ● *vi* (*sound*) trasmettersi. **carry off** *vt* portare via; vincere (*prize*). **carry on** *vi* continuare; (*fam: make scene*) fare delle storie; ~ **on with sth** continuare qcsa; ~ **on with sb** *fam* intendersela con qcno ● *vt* mantenere (*business*). **carry out** *vt* portare fuori; eseguire (*instructions, task*); mettere in atto (*threat*); effettuare (*experiment, survey*)

'**carry-cot** *n* porte-enfant *m inv*

cart /kɑːt/ *n* carretto *m* ● *vt* (*fam: carry*) portare

cartilage /ˈkɑːtɪlɪdʒ/ *n Anat* cartilagine *f*

carton /ˈkɑːtn/ *n* scatola *f* di cartone; (*for drink*) cartone *m*; (*of cream, yoghurt*) vasetto *m*; (*of cigarettes*) stecca *f*

cartoon /kɑːˈtuːn/ *n* vignetta *f*; (*strip*) vignette *fpl*; (*film*) cartone *m* animato; (*in art*) bozzetto *m*. ~**ist** *n* vignettista *mf*; (*for films*) disegnatore, -trice *mf* di cartoni animati

cartridge /ˈkɑːtrɪdʒ/ *n* cartuccia *f*; (*for film*) bobina *f*; (*of record player*) testina *f*

carve /kɑːv/ *vt* scolpire; tagliare (*meat*)

carving /'kɑːvɪŋ/ n scultura f. **~-knife** n trinciante m

'car wash n autolavaggio m inv

case¹ /keɪs/ n caso m; **in any ~** in ogni caso; **in that ~** in questo caso; **just in ~** per sicurezza; **in ~ he comes** nel caso in cui venisse

case² n (container) scatola f; (crate) cassa f; (for spectacles) astuccio m; (suitcase) valigia f; (for display) vetrina f

cash /kæʃ/ n denaro m contante; (fam: money) contanti mpl; **pay [in] ~** pagare in contanti; **~ on delivery** pagamento alla consegna ● vt incassare (cheque). **~ desk** n cassa f

cashier /kæ'ʃɪə(r)/ n cassiere, -a mf

'cash register n registratore m di cassa

casino /kə'siːnəʊ/ n casinò m inv

casket /'kɑːskɪt/ n scrigno m; (Am: coffin) bara f

casserole /'kæsərəʊl/ n casseruola f; (stew) stufato m

cassette /kə'set/ n cassetta f. **~ recorder** n registratore m (a cassette)

cast /kɑːst/ n (mould) forma f; Theat cast m inv; [plaster] ~ Med ingessatura f ● vt (pt/pp cast) dare (vote); Theat assegnare le parti di (play); fondere (metal); (throw) gettare; **~ an actor as** dare ad un attore il ruolo di; **~ a glance at** lanciare uno sguardo a. **cast off** vi Naut sganciare gli ormeggi ● vt (in knitting) diminuire. **cast on** vt (in knitting) avviare

castaway /'kɑːstəweɪ/ n naufrago, -a mf

caste /kɑːst/ n casta f

caster /'kɑːstə(r)/ n (wheel) rotella f. **~ sugar** n zucchero m raffinato

cast 'iron n ghisa f

cast-'iron a di ghisa; fig solido

castle /'kɑːsl/ n castello m; (in chess) torre f

'cast-offs npl abiti mpl smessi

castor /'kɑːstə(r)/ n (wheel) rotella f. **~ oil** n olio m di ricino. **~ sugar** n zucchero m raffinato

castrat|e /kæ'streɪt/ vt castrare. **~ion** /-eɪʃn/ n castrazione f

casual /'kæʒʊəl/ a (chance) casuale; (remark) senza importanza; (glance) di sfuggita; (attitude, approach) disinvolto; (chat) informale; (clothes) casual inv; (work) saltuario; **~ wear** abbigliamento m casual. **~ly** adv (dress) casual; (meet) casualmente

casualty /'kæʒʊəltɪ/ n (injured person) ferito m; (killed) vittima f. **~ [department]** n pronto soccorso m

cat /kæt/ n gatto m; pej arpia f

catalogue /'kætəlɒg/ n catalogo m ● vt catalogare

catalyst /'kætəlɪst/ n Chem & fig catalizzatore m

catalytic /kætə'lɪtɪk/ a **~ converter** Auto marmitta f catalitica

catapult /'kætəpʌlt/ n catapulta f; (child's) fionda f ● vt/ig catapultare

cataract /'kætərækt/ n Med cataratta f

catarrh /kə'tɑː(r)/ n catarro m

catastroph|e /kə'tæstrəfɪ/ n catastrofe f. **~ic** /kætə'strɒfɪk/ a catastrofico

catch /kætʃ/ n (of fish) pesca f; (fastener) fermaglio m; (on door) fermo m; (on window) gancio m; (fam: snag) tranello m ● v (pt/pp caught) ● vt acchiappare (ball); (grab) afferrare; prendere (illness, fugitive, train); **~ a cold** prendersi un raffreddore; **~ sight of** scorgere; **I caught him stealing** l'ho sorpreso mentre rubava; **~ one's finger in the door** chiudersi il dito nella porta; **~ sb's eye** or **attention** attirare l'attenzione di qcno ● vi (fire:) prendere; (get stuck) impigliarsi. **catch on** vi fam (understand) afferrare; (become popular) diventare popolare. **catch up** vt raggiungere ● vi recuperare; (runner:) riguadagnare terreno; **~ up with** raggiungere (sb); mettersi in pari con (work)

catching /'kætʃɪŋ/ a contagioso

catch: **~-phrase** n tormentone m. **~word** n slogan m inv

catchy /'kætʃɪ/ a (-ier, -iest) orecchiabile

categor|ical /kætɪ'gɒrɪkl/ a categorico. **~y** /'kætɪgərɪ/ n categoria f

cater /'keɪtə(r)/ vi **~ for** provvedere a (needs); fig venire incontro alle esigenze di. **~ing** n (trade) ristorazione f; (food) rinfresco m

caterpillar /'kætəpɪlə(r)/ n bruco m

cathedral /kə'θiːdrl/ n cattedrale f

Catholic /'kæθəlɪk/ a & n cattolico, -a mf. **~ism** /kə'θɒlɪsɪzm/ n cattolicesimo m

cat's eyes npl catarifrangente msg (inserito nell'asfalto)

cattle /'kætl/ npl bestiame msg

catty /'kætɪ/ a (-ier, -iest) dispettoso

catwalk /'kætwɔːk/ n passerella f

caught /kɔːt/ see **catch**

cauliflower /'kɒlɪ-/ n cavolfiore m

cause /kɔːz/ n causa f ● vt causare; **~ sb to do sth** far fare qcsa a qcno

'causeway /n strada f sopraelevata

caustic /'kɔːstɪk/ a caustico

caution /'kɔːʃn/ n cautela f; (warning) ammonizione f ● vt mettere in guardia; Jur ammonire

cautious /'kɔːʃəs/ a cauto

cavalry /'kævəlrɪ/ n cavalleria f

cave /keɪv/ n caverna f ● **cave in** vi (roof:) crollare; (fig: give in) capitolare

cavern /'kævən/ n caverna f

caviare /'kævɪɑː(r)/ n caviale m

caving /'keɪvɪŋ/ n speleologia f

cavity /'kævətɪ/ n cavità f inv; (in tooth) carie f inv

cavort /kə'vɔːt/ vi saltellare

CD n CD m inv. **~ player** n lettore m [di] compact

CD-Rom /siːdiː'rɒm/ n CD-Rom m inv. **~ drive** n lettore m [di] CD-Rom

cease /siːs/ n without ● incessantemente ● vt/i cessare. **~-fire** n cessate il fuoco m inv. **~less** a incessante

cedar /'siːdə(r)/ n cedro m

cede /siːd/ vt cedere

ceiling /'siːlɪŋ/ n soffitto m; fig tetto m [massimo]

celebrat|e /'selɪbreɪt/ vt festeggiare (birthday, victory) ● vi far festa. **~ed** a celebre (for per). **~ion** /-'breɪʃn/ n celebrazione f

celebrity /sɪ'lebrətɪ/ n celebrità f inv

celery /'selərɪ/ n sedano m

celiba|cy /'selɪbəsɪ/ n celibato m. **~te** a (man) celibe; (woman) nubile

cell /sel/ n cella f; Biol cellula f

cellar /'selə(r)/ n scantinato m; (for wine) cantina f

cellist /'tʃelɪst/ n violoncellista mf

cello /'tʃeləʊ/ n violoncello m

Cellophane® /'seləfeɪn/ n cellofan m inv

cellular phone /seljʊlə'fəʊn/ n [telefono m] cellulare m

celluloid /'seljʊlɔɪd/ n celluloide f

Celsius /'selsɪəs/ a Celsius

Celt /kelt/ n celta mf. **~ic** a celtico

cement /sɪ'ment/ n cemento m; (adhesive) mastice m ● vt cementare; fig consolidare

cemetery /'semətrɪ/ n cimitero m

censor /'sensə(r)/ n censore m ● vt censurare. **~ship** n censura f

censure /'senʃə(r)/ vt biasimare

census /'sensəs/ n censimento m

cent /sent/ n (coin) centesimo m

centenary /sen'tiːnərɪ/ n, Am **centennial** /sen'tenɪəl/ n centenario m

center /'sentə(r)/ n Am = **centre**

centi|grade /'sentɪ-/ a centigrado. **~metre** n centimetro m. **~pede** /-piːd/ n centopiedi m inv

central /'sentrəl/ a centrale. **~ 'heating** n riscaldamento m autonomo. **~ize** vt centralizzare. **~ly** adv al centro; **~ly heated** con riscaldamento autonomo. **~ reser'vation** n Auto banchina f spartitraffico

centre /'sentə(r)/ n centro m ● v (pt/pp **centred**) ● vt centrare ● vi **~ on** fig incentrarsi su. **~-'forward** n centravanti m inv

centrifugal /sentrɪ'fjuːgl/ a **~ force** forza f centrifuga

century /'sentʃərɪ/ n secolo m

ceramic /sɪ'ræmɪk/ a ceramico. **~s** n (art) ceramica fsg; (objects) ceramiche fpl

cereal /'sɪərɪəl/ n cereale m

cerebral /'serɪbrl/ a cerebrale

ceremon|ial /serɪ'məʊnɪəl/ a da cerimonia ● n cerimoniale m. **~ious** /-əs/ a cerimonioso

ceremony /'serɪmənɪ/ n cerimonia f

certain /'sɜːtn/ a certo; **for ~** di sicuro; **make ~** accertarsi : **he is ~ to win** è certo di vincere; **it's not ~ whether he'll come** non è sicuro che venga. **~ly** adv certamente; **~ly not!** no di certo! **~ty** n certezza f; **it's a ~ty** è una cosa certa

certificate /sə'tɪfɪkət/ n certificato m

certify /'sɜːtɪfaɪ/ vt (pt/pp **-ied**) certificare; (declare insane) dichiarare malato di mente

cessation /se'seɪʃn/ n cessazione f

cesspool /'ses-/ n pozzo m nero

cf abbr (**compare**) cf. cfr

chafe /tʃeɪf/ vt irritare

chain /tʃeɪn/ n catena f ● vt incatenare (prisoner); attaccare con la catena (dog) (**to** a). **chain up** vt legare alla catena (dog)

chain: ~ re'action n reazione f a catena. **~-smoke** vi fumare una sigaretta dopo l'altra. **~-smoker** n fumatore, -trice mf accanito, -a. **~ store** n negozio m appartenente a una catena

chair /tʃeə(r)/ n sedia f; Univ cattedra f ● vt presiedere. **~-lift** n seggiovia f. **~man** n presidente m

chalet /'ʃæleɪ/ n chalet m inv; (in holiday camp) bungalow m inv

chalice /'tʃælɪs/ n Relig calice m

chalk /tʃɔːk/ n gesso m. **~y** a gessoso

challeng|e /'tʃælɪndʒ/ n sfida f; Mil intimazione f ● vt sfidare; Mil intimare il

chi va là a; *fig* mettere in dubbio
⟨*statement*⟩. **~er** *n* sfidante *mf*. **~ing** *a*
⟨*job*⟩ impegnativo

chamber /ˈtʃeɪmbə(r)/ *n* **C~ of
Commerce** camera *f* di commercio

chamber: **~maid** *n* cameriera *f* [d'albergo]. **~ music** *n* musica *f* da camera

chamois¹ /ˈʃæmwɑː/ *n inv* ⟨*animal*⟩ camoscio *m*

chamois² /ˈʃæmɪ/ *n* **~[-leather]** [pelle
f di] camoscio *m*

champagne /ʃæmˈpeɪn/ *n* champagne
m inv

champion /ˈtʃæmpɪən/ *n Sport* campione *m*; ⟨*of cause*⟩ difensore,
difenditrice *mf* ● *vt* ⟨*defend*⟩ difendere;
⟨*fight for*⟩ lottare per. **~ship** *n Sport*
campionato *m*

chance /tʃɑːns/ *n* caso *m*; ⟨*possibility*⟩
possibilità *f inv*; ⟨*opportunity*⟩ occasione *f*; **by ~** per caso; **take a ~** rischiare;
give sb a second ~ dare un'altra possibilità a qcno ● *attrib* fortuito ● *vt* **I'll
~ it** *fam* corro il rischio

chancellor /ˈtʃɑːnsələ(r)/ *n* cancelliere *m*; *Univ* rettore *m*; **C~ of the
Exchequer** ≈ ministro *m* del tesoro

chancy /ˈtʃɑːnsɪ/ *a* rischioso

chandelier /ʃændəˈlɪə(r)/ *n* lampadario *m*

change /tʃeɪndʒ/ *n* cambiamento *m*;
⟨*money*⟩ resto *m*; ⟨*small coins*⟩ spiccioli
mpl; **for a ~** tanto per cambiare; **a ~ of
clothes** un cambio di vestiti; **the ~** [**of
life**] la menopausa ● *vt* cambiare;
⟨*substitute*⟩ scambiare (**for** con); **~
one's clothes** cambiarsi [i vestiti]; **~
trains** cambiare treno ● *vi* cambiare;
⟨*~ clothes*⟩ cambiarsi; **all ~!** stazione
terminale!

changeable /ˈtʃeɪndʒəbl/ *a* mutevole;
⟨*weather*⟩ variabile

'**changing-room** *n* camerino *m*; ⟨*for
sports*⟩ spogliatoio *m*

channel /ˈtʃænl/ *n* canale *m*; **the
[English] C~** la Manica; **the C~
Islands** le Isole del Canale ● *vt* (*pt/pp*
channelled) **~ one's energies into
sth** convogliare le proprie energie in
qcsa

chant /tʃɑːnt/ *n* cantilena *f*; ⟨*of
demonstrators*⟩ slogan *m inv* di protesta
● *vt* cantare; ⟨*demonstrators:*⟩ gridare

chao|s /ˈkeɪɒs/ *n* caos *m*. **~tic** /-ˈɒtɪk/ *a*
caotico

chap /tʃæp/ *n fam* tipo *m*

chapel /ˈtʃæpl/ *n* cappella *f*

chaperon /ˈʃæpərəʊn/ *n* chaperon *f
inv* ● *vt* fare da chaperon a ⟨*sb*⟩

chaplain /ˈtʃæplɪn/ *n* cappellano *m*

chapped /tʃæpt/ *a* ⟨*skin, lips*⟩ screpolato

chapter /ˈtʃæptə(r)/ *n* capitolo *m*

char¹ /tʃɑː(r)/ *n fam* donna *f* delle pulizie

char² *vt* (*pt/pp* **charred**) ⟨*burn*⟩ carbonizzare

character /ˈkærɪktə(r)/ *n* carattere *m*;
⟨*in novel, play*⟩ personaggio *m*; **quite a
~** *fam* un tipo particolare

characteristic /kærɪktəˈrɪstɪk/ *a* caratteristico ● *n* caratteristica *f*. **~ally**
adv tipicamente

characterize /ˈkærɪktəraɪz/ *vt* caratterizzare

charade /ʃəˈrɑːd/ *n* farsa *f*

charcoal /ˈtʃɑː-/ *n* carbonella *f*

charge /tʃɑːdʒ/ *n* ⟨*cost*⟩ prezzo *m*;
Electr, Mil carica *f*; *Jur* accusa *f*; **free of
~** gratuito; **be in ~** essere responsabile
⟨**of** di⟩; **take ~** assumersi la responsabilità; **take ~ of** occuparsi di ● *vt* far
pagare ⟨*fee*⟩; far pagare a ⟨*person*⟩;
Electr, Mil caricare; *Jur* accusare (**with**
di); **~ sb for sth** far pagare qcsa a
qcno; **~ it to my account** lo addebiti
sul mio conto ● *vi* ⟨*attack*⟩ caricare

chariot /ˈtʃærɪət/ *n* cocchio *m*

charisma /kəˈrɪzmə/ *n* carisma *m*.
~tic /kærɪzˈmætɪk/ *a* carismatico

charitable /ˈtʃærɪtəbl/ *a* caritatevole;
⟨*kind*⟩ indulgente

charity /ˈtʃærətɪ/ *n* carità *f*;
⟨*organization*⟩ associazione *f* di beneficenza; **concert given for ~** concerto
m di beneficenza; **live on ~** vivere di
elemosina

charm /tʃɑːm/ *n* fascino *m*; ⟨*object*⟩
ciondolo *m* ● *vt* affascinare. **~ing** *a* affascinante

chart /tʃɑːt/ *n* carta *f* nautica; ⟨*table*⟩
tabella *f*

charter /ˈtʃɑːtə(r)/ *n* **~ [flight]** [volo
m] charter *m inv* ● *vt* noleggiare. **~ed
accountant** *n* commercialista *mf*

charwoman /ˈtʃɑː-/ *n* donna *f* delle
pulizie

chase /tʃeɪs/ *n* inseguimento *m* ● *vt* inseguire. **chase away** *or* **off** *vt* cacciare
via

chasm /ˈkæz(ə)m/ *n* abisso *m*

chassis /ˈʃæsɪ/ *n* (*pl* **chassis** /-sɪz/) telaio *m*

chaste /tʃeɪst/ *a* casto

chastity /ˈtʃæstətɪ/ *n* castità *f*

chat /tʃæt/ n chiacchierata f; **have a ~
with** fare quattro chiacchere con ● vi
(pt/pp **chatted**) chiacchierare. ~
show n talk show m inv

chatter /'tʃætə(r)/ n chiacchiere fpl
● vi chiacchierare; ⟨teeth:⟩ battere.
~**box** n fam chiacchierone, -a mf

chatty /'tʃæti/ a (-ier, -iest) chiacchierone; ⟨style⟩ familiare

chauffeur /'ʃəʊfə(r)/ n autista mf

chauvin|ism /'ʃəʊvɪnɪzm/ n scio-
vinismo m. ~**ist** n sciovinista mf. **male
~ist** n fam maschilista m

cheap /tʃiːp/ a a buon mercato; ⟨rate⟩
economico; ⟨vulgar⟩ grossolano; (of
poor quality) scadente ● adv a buon
mercato. ~**ly** adv a buon mercato

cheat /tʃiːt/ n imbroglione, -a mf; (at
cards) baro m ● vt imbrogliare; ~ **sb
out of sth** sottrarre qcsa a qcno con
l'inganno ● vi imbrogliare; (at cards)
barare. **cheat on** vt fam tradire ⟨wife⟩

check¹ /tʃek/ a ⟨pattern⟩ a quadri ● n
disegno m a quadri

check² n verifica f; (of tickets) controllo m; (in chess) scacco m; (Am: bill) conto m; (Am: cheque) assegno m; (Am: tick)
segnetto m; **keep a ~ on** controllare;
keep in ~ tenere sotto controllo ● vt
verificare;   controllare   ⟨tickets⟩;
⟨restrain⟩ contenere; (stop) bloccare
● vi controllare; ~ **on sth** controllare
qcsa. **check in** vi registrarsi all'arrivo
(in albergo); Aeron fare il check-in ● vt
registrare   all'arrivo   (in   albergo).
check out vi (of hotel) saldare il conto
● vt (fam: investigate) controllare.
check up vi accertarsi; ~ **up on** prendere informazioni su

check|ed /tʃekt/ a a quadri. ~**ers** n
Am dama f

check: ~**-in** n (in airport: place) banco
m accettazione, check-in m inv; ~**-in
time** check-in m inv. ~ **mark** n Am
segnetto m. ~**mate** int scacco matto!
~**-out** n (in supermarket) cassa f.
~**room** n Am deposito m bagagli. ~**-up**
n Med visita f di controllo, check-up m
inv

cheek /tʃiːk/ n guancia f; (impudence)
sfacciataggine f. ~**y** a sfacciato

cheep /tʃiːp/ vi pigolare

cheer /tʃɪə(r)/ n evviva m inv; **three
~s** tre urrà; ~**s!** salute!; (goodbye) arrivederci!; (thanks) grazie! ● vt/i acclamare. **cheer up** vt tirare su [di morale]
● vi tirarsi su [di morale]; ~ **up!** su con

la vita!. ~**ful** a allegro. ~**fulness** n alle-
gria f. ~**ing** n acclamazione f

cheerio /tʃɪərɪ'əʊ/ int fam arrivederci

'cheerless a triste, tetro

cheese /tʃiːz/ n formaggio m. ~**cake**
n dolce m al formaggio

chef /ʃef/ n cuoco, chef mf inv

chemical /'kemɪkl/ a chimico ● n prodotto m chimico

chemist /'kemɪst/ n (pharmacist) farmacista mf; (scientist) chimico, -a mf;
~**'s [shop]** farmacia f. ~**ry** n chimica f

cheque /tʃek/ n assegno m. ~**-book** n
libretto m degli assegni. ~ **card** n carta
f assegni

cherish /'tʃerɪʃ/ vt curare teneramente; (love) avere caro; nutrire ⟨hope⟩

cherry /'tʃerɪ/ n ciliegia f; (tree) cilie-
gio m

cherub /'tʃerəb/ n cherubino m

chess /tʃes/ n scacchi mpl

chess: ~**board** n scacchiera f. ~**-man**
n pezzo m degli scacchi. ~**player** n
scacchista mf

chest /tʃest/ n petto m; (box) cassapan-
ca f

chestnut /'tʃesnʌt/ n castagna f; (tree)
castagno m

chest of 'drawers n cassettone m

chew /tʃuː/ vt masticare. ~**ing-gum** n
gomma f da masticare

chic /ʃiːk/ a chic inv

chick /tʃɪk/ n pulcino m, (fam: girl) ragazza f

chicken /'tʃɪkn/ n pollo m ● attrib
⟨soup, casserole⟩ di pollo ● a fam fifone
● **chicken out** vi fam **he ~ed out** gli è
venuta fifa. ~**pox** n varicella f

chicory /'tʃɪkərɪ/ n cicoria f

chief /tʃiːf/ a principale ● n capo m.
~**ly** adv principalmente

chilblain /'tʃɪlbleɪn/ n gelone m

child /tʃaɪld/ n (pl ~**ren**) bambino, -a
mf; (son/daughter) figlio, -a mf

child: ~**birth** n parto m. ~**hood** n infanzia f. ~**ish** a infantile. ~**ishness** n
puerilità f. ~**less** a senza figli. ~**like** a
ingenuo. ~**-minder** n baby-sitter mf inv

children /'tʃɪldrən/ see **child**

Chile /'tʃɪlɪ/ n Cile m. ~**an** a & n cileno,
-a mf

chill /tʃɪl/ n freddo m; (illness) infredda-
tura f ● vt raffreddare

chilli /'tʃɪlɪ/ n (pl -es) ~ **[pepper]**
peperoncino m

chilly /'tʃɪlɪ/ a freddo

chime /tʃaɪm/ vi suonare

chimney /'tʃɪmnɪ/ n camino m. ~**-pot**

n comignolo *m*. **~-sweep** *n* spazzacamino *m*

chimpanzee /tʃimpænˈziː/ *n* scimpanzé *m inv*

chin /tʃin/ *n* mento *m*

china /ˈtʃaɪnə/ *n* porcellana *f*

China *n* Cina *f*. **~ese** /-ˈniːz/ *a & n* cinese *mf*. *(language)* cinese *m*: **the ~ese** *pl* i cinesi

chink¹ /tʃiŋk/ *n (slit)* fessura *f*

chink² /tʃiŋk/ *n (noise)* tintinnio *m*

chip /tʃip/ *n (fragment)* scheggia *f*; *(in china, paintwork)* scheggiatura *f*; *Comput* chip *m inv*; *(in gambling)* fiche *f inv*; **~s** *pl Br Culin* patatine *fpl* fritte; *Am Culin* patatine *fpl* ● *vt (pt/pp chipped) (damage)* scheggiare. **chip in** *vi fam* intromettersi; *(with money)* contribuire. **~ped** *a (damaged)* scheggiato

chiropodist /kɪˈrɒpədist/ *n* podiatra *mf inv*. **~y** *n* podiatria *f*

chirp /tʃɜːp/ *vi* cinguettare; *(cricket:)* fare cri cri. **~y** *a fam* pimpante

chisel /ˈtʃizl/ *n* scalpello *m*

chivalrous /ˈʃivlrəs/ *a* cavalleresco. **~ry** *n* cavalleria *f*

chives /tʃaivz/ *npl* erba *f* cipollina

chlorine /ˈklɔːriːn/ *n* cloro *m*

chloroform /ˈklɒrəfɔːm/ *n* cloroformio *m*

chock-a-block /tʃɒkəˈblɒk/, **chock-full** /tʃɒkˈfʊl/ *a* pieno zeppo

chocolate /ˈtʃɒkələt/ *n* cioccolato *m*; *(drink)* cioccolata *f*; **a ~** un cioccolatino

choice /tʃɔɪs/ *n* scelta *f* ● *a* scelto

choir /ˈkwaɪə(r)/ *n* coro *m*. **~boy** *n* corista *m*

choke /tʃəʊk/ *n Auto* aria *f* ● *vt/i* soffocare

cholera /ˈkɒlərə/ *n* colera *m*

cholesterol /kəˈlestərɒl/ *n* colesterolo *m*

choose /tʃuːz/ *vt/i (pt chose, pp chosen)* scegliere; **as you ~** come vuoi

choosey /ˈtʃuːzi/ *a fam* difficile

chop /tʃɒp/ *n (blow)* colpo *m (d'ascia)*; *Culin* costata *f* ● *vt (pt/pp chopped)* tagliare. **chop down** *vt* abbattere *(tree)*. **chop off** *vt* spaccare

chopper /ˈtʃɒpə(r)/ *n* accetta *f*; *fam* elicottero *m*. **~py** *a* increspato

chopsticks *npl* bastoncini *mpl* cinesi

choral /ˈkɔːrəl/ *a* corale

chord /kɔːd/ *n Mus* corda *f*

chore /tʃɔː(r)/ *n* corvè *f inv*; [**household**] **~s** faccende *fpl* domestiche

choreographer /kɒriˈɒɡrəfə(r)/ *n* coreografo, -a *mf*. **~y** /-ɪ/ *n* coreografia *f*

chortle /ˈtʃɔːtl/ *vi* ridacchiare

chorus /ˈkɔːrəs/ *n* coro *m*; *(of song)* ritornello *m*

chose, chosen /tʃəʊz, ˈtʃəʊzn/ *see* **choose**

Christ /kraɪst/ *n* Cristo *m*

christen /ˈkrisn/ *vt* battezzare. **~ing** *n* battesimo *m*

Christian /ˈkristʃən/ *a & n* cristiano, -a *mf*. **~ity** /-stɪˈænəti/ *n* cristianesimo *m*. **~ name** *n* nome *m* di battesimo

Christmas /ˈkrisməs/ *n* Natale *m* ● *attrib* di Natale. **'~ card** *n* biglietto *m* d'auguri di Natale. **~ 'Day** *n* il giorno di Natale. **~ 'Eve** *n* la vigilia di Natale. **~ present** *n* regalo *m* di Natale. **~ 'pudding** *dolce m natalizio a base di frutta candita e liquore*. **'~ tree** *n* albero *m* di Natale

chrome /krəʊm/ *n*, **chromium** /ˈkrəʊmɪəm/ *n* cromo *m*

chromosome /ˈkrəʊməsəʊm/ *n* cromosoma *m*

chronic /ˈkrɒnik/ *a* cronico

chronicle /ˈkrɒnikl/ *n* cronaca *f*

chronological /krɒnəˈlɒdʒikl/ *a* cronologico. **~ly** *adv (ordered)* in ordine cronologico

chrysanthemum /krɪˈsænθəməm/ *n* crisantemo *m*

chubby /ˈtʃʌbi/ *a (-ier, -iest)* paffuto

chuck /tʃʌk/ *vt fam* buttare. **chuck out** *vt fam* buttare via *(object)*; buttare fuori *(person)*

chuckle /ˈtʃʌkl/ *vi* ridacchiare

chug /tʃʌɡ/ *vi (pt/pp chugged)* **the train ~ged out of the station** il treno è uscito dalla stazione sbuffando

chum /tʃʌm/ *n* amico, -a *mf*. **~my** *a fam* **be ~my with** essere amico di

chunk /tʃʌŋk/ *n* grosso pezzo *m*

church /tʃɜːtʃ/ *n* chiesa *f*. **~yard** *n* cimitero *m*

churlish /ˈtʃɜːliʃ/ *a* sgarbato

churn /tʃɜːn/ *vt* **churn out** sfornare

chute /ʃuːt/ *n* scivolo *m*; *(for rubbish)* canale *m* di scarico

CID *n abbr* (**Criminal Investigation Department**) polizia *f* giudiziaria

cider /ˈsaɪdə(r)/ *n* sidro *m*

cigar /sɪˈɡɑː(r)/ *n* sigaro *m*

cigarette /sɪɡəˈret/ *n* sigaretta *f*

cine-camera /ˈsini-/ *n* cinepresa *f*

cinema /ˈsinimə/ *n* cinema *m inv*

cinnamon /ˈsinəmən/ *n* cannella *f*

circle /ˈsɜːkl/ *n* cerchio *m*; *Theat* galleria *f*; **in a ~** in cerchio ● *vt* girare intorno a; cerchiare ⟨*mistake*⟩ ● *vi* descrivere dei cerchi

circuit /ˈsɜːkɪt/ *n* circuito *m*; ⟨*lap*⟩ giro *m*; **~ board** *n* circuito *m* stampato. **~ous** /səˈkjuːɪtəs/ *a* **~ous route** percorso *m* lungo e indiretto

circular /ˈsɜːkjʊlə(r)/ *a* circolare ● *n* circolare *f*

circulat|e /ˈsɜːkjʊleɪt/ *vt* far circolare ● *vi* circolare. **~ion** /-ˈleɪʃn/ *n* circolazione *f*; ⟨*of newspaper*⟩ tiratura *f*

circumcis|e /ˈsɜːkəmsaɪz/ *vt* circoncidere. **~ion** /-ˈsɪʒn/ *n* circoncisione *f*

circumference /səˈkʌmfərəns/ *n* conconferenza *f*

circumstance /ˈsɜːkəmstəns/ *n* circostanza *f*; **~s** *pl* ⟨*financial*⟩ condizioni *fpl* finanziarie

circus /ˈsɜːkəs/ *n* circo *m*

CIS *n abbr* (**Commonwealth of Independent States**) CSI *f*

cistern /ˈsɪstən/ *n* ⟨*tank*⟩ cisterna *f*; ⟨*of WC*⟩ serbatoio *m*

cite /saɪt/ *vt* citare

citizen /ˈsɪtɪzn/ *n* cittadino, -a *mf*; ⟨*of town*⟩ abitante *mf*. **~ship** *n* cittadinanza *f*

citrus /ˈsɪtrəs/ *n* [**fruit**] agrume *m*

city /ˈsɪtɪ/ *n* città *f inv*; **the C~** la City ⟨*di Londra*⟩

civic /ˈsɪvɪk/ *a* civico

civil /ˈsɪvl/ *a* civile

civilian /sɪˈvɪljən/ *a* civile; **in ~ clothes** in borghese ● *n* civile *mf*

civiliz|ation /sɪvɪlaɪˈzeɪʃn/ *n* civiltà *f inv*. **~e** /ˈsɪvɪlaɪz/ *vt* civilizzare

civil: ~ servant *n* impiegato, -a *mf* statale. **C~ 'Service** *n* pubblica amministrazione *f*

clad /klæd/ *a* vestito (**in** di)

claim /kleɪm/ *n* richiesta *f*; ⟨*right*⟩ diritto *m*; ⟨*assertion*⟩ dichiarazione *f*; **lay to sth** rivendicare qcsa ● *vt* richiedere; reclamare ⟨*lost property*⟩; rivendicare ⟨*ownership*⟩; **~ that** sostenere che. **~ant** *n* richiedente *mf*

clairvoyant /kleəˈvɔɪənt/ *n* chiaroveggente *mf*

clam /klæm/ *n* Culin vongola *f* ● **clam up** *vi* ⟨*pt/pp* clammed⟩ zittirsi

clamber /ˈklæmbə(r)/ *vi* arrampicarsi

clammy /ˈklæmɪ/ *a* (**-ier, -iest**) appiccicaticcio

clamour /ˈklæmə(r)/ *n* ⟨*protest*⟩ rimostranza *f* ● *vi* **~ for** chiedere a gran voce

clamp /klæmp/ *n* morsa *f* ● *vt* ammorsare; *Auto* mettere i ceppi bloccaruote a. **clamp down** *vi fam* essere duro; **~ down on** reprimere

clan /klæn/ *n* clan *m inv*

clandestine /klænˈdestɪn/ *a* clandestino

clang /klæŋ/ *n* suono *m* metallico. **~er** *n fam* gaffe *f inv*

clank /klæŋk/ *n* rumore *m* metallico

clap /klæp/ *n* give sb a ~ applaudire qcno; **~ of thunder** tuono *m* ● *vt/i* ⟨*pt/pp* clapped⟩ applaudire; **~ one's hands** applaudire. **~ping** *n* applausi *mpl*

clari|fication /klærɪfɪˈkeɪʃn/ *n* chiarimento *m*. **~fy** /ˈklærɪfaɪ/ *vt/i* ⟨*pt/pp* -ied⟩ chiarire

clarinet /klærɪˈnet/ *n* clarinetto *m*

clarity /ˈklærətɪ/ *n* chiarezza *f*

clash /klæʃ/ *n* scontro *m*; ⟨*noise*⟩ fragore *m* ● *vi* scontrarsi; ⟨*colours:*⟩ stonare; ⟨*events:*⟩ coincidere

clasp /klɑːsp/ *n* chiusura *f* ● *vt* agganciare; ⟨*hold*⟩ stringere

class /klɑːs/ *n* classe *f*; ⟨*lesson*⟩ corso *m* ● *vt* classificare

classic /ˈklæsɪk/ *a* classico ● *n* classico *m*; **~s** *pl Univ* lettere *fpl* classiche. **~al** *a* classico

classi|fication /klæsɪfɪˈkeɪʃn/ *n* classificazione *f*. **~fy** /ˈklæsɪfaɪ/ *vt* ⟨*pt/pp* -ied⟩ classificare

classroom *n* aula *f*

classy /ˈklɑːsɪ/ *a* (**-ier, -iest**) *fam* d'alta classe

clatter /ˈklætə(r)/ *n* fracasso *m* ● *vi* far fracasso

clause /klɔːz/ *n* clausola *f*; *Gram* proposizione *f*

claustrophob|ia /klɔːstrəˈfəʊbɪə/ *n* claustrofobia *f*

claw /klɔː/ *n* artiglio *m*; ⟨*of crab, lobster & Techn*⟩ tenaglia *f* ● *vt* ⟨*cat:*⟩ graffiare

clay /kleɪ/ *n* argilla *f*

clean /kliːn/ *a* pulito, lindo ● *adv* completamente ● *vt* pulire ⟨*shoes, windows*⟩; **~ one's teeth** lavarsi i denti; **have a coat ~ed** portare un cappotto in lavanderia. **clean up** *vt* pulire ● *vi* far pulizia

cleaner /ˈkliːnə(r)/ *n* uomo *m*/donna *f* delle pulizie; ⟨*substance*⟩ detersivo *m*; [**dry**] **~'s** lavanderia *f*, tintoria *f*

cleanliness /ˈklenlɪnɪs/ *n* pulizia *f*

cleanse /klenz/ *vt* pulire. **~r** *n* detergente *m*

clean-shaven *a* sbarbato

cleansing cream /'klenz-/ n latte m detergente

clear /klɪə(r)/ a chiaro; ⟨conscience⟩ pulito; ⟨road⟩ libero; ⟨profit, advantage, majority⟩ netto; ⟨sky⟩ sereno; ⟨water⟩ limpido; ⟨glass⟩ trasparente; **make sth ~** mettere qcsa in chiaro; **have I made myself ~?** mi sono fatto capire?; **five ~ days** cinque giorni buoni ●adv **stand ~ of** allontanarsi da; **keep ~ of** tenersi alla larga da ●vt sgombrare ⟨room, street⟩; sparecchiare ⟨table⟩; ⟨acquit⟩ scagionare; ⟨authorize⟩ autorizzare; scavalcare senza toccare ⟨fence, wall⟩; guadagnare ⟨sum of money⟩; passare ⟨Customs⟩; **~ one's throat** schiarirsi la gola ●vi ⟨face, sky:⟩ rasserenarsi; ⟨fog:⟩ dissiparsi. **clear away** vt metter via. **clear off** vi fam filar via. **clear out** vt sgombrare ●vi fam filar via. **clear up** vt ⟨tidy⟩ mettere a posto; chiarire ⟨mystery⟩ ●vi ⟨weather:⟩ schiarirsi

clearance /'klɪərəns/ n ⟨space⟩ spazio m libero; ⟨authorization⟩ autorizzazione f; ⟨Customs⟩ sdoganamento m. **~ sale** n liquidazione f

clear|ing /'klɪərɪŋ/ n radura f. **~ly** adv chiaramente. **~ way** n Auto strada f con divieto di sosta

cleavage /'kliːvɪdʒ/ n ⟨woman's⟩ décolleté m inv

cleft /kleft/ n fenditura f

clench /klentʃ/ vt serrare

clergy /'klɜːdʒɪ/ npl clero m. **~man** n ecclesiastico m

cleric /'klerɪk/ n ecclesiastico m. **~al** a impiegatizio; Relig clericale

clerk /klɑːk/, Am /klɜːk/ n impiegato, -a mf; ⟨Am: shop assistant⟩ commesso, -a mf

clever /'klevə(r)/ a intelligente; ⟨skilful⟩ abile

cliché /'kliːʃeɪ/ n cliché m inv

click /klɪk/ vi scattare ●n Comput click m. **click on** vt Comput cliccare su

client /'klaɪənt/ n cliente mf

clientele /kliːɒn'tel/ n clientela f

cliff /klɪf/ n scogliera f

climat|e /'klaɪmət/ n clima f. **~ic** /-'mætɪk/ a climatico

climax /'klaɪmæks/ n punto m culminante

climb /klaɪm/ n salita f ●vt scalare ⟨mountain⟩; arrampicarsi su ⟨ladder, tree⟩ ●vi arrampicarsi; ⟨rise⟩ salire; ⟨road:⟩ salire. **climb down** vi scendere; ⟨from ladder, tree⟩ scendere; fig tornare sui propri passi

climber /'klaɪmə(r)/ n alpinista mf; ⟨plant⟩ rampicante m

clinch /klɪntʃ/ vt fam concludere ⟨deal⟩ ●n ⟨in boxing⟩ clinch m inv

cling /klɪŋ/ vi (pt/pp clung) aggrapparsi; ⟨stick⟩ aderire. **~ film** n pellicola f trasparente

clinic /'klɪnɪk/ n ambulatorio m. **~al** a clinico

clink /klɪŋk/ n tintinnio m; ⟨fam: prison⟩ galera f ●vi tintinnare

clip¹ /klɪp/ n fermaglio m; ⟨jewellery⟩ spilla f ●vt (pt/pp clipped) attaccare

clip² n ⟨extract⟩ taglio m ●vt obliterare ⟨ticket⟩. **~board** n fermabloc m inv. **~pers** npl ⟨for hair⟩ rasoio m; ⟨for hedge⟩ tosasiepi m inv; ⟨for nails⟩ tronchesina f. **~ping** n ⟨from newspaper⟩ ritaglio m

clique /kliːk/ n cricca f

cloak /kləʊk/ n mantello m. **~room** n guardaroba m inv; ⟨toilet⟩ bagno m

clock /klɒk/ n orologio m; ⟨fam: speedometer⟩ tachimetro m ●**clock in** vi attaccare. **clock out** vi staccare

clock: **~ tower** n torre f dell'orologio. **~wise** a & adv in senso orario. **~work** n meccanismo m

clod /klɒd/ n zolla f

clog /klɒg/ n zoccolo m ●vt (pt/pp clogged) **~ [up]** intasare ⟨drain⟩; inceppare ⟨mechanism⟩ ●vi ⟨drain:⟩ intasarsi

cloister /'klɔɪstə(r)/ n chiostro m

clone /kləʊn/ n clone m

close¹ /kləʊs/ a vicino; ⟨friend⟩ intimo; ⟨weather⟩ afoso; **have a ~ shave** fam scamparla bella; **be ~ to sb** essere unito a qcno ●adv vicino; **~ by** vicino; **it's ~ on five o'clock** sono quasi le cinque

close² /kləʊz/ n fine f ●vt chiudere ●vi chiudersi; ⟨shop:⟩ chiudere. **close down** vt chiudere ●vi ⟨TV station:⟩ interrompere la trasmissione; ⟨factory:⟩ chiudere

closely /'kləʊslɪ/ adv da vicino; ⟨watch, listen⟩ attentamente

closet /'klɒzɪt/ n Am armadio m

close-up /'kləʊs-/ n primo piano m

closure /'kləʊʒə(r)/ n chiusura f

clot /klɒt/ n grumo m; ⟨fam: idiot⟩ tonto, -a mf ●vi (pt/pp clotted) ⟨blood:⟩ coagularsi

cloth /klɒθ/ n ⟨fabric⟩ tessuto m; ⟨duster etc⟩ straccio m

clothe /kləʊð/ vt vestire

clothes /kləʊðz/ npl vestiti mpl, abiti

mpl. **~-brush** *n* spazzola *f* per abiti.
~-line *n* corda *f* stendibiancheria
clothing /'kləʊðɪŋ/ *n* abbigliamento *m*
cloud /klaʊd/ *n* nuvola *f* ● **cloud over**
vi rannuvolarsi. **~burst** *n* acquazzone *m*
cloudy /'klaʊdɪ/ *a* (**-ier, -iest**) nuvolo-
so; ⟨*liquid*⟩ torbido
clout /klaʊt/ *n fam* colpo *m*; (*influence*)
impatto *m* (**with** su) ● *vt fam* colpire
clove /kləʊv/ *n* chiodo *m* di garofano; **~
of garlic** spicchio *m* d'aglio
clover /'kləʊvə(r)/ *n* trifoglio *m*
clown /klaʊn/ *n* pagliaccio *m* ● *vi* **~
[about]** fare il pagliaccio
club /klʌb/ *n* club *m inv*; (*weapon*) clava
f; *Sport* mazza *f*; **~s** *pl* (*Cards*) fiori *mpl*
● *v* (*pt/pp* **clubbed**) ● *vt* bastonare.
club together *vi* unirsi
cluck /klʌk/ *vi* chiocciare
clue /kluː/ *n* indizio *m*; (*in crossword*)
definizione *f*; **I haven't a ~** *fam* non ne
ho idea
clump /klʌmp/ *n* gruppo *m*
clumsiness /'klʌmzɪnɪs/ *n* goffaggi-
ne *f*
clumsy /'klʌmzɪ/ *a* (**-ier, -iest**) malde-
stro; ⟨*tool*⟩ scomodo; ⟨*remark*⟩ senza tatto
clung /klʌŋ/ *see* **cling**
cluster /'klʌstə(r)/ *n* gruppo *m* ● *vi*
raggrupparsi (**round** intorno a)
clutch /klʌtʃ/ *n* stretta *f*; *Auto* frizione
f; **be in sb's ~es** essere in balia di qcno
● *vt* stringere; (*grab*) afferrare ● *vi* **~
at** afferrare
clutter /'klʌtə(r)/ *n* caos *m* ● *vt* **~ [up]**
ingombrare
c/o *abbr* (**care of**) c/o, presso
coach /kəʊtʃ/ *n* pullman *m inv*; *Rail*
vagone *m*; (*horse-drawn*) carrozza *f*;
Sport allenatore, -trice *mf* ● *vt* fare
esercitare; *Sport* allenare
coagulate /kəʊ'ægjʊleɪt/ *vi* coagularsi
coal /kəʊl/ *n* carbone *m*
coalition /kəʊə'lɪʃn/ *n* coalizione *f*
'coal-mine *n* miniera *f* di carbone
coarse /kɔːs/ *a* grossolano; ⟨*joke*⟩ spinto
coast /kəʊst/ *n* costa *f* ● *vi* (*freewheel*)
scendere a ruota libera; *Auto* scendere
in folle. **~al** *a* costiero. **~er** *n* (*mat*)
sottobicchiere *m inv*
coast: **~guard** *n* guardia *f* costiera.
~line *n* litorale *m*
coat /kəʊt/ *n* cappotto *m*; (*of animal*)
manto *m*; (*of paint*) mano *f*; **~ of arms**

stemma *f* ● *vt* coprire; (*with paint*) ricoprire. **~-hanger** *n* gruccia *f*. **~-hook** *n*
gancio *m* [appendiabiti]
coating /'kəʊtɪŋ/ *n* rivestimento *m*; (*of
paint*) stato *m*
coax /kəʊks/ *vt* convincere con le moine
cob /kɒb/ *n* (*of corn*) pannocchia *f*
cobble /'kɒbl/ *vt* **~ together** raffazzo-
nare. **~r** *n* ciabattino *m*
'cobblestones *npl* ciottolato *msg*
cobweb /'kɒb-/ *n* ragnatela *f*
cocaine /kə'keɪn/ *n* cocaina *f*
cock /kɒk/ *n* gallo *m*; (*any male bird*)
maschio *m* ● *vt* sollevare il grilletto di
⟨*gun*⟩; **~ its ears** ⟨*animal:*⟩ drizzare le
orecchie
cockerel /'kɒkərəl/ *n* galletto *m*
cock-'eyed *a fam* storto; (*absurd*) assurdo
cockle /'kɒkl/ *n* cardio *m*
cockney /'kɒknɪ/ *n* (*dialect*) dialetto *m*
londinese; (*person*) abitante *mf* dell'est
di Londra
cock: **~pit** *n Aeron* cabina *f*. **~roach**
/-rəʊtʃ/ *n* scarafaggio *m*. **~tail** *n* cocktail *m inv*. **~-up** *n sl* **make a ~-up** fare
un casino (**of** con)
cocky /'kɒkɪ/ *a* (**-ier, -iest**) *fam* presuntuoso
cocoa /'kəʊkəʊ/ *n* cacao *m*
coconut /'kəʊkənʌt/ *n* noce *f* di cocco
cocoon /kə'kuːn/ *n* bozzolo *m*
cod /kɒd/ *n inv* merluzzo *m*
COD *abbr* (**cash on delivery**) pagamento *m* alla consegna
code /kəʊd/ *n* codice *m*. **~d** *a* codificato
coedu'cational /kəʊ-/ *a* misto
coerc|e /kəʊ'ɜːs/ *vt* costringere. **~ion**
/-'ɜːʃn/ *n* coercizione *f*
coe'xist *vi* coesistere. **~ence** *n*
coesistenza *f*
coffee /'kɒfɪ/ *n* caffè *m inv*
coffee: **~-grinder** *n* macinacaffè *m
inv*. **~-pot** *n* caffettiera *f*. **~-table** *n* ta-
volino *m*
coffin /'kɒfɪn/ *n* bara *f*
cog /kɒg/ *n Techn* dente *m* (*di ruota*)
cogent /'kəʊdʒənt/ *a* convincente
cog-wheel *n* ruota *f* dentata
cohabit /kəʊ'hæbɪt/ *vi Jur* convivere
coherent /kəʊ'hɪərənt/ *a* coerente;
(*when speaking*) logico
coil /kɔɪl/ *n* rotolo *m*; *Electr* bobina *f*;
~s *pl* spire *fpl* ● *vt* **~ [up]** avvolgere
coin /kɔɪn/ *n* moneta *f* ● *vt* coniare
⟨*word*⟩
coincide /kəʊɪn'saɪd/ *vi* coincidere

coinciden|ce /kəʊˈɪnsɪdəns/ n coincidenza f. **~tal** /-ˈdentl/ a casuale. **~tally** adv casualmente

coke /kəʊk/ n [carbone m] coke m

Coke® n Coca[-cola]® f

cold /kəʊld/ a freddo; **I'm ~** ho freddo ● n freddo m; Med raffreddore m

cold: ~-'blooded a spietato. **~-'hearted** a insensibile. **~ly** adv fig freddamente. **~ meat** n salumi mpl. **~ness** n freddezza f

coleslaw /ˈkəʊlslɔː/ n insalata f di cavolo crudo, cipolle e carote in maionese

colic /ˈkɒlɪk/ n colica f

collaborat|e /kəˈlæbəreɪt/ vi collaborare; **~e on sth** collaborare in qcsa. **~ion** /-ˈreɪʃn/ n collaborazione f; (with enemy) collaborazionismo m. **~or** n collaboratore, -trice mf; (with enemy) collaborazionista m

collaps|e /kəˈlæps/ n crollo m ● vi (person:) svenire; (roof, building:) crollare. **~ible** a pieghevole

collar /ˈkɒlə(r)/ n colletto m; (for animal) collare m. **~-bone** n clavicola f

colleague /ˈkɒliːg/ n collega mf

collect /kəˈlekt/ vt andare a prendere (person); ritirare (parcel, tickets); riscuotere (taxes); raccogliere (rubbish); (as hobby) collezionare ● vi riunirsi ● adv call ~ Am telefonare a carico del destinatario. **~ed** /-ɪd/ a controllato

collection /kəˈlekʃn/ n collezione f; (in church) questua f; (of rubbish) raccolta f; (of post) levata f

collective /kəˈlektɪv/ a collettivo

collector /kəˈlektə(r)/ n (of stamps etc) collezionista mf

college /ˈkɒlɪdʒ/ n istituto m parauniversitario; **C~ of...** Scuola f di...

collide /kəˈlaɪd/ vi scontrarsi

colliery /ˈkɒliəri/ n miniera f di carbone

collision /kəˈlɪʒn/ n scontro m

colloquial /kəˈləʊkwɪəl/ a colloquiale. **~ism** n espressione f colloquiale

cologne /kəˈləʊn/ n colonia f

colon /ˈkəʊlən/ n due punti mpl; Anat colon m inv

colonel /ˈkɜːnl/ n colonnello m

colonial /kəˈləʊnɪəl/ a coloniale

colon|ize /ˈkɒlənaɪz/ vt colonizzare. **~y** n colonia f

colossal /kəˈlɒsl/ a colossale

colour /ˈkʌlə(r)/ n colore m; (complexion) colorito m; **~s** pl (flag) bandiera fsg; **off ~** fam giù di tono ● vt colorare; **~ [in]** colorare ● vi (blush) arrossire

colour: ~ bar n discriminazione f razziale. **~-blind** a daltonico. **~ed** a colorato; (person) di colore ● n (person) persona f di colore. **~-fast** a dai colori resistenti. **~ film** n film m inv a colori. **~ful** a pieno di colore. **~less** a incolore. **~ television** n televisione f a colori

colt /kəʊlt/ n puledro m

column /ˈkɒləm/ n colonna f. **~ist** /-nɪst/ n giornalista mf che cura una rubrica

coma /ˈkəʊmə/ n coma m inv

comb /kəʊm/ n pettine m; (for wearing) pettinino m ● vt pettinare; (fig: search) setacciare; **~ one's hair** pettinarsi i capelli

combat /ˈkɒmbæt/ n combattimento m ● vt (pt/pp combated) combattere

combination /kɒmbɪˈneɪʃn/ n combinazione f

combine¹ /kəmˈbaɪn/ vt unire; **~ a job with being a mother** conciliare il lavoro con il ruolo di madre ● vi (chemical elements:) combinarsi

combine² /ˈkɒmbaɪn/ n Comm associazione f. **~ [harvester]** n mietitrebbia f

combustion /kəmˈbʌstʃn/ n combustione f

come /kʌm/ vi (pt came, pp come) venire; **where do you ~ from?** da dove vieni?; **~ to** (reach) arrivare a; **that ~s to £10** fanno 10 sterline; **~ into money** ricevere dei soldi; **~ true/open** verificarsi/aprirsi; **~ first** arrivare primo; fig venire prima di tutto; **~ in two sizes** esistere in due misure; **the years to ~** gli anni a venire; **how ~?** fam come mai? **come about** vi succedere. **come across** vi ~ **across as being** fam dare l'impressione di essere ● vt (find) imbattersi in. **come along** vi venire; (job, opportunity:) presentarsi; (progress) andare bene. **come apart** vi smontarsi; (break) rompersi. **come away** vi venir via; (button, fastener:) staccarsi. **come back** vi ritornare. **come by** vi passare ● vt (obtain) avere. **come down** vi scendere; **~ down to** (reach) arrivare a. **come in** vi entrare; (in race) arrivare; (tide:) salire. **come in for** vt ~ **in for criticism** essere criticato. **come off** vi staccarsi; (take place) esserci; (succeed) riuscire. **come on** vi (make progress) migliorare; **~ on!** (hurry) dai!; (indicating disbelief) ma va là!. **come out** vi venir fuori: ⟨book, sun:⟩ uscire; ⟨stain:⟩ andar via. **come over** vi venire. **come round** vi venire; (after fainting) riaversi; (change one's mind) farsi convincere. **come to** vi (after fainting) riaversi. **come up** vi salire; ⟨sun:⟩ sorgere; ⟨plant:⟩ crescere; **something came up** (I was prevented) ho avuto un imprevisto. **come up with** vt tirar fuori

'**come-back** n ritorno m
comedian /kə'mi:dɪən/ n comico m
'**come-down** n passo m indietro
comedy /'kɒmədɪ/ n commedia f
comet /'kɒmɪt/ n cometa f
come-uppance /kʌm'ʌpəns/ n **get one's ~** fam avere quel che si merita
comfort /'kʌmfət/ n benessere m; (consolation) conforto m ●vt confortare
comfortabl|e /'kʌmfətəbl/ a comodo; **be ~e** ⟨person:⟩ stare comodo; (fig: in situation) essere a proprio agio; (financially) star bene. **~y** adv comodamente
'**comfort station** n Am bagno m pubblico
comfy /'kʌmfɪ/ a fam comodo
comic /'kɒmɪk/ a comico ●n comico m; (periodical) fumetto m. **~al** a comico. **~ strip** n striscia f di fumetti
coming /'kʌmɪŋ/ n venuta f; **~s and goings** viavai m
comma /'kɒmə/ n virgola f
command /kə'mɑ:nd/ n comando m; (order) ordine m; (mastery) padronanza f ●vt ordinare; comandare ⟨army⟩
commandeer /kɒmən'dɪə(r)/ vt requisire
command|er /kə'mɑ:ndə(r)/ n comandante m. **~ing** a ⟨view⟩ imponente; ⟨lead⟩ dominante. **~ing officer** n comandante m. **~ment** n comandamento m
commemorat|e /kə'meməreɪt/ vt commemorare. **~ion** /-'reɪʃn/ n commemorazione f. **~ive** /-ətɪv/ a commemorativo
commence /kə'mens/ vt/i cominciare. **~ment** n inizio m
commend /kə'mend/ vt complimentarsi con (**on** per); (recommend) raccomandare (**to** a). **~able** /-əbl/ a lodevole
commensurate /kə'menʃərət/ a proporzionato (**with** a)
comment /'kɒment/ n commento m ●vi fare commenti (**on** su)
commentary /'kɒməntrɪ/ n commento m; ⟨running⟩ **~** (on radio, TV) cronaca f diretta
commentat|e /'kɒmənteɪt/ vt **~e on**

TV, Radio fare la cronaca di. **~or** n cronista mf
commerce /'kɒmɜ:s/ n commercio m
commercial /kə'mɜ:ʃl/ a commerciale ●n TV pubblicità f inv. **~ize** vt commercializzare
commiserate /kə'mɪzəreɪt/ vi esprimere il proprio rincrescimento (**with** a)
commission /kə'mɪʃn/ n commissione f; **receive one's ~** Mil essere promosso ufficiale; **out of ~** fuori uso ●vt commissionare
commissionaire /kəmɪʃə'neə(r)/ n portiere m
commissioner /kə'mɪʃənə(r)/ n commissario m
commit /kə'mɪt/ vt (pt/pp committed) commettere; (to prison, hospital) affidare (**to** a); impegnare ⟨funds⟩; **~ oneself** impegnarsi. **~ment** n impegno m; (involvement) compromissione f. **~ted** a impegnato
committee /kə'mɪtɪ/ n comitato m
commodity /kə'mɒdətɪ/ n prodotto m
common /'kɒmən/ a comune; (vulgar) volgare ●n prato m pubblico; **have in ~** avere in comune; **House of C~s** Camera f dei Comuni. **~er** n persona f non nobile
common: ~ law n diritto m consuetudinario. **~ly** adv comunemente. **C~ 'Market** n Mercato m Comune. **~place** a banale. **~-room** n sala f dei professori/degli studenti. **~ 'sense** n buon senso m
commotion /kə'məʊʃn/ n confusione f
communal /'kɒmjʊnl/ a comune
communicate /kə'mju:nɪkeɪt/ vt/i municare
communication /kəmju:nɪ'keɪʃn/ n comunicazione f; (of disease) trasmissione f; **be in ~ with** sb essere in contatto con qcno; **~s** pl (technology) telecomunicazioni fpl. **~ cord** n fermata f d'emergenza
communicative /kə'mju:nɪkətɪv/ a comunicativo
Communion /kə'mju:nɪən/ n [Holy] **~** comunione f
communiqué /kə'mju:nɪkeɪ/ n comunicato m stampa
Communis|m /'kɒmjʊnɪzm/ n comunismo m. **~t** /-ɪst/ a & n comunista mf
community /kə'mju:nətɪ/ n comunità f. **~ centre** n centro m sociale
commute /kə'mju:t/ vi fare il pendolare ●vt Jur commutare. **~r** n pendolare mf

compact[1] /kəm'pækt/ a compatto

compact[2] /'kɒmpækt/ n portacipria m inv. ~ **disc** n compact disc m inv

companion /kəm'pænjən/ n compagno, -a mf. ~**ship** n compagnia f

company /'kʌmpənɪ/ n compagnia f; (guests) ospiti mpl. ~ **car** n macchina f della ditta

comparable /'kɒmpərəbl/ a paragonabile

comparative /kəm'pærətɪv/ a comparativo; (relative) relativo ● n Gram comparativo m. ~**ly** adv relativamente

compare /kəm'peə(r)/ vt paragonare (**with/to** a) ● vi essere paragonato

comparison /kəm'pærɪsn/ n paragone m

compartment /kəm'pɑːtmənt/ n compartimento m; Rail scompartimento m

compass /'kʌmpəs/ n bussola f. ~**es** npl, **pair of** ~**es** compasso msg

compassion /kəm'pæʃn/ n compassione f. ~**ate** /-'ʃənət/ a compassionevole

compatible /kəm'pætəbl/ a compatibile

compatriot /kəm'pætrɪət/ n compatriota mf

compel /kəm'pel/ vt (pt/pp **compelled**) costringere. ~**ling** a (reason) inconfutabile

compensat|e /'kɒmpənseɪt/ vt risarcire ● vi ~**e for** fig compensare di. ~**ion** /-'seɪʃn/ n risarcimento m; (fig: comfort) consolazione f

compère /'kɒmpeə(r)/ n presentatore, -trice mf

compete /kəm'piːt/ vi competere; (take part) gareggiare

competen|ce /'kɒmpɪtəns/ n competenza f. ~**t** a competente

competition /kɒmpə'tɪʃn/ n concorrenza f; (contest) gara f

competitive /kəm'petɪtɪv/ a competitivo; ~ **prices** prezzi mpl concorrenziali

competitor /kəm'petɪtə(r)/ n concorrente mf

complacen|cy /kəm'pleɪsənsɪ/ n compiacimento m. ~**t** a compiaciuto

complain /kəm'pleɪn/ vi lamentarsi (**about** di); (formally) reclamare; ~ **of** Med accusare. ~**t** n lamentela f; (formal) reclamo m; Med disturbo m

complement[1] /'kɒmplɪmənt/ n complemento m

complement[2] /'kɒmplɪment/ vt complementare; ~ **each other** complementarsi a vicenda. ~**ary** /-'mentərɪ/ a complementare

complete /kəm'pliːt/ a completo; (utter) finito ● vt completare; compilare (form). ~**ly** adv completamente

completion /kəm'pliːʃn/ n fine f

complex /'kɒmpleks/ a complesso ● n complesso m

complexion /kəm'plekʃn/ n carnagione f

complexity /kəm'pleksətɪ/ n complessità f inv

compliance /kəm'plaɪəns/ n accettazione f; (with rules) osservanza f; **in** ~ **with** in osservanza a (law); conformemente a (request)

complicat|e /'kɒmplɪkeɪt/ vt complicare. ~**ed** a complicato. ~**ion** /-'keɪʃn/ n complicazione f

compliment /'kɒmplɪmənt/ n complimento m; ~**s** pl omaggi mpl ● vt complimentare. ~**ary** /-'mentərɪ/ a complimentoso; (given free) in omaggio

comply /kəm'plaɪ/ vi (pt/pp -**ied**) ~ **with** conformarsi a

component /kəm'pəʊnənt/ a & n ~ [**part**] componente m

compose /kəm'pəʊz/ vt comporre; ~ **oneself** ricomporsi; **be** ~**d of** essere composto da. ~**d** a (calm) composto. ~**r** n compositore, -trice mf

composition /kɒmpə'zɪʃn/ n composizione f; (essay) tema m

compost /'kɒmpɒst/ n composta f

composure /kəm'pəʊʒə(r)/ n calma f

compound /'kɒmpaʊnd/ a composto. ~ **fracture** n frattura f esposta. ~ **interest** n interesse m composto ● n Chem composto m; Gram parola f composta; (enclosure) recinto m

comprehen|d /kɒmprɪ'hend/ vt comprendere. ~**sible** /-'hensəbl/ a comprensibile. ~**sion** /-'henʃn/ n comprensione f

comprehensive /kɒmprɪ'hensɪv/ a & n comprensivo; ~ [**school**] scuola f media in cui gli allievi hanno capacità d'apprendimento diverse. ~ **insurance** n Auto polizza f casco

compress[1] /'kɒmpres/ n compressa f

compress[2] /kəm'pres/ vt comprimere; ~**ed air** aria f compressa

comprise /kəm'praɪz/ vt comprendere; (form) costituire

compromise /'kɒmprəmaɪz/ n compromesso m ● vt compromettere ● vi fare un compromesso compuls|ion /kəm'pʌlʃn/ n desiderio m irresistibile. ~ive /-sɪv/ a Psych patologico. ~ive eating voglia f ossessiva di mangiare. ~ory /-sərɪ/ a obbligatorio

comput|er /kəm'pju:tə(r)/ n computer m inv. ~erize vt computerizzare. ~ing n informatica f

comrade /'kɒmreɪd/ n camerata m; Pol compagno, -a mf. ~ship n cameratismo m

con¹ /kɒn/ see pro

con² n fam fregatura f ● vt (pt/pp conned) fam fregare

concave /'kɒnkeɪv/ a concavo

conceal /kən'si:l/ vt nascondere

concede /kən'si:d/ vt (admit) ammettere; (give up) rinunciare a; lasciar fare (goal)

conceit /kən'si:t/ n presunzione f. ~ed a presuntuoso

conceivable /kən'si:vəbl/ a concepibile

conceive /kən'si:v/ vt Biol concepire ● vi aver figli. conceive of vt fig concepire

concentrat|e /'kɒnsəntreɪt/ vt concentrare ● vi concentrarsi. ~ion /-'treɪʃn/ n concentrazione f. ~ion camp n campo m di concentramento

concept /'kɒnsept/ n concetto m. ~ion /kən'sepʃn/ n concezione f; (idea) idea f

concern /kən'sɜ:n/ n preoccupazione f; Comm attività f inv ● vt (be about, affect) riguardare; (worry) preoccupare; be ~ed about essere preoccupato per; ~ oneself with preoccuparsi di; as far as I am ~ed per quanto mi riguarda. ~ing prep riguardo a

concert /'kɒnsət/ n concerto m. ~ed /kən'sɜ:tɪd/ a collettivo

concertina /kɒnsə'ti:nə/ n piccola fisarmonica f

'concertmaster n Am primo violino m

concerto /kən'tʃeətəʊ/ n concerto m

concession /kən'seʃn/ n concessione f; (reduction) sconto m. ~ary a (reduced) scontato

conciliation /kənsɪlɪ'eɪʃn/ n conciliazione f

concise /kən'saɪs/ a conciso

conclu|de /kən'klu:d/ vt concludere ● vi concludersi. ~ding a finale

conclusion /kən'klu:ʒn/ n conclusione f, in ~ per concludere

conclusive /kən'klu:sɪv/ a definitivo. ~ly adv in modo definitivo

concoct /kən'kɒkt/ vt confezionare; fig inventare. ~ion /-'ɒkʃn/ n mistura f; (drink) intruglio m

concourse /'kɒnkɔ:s/ n atrio m

concrete /'kɒnkri:t/ a concreto ● n calcestruzzo m

concur /kən'kɜ:(r)/ vi (pt/pp concurred) essere d'accordo

concurrently /kən'kʌrəntlɪ/ adv contemporaneamente

concussion /kən'kʌʃn/ n commozione f cerebrale

condemn /kən'dem/ vt condannare; dichiarare inagibile (building). ~ation /kɒndem'neɪʃn/ n condanna f

condensation /kɒnden'seɪʃn/ n condensazione f

condense /kən'dens/ vt condensare; Phys condensare ● vi condensarsi. ~d milk n latte m condensato

condescend /kɒndɪ'send/ vi degnarsi. ~ing a condiscendente

condition /kən'dɪʃn/ n condizione f; on ~ that a condizione che ● vt Psych condizionare. ~al (acceptance) condizionato; Gram condizionale ● n Gram condizionale m. ~er n balsamo m; (for fabrics) ammorbidente m

condolences /kən'dəʊlənsɪz/ npl condoglianze fpl

condom /'kɒndəm/ n preservativo m

condo[minium] /'kɒndə(mɪnɪəm)/ n Am condominio m

condone /kən'dəʊn/ vt passare sopra a

conducive /kən'dju:sɪv/ a be ~ to contribuire a

conduct¹ /'kɒndʌkt/ n condotta f

conduct² /kən'dʌkt/ vt condurre; dirigere (orchestra). ~or n direttore m d'orchestra; (of bus) bigliettaio m; Phys conduttore m. ~ress n bigliettaia f

cone /kəʊn/ n cono m; Bot pigna f; Auto birillo m ● cone off vt be ~d off Auto essere chiuso da birilli

confectioner /kən'fekʃənə(r)/ n pasticciere, -a mf. ~y n pasticceria f

confederation /kənfedə'reɪʃn/ n confederazione f

confer /kən'fɜ:(r)/ v (pt/pp conferred) ● vt conferire (on a) ● vi (discuss) conferire

conference /'kɒnfərəns/ n conferenza f

confess /kən'fes/ vt confessare ● vi confessare; Relig confessarsi. ~ion /-eʃn/ n confessione f. ~ional /-eʃənəl/ n confessionale m. ~or n confessore m

confetti /kən'fetɪ/ n coriandoli mpl

confide /kənˈfaɪd/ vt confidare. **confide in** vt ~ **in sb** fidarsi di qcno

confidence /ˈkɒnfɪdəns/ n (trust) fiducia f; (self-assurance) sicurezza f di sé; (secret) confidenza f; **in** ~ in confidenza. ~ **trick** n truffa f

confident /ˈkɒnfɪdənt/ a fiducioso; (self-assured) sicuro di sé. ~**ly** adv con aria fiduciosa

confidential /kɒnfɪˈdenʃl/ a confidenziale

confine /kənˈfaɪn/ vt rinchiudere; (limit) limitare; **be ~d to bed** essere confinato a letto. ~**d** a (space) limitato. ~**ment** n detenzione f; Med parto m

confines /ˈkɒnfaɪnz/ npl confini mpl

confirm /kənˈfɜːm/ vt confermare; Relig cresimare. ~**ation** /kɒnfəˈmeɪʃn/ n conferma f; Relig cresima f. ~**ed** a incallito; ~**ed bachelor** scapolo m impenitente

confiscate /ˈkɒnfɪskeɪt/ vt confiscare. ~**ion** /-ˈkeɪʃn/ n confisca f

conflict¹ /ˈkɒnflɪkt/ n conflitto m

conflict² /kənˈflɪkt/ vi essere in contraddizione. ~**ing** a contraddittorio

conform /kənˈfɔːm/ vi (person:) conformarsi; (thing:) essere conforme (**to** a). ~**ist** n conformista mf

confounded /kənˈfaʊndɪd/ a fam maledetto

confront /kənˈfrʌnt/ vt affrontare; **the problems ~ing us** i problemi che dobbiamo affrontare. ~**ation** /kɒnfrʌnˈteɪʃn/ n confronto m

confuse /kənˈfjuːz/ vt confondere. ~**ing** a che confonde. ~**ion** /-juːʒn/ n confusione f

congeal /kənˈdʒiːl/ vi (blood:) coagularsi

congenial /kənˈdʒiːnɪəl/ a congeniale

congenital /kənˈdʒenɪtl/ a congenito

congested /kənˈdʒestɪd/ a congestionato. ~**ion** /-estʃn/ n congestione f

congratulate /kənˈgrætjʊleɪt/ vt congratularsi con (**on** per). ~**ions** /-ˈeɪʃnz/ npl congratulazioni fpl

congregate /ˈkɒŋgrɪgeɪt/ vi radunarsi. ~**ion** /-ˈgeɪʃn/ n Relig assemblea f

congress /ˈkɒŋgres/ n congresso m. ~**man** n Am Pol membro m del congresso

conical /ˈkɒnɪkl/ a conico

conifer /ˈkɒnɪfə(r)/ n conifera f

conjecture /kənˈdʒektʃə(r)/ n congettura f

conjugal /ˈkɒndʒʊgl/ a coniugale

conjugate /ˈkɒndʒʊgeɪt/ vt coniugare. ~**ion** /-ˈgeɪʃn/ n coniugazione f

conjunction /kənˈdʒʌŋkʃn/ n congiunzione f; **in** ~ **with** insieme a

conjunctivitis /kəndʒʌŋktɪˈvaɪtɪs/ n congiuntivite f

conjur|e /ˈkʌndʒə(r)/ vi ~**ing tricks** npl giochi mpl di prestigio. ~**or** n prestigiatore, -trice mf. **conjure up** vt evocare (image); tirar fuori dal nulla (meal)

conk /kɒŋk/ vi ~ **out** fam (machine:) guastarsi; (person:) crollare

'**con-man** n fam truffatore m

connect /kəˈnekt/ vt collegare; **be ~ed with** avere legami con; (be related to) essere imparentato con; **be well ~ed** aver conoscenze influenti ● vi essere collegato (**with** a); (train:) fare coincidenza

connection /kəˈnekʃn/ n (between ideas) nesso m; (in travel) coincidenza f; Electr collegamento m; **in** ~ **with** con riferimento a. ~**s** pl (people) conoscenze fpl

connoisseur /kɒnəˈsɜː(r)/ n intenditore, -trice mf

conquer /ˈkɒŋkə(r)/ vt conquistare; fig superare (fear). ~**or** n conquistatore m

conquest /ˈkɒŋkwest/ n conquista f

conscience /ˈkɒnʃəns/ n coscienza f

conscientious /kɒnʃɪˈenʃəs/ a coscienzioso. ~ **objector** n obiettore m di coscienza

conscious /ˈkɒnʃəs/ a conscio; (decision) meditato; [**fully**] ~ cosciente; **be/become** ~ **of sth** rendersi conto di qcsa. ~**ly** adv consapevolmente. ~**ness** n consapevolezza f; Med conoscenza f

conscript¹ /ˈkɒnskrɪpt/ n coscritto m

conscript² /kənˈskrɪpt/ vt Mil chiamare alle armi. ~**ion** /-ɪpʃn/ n coscrizione f, leva f

consecrate /ˈkɒnsɪkreɪt/ vt consacrare. ~**ion** /-ˈkreɪʃn/ n consacrazione f

consecutive /kənˈsekjʊtɪv/ a consecutivo

consensus /kənˈsensəs/ n consenso m

consent /kənˈsent/ n consenso m ● vi acconsentire

consequen|ce /ˈkɒnsɪkwəns/ n conseguenza f; (importance) importanza f. ~**t** a conseguente. ~**tly** adv di conseguenza

conservation /kɒnsəˈveɪʃn/ n conservazione f. ~**ist** n fautore, -trice mf della tutela ambientale

conservative /kənˈsɜːvətɪv/ a conservativo; (estimate) ottimistico. **C** ~

Pol a conservatore ● *n* conservatore, -trice *mf*

conservatory /kən'sɜː:vətrɪ/ *n* spazio *m* chiuso da vetrate adiacente alla casa

conserve /kən'sɜː:v/ *vt* conservare

consider /kən'sɪdə(r)/ *vt* considerare; ~ **doing sth** considerare la possibilità di fare qcsa. ~**able** /-əbl/ *a* considerevole. ~**ably** *adv* considerevolmente

consider|ate /kən'sɪdərət/ *a* pieno di riguardo. ~**ately** *adv* con riguardo. ~**ation** /-'reɪʃn/ *n* considerazione *f*; (*thoughtfulness*) attenzione *f*; (*respect*) riguardo *m*; (*payment*) compenso *m*; **take into** ~**ation** prendere in considerazione. ~**ing** *prep* considerando

consign /kən'saɪn/ *vt* affidare. ~**ment** *n* consegna *f*

consist /kən'sɪst/ *vi* ~ **of** consistere di

consisten|cy /kən'sɪstənsɪ/ *n* coerenza *f*; (*density*) consistenza *f*. ~**t** *a* coerente; ⟨loyalty⟩ costante. ~**tly** *adv* coerentemente; ⟨late, loyal⟩ costantemente

consolation /kɒnsə'leɪʃn/ *n* consolazione *f*. ~ **prize** *n* premio *m* di consolazione

console /kən'səʊl/ *vt* consolare

consolidate /kən'sɒlɪdeɪt/ *vt* consolidare

consonant /'kɒnsənənt/ *n* consonante *f*

consort /kən'sɔ:t/ *vi* ~ **with** frequentare

consortium /kən'sɔ:tɪəm/ *n* consorzio *m*

conspicuous /kən'spɪkjʊəs/ *a* facilmente distinguibile

conspiracy /kən'spɪrəsɪ/ *n* cospirazione *f*

conspire /kən'spaɪə(r)/ *vi* cospirare

constable /'kʌnstəbl/ *n* agente *m* [di polizia]

constant /'kɒnstənt/ *a* costante. ~**ly** *adv* costantemente

constellation /kɒnstə'leɪʃn/ *n* costellazione *f*

consternation /kɒnstə'neɪʃn/ *n* costernazione *f*

constipat|ed /'kɒnstɪpeɪtɪd/ *a* stitico. ~**ion** /-'peɪʃn/ *n* stitichezza *f*

constituency /kən'stɪtjʊənsɪ/ *n* area *f* elettorale di un deputato nel Regno Unito

constituent /kən'stɪtjʊənt/ *n* costituente *m*; *Pol* elettore, -trice *mf*

constitut|e /'kɒnstɪtjuːt/ *vt* costituire. ~**ion** /-'tjuːʃn/ *n* costituzione *f*. ~**ional** /-'tjuːʃənl/ *a* costituzionale

constrain /kən'streɪn/ *vt* costringere.

~**t** *n* costrizione *f*; (*restriction*) restrizione *f*; (*strained manner*) disagio *m*

construct /kən'strʌkt/ *vt* costruire. ~**ion** /-ʌkʃn/ *n* costruzione *f*; **under** ~**ion** in costruzione. ~**ive** /-ɪv/ *a* costruttivo

construe /kən'struː/ *vt* interpretare

consul /'kɒnsl/ *n* console *m*. ~**ar** /'kɒnsjʊlə(r)/ *a* consolare. ~**ate** /'kɒnsjʊlət/ *n* consolato *m*

consult /kən'sʌlt/ *vt* consultare. ~**ant** *n* consulente *mf*; *Med* specialista *mf*. ~**ation** /kɒnsl'teɪʃn/ *n* consultazione *f*; *Med* consulto *m*

consume /kən'sjuːm/ *vt* consumare. ~**r** *n* consumatore, -trice *mf*. ~**r goods** *npl* beni *mpl* di consumo. ~**er organization** *n* organizzazione *f* per la tutela dei consumatori

consumerism /kən'sjuːmərɪzm/ *n* consumismo *m*

consummate /'kɒnsəmeɪt/ *vt* consumare

consumption /kən'sʌmpʃn/ *n* consumo *m*

contact /'kɒntækt/ *n* contatto *m*; (*person*) conoscenza *f* ● *vt* mettersi in contatto con. ~ **lenses** *npl* lenti *fpl* a contatto

contagious /kən'teɪdʒəs/ *a* contagioso

contain /kən'teɪn/ *vt* contenere; ~ **oneself** controllarsi. ~**er** *n* recipiente *m*; (*for transport*) container *m inv*

contaminat|e /kən'tæmɪneɪt/ *vt* contaminare. ~**ion** /-'neɪʃn/ *n* contaminazione *f*

contemplat|e /'kɒntəmpleɪt/ *vt* contemplare; (*consider*) considerare; ~**e doing sth** considerare di fare qcsa. ~**ion** /-'pleɪʃn/ *n* contemplazione *f*

contemporary /kən'tempərərɪ/ *a & n* contemporaneo, -a *mf*

contempt /kən'tempt/ *n* disprezzo *m*; **beneath** ~ più che vergognoso; ~ **of court** oltraggio *m* alla Corte. ~**ible** /-əbl/ *a* spregevole. ~**uous** /-tjʊəs/ *a* sprezzante

contend /kən'tend/ *vi* ~ **with** occuparsi di ● *vt* (*assert*) sostenere. ~**er** *n* concorrente *mf*

content[1] /'kɒntent/ *n* contenuto *m*

content[2] /kən'tent/ *a* soddisfatto ● *vt* ~ **oneself** accontentarsi (**with** di). ~**ed** *a* soddisfatto. ~**edly** *adv* con aria soddisfatta

contention /kən'tenʃn/ *n* (*assertion*) opinione *f*

contentment /kən'tentmənt/ n soddi-sfazione f

contents /'kɒntents/ npl contenuto m

contest¹ /'kɒntest/ n gara f

contest² /kən'test/ vt contestare ⟨statement⟩; impugnare ⟨will⟩; Pol ⟨candidates:⟩ contendersi; ⟨one candidate:⟩ aspirare a. ~ant n concorrente mf

context /'kɒntekst/ n contesto m

continent /'kɒntɪnənt/ n continente m; **the C~** l'Europa f continentale

continental /kɒntɪ'nentl/ a continentale. ~ **breakfast** n prima colazione f a base di pane, burro, marmellata, croissant, ecc. ~ **quilt** n piumone m

contingency /kən'tɪndʒənsɪ/ n eventualità f inv

continual /kən'tɪnjʊəl/ a continuo

continuation /kəntɪnjʊ'eɪʃn/ n continuazione f

continue /kən'tɪnjuː/ vt continuare; ~ **doing** or **to do sth** continuare a fare qcsa; **to be ~d** continua ● vi continuare. ~**d** a continuo

continuity /kɒntɪ'njuːətɪ/ n continuità f

continuous /kən'tɪnjʊəs/ a continuo

contort /kən'tɔːt/ vt contorcere. ~**ion** /-ɔːʃn/ n contorsione f. ~**ionist** n contorsionista mf

contour /'kɒntʊə(r)/ n contorno m; ⟨line⟩ curva f di livello

contraband /'kɒntrəbænd/ n contrabbando m

contracep|tion /kɒntrə'sepʃn/ n contraccezione f. ~**tive** /-tɪv/ n contraccettivo m

contract¹ /'kɒntrækt/ n contratto m

contract² /kən'trækt/ vi ⟨get smaller⟩ contrarsi ● vt contrarre ⟨illness⟩. ~**ion** /-ækʃn/ n contrazione f. ~**or** n imprenditore, -trice mf

contradict /kɒntrə'dɪkt/ vt contraddire. ~**ion** /-ɪkʃn/ n contraddizione f. ~**ory** a contraddittorio

contra-flow /'kɒntrəfləʊ/ n utilizzazione f di una corsia nei due sensi di marcia durante lavori stradali

contralto /kən'træltəʊ/ n contralto m

contraption /kən'træpʃn/ n fam aggeggio m

contrary¹ /'kɒntrərɪ/ a contrario ● adv ~ **to** contrariamente a ● n contrario m; **on the ~** al contrario

contrary² /kən'treərɪ/ a disobbediente

contrast¹ /'kɒntrɑːst/ n contrasto m

contrast² /kən'trɑːst/ vt confrontare ● vi contrastare. ~**ing** a contrastante

contraven|e /kɒntrə'viːn/ vt trasgredire. ~**tion** /-'venʃn/ n trasgressione f

contribut|e /kən'trɪbjuːt/ vt/i contribuire. ~**ion** /kɒntrɪ'bjuːʃn/ n contribuzione f; ⟨what is contributed⟩ contributo m. ~**or** n contributore, -trice mf

contrive /kən'traɪv/ vt escogitare; ~ **to do sth** riuscire a fare qcsa

control /kən'trəʊl/ n controllo m; ~**s** pl ⟨of car, plane⟩ comandi mpl; **get out of ~** sfuggire al controllo ● vt ⟨pt/pp **controlled**⟩ controllare; ~ **oneself** controllarsi

controvers|ial /kɒntrə'vɜːʃl/ a controverso. ~**y** /'kɒntrəvɜːsɪ/ n controversia f

conurbation /kɒnɜː'beɪʃn/ n conurbazione f

convalesce /kɒnvə'les/ vi essere in convalescenza

convalescent /kɒnvə'lesənt/ a convalescente. ~ **home** n convalescenziario m

convector /kən'vektə(r)/ n ~ [**heater**] convettore m

convene /kən'viːn/ vt convocare ● vi riunirsi

convenience /kən'viːnɪəns/ n convenienza f; [**public**] ~ gabinetti mpl pubblici; **with all modern ~s** con tutti i comfort

convenient /kən'viːnɪənt/ a comodo; **be ~ for sb** andar bene per qcno; **if it is ~ [for you]** se ti va bene. ~**ly** adv comodamente; ~**ly located** in una posizione comoda

convent /'kɒnvənt/ n convento m

convention /kən'venʃn/ n convenzione f; ⟨assembly⟩ convegno m. ~**al** a convenzionale

converge /kən'vɜːdʒ/ vi convergere

conversant /kən'vɜːsənt/ a ~ **with** pratico di

conversation /kɒnvə'seɪʃn/ n conversazione f. ~**al** a di conversazione. ~**alist** n conversatore, -trice mf

converse¹ /kən'vɜːs/ vi conversare

converse² /'kɒnvɜːs/ n inverso m. ~**ly** adv viceversa

conversion /kən'vɜːʃn/ n conversione f

convert¹ /'kɒnvɜːt/ n convertito, -a mf

convert² /kən'vɜːt/ vt convertire ⟨into in⟩; sconsacrare ⟨church⟩. ~**ible** /-əbl/ a convertibile ● n Auto macchina f decappottabile

convex /'kɒnveks/ a convesso

convey /kən'veɪ/ vt portare; trasmettere ‹*idea, message*›. **~or belt** n nastro m trasportatore

convict¹ /'kɒnvɪkt/ n condannato, -a mf

convict² /kən'vɪkt/ vt giudicare colpevole. **~ion** /-ɪkʃn/ n condanna f; (*belief*) convinzione f; **previous ~ion** precedente m penale

convinc|e /kən'vɪns/ vt convincere. **~ing** a convincente

convivial /kən'vɪvɪəl/ a conviviale

convoluted /'kɒnvəluːtɪd/ a contorto

convoy /'kɒnvɔɪ/ n convoglio m

convuls|e /kən'vʌls/ vt sconvolgere; **be ~ed with laughter** contorcersi dalle risa. **~ion** /-ʌlʃn/ n convulsione f

coo /kuː/ vi tubare

cook /kʊk/ n cuoco, -a mf ● vt cucinare; **is it ~ed?** è cotto?; **~ the books** fam truccare i libri contabili ● vi ‹*food*:› cuocere; ‹*person*:› cucinare. **~book** n libro m di cucina

cooker /'kʊkə(r)/ n cucina f; (*apple*) mela f da cuocere. **~y** n cucina f. **~y book** n libro m di cucina

cookie /'kʊkɪ/ n Am biscotto m

cool /kuːl/ a fresco; (*calm*) calmo; (*unfriendly*) freddo ● n fresco m ● vt rinfrescare ● vi rinfrescarsi. **~-box** n borsa f termica. **~ness** n freddezza f

coop /kuːp/ n stia f ● vt **~ up** rinchiudere

co-operat|e /kəʊ'ɒpəreɪt/ vi cooperare. **~ion** /-'reɪʃn/ n cooperazione f

co-operative /kəʊ'ɒpərətɪv/ a cooperativo ● n cooperativa f

co-opt /kəʊ'ɒpt/ vt eleggere

co-ordinat|e /kəʊ'ɔːdɪneɪt/ vt coordinare. **~ion** /-'neɪʃn/ n coordinazione f

cop /kɒp/ n fam poliziotto m

cope /kəʊp/ vi fam farcela; **can she ~ by herself?** ce la fa da sola?; **~ with** farcela con

copious /'kəʊpɪəs/ a abbondante

copper¹ /'kɒpə(r)/ n rame m; **~s** pl monete fpl da uno o due pence ● attrib di rame

copper² n fam poliziotto m

coppice /'kɒpɪs/ n, **copse** /kɒps/ n boschetto m

copulat|e /'kɒpjʊleɪt/ vi accoppiarsi. **~ion** /-'leɪʃn/ n copulazione f

copy /'kɒpɪ/ n copia f ● vt (pt/pp -ied) copiare

copy: ~right n diritti mpl d'autore. **~-writer** n copywriter mf inv

coral /'kɒrəl/ n corallo m

cord /kɔːd/ n corda f; (*thinner*) cordon-

cino m; (*fabric*) velluto m a coste; **~s** pl pantaloni mpl di velluto a coste

cordial /'kɔːdɪəl/ a cordiale ● n analcolico m

cordon /'kɔːdn/ n cordone m (*di persone*) ● **cordon off** vt mettere un cordone (*di persone*) intorno a

corduroy /'kɔːdərɔɪ/ n velluto m a coste

core /kɔː(r)/ n (*of apple, pear*) torsolo m; (*fig: of organization*) cuore m; (*of problem, theory*) nocciolo m

cork /kɔːk/ n sughero m; (*for bottle*) turacciolo m. **~screw** n cavatappi m inv

corn¹ /kɔːn/ n grano m; (*Am: maize*) granturco m

corn² n Med callo m

cornea /'kɔːnɪə/ n cornea f

corned beef /kɔːnd'biːf/ n manzo m sotto sale

corner /'kɔːnə(r)/ n angolo m; (*football*) calcio m d'angolo, corner m inv ● vt bloccare; Comm accaparrarsi (*market*)

cornet /'kɔːnɪt/ n Mus cornetta f; (*for ice-cream*) cono m

corn: ~flour n, Am **~starch** n farina f di granturco

corny /'kɔːnɪ/ a (-ier, -est) (*fam: joke, film*) scontato; (*person*) banale; (*sentimental*) sdolcinato

coronary /'kɒrənərɪ/ a coronario ● n **~** [**thrombosis**] trombosi f coronarica

coronation /kɒrə'neɪʃn/ n incoronazione f

coroner /'kɒrənə(r)/ n coroner m inv (*nel diritto britannico, ufficiale incaricato delle indagini su morti sospette*)

corporal¹ /'kɔːpərəl/ n Mil caporale m

corporal² a corporale; **~ punishment** punizione f corporale

corporate /'kɔːpərət/ a (*decision, policy, image*) aziendale; **~ life** la vita in un'azienda

corporation /kɔːpə'reɪʃn/ n ente m; (*of town*) consiglio m comunale

corps /kɔː(r)/ n (pl **corps** /kɔːz/) corpo m

corpse /kɔːps/ n cadavere m

corpulent /'kɔːpjʊlənt/ a corpulento

corpuscle /'kɔːpʌsl/ n globulo m

correct /kə'rekt/ a corretto; **be ~** ‹*person*:› aver ragione; **~!** esatto! ● vt correggere. **~ion** /-ekʃn/ n correzione f. **~ly** adv correttamente

correlation /kɒrə'leɪʃn/ n correlazione f

correspond /kɒrɪ'spɒnd/ vi corrispondere (**to** a); (*two things*:) corrispondere; (*write*) scriversi. **~ence** *n* corrispondenza *f*. **~ent** *n* corrispondente *mf*. **~ing** *a* corrispondente. **~ingly** *adv* in modo corrispondente

corridor /'kɒrɪdɔ:(r)/ *n* corridoio *m*

corroborate /kə'rɒbəreɪt/ *vt* corroborare

corro|de /kə'rəʊd/ *vt* corrodere ● *vi* corrodersi. **~sion** /-'rəʊʒn/ *n* corrosione *f*

corrugated /'kɒrəgeɪtɪd/ *a* ondulato. **~ iron** *n* lamiera *f* ondulata

corrupt /kə'rʌpt/ *a* corrotto ● *vt* corrompere. **~ion** /-ʌpʃn/ *n* corruzione *f*

corset /'kɔ:sɪt/ *n* &-**s** *pl* busto *m*

Corsica /'kɔ:sɪkə/ *n* Corsica *f*. **~n** *a* & *n* corso, -a *mf*

cortège /kɔ:'teɪʒ/ *n* [**funeral**] ~ corteo *m* funebre

cosh /kɒʃ/ *n* randello *m*

cosmetic /kɒz'metɪk/ *a* cosmetico ● *n* ~**s** *pl* cosmetici *mpl*

cosmic /'kɒzmɪk/ *a* cosmico

cosmonaut /'kɒzmənɔ:t/ *n* cosmonauta *mf*

cosmopolitan /kɒzmə'pɒlɪtən/ *a* cosmopolita

cosmos /'kɒzmɒs/ *n* cosmo *m*

cosset /'kɒsɪt/ *vt* coccolare

cost /kɒst/ *n* costo *m*; ~**s** *pl* Jur spese *fpl* processuali; **at all ~s** a tutti i costi; **I learnt to my ~** ho imparato a mie spese ● *vt* (*pt/pp* **cost**) costare; **it ~ me £20** mi è costato 20 sterline ● *vt* (*pt/pp* **costed**) ~ [**out**] stabilire il prezzo di

costly /'kɒstlɪ/ *a* (**-ier, -iest**) costoso

cost: ~ **of 'living** *n* costo *m* della vita. ~ **price** *n* prezzo *m* di costo

costume /'kɒstju:m/ *n* costume *m*. ~ **jewellery** *n* bigiotteria *f*

cosy /'kəʊzɪ/ *a* (**-ier, -iest**) (*pub, chat*) intimo; **it's nice and ~ in here** si sta bene qui

cot /kɒt/ *n* lettino *m*; (*Am: camp-bed*) branda *f*

cottage /'kɒtɪdʒ/ *n* casetta *f*. ~ **'cheese** *n* fiocchi *mpl* di latte

cotton /'kɒtn/ *n* cotone *m* ● *attrib* di cotone ● **cotton on** *vi fam* capire

cotton 'wool *n* cotone *m* idrofilo

couch /kaʊtʃ/ *n* divano *m*. ~ **potato** *n* pantofolaio, -a *mf*

couchette /ku:'ʃet/ *n* cuccetta *f*

cough /kɒf/ *n* tosse *f* ● *vi* tossire. **cough up** *vt/i* sputare; (*fam: pay*) sborsare

'cough mixture *n* sciroppo *m* per la tosse

could /kʊd/, *atono* /kəd/ *v aux* (*see also*

can²) ~ **I have a glass of water?** potrei avere un bicchier d'acqua?; **I ~n't do it even if I wanted to** non potrei farlo nemmeno se lo volessi; **I ~n't care less** non potrebbe importarmene di meno; **he ~n't have done it without help** non avrebbe potuto farlo senza aiuto; **you ~ have phoned** avresti potuto telefonare

council /'kaʊnsl/ *n* consiglio *m*. ~ **house** *n* casa *f* popolare

councillor /'kaʊnsələ(r)/ *n* consigliere, -a *mf*

'council tax *n* imposta *f* locale sugli immobili

counsel /'kaʊnsl/ *n* consigli *mpl*; Jur avvocato *m* ● *vt* (*pt/pp* **counselled**) consigliare a (*person*). **~lor** *n* consigliere, -a *mf*

count¹ /kaʊnt/ *n* (*nobleman*) conte *m*

count² *n* conto *m*; **keep** ~ tenere il conto ● *vt/i* contare. **count on** *vt* contare su

countdown /'kaʊntdaʊn/ *n* conto *m* alla rovescia

countenance /'kaʊntənəns/ *n* espressione *f* ● *vt* approvare

counter¹ /'kaʊntə(r)/ *n* banco *m*; (*in games*) gettone *m*

counter² *adv* ~ **to** contro, in contrasto a; **go** ~ **to sth** andare contro qcsa ● *vt/i* opporre (*measure, effect*); parare (*blow*)

counter'act *vt* neutralizzare

'counter-attack *n* contrattacco *m*

counter-'espionage *n* controspionaggio *m*

counterfeit /-fɪt/ *a* contraffatto ● *n* contraffazione *f* ● *vt* contraffare

'counterfoil *n* matrice *f*

'counterpart *n* equivalente *mf*

counter-pro'ductive *a* controproduttivo

'countersign *vt* controfirmare

countess /'kaʊntɪs/ *n* contessa *f*

countless /'kaʊntlɪs/ *a* innumerevole

country /'kʌntrɪ/ *n* nazione *f*, paese *m*; (*native land*) patria *f*; (*countryside*) campagna *f*; **in the** ~ in campagna; **go to the** ~ andare in campagna; *Pol* indire le elezioni politiche. **~man** *n* uomo *m* di campagna; (*fellow ~man*) compatriota *m*. **~side** *n* campagna *f*

county /'kaʊntɪ/ *n* contea *f* (*unità amministrativa britannica*)

coup /ku:/ *n* Pol colpo *m* di stato

couple /'kʌpl/ *n* coppia *f*; **a** ~ **of** un paio di

coupon /'ku:pɒn/ *n* tagliando *m*; (*for discount*) buono *m* sconto

courage /'kʌrɪdʒ/ n coraggio m. **~ous** /kə'reɪdʒəs/ a coraggioso

courgette /kʊə'ʒet/ n zucchino m

courier /'kʊrɪə(r)/ n corriere m; (for tourists) guida f

course /kɔːs/ n Sch corso m; Naut rotta f; Culin portata f; (for golf) campo m; **~ of treatment** Med serie f inu di cure; **of ~** naturalmente; **in the ~ of** durante; **in due ~** a tempo debito

court /kɔːt/ n tribunale m; Sport campo m; **take sb to ~** citare qcno in giudizio ●vt fare la corte a (woman); **~ing couples** coppiette fpl

courteous /'kɜːtɪəs/ a cortese

courtesy /'kɜːtəsɪ/ n cortesia f

court: ~ 'martial n (pl **~s martial**) corte f marziale ●**~-martial** vt (pt **~-martialled**) portare davanti alla corte marziale; **~yard** n cortile m

cousin /'kʌzn/ n cugino, -a

cove /kəʊv/ n insenatura f

cover /'kʌvə(r)/ n copertura f; (of cushion, to protect sth) fodera f; (of book, magazine) copertina f; **take ~** mettersi al riparo; **under separate ~** a parte ●vt coprire; foderare (cushion); Journ fare un servizio su. **cover up** vt coprire; fig soffocare (scandal)

coverage /'kʌvərɪdʒ/ n Journ **it got a lot of ~** i media gli hanno dedicato molto spazio

cover: ~ charge n coperto m. **~ing** n copertura f; (for floor) rivestimento m; **~ing letter** lettera f d'accompagnamento. **~-up** n messa f a tacere

covet /'kʌvɪt/ vt bramare

cow /kaʊ/ n vacca f, mucca f

coward /'kaʊəd/ n vigliacco, -a mf. **~ice** /-ɪs/ n vigliaccheria f. **~ly** a da vigliacco

'cowboy n cowboy m inv, buffone m fam

cower /'kaʊə(r)/ vi acquattarsi

'cowshed n stalla f

cox /kɒks/ n, **coxswain** /'kɒksn/ n timoniere, -a mf

coy /kɔɪ/ a falsamente timido; (flirtatiously) civettuolo; **be ~ about sth** essere evasivo su qcsa

crab /kræb/ n granchio m

crack /kræk/ n (in wall) crepa f; (in china, glass, bone) incrinatura f; (noise) scoppio m; (fam: joke) battuta f; **have a ~** (try) fare un tentativo ●a (fam: best) di prim'ordine ●vt incrinare (china, glass); schiacciare (nut); decifrare (code); fam risolvere (problem); **~ a joke** fam fare una battuta ●vi (china,

glass:) incrinarsi; (whip:) schioccare. **crack down** vi fam prendere seri provvedimenti. **crack down on** vt fam prendere seri provvedimenti contro

cracked /krækt/ a (plaster) crepato; (skin) screpolato; (rib) incrinato; (fam: crazy) svitato

cracker /'krækə(r)/ n (biscuit) cracker m inv; (firework) petardo m; **[Christmas] ~** tubo m di cartone colorato contenente una sorpresa

crackers /'krækəz/ a fam matto

crackle /'krækl/ vi crepitare

cradle /'kreɪdl/ n culla f

craft¹ /krɑːft/ n inv (boat) imbarcazione f

craft² n mestiere m; (technique) arte f. **~sman** n artigiano m

crafty /'krɑːftɪ/ a (-ier, -iest) astuto

crag /kræg/ n rupe f. **~gy** a scosceso; (face) dai lineamenti marcati

cram /kræm/ v (pt/pp **crammed**) ●vt stipare (**into** in) ●vi (for exams) sgobbare

cramp /kræmp/ n crampo m. **~ed** a (room) stretto; (handwriting) appiccicato

crampon /'kræmpən/ n rampone f

cranberry /'krænbərɪ/ n Culin mirtillo m rosso

crane /kreɪn/ n (at docks, bird) gru f inv ●vt **~ one's neck** allungare il collo

crank¹ /kræŋk/ n tipo, -a mf strampalato, -a

crank² /kræŋk/ n Techn manovella f. **~shaft** n albero m a gomiti

cranky /'kræŋkɪ/ a strampalato; (Am: irritable) irritabile

cranny /'krænɪ/ n fessura f

crash /kræʃ/ n (noise) fragore m; Auto, Aeron incidente m; Comm crollo m ●vi schiantarsi (**into** contro); (plane:) precipitare ●vt schiantare (car)

crash: ~ course n corso m intensivo. **~-helmet** n casco m. **~-landing** n atterraggio m di fortuna

crate /kreɪt/ n (for packing) cassa f

crater /'kreɪtə(r)/ n cratere m

crav|e /kreɪv/ vt morire dalla voglia di. **~ing** n voglia f smodata

crawl /krɔːl/ n (swimming) stile m libero; **do the ~** nuotare a stile libero; **at a ~** a passo di lumaca ●vi andare carponi; **~ with** brulicare di. **~er lane** n Auto corsia f riservata al traffico lento

crayon /'kreɪən/ n pastello m a cera; (pencil) matita f colorata

craze /kreɪz/ n mania f

crazy /'kreɪzɪ/ a (-ier, -iest) matto; be ~ **about** andar matto per

creak /kriːk/ n scricchiolio m ●vi scricchiolare

cream /kriːm/ n crema f; (fresh) panna f ●a (colour) [bianco] panna inv ●vt Culin sbattere. ~ '**cheese** n formaggio m cremoso. ~y a cremoso

crease /kriːs/ n piega f ●vt stropicciare ●vi stropicciarsi. ~-**resistant** a che non si stropiccia

creat|e /kriː'eɪt/ vt creare. ~**ion** /-'eɪʃn/ n creazione f. ~**ive** /-tɪv/ a creativo. ~**or** n creatore, -trice

creature /'kriːtʃə(r)/ n creatura f

crèche /kreʃ/ n asilo m nido

credentials /krɪ'denʃlz/ npl credenziali fpl

credibility /kredə'bɪlətɪ/ n credibilità f

credible /'kredəbl/ a credibile

credit /'kredɪt/ n credito m; (honour) merito m; **take the ~ for** prendersi il merito di ●vt (pt/pp **credited**) accreditare; ~ **sb with sth** Comm accreditare qcsa a qcno; fig attribuire qcsa a qcno. ~**able** /-əbl/ a lodevole

credit: ~ **card** n carta f di credito. ~**or** n creditore, -trice mf

creed /kriːd/ n credo m inv

creek /kriːk/ n insenatura f; (Am: stream) torrente m

creep /kriːp/ vi (pt/pp **crept**) muoversi furtivamente ●n fam tipo m viscido. ~**er** n pianta f rampicante. ~**y** a che fa venire i brividi

cremat|e /krɪ'meɪt/ vt cremare. ~**ion** /-eɪʃn/ n cremazione f

crematorium /kremə'tɔːrɪəm/ n crematorio m

crêpe /kreɪp/ n (fabric) crespo m

crept /krept/ see **creep**

crescent /'kresənt/ n mezzaluna f

cress /kres/ n crescione m

crest /krest/ n cresta f; (coat of arms) cimiero m

Crete /kriːt/ n Creta f

crevasse /krɪ'væs/ n crepaccio m

crevice /'krevɪs/ n crepa f

crew /kruː/ n equipaggio m; (gang) équipe f inv. ~ **cut** n capelli mpl a spazzola. ~ **neck** n girocollo m

crib[1] /krɪb/ n (for baby) culla f

crib[2] vt/i (pt/pp **cribbed**) fam copiare

crick /krɪk/ n ~ **in the neck** torcicollo m

cricket[1] /'krɪkɪt/ n (insect) grillo m

cricket[2] n cricket m. ~**er** n giocatore m di cricket

crime /kraɪm/ n crimine m; (criminality) criminalità f

criminal /'krɪmɪnl/ a criminale; (law, court) penale ●n criminale mf

crimson /'krɪmzn/ a cremisi inv

cringe /krɪndʒ/ vi (cower) acquattarsi; (at bad joke etc) fare una smorfia

crinkle /'krɪŋkl/ vt spiegazzare ●vi spiegazzarsi

cripple /'krɪpl/ n storpio, -a mf ●vt storpiare; fig danneggiare. ~**d** a (person) storpio; (ship) danneggiato

crisis /'kraɪsɪs/ n (pl -**ses** /-siːz/) crisi f inv

crisp /krɪsp/ a croccante; (air) frizzante; (style) incisivo. ~**bread** n crostini mpl di pane. ~**s** npl patatine fpl

criterion /kraɪ'tɪərɪən/ n (pl -**ria** /-rɪə/) criterio m

critic /'krɪtɪk/ n critico, -a mf. ~**al** a critico. ~**ally** adv in modo critico; ~**ally ill** gravemente malato

criticism /'krɪtɪsɪzm/ n critica f; **he doesn't like** ~ non ama le critiche

criticize /'krɪtɪsaɪz/ vt criticare

croak /krəʊk/ vi gracchiare; (frog:) gracidare

crochet /'krəʊʃeɪ/ n lavoro m all'uncinetto ●vt fare all'uncinetto. ~-**hook** n uncinetto m

crock /krɒk/ n fam **old** ~ (person) rudere m; (car) macinino m

crockery /'krɒkərɪ/ n terrecotte fpl

crocodile /'krɒkədaɪl/ n coccodrillo m. ~ **tears** lacrime fpl di coccodrillo

crocus /'krəʊkəs/ n (pl -**es**) croco m

crony /'krəʊnɪ/ n compare m

crook /krʊk/ n (fam: criminal) truffatore, -trice mf

crooked /'krʊkɪd/ a storto; (limb) storpiato; (fam: dishonest) disonesto

crop /krɒp/ n raccolto m; fig quantità f inv ●v (pt/pp **cropped**) ●vt coltivare. **crop up** vi far presentarsi

croquet /'krəʊkeɪ/ n croquet m

croquette /krəʊ'ket/ n crocchetta f

cross /krɒs/ a (annoyed) arrabbiato; **talk at ~ purposes** fraintendersi ●n croce f; Bot, Zool incrocio m ●vt sbarrare (cheque); incrociare (road, animals); ~ **oneself** farsi il segno della croce; ~ **one's arms** incrociare le braccia; ~ **one's legs** accavallare le gambe; **keep one's fingers ~ed for sb** tenere le dita incrociate per qcno; **it ~ed my mind** mi è venuto in mente ●vi (go across) attraversare; (lines:) incrociarsi. **cross out** vt depennare

cross: **~bar** n (of goal) traversa f; (on bicycle) canna f. **~·'country** n Sport corsa f campestre. **~·ex'amine** vt sottoporre a controinterrogatorio. **~-exami'nation** n controinterrogatorio m. **~·'eyed** a strabico. **~fire** n fuoco m incrociato. **~ing** n (for pedestrians) passaggio m pedonale; (sea journey) traversata f. **~·'reference** n rimando m. **~roads** n incrocio m. **~·'section** n sezione f; (of community) campione m. **~wise** adv in diagonale. **~word** n **~word** [puzzle] parole fpl crociate

crotchet /'krɒtʃɪt/ n Mus semiminima f

crotchety /'krɒtʃɪtɪ/ a irritabile

crouch /krautʃ/ vi accovacciarsi

crow /krəʊ/ n corvo m; **as the ~ flies** in linea d'aria ●vi cantare. **~bar** n piede m di porco

crowd /kraud/ n folla f ●vt affollare ●vi affollarsi. **~ed** /'kraudɪd/ a affollato

crown /kraʊn/ n corona f ●vt incoronare; incapsulare (tooth)

crucial /'kru:ʃl/ a cruciale

crucifix /'kru:sɪfɪks/ n crocifisso m

crucif|ixion /kru:sɪ'fɪkʃn/ n crocifissione f. **~y** /'kru:sɪfaɪ/ vt (pt/pp -ied) crocifiggere

crude /kru:d/ a (oil) greggio; (language) crudo; (person) rozzo

cruel /'kru:əl/ a (crueller, cruellest) crudele (to verso). **~ly** adv con crudeltà. **~ty** n crudeltà f

cruis|e /kru:z/ n crociera f ●vi fare una crociera; (car:) andare a velocità di crociera. **~er** n Mil incrociatore m; (motor boat) motoscafo m. **~ing speed** n velocità m inv di crociera

crumb /krʌm/ n briciola f

crumb|le /'krʌmbl/ vt sbriciolare ●vi sbriciolarsi; (building, society:) sgretolarsi. **~ly** a friabile

crumple /'krʌmpl/ vt spiegazzare ●vi spiegazzarsi

crunch /krʌntʃ/ n fam **when it comes to the ~** quando si viene al dunque ●vt sgranocchiare ●vi (snow:) scricchiolare

crusade /kru:'seɪd/ n crociata f. **~r** n crociato m

crush /krʌʃ/ n (crowd) calca f; **have a ~ on sb** essersi presa una cotta per qcno ●vt schiacciare; sgualcire (clothes)

crust /krʌst/ n crosta f

crutch /krʌtʃ/ n gruccia f; Anat inforcatura f

crux /krʌks/ n fig punto m cruciale

cry /kraɪ/ n grido m; **have a ~** farsi un pianto; **a far ~ from** fig tutta un'altra cosa rispetto a ●vi (pt/pp cried) (weep) piangere; (call) gridare

crypt /krɪpt/ n cripta f. **~ic** a criptico

crystal /'krɪstl/ n cristallo m; (glassware) cristalli mpl. **~lize** vi (become clear) concretizzarsi

cub /kʌb/ n (animal) cucciolo m; **C~** [Scout] lupetto m

Cuba /'kju:bə/ n Cuba f

cubby-hole /'kʌbɪ-/ n (compartment) scomparto m; (room) ripostiglio m

cub|e /kju:b/ n cubo m. **~ic** a cubico

cubicle /'kju:bɪkl/ n cabina f

cuckoo /'kuku:/ n cuculo m. **~ clock** n orologio m a cucù

cucumber /'kju:kʌmbə(r)/ n cetriolo m

cuddl|e /'kʌdl/ vt coccolare ●vi **~e up to** starsene accoccolato insieme a ●n **have a ~e** (child:) farsi coccolare; (lovers:) abbracciarsi. **~y** a tenerone; (wanting cuddles) coccolone. **~y 'toy** n peluche m inv

cudgel /'kʌdʒl/ n randello m

cue¹ /kju:/ n segnale m; Theat battuta f d'entrata

cue² n (in billiards) stecca f. **~ ball** n pallino m

cuff /kʌf/ n polsino m; (Am: turn-up) orlo m; (blow) scapaccione m; **off the ~** improvvisando ●vt dare una pacca a. **~-link** n gemello m

cul-de-sac /'kʌldəsæk/ n vicolo m cieco

culinary /'kʌlɪnərɪ/ a culinario

cull /kʌl/ vt scegliere (flowers); (kill) selezionare e uccidere

culminat|e /'kʌlmɪneɪt/ vi culminare. **~ion** /-'neɪʃn/ n culmine m

culottes /kju:'lɒts/ npl gonna fsg pantalone

culprit /'kʌlprɪt/ n colpevole mf

cult /kʌlt/ n culto m

cultivate /'kʌltɪveɪt/ vt coltivare; fig coltivarsi (person)

cultural /'kʌltʃərəl/ a culturale

culture /'kʌltʃə(r)/ n cultura f. **~d** a colto

cumbersome /'kʌmbəsəm/ a ingombrante

cumulative /'kju:mjʊlətɪv/ a cumulativo

cunning /'kʌnɪŋ/ a astuto ●n astuzia f

cup /kʌp/ n tazza f; (prize, of bra) coppa f

cupboard /'kʌbəd/ n armadio m. **~ love** n fam amore m interessato

Cup 'Final n finale f di coppa

Cupid /'kju:pɪd/ n Cupido m

curable /'kjʊərəbl/ a curabile

curate /'kjʊərət/ n curato m

curator /kjʊə'reɪtə(r)/ n direttore. -trice mf (di museo)

curb /kɜ:b/ vt tenere a freno

curdle /'kɜ:dl/ vi coagularsi

cure /kjʊə(r)/ n cura f ● vt curare; (salt) mettere sotto sale; (smoke) affumicare

curfew /'kɜ:fju:/ n coprifuoco m

curio /'kjʊərɪəʊ/ n curiosità f inv

curiosity /kjʊərɪ'ɒsətɪ/ n curiosità f

curious /'kjʊərɪəs/ a curioso. ~ly adv curiosamente

curl /kɜ:l/ n ricciolo m ● vt arricciare ● vi arricciarsi. **curl up** vi raggomitolarsi

curler /'kɜ:lə(r)/ n bigodino m

curly /'kɜ:lɪ/ a (-ier, -iest) riccio

currant /'kʌrənt/ n (dried) uvetta f

currency /'kʌrənsɪ/ n valuta f; (of word) ricorrenza f. **foreign ~** valuta f estera

current /'kʌrənt/ a corrente ● n corrente f. ~ **affairs** or **events** npl attualità fsg. ~ly adv attualmente

curriculum /kə'rɪkjʊləm/ n programma m di studi. ~ **vitae** /'vi:taɪ/ n curriculum vitae m inv

curry /'kʌrɪ/ n curry m inv; (meal) piatto m cucinato nel curry ● vt (pt/pp -ied) ~ **favour** with **sb** cercare d'ingraziarsi qcno

curse /kɜ:s/ n maledizione f; (oath) imprecazione f ● vt maledire ● vi imprecare

cursor /'kɜ:sə(r)/ n cursore m

cursory /'kɜ:sərɪ/ a sbrigativo

curt /kɜ:t/ a brusco

curtail /kɜ:'teɪl/ vt ridurre

curtain /'kɜ:tn/ n tenda f; Theat sipario m

curtsy /'kɜ:tsɪ/ n inchino m ● vi (pt/pp -ied) fare l'inchino

curve /kɜ:v/ n curva f ● vi curvare; ~ **to the right/left** curvare a destra/sinistra. ~d a curvo

cushion /'kʊʃn/ n cuscino m ● vt attutire; (protect) proteggere

cushy /'kʊʃɪ/ a (-ier, -iest) fam facile

custard /'kʌstəd/ n (liquid) crema f pasticciera

custodian /kʌ'stəʊdɪən/ n custode mf

custody /'kʌstədɪ/ n (of child) custodia f; (imprisoning) detenzione f preventiva

custom /'kʌstəm/ n usanza f; Jur consuetudine f; Comm clientela f. ~ary a (habitual) abituale; (usual) ... è consuetudine.... ~er n cliente mf

customs /'kʌstəmz/ npl dogana f. ~ **officer** n doganiere m

cut /kʌt/ n (with knife etc, of clothes) taglio m; (reduction) riduzione f; (in public spending) taglio m ● vt/i (pt/pp **cut**, pres p **cutting**) tagliare; (reduce) ridurre; ~ **one's finger** tagliarsi il dito; ~ **sb's hair** tagliare i capelli a qcno ● vi (with cards) alzare. **cut back** vt tagliare (hair); (reduce) ridurre. **cut down** vt abbattere (tree); (reduce) ridurre. **cut off** vt tagliar via; (disconnect) interrompere; fig isolare; **I was ~ off** Teleph la linea è caduta. **cut out** vt ritagliare; (delete) eliminare; **be ~ out for** fam essere tagliato per; ~ **it out!** fam dacci un taglio!. **cut up** vt (slice) tagliare a pezzi

'**cut-back** n riduzione f; (in government spending) taglio m

cute /kju:t/ a fam (in appearance) carino; (clever) acuto

cuticle /'kju:tɪkl/ n cuticola f

cutlery /'kʌtlərɪ/ n posate fpl

cutlet /'kʌtlɪt/ n cotoletta f

'**cut-price** a a prezzo ridotto; (shop) che fa prezzi ridotti

'**cut-throat** a spietato

cutting /'kʌtɪŋ/ a (remark) tagliente ● n (from newspaper) ritaglio m; (of plant) talea f

CV n abbr **curriculum vitae**

cyanide /'saɪənaɪd/ n cianuro m

cybernetics /saɪbə'netɪks/ n cibernetica f

cycle /'saɪkl/ n ciclo m; (bicycle) bicicletta f, bici f inv fam ● vi andare in bicicletta. ~ing n ciclismo m. ~ist n ciclista m

cyclone /'saɪkləʊn/ n ciclone m

cylinder /'sɪlɪndə(r)/ n cilindro m. ~rical /-'lɪndrɪkl/ a cilindrico

cymbals /'sɪmblz/ npl Mus piatti mpl

cynic /'sɪnɪk/ n cinico, -a mf. ~al a cinico. ~ism /-sɪzm/ n cinismo m

cypress /'saɪprəs/ n cipresso m

Cypriot /'sɪprɪət/ n cipriota mf

Cyprus /'saɪprəs/ n Cipro m

cyst /sɪst/ n ciste f. ~itis /-'staɪtɪs/ n cistite f

Czech /tʃek/ a ceco; ~ **Republic** Repubblica f Ceca ● n ceco, -a mf

Czechoslovak /tʃekə'sləʊvæk/ a cecoslovacco. ~ia /-'vækɪə/ n Cecoslovacchia f

Dd

dab /dæb/ n colpetto m; **a ~ of** un pochino di ● vt (pt/pp **dabbed**) toccare leggermente ‹eyes›. **dab on** vt mettere un po' di ‹paint etc›

dabble /'dæbl/ vi **~ in sth** fig occuparsi di qcsa a tempo perso

dachshund /'dækshʊnd/ n bassotto m

dad[dy] /'dæd[ɪ]/ n fam papà m inv, babbo m

daddy-'long-legs n zanzarone m [dei boschi]; ‹Am: spider› ragno m

daffodil /'dæfədɪl/ n giunchiglia f

daft /dɑːft/ a sciocco

dagger /'dægə(r)/ n stiletto m

dahlia /'deɪlɪə/ n dalia f

daily /'deɪlɪ/ a giornaliero ● adv giornalmente ● n ‹newspaper› quotidiano m; ‹fam: cleaner› donna f delle pulizie

dainty /'deɪntɪ/ a (**-ier, -iest**) grazioso; ‹movement› delicato

dairy /'deərɪ/ n caseificio m; ‹shop› latteria f. **~ cow** n mucca f da latte. **~ products** npl latticini mpl

dais /'deɪs/ n pedana f

daisy /'deɪzɪ/ n margheritina f; ‹larger› margherita f

dale /deɪl/ n liter valle f

dam /dæm/ n diga f ● vt (pt/pp **dammed**) costruire una diga su

damag|e /'dæmɪdʒ/ n danno m (**to** a); **~es** pl Jur risarcimento msg ● vt danneggiare; fig nuocere a. **~ing** a dannoso

dame /deɪm/ n liter dama f; Am sl donna f

damn /dæm/ a fam maledetto ● adv ‹lucky, late› maledettamente ● n **I don't care** or **give a ~** fam non me ne frega un accidente ● vt dannare. **~ation** /-'neɪʃn/ n dannazione f ● int fam accidenti!

damp /dæmp/ a umido ● n umidità f ● vt = **dampen**

damp|en /'dæmpən/ vt inumidire; fig raffreddare ‹enthusiasm›. **~ness** n umidità f

dance /dɑːns/ n ballo m ● vt/i ballare. **~-hall** n sala f da ballo. **~ music** n musica f da ballo

dancer /'dɑːnsə(r)/ n ballerino, -a mf

dandelion /'dændɪlaɪən/ n dente m di leone

dandruff /'dændrʌf/ n forfora f

Dane /deɪn/ n danese mf; **Great ~** danese m

danger /'deɪndʒə(r)/ n pericolo m; **in/out of ~** in/fuori pericolo. **~ous** /-rəs/ a pericoloso. **~ously** adv pericolosamente; **~ously ill** in pericolo di vita

dangle /'dæŋgl/ vi penzolare ● vt far penzolare

Danish /'deɪnɪʃ/ a & n danese. **~ 'pastry** n dolce m a base di pasta sfoglia contenente pasta di mandorle, mele ecc

dank /dæŋk/ a umido e freddo

Danube /'dænjuːb/ n Danubio m

dare /deə(r)/ vt/i osare; ‹challenge› sfidare (**to** a); **~ [to] do sth** osare fare qcsa; **I ~ say!** molto probabilmente!
● n sfida f. **~devil** n spericolato, -a mf

daring /'deərɪŋ/ a audace ● n audacia f

dark /dɑːk/ a buio; **~ blue/brown** blu/marrone scuro; **it's getting ~** sta cominciando a fare buio; **~ horse** fig ‹in race, contest› vincitore m imprevisto; ‹not much known about› misterioso m; **keep sth ~** fig tenere qcsa nascosto ● n **after ~** col buio; **in the ~** al buio; **keep sb in the ~** fig tenere qcno all'oscuro

dark|en /'dɑːkn/ vt oscurare ● vi oscurarsi. **~ness** n buio m

'dark-room n camera f oscura

darling /'dɑːlɪŋ/ a adorabile; **my ~ Joan** carissima Joan ● n tesoro m

darn /dɑːn/ vt rammendare. **~ing-needle** n ago m da rammendo

dart /dɑːt/ n dardo m; ‹in sewing› pince f inv; **~s** sg ‹game› freccette fpl ● vi lanciarsi

dartboard /'dɑːtbɔːd/ n bersaglio m [per freccette]

dash /dæʃ/ n Typ trattino m; ‹in Morse› linea f; **a ~ of milk** un goccio di latte; **make a ~ for** lanciarsi verso ● vi **I must ~** devo scappare ● vt far svanire ‹hopes›. **dash off** vi scappar via ● vt (*write quickly*) buttare giù. **dash out** *vi* uscire di corsa

'dashboard *n* cruscotto *m*

dashing /'dæʃɪŋ/ *a* (*bold*) ardito; (*in appearance*) affascinante

data /'deɪtə/ *npl & sg* dati *mpl*. **~base** *n* base [di] dati *f*, database *m* *inv*. **~comms** /'kɒmz/ *n* telematica *f*. **~ processing** *n* elaborazione *f* [di] dati

date¹ /deɪt/ *n* (*fruit*) dattero *m*

date² *n* data *f*; (*meeting*) appuntamento *m*; **to ~** fino ad oggi; **out of ~** (*not fashionable*) fuori moda; (*expired*) scaduto; ⟨*information*⟩ non aggiornato; **make a ~ with sb** dare un appuntamento a qcno; **be up to ~** essere aggiornato ●*vt/i* datare; (*go out with*) uscire con. **date back to** *vi* risalire a

dated /'deɪtɪd/ *a* fuori moda; ⟨*language*⟩ antiquato

'date-line *n* linea *f* [del cambiamento] di data

daub /dɔːb/ *vt* imbrattare ⟨*walls*⟩

daughter /'dɔːtə(r)/ *n* figlia *f*. **~-in-law** *n* (*pl* **~s-in-law**) nuora *f*

daunt /dɔːnt/ *vt* scoraggiare; **nothing ~ed** per niente scoraggiato. **~less** *a* intrepido

dawdle /'dɔːdl/ *vi* bighellonare; (*over work*) cincischiarsi

dawn /dɔːn/ *n* alba *f*; **at ~** all'alba ●*vi* albeggiare; **it ~ed on me** *fig* mi è apparso chiaro

day /deɪ/ *n* giorno *m*; (*whole day*) giornata *f*; (*period*) epoca *f*; **these ~s** oggigiorno; **in those ~s** a quei tempi; **it's had its ~** *fam* ha fatto il suo tempo

day: **~break** *n* **at ~break** allo spuntar del giorno. **~-dream** *n* sogno *m* ad occhi aperti ●*vi* sognare ad occhi aperti. **~light** *n* luce *f* del giorno. **~re'turn** *n* (*ticket*) biglietto *m* di andata e ritorno con validità giornaliera. **~time** *n* giorno *m*; **in the ~time** di giorno

daze /deɪz/ *n* **in a ~** stordito; *fig* sbalordito. **~d** *a* stordito; *fig* sbalordito

dazzle /'dæzl/ *vt* abbagliare

deacon /'diːkn/ *n* diacono *m*

dead /ded/ *a* morto; (*numb*) intorpidito; **~ body** morto *m*; **~ centre** pieno centro *m* ●*adv* **~ tired** stanco morto; **~ slow/easy** lentissimo/facilissimo; **you're ~ right** hai perfettamente ragione; **stop ~** fermarsi di colpo; **be ~ on time** essere in perfetto orario ●*n* **the ~** *pl* i morti; **in the ~ of night** nel cuore della notte

deaden /'dedn/ *vt* attutire ⟨*sound*⟩; calmare ⟨*pain*⟩

dead: **~ 'end** *n* vicolo *m* cieco. **~ 'heat** *n* **it was a ~ heat** è finita a pari merito. **~line** *n* scadenza *f*. **~lock** *n* **reach ~lock** *fig* giungere a un punto morto

deadly /'dedlɪ/ *a* (**-ier, -iest**) mortale; (*fam: dreary*) barboso; **~ sins** peccati *mpl* capitali

deadpan /'dedpæn/ *a* impassibile; ⟨*humour*⟩ all'inglese

deaf /def/ *a* sordo; **~ and dumb** sordomuto. **~-aid** *n* apparecchio *m* acustico

deaf|en /'defn/ *vt* assordare; (*permanently*) render sordo. **~ening** *a* assordante. **~ness** *n* sordità *f*

deal /diːl/ *n* (*agreement*) patto *m*; (*in business*) accordo *m*; (*in cards*) a chi tocca dare le carte?; **a good** or **great ~** molto; **get a raw ~** *fam* ricevere un trattamento ingiusto ●*vt* (*pt/pp* **dealt** /delt/) (*in cards*) dare; **~ sb a blow** dare un colpo a qcno. **deal in** *vt* trattare in. **deal out** *vt* (*hand out*) distribuire. **deal with** *vt* (*handle*) occuparsi di; trattare con ⟨*company*⟩; (*be about*) trattare di; **that's been ~t with** è stato risolto

deal|er /'diːlə(r)/ *n* commerciante *mf*; (*in drugs*) spacciatore, -trice *mf*. **~ings** *npl* **have ~ings with** avere a che fare con

dean /diːn/ *n* decano *m*; *Univ* ≈ preside *mf* di facoltà

dear /dɪə(r)/ *a* caro; (*in letter*) Caro; (*formal*) Gentile ●*n* caro, -a *mf* ●*int* **oh ~!** Dio mio!. **~ly** *adv* ⟨*love*⟩ profondamente; ⟨*pay*⟩ profumatamente

dearth /dɜːθ/ *n* penuria *f*

death /deθ/ *n* morte *f*. **~ certificate** *n* certificato *m* di morte. **~ duty** *n* tassa *f* di successione

deathly /'deθlɪ/ *a* **~ silence** silenzio *m* di tomba ●*adv* **~ pale** di un pallore cadaverico

death: **~ penalty** *n* pena *f* di morte. **~-trap** *n* trappola *f* mortale

debar /dɪ'bɑː(r)/ *vt* (*pt/pp* **debarred**) escludere

debase /dɪ'beɪs/ *vt* degradare

debatable /dɪ'beɪtəbl/ *a* discutibile

debate /dɪ'beɪt/ *n* dibattito *m* ●*vt* discutere; (*in formal debate*) dibattere ●*vi* **~ whether to...** considerare se...

debauchery /dɪ'bɔːtʃərɪ/ *n* dissolutezza *f*

debility /dɪ'bɪlɪtɪ/ *n* debilitazione *f*

debit /'debit/ n debito m ●vt (pt/pp **debited**) Comm addebitare ⟨sum⟩

debris /'debri:/ n macerie fpl

debt /det/ n debito m; **be in** ~ avere dei debiti. **~or** n debitore, -trice mf

début /'deibu:/ n debutto m

decade /'dekeid/ n decennio m

decaden|ce /'dekədəns/ n decadenza f. **~t** a decadente

decaffeinated /di:'kæfineitid/ a decaffeinato

decant /di'kænt/ vt travasare. **~er** n caraffa f ⟨di cristallo⟩

decapitate /di'kæpiteit/ vt decapitare

decay /di'kei/ n (also fig) decadenza f; ⟨rot⟩ decomposizione f; ⟨of tooth⟩ carie f inv ●vi imputridire; ⟨rot⟩ decomporsi; ⟨tooth:⟩ cariarsi

deceased /di'si:st/ a defunto ●n **the** ~**d** il defunto; la defunta

deceit /di'si:t/ n inganno m. **~ful** a falso

deceive /di'si:v/ vt ingannare

December /di'sembə(r)/ n dicembre m

decency /'di:sənsi/ n decenza f

decent /'di:sənt/ a decente; ⟨respectable⟩ rispettabile; **very** ~ **of you** molto gentile da parte tua. **~ly** adv decentemente; ⟨kindly⟩ gentilmente

decentralize /di:'sentrəlaiz/ vt decentrare

decept|ion /di'sepʃn/ n inganno m. **~ive** /-tiv/ a ingannevole. **~ively** adv ingannevolmente; **it looks ~ively easy** sembra facile, ma non lo è

decibel /'desibel/ n decibel m inv

decide /di'said/ vt decidere ●vi decidere (**on** di)

decided /di'saidid/ a risoluto. **~ly** adv risolutamente; ⟨without doubt⟩ senza dubbio

deciduous /di'sidjʊəs/ a a foglie decidue

decimal /'desiml/ a decimale ●n numero m decimale. ~ **'point** n virgola f

decimate /'desimeit/ vt decimare

decipher /di'saifə(r)/ vt decifrare

decision /di'siʒn/ n decisione f

decisive /di'saisiv/ a decisivo

deck[1] /dek/ vt abbigliare

deck[2] n Naut ponte m; **on** ~ in coperta; **top** ~ ⟨of bus⟩ piano m di sopra; ~ **of cards** mazzo m. **~-chair** n [sedia f a] sdraio f inv

declaration /deklə'reiʃn/ n dichiarazione f

declare /di'kleə(r)/ vt dichiarare; **anything to** ~? niente da dichiarare?

declension /di'klenʃn/ n declinazione f

decline /di'klain/ n declino m ●vt also Gram declinare ●vi ⟨decrease⟩ diminuire; ⟨health:⟩ deperire; ⟨say no⟩ rifiutare

decode /di:'kəʊd/ vt decifrare; Comput decodificare

decompose /di:kəm'pəʊz/ vi decomporsi

décor /'deikɔ:(r)/ n decorazione f; ⟨including furniture⟩ arredamento m

decorat|e /'dekəreit/ vt decorare; ⟨paint⟩ pitturare; ⟨wallpaper⟩ tappezzare. **~ion** /-'reiʃn/ n decorazione f. **~ive** /-rətiv/ a decorativo. **~or** n **painter and ~or** imbianchino m

decorum /di'kɔ:rəm/ n decoro m

decoy[1] /'di:kɔi/ n esca f

decoy[2] /di'kɔi/ vt adescare

decrease[1] /'di:kri:s/ n diminuzione f

decrease[2] /di'kri:s/ vt/i diminuire

decree /di'kri:/ n decreto m ●vt (pt/pp **decreed**) decretare

decrepit /di'krepit/ a decrepito

dedicat|e /'dedikeit/ vt dedicare. **~ed** a ⟨person⟩ scrupoloso. **~ion** /-'keiʃn/ n dedizione f; ⟨in book⟩ dedica f

deduce /di'dju:s/ vt dedurre (**from** da)

deduct /di'dʌkt/ vt dedurre

deduction /di'dʌkʃn/ n deduzione f

deed /di:d/ n azione f; Jur atto m di proprietà

deem /di:m/ vt ritenere

deep /di:p/ a profondo; **go off the** ~ **end** fam arrabbiarsi

deepen /'di:pn/ vt approfondire; scavare più profondamente ⟨trench⟩ ●vi approfondirsi; ⟨fig: mystery:⟩ infittirsi

deep-'freeze n congelatore m

deeply /'di:pli/ adv profondamente

deer /diə(r)/ n inv cervo m

deface /di'feis/ vt sfigurare ⟨picture⟩; deturpare ⟨monument⟩

defamat|ion /defə'meiʃn/ n diffamazione f. **~ory** /di'fæmətəri/ a diffamatorio

default /di'fɔ:lt/ n ⟨Jur: non-payment⟩ morosità f; ⟨failure to appear⟩ contumacia f; **win by** ~ Sport vincere per abbandono dell'avversario; **in** ~ **of** per mancanza di ●a ~ **drive** Comput lettore m di default ●vi ⟨not pay⟩ venir meno a un pagamento

defeat /di'fi:t/ n sconfitta f ●vt sconfiggere; ⟨frustrate⟩ vanificare ⟨attempts⟩; **that** ~**s the object** questo fa fallire l'obiettivo

defect[1] /di'fekt/ vi Pol fare defezione

defect[2] /'di:fekt/ n difetto m. **~ive** /dɪ'fektɪv/ a difettoso

defence /dɪ'fens/ n difesa f. **~less** a indifeso

defend /dɪ'fend/ vt difendere; (justify) giustificare. **~ant** n Jur imputato, -a mf

defensive /dɪ'fensɪv/ a difensivo ● n difensiva f; **on the ~** sulla difensiva

defer /dɪ'fɜ:(r)/ v (pt/pp **deferred**) ● vt (postpone) rinviare ● vi **~ to sb** rimettersi a qcno

deferen|ce /'defərəns/ n deferenza f. **~tial** /-'renʃl/ a deferente

defian|ce /dɪ'faɪəns/ n sfida f; **in ~ce of** sfidando. **~t** a (person) ribelle; (gesture, attitude) di sfida. **~tly** adv con aria di sfida

deficien|cy /dɪ'fɪʃənsɪ/ n insufficienza f. **~t** a insufficiente; **be ~t in** mancare di

deficit /'defɪsɪt/ n deficit m inv

defile /dɪ'faɪl/ vt fig contaminare

define /dɪ'faɪn/ vt definire

definite /'defɪnɪt/ a definito; (certain) (answer, yes) definitivo; (improvement, difference) netto; **he was ~ about it** è stato chiaro in proposito. **~ly** adv sicuramente

definition /defɪ'nɪʃn/ n definizione f

definitive /dɪ'fɪnɪtɪv/ a definitivo

deflat|e /dɪ'fleɪt/ vt sgonfiare. **~ion** /-eɪʃn/ n Comm deflazione f

deflect /dɪ'flekt/ vt deflettere

deform|ed /dɪ'fɔːmd/ a deforme. **~ity** n deformità f inv

defraud /dɪ'frɔːd/ vt defraudare

defrost /di:'frɒst/ vt sbrinare (fridge); scongelare (food)

deft /deft/ a abile

defunct /dɪ'fʌŋkt/ a morto e sepolto; (law) caduto in disuso

defuse /di:'fju:z/ vt disinnescare; calmare (situation)

defy /dɪ'faɪ/ vt (pt/pp **-ied**) (challenge) sfidare; resistere a (attempt); (not obey) disobbedire a

degenerate[1] /dɪ'dʒenəreɪt/ vi degenerare; **~ into** fig degenerare in

degenerate[2] /dɪ'dʒenərət/ a degenerato

degrading /dɪ'greɪdɪŋ/ a degradante

degree /dɪ'griː/ n grado m; Univ laurea f; **20 ~s** 20 gradi; **not to the same ~** non allo stesso livello

dehydrate /di:'haɪdreɪt/ vt disidratare. **~d** /-ɪd/ a disidratato

de-ice /di:'aɪs/ vt togliere il ghiaccio da

deign /deɪn/ vi **~ to do sth** degnarsi di fare qcsa

deity /'di:ɪtɪ/ n divinità f inv

dejected /dɪ'dʒektɪd/ a demoralizzato

delay /dɪ'leɪ/ n ritardo m; **without ~** senza indugio ● vt ritardare; **be ~ed** (person:) essere trattenuto; (train, aircraft:) essere in ritardo ● vi indugiare

delegate[1] /'delɪgət/ n delegato, -a mf

delegat|e[2] /'delɪgeɪt/ vt delegare. **~ion** /-'geɪʃn/ n delegazione f

delet|e /dɪ'liːt/ vt cancellare. **~ion** /-i:ʃn/ n cancellatura f

deliberate[1] /dɪ'lɪbərət/ a deliberato; (slow) posato. **~ly** adv deliberatamente; (slowly) in modo posato

deliberat|e[2] /dɪ'lɪbəreɪt/ vt/i deliberare. **~ion** /-'reɪʃn/ n deliberazione f

delicacy /'delɪkəsɪ/ n delicatezza f; (food) prelibatezza f

delicate /'delɪkət/ a delicato

delicatessen /delɪkə'tesn/ n negozio m di specialità gastronomiche

delicious /dɪ'lɪʃəs/ a delizioso

delight /dɪ'laɪt/ n piacere m ● vt deliziare ● vi **~ in** dilettarsi con. **~ed** a lieto. **~ful** a delizioso

delinquen|cy /dɪ'lɪŋkwənsɪ/ n delinquenza f. **~t** a delinquente ● n delinquente mf

deli|rious /dɪ'lɪrɪəs/ a **be ~rious** delirare; (fig: very happy) essere pazzo di gioia. **~rium** /-rɪəm/ n delirio m

deliver /dɪ'lɪvə(r)/ vt consegnare; recapitare (post, newspaper); tenere (speech); dare (message); tirare (blow); (set free) liberare; **~ a baby** far nascere un bambino. **~ance** n liberazione f. **~y** n consegna f; (of post) distribuzione f; Med parto m; **cash on ~y** pagamento m alla consegna

delude /dɪ'luːd/ vt ingannare; **~ oneself** illudersi

deluge /'deljuːdʒ/ n diluvio m ● vt (fig: with requests etc) inondare

delusion /dɪ'luːʒn/ n illusione f

de luxe /də'lʌks/ a di lusso

delve /delv/ vi **~ into** (into pocket etc) frugare in; (into notes, the past) fare ricerche in

demand /dɪ'mɑːnd/ n richiesta f; Comm domanda f; **in ~** richiesto; **on ~** a richiesta ● vt esigere (of/from da). **~ing** a esigente

demarcation /di:mɑː'keɪʃn/ n demarcazione f

demean /dɪ'miːn/ vt ~ **oneself** abbassarsi (**to** a)

demeanour /dɪ'miːnə(r)/ n comportamento m

demented /dɪ'mentɪd/ a demente

demise /dɪ'maɪz/ n decesso m

demister /diː'mɪstə(r)/ n Auto sbrinatore m

demo /'deməʊ/ n (pl ~s) fam manifestazione f. ~ **disk** Comput demodisk m inv

democracy /dɪ'mɒkrəsɪ/ n democrazia f

democrat /'deməkræt/ n democratico. ~a mf. ~ic /-'krætɪk/ a democratico

demolish /dɪ'mɒlɪʃ/ vt demolire. ~lition /demə'lɪʃn/ n demolizione f

demon /'diːmən/ n demonio m

demonstrate /'demənstreɪt/ vt dimostrare; fare una dimostrazione sull'uso di ⟨appliance⟩ ●vi Pol manifestare. ~ion /-'streɪʃn/ n dimostrazione f; Pol manifestazione f

demonstrative /dɪ'mɒnstrətɪv/ a Gram dimostrativo; **be ~** essere espansivo

demonstrator /'demənstreɪtə(r)/ n Pol manifestante mf; (for product) dimostratore. ·trice mf

demoralize /dɪ'mɒrəlaɪz/ vt demoralizzare

demote /dɪ'məʊt/ vt retrocedere di grado; Mil degradare

demure /dɪ'mjʊə(r)/ a schivo

den /den/ n tana f; (room) rifugio m

denial /dɪ'naɪəl/ n smentita f

denim /'denɪm/ n [tessuto m] jeans m; ~s pl [blue]jeans mpl

Denmark /'denmɑːk/ n Danimarca f

denomination /dɪnɒmɪ'neɪʃn/ n Relig confessione f; (money) valore f

denounce /dɪ'naʊns/ vt denunciare

dense /dens/ a denso; ⟨crowd, forest⟩ fitto; (stupid) ottuso. ~ely adv (populated) densamente; ~ely **wooded** fittamente ricoperto di alberi. ~ity n densità f inv; (of forest) fittezza f

dent /dent/ n ammaccatura f ●vt ammaccare; ~ed a ammaccato

dental /'dentl/ a dei denti; (treatment) dentistico; (hygiene) dentale. ~ **surgeon** n odontoiatra mf; medico m dentista

dentist /'dentɪst/ n dentista mf. ~ry n odontoiatria f

dentures /'dentʃəz/ npl dentiera fsg

denunciation /dɪnʌnsɪ'eɪʃn/ n denuncia f

deny /dɪ'naɪ/ vt (pt/pp -ied) negare; (officially) smentire; ~ **sb sth** negare qcsa a qcno

deodorant /diː'əʊdərənt/ n deodorante m

depart /dɪ'pɑːt/ vi ⟨plane, train:⟩ partire; ⟨liter: person⟩ andare via; (deviate) allontanarsi (**from** da)

department /dɪ'pɑːtmənt/ n reparto m; Pol ministero m; (of company) sezione f; Univ dipartimento m. ~ **store** n grande magazzino m

departure /dɪ'pɑːtʃə(r)/ n partenza f; (from rule) allontanamento m; **new ~** svolta f

depend /dɪ'pend/ vi dipendere (**on** da); (rely) contare (**on** su); **it all** ~s dipende; ~ing **on what he says** a seconda di quello che dice. ~**able** /-əbl/ a fidato. ~**ant** n persona f a carico. ~**ence** n dipendenza f. ~**ent** a dipendente (**on** da)

depict /dɪ'pɪkt/ vt (in writing) dipingere; (with picture) rappresentare

depilatory /dɪ'pɪlətərɪ/ n (cream) crema f depilatoria

deplete /dɪ'pliːt/ vt ridurre; **totally ~d** completamente esaurito

deplorable /dɪ'plɔːrəbl/ a deplorevole. ~e vt deplorare

deploy /dɪ'plɔɪ/ vt Mil spiegare ●vi schierarsi

deport /dɪ'pɔːt/ vt deportare. ~**ation** /diːpɔː'teɪʃn/ n deportazione f

depose /dɪ'pəʊz/ vt deporre

deposit /dɪ'pɒzɪt/ n deposito m; (against damage) cauzione f; (first instalment) acconto m ●vt (pt/pp **deposited**) depositare. ~ **account** n libretto m di risparmio; (without instant access) conto m vincolato

depot /'depəʊ/ n deposito m; Am Rail stazione f ferroviaria

deprave /dɪ'preɪv/ vt depravare. ~**ed** a depravato. ~**ity** /-'prævətɪ/ n depravazione f

depreciate /dɪ'priːʃɪeɪt/ vi deprezzarsi. ~**ion** /-'eɪʃn/ n deprezzamento m

depress /dɪ'pres/ vt deprimere; (press down) premere. ~**ed** a depresso; ~**ed area** zona f depressa. ~**ing** a deprimente. ~**ion** /-eʃn/ n depressione f

deprivation /deprɪ'veɪʃn/ n privazione f

deprive /dɪ'praɪv/ vt ~ **sb of sth** privare qcno di qcsa. ~**d** a ⟨area, childhood⟩ disagiato

depth /depθ/ n profondità f inv; **in ~** ⟨study, analyse⟩ in modo approfondito;

in the ~s of winter in pieno inverno; **be out of one's ~** ⟨*in water*⟩ non toccare il fondo; *fig* sentirsi in alto mare

deputation /depjʊ'teɪʃn/ *n* deputazione *f*

deputize /'depjʊtaɪz/ *vi* **~ for** fare le veci di

deputy /'depjʊtɪ/ *n* vice *mf*; ⟨*temporary*⟩ sostituto, -a *mf* ●*attrib* **~ leader** vicesegretario, -a *mf*; **~ chairman** vicepresidente *mf*

derail /dɪ'reɪl/ *vt* **be ~ed** ⟨*train:*⟩ essere deragliato. **~ment** *n* deragliamento *m*

deranged /dɪ'reɪndʒd/ *a* squilibrato

derelict /'derəlɪkt/ *a* abbandonato

deri|de /dɪ'raɪd/ *vt* deridere. **~sion** /-'rɪʒn/ *n* derisione *f*

derisory /dɪ'raɪsərɪ/ *a* ⟨*laughter*⟩ derisorio; ⟨*offer*⟩ irrisorio

derivation /derɪ'veɪʃn/ *n* derivazione *f*

derivative /dɪ'rɪvətɪv/ *a* derivato ●*n* derivato *m*

derive /dɪ'raɪv/ *vt* ⟨*obtain*⟩ derivare; **be ~d from** ⟨*word:*⟩ derivare da

dermatologist /dɜ:mə'tɒlədʒɪst/ *n* dermatologo, -a *mf*

derogatory /dɪ'rɒgətrɪ/ *a* ⟨*comments*⟩ peggiorativo

descend /dɪ'send/ *vi* scendere ●*vt* scendere da; **be ~ed from** discendere da. **~ant** *n* discendente *mf*

descent /dɪ'sent/ *n* discesa *f*; ⟨*lineage*⟩ origine *f*

describe /dɪ'skraɪb/ *vt* descrivere

descrip|tion /dɪ'skrɪpʃn/ *n* descrizione *f*; **they had no help of any ~tion** non hanno avuto proprio nessun aiuto. **~tive** /-tɪv/ *a* descrittivo; ⟨*vivid*⟩ vivido

desecrat|e /'desɪkreɪt/ *vt* profanare. **~ion** /-'kreɪʃn/ *n* profanazione *f*

desert[1] /'dezət/ *n* deserto *m* ●*a* deserto; **~ island** isola *f* deserta

desert[2] /dɪ'zɜ:t/ *vt* abbandonare ●*vi* disertare. **~ed** a deserto. **~er** *n* *Mil* disertore *m*. **~ion** /-'zɜ:ʃn/ *n* *Mil* diserzione *f*; ⟨*of family*⟩ abbandono *m*

deserts /dɪ'zɜ:ts/ *npl* **get one's just ~** ottenere ciò che ci si merita

deserv|e /dɪ'zɜ:v/ *vt* meritare. **~ing** *a* meritevole; **~ing cause** opera *f* meritoria

design /dɪ'zaɪn/ *n* progettazione *f*; ⟨*fashion ~, appearance*⟩ design *m inv*; ⟨*pattern*⟩ modello *m*; ⟨*aim*⟩ proposito *m* ●*vt* progettare; disegnare ⟨*clothes, furniture, models*⟩; **be ~ed for** essere fatto per

designat|e /'dezɪgneɪt/ *vt* designare. **~ion** /-'neɪʃn/ *n* designazione *f*

designer /dɪ'zaɪnə(r)/ *n* progettista *mf*; ⟨*of clothes*⟩ stilista *mf*; ⟨*Theat: of set*⟩ scenografo, -a *mf*

desirable /dɪ'zaɪərəbl/ *a* desiderabile

desire /dɪ'zaɪə(r)/ *n* desiderio *m* ●*vt* desiderare

desk /desk/ *n* scrivania *f*; ⟨*in school*⟩ banco *m*; ⟨*in hotel*⟩ reception *f inv*; ⟨*cash ~*⟩ cassa *f*. **~top 'publishing** *n* desktop publishing *m*, editoria *f* da tavolo

desolat|e /'desələt/ *a* desolato. **~ion** /-'leɪʃn/ *n* desolazione *f*

despair /dɪ'speə(r)/ *n* disperazione *f*; **in ~** disperato; ⟨*say*⟩ per disperazione ●*vi* **I ~ of that boy** quel ragazzo mi fa disperare

desperat|e /'despərət/ *a* disperato; **be ~e** ⟨*criminal:*⟩ essere un disperato; **be ~e for sth** morire dalla voglia di. **~ely** *adv* disperatamente; **he said ~ely** ha detto, disperato. **~ion** /-'reɪʃn/ *n* disperazione *f*; **in ~ion** per disperazione

despicable /dɪ'spɪkəbl/ *a* disprezzevole

despise /dɪ'spaɪz/ *vt* disprezzare

despite /dɪ'spaɪt/ *prep* malgrado

despondent /dɪ'spɒndənt/ *a* abbattuto

despot /'despɒt/ *n* despota *m*

dessert /dɪ'zɜ:t/ *n* dolce *m*. **~ spoon** *n* cucchiaio *m* da dolce

destination /destɪ'neɪʃn/ *n* destinazione *f*

destine /'destɪn/ *vt* destinare; **be ~d for sth** essere destinato a qcsa

destiny /'destɪnɪ/ *n* destino *m*

destitute /'destɪtju:t/ *a* bisognoso

destroy /dɪ'strɔɪ/ *vt* distruggere. **~er** *n* *Naut* cacciatorpediniere *m*

destruc|tion /dɪ'strʌkʃn/ *n* distruzione *f*. **~tive** /-tɪv/ *a* distruttivo; ⟨*fig: criticism*⟩ negativo

detach /dɪ'tætʃ/ *vt* staccare. **~able** /-əbl/ *a* separabile. **~ed** *a fig* distaccato; **~ed house** villetta *f*

detachment /dɪ'tætʃmənt/ *n* distacco *m*; *Mil* distaccamento *m*

detail /'di:teɪl/ *n* particolare *m*, dettaglio *m*; **in ~** particolareggiatamente ●*vt* esporre con tutti i particolari; *Mil* assegnare. **~ed** *a* particolareggiato, dettagliato

detain /dɪ'teɪn/ *vt* ⟨*police:*⟩ trattenere; ⟨*delay*⟩ far ritardare. **~ee** /dɪtɪ'ni:/ *n* detenuto, -a *mf*

detect /dɪ'tekt/ *vt* individuare;

(*perceive*) percepire. **~ion** /-'ekʃn/ *n* scoperta *f*

detective /dɪ'tektɪv/ *n* investigatore, -trice *mf*. **~ story** *n* racconto *m* poliziesco

detector /dɪ'tektə(r)/ *n* (*for metal*) metal detector *m inv*

detention /dɪ'tenʃn/ *n* detenzione *f*; *Sch* punizione *f*

deter /dɪ'tɜ:(r)/ *vt* (*pt/pp* **deterred**) impedire; **~ sb from doing sth** impedire a qcno di fare qcsa

detergent /dɪ'tɜ:dʒənt/ *n* detersivo *m*

deteriorat|e /dɪ'tɪərɪəreɪt/ *vi* deteriorarsi. **~ion** /-'reɪʃn/ *n* deterioramento *m*

determination /dɪtɜ:mɪ'neɪʃn/ *n* determinazione *f*

determine /dɪ'tɜ:mɪn/ *vt* (*ascertain*) determinare; **~ to** (*resolve*) decidere di. **~d** *a* deciso

deterrent /dɪ'terənt/ *n* deterrente *m*

detest /dɪ'test/ *vt* detestare. **~able** /-əbl/ *a* detestabile

detonat|e /'detəneɪt/ *vt* far detonare ● *vi* detonare. **~or** *n* detonatore *m*

detour /'di:toə(r)/ *n* deviazione *f*

detract /dɪ'trækt/ *vi* **~ from** sminuire (*merit*); rovinare (*pleasure, beauty*)

detriment /'detrɪmənt/ *n* **to the ~ of** a danno di. **~al** /-'mentl/ *a* dannoso

deuce /dju:s/ *n Tennis* deuce *m inv*

devaluation /di:vælju'eɪʃn/ *n* svalutazione *f*

de'value *vt* svalutare (*currency*)

devastat|e /'devəsteɪt/ *vt* devastare. **~ed** *a fam* sconvolto. **~ing** *a* devastante; (*news*) sconvolgente. **~ion** /-'steɪʃn/ *n* devastazione *f*

develop /dɪ'veləp/ *vt* sviluppare; contrarre (*illness*); (*add to value of*) valorizzare (*area*) ● *vi* svilupparsi; **~ into** divenire. **~er** *n* [**property**] **~er** imprenditore, -trice *mf* edile

de'veloping country *n* paese *m* in via di sviluppo

development /dɪ'veləpmənt/ *n* sviluppo *m*; (*of vaccine etc*) messa *f* a punto

deviant /'di:vɪənt/ *a* deviato

deviat|e /'di:vɪeɪt/ *vi* deviare. **~ion** /-'eɪʃn/ *n* deviazione *f*

device /dɪ'vaɪs/ *n* dispositivo *m*

devil /'devl/ *n* diavolo *m*

devious /'di:vɪəs/ *a* (*person*) subdolo; (*route*) tortuoso

devise /dɪ'vaɪz/ *vt* escogitare

devoid /dɪ'vɔɪd/ *a* **~ of** privo di

devolution /di:və'lu:ʃn/ *n* (*of power*) decentramento *m*

devot|e /dɪ'vəʊt/ *vt* dedicare. **~ed** *a* (*daughter etc*) affezionato; **be ~ed to sth** consacrarsi a qcsa. **~ee** /devə'ti:/ *n* appassionato, -a *mf*

devotion /dɪ'vəʊʃn/ *n* dedizione *f*; **~s** *pl Relig* devozione *fsg*

devour /dɪ'vaʊə(r)/ *vt* divorare

devout /dɪ'vaʊt/ *a* devoto

dew /dju:/ *n* rugiada *f*

dexterity /dek'sterəti/ *n* destrezza *f*

diabet|es /daɪə'bi:ti:z/ *n* diabete *m*. **~ic** /-'betɪk/ *a* diabetico ● *n* diabetico, -a *mf*

diabolical /daɪə'bɒlɪkl/ *a* diabolico

diagnose /daɪəg'nəʊz/ *vt* diagnosticare

diagnosis /daɪəg'nəʊsɪs/ *n* (*pl* **-oses** /-si:z/) diagnosi *f inv*

diagonal /daɪ'ægənl/ *a* diagonale ● *n* diagonale *f*

diagram /'daɪəgræm/ *n* diagramma *m*

dial /'daɪəl/ *n* (*of clock, machine*) quadrante *m*; *Teleph* disco *m* combinatore ● *v* (*pt/pp* **dialled**) ● *vi Teleph* fare il numero; **~ direct** chiamare in teleselezione ● *vt* fare (*number*)

dialect /'daɪəlekt/ *n* dialetto *m*

dialling: **~ code** *n* prefisso *m*. **~ tone** *n* segnale *m* di linea libera

dialogue /'daɪəlɒg/ *n* dialogo *m*

'dial tone *n Am Teleph* segnale *m* di linea libera

diameter /daɪ'æmɪtə(r)/ *n* diametro *m*

diametrically /daɪə'metrɪklɪ/ *adv* **~ opposed** diametralmente opposto

diamond /'daɪəmənd/ *n* diamante *m*, brillante *m*; (*shape*) losanga *f*; **~s** *pl* (*in cards*) quadri *mpl*

diaper /'daɪəpə(r)/ *n Am* pannolino *m*

diaphragm /'daɪəfræm/ *n* diaframma *m*

diarrhoea /daɪə'ri:ə/ *n* diarrea *f*

diary /'daɪərɪ/ *n* (*for appointments*) agenda *f*; (*for writing in*) diario *m*

dice /daɪs/ *n inv* dadi *mpl* ● *vt Culin* tagliare a dadini

dicey /'daɪsɪ/ *a fam* rischioso

dictat|e /dɪk'teɪt/ *vt/i* dettare. **~ion** /-eɪʃn/ *n* dettato *m*

dictator /dɪk'teɪtə(r)/ *n* dittatore *m*. **~ial** /-tə'tɔ:rɪəl/ *a* dittatoriale. **~ship** *n* dittatura *f*

dictionary /'dɪkʃənrɪ/ *n* dizionario *m*

did /dɪd/ *see* **do**

didactic /dɪ'dæktɪk/ *a* didattico

diddle /'dɪdl/ *vt fam* gabbare

didn't /'dɪdnt/ = **did not**

die /daɪ/ *vi* (*pres p* **dying**) morire (**of** di); **be dying to do sth** *fam* morire dalla voglia di fare qcsa. **die down** *vi* calmarsi; *(fire, flames:)* spegnersi. **die out** *vi* estinguersi; *(custom:)* morire

diesel /'di:zl/ *n* diesel *m*

diet /'daɪət/ *n* regime *m* alimentare; *(restricted)* dieta *f*: **be on a ~** essere a dieta ● *vi* essere a dieta

differ /'dɪfə(r)/ *vi* differire; *(disagree)* non essere d'accordo

difference /'dɪfrəns/ *n* differenza *f*; *(disagreement)* divergenza *f*

different /'dɪfrənt/ *a* diverso, differente; *(various)* diversi: **be ~ from** essere diverso da

differential /dɪfə'renʃl/ *a* differenziale ● *n* differenziale *m*

differentiate /dɪfə'renʃɪeɪt/ *vt* distinguere **(between** fra); *(discriminate)* discriminare **(between** fra); *(make differ)* differenziare

differently /'dɪfrəntlɪ/ *adv* in modo diverso; **~ from** diversamente da

difficult /'dɪfɪkəlt/ *a* difficile. **~y** *n* difficoltà *f inv*: **with ~y** con difficoltà

diffuse[1] /dɪ'fju:s/ *a* diffuso; *(wordy)* prolisso

diffuse[2] /dɪ'fju:z/ *vt* Phys diffondere

dig /dɪg/ *n (poke)* spinta *f*; *(remark)* frecciata *f*; Archaeol scavo *m*; **~s** *pl fam* camera *fsg* ammobiliata ● *vt/i (pt/pp* **dug,** *pres p* **digging)** scavare *(hole)*; vangare *(garden)*; *(thrust)* conficcare: **~ sb in the ribs** dare una gomitata a qcno. **dig out** *vt fig* tirar fuori. **dig up** *vt* scavare *(garden, street, object)*; sradicare *(tree, plant)*; *(fig: find)* scovare

digest[1] /'daɪdʒest/ *n* compendio *m*

digest[2] /daɪ'dʒest/ *vt* digerire. **~ible** *a* digeribile. **~ion** /-estʃn/ *n* digestione *f*

digger /'dɪgə(r)/ *n Techn* scavatrice *f*

digit /'dɪdʒɪt/ *n* cifra *f*; *(finger)* dito *m*

digital /'dɪdʒɪtl/ *a* digitale; **~ clock** orologio *m* digitale

dignified /'dɪgnɪfaɪd/ *a* dignitoso

dignitary /'dɪgnɪtərɪ/ *n* dignitario *m*

dignity /'dɪgnɪtɪ/ *n* dignità *f*

digress /daɪ'gres/ *vi* divagare. **~ion** /-eʃn/ *n* digressione *f*

dike /daɪk/ *n* diga *f*

dilapidated /dɪ'læpɪdeɪtɪd/ *a* cadente

dilate /daɪ'leɪt/ *vi* dilatarsi

dilemma /dɪ'lemə/ *n* dilemma *m*

dilettante /dɪlɪ'tæntɪ/ *n* dilettante *mf*

dilly-dally /'dɪlɪdælɪ/ *vi (pt/pp* **-ied)** *fam* tentennare

dilute /daɪ'lu:t/ *vt* diluire

dim /dɪm/ *a* **(dimmer, dimmest)** debole *(light)*; *(dark)* scuro; *(prospect,*

chance) scarso; *(indistinct)* impreciso; *(fam: stupid)* tonto ● *vt/i (pt/pp* **dimmed)** affievolire. **~ly** *adv (see, remember)* indistintamente; *(shine)* debolmente

dime /daɪm/ *n Am* moneta *f* da dieci centesimi

dimension /daɪ'menʃn/ *n* dimensione *f*

diminish /dɪ'mɪnɪʃ/ *vt/i* diminuire

diminutive /dɪ'mɪnjʊtɪv/ *a* minuscolo ● *n* diminutivo *m*

dimple /'dɪmpl/ *n* fossetta *f*

din /dɪn/ *n* baccano *m*

dine /daɪn/ *vi* pranzare. **~r** *n (Am: restaurant)* tavola *f* calda; **the last ~r in the restaurant** l'ultimo cliente nel ristorante

dinghy /'dɪŋgɪ/ *n* dinghy *m*; *(inflatable)* canotto *m* pneumatico

dingy /'dɪndʒɪ/ *a* **(-ier, -iest)** squallido e tetro

dining /'daɪnɪŋ/: **~-car** *n* carrozza *f* ristorante. **~-room** *n* sala *f* da pranzo. **~-table** *n* tavolo *m* da pranzo

dinner /'dɪnə(r)/ *n* cena *f*; *(at midday)* pranzo *m*. **~-jacket** *n* smoking *m*

dinosaur /'daɪnəsɔ:(r)/ *n* dinosauro *m*

dint /dɪnt/ *n* **by ~ of** a forza di

diocese /'daɪəsɪs/ *n* diocesi *f inv*

dip /dɪp/ *n (in ground)* inclinazione *f*; *Culin* salsina *f*; **go for a ~** andare a fare una nuotata ● *v (pt/pp* **dipped)** ● *vt (in liquid)* immergere; abbassare *(head, headlights)* ● *vi (land:)* formare un avvallamento. **dip into** *vt* scorrere *(book)*

diphtheria /dɪf'θɪərɪə/ *n* difterite *f*

diphthong /'dɪfθɒŋ/ *n* dittongo *m*

diploma /dɪ'pləʊmə/ *n* diploma *m*

diplomacy /dɪ'pləʊməsɪ/ *n* diplomazia *f*

diplomat /'dɪpləmæt/ *n* diplomatico, -a *mf*. **~ic** /-'mætɪk/ *a* diplomatico. **~ically** *adv* con diplomazia

'dip-stick *n Auto* astina *f* dell'olio

dire /'daɪə(r)/ *a (situation, consequences)* terribile

direct /dɪ'rekt/ *a* diretto ● *adv* direttamente ● *vt (aim)* rivolgere *(attention, criticism)*; *(control)* dirigere; fare la regia di *(film, play)*; **~ sb** *(show the way)* indicare la strada a qcno; **~ sb to do sth** ordinare a qcno di fare qcsa. **~ 'current** *n* corrente *m* continua

direction /dɪ'rekʃn/ *n* direzione *f*; *(of play, film)* regia *f*; **~s** *pl* indicazioni *fpl*

directly /dɪ'rektlɪ/ *adv* direttamente; *(at once)* immediatamente ● *conj* [non] appena

director /dɪˈrektə(r)/ n Comm direttore, -trice mf; (of play, film) regista mf

directory /dɪˈrektərɪ/ n elenco m; Teleph elenco m [telefonico]; (of streets) stradario m

dirt /dɜːt/ n sporco m; ~ **cheap** fam a [un] prezzo stracciato

dirty /ˈdɜːtɪ/ a (-ier, -iest) sporco; ~ **trick** brutto scherzo m; ~ **word** parolaccia f ● vt (pt/pp -ied) sporcare

dis|**a**|**bility** /dɪs-/ n infermità f inv. ~**abled** /dɪˈseɪbld/ a invalido

disad|**van**|**tage** n svantaggio m; **at a** ~**tage** in una posizione di svantaggio. ~**taged** a svantaggiato. ~**tageous** a svantaggioso

disa|**gree** vi non essere d'accordo; ~ **with** (food:) far male a

disa|**greeable** a sgradevole

disa|**greement** n disaccordo m; (quarrel) dissidio m

disal|**low** vt annullare (goal)

disap|**pear** vi scomparire. ~**ance** n scomparsa f

disap|**point** vt deludere; **I'm** ~**ed** sono deluso. ~**ing** a deludente. ~**ment** n delusione f

disap|**proval** n disapprovazione f

disap|**prove** vi disapprovare; ~ **of sb/sth** disapprovare qcno/qcsa

dis|**arm** vt disarmare ● vi Mil disarmarsi. ~**ament** n disarmo m. ~**ing** a (frankness etc) disarmante

disar|**ray** n **in** ~ in disordine

disast|**er** /dɪˈzɑːstə(r)/ n disastro m. ~**rous** /-rəs/ a disastroso

dis|**band** vt sciogliere; smobilitare (troops) ● vi sciogliersi; (regiment:) essere smobilitato

disbe|**lief** n incredulità f; **in** ~ con incredulità

disc /dɪsk/ n disco m; (CD) compact disc m inv

discard /dɪˈskɑːd/ vt scartare; (throw away) eliminare; scaricare (boyfriend)

discern /dɪˈsɜːn/ vt discernere. ~**ible** a discernibile. ~**ing** a perspicace

discharge[1] n Electr scarica f; (dismissal) licenziamento m; Mil congedo m; (Med: of blood) emissione f; (of cargo) scarico m

dis|**charge**[2] vt scaricare (battery, cargo); (dismiss) licenziare; Mil congedare; Jur assolvere (accused); dimettere (patient) ● vi Electr scaricarsi

disciple /dɪˈsaɪpl/ n discepolo m

disciplinary /ˈdɪsɪplɪnərɪ/ a disciplinare

discipline /ˈdɪsɪplɪn/ n disciplina f ● vt disciplinare; (punish) punire

disc jockey n disc jockey m inv

dis|**claim** vt disconoscere. ~**er** n rifiuto m

dis|**clos**|**e** vt svelare. ~**ure** n rivelazione f

disco /ˈdɪskəʊ/ n discoteca f

dis|**colour** vt scolorire ● vi scolorirsi

dis|**comfort** n scomodità f, fig disagio m

disconcert /dɪskənˈsɜːt/ vt sconcertare

discon|**nect** vt disconnettere

disconsolate /dɪsˈkɒnsələt/ a sconsolato

discon|**tent** n scontentezza f. ~**ed** a scontento

discon|**tinue** vt cessare, smettere; Comm sospendere la produzione di; ~**d line** fine f serie

discord n discordia f; Mus dissonanza f. ~**ant** /dɪˈskɔːdənt/ a ~**ant note** nota f discordante

discothèque /ˈdɪskətek/ n discoteca f

discount[1] n sconto m

dis|**count**[1] vt (not believe) non credere a; (leave out of consideration) non tener conto di

dis|**courage** vt scoraggiare; (dissuade) dissuadere

discourse n discorso m

dis|**courteous** a scortese

discover /dɪˈskʌvə(r)/ vt scoprire. ~**y** n scoperta f

dis|**credit** n discredito m ● vt (pt/pp discredited) screditare

discreet /dɪˈskriːt/ a discreto

discrepancy /dɪˈskrepənsɪ/ n discrepanza f

discretion /dɪˈskreʃn/ n discrezione f

discriminat|**e** /dɪˈskrɪmɪneɪt/ vi discriminare (**against** contro); ~**e between** distinguere tra. ~**ing** a esigente. ~**ion** /-ˈneɪʃn/ n discriminazione f; (quality) discernimento m

discus /ˈdɪskəs/ n disco m

discuss /dɪˈskʌs/ vt discutere; (examine critically) esaminare. ~**ion** /-ˈʌʃn/ n discussione f

disdain /dɪsˈdeɪn/ n sdegno f ● vt sdegnare. ~**ful** a sdegnoso

disease /dɪˈziːz/ n malattia f. ~**d** a malato

disem|**bark** vi sbarcare

disen|**chant** vt disincantare. ~**ment** n disincanto m

disen|**gage** vt disimpegnare; disinnestare (clutch)

disen'tangle vt districare

dis'favour n sfavore m

dis'figure vt deformare

dis'grace n vergogna f; **I am in ~** sono caduto in disgrazia; **it's a ~** è una vergogna ● vt disonorare. **~ful** a vergognoso

disgruntled /dɪsˈɡrʌntld/ a malcontento

disguise /dɪsˈɡaɪz/ n travestimento m; **in ~** travestito ● vt contraffare ⟨voice⟩; dissimulare ⟨emotions⟩; **~d as** travestito da

disgust /dɪsˈɡʌst/ n disgusto m; **in ~** con aria disgustata ● vt disgustare. **~ing** a disgustoso

dish /dɪʃ/ n piatto m; **do the ~es** lavare i piatti ● **dish out** vt ⟨serve⟩ servire; ⟨distribute⟩ distribuire. **dish up** vt servire

'dishcloth n strofinaccio m

dis'hearten vt scoraggiare

dishevelled /dɪˈʃevld/ a scompigliato

dis'honest a disonesto. **~y** n disonestà f

dis'honour n disonore m ● vt disonorare ⟨family⟩; non onorare ⟨cheque⟩. **~able** a disonorevole. **~ably** adv in modo disonorevole

'dishwasher n lavapiatti f inv

disil'lusion vt disilludere. **~ment** n disillusione f

disin'fect vt disinfettare. **~ant** n disinfettante m

disin'herit vt diseredare

dis'integrate vi disintegrarsi

dis'interested a disinteressato

dis'jointed a sconnesso

disk /dɪsk/ n Comput disco m; ⟨diskette⟩ dischetto m

dis'like n avversione f; **your likes and ~s** i tuoi gusti ● vt **I ~ him/it** non mi piace; **I don't ~ him/it** non mi dispiace

dislocate /ˈdɪsləkeɪt/ vt slogare; **~ one's shoulder** slogarsi una spalla

dis'lodge vt sloggiare

dis'loyal a sleale. **~ty** n slealtà f

dismal /ˈdɪzml/ a ⟨person⟩ abbacchiato; ⟨news, weather⟩ deprimente; ⟨performance⟩ mediocre

dismantle /dɪsˈmæntl/ vt smontare ⟨tent, machine⟩; fig smantellare

dis'may n sgomento m. **~ed** a sgomento

dis'miss vt licenziare ⟨employee⟩; ⟨reject⟩ scartare ⟨idea, suggestion⟩. **~al** n licenziamento m

dis'mount vi smontare

diso'bedien|ce n disubbidienza f. **~t** a disubbidiente

diso'bey vt disubbidire a ⟨rule⟩ ● vi disubbidire

dis'order n disordine m; Med disturbo m. **~ly** a disordinato; ⟨crowd⟩ turbolento; **~ly conduct** turbamento m della quiete pubblica

dis'organized a disorganizzato

dis'orientate vt disorientare

dis'own vt disconoscere

disparaging /dɪˈspærɪdʒɪŋ/ a sprezzante

disparity /dɪˈspærətɪ/ n disparità f inv

dispassionate /dɪsˈpæʃənət/ a spassionato

dispatch /dɪˈspætʃ/ n Comm spedizione f; ⟨Mil, report⟩ dispaccio m; **with ~** con prontezza ● vt spedire; ⟨kill⟩ spedire al creatore

dispel /dɪˈspel/ vt (pt/pp **dispelled**) dissipare

dispensable /dɪˈspensəbl/ a dispensabile

dispensary /dɪˈspensərɪ/ n farmacia f

dispense /dɪˈspens/ vt distribuire; **~ with** fare a meno di; **dispensing chemist** farmacista mf; ⟨shop⟩ farmacia f. **~r** n ⟨device⟩ distributore m

dispers|al /dɪˈspɜːsl/ n dispersione f. **~e** /dɪˈspɜːs/ vt disperdere ● vi disperdersi

dispirited /dɪˈspɪrɪtɪd/ a scoraggiato

dis'place vt spostare; **~d person** profugo, -a mf

display /dɪˈspleɪ/ n mostra f; Comm esposizione f; ⟨of feelings⟩ manifestazione f; pej ostentazione f; Comput display m inv ● vt mostrare; esporre ⟨goods⟩; manifestare ⟨feelings⟩; Comput visualizzare

dis'please vt non piacere a; **be ~d with** essere scontento di

dis'pleasure n malcontento m

disposable /dɪˈspəʊzəbl/ a ⟨throwaway⟩ usa e getta; ⟨income⟩ disponibile

disposal /dɪˈspəʊzl/ n ⟨getting rid of⟩ eliminazione f; **be at sb's ~** essere a disposizione di qcno

dispose /dɪˈspəʊz/ vi **~ of** ⟨get rid of⟩ disfarsi di; **be well ~d** essere ben disposto (**to** verso)

disposition /dɪspəˈzɪʃn/ n disposizione f; ⟨nature⟩ indole f

disproportionate /dɪsprəˈpɔːʃənət/ a sproporzionato

dis'prove vt confutare

dispute /dɪˈspjuːt/ n disputa f;

(industrial) contestazione *f* ● *vt* contestare *(statement)*

disqualifi'cation *n* squalifica *f*; *(from driving)* ritiro *m* della patente

dis'qualify *vt* *(pt/pp* **-ied)** escludere; *Sport* squalificare; ~ **sb from driving** ritirare la patente a qcno

disquieting /dɪs'kwaɪətɪŋ/ *a* allarmante

disre'gard *n* mancanza *f* di considerazione ● *vt* ignorare

disre'pair *n* **fall into** ~ deteriorarsi; **in a state of** ~ in cattivo stato

dis'reputable *a* malfamato

disre'pute *n* discredito *m*; **bring sb into** ~ rovinare la reputazione a qcno

disre'spect *n* mancanza *f* di rispetto. ~**ful** *a* irrispettoso

disrupt /dɪs'rʌpt/ *vt* creare scompiglio in; sconvolgere *(plans)*. ~**ion** /-ʌpʃn/ *n* scompiglio *m*; *(of plans)* sconvolgimento *m*. ~**ive** /-tɪv/ *a (person, behaviour)* indisciplinato

dissatis'faction *n* malcontento *m*

dis'satisfied *a* scontento

dissect /dɪ'sekt/ *vt* sezionare. ~**ion** /-ekʃn/ *n* dissezione *f*

dissent /dɪ'sent/ *n* dissenso *m* ● *vi* dissentire

dissertation /dɪsə'teɪʃn/ *n* tesi *f inv*

dis'service *n* **do sb/oneself a** ~ rendere un cattivo servizio a qcno/se stesso

dissident /'dɪsɪdənt/ *n* dissidente *mf*

dis'similar *a* dissimile **(to** da)

dissociate /dɪ'səʊʃɪeɪt/ *vt* dissociare; ~ **oneself from** dissociarsi da

dissolute /'dɪsəluːt/ *a* dissoluto

dissolution /dɪsə'luːʃn/ *n* scioglimento *m*

dissolve /dɪ'zɒlv/ *vt* dissolvere ● *vi* dissolversi

dissuade /dɪ'sweɪd/ *vt* dissuadere

distance /'dɪstəns/ *n* distanza *f*; **it's a short** ~ **from here to the station** la stazione non è lontana da qui; **in the** ~ in lontananza; **from a** ~ da lontano

distant /'dɪstənt/ *a* distante; *(relative)* lontano

dis'taste *n* avversione *f*. ~**ful** *a* spiacevole

distil /dɪ'stɪl/ *vt* *(pt/pp* **distilled)** distillare. ~**lation** /-'leɪʃn/ *n* distillazione *f*. ~**lery** /-ərɪ/ *n* distilleria *f*

distinct /dɪ'stɪŋkt/ *a* chiaro; *(different)* distinto. ~**ion** /ɪŋkʃn/ *n* distinzione *f*; *Sch* massimo *m* dei voti. ~**ive** /-tɪv/ *a* caratteristico. ~**ly** *adv* chiaramente

distinguish /dɪ'stɪŋgwɪʃ/ *vt/i* distin-

guere; ~ **oneself** distinguersi. ~**ed** *a* rinomato; *(appearance)* distinto; *(career)* brillante

distort /dɪ'stɔːt/ *vt* distorcere. ~**ion** /-ɔːʃn/ *n* distorsione *f*

distract /dɪ'strækt/ *vt* distrarre. ~**ed** /-ɪd/ *a* assente; *(fam: worried)* preoccupato. ~**ing** *a* che distoglie. ~**ion** /-ækʃn/ *n* distrazione *f*; *(despair)* disperazione *f*; **drive sb to** ~ portare qcno alla disperazione

distraught /dɪ'strɔːt/ *a* sconvolto

distress /dɪ'stres/ *n* angoscia *f*; *(pain)* sofferenza *f*; *(danger)* difficoltà *f* ● *vt* sconvolgere; *(sadden)* affliggere. ~**ing** *a* penoso; *(shocking)* sconvolgente. ~ **signal** *n* segnale *m* di richiesta di soccorso

distribute /dɪ'strɪbjuːt/ *vt* distribuire. ~**ion** /-'bjuːʃn/ *n* distribuzione *f*. ~**or** *n* distributore *m*

district /'dɪstrɪkt/ *n* regione *f*; *Admin* distretto *m*. ~ **nurse** *n* infermiere, -a *mf* che fa visite a domicilio

dis'trust *n* sfiducia *f* ● *vt* non fidarsi di. ~**ful** *a* diffidente

disturb /dɪ'stɜːb/ *vt* disturbare; *(emotionally)* turbare; spostare *(papers)*. ~**ance** *n* disturbo *m*; ~**ances** *(pl: rioting etc)* disordini *mpl*. ~**ed** *a* turbato; *(mentally)* ~**ed** malato di mente. ~**ing** *a* inquietante

dis'used *a* non utilizzato

ditch /dɪtʃ/ *n* fosso *m* ● *vt (fam: abandon)* abbandonare *(plan, car)*; piantare *(lover)*

dither /'dɪðə(r)/ *vi* titubare

divan /dɪ'væn/ *n* divano *m*

dive /daɪv/ *n* tuffo *m*; *Aeron* picchiata *f*; *(fam: place)* bettola *f* ● *vi* tuffarsi; *(when in water)* immergersi; *Aeron* scendere in picchiata; *(fam: rush)* precipitarsi

diver /'daɪvə(r)/ *n* *(from board)* tuffatore, -trice *mf*; *(scuba)* sommozzatore, -trice *mf*; *(deep sea)* palombaro *m*

diverge /daɪ'vɜːdʒ/ *vi* divergere. ~**gent** /-ənt/ *a* divergente

diverse /daɪ'vɜːs/ *a* vario

diversify /daɪ'vɜːsɪfaɪ/ *vt/i* *(pt/pp* **-ied)** diversificare

diversion /daɪ'vɜːʃn/ *n* deviazione *f*; *(distraction)* diversivo *m*

diversity /daɪ'vɜːsətɪ/ *n* varietà *f*

divert /daɪ'vɜːt/ *vt* deviare *(traffic)*; distogliere *(attention)*

divest /daɪ'vest/ *vt* privare **(of** di)

divide /dɪˈvaɪd/ vt dividere (**by** per); **six ~d by two** sei diviso due ● vi dividersi

dividend /ˈdɪvɪdend/ n dividendo m; **pay ~s** fig ripagare

divine /dɪˈvaɪn/ a divino

diving /ˈdaɪvɪŋ/ n (from board) tuffi mpl; (scuba) immersione f. **~-board** n trampolino m. **~ mask** n maschera f [subacquea]. **~-suit** n muta f; (deep sea) scafandro m

divinity /dɪˈvɪnətɪ/ n divinità f inv; (subject) teologia f; (at school) religione f

divisible /dɪˈvɪzɪbl/ a divisibile (**by** per)

division /dɪˈvɪʒn/ n divisione f; (in sports league) serie f

divorce /dɪˈvɔːs/ n divorzio m ● vt divorziare da. **~d** a divorziato; **get ~d** divorziare

divorcee /dɪvɔːˈsiː/ n divorziato, -a mf

divulge /daɪˈvʌldʒ/ vt rendere pubblico

DIY n abbr do-it-yourself

dizziness /ˈdɪzɪnɪs/ n giramenti mpl di testa

dizzy /ˈdɪzɪ/ a (-ier, -iest) vertiginoso; **I feel ~** mi gira la testa

do /duː/ n (pl dos or do's) fam festa f ● v (3 sg pres tense **does**; pt did; pp **done**) ● vt fare; (fam: cheat) fregare; **be done** Culin essere cotto; **well done** bravo; Culin ben cotto; **do the flowers** sistemare i fiori; **do the washing up** lavare i piatti; **do one's hair** farsi i capelli ● vi (be suitable) andare; (be enough) bastare; **this will do** questo va bene; **that will do!** basta così!; **do well/badly** cavarsela bene/male; **how is he doing?** come sta? ● v aux **do you speak Italian?** parli italiano?; **you don't like him, do you?** non ti piace, vero?; (expressing astonishment) non dirmi che ti piace!; **yes, I do** sì; (emphatic) invece sì; **no, I don't** no, non mi piace; **I don't smoke** non fumo; **don't you/doesn't he?** vero?; **so do I** anch'io; **come in, John** entra, John; **how do you do?** piacere. **do away with** vt abolire (rule). **do for** vt **done for** fam rovinato. **do in** vt (fam: kill) uccidere; farsi male a (back); **done in** fam esausto. **do up** vt (fasten) abbottonare; (renovate) rimettere a nuovo; (wrap) avvolgere. **do with** vt **I could do with a spanner** mi ci vorrebbe una chiave inglese. **do without** vt fare a meno di

docile /ˈdəʊsaɪl/ a docile

dock¹ /dɒk/ n Jur banco m degli imputati

dock² n Naut bacino m ● vi entrare in porto; (spaceship:) congiungersi. **~er** n portuale m. **~s** npl porto m. **~yard** n cantiere m navale

doctor /ˈdɒktə(r)/ n dottore m, dottoressa f ● vt alterare (drink); castrare (cat). **~ate** /-ət/ n dottorato m

doctrine /ˈdɒktrɪn/ n dottrina f

document /ˈdɒkjʊmənt/ n documento m. **~ary** /-ˈmentərɪ/ a documentario ● n documentario m

doddery /ˈdɒdərɪ/ a fam barcollante

dodge /dɒdʒ/ n fam trucco m ● vt schivare (blow); evitare (person) ● vi scansarsi; **~ out of the way** scansarsi

dodgems /ˈdɒdʒəmz/ npl auto-scontro msg

dodgy /ˈdɒdʒɪ/ a (-ier, -iest) (fam: dubious) sospetto

doe /dəʊ/ n femmina f (di daino, renna, lepre); (rabbit) coniglia f

does /dʌz/ see do

doesn't /ˈdʌznt/ = does not

dog /dɒg/ n cane m ● vt (pt/pp **dogged**) (illness, bad luck:) perseguitare

dog: **~-biscuit** n biscotto m per cani. **~-collar** n collare m (per cani); Relig fam collare m del prete. **~-eared** a con le orecchie

dogged /ˈdɒgɪd/ a ostinato

'dog house n **in the ~** fam in disgrazia

dogma /ˈdɒgmə/ n dogma m. **~tic** /-ˈmætɪk/ a dogmatico

'dogsbody n fam tirapiedi mf inv

doily /ˈdɔɪlɪ/ n centrino m

do-it-yourself /duːɪtjəˈself/ n fai da te m, bricolage m. **~ shop** n negozio m di bricolage

doldrums /ˈdɒldrəmz/ npl **be in the ~** essere giù di corda; (business:) essere in fase di stasi

dole /dəʊl/ n sussidio m di disoccupazione; **be on the ~** essere disoccupato ● **dole out** vt distribuire

doleful /ˈdəʊlfl/ a triste

doll /dɒl/ n bambola f ● **doll oneself up** vt fam mettersi in ghingheri

dollar /ˈdɒlə(r)/ n dollaro m

dollop /ˈdɒləp/ n fam cucchiaiata f

dolphin /ˈdɒlfɪn/ n delfino m

dome /dəʊm/ n cupola f

domestic /dəˈmestɪk/ a domestico; Pol interno; Comm nazionale. **~ animal** n animale m domestico

domesticated /dəˈmestɪkeɪtɪd/ a (animal) addomesticato

domestic: ~ **flight** n volo m nazionale. ~ 'servant n domestico, -a mf

dominant /'dɒminənt/ a dominante

dominat|e /'dɒmineit/ vt/i dominare. ~ion /-'neiʃn/ n dominio m

domineering /dɒmi'niəriŋ/ a autoritario

dominion /də'minjən/ n Br Pol dominion m inv

domino /'dɒminəʊ/ n (pl -es) tessera f del domino; ~es sg (game) domino m

don[1] /dɒn/ vt (pt/pp donned) liter indossare

don[2] n docente mf universitario, -a

donat|e /dəʊ'neit/ vt donare. ~ion /-eiʃn/ n donazione f

done /dʌn/ see do

donkey /'dɒŋki/ n asino m; ~'s years fam secoli mpl. ~-work n sgobbata f

donor /'dəʊnə(r)/ n donatore, -trice mf

don't /dəʊnt/ = do not

doodle /'du:dl/ vi scarabocchiare

doom /du:m/ n fato m; (ruin) rovina f ● vt be ~ed [to failure] essere destinato al fallimento; ~ed (ship) destinato ad affondare

door /dɔ:(r)/ n porta f; (of car) portiera f; out of ~s all'aperto

door: ~man n portiere m. ~mat n zerbino m. ~step n gradino m della porta. ~way n vano m della porta

dope /dəʊp/ n fam (drug) droga f leggera; (information) indiscrezioni fpl; (idiot) idiota mf ● vt drogare; Sport dopare

dopey /'dəʊpi/ a fam addormentato

dormant /'dɔ:mənt/ a latente; (volcano) inattivo

dormer /'dɔ:mə(r)/ n ~ [window] abbaino m

dormitory /'dɔ:mitəri/ n dormitorio m

dormouse /'dɔ:-/ n ghiro m

dosage /'dəʊsidʒ/ n dosaggio m

dose /dəʊs/ n dose f

doss /dɒs/ vi sl accamparsi. ~er n barbone, -a mf. ~-house n dormitorio m pubblico

dot /dɒt/ n punto m; at 8 o'clock on the ~ alle 8 in punto

dote /dəʊt/ vi ~ on stravedere per

dotted /'dɒtid/ a ~ line linea f punteggiata; be ~ with essere punteggiato di

dotty /'dɒti/ a (-ier, -iest) fam tocco; (idea) folle

double /'dʌbl/ a doppio ● adv cost ~ costare il doppio; see ~ vedere doppio; ~ the amount la quantità doppia ● n doppio m; (person) sosia m inv; ~s pl

Tennis doppio m; at the ~ di corsa ● vt raddoppiare; (fold) piegare in due ● vi raddoppiare. **double back** vi (go back) fare dietro front. **double up** vi (bend over) piegarsi in due (with per); (share) dividere una stanza

double: ~-bass n contrabbasso m. ~ 'bed n letto m matrimoniale. ~-breasted a a doppio petto. ~ 'chin n doppio mento m. ~-'cross vt ingannare. ~-'decker n autobus m inv a due piani. ~ 'Dutch n fam ostrogoto m. ~ 'glazing n doppiovetro m. ~ 'room n camera f doppia

doubly /'dʌbli/ adv doppiamente

doubt /daʊt/ n dubbio m ● vt dubitare di. ~ful a dubbio; (having doubts) in dubbio. ~fully adv con aria dubbiosa. ~less adv indubbiamente

dough /dəʊ/ n pasta f; (for bread) impasto m; (fam: money) quattrini mpl. ~nut n bombolone m, krapfen m inv

douse /daʊs/ vt spegnere

dove /dʌv/ n colomba f. ~tail n Techn incastro m a coda di rondine

dowdy /'daʊdi/ a (-ier, -iest) trasandato

down[1] /daʊn/ n (feathers) piumino m

down[2] adv giù; go/come ~ scendere; ~ there laggiù; sales are ~ le vendite sono diminuite; **£50** ~ 50 sterline d'acconto; ~ **10%** ridotto del 10%; ~ with...! abbasso...! ● prep walk ~ the road camminare per strada; ~ the stairs giù per le scale; fall ~ the stairs cadere giù dalle scale; get that ~ you! fam butta giù!; be ~ the pub fam essere al pub ● vt bere tutto d'un fiato (drink)

down: ~-and-'out n spiantato, -a mf. ~cast a abbattuto. ~fall n caduta f; (of person) rovina f. ~-'grade vt (in seniority) degradare. ~-'hearted a scoraggiato. ~ hill adv in discesa; go ~hill fig essere in declino. ~ payment n deposito m. ~pour n acquazzone m. ~right a (absolute) totale; (lie) bell'e buono; (idiot) perfetto ● adv (completely) completamente. ~'stairs adv al piano di sotto ● a /'-/ del piano di sotto. ~'stream adv a valle. ~-to-'earth a (person) con i piedi per terra. ~town adv Am in centro. ~trodden a oppresso. ~ward[s] a verso il basso; (slope) in discesa ● adv verso il basso

dowry /'daʊri/ n dote f

doze /dəʊz/ n sonnellino m ● vi sonnecchiare. **doze off** vi assopirsi

dozen /'dʌzn/ n dozzina f; ~s of books libri a dozzine

Dr abbr doctor

drab /dræb/ a spento

draft¹ /drɑːft/ n abbozzo m; Comm cambiale f; Am Mil leva f ●vt abbozzare; Am Mil arruolare

draft² n Am = draught

drag /dræg/ n fam scocciatura f; in ~ fam (man) travestito da donna ●vt (pt/pp dragged) trascinare; dragare (river). **drag on** vi (time, meeting:) trascinarsi

dragon /'drægən/ n drago m. ~-fly n libellula f

drain /dreɪn/ n tubo m di scarico; (grid) tombino m; **the ~s** pl le fognature; **be a ~ on sb's finances** prosciugare le finanze di qcno ●vt drenare (land, wound); scolare (liquid, vegetables); svuotare (tank, glass, person) ●vi [away] andar via

drain|age /'dreɪnɪdʒ/ n (system) drenaggio m; (of land) scolo m. ~ing board n scolapiatti m inv. ~-pipe n tubo m di scarico

drake /dreɪk/ n maschio m dell'anatra

drama /'drɑːmə/ n arte f drammatica; (play) opera f teatrale; (event) dramma m

dramatic /drə'mætɪk/ a drammatico

dramat|ist /'dræmətɪst/ n drammaturgo, -a mf. ~ize vt adattare per il teatro; fig drammatizzare

drank /dræŋk/ see drink

drape /dreɪp/ n Am tenda f ●vt appoggiare (over su)

drastic /'dræstɪk/ a drastico; ~ally adv drasticamente

draught /drɑːft/ n corrente f [d'aria]; ~s sg (game) [gioco m della] dama fsg

draught: ~ **beer** n birra f alla spina. ~sman n disegnatore, -trice mf

draughty /'drɑːftɪ/ a pieno di correnti d'aria; **it's** ~ c'è corrente

draw /drɔː/ n (attraction) attrazione f; Sport pareggio m; (in lottery) sorteggio m ●v (pt drew, pp drawn) ●vt tirare; (attract) attirare; disegnare (picture); tracciare (line); ritirare (money); ~ lots tirare a sorte ●vi (tea:) essere in infusione; Sport pareggiare; ~ near avvicinarsi. **draw back** vt tirare indietro; ritirare (hand); tirare (curtains) ●vi (recoil) tirarsi indietro. **draw in** vt ritrarre (claws etc) ●vi (train:) arrivare; (days:) accorciarsi. **draw out** vt (pull out) tirar fuori; ritirare (money) ●vi

(train:) partire; (days:) allungarsi. **draw up** vt redigere (document); accostare (chair); ~ **oneself up to one's full height** farsi grande ●vi (stop) fermarsi

draw: ~back n inconveniente m. ~bridge n ponte m levatoio

drawer /drɔː(r)/ n cassetto m

drawing /'drɔːɪŋ/ n disegno m

drawing: ~-board n tavolo m da disegno; fig **go back to the ~-board** ricominciare da capo. ~-pin n puntina f. ~-room n salotto m

drawl /drɔːl/ n pronuncia f strascicata

drawn /drɔːn/ see draw

dread /dred/ n terrore m ●vt aver il terrore di

dreadful /'dredfʊl/ a terribile. ~ly adv terribilmente

dream /driːm/ n sogno m ●attrib di sogno ●vt/i (pt/pp dreamt /dremt/ or dreamed) sognare (**about/of** di)

dreary /'drɪərɪ/ a (-ier, -iest) tetro; (boring) monotono

dredge /dredʒ/ vt/i dragare

dregs /dregz/ npl feccia fsg

drench /drentʃ/ vt **get ~ed** inzupparsi; ~ed zuppo

dress /dres/ n (woman's) vestito m; (clothing) abbigliamento m ●vt vestire; (decorate) adornare; Culin condire; Med fasciare; ~ **oneself, get ~ed** vestirsi ●vi vestirsi. **dress up** vi mettersi elegante; (in disguise) travestirsi (**as** da)

dress: ~ **circle** n Theat prima galleria f. ~er n (furniture) credenza f; (Am: dressing-table) toilette f inv

dressing /'dresɪŋ/ n Culin condimento m; Med fasciatura f

dressing: ~-gown n vestaglia f. ~-room n (in gym) spogliatoio m; Theat camerino m. ~-table n toilette f inv

dress: ~maker n sarta f. ~ **rehearsal** n prova f generale

dressy /'dresɪ/ a (-ier, -iest) elegante

drew /druː/ see draw

dribble /'drɪbl/ vi gocciolare; (baby:) sbavare; Sport dribblare

dribs and drabs /drɪbzən'dræbz/ npl **in** ~ alla spicciolata

dried /draɪd/ a (food) essiccato

drier /'draɪə(r)/ n asciugabiancheria m inv

drift /drɪft/ n movimento m lento; (of snow) cumulo m; (meaning) senso m ●vi (off course) andare alla deriva; (snow:) accumularsi; (fig: person:) procedere senza meta. **drift apart** vi ⟨people:⟩ allontanarsi l'uno dall'altro

drill /drɪl/ n trapano m; Mil esercitazione f ● vt trapanare; Mil fare esercitare ● vi Mil esercitarsi; ~ **for oil** trivellare in cerca di petrolio

drily /'draɪlɪ/ adv seccamente

drink /drɪŋk/ n bevanda f; ⟨alcoholic⟩ bicchierino m; **have a** ~ bere qualcosa; **a** ~ **of water** un po' d'acqua ● vt/i (pt **drank**, pp **drunk**) bere. **drink up** vt finire ● vi finire il bicchiere

drink|able /'drɪŋkəbl/ a potabile. **~er** n bevitore, -trice mf

drinking-water n acqua f potabile

drip /drɪp/ n gocciolamento m; ⟨drop⟩ goccia f; Med flebo f inv; ⟨fam: person⟩ mollaccione, -a mf ● vi (pt/pp **dripped**) gocciolare. **~-'dry** a che non si stira. **~ping** n ⟨from meat⟩ grasso m d'arrosto ● a **~ping** [**wet**] fradicio

drive /draɪv/ n ⟨in car⟩ giro m; ⟨entrance⟩ viale m; ⟨energy⟩ grinta f; Psych pulsione f; ⟨organized effort⟩ operazione f; Techn motore m; Comput lettore m ● v (pt **drove**, pp **driven**) ● vt portare ⟨person by car⟩; guidare ⟨car⟩; ⟨Sport: hit⟩ mandare; Techn far funzionare; ~ **sb mad** far diventare matto qcno ● vi guidare. **drive at** vt **what are you driving at?** dove vuoi arrivare? **drive away** vt portare via in macchina; ⟨chase⟩ cacciare ● vi andare via in macchina. **drive in** vt piantare ⟨nail⟩ ● vi arrivare [in macchina]. **drive off** vt portare via in macchina; ⟨chase⟩ cacciare ● vi andare via in macchina. **drive on** vi proseguire ⟨in macchina⟩. **drive up** vi arrivare ⟨in macchina⟩

drivel /'drɪvl/ n fam sciocchezze fpl

driven /'drɪvn/ see **drive**

driver /'draɪvə(r)/ n guidatore, -trice mf; ⟨of train⟩ conducente mf

driving /'draɪvɪŋ/ a ⟨rain⟩ violento; ⟨force⟩ motore ● n guida f

driving: ~ **lesson** n lezione f di guida. ~ **licence** n patente f di guida. ~ **school** n scuola f guida. ~ **test** n esame m di guida

drizzle /'drɪzl/ n pioggerella f ● vi piovigginare

drone /drəʊn/ n ⟨bee⟩ fuco m; ⟨sound⟩ ronzio m

droop /druːp/ vi abbassarsi; ⟨flowers:⟩ afflosciarsi

drop /drɒp/ n ⟨of liquid⟩ goccia f; ⟨fall⟩ caduta f; ⟨in price, temperature⟩ calo m ● v (pt/pp **dropped**) ● vt far cadere;

sganciare ⟨bomb⟩; ⟨omit⟩ omettere; ⟨give up⟩ abbandonare ● vi cadere; ⟨price, temperature, wind:⟩ calare; ⟨ground:⟩ essere in pendenza. **drop in** vi passare. **drop off** vt depositare ⟨person⟩ ● vi cadere; ⟨fall asleep⟩ assopirsi. **drop out** vi cadere; ⟨of race, society⟩ ritirarsi; ~ **out of school** lasciare la scuola

drop-out n persona f contro il sistema sociale

droppings /'drɒpɪŋz/ npl sterco m

drought /draʊt/ n siccità f

drove /drəʊv/ see **drive**

droves /drəʊvz/ npl **in** ~ in massa

drown /draʊn/ vi annegare ● vt annegare; coprire ⟨noise⟩; **he was ~ed** è annegato

drowsy /'draʊzɪ/ a sonnolento

drudgery /'drʌdʒərɪ/ n lavoro m pesante e noioso

drug /drʌg/ n droga f; Med farmaco m; **take** ~**s** drogarsi ● vt (pt/pp **drugged**) drogare

drug: ~ **addict** n tossicomane, -a mf. ~ **dealer** n spacciatore, -trice mf [di droga]. **~gist** n Am farmacista mf. **~store** n Am negozio m di generi vari, inclusi medicinali, che funge anche da bar; ⟨dispensing⟩ farmacia f

drum /drʌm/ n tamburo m; ⟨for oil⟩ bidone m; ~**s** (pl: in pop-group) batteria f ● v (pt/pp **drummed**) ● vi suonare il tamburo; ⟨in pop-group⟩ suonare la batteria ● vt ~ **sth into sb** fam ripetere qcsa a qcno cento volte. **~mer** n percussionista mf; ⟨in pop-group⟩ batterista mf. **~stick** n bacchetta f; ⟨of chicken, turkey⟩ coscia f

drunk /drʌŋk/ see **drink** ● a ubriaco; **get** ~ ubriacarsi ● n ubriaco, -a mf

drunk|ard /'drʌŋkəd/ n ubriacone, -a mf. **~en** a ubriaco; **~en driving** guida f in stato di ebbrezza

dry /draɪ/ a (**drier, driest**) asciutto; ⟨climate, country⟩ secco ● vt/i (pt/pp **dried**) asciugare; ~ **one's eyes** asciugarsi le lacrime. **dry up** vi seccarsi; ⟨fig: source⟩ prosciugarsi; ⟨fam: be quiet⟩ stare zitto; ⟨do dishes⟩ asciugare i piatti

dry: **~-'clean** vt pulire a secco. **~-'cleaner's** n ⟨shop⟩ tintoria f. **~ness** n secchezza f

DTP n abbr (**desktop publishing**) desktop publishing m

dual /'djuːəl/ a doppio

dual: '**carriageway** n strada f a due carreggiate. **~-'purpose** a a doppio uso

dub /dʌb/ vt (pt/pp **dubbed**) doppiare ⟨film⟩; ⟨name⟩ soprannominare

dubious /'dju:bɪəs/ a dubbio; **be ~ about** avere dei dubbi riguardo

duchess /'dʌtʃɪs/ n duchessa f

duck /dʌk/ n anatra f ● vt (in water) immergere; **~ one's head** abbassare la testa ● vi abbassarsi. **~ling** n anatroccolo m

duct /dʌkt/ n condotto m; Anat dotto m

dud /dʌd/ fam a Mil disattivato; ⟨coin⟩ falso; ⟨cheque⟩ a vuoto ● n (banknote) banconota f falsa

due /dju:/ a dovuto; **be ~** ⟨train:⟩ essere previsto; **the baby is ~ next week** il bambino dovrebbe nascere la settimana prossima; **~ to** (owing to) a causa di; **be ~ to** (causally) essere dovuto a; **I'm ~ to...** dovrei...; **in ~ course** a tempo debito ● adv **~ north** direttamente a nord

duel /'dju:əl/ n duello m

dues /dju:z/ npl quota f [di iscrizione]

duet /dju:'et/ n duetto m

dug /dʌg/ see **dig**

duke /dju:k/ n duca m

dull /dʌl/ a (overcast, not bright) cupo; (not shiny) opaco; ⟨sound⟩ soffocato; (boring) monotono; (stupid) ottuso ● vt intorpidire ⟨mind⟩; attenuare ⟨pain⟩

duly /'dju:lɪ/ adv debitamente

dumb /dʌm/ a muto; (fam: stupid) ottuso. **~founded** /dʌm'faʊndɪd/ a sbigottito

dummy /'dʌmɪ/ n (tailor's) manichino m; (for baby) succhiotto m; (model) riproduzione f

dump /dʌmp/ n (for refuse) scarico m; (fam: town) mortorio m; **be down in the ~s** fam essere depresso ● vt scaricare; (fam: put down) lasciare; (fam: get rid of) liberarsi di

dumpling /'dʌmplɪŋ/ n gnocco m

dunce /dʌns/ n zuccone, -a mf

dune /dju:n/ n duna f

dung /dʌŋ/ n sterco m

dungarees /dʌŋgə'ri:z/ npl tuta fsg

dungeon /'dʌndʒən/ n prigione f sotterranea

duo /'dju:əʊ/ n duo m inv; Mus duetto m

duplicate¹ /'dju:plɪkət/ a doppio ● n duplicato m; ⟨document⟩ copia f; **in ~** in duplicato

duplicat|e² /'dju:plɪkeɪt/ vt fare un duplicato di; ⟨research:⟩ essere una ripetizione di ⟨work⟩

durable /'djʊərəbl/ a resistente; durevole ⟨basis, institution⟩

duration /djʊə'reɪʃn/ n durata f

duress /djʊə'res/ n costrizione f; **under ~** sotto minaccia

during /'djʊərɪŋ/ prep durante

dusk /dʌsk/ n crepuscolo m

dust /dʌst/ n polvere f ● vt spolverare; (sprinkle) cospargere ⟨cake⟩ (**with** di) ● vi spolverare

dust: ~bin n pattumiera f. **~-cart** n camion m della nettezza urbana. **~er** n strofinaccio m. **~-jacket** n sopraccoperta f. **~man** n spazzino m. **~pan** n paletta f per la spazzatura

dusty /'dʌstɪ/ a (-ier, -iest) polveroso

Dutch /dʌtʃ/ a olandese; **go ~** fam fare alla romana ● n (language) olandese m; **the ~** pl gli olandesi. **~man** n olandese m

dutiable /'dju:tɪəbl/ a soggetto a imposta

dutiful /'dju:tɪfl/ a rispettoso

duty /'dju:tɪ/ n dovere m; (task) compito m; (tax) dogana f; **be on ~** essere di servizio. **~-free** a esente da dogana

duvet /'du:veɪ/ n piumone m

dwarf /dwɔ:f/ n (pl -s or **dwarves**) nano, -a mf ● vt rimpicciolire

dwell /dwel/ vi (pt/pp **dwelt**) liter dimorare. **dwell on** vt fig soffermarsi su. **~ing** n abitazione f

dwindle /'dwɪndl/ vi diminuire

dye /daɪ/ n tintura f ● vt (pres p **dyeing**) tingere

dying /'daɪɪŋ/ see **die²**

dynamic /daɪ'næmɪk/ a dinamico

dynamite /'daɪnəmaɪt/ n dinamite f

dynamo /'daɪnəməʊ/ n dinamo f inv

dynasty /'dɪnəstɪ/ n dinastia f

dysentery /'dɪsəntrɪ/ n dissenteria f

dyslex|ia /dɪs'leksɪə/ n dislessia f. **~ic** a dislessico

Ee

each /iːtʃ/ a ogni ● pron ognuno; **£1 ~** una sterlina ciascuno; **they love/hate ~ other** si amano/odiano; **we lend ~ other money** ci prestiamo i soldi

eager /'iːgə(r)/ a ansioso **(to do di** fare); ⟨pupil⟩ avido di sapere. **~ly** adv ⟨wait⟩ ansiosamente; ⟨offer⟩ premurosamente. **~ness** n premura f

eagle /'iːgl/ n aquila f

ear¹ /ɪə(r)/ n (of corn) spiga f

ear² n orecchio m. **~ache** n mal m d'orecchi. **~-drum** n timpano m

earl /ɜːl/ n conte m

early /'ɜːlɪ/ a (-ier, -iest) (before expected time) in anticipo; ⟨spring⟩ prematuro; ⟨reply⟩ pronto; ⟨works, writings⟩ primo; **be here ~!** sii puntuale!; **you're ~!** sei in anticipo!; **~ morning walk** passeggiata f mattutina; **in the ~ morning** la mattina presto; **in the ~ spring** all'inizio della primavera; **~ retirement** prepensionamento m ● adv presto; (ahead of time) in anticipo; **~ in the morning** la mattina presto

'**earmark** vt riservare (**for** a)

earn /ɜːn/ vt guadagnare; (deserve) meritare

earnest /'ɜːnɪst/ a serio ● n **in ~** sul serio. **~ly** adv con aria seria

earnings /'ɜːnɪŋz/ npl guadagni mpl; (salary) stipendio m

ear: ~phones npl cuffia fsg. **~-ring** n orecchino m. **~shot** n **within ~shot** a portata d'orecchio; **he is out of ~shot** non può sentire

earth /ɜːθ/ n terra f **where/what on ~?** dove/che diavolo? ● vt Electr mettere a terra

earthenware /'ɜːθn-/ n terraglia f

earthly /'ɜːθlɪ/ a terrestre; **be no ~ use** fam essere perfettamente inutile

'**earthquake** n terremoto m

earthy /'ɜːθɪ/ a terroso; (coarse) grossolano

earwig /'ɪəwɪg/ n forbicina f

ease /iːz/ n **at ~** a proprio agio; **at ~!** Mil riposo!; **ill at ~** a disagio; **with ~** con facilità ● vt calmare ⟨pain⟩; alleviare ⟨tension, shortage⟩; (slow down) rallentare; (loosen) allentare ● vi ⟨pain, situation, wind⟩ calmarsi

easel /'iːzl/ n cavalletto m

easily /'iːzɪlɪ/ adv con facilità; **~ the best** certamente il meglio

east /iːst/ n est m; **to the ~ of** è a est di ● a dell'est ● adv verso est

Easter /'iːstə(r)/ n Pasqua f. **~ egg** n uovo m di Pasqua

east|erly /'iːstəlɪ/ a da levante. **~ern** a orientale. **~ward[s]** /-wəd[z]/ adv verso est

easy /'iːzɪ/ a (-ier, -iest) facile; **take it or things ~** prendersela con calma; **take it ~!** (don't get excited) calma!; **go ~ with** andarci piano con

easy: ~ chair n poltrona f. **~ going** a conciliante; **too ~going** troppo accomodante

eat /iːt/ vt/i (pt **ate**, pp **eaten**) mangiare. **eat into** vt intaccare. **eat up** vt mangiare tutto ⟨food⟩; fig inghiottire ⟨profits⟩

eat|able /'iːtəbl/ a mangiabile. **~er** n (apple) mela f da tavola; **be a big ~er** ⟨person:⟩ essere una buona forchetta

eau-de-Cologne /əʊdəkə'ləʊn/ n acqua f di Colonia

eaves /iːvz/ npl cornicione msg. **~drop** vi (pt/pp **~dropped**) origliare; **~drop on** ascoltare di nascosto

ebb /eb/ n (tide) riflusso m; **at a low ~** fig a terra ● vi rifluire; fig declinare

ebony /'ebənɪ/ n ebano m

EC n abbr (**European Community**) CE f

eccentric /ɪk'sentrɪk/ a & n eccentrico, -a mf

ecclesiastical /ɪkliːzɪ'æstɪkl/ a ecclesiastico

echo /'ekəʊ/ n (pl -es) eco f or m ● v (pt/pp **echoed**, pres p **echoing**) ● vt echeggiare; ripetere ⟨words⟩ ● vi risuonare (**with** di)

eclipse /ɪ'klɪps/ n Astr eclissi f inv ● vt fig eclissare

ecolog|ical /iːkə'lɒdʒɪkl/ a ecologico. **~y** /ɪ'kɒlədʒɪ/ n ecologia f

economic /iːkə'nɒmɪk/ a economico.

~al a economico. **~ally** adv economicamente; (thriftily) in economia. **~s** n economia f

economist /ɪ'kɒnəmɪst/ n economista mf

economize /ɪ'kɒnəmaɪz/ vi economizzare (**on** su)

economy /ɪ'kɒnəmɪ/ n economia f

ecstasy /'ekstəsɪ/ n estasi f inv; (drug) ecstasy f

ecstatic /ɪk'stætɪk/ a estatico

ecu /'eɪkjuː/ n ecu m inv

eczema /'eksɪmə/ n eczema m

edge /edʒ/ n bordo m; (of knife) filo m; (of road) ciglio m; **on** ~ con i nervi tesi; **have the** ~ **on** fam avere un vantaggio su ● vt bordare. **edge forward** vi avanzare lentamente

edgeways /'edʒweɪz/ adv di fianco; **I couldn't get a word in** ~ non ho potuto infilare neanche mezza parola nel discorso

edging /'edʒɪŋ/ n bordo m

edgy /'edʒɪ/ a nervoso

edible /'edɪbl/ a commestibile; **this pizza's not** ~ questa pizza è immangiabile

edict /'iːdɪkt/ n editto m

edify /'edɪfaɪ/ vt (pt/pp -ied) edificare. **~ing** a edificante

edit /'edɪt/ vt (pt/pp edited) far la revisione di (text); curare l'edizione di (anthology, dictionary); dirigere (newspaper); montare (film); editare (tape). **~ed by** (book) a cura di

edition /ɪ'dɪʃn/ n edizione f

editor /'edɪtə(r)/ n (of anthology, dictionary) curatore, -trice mf; (of newspaper) redattore, -trice mf; (of film) responsabile mf del montaggio

editorial /edɪ'tɔːrɪəl/ a redazionale ● n Journ editoriale m

educate /'edjʊkeɪt/ vt istruire; educare (public, mind); **be ~d at Eton** essere educato a Eton. **~d** a istruito

education /edjʊ'keɪʃn/ n istruzione f; (culture) cultura f, educazione f. **~al** a istruttivo; (visit) educativo; (publishing) didattico

eel /iːl/ n anguilla f

eerie /'ɪərɪ/ a (-ier, -iest) inquietante

effect /ɪ'fekt/ n effetto m; **in** ~ in effetti; **take** ~ (law:) entrare in vigore; (medicine:) fare effetto ● vt effettuare

effective /ɪ'fektɪv/ a efficace; (striking) che colpisce; (actual) di fatto; ~ **from** in vigore a partire da. **~ly** adv efficacemente; (actually) di fatto. **~ness** n efficacia f

effeminate /ɪ'femɪnət/ a effeminato

effervescent /efə'vesnt/ a effervescente

efficiency /ɪ'fɪʃənsɪ/ n efficienza f; (of machine) rendimento m

efficient /ɪ'fɪʃənt/ a efficiente. **~ly** adv efficientemente

effort /'efət/ n sforzo m; **make an** ~ sforzarsi. **~less** a facile. **~lessly** adv con facilità

effrontery /ɪ'frʌntərɪ/ n sfrontatezza f

effusive /ɪ'fjuːsɪv/ a espansivo; (speech) caloroso

e.g. abbr (exempli gratia) per es.

egalitarian /ɪgælɪ'teərɪən/ a egalitario

egg¹ /eg/ vt ~ **on** fam incitare

egg² n uovo m. **~-cup** n portauovo m inv. **~-shell** n guscio m d'uovo. **~-timer** n clessidra f per misurare il tempo di cottura delle uova

ego /'iːgəʊ/ n ego m. **~centric** /-'sentrɪk/ a egocentrico. **~ism** n egoismo m. **~ist** n egoista mf. **~tism** n egotismo m. **~tist** n egotista mf

Egypt /'iːdʒɪpt/ n Egitto m. **~ian** /ɪ'dʒɪpʃn/ a & n egiziano, -a mf

eiderdown /'aɪdə-/ n (quilt) piumino m

eigh|t /eɪt/ a otto ● n otto m. **~'teen** a & n diciotto m. **~'teenth** a & n diciottesimo, -a mf

eighth /eɪtθ/ a ottavo ● n ottavo m

eightieth /'eɪtɪɪθ/ a & n ottantesimo, -a mf

eighty /'eɪtɪ/ a & n ottanta m

either /'aɪðə(r)/ a & pron ~ [of them] l'uno o l'altro; **I don't like** ~ [of them] non mi piace né l'uno né l'altro; **on** ~ **side** da tutte e due le parti ● adv **I don't** ~ nemmeno io; **I don't like John or his brother** ~ non mi piace John e nemmeno suo fratello ● conj ~ **John or his brother will be there** ci saranno o John o suo fratello; **I don't like** ~ **John or his brother** non mi piacciono né John né suo fratello; **you go to bed or [else]...** o vai a letto o [altrimenti]..

eject /ɪ'dʒekt/ vt eiettare (pilot); espellere (tape, drunk)

eke /iːk/ vt ~ **out** far bastare; (increase) arrotondare; ~ **out a living** arrangiarsi

elaborate¹ /ɪ'læbərət/ a elaborato

elaborate² /ɪ'læbəreɪt/ vi entrare nei particolari (**on** di)

elapse /ɪ'læps/ vi trascorrere

elastic /ɪ'læstɪk/ a elastico ● n elastico m. ~ '**band** n elastico m

elasticity /ɪlæs'tɪsətɪ/ n elasticità f

elated /ɪ'leɪtɪd/ a esultante

elbow /'elbəʊ/ n gomito m

elder[1] /'eldə(r)/ n (tree) sambuco m

eld|er[2] a maggiore ● n **the ~** il/la maggiore. **~erly** a anziano. **~est** a maggiore ● n **the ~est** il/la maggiore

elect /ɪ'lekt/ a **the president ~** il futuro presidente ● vt eleggere; **~ to do sth** decidere di fare qcsa. **~ion** /-ekʃn/ n elezione f

elector /ɪ'lektə(r)/ n elettore, -trice mf. **~al** a elettorale; **~al roll** liste fpl elettorali. **~ate** /-rət/ n elettorato m

electric /ɪ'lektrɪk/ a elettrico

electrical /ɪ'lektrɪkl/ a elettrico; **~ engineering** elettrotecnica f

electric: ~ 'blanket n termocoperta f. **~ 'fire** n stufa f elettrica

electrician /ɪlek'trɪʃn/ n elettricista m

electricity /ɪlek'trɪsətɪ/ n elettricità f

electrify /ɪ'lektrɪfaɪ/ vt (pt/pp -ied) elettrificare; fig elettrizzare. **~ing** a fig elettrizzante

electrocute /ɪ'lektrəkjuːt/ vt fulminare, (execute) giustiziare sulla sedia elettrica

electrode /ɪ'lektrəʊd/ n elettrodo m

electron /ɪ'lektrɒn/ n elettrone m

electronic /ɪlek'trɒnɪk/ a elettronico. **~ mail** n posta f elettronica. **~s** n elettronica f

elegance /'elɪgəns/ n eleganza f

elegant /'elɪgənt/ a elegante

elegy /'elɪdʒɪ/ n elegia f

element /'elɪmənt/ n elemento m. **~ary** /-'mentərɪ/ a elementare

elephant /'elɪfənt/ n elefante m

elevat|e /'elɪveɪt/ vt elevare. **~ion** /-'veɪʃn/ n elevazione f; (height) altitudine f; (angle) alzo m

elevator /'elɪveɪtə(r)/ n Am ascensore m

eleven /ɪ'levn/ a & n undici m ● a. **~th** a & n undicesimo, -a mf; **at the ~th hour** fam all'ultimo momento

elf /elf/ n (pl elves) elfo m

elicit /ɪ'lɪsɪt/ vt ottenere

eligible /'elɪdʒəbl/ a eleggibile; **~ young man** buon partito; **be ~ for** aver diritto a

eliminate /ɪ'lɪmɪneɪt/ vt eliminare

élite /eɪ'liːt/ n fior fiore m

ellip|se /ɪ'lɪps/ n ellisse f. **~tical** a ellittico

elm /elm/ n olmo m

elocution /elə'kjuːʃn/ n elocuzione f

elope /ɪ'ləʊp/ vi fuggire [per sposarsi]

eloquen|ce /'eləkwəns/ n eloquenza f. **~t** a eloquente. **~tly** adv con eloquenza

else /els/ adv altro; **who ~?** e chi altro?; **he did of course, who ~?** l'ha fatto lui e chi, se no?; **nothing ~** nient'altro; **or ~** altrimenti; **someone ~** qualcun altro; **somewhere ~** da qualche altra parte; **anyone ~** chiunque altro; (as question) nessun'altro?; **anything ~** qualunque altra cosa; (as question) altro?. **~where** adv altrove

elucidate /ɪ'luːsɪdeɪt/ vt delucidare

elude /ɪ'luːd/ vt eludere; (avoid) evitare; **the name ~s me** il nome mi sfugge

elusive /ɪ'luːsɪv/ a elusivo

emaciated /ɪ'meɪsɪeɪtɪd/ a emaciato

e-mail /'iːmeɪl/ n posta f elettronica ● vt spedire via posta elettronica

emanate /'eməneɪt/ vi emanare

emancipat|ed /ɪ'mænsɪpeɪtɪd/ a emancipato. **~ion** /-'peɪʃn/ n emancipazione f; (of slaves) liberazione f

embankment /ɪm'bæŋkmənt/ n argine m; Rail massicciata f

embargo /em'bɑːgəʊ/ n (pl -es) embargo m

embark /ɪm'bɑːk/ vi imbarcarsi; **~ on** intraprendere. **~ation** /emba:'keɪʃn/ n imbarco m

embarrass /em'bærəs/ vt imbarazzare. **~ed** a imbarazzato. **~ing** a imbarazzante. **~ment** n imbarazzo m

embassy /'embəsɪ/ n ambasciata f

embedded /ɪm'bedɪd/ a (in concrete) cementato; (traditions, feelings) radicato

embellish /ɪm'belɪʃ/ vt abbellire

embers /'embəz/ npl braci fpl

embezzle /ɪm'bezl/ vt appropriarsi indebitamente di. **~ment** n appropriazione f indebita

embitter /ɪm'bɪtə(r)/ vt amareggiare

emblem /'embləm/ n emblema m

embody /ɪm'bɒdɪ/ vt (pt/pp -ied) incorporare; **~ what is best in...** rappresentare quanto c'è di meglio di...

emboss /ɪm'bɒs/ vt sbalzare (metal); stampare in rilievo (paper). **~ed** a in rilievo

embrace /ɪm'breɪs/ n abbraccio m ● vt abbracciare ● vi abbracciarsi

embroider /ɪm'brɔɪdə(r)/ vt ricamare (design); fig abbellire. **~y** n ricamo m

embryo /'embrɪəʊ/ n embrione m

emerald /'emərəld/ n smeraldo m

emer|ge /ɪ'mɜːdʒ/ vi emergere; (come into being: nation) nascere; (sun, *flowers*) spuntare fuori. **~gence** /-əns/ n emergere m; (*of new country*) nascita f

emergency /ı'mɜːdʒənsı/ n emergenza f; **in an ~** in caso di emergenza. **~ exit** n uscita f di sicurezza

emery /'emərı/ : **~ board** n limetta f [per le unghie]

emigrant /'emıgrənt/ n emigrante mf

emigrat|e /'emıgreıt/ vi emigrare. **~ion** /-'greıʃn/ n emigrazione f

eminent /'emınənt/ a eminente. **~ly** adv eminentemente

emission /ı'mıʃn/ n emissione f; (*of fumes*) esalazione f

emit /ı'mıt/ vt (pt/pp **emitted**) emettere; esalare (*fumes*)

emotion /ı'məʊʃn/ n emozione f. **~al** a denso di emozione; (*person, reaction*) emotivo; **become ~al** avere una reazione emotiva

emotive /ı'məʊtıv/ a emotivo

empathize /'empəθaız/ vi **~ with sb** immedesimarsi nei problemi di qcno

emperor /'empərə(r)/ n imperatore m

emphasis /'emfəsıs/ n enfasi f; **put the ~ on sth** accentuare qcsa

emphasize /'emfəsaız/ vt accentuare (*word, syllable*); sottolineare (*need*)

emphatic /ım'fætık/ a categorico

empire /'empaıə(r)/ n impero m

empirical /em'pırıkl/ a empirico

employ /ım'plɔı/ vt impiegare; fig usare (*tact*). **~ee** /emplɔı'iː/ n impiegato, -a mf. **~er** n datore m di lavoro. **~ment** n occupazione f; (*work*) lavoro m. **~ment agency** n ufficio m di collocamento

empower /ım'paʊə(r)/ vt autorizzare; (*enable*) mettere in grado

empress /'emprıs/ n imperatrice f

empties /'emptız/ npl vuoti mpl

emptiness /'emptınıs/ n vuoto m

empty /'emptı/ a vuoto; (*promise, threat*) vano ●v (pt/pp **-ied**) ●vt vuotare (*container*) ●vi vuotarsi

emulate /'emjʊleıt/ vt emulare

emulsion /ı'mʌlʃn/ n emulsione f

enable /ı'neıbl/ vt **~ sb to** mettere qcno in grado di

enact /ı'nækt/ vt Theat rappresentare; decretare (*law*)

enamel /ı'næml/ n smalto m ●vt (pt/pp **enamelled**) smaltare

enchant /ın'tʃɑːnt/ vt incantare. **~ing** a incantevole. **~ment** n incanto m

encircle /ın'sɜːkl/ vt circondare

enclave /'enkleıv/ n enclave f inv; fig territorio m

enclos|e /ın'kləʊz/ vt circondare

(*land*); (*in letter*) allegare (**with** a). **~ed** a (*space*) chiuso; (*in letter*) allegato. **~ure** /-ʒə(r)/ n (*at zoo*) recinto m; (*in letter*) allegato m

encompass /ın'kʌmpəs/ vt (*include*) comprendere

encore /'ɒŋkɔː(r)/ n & int bis m inv

encounter /ın'kaʊntə(r)/ n incontro m; (*battle*) scontro m ●vt incontrare

encourag|e /ın'kʌrıdʒ/ vt incoraggiare; promuovere (*the arts, independence*). **~ement** n incoraggiamento m; (*of the arts*) promozione f. **~ing** a incoraggiante; (*smile*) di incoraggiamento

encroach /ın'krəʊtʃ/ vt **~ on** invadere (*land, privacy*); abusare di (*time*); interferire con (*rights*)

encumb|er /ın'kʌmbə(r)/ vt **~ered with** essere carico di (*children, suitcases*); ingombro di (*furniture*). **~rance** /-rəns/ n peso m

encyclop[a]ed|ia /ınsaıklə'piːdıə/ n enciclopedia f. **~ic** a enciclopedico

end /end/ n fine f; (*of box, table, piece of string*) estremità f; (*of town, room*) parte f; (*purpose*) fine m; **in the ~** alla fine; **at the ~ of May** alla fine di maggio; **at the ~ of the street/garden** in fondo alla strada/al giardino; **on ~** (*upright*) in piedi; **for days on ~** per giorni e giorni; **for six days on ~** per sei giorni di fila; **put an ~ to sth** mettere fine a qcsa; **make ~s meet** fam sbarcare il lunario; **no ~ of** fam un sacco di ●vt/i finire. **end up** vi finire; **~ up doing sth** finire col fare qcsa

endanger /ın'deındʒə(r)/ vt rischiare (*one's life*); mettere a repentaglio (*sb else, success of sth*)

endear|ing /ın'dıərıŋ/ a accattivante. **~ment** n term of **~ment** vezzeggiativo m

endeavour /ın'devə(r)/ n tentativo m ●vi sforzarsi (**to** di)

ending /'endıŋ/ n fine f; Gram desinenza f

endive /'endaıv/ n indivia f

endless /'endlıs/ a interminabile; (*patience*) infinito. **~ly** adv continuamente; (*patient*) infinitamente

endorse /en'dɔːs/ vt girare (*cheque*); (*sports personality:*) fare pubblicità a (*product*); approvare (*plan*). **~ment** n (*of cheque*) girata f; (*of plan*) conferma f; (*on driving licence*) registrazione f su patente di un'infrazione

endow /ın'daʊ/ vt dotare

endur|able /ın'djʊərəbl/ a sopportabile. **~ance** /-rəns/ n resistenza f; **it is beyond ~ance** è insopportabile

endur|e /ɪnˈdjʊə(r)/ vt sopportare ● vi durare. **~ing** a duraturo

'end user n utente m finale

enemy /ˈenəmɪ/ n nemico, -a mf ● attrib nemico

energetic /enəˈdʒetɪk/ a energico

energy /ˈenədʒɪ/ n energia f

enforce /ɪnˈfɔːs/ vt far rispettare ⟨law⟩. **~d** a forzato

engage /ɪnˈgeɪdʒ/ vt assumere ⟨staff⟩; Theat ingaggiare; Auto ingranare ⟨gear⟩ ● vi Techn ingranare; **~ in** impegnarsi in. **~d** a ⟨in use, busy⟩ occupato; ⟨person⟩ impegnato; ⟨to be married⟩ fidanzato; **get ~d** fidanzarsi (**to** con); **~d tone** Teleph segnale m di occupato. **~ment** n fidanzamento m; ⟨appointment⟩ appuntamento m; Mil combattimento m; **~ment ring** anello m di fidanzamento

engaging /ɪnˈgeɪdʒɪŋ/ a attraente

engender /ɪnˈdʒendə(r)/ vt fig generare

engine /ˈendʒɪn/ n motore m; Rail locomotrice f. **~-driver** n macchinista m

engineer /endʒɪˈnɪə(r)/ n ingegnere m; ⟨service, installation⟩ tecnico m; Naut, Am Rail macchinista m ● vt fig architettare. **~ing** n ingegneria f

England /ˈɪŋglənd/ n Inghilterra f

English /ˈɪŋglɪʃ/ a inglese; **the ~ Channel** la Manica ● n ⟨language⟩ inglese m; **the ~** pl gli inglesi. **~man** n inglese m. **~woman** n inglese f

engrav|e /ɪnˈgreɪv/ vt incidere. **~ing** n incisione f

engross /ɪnˈgrəʊs/ vt **~ed in** assorto in

engulf /ɪnˈgʌlf/ vt ⟨fire, waves⟩ inghiottire

enhance /ɪnˈhɑːns/ vt accrescere ⟨beauty, reputation⟩; migliorare ⟨performance⟩

enigma /ɪˈnɪgmə/ n enigma m. **~tic** /enɪgˈmætɪk/ a enigmatico

enjoy /ɪnˈdʒɔɪ/ vt godere di ⟨good health⟩; **~ oneself** divertirsi; **I ~ cooking/painting** mi piace cucinare/dipingere; **~ your meal** buon appetito. **~able** /-əbl/ a piacevole. **~ment** n piacere m

enlarge /ɪnˈlɑːdʒ/ vt ingrandire ● vi **~ upon** dilungarsi su. **~ment** n ingrandimento m

enlighten /ɪnˈlaɪtn/ vt illuminare.

~ed a progressista. **~ment** n The E~ment l'Illuminismo m

enlist /ɪnˈlɪst/ vt Mil reclutare; **~ sb's help** farsi aiutare da qcno ● vi Mil arruolarsi

enliven /ɪnˈlaɪvn/ vt animare

enmity /ˈenmətɪ/ n inimicizia f

enormity /ɪˈnɔːmətɪ/ n enormità f

enormous /ɪˈnɔːməs/ a enorme. **~ly** adv estremamente; ⟨grateful⟩ infinitamente

enough /ɪˈnʌf/ a & n abbastanza; **I didn't bring ~ clothes** non ho portato abbastanza vestiti; **have you had ~?** ⟨to eat/drink⟩ hai mangiato/bevuto abbastanza?; **I've had ~!** fam ne ho abbastanza!; **is that ~?** basta?; **that's ~!** basta così!; **£50 isn't ~** 50 sterline non sono sufficienti ● adv abbastanza; **you're not working fast ~** non lavori abbastanza in fretta; **funnily ~** stranamente

enquir|e /ɪnˈkwaɪə(r)/ vi domandare; **~e about** chiedere informazioni su. **~y** n domanda f; ⟨investigation⟩ inchiesta f

enrage /ɪnˈreɪdʒ/ vt fare arrabbiare

enrich /ɪnˈrɪtʃ/ vt arricchire; ⟨improve⟩ migliorare ⟨vocabulary⟩

enrol /ɪnˈrəʊl/ vi ⟨pt/pp **-rolled**⟩ ⟨for exam, in club⟩ iscriversi (**for, in** a). **~ment** n iscrizione f

ensemble /ɒnˈsɒmbl/ n ⟨clothing & Mus⟩ complesso m

enslave /ɪnˈsleɪv/ vt render schiavo

ensu|e /ɪnˈsjuː/ vi seguire; **the ~ing discussion** la discussione che ne è seguita

ensure /ɪnˈʃʊə(r)/ vt assicurare; **~ that** ⟨person⟩ assicurarsi che, ⟨measure⟩ garantire che

entail /ɪnˈteɪl/ vt comportare; **what does it ~?** in che cosa consiste?

entangle /ɪnˈtæŋgl/ vt **get ~d in** rimanere impigliato in; fig rimanere coinvolto in

enter /ˈentə(r)/ vt entrare in; iscrivere ⟨horse, runner in race⟩; cominciare ⟨university⟩; partecipare a ⟨competition⟩; Comput immettere ⟨data⟩; ⟨write down⟩ scrivere ● vi entrare; Theat entrare in scena; ⟨register as competitor⟩ iscriversi; ⟨take part⟩ partecipare (**in** a)

enterpris|e /ˈentəpraɪz/ n impresa f; ⟨quality⟩ iniziativa f. **~ing** a intraprendente

entertain /entəˈteɪn/ vt intrattenere;

(invite) ricevere; nutrire *(ideas, hopes)*; prendere in considerazione *(possibility)* ● *vi* intrattenersi; *(have guests)* ricevere. **~er** *n* artista *mf.* **~ing** *a (person)* di gradevole compagnia; *(evening, film, play)* divertente. **~ment** *n (amusement)* intrattenimento *m*

enthral /ɪn'θrɔːl/ *vt (pt/pp* **enthralled)** be **~led** essere affascinato *(by* da)

enthusias|m /ɪn'θjuːzɪæzm/ *n* entusiasmo *m.* **~t** *n* entusiasta *mf.* **~tic** /-'æstɪk/ *a* entusiastico

entice /ɪn'taɪs/ *vt* attirare. **~ment** *n (incentive)* incentivo *m*

entire /ɪn'taɪə(r)/ *a* intero. **~ly** *adv* del tutto; **I'm not ~ly satisfied** non sono completamente soddisfatto. **~ty** /-rətɪ/ *n* in its **~ty** nell'insieme

entitled /ɪn'taɪtld/ *a (book)* intitolato; be **~ to sth** aver diritto a qcsa

entitlement /ɪn'taɪtlmənt/ *n* diritto *m*

entity /'entətɪ/ *n* entità *f*

entrance[1] /'entrəns/ *n* entrata *f; Theat* entrata *f* in scena; *(right to enter)* ammissione *f;* '**no ~**' 'ingresso vietato'. **~ examination** *n* esame *m* di ammissione. **~ fee** *n* **how much is the ~ fee?** quanto costa il biglietto di ingresso?

entrance[2] /ɪn'trɑːns/ *vt* estasiare

entrant /'entrənt/ *n* concorrente *mf*

entreat /ɪn'triːt/ *vt* supplicare

entrenched /ɪn'trentʃt/ *a (ideas, views)* radicato

entrust /ɪn'trʌst/ *vt* **~ sb with sth, ~ sth to sb** affidare qcsa a qcno

entry /'entrɪ/ *n* ingresso *m; (way in)* entrata *f; (in directory etc)* voce *f; (in appointment diary)* appuntamento *m;* **no ~** ingresso vietato; *Auto* accesso vietato. **~ form** *n* modulo *m* di ammissione. **~ visa** *n* visto *m* di ingresso

enumerate /ɪ'njuːməreɪt/ *vt* enumerare

enunciate /ɪ'nʌnsɪeɪt/ *vt* enunciare

envelop /ɪn'veləp/ *vt (pt/pp* **enveloped)** avviluppare

envelope /'envələʊp/ *n* busta *f*

enviable /'envɪəbl/ *a* invidiabile

envious /'envɪəs/ *a* invidioso. **~ly** *adv* con invidia

environment /ɪn'vaɪrənmənt/ *n* ambiente *m*

environmental /ɪnvaɪrən'mentl/ *a* ambientale. **~ist** *n* ambientalista *mf.* **~ly** *adv* **~ly friendly** che rispetta l'ambiente

envisage /ɪn'vɪzɪdʒ/ *vt* prevedere

envoy /'envɔɪ/ *n* inviato, -a *mf*

envy /'envɪ/ *n* invidia *f* ● *vt (pt/pp* **-ied)** **~ sb sth** invidiare qcno per qcsa

enzyme /'enzaɪm/ *n* enzima *m*

epic /'epɪk/ *a* epico ● *n* epopea *f*

epidemic /epɪ'demɪk/ *n* epidemia *f*

epilep|sy /'epɪlepsɪ/ *n* epilessia *f.* **~tic** /-'leptɪk/ *a & n* epilettico, -a *mf*

epilogue /'epɪlɒg/ *n* epilogo *m*

episode /'epɪsəʊd/ *n* episodio *m*

epitaph /'epɪtɑːf/ *n* epitaffio *m*

epithet /'epɪθet/ *n* epiteto *m*

epitom|e /ɪ'pɪtəmɪ/ *n* epitome *f.* **~ize** *vt* essere il classico esempio di

epoch /'iːpɒk/ *n* epoca *f*

equal /'iːkwl/ *a (parts, amounts)* uguale; **of ~ height** della stessa altezza; **be ~ to the task** essere a l'altezza del compito ● *n* pari *m inv* ● *vt (pt/pp* **equalled)** *(be same in quantity as)* essere pari a; *(rival)* uguagliare; **5 plus 5 ~s 10** 5 più 5 [è] uguale a 10. **~ity** /ɪ'kwɒlətɪ/ *n* uguaglianza *f*

equalize /'iːkwəlaɪz/ *vi Sport* pareggiare. **~r** *n Sport* pareggio *m*

equally /'iːkwəlɪ/ *adv (divide)* in parti uguali; **~ intelligent** della stessa intelligenza; **~,...** allo stesso tempo...

equanimity /ekwə'nɪmətɪ/ *n* equanimità *f*

equat|e /ɪ'kweɪt/ *vt* **~e sth with sth** equiparare qcsa a qcsa. **~ion** /-eɪʒn/ *n Math* equazione *f*

equator /ɪ'kweɪtə(r)/ *n* equatore *m*

equestrian /ɪ'kwestrɪən/ *a* equestre

equilibrium /iːkwɪ'lɪbrɪəm/ *n* equilibrio *m*

equinox /'iːkwɪnɒks/ *n* equinozio *m*

equip /ɪ'kwɪp/ *vt (pt/pp* **equipped)** equipaggiare; attrezzare *(kitchen, office).* **~ment** *n* attrezzatura *f*

equitable /'ekwɪtəbl/ *a* giusto

equity /'ekwɪtɪ/ *n (justness)* equità *f; Comm* azioni *fpl*

equivalent /ɪ'kwɪvələnt/ *a* equivalente; **be ~ to** equivalere a ● *n* equivalente *m*

equivocal /ɪ'kwɪvəkl/ *a* equivoco

era /'ɪərə/ *n* età *f; (geological)* era *f*

eradicate /ɪ'rædɪkeɪt/ *vt* eradicare

erase /ɪ'reɪz/ *vt* cancellare. **~r** *n* gomma *f* [da cancellare]; *(for blackboard)* cancellino *m*

erect /ɪ'rekt/ *a* eretto ● *vt* erigere. **~ion** /-ekʃn/ *n* erezione *f*

ero|de /ɪ'rəʊd/ *vt (water:)* erodere; *(acid:)* corrodere. **~sion** /-əʊʒn/ *n* erosione *f; (by acid)* corrosione *f*

erotic /ɪ'rɒtɪk/ *a* erotico. **~ism** /-tɪsɪzm/ *n* erotismo *m*

err /ɜ:(r)/ *vi* errare; (*sin*) peccare

errand /'erənd/ *n* commissione *f*

erratic /ɪ'rætɪk/ *a* irregolare; (*person, moods*) imprevedibile; (*exchange rate*) incostante

erroneous /ɪ'rəʊnɪəs/ *a* erroneo

error /'erə(r)/ *n* errore *m*; **in** ~ per errore

erudit|e /'erʊdaɪt/ *a* erudito. ~**ion** /-'dɪʃn/ *n* erudizione *f*

erupt /ɪ'rʌpt/ *vi* eruttare; (*spots:*) spuntare; (*fig: in anger*) dare in escandescenze. ~**ion** /-ʌpʃn/ *n* eruzione *f*; *fig* scoppio *m*

escalat|e /'eskəleɪt/ *vi* intensificarsi •*vt* intensificare. ~**ion** /-'leɪʃn/ *n* escalation *f inv*. ~**or** *n* scala *f* mobile

escapade /'eskəpeɪd/ *n* scappatella *f*

escape /ɪ'skeɪp/ *n* fuga *f*; (*from prison*) evasione *f*; **have a narrow** ~ cavarsela per un pelo •*vi* (*prisoner:*) evadere (**from**da); sfuggire (**from sb**alla sorveglianza di qcno); (*animal:*) scappare; (*gas:*) fuoriuscire •*vt* ~ **notice** passare inosservato; **the name** ~**s me** mi sfugge il nome

escapism /ɪ'skeɪpɪzm/ *n* evasione *f* [dalla realtà]

escort[1] /'eskɔ:t/ *n* (*of person*) accompagnatore, -trice *mf*; *Mil etc* scorta *f*

escort[2] /ɪ'skɔ:t/ *vt* accompagnare; *Mil etc* scortare

Eskimo /'eskɪməʊ/ *n* esquimese *mf*

esoteric /esə'terɪk/ *a* esoterico

especial /ɪ'speʃl/ *a* speciale. ~**ly** *adv* specialmente; (*kind*) particolarmente

espionage /'espɪənɑ:ʒ/ *n* spionaggio *m*

essay /'eseɪ/ *n* saggio *m*; *Sch* tema *f*

essence /'esns/ *n* essenza *f*; **in** ~ in sostanza

essential /ɪ'senʃl/ *a* essenziale •*n* **the** ~**s** *pl* l'essenziale *m*. ~**ly** *adv* essenzialmente

establish /ɪ'stæblɪʃ/ *vt* stabilire (*contact, lead*); fondare (*firm*); (*prove*) accertare. ~ **oneself as** affermarsi come. ~**ment** *n* (*firm*) azienda *f*; **the E**~**ment** l'ordine *m* costituito

estate /ɪ'steɪt/ *n* tenuta *f*; (*possessions*) patrimonio *m*; (*housing*) quartiere *m* residenziale. ~ **agent** *n* agente *m* immobiliare. ~ **car** *n* giardiniera *f*

esteem /ɪ'sti:m/ *n* stima *f* •*vt* stimare; (*consider*) giudicare

estimate[1] /'estɪmət/ *n* valutazione *f*; *Comm* preventivo *m*; **at a rough** ~ a occhio e croce

estimate[2] /'estɪmeɪt/ *vt* stimare. ~**ion** /-'meɪʃn/ *n* (*esteem*) stima *f*; **in my** ~**ion** (*judgement*) a mio giudizio

estuary /'estjʊərɪ/ *n* estuario *m*

etc /et'setərə/ *abbr* (**et cetera**) ecc

etching /'etʃɪŋ/ *n* acquaforte *f*

eternal /ɪ'tɜ:nl/ *a* eterno

eternity /ɪ'tɜ:nətɪ/ *n* eternità *f*

ethic /'eθɪk/ *n* etica *f*. ~**al** *a* etico. ~**s** *n* etica *f*

Ethiopia /i:θɪ'əʊpɪə/ *n* Etiopia *f*

ethnic /'eθnɪk/ *a* etnico

etiquette /'etɪket/ *n* etichetta *f*

EU *n abbr* (**European Union**) UE *f*

eucalyptus /ju:kə'lɪptəs/ *n* eucalipto *m*

eulogy /'ju:lədʒɪ/ *n* elogio *m*

euphemis|m /'ju:fəmɪzm/ *n* eufemismo *m*. ~**tic** /-'mɪstɪk/ *a* eufemistico

euphoria /ju:'fɔ:rɪə/ *n* euforia *f*

Euro+ /'jʊərəʊ-/ *pref* ~**cheque** *n* eurochèque *m inv*. ~**dollar** *n* eurodollaro *m*

Europe /'jʊərəp/ *n* Europa *f*

European /jʊərə'pɪən/ *a* europeo; ~ **Community** Comunità *f* Europea; ~ **Union** Unione *f* Europea •*n* europeo, -a *mf*

evacuat|e /ɪ'vækjʊeɪt/ *vt* evacuare (*building, area*). ~**ion** /-'eɪʃn/ *n* evacuazione *f*

evade /ɪ'veɪd/ *vt* evadere (*taxes*); evitare (*the enemy, authorities*); ~ **the issue** evitare l'argomento

evaluate /ɪ'væljʊeɪt/ *vt* valutare

evangelical /i:væn'dʒelɪkl/ *a* evangelico. ~**list** /ɪ'vændʒəlɪst/ *n* evangelista *m*

evaporat|e /ɪ'væpəreɪt/ *vi* evaporare; *fig* svanire. ~**ion** /-'reɪʃn/ *n* evaporazione *f*

evasion /ɪ'veɪʒn/ *n* evasione *f*

evasive /ɪ'veɪsɪv/ *a* evasivo

eve /i:v/ *n liter* vigilia *f*

even /'i:vn/ *a* (*level*) piatto; (*same, equal*) uguale; (*regular*) regolare; (*number*) pari; **get** ~ **with** vendicarsi di; **now we're** ~ adesso siamo pari •*adv* anche, ancora; ~ **if** anche se; ~ **so** con tutto ciò; **not** ~ nemmeno; ~ **bigger/hotter** ancora più grande/caldo •*vt* ~ **the score** *Sport* pareggiare. **even out** *vi* livellarsi. **even up** *vt* livellare

evening /'i:vnɪŋ/ *n* sera *f*; (*whole evening*) serata *f*; **this** ~ stasera; **in the** ~ la sera. ~ **class** *n* corso *m* serale. ~ **dress** *n* (*man's*) abito *m* scuro; (*woman's*) abito *m* da sera

evenly /'i:vnlɪ/ *adv* (*distributed*) uniformemente; ⟨*breathe*⟩ regolarmente; ⟨*divided*⟩ in uguali parti

event /ɪ'vent/ n avvenimento m; ⟨*function*⟩ manifestazione f; *Sport* gara f; **in the ~ of** nell'eventualità di; **in the ~** alla fine. **~ful** a movimentato

eventual /ɪ'ventjʊəl/ a **the ~ winner was...** alla fine il vincitore è stato.... **~ity** /-'ælətɪ/ n eventualità f. **~ly** adv alla fine; **~ly!** finalmente!

ever /'evə(r)/ adv mai; **I haven't ~...** non ho mai...; **for ~** per sempre; **hardly ~** quasi mai; **~ since** da quando; ⟨*since that time*⟩ da allora; **~ so** fam veramente

'**evergreen** n sempreverde m

ever'**lasting** a eterno

every /'evrɪ/ a ogni; **~ one** ciascuno; **~ other day** un giorno si un giorno no

every: **~body** pron tutti pl. **~day** a quotidiano, di ogni giorno. **~one** pron tutti pl; **~one else** tutti gli altri. **~thing** pron tutto; **~thing else** tutto il resto. **~where** adv dappertutto; ⟨*wherever*⟩ dovunque

evict /ɪ'vɪkt/ vt sfrattare. **~ion** /-ɪkʃn/ n sfratto m

eviden|ce /'evɪdəns/ n evidenza f; *Jur* testimonianza f; **give ~ce** testimoniare. **~t** a evidente. **~tly** adv evidentemente

evil /'iːvl/ a cattivo ● n male m

evocative /ɪ'vɒkətɪv/ a evocativo; **be ~ of** evocare

evoke /ɪ'vəʊk/ vt evocare

evolution /iːvə'luːʃn/ n evoluzione f

evolve /ɪ'vɒlv/ vt evolvere ● vi evolversi

ewe /juː/ n pecora f

exacerbate /ɪg'zæsəbeɪt/ vt esacerbare ⟨*situation*⟩

exact /ɪg'zækt/ a esatto ● vt esigere. **~ing** a esigente. **~itude** /-ɪtjuːd/ n esattezza f. **~ly** adv esattamente; **not ~ly** non proprio. **~ness** n precisione f

exaggerat|e /ɪg'zædʒəreɪt/ vt/i esagerare. **~ion** /-'reɪʃn/ n esagerazione f

exam /ɪg'zæm/ n esame m

examination /ɪgzæmɪ'neɪʃn/ n esame m; ⟨*of patient*⟩ visita f

examine /ɪg'zæmɪn/ vt esaminare; visitare ⟨*patient*⟩. **~r** n *Sch* esaminatore, -trice mf

example /ɪg'zɑːmpl/ n esempio m; **for ~** per esempio; **make an ~ of sb** punire qcno per dare un esempio; **be an ~ to sb** dare il buon esempio a qcno

exasperat|e /ɪg'zæspəreɪt/ vt esasperare. **~ion** /-'reɪʃn/ n esasperazione f

excavat|e /'ekskəveɪt/ vt scavare; *Archaeol* fare gli scavi di. **~ion** /-'veɪʃn/ n scavo m

exceed /ɪk'siːd/ vt eccedere. **~ingly** adv estremamente

excel /ɪk'sel/ v (pt/pp **excelled**) ● vi eccellere ● vt **~ oneself** superare se stessi

excellen|ce /'eksələns/ n eccellenza f. **E~cy** n ⟨*title*⟩ Eccellenza f. **~t** a eccellente

except /ɪk'sept/ prep eccetto, tranne; **~ for** eccetto, tranne; **~ that...** eccetto che... ● vt eccettuare. **~ing** prep eccetto, tranne

exception /ɪk'sepʃn/ n eccezione f; **take ~ to** fare obiezioni a. **~al** a eccezionale. **~ally** adv eccezionalmente

excerpt /'eksɜːpt/ n estratto m

excess /ɪk'ses/ n eccesso m; **in ~ of** oltre. **~ baggage** n bagaglio m in eccedenza. **~ fare** n supplemento m

excessive /ɪk'sesɪv/ a eccessivo. **~ly** adv eccessivamente

exchange /ɪks'tʃeɪndʒ/ n scambio m; *Teleph* centrale f; *Comm* cambio m; [stock] **~** borsa f valori; **in ~** in cambio (**for** di) ● vt scambiare (**for** con); cambiare ⟨*money*⟩. **~ rate** n tasso m di cambio

exchequer /ɪks'tʃekə(r)/ n *Pol* tesoro m

excise[1] /'eksaɪz/ n dazio m; **~ duty** dazio m

excise[2] /ɪk'saɪz/ vt recidere

excitable /ɪk'saɪtəbl/ a eccitabile

excit|e /ɪk'saɪt/ vt eccitare. **~ed** a eccitato; **get ~ed** eccitarsi. **~edly** adv tutto eccitato. **~ement** n eccitazione f. **~ing** a eccitante; ⟨*story, film*⟩ appassionante; ⟨*holiday*⟩ entusiasmante

exclaim /ɪk'skleɪm/ vt/i esclamare

exclamation /eksklə'meɪʃn/ n esclamazione f; **~ mark** n, *Am* **~ point** n punto m esclamativo

exclu|de /ɪk'skluːd/ vt escludere. **~ding** prep escluso. **~sion** /-ʒn/ n esclusione f

exclusive /ɪk'skluːsɪv/ a ⟨*rights, club*⟩ esclusivo; ⟨*interview*⟩ in esclusiva; **~ of...** ...escluso. **~ly** adv esclusivamente

excommunicate /ekskə'mjuːnɪkeɪt/ vt scomunicare

excrement /'ekskrɪmənt/ n escremento m

excruciating /ɪk'skruːʃɪeɪtɪŋ/ a atroce ⟨*pain*⟩; ⟨*fam: very bad*⟩ spaventoso

excursion /ɪkˈskɜːʃn/ n escursione f
excusable /ɪkˈskjuːzəbl/ a perdonabile
excuse[1] /ɪkˈskjuːs/ n scusa f
excuse[2] /ɪkˈskjuːz/ vt scusare; ~ **from** esonerare da; ~ **me!** (to get attention) scusi!; (to get past) permesso!, scusi!; (indignant) come ha detto?
ex-directory a be ~ non figurare sull'elenco telefonico
execute /ˈeksɪkjuːt/ vt eseguire; (put to death) giustiziare; attuare (plan)
execution /eksɪˈkjuːʃn/ n esecuzione f; (of plan) attuazione f. ~**er** n boia m inv
executive /ɪgˈzekjʊtɪv/ a esecutivo ●n dirigente mf; Pol esecutivo m
executor /ɪgˈzekjʊtə(r)/ n Jur esecutore, -trice mf
exemplary /ɪgˈzemplərɪ/ a esemplare
exemplify /ɪgˈzemplɪfaɪ/ vt (pt/pp -ied) esemplificare
exempt /ɪgˈzempt/ a esente ●vt esentare (from da). ~**ion** /-empʃn/ n esenzione f
exercise /ˈeksəsaɪz/ n esercizio m; Mil esercitazione f; **physical** ~**s** ginnastica f; **take** ~ fare del moto ●vt esercitare (muscles, horse); portare a spasso (dog); mettere in pratica (skills) ●vi esercitarsi. ~ **book** n quaderno m
exert /ɪgˈzɜːt/ vt esercitare; ~ **oneself** sforzarsi. ~**ion** /-ɜːʃn/ n sforzo m
exhale /eksˈheɪl/ vt/i esalare
exhaust /ɪgˈzɔːst/ n Auto scappamento m; (pipe) tubo m di scappamento; ~ **fumes** fumi mpl di scarico m ●vt esaurire. ~**ed** a esausto. ~**ing** a estenuante; (climate, person) sfibrante. ~**ion** /-ɔːstʃn/ n esaurimento m. ~**ive** /-ɪv/ a fig esauriente
exhibit /ɪgˈzɪbɪt/ n oggetto m esposto; Jur reperto m ●vt esporre; fig dimostrare
exhibition /eksɪˈbɪʃn/ n mostra f; (of strength, skill) dimostrazione f. ~**ist** n esibizionista mf
exhibitor /ɪgˈzɪbɪtə(r)/ n espositore, -trice mf
exhilarat|ed /ɪgˈzɪləreɪtɪd/ a rallegrato. ~**ing** a stimolante; (mountain air) tonificante. ~**ion** /-ˈreɪʃn/ n allegria f
exhort /ɪgˈzɔːt/ vt esortare
exhume /eksˈzjuːm/ vt esumare
exile /ˈeksaɪl/ n esilio m; (person) esule mf ●vt esiliare
exist /ɪgˈzɪst/ vi esistere. ~**ence** /-əns/

n esistenza f; **in** ~ esistente; **be in** ~**ence** esistere. ~**ing** a attuale
exit /ˈeksɪt/ n uscita f; Theat uscita f di scena ●vi Theat uscire di scena; Comput uscire
exonerate /ɪgˈzɒnəreɪt/ vt esonerare
exorbitant /ɪgˈzɔːbɪtənt/ a esorbitante
exorcize /ˈeksɔːsaɪz/ vt esorcizzare
exotic /ɪgˈzɒtɪk/ a esotico
expand /ɪkˈspænd/ vt espandere ●vi espandersi; Comm svilupparsi; (metal) dilatarsi; ~ **on** (fig: explain better) approfondire
expans|e /ɪkˈspæns/ n estensione f. ~**ion** /-ænʃn/ n espansione f; Comm sviluppo m; (of metal) dilatazione f. ~**ive** /-ɪv/ a espansivo
expatriate /eksˈpætrɪət/ n espatriato, -a mf
expect /ɪkˈspekt/ vt aspettare (letter, baby); (suppose) pensare; (demand) esigere; **I** ~ **so** penso di sì; **be** ~**ing** essere in stato interessante
expectan|cy /ɪkˈspektənsɪ/ n aspettativa f. ~**t** a in attesa; ~**t mother** donna f incinta. ~**tly** adv con impazienza
expectation /ekspekˈteɪʃn/ n aspettativa f, speranza f
expedient /ɪkˈspiːdɪənt/ a conveniente ●n espediente m
expedition /ekspɪˈdɪʃn/ n spedizione f. ~**ary** a Mil di spedizione
expel /ɪkˈspel/ vt (pt/pp **expelled**) espellere
expend /ɪkˈspend/ vt consumare. ~**able** /-əbl/ a sacrificabile
expenditure /ɪkˈspendɪtʃə(r)/ n spesa f
expense /ɪkˈspens/ n spesa f; **business** ~**s** pl spese fpl; **at my** ~ a mie spese; **at the** ~ **of** fig a spese di
expensive /ɪkˈspensɪv/ a caro, costoso. ~**ly** adv costosamente
experience /ɪkˈspɪərɪəns/ n esperienza f ●vt provare (sensation); avere (problem). ~**d** a esperto
experiment /ɪkˈsperɪmənt/ n esperimento m ●/-ment/ vi sperimentare. ~**al** /-ˈmentl/ a sperimentale
expert /ˈekspɜːt/ a & n esperto, -a mf. ~**ly** adv abilmente
expertise /ekspɜːˈtiːz/ n competenza f
expire /ɪkˈspaɪə(r)/ vi scadere
expiry /ɪkˈspaɪərɪ/ n scadenza f. ~ **date** n data f di scadenza
explain /ɪkˈspleɪn/ vt spiegare
explana|tion /ekspləˈneɪʃn/ n spiegazione f. ~**tory** /ɪkˈsplænətərɪ/ a esplicativo

expletive /ɪk'spliːtɪv/ n imprecazione f

explicit /ɪk'splɪsɪt/ a esplicito. ~**ly** adv esplicitamente

explode /ɪk'spləʊd/ vi esplodere ● vt fare esplodere

exploit[1] /'eksplɔɪt/ n impresa f

exploit[2] /ɪk'splɔɪt/ vt sfruttare. ~**ation** /eksplɔɪ'teɪʃn/ n sfruttamento m

explora|tion /eksplə'reɪʃn/ n esplorazione f. ~**tory** /ɪk'splɒrətərɪ/ a esplorativo

explore /ɪk'splɔː(r)/ vt esplorare; fig studiare ⟨implications⟩. ~**r** n esploratore, -trice mf

explos|ion /ɪk'spləʊʒn/ n esplosione f. ~**ive** /-sɪv/ a & n esplosivo m

exponent /ɪk'spəʊnənt/ n esponente mf

export /'ekspɔːt/ n esportazione f ● vt /-'spɔːt/ esportare. ~**er** n esportatore, -trice mf

expos|e /ɪk'spəʊz/ vt esporre; ⟨reveal⟩ svelare; smascherare ⟨traitor etc⟩. ~**ure** /-ʒə(r)/ n esposizione f; Med esposizione f prolungata al freddo/caldo; ⟨of crimes⟩ smascheramento m; **24** ~**ures** Phot 24 pose

expound /ɪk'spaʊnd/ vt esporre

express /ɪk'spres/ a espresso ● adv ⟨send⟩ per espresso ● n ⟨train⟩ espresso m ● vt esprimere; ~ **oneself** esprimersi. ~**ion** /-ʃn/ n espressione f. ~**ive** /-ɪv/ a espressivo. ~**ly** adv espressamente

expulsion /ɪk'spʌlʃn/ n espulsione f

exquisite /ek'skwɪzɪt/ a squisito

ex-'serviceman n ex-combattente m

extend /ɪk'stend/ vt prolungare ⟨visit, road⟩; prorogare ⟨visa, contract⟩; ampliare ⟨building, knowledge⟩; ⟨stretch out⟩ allungare; tendere ⟨hand⟩ ● vi ⟨garden, knowledge:⟩ estendersi

extension /ɪk'stenʃn/ n prolungamento m; ⟨of visa, contract⟩ proroga f; ⟨of treaty⟩ ampliamento m; ⟨part of building⟩ annesso m; ⟨length of cable⟩ prolunga f; Teleph interno m; ~ **226** interno 226

extensive /ɪk'stensɪv/ a ampio, vasto. ~**ly** adv ampiamente

extent /ɪk'stent/ n ⟨scope⟩ portata f; **to a certain** ~ fino a un certo punto; **to such an** ~ **that...** fino al punto che...

extenuating /ɪk'stenjʊeɪtɪŋ/ a ~ **circumstances** /ɪk'stenjʊeɪtɪŋ/ attenuanti fpl

exterior /ɪk'stɪərɪə(r)/ a & n esterno m

exterminat|e /ɪk'stɜːmɪneɪt/ vt sterminare. ~**ion** /-'neɪʃn/ n sterminio m

external /ɪk'stɜːnl/ a esterno; **for** ~ **use only** Med per uso esterno. ~**ly** adv esternamente

extinct /ɪk'stɪŋkt/ a estinto. ~**ion** /-ɪŋkʃn/ n estinzione f

extinguish /ɪk'stɪŋgwɪʃ/ vt estinguere. ~**er** n estintore m

extort /ɪk'stɔːt/ vt estorcere. ~**ion** /-ɔːʃn/ n estorsione f

extortionate /ɪk'stɔːʃənət/ a esorbitante

extra /'ekstrə/ a in più; ⟨train⟩ straordinario; **an** ~ **£10** 10 sterline extra, 10 sterline in più ● adv in più; ⟨especially⟩ più; **pay** ~ pagare in più, pagare extra; ~ **strong/busy** fortissimo/occupatissimo ● n Theat comparsa f; ~**s** pl extra mpl

extract[1] /'ekstrækt/ n estratto m

extract[2] /ɪk'strækt/ vt estrarre ⟨tooth, oil⟩; strappare ⟨secret⟩; ricavare ⟨truth⟩. ~**or** [**fan**] n aspiratore m

extradit|e /'ekstrədaɪt/ Jur vt estradare. ~**ion** /-'dɪʃn/ n estradizione f

extra'marital a extraconiugale

extra'ordinar|y /ɪk'strɔːdɪnərɪ/ a straordinario. ~**ily** /-ɪlɪ/ adv straordinariamente

extravagan|ce /ɪk'strævəgəns/ n ⟨with money⟩ prodigalità f; ⟨of behaviour⟩ stravaganza f. ~**t** a spendaccione; ⟨bizarre⟩ stravagante; ⟨claim⟩ esagerato

extrem|e /ɪk'striːm/ a estremo ● n estremo m; **in the** ~**e** al massimo. ~**ely** adv estremamente. ~**ist** n estremista mf

extremity /ɪk'stremətɪ/ n ⟨end⟩ estremità f inv

extricate /'ekstrɪkeɪt/ vt districare

extrovert /'ekstrəvɜːt/ n estroverso, -a mf

exuberant /ɪg'zjuːbərənt/ a esuberante

exude /ɪg'zjuːd/ vt also fig trasudare

exult /ɪg'zʌlt/ vi esultare

eye /aɪ/ n occhio m; ⟨of needle⟩ cruna f; **keep an** ~ **on** tener d'occhio; **see** ~ **to** ~ aver le stesse idee ● vt ⟨pt/pp **eyed**, pres p **ey[e]ing**⟩ guardare

eye: ~**ball** n bulbo m oculare. ~ **brow** n sopracciglio m ⟨pl sopracciglia f⟩. ~**lash** n ciglio m ⟨pl ciglia f⟩. ~**lid** n palpebra f. ~**-opener** n rivelazione f. ~**-shadow** n ombretto m. ~**sight** n vista f. ~**sore** n fam pugno m nell'occhio. ~**witness** n testimone mf oculare

Ff

fable /'feɪbl/ n favola f

fabric /'fæbrɪk/ n also fig tessuto m

fabrication /fæbrɪ'keɪʃn/ n invenzione f; (manufacture) fabbricazione f

fabulous /'fæbjʊləs/ a fam favoloso

façade /fə'sɑːd/ n (of building, person) facciata f

face /feɪs/ n faccia f, viso m; (grimace) smorfia f; (surface) faccia f; (of clock) quadrante m; **pull ~s** far boccacce; **in the ~ of** di fronte a; **on the ~ of it** in apparenza ●vt essere di fronta a; (confront) affrontare; **~ north** (house:) dare a nord; **~ the fact that** arrendersi al fatto che. **face up to** vt accettare (facts); affrontare (person)

face: **~flannel** n guanto m di spugna. **~less** a anonimo. **~lift** n plastica f facciale

facet /'fæsɪt/ n sfaccettatura f; fig aspetto m

facetious /fə'siːʃəs/ a spiritoso. **~ remarks** spiritosaggini mpl

'**face value** n (of money) valore m nominale; **take sb/sth at ~** fermarsi alle apparenze

facial /'feɪʃl/ a facciale ●n trattamento m di bellezza al viso

facile /'fæsaɪl/ a semplicistico

facilitate /fə'sɪlɪteɪt/ vt rendere possibile; (make easier) facilitare

facility /fə'sɪlətɪ/ n facilità f; **~ies** pl (of area, in hotel etc) attrezzature fpl

facing /'feɪsɪŋ/ prep ~ **the sea** (house) che dà sul mare; **the person ~ me** la persona di fronte a me

facsimile /fæk'sɪmɪlɪ/ n facsimile m

fact /fækt/ n fatto m; **in ~** infatti

faction /'fækʃn/ n fazione f

factor /'fæktə(r)/ n fattore m

factory /'fæktərɪ/ n fabbrica f

factual /'fæktʃʊəl/ a **be ~** attenersi ai fatti. **~ly** adv (inaccurate) dal punto di vista dei fatti

faculty /'fækəltɪ/ n facoltà f inv

fad /fæd/ n capriccio m

fade /feɪd/ vi sbiadire; (sound, light:) affievolirsi; (flower:) appassire. **fade** in vt cominciare in dissolvenza (picture).

fade out vt finire in dissolvenza (picture)

fag /fæg/ n (chore) fatica f; (fam: cigarette) sigaretta f; (Am sl: homosexual) frocio m. **~ end** n fam cicca f

fagged /fægd/ a **~ out** fam stanco morto

Fahrenheit /'færənhaɪt/ a Fahrenheit

fail /feɪl/ n **without ~** senz'altro ●vi (attempt:) fallire; (eyesight, memory:) indebolirsi; (engine, machine:) guastarsi; (marriage:) andare a rotoli; (in exam) essere bocciato; **~ to do sth** non fare qcsa; **I tried but I ~ed** ho provato ma non ci sono riuscito ●vt non superare (exam); bocciare (candidate); (disappoint) deludere; **words ~ me** mi mancano le parole

failing /'feɪlɪŋ/ n difetto m ●prep ~ **that** altrimenti

failure /'feɪljə(r)/ n fallimento m; (mechanical) guasto m; (person) incapace mf

faint /feɪnt/ a leggero; (memory) vago; **feel ~** sentirsi mancare ●n svenimento m ●vi svenire

faint: **~-'hearted** a timido. **~ly** adv (slightly) leggermente. **~ness** n (physical) debolezza f

fair¹ /feə(r)/ n fiera f

fair² /feə(r)/ a (hair, person) biondo; (skin) chiaro; (weather) bello; (just) giusto; (quite good) discreto; Sch abbastanza bene; **a ~ amount** abbastanza ●adv **play ~** fare un gioco pulito. **~ly** adv con giustizia; (rather) discretamente, abbastanza. **~ness** n giustizia f. **~ play** n fair play m inv

fairy /'feərɪ/ n fata f; **~ story, ~-tale** n fiaba f

faith /feɪθ/ n fede f; (trust) fiducia f; **in good/bad ~** in buona/mala fede

faithful /'feɪθfl/ a fedele. **~ly** adv fedelmente; **yours ~ly** distinti saluti. **~ness** n fedeltà f

'**faith-healer** n guaritore, -trice mf

fake /feɪk/ a falso ●n falsificazione f;

(*person*) impostore *m* ●*vt* falsificare; (*pretend*) fingere

falcon /'fɔːlkən/ *n* falcone *m*

fall /fɔːl/ *n* caduta *f*; (*in prices*) ribasso *m*; (*Am: autumn*) autunno *m*; **have a ~** fare una caduta ●*vi* (*pt* **fell**, *pp* **fallen**) cadere; (*night:*) scendere; **~ in love** innamorarsi. **fall about** *vi* (*with laughter*) morire dal ridere. **fall back on** *vt* ritornare su. **fall for** *vt fam* innamorarsi di (*person*); cascarci (*sth, trick*). **fall down** *vi* cadere; (*building:*) crollare. **fall in** *vi* cadere dentro; (*collapse*) crollare; *Mil* mettersi in riga; **~ in with** concordare con (*suggestion, plan*). **fall off** *vi* cadere; (*diminish*) diminuire. **fall out** *vi* (*quarrel*) litigare; **his hair is ~ing out** perde i capelli. **fall over** *vi* cadere. **fall through** *vi* (*plan:*) andare a monte

fallacy /'fæləsɪ/ *n* errore *m*

fallible /'fæləbl/ *a* fallibile

'fall-out *n* pioggia *f* radioattiva

false /fɔːls/ *a* falso; **~ bottom** doppio fondo *m*. **~ start** *Sport* falsa partenza *f*. **~hood** *n* menzogna *f*. **~ness** *n* falsità *f*

false 'teeth *npl* dentiera *f*

falsify /'fɔːlsɪfaɪ/ *vt* (*pt/pp* **-ied**) falsificare

falter /'fɔːltə(r)/ *vi* vacillare; (*making speech*) esitare

fame /feɪm/ *n* fama *f*

familiar /fə'mɪljə(r)/ *a* familiare; **be ~ with** (*know*) conoscere. **~ity** /-lɪ'ærɪtɪ/ *n* familiarità *f*. **~ize** *vt* familiarizzare; **~ize oneself with** familiarizzarsi con

family /'fæməlɪ/ *n* famiglia *f*

family: **~ al'lowance** *n* assegni *mpl* familiari. **~ 'doctor** *n* medico *m* di famiglia. **~ 'life** *n* vita *f* familiare. **~ 'planning** *n* pianificazione *f* familiare. **~ 'tree** *n* albero *m* genealogico

famine /'fæmɪn/ *n* carestia *f*

famished /'fæmɪʃt/ *a* **be ~** *fam* avere una fame da lupo

famous /'feɪməs/ *a* famoso

fan¹ /fæn/ *n* ventilatore *m*; (*handheld*) ventaglio *m* ●*vt* (*pt/pp* **fanned**) far vento a; **~ oneself** sventagliarsi; *fig* **~ the flames** soffiare sul fuoco. **fan out** *vi* spiegarsi a ventaglio

fan² *n* (*admirer*) ammiratore, -trice *mf*; *Sport* tifoso *m*; (*of Verdi etc*) appassionato, -a *mf*

fanatic /fə'nætɪk/ *n* fanatico, -a *mf*. **~al** *a* fanatico. **~ism** /-sɪzm/ *n* fanatismo *m*

'fan belt *n* cinghia *f* per ventilatore

fanciful /'fænsɪfl/ *a* fantasioso

fancy /'fænsɪ/ *n* fantasia *f*; **I've taken a real ~ to him** mi è molto simpatico; **as the ~ takes you** come ti pare ●*a* [a] fantasia ●*vt* (*pt/pp* **-ied**) (*believe*) credere; (*fam: want*) aver voglia di; **he fancies you** *fam* gli piaci; **~ that!** ma guarda un po'! **~ 'dress** *n* costume *m* (*per maschera*)

fanfare /'fænfeə(r)/ *n* fanfara *f*

fang /fæŋ/ *n* zanna *f*; (*of snake*) dente *m*

fan: **~ heater** *n* termoventilatore *m*. **~light** *n* lunetta *f*

fantas|ize /'fæntəsaɪz/ *vi* fantasticare. **~tic** /-'tæstɪk/ *a* fantastico. **~y** *n* fantasia *f*

far /fɑː(r)/ *adv* lontano; (*much*) molto; **by ~** di gran lunga; **~ away** lontano; **as ~ as the church** fino alla chiesa; **how ~ is it from here?** quanto dista da qui?; **as ~ as I know** per quanto io sappia ●*a* (*end, side*) altro; **the F~ East** l'Estremo Oriente *m*

farce /fɑːs/ *n* farsa *f*. **~ical** *a* ridicolo

fare /feə(r)/ *n* tariffa *f*; (*food*) vitto *m*. **~-dodger** /-dɒdʒə(r)/ *n* passeggero, -a *mf* senza biglietto

farewell /feə'wel/ *int liter* addio! ●*n* addio *m*

far-'fetched *a* improbabile

farm /fɑːm/ *n* fattoria *f* ●*vi* fare l'agricoltore ●*vt* coltivare (*land*). **~er** *n* agricoltore *m*

farm: **~house** *n* casa *f* colonica. **~ing** *n* agricoltura *f*. **~yard** *n* aia *f*

far: **~-'reaching** *a* di larga portata. **~-'sighted** *a* *fig* prudente; (*Am: long-sighted*) presbite

fart /fɑːt/ *fam* *n* scoreggia *f* ●*vi* scoreggiare

farther /'fɑːðə(r)/ *adv* più lontano ●*a* **at the ~ end of** all'altra estremità di

fascinat|e /'fæsɪneɪt/ *vt* affascinare. **~ing** *a* affascinante. **~ion** /-'neɪʃn/ *n* fascino *m*

fascis|m /'fæʃɪzm/ *n* fascismo *m*. **~t** *n* fascista *mf* ●*a* fascista

fashion /'fæʃn/ *n* moda *f*; (*manner*) maniera *f* ●*vt* modellare. **~able** /-əbl/ *a* di moda; **be ~able** essere alla moda. **~ably** *adv* alla moda

fast¹ /fɑːst/ *a* veloce; (*colour*) indelebile; **be ~** (*clock:*) andare avanti ●*adv* velocemente; (*firmly*) saldamente; **~er!** più in fretta!; **be ~ asleep** dormire profondamente

fast² *n* digiuno *m* ●*vi* digiunare

fasten /'fɑːsn/ *vt* allacciare; chiudere (*window*); (*stop flapping*) mettere un fermo /a ●*vi* allacciarsi. ~**er** *n*. ~**ing** *n* chiusura *f*

fastidious /fə'stɪdɪəs/ *a* esigente

fat /fæt/ *a* (**fatter, fattest**) ⟨*person, cheque*⟩ grasso ●*n* grasso *m*

fatal /'feɪtl/ *a* mortale; ⟨*error*⟩ fatale. ~**ism** /-təlɪzm/ *n* fatalismo *m*. ~**ist** /-təlɪst/ *n* fatalista *mf*. ~**ity** /fə'tælətɪ/ *n* morte *f*. ~**ly** *adv* mortalmente

fate /feɪt/ *n* destino *m*. ~**ful** *a* fatidico

'**fat-head** *n fam* zuccone. -a *mf*

father /'fɑ:ðə(r)/ *n* padre *m*; **F~ Christmas** Babbo *m* Natale ●*vt* generare ⟨*child*⟩

father: ~**hood** *n* paternità *f*. ~**-in-law** *n* (*pl* ~**s-in-law**) suocero *m*. ~**ly** *a* paterno

fathom /'fæð(ə)m/ *n Naut* braccio *m* ●*vt* ~ [**out**] comprendere

fatigue /fə'ti:g/ *n* fatica *f*

fatten /'fætn/ *vt* ingrassare ⟨*animal*⟩. ~**ing** *a* **cream is** ~**ing** la panna fa ingrassare

fatty /'fætɪ/ *a* grasso ●*n fam* ciccione, a *mf*

fatuous /'fætjʊəs/ *a* fatuo

faucet /'fɔ:sɪt/ *n Am* rubinetto *m*

fault /fɔ:lt/ *n* difetto *m*; *Geol* faglia *f*; *Tennis* fallo *m*: **be at** ~ avere torto; **find** ~ **with** trovare da ridire su; **it's your** ~ è colpa tua ●*vt* criticare. ~**less** *a* impeccabile

faulty /'fɔ:ltɪ/ *a* difettoso

fauna /'fɔ:nə/ *n* fauna *f*

favour /'feɪvə(r)/ *n* favore *m*; **be in** ~ **of sth** essere a favore di qcsa; **do sb a** ~ fare un piacere a qcno ●*vt* (*prefer*) preferire. ~**able** /-əbl/ *a* favorevole

favourit|e /'feɪv(ə)rɪt/ *a* preferito ●*n* preferito, -a *mf*; *Sport* favorito, -a *mf*. ~**ism** *n* favoritismo *m*

fawn /fɔ:n/ *a* fulvo ●*n* ⟨*animal*⟩ cerbiatto *m*

fax /fæks/ *n* ⟨*document, machine*⟩ fax *m inv*; **by** ~ per fax *m inv*. ~ **machine** *n* fax *m inv*. ~**-modem** *n* modem-fax *m inv*, fax-modem *m inv*

fear /fɪə(r)/ *n* paura *f*; **no** ~! *fam* vai tranquillo! ●*vt* temere ●*vi* ~ **for sth** temere per qcsa

fear|ful /'fɪəfl/ *a* pauroso; ⟨*awful*⟩ terribile. ~**less** *a* impavido. ~**some** /-səm/ *a* spaventoso

feas|ibility /fi:zɪ'bɪlɪtɪ/ *n* praticabilità *f*. ~**ible** /-əbl/ *a* fattibile; (*possible*) probabile

feast /fi:st/ *n* festa *f*; (*banquet*) banchetto *m* ●*vi* banchettare; ~ **on** godersi

feat /fi:t/ *n* impresa *f*

feather /'feðə(r)/ *n* piuma *f*

feature /'fi:tʃə(r)/ *n* (*quality*) caratteristica *f*; *Journ* articolo *m*; ~**s** (*pl: of face*) lineamenti *mpl* ●*vt* ⟨*film:*⟩ avere come protagonista ●*vi* (*on a list etc*) comparire. ~ **film** *n* lungometraggio *m*

February /'februərɪ/ *n* febbraio *m*

fed /fed/ *see* **feed** ●*a* **be** ~ **up** *fam* essere stufo (**with** di)

federal /'fed(ə)rəl/ *a* federale

federation /fedə'reɪʃn/ *n* federazione *f*

fee /fi:/ *n* tariffa *f*; (*lawyer's, doctor's*) onorario *m*; (*for membership, school*) quota *f*

feeble /'fi:bl/ *a* debole; (*excuse*) fiacco

feed /fi:d/ *n* mangiare *m*; (*for baby*) pappa *f* ●*v* (*pt/pp* **fed**) ●*vt* dar da mangiare a ⟨*animal*⟩; (*support*) nutrire; ~ **sth into sth** inserire in qcsa ●*vi* mangiare

'**feedback** *n* controreazione *f*; (*of information*) reazione *f*, feedback *m*

feel /fi:l/ *v* (*pt/pp* **felt**) ●*vt* sentire; (*experience*) provare; (*think*) pensare; (*touch: searching*) tastare; (*touch: for texture*) toccare ●*vi* ~ **soft/hard** essere duro/morbido al tatto; ~ **hot/hungry** aver caldo/fame; ~ **ill** sentirsi male; **I don't** ~ **like it** non ne ho voglia; **how do you** ~ **about it?** (*opinion*) che te ne pare?; **it doesn't** ~ **right** non mi sembra giusto. ~**er** *n* (*of animal*) antenna *f*; **put out** ~**ers** *fig* tastare il terreno. ~**ing** *n* sentimento *m*; (*awareness*) sensazione *f*

feet /fi:t/ *see* **foot**

feign /feɪn/ *vt* simulare

feline /'fi:laɪn/ *a* felino

fell[1] /fel/ *vt* (*knock down*) abbattere

fell[2] *see* **fall**

fellow /'feləʊ/ *n* (*of society*) socio *m*; (*fam: man*) tipo *m*

fellow: ~-**countryman** *n* compatriota *m*. ~-**men** *npl* prossimi *mpl*. ~**ship** *n* cameratismo *m*; (*group*) associazione *f*; *Univ* incarico *m* di ricercatore, -trice

felony /'felənɪ/ *n* delitto *m*

felt[1] /felt/ *see* **feel**

felt[2] *n* feltro *m*. ~[-**tipped**] '**pen** /[-'tɪpt]/ *n* pennarello *m*

female /'fi:meɪl/ *a* femminile; **the** ~ **antelope** l'antilope femmina ●*n* femmina *f*

femin|ine /'femɪnɪn/ *a* femminile ●*n Gram* femminile *m*. ~**inity** /-'nɪnətɪ/ *n* femminilità *f*. ~**ist** *a* & *n* femminista *mf*

fenc|e /fens/ *n* recinto *m*; (*fam: person*)

ricettatore *m* ●*vi Sport* tirar di scherma. **fence in** *vt* chiudere in un recinto. **~er** *n* schermidore *m*. **~ing** *n* steccato *m*; *Sport* scherma *f*

fend /fend/ *vi* **~ for oneself** badare a se stesso. **fend off** *vt* parare; difendersi da ‹*criticisms*›

fender /'fendə(r)/ *n* parafuoco *m inv*; (*Am: on car*) parafango *m*

fennel /'fenl/ *n* finocchio *m*

ferment¹ /'fɜːment/ *n* fermento *m*

ferment² /fə'ment/ *vi* fermentare ●*vt* far fermentare. **~ation** /fɜːmen'teɪʃn/ *n* fermentazione *f*

fern /fɜːn/ *n* felce *f*

feroc|ious /fə'rəʊʃəs/ *a* feroce. **~ity** /-'rɒsəti/ *n* ferocia *f*

ferret /'ferɪt/ *n* furetto *m* ● **ferret out** *vt* scovare

ferry /'ferɪ/ *n* traghetto *m* ●*vt* traghettare

fertil|e /'fɜːtaɪl/ *a* fertile. **~ity** /fɜː'tɪlətɪ/ *n* fertilità *f*

fertilize /'fɜːtɪlaɪz/ *vt* fertilizzare ‹*land, ovum*›. **~r** *n* fertilizzante *m*

fervent /'fɜːvənt/ *a* fervente

fervour /'fɜːvə(r)/ *n* fervore *m*

fester /'festə(r)/ *vi* suppurare

festival /'festɪvl/ *n Mus, Theat* festival *m*; *Relig* festa *f*

festiv|e /'festɪv/ *a* festivo; **~e season** periodo *m* delle feste natalizie. **~ities** /fe'stɪvətɪz/ *npl* festeggiamenti *mpl*

festoon /fe'stuːn/ *vt* **~ with** ornare di

fetch /fetʃ/ *vt* andare/venire a prendere; (*be sold for*) raggiungere [il prezzo di]

fetching /'fetʃɪŋ/ *a* attraente

fête /feɪt/ *n* festa *f* ●*vt* festeggiare

fetish /'fetɪʃ/ *n* feticcio *m*

fetter /'fetə(r)/ *vt* incatenare

fettle /'fetl/ *n* **in fine ~** in buona forma

feud /fjuːd/ *n* faida *f*

feudal /'fjuːdl/ *a* feudale

fever /'fiːvə(r)/ *n* febbre *f*. **~ish** *a* febbricitante; *fig* febbrile

few /fjuː/ *a* pochi; **every ~ days** ogni due o tre giorni; **a ~ people** alcuni; **~er reservations** meno prenotazioni; **the ~est number** il numero più basso ●*pron* pochi; **~ of us** pochi di noi; **a ~** alcuni; **quite a ~** parecchi; **~er than** last year meno dell'anno scorso

fiancé /fɪ'ɒnseɪ/ *n* fidanzato *m*. **~e** *n* fidanzata *f*

fiasco /fɪ'æskəʊ/ *n* fiasco *m*

fib /fɪb/ *n* storia *f*; **tell a ~** raccontare una storia

fibre /'faɪbə(r)/ *n* fibra *f*. **~glass** *n* fibra *f* di vetro

fickle /'fɪkl/ *a* incostante

fiction /'fɪkʃn/ *n* [**works of**] **~** narrativa *f*; (*fabrication*) finzione *f*. **~al** *a* immaginario

fictitious /fɪk'tɪʃəs/ *a* fittizio

fiddle /'fɪdl/ *n fam* violino *m*; (*cheating*) imbroglio *m* ●*vi* gingillarsi (**with** con) ●*vt fam* truccare ‹*accounts*›

fiddly /'fɪdlɪ/ *a* intricato

fidelity /fɪ'delətɪ/ *n* fedeltà *f*

fidget /'fɪdʒɪt/ *vi* agitarsi. **~y** *a* agitato

field /fiːld/ *n* campo *m*

field: ~ events *npl* atletica *fsg* leggera. **~-glasses** *npl* binocolo *msg*. F**~ 'Marshal** *n* feldmaresciallo *m*. **~work** *n* ricerche *fpl* sul terreno

fiend /fiːnd/ *n* demonio *m*

fierce /fɪəs/ *a* feroce. **~ness** *n* ferocia *f*

fiery /'faɪərɪ/ *a* (**-ier, -iest**) focoso

fifteen /fɪf'tiːn/ *a & n* quindici *m*. **~th** *a & n* quindicesimo, -a *mf*

fifth /fɪfθ/ *a & n* quinto, -a *mf*

fiftieth /'fɪftɪɪθ/ *a & n* cinquantesimo, -a *mf*

fifty /'fɪftɪ/ *a & n* cinquanta *m*

fig /fɪg/ *n* fico *m*

fight /faɪt/ *n* lotta *f*; (*brawl*) zuffa *f*; (*argument*) litigio *m*; (*boxing*) incontro *m* ●*v* (*pt/pp* **fought**) ●*vt also fig* combattere ●*vi* combattere; (*brawl*) azzuffarsi; (*argue*) litigare. **~er** *n* combattente *mf*; *Aeron* caccia *m inv*. **~ing** *n* combattimento *m*

figment /'fɪgmənt/ *n* **it's a ~ of your imagination** questo è tutta una tua invenzione

figurative /'fɪgjərətɪv/ *a* ‹*sense*› figurato; ‹*art*› figurativo

figure /'fɪgə(r)/ *n* (*digit*) cifra *f*; (*carving, sculpture, illustration, form*) figura *f*; (*body shape*) linea *f*; **~ of speech** modo *m* di dire ●*vi* (*appear*) figurare ●*vt* (*Am: think*) pensare. **figure out** *vt* dedurre; capire ‹*person*›

figure: ~-head *n* figura *f* simbolica. **~ skating** *n* pattinaggio *m* artistico

file¹ /faɪl/ *n* scheda *f*; (*set of documents*) incartamento *m*; (*folder*) cartellina *f*; *Comput* file *m inv* ●*vt* archiviare ‹*documents*›

file² /faɪl/ *n* (*line*) fila *f*; **in single ~** in fila

file³ /faɪl/ *n Techn* lima *f* ●*vt* limare

filing cabinet /'faɪlɪŋkæbɪnət/ *n* schedario *m*, classificatore *m*

filings /'faɪlɪŋz/ *npl* limatura *fsg*

fill /fɪl/ *n* **eat one's ~** mangiare a

sazietà ●vt riempire; otturare ⟨tooth⟩ ●vi riempirsi. **fill in** vt compilare ⟨form⟩. **fill out** vt compilare ⟨form⟩. **fill up** vi ⟨room, tank:⟩ riempirsi; Auto far il pieno ●vt riempire

fillet /'filɪt/ n filetto m ●vt ⟨pt/pp **filleted**⟩ disossare

filling /'filɪŋ/ n Culin ripieno m; ⟨of tooth⟩ piombatura f. ~ **station** stazione f di rifornimento

filly /'filɪ/ n puledra f

film /film/ n Cinema film m inv; Phot pellicola f; [**cling**] ~ pellicola f per alimenti ●vt/i filmare. ~ **star** n star f inv, divo, -a mf

filter /'filtə(r)/ n filtro m ●vt filtrare. **filter through** vi ⟨news:⟩ trapelare. ~ **tip** n filtro m; ⟨cigarette⟩ sigaretta f col filtro

filth /filθ/ n sudiciume m. ~**y** a ⟨-ier, -iest⟩ sudicio; ⟨language⟩ sconcio

fin /fin/ n pinna f

final /'faɪnl/ a finale; ⟨conclusive⟩ decisivo ●n Sport finale f; ~**s** pl Univ esami mpl finali

finale /fɪ'nɑːlɪ/ n finale m

finalist /'faɪnəlɪst/ n finalista mf. ~**ity** /-'nælətɪ/ n finalità f

finalize /'faɪnəlaɪz/ vt mettere a punto ⟨text⟩; definire ⟨agreement⟩. ~**ly** adv ⟨at last⟩ finalmente; ⟨at the end⟩ alla fine; ⟨to conclude⟩ per finire

finance /'faɪnæns/ n finanza f ●vt finanziare

financial /faɪ'nænʃl/ a finanziario

finch /fintʃ/ n fringuello m

find /faɪnd/ n scoperta f ●vt ⟨pt/pp **found**⟩ trovare; ⟨establish⟩ scoprire; ~ **sb guilty** Jur dichiarare qcno colpevole. **find out** vt scoprire ●vi ⟨enquire⟩ informarsi

findings /'faɪndɪŋz/ npl conclusioni fpl

fine[1] /faɪn/ n ⟨penalty⟩ multa f ●vt multare

fine[2] a bello; ⟨slender⟩ fine; **he's** ~ ⟨in health⟩ sta bene; ~ **arts** belle arti fpl ●adv bene; **that's cutting it** ~ non ci lascia molto tempo ●int [va] bene. ~**ly** adv ⟨cut⟩ finemente

finery /'faɪnərɪ/ n splendore m

finesse /fɪ'nes/ n finezza f

finger /'fiŋgə(r)/ n dito m ⟨pl dita f⟩ ●vt tastare

finger: ~-**mark** n ditata f. ~-**nail** n unghia f. ~-**print** n impronta f digitale. ~**tip** n punta f del dito; **have sth at one's** ~**tips** sapere qcsa a menadito;

⟨close at hand⟩ avere qcsa a portata di mano

finicky /'fɪnɪkɪ/ a ⟨person⟩ pignolo; ⟨task⟩ intricato

finish /'fɪnɪʃ/ n fine f; ⟨finishing line⟩ traguardo m; ⟨of product⟩ finitura f; **have a good** ~ ⟨runner:⟩ avere un buon finale ●vt finire; ~ **reading** finire di leggere ●vi finire

finite /'faɪnaɪt/ a limitato

Finland /'finlənd/ n Finlandia f

Finn /fin/ n finlandese mf. ~**ish** a finlandese ●n ⟨language⟩ finnico m

fiord /fjɔːd/ n fiordo m

fir /fɜː(r)/ n abete m

fire /'faɪə(r)/ n fuoco m; ⟨forest, house⟩ incendio m; **be on** ~ bruciare; **catch** ~ prendere fuoco; **set** ~ **to** dar fuoco a; **under** ~ sotto il fuoco ●vt cuocere ⟨pottery⟩; sparare ⟨shot⟩; tirare ⟨gun⟩; ⟨fam: dismiss⟩ buttar fuori ●vi sparare ⟨at a⟩

fire: ~ **alarm** n allarme m antincendio. ~**arm** n arma f da fuoco. ~ **brigade** n vigili mpl del fuoco. ~-**engine** n autopompa f. ~-**escape** n uscita f di sicurezza. ~ **extinguisher** n estintore m. ~**man** n pompiere m, vigile m del fuoco. ~**place** n caminetto m. ~**side** n by or at the ~**side** accanto al fuoco. ~ **station** n caserma f dei pompieri. ~**wood** n legna f ⟨da ardere⟩. ~**work** n fuoco m d'artificio; ~**works** pl ⟨display⟩ fuochi mpl d'artificio

'**firing squad** n plotone m d'esecuzione

firm[1] /fɜːm/ n ditta f, azienda f

firm[2] a fermo; ⟨soil⟩ compatto; ⟨stable, fixed⟩ solido; ⟨resolute⟩ risoluto. ~**ly** adv ⟨hold⟩ stretto; ⟨say⟩ con fermezza

first /fɜːst/ a & n primo, -a mf; **at** ~ all'inizio; **who's** ~? chi è il primo?; **from the** ~ [fin] dall'inizio ●adv ⟨arrive, leave⟩ per primo; ⟨beforehand⟩ prima; ⟨in listing⟩ prima di tutto, innanzitutto

first: ~ **aid** n pronto soccorso m. ~-'**aid kit** n cassetta f di pronto soccorso. ~-**class** a di prim'ordine; Rail di prima classe ●adv ⟨travel⟩ in prima classe. ~ '**floor** n primo piano m; ⟨Am: ground floor⟩ pianterreno m. ~**ly** adv in primo luogo. ~ **name** n nome m di battesimo. ~-**rate** a ottimo

fish /fiʃ/ n pesce m ●vt/i pescare. **fish out** vt tirar fuori

fish: ~-**bone** n lisca f. ~**erman** n pescatore m. ~-**farm** n vivaio m. ~ '**finger** n bastoncino m di pesce

fishing /'fɪʃɪŋ/ n pesca f. ~ **boat** n pescereccio m. ~**-rod** n canna f da pesca

fish: ~**monger** /-mʌŋɡə(r)/ n pescivendolo m. ~**-slice** n paletta f per fritti. ~**y** a ⟨fam: suspicious⟩ sospetto

fission /'fɪʃn/ n Phys fissione f

fist /fɪst/ n pugno m

fit[1] /fɪt/ n ⟨attack⟩ attacco m; ⟨of rage⟩ accesso m; ⟨of generosity⟩ slancio m

fit[2] a ⟨**fitter, fittest**⟩ ⟨suitable⟩ adatto; ⟨healthy⟩ in buona salute; Sport in forma; **be ~ to do sth** essere in grado di fare qcsa; ~ **to eat** buono da mangiare; **keep ~** tenersi in forma

fit[3] n ⟨of clothes⟩ taglio m; **it's a good ~** ⟨coat etc:⟩ ti/le sta bene ●v ⟨pt/pp **fitted**⟩ ●vi ⟨be the right size⟩ andare bene; **it won't ~** ⟨no room⟩ non ci sta ●vt ⟨fix⟩ applicare (**to** a); ⟨install⟩ installare; **it doesn't ~ me** ⟨coat etc:⟩ non mi va bene; ~ **with** fornire di. **fit in** vi ⟨person:⟩ adattarsi; **it won't ~ in** ⟨no room⟩ non ci sta ●vt ⟨in schedule, vehicle⟩ trovare un buco per

fit|**ful** /'fɪtfl/ a irregolare. ~**fully** adv a sprazzi. ~**ments** npl ⟨in house⟩ impianti mpl fissi. ~**ness** n ⟨suitability⟩ capacità f; [**physical**] ~**ness** forma f, fitness m

fitted: ~'**carpet** n moquette f inv. ~'**cupboard** n armadio m a muro; ⟨smaller⟩ armadietto m a muro. ~'**kitchen** n cucina f componibile. ~'**sheet** n lenzuolo m con angoli

fitter /'fɪtə(r)/ n installatore, -trice mf

fitting /'fɪtɪŋ/ a appropriato ●n ⟨of clothes⟩ prova f; Techn montaggio m; ~**s** pl accessori mpl. ~ **room** n camerino m

five /faɪv/ a & n cinque m. ~**r** n fam biglietto m da cinque sterline

fix /fɪks/ n ⟨sl: drugs⟩ pera f; **be in a ~** fam essere nei guai ●vt fissare; ⟨repair⟩ aggiustare; preparare ⟨meal⟩. **fix up** vt fissare ⟨meeting⟩

fixation /fɪk'seɪʃn/ n fissazione f

fixed /fɪkst/ a fisso

fixture /'fɪkstʃə(r)/ n Sport incontro m; ~**s and fittings** impianti mpl fissi

fizz /fɪz/ vi frizzare

fizzle /'fɪzl/ vi ~ **out** finire in nulla

fizzy /'fɪzɪ/ a gassoso. ~ **drink** n bibita f gassata

flabbergasted /'flæbəɡɑːstɪd/ a **be ~** rimanere a bocca aperta

flabby /'flæbɪ/ a floscio

flag[1] /flæɡ/ n bandiera f ● **flag down** vt ⟨pt/pp **flagged**⟩ far segno di fermarsi a ⟨taxi⟩

flag[2] vi ⟨pt/pp **flagged**⟩ cedere

'**flag-pole** n asta f della bandiera

flagrant /'fleɪɡrənt/ a flagrante

'**flagship** n Naut nave f ammiraglia; fig fiore m all'occhiello

'**flagstone** n pietra f da lastricare

flair /fleə(r)/ n ⟨skill⟩ talento m; ⟨style⟩ stile m

flake /fleɪk/ n fiocco m ●vi ~ [**off**] cadere in fiocchi

flaky /'fleɪkɪ/ a a scaglie. ~ **pastry** n pasta f sfoglia

flamboyant /flæm'bɔɪənt/ a ⟨personality⟩ brillante; ⟨tie⟩ sgargiante

flame /fleɪm/ n fiamma f

flammable /'flæməbl/ a infiammabile

flan /flæn/ n ⟨fruit⟩ ~ crostata f

flank /flæŋk/ n fianco m ●vt fiancheggiare

flannel /'flænl/ n flanella f; ⟨for washing⟩ guanto m di spugna; ~**s** ⟨trousers⟩ pantaloni mpl di flanella

flannelette /flænə'let/ n flanella f di cotone

flap /flæp/ n ⟨of pocket, envelope⟩ risvolto m; ⟨of table⟩ ribalta f; **in a ~** fam in grande agitazione ●v ⟨pt/pp **flapped**⟩ ●vi sbattere; fam agitarsi ●vt ~ **its wings** battere le ali

flare /fleə(r)/ n fiammata f; ⟨device⟩ razzo m ● **flare up** vi ⟨rash:⟩ venire fuori; ⟨fire:⟩ fare una fiammata; ⟨person, situation:⟩ esplodere. ~**d** a ⟨garment⟩ svasato

flash /flæʃ/ n lampo m; **in a ~** fam in un attimo ●vi lampeggiare; ~ **past** passare come un bolide ●vt lanciare ⟨smile⟩; ~ **one's head-lights** lampeggiare; ~ **a torch** at puntare una torcia su

flash: ~**back** n scena f retrospettiva. ~**bulb** n Phot flash m inv. ~**er** n Auto lampeggiatore m. ~**light** n Phot flash m inv; ⟨Am: torch⟩ torcia f[elettrica]. ~**y** a vistoso

flask /flɑːsk/ n fiasco m; ⟨vacuum ~⟩ termos m inv

flat /flæt/ a ⟨**flatter, flattest**⟩ piatto; ⟨refusal⟩ reciso; ⟨beer⟩ sgassato; ⟨battery⟩ scarico; ⟨tyre⟩ a terra; **A ~** Mus la bemolle ●n appartamento m; Mus bemolle m; ⟨puncture⟩ gomma f a terra

flat: ~**feet** npl piedi mpl piatti. ~**-fish** n pesce m piatto. ~**ly** adv ⟨refuse⟩ categoricamente. ~ **rate** n tariffa f unica

flatten /'flætn/ vt appiattire

flatter /'flætə(r)/ vt adulare. ~**ing** a ⟨comments⟩ lusinghiero; ⟨colour, dress⟩

che fa sembrare più bello. **~y** *n* adulazione *f*

flat 'tyre *n* gomma *f* a terra

flaunt /flɔ:nt/ *vt* ostentare

flautist /'flɔ:tɪst/ *n* flautista *mf*

flavour /'fleɪvə(r)/ *n* sapore *m* ●*vt* condire: **chocolate ~ed** al sapore di cioccolato. **~ing** *n* condimento *m*

flaw /flɔ:/ *n* difetto *m*. **~less** *a* perfetto

flax /flæks/ *n* lino *m*. **~en** *⟨hair⟩* biondo platino

flea /fli:/ *n* pulce *f*. **~ market** *n* mercato *m* delle pulci

fleck /flek/ *n* macchiolina *f*

fled /fled/ *see* **flee**

flee /fli:/ *vt/i* *(pt/pp* **fled**) fuggire (**from** da)

fleec|e /fli:s/ *n* pelliccia *f* ●*vt fam* spennare. **~y** *a* ⟨*lining*⟩ felpato

fleet /fli:t/ *n* flotta *f*; *(of cars)* parco *m*

fleeting /'fli:tɪŋ/ *a* **catch a ~ glance of sth** intravedere qcsa: **for a ~ moment** per un attimo

flesh /fleʃ/ *n* carne *f*; **in the ~** in persona. **~y** *a* carnoso

flew /flu:/ *see* **fly²**

flex¹ /fleks/ *vt* flettere ⟨*muscle*⟩

flex² *n* *Electr* filo *m*

flexib|ility /fleksɪ'bɪlətɪ/ *n* flessibilità *f*. **~le** *a* flessibile

'flexitime /'fleksɪ-/ *n* orario *m* flessibile

flick /flɪk/ *vt* dare un buffetto a: **~ sth off sth** togliere qcsa da qcsa con un colpetto. **flick through** *vt* sfogliare

flicker /'flɪkə(r)/ *vi* tremolare

flier /'flaɪə(r)/ *n* = **flyer**

flight¹ /flaɪt/ *n* ⟨*fleeing*⟩ fuga *f*. **take ~** darsi alla fuga

flight² *n* ⟨*flying*⟩ volo *m*; **~ of stairs** rampa *f*

flight: ~ path *n* traiettoria *f* di volo. **~ recorder** *n* registratore *m* di volo

flighty /'flaɪtɪ/ *a* (**-ier**, **-iest**) frivolo

flimsy /'flɪmzɪ/ *a* (**-ier**, **-iest**) ⟨*material*⟩ leggero; ⟨*shelves*⟩ poco robusto; ⟨*excuse*⟩ debole

flinch /flɪntʃ/ *vi* ⟨*wince*⟩ sussultare; ⟨*draw back*⟩ ritirarsi; **~ from a task** *fig* sottrarsi a un compito

fling /flɪŋ/ *n* **have a ~** ⟨*fam: affair*⟩ aver un'avventura ●*vt* *(pt/pp* **flung**) gettare

flint /flɪnt/ *n* pietra *f* focaia; *(for lighter)* pietrina *f*

flip /flɪp/ *v* *(pt/pp* **flipped**) ●*vt* dare un colpetto a; buttare in aria ⟨*coin*⟩ ●*vi fam* uscire dai gangheri; ⟨*go mad*⟩ impazzire. **flip through** *vt* sfogliare

flippant /'flɪpənt/ *a* irriverente

flipper /'flɪpə(r)/ *n* pinna *f*

flirt /flɜ:t/ *n* civetta *f* ●*vi* flirtare

flirtat|ion /flɜ:'teɪʃn/ *n* flirt *m* inv. **~ious** /-ʃəs/ *a* civettuolo

flit /flɪt/ *vi* *(pt/pp* **flitted**) volteggiare

float /fləʊt/ *n* galleggiante *m*; *(in procession)* carro *m*; *(money)* riserva *f* di cassa ●*vi* galleggiare; *Fin* fluttuare

flock /flɒk/ *n* gregge *m*; *(of birds)* stormo *m* ●*vi* affollarsi

flog /flɒg/ *vt* *(pt/pp* **flogged**) bastonare; *(fam: sell)* vendere

flood /flʌd/ *n* alluvione *f*: *(of river)* straripamento *m*; *(fig: of letters, tears)* diluvio *m*; **be in ~** ⟨*river:*⟩ essere straripato ●*vt* allagare ●*vi* ⟨*river:*⟩ straripare

'floodlight *n* riflettore *m* ●*vt* *(pt/pp* **floodlit**) illuminare con riflettori

floor /flɔ:(r)/ *n* pavimento *m*; *(storey)* piano *m*; *(for dancing)* pista *f* ●*vt* *(baffle)* confondere; *(knock down)* stendere ⟨*person*⟩

floor: ~ board *n* asse *f* del pavimento. **~polish** *n* cera *f* per il pavimento. **~ show** *n* spettacolo *m* di varietà

flop /flɒp/ *n fam* ⟨*failure*⟩ tonfo *m*; *Theat* fiasco *m* ●*vi* *(pt/pp* **flopped**) *(fam: fail)* far fiasco. **flop down** *vi* accasciarsi

floppy /'flɒpɪ/ *a* floscio. **~ 'disk** *n* floppy disk *m inv.* **~ [disk] drive** *n* lettore di floppy *m*

flora /'flɔ:rə/ *n* flora *f*

floral /'flɔ:rəl/ *a* floreale

Florence /'flɒrəns/ *n* Firenze *f*

florid /'flɒrɪd/ *a* ⟨*complexion*⟩ florido; ⟨*style*⟩ troppo ricercato

florist /'flɒrɪst/ *n* fioraio. a *mf*

flounce /flaʊns/ *n* balza *f* ●*vi* **~ out** uscire con aria melodrammatica

flounder¹ /'flaʊndə(r)/ *vi* dibattersi; ⟨*speaker:*⟩ impappinarsi

flounder² *n* ⟨*fish*⟩ passera *f* di mare

flour /'flaʊə(r)/ *n* farina *f*

flourish /'flʌrɪʃ/ *n* gesto *m* drammatico; *(scroll)* ghirigoro *m* ●*vi* prosperare ●*vt* brandire

floury /'flaʊərɪ/ *a* farinoso

flout /flaʊt/ *vt* fregarsene di ⟨*rules*⟩

flow /fləʊ/ *n* flusso *m* ●*vi* scorrere; *(hang loosely)* ricadere

flower /'flaʊə(r)/ *n* fiore *m* ●*vi* fiorire

flower: ~-bed *n* aiuola *f*. **~ed** *a* a fiori. **~pot** *n* vaso *m* [per i fiori]. **~y** *a* fiorito

flown /fləʊn/ *see* **fly²**

flu /flu:/ *n* influenza *f*

fluctuat|e /'flʌktjʊeɪt/ *vi* fluttuare. **~ion** /-'eɪʃn/ *n* fluttuazione *f*

fluent /'fluːənt/ *a* spedito; **speak ~ Italian** parlare correntemente l'italiano. **~ly** *adv* speditamente

fluff /flʌf/ *n* peluria *f*. **~y** *a* (**-ier, -iest**) vaporoso; ⟨*toy*⟩ di peluche

fluid /'fluːɪd/ *a* fluido ●*n* fluido *m*

fluke /fluːk/ *n* colpo *m* di fortuna

flung /flʌŋ/ *see* **fling**

flunk /flʌŋk/ *vt Am fam* essere bocciato in

fluorescent /flʊə'resnt/ *a* fluorescente

fluoride /'flʊəraɪd/ *n* fluoruro *m*

flurry /'flʌrɪ/ *n* ⟨*snow*⟩ raffica *f*; *fig* agitazione *f*

flush /flʌʃ/ *n* ⟨*blush*⟩ [vampata *f* di] rossore *m* ●*vi* arrossire ●*vt* lavare con un getto d'acqua; **~ the toilet** tirare l'acqua ●*a* a livello (**with** di); ⟨*fam: affluent*⟩ a soldi

flustered /'flʌstəd/ *a* in agitazione; **get ~** mettersi in agitazione

flute /fluːt/ *n* flauto *m*

flutter /'flʌtə(r)/ *n* battito *m* ●*vi* svolazzare

flux /flʌks/ *n* **in a state of ~** in uno stato di flusso

fly¹ /flaɪ/ *n* (*pl* **flies**) mosca *f*

fly² *v* (*pt* **flew**, *pp* **flown**) ●*vi* volare; ⟨*go by plane*⟩ andare in aereo; ⟨*flag:*⟩ sventolare; ⟨*rush*⟩ precipitarsi; **~ open** spalancarsi ●*vt* pilotare ⟨*plane*⟩; trasportare [in aereo] ⟨*troops, supplies*⟩; volare con ⟨*Alitalia etc*⟩

fly³ *n* & **flies** *pl* ⟨*on trousers*⟩ patta *f*

flyer /'flaɪə(r)/ *n* aviatore *m*; ⟨*leaflet*⟩ volantino *m*

flying /'flaɪɪŋ/: **~ 'buttress** *n* arco *m* rampante. **~ 'colours**: **with ~ colours** a pieni voti. **~ 'saucer** *n* disco *m* volante. **~ 'start** *n* **get off to a ~ start** fare un'ottima partenza. **~ 'visit** *n* visita *f* lampo

fly: **~ leaf** *n* risguardo *m*. **~over** *n* cavalcavia *m inv*

foal /fəʊl/ *n* puledro *m*

foam /fəʊm/ *n* schiuma *f*; ⟨*synthetic*⟩ gommapiuma® *f* ●*vi* spumare; **~ at the mouth** fare la bava alla bocca. **~ 'rubber** *n* gommapiuma® *f*

fob /fɒb/ *vt* (*pt/pp* **fobbed**) **~ sth off** affibbiare qcsa (**on sb** a qcno); **~ sb off** liquidare qcno

focal /'fəʊkl/ *a* focale

focus /'fəʊkəs/ *n* fuoco *m*; **in ~** a fuoco; **out of ~** sfocato ●*v* (*pt/pp* **focused** or

focussed) ●*vt fig* concentrare (**on** su) ●*vi Phot* **~ on** mettere a fuoco; *fig* concentrarsi (**on** su)

fodder /'fɒdə(r)/ *n* foraggio *m*

foe /fəʊ/ *n* nemico, -a *mf*

foetus /'fiːtəs/ *n* (*pl* **-tuses**) feto *m*

fog /fɒg/ *n* nebbia *f*

fogey /'fəʊgɪ/ *n* **old ~** persona *f* antiquata

foggy /'fɒgɪ/ *a* (**foggier, foggiest**) nebbioso; **it's ~** c'è nebbia

'fog-horn *n* sirena *f* da nebbia

foil¹ /fɔɪl/ *n* lamina *f* di metallo

foil² *vt* ⟨*thwart*⟩ frustrare

foil³ *n* ⟨*sword*⟩ fioretto *m*

foist /fɔɪst/ *vt* appioppare (**on sb** a qcno)

fold¹ /fəʊld/ *n* ⟨*for sheep*⟩ ovile *m*

fold² *n* piega *f* ●*vt* piegare; **~ one's arms** incrociare le braccia ●*vi* piegarsi; ⟨*fail*⟩ crollare. **fold up** *vt* ripiegare ⟨*chair*⟩ ●*vi* essere pieghevole; ⟨*fam: business:*⟩ collassare

fold|er /'fəʊldə(r)/ *n* cartella *f*. **~ing** *a* pieghevole

foliage /'fəʊlɪɪdʒ/ *n* fogliame *m*

folk /fəʊk/ *npl* gente *f*; **my ~s** ⟨*family*⟩ i miei; **hello there ~s** ciao a tutti

folk: **~-dance** *n* danza *f* popolare. **~lore** *n* folclore *m*. **~-song** *n* canto *m* popolare

follow /'fɒləʊ/ *vt/i* seguire; **it doesn't ~** non è necessariamente così; **~ suit** *fig* fare lo stesso; **as ~s** come segue. **follow up** *vt* fare seguito a ⟨*letter*⟩

follow|er /'fɒləʊə(r)/ *n* seguace *mf*. **~ing** *a* seguente ●*n* seguito *m*; ⟨*supporters*⟩ seguaci *mpl* ●*prep* in seguito a

folly /'fɒlɪ/ *n* follia *f*

fond /fɒnd/ *a* affezionato *a*; ⟨*hope*⟩ vivo; **be ~ of** essere appassionato di ⟨*music*⟩; **I'm ~ of...** ⟨*food, person*⟩ mi piace moltissimo...

fondle /'fɒndl/ *vt* coccolare

fondness /'fɒndnɪs/ *n* affetto *m*; ⟨*for things*⟩ amore *m*

font /fɒnt/ *n* fonte *f* battesimale; *Typ* carattere *m* di stampa

food /fuːd/ *n* cibo *m*; ⟨*for animals, groceries*⟩ mangiare *m*; **let's buy some ~** compriamo qualcosa da mangiare

food: **~ mixer** *n* frullatore *m*. **~ poisoning** *n* intossicazione *f* alimentare. **~ processor** *n* tritatutto *m inv* elettrico

fool¹ /fuːl/ *n* sciocco, -a *mf*; **she's no ~** non è una stupida; **make a ~ of**

oneself rendersi ridicolo ● *vt* prendere in giro ● *vi* ~ **around** giocare; ⟨husband, wife⟩ avere l'amante

fool² *n* Culin crema *f*

'**fool**|**hardy** *a* temerario. ~**ish** *a* stolto. ~**ishly** *adv* scioccamente. ~**ishness** *n* sciocchezza *f*. ~**proof** *a* facilissimo

foot /fʊt/ *n* (*pl* **feet**) piede *m*; (*of animal*) zampa *f*; (*measure*) piede *m* (= 30,48 cm); **on** ~ a piedi; **on one's feet** in piedi; **put one's** ~ **in it** *fam* fare una gaffe

foot: ~-**and**-'**mouth disease** *n* afta *f* epizootica. ~**ball** *n* calcio *m*; (*ball*) pallone *m*. ~**baller** *n* giocatore *m* di calcio. ~**ball pools** *npl* ≈ totocalcio *m*. ~-**brake** *n* freno *m* a pedale. ~-**bridge** *n* passerella *f*. ~-**hills** *npl* colline *fpl* pedemontane. ~**hold** *n* punto *m* d'appoggio. ~**ing** *n* lose one's ~**ing** perdere l'appiglio; **on an equal** ~**ing** in condizioni di parità. ~**man** *n* valletto *m*. ~**note** *n* nota *f* a piè di pagina. ~**path** *n* sentiero *m*. ~**print** *n* orma *f*. ~**step** *n* passo *m*; **follow in sb's** ~**steps** *fig* seguire l'esempio di qcno. ~**stool** *n* sgabellino *m*. ~**wear** *n* calzature *fpl*

for /fə(r)/, *accentato* /fɔ:(r)/ *prep* per; ~ **this reason** per questa ragione; **I have lived here** ~ **ten years** vivo qui da dieci anni; ~ **supper** per cena; ~ **all that** nonostante questo; **what** ~? a che scopo?; **send** ~ **a doctor** chiamare un dottore; **fight** ~ **a cause** lottare per una causa; **go** ~ **a walk** andare a fare una passeggiata; **there's no need** ~ **you to go** non c'è bisogno che tu vada; **it's not** ~ **me to say** no sta a me dirlo; **now you're** ~ **it** ora sei nei pasticci ● *conj* poiché, perché

forage /'fɒrɪdʒ/ *n* foraggio *m* ● *vi* ~ **for** cercare

forbade /fə'bæd/ *see* **forbid**

forbear|**ance** /fɔ:'beərəns/ *n* pazienza *f*. ~**ing** *a* tollerante

forbid /fə'bɪd/ *vt* (*pt* **forbade**, *pp* **forbidden**) proibire. ~**ding** *a* ⟨prospect⟩ che spaventa; ⟨stern⟩ severo

force /fɔ:s/ *n* forza *f*; **in** ~ in vigore; (*in large numbers*) in massa; **come into** ~ entrare in vigore; **the** [**armed**] ~**s** *pl* le forze armate ● *vt* forzare; ~ **sth on sb** ⟨decision⟩ imporre qcsa a qcno; ⟨drink⟩ costringere qcno a fare qcsa

forced /fɔ:st/ *a* forzato

force: ~-'**feed** *vt* (*pt*/*pp* -**fed**) nutrire a forza. ~**ful** *a* energico. ~**fully** *adv* ⟨say, argue⟩ con forza

forceps /'fɔ:seps/ *npl* forcipe *m*

forcible /'fɔ:sɪbl/ *a* forzato

ford /fɔ:d/ *n* guado *m* ● *vt* guadare

fore /fɔ:(r)/ *n* **to the** ~ in vista; **come to the** ~ salire alla ribalta

fore: ~**arm** *n* avambraccio *m*. ~**boding** /-'bəʊdɪŋ/ *n* presentimento *m*. ~**cast** *n* previsione *f* ● *vt* (*pt*/*pp* ~**cast**) prevedere. ~**court** *n* cortile *m* anteriore. ~**fathers** *npl* antenati *mpl*. ~**finger** *n* [dito *m*] indice *m*. ~**front** *n* **be in the** ~**front** essere all'avanguardia. ~**gone** *a* **be a** ~**gone conclusion** essere una cosa scontata. ~**ground** *n* primo piano *m*. ~**head** /'fɔ:hed, 'fɒrɪd/ *n* fronte *f*. ~**hand** *n* Tennis diritto *m*

foreign /'fɒrən/ *a* straniero; ⟨trade⟩ estero; (*not belonging*) estraneo; **he is** ~ è uno straniero. ~ **currency** *n* valuta *f* estera. ~**er** *n* straniero, -a *mf*. ~ **language** *n* lingua *f* straniera

Foreign: ~ **Office** *n* ministero *m* degli [affari] esteri. ~ '**Secretary** *n* ministro *m* degli esteri

fore: ~**man** *n* caporeparto *m*. ~**most** *a* principale ● *adv* **first and** ~**most** in primo luogo. ~**name** *n* nome *m* di battesimo

forensic /fə'rensɪk/ *a* ~ **medicine** medicina *f* legale

'**forerunner** *n* precursore *m*

fore'**see** *vt* (*pt* -**saw**, *pp* -**seen**) prevedere. ~**able** /-əbl/ *a* **in the** ~**able future** in futuro per quanto si possa prevedere

'**foresight** *n* previdenza *f*

forest /'fɒrɪst/ *n* foresta *f*. ~**er** *n* guardia *f* forestale

fore'**stall** *vt* prevenire

forestry /'fɒrɪstrɪ/ *n* silvicoltura *f*

'**foretaste** *n* pregustazione *f*

fore'**tell** *vt* (*pt*/*pp* -**told**) predire

forever /fə'revə(r)/ *adv* per sempre; **he's** ~ **complaining** si lamenta sempre

fore'**warn** *vt* avvertire

'**foreword** *n* prefazione *f*

forfeit /'fɔ:fɪt/ *n* (*in game*) pegno *m*; Jur penalità *f* ● *vt* perdere

forgave /fə'geɪv/ *see* **forgive**

forge¹ /fɔ:dʒ/ *vi* ~ **ahead** ⟨runner:⟩ lasciarsi indietro gli altri; *fig* farsi strada

forge² *n* fucina *f* ● *vt* fucinare; (*counterfeit*) contraffare. ~**r** *n* contraffattore *m*. ~**ry** *n* contraffazione *f*

forget /fə'get/ *vt*/*i* (*pt* -**got**, *pp* -**gotten**, *pres p* -**getting**) dimenticare; dimenticarsi di ⟨language, skill⟩. ~**table** /-əbl/

a ⟨day, film⟩ da dimenticare. **~ful** a smemorato. **~fulness** n smemoratezza f. **~-me-not** n non-ti-scordar-dimé m inv

forgive /fə'gɪv/ vt ⟨pt **-gave**, pp **-given**⟩ **~ sb for sth** perdonare qcno per qcsa. **~ness** n perdono m

forgo /fɔː'gəʊ/ vt ⟨pt **-went**, pp **-gone**⟩ rinunciare a

forgot(ten) /fə'gɒt(n)/ see forget

fork /fɔːk/ n forchetta f; ⟨for digging⟩ forca f; ⟨in road⟩ bivio m ● vi ⟨road:⟩ biforcarsi: **~ right** prendere a destra. **fork out** vt fam sborsare

fork-lift 'truck n elevatore m

forlorn /fə'lɔːn/ a ⟨look⟩ perduto; ⟨place⟩ derelitto; **~ hope** speranza f vana

form /fɔːm/ n forma f; ⟨document⟩ modulo m; Sch classe f ● vt formare; formulare ⟨opinion⟩ ● vi formarsi

formal /'fɔːml/ a formale. **~ity** /-'mælətɪ/ n formalità f inv. **~ly** adv in modo formale; ⟨officially⟩ ufficialmente

format /'fɔːmæt/ n formato m ● vt formattare ⟨disk, page⟩

formation /fɔː'meɪʃn/ n formazione f

formative /'fɔːmətɪv/ a **~ years** anni mpl formativi

former /'fɔːmə(r)/ a precedente; ⟨PM, colleague⟩ ex; **the ~, the latter** il primo, l'ultimo. **~ly** adv precedentemente; ⟨in olden times⟩ in altri tempi

formidable /'fɔːmɪdəbl/ a formidabile

formula /'fɔːmjʊlə/ n ⟨pl **-ae** /-liː/ or **-s**⟩ formula f

formulate /'fɔːmjʊleɪt/ vt formulare

forsake /fə'seɪk/ vt ⟨pt **-sook** /-sʊk/, pp **-saken**⟩ abbandonare

fort /fɔːt/ n Mil forte m

forte /'fɔːteɪ/ n [pezzo f] forte m

forth /fɔːθ/ adv back and **~** avanti e indietro; **and so ~** e così via

forth: **~'coming** a prossimo; ⟨communicative⟩ comunicativo; **no response was ~** non arrivava nessuna risposta. **~right** a schietto. **~'with** adv immediatamente

fortieth /'fɔːtɪθ/ a & n quarantesimo, -a mf

fortification /fɔːtɪfɪ'keɪʃn/ n fortificazione f

fortify /'fɔːtɪfaɪ/ vt ⟨pt/pp **-ied**⟩ fortificare; fig rendere forte

fortnight /'fɔːt-/ Br n quindicina f. **~ly** a bimensile ● adv ogni due settimane

fortress /'fɔːtrɪs/ n fortezza f

fortuitous /fɔː'tjuːɪtəs/ a fortuito

fortunate /'fɔːtʃənət/ a fortunato;

that's **~**! meno male!. **~ly** adv fortunatamente

fortune /'fɔːtʃuːn/ n fortuna f. **~-teller** n indovino, -a mf

forty /'fɔːtɪ/ a & n quaranta m

forum /'fɔːrəm/ n foro m

forward /'fɔːwəd/ adv avanti; ⟨towards the front⟩ in avanti ● a in avanti; ⟨presumptuous⟩ sfacciato ● n Sport attaccante m ● vt inoltrare ⟨letter⟩; spedire ⟨goods⟩. **~s** adv avanti

fossil /'fɒsl/ n fossile m. **~ized** a fossile; ⟨ideas⟩ fossilizzato

foster /'fɒstə(r)/ vt allevare ⟨child⟩. **~-child** n figlio, -a mf in affidamento. **~-mother** n madre f affidataria

fought /fɔːt/ see fight

foul /faʊl/ a ⟨smell, taste⟩ cattivo; ⟨air⟩ viziato; ⟨language⟩ osceno; ⟨mood, weather⟩ orrendo; **~ play** Jur delitto m ● n Sport fallo m ● vt inquinare ⟨water⟩; Sport commettere un fallo contro; ⟨nets, rope:⟩ impigliarsi in. **~-smelling** a puzzo

found[1] /faʊnd/ see find

found[2] vt fondare

foundation /faʊn'deɪʃn/ n ⟨basis⟩ fondamento m; ⟨charitable⟩ fondazione f; **~s** pl ⟨of building⟩ fondamenta fpl; **lay the ~-stone** porre la prima pietra

founder[1] /'faʊndə(r)/ n fondatore, -trice mf

founder[2] vi ⟨ship:⟩ affondare

foundry /'faʊndrɪ/ n fonderia f

fountain /'faʊntɪn/ n fontana f. **~-pen** n penna f stilografica

four /fɔː(r)/ a & n quattro m

four: **~-'poster** n letto m a baldacchino. **~some** /'fɔːsəm/ n quartetto m. **~'teen** a & n quattordici m. **~'teenth** a & n quattordicesimo, -a mf

fourth /fɔːθ/ a & n quarto, -a mf

fowl /faʊl/ n pollame m

fox /fɒks/ n volpe f ● vt ⟨puzzle⟩ ingannare

foyer /'fɔɪeɪ/ n Theat ridotto m; ⟨in hotel⟩ salone m d'ingresso

fraction /'frækʃn/ n frazione f

fracture /'fræktʃə(r)/ n frattura f ● vt fratturare ● vi fratturarsi

fragile /'frædʒaɪl/ a fragile

fragment /'frægmənt/ n frammento m. **~ary** a frammentario

fragran|ce /'freɪɡrəns/ n fragranza f. **~t** a fragrante

frail /freɪl/ a gracile

frame /freɪm/ n ⟨of picture, door, window⟩ cornice f; ⟨of spectacles⟩ montatura f; Anat ossatura f; (structure, of bike) telaio m; ~ **of mind** stato m d'animo ● vt incorniciare (picture); fig formulare; (sl: incriminate) montare. ~**work** n struttura f

franc /fræŋk/ n franco m

France /frɑːns/ n Francia f

franchise /ˈfræntʃaɪz/ n Pol diritto m di voto; Comm franchigia f

frank¹ /fræŋk/ vt affrancare (letter)

frank² a franco. ~**ly** adv francamente

frankfurter /ˈfræŋkfɜːtə(r)/ n würstel m inv

frantic /ˈfræntɪk/ a frenetico; **be ~ with worry** essere agitatissimo. ~**ally** adv freneticamente

fraternal /frəˈtɜːnl/ a fraterno

fraud /frɔːd/ n frode f; (person) impostore m. ~**ulent** /-jʊlənt/ a fraudolento

fraught /frɔːt/ a ~ **with** pieno di

fray¹ /freɪ/ n mischia f

fray² vi sfilacciarsi

frayed /freɪd/ a (cuffs) sfilacciato; (nerves) a pezzi

freak /friːk/ n fenomeno m; (person) scherzo m di natura; (fam; weird person) tipo m strambo ● a anormale. ~**ish** a strambo

freckle /ˈfrekl/ n lentiggine f. ~**d** a lentigginoso

free /friː/ a (**freer, freest**) libero; (ticket, copy) gratuito; (lavish) generoso; ~ **of charge** gratuito; **set** ~ liberare ● vt (pt/pp **freed**) liberare

free: ~dom n libertà f. ~**hand** adv a mano libera. ~**hold** n proprietà f [fondiaria] assoluta. ~ **'kick** n calcio m di punizione. ~**lance** a & adv indipendente.   ~**ly** adv liberamente; (generously) generosamente; **I ~ly admit that...** devo ammettere che.... **F~mason** n massone m. ~**-range** a ~**-range egg** uovo m di gallina ruspante. ~'**sample** n campione m gratuito. ~'**style** n stile m libero. ~**way** n Am autostrada f. ~'**wheel** vi (car:) (in neutral) andare in folle; (with engine switched off) andare a motore spento; (bicycle:) andare a ruota libera

freeze /friːz/ vt (pt **froze**, pp **frozen**) gelare; bloccare (wages) ● vi (water:) gelare; **it's ~ing** si gela; **my hands are ~ing** ho le mani congelate

freez|er /ˈfriːzə(r)/ n freezer m inv, congelatore m. ~**ing** a gelido ● n **below ~ing** sotto zero

freight /freɪt/ n carico m. ~**er** n nave f da carico. ~ **train** n Am treno m merci

French /frentʃ/ a francese ● n (language) francese m; **the ~** pl i francesi mpl

French: ~ 'beans npl fagiolini mpl [verdi]. ~ '**bread** n filone m (di pane). ~ '**fries** npl patate fpl fritte. ~**man** n francese m. ~ '**window** n porta-finestra f. ~**woman** n francese f

frenzied /ˈfrenzɪd/ a frenetico

frenzy /ˈfrenzɪ/ n frenesia f

frequency /ˈfriːkwənsɪ/ n frequenza f

frequent¹ /ˈfriːkwənt/ a frequente. ~**ly** adv frequentemente

frequent² /frɪˈkwent/ vt frequentare

fresco /ˈfreskəʊ/ n affresco m

fresh /freʃ/ a fresco; (new) nuovo; (Am: cheeky) sfacciato. ~**ly** adv di recente

freshen /ˈfreʃn/ vi (wind:) rinfrescare. **freshen up** vt dare una rinfrescata a ● vi rinfrescarsi

freshness /ˈfreʃnɪs/ n freschezza f

'**freshwater** a di acqua dolce

fret /fret/ vi (pt/pp **fretted**) inquietarsi. ~**ful** a irritabile

'**fretsaw** n seghetto m da traforo

friar /ˈfraɪə(r)/ n frate m

friction /ˈfrɪkʃn/ n frizione f

Friday /ˈfraɪdeɪ/ n venerdì m inv

fridge /frɪdʒ/ n frigo m

fried /fraɪd/ see **fry** ● a fritto; ~ **egg** uovo m fritto

friend /frend/ n amico, -a mf. ~**ly** a (**-ier, -iest**) (relations, meeting, match) amichevole; (neighbourhood, smile) piacevole; (software) di facile uso; **be ~ly with** essere amico di. ~**ship** n amicizia f

frieze /friːz/ n fregio m

fright /fraɪt/ n paura f; **take ~** spaventarsi

frighten /ˈfraɪtn/ vt spaventare. ~**ed** a spaventato; **be ~ed** aver paura (**of** di). ~**ing** a spaventoso

frightful /ˈfraɪtfʊl/ a terribile

frigid /ˈfrɪdʒɪd/ a frigido. ~**ity** /-ˈdʒɪdətɪ/ n freddezza f; Psych frigidità f

frill /frɪl/ n volant m inv. ~**y** a (dress) con tanti volant

fringe /frɪndʒ/ n frangia f; (of hair) frangetta f; (fig: edge) margine m. ~ **benefits** npl benefici mpl supplementari

frisk /frɪsk/ vt (search) perquisire

frisky /ˈfrɪskɪ/ a (**-ier, -iest**) vispo

fritter /ˈfrɪtə(r)/ n frittella f ● **fritter away** vt sprecare

frivol|ity /frɪˈvɒlətɪ/ n frivolezza f. ~**ous** /ˈfrɪvələs/ a frivolo

frizzy /ˈfrɪzɪ/ a crespo

fro /frəʊ/ see **to**

frock /frɒk/ n abito m

frog /frɒg/ n rana f. **~man** n uomo m rana

frolic /ˈfrɒlɪk/ vi (pt/pp **frolicked**) ⟨lambs:⟩ sgambettare; ⟨people:⟩ folleggiare

from /frɒm/ prep da; **~ Monday** da lunedì; **~ that day** da quel giorno; **he's ~ London** è di Londra; **this is a letter ~ my brother** questa è una lettera di mio fratello; **documents ~ the 16th century** documenti del XVI secolo; **made ~** fatto con; **she felt ill ~ fatigue** si sentiva male dalla stanchezza; **~ now on** d'ora in poi

front /frʌnt/ n parte f anteriore; ⟨fig: organization etc⟩ facciata f; ⟨of garment⟩ davanti m; ⟨sea~⟩ lungomare m; Mil, Pol, Meteorol fronte m; **in ~ of** davanti a; **in** or **at the ~** davanti; **to the ~** avanti ●a davanti; ⟨page, row, wheel⟩ anteriore

frontal /ˈfrʌntl/ a frontale

front: **~ 'door** n porta f d'entrata. **~ 'garden** n giardino m d'avanti

frontier /ˈfrʌntɪə(r)/ n frontiera f

front-wheel 'drive n trazione f anteriore

frost /frɒst/ n gelo m; ⟨hoar~⟩ brina f. **~bite** n congelamento m. **~bitten** a congelato

frost|ed /ˈfrɒstɪd/ a **~ed glass** vetro m smerigliato. **~ily** adv gelidamente. **~ing** n Am Culin glassa f. **~y** a also fig gelido

froth /frɒθ/ n schiuma f ●vi far schiuma. **~y** a schiumoso

frown /fraʊn/ n cipiglio m ●vi aggrottare le sopracciglia. **frown on** vt disapprovare

froze /frəʊz/ see **freeze**

frozen /ˈfrəʊzn/ see **freeze** ●a ⟨corpse, hand⟩ congelato; ⟨wastes⟩ gelido; Culin surgelato; **I'm ~** sono gelato. **~ food** n surgelati mpl

frugal /ˈfruːgl/ a frugale

fruit /fruːt/ n frutto m; ⟨collectively⟩ frutta f; **eat more ~** mangia più frutta. **~ cake** n dolce m con frutta candita

fruit|erer /ˈfruːtərə(r)/ n fruttivendolo, -a mf. **~ful** a fig fruttuoso

fruition /fruːˈɪʃn/ n **come to ~** dare dei frutti

fruit: **~ juice** n succo m di frutta. **~less** a infruttuoso. **~ machine** n

macchinetta f mangiasoldi. **~ 'salad** n macedonia f [di frutta]

frumpy /ˈfrʌmpɪ/ a scialbo

frustrat|e /frʌˈstreɪt/ vt frustrare; rovinare ⟨plans⟩. **~ing** a frustrante. **~ion** /-eɪʃn/ n frustrazione f

fry¹ vt/i (pt/pp **fried**) friggere

fry² /fraɪ/ n inv **small ~** fig pesce m piccolo

frying pan n padella f

fuck /fʌk/ vulg vt/i scopare ●int cazzo. **~ing** a del cazzo

fuddy-duddy /ˈfʌdɪdʌdɪ/ n fam matusa mf inv

fudge /fʌdʒ/ n caramella f a base di zucchero, burro e latte

fuel /ˈfjuːəl/ n carburante m; fig nutrimento m ●vt fig alimentare

fugitive /ˈfjuːdʒɪtɪv/ n fuggiasco, -a mf

fugue /fjuːg/ n Mus fuga f

fulfil /fʊlˈfɪl/ vt (pt/pp **-filled**) soddisfare ⟨conditions, need⟩; realizzare ⟨dream, desire⟩; **~ oneself** realizzarsi. **~ing** a soddisfacente. **~ment** n **sense of ~ment** senso m di appagamento

full /fʊl/ a pieno (**of**); ⟨detailed⟩ esauriente; ⟨bus, hotel⟩ completo; ⟨skirt⟩ ampio; **at ~ speed** a tutta velocità; **in ~ swing** in pieno fervore ●n **in ~** per intero

full: **~ 'moon** n luna f piena. **~-scale** a ⟨model⟩ in scala reale; ⟨alert⟩ di massima gravità. **~ 'stop** n punto m. **~-time** a & adv a tempo pieno

fully /ˈfʊlɪ/ adv completamente; ⟨in detail⟩ dettagliatamente; **~ booked** ⟨hotel, restaurant⟩ tutto prenotato

fumble /ˈfʌmbl/ vi **~ in** rovistare in; **~ with** armeggiare con; **~ for one's keys** rovistare alla ricerca delle chiavi

fume /fjuːm/ vi ⟨be angry⟩ essere furioso

fumes /fjuːmz/ npl fumi mpl; ⟨from car⟩ gas mpl di scarico

fumigate /ˈfjuːmɪgeɪt/ vt suffumicare

fun /fʌn/ n divertimento m; **for ~** per ridere; **make ~ of** prendere in giro; **have ~** divertirsi

function /ˈfʌŋkʃn/ n funzione f; ⟨event⟩ cerimonia f ●vi funzionare; **~ as** ⟨serve as⟩ funzionare da. **~al** a funzionale

fund /fʌnd/ n fondo m; fig pozzo m; **~s** pl fondi mpl ●vt finanziare

fundamental /fʌndəˈmentl/ a fondamentale

funeral /ˈfjuːnərəl/ n funerale m

funeral: **~ directors** n impresa f di pompe funebri. **~ home** Am, **~**

parlour n camera f ardente. **~ march** n marcia f funebre. **~ service** n rito m funebre

'funfair n luna park m inv

fungus /'fʌŋɡəs/ n (pl **-gi** /-ɡaɪ/) fungo m

funicular /fju:'nɪkjʊlə(r)/ n funicolare f

funnel /'fʌnl/ n imbuto m; (on ship) ciminiera f

funnily /'fʌnɪlɪ/ adv comicamente; (oddly) stranamente; **~ enough** strano a dirsi

funny /'fʌnɪ/ a (**-ier, -iest**) buffo; (odd) strano. **~ business** n affare m losco

fur /fɜ:(r)/ n pelo m; (for clothing) pelliccia f; (in kettle) deposito m. **~ 'coat** n pelliccia f

furious /'fjʊərɪəs/ a furioso

furnace /'fɜ:nɪs/ n fornace f

furnish /'fɜ:nɪʃ/ vt ammobiliare (flat); fornire (supplies). **~ed** a **~ed room** stanza f ammobiliata. **~ings** npl mobili mpl

furniture /'fɜ:nɪtʃə(r)/ n mobili mpl

furred /fɜ:d/ a (tongue) impastato

furrow /'fʌrəʊ/ n solco m

furry /'fɜ:rɪ/ a (animal) peloso; (toy) di peluche

further /'fɜ:ðə(r)/ a (additional) ulteriore; **at the ~ end** all'altra estremità; **until ~ notice** fino a nuovo avviso ● adv più lontano; **~,...** inoltre,...; **~ off** più lontano ● vt promuovere

further: ~ edu'cation n ≈ formazione f parauniversitaria. **~'more** adv per di più

furthest /'fɜ:ðɪst/ a più lontano ● adv più lontano

furtive /'fɜ:tɪv/ a furtivo

fury /'fjʊərɪ/ n furore m

fuse¹ /fju:z/ n (of bomb) detonatore m; (cord) miccia f

fuse² n Electr fusibile m ● vt fondere; Electr far saltare ● vi fondersi; Electr saltare; **the lights have ~d** sono saltate le luci. **~-box** n scatola f dei fusibili

fuselage /'fju:zəlɑ:ʒ/ n Aeron fusoliera f

fusion /'fju:ʒn/ n fusione f

fuss /fʌs/ n storie fpl; **make a ~** fare storie; **make a ~ of** colmare di attenzioni ● vi fare storie

fussy /'fʌsɪ/ a (**-ier, -iest**) (person) difficile da accontentare; (clothes etc) pieno di fronzoli

fusty /'fʌstɪ/ a che odora di stantio; (smell) di stantio

futile /'fju:taɪl/ a inutile. **~ity** /-'tɪlətɪ/ n futilità f

future /'fju:tʃə(r)/ a & n futuro; **in ~** in futuro. **~ perfect** futuro m anteriore

futuristic /fju:tʃə'rɪstɪk/ a futuristico

fuzz /fʌz/ n **the ~** (sl: police) la pula

fuzzy /'fʌzɪ/ a (**-ier, -iest**) (hair) crespo; (photo) sfuocato

Gg

gab /ɡæb/ n fam **have the gift of the ~** avere la parlantina

gabble /'ɡæb(ə)l/ vi parlare troppo in fretta

gad /ɡæd/ vi (pt/pp **gadded**) **~ about** andarsene in giro

gadget /'ɡædʒɪt/ n aggeggio m

Gaelic /'ɡeɪlɪk/ a & n gaelico m

gaffe /ɡæf/ n gaffe f inv

gag /ɡæɡ/ n bavaglio m; (joke) battuta f ● vt (pt/pp **gagged**) imbavagliare

gaily /'ɡeɪlɪ/ adv allegramente

gain /ɡeɪn/ n guadagno m; (increase) aumento m ● vt acquisire; **~ weight** aumentare di peso; **~ access** accedere

● vi (clock:) andare avanti. **~ful** a **~ful employment** lavoro m remunerativo

gait /ɡeɪt/ n andatura f

gala /'ɡɑ:lə/ n gala f; **swimming ~** manifestazione f di nuoto ● attrib di gala

galaxy /'ɡæləksɪ/ n galassia f

gale /ɡeɪl/ n bufera f

gall /ɡɔ:l/ n (impudence) impudenza f

gallant /'ɡælənt/ a coraggioso; (chivalrous) galante. **~ry** n coraggio m

'gall-bladder n cistifellea f

gallery /'ɡælərɪ/ n galleria f

galley /'ɡælɪ/ n (ship's kitchen) cambusa f; **~ [proof]** bozza f in colonna

gallivant /'ɡælɪvænt/ vi fam andare in giro

gallon /'gælən/ n gallone m (= 4,5 l; Am = 3,7 l)

gallop /'gæləp/ n galoppo m ● vi galoppare

gallows /'gæləʊz/ n forca f

'gallstone n calcolo m biliare

galore /gə'lɔ:(r)/ adv a bizzeffe

galvanize /'gælvənaɪz/ vt Techn galvanizzare; fig stimolare (**into** a)

gambit /'gæmbɪt/ n prima mossa f

gamb|le /'gæmbl/ n (risk) azzardo m ● vi giocare; (on Stock Exchange) speculare; ~**e on** (rely) contare su. ~**er** n giocatore, -trice mf [d'azzardo]. ~**ing** n gioco m [d'azzardo]

game /geɪm/ n gioco m; (match) partita f; (animals, birds) selvaggina f; ~**s** Sch ≈ ginnastica f ● a (brave) coraggioso; **are you ~?** ti va?; **be ~ for** essere pronto per. ~**keeper** n guardacaccia m inv

gammon /'gæmən/ n coscia f di maiale

gamut /'gæmət/ n fig gamma f

gander /'gændə(r)/ n oca f maschio

gang /gæŋ/ n banda f; (of workmen) squadra f ● **gang up** vi far comunella (**on** contro)

gangling /'gæŋglɪŋ/ a spilungone

gangrene /'gæŋgri:n/ n cancrena f

gangster /'gæŋstə(r)/ n gangster m inv

gangway /'gæŋweɪ/ n passaggio m; Naut, Aeron passerella f

gaol /dʒeɪl/ n carcere m ● vt incarcerare. ~**er** n carceriere m

gap /gæp/ n spazio m; (in ages, between teeth) scarto m; (in memory) vuoto m; (in story) punto m oscuro

gap|e /geɪp/ vi stare a bocca aperta; (be wide open) spalancarsi; ~**e at** guardare a bocca aperta. ~**ing** a aperto

garage /'gæra:ʒ/ n garage m inv; (for repairs) meccanico m; (for petrol) stazione f di servizio

garbage /'gɑ:bɪdʒ/ n immondizia f; (nonsense) idiozie fpl. ~ **can** n Am bidone m dell'immondizia

garbled /'gɑ:bld/ a confuso

garden /'gɑ:dn/ n giardino m; [public] ~**s** pl giardini mpl pubblici ● vi fare giardinaggio. ~ **centre** n negozio m di piante e articoli da giardinaggio. ~**er** n giardiniere, -a mf. ~**ing** n giardinaggio m

gargle /'gɑ:gl/ n gargarismo m ● vi fare gargarismi

gargoyle /'gɑ:gɔɪl/ n gargouille f inv

garish /'geərɪʃ/ a sgargiante

garland /'gɑ:lənd/ n ghirlanda f

garlic /'gɑ:lɪk/ n aglio m. ~ **bread** n pane m condito con aglio

garment /'gɑ:mənt/ n indumento m

garnish /'gɑ:nɪʃ/ n guarnizione f ● vt guarnire

garrison /'gærɪsn/ n guarnigione f

garter /'gɑ:tə(r)/ n giarrettiera f; (Am: on man's sock) reggicalze m inv da uomo

gas /gæs/ n gas m inv; (Am fam: petrol) benzina f ● v (pt/pp **gassed**) ● vt asfissiare ● vi fam blaterare. ~ **cooker** n cucina f a gas. ~ **fire** n stufa f a gas

gash /gæʃ/ n taglio m ● vt tagliare

gasket /'gæskɪt/ n Techn guarnizione f

gas: ~ **mask** n maschera f antigas. ~-**meter** n contatore m del gas

gasoline /'gæsəli:n/ n Am benzina f

gasp /gɑ:sp/ vi avere il fiato mozzato

'gas station n Am distributore m di benzina

gastric /'gæstrɪk/ a gastrico. ~ '**flu** n influenza f gastro-intestinale. ~ '**ulcer** n ulcera f gastrica

gastronomy /gæ'strɒnəmɪ/ n gastronomia f

gate /geɪt/ n cancello m; (at airport) uscita f

gâteau /'gætəʊ/ n torta f

gate: ~**crash** vt entrare senza invito a. ~**crasher** n intruso, -a mf. ~**way** n ingresso m

gather /'gæðə(r)/ vt raccogliere; (conclude) dedurre; (in sewing) arricciare; ~ **speed** acquistare velocità; ~ **together** radunare (people, belongings); (obtain gradually) acquistare ● vi (people:) radunarsi. ~**ing** n family ~**ing** ritrovo m di famiglia

gaudy /'gɔ:dɪ/ a (-ier, -iest) pacchiano

gauge /geɪdʒ/ n calibro m; Rail scartamento m; (device) indicatore m ● vt misurare; fig stimare

gaunt /gɔ:nt/ a (thin) smunto

gauze /gɔ:z/ n garza f

gave /geɪv/ see give

gawky /'gɔ:kɪ/ a (-ier, -iest) sgraziato

gawp /gɔ:p/ vi ~ [**at**] fam guardare con aria da ebete

gay /geɪ/ a gaio; (homosexual) omosessuale; (bar, club) gay

gaze /geɪz/ n sguardo m fisso ● vi guardare; ~ **at** fissare

GB abbr (**Great Britain**) GB

gear /gɪə(r)/ n equipaggiamento m; Techn ingranaggio m; Auto marcia f; **in** ~ con la marcia innestata; **change** ~ cambiare marcia ● vt finalizzare (**to** a)

gear: ~**box** n Auto scatola f del

cambio. **~-lever** *n*. *Am* **~-shift** *n* leva *f* del cambio

geese /giːs/ *see* **goose**

geezer /'giːzə(r)/ *n sl* tipo *m*

gel /dʒel/ *n* gel *m inv*

gelatine /'dʒelətɪn/ *n* gelatina *f*

gelignite /'dʒelɪɡnaɪt/ *n* gelatina *f* esplosiva

gem /dʒem/ *n* gemma *f*

Gemini /'dʒemɪnaɪ/ *n* *Astr* Gemelli *mpl*

gender /'dʒendə(r)/ *n* *Gram* genere *m*

gene /dʒiːn/ *n* gene *m*

genealogy /dʒiːnɪˈælədʒɪ/ *n* genealogia *f*

general /'dʒenrəl/ *a* generale ● *n* generale *m*; **in ~** in generale. **~ e'lection** *n* elezioni *fpl* politiche

generaliz|ation /dʒenrəlaɪˈzeɪʃn/ *n* generalizzazione *f*. **~e** /'dʒenrəlaɪz/ *vi* generalizzare

generally /'dʒenrəlɪ/ *adv* generalmente

general prac'titioner *n* medico *m* generico

generate /'dʒenəreɪt/ *vt* generare

generation /dʒenəˈreɪʃn/ *n* generazione *f*

generator /'dʒenəreɪtə(r)/ *n* generatore *m*

generic /dʒɪˈnerɪk/ *a* **~ term** termine *m* generico

generosity /dʒenəˈrɒsɪtɪ/ *n* generosità *f*

generous /'dʒenərəs/ *a* generoso. **~ly** *adv* generosamente

genetic /dʒɪˈnetɪk/ *a* genetico. **~ engineering** *n* ingegneria *f* genetica. **~s** *n* genetica *f*

Geneva /dʒɪˈniːvə/ *n* Ginevra *f*

genial /'dʒiːnɪəl/ *a* gioviale

genitals /'dʒenɪtlz/ *npl* genitali *mpl*

genitive /'dʒenɪtɪv/ *a* & *n* **~ [case]** genitivo *m*

genius /'dʒiːnɪəs/ *n* (*pl* **-uses**) genio *m*

genocide /'dʒenəsaɪd/ *n* genocidio *m*

genre /'ʒɒrə/ *n* genere *m* [letterario]

gent /dʒent/ *n fam* signore *m*; **the ~s** *sg* il bagno per uomini

genteel /dʒenˈtiːl/ *a* raffinato

gentle /'dʒentl/ *a* delicato; ⟨*breeze, tap, slope*⟩ leggero

gentleman /'dʒentlmən/ *n* signore *m*; ⟨*well-mannered*⟩ gentiluomo *m*

gent|leness /'dʒentlnɪs/ *n* delicatezza *f*. **~ly** *adv* delicatamente

genuine /'dʒenjuɪn/ *a* genuino. **~ly** *adv* ⟨*sorry*⟩ sinceramente

geograph|ical /dʒɪəˈɡræfɪkl/ *a* geografico. **~y** /dʒɪˈɒɡrəfɪ/ *n* geografia *f*

geological /dʒɪəˈlɒdʒɪkl/ *a* geologico

geolog|ist /dʒɪˈɒlədʒɪst/ *n* geologo. **-a** *mf*. **~y** *n* geologia *f*

geometr|ic[al] /dʒɪəˈmetrɪk(l)/ *a* geometrico. **~y** /dʒɪˈɒmətrɪ/ *n* geometria *f*

geranium /dʒəˈreɪnɪəm/ *n* geranio *m*

geriatric /dʒerɪˈætrɪk/ *a* geriatrico; **~ward** *n* reparto *m* geriatria. **~s** *n* geriatria *f*

germ /dʒɜːm/ *n* germe *m*; **~s** *pl* microbi *mpl*

German /'dʒɜːmən/ *n* & *a* tedesco. **-a** *mf*. (*language*) tedesco *m*

Germanic /dʒəˈmænɪk/ *a* germanico

German: **~ 'measles** *n* rosolia *f*. **~ 'shepherd** *n* pastore *m* tedesco

Germany /'dʒɜːmənɪ/ *n* Germania *f*

germinate /'dʒɜːmɪneɪt/ *vi* germogliare

gesticulate /dʒeˈstɪkjʊleɪt/ *vi* gesticolare

gesture /'dʒestʃə(r)/ *n* gesto *m*

get /ɡet/ *v* (*pt/pp* **got**, *pp Am also* **gotten**, *pres p* **getting**) ● *vt* (*receive*) ricevere; (*obtain*) ottenere; trovare ⟨*job*⟩; ⟨*buy, catch, fetch*⟩ prendere; (*transport, deliver to airport etc*) portare; (*reach on telephone*) trovare; (*fam: understand*) comprendere; preparare ⟨*meal*⟩; **~ sb to do sth** far fare qcsa a qcno ● *vi* (*become*) **~ tired/bored/angry** stancarsi/annoiarsi/arrabbiarsi; **I'm ~ting hungry** mi sta venendo fame; **~ dressed/married** vestirsi/sposarsi; **~ sth ready** preparare qcsa; **~ nowhere** non concludere nulla; **this is ~ting us nowhere** questo non ci è di nessun aiuto; **~ to** (*reach*) arrivare a. **get at** *vi* (*criticize*) criticare; **I see what you're ~ting at** ho capito cosa vuoi dire; **what are you ~ting at?** dove vuoi andare a parare?. **get away** *vi* (*leave*) andarsene; (*escape*) scappare. **get back** *vi* tornare ● *vt* (*recover*) riavere; **~ one's own back** rifarsi. **get by** *vi* passare; (*manage*) cavarsela. **get down** *vi* scendere; **~ down to work** mettersi al lavoro ● *vt* (*depress*) buttare giù. **get in** *vi* entrare ● *vt* mettere dentro ⟨*washing*⟩; far venire ⟨*plumber*⟩. **get off** *vi* scendere; (*from work*) andarsene; *Jur* essere assolto; **~ off the bus/one's bike** scendere dal pullman/dalla bici ● *vt* (*remove*) togliere. **get on** *vi* salire; (*be on good terms*) andare d'accordo; (*make progress*) andare avanti; (*in life*) riuscire; **~ on the bus/one's bike** salire sul pullman/sulla bici; **how are you**

~ting on? come va?. **get out** vi uscire; (of car) scendere; **~ out!** fuori!; **~ out of** (avoid doing) evitare ● vt togliere (cork, stain). **get over** vi andare al di là ● vt fig riprendersi da (illness). **get round** vt aggirare (rule); rigirare (person) ● vi **I never ~ round to it** non mi sono mai deciso a farlo. **get through** vi (on telephone) prendere la linea. **get up** vi alzarsi; (climb) salire; **~ up a hill** salire su una collina

get: ~away n fuga f. **~-up** n tenuta f

geyser /'giːzə(r)/ n scaldabagno m; Geol geyser m inv

ghastly /'gɑːstlɪ/ a (-ier, -iest) terribile; **feel ~** sentirsi da cani

gherkin /'gɜːkɪn/ n cetriolino m

ghetto /'getəʊ/ n ghetto m

ghost /gəʊst/ n fantasma m. **~ly** a spettrale

ghoulish /'guːlɪʃ/ a macabro

giant /'dʒaɪənt/ n gigante m ● a gigante

gibberish /'dʒɪbərɪʃ/ n stupidaggini fpl

gibe /dʒaɪb/ n malignità f inv

giblets /'dʒɪblɪts/ npl frattaglie fpl

giddiness /'gɪdɪnɪs/ n vertigini fpl

giddy /'gɪdɪ/ a (-ier, -iest) vertiginoso; **feel ~** avere le vertigini

gift /gɪft/ n dono m; (to charity) donazione f. **~ed** /-ɪd/ a dotato. **~-wrap** vt impacchettare in carta da regalo

gig /gɪg/ n Mus fam concerto m

gigantic /dʒaɪˈgæntɪk/ a gigantesco

giggle /'gɪgl/ n risatina f ● vi ridacchiare

gild /gɪld/ vt dorare

gills /gɪlz/ npl branchia fsg

gilt /gɪlt/ a dorato ● n doratura f. **~-edged stock** n investimento m sicuro

gimmick /'gɪmɪk/ n trovata f

gin /dʒɪn/ n gin m inv

ginger /'dʒɪndʒə(r)/ a rosso fuoco inv; (cat) rosso ● n zenzero m. **~ ale** n, **~ beer** n bibita f allo zenzero. **~bread** n panpepato m

gingerly /'dʒɪndʒəlɪ/ adv con precauzione

gipsy /'dʒɪpsɪ/ n = **gypsy**

giraffe /dʒɪˈrɑːf/ n giraffa f

girder /'gɜːdə(r)/ n Techn trave f

girl /gɜːl/ n ragazza f; (female child) femmina f. **~friend** n amica f; (of boy) ragazza f. **~ish** a da ragazza

giro /'dʒaɪərəʊ/ n bancogiro m; (cheque) sussidio m di disoccupazione

girth /gɜːθ/ n circonferenza f

gist /dʒɪst/ n **the ~** la sostanza

give /gɪv/ n elasticità f ● v (pt **gave**, pp **given**) ● vt dare; (as present) regalare (to a); fare (lecture, present, shriek); donare (blood); **~ birth** partorire ● vi (to charity) fare delle donazioni; (yield) cedere. **give away** vt dar via; (betray) tradire; (distribute) assegnare; **~ away the bride** portare la sposa all'altare. **give back** vt restituire. **give in** vt consegnare ● vi (yield) arrendersi. **give off** vt emanare. **give over** vi **~ over!** piantala!. **give up** vt rinunciare a; **~ oneself up** arrendersi ● vi rinunciare. **give way** vi cedere; Auto dare la precedenza; (collapse) crollare

given /'gɪvn/ see **give** ● a **~ name** nome m di battesimo

glacier /'glæsɪə(r)/ n ghiacciaio m

glad /glæd/ a contento (of di). **~den** /'glædn/ vt rallegrare

glade /gleɪd/ n radura f

gladly /'glædlɪ/ adv volentieri

glamor|ize /'glæməraɪz/ vt rendere affascinante. **~ous** a affascinante

glamour /'glæmə(r)/ n fascino m

glance /glɑːns/ n sguardo m ● vi **~ at** dare un'occhiata a. **glance up** vi alzare gli occhi

gland /glænd/ n glandola f

glandular /'glændjʊlə(r)/ a ghiandolare. **~ fever** n mononucleosi f

glare /gleə(r)/ n bagliore m; (look) occhiataccia f ● vi **~ at** dare un'occhiataccia a

glaring /'gleərɪŋ/ a sfolgorante; (mistake) madornale

glass /glɑːs/ n vetro m; (for drinking) bicchiere m; **~es** pl (spectacles) occhiali mpl. **~y** a vitreo

glaze /gleɪz/ n smalto m ● vt mettere i vetri a (door, window); smaltare (pottery); Culin spennellare. **~d** (eyes) vitreo

glazier /'gleɪzɪə(r)/ n vetraio m

gleam /gliːm/ n luccichio m ● vi luccicare

glean /gliːn/ vt racimolare (information)

glee /gliː/ n gioia f. **~ful** a gioioso

glen /glen/ n vallone m

glib /glɪb/ a pej insincero

glid|e /glaɪd/ vi scorrere; (through the air) planare. **~er** n aliante m

glimmer /'glɪmə(r)/ n barlume m ● vi emettere un barlume

glimpse /glɪmps/ n occhiata f; **catch a ~ of** intravedere ● vt intravedere

glint /glɪnt/ n luccichio m ● vi luccicare

glisten /'glɪsn/ vi luccicare

glitter /'glɪtə(r)/ vi brillare

gloat /gləʊt/ vi gongolare (**over** su)

global /'gləʊbl/ a mondiale

globe /gləʊb/ n globo m; (map) mappamondo m

gloom /glu:m/ n oscurità f; (sadness) tristezza f. **~ily** adv (sadly) con aria cupa

gloomy /'glu:mɪ/ a (**-ier, -iest**) cupo

glorif|y /'glɔ:rɪfaɪ/ vt (pt/pp **-ied**) glorificare; **a ~ied waitress** niente più che una cameriera

glorious /'glɔ:rɪəs/ a splendido; (deed, hero) glorioso

glory /'glɔ:rɪ/ n gloria f; (splendour) splendore m; (cause for pride) vanto m ● vi (pt/pp **-ied**) ~ **in** vantarsi di

gloss /glɒs/ n lucentezza f. **~ paint** n vernice f lucida ● **gloss over** vt sorvolare su

glossary /'glɒsərɪ/ n glossario m

glossy /'glɒsɪ/ a (**-ier, -iest**) lucido; ~ [**magazine**] rivista f femminile

glove /glʌv/ n guanto m. ~ **compartment** n Auto cruscotto m

glow /gləʊ/ n splendore m; (in cheeks) rossore m; (of candle) luce f soffusa ● vi risplendere; (candle:) brillare; (person:) avvampare. **~ing** a ardente; (account) entusiastico

'glow-worm n lucciola f

glucose /'glu:kəʊs/ n glucosio m

glue /glu:/ n colla f ● vt (pres p **gluing**) incollare

glum /glʌm/ a (**glummer, glummest**) tetro

glut /glʌt/ n eccesso m

glutton /'glʌtən/ n ghiottone, -a mf. **~ous** /-əs/ a ghiotto. **~y** n ghiottoneria f

gnarled /nɑ:ld/ a nodoso

gnash /næʃ/ vt ~ **one's teeth** digrignare i denti

gnat /næt/ n moscerino m

gnaw /nɔ:/ vt rosicchiare

gnome /nəʊm/ n gnomo m

go /gəʊ/ n (pl **goes**) energia f; (attempt) tentativo m; **on the go** in movimento; **at one go** in una sola volta; **it's your go** tocca a te; **make a go of it** riuscire ● vi (pt **went**, pp **gone**) andare; (leave) andar via; (vanish) sparire; (become) diventare; (be sold) vendersi; **go and see** andare a vedere; **go swimming/shopping** andare a nuotare/fare spese; **where's the time gone?** come ha fatto il tempo a volare così?; **it's all gone** è fi-

nito; **be going to do** stare per fare; **I'm not going to** non ne ho nessuna intenzione; **to go** (Am: hamburgers etc) da asporto; **a coffee to go** un caffè da portar via. **go about** vi andare in giro. **go away** vi andarsene. **go back** vi ritornare. **go by** vi passare. **go down** vi scendere; (sun:) tramontare; (ship:) affondare; (swelling:) diminuire. **go for** vt andare a prendere; andare a cercare (doctor); (choose) optare per; (fam: attack) aggredire; **he's not the kind I go for** non è il genere che mi attira. **go in** vi entrare. **go in for** vt partecipare a (competition); darsi a (tennis). **go off** vi andarsene; (alarm:) scattare; (gun, bomb:) esplodere; (food, milk:) andare a male; **go off well** riuscire. **go on** vi andare avanti; **what's going on?** cosa succede? **go on at** vt fam scocciare. **go out** vi uscire; (light, fire:) spegnersi. **go over** vi andare ● vt (check) controllare. **go round** vi andare in giro; (visit) andare; (turn) girare; **is there enough to go round?** ce n'è abbastanza per tutti? **go through** vi (bill, proposal:) passare ● vt (suffer) subire; (check) controllare; (read) leggere. **go under** vi passare sotto; (ship, swimmer:) andare sott'acqua; (fail) fallire. **go up** vi salire; (Theat: curtain:) aprirsi. **go with** vt accompagnare. **go without** vt fare a meno di (supper, sleep) ● vi fare senza

goad /gəʊd/ vt spingere (**into** a); (taunt) spronare

'go-ahead a (person, company) intraprendente ● n okay m

goal /gəʊl/ n porta f; (point scored) gol m inv; (in life) obiettivo m; **score a ~** segnare. **~ie** fam, **~keeper** n portiere m. **~-post** n palo m

goat /gəʊt/ n capra f

gobble /'gɒbl/ vt ~ [**down, up**] tranguggiare

'go-between n intermediario, -a mf

God, god /gɒd/ n Dio m, dio m

god: **~child** n figlioccio, -a mf. **~-daughter** n figlioccia f. **~dess** n dea f. **~father** n padrino m. **~-fearing** a timorato di Dio. **~-forsaken** a dimenticato da Dio. **~mother** n madrina f. **~parents** npl padrino m e madrina f. **~send** n manna f. **~son** n figlioccio m

go-getter /'gəʊgetə(r)/ n ambizioso, -a mf

goggle /'gɒgl/ vi fam ~ **at** fissare con gli occhi sgranati. **~s** npl occhiali mpl;

going | graft

(of swimmer) occhialini mpl [da piscina]; (of worker) occhiali mpl protettivi

going /'gəʊɪŋ/ a ⟨price, rate⟩ corrente; ~ **concern** azienda f florida ● n it's hard ~ è una faticaccia; while the ~ is good finché si può. ~s-'on npl avvenimenti mpl

gold /gəʊld/ n oro m ● a d'oro

golden /'gəʊldn/ a dorato. ~ 'handshake n buonuscita f (al termine di un rapporto di lavoro). ~ **mean** n giusto mezzo m. ~ 'wedding n nozze fpl d'oro

gold: ~fish n inv pesce m rosso. ~-mine n miniera f d'oro. ~-plated a placcato d'oro. ~smith n orefice m

golf /gɒlf/ n golf m

golf: ~-club n circolo m di golf; (implement) mazza f da golf. ~-course n campo m di golf. ~er n giocatore. trice mf di golf

gondo·la /'gɒndələ/ n gondola f. ~lier /·'lɪə(r)/ n gondoliere m

gone /gɒn/ see **go**

gong /gɒŋ/ n gong m inv

good /gʊd/ a (better, best) buono; ⟨child, footballer, singer⟩ bravo; ⟨holiday, film⟩ bello; ~ at bravo in; a ~ deal of anger molta rabbia; as ~ as (almost) quasi; ~ morning, ~ afternoon buon giorno; ~ evening buona sera; ~ night buonanotte; have a ~ time divertirsi ● n bene m; for ~ per sempre; do ~ far del bene; do sb ~ far bene a qcno; it's no ~ è inutile; be up to no ~ combinare qualcosa

goodbye /gʊd'baɪ/ int arrivederci

good: ~-for-nothing a buono, -a mf a nulla. G~ 'Friday n Venerdì m Santo

good: ~-'looking a bello. ~-'natured a be ~-natured avere un buon carattere

goodness /'gʊdnɪs/ n bontà f; my ~! santo cielo!; thank ~! grazie al cielo!

goods /gʊdz/ npl prodotti mpl. ~ train n treno m merci

good'will n buona volontà f; Comm avviamento m

goody /'gʊdi/ n ⟨fam: person⟩ buono m. ~-goody n santarellino, -a mf

gooey /'guːɪ/ a fam appiccicaticcio; fig sdolcinato

goof /guːf/ vi fam cannare

goose /guːs/ n (pl geese) oca f

gooseberry /'gʊzbərɪ/ n uva f spina

goose /guːs/ ~-flesh n, ~-pimples npl pelle fsg d'oca

gore¹ /gɔː(r)/ n sangue m

gore² vt incornare

gorge /gɔːdʒ/ n Geog gola f ● vt ~ oneself ingozzarsi

gorgeous /'gɔːdʒəs/ a stupendo

gorilla /gə'rɪlə/ n gorilla m inv

gormless /'gɔːmlɪs/ a fam stupido

gorse /gɔːs/ n ginestrone m

gory /'gɔːrɪ/ a (-ier, -iest) cruento

gosh /gɒʃ/ int fam caspita

gospel /'gɒspl/ n vangelo m. ~ truth n sacrosanta verità f

gossip /'gɒsɪp/ n pettegolezzi mpl; (person) pettegolo, -a mf ● vi pettegolare. ~y a pettegolo

got /gɒt/ see **get**; have ~ avere; have ~ to do sth dover fare qcsa

Gothic /'gɒθɪk/ a gotico

gotten /'gɒtn/ Am see **get**

gouge /gaʊdʒ/ vt ~ out cavare

gourmet /'gʊəmeɪ/ n buongustaio, -a mf

gout /gaʊt/ n gotta f

govern /'gʌv(ə)n/ vt/i governare; (determine) determinare

government /'gʌvnmənt/ n governo m. ~al /·'mentl/ a governativo

governor /'gʌvənə(r)/ n governatore m; (of school) membro m de consiglio di istituto; (of prison) direttore, -trice mf; (fam: boss) capo m

gown /gaʊn/ n vestito m; Univ, Jur toga f

GP n abbr **general practitioner**

grab /græb/ vt (pt/pp grabbed) ~ [hold of] afferrare

grace /greɪs/ n grazia f; (before meal) benedicite m inv; with good ~ volentieri; three days' ~ tre giorni di proroga. ~ful a aggraziato. ~fully adv con grazia

gracious /'greɪʃəs/ a cortese; (elegant) lussuoso

grade /greɪd/ n livello m; Comm qualità f; Sch voto m; (Sch: class) classe f; Am = gradient ● vt Comm classificare; Sch dare il voto a. ~ crossing n Am passaggio m a livello

gradient /'greɪdɪənt/ n pendenza f

gradual /'grædʒʊəl/ a graduale. ~ly adv gradualmente

graduate¹ /'grædʒʊət/ n laureato, -a mf

graduate² /'grædʒʊeɪt/ vi Univ laurearsi

graduation /grædʒʊ'eɪʃn/ n laurea f

graffiti /grə'fiːtɪ/ npl graffiti mpl

graft /grɑːft/ n (Bot, Med) innesto m; (Med: organ) trapianto m; (fam: hard work) duro lavoro m; (fam: corruption) corruzione f ● vt innestare; trapiantare ⟨organ⟩

grain /greɪn/ n ⟨of sand, salt⟩ granello m; ⟨of rice⟩ chicco m; ⟨cereals⟩ cereali mpl; ⟨in wood⟩ venatura f; **it goes against the ~** fig è contro la mia/sua natura

gram /græm/ n grammo m

grammar /'græmə(r)/ n grammatica f. **~ school** m ≈ liceo m

grammatical /grə'mætɪkl/ a grammaticale

granary /'grænərɪ/ n granaio m

grand /grænd/ a grandioso; fam eccellente

grandad /'grændæd/ n fam nonno m

'grandchild n nipote mf

'granddaughter n nipote f

grandeur /'grændʒə(r)/ n grandiosità f

'grandfather n nonno m. **~ clock** n pendolo m ⟨che poggia a terra⟩

grandiose /'grændɪəʊs/ a grandioso

grand: **~mother** n nonna f. **~parents** npl nonni mpl. **~ pi'ano** n pianoforte m a coda. **~son** n nipote m. **~stand** n tribuna f

granite /'grænɪt/ n granito m

granny /'grænɪ/ n fam nonna f

grant /grɑ:nt/ n ⟨money⟩ sussidio m; Univ borsa f di studio ● vt accordare; ⟨admit⟩ ammettere; **take sth for ~ed** dare per scontato qcsa

granulated /'grænjʊleɪtɪd/ a **~ sugar** zucchero m semolato

granule /'grænju:l/ n granello m

grape /greɪp/ n acino m; **~s** pl uva fsg

grapefruit /greɪp-/ n inv pompelmo m

graph /grɑ:f/ n grafico m

graphic /'græfɪk/ a grafico; ⟨vivid⟩ vivido. **~s** n grafica f

'graph paper n carta f millimetrata

grapple /'græpl/ vi **~ with** also fig essere alle prese con

grasp /grɑ:sp/ n stretta f; ⟨understanding⟩ comprensione f ● vt afferrare. **~ing** a avido

grass /grɑ:s/ n erba f; **at the ~ roots** alla base. **~hopper** n cavalletta f. **~land** n prateria f

grassy /'grɑ:sɪ/ a erboso

grate[1] /greɪt/ n grata f

grate[2] vt Culin grattugiare ● vi stridere

grateful /'greɪtfl/ a grato. **~ly** adv con gratitudine

grater /'greɪtə(r)/ n Culin grattugia f

gratify /'grætɪfaɪ/ vt ⟨pt/pp -ied⟩ appagare. **~ied** a appagato. **~ying** a appagante

grating /'greɪtɪŋ/ n grata f

gratis /'grɑ:tɪs/ adv gratis

gratitude /'grætɪtju:d/ n gratitudine f

gratuitous /grə'tju:ɪtəs/ a gratuito

gratuity /grə'tju:ɪtɪ/ n gratifica f

grave[1] /greɪv/ a grave

grave[2] n tomba f

gravel /'grævl/ n ghiaia f

grave: **~stone** n lapide f. **~yard** n cimitero m

gravitate /'grævɪteɪt/ vi gravitare

gravity /'grævɪtɪ/ n gravità f

gravy /'greɪvɪ/ n sugo m della carne

gray /greɪ/ a Am = **grey**

graze[1] /greɪz/ vi ⟨animal⟩ pascolare

graze[2] n escoriazione f ● vt ⟨touch lightly⟩ sfiorare; ⟨scrape⟩ escoriare; sbucciarsi ⟨knee⟩

grease /gri:s/ n grasso m ● vt ungere. **~-proof 'paper** n carta f oleata

greasy /'gri:sɪ/ a ⟨-ier, -iest⟩ untuoso; ⟨hair, skin⟩ grasso

great /greɪt/ a grande; ⟨fam: marvellous⟩ eccezionale

great: **~-'aunt** n prozia f. **G~ 'Britain** n Gran Bretagna f. **~'grandchildren** npl pronipoti mpl. **~-'grandfather** n bisnonno m. **~-'grandmother** n bisnonna f

great|ly /'greɪtlɪ/ adv enormemente. **~ness** n grandezza f

great-'uncle n prozio m

Greece /gri:s/ n Grecia f

greed /gri:d/ n avidità f; ⟨for food⟩ ingordigia f

greedily /'gri:dɪlɪ/ adv avidamente; ⟨eat⟩ con ingordigia

greedy /'gri:dɪ/ a ⟨-ier, -iest⟩ avido; ⟨for food⟩ ingordo

Greek /gri:k/ a & n greco, -a mf; ⟨language⟩ greco m

green /gri:n/ a verde; ⟨fig: inexperienced⟩ immaturo ● n verde m; **~s** pl verdura f; **the G~s** pl Pol i verdi. **~ belt** n zona f verde intorno a una città. **~ card** n Auto carta f verde

greenery /'gri:nərɪ/ n verde m

green fingers npl **have ~ ~** avere il police verde

'greenfly n afide m

green: **~grocer** n fruttivendolo, -a mf. **~house** n serra f. **~house effect** n effetto m serra. **~ light** n fam verde m

greet /gri:t/ vt salutare; ⟨welcome⟩ accogliere. **~ing** n saluto m; ⟨welcome⟩ accoglienza f. **~ings card** n biglietto m d'auguri

gregarious /grɪˈɡeərɪəs/ a gregario; (*person*) socievole

grenade /grɪˈneɪd/ n granata f

grew /gru:/ see **grow**

grey /greɪ/ a grigio; (*hair*) bianco ● n grigio m. **~hound** n levriero m

grid /grɪd/ n griglia f; (*on map*) reticolato m; *Electr* rete f

grief /gri:f/ n dolore m; **come to ~** (*plans:*) naufragare

grievance /ˈɡriːvəns/ n lamentela f

grieve /griːv/ vt addolorare ● vi essere addolorato

grill /grɪl/ n graticola f; (*for grilling*) griglia f; **mixed ~** grigliata f mista ● vt/i cuocere alla griglia; (*interrogate*) sottoporre al terzo grado

grille /grɪl/ n grata f

grim /grɪm/ a (**grimmer, grimmest**) arcigno; (*determination*) accanito

grimace /grɪˈmeɪs/ n smorfia f ● vi fare una smorfia

grime /graɪm/ n sudiciume m

grimy /ˈɡraɪmɪ/ a (**-ier, -iest**) sudicio

grin /grɪn/ n sorriso m ● vi (*pt/pp* **grinned**) fare un gran sorriso

grind /graɪnd/ n (*fam: hard work*) sfacchinata f ● vt (*pt/pp* **ground**) macinare; affilare (*knife*); (*Am: mince*) tritare; **~ one's teeth** digrignare i denti

grip /grɪp/ n presa f; *fig* controllo m; (*bag*) borsone m; **get a ~ of oneself** controllarsi ● vt (*pt/pp* **gripped**) afferrare; (*tyres:*) far presa su; tenere avvinto (*attention*)

gripe /graɪp/ vi (*fam: grumble*) lagnarsi

gripping /ˈɡrɪpɪŋ/ a avvincente

grisly /ˈɡrɪzlɪ/ a (**-ier, -iest**) raccapricciante

gristle /ˈɡrɪsl/ n cartilagine f

grit /grɪt/ n graniglia f; (*for roads*) sabbia f; (*courage*) coraggio m ● vt (*pt/pp* **gritted**) spargere sabbia su (*road*); **~ one's teeth** serrare i denti

grizzle /ˈɡrɪzl/ vi piagnucolare

groan /ɡrəʊn/ n gemito m ● vi gemere

grocer /ˈɡrəʊsə(r)/ n droghiere, -a mf; **~'s** [**shop**] drogheria f. **~ies** npl generi mpl alimentari

groggy /ˈɡrɒɡɪ/ a (**-ier, -iest**) stordito; (*unsteady*) barcollante

groin /grɔɪn/ n *Anat* inguine m

groom /ɡruːm/ n sposo m; (*for horse*) stalliere m ● vt strigliare (*horse*); *fig* preparare; **well-~ed** ben curato

groove /ɡruːv/ n scanalatura f

grope /ɡrəʊp/ vi brancolare; **~ for** cercare a tastoni

gross /ɡrəʊs/ a obeso; (*coarse*) volgare; (*glaring*) grossolano; (*salary, weight*) lordo ● n inv grossa f. **~ly** adv (*very*) enormemente

grotesque /ɡrəʊˈtesk/ a grottesco

grotto /ˈɡrɒtəʊ/ n (*pl*-es) grotta f

grotty /ˈɡrɒtɪ/ a (**-ier, -iest**) (*fam: flat, street*) squallido

ground[1] /ɡraʊnd/ see **grind**

ground[2] n terra f; *Sport* terreno m; (*reason*) ragione f; **~s** pl (*park*) giardini mpl; (*of coffee*) fondi mpl ● vi (*ship:*) arenarsi ● vt bloccare a terra (*aircraft*); *Am Electr* mettere a terra

ground: ~ floor n pianterreno m. **~ing** n base f. **~less** a infondato. **~sheet** n telone m impermeabile. **~work** n lavoro m di preparazione

group /ɡruːp/ n gruppo m ● vt raggruppare ● vi raggrupparsi

grouse[1] /ɡraʊs/ n inv gallo m cedrone

grouse[2] vi fam brontolare

grovel /ˈɡrɒvl/ vi (*pt/pp* **grovelled**) strisciare. **~ling** a leccapiedi inv

grow /ɡrəʊ/ v (*pt* **grew**, *pp* **grown**) ● vi crescere; (*become*) diventare; (*unemployment, fear:*) aumentare; (*town:*) ingrandirsi ● vt coltivare; **~ one's hair** farsi crescere i capelli. **grow up** vi crescere; (*town:*) svilupparsi

growl /ɡraʊl/ n grugnito m ● vi ringhiare

grown /ɡrəʊn/ see **grow** ● a adulto. **~-up** a & n adulto, -a mf

growth /ɡrəʊθ/ n crescita f; (*increase*) aumento m; *Med* tumore m

grub /ɡrʌb/ n larva f; (*fam: food*) mangiare m

grubby /ˈɡrʌbɪ/ a (**-ier, -iest**) sporco

grudge /ɡrʌdʒ/ n rancore m; **bear sb a ~e** portare rancore a qcno ● vt dare a malincuore. **~ing** a reluttante. **~ingly** adv a malincuore

gruelling /ˈɡruːəlɪŋ/ a estenuante

gruesome /ˈɡruːsəm/ a macabro

gruff /ɡrʌf/ a burbero

grumble /ˈɡrʌmbl/ vi brontolare (**at** contro)

grumpy /ˈɡrʌmpɪ/ a (**-ier, -iest**) scorbutico

grunt /ɡrʌnt/ n grugnito m ● vi fare un grugnito

guarantee /ɡærənˈtiː/ n garanzia f ● vt garantire. **~or** n garante mf

guard /ɡɑːd/ n guardia f; (*security*) guardiano m; (*on train*) capotreno m;

Techn schermo *m* protettivo; **be on ~** essere di guardia ● *vt* sorvegliare; (*protect*) proteggere. **guard against** *vt* guardarsi da. **~-dog** *n* cane *m* da guardia

guarded /'gɑːdɪd/ *a* guardingo

guardian /'gɑːdɪən/ *n* (*of minor*) tutore, -trice *mf*

guerrilla /gə'rɪlə/ *n* guerrigliero, -a *mf*. **~ warfare** *n* guerriglia *f*

guess /ges/ *n* supposizione *f* ● *vt* indovinare ● *vi* indovinare; (*Am: suppose*) supporre. **~work** *n* supposizione *f*

guest /gest/ *n* ospite *mf*; (*in hotel*) cliente *mf*. **~-house** *n* pensione *f*

guffaw /gʌ'fɔː/ *n* sghignazzata *f* ● *vi* sghignazzare

guidance /'gaɪdəns/ *n* guida *f*; (*advice*) consigli *mpl*

guide /gaɪd/ *n* guida *f*; [**Girl**] **G~** giovane esploratrice *f* ● *vt* guidare. **~book** *n* guida *f* turistica

guided /'gaɪdɪd/ *a* **~ missile** missile *m* teleguidato; **~ tour** giro *m* guidato

guide: ~-dog *n* cane *m* per ciechi. **~lines** *npl* direttive *fpl*

guild /gɪld/ *n* corporazione *f*

guile /gaɪl/ *n* astuzia *f*

guillotine /'gɪləti:n/ *n* ghigliottina *f*; (*for paper*) taglierina *f*

guilt /gɪlt/ *n* colpa *f*. **~ily** *adv* con aria colpevole

guilty /'gɪltɪ/ *a* (**-ier, -iest**) colpevole; **have a ~ conscience** avere la coscienza sporca

guinea-pig /'gɪnɪ-/ *n* porcellino *m* d'India; (*in experiments*) cavia *f*

guise /gaɪz/ *n* **in the ~ of** sotto le spoglie di

guitar /gɪ'tɑː(r)/ *n* chitarra *f*. **~ist** *n* chitarrista *mf*

gulf /gʌlf/ *n Geog* golfo *m*; *fig* abisso *m*

gull /gʌl/ *n* gabbiano *m*

gullet /'gʌlɪt/ *n* esofago *m*; (*throat*) gola *f*

gullible /'gʌlɪbl/ *a* credulone

gully /'gʌlɪ/ *n* burrone *m*; (*drain*) canale *m* di scolo

gulp /gʌlp/ *n* azione *f* di deglutire; (*of food*) boccone *m*; (*of liquid*) sorso *m* ● *vi*

deglutire. **gulp down** *vt* tranguggiare (*food*); scolarsi (*liquid*)

gum¹ /gʌm/ *n Anat* gengiva *f*

gum² *n* gomma *f*; (*chewing-gum*) gomma *f* da masticare, chewing-gum *m inv* ● *vt* (*pt/pp* gummed) ingommare (**to** a)

gummed /gʌmd/ *see* **gum²** ● *a* (*label*) adesivo

gumption /'gʌmpʃn/ *n fam* buon senso *m*

gun /gʌn/ *n* pistola *f*; (*rifle*) fucile *m*; (*cannon*) cannone *m* ● **gun down** *vt* (*pt/pp* gunned) freddare

gun: ~fire *n* spari *mpl*; (*of cannon*) colpi *mpl* [di cannone]. **~man** uomo *m* armato

gun: ~powder *n* polvere *f* da sparo. **~shot** *n* colpo *m* [di pistola]

gurgle /'gɜːgl/ *vi* gorgogliare; (*baby:*) fare degli urletti

gush /gʌʃ/ *vi* sgorgare; (*enthuse*) parlare con troppo entusiasmo (**over** di). **gush out** *vi* sgorgare. **~ing** *a* eccessivamente entusiastico

gust /gʌst/ *n* (*of wind*) raffica *f*

gusto /'gʌstəʊ/ *n* **with ~** con trasporto

gusty /'gʌstɪ/ *a* ventoso

gut /gʌt/ *n* intestino *m*; **~s** *pl* pancia *f*; (*fam: courage*) fegato *m* ● *vt* (*pt/pp* gutted) *Culin* svuotare delle interiora; **~ted by fire** sventrato da un incendio

gutter /'gʌtə(r)/ *n* canale *m* di scolo; (*on roof*) grondaia *f*; *fig* bassifondi *mpl*

guttural /'gʌtərəl/ *a* gutturale

guy /gaɪ/ *n fam* tipo *m*, tizio *m*

guzzle /'gʌzl/ *vt* ingozzarsi con (*food*); **he's ~d the lot** si è sbafato tutto

gym /dʒɪm/ *n fam* palestra *f*; (*gymnastics*) ginnastica *f*

gymnasium /dʒɪm'neɪzɪəm/ *n* palestra *f*

gymnast /'dʒɪmnæst/ *n* ginnasta *mf*. **~ics** /-'næstɪks/ *n* ginnastica *f*

gym: ~ shoes *npl* scarpe *fpl* da ginnastica. **~-slip** *n Sch* ≈ grembiule *m* (*da bambina*)

gynaecolog|ist /gaɪnɪ'kɒlədʒɪst/ *n* ginecologo, -a *mf*. **~y** *n* ginecologia *f*

gypsy /'dʒɪpsɪ/ *n* zingaro, -a *mf*

gyrate /dʒaɪ'reɪt/ *vi* roteare

Hh

haberdashery /hæbə'dæʃərɪ/ n merceria f; Am negozio m d'abbigliamento da uomo

habit /'hæbɪt/ n abitudine f; (Relig: costume) tonaca f; **be in the ~ of doing sth** avere l'abitudine di fare qcsa

habitable /'hæbɪtəbl/ a abitabile

habitat /'hæbɪtæt/ n habitat m inv

habitation /hæbɪ'teɪʃn/ n **unfit for human ~** inagibile

habitual /hə'bɪtjʊəl/ a abituale; ⟨smoker, liar⟩ inveterato. **~ly** adv regolarmente

hack[1] /hæk/ n (writer) scribacchino, -a mf

hack[2] vt tagliare; **~ to pieces** tagliare a pezzi

hackneyed /'hæknɪd/ a trito [e ritrito]

'hacksaw n seghetto m

had /hæd/ see **have**

haddock /'hædək/ n inv eglefino m

haemorrhage /'hemərɪdʒ/ n emorragia f

haemorrhoids /'hemərɔɪdz/ npl emorroidi fpl

hag /hæg/ n old ~ vecchia befana f

haggard /'hægəd/ a sfatto

haggle /'hægl/ vi contrattare (**over** per)

hail[1] /heɪl/ vt salutare; far segno a ⟨taxi⟩ ● vi ~ **from** provenire da

hail[2] n grandine f ● vi grandinare. **~stone** n chicco m di grandine. **~storm** n grandinata f

hair /heə(r)/ n capelli mpl; (on body, of animal) pelo m

hair: **~brush** n spazzola f per capelli. **~cut** n taglio m di capelli; **have a ~cut** farsi tagliare i capelli. **~-do** n fam pettinatura f. **~dresser** n parrucchiere, -a mf. **~dryer** n fon m inv; (with hood) casco m [asciugacapelli]. **~grip** n molletta f. **~pin** n forcina f. **~pin 'bend** n tornante m, curva f a gomito. **~raising** a terrificante. **~style** n acconciatura f

hairy /'heərɪ/ a (-ier, -iest) peloso; (fam: frightening) spaventoso

hale /heɪl/ a ~ **and hearty** in piena forma

half /hɑːf/ n (pl **halves**) metà f inv; **cut in ~** tagliare a metà; **one and a ~** uno e mezzo; **~ a dozen** mezza dozzina; **~ an hour** mezz'ora ● a mezzo; [at] **~ price** [a] metà prezzo ● adv a metà; **~ past two** le due e mezza

half: ~ **board** n mezza pensione f. **~-'hearted** a esitante. **~-'hourly** a & adv ogni mezz'ora. ~ **'mast** n **at ~ mast** a mezz'asta. ~ **measures** npl mezze misure fpl. '**~-open** a socchiuso. **~-'term** n vacanza f di metà trimestre. **~-'time** n Sport intervallo m. ~ **'way** a the **~way mark/stage** il livello intermedio ● adv a metà strada; **get ~way** fig arrivare a metà. **~wit** n idiota mf

hall /hɔːl/ n (entrance) ingresso m; (room) sala f; (mansion) residenza f di campagna; ~ **of residence** Univ casa f dello studente

'hallmark n marchio m di garanzia; fig marchio m

hallo /hə'ləʊ/ int ciao!; (on telephone) pronto!; **say ~ to** salutare

Hallowe'en /hæləʊ'iːn/ n vigilia f d'Ognissanti e notte delle streghe, celebrata soprattutto dai bambini

hallucination /həluːsɪ'neɪʃn/ n allucinazione f

halo /'heɪləʊ/ n (pl **-es**) aureola f; Astr alone m

halt /hɔːlt/ n alt m inv; **come to a ~** fermarsi; ⟨traffic:⟩ bloccarsi ● vi fermarsi; ~! alt! ● vt fermare. **~ing** a esitante

halve /hɑːv/ vt dividere a metà; (reduce) dimezzare

ham /hæm/ n prosciutto m; Theat attore, -trice mf da strapazzo

hamburger /'hæmbɜːgə(r)/ n hamburger m inv

hamlet /'hæmlɪt/ n paesino m

hammer /'hæmə(r)/ n martello m ● vt martellare ● vi ~ **at/on** picchiare a

hammock /'hæmək/ n amaca f

hamper[1] /'hæmpə(r)/ n cesto m; [gift] ~ cestino m

hamper² *vt* ostacolare

hamster /'hæmstə(r)/ *n* criceto *m*

hand /hænd/ *n* mano *f*; (*of clock*) lancetta *f*; (*writing*) scrittura *f*; (*worker*) manovale *m*; **at ~, to ~** a portata di mano; **on the one ~** da un lato; **on the other ~** d'altra parte; **out of ~** incontrollabile; (*summarily*) su due piedi; **give sb a ~** dare una mano a qcno ● *vt* porgere. **hand down** *vt* tramandare. **hand in** *vt* consegnare. **hand out** *vt* distribuire. **hand over** *vt* passare; (*to police*) consegnare

hand: **~bag** *n* borsa *f* (*da signora*). **~book** *n* manuale *m*. **~brake** *n* freno *m* a mano. **~cuffs** *npl* manette *fpl*. **~ful** *n* manciata *f*; **be ⟨quite⟩ a ~ful** *fam* essere difficile da tenere a freno

handicap /'hændɪkæp/ *n* handicap *m inv*. **~ped** *a* **mentally physically ~ped** mentalmente/fisicamente handicappato

handi|craft /'hændɪkrɑːft/ *n* artigianato *m*. **~work** *n* opera *f*

handkerchief /'hæŋkətʃɪf/ *n* (*pl* **~s** & **-chieves**) fazzoletto *m*

handle /'hændl/ *n* manico *m*; (*of door*) maniglia *f*; **fly off the ~** *fam* perdere le staffe ● *vt* maneggiare; occuparsi di (*problem, customer*); prendere (*difficult person*); trattare (*subject*). **~bars** *npl* manubrio *m*

hand: **~luggage** *n* bagaglio *m* a mano. **~made** *a* fatto a mano. **~out** *n* (*at lecture*) foglio *m* informativo; (*fam: money*) elemosina *f*. **~rail** *n* corrimano *m*. **~shake** *n* stretta *f* di mano

handsome /'hænsəm/ *a* bello; (*fig: generous*) generoso

hand: **~stand** *n* verticale *f*. **~writing** *n* calligrafia *f*. **~-written** *a* scritto a mano

handy /'hændɪ/ *a* (**-ier, -iest**) utile; (*person*) abile; **have/keep ~** avere/tenere a portata di mano. **~man** *n* tuttofare *m inv*

hang /hæŋ/ *vt* (*pt/pp* **hung**) appendere (*picture*); (*pt/pp* **hanged**) impiccare (*criminal*); **~ oneself** impiccarsi ● *vi* (*pt/pp* **hung**) pendere; (*hair:*) scendere ● *n* **get the ~ of it** *fam* afferrare. **hang about** *vi* gironzolare. **hang on** *vi* tenersi stretto; (*fam: wait*) aspettare; *Teleph* restare in linea. **hang on to** *vt* tenersi stretto a; (*keep*) tenere. **hang out** *vi* spuntare; **where does he usually ~ out?** *fam* dove bazzica di solito? ● *vt* stendere (*washing*). **hang up** *vt* appen-

dere; *Teleph* riattaccare ● *vi* essere appeso; *Teleph* riattaccare

hangar /'hæŋə(r)/ *n* hangar *m inv*

hanger /'hæŋə(r)/ *n* gruccia *f*. **~-on** *n* leccapiedi *mf*

hang: **~-glider** *n* deltaplano *m*. **~-gliding** *n* deltaplano *m*. **~man** *n* boia *m*. **~over** *n* *fam* postumi *mpl* da sbornia. **~-up** *n* *fam* complesso *m*

hanker /'hæŋkə(r)/ *vi* **~ after sth** smaniare per qcsa

hanky /'hæŋkɪ/ *n* *fam* fazzoletto *m*

hanky-panky /hæŋkɪ'pæŋkɪ/ *n* *fam* qualcosa *m* di losco

haphazard /hæp'hæzəd/ *a* a casaccio

happen /'hæpn/ *vi* capitare, succedere; **as it ~s** per caso; **I ~ed to meet him** mi è capitato di incontrarlo; **what has ~ed to him?** cosa gli è capitato?; (*become of*) che fine ha fatto? **~ing** *n* avvenimento *m*

happi|ly /'hæpɪlɪ/ *adv* felicemente; (*fortunately*) fortunatamente. **~ness** *n* felicità *f*

happy /'hæpɪ/ *a* (**-ier, -iest**) contento, felice. **~-go-'lucky** *a* spensierato

harass /'hærəs/ *vt* perseguitare. **~ed** *a* stressato. **~ment** *n* persecuzione *f*; **sexual ~ment** molestie *fpl* sessuali

harbour /'hɑːbə(r)/ *n* porto *m* ● *vt* dare asilo a; nutrire (*grudge*)

hard /hɑːd/ *a* duro; (*question, problem*) difficile; **~ of hearing** duro d'orecchi; **be ~ on sb** (*person:*) essere duro con qcno ● *adv* (*work*) duramente; (*pull, hit, rain, snow*) forte; **~ hit by unemployment** duramente colpito dalla disoccupazione; **take sth ~** non accettare qcsa; **think ~!** pensaci bene!; **try ~** mettercela tutta; **try ~er** metterci più impegno; **~ done by** *fam* trattato ingiustamente

hard: **~back** *n* edizione *f* rilegata. **~-boiled** *a* (*egg*) sodo. **~ copy** *n* copia *f* stampata. **~ disk** *n* hard disk *m inv*, disco *m* rigido

harden /'hɑːdn/ *vi* indurirsi

hard: **~-headed** *a* (*businessman*) dal sangue freddo. **~-hearted** *a* dal cuore duro. **~ line** *n* linea *f* dura; **~ lines!** che sfortuna!. **~ line** *a* duro. **~liner** *n* fautore, -trice *mf* della linea dura. **~ luck** *n* sfortuna *f*

hard|ly /'hɑːdlɪ/ *adv* appena; **~ly ever** quasi mai. **~ness** *n* durezza *f*. **~ship** *n* avversità *f inv*

hard: **~ 'shoulder** *n* *Auto* corsia *f* d'emergenza. **~ up** *a* *fam* a corto di sol-

di; ~ **up for sth** a corto di qcsa. **~ware**
n ferramenta fpl; Comput hardware m
inv. **~·'working** abe **~-working** essere un
gran lavoratore

hardy /'hɑːdɪ/ a (**-ier, -iest**) dal fisico
resistente; ⟨plant⟩ che sopporta il gelo

hare /heə(r)/ n lepre f. **~-brained** a
fam ⟨scheme⟩ da scervellati

hark /hɑːk/ vi ~ **back to** fig ritornare
su

harm /hɑːm/ n male m; ⟨damage⟩ danni
mpl; out of ~'s way in un posto sicuro;
it won't do any ~ non farà certo male
● vt far male a; ⟨damage⟩ danneggiare.
~ful a dannoso. **~less** a innocuo

harmonica /hɑːˈmɒnɪkə/ n armonica
f ⟨a bocca⟩

harmonious /hɑːˈməʊnɪəs/ a armo-
nioso. **~ly** adv in armonia

harmon|ize /ˈhɑːmənaɪz/ vi fig armo-
nizzare. **~y** n armonia f

harness /ˈhɑːnɪs/ n finimenti mpl; ⟨of
parachute⟩ imbracatura f ● vt bardare
⟨horse⟩; sfruttare ⟨resources⟩

harp /hɑːp/ n arpa f ● **harp on** vi fam
insistere (**about** su). **~ist** n arpista mf

harpoon /hɑːˈpuːn/ n arpione m

harpsichord /ˈhɑːpsɪkɔːd/ n clavicem-
balo m

harrowing /ˈhærəʊɪŋ/ a straziante

harsh /hɑːʃ/ a duro; ⟨light⟩ abbaglian-
te. **~ness** n durezza f

harvest /ˈhɑːvɪst/ n raccolta f; ⟨of
grapes⟩ vendemmia f; ⟨crop⟩ raccolto m
● vt raccogliere

has /hæz/ see **have**

hash /hæʃ/ n make a ~ of fam fare un
casino con

hashish /ˈhæʃɪʃ/ n hascish m

hassle /ˈhæsl/ n fam rottura f ● vt
rompere le scatole a

haste /heɪst/ n fretta f

hast|y /ˈheɪstɪ/ a (**-ier, -iest**) frettoloso;
⟨decision⟩ affrettato. **~ily** adv frettolo-
samente

hat /hæt/ n cappello m

hatch¹ /hætʃ/ n ⟨for food⟩ sportello m
passavivande; Naut boccaporto m

hatch² /hætʃ/ vi ~ [**out**] rompere il guscio;
⟨egg:⟩ schiudersi ● vt covare; tramare
⟨plot⟩

hatchback n tre/cinque porte m inv;
⟨door⟩ porta f del bagagliaio

hatchet /ˈhætʃɪt/ n ascia f

hate /heɪt/ n odio m ● vt odiare. **~ful** a
odioso

hatred /ˈheɪtrɪd/ n odio m

haught|y /ˈhɔːtɪ/ a (**-ier, -iest**) altezzo-
so. **~ily** adv altezzosamente

haul /hɔːl/ n ⟨fish⟩ pescata f; ⟨loot⟩ bottino m; ⟨pull⟩ tirata f ● vt tirare; trasportare ⟨goods⟩ ● vi ~ **on** tirare. **~age**
/-ɪdʒ/ n trasporto m. **~ier** /-ɪə(r)/ n
autotrasportatore m

haunt /hɔːnt/ n ritrovo m ● vt frequentare; ⟨linger in the mind⟩ perseguitare;
this house is ~ed questa casa è abita-
ta da fantasmi

have /hæv/ vt (3 sg pres tense **has**; pt/pp
had) avere; fare ⟨breakfast, bath, walk
etc⟩; ~ **a drink** bere qualcosa; ~
lunch/dinner pranzare/cenare; ~ **a
rest** riposarsi; **I had my hair cut** mi
sono tagliata i capelli; **we had the
house painted** abbiamo fatto
tinteggiare la casa; **I had it made** l'ho
fatto fare; ~ **to do sth** dover fare qcsa;
~ **him telephone me tomorrow** digli
di telefonarmi domani; **he has** or **he's
got two houses** ha due case; **you've
got the money, ~n't you?** hai i soldi,
no? ● v aux avere; ⟨with verbs of motion
& some others⟩ essere; **I ~ seen him**
l'ho visto; **he has never been there**
non ci è mai stato. **have on** vt ⟨be
wearing⟩ portare; ⟨dupe⟩ prendere in
giro; **I've got something on tonight**
ho un impegno stasera. **have out** vt ~
it out with sb chiarire le cose con qcno
● npl **the ~s and the ~-nots** i ricchi e
i poveri

haven /ˈheɪvn/ n fig rifugio m

haversack /ˈhævə-/ n zaino m

havoc /ˈhævək/ n strage f; **play ~ with**
fig scombussolare

haw /hɔː/ see **hum**

hawk /hɔːk/ n falco m

hay /heɪ/ n fieno m. ~ **fever** n raffreddore m da fieno. **~stack** n pagliaio m

haywire a fam **go ~** dare i numeri;
⟨plans:⟩ andare all'aria

hazard /ˈhæzəd/ n ⟨risk⟩ rischio m ● vt
rischiare; ~ **a guess** azzardare un'ipotesi. **~ous** /-əs/ a rischioso. ~
[**warning**] **lights** npl Auto luci fpl
d'emergenza

haze /heɪz/ n foschia f

hazel /ˈheɪz(ə)l/ n nocciolo m; ⟨colour⟩
[color m] nocciola m. **~-nut** n nocciola f

hazy /ˈheɪzɪ/ a (**-ier, -iest**) nebbioso;
⟨fig: person⟩ confuso; ⟨memories⟩ vago

he /hiː/ pron lui; **he's tired** è stanco;
I'm going but he's not io vengo, ma
lui no

head /hed/ n testa f; ⟨of firm⟩ capo m;

(of primary school) direttore, -trice mf; (of secondary school) preside mf; (on beer) schiuma f; **be off one's** ~ essere fuori di testa; **have a good** ~ **for business** avere il senso degli affari; **have a good** ~ **for heights** non soffrire di vertigini; **10 pounds a** ~ 10 sterline a testa; **20** ~ **of cattle** 20 capi di bestiame; ~ **first** a capofitto; ~ **over heels in love** innamorato pazzo; ~**s or tails?** testa o croce? ● vt essere a capo di; essere in testa a ⟨list⟩; colpire di testa ⟨ball⟩ ● vi ~ **for** dirigersi verso.

head: ~**ache** n mal m di testa. ~**-dress** n acconciatura f. ~**er** /'hedə(r)/ n rinvio m di testa; ⟨dive⟩ tuffo m di testa. ~**hunter** n cacciatore, -trice mf di teste. ~**ing** n (in list etc) titolo m. ~**lamp** n Auto fanale m. ~**land** n promontorio m. ~**light** n Auto fanale m. ~**line** n titolo m. ~**long** a & adv a capofitto. ~'**master** n (of primary school) direttore m; (of secondary school) preside m. ~'**mistress** n (of primary school) direttrice f; (of secondary school) preside f. ~ **office** n sede f centrale. ~**-on** a frontale ● adv frontalmente. ~**phones** npl cuffie fpl. ~**quarters** npl sede fsg; Mil quartier m generale msg. ~**-rest** n poggiatesta m inv. ~**room** n sottotetto m; (of bridge) altezza f libera di passaggio. ~**scarf** n foulard m inv, fazzoletto m. ~**strong** a testardo. ~'**waiter** n capocameriere m. ~**way** n progresso m. ~**wind** n vento m di prua

heady /'hedɪ/ a che dà alla testa

heal /hiːl/ vt/i guarire

health /helθ/ n salute f

health: ~ **farm** n centro m di rimessa in forma. ~ **foods** npl alimenti mpl macrobiotici. ~**-food shop** n negozio m di macrobiotica. ~ **insurance** n assicurazione f contro malattie

healthy /'helθɪ/ a (-ier, -iest) sano. ~**ily** adv in modo sano

heap /hiːp/ n mucchio m; ~**s of** fam un sacco di ● vt ~ **[up]** ammucchiare; ~**ed teaspoon** un cucchiaino abbondante

hear /hɪə(r)/ vt/i (pt/pp **heard**) sentire; ~, ~! bravo! ~ **from** vi aver notizie di. **hear of** vi sentir parlare di; **he would not** ~ **of it** non ne ha voluto sentir parlare

hearing /'hɪərɪŋ/ n udito m; Jur udienza f. ~**-aid** n apparecchio m acustico

'**hearsay** n **from** ~ per sentito dire

hearse /hɜːs/ n carro m funebre

heart /hɑːt/ n cuore m; ~**s** pl (in cards) cuori mpl; **by** ~ a memoria

heart: ~**ache** n pena f. ~ **attack** n infarto m. ~**beat** n battito m cardiaco. ~**break** n afflizione f. ~**breaking** a straziante. ~**broken** a **be** ~**broken** avere il cuore spezzato. ~**burn** n mal m di stomaco. ~**en** vt rincuorare. ~**felt** a di cuore

hearth /hɑːθ/ n focolare m

heart|ily /'hɑːtɪlɪ/ adv di cuore; ⟨eat⟩ con appetito; **be** ~**ily sick of sth** non poterne più di qcsa. ~**less** a spietato. ~**-searching** n esame m di coscienza. ~**-to-** n conversazione f a cuore aperto ● a a cuore aperto. ~**y** a caloroso; ⟨meal⟩ copioso; ⟨person⟩ gioviale

heat /hiːt/ n calore m; Sport prova f eliminatoria ● vt scaldare ● vi scaldarsi. ~**ed** a ⟨swimming pool⟩ riscaldato; ⟨discussion⟩ animato. ~**er** n (for room) stufa f; (for water) boiler m inv; Auto riscaldamento m

heath /hiːθ/ n brughiera f

heathen /'hiːðn/ a & n pagano, -a mf

heather /'heðə(r)/ n erica f

heating /'hiːtɪŋ/ n riscaldamento m

heat: ~**-stroke** n colpo m di sole. ~**wave** n ondata f di calore

heave /hiːv/ vt tirare; (lift) tirare su; (fam: throw) gettare; emettere ⟨sigh⟩ ● vi tirare

heaven /'hevn/ n paradiso m; ~ **help you if...** Dio ti scampi se...; **H**~**s!** santo cielo!. ~**ly** a celeste; fam delizioso

heav|y /'hevɪ/ a (-ier, -iest) pesante; ⟨traffic⟩ intenso; ⟨rain, cold⟩ forte; **be a** ~**y smoker/drinker** essere un gran fumatore/bevitore. ~**ily** adv pesantemente; ⟨smoke, drink etc⟩ molto. ~**yweight** n peso m massimo

Hebrew /'hiːbruː/ a ebreo

heckle /'hekl/ vt interrompere di continuo. ~**r** n disturbatore, -trice mf

hectic /'hektɪk/ a frenetico

hedge /hedʒ/ n siepe f ● vi fig essere evasivo. ~**hog** n riccio m

heed /hiːd/ n **pay** ~ to prestare ascolto a ● vt prestare ascolto a. ~**less** a noncurante

heel¹ /hiːl/ n tallone m; (of shoe) tacco m; **take to one's** ~**s** fam darsela a gambe

heel² vi ~ **over** Naut inclinarsi

hefty /'heftɪ/ a (-ier, -iest) massiccio

heifer /'hefə(r)/ n giovenca f

height /haɪt/ n altezza f; (of plane) altitudine f; (of season, fame) culmine m. ~**en** vt fig accrescere

heir /eə(r)/ n erede mf. ~**ess** n ereditiera f. ~**loom** n cimelio m di famiglia

held /held/ see **hold²**

helicopter /'helɪkɒptə(r)/ n elicottero m

hell /hel/ n inferno m; **go to ~!** sl va' al diavolo! ● int porca miseria!

hello /hə'ləʊ/ int & n = **hallo**

helm /helm/ n timone m; **at the ~** fig al timone

helmet /'helmɪt/ n casco m

help /help/ n aiuto m; (employee) aiuto m domestico; **that's no ~** non è d'aiuto ● vt aiutare; ~ **oneself to sth** servirsi di qcsa; ~ **yourself** (at table) servíti pure; **I could not ~ laughing** non ho potuto trattenermi dal ridere; **it cannot be ~ed** non c'è niente da fare; **I can't ~ it** non ci posso far niente ● vi aiutare

help|er /'helpə(r)/ n aiutante mf. ~**ful** a ⟨person⟩ di aiuto; ⟨advice⟩ utile. ~**ing** n porzione f. ~**less** a (unable to manage) incapace; (powerless) impotente

helter-skelter /heltə'skeltə(r)/ adv in fretta e furia ● n scivolo m a spirale nei luna park

hem /hem/ n orlo m ● vt (pt/pp hemmed) orlare. **hem in** vt intrappolare

hemisphere /'hemɪ-/ n emisfero m

hemp /hemp/ n canapa f

hen /hen/ n gallina f; (any female bird) femmina f

hence /hens/ adv (for this reason) quindi. ~ **forth** adv d'ora innanzi

henchman /'hentʃmən/ n pej tirapiedi m

hen: ~**-party** n fam festa f di addio al celibato per sole donne. ~**pecked** a tiranneggiato dalla moglie

her /hɜ:(r)/ poss a il suo m, la sua f, i suoi mpl, le sue fpl; ~ **mother father** sua madre/suo padre ● pers pron (direct object) la; (indirect object) le; (after prep) lei; **I know ~** la conosco; **give ~ the money** dale i soldi; **give it to ~** daglielo; **I came with ~** sono venuto con lei; **it's ~** è lei; **I've seen ~** l'ho vista; **I've seen ~, but not him** ho visto lei, ma non lui

herald /'herəld/ vt annunciare

herb /hɜ:b/ n erba f

herbal /'hɜ:b(ə)l/ a alle erbe; ~ **tea** tisana f

herbs /hɜ:bz/ npl (for cooking) aromi mpl [da cucina]; (medicinal) erbe fpl

herd /hɜ:d/ n gregge m ● vt (tend) sorvegliare; (drive) far muovere; fig ammassare

here /hɪə(r)/ adv qui, qua; **in ~** qui dentro; **come/bring ~** vieni/porta qui; ~ **is..., ~ are...** ecco...; ~ **you are!** ecco qua!. ~ **after** adv in futuro. ~ **by** adv con la presente

heredit|ary /hə'redɪtəri/ a ereditario. ~**y** n eredità f

here|sy /'herəsi/ n eresia f. ~**tic** n eretico, -a mf

here with adv Comm con la presente

heritage /'herɪtɪdʒ/ n eredità f

hermetic /hɜ:'metɪk/ a ermetico. ~**ally** adv ermeticamente

hermit /'hɜ:mɪt/ n eremita mf

hernia /'hɜ:nɪə/ n ernia f

hero /'hɪərəʊ/ n (pl -es) eroe m

heroic /hɪ'rəʊɪk/ a eroico

heroin /'herəʊɪn/ n eroina f (droga)

hero|ine /'herəʊɪn/ n eroina f. ~**ism** n eroismo m

heron /'herən/ n airone m

herring /'herɪŋ/ n aringa f

hers /hɜ:z/ poss pron il suo m, la sua f, i suoi mpl, le sue fpl; **a friend of ~** un suo amico; **friends of ~** dei suoi amici; **that is ~** quello è suo; (as opposed to mine) quello è il suo

her self pers pron (reflexive) si; (emphatic) lei stessa; (after prep) sé, se stessa; **she poured ~ a drink** si è versata da bere; **she told me so** ~ me lo ha detto lei stessa; **she's proud of ~** è fiera di sé; **by ~** da sola

hesitant /'hezɪtənt/ a esitante. ~**ly** adv con esitazione

hesitat|e /'hezɪteɪt/ vi esitare. ~**ion** /-'teɪʃn/ n esitazione f

het /het/ a ~ **up** fam agitato

hetero sexual /hetərəʊ-/ a eterosessuale

hexagon /'heksəgən/ n esagono m. ~**al** /hek'sægənl/ a esagonale

hey /heɪ/ int ehi

heyday /'heɪ-/ n tempi mpl d'oro

hi /haɪ/ int ciao!

hiatus /haɪ'eɪtəs/ n (pl -tuses) iato m

hibernat|e /'haɪbəneɪt/ vi andare in letargo. ~**ion** /-'neɪʃn/ n letargo m

hiccup /'hɪkʌp/ n singhiozzo m; (fam: hitch) intoppo m ● vi fare un singhiozzo

hid /hɪd/, **hidden** /'hɪdn/ see **hide²**

hide¹ /haɪd/ n (leather) pelle f (di animale)

hide² *vt* (*pt* **hid**, *pp* **hidden**) nascondere ● *vi* nascondersi. **~-and-seek** *n* **play ~-and-seek** giocare a nascondino

hideous /'hɪdɪəs/ *a* orribile

'**hide-out** *n* nascondiglio *m*

hiding¹ /'haɪdɪŋ/ *n* (*fam: beating*) bastonata *f*; (*defeat*) batosta *f*

hiding² *n* **go into ~** sparire dalla circolazione

hierarchy /'haɪərɑːkɪ/ *n* gerarchia *f*

hieroglyphics /haɪərə'glɪfɪks/ *npl* geroglifici *mpl*

hi-fi /'haɪfaɪ/ *n fam* stereo *m*, hi-fi *m inv* ● *a fam* ad alta fedeltà

higgledy-piggledy /hɪgldɪ'pɪgldɪ/ *adv* alla rinfusa

high /haɪ/ *a* alto; (*meat*) che comincia ad andare a male; (*wind*) forte; (*on drugs*) fatto; **it's ~ time we did something about it** è ora di fare qualcosa in proposito ● *adv* in alto; **~ and low** in lungo e in largo ● *n* massimo *m*; (*temperature*) massima *f*; **be on a ~** *fam* essere fatto

high: ~brow *a & n* intellettuale *mf*. **~ chair** *n* seggiolone *m*. **~er education** *n* formazione *f* universitaria. **~-handed** *a* dispotico. **~-heeled** *a* coi tacchi alti. **~ heels** *npl* tacchi *mpl* alti. **~ jump** *n* salto *m* in alto

highlight /'haɪlaɪt/ *n fig* momento *m* clou; **~s** *pl* (*in hair*) mèche *fpl* ● *vt* (*emphasize*) evidenziare. **~er** *n* (*marker*) evidenziatore *m*

highly /'haɪlɪ/ *adv* molto; **speak ~ of** lodare; **think ~ of** avere un'alta opinione di. **~-strung** *a* nervoso

Highness /'haɪnɪs/ *n* altezza *f*; **Your ~** Sua Altezza

high: ~-rise *a* (*building*) molto alto ● *n* edificio *m* molto alto. **~ school** *n* scuola *f* superiore. **~ season** *n* alta stagione *f*. **~ street** *n* strada *f* principale. **~ tea** *n* pasto *m* pomeridiano servito insieme al tè. **~ tide** *n* alta marea *f*. **~way code** *n* codice *m* stradale

hijack /'haɪdʒæk/ *vt* dirottare ● *n* dirottamento *m*. **~er** *n* dirottatore, -trice *mf*

hike /haɪk/ *n* escursione *f* a piedi ● *vi* fare un'escursione a piedi. **~r** *n* escursionista *mf*

hilarious /hɪ'leərɪəs/ *a* esilarante

hill /hɪl/ *n* collina *f*; (*mound*) collinetta *f*; (*slope*) altura *f*

hill: ~side *n* pendio *m*. **~y** *a* collinoso

hilt /hɪlt/ *n* impugnatura *f*; **to the ~**

(*fam: support*) fino in fondo; (*mortgaged*) fino al collo

him /hɪm/ *pers pron* (*direct object*) lo; (*indirect object*) gli; (*with prep*) lui; **I know ~** lo conosco; **give ~ the money** dagli i soldi; **give it to ~** daglielo; **I spoke to ~** gli ho parlato; **it's ~** è lui; **she loves ~** lo ama; **she loves ~, not you** ama lui, non te. **~'self** *pers pron* (*reflexive*) si; (*emphatic*) lui stesso; (*after prep*) sé, se stesso; **he poured ~ a drink** si è versato da bere; **he told me so ~self** me lo ha detto lui stesso; **he's proud of ~self** è fiero di sé; **by ~self** da solo

hind /haɪnd/ *a* posteriore

hind|er /'hɪndə(r)/ *vt* intralciare. **~rance** /-rəns/ *n* intralcio *m*

hindsight /'haɪnd-/ *n* **with ~** con il senno del poi

Hindu /'hɪnduː/ *n* indù *mf inv* ● *a* indù. **~ism** *n* induismo *m*

hinge /hɪndʒ/ *n* cardine *m* ● *vi* **~ on** *fig* dipendere da

hint /hɪnt/ *n* (*clue*) accenno *m*; (*advice*) suggerimento *m*; (*indirect suggestion*) allusione *f*; (*trace*) tocco *m* ● *vt* **~ that...** far capire che... ● *vi* **~ at** alludere a

hip /hɪp/ *n* fianco *m*

hippie /'hɪpɪ/ *n* hippy *mf inv*

hippo /'hɪpəʊ/ *n* ippopotamo *m*

hip 'pocket *n* tasca *f* posteriore

hippopotamus /hɪpə'pɒtəməs/ *n* (*pl* **-muses** *or* **-mi** /-maɪ/) ippopotamo *m*

hire /'haɪə(r)/ *vt* affittare; assumere (*person*); **~ |out|** affittare ● *n* noleggio *m*; '**for ~**' 'affittasi'. **~ car** *n* macchina *f* a noleggio. **~ purchase** *n* acquisto *m* rateale

his /hɪz/ *poss a* il suo *m*, la sua *f*, i suoi *mpl*, le sue *fpl*; **~ mother/father** sua madre/suo padre ● *poss pron* il suo *m*, la sua *f*, i suoi *mpl*, le sue *fpl*; **a friend of ~** un suo amico; **friends of ~** dei suoi amici; **that is ~** questo è suo; (*as opposed to mine*) questo è il suo

hiss /hɪs/ *n* sibilo *m*; (*of disapproval*) fischio *m* ● *vt* fischiare ● *vi* sibilare; (*in disapproval*) fischiare

historian /hɪ'stɔːrɪən/ *n* storico, -a *mf*

historic /hɪ'stɒrɪk/ *a* storico. **~al** *a* storico. **~ally** *adv* storicamente

history /'hɪstərɪ/ *n* storia *f*; **make ~** passare alla storia

hit /hɪt/ *n* (*blow*) colpo *m*; (*fam: success*) successo *m*; **score a direct ~** (*missile:*) colpire in pieno ● *vt/i* (*pt/pp* **hit**, *pres p* hitting) colpire; **~ one's head on the table** battere la testa contro il tavolo; **the car ~ the wall** la macchina ha sbattuto contro il muro; **~ the roof** *fam* perdere le staffe. **hit off** *vt* **~ it off** andare d'accordo. **hit on** *vt fig* trovare

hitch /hɪtʃ/ *n* intoppo *m*; **technical ~** problema *m* tecnico ● *vt* attaccare; **~ a lift** chiedere un passaggio. **hitch up** *vt* tirarsi su ⟨*trousers*⟩. **~-hike** *vi* fare l'autostop. **~-hiker** *n* autostoppista *mf*

hit-or-'miss *a* **on a very ~ basis** all'improvvisata

hither /'hɪðə(r)/ *adv* **~ and thither** di qua e di là. **~'to** *adv* finora

hive /haɪv/ *n* alveare *m*; **~ of industry** fucina *f* di lavoro ● **hive off** *vt Comm* separare

hoard /hɔːd/ *n* provvista *f*; ⟨*of money*⟩ gruzzolo *m* ● *vt* accumulare

hoarding /'hɔːdɪŋ/ *n* palizzata *f*; ⟨*with advertisements*⟩ tabellone *m* per manifesti pubblicitari

hoarse /hɔːs/ *a* rauco. **~ly** *adv* con voce rauca. **~ness** *n* raucedine *f*

hoax /həʊks/ *n* scherzo *m*; ⟨*false alarm*⟩ falso allarme *m*. **~er** *n* burlone, -a *mf*

hob /hɒb/ *n* piano *m* di cottura

hobble /'hɒbl/ *vi* zoppicare

hobby /'hɒbɪ/ *n* hobby *m inv*. **~-horse** *n fig* fissazione *f*

hockey /'hɒkɪ/ *n* hockey *m*

hoe /həʊ/ *n* zappa *f*

hog /hɒg/ *n* maiale *m* ● *vt* ⟨*pt/pp* **hogged**⟩ *fam* monopolizzare

hoist /hɔɪst/ *n* montacarichi *m inv*; ⟨*fam: push*⟩ spinta *f* in su ● *vt* sollevare; innalzare ⟨*flag*⟩; levare ⟨*anchor*⟩

hold[1] /həʊld/ *n Naut, Aeron* stiva *f*

hold[2] *n* presa *f*; ⟨*fig: influence*⟩ ascendente *m*; **get ~ of** trovare; procurarsi ⟨*information*⟩ ● *v* ⟨*pt/pp* **held**⟩ ● *vt* tenere; ⟨*container*⟩ contenere; essere titolare di ⟨*licence, passport*⟩; trattenere ⟨*breath, suspect*⟩; mantenere vivo ⟨*interest*⟩; ⟨*civil servant etc:*⟩ occupare ⟨*position*⟩; ⟨*retain*⟩ mantenere; **~ sb's hand** tenere qcno per mano; **~ one's tongue** tenere la bocca chiusa; **~ sb responsible** considerare qcno responsabile; **~ that** ⟨*believe*⟩ ritenere che ● *vi* tenere; ⟨*weather, luck:*⟩ durare; ⟨*offer:*⟩ essere valido; *Teleph* restare in linea; **I don't ~ with the idea that** *fam* non sono d'accordo sul fatto che. **hold back** *vt* rallentare ● *vi* esitare. **hold down** *vt* tenere a bada ⟨*sb*⟩. **hold on** *vi* ⟨*wait*⟩ attendere; *Teleph* restare in linea. **hold

on to** *vt* aggrapparsi a; ⟨*keep*⟩ tenersi. **hold out** *vt* porgere ⟨*hand*⟩; *fig* offrire ⟨*possibility*⟩ ● *vi* ⟨*resist*⟩ resistere. **hold up** *vt* tenere su; ⟨*delay*⟩ rallentare; ⟨*rob*⟩ assalire; **~ one's head up** *fig* tenere la testa alta

'hold: ~all *n* borsone *m*. **~er** *n* titolare *mf*; ⟨*of record*⟩ detentore, -trice *mf*; ⟨*container*⟩ astuccio *m*. **~ing** *n* ⟨*land*⟩ terreno *m* in affitto; *Comm* azioni *fpl*. **~-up** *n* ritardo *m*; ⟨*attack*⟩ rapina *f* a mano armata

hole /həʊl/ *n* buco *m*

holiday /'hɒlɪdeɪ/ *n* vacanza *f*; ⟨*public*⟩ giorno *m* festivo; ⟨*day off*⟩ giorno *m* di ferie; **go on ~** andare in vacanza ● *vi* andare in vacanza. **~-maker** *n* vacanziere *mf*

holiness /'həʊlɪnɪs/ *n* santità *f*; **Your H~** Sua Santità

Holland /'hɒlənd/ *n* Olanda *f*

hollow /'hɒləʊ/ *a* cavo; ⟨*promise*⟩ a vuoto; ⟨*voice*⟩ assente; ⟨*cheeks*⟩ infossato ● *n* cavità *f inv*; ⟨*in ground*⟩ affossamento *m*

holly /'hɒlɪ/ *n* agrifoglio *m*

holocaust /'hɒləkɔːst/ *n* olocausto *m*

hologram /'hɒləgræm/ *n* ologramma *m*

holster /'həʊlstə(r)/ *n* fondina *f*

holy /'həʊlɪ/ *a* (**-ier, -est**) santo; ⟨*water*⟩ benedetto. **H~ Ghost** *or* **Spirit** *n* Spirito *m* Santo. **H~ Scriptures** *npl* sacre scritture *fpl*. **H~ Week** *n* settimana *f* santa

homage /'hɒmɪdʒ/ *n* omaggio *m*; **pay ~ to** rendere omaggio a

home /həʊm/ *n* casa *f*; ⟨*for children*⟩ istituto *m*; ⟨*for old people*⟩ casa *f* di riposo; ⟨*native land*⟩ patria *f* ● *adv* **at ~** a casa; ⟨*football*⟩ in casa; **feel at ~** sentirsi a casa propria; **come/go ~** venire/andare a casa; **drive a nail ~** piantare un chiodo a fondo ● *a* domestico; ⟨*movie, video*⟩ casalingo; ⟨*team*⟩ ospitante; *Pol* nazionale

home: ~ ad'dress *n* indirizzo *m* di casa. **~ com'puter** *n* computer *m inv* da casa. **H~ Counties** *npl* contee *fpl* intorno a Londra. **~ game** *n* gioco *m* in casa. **~ help** *n* aiuto *m* domestico ⟨*per persone non autosufficienti*⟩. **~land** *n* patria *f*. **~less** *a* senza tetto

homely /'həʊmlɪ/ *a* (**-ier, -iest**) semplice; ⟨*atmosphere*⟩ familiare; ⟨*Am: ugly*⟩ bruttino

home: ~-'made *a* fatto in casa. **H~ Office** *n Br* ministero *m* degli interni. **H~ 'Secretary** *n Br* ministro *m* degli interni. **~sick** *a* **be ~sick** avere nostalgia (**for** di). **~sickness** *n* nostalgia *f* di casa. **~ 'town** *n* città *f inv* natia. **~ward** *a* di ritorno ● *adv* verso casa. **~work** *n Sch* compiti *mpl*

homicide /'hɒmɪsaɪd/ *n* (*crime*) omicidio *m*

homoeopath|ic /həʊmɪə'pæθɪk/ *a* omeopatico. **~y** /-'ɒpəθɪ/ *n* omeopatia *f*

homogeneous /hɒmə'dʒiːnɪəs/ *a* omogeneo

homo'sexual *a & n* omosessuale *mf*

honest /'ɒnɪst/ *a* onesto; (*frank*) sincero. **~ly** *adv* onestamente; (*frankly*) sinceramente; **~ly!** ma insomma!. **~y** *n* onestà *f*; (*frankness*) sincerità *f*

honey /'hʌnɪ/ *n* miele *m*; (*fam: darling*) tesoro *m*

honey: ~comb *n* favo *m*. **~moon** *n* luna *f* di miele. **~suckle** *n* caprifoglio *m*

honk /hɒŋk/ *vi Aut* clacsonare

honorary /'ɒnərərɪ/ *a* onorario

honour /'ɒnə(r)/ *n* onore *m* ● *vt* onorare. **~able** /-əbl/ *a* onorevole. **~ably** *adv* con onore. **~s degree** *n* ≈ diploma *m* di laurea

hood /hʊd/ *n* cappuccio *m*; (*of pram*) tettuccio *m*; (*over cooker*) cappa *f*; *Am Auto* cofano *m*

hoodlum /'huːdləm/ *n* teppista *m*

'hoodwink *vt fam* infinocchiare

hoof /huːf/ *n* (*pl* **~s** *or* **hooves**) zoccolo *m*

hook /hʊk/ *n* gancio *m*; (*for fishing*) amo *m*; **off the ~** *Teleph* staccato; *fig* fuori pericolo ● *vt* agganciare ● *vi* agganciarsi

hook|ed /hʊkt/ *a* (*nose*) adunco; **~ed on** (*fam: drugs*) dedito a; **be ~ed on skiing** essere un fanatico dello sci. **~er** *n Am sl* battona *f*

hookey /'hʊkɪ/ *n* **play ~** *Am fam* marinare la scuola

hooligan /'huːlɪgən/ *n* teppista *mf*. **~ism** *n* teppismo *m*

hoop /huːp/ *n* cerchio *m*

hooray /hʊ'reɪ/ *int & n* = **hurrah**

hoot /huːt/ *n* colpo *m* di clacson; (*of siren*) ululato *m*; (*of owl*) grido *m* ● *vi* (*owl:*) gridare; (*car:*) clacsonare; (*siren:*) ululare; (*jeer*) fischiare. **~er** *n* (*of factory*) sirena *f*; *Auto* clacson *m inv*

hoover® /'huːvə(r)/ *n* aspirapolvere *m inv* ● *vt* passare l'aspirapolvere su (*carpet*); passare l'aspirapolvere in (*room*)

hop /hɒp/ *n* saltello *m* ● *vi* (*pt/pp*

hopped) saltellare; **~ it!** *fam* tela!. **hop in** *vi fam* saltar su

hope /həʊp/ *n* speranza *f* ● *vi* sperare (**for** in); **I ~ so/not** spero di sì/no ● *vt* **~ that** sperare che

hope|ful /'həʊpfl/ *a* pieno di speranza; (*promising*) promettente; **be ~ful that** avere buone speranze che. **~fully** *adv* con speranza; (*it is hoped*) se tutto va bene. **~less** *a* senza speranze; (*useless*) impossibile; (*incompetent*) incapace. **~lessly** *adv* disperatamente; (*inefficient, lost*) completamente. **~lessness** *n* disperazione *f*

horde /hɔːd/ *n* orda *f*

horizon /hə'raɪzn/ *n* orizzonte *m*

horizontal /hɒrɪ'zɒntl/ *a* orizzontale

hormone /'hɔːməʊn/ *n* ormone *m*

horn /hɔːn/ *n* corno *m*; *Auto* clacson *m inv*

horny /'hɔːnɪ/ *a* calloso; *fam* arrapato

horoscope /'hɒrəskəʊp/ *n* oroscopo *m*

horribl|e /'hɒrɪbl/ *a* orribile. **~y** *adv* spaventosamente

horrid /'hɒrɪd/ *a* orrendo

horrific /hə'rɪfɪk/ *a* raccapricciante; (*fam: accident, prices, story*) terrificante

horrify /'hɒrɪfaɪ/ *vt* (*pt/pp* **-ied**) far inorridire; **I was horrified** ero sconvolto. **~ing** *a* terrificante

horror /'hɒrə(r)/ *n* orrore *m*. **~ film** *n* film *m* dell'orrore

hors-d'œuvre /ɔː'dɜːvr/ *n* antipasto *m*

horse /hɔːs/ *n* cavallo *m*

horse: ~back *n* **on ~back** a cavallo. **~man** *n* cavaliere *m*. **~play** *n* gioco *m* pesante. **~power** *n* cavallo *m* [vapore]. **~-racing** *n* corse *fpl* di cavalli. **~shoe** *n* ferro *m* di cavallo

horti'cultural /hɔːtɪ-/ *a* di orticoltura

'horticulture *n* orticoltura *f*

hose /həʊz/ *n* (*pipe*) manichetta *f* ● **hose down** *vt* lavare con la manichetta

hospice /'hɒspɪs/ *n* (*for the terminally ill*) ospedale *m* per i malati in fase terminale

hospitabl|e /hɒ'spɪtəbl/ *a* ospitale. **~y** *adv* con ospitalità

hospital /'hɒspɪtl/ *n* ospedale *m*

hospitality /hɒspɪ'tælətɪ/ *n* ospitalità *f*

host¹ /həʊst/ *n* **a ~ of** una moltitudine di

host² *n* ospite *m*

host³ *n Relig* ostia *f*

hostage /'hɒstɪdʒ/ *n* ostaggio *m*; **hold sb ~** tenere qcno in ostaggio

hostel /'hɒstl/ *n* ostello *m*

hostess /'həʊstɪs/ n padrona f di casa; *Aeron* hostess f inv

hostile /'hɒstaɪl/ a ostile

hostilit|y /hɒ'stɪlətɪ/ n ostilità f; **~ies** pl ostilità fpl

hot /hɒt/ a (**hotter, hottest**) caldo; ⟨spicy⟩ piccante; **I am** or **feel ~** ho caldo; **it is ~** fa caldo

'hotbed n fig focolaio m

hotchpotch /'hɒtʃpɒtʃ/ n miscuglio m

'hot-dog n hot dog m inv

hotel /həʊ'tel/ n albergo m. **~ier** /-ɪə(r)/ n albergatore, -trice mf

hot: **~head** n persona f impetuosa. **~house** n serra f. **~ly** adv fig accanitamente. **~plate** n piastra f riscaldante ~ **tap** n rubinetto m dell'acqua calda. **~-'tempered** a irascibile. **~-'water bottle** n borsa f dell'acqua calda

hound /haʊnd/ n cane m da caccia ● vt fig perseguire

hour /'aʊə(r)/ n ora f. **~ly** a ad ogni ora; ⟨pay, rate⟩ a ora ● adv ogni ora

house¹ /haʊs/ n casa f; *Pol* camera f; *Theat* sala f; **at my ~** a casa mia, da me

house² /haʊz/ vt alloggiare ⟨person⟩

house /haʊs/: **~boat** n casa f galleggiante. **~breaking** n furto m con scasso. **~hold** n casa f, famiglia f. **~holder** n capo m di famiglia. **~keeper** n governante f di casa. **~keeping** n governo m della casa; ⟨money⟩ soldi mpl per le spese di casa. **~plant** n pianta f da appartamento. **~trained** a che non sporca in casa. **~-warming [party]** n festa f di inaugurazione della nuova casa. **~wife** n casalinga f. **~work** n lavoro m domestico

housing /'haʊzɪŋ/ n alloggio m. **~ estate** n zona f residenziale

hovel /'hɒvl/ n tugurio m

hover /'hɒvə(r)/ vi librarsi; ⟨linger⟩ indugiare. **~craft** n hovercraft m inv

how /haʊ/ adv come; **~ are you?** come stai?; **~ about a coffee/going on holiday?** che ne diresti di un caffè/di andare in vacanza?; **~ do you do?** molto lieto!; **~ old are you?** quanti anni hai?; **~ long** quanto tempo; **~ many** quanti; **~ much** quanto; **~ often** ogni quanto; **and ~!** eccome!; **~ odd!** che strano!

how'ever adv ⟨nevertheless⟩ comunque; **~ small** per quanto piccolo

howl /haʊl/ n ululato m ● vi ululare; ⟨cry, with laughter⟩ singhiozzare. **~er** n fam strafalcione m

HP n abbr **hire purchase**; n abbr ⟨**horse power**⟩ C.V.

hub /hʌb/ n mozzo m; fig centro m

hubbub /'hʌbʌb/ n baccano m

'hub-cap n coprimozzo m

huddle /'hʌdl/ vi **~ together** rannicchiarsi

hue¹ /hju:/ n colore m

hue² n **~ and cry** clamore m

huff /hʌf/ n **be in/go into a ~** fare il broncio

hug /hʌg/ n abbraccio m ● vt (pt/pp **hugged**) abbracciare; ⟨keep close to⟩ tenersi vicino a

huge /hju:dʒ/ a enorme

hulking /'hʌlkɪŋ/ a fam grosso

hull /hʌl/ n Naut scafo m

hullo /hə'ləʊ/ int = hallo

hum /hʌm/ n ronzio m ● v (pt/pp **hummed**) ● vt canticchiare ● vi ⟨motor:⟩ ronzare; fig fervere ⟨di attività⟩; **~ and haw** esitare

human /'hju:mən/ a umano ● n essere m umano. **~ 'being** n essere m umano

humane /hju:'meɪn/ a umano

humanitarian /hju:mænɪ'teərɪən/ a & n umanitario, -a mf

humanit|y /hju:'mænətɪ/ n umanità f; **~ies** pl Univ dottrine fpl umanistiche

humbl|e /'hʌmbl/ a umile ● vt umiliare

'humdrum a noioso

humid /'hju:mɪd/ a umido. **~ifier** /-'mɪdɪfaɪə(r)/ n umidificatore m. **~ity** /-'mɪdətɪ/ n umidità f

humiliat|e /hju:'mɪlɪeɪt/ vt umiliare. **~ion** /-'eɪʃn/ n umiliazione f

humility /hju:'mɪlətɪ/ n umiltà f

humorous /'hju:mərəs/ a umoristico. **~ly** adv con spirito

humour /'hju:mə(r)/ n umorismo m; ⟨mood⟩ umore m; **have a sense of ~** avere il senso dell'umorismo ● vt compiacere

hump /hʌmp/ n protuberanza f; ⟨of camel, hunchback⟩ gobba f

hunch /hʌntʃ/ n ⟨idea⟩ intuizione f

'hunchback n gobbo, -a mf. **~ed** a **~ed up** incurvato

hundred /'hʌndrəd/ a **one/a ~** cento ● n cento m; **~s of** centinaia di. **~th** a centesimo ● n centesimo m. **~weight** n cinquanta chili m

hung /hʌŋ/ see **hang**

Hungarian /hʌŋ'geərɪən/ a & n ungherese mf; ⟨language⟩ ungherese m

Hungary /'hʌŋgərɪ/ n Ungheria f

351

hunger | icing

hunger /'hʌŋgə(r)/ *n* fame *f.* **~-strike** *n* sciopero *m* della fame *m*

hungry /'hʌŋgrɪ/ *a* (**-ier, -iest**) affamato; **be ~y** aver fame. **~ily** *adv* con appetito

hunk /hʌŋk/ *n* [grosso] pezzo *m*

hunt /hʌnt/ *n* caccia *f*● *vt* andare a caccia di ‹*animal*›; dare la caccia a ‹*criminal*› ● *vi* andare a caccia; **~ for** cercare. **~er** *n* cacciatore *m*. **~ing** *n* caccia *f*

hurdle /'hɜ:dl/ *n Sport & fig* ostacolo *m*. **~r** *n* ostacolista *mf*

hurl /hɜ:l/ *vt* scagliare

hurrah /hʊ'rɑ:/, **hurray** /hʊ'reɪ/ *int* urrà! ● *n* urrà *m*

hurricane /'hʌrɪkən/ *n* uragano *m*

hurried /'hʌrɪd/ *a* affrettato; ‹*job*› fatto in fretta. **~ly** *adv* in fretta

hurry /'hʌrɪ/ *n* fretta *f*; **be in a ~** aver fretta ● *vi* (*pt/pp* **-ied**) affrettarsi. **hurry up** *vi* sbrigarsi ● *vt* fare sbrigare ‹*person*›; accelerare ‹*things*›

hurt /hɜ:t/ *v* (*pt/pp* **hurt**) ● *vt* far male a; ‹*offend*› ferire ● *vi* far male; **my leg ~s** mi fa male la gamba. **~ful** *a fig* offensivo

hurtle /'hɜ:tl/ *vi* **~ along** andare a tutta velocità

husband /'hʌzbənd/ *n* marito *m*

hush /hʌʃ/ *n* silenzio *m* ● **hush up** *vt* mettere a tacere. **~ed** *a* ‹*voice*› sommesso. **~-'hush** *a fam* segretissimo

husky /'hʌskɪ/ *a* (**-ier, -iest**) ‹*voice*› rauco

hustle /'hʌsl/ *vt* affrettare ● *n* attività *f* incessante; **~ and bustle** trambusto *m*

hut /hʌt/ *n* capanna *f*

hybrid /'haɪbrɪd/ *a* ibrido ● *n* ibrido *m*

hydrant /'haɪdrənt/ *n* [**fire**] **~** idrante *m*

hydraulic /haɪ'drɔ:lɪk/ *a* idraulico

hydroe'lectric /haɪdrəʊ-/ *a* idroelettrico

hydrofoil /'haɪdrə-/ *n* aliscafo *m*

hydrogen /'haɪdrədʒən/ *n* idrogeno *m*

hyena /haɪ'i:nə/ *n* iena *f*

hygien|e /'haɪdʒi:n/ *n* igiene *f.* **~ic** /haɪ'dʒi:nɪk/ *a* igienico

hymn /hɪm/ *n* inno *m.* **~-book** *n* libro *m* dei canti

hypermarket /'haɪpəmɑ:kɪt/ *n* ipermercato *m*

hyphen /'haɪfn/ *n* lineetta *f.* **~ate** *vt* unire con lineetta

hypno|sis /hɪp'nəʊsɪs/ *n* ipnosi *f.* **~tic** /-'nɒtɪk/ *a* ipnotico

hypno|tism /'hɪpnətɪzm/ *n* ipnotismo *m.* **~tist** /-tɪst/ *n* ipnotizzatore, -trice *mf.* **~tize** *vt* ipnotizzare

hypochondriac /haɪpə'kɒndrɪæk/ *a* ipocondriaco ● *n* ipocondriaco, -a *mf*

hypocrisy /hɪ'pɒkrəsɪ/ *n* ipocrisia *f*

hypocrit|e /'hɪpəkrɪt/ *n* ipocrita *mf.* **~ical** /-'krɪtɪkl/ *a* ipocrita

hypodermic /haɪpə'dɜ:mɪk/ *a & n* **~** [**syringe**] siringa *f* ipodermica

hypothe|sis /haɪ'pɒθəsɪs/ *n* ipotesi *f inv.* **~tical** /-ə'θetɪkl/ *a* ipotetico. **~tically** *adv* in teoria; ‹*speak*› per ipotesi

hyster|ia /hɪ'stɪərɪə/ *n* isterismo *m.* **~ical** /-'sterɪkl/ *a* isterico. **~ically** *adv* istericamente; **~ically funny** da morir dal ridere. **~ics** /hɪ'sterɪks/ *npl* attacco *m* isterico

---

Ii

I /aɪ/ *pron* io; **I'm tired** sono stanco; **he's going, but I'm not** lui va, ma io no

ice /aɪs/ *n* ghiaccio *m* ● *vt* glassare ‹*cake*›. **ice over/up** *vi* ghiacciarsi

ice: ~ age *n* era *f* glaciale. **~-axe** *n* piccozza *f* per il ghiaccio. **~berg** /-bɜ:g/ *n* iceberg *m inv.* **~box** *n Am* frigorifero *m.* **~-'cream** *n* gelato *m.* **~-'cream parlour** *n* gelateria *f.* **~-cube** *n* cubetto *m* di ghiaccio. **~ hockey** *n* hockey *m* su ghiaccio.

ice: ~ 'lolly *n* ghiacciolo *m.* **~ rink** *n* pista *f* di pattinaggio. **~ skater** pattinatore, -trice *mf* sul ghiaccio. **~ skating** pattinaggio *m* sul ghiaccio

icicle /'aɪsɪkl/ *n* ghiacciolo *m*

icily /'aɪsɪlɪ/ *adv* gelidamente

icing /'aɪsɪŋ/ *n* glassa *f.* **~ sugar** *n* zucchero *m* a velo

icon /'aɪkɒn/ n icona f

icy /'aɪsɪ/ a (-ier, -iest) ghiacciato; fig gelido

idea /aɪ'dɪə/ n idea f; **I've no ~!** non ne ho idea!

ideal /aɪ'dɪəl/ a ideale ● n ideale m. **~ism** n idealismo m. **~ist** n idealista mf. **~istic** /-'lɪstɪk/ a idealistico. **~ize** vt idealizzare. **~ly** adv idealmente

identical /aɪ'dentɪkl/ a identico

identi|fication /aɪdentɪfɪ'keɪʃn/ n identificazione f; (proof of identity) documento m di riconoscimento. **~fy** /aɪ'dentɪfaɪ/ vt (pt/pp -ied) identificare

identikit® /aɪ'dentɪkɪt/ n identikit m inv

identity /aɪ'dentətɪ/ n identità f inv. **~ card** n carta f d'identità

ideolog|ical /aɪdɪə'lɒdʒɪkl/ a ideologico. **~y** /aɪdɪ'ɒlədʒɪ/ n ideologia f

idiom /'ɪdɪəm/ n idioma f. **~atic** /-'mætɪk/ a idiomatico

idiosyncrasy /ɪdɪə'sɪŋkrəsɪ/ n idiosincrasia f

idiot /'ɪdɪət/ n idiota mf. **~ic** /-'ɒtɪk/ a idiota

idl|e /'aɪd(ə)l/ a (lazy) pigro, ozioso; (empty) vano; (machine:) fermo ● vi oziare; (engine:) girare a vuoto. **~eness** n ozio m. **~y** adv oziosamente

idol /'aɪdl/ n idolo m. **~ize** /'aɪdəlaɪz/ vt idolatrare

idyllic /ɪ'dɪlɪk/ a idillico

i.e. abbr (id est) cioè

if /ɪf/ conj se; **as if** come se

ignite /ɪg'naɪt/ vt dar fuoco a ● vi prender fuoco

ignition /ɪg'nɪʃn/ n Auto accensione f. **~ key** n chiave f d'accensione

ignoramus /ɪgnə'reɪməs/ n ignorante mf

ignoran|ce /'ɪgnərəns/ n ignoranza f. **~t** a (lacking knowledge) ignaro; (rude) ignorante

ignore /ɪg'nɔː(r)/ vt ignorare

ill /ɪl/ a ammalato; **feel ~ at ease** sentirsi a disagio ● adv male ● n male m. **~-advised** a avventato. **~-bred** a maleducato

illegal /ɪ'liːgl/ a illegale

illegibl|e /ɪ'ledʒɪbl/ a illeggibile

illegitima|cy /ɪlɪ'dʒɪtɪməsɪ/ n illegittimità f. **~te** /-mət/ a illegittimo

illicit /ɪ'lɪsɪt/ a illecito

illitera|cy /ɪ'lɪtərəsɪ/ n analfabetismo m. **~te** /-rət/ a & n analfabeta mf

illness /'ɪlnɪs/ n malattia f

illogical /ɪ'lɒdʒɪkl/ a illogico

ill-treat /ɪl'triːt/ vt maltrattare. **~ment** n maltrattamento m

illuminat|e /ɪ'luːmɪneɪt/ vt illuminare. **~ing** a chiarificatore. **~ion** /-'neɪʃn/ n illuminazione f

illusion /ɪ'luːʒn/ n illusione f; **be under the ~ that** avere l'illusione che

illusory /ɪ'luːsərɪ/ a illusorio

illustrat|e /'ɪləstreɪt/ vt illustrare. **~ion** /-'streɪʃn/ n illustrazione f. **~or** n illustratore, -trice mf

illustrious /ɪ'lʌstrɪəs/ a illustre

ill 'will n malanimo m

image /'ɪmɪdʒ/ n immagine f; (exact likeness) ritratto m

imagin|able /ɪ'mædʒɪnəbl/ a immaginabile. **~ary** /-ərɪ/ a immaginario

imaginat|ion /ɪmædʒɪ'neɪʃn/ n immaginazione f, fantasia f; **it's your ~ion** è solo una tua idea. **~ive** /ɪ'mædʒɪnətɪv/ a fantasioso. **~ively** adv con fantasia or immaginazione

imagine /ɪ'mædʒɪn/ vt immaginare; (wrongly) inventare

im'balance n squilibrio m

imbecile /'ɪmbəsiːl/ n imbecille mf

imbibe /ɪm'baɪb/ vt ingerire

imbue /ɪm'bjuː/ vt **~d with** impregnato di

imitat|e /'ɪmɪteɪt/ vt imitare. **~ion** /-'teɪʃn/ n imitazione f. **~or** n imitatore, -trice mf

immaculate /ɪ'mækjʊlət/ a immacolato. **~ly** adv immacolatamente

imma'terial a (unimportant) irrilevante

imma'ture a immaturo

immediate /ɪ'miːdɪət/ a immediato; (relative) stretto; **in the ~ vicinity** nelle immediate vicinanze. **~ly** adv immediatamente; **~ly next to** subito accanto a ● conj [non] appena

immemorial /ɪmɪ'mɔːrɪəl/ a **from time ~** da tempo immemorabile

immense /ɪ'mens/ a immenso

immers|e /ɪ'mɜːs/ vt immergere; **be ~ed in** fig essere immerso in. **~ion** /-ɜːʃn/ n immersione f. **~ion heater** n scaldabagno m elettrico

immigrant /'ɪmɪgrənt/ n immigrante mf

immigrat|e /'ɪmɪgreɪt/ vi immigrare. **~ion** /-'greɪʃn/ n immigrazione f

imminent /'ɪmɪnənt/ a imminente

immobil|e /ɪ'məʊbaɪl/ a immobile. **~ize** /-bɪlaɪz/ vt immobilizzare

immoderate /ɪ'mɒdərət/ a smodato

immodest /ɪ'mɒdɪst/ a immodesto

immoral /ɪˈmɒrəl/ a immorale. **~ity** /ɪməˈrælətɪ/ n immoralità f

immortal /ɪˈmɔːtl/ a immortale. **~ity** /-ˈtælətɪ/ n immortalità f. **~ize** vt immortalare

immovable /ɪˈmuːvəbl/ a fig irremovibile

immune /ɪˈmjuːn/ a immune (**to/from** da). **~ system** n sistema m immunitario

immunity /ɪˈmjuːnətɪ/ n immunità f

immuniz|e /ˈɪmjʊnaɪz/ vt immunizzare

imp /ɪmp/ n diavoletto m

impact /ˈɪmpækt/ n impatto m

impair /ɪmˈpeə(r)/ vt danneggiare

impale /ɪmˈpeɪl/ vt impalare

impart /ɪmˈpɑːt/ vt impartire

im'parti|al a imparziale. **~'ality** n imparzialità f

im'passable a impraticabile

impasse /æmˈpɑːs/ n fig impasse f inv

impassioned /ɪmˈpæʃnd/ a appassionato

im'passive a impassibile

im'patien|ce n impazienza f. **~t** a impaziente. **~tly** adv impazientemente

impeccabl|e /ɪmˈpekəbl/ a impeccabile. **~y** adv in modo impeccabile

impede /ɪmˈpiːd/ vt impedire

impediment /ɪmˈpedɪmənt/ n impedimento m; (in speech) difetto m

impel /ɪmˈpel/ vt (pt/pp **impelled**) costringere; **feel ~led to** sentire l'obbligo di

impending /ɪmˈpendɪŋ/ a imminente

impenetrable /ɪmˈpenɪtrəbl/ a impenetrabile

imperative /ɪmˈperətɪv/ a imperativo ● n Gram imperativo m

imper'ceptible a impercettibile

im'perfect a imperfetto; (faulty) difettoso ● n Gram imperfetto m. **~ion** /-ˈfekʃn/ n imperfezione f

imperial /ɪmˈpɪərɪəl/ a imperiale. **~ism** n imperialismo m. **~ist** n imperialista mf

imperious /ɪmˈpɪərɪəs/ a imperioso

im'personal a impersonale

impersonat|e /ɪmˈpɜːsəneɪt/ vt impersonare. **~or** n imitatore, -trice mf

impertinen|ce /ɪmˈpɜːtɪnəns/ n impertinenza f. **~t** a impertinente

imperturbable /ɪmpəˈtɜːbəbl/ a imperturbabile

impervious /ɪmˈpɜːvɪəs/ a **~ to** fig in differente a

impetuous /ɪmˈpetjʊəs/ a impetuoso. **~ly** adv impetuosamente

impetus /ˈɪmpɪtəs/ n impeto m

implacable /ɪmˈplækəbl/ a implacabile

im'plant¹ vt trapiantare; fig inculcare

'implant² n trapianto m

implement¹ /ˈɪmplɪmənt/ n attrezzo m

implement² /ˈɪmplɪment/ vt mettere in atto

implicat|e /ˈɪmplɪkeɪt/ vt implicare. **~ion** /-ˈkeɪʃn/ n implicazione f; **by ~ion** implicitamente

implicit /ɪmˈplɪsɪt/ a implicito; (absolute) assoluto

implore /ɪmˈplɔː(r)/ vt implorare

imply /ɪmˈplaɪ/ vt (pt/pp -ied) implicare; **what are you ~ing?** che cosa vorresti insinuare?

impo'lite a sgarbato

import¹ /ˈɪmpɔːt/ n Comm importazione f

import² /ɪmˈpɔːt/ vt importare

importan|ce /ɪmˈpɔːtəns/ n importanza f. **~t** a importante

importer /ɪmˈpɔːtə(r)/ n importatore, -trice mf

impos|e /ɪmˈpəʊz/ vt imporre (**on** a) ● vi imporsi; **~e on** abusare di. **~ing** a imponente. **~ition** /ɪmpəˈzɪʃn/ n imposizione f

impossi'bility n impossibilità f

im'possibl|e a impossibile

impostor /ɪmˈpɒstə(r)/ n impostore, -trice mf

impoten|ce /ˈɪmpətəns/ n impotenza f. **~t** a impotente

impound /ɪmˈpaʊnd/ vt confiscare

impoverished /ɪmˈpɒvərɪʃt/ a impoverito

im'practicable a impraticabile

im'practical a non pratico

impre'cise a impreciso

impregnable /ɪmˈpregnəbl/ a imprendibile

impregnate /ˈɪmpregneɪt/ vt impregnare (**with** di); Biol fecondare

im'press vt imprimere; fig colpire (positivamente); **~ sth [up]on sb** fare capire qcsa a qcno

impression /ɪmˈpreʃn/ n impressione f; (imitation) imitazione f. **~able** a (child, mind) influenzabile. **~ism** n impressionismo m. **~ist** n imitatore, -trice mf; (artist) impressionista mf

impressive /ɪmˈpresɪv/ a imponente

'imprint¹ n impressione f

im'print² vt imprimere; **~ed on my mind** impresso nella mia memoria

im'prison vt incarcerare. ~ment n reclusione f

im'probable a improbabile

impromptu /ɪm'prɒmptjuː/ a improvvisato

im'proper a ⟨use⟩ improprio; ⟨behaviour⟩ scorretto. ~ly adv scorrettamente

impro'priety n scorrettezza f

improve /ɪm'pruːv/ vt/i migliorare. **improve** |up**on** vt perfezionare. ~ment /-mənt/ n miglioramento m

improvis|e /'ɪmprəvaɪz/ vt/i improvvisare

im'prudent a imprudente

impuden|ce /'ɪmpjʊdəns/ n sfrontatezza f. ~t a sfrontato

impuls|e /'ɪmpʌls/ n impulso m; on |an| ~e impulsivamente. ~ive /-'pʌlsɪv/ a impulsivo

impunity /ɪm'pjuːnətɪ/ n with ~ impunemente

im'pur|e a impuro. ~ity n impurità f inv. ~ities pl impurità fpl

impute /ɪm'pjuːt/ vt imputare (**to** a)

in /ɪn/ prep in; ⟨with names of towns⟩ a; **in the garden** in giardino; **in the street** in or per strada; **in bed/hospital** a letto/all'ospedale; **in the world** nel mondo; **in the rain** sotto la pioggia; **in the sun** al sole; **in this heat** con questo caldo; **in summer/winter** in estate/inverno; **in 1995** nel 1995; **in the evening** la sera; **he's arriving in two hours' time** arriva fra due ore; **deaf in one ear** sordo da un orecchio; **in the army** nell'esercito; **in English/Italian** in inglese/italiano; **in ink/pencil** a penna/matita; **in red** ⟨dressed, circled⟩ di rosso; **the man in the raincoat** l'uomo con l'impermeabile; **in a soft/loud voice** a voce bassa/alta; **one in ten people** una persona su dieci; **in doing this, he...** nel far questo....; **in itself** in sé; **in that** in quanto ● adv ⟨at home⟩ a casa; ⟨indoors⟩ dentro; **he's not in yet** non è ancora arrivato; **in there/here** li/qui dentro; **ten in all** dieci in tutto; **day in, day out** giorno dopo giorno; **have it in for sb** fam avercela con qcno; **send him in** fallo entrare; **come in** entrare; **bring in the washing** portare dentro i panni ● a ⟨fam: in fashion⟩ di moda ● n the **ins and outs** i dettagli

ina'bility n incapacità f

inac'cessible a inaccessibile

in'accura|cy n inesattezza f. ~te a inesatto

in'ac|tive a inattivo. ~'tivity n inattività f

in'adequate a inadeguato. ~ly adv inadeguatamente

inad'missible a inammissibile

inadvertently /ɪnəd'vɜːtəntlɪ/ adv inavvertitamente

inad'visable a sconsigliabile

inane /ɪ'neɪn/ a stupido

in'animate a esanime

in'applicable a inapplicabile

inap'propriate a inadatto

inar'ticulate a inarticolato

inat'tentive a disattento

in'audibl|e a impercettibile

inaugural /ɪ'nɔːgjʊrəl/ a inaugurale

inaugurat|e /ɪ'nɔːgjʊreɪt/ vt inaugurare. ~ion /-'reɪʃn/ n inaugurazione f

inau'spicious a infausto

inborn /'ɪnbɔːn/ a innato

inbred /ɪn'bred/ a congenito

incalculable /ɪn'kælkjʊləbl/ a incalcolabile

in'capable a incapace

incapacitate /ɪnkə'pæsɪteɪt/ vt rendere incapace

incarnat|e /ɪn'kɑːnət/ a **the devil ~e** il diavolo in carne e ossa

incendiary /ɪn'sendɪərɪ/ a incendiario

incense¹ /'ɪnsens/ n incenso m

incense² /ɪn'sens/ vt esasperare

incentive /ɪn'sentɪv/ n incentivo m

incessant /ɪn'sesənt/ a incessante

incest /'ɪnsest/ n incesto m

inch /ɪntʃ/ n pollice m (= 2.54 cm) ● vi ~ **forward** avanzare gradatamente

inciden|ce /'ɪnsɪdəns/ n incidenza f. ~t n incidente m

incidental /ɪnsɪ'dentl/ a incidentale; ~ **expenses** spese fpl accessorie. ~ly adv incidentalmente; ⟨by the way⟩ a proposito

incinerat|e /ɪn'sɪnəreɪt/ vt incenerire. ~or n inceneritore m

incision /ɪn'sɪʒn/ n incisione f

incisive /ɪn'saɪsɪv/ a incisivo

incisor /ɪn'saɪzə(r)/ n incisivo m

incite /ɪn'saɪt/ vt incitare. ~ment n incitamento m

inclination /ɪnklɪ'neɪʃn/ n inclinazione f

incline¹ /ɪn'klaɪn/ vt inclinare; **be ~d to do sth** essere propenso a fare qcsa

incline² /'ɪnklaɪn/ n pendio m

inclu|de /ɪn'kluːd/ vt includere. ~ding prep incluso. ~sion /-uːʒn/ n inclusione f

inclusive /ɪn'klu:sɪv/ a incluso; ~ of comprendente; **be ~ of** comprendere ● adv incluso

incognito /ɪnkɒg'ni:təʊ/ adv incognito

inco'herent a incoerente; (because drunk etc) incomprensibile

income /'ɪnkʌm/ n reddito m. ~ **tax** n imposta f sul reddito

'incoming a in arrivo. ~ **tide** n marea f montante

in'comparable a incomparabile

incompati'bility n incompatibilità f

incom'patible a incompatibile

incom'peten|ce n incompetenza f. ~**t** a incompetente

incom'plete a incompleto

incompre'hensible a incomprensibile

incon'ceivable a inconcepibile

incon'clusive a inconcludente

incongruous /ɪn'kɒŋgrʊəs/ a contrastante

inconsequential /ɪnkɒnsɪ'kwenʃl/ a senza importanza

incon'siderate a trascurabile

incon'sistency n incoerenza f

incon'sistent a incoerente; **be ~ with** non essere coerente con. ~**ly** adv in modo incoerente

inconsolable /ɪnkən'səʊləbl/ a inconsolabile

incon'spicuous a non appariscente. ~**ly** adv modestamente

incontinen|ce /ɪn'kɒntɪnəns/ n incontinenza f. ~**t** a incontinente

incon'venien|ce n scomodità f; (drawback) inconveniente m; **put sb to ~ce** dare disturbo a qcno. ~**t** a scomodo; (time, place) inopportuno. ~**tly** adv in modo inopportuno

incorporate /ɪn'kɔ:pəreɪt/ vt incorporare; (contain) comprendere

incor'rect a incorretto. ~**ly** adv scorrettamente

incorrigible /ɪn'kɒrɪdʒəbl/ a incorreggibile

incorruptible /ɪnkə'rʌptəbl/ a incorruttibile

increase¹ /'ɪnkri:s/ n aumento m; **on the ~** in aumento

increas|e² /ɪn'kri:s/ vt/i aumentare. ~**ing** a (impatience etc) crescente; (numbers) in aumento. ~**ingly** adv sempre più

in'credible a incredibile

incredulous /ɪn'kredjʊləs/ a incredulo

increment /'ɪnkrɪmənt/ n incremento m

incriminate /ɪn'krɪmɪneɪt/ vt Jur incriminare

incubat|e /'ɪŋkjʊbeɪt/ vt incubare. ~**ion** /-'beɪʃn/ n incubazione f. ~**ion period** n Med periodo m di incubazione. ~**or** n (for baby) incubatrice f

incumbent /ɪn'kʌmbənt/ a **be ~ on sb** incombere a qcno

incur /ɪn'kɜ:(r)/ vt (pt/pp **incurred**) incorrere; contrarre (debts)

in'curable a incurabile

incursion /ɪn'kɜ:ʃn/ n incursione f

indebted /ɪn'detɪd/ a obbligato (to verso)

in'decent a indecente

inde'cision n indecisione f

inde'cisive a indeciso. ~**ness** n indecisione f

indeed /ɪn'di:d/ adv (in fact) difatti; **yes ~!** sì, certamente!; ~ **I am/do** veramente!; **very much ~** moltissimo; **thank you very much ~** grazie infinite; ~**?** davvero?

indefatigable /ɪndɪ'fætɪgəbl/ a instancabile

inde'finable a indefinibile

in'definite a indefinito. ~**ly** adv indefinitamente; (postpone) a tempo indeterminato

indelible /ɪn'delɪbl/ a indelebile

indemnity /ɪn'demnɪtɪ/ n indennità f inv

indent¹ /'ɪndent/ n Typ rientranza f dal margine

indent² /ɪn'dent/ vt Typ fare rientrare dal margine. ~**ation** /-'teɪʃn/ n (notch) intaccatura f

inde'penden|ce n indipendenza f. ~**t** a indipendente. ~**tly** adv indipendentemente

indescribable /ɪndɪ'skraɪbəbl/ a indescrivibile

indestructible /ɪndɪ'strʌktəbl/ a indistruttibile

indeterminate /ɪndɪ'tɜ:mɪnət/ a indeterminato

index /'ɪndeks/ n indice m

index: ~ card n scheda f. ~ **finger** n dito m indice. ~**-linked** a (pension) legato al costo della vita

India /'ɪndɪə/ n India f. ~**n** a indiano; (American) indiano [d'America] ● n indiano, -a mf, (American) indiano, -a mf [d'America], pellerossa mf inv

indicat|e /'ɪndɪkeɪt/ vt indicare;

(*register*) segnare ● *vi Auto* mettere la freccia. **~ion** /-'keɪʃn/ *n* indicazione *f*

indicative /ɪn'dɪkətɪv/ *a* **be ~ of** essere indicativo di ● *n Gram* indicativo *m*

indicator /'ɪndɪkeɪtə(r)/ *n Auto* freccia *f*

indict /ɪn'daɪt/ *vt* accusare. **~ment** *n* accusa *f*

in'differen|ce *n* indifferenza *f*. **~t** *a* indifferente; (*not good*) mediocre

indigenous /ɪn'dɪdʒɪnəs/ *a* indigeno

indi'gest|ible *a* indigesto. **~ion** *n* indigestione *f*

indigna|nt /ɪn'dɪgnənt/ *a* indignato. **~ntly** *adv* con indignazione. **~tion** /-'neɪʃn/ *n* indignazione *f*

in'dignity *n* umiliazione *f*

indi'rect *a* indiretto. **~ly** *adv* indirettamente

indi'screet *a* indiscreto

indis'cretion *n* indiscrezione *f*

indiscriminate /ɪndɪ'skrɪmɪnət/ *a* indiscriminato. **~ly** *adv* senza distinzione

indi'spensable *a* indispensabile

indisposed /ɪndɪ'spəʊzd/ *a* indisposto

indisputable /ɪndɪ'spjuːtəbl/ *a* indisputabile

indi'stinct *a* indistinto

indistinguishable /ɪndɪ'stɪŋgwɪʃəbl/ *a* indistinguibile

individual /ɪndɪ'vɪdjʊəl/ *a* individuale ● *n* individuo *m*. **~ity** /-'ælətɪ/ *n* individualità *f*

indi'visible *a* indivisibile

indoctrinate /ɪn'dɒktrɪneɪt/ *vt* indottrinare

indomitable /ɪn'dɒmɪtəbl/ *a* indomito

indoor /'ɪndɔː(r)/ *a* interno; (*shoes*) per casa; (*plant*) da appartamento; (*swimming pool etc*) coperto. **~s** /-'dɔːz/ *adv* dentro

induce /ɪn'djuːs/ *vt* indurre (**to** a); (*produce*) causare. **~ment** *n* (*incentive*) incentivo *m*

indulge /ɪn'dʌldʒ/ *vt* soddisfare; viziare (*child*) ● *vi* ~ **in** concedersi. **~nce** /-əns/ *n* lusso *m*; (*leniency*) indulgenza *f*. **~nt** *a* indulgente

industrial /ɪn'dʌstrɪəl/ *a* industriale; **take ~ action** scioperare. **~ist** *n* industriale *mf*. **~ized** *a* industrializzato

industr|ious /ɪn'dʌstrɪəs/ *a* industrioso. **~y** /'ɪndəstrɪ/ *n* industria *f*; (*zeal*) operosità *f*

inebriated /ɪ'niːbrɪeɪtɪd/ *a* ebbro

in'edible *a* immangiabile

inef'fective *a* inefficace

ineffectual /ɪnɪ'fektʃʊəl/ *a* inutile; (*person*) inconcludente

inef'ficien|cy *n* inefficienza *f*. **~t** *a* inefficiente

in'eligible *a* inadatto

inept /ɪ'nept/ *a* inetto

ine'quality *n* ineguaglianza *f*

inert /ɪ'nɜːt/ *a* inerte. **~ia** /ɪ'nɜːʃə/ *n* inerzia *f*

inescapable /ɪnɪ'skeɪpəbl/ *a* inevitabile

inestimable /ɪn'estɪməbl/ *a* inestimabile

inevitab|le /ɪn'evɪtəbl/ *a* inevitabile. **~y** *adv* inevitabilmente

ine'xact *a* inesatto

inex'cusable *a* imperdonabile

inexhaustible /ɪnɪg'zɔːstəbl/ *a* inesauribile

inexorable /ɪn'eksərəbl/ *a* inesorabile

inex'pensive *a* poco costoso

inex'perience *n* inesperienza *f*. **~d** *a* inesperto

inexplicable /ɪnɪk'splɪkəbl/ *a* inesplicabile

in'fallible *a* infallibile

infam|ous /'ɪnfəməs/ *a* infame; (*person*) famigerato. **~y** *n* infamia *f*

infan|cy /'ɪnfənsɪ/ *n* infanzia *f*; **in its ~cy** *fig* agli inizi. **~t** *n* bambino, -a *mf* piccolo, -a. **~tile** *a* infantile

infantry /'ɪnfəntrɪ/ *n* fanteria *f*

infatuat|ed /ɪn'fætʃʊeɪtɪd/ *a* infatuato (**with** di). **~ion** *n* infatuazione *f*

infect /ɪn'fekt/ *vt* infettare; **become ~ed** (*wound:*) infettarsi. **~ion** /-'fekʃn/ *n* infezione *f*. **~ious** /-'fekʃəs/ *a* infettivo

infer /ɪn'fɜː(r)/ *vt* (*pt*/*pp* **inferred**) dedurre (**from** da); (*imply*) implicare. **~ence** /'ɪnfərəns/ *n* deduzione *f*

inferior /ɪn'fɪərɪə(r)/ *a* inferiore; (*goods*) scadente; (*in rank*) subalterno ● *n* inferiore *mf*; (*in rank*) subalterno, -a *mf*

inferiority /ɪnfɪərɪ'ɒrətɪ/ *n* inferiorità *f*. **~ complex** *n* complesso *m* di inferiorità

infern|al /ɪn'fɜːnl/ *a* infernale. **~o** *n* inferno *m*

in'fertile *a* sterile. **~'tility** *n* sterilità *f*

infest /ɪn'fest/ *vt* **be ~ed with** essere infestato di

infi'delity *n* infedeltà *f*

infighting /'ɪnfaɪtɪŋ/ *n fig* lotta *f* per il potere

infiltrate /'ɪnfɪltreɪt/ *vt* infiltrare; *Pol* infiltrarsi in

infinite /'ɪnfɪnət/ *a* infinito

infinitive /ɪnˈfɪnətɪv/ *n Gram* infinito *m*

infinity /ɪnˈfɪnəti/ *n* infinità *f*

infirm /ɪnˈfɜːm/ *a* debole. **~ary** *n* infermeria *f*. **~ity** *n* debolezza *f*

inflame /ɪnˈfleɪm/ *vt* infiammare. **~d** *a* infiammato; **become ~d** infiammarsi

in'flammable *a* infiammabile

inflammation /ɪnfləˈmeɪʃn/ *n* infiammazione *f*

inflammatory /ɪnˈflæmətri/ *a* incendiario

inflatable /ɪnˈfleɪtəbl/ *a* gonfiabile

inflat|e /ɪnˈfleɪt/ *vt* gonfiare. **~ion** /-eɪʃn/ *n* inflazione *f*. **~ionary** /-eɪʃənəri/ *a* inflazionario

in'flexible *a* inflessibile

inflexion /ɪnˈflekʃn/ *n* inflessione *f*

inflict /ɪnˈflɪkt/ *vt* infliggere (**on** a)

influen|ce /ˈɪnflʊəns/ *n* influenza *f*. **●** *vt* influenzare. **~tial** /-ˈenʃl/ *a* influente

influenza /ɪnflʊˈenzə/ *n* influenza *f*

influx /ˈɪnflʌks/ *n* affluenza *f*

inform /ɪnˈfɔːm/ *vt* informare; **keep sb ~ed** tenere qcno al corrente **●** *vi* **against** denunziare

in'for|mal *a* informale; ⟨agreement⟩ ufficioso. **~mally** *adv* in modo informale. **~mality** *n* informalità *f inv*

informant /ɪnˈfɔːmənt/ *n* informatore, -trice *mf*

informat|ion /ɪnfəˈmeɪʃn/ *n* informazioni *fpl*; **a piece of ~ion** un'informazione. **~ion highway** *n* autostrada *f* telematica. **~ion technology** *n* informatica *f*. **~ive** /ɪnˈfɔːmətɪv/ *a* informativo; ⟨film, book⟩ istruttivo

informer /ɪnˈfɔːmə(r)/ *n* informatore, -trice *mf*; *Pol* delatore, -trice *mf*

infra-'red /ɪnfrə-/ *a* infrarosso

infrastructure /ˈɪnfrəstrʌktʃə(r)/ *n* infrastruttura *f*

infringe /ɪnˈfrɪndʒ/ *vt* **~ on** usurpare. **~ment** *n* violazione *f*

infuriat|e /ɪnˈfjʊərieɪt/ *vt* infuriare. **~ing** *a* esasperante

infusion /ɪnˈfjuːʒn/ *n* ⟨drink⟩ infusione *f*; ⟨of capital, new blood⟩ afflusso *m*

ingenious /ɪnˈdʒiːnɪəs/ *a* ingegnoso

ingenuity /ɪndʒɪˈnjuːəti/ *n* ingegnosità *f*

ingenuous /ɪnˈdʒenjʊəs/ *a* ingenuo

ingot /ˈɪŋgət/ *n* lingotto *m*

ingrained /ɪnˈgreɪnd/ *a* (in person) radicato; ⟨dirt⟩ incrostato

ingratiate /ɪnˈgreɪʃɪeɪt/ *vt* **~ oneself with sb** ingraziarsi qcno

in'gratitude *n* ingratitudine *f*

ingredient /ɪnˈgriːdɪənt/ *n* ingrediente *m*

ingrowing /ˈɪngrəʊɪŋ/ *a* ⟨nail⟩ incarnito

inhabit /ɪnˈhæbɪt/ *vt* abitare. **~ant** *n* abitante *mf*

inhale /ɪnˈheɪl/ *vt* aspirare; *Med* inalare **●** *vi* inspirare; (when smoking) aspirare. **~r** *n* (device) inalatore *m*

inherent /ɪnˈhɪərənt/ *a* inerente

inherit /ɪnˈherɪt/ *vt* ereditare. **~ance** /-əns/ *n* eredità *f inv*

inhibit /ɪnˈhɪbɪt/ *vt* inibire. **~ed** *a* inibito. **~ion** /-ˈbɪʃn/ *n* inibizione *f*

inho'spitable *a* inospitale

in'human *a* disumano

initial /ɪˈnɪʃl/ *a* iniziale **●** *n* iniziale *f* **●** *vt* (pt/pp **initialled**) siglare. **~ly** *adv* all'inizio

initiat|e /ɪˈnɪʃɪeɪt/ *vt* iniziare. **~ion** /-ˈeɪʃn/ *n* iniziazione *f*

initiative /ɪˈnɪʃətɪv/ *n* iniziativa *f*

inject /ɪnˈdʒekt/ *vt* iniettare. **~ion** /-ekʃn/ *n* iniezione *f*

injur|e /ˈɪndʒə(r)/ *vt* ferire; (wrong) nuocere. **~y** *n* ferita *f*; (wrong) torto *m*

in'justice *n* ingiustizia *f*; **do sb an ~** giudicare qcno in modo sbagliato

ink /ɪŋk/ *n* inchiostro *m*

inkling /ˈɪŋklɪŋ/ *n* sentore *m*

inlaid /ɪnˈleɪd/ *a* intarsiato

inland /ˈɪnlənd/ *a* interno **●** *adv* all'interno. **I~ Revenue** *n* fisco *m*

in-laws /ˈɪnlɔːz/ *npl fam* parenti *mpl* acquisiti

inlay /ˈɪnleɪ/ *n* intarsio *m*

inlet /ˈɪnlet/ *n* insenatura *f*; *Techn* entrata *f*

inmate /ˈɪnmeɪt/ *n* (of hospital) degente *mf*; (of prison) carcerato, -a *mf*

inn /ɪn/ *n* locanda *f*

innate /ɪˈneɪt/ *a* innato

inner /ˈɪnə(r)/ *a* interno. **~most** *a* il più profondo. **~ tube** *n* camera *f* d'aria

'innkeeper *n* locandiere, -a *mf*

innocen|ce /ˈɪnəsəns/ *n* innocenza *f*. **~t** *a* innocente

innocuous /ɪˈnɒkjʊəs/ *a* innocuo

innovat|e /ˈɪnəveɪt/ *vi* innovare. **~ion** /-ˈveɪʃn/ *n* innovazione *f*. **~ive** /ˈɪnəvətɪv/ *a* innovativo. **~or** /ˈɪnəveɪtə(r)/ *n* innovatore, -trice *mf*

innuendo /ɪnjʊˈendəʊ/ *n* (pl -es) insinuazione *f*

innumerable /ɪˈnjuːmərəbl/ *a* innumerevole

inoculat|e /ɪˈnɒkjʊleɪt/ *vt* vaccinare. **~ion** /-ˈleɪʃn/ *n* vaccinazione *f*

inof'fensive a inoffensivo

in'operable a inoperabile

in'opportune a inopportuno

inordinate /ɪˈnɔːdɪnət/ a smodato

inor'ganic a inorganico

'in-patient n degente mf

input /ˈɪnpʊt/ n input m inv, ingresso m

inquest /ˈɪnkwest/ n inchiesta f

inquire /ɪnˈkwaɪə(r)/ vi informarsi (**about** su); **~e into** far indagini su ● vt domandare. **~y** n domanda f; (investigation) inchiesta f

inquisitive /ɪnˈkwɪzətɪv/ a curioso

inroad /ˈɪnrəʊd/ n make **~s into** intaccare (savings); cominciare a risolvere (problem)

in'sane a pazzo; fig insensato

in'sanitary a malsano

in'sanity n pazzia f

insatiable /ɪnˈseɪʃəbl/ a insaziabile

inscri|be /ɪnˈskraɪb/ vt iscrivere. **~ption** /-ˈskrɪpʃn/ n iscrizione f

inscrutable /ɪnˈskruːtəbl/ a impenetrabile

insect /ˈɪnsekt/ n insetto m. **~icide** /-ˈsektɪsaɪd/ n insetticida m

inse'cur|e a malsicuro; (fig: person) insicuro. **~ity** n mancanza f di sicurezza

insemination /ɪnsemɪˈneɪʃn/ n inseminazione f

in'sensitive a insensibile

in'separable a inseparabile

insert¹ /ˈɪnsɜːt/ n inserto m

insert² /ɪnˈsɜːt/ vt inserire. **~ion** /-ɜːʃn/ n inserzione f

inside /ɪnˈsaɪd/ n interno m. **~s** npl fam pancia f ● attrib Aut **~ lane** n corsia f interna ● adv dentro; **~ out** a rovescio; (thoroughly) a fondo ● prep dentro; (of time) entro

insidious /ɪnˈsɪdɪəs/ a insidioso

insight /ˈɪnsaɪt/ n intuito m (**into** per); **an ~ into** un quadro di

insignia /ɪnˈsɪgnɪə/ npl insegne fpl

insig'nificant a insignificante

insin'cer|e a poco sincero. **~ity** /-ˈserɪtɪ/ n mancanza f di sincerità

insinuat|e /ɪnˈsɪnjʊeɪt/ vt insinuare. **~ion** /-ˈeɪʃn/ n insinuazione f

insipid /ɪnˈsɪpɪd/ a insipido

insist /ɪnˈsɪst/ vi insistere (**on** per) ● vt **~ that** insistere che. **~ence** n insistenza f. **~ent** a insistente

insole n soletta f

insolen|ce /ˈɪnsələns/ n insolenza f. **~t** a insolente

in'soluble a insolubile

in'solven|cy n insolvenza f. **~t** a insolvente

insomnia /ɪnˈsɒmnɪə/ n insonnia f

inspect /ɪnˈspekt/ vt ispezionare; controllare (ticket). **~ion** /-ekʃn/ n ispezione f; (of ticket) controllo m. **~or** n ispettore, -trice mf; (of tickets) controllore m

inspiration /ɪnspəˈreɪʃn/ n ispirazione f

inspire /ɪnˈspaɪə(r)/ vt ispirare

insta'bility n instabilità f

install /ɪnˈstɔːl/ vt installare. **~ation** /-stəˈleɪʃn/ n installazione f

instalment /ɪnˈstɔːlmənt/ n Comm rata f; (of serial) puntata f; (of publication) fascicolo m

instance /ˈɪnstəns/ n (case) caso m; (example) esempio m; **in the first ~** in primo luogo; **for ~** per esempio

instant /ˈɪnstənt/ a immediato; Culin espresso ● n istante m. **~aneous** /-ˈteɪnɪəs/ a istantaneo

instant 'coffee n caffè m inv solubile

instantly /ˈɪnstəntlɪ/ adv immediatamente

instead /ɪnˈsted/ adv invece; **~ of doing** anziché fare; **~ of me** al mio posto; **~ of going** invece di andare

'instep n collo m del piede

instigat|e /ˈɪnstɪgeɪt/ vt istigare. **~ion** /-ˈgeɪʃn/ n istigazione f; **at his ~ion** dietro suo suggerimento. **~or** n istigatore, -trice mf

instil /ɪnˈstɪl/ vt (pt/pp **instilled**) inculcare (**into** in)

instinct /ˈɪnstɪŋkt/ n istinto m. **~ive** /ɪnˈstɪŋktɪv/ a istintivo

institut|e /ˈɪnstɪtjuːt/ n istituto m ● vt istituire (scheme); iniziare (search); intentare (legal action). **~ion** /-ˈtjuːʃn/ n istituzione f; (home for elderly) istituto m per anziani; (for mentally ill) istituto m per malati di mente

instruct /ɪnˈstrʌkt/ vt istruire; (order) ordinare. **~ion** /-ʌkʃn/ n istruzione f. **~s** (pl: orders) ordini mpl. **~ive** /-ɪv/ a istruttivo. **~or** n istruttore, -trice mf

instrument /ˈɪnstrʊmənt/ n strumento m. **~al** /-ˈmentl/ a strumentale; **be ~al in** contribuire a. **~alist** n strumentista mf

insu'bordi|nate a insubordinato. **~nation** /-ˈneɪʃn/ n insubordinazione f

in'sufferable a insopportabile

insuf'ficient a insufficiente

insular /ˈɪnsjʊlə(r)/ a fig gretto

insulat|e /ˈɪnsjʊleɪt/ vt isolare. **~ing**

tape *n* nastro *m* isolante. **~ion** /·'leɪʃn/ *n* isolamento *m*

insulin /'ɪnsjʊlɪn/ *n* insulina *f*

insult¹ /'ɪnsʌlt/ *n* insulto *m*

insult² /ɪn'sʌlt/ *vt* insultare

insuperable /ɪn'su:pərəbl/ *a* insuperabile

insur|ance /ɪn'ʃʊərəns/ *n* assicurazione *f*. **~e** *vt* assicurare

insurrection /ɪnsə'rekʃn/ *n* insurrezione *f*

intact /ɪn'tækt/ *a* intatto

intake /'ɪnteɪk/ *n* immissione *f*; (*of food*) consumo *m*

in'tangible *a* intangibile

integral /'ɪntɪgrəl/ *a* integrale

integrat|e /'ɪntɪgreɪt/ *vt* integrare ● *vi* integrarsi. **~ion** /·'greɪʃn/ *n* integrazione *f*

integrity /ɪn'tegrəti/ *n* integrità *f*

intellect /'ɪntəlekt/ *n* intelletto *m*. **~ual** /·'lektjʊəl/ *a & n* intellettuale *mf*

intelligen|ce /ɪn'telɪdʒəns/ *n* intelligenza *f*; *Mil* informazioni *fpl*. **~t** *a* intelligente

intelligentsia /ɪntelɪ'dʒentsɪə/ *n* intellighenzia *f*

intelligible /ɪn'telɪdʒəbl/ *a* intelligibile

intend /ɪn'tend/ *vt* destinare; (*have in mind*) aver intenzione di; **be ~ed for** essere destinato a. **~ed** *a* (*effect*) voluto ● *n* **my ~ed** *fam* il mio/la mia fidanzato, ·a

intense /ɪn'tens/ *a* intenso; (*person*) dai sentimenti intensi. **~ly** *adv* intensamente; (*very*) estremamente

intensi|fication /ɪntensɪfɪ'keɪʃn/ *n* intensificazione *f*. **~fy** /·'tensɪfaɪ/ *v* (*pt/pp* **-ied**) ● *vt* intensificare ● *vi* intensificarsi

intensity /ɪn'tensəti/ *n* intensità *f*

intensive /ɪn'tensɪv/ *a* intensivo. **~ care** (*for people in coma*) rianimazione *f*; **~ care** [**unit**] terapia *f* intensiva

intent /ɪn'tent/ *a* intento; **~ on** (*absorbed in*) preso da; **be ~ on doing sth** essere intento a fare qcsa ● *n* intenzione *f*; **to all ~s and purposes** a tutti gli effetti. **~ly** *adv* attentamente

intention /ɪn'tenʃn/ *n* intenzione *f*. **~al** *a* intenzionale. **~ally** *adv* intenzionalmente

inter'acti|on *n* cooperazione *f*. **~ve** *a* interattivo

intercede /ɪntə'si:d/ *vi* intercedere (**on behalf of** a favore di)

intercept /ɪntə'sept/ *vt* intercettare

interchange *n* scambio *m*; *Auto* raccordo *m* [autostradale]

inter'changeable *a* interscambiabile

intercom /'ɪntəkɒm/ *n* citofono *m*

intercourse *n* (*sexual*) rapporti *mpl* [sessuali]

interest /'ɪntrəst/ *n* interesse *m*; **have an ~ in** *Comm* essere cointeressato in; **be of ~** essere interessante; **~ rate** *n* tasso *m* di interesse ● *vt* interessare. **~ed** *a* interessato. **~ing** *a* interessante

interface /'ɪntəfeɪs/ *n* interfaccia *f* ● *vt* interfacciare ● *vi* interfacciarsi

interfere /ɪntə'fɪə(r)/ *vi* interferire; **~ with** interferire con. **~nce** /·əns/ *n* interferenza *f*

interim /'ɪntərɪm/ *a* temporaneo; **~ payment** acconto *m* ● *n* **in the ~** nel frattempo

interior /ɪn'tɪərɪə(r)/ *a* interiore ● *n* interno *m*. **~ designer** *n* arredatore, ·trice *mf*

interject /ɪntə'dʒekt/ *vt* intervenire. **~ion** /·ekʃn/ *n* *Gram* interiezione *f*; (*remark*) intervento *m*

interloper /'ɪntələʊpə(r)/ *n* intruso, ·a *mf*

interlude /'ɪntəlu:d/ *n* intervallo *m*

inter'marry *vi* sposarsi tra parenti; (*different groups:*) contrarre matrimoni misti

intermediary /ɪntə'mi:dɪəri/ *n* intermediario, ·a *mf*

intermediate /ɪntə'mi:dɪət/ *a* intermedio

interminable /ɪn'tɜ:mɪnəbl/ *a* interminabile

intermission /ɪntə'mɪʃn/ *n* intervallo *m*

intermittent /ɪntə'mɪtənt/ *a* intermittente

intern /ɪn'tɜ:n/ *vt* internare

internal /ɪn'tɜ:nl/ *a* interno. **~ly** *adv* internamente; (*deal with*) all'interno

inter'national *a* internazionale ● *n* (*game*) incontro *m* internazionale; (*player*) competitore, ·trice *mf* in gare internazionali. **~ly** *adv* internazionalmente

Internet /'ɪntənet/ *n* Internet *m*

internist /ɪn'tɜ:nɪst/ *n* *Am* internista *mf*

internment /ɪn'tɜ:nmənt/ *n* internamento *m*

interplay *n* azione *f* reciproca

interpret /ɪn'tɜ:prɪt/ *vt* interpretare

● *vi* fare l'interprete. **~ation** /-'teɪʃn/ *n* interpretazione *f*. **~er** *n* interprete *mf*

interre'lated *a* (facts) in correlazione

interrogat|e /ɪn'terəgeɪt/ *vt* interrogare. **~ion** /-'geɪʃn/ *n* interrogazione *f*; (by police) interrogatorio *m*

interrogative /ɪntə'rɒgətɪv/ *a* & *n* **~ [pronoun]** interrogativo *m*

interrupt /ɪntə'rʌpt/ *vt/i* interrompere. **~ion** /-ʌpʃn/ *n* interruzione *f*

intersect /ɪntə'sekt/ *vi* intersecarsi ● *vt* intersecare. **~ion** /-ekʃn/ *n* intersezione *f*; (of street) incrocio *m*

interspersed /ɪntə'spɜ:st/ *a* **~ with** inframmezzato a

inter'twine *vi* attorcigliarsi

interval /'ɪntəvl/ *n* intervallo *m*; **bright ~s** *pl* schiarite *fpl*

interven|e /ɪntə'vi:n/ *vi* intervenire. **~tion** /-'venʃn/ *n* intervento *m*

interview /'ɪntəvju:/ *n* Journ intervista *f*; (for job) colloquio *m* [di lavoro] ● *vt* intervistare. **~er** *n* intervistatore, -trice *mf*

intestin|e /ɪn'testɪn/ *n* intestino *m*. **~al** *a* intestinale

intimacy /'ɪntɪməsɪ/ *n* intimità *f*

intimate[1] /'ɪntɪmət/ *a* intimo. **~ly** *adv* intimamente

intimate[2] /'ɪntɪmeɪt/ *vt* far capire; (imply) suggerire

intimidat|e /ɪn'tɪmɪdeɪt/ *vt* intimidire. **~ion** /-'deɪʃn/ *n* intimidazione *f*

into /'ɪntə/, *di fronte a una vocale* /'ɪntʊ/ *prep* dentro, in; **go ~ the house** andare dentro [casa] *o* in casa; **be ~** (fam: like) essere appassionato di; **I'm not ~ that** questo non mi piace; **7 ~ 21 goes 3** il 7 nel 21 ci sta 3 volte; **translate ~ French** tradurre in francese; **get ~ trouble** mettersi nei guai

in'tolerable *a* intollerabile

in'toleran|ce *n* intolleranza *f*. **~t** *a* intollerante

intonation /ɪntə'neɪʃn/ *n* intonazione *f*

intoxicat|ed /ɪn'tɒksɪkeɪtɪd/ *a* inebriato. **~ion** /-'keɪʃn/ *n* ebbrezza *f*

intractable /ɪn'træktəbl/ *a* intrattabile; (problem) insolubile

intransigent /ɪn'trænzɪdʒənt/ *a* intransigente

in'transitive *a* intransitivo

intravenous /ɪntrə'vi:nəs/ *a* endovenoso. **~ly** *adv* per via endovenosa

intrepid /ɪn'trepɪd/ *a* intrepido

intricate /'ɪntrɪkət/ *a* complesso

intrigu|e /ɪn'tri:g/ *n* intrigo *m* ● *vt* intrigare ● *vi* tramare. **~ing** *a* intrigante

intrinsic /ɪn'trɪnsɪk/ *a* intrinseco

introduce /ɪntrə'dju:s/ *vt* presentare; (bring in, insert) introdurre

introduct|ion /ɪntrə'dʌkʃn/ *n* introduzione *f*; (to person) presentazione *f*; (to book) prefazione *f*. **~ory** /-tərɪ/ *a* introduttivo

introspective /ɪntrə'spektɪv/ *a* introspettivo

introvert /'ɪntrəvɜ:t/ *n* introverso, -a *mf*

intru|de /ɪn'tru:d/ *vi* intromettersi. **~der** *n* intruso, -a *mf*. **~sion** /-u:ʒn/ *n* intrusione *f*

intuit|ion /ɪntju'ɪʃn/ *n* intuito *m*. **~ive** /-'tju:ɪtɪv/ *a* intuitivo

inundate /'ɪnəndeɪt/ *vt* fig inondare (with di)

invade /ɪn'veɪd/ *vt* invadere. **~r** *n* invasore *m*

invalid[1] /'ɪnvəlɪd/ *n* invalido, -a *mf*

invalid[2] /ɪn'vælɪd/ *a* non valido. **~ate** *vt* invalidare

in'valuable *a* prezioso; (priceless) inestimabile

in'variab|le *a* invariabile. **~y** *adv* invariabilmente

invasion /ɪn'veɪʒn/ *n* invasione *f*

invective /ɪn'vektɪv/ *n* invettiva *f*

invent /ɪn'vent/ *vt* inventare. **~ion** /-enʃn/ *n* invenzione *f*. **~ive** /-tɪv/ *a* inventivo. **~or** *n* inventore, -trice *mf*

inventory /'ɪnvəntrɪ/ *n* inventario *m*

inverse /ɪn'vɜ:s/ *a* inverso ● *n* inverso *m*

invert /ɪn'vɜ:t/ *vt* invertire; **in ~ed commas** tra virgolette

invest /ɪn'vest/ *vt* investire ● *vi* fare investimenti; **~ in** (fam: buy) comprarsi

investigat|e /ɪn'vestɪgeɪt/ *vt* investigare. **~ion** /-'geɪʃn/ *n* investigazione *f*

invest|ment /ɪn'vestmənt/ *n* investimento *m*. **~or** *n* investitore, -trice *mf*

inveterate /ɪn'vetərət/ *a* inveterato

invidious /ɪn'vɪdɪəs/ *a* ingiusto; (position) antipatico

invigilat|e /ɪn'vɪdʒɪleɪt/ *vi* Sch sorvegliare lo svolgimento di un esame. **~or** *n* persona *f* che sorveglia lo svolgimento di un esame

invigorate /ɪn'vɪgəreɪt/ *vt* rinvigorire

invigorating /ɪn'vɪgəreɪtɪŋ/ *a* tonificante

invincible /ɪn'vɪnsəbl/ *a* invincibile

inviolable /ɪn'vaɪələbl/ *a* inviolabile

in'visible *a* invisibile

invitation /ɪnvɪ'teɪʃn/ *n* invito *m*

invit|e /ɪn'vaɪt/ *vt* invitare; (attract) attirare. **~ing** *a* invitante

invoice /'ɪnvɔɪs/ *n* fattura *f* ● *vt* ~ **sb** emettere una fattura a qcno

invoke /ɪn'vəʊk/ *vt* invocare

in'voluntar|y *a* involontario

involve /ɪn'vɒlv/ *vt* comportare; ⟨*affect, include*⟩ coinvolgere; ⟨*entail*⟩ implicare; **get ~d with sb** legarsi a qcno; ⟨*romantically*⟩ legarsi sentimentalmente a qcno. **~d** *a* complesso. **~ment** *n* coinvolgimento *m*

in'vulnerable *a* invulnerabile; ⟨*position*⟩ inattaccabile

inward /'ɪnwəd/ *a* interno; ⟨*thoughts etc*⟩ interiore; ~ **investment** *Comm* investimento *m* di capitali stranieri. **~ly** *adv* interiormente. **~[s]** *adv* verso l'interno

iodine /'aɪədiːn/ *n* iodio *m*

iota /aɪ'əʊtə/ *n* briciolo *m*

IOU *n abbr* (**I owe you**) pagherò *m inv*

IQ *n abbr* (**intelligence quotient**) Q.I.

IRA *n abbr* (**Irish Republican Army**) I.R.A.*f*

Iran /ɪ'rɑːn/ *n* Iran *m*. **~ian** /ɪ'reɪnɪən/ *a & n* iraniano, -a *mf*

Iraq /ɪ'rɑːk/ *n* Iràq *m*. **~i** /ɪ'ru:kɪ/ *a & n* iracheno, -a *mf*

irascible /ɪ'ræsəbl/ *a* irascibile

irate /aɪ'reɪt/ *a* adirato

Ireland /'aɪələnd/ *n* Irlanda *f*

iris /'aɪrɪs/ *n Anat* iride *f*; *Bot* iris *f inv*

Irish /'aɪrɪʃ/ *a* irlandese ● *npl* **the** ~ gli irlandesi. **~man** *n* irlandese *m*. **~woman** *n* irlandese *f*

iron /'aɪən/ *a* di ferro. **I~ Curtain** *n* cortina *f* di ferro ● *n* ferro *m*; ⟨*appliance*⟩ ferro *m* [da stiro] ● *vt*/*i* stirare. **iron out** *vt* eliminare stirando; *fig* appianare

ironic[al] /aɪ'rɒnɪk[l]/ *a* ironico

ironing /'aɪənɪŋ/ *n* stirare *m*; ⟨*articles*⟩ roba *f* da stirare; **do the** ~ stirare. **~-board** *n* asse *f* da stiro

ironmonger /-mʌŋgə(r)/ *n* **~'s [shop]** negozio *m* di ferramenta

irony /'aɪrənɪ/ *n* ironia *f*

irradiate /ɪ'reɪdɪeɪt/ *vt* irradiare

irrational /ɪ'ræʃənl/ *a* irrazionale

irreconcilable /ɪ'rekənsaɪləbl/ *a* irreconciliabile

irrefutable /ɪrɪ'fju:təbl/ *a* irrefutabile

irregular /ɪ'regjʊlə(r)/ *a* irregolare. **~ity** /-'lærətɪ/ *n* irregolarità *f inv*

irrelevant /ɪ'reləvənt/ *a* non pertinente

irreparabl|e /ɪ'repərəbl/ *a* irreparabile. **~y** *adv* irreparabilmente

irreplaceable /ɪrɪ'pleɪsəbl/ *a* insostituibile

irrepressible /ɪrɪ'presəbl/ *a* irrefrenabile; ⟨*person*⟩ incontenibile

irresistible /ɪrɪ'zɪstəbl/ *a* irresistibile

irresolute /ɪ'rezəlu:t/ *a* irresoluto

irrespective /ɪrɪ'spektɪv/ *a* ~ **of** senza riguardo per

irresponsible /ɪrɪ'spɒnsɪbl/ *a* irresponsabile

irreverent /ɪ'revərənt/ *a* irreverente

irreversible /ɪrɪ'vɜ:səbl/ *a* irreversibile

irrevocabl|e /ɪ'revəkəbl/ *a* irrevocabile. **~y** *adv* irrevocabilmente

irrigat|e /'ɪrɪgeɪt/ *vt* irrigare. **~ion** /-'geɪʃn/ *n* irrigazione *f*

irritability /ɪrɪtə'bɪlətɪ/ *n* irritabilità *f*

irritable /'ɪrɪtəbl/ *a* irritabile

irritant /'ɪrɪtənt/ *n* sostanza *f* irritante

irritat|e /'ɪrɪteɪt/ *vt* irritare. **~ing** *a* irritante. **~ion** /-'teɪʃn/ *n* irritazione *f*

is /ɪz/ *see* **be**

Islam /'ɪzlɑːm/ *n* Islam *m*. **~ic** /-'læmɪk/ *a* islamico

island /'aɪlənd/ *n* isola *f*; ⟨*in road*⟩ isola *f* spartitraffico. **~er** *n* isolano, -a *mf*

isle /aɪl/ *n liter* isola *f*

isolat|e /'aɪsəleɪt/ *vt* isolare. **~ed** *a* isolato. **~ion** /-'leɪʃn/ *n* isolamento *m*

Israel /'ɪzreɪl/ *n* Israele *m*. **~i** /ɪz'reɪlɪ/ *a & n* israeliano, -a *mf*

issue /'ɪʃu:/ *n* ⟨*outcome*⟩ risultato *m*; ⟨*of magazine*⟩ numero *m*; ⟨*of stamps etc*⟩ emissione *f*; ⟨*offspring*⟩ figli *mpl*; ⟨*matter, question*⟩ questione *f*; **at** ~ in questione; **take** ~ **with sb** prendere posizione contro qcno ● *vt* distribuire ⟨*supplies*⟩; rilasciare ⟨*passport*⟩; emettere ⟨*stamps, order*⟩; pubblicare ⟨*book*⟩; **be ~d with sth** ricevere qcsa ● *vi* ~ **from** uscire da

isthmus /'ɪsməs/ *n* (*pl* **-muses**) istmo *m*

it /ɪt/ *pron* ⟨*direct object*⟩ lo *m*, la *f*; ⟨*indirect object*⟩ gli *m*, le *f*; **it's** rotto/rotta; **will it be enough?** basterà?; **it's hot** fa caldo; **it's raining** piove; **it's me** sono io; **who is it?** chi è?; **it's two o'clock** sono le due; **I doubt it** ne dubito; **take it with you** prendilo con te; **give it a wipe** dagli una pulita

Italian /ɪ'tæljən/ *a & n* italiano, -a *mf*; ⟨*language*⟩ italiano *m*

italic /ɪ'tælɪk/ *a* in corsivo. **~s** *npl* corsivo *msg*

Italy /'ɪtəlɪ/ *n* Italia *f*

itch /ɪtʃ/ *n* prurito *m* ● *vi* avere prurito, prudere; **be ~ing to** *fam* avere una voglia matta di. **~y** *a* che prude; **my foot is ~y** ho prurito al piede

item /'aɪtəm/ n articolo m; (on agenda, programme) punto m; (on invoice) voce f; ~ **[of news]** notizia f. **~ize** vt dettagliare ⟨bill⟩

itinerant /aɪ'tɪnərənt/ a itinerante

itinerary /aɪ'tɪnərərɪ/ n itinerario m

its /ɪts/ poss pron suo m, sua f, suoi mpl, sue fpl; ~ **mother/cage** sua madre/la sua gabbia

it's = it is, it has

itself /ɪt'self/ pron (reflexive) si; (emphatic) essa stessa; **the baby looked at ~ in the mirror** il bambino si è guardato nello specchio; **by ~** da solo; **the machine in ~ is simple** la macchina di per sé è semplice

ITV n abbr (**Independent Television**) stazione f televisiva privata britannica

ivory /'aɪvərɪ/ n avorio m

ivy /'aɪvɪ/ n edera f

Jj

jab /dʒæb/ n colpo m secco; (fam: injection) puntura f ● vt (pt/pp **jabbed**) punzecchiare

jabber /'dʒæbə(r)/ vi borbottare

jack /dʒæk/ n Auto cric m inv; (in cards) fante m, jack m inv ● **jack up** vt Auto sollevare [con il cric]

jackdaw /'dʒækdɔ:/ n taccola f

jacket /'dʒækɪt/ n giacca f; (of book) sopraccoperta f. ~ **po'tato** n patata f cotta al forno con la buccia

'jackpot n premio m (di una lotteria); **win the ~** vincere alla lotteria; **hit the ~** fig fare un colpo grosso

jade /dʒeɪd/ n giada f ● attrib di giada

jaded /'dʒeɪdɪd/ a spossato

jagged /'dʒægɪd/ a dentellato

jail /dʒeɪl/ = **gaol**

jalopy /dʒə'lɒpɪ/ n fam vecchia carretta f

jam¹ /dʒæm/ n marmellata f

jam² n Auto ingorgo m; (fam: difficulty) guaio m ● v (pt/pp **jammed**) ● vt (cram) pigiare; disturbare ⟨broadcast⟩; inceppare ⟨mechanism, drawer etc⟩; **be ~med** ⟨roads:⟩ essere congestionato ● vi ⟨mechanism:⟩ incepparsi; ⟨window, drawer:⟩ incastrarsi

Jamaica /dʒə'meɪkə/ n Giamaica f. ~**n** a & n giamaicano, -a mf

jam-'packed a fam pieno zeppo

jangle /'dʒæŋgl/ vt far squillare ● vi squillare

janitor /'dʒænɪtə(r)/ n (caretaker) custode m; (in school) bidello, -a mf

January /'dʒænjʊərɪ/ n gennaio m

Japan /dʒə'pæn/ n Giappone m. ~**ese** /dʒæpə'ni:z/ a & n giapponese mf; (language) giapponese m

jar¹ /dʒɑ:(r)/ n (glass) barattolo m

jar² vi (pt/pp **jarred**) ⟨sound:⟩ stridere

jargon /'dʒɑ:gən/ n gergo m

jaundice /'dʒɔ:ndɪs/ n itterizia f. ~**d** a fig inacidito

jaunt /dʒɔ:nt/ n gita f

jaunty /'dʒɔ:ntɪ/ a (-ier, -iest) sbarazzino

javelin /'dʒævlɪn/ n giavellotto m

jaw /dʒɔ:/ n mascella f; (bone) mandibola f

jay-walker /'dʒeɪwɔ:kə(r)/ n pedone m indisciplinato

jazz /dʒæz/ n jazz m ● **jazz up** vt ravvivare. ~**y** a vistoso

jealous /'dʒeləs/ a geloso. ~**y** n gelosia f

jeans /dʒi:nz/ npl [blue] jeans mpl

jeep /dʒi:p/ n jeep f inv

jeer /dʒɪə(r)/ n scherno m ● vi schernire; ~ **at** prendersi gioco di ● vt (boo) fischiare

jell /dʒel/ vi concretarsi

jelly /'dʒelɪ/ n gelatina f. ~**-fish** n medusa f

jeopardize /'dʒepədaɪz/ vt mettere in pericolo. ~**dy** /-dɪ/ n **in ~dy** in pericolo

jerk /dʒɜ:k/ n scatto m, scossa f ● vt scattare ● vi sobbalzare; ⟨limb, muscle:⟩ muoversi a scatti. ~**ily** adv a scatti. ~**y** a traballante

jersey /'dʒɜ:zɪ/ n maglia f; Sport maglietta f; (fabric) jersey m

jest /dʒest/ n scherzo m; **in ~** per scherzo ● vi scherzare

Jesus /'dʒi:zəs/ n Gesù m

jet¹ /dʒet/ n (stone) giaietto m

jet² n (of water) getto m; (nozzle) becco m; (plane) aviogetto m, jet m inv

jet: ~-·black *a* nero ebano. ~lag *n* scombussolamento *m* da fuso orario. ~-pro·pelled *a* a reazione

jettison /'dʒetɪsn/ *vt* gettare a mare; *fig* abbandonare

jetty /'dʒetɪ/ *n* molo *m*

Jew /dʒuː/ *n* ebreo *m*

jewel /'dʒuːəl/ *n* gioiello *m*. ~ler *n* gioielliere *m*; ~ler's |shop| gioielleria *f*. ~lery *n* gioielli *mpl*

Jew|ess /'dʒuːɪs/ *n* ebrea *f*. ~ish *a* ebreo

jiffy /'dʒɪfɪ/ *n fam* **in a ~** in un batter d'occhio

jigsaw /'dʒɪgsɔː/ *n* ~ |puzzle| puzzle *m inv*

jilt /dʒɪlt/ *vt* piantare

jingle /'dʒɪŋgl/ *n (rhyme)* canzoncina *f* pubblicitaria ● *vi* tintinnare

jinx /dʒɪŋks/ *n (person)* iettatore, -trice *mf*; **it's got a ~ on it** è iellato

jitter|s /'dʒɪtəz/ *npl fam* **have the ~s** aver una gran fifa. ~y *a fam* in preda alla fifa

job /dʒɒb/ *n* lavoro *m*; **this is going to be quite a ~** *fam* [questa] non sarà un'impresa facile; **it's a good ~ that....** meno male che.... **~ centre** *n* ufficio *m* statale di collocamento. **~less** *a* senza lavoro

jockey /'dʒɒkɪ/ *n* fantino *m*

jocular /'dʒɒkjʊlə(r)/ *a* scherzoso

jog /dʒɒg/ *n* colpetto *m*; **at a ~** in un balzo; *Sport* **go for a ~** andare a fare jogging ● *v (pt/pp* **jogged)** ● *vt (hit)* urtare; **~ sb's memory** farlo ritornare in mente a qcno ● *vi Sport* fare jogging. **~ging** *n* jogging *m*

john /dʒɒn/ *n (Am fam: toilet)* gabinetto *m*

join /dʒɔɪn/ *n* giuntura *f* ● *vt* raggiungere, unire; raggiungere *(person)*; *(become member of)* iscriversi a; entrare in *(firm)* ● *vi (roads:)* congiungersi. **join in** *vi* partecipare. **join up** *vi Mil* arruolarsi ● *vt* unire

joiner /'dʒɔɪnə(r)/ *n* falegname *m*

joint /dʒɔɪnt/ *a* comune ● *n* articolazione *f*; *(in wood, brickwork)* giuntura *f*; *Culin* arrosto *m*; *(fam: bar)* bettola *f*; *(sl:drug)* spinello *m*. **~ly** *adv* unitamente

joist /dʒɔɪst/ *n* travetto *m*

jok|e /dʒəʊk/ *n (trick)* scherzo *m*; *(funny story)* barzelletta *f* ● *vi* scherzare. **~er** *n* burlone, -a *mf*; *(in cards)* jolly *m inv*. **~ing** *n* **~ing apart** scherzi a parte **~ingly** *adv* per scherzo

jolly /'dʒɒlɪ/ *a* **(-ier,·-iest)** allegro ● *adv fam* molto

jolt /dʒəʊlt/ *n* scossa *f*, sobbalzo *m* ● *vt* far sobbalzare ● *vi* sobbalzare

Jordan /'dʒɔːdn/ *n* Giordania *f*; *(river)* Giordano *m*. **~ian** /-'deɪnɪən/ *a* & *n* giordano, -a *mf*

jostle /'dʒɒsl/ *vt* spingere

jot /dʒɒt/ *n* nulla *f* ● **jot down** *vt (pt/pp* **jotted)** annotare. **~ter** *n* taccuino *m*; *(with a spine)* quaderno *m*

journal /'dʒɜːnl/ *n* giornale *m*; *(diary)* diario *m*. **~ese** /-ə'liːz/ *n* gergo *m* giornalistico. **~ism** *n* giornalismo *m*. **~ist** *n* giornalista *mf*

journey /'dʒɜːnɪ/ *n* viaggio *m*

jovial /'dʒəʊvɪəl/ *a* gioviale

joy /dʒɔɪ/ *n* gioia *f*. **~ful** *a* gioioso. **~ride** *n fam* giro *m* con una macchina rubata. **~stick** *n Comput* joystick *m inv*

jubil|ant /'dʒuːbɪlənt/ *a* giubilante. **~ation** /-'leɪʃn/ *n* giubilo *m*

jubilee /'dʒuːbɪliː/ *n* giubileo *m*

judder /'dʒʌdə(r)/ *vi* vibrare violentemente

judge /dʒʌdʒ/ *n* giudice *m* ● *vt* giudicare; *(estimate)* valutare; *(consider)* ritenere ● *vi* giudicare **(by** da). **~ment** *n* giudizio *m*; *Jur* sentenza *f*

judic|ial /dʒuː'dɪʃl/ *a* giudiziario. **~iary** /-ʃərɪ/ *n* magistratura *f*. **~ious** /-ʃəs/ *a* giudizioso

judo /'dʒuːdəʊ/ *n* judo *m*

jug /dʒʌg/ *n* brocca *f*; *(small)* bricco *m*

juggernaut /'dʒʌgənɔːt/ *n fam* grosso autotreno *m*

juggle /'dʒʌgl/ *vi* fare giochi di destrezza. **~r** *n* giocoliere, -a *mf*

juice /dʒuːs/ *n* succo *m*

juicy /'dʒuːsɪ/ *a* **(-ier, -iest)** succoso; *(fam: story)* piccante

juke-box /'dʒuːk-/ *n* juke-box *m inv*

July /dʒʊ'laɪ/ *n* luglio *m*

jumble /'dʒʌmbl/ *n* accozzaglia *f* ● *vt* ~ |up| mischiare. **~ sale** *n* vendita *f* di beneficenza

jumbo /'dʒʌmbəʊ/ *n* ~ |jet| jumbo jet *m inv*

jump /dʒʌmp/ *n* salto *m*; *(in prices)* balzo *m*; *(in horse racing)* ostacolo *m* ● *vi* saltare; *(with fright)* sussultare; *(prices:)* salire rapidamente; ~ **to conclusions** saltare alle conclusioni ● *vt* saltare; ~ **the gun** *fig* precipitarsi; ~ **the queue** non rispettare la fila.

jump at *vt fig* accettare con entusiasmo *(offer)*. **jump up** *vi* rizzarsi in piedi

jumper /'dʒʌmpə(r)/ n (sweater) golf m inv

jumpy /'dʒʌmpɪ/ a nervoso

junction /'dʒʌŋkʃn/ n (of roads) incrocio m; (of motorway) uscita f; Rail nodo m ferroviario

juncture /'dʒʌŋktʃə(r)/ n at this ~ a questo punto

June /dʒuːn/ n giugno m

jungle /'dʒʌŋgl/ n giungla f

junior /'dʒuːnɪə(r)/ a giovane; (in rank) subalterno; Sport junior inv ● npl the ~s Sch i più giovani. ~ school n scuola f elementare

junk /dʒʌŋk/ n cianfrusaglie fpl. ~ food n fam cibo m poco sano, porcherie fpl. ~ mail posta f spazzatura

junkie /'dʒʌŋkɪ/ n sl tossico, -a mf

'junk-shop n negozio m di rigattiere

jurisdiction /dʒʊərɪs'dɪkʃn/ n giurisdizione f

juror /'dʒʊərə(r)/ n giurato, -a mf

jury /'dʒʊərɪ/ n giuria f; Jur giuria f [popolare]

just /dʒʌst/ a giusto ● adv (barely) appena; (simply) solo; (exactly) esattamente; ~ as tall altrettanto alto; ~ as I was leaving proprio quando stavo andando via; I've ~ seen her l'ho appena vista; it's ~ as well meno male; ~ at that moment proprio in quel momento; ~ listen! ascolta!; I'm ~ going sto andando proprio ora

justice /'dʒʌstɪs/ n giustizia f; do ~ to rendere giustizia a; J~ of the Peace giudice m conciliatore

justifiabl|e /'dʒʌstɪfaɪəbl/ a giustificabile

justi|fication /dʒʌstɪfɪ'keɪʃn/ n giustificazione f. ~fy /'dʒʌstɪfaɪ/ vt (pt/pp -ied) giustificare

justly /'dʒʌstlɪ/ adv giustamente

jut /dʒʌt/ vi (pt/pp jutted) ~ out sporgere

juvenile /'dʒuːvənaɪl/ a giovanile; (childish) infantile; (for the young) per i giovani ● n giovane mf. ~ delinquency n delinquenza f giovanile

juxtapose /dʒʌkstə'pəʊz/ vt giustapporre

Kk

kangaroo /kæŋgə'ruː/ n canguro m

karate /kə'rɑːtɪ/ n karate m

kebab /kɪ'bæb/ n Culin spiedino m di carne

keel /kiːl/ n chiglia f ● keel over vi capovolgersi

keen /kiːn/ a (intense) acuto; (interest) vivo; (eager) entusiastico; (competition) feroce; (wind, knife) tagliente; ~ on entusiasta di; she's ~ on him le piace molto; be ~ to do sth avere voglia di fare qcsa. ~ness n entusiasmo m

keep /kiːp/ n (maintenance) mantenimento m; (of castle) maschio m; for ~s per sempre ● v (pt/pp kept) ● vt tenere; (not throw away) conservare; (detain) trattenere; mantenere (family, promise); avere (shop); allevare (animals); rispettare (law, rules); ~ sth hot tenere qcsa in caldo; ~ sb from doing sth impedire a qcno di fare qcsa; ~ sb waiting far aspettare qcno; ~ sth to oneself tenere qcsa per sé; ~ sth from sb tenere nascosto qcsa a qcno ● vi (remain) rimanere; (food:) conservarsi; ~ calm rimanere calmo; ~ left/right tenere la sinistra/destra; ~ [on] doing sth continuare a fare qcsa. keep back vt trattenere (person); ~ sth back from sb tenere nascosto qcsa a qcno. keep in with vt mantenersi in buoni rapporti con. keep on vi fam assillare (at sb qcno). keep up vi stare al passo ● vt (continue) continuare

keep|er /'kiːpə(r)/ n custode mf. ~-fit n ginnastica f. ~ing n custodia f; be in ~ing with essere in armonia con. ~sake n ricordo m

keg /keg/ n barilotto m

kennel /'kenl/ n canile m; ~s pl (boarding) canile m; (breeding) allevamento m di cani

Kenya /'kenjə/ n Kenia m. ~n a & n keniota mf

kept /kept/ *see* **keep**

kerb /kɜ:b/ *n* bordo *m* del marciapiede

kernel /'kɜ:nl/ *n* nocciolo *m*

kerosene /'kerəsi:n/ *n Am* cherosene *m*

ketchup /'ketʃʌp/ *n* ketchup *m*

kettle /'ket(ə)l/ *n* bollitore *m*; **put the ~ on** mettere l'acqua a bollire

key /ki:/ *n also Mus* chiave *f*; (*of piano, typewriter*) tasto *m* ● *vt* ~ [**in**] digitare ⟨*character*⟩; **could you ~ this?** puoi battere questo?

key: ~**board** *n Comput, Mus* tastiera *f*. ~**boarder** *vi Sport* tastierista *mf*. ~**ed-up** *a* ⟨*anxious*⟩ estremamente agitato; (*ready to act*) psicologicamente preparato. ~**hole** *n* buco *m* della serratura. ~**-ring** *n* portachiavi *m inv*

khaki /'kɑ:kɪ/ *a* cachi *inv* ● *n* cachi *m*

kick /kɪk/ *n* calcio *m*; (*fam: thrill*) piacere *m*; **for ~s** fam per spasso ● *vt* dar calci a; ~ **the bucket** fam crepare ● *vi* ⟨*animal:*⟩ scalciare; ⟨*person:*⟩ dare calci. **kick off** *vi Sport* dare il calcio d'inizio; *fam* iniziare. **kick up** *vt* ~ **up a row** fare una scenata

'**kickback** *n* ⟨*fam: percentage*⟩ tangente *f*

'**kick-off** *n Sport* calcio *m* d'inizio

kid /kɪd/ *n* capretto *m*; (*fam: child*) ragazzino, -a *mf* ● *v* (*pt/pp* **kidded**) ● *vt fam* prendere in giro ● *vi fam* scherzare

kidnap /'kɪdnæp/ *vt* (*pt/pp* **-napped**) rapire, sequestrare. ~**per** *n* sequestratore, -trice *mf*, rapitore, -trice *mf*. ~**ping** *n* rapimento *m*, sequestro *m* [di persona]

kidney /'kɪdnɪ/ *n* rene *m*; *Culin* rognone *m*. ~ **machine** *n* rene *m* artificiale

kill /kɪl/ *vt* uccidere; *fig* metter fine a; ammazzare ⟨*time*⟩. ~**er** *n* assassino, -a *mf*. ~**ing** *n* uccisione *f*; (*murder*) omicidio *m*; **make a ~ing** *fig* fare un colpo grosso

'**killjoy** *n* guastafeste *mf inv*

kiln /kɪln/ *n* fornace *f*

kilo /'ki:ləʊ/ *n* chilo *m*

kilo /'kɪlə/: ~**byte** *n* kilobyte *m inv*. ~**gram** *n* chilogrammo *m*. ~**metre** /kɪ'lɒmɪtə(r)/ *n* chilometro *m*. ~**watt** *n* chilowatt *m inv*

kilt /kɪlt/ *n* kilt *m inv* (*gonnellino degli scozzesi*)

kin /kɪn/ *n* congiunti *mpl*; **next of ~** parente *m* stretto; parenti *mpl* stretti

kind[1] /kaɪnd/ *n* genere *m*, specie *f*; (*brand, type*) tipo *m*; ~ **of** fam alquanto; **two of a ~** due della stessa specie

kind[2] *a* gentile, buono; ~ **to animals** amante degli animali; ~ **regards** cordiali saluti

kindergarten /'kɪndəgɑ:tn/ *n* asilo *m* infantile

kindle /'kɪndl/ *vt* accendere

kind|ly /'kaɪndlɪ/ *a* (**-ier, -iest**) benevolo ● *adv* gentilmente; (*if you please*) per favore. ~**ness** *n* gentilezza *f*

kindred /'kɪndrɪd/ *a* **she's a ~ spirit** è la mia/sua/tua anima gemella

kinetic /kɪ'netɪk/ *a* cinetico

king /kɪŋ/ *n* re *m inv*. ~**dom** *n* regno *m*

king: ~**fisher** *n* martin *m inv* pescatore. ~**-sized** *a* ⟨*cigarette*⟩ king-size *inv*, lungo; ⟨*bed*⟩ matrimoniale grande

kink /kɪŋk/ *n* attorcigliamento *m*. ~**y** *a* fam bizzarro

kiosk /'ki:ɒsk/ *n* chiosco *m*; *Teleph* cabina *f* telefonica

kip /kɪp/ *n fam* pisolino *m*; **have a ~** schiacciare un pisolino ● *vi* (*pt/pp* **kipped**) fam dormire

kipper /'kɪpə(r)/ *n* aringa *f* affumicata

kiss /kɪs/ *n* bacio *m*; ~ **of life** respirazione *f* bocca a bocca ● *vt* baciare ● *vi* baciarsi

kit /kɪt/ *n* equipaggiamento *m*, kit *m inv*; (*tools*) attrezzi *mpl*; (*construction ~*) pezzi *mpl* da montare, kit *m inv* ● **kit out** *vt* (*pt/pp* **kitted**) equipaggiare. ~**bag** *n* sacco *m* a spalla

kitchen /'kɪtʃɪn/ *n* cucina *f* ● *attrib* di cucina. ~**ette** /kɪtʃɪ'net/ *n* cucinino *m*

kitchen: ~'**garden** *n* orto *m*. ~ **roll** *or* **towel** Scottex® *m inv*. ~'**sink** *n* lavello *m*

kite /kaɪt/ *n* aquilone *m*

kitten /'kɪtn/ *n* gattino *m*

kitty /'kɪtɪ/ *n* (*money*) cassa *f* comune

kleptomaniac /kleptə'meɪnɪæk/ *n* cleptomane *mf*

knack /næk/ *n* tecnica *f*; **have the ~ for doing sth** avere la capacità di fare qcsa

knead /ni:d/ *vt* impastare

knee /ni:/ *n* ginocchio *m*. ~**cap** *n* rotula *f*

kneel /ni:l/ *vi* (*pt/pp* **knelt**) ~ [**down**] inginocchiarsi; **be ~ing** essere inginocchiato

knelt /nelt/ *see* **kneel**

knew /nju:/ *see* **know**

knickers /'nɪkəz/ *npl* mutandine *fpl*

knick-knacks /'nɪknæks/ *npl* ninnoli *mpl*

knife /naɪf/ *n* (*pl* **knives**) coltello *m* ● *vt fam* accoltellare

knight /naɪt/ n cavaliere m; (in chess) cavallo m ● vt nominare cavaliere

knit /nɪt/ vt/i (pt/pp **knitted**) lavorare a maglia; **~ one, purl one** un diritto, un rovescio. **~ting** n lavorare m a maglia; (product) lavoro m a maglia. **~ting-needle** n ferro m da calza. **~wear** n maglieria f

knives /naɪvz/ see **knife**

knob /nɒb/ n pomello m; (of stick) pomo m; (of butter) noce f. **~bly** a nodoso; (bony) spigoloso

knock /nɒk/ n colpo m; **there was a ~ at the door** hanno bussato alla porta ● vt bussare a (door); (fam: criticize) denigrare; **~ a hole in sth** fare un buco in qcsa; **~ one's head** battere la testa (**on** contro) ● vi (at door) bussare. **knock about** vt malmenare ● vi fam girovagare. **knock down** vt far cadere; (with fist) stendere con un pugno; (in car) investire; (demolish) abbattere; (fam: reduce) ribassare (price). **knock off** vt (fam: steal) fregare; (fam: complete quickly) fare alla bell'e meglio ● vi (fam: cease work) staccare. **knock out** vt eliminare; (make unconscious) mettere K.O.; (fam: anaesthetize) addormentare. **knock over** vt rovesciare; (in car) investire

knock: ~-down a **~-down price** prezzo m stracciato. **~er** n battente m. **~-kneed** /-'ni:d/ a con gambe storte. **~-out** n (in boxing) knock-out m inv

knot /nɒt/ n nodo m ● vt (pt/pp **knotted**) annodare

knotty /'nɒtɪ/ a (-ier, -iest) fam spinoso

know /nəʊ/ v (pt **knew**, pp **known**) ● vt sapere; conoscere (person, place); (recognize) riconoscere; **get to ~ sb** conoscere qcno; **~ how to swim** sapere nuotare ● vi sapere; **did you ~ about this?** lo sapevi? ● n **in the ~** fam al corrente

know: ~-all n fam sapientone, -a mf. **~-how** n abilità f. **~ing** a d'intesa. **~ingly** adv (intentionally) consapevolmente; (smile etc) con un'aria d'intesa

knowledge /'nɒlɪdʒ/ n conoscenza f. **~able** /-abl/ a ben informato

known /nəʊn/ see **know** ● a noto

knuckle /'nʌkl/ n nocca f ● **knuckle down** vi darci sotto (**to** con). **knuckle under** vi sottomettersi

Koran /kə'rɑ:n/ n Corano m

Korea /kə'rɪə/ n Corea f. **~n** a & n coreano, -a mf

kosher /'kəʊʃə(r)/ a kasher inv

kowtow /kaʊ'taʊ/ vi piegarsi

kudos /'kju:dɒs/ n fam gloria f

lab /læb/ n fam laboratorio m

label /'leɪbl/ n etichetta f ● vt (pt/pp **labelled**) mettere un'etichetta a; fig etichettare (person)

laboratory /lə'bɒrətrɪ/ n laboratorio m

laborious /lə'bɔ:rɪəs/ a laborioso

labour /'leɪbə(r)/ n lavoro m; (workers) manodopera f; Med doglie fpl; **be in ~** avere le doglie; **L~** Pol partito m laburista ● attrib Pol laburista ● vi lavorare ● vt **~ the point** fig ribadire il concetto. **~er** n manovale m

'labour-saving a che fa risparmiare lavoro e fatica

labyrinth /'læbərɪnθ/ n labirinto m

lace /leɪs/ n pizzo m; (of shoe) laccio m ● attrib di pizzo ● vt allacciare (shoes); correggere (drink)

lacerate /'læsəreɪt/ vt lacerare

lack /læk/ n mancanza f ● vt mancare di; **I ~ the time** mi manca il tempo ● vi be **~ing** mancare; **be ~ing in sth** mancare di qcsa

lackadaisical /lækə'deɪzɪkl/ a senza entusiasmo

laconic /lə'kɒnɪk/ a laconico

lacquer /'lækə(r)/ n lacca f

lad /læd/ n ragazzo m

ladder /'lædə(r)/ n scala f; (in tights) sfilatura f

laden /'leɪdn/ a carico (**with** di)

ladle /'leɪdl/ n mestolo m ● vt ~ [out] versare (col mestolo)

lady /'leɪdɪ/ n signora f; (title) Lady f; **ladies [room]** bagno m per donne

lady: ~**bird** n, Am ~**bug** n coccinella f.
~**like** a signorile
lag¹ /læg/ vi (pt/pp **lagged**) ~ **behind**
restare indietro
lag² vt (pt/pp **lagged**) isolare ‹pipes›
lager /ˈlɑːɡə(r)/ n birra f chiara
lagoon /ləˈɡuːn/ n laguna f
laid /leɪd/ see **lay³**
lain /leɪn/ see **lie²**
lair /ˈleə(r)/ n tana f
lake /leɪk/ n lago m
lamb /læm/ n agnello m
lame /leɪm/ a zoppo; fig ‹argument› zoppicante; ‹excuse› traballante
lament /ləˈment/ n lamento m ● vt lamentare ● vi lamentarsi
lamentable /ˈlæməntəbl/ a deplorevole
laminated /ˈlæmɪneɪtɪd/ a laminato
lamp /læmp/ n lampada f; (in street)
lampione m. ~**post** n lampione m.
~**shade** n paralume m
lance /lɑːns/ n lancia f ● vt Med incidere. ~**-corporal** n appuntato m
land /lænd/ n terreno m; (country) paese m; (as opposed to sea) terra f; **plot of**
~ pezzo m di terreno ● vt Naut sbarcare; ‹fam: obtain› assicurarsi; **be** ~**ed**
with sth fam ritrovarsi fra capo e collo
qcsa ● vi Aeron atterrare; ‹fall› cadere.
land up vi fam finire
landing /ˈlændɪŋ/ n Naut sbarco m;
Aeron atterraggio m; (top of stairs) pia-
nerottolo m. ~**-stage** n pontile m da
sbarco. ~ **strip** n pista f d'atterraggio
land: ~**lady** n proprietaria f; (of flat)
padrona f di casa. ~**-locked** a privo di
sbocco sul mare. ~**lord** n proprietario
m; (of flat) padrone m di casa. ~**mark** n
punto m di riferimento; fig pietra f miliare. ~**owner** n proprietario, -a mf
terriero, -a. ~**scape** /-skeɪp/ n paesaggio m. ~**slide** n frana f; Pol valanga f di
voti
lane /leɪn/ n sentiero m; Auto, Sport
corsia f
language /ˈlæŋɡwɪdʒ/ n lingua f;
(speech, style) linguaggio m. ~ **laboratory** n laboratorio m linguistico
languid /ˈlæŋɡwɪd/ a languido
languish /ˈlæŋɡwɪʃ/ vi languire
lank /læŋk/ a ‹hair› diritto
lanky /ˈlæŋkɪ/ a (-**ier**, -**iest**) allampa-
nato
lantern /ˈlæntən/ n lanterna f
lap¹ /læp/ n grembo m
lap² n (of journey) tappa f; Sport giro m

● v (pt/pp **lapped**) ● vi ‹water:› ~
against lambire ● vt Sport doppiare
lap³ vt (pt/pp **lapped**) ~ **up** bere avidamente; bersi completamente ‹lies›; credere ciecamente a ‹praise›
lapel /ləˈpel/ n bavero m
lapse /læps/ n sbaglio m; (moral)
sbandamento m [morale]; (of time) intervallo m ● vi ‹expire› scadere;
(morally) scivolare; ~ **into** cadere in
laptop /ˈlæptɒp/ n ~ [**computer**] computer m inv portabile, laptop m inv
larceny /ˈlɑːsənɪ/ n furto m
lard /lɑːd/ n strutto m
larder /ˈlɑːdə(r)/ n dispensa f
large /lɑːdʒ/ a grande; ‹number,
amount› grande, grosso; **by and** ~ in
complesso; **at** ~ in libertà; (in general)
ampiamente. ~**ly** adv ampiamente; ~**ly**
because of in gran parte a causa di
lark¹ /lɑːk/ n ‹bird› allodola f
lark² n ‹joke› burla f ● **lark about** vi
giocherellare
larva /ˈlɑːvə/ n (pl -**vae** /-viː/) larva f
laryngitis /lærɪnˈdʒaɪtɪs/ n laringite f
larynx /ˈlærɪŋks/ n laringe f
lascivious /ləˈsɪvɪəs/ a lascivo
laser /ˈleɪzə(r)/ n laser m inv. ~
[**printer**] n stampante f laser
lash /læʃ/ n frustata f; (eyelash) ciglio m
● vt (whip) frustare; (tie) legare fermamente. **lash out** vi attaccare; (spend)
sperperare (**on** in)
lashings /ˈlæʃɪŋz/ npl ~ **of** fam una
marea di
lass /læs/ n ragazzina f
lasso /ləˈsuː/ n lazo m
last /lɑːst/ a (final) ultimo; (recent)
scorso; ~ **year** l'anno scorso; ~ **night**
ieri sera; **at** ~ alla fine; **at** ~**!** finalmente!; **that's the** ~ **straw** fam questa è
l'ultima goccia ● n ultimo, -a mf; **the** ~
but one il penultimo ● adv per ultimo;
(last time) l'ultima volta ● vi durare.
~**ing** a durevole. ~**ly** adv infine
late /leɪt/ a (delayed) in ritardo; (at a
late hour) tardo; (deceased) defunto; **it's**
~ (at night) è tardi; **in** ~ **November**
alla fine di Novembre ● adv tardi; **stay**
up ~ stare alzati fino a tardi. ~**comer**
n ritardatario, -a mf; (to political party
etc) nuovo, -a arrivato, -a mf. ~**ly** adv recentemente. ~**ness** n ora f tarda;
(delay) ritardo m
latent /ˈleɪtnt/ a latente
later /ˈleɪtə(r)/ a (train) che parte più
tardi; (edition) più recente ● adv più
tardi; ~ **on** più tardi, dopo

lateral /'lætərəl/ a laterale

latest /'leɪtɪst/ a ultimo; (most recent) più recente; **the ~** [news] le ultime notizie ● n **six o'clock at the ~** alle sei al più tardi

lathe /leɪð/ n tornio m

lather /'lɑːðə(r)/ n schiuma f ● vt insaponare ● vi far schiuma

Latin /'lætɪn/ a latino ● n latino m. **~ A'merica** n America f Latina. **~ A'merican** a & n latino-americano, -a mf

latitude /'lætɪtjuːd/ n Geog latitudine f; fig libertà f d'azione

latter /'lætə(r)/ a ultimo ● n **the ~** quest'ultimo. **~ly** adv ultimamente

lattice /'lætɪs/ n traliccio m

Latvia /'lætvɪə/ n Lettonia f. **~n** a & n lettone mf

laudable /'lɔːdəbl/ a lodevole

laugh /lɑːf/ n risata f ● vi ridere (at/about di); **~ at sb** (mock) prendere in giro qcno. **~able** /-əbl/ a ridicolo. **~ing-stock** n zimbello m

laughter /'lɑːftə(r)/ n risata f

launch[1] /lɔːntʃ/ n (boat) lancia f

launch[2] n lancio m; (of ship) varo m ● vt lanciare (rocket, product); varare (ship); sferrare (attack)

launder /'lɔːndə(r)/ vt lavare e stirare; **~ money** fig riciclare denaro sporco. **~ette** /-'dret/ n lavanderia f automatica

laundry /'lɔːndrɪ/ n lavanderia f; (clothes) bucato m

laurel /'lɒrəl/ n lauro m; **rest on one's ~s** fig dormire sugli allori

lava /'lɑːvə/ n lava f

lavatory /'lævətrɪ/ n gabinetto m

lavender /'lævəndə(r)/ n lavanda f

lavish /'lævɪʃ/ a copioso; (wasteful) prodigo; **on a ~ scale** su vasta scala ● vt **~ sth on sb** ricoprire qcno di qcsa. **~ly** adv copiosamente

law /lɔː/ n legge f; **study ~** studiare giurisprudenza, studiare legge; **~ and order** ordine m pubblico

law: ~-abiding a che rispetta la legge. **~court** n tribunale m. **~ful** a legittimo. **~less** a senza legge. **~ school** n facoltà f di giurisprudenza

lawn /lɔːn/ n prato m [all'inglese]. **~-mower** n tosaerba m inv

'law suit n causa f

lawyer /'lɔːjə(r)/ n avvocato m

lax /læks/ a negligente; (morals etc) lassista

laxative /'læksətɪv/ n lassativo m

laxity /'læksətɪ/ n lassismo m

lay[1] /leɪ/ a laico; fig profano

lay[2] see **lie**[2]

lay[3] vt (pt/pp laid) porre, mettere; apparecchiare (table); fare le uova. **lay down** vt posare; stabilire (rules, conditions). **lay off** vt licenziare (workers) ● vi (fam: stop) **~ off!** smettila! **lay out** vt (display, set forth) esporre; (plan) pianificare (garden); (spend) sborsare; Typ impaginare

lay: ~about n fannullone, -a mf. **~-by** n piazzola f di sosta

layer /'leɪə(r)/ n strato m

lay: ~man n Typ profano m. **~out** n disposizione f; Typ impaginazione f, layout m inv

laze /leɪz/ vi [about] oziare

laziness /'leɪzɪnɪs/ n pigrizia f

lazy /'leɪzɪ/ a (-ier, -iest) pigro. **~-bones** n poltrone, -a mf

lb abbr (pound) libbra

lead[1] /led/ n piombo m; (of pencil) mina f

lead[2] /liːd/ n guida f; (leash) giunzaglio m; (flex) filo m; (clue) indizio m; Theat parte f principale; (distance ahead) distanza f (over su); **in the ~** in testa ● v (pt/pp led) vt condurre; dirigere (expedition, party etc); (induce) indurre; **~ the way** mettersi in testa ● vi (be in front) condurre; (in race, competition) essere in testa; (at cards) giocare (per primo). **lead away** vt portar via. **lead to** vt portare a. **lead up to** vt preludere; **what's this ~ing up to?** dove porta questo?

leaded /'ledɪd/ a con piombo

leader /'liːdə(r)/ n capo m; (of orchestra) primo violino m; (in newspaper) articolo m di fondo. **~ship** n direzione f, leadership f inv; **show ~ship** mostrare capacità di comando

lead-free a senza piombo

leading /'liːdɪŋ/ a principale; **~ lady/man** n attrice f/attore m principale; **~ question** domanda f tendenziosa

leaf /liːf/ n (pl leaves) foglia f; (of table) asse f ● leaf through vt sfogliare. **~let** n dépliant m inv; (advertising) dépliant m inv pubblicitario; (political) manifestino m

league /liːg/ n lega f; Sport campionato m; **be in ~ with** essere in combutta con

leak /liːk/ n (hole) fessura f; Naut falla f; (of gas & fig) fuga f ● vi colare; (ship:) fare acqua; (liquid, gas:) fuoriuscire ● vt **~ sth to sb** fig far trapelare qcsa a qcno. **~y** a che perde; Naut che fa acqua

lean¹ /liːn/ a magro

lean² v (pt/pp **leaned** or **leant** /lent/) ● vt appoggiare (**against/on** contro/su) ● vi appoggiarsi (**against/on** contro/su); (not be straight) pendere; **be ~ing against** essere appoggiato contro; **~ on sb** (depend on) appoggiarsi a qcno; (fam: exert pressure on) stare alle calcagne di qcno. **lean back** vi sporgersi indietro. **lean forward** vi piegarsi in avanti. **lean out** vi sporgersi. **lean over** vi piegarsi

leaning /ˈliːnɪŋ/ a pendente; **the L~ Tower of Pisa** la torre di Pisa, la torre pendente ● n tendenza f

leap /liːp/ n salto m ● vi (pt/pp **leapt** /lept/ or **leaped**) saltare; **he leapt at it** fam l'ha preso al volo. **~-frog** n cavallina f. **~ year** n anno m bisestile

learn /lɜːn/ v (pt/pp **learnt** or **learned**) ● vt imparare; **~ to swim** imparare a nuotare; **I have ~ed that...** (heard) sono venuto a sapere che... ● vi imparare

learn|ed /ˈlɜːnɪd/ a colto. **~er** n also Auto principiante mf. **~ing** n cultura f

lease /liːs/ n contratto m d'affitto; (rental) affitto m ● vt affittare

leash /liːʃ/ n guinzaglio m

least /liːst/ a più piccolo; (amount) minore; **you've got ~ luggage** hai meno bagagli di tutti ● n **the ~** il meno; **at ~** almeno; **not in the ~** niente affatto ● adv meno; **the ~ expensive wine** il vino meno caro

leather /ˈleðə(r)/ n pelle f; (of soles) cuoio m ● attrib di pelle/cuoio. **~y** a (meat, skin) duro

leave /liːv/ n (holiday) congedo m; Mil licenza f; **on ~** in congedo/licenza ● v (pt/pp **left**) ● vt lasciare; uscire da (house, office); (forget) dimenticare; **there is nothing left** non è rimasto niente ● vi andare via; (train, bus:) partire. **leave behind** vt lasciare; (forget) dimenticare. **leave out** vt omettere; (not put away) lasciare fuori

leaves /liːvz/ see **leaf**

Leban|on /ˈlebənən/ n Libano m **~ese** /-ˈniːz/ a & n libanese mf

lecherous /ˈletʃərəs/ a lascivo

lectern /ˈlektɜːn/ n leggio m

lecture /ˈlektʃə(r)/ n conferenza f; Univ lezione f; (reproof) ramanzina f ● vi fare una conferenza (**on** su); Univ insegnare (**on sth** qcsa) ● vt **~ sb** rimproverare qcno. **~r** n conferenziere, -a mf; Univ docente mf universitario, -a

led /led/ see **lead²**

ledge /ledʒ/ n cornice f; (of window) davanzale m

ledger /ˈledʒə(r)/ n libro m mastro

leech /liːtʃ/ n sanguisuga f

leek /liːk/ n porro m

leer /lɪə(r)/ n sguardo m libidinoso ● vi **~ [at]** guardare in modo libidinoso

leeway /ˈliːweɪ/ n fig libertà f di azione

left¹ /left/ see **leave**

left² a sinistro ● adv a sinistra ● n also Pol sinistra f; **on the ~** a sinistra

left: ~-handed a mancino. **~-luggage [office]** n deposito m bagagli. **~overs** npl rimasugli mpl. **~-wing** a Pol di sinistra

leg /leg/ n gamba f; (of animal) zampa f; (of journey) tappa f; Culin (of chicken) coscia f; (of lamb) cosciotto m

legacy /ˈlegəsɪ/ n lascito m

legal /ˈliːgl/ a legale; **take ~ action** intentare un'azione legale. **~ly** adv legalmente

legality /lɪˈgælətɪ/ n legalità f

legalize /ˈliːgəlaɪz/ vt legalizzare

legend /ˈledʒənd/ n leggenda f **~ary** a leggendario

legib|le /ˈledʒəbl/ a leggibile. **~ly** adv in modo leggibile

legislat|e /ˈledʒɪsleɪt/ vi legiferare. **~ion** /-ˈleɪʃn/ n legislazione f

legislat|ive /ˈledʒɪslətɪv/ a legislativo. **~ure** /-leɪtʃə(r)/ n legislatura f

legitima|te /lɪˈdʒɪtɪmət/ a legittimo; (excuse) valido

leisure /ˈleʒə(r)/ n tempo m libero; **at your ~** con comodo. **~ly** a senza fretta

lemon /ˈlemən/ n limone m. **~ade** /-ˈneɪd/ n limonata f

lend /lend/ vt (pt/pp **lent**) prestare; **~ a hand** fig dare una mano. **~ing library** n biblioteca f per il prestito

length /leŋθ/ n lunghezza f; (piece) pezzo m; (of wallpaper) parte f; (of visit) durata f; **at ~** a lungo; (at last) alla fine

length|en /ˈleŋθən/ vt allungare ● vi allungarsi. **~ways** adv per lungo

lengthy /ˈleŋθɪ/ a (-ier, -iest) lungo

lenien|ce /ˈliːnɪəns/ n indulgenza f. **~t** a indulgente

lens /lenz/ n lente f; Phot obiettivo m; (of eye) cristallino m

Lent /lent/ n Quaresima f

lent see **lend**

lentil /ˈlentl/ n Bot lenticchia f

Leo /ˈliːəʊ/ n Astr Leone m

leopard /ˈlepəd/ n leopardo m

leotard /ˈliːətɑːd/ n body m inv

leprosy /'leprəsɪ/ n lebbra f
lesbian /'lezbɪən/ a lesbico ● n lesbica f
less /les/ a meno di; **~ and ~** sempre meno ● adv & prep meno ● n meno m
lessen /'lesn/ vt/i diminuire
lesser /'lesə(r)/ a minore
lesson /'lesn/ n lezione f
lest /lest/ conj liter per timore che
let /let/ vt (pt/pp **let**, pres p **letting**) lasciare, permettere; (rent) affittare; '(rent)' affittasi'; **~ us go** andiamo; **~ sb do sth** lasciare fare qcsa a qcno, permettere a qcno di fare qcsa; **~ me know I'm** just **~ him try!** che ci provi solamente!'; **~ oneself in for sth** fam impelagarsi in qcsa. **let down** vt sciogliersi ⟨hair⟩; abbassare ⟨blinds⟩; (lengthen) allungare; (disappoint) deludere; **don't ~ me down** conto su di te. **let in** vt far entrare. **let off** vt far partire; (not punish) perdonare; **~ sb off doing sth** abbonare qcsa a qcno. **let out** vt far uscire; (make larger) allargare; emettere ⟨scream, groan⟩. **let through** vt far passare. **let up** vi fam diminuire
'let-down n delusione f
lethal /'li:θl/ a letale
letharg|ic /lɪ'θɑ:dʒɪk/ a apatico. **~y** /'leθədʒɪ/ n apatia f
letter /'letə(r)/ n lettera f. **~-box** n buca f per le lettere. **~-head** n carta f intestata. **~ing** n caratteri mpl
lettuce /'letɪs/ n lattuga f
'let-up n fam pausa f
leukaemia /lu:'ki:mɪə/ n leucemia f
level /'levl/ a piano; (in height, competition) allo stesso livello; ⟨spoonful⟩ raso; **draw ~ with sb** affiancare qcno ● n livello m; **on the ~** fam giusto ● vt (pt/pp **levelled**) livellare; (aim) puntare ⟨at su⟩
level: ~ 'crossing n passaggio m a livello. **~-'headed** a posato
lever /'li:və(r)/ n leva f ● **lever up** vt sollevare ⟨con una leva⟩. **~age** /-rɪdʒ/ n azione f di una leva; fig influenza f
levy /'levɪ/ vt (pt/pp **levied**) imporre ⟨tax⟩
lewd /lju:d/ a osceno
liabilit|y /laɪə'bɪlətɪ/ n responsabilità f; (fam: burden) peso m; **~ies** pl debiti mpl
liable /'laɪəbl/ a responsabile (**for** di); **be ~ to** ⟨rain, break etc⟩ rischiare di; (tend to) tendere a
liaise /lɪ'eɪz/ vi fam essere in contatto

liaison /lɪ'eɪzɒn/ n contatti mpl; Mil collegamento m; (affair) relazione f
liar /'laɪə(r)/ n bugiardo, -a mf
libel /'laɪbl/ n diffamazione f ● vt (pt/pp **libelled**) diffamare. **~lous** a diffamatorio
liberal /'lɪb(ə)rəl/ a (tolerant) di larghe vedute; (generous) generoso. **L~** a Pol liberale ● n liberale mf
liberat|e /'lɪbəreɪt/ vt liberare. **~ed** a ⟨woman⟩ emancipata. **~ion** /-'reɪʃn/ n liberazione f; (of women) emancipazione f. **~or** n liberatore, -trice mf
liberty /'lɪbətɪ/ n libertà f; **take the ~ of doing sth** prendersi la libertà di fare qcsa; **be at ~ to do sth** essere libero di fare qcsa
Libra /'li:brə/ n Astr Bilancia f
librarian /laɪ'breərɪən/ n bibliotecario, -a mf
library /'laɪbrərɪ/ n biblioteca f
Libya /'lɪbɪə/ n Libia f. **~n** a & n libico, -a mf
lice /laɪs/ see louse
licence /'laɪsns/ n licenza f; (for TV) canone m televisivo; (for driving) patente f; (freedom) sregolatezza f. **~-plate** n targa f
license /'laɪsns/ vt autorizzare; **be ~d** ⟨car:⟩ avere il bollo; ⟨restaurant:⟩ essere autorizzato alla vendita di alcolici
licentious /laɪ'senʃəs/ a licenzioso
lick /lɪk/ n leccata f; **a ~ of paint** una passata leggera di pittura ● vt leccare; (fam: defeat) battere; leccarsi ⟨lips⟩
lid /lɪd/ n coperchio m; (of eye) palpebra f
lie¹ /laɪ/ n bugia f; **tell a ~** mentire ● vi (pt/pp **lied**, pres p **lying**) mentire
lie² vi (pt **lay**, pp **lain**, pres p **lying**) ⟨person:⟩ sdraiarsi; ⟨object:⟩ stare; (remain) rimanere; **leave sth lying about** or **around** lasciare qcsa in giro. **lie down** vi sdraiarsi
'lie: ~-down n **have a ~-down** fare un riposino. **~-in** n fam **have a ~-in** restare a letto fino a tardi
lieu /lju:/ n **in ~ of** in luogo di
lieutenant /lef'tenənt/ n tenente m
life /laɪf/ n (pl **lives**) vita f
life: ~belt n salvagente m. **~-boat** n lancia f di salvataggio; (on ship) scialuppa f di salvataggio. **~buoy** n salvagente m. **~-guard** n bagnino m. **~ insurance** n assicurazione f sulla vita. **~-jacket** n giubbotto m di salvataggio. **~less** a inanimato. **~like** a realistico. **~long** a di tutta la vita. **~-size[d]** a in grandezza naturale. **~time** n vita f; **the**

chance of a ~time un'occasione unica

lift /lɪft/ n ascensore m; Auto passaggio m ●vt sollevare; revocare ⟨restrictions⟩; ⟨fam: steal⟩ rubare ●vi ⟨fog:⟩ alzarsi. **lift up** vt sollevare

'**lift-off** n decollo m (di razzo)

ligament /'lɪgəmənt/ n Anat legamento m

light¹ /laɪt/ a ⟨not dark⟩ luminoso; **~ green** verde chiaro ●n luce f; ⟨lamp⟩ lampada f; **in the ~ of** fig alla luce di; **have you got a ~?** ha da accendere?; **come to ~** essere rivelato ●vt ⟨pt/pp **lit** or **lighted**⟩ accendere; ⟨illuminate⟩ illuminare. **light up** vi ⟨face:⟩ illuminarsi

light² a ⟨not heavy⟩ leggero ●adv **travel ~** viaggiare con poco bagaglio

'**light-bulb** n lampadina f

lighten¹ /'laɪtn/ vt illuminare

lighten² vt alleggerire ⟨load⟩

lighter /'laɪtə(r)/ n accendino m

light: ~-'fingered a svelto di mano. **~-'headed** a sventato. **~-'hearted** a spensierato. '**~house** n faro m. **~ing** n illuminazione f. **~ly** adv leggermente; ⟨accuse⟩ con leggerezza; ⟨without concern⟩ senza dare importanza alla cosa; **get off ~ly** cavarsela a buon mercato. **~ness** n leggerezza f

lightning /'laɪtnɪŋ/ n lampo m, fulmine m. **~-conductor** n parafulmine m

light: ~weight a leggero ●n ⟨in boxing⟩ peso m leggero. **~ year** n anno m luce

like¹ /laɪk/ a simile ●prep come; **~ this/ that** così; **what's he ~?** com'è? ●conj ⟨fam: as⟩ come; ⟨Am: as if⟩ come se

like² vt piacere, gradire; **I should or would ~** vorrei, gradirei; **I ~ him** mi piace; **I ~ this car** mi piace questa macchina; **I ~ dancing** mi piace ballare; **I ~ that!** fam questa mi è piaciuta! ●n **~s and dislikes** pl gusti mpl

like|able /'laɪkəbl/ a simpatico. **~lihood** /-lɪhʊd/ n probabilità f. **~ly** a (-ier, -iest) probabile ●adv probabilmente; **not ~ly!** fam neanche per sogno!

like-'minded a con gusti affini

liken /'laɪkən/ vt paragonare ⟨to a⟩

like|ness /'laɪknɪs/ n somiglianza f. '**~wise** adv lo stesso

liking /'laɪkɪŋ/ n gusto m; **is it to your ~?** è di suo gusto? **take a ~ to sb** prendere qcno in simpatia

lilac /'laɪlək/ n lillà m ●a color lillà

lily /'lɪlɪ/ n giglio m. **~ of the valley** n mughetto m

limb /lɪm/ n arto m

limber /'lɪmbə(r)/ vi **~ up** sciogliersi i muscoli

lime¹ /laɪm/ n ⟨fruit⟩ cedro m; ⟨tree⟩ tiglio m

lime² n calce f. '**~light** n **be in the ~light** essere molto in vista. '**~stone** n calcare m

limit /'lɪmɪt/ n limite m; **that's the ~!** fam questo è troppo! ●vt limitare ⟨to a⟩. **~ation** /-ɪ'teɪʃn/ n limite m. **~ed** a ristretto; **~ed company** società f inv a responsabilità limitata

limousine /'lɪməziːn/ n limousine f inv

limp¹ /lɪmp/ n andatura f zoppicante; **have a ~** zoppicare ●vi zoppicare

limp² a floscio

line¹ /laɪn/ n linea f; ⟨length of rope, cord⟩ filo m; ⟨of writing⟩ riga f; ⟨of poem⟩ verso m; ⟨row⟩ fila f; ⟨wrinkle⟩ ruga f; ⟨of business⟩ settore m; ⟨Am: queue⟩ coda f; **in ~ with** in conformità con ●vt segnare; fiancheggiare ⟨street⟩. **line up** vi allinearsi ●vt allineare

line² vt foderare ⟨garment⟩

linear /'lɪnɪə(r)/ a lineare

lined¹ /laɪnd/ a ⟨face⟩ rugoso; ⟨paper⟩ a righe

lined² a ⟨garment⟩ foderato

linen /'lɪnɪn/ n lino m; ⟨articles⟩ biancheria f ●attrib di lino

liner /'laɪnə(r)/ n nave f di linea

linesman n Sport guardalinee m inv

linger /'lɪŋgə(r)/ vi indugiare

lingerie /'lɒʒərɪ/ n biancheria f intima ⟨da donna⟩

linguist /'lɪŋgwɪst/ n linguista mf

linguistic /lɪŋ'gwɪstɪk/ a linguistico. **~s** n linguistica fsg

lining /'laɪnɪŋ/ n ⟨of garment⟩ fodera f; ⟨of brakes⟩ guarnizione f

link /lɪŋk/ n ⟨of chain⟩ anello m; fig legame m ●vt collegare. **link up** vi unirsi ⟨with a⟩; TV collegarsi

lino /'laɪnəʊ/ n, **linoleum** /lɪ'nəʊlɪəm/ n linoleum m

lint /lɪnt/ n garza f

lion /'laɪən/ n leone m. **~ess** n leonessa f

lip /lɪp/ n labbro m ⟨pl labbra f⟩; ⟨edge⟩ bordo m

lip: ~-read vi leggere le labbra; **~-reading** n lettura f delle labbra. **~-service** n **pay ~-service to** approvare soltanto a parole. **~salve** n burro m [di] cacao. **~stick** n rossetto m

liqueur /lɪˈkjʊə(r)/ n liquore m
liquid /ˈlɪkwɪd/ n liquido m ●a liquido
liquidat|e /ˈlɪkwɪdeɪt/ vt liquidare.
~ion /-ˈdeɪʃn/ n liquidazione f; **go into**
~ion Comm andare in liquidazione
liquidize /ˈlɪkwɪdaɪz/ vt rendere liquido. ~r n Culin frullatore m
liquor /ˈlɪkə(r)/ n bevanda f alcoolica
liquorice /ˈlɪkərɪs/ n liquirizia f
liquor store n Am negozio m di alcolici
lisp /lɪsp/ n pronuncia f con la lisca ●vi
parlare con la lisca
list¹ /lɪst/ n lista f ●vt elencare
list² vi inclinarsi
listen /ˈlɪsn/ vi ascoltare; ~ **to** ascoltare. ~er n ascoltatore, -trice mf
listings /ˈlɪstɪŋz/ npl TV programma m
tv
listless /ˈlɪstlɪs/ a svogliato
lit /lɪt/ see **light¹**
literacy /ˈlɪtərəsɪ/ n alfabetizzazione f
literal /ˈlɪtərəl/ a letterale. ~ly adv let-
teralmente
literary /ˈlɪtərərɪ/ a letterario
literate /ˈlɪtərət/ a be ~ saper leggere
e scrivere
literature /ˈlɪtrətʃə(r)/ n letteratura f
Lithuania /lɪθjʊˈeɪnɪə/ n Lituania f. ~n
a & n lituano, -a mf
litigation /lɪtɪˈgeɪʃn/ n causa f
[giudiziaria]
litre /ˈliːtə(r)/ n litro m
litter /ˈlɪtə(r)/ n immondizie fpl; Zool
figliata f ●vt be ~ed with essere in-
gombrato di. ~-bin n bidone m della
spazzatura
little /ˈlɪtl/ a piccolo; (not much) poco
●adv & n poco m; a ~ un po'; a ~
water un po' d'acqua; a ~ **better** un
po' meglio; ~ **by** ~ a poco a poco
liturgy /ˈlɪtədʒɪ/ n liturgia f
live¹ /laɪv/ a vivo; ⟨ammunition⟩ carico;
~ **broadcast** trasmissione f in diretta;
be ~ Electr essere sotto tensione; ~
wire n fig persona f dinamica ●adv
⟨broadcast⟩ in diretta
live² /lɪv/ vi vivere; (reside) abitare; ~
with convivere con. **live down** vt far dimenticare. **live off** vt vivere alle spalle
di. **live on** vt vivere di ●vi sopravvivere. **live up** vt ~ **it up** far la bella vita.
live up to vt essere all'altezza di
liveli|hood /ˈlaɪvlɪhʊd/ n mezzi mpl di
sostentamento. ~ness n vivacità f
lively /ˈlaɪvlɪ/ a (-ier, -iest) vivace
liven /ˈlaɪvn/ vt ~ **up** vivacizzare ●vi
vivacizzarsi

liver /ˈlɪvə(r)/ n fegato m
lives /laɪvz/ see **life**
livestock /ˈlaɪv-/ n bestiame m
livid /ˈlɪvɪd/ a fam livido
living /ˈlɪvɪŋ/ a vivo ●n **earn one's** ~
guadagnarsi da vivere; **the** ~ pl i vivi.
~-**room** n soggiorno m
lizard /ˈlɪzəd/ n lucertola f
load /ləʊd/ n carico m; ~**s of** fam un
sacco di ●vt caricare. ~**ed** a carico;
(fam: rich) ricchissimo
loaf¹ /ləʊf/ n (pl **loaves**) pagnotta f
loaf² vi oziare
loan /ləʊn/ n prestito m; **on** ~ in prestito ●vt prestare
loath /ləʊθ/ a **be** ~ **to do sth** essere
restio a fare qcsa
loath|e /ləʊð/ vt detestare. ~**ing** n di-
sgusto m. ~**some** a disgustoso
loaves /ləʊvz/ see **loaf**
lobby /ˈlɒbɪ/ n atrio m; Pol gruppo m di
pressione, lobby m inv
lobster /ˈlɒbstə(r)/ n aragosta f
local /ˈləʊkl/ a locale; **I'm not** ~ non
sono del posto ●n abitante mf del
luogo; (fam: public house) pub m inv
locale. ~ **au'thority** n autorità f locale.
~ **call** n Teleph telefonata f urbana. ~
government n autorità f inv locale
locality /ləʊˈkælətɪ/ n zona f
localized /ˈləʊkəlaɪzd/ a localizzato
locally /ˈləʊkəlɪ/ adv localmente; ⟨live,
work⟩ nei paraggi
'**local network** n Comput rete f locale
locat|e /ləʊˈkeɪt/ vt situare; trovare
⟨person⟩; **be** ~**ed** essere situato. ~**ion**
/-ˈkeɪʃn/ n posizione f; **filmed on** ~**ion**
girato in esterni
lock¹ /lɒk/ n (of hair) ciocca f
lock² n (on door) serratura f; (on canal)
chiusa f ●vt chiudere a chiave;
bloccare ⟨wheels⟩ ●vi chiudersi. **lock
in** vt chiudere dentro. **lock out** vt
chiudere fuori. **lock up** vt (in prison)
mettere dentro ●vi chiudere
locker /ˈlɒkə(r)/ n armadietto m
locket /ˈlɒkɪt/ n medaglione m
lock: ~-**out** n serrata f. ~**smith** n fabbro m
locomotive /ləʊkəˈməʊtɪv/ n locomotiva f
locum /ˈləʊkəm/ n sostituto, -a mf
locust /ˈləʊkəst/ n locusta f
lodge /lɒdʒ/ n (porter's) portineria f;
(masonic) loggia f ●vt presentare
⟨claim, complaint⟩; (with bank, solicitor)
depositare; **be** ~**d** essersi conficcato

● *vi* essere a pensione (**with** da); (*become fixed*) conficcarsi. **~r** *n* inquilino, -a *mf*

lodgings /'lɒdʒɪŋz/ *npl* camere *fpl* in affitto

loft /lɒft/ *n* soffitta *f*

lofty /'lɒftɪ/ *a* (**-ier**, **-iest**) alto; (*haughty*) altezzoso

log /lɒg/ *n* ceppo *m*; *Auto* libretto *m* di circolazione; *Naut* giornale *m* di bordo ● *vt* (*pt/pp* **logged**) registrare. **log on to** *vt Comput* connettersi a

logarithm /'lɒgərɪðm/ *n* logaritmo *m*

'log-book *n Naut* giornale *m* di bordo; *Auto* libretto *m* di circolazione

loggerheads /'lɒgə-/ *npl* **be at ~** *fam* essere in totale disaccordo

logic /'lɒdʒɪk/ *n* logica *f*. **~al** *a* logico. **~ally** *adv* logicamente

logistics /lə'dʒɪstɪks/ *npl* logistica *f*

logo /'ləʊgəʊ/ *n* logo *m* *inv*

loin /lɔɪn/ *n Culin* lombata *f*

loiter /'lɔɪtə(r)/ *vi* gironzolare

lollipop /'lɒlɪpɒp/ *n* lecca-lecca *m* *inv*. **~y** *n* lecca-lecca *m* *inv*; (*fam: money*) quattrini *mpl*

London /'lʌndən/ *n* Londra *f* ● *attrib* londinese, di Londra. **~er** *n* londinese *mf*

lone /ləʊn/ *a* solitario. **~liness** *n* solitudine *f*

lonely /'ləʊnlɪ/ *a* (**-ier**, **-iest**) solitario; (*person*) solo

loner /'ləʊnə(r)/ *n* persona *f* solitaria. **~some** *a* solo

long¹ /lɒŋ/ *a* lungo; **a ~ time** molto tempo; **a ~ way** distante; **in the ~ run** a lungo andare; (*in the end*) alla fin fine ● *adv* a lungo, lungamente; **how ~ is it?** quanto è lungo?; (*in time*) quanto dura?; **all day ~** tutto il giorno; **not ~ ago** non molto tempo fa; **before ~** fra breve; **he's no ~er here** non è più qui; **as** *or* **so ~as** finché; (*provided that*) purché; **so ~!** *fam* ciao!; **will you be ~?** [ti] ci vuole molto?

long² *vi* **~ for** desiderare ardentemente

long-'distance *a* a grande distanza; *Sport* di fondo; (*call*) interurbano

longhand *n* **in ~** in scrittura ordinaria

longing /'lɒŋɪŋ/ *a* desideroso ● *n* brama *f*. **~ly** *adv* con desiderio

longitude /'lɒŋgɪtjuːd/ *n Geog* longitudine *f*

long: ~ jump *n* salto *m* in lungo. **~-life 'milk** *n* latte *m* a lunga conservazione. **~-lived** /-lɪvd/ *a* longevo. **~-range** *a* *Mil, Aeron* a lunga portata; (*forecast*) a

lungo termine. **~-sighted** *a* presbite. **~-sleeved** *a* a maniche lunghe. **~-suffering** *a* infinitamente paziente. **~-term** *a* a lunga scadenza. **~ wave** *n* onde *fpl* lunghe. **~-winded** /-'wɪndɪd/ *a* prolisso

loo /luː/ *n fam* gabinetto *m*

look /lʊk/ *n* occhiata *f*; (*appearance*) aspetto *m*; [**good**] **~s** *pl* bellezza *f*; **have a ~ at** dare un'occhiata a ● *vi* guardare; (*seem*) sembrare; **~ here!** mi ascolti bene!; **~ at** guardare; **~ for** cercare; **~ like** (*resemble*) assomigliare a. **look after** *vt* badare a. **look down** *vi* guardare in basso; **~ down on sb** *fig* guardare dall'alto in basso qcno. **look forward to** *vt* essere impaziente di. **look in** *vt* passare da. **look into** *vt* (*examine*) esaminare. **look on to** *vt* (*room:*) dare su. **look out** *vi* guardare fuori; (*take care*) fare attenzione; **~ out for** cercare; **~ out!** attento! **look round** *vi* girarsi; (*in shop, town etc*) dare un'occhiata. **look through** *vt* dare un'occhiata a (*script, notes*). **look up** *vi* guardare in alto; **~ up to sb** *fig* rispettare qcno ● *vt* cercare [nel dizionario] (*word*); (*visit*) andare a trovare

'look-out /'lʊkaʊt/ *n* guardia *f*; (*prospect*) prospettiva *f*; **be on the ~ for** tenere gli occhi aperti per

loom /luːm/ *vi* apparire; *fig* profilarsi

loony /'luːnɪ/ *a & n fam* matto, -a *mf*. **~ bin** *n* manicomio *m*

loop /luːp/ *n* cappio *m*; (*on garment*) passante *m*. **~hole** *n* (*in the law*) scappatoia *f*

loose /luːs/ *a* libero; ⟨*knot*⟩ allentato; ⟨*page*⟩ staccato; ⟨*clothes*⟩ largo; ⟨*morals*⟩ dissoluto; (*inexact*) vago; **be at a ~ end** non sapere cosa fare; **come ~** ⟨*knot*:⟩ sciogliersi; **set ~** liberare. **'change** *n* spiccioli *mpl*. **~ly** *adv* scorrevolmente; ⟨*defined*⟩ vagamente

loosen /'luːsn/ *vt* sciogliere

loot /luːt/ *n* bottino *m* ● *vt/i* depredare. **~er** *n* predatore, -trice *mf*. **~ing** *n* saccheggio *m*

lop /lɒp/ **~ off** *vt* (*pt/pp* **lopped**) potare

lop'sided *a* sbilenco

lord /lɔːd/ *n* signore *m*; (*title*) Lord *m*; **House of L~s** Camera *f* dei Lords; **the L~'s Prayer** il Padrenostro; **good L~!** Dio mio!

lore /lɔː(r)/ *n* tradizioni *fpl*

lorry /'lɒrɪ/ *n* camion *m* *inv*; **~ driver** camionista *mf*

lose /luːz/ *v* (*pt/pp* **lost**) ● *vt* perdere

●*vi* perdere; *(clock:)* essere indietro; **get lost** perdersi; **get lost!** *fam* va a quel paese! **~r** *n* perdente *mf*

loss /lɒs/ *n* perdita *f*; **~es** *pl Comm* perdite *fpl*; **be at a ~** essere perplesso; **be at a ~ for words** non trovare le parole

lost /lɒst/ *see* **lose** ●*a* perduto. **~ 'property office** *n* ufficio *m* oggetti smarriti

lot¹ /lɒt/ *n* (*at auction*) lotto *m*; **draw ~s** tirare a sorte

lot² *n* **the ~** il tutto; **a ~ of**, **~s of** molto/i; **the ~ of you** tutti voi; **it has changed a ~** è cambiato molto

lotion /ˈləʊʃn/ *n* lozione *f*

lottery /ˈlɒtərɪ/ *n* lotteria *f*. **~ ticket** *n* biglietto *m* della lotteria

loud /laʊd/ *a* sonoro, alto; *(colours)* sgargiante ●*adv* forte; **out ~** ad alta voce. **~ 'hailer** *n* megafono *m*. **~ly** *adv* forte. **~ 'speaker** *n* altoparlante *m*

lounge /laʊndʒ/ *n* salotto *m*; (*in hotel*) salone *m* ●*vi* poltrire. **~ suit** *n* vestito *m* da uomo, completo *m* da uomo

louse /laʊs/ *n* (*pl* **lice**) pidocchio *m*

lousy /ˈlaʊzɪ/ *a* (**-ier, -iest**) *fam* schifoso

lout /laʊt/ *n* zoticone *m*. **~ish** *a* rozzo

lovable /ˈlʌvəbl/ *a* adorabile

love /lʌv/ *n* amore *m*; *Tennis* zero *m*; **in ~** innamorato (**with** di) ●*vt* amare *(person, country)*; **I ~ watching tennis** mi piace molto guardare il tennis. **~-affair** *n* relazione *f* [sentimentale]. **~ letter** *n* lettera *f* d'amore

lovely /ˈlʌvlɪ/ *a* (**-ier, -iest**) bello; (*in looks*) bello, attraente; (*in character*) piacevole; *(meal)* delizioso; **have a ~ time** divertirsi molto

lover /ˈlʌvə(r)/ *n* amante *mf*

love: **~ song** *n* canzone *f* d'amore. **~ story** *n* storia *f* d'amore

loving /ˈlʌvɪŋ/ *a* affettuoso

low /ləʊ/ *a* basso; (*depressed*) giù *inv* ●*adv* basso; **feel ~** sentirsi giù ●*n* minimo *m*; *Meteorol* depressione *f*; **at an all-time ~** *(prices etc)* al livello minimo

low: **~-brow** *a* di scarsa cultura. **~-cut** *a* *(dress)* scollato

lower /ˈləʊə(r)/ *a* & *adv* see **low** ●*vt* abbassare; **~ oneself** abbassarsi

low: **~-'fat** *a* magro. **~-'grade** *a* di qualità inferiore. **~-key** *fig* moderato. **~lands** /-ləndz/ *npl* pianure *fpl*. **~ 'tide** *n* bassa marea *f*

loyal /ˈlɔɪəl/ *a* leale. **~ty** *n* lealtà *f*

lozenge /ˈlɒzɪndʒ/ *n* losanga *f*; (*tablet*) pastiglia *f*

LP *n abbr* **long-playing record**

Ltd *abbr* (**Limited**) s.r.l.

lubricant /ˈluːbrɪkənt/ *n* lubrificante *m*

lubricat|e /ˈluːbrɪkeɪt/ *vt* lubrificare. **~ion** /-ˈkeɪʃn/ *n* lubrificazione *f*

lucid /ˈluːsɪd/ *a* (*explanation*) chiaro; (*sane*) lucido. **~ity** /-ˈsɪdətɪ/ *n* lucidità *f*; (*of explanation*) chiarezza *f*

luck /lʌk/ *n* fortuna *f*; **bad ~** sfortuna *f*; **good ~!** buona fortuna! **~ily** *adv* fortunatamente

lucky /ˈlʌkɪ/ *a* (**-ier, -iest**) fortunato; **be ~** essere fortunato; *(thing:)* portare fortuna. **~ 'charm** *n* portafortuna *m inv*

lucrative /ˈluːkrətɪv/ *a* lucrativo

ludicrous /ˈluːdɪkrəs/ *a* ridicolo. **~ly** *adv* (*expensive, complex*) eccessivamente

lug /lʌg/ *vt* (*pt/pp* **lugged**) *fam* trascinare

luggage /ˈlʌgɪdʒ/ *n* bagaglio *m*. **~-rack** *n* portabagagli *m inv*. **~ trolley** *n* carrello *m* portabagagli. **~-van** *n* bagagliaio *m*

lukewarm /ˈluːk-/ *a* tiepido; *fig* poco entusiasta

lull /lʌl/ *n* pausa *f* ●*vt* **~ to sleep** cullare

lullaby /ˈlʌləbaɪ/ *n* ninnananna *f*

lumbago /lʌmˈbeɪgəʊ/ *n* lombaggine *f*

lumber /ˈlʌmbə(r)/ *n* cianfrusaglie *fpl*; (*Am: timber*) legname *m* ●*vt fam* **~ sb with sth** affibbiare qcsa a qcno. **~ jack** *n* tagliaboschi *m inv*

luminous /ˈluːmɪnəs/ *a* luminoso

lump¹ /lʌmp/ *n* (*of sugar*) zolletta *f*; (*swelling*) gonfiore *m*; (*in breast*) nodulo *m*; (*in sauce*) grumo *m* ●*vt* **~ together** ammucchiare

lump² *vt* **~ it** *fam* **you'll just have to ~ it** che ti piaccia o no è così

lump sum *n* somma *f* globale

lumpy /ˈlʌmpɪ/ *a* (**-ier, -iest**) grumoso

lunacy /ˈluːnəsɪ/ *n* follia *f*

lunar /ˈluːnə(r)/ *a* lunare

lunatic /ˈluːnətɪk/ *n* pazzo, -a *mf*

lunch /lʌntʃ/ *n* pranzo *m* ●*vi* pranzare

luncheon /ˈlʌntʃn/ *n* (*formal*) pranzo *m*. **~ meat** *n* carne *f* in scatola. **~ voucher** *n* buono *m* pasto

lunch: **~-hour** *n* intervallo *m* per il pranzo. **~-time** *n* ora *f* di pranzo

lung /lʌŋ/ *n* polmone *m*. **~ cancer** *n* cancro *m* al polmone

lunge /lʌndʒ/ *vi* lanciarsi (**at** su)

lurch¹ /lɜːtʃ/ *n* **leave in the ~** *fam* lasciare nei guai

lurch² *vi* barcollare

lure /lʊə(r)/ *n* esca *f*; *fig* lusinga *f* ●*vt* adescare

lurid /'lʊərɪd/ a (gaudy) sgargiante; (sensational) sensazionalistico
lurk /lɜ:k/ vi appostarsi
luscious /'lʌʃəs/ a saporito; fig sexy inv
lush /lʌʃ/ a lussureggiante
lust /lʌst/ n lussuria ● vi ~ after desiderare [fortemente]. ~ful a lussurioso
lusty /'lʌstɪ/ a (-ier, -iest) vigoroso
lute /lu:t/ n liuto m
luxuriant /lʌg'ʒʊərɪənt/ a lussureggiante

luxurious /lʌg'ʒʊərɪəs/ a lussuoso
luxury /'lʌkʃərɪ/ n lusso m ● attrib di lusso
lying /'laɪɪŋ/ see lie¹ & ² ● n mentire m
lymph gland /'lɪmf/ n linfoghiandola f
lynch /lɪntʃ/ vt linciare
lynx /lɪŋks/ n lince f
lyric /'lɪrɪk/ a lirico. ~al a lirico; (fam: enthusiastic) entusiasta. ~s npl parole fpl

Mm

mac /mæk/ n fam impermeabile m
macabre /mə'kɑ:br/ a macabro
macaroni /mækə'rəʊnɪ/ n maccheroni mpl
mace¹ /meɪs/ n (staff) mazza f
mace² n (spice) macis m o f
machinations /mækɪ'neɪʃnz/ npl macchinazioni fpl
machine /mə'ʃi:n/ n macchina f ● vt (sew) cucire a macchina; Techn lavorare a macchina. ~-gun n mitragliatrice f
machinery /mə'ʃi:nərɪ/ n macchinario m
machinist /mə'ʃi:nɪst/ n macchinista mf; (on sewing machine) lavorante mf adetto, -a alla macchina da cucire
machismo /mæ'tʃɪzməʊ/ n machismo m
macho /'mætʃəʊ/ a macho inv
mackerel /'mækr(ə)l/ n inv sgombro m
mackintosh /'mækɪntɒʃ/ n impermeabile m
mad /mæd/ a (madder, maddest) pazzo, matto; (fam: angry) furioso (at con); like ~ fam come un pazzo; be ~ about sb sth (fam: keen on) andare matto per qcno/qcsa
madam /'mædəm/ n signora f
madden /'mædən/ vt (make angry) far diventare matto
made /meɪd/ see make ~ to measure [fatto] su misura
Madeira cake /mə'dɪərə/ n dolce m di pan di Spagna
madly /'mædlɪ/ adv fam follemente; ~ly in love innamorato follemente. ~man n pazzo m. ~ness n pazzia f
madonna /mə'dɒnə/ n madonna f

magazine /mægə'zi:n/ n rivista f; Mil, Phot magazzino m
maggot /'mægət/ n verme m
Magi /'meɪdʒaɪ/ npl the ~ i Re Magi
magic /'mædʒɪk/ n magia f; (tricks) giochi mpl di prestigio ● a magico; (trick) di prestigio. ~al a magico
magician /mə'dʒɪʃn/ n mago, -a mf; (entertainer) prestigiatore, -trice mf
magistrate /'mædʒɪstreɪt/ n magistrato m
magnanim|ity /mægnə'nɪmətɪ/ n magnanimità f. ~ous /·'næmɪməs/ a magnanimo
magnet /'mægnɪt/ n magnete m, calamita f. ~ic /·'netɪk/ a magnetico. ~ism n magnetismo m
magnification /mægnɪfɪ'keɪʃn/ n ingrandimento m
magnificen|ce /mæg'nɪfɪsəns/ n magnificenza f. ~t a magnifico
magnify /'mægnɪfaɪ/ vt (pt/pp -ied) ingrandire; (exaggerate) ingigantire. ~ing glass n lente f d'ingrandimento
magnitude /'mægnɪtju:d/ n grandezza f; (importance) importanza f
magpie /'mægpaɪ/ n gazza f
mahogany /mə'hɒgənɪ/ n mogano m ● a di mogano
maid /meɪd/ n cameriera f; old ~ pej zitella f
maiden /'meɪdn/ n liter fanciulla f ● a (speech, voyage) inaugurale. ~ 'aunt n zia f zitella. ~ name n nome m da ragazza
mail /meɪl/ n posta f ● vt impostare
mail: ~-bag n sacco m postale. ~box n

Am cassetta *f* delle lettere; *(e-mail)* casella *f* di posta elettronica. **~ing list** *n* elenco *m* d'indirizzi per un mailing. **~man** *n Am* postino *m.* **~ order** *n* vendita *f* per corrispondenza. **~-order firm** *n* ditta *f* di vendita per corrispondenza

mailshot /ˈmeɪlʃɒt/ *n* mailing *m inv*

maim /meɪm/ *vt* menomare

main¹ /meɪn/ *n (water, gas, electricity)* conduttura *f* principale

main² *a* principale; **the ~ thing is to...** la cosa essenziale è di... ● *n* **in the ~** in complesso

main: ~land /-lənd/ *n* continente *m.* **~ly** *adv* principalmente. **~stay** *n fig* pilastro *m.* **~ street** *n* via *f* principale

maintain /meɪnˈteɪn/ *vt* mantenere; *(keep in repair)* curare la manutenzione di; *(claim)* sostenere

maintenance /ˈmeɪntənəns/ *n* mantenimento *m*; *(care)* manutenzione *f*; *(allowance)* alimenti *mpl*

maisonette /meɪzəˈnet/ *n* appartamento *m* a due piani

majestic /məˈdʒestɪk/ *a* maestoso

majesty /ˈmædʒəstɪ/ *n* maestà *f inv*; **His/Her M~** Sua Maestà

major /ˈmeɪdʒə(r)/ *a* maggiore; **~ road** strada *f* con diritto di precedenza ● *n Mil, Mus* maggiore *m* ● *vi Am* **~ in** specializzarsi in

Majorca /məˈjɔːkə/ *n* Maiorca *f*

majority /məˈdʒɒrətɪ/ *n* maggioranza *f*; **be in the ~** avere la maggioranza

make /meɪk/ *n (brand)* marca *f* ● *vt (pt/pp* made) ● *vt* fare; *(earn)* guadagnare; *(render)* rendere ‹*happy, clear*›; prendere ‹*decision*›; **~ sb laugh** far ridere qcno; **~ sb do sth** far fare qcsa a qcno; **~ it** *(to party, top of hill etc)* farcela; **what time do you ~ it?** che ore fai? ● *vi* **~ as if to** fare per. **make do** *vi* arrangiarsi. **make for** *vt* dirigersi verso. **make off** *vi* fuggire. **make out** *vt (distinguish)* distinguere; *(write out)* rilasciare ‹*cheque*›; compilare ‹*list*›; *(claim)* far credere. **make over** *vt* cedere. **make up** *vt (constitute)* comporre; *(complete)* completare; *(invent)* inventare; *(apply cosmetics to)* truccare; fare ‹*parcel*›; **~ up one's mind** decidersi; **~ it up** *(after quarrel)* riconciliarsi ● *vi (after quarrel)* fare la pace; **~ up for** compensare; **~ up for lost time** recuperare il tempo perso

'make-believe *n* finzione *f*

maker /ˈmeɪkə(r)/ *n* fabbricante *mf*; **M~** *Relig* Creatore *m*

make: ~ shift *a* di fortuna ● *n* espediente *m.* **~-up** *n* trucco *m*; *(character)* natura *f*

making /ˈmeɪkɪŋ/ *n* **have the ~s of** aver la stoffa di

maladjust|ed /mæləˈdʒʌstɪd/ *a* disadattato

malaise /məˈleɪz/ *n fig* malessere *m*

malaria /məˈleərɪə/ *n* malaria *f*

Malaysia /məˈleɪzɪə/ *n* Malesia *f*

male /meɪl/ *a* maschile ● *n* maschio *m.* **~ nurse** *n* infermiere *m*

malevolen|ce /məˈlevələns/ *n* malevolenza *f.* **~t** *a* malevolo

malfunction /mælˈfʌŋkʃn/ *n* funzionamento *m* imperfetto ● *vi* funzionare male

malice /ˈmælɪs/ *n* malignità *f*; **bear sb ~** voler del male a qcno

malicious /məˈlɪʃəs/ *a* maligno

malign /məˈlaɪn/ *vt* malignare su

malignan|cy /məˈlɪgnənsɪ/ *n* malignità *f.* **~t** *a* maligno

malinger /məˈlɪŋgə(r)/ *vi* fingersi malato. **~er** *n* scansafatiche *mf inv*

malleable /ˈmælɪəbl/ *a* malleabile

mallet /ˈmælɪt/ *n* martello *m* di legno

malnu'trition /mæl-/ *n* malnutrizione *f*

mal'practice *n* negligenza *f*

malt /mɔːlt/ *n* malto *m*

Malta /ˈmɔːltə/ *n* Malta *f.* **~ese** /-ˈiːz/ *a & n* maltese *mf*

mal'treat /mæl-/ *vt* maltrattare. **~ment** *n* maltrattamento *m*

mammal /ˈmæml/ *n* mammifero *m*

mammoth /ˈmæməθ/ *a* mastodontico ● *n* mammut *m inv*

man /mæn/ *n (pl* men) uomo *m*; *(chess, draughts)* pedina *f* ● *vt (pt/pp* **manned**) equipaggiare; essere di servizio a ‹*counter, telephones*›

manage /ˈmænɪdʒ/ *vt* dirigere; gestire ‹*shop, affairs*›; *(cope with)* farcela; **~ to do sth** riuscire a fare qcsa ● *vi* riuscire; *(cope)* farcela **(on** con). **~able** /-əbl/ *a (hair)* docile; *(size)* maneggevole. **~ment** /-mənt/ *n* gestione *f*; **the ~ment** la direzione

manager /ˈmænɪdʒə(r)/ *n* direttore *m*; *(of shop, bar)* gestore *m*; *Sport* manager *m inv.* **~ess** /-ˈres/ *n* direttrice *f.* **~ial** /-ˈdʒɪərɪəl/ *a* **~ial staff** personale *m* direttivo

managing /ˈmænɪdʒɪŋ/ *a* **~ director** direttore, -trice *mf* generale

mandarin /ˈmændərɪn/ *n* **~ [orange]** mandarino *m*

mandat|e /'mændeɪt/ *n* mandato *m*. **~ory** /-dətrɪ/ *a* obbligatorio

mane /meɪn/ *n* criniera *f*

mangle /'mæŋgl/ *vt* (*damage*) maciullare

mango /'mæŋgəʊ/ *n* (*pl* -**es**) mango *m*

mangy /'meɪndʒɪ/ *a* (*dog*) rognoso

man: **~'handle** *vt* malmenare. **~hole** *n* botola *f*. **~hole cover** *n* tombino *m*. **~hood** *n* età *f* adulta; (*quality*) virilità *f*. **~-hour** *n* ora *f* lavorativa. **~-hunt** *n* caccia *f* all'uomo

man|ia /'meɪnɪə/ *n* mania *f*. **~iac** /-ɪæk/ *n* maniaco, -a *mf*

manicure /'mænɪkjʊə(r)/ *n* manicure *f inv* ● *vt* fare la manicure a

manifest /'mænɪfest/ *a* manifesto ● *vt* **~ itself** manifestarsi. **~ly** *adv* palesemente

manifesto /mænɪ'festəʊ/ *n* manifesto *m*

manifold /'mænɪfəʊld/ *a* molteplice

manipulat|e /mə'nɪpjʊleɪt/ *vt* manipolare. **~ion** /-'leɪʃn/ *n* manipolazione *f*

man'kind *n* genere *m* umano

manly /'mænlɪ/ *a* virile

'man-made *a* artificiale. **~ fibre** *n* fibra *f* sintetica

manner /'mænə(r)/ *n* maniera *f*; **in this ~** in questo modo; **have no ~s** avere dei pessimi modi; **good/bad ~s** buone/cattive maniere *fpl*. **~ism** *n* affettazione *f*

manœuvre /mə'nu:və(r)/ *n* manovra *f* ● *vt* fare manovra con (*vehicle*); manovrare (*person*)

manor /'mænə(r)/ *n* maniero *m*

'manpower *n* manodopera *f*

mansion /'mænʃn/ *n* palazzo *m*

'manslaughter *n* omicidio *m* colposo

mantelpiece /'mæntl-/ *n* mensola *f* di caminetto

manual /'mænjʊəl/ *a* manuale ● *n* manuale *m*

manufacture /mænjʊ'fæktʃə(r)/ *vt* fabbricare ● *n* manifattura *f*. **~r** *n* fabbricante *m*

manure /mə'njʊə(r)/ *n* concime *m*

manuscript /'mænjʊskrɪpt/ *n* manoscritto *m*

many /'menɪ/ *a & pron* molti; **there are as ~ boys as girls** ci sono tanti ragazzi quante ragazze; **as ~ as 500** ben 500; **as ~ as that** così tanti; **as ~** altrettanti, **very ~**, **a good/great ~** moltissimi; **~ a time** molte volte

map /mæp/ *n* carta *f* geografica; (*of town*) mappa *f* ● **map out** *vt* (*pt/pp* **mapped**) *fig* programmare

maple /'meɪpl/ *n* acero *m*

mar /mɑ:(r)/ *vt* (*pt/pp* **marred**) rovinare

marathon /'mærəθən/ *n* maratona *f*

marble /'mɑ:bl/ *n* marmo *m*; (*for game*) pallina *f* ● *attrib* di marmo

March /mɑ:tʃ/ *n* marzo *m*

march *n* marcia *f*; (*protest*) dimostrazione *f* ● *vi* marciare ● *vt* far marciare; **~ sb off** scortare qcno fuori

mare /meə(r)/ *n* giumenta *f*

margarine /mɑ:dʒə'ri:n/ *n* margarina *f*

margin /'mɑ:dʒɪn/ *n* margine *m*. **~al** *a* marginale. **~ally** *adv* marginalmente

marigold /'mærɪgəʊld/ *n* calendula *f*

marijuana /mærʊ'wɑ:nə/ *n* marijuana *f*

marina /mə'ri:nə/ *n* porticciolo *m*

marinade /mærɪ'neɪd/ *n* marinata *f* ● *vt* marinare

marine /mə'ri:n/ *a* marino ● *n* (*sailor*) soldato *m* di fanteria marina

marionette /mærɪə'net/ *n* marionetta *f*

marital /'mærɪtl/ *a* coniugale. **~ status** stato *m* civile

maritime /'mærɪtaɪm/ *a* marittimo

mark¹ /mɑ:k/ *n* (*currency*) marco *m*

mark² *n* (*stain*) macchia *f*; (*sign, indication*) segno *m*; *Sch* voto *m* ● *vt* segnare; (*stain*) macchiare; *Sch* correggere; *Sport* marcare; **~ time** *Mil* segnare il passo; *fig* non far progressi; **~ my words** ricordati quello che dico. **mark out** *vt* delimitare; *fig* designare

marked /mɑ:kt/ *a* marcato. **~ly** -kɪdlɪ/ *adv* notevolmente

marker /'mɑ:kə(r)/ *n* (*for highlighting*) evidenziatore *m*; *Sport* marcatore *m*; (*of exam*) esaminatore, -trice *mf*

market /'mɑ:kɪt/ *n* mercato *m* ● *vt* vendere al mercato; (*launch*) commercializzare; **on the ~** sul mercato. **~ing** *n* marketing *m*. **~ re'search** *n* ricerca *f* di mercato

marksman /'mɑ:ksmən/ *n* tiratore *m* scelto

marmalade /'mɑ:məleɪd/ *n* marmellata *f* d'arance

maroon /mə'ru:n/ *a* marrone rossastro

marooned /mə'ru:nd/ *a* abbandonato

marquee /mɑ:'ki:/ *n* tendone *m*

marquis /'mɑ:kwɪs/ *n* marchese *m*

marriage /'mærɪdʒ/ *n* matrimonio *m*

married /'mærɪd/ *a* sposato; (*life*) coniugale

marrow /'mærəʊ/ n Anat midollo m; (vegetable) zucca f

marr|y /'mærɪ/ vt (pt/pp -ied) sposare; **get ~ied** sposarsi ● vi sposarsi

marsh /mɑːʃ/ n palude f

marshal /'mɑːʃl/ n (steward) cerimoniere m ● vt (pt/pp **marshalled**) fig organizzare (arguments)

marshy /'mɑːʃɪ/ a paludoso

marsupial /mɑː'suːpɪəl/ n marsupiale m

martial /'mɑːʃl/ a marziale

martyr /'mɑːtə(r)/ n martire mf ● vt martirizzare. **~dom** /-dəm/ n martirio m. **~ed** a fam da martire

marvel /'mɑːvl/ n meraviglia f ● vi (pt/pp **marvelled**) meravigliarsi (at di). **~lous** /-vələs/ a meraviglioso

Marxis|m /'mɑːksɪzm/ n marxismo m. **~t** a & n marxista mf

marzipan /'mɑːzɪpæn/ n marzapane m

mascara /mæ'skɑːrə/ n mascara m inv

mascot /'mæskət/ n mascotte f inv

masculin|e /'mæskjʊlɪn/ a maschile ● n Gram maschile m. **~ity** /-'lɪnətɪ/ n mascolinità f

mash /mæʃ/ vt impastare. **~ed potatoes** npl purè m inv di patate

mask /mɑːsk/ n maschera f ● vt mascherare

masochis|m /'mæsəkɪzm/ n masochismo m. **~t** /-ɪst/ n masochista mf

mason /'meɪsn/ n muratore m

Mason n massone m. **~ic** /mə'sɒnɪk/ a massonico

masonry /'meɪsnrɪ/ n massoneria f

masquerade /mæskə'reɪd/ n fig mascherata f ● vi ~ **as** (pose) farsi passare per

mass¹ /mæs/ n Relig messa f

mass² n massa f; **~es of** fam un sacco di ● vi ammassarsi

massacre /'mæsəkə(r)/ n massacro m ● vt massacrare

massage /'mæsɑːʒ/ n massaggio m ● vt massaggiare; fig manipolare (statistics)

masseu|r /mæ'sɜː(r)/ n massaggiatore m. **~se** /-'sɜːz/ n massaggiatrice f

massive /'mæsɪv/ a enorme

mass: ~ **media** npl mpl di comunicazione di massa, mass media mpl. **~-pro'duce** vt produrre in serie. **~-pro'duction** n produzione f in serie

mast /mɑːst/ n Naut albero m; (for radio) antenna f

master /'mɑːstə(r)/ n maestro m, padrone m; (teacher) professore m; (of ship) capitano m; **M~** (boy) signorino m

master: ~**-key** n passe-partout m inv. **~ly** a magistrale. **~-mind** n cervello m ● vt ideare e dirigere. **~piece** n capolavoro m. **~-stroke** n colpo m da maestro. **~y** n (of subject) padronanza f

masturbat|e /'mæstəbeɪt/ vi masturbarsi. **~ion** /-'beɪʃn/ n masturbazione f

mat /mæt/ n stuoia f; (on table) sottopiatto m

match¹ /mætʃ/ n Sport partita f; (equal) uguale mf; (marriage) matrimonio m; (person to marry) partito m; **be a good ~** (colours:) intonarsi bene; **be no ~ for** non essere dello stesso livello di ● vt (equal) uguagliare; (be like) andare bene con ● vi intonarsi

match² n fiammifero m. **~box** n scatola f di fiammiferi

matching /'mætʃɪŋ/ a intonato

mate¹ /meɪt/ n compagno, -a mf; (assistant) aiuto m; Naut secondo m; (fam: friend) amico, -a mf ● vi accoppiarsi ● vt accoppiare

mate² n (in chess) scacco m matto

material /mə'tɪərɪəl/ n materiale m; (fabric) stoffa f; **raw ~s** pl materie fpl prime ● a materiale

material|ism /mə'tɪərɪəlɪzm/ n materialismo m. **~istic** /-'lɪstɪk/ a materialistico. **~ize** /-laɪz/ vi materializzarsi

maternal /mə'tɜːnl/ a materno

maternity /mə'tɜːnətɪ/ n maternità f. ~ **clothes** npl abiti mpl pre-maman. ~ **ward** n maternità f inv

matey /'meɪtɪ/ a fam amichevole

mathematic|al /mæθə'mætɪkl/ a matematico. **~ian** /-mə'tɪʃn/ n matematico, -a mf

mathematics /mæθə'mætɪks/ n matematica fsg

maths /mæθs/ n fam matematica fsg

matinée /'mætɪneɪ/ n Theat matinée f inv

mating /'meɪtɪŋ/ n accoppiamento m; ~ **season** stagione f degli amori

matriculat|e /mə'trɪkjʊleɪt/ vi immatricolarsi. **~ion** /-'leɪʃn/ n immatricolazione f

matrix /'meɪtrɪks/ n (pl **matrices** /-sɪːz/) n matrice f

matted /'mætɪd/ a ~ **hair** capelli mpl tutti appiccicati tra loro

matter /'mætə(r)/ n (affair) faccenda f; (question) questione f; (pus) pus m; (phys: substance) materia f; **as a ~ of fact** a dire la verità; **what is the ~?** che cosa c'è? ● vi importare; ~ **to sb**

essere importante per qcno; **it doesn't ~** non importa. **~-of-fact** a pratico

mattress /'mætrɪs/ n materasso m

matur|e /mə'tʃʊə(r)/ a maturo; *Comm* in scadenza ● vi maturare ● vt far maturare. **~ity** n maturità f; *Fin* maturazione f

maul /mɔ:l/ vt malmenare

Maundy /'mɔ:ndɪ/ n ~ **Thursday** giovedì m santo

mauve /məʊv/ a malva

maxim /'mæksɪm/ n massima f

maximum /'mæksɪməm/ a massimo; **ten minutes ~** dieci minuti al massimo ● n (pl **-ima**) massimo m

May /meɪ/ n maggio m

may /meɪ/ v aux (solo al presente) potere; **~ I come in?** posso entrare?; **if I ~ say so** se mi posso permettere; **~ you both be very happy** siate felici; **I ~ as well stay** potrei anche rimanere; **it ~ be true** potrebbe esser vero; **she ~ be old, but...** sarà anche vecchia, ma...

maybe /'meɪbɪ/ adv forse, può darsi

'May Day n il primo maggio

mayonnaise /meɪə'neɪz/ n maionese f

mayor /'meə(r)/ n sindaco m. **~ess** n sindaco m; (wife of mayor) moglie f del sindaco

maze /meɪz/ n labirinto m

me /mi:/ pron (object) mi; (with preposition) me; **she called me** mi ha chiamato; **she called me, not you** ha chiamato me, non te; **give me the money** dammi i soldi; **give it to me** dammelo; **he gave it to me** me lo ha dato; **it's ~** sono io

meadow /'medəʊ/ n prato m

meagre /'mi:gə(r)/ a scarso

meal¹ /mi:l/ n pasto m

meal² n (grain) farina f

mealy-mouthed /mi:lɪ'maʊðd/ a ambiguo

mean¹ /mi:n/ a avaro; (unkind) meschino

mean² a medio ● n (average) media f; **Greenwich ~ time** ora f media di Greenwich

mean³ vt (pt/pp **meant**) voler dire; (signify) significare; (intend) intendere; **I ~ it** lo dico seriamente; **~ well** avere buone intenzioni; **be ~t for** ⟨present:⟩ essere destinato a; ⟨remark:⟩ essere riferito a

meander /mɪ'ændə(r)/ vi vagare

meaning /'mi:nɪŋ/ n significato m. **~ful** a significativo. **~less** a senza senso

means /mi:nz/ n mezzo m; **~ of transport** mezzo m di trasporto; **by ~ of** per mezzo di; **by all ~!** certamente!; **by no ~** niente affatto ● npl (resources) mezzi mpl

meant /ment/ see **mean³**

'meantime n **in the ~** nel frattempo ● adv intanto

'meanwhile adv intanto

measles /'mi:zlz/ nsg morbillo m

measly /'mi:zlɪ/ a fam misero

measurable /'meʒərəbl/ a misurabile

measure /'meʒə(r)/ n misura f ● vt/i misurare. **measure up to** vt fig essere all'altezza di. **~d** a misurato. **~ment** /-mənt/ n misura f

meat /mi:t/ n carne f. **~ ball** n Culin polpetta f di carne. **~ loaf** n polpettone m

mechan|ic /mɪ'kænɪk/ n meccanico m. **~ical** a meccanico; **~ical engineering** ingegneria f meccanica. **~ically** adv meccanicamente. **~ics** n meccanica f ● npl meccanismo msg

mechan|ism /'mekənɪzm/ n meccanismo m. **~ize** vt meccanizzare

medal /'medl/ n medaglia f

medallion /mɪ'dælɪən/ n medaglione m

medallist /'medəlɪst/ n vincitore, -trice mf di una medaglia

meddle /'medl/ vi immischiarsi (**in** di); (tinker) armeggiare (**with** con)

media /'mi:dɪə/ npl **the ~** i mass media. **~ studies** npl scienze fpl della comunicazione

median /'mi:dɪən/ a **~ strip** Am banchina f spartitraffico

mediat|e /'mi:dɪeɪt/ vi fare da mediatore. **~ion** /-'eɪʃn/ n mediazione f. **~or** n mediatore, -trice mf

medical /'medɪkl/ a medico ● n visita f medica. **~ insurance** n assicurazione f sanitaria. **~ student** n studente, -essa mf di medicina

medicat|ed /'medɪkeɪtɪd/ a medicato. **~ion** /-'keɪʃn/ n (drugs) medicinali mpl

medicinal /mɪ'dɪsɪnl/ a medicinale

medicine /'medsən/ n medicina f

medieval /medr'i:vl/ a medievale

mediocr|e /mi:dɪ'əʊkə(r)/ a mediocre. **~ity** /-'ɒkrətɪ/ n mediocrità f

meditat|e /'medɪteɪt/ vi meditare (**on** su). **~ion** /-'teɪʃn/ n meditazione f

Mediterranean /medɪtə'reɪnɪən/ n **the ~ [Sea]** il [mare] Mediterraneo ● a mediterraneo

medium /'mi:dɪəm/ a medio; Culin di media cottura ● n (pl **media**) mezzo m; (pl **-s**) (person) medium mf inv

medium: ~**-sized** a di taglia media. ~ **wave** n onde fpl medie

medley /'medlɪ/ n miscuglio m; *Mus* miscellanea f

meek /miːk/ a mite, mansueto. ~**ly** adv docilmente

meet /miːt/ v (pt/pp met) ● vt incontrare; (at station, airport) andare incontro a; (for first time) far la conoscenza di; pagare (bill); soddisfare (requirements) ● vi incontrarsi; (committee:) riunirsi; ~ **with** incontrare (problem); incontrarsi con (person) ● n raduno m [sportivo]

meeting /'miːtɪŋ/ n riunione f, meeting m inv; (large) assemblea f; (by chance) incontro m

megabyte /'megəbaɪt/ n megabyte m

megalomania /megələ'meɪnɪə/ n megalomania f

megaphone /'megəfəʊn/ n megafono m

melancholy /'melənkəlɪ/ a malinconico ● n malinconia f

mellow /'meləʊ/ a (wine) generoso; (sound, colour) caldo; (person) dolce ● vi (person:) addolcirsi

melodic /mɪ'lɒdɪk/ a melodico

melodrama /'melə-/ n melodramma m. ~**tic** /-drə'mætɪk/ a melodrammatico

melody /'melədɪ/ n melodia f

melon /'melən/ n melone m

melt /melt/ vt sciogliere ● vi sciogliersi. **melt down** vt fondere. ~**ing-pot** n fig crogiuolo m

member /'membə(r)/ n membro m; ~ **countries** paesi mpl membri; **M~ of Parliament** deputato, -a mf; **M~ of the European Parliament** eurodeputato, -a mf. ~**ship** n iscrizione f; (members) soci mpl

membrane /'membreɪn/ n membrana f

memo /'meməʊ/ n promemoria m inv

memoirs /'memwɑːz/ npl ricordi mpl

memorable /'memərəbl/ a memorabile

memorandum /memə'rændəm/ n promemoria m inv

memorial /mɪ'mɔːrɪəl/ n monumento m. ~ **service** n funzione f commemorativa

memorize /'meməraɪz/ vt memorizzare

memory /'memərɪ/ n also Comput memoria f; (thing remembered) ricordo m; **from** ~ a memoria; **in** ~ **of** in ricordo di

men /men/ see **man**

menace /'menəs/ n minaccia f; (nuisance) piaga f ● vt minacciare. ~**ing** a minaccioso

mend /mend/ vt riparare; (darn) rammendare ● n **on the** ~ in via di guarigione

'menfolk n uomini mpl

menial /'miːnɪəl/ a umile

meningitis /menɪn'dʒaɪtɪs/ n meningite f

menopause /'menə-/ n menopausa f

menstruat|e /'menstrʊeɪt/ vi mestruare. ~**ion** /-'eɪʃn/ n mestruazione f

mental /'mentl/ a mentale; (fam: mad) pazzo. ~ **a'rithmetic** n calcolo m mentale. ~ **'illness** n malattia f mentale

mental|ity /men'tæləti/ n mentalità f inv. ~**ly** adv mentalmente; ~**ly ill** malato di mente

mention /'menʃn/ n menzione f ● vt menzionare; **don't** ~ **it** non c'è di che

menu /'menjuː/ n menu m inv

MEP n abbr **Member of the European Parliament**

mercenary /'mɜːsɪnərɪ/ a mercenario ● n mercenario m

merchandise /'mɜːtʃəndaɪz/ n merce f

merchant /'mɜːtʃənt/ n commerciante mf. ~ **bank** n banca f d'affari. ~ **'navy** n marina f mercantile

merci|ful /'mɜːsɪfl/ a misericordioso. ~**fully** adv fam grazie a Dio. ~**less** a spietato

mercury /'mɜːkjʊrɪ/ n mercurio m

mercy /'mɜːsɪ/ n misericordia f; **be at sb's** ~ essere alla mercé di qcno, essere in balia di qcno

mere /mɪə(r)/ a solo. ~**ly** adv solamente

merest /'mɪərɪst/ a minimo

merge /mɜːdʒ/ vi fondersi

merger /'mɜːdʒə(r)/ n fusione f

meringue /mə'ræŋ/ n meringa f

merit /'merɪt/ n merito m; (advantage) qualità f inv ● vt meritare

mermaid /'mɜːmeɪd/ n sirena f

merri|ly /'merɪlɪ/ adv allegramente. ~**ment** /-mənt/ n baldoria f

merry /'merɪ/ a (-ier, -iest) allegro; ~ **Christmas!** Buon Natale!

merry: ~**-go-round** n giostra f. ~**-making** n festa f

mesh /meʃ/ n maglia f

mesmerize /'mezmərаɪz/ vt ipnotizzare. ~**d** a fig ipnotizzato

mess /mes/ n disordine m, casino m fam; (trouble) guaio m; (something spilt) sporco m; Mil mensa f; **make a** ~ **of**

(*botch*) fare un pasticcio di ● **mess about** *vi* perder tempo; ~ **about with** armeggiare con ● *vt* prendere in giro (*person*). **mess up** *vt* mettere in disordine, incasinare *fam*; (*botch*) mandare all'aria

message /'mesɪdʒ/ *n* messaggio *m*

messenger /'mesɪndʒə(r)/ *n* messaggero *m*

Messiah /mɪ'saɪə/ *n* Messia *m*

Messrs /'mesəz/ *npl* (*on letter*) ~ **Smith** Spett. ditta Smith

messy /'mesɪ/ *a* (**-ier, -iest**) disordinato; (*in dress*) sciatto

met /met/ *see* **meet**

metal /'metl/ *n* metallo *m* ● *a* di metallo. ~**lic** /mɪ'tælɪk/ *a* metallico

metamorphosis /metə'mɔ:fəsɪs/ *n* (*pl* **-phoses** /-si:z/) metamorfosi *f inv*

metaphor /'metəfə(r)/ *n* metafora *f*. ~**ical** /-'fɒrɪkl/ *a* metaforico

meteor /'mi:tɪə(r)/ *n* meteora *f*. ~**ic** /-'ɒrɪk/ *a* fulmineo

meteorological /mi:tɪərə'lɒdʒɪkl/ *a* meteorologico

meteorolog|ist /mi:tɪə'rɒlədʒɪst/ *n* meteorologo, -a *mf*. ~**y** *n* meteorologia *f*

meter[1] /'mi:tə(r)/ *n* contatore *m*

meter[2] *n* *Am* = **metre**

method /'meθəd/ *n* metodo *m*

methodical /mɪ'θɒdɪkl/ *a* metodico. ~**ly** *adv* metodicamente

Methodist /'meθədɪst/ *n* metodista *mf*

meths /meθs/ *n fam* alcol *m* denaturato

methylated /'meθɪleɪtɪd/ *a* ~ **spirit**[s] alcol *m* denaturato

meticulous /mɪ'tɪkjʊləs/ *a* meticoloso. ~**ly** *adv* meticolosamente

metre /'mi:tə(r)/ *n* metro *m*

metric /'metrɪk/ *a* metrico

metropolis /mɪ'trɒpəlɪs/ *n* metropoli *f inv*

metropolitan /metrə'pɒlɪtən/ *a* metropolitano

mew /mju:/ *n* miao *m* ● *vi* miagolare

Mexican /'meksɪkən/ *a & n* messicano, -a *mf*. '**Mexico** *n* Messico *m*

miaow /mɪ'aʊ/ *n* miao *m* ● *vi* miagolare

mice /maɪs/ *see* **mouse**

mickey /'mɪkɪ/ *n* **take the ~ out of** prendere in giro

microbe /'maɪkrəʊb/ *n* microbo *m*

micro /'maɪkrəʊ/: ~**chip** *n* microchip *m inv*. ~**computer** *n* microcomputer *m inv*. ~**film** *n* microfilm *m inv*. ~**phone** *n* microfono *m*. ~**processor** *n* microprocessore *m*. ~**scope** *n* microscopio *m*. ~**scopic** /-'skɒpɪk/ *a* microscopico.

~**wave** *n* microonda *f*; (*oven*) forno *m* a microonde

mid /mɪd/ *a* ~ **May** metà maggio; **in ~ air** a mezz'aria

midday /mɪd'deɪ/ *n* mezzogiorno *m*

middle /'mɪdl/ *a* di centro; **the M~ Ages** il medioevo; **the ~ class[es]** la classe media; **the M~ East** il Medio Oriente ● *n* mezzo *m*; **in the ~ of** (*room, floor etc*) in mezzo a; **in the ~ of the night** nel pieno della notte, a notte piena

middle: ~-aged *a* di mezza età. ~**-class** *a* borghese. ~**man** *n Comm* intermediario *m*

middling /'mɪdlɪŋ/ *a* discreto

midge /mɪdʒ/ *n* moscerino *m*

midget /'mɪdʒɪt/ *n* nano, -a *mf*

Midlands /'mɪdləndz/ *npl* **the ~** l'Inghilterra *fsg* centrale

midnight *n* mezzanotte *f*

midriff /'mɪdrɪf/ *n* diaframma *m*

midst /mɪdst/ *n* **in the ~ of** in mezzo a; **in our ~** fra di noi, in mezzo a noi

mid: ~**summer** *n* mezza estate *f*. ~**way** *adv* a metà strada. ~**wife** *n* ostetrica *f*. ~**wifery** /-'wɪfrɪ/ *n* ostetricia *f*. ~'**winter** *n* pieno inverno *m*

might[1] /maɪt/ *v aux* **I ~** potrei; **will you come? - I ~** vieni? - può darsi; **it ~ be true** potrebbe essere vero; **I ~ as well stay** potrei anche restare; **you ~ have drowned** avresti potuto affogare; **you ~ have said so!** avresti potuto dirlo!

might[2] *n* potere *m*

mighty /'maɪtɪ/ *a* (**-ier, -iest**) potente ● *adv fam* molto

migraine /'mi:greɪn/ *n* emicrania *f*

migrant /'maɪgrənt/ *a* migratore ● *n* (*bird*) migratore, -trice *mf*; (*person: for work*) emigrante *mf*

migrat|e /maɪ'greɪt/ *vi* migrare. ~**ion** /-'greɪʃn/ *n* migrazione *f*

mike /maɪk/ *n fam* microfono *f*

Milan /mɪ'læn/ *n* Milano *f*

mild /maɪld/ *a* (*weather*) mite; (*person*) dolce; (*flavour*) delicato; (*illness*) leggero

mildew /'mɪldju:/ *n* muffa *f*

mild|ly /'maɪldlɪ/ *adv* moderatamente; (*say*) dolcemente; **to put it ~ly** a dir poco, senza esagerazione. ~**ness** *n* (*of person, words*) dolcezza *f*; (*of weather*) mitezza *f*

mile /maɪl/ *n* miglio *m* (= 1,6 km); ~**s nicer** *fam* molto più bello

mile|age /-ɪdʒ/ *n* chilometraggio *m*.
~stone *n* pietra *f* miliare

militant /'mɪlɪtənt/ *a* & *n* militante *mf*

military /'mɪlɪtrɪ/ *a* militare. **~
service** *n* servizio *m* militare

militate /'mɪlɪteɪt/ *vi* ~ **against** opporsi a

militia /mɪ'lɪʃə/ *n* milizia *f*

milk /mɪlk/ *n* latte *m* ● *vt* mungere

milk: **~man** *n* lattaio *m*. **~ shake** *n*
frappé *m inv*

milky /'mɪlkɪ/ *a* (**-ier, -iest**) latteo; *(tea
etc)* con molto latte. **M~ Way** *n* Astr Via
f Lattea

mill /mɪl/ *n* mulino *m*; *(factory)* fabbrica
f; *(for coffee etc)* macinino *m* ● *vt* macinare *(grain)*. **mill about, mill around**
vi brulicare

millennium /mɪ'lenɪəm/ *n* millennio *m*

miller /'mɪlə(r)/ *n* mugnaio *m*

milli|gram /'mɪlɪ-/ *n* milligrammo *m*.
~metre *n* millimetro *m*

million /'mɪljən/ *a* & *n* milione *m*; **a ~
pounds** un milione di sterline. **~aire**
/-'neə(r)/ *n* miliardario, -a *mf*

millstone *n fig* peso *m*

mime /maɪm/ *n* mimo *m* ● *vt* mimare

mimic /'mɪmɪk/ *n* imitatore, -trice *mf*
● *vt* (*pt/pp* **mimicked**) imitare. **~ry** *n*
mimetismo *m*

mimosa /mɪ'məʊzə/ *n* mimosa *f*

mince /mɪns/ *n* carne *f* tritata ● *vt*
Culin tritare; **not ~ one's words** parlare senza mezzi termini

mince: **~meat** *n* miscuglio *m* di frutta
secca; **make ~meat of** *fig* demolire.
~ pie *n* pasticcino *m* a base di frutta secca

mincer /'mɪnsə(r)/ *n* tritacarne *m inv*

mind /maɪnd/ *n* mente *f*; *(sanity)* ragione *f*; **to my ~** a mio parere; **give sb a
piece of one's ~** dire chiaro e tondo a
qcno quello che si pensa; **make up
one's ~** decidersi; **have sth in ~** avere
qcsa in mente; **bear sth in ~** tenere
presente qcsa; **have something on
one's ~** essere preoccupato; **have a
good ~ to** avere una gran voglia di; **I
have changed my ~** ho cambiato
idea; **in two ~s** indeciso; **are you out
of your ~?** sei diventato matto? ● *vt*
(look after) occuparsi di; **I don't ~ the
noise** il rumore non mi dà fastidio; **I
don't ~ what we do** non mi importa
quello che facciamo; **~ the step!** attenzione al gradino! ● *vi* I don't ~ non mi
importa; **never ~!** non importa!; **do**

you ~ if...? ti dispiace se...? **mind out**
vi ~ **out!** [fai] attenzione!

minder /'maɪndə(r)/ *n* (*Br: bodyguard*)
gorilla *m inv*; *(for child)* baby-sitter *mf
inv*

mind|ful *a* **~ful of** attento a. **~less** *a*
noncurante

mine[1] /maɪn/ *poss pron* il mio *m*, la mia
f, i miei *mpl*, le mie *fpl*; **a friend of ~**
un mio amico; **friends of ~** dei miei
amici; **that is ~** questo è mio; *(as
opposed to yours)* questo è il mio

mine[2] *n* miniera *f*; *(explosive)* mina *f*
● *vt* estrarre; *Mil* minare. **~ detector**
n rivelatore *m* di mine. **~field** *n* campo
m minato

miner /'maɪnə(r)/ *n* minatore *m*

mineral /'mɪnərəl/ *n* minerale *m* ● *a*
minerale. **~ water** *n* acqua *f* minerale

minesweeper /'maɪn-/ *n* dragamine
m inv

mingle /'mɪŋgl/ *vi* ~ **with** mescolarsi a

mini /'mɪnɪ/ *n* (*skirt*) mini *f*

miniature /'mɪnɪtʃə(r)/ *a* in miniatura
● *n* miniatura *f*

mini|bus /'mɪnɪ-/ *n* minibus *m inv*, pulmino *m*. **~cab** *n* taxi *m inv*

minim /'mɪnɪm/ *n* Mus minima *f*

minim|al /'mɪnɪməl/ *a* minimo. **~ize** *vt*
minimizzare. **~um** *n* (*pl-ima*) minimo
m ● *a* minimo; **ten minutes ~um** minimo dieci minuti

mining /'maɪnɪŋ/ *n* estrazione *f* ● *a*
estrattivo

miniskirt /'mɪnɪ-/ *n* minigonna *f*

minist|er /'mɪnɪstə(r)/ *n* ministro *m*;
Relig pastore *m*. **~erial** /-'stɪərɪəl/ *a*
ministeriale

ministry /'mɪnɪstrɪ/ *n* Pol ministero *m*;
the ~ Relig il ministero sacerdotale

mink /mɪŋk/ *n* visone *m*

minor /'maɪnə(r)/ *a* minore ● *n* minorenne *mf*

minority /maɪ'nɒrətɪ/ *n* minoranza *f*;
(age) minore età *f*

minor road *n* strada *f* secondaria

mint[1] /mɪnt/ *n fam* patrimonio *m* ● *a* **in
~ condition** in condizione perfetta

mint[2] *n* (*herb*) menta *f*

minus /'maɪnəs/ *prep* meno; *(fam:
without)* senza ● *n* ~ [**sign**] meno *m*

minute[1] /'mɪnɪt/ *n* minuto *m*; **in a ~**
(shortly) in un minuto; **~s** *pl* (*of meeting*) verbale *msg*

minute[2] /maɪ'njuːt/ *a* minuto; *(precise)*
minuzioso

mirac|le /'mɪrəkl/ *n* miracolo *m*.
~ulous /-'rækjʊləs/ *a* miracoloso

mirage /'mɪrɑːʒ/ n miraggio m
mirror /'mɪrə(r)/ n specchio m ● vt rispecchiare
mirth /mɜːθ/ n ilarità f
misad'venture /mɪs-/ n disavventura f
misanthropist /mɪ'zænθrəpɪst/ n misantropo, -a mf
misappre'hension n malinteso m; **be under a ~** avere frainteso
misbe'have vi comportarsi male
mis'calcu|late vt/i calcolare male. **~lation** n calcolo m sbagliato
'miscarriage n aborto m spontaneo; **~ of justice** errore m giudiziario. **mis'carry** vi abortire
miscellaneous /mɪsə'leɪnɪəs/ a assortito
mischief /'mɪstʃɪf/ n malefatta f; (harm) danno m
mischievous /'mɪstʃɪvəs/ a (naughty) birichino; (malicious) dannoso
miscon'ception n concetto m erroneo
mis'conduct n cattiva condotta f
misde'meanour n reato m
miser /'maɪzə(r)/ n avaro m
miserabl|e /'mɪzrəbl/ a (unhappy) infelice; (wretched) miserabile; (fig: weather) deprimente. **~y** adv (live, fail) miseramente; (say) tristemente
miserly /'maɪzəlɪ/ a avaro; (amount) ridicolo
misery /'mɪzərɪ/ n miseria f; (fam: person) piagnone, -a mf
mis'fire vi (gun:) far cilecca; (plan etc:) non riuscire
'misfit n disadattato, -a mf
mis'fortune n sfortuna f
mis'givings npl dubbi mpl
mis'guided a fuorviato
mishap /'mɪshæp/ n disavventura f
misin'terpret vt fraintendere
mis'judge vt giudicar male; (estimate wrongly) valutare male
mis'lay vt (pt/pp -laid) smarrire
mis'lead vt (pt/pp -led) fuorviare. **~ing** a fuorviante
mis'manage vt amministrare male. **~ment** n cattiva amministrazione f
misnomer /mɪs'nəʊmə(r)/ n termine m improprio
'misprint n errore m di stampa
mis'quote vt citare erroneamente
misrepre'sent vt rappresentare male
miss /mɪs/ n colpo m mancato ● vt (fail to hit or find) mancare; perdere (train, bus, class); (feel the loss of) sentire la mancanza di; **I ~ed that part** (failed to

notice) mi è sfuggita quella parte ● vi but he **~ed** (failed to hit) ma l'ha mancato. **miss out** vt saltare, omettere
Miss n (pl -es) signorina f
misshapen /mɪs'ʃeɪpən/ a malformato
missile /'mɪsaɪl/ n missile m
missing /'mɪsɪŋ/ a mancante; (person) scomparso; Mil disperso; **be ~** essere introvabile
mission /'mɪʃn/ n missione f
missionary /'mɪʃənrɪ/ n missionario, -a mf
mis'spell vt (pt/pp -spelled, -spelt) sbagliare l'ortografia di
mist /mɪst/ n (fog) foschia f ● **mist up** vi appannarsi, annebbiarsi
mistake /mɪ'steɪk/ n sbaglio m; **by ~** per sbaglio ● vt (pt mistook, pp mistaken) sbagliare (road, house); fraintendere (meaning, words); **~ for** prendere per
mistaken /mɪ'steɪkən/ a sbagliato; **be ~** sbagliarsi; **~ identity** errore m di persona. **~ly** adv erroneamente
mistletoe /'mɪsltəʊ/ n vischio m
mistress /'mɪstrɪs/ n padrona f; (teacher) maestra f; (lover) amante f
mis'trust n sfiducia f ● vt non aver fiducia in
misty /'mɪstɪ/ a (-ier, -iest) nebbioso
misunder'stand vt (pt/pp -stood) fraintendere. **~ing** n malinteso m
misuse¹ /mɪs'juːz/ vt usare male
misuse² /mɪs'juːs/ n cattivo uso m
mite /maɪt/ n (child) piccino, -a mf
mitigat|e /'mɪtɪgeɪt/ vt attenuare. **~ing** a attenuante
mitten /'mɪtn/ n manopola f, muffola f
mix /mɪks/ n (combination) mescolanza f; Culin miscuglio m; (ready-made) preparato m ● vt mischiare ● vi mischiarsi; (person:) inserirsi; **~ with** (associate with) frequentare. **mix up** vt mescolare (papers); (confuse, mistake for) confondere
mixed /mɪkst/ a misto; **~ up** (person) confuso
mixer /'mɪksə(r)/ n Culin frullatore m, mixer m inv; **he's a good ~** è un tipo socievole
mixture /'mɪkstʃə(r)/ n mescolanza f; (medicine) sciroppo m; Culin miscela f
'mix-up n (confusion) confusione f; (mistake) pasticcio m
moan /məʊn/ n lamento m ● vi lamentarsi; (complain) lagnarsi
moat /məʊt/ n fossato m

mob /mɒb/ n folla f; (rabble) gentaglia f; (fam: gang) banda f ● vt (pt/pp mobbed) assalire

mobile /'məʊbaɪl/ a mobile ● n composizione f mobile. ~ 'home n casa f roulotte. ~ [**phone**] n [telefono m] cellulare m

mobility /mə'bɪlətɪ/ n mobilità f

mock /mɒk/ a finto ● vt canzonare. ~ery n derisione f

'**mock-up** n modello m in scala

mode /məʊd/ n modo m; Comput modalità f

model /'mɒdl/ n modello m; [fashion] ~ indossatore, -trice mf, modello, -a mf ● a (yacht, plane) in miniatura; (pupil, husband) esemplare, modello ● v (pt/pp modelled) ● vt indossare (clothes) ● vi fare l'indossatore, -trice mf; (for artist) posare

modem /'məʊdem/ n modem m inv

moderate¹ /'mɒdəreɪt/ vt moderare ● vi moderarsi

moderate² /'mɒdərət/ a moderato ● n Pol moderato, -a mf. ~ly adv (drink, speak etc) moderatamente; (good, bad etc) relativamente

moderation /mɒdə'reɪʃn/ n moderazione f; in ~ con moderazione

modern /'mɒdn/ a moderno. ~ize vt modernizzare

modest /'mɒdɪst/ a modesto. ~y n modestia f

modicum /'mɒdɪkəm/ n a ~ of un po' di

modif|ication /mɒdɪfɪ'keɪʃn/ n modificazione f. ~y /'mɒdɪfaɪ/ vt (pt/pp -fied) modificare

module /'mɒdjuːl/ n modulo m

moist /mɔɪst/ a umido

moisten /'mɔɪsn/ vt inumidire

moistur|e /'mɔɪstʃə(r)/ n umidità f. ~izer n [crema f] idratante m

molar /'məʊlə(r)/ n molare m

molasses /mə'læsɪz/ n Am melassa f

mole¹ /məʊl/ n (on face etc) neo m

mole² n Zool talpa f

molecule /'mɒlɪkjuːl/ n molecola f

molest /mə'lest/ vt molestare

mollycoddle /'mɒlɪkɒdl/ vt tenere nella bambagia

molten /'məʊltən/ a fuso

mom /mɒm/ n Am fam mamma f

moment /'məʊmənt/ n momento m; at the ~ in questo momento. ~arily adv momentaneamente. ~ary a momentaneo

momentous /mə'mentəs/ a molto importante

momentum /mə'mentəm/ n impeto m

monarch /'mɒnək/ n monarca m. ~y n monarchia f

monast|ery /'mɒnəstrɪ/ n monastero m. ~ic /mə'næstɪk/ a monastico

Monday /'mʌndeɪ/ n lunedì m inv

monetary /'mʌnɪtrɪ/ a monetario

money /'mʌnɪ/ n denaro m

money: ~-box n salvadanaio m. ~-lender n usuraio m

mongrel /'mʌŋgrəl/ n bastardo m

monitor /'mɒnɪtə(r)/ n Techn monitor m inv ● vt controllare

monk /mʌŋk/ n monaco m

monkey /'mʌŋkɪ/ n scimmia f. ~-nut n nocciolina f americana. ~-wrench n chiave f inglese a rullino

mono /'mɒnəʊ/ n mono m

monogram /'mɒnəgræm/ n monogramma m

monologue /'mɒnəlɒg/ n monologo m

monopol|ize /mə'nɒpəlaɪz/ vt monopolizzare. ~y n monopolio m

monosyllabic /mɒnəsɪ'læbɪk/ a monosillabico

monotone /'mɒnətəʊn/ n **speak in a** ~ parlare con tono monotono

monoton|ous /mə'nɒtənəs/ a monotono. ~y n monotonia f

monsoon /mɒn'suːn/ n monsone m

monster /'mɒnstə(r)/ n mostro m

monstrosity /mɒn'strɒsətɪ/ n mostruosità f

monstrous /'mɒnstrəs/ a mostruoso

month /mʌnθ/ n mese m. ~ly a mensile ● adv mensilmente ● n (periodical) mensile m

monument /'mɒnjʊmənt/ n monumento m. ~al /-'mentl/ a fig monumentale

moo /muː/ n muggito m ● vi (pt/pp mooed) muggire

mooch /muːtʃ/ vi ~ about fam gironzolare (**the house** per casa)

mood /muːd/ n umore m; be in a good/bad ~ essere di buon/cattivo umore; be in the ~ for essere in vena di

moody /'muːdɪ/ a (-ier, -iest) (variable) lunatico; (bad-tempered) di malumore

moon /muːn/ n luna f; over the ~ fam al settimo cielo

moon: ~light n chiaro m di luna ● vi fam lavorare in nero. ~lit a illuminato dalla luna

moor¹ /mʊə(r)/ n brughiera f

385

moor² *vt Naut* ormeggiare
moose /muːs/ *n* (*pl* **moose**) alce *m*
moot /muːt/ *a* **it's a ~ point**è un punto controverso
mop /mɒp/ *n* mocio® *m* ; **~ of hair**zazzera *f* ●*vt* (*pt/pp* **mopped**) lavare con il mocio. **mop up**vt (*dry*) asciugare con lo straccio; (*clean*) pulire con lo straccio
mope /məʊp/ *vi* essere depresso
moped /ˈməʊped/ *n* ciclomotore *m*
moral /ˈmɒrəl/ *a* morale ●*n* morale *f*. **~ly**adv moralmente. **~s** *pl* moralità *f*
morale /məˈrɑːl/ *n* morale *m*
morality /məˈrælətɪ/ *n* moralità *f*
morbid /ˈmɔːbɪd/ *a* morboso
more /mɔː(r)/ *a* più; **a few ~ books**un po' più di libri; **some ~ tea?** ancora un po' di tè?; **there's no ~ bread** non c'è più pane; **there are no ~ apples** non ci sono più mele; **one ~ word and...** ancora una parola e... ●*pron* di più; **would you like some ~?**ne vuoi ancora?; **no ~, thank you** non ne voglio più, grazie ●*adv* più; **~ interesting** più interessante; **~ [and ~]** quickly [sempre] più veloce; **~ than** più di; **I don't love him any ~** no lo amo più; **once ~** ancora una volta; **~ or less** più o meno; **the ~ I see him, the ~ I like him**più lo vedo, più mi piace
moreover /mɔːˈrəʊvə(r)/ *adv* inoltre
morgue /mɔːg/ *n* obitorio *m*
moribund /ˈmɒrɪbʌnd/ *a* moribondo
morning /ˈmɔːnɪŋ/ *n* mattina *f*; **in the ~** del mattino; (*tomorrow*) domani mattina
Morocc|o /məˈrɒkəʊ/ *n* Marocco *m* ●*a* **~an**a & *n* marocchino, -a *mf*
moron /ˈmɔːrɒn/ *n fam* deficiente *mf*
morose /məˈrəʊs/ *a* scontroso
morphine /ˈmɔːfiːn/ *n* morfina *f*
Morse /mɔːs/ *n* ~ [code] [codice *m*] Morse *m*
morsel /ˈmɔːsl/ *n* (*food*) boccone *m*
mortal /ˈmɔːtl/ *a & n* mortale *mf*. **~ity** /mɔːˈtælətɪ/ *n* mortalità *f*. **~ly** *adv* (*wounded, offended*) a morte; (*afraid*) da morire
mortar /ˈmɔːtə(r)/ *n* mortaio *m*
mortgage /ˈmɔːgɪdʒ/ *n* mutuo *m*; (*on property*) ipoteca *f* ●*vt* ipotecare
mortuary /ˈmɔːtjʊərɪ/ *n* camera *f* mortuaria
mosaic /məʊˈzeɪɪk/ *n* mosaico *m*.
Moscow /ˈmɒskəʊ/ *n* Mosca *f*
Moslem /ˈmʊzlɪm/ *a & n* musulmano, -a *mf*

mosque /mɒsk/ *n* moschea *f*
mosquito /mɒsˈkiːtəʊ/ *n* (*pl* **-es**) zanzara *f*
moss /mɒs/ *n* muschio *m*. **~y** *a* muschioso
most /məʊst/ *a* (*majority*) la maggior parte di; **for the ~ part** per lo più ●*adv* più, maggiormente; (*very*) estremamente, molto; **the ~ interesting day** la giornata più interessante; **a ~ interesting day**una giornata estremamente interessante; **the ~ beautiful woman in the world**la donna più bella del mondo; **~ unlikely** veramente improbabile ●*pron* ~ **of them** la maggior parte di loro; **at [the] ~** al massimo; **make the ~ of**sfruttare al massimo; **~ of the time** la maggior parte del tempo. **~ly**adv per lo più
MOT *n Br* revisione *f* obbligatoria di autoveicoli
motel /məʊˈtel/ *n* motel *m inv*
moth /mɒθ/ *n* falena *f*; [clothes-] ~ tarma *f*
moth: **~ball** *n* pallina *f* di naftalina. **~-eaten** *a* tarmato
mother /ˈmʌðə(r)/ *n* madre *f*; **M~'s Day** la festa della mamma ●*vt* fare da madre a:
mother: **~board** *n Comput* scheda *f* madre. **~hood** *n* maternità *f*. **~-in-law** *n* (*pl* ~ **s-in-law**) suocera *f*. **~-land** *n* madrepatria *f*. **~-of-pearl** *n* madreperla *f*. **~-to-be** *n* futura mamma *f*. ~ **tongue** *n* madrelingua *f*
mothproof /ˈmɒθ-/ *a* antitarmico
motif /məʊˈtiːf/ *n* motivo *m*
motion /ˈməʊʃn/ *n* moto *m*; (*proposal*) mozione *f*; (*gesture*) gesto *m* ●*vt/i* ~ [to] sb to come in fare segno a qcno di entrare. **~less** *a* immobile. **~lessly** *adv* senza alcun movimento
motivat|e /ˈməʊtɪveɪt/ *vt* motivare. **~ion** /-ˈveɪʃn/ *n* motivazione *f*
motive /ˈməʊtɪv/ *n* motivo *m*
motley /ˈmɒtlɪ/ *a* disparato
motor /ˈməʊtə(r)/ *n* motore *m*; (*car*) macchina *f* ●*a* a motore; *Anat* motore ●*vi* andare in macchina
Motorail /ˈməʊtəreɪl/ *n* treno *m* per trasporto auto
motor: **~ bike** *n fam* moto *f inv*. **~ boat** *n* motoscafo *m*. **~cade** /-keɪd/ *n Am* corteo *m* di auto. ~ **car** *n* automobile *f*. ~ **cycle** *n* motocicletta *f*. **~cyclist** *n* motociclista *mf*. **~ing** *n* automobilismo *m*. **~ist** *n* automobilista *mf*. ~ **racing** *n* corse *fpl* automobilistiche. ~

vehicle *n* autoveicolo *m.* ~**way** *n* autostrada *f*

mottled /'mɒtld/ *a* chiazzato

motto /'mɒtəʊ/ *n* (*pl* -**es**) motto *m*

mould[1] /məʊld/ *n* (*fungus*) muffa *f*

mould[2] *n* stampo *m* ● *vt* foggiare; *fig* formare. ~**ing** *n Archit* cornice *f*

mouldy /'məʊldɪ/ *a* ammuffito; (*fam: worthless*) ridicolo

moult /məʊlt/ *vi* (*bird:*) fare la muta; (*animal:*) perdere il pelo

mound /maʊnd/ *n* mucchio *m*; (*hill*) collinetta *f*

mount /maʊnt/ *n* (*horse*) cavalcatura *f*; (*of jewel, photo, picture*) montatura *f* ● *vt* montare a (*horse*); salire su (*bicycle*); incastonare (*jewel*); incorniciare (*photo, picture*) ● *vi* aumentare. **mount up** *vi* aumentare

mountain /'maʊntɪn/ *n* montagna *f.* ~**bike** *n* mountain bike *f inv*

mountaineer /maʊntɪ'nɪə(r)/ *n* alpinista *mf.* ~**ing** *n* alpinismo *m*

mountainous /'maʊntɪnəs/ *a* montagnoso

mourn /mɔːn/ *vt* lamentare ● *vi* ~ **for** piangere la morte di. ~**er** *n* persona *f* che partecipa a un funerale. ~**ful** *a* triste. ~**ing** *n* in ~**ing** in lutto

mouse /maʊs/ *n* (*pl* **mice**) topo *m*; *Comput* mouse *m inv.* ~**trap** *n* trappola *f* [per topi]

mousse /muːs/ *n Culin* mousse *f inv*

moustache /məˈstɑːʃ/ *n* baffi *mpl*

mousy /'maʊsɪ/ *a* (*colour*) grigio topo

mouth[1] /maʊð/ *vt* ~ **sth** dire qcsa silenziosamente muovendo solamente le labbra

mouth[2] /maʊθ/ *n* bocca *f*; (*of river*) foce *f*

mouth: ~**ful** *n* boccone *m.* ~-**organ** *n* armonica *f* [a bocca]. ~**piece** *n* imboccatura *f*; (*fig: person*) portavoce *m inv.* ~**wash** *n* acqua *f* dentifricia. ~-**watering** *a* che fa venire l'acquolina in bocca

movable /'muːvəbl/ *a* movibile

move /muːv/ *n* mossa *f*; (*moving house*) trasloco *m*; **on the** ~ in movimento; **get a** ~ **on** *fam* darsi una mossa ● *vt* muovere; (*emotionally*) commuovere; spostare (*car, furniture*); (*transfer*) trasferire; (*propose*) proporre; ~ **house** traslocare ● *vi* muoversi; (*move house*) traslocare. **move along** *vi* andare avanti ● *vt* muovere in avanti. **move away** *vi* allontanarsi; (*move house*) trasferirsi ● *vt* allontanare. **move forward** *vi* avanzare ● *vt* spostare avanti. **move in**

vi (*to a house*) trasferirsi. **move off** *vi* (*vehicle:*) muoversi. **move out** *vi* (*of house*) andare via. **move over** *vi* spostarsi ● *vt* spostare. **move up** *vi* muoversi; (*advance, increase*) avanzare

movement /'muːvmənt/ *n* movimento *m*

movie /'muːvɪ/ *n* film *m inv*; **go to the** ~**s** andare al cinema

moving /'muːvɪŋ/ *a* mobile; (*touching*) commovente

mow /məʊ/ *vt* (*pt* **mowed**, *pp* **mown** or **mowed**) tagliare (*lawn*). **mow down** *vt* (*destroy*) sterminare

mower /'məʊə(r)/ *n* tosaerba *m inv*

MP *n abbr* **Member of Parliament**

Mr /'mɪstə(r)/ *n* (*pl* **Messrs**) Signor *m*

Mrs /'mɪsɪz/ *n* Signora *f*

Ms /mɪz/ *n* Signora *f* (*modo m formale di rivolgersi ad una donna quando non si vuole connotarla come sposata o nubile*)

much /mʌtʃ/ *a, adv & pron* molto; ~ **as** per quanto; **I love you just as** ~ **as before/him** ti amo quanto prima/lui; **as** ~ **as £5 million** ben cinque milioni di sterline; **as** ~ **as that** così tanto; **very** ~ tantissimo, moltissimo; ~ **the same** quasi uguale

muck /mʌk/ *n* (*dirt*) sporcizia *f*; (*farming*) letame *m*; (*fam: filth*) porcheria *f.* **muck about** *vi fam* perder tempo; ~ **about with** trafficare con. **muck up** *vt fam* rovinare; (*make dirty*) sporcare

mucky /'mʌkɪ/ *a* (-**ier**, -**iest**) sudicio

mucus /'mjuːkəs/ *n* muco *m*

mud /mʌd/ *n* fango *m*

muddle /'mʌdl/ *n* disordine *m*; (*mix-up*) confusione *f* ● *vt* ~ [**up**] confondere (*dates*)

muddy /'mʌdɪ/ *a* (-**ier**, -**iest**) (*path*) fangoso; (*shoes*) infangato

mudguard *n* parafango *m*

muesli /'muːzlɪ/ *n* muesli *m inv*

muffle /'mʌfl/ *vt* smorzare (*sound*). **muffle** [**up**] *vt* (*for warmth*) imbacuccare

muffler /'mʌflə(r)/ *n* sciarpa *f*; *Am Auto* marmitta *f*

mug[1] /mʌg/ *n* tazza *f*; (*for beer*) boccale *m*; (*fam: face*) muso *m*; (*fam: simpleton*) pollo *m*

mug[2] *vt* (*pt/pp* **mugged**) aggredire e derubare. ~**ger** *n* assalitore, -trice *mf.* ~**ging** *n* aggressione *f* per furto

muggy /'mʌgɪ/ *a* (-**ier**, -**iest**) afoso

mule /mjuːl/ *n* mulo *m*

mull /mʌl/ *vt* ~ **over** rimuginare su

mulled /mʌld/ a ~ **wine** vin brûlé m inv

multi /'mʌltɪ/: ~**coloured** a variopinto. ~**lingual** /-'lɪŋgwəl/ a multilingue inv. ~**media** n multimedia mpl ● a multimediale. ~**national** a multinazionale ● n multinazionale f

multiple /'mʌltɪpl/ a multiplo

multiplication /mʌltɪplɪ'keɪʃn/ n moltiplicazione f

multiply /'mʌltɪplaɪ/ v (pt/pp -ied) ● vt moltiplicare (**by** per) ● vi moltiplicarsi

multi'storey a ~ **car park** parcheggio m a più piani

mum[1] /mʌm/ a **keep** ~ **fam** non aprire bocca

mum[2] n fam mamma f

mumble /'mʌmbl/ vt/i borbottare

mummy[1] /'mʌmɪ/ n fam mamma f

mummy[2] n Archæol mummia f

mumps /mʌmps/ n orecchioni mpl

munch /mʌntʃ/ vt/i sgranocchiare

mundane /mʌn'deɪn/ a (everyday) banale

municipal /mju'nɪsɪpl/ a municipale

mural /'mjʊərəl/ n dipinto m murale

murder /'mɜːdə(r)/ n assassinio m ● vt assassinare; (fam: ruin) massacrare. ~**er** n assassino, -a mf. ~**ous** /-rəs/ a omicida

murky /'mɜːkɪ/ a (-ier, -iest) oscuro

murmur /'mɜːmə(r)/ n mormorio m ● vt/i mormorare

muscle /'mʌsl/ n muscolo m ● **muscle in** vi sl intromettersi (**on** in)

muscular /'mʌskjʊlə(r)/ a muscolare; (strong) muscoloso

muse /mjuːz/ vi meditare (**on** su)

museum /mju'zɪəm/ n museo m

mushroom /'mʌʃrʊm/ n fungo m ● vi fig spuntare come funghi

music /'mjuːzɪk/ n musica f; (written) spartito m.

musical /'mjuːzɪkl/ a musicale; (person) dotato di senso musicale ● n commedia f musicale. ~ **box** n carillon m inv. ~ **instrument** n strumento m musicale

music: ~ **box** n carillon m inv. ~ **centre** n impianto m stereo; '~-**hall** n teatro m di varietà

musician /mju'zɪʃn/ n musicista mf

Muslim /'mʊzlɪm/ a & n musulmano, -a mf

mussel /'mʌsl/ n cozza f

must /mʌst/ v aux (solo al presente) dovere; **you** ~ **not be late** non devi essere in ritardo; **she** ~ **have finished by now** (probability) deve aver finito ormai ● n a ~ fam una cosa da non perdere

mustard /'mʌstəd/ n senape f

musty /'mʌstɪ/ a (-ier, -iest) stantio

mutation /mju'teɪʃn/ n Biol mutazione f

mute /mjuːt/ a muto

muted /'mjuːtɪd/ a smorzato

mutilat|e /'mjuːtɪleɪt/ vt mutilare. ~**ion** /-'leɪʃn/ n mutilazione f

mutin|ous /'mjuːtɪnəs/ a ammutinato. ~**y** n ammutinamento m ● vi (pt/pp -ied) ammutinarsi

mutter /'mʌtə(r)/ vt/i borbottare

mutton /'mʌtn/ n carne f di montone

mutual /'mjuːtjʊəl/ a reciproco; (fam: common) comune. ~**ly** adv reciprocamente

muzzle /'mʌzl/ n (of animal) muso m; (of firearm) bocca f; (for dog) museruola f ● vt fig mettere il bavaglio a

my /maɪ/ poss a il mio m, la mia f, i miei mpl, le mie fpl; **my mother/father** mia madre/mio padre

myself /maɪ'self/ pers pron (reflexive) mi; (emphatic) me stesso; (after prep) me; **I've seen it** ~ l'ho visto io stesso; **by** ~ da solo; **I thought to** ~ ho pensato tra me e me; **I'm proud of** ~ sono fiero di me

mysterious /mɪ'stɪərɪəs/ a misterioso. ~**ly** adv misteriosamente

mystery /'mɪstərɪ/ n mistero m; ~ [**story**] racconto m del mistero

mysti|c[al] /'mɪstɪk[l]/ a mistico. ~**cism** /-sɪzm/ n misticismo f

mystified /'mɪstɪfaɪd/ a disorientato

mystify /'mɪstɪfaɪ/ vt (pt/pp -ied) disorientare

mystique /mɪ'stiːk/ n mistica f

myth /mɪθ/ n mito m. ~**ical** a mitico

mythology /mɪ'θɒlədʒɪ/ n mitologia f

Nn

nab /næb/ *vt* (*pt/pp* **nabbed**) *fam* beccare

naff /næf/ *a Br fam* banale

nag¹ /næg/ *n* (*horse*) ronzino *m*

nag² *v* (*pt/pp* **nagged**) ● *vt* assillare ● *vi* essere insistente ● *n* (*person*) brontolone, -a *mf*. **~ging** *a* (*pain*) persistente

nail /neɪl/ *n* chiodo *m*; (*of finger, toe*) unghia *f* ● **nail down** *vt* inchiodare; **~ sb down to a time/price** far fissare a qcno un'ora/un prezzo

nail: **~-brush** *n* spazzolino *m* da unghie. **~-file** *n* limetta *f* da unghie. **~ polish** *n* smalto *m* [per unghie]. **~ scissors** *npl* forbicine *fpl* da unghie. **~ varnish** *n* smalto *m* [per unghie]

naïve /narʼiːv/ *a* ingenuo. **~ly** /-ətɪ/ *n* ingenuità *f*

naked /ˈneɪkɪd/ *a* nudo; **with the ~ eye** a occhio nudo

name /neɪm/ *n* nome *m*; **what's your ~?** come ti chiami?; **my ~ is Matthew** mi chiamo Matthew; **I know her by ~** la conosco di nome; **by the ~ of Bates** di nome Bates; **call sb ~s** *fam* insultare qcno ● *vt* (*to position*) nominare; chiamare (*baby*); (*identify*) citare; **be ~d after** essere chiamato col nome di. **~less** *a* senza nome. **~ly** *adv* cioè

name: **~-plate** *n* targhetta *f*. **~sake** *n* omonimo, -a *mf*

nanny /ˈnænɪ/ *n* bambinaia *f*. **~-goat** *n* capra *f*

nap /næp/ *n* pisolino *m*; **have a ~** fare un pisolino ● *vi* (*pt/pp* **napped**) **catch sb ~ping** cogliere qcno alla sprovvista

nape /neɪp/ *n* ~ [**of the neck**] nuca *f*

napkin /ˈnæpkɪn/ *n* tovagliolo *m*

Naples /ˈneɪplz/ *n* Napoli *f*

nappy /ˈnæpɪ/ *n* pannolino *m*

narcotic /nɑːˈkɒtɪk/ *a & n* narcotico *m*

narrat|e /nəˈreɪt/ *vt* narrare. **~ion** /-eɪʃn/ *n* narrazione *f*

narrative /ˈnærətɪv/ *a* narrativo ● *n* narrazione *f*

narrator /nəˈreɪtə(r)/ *n* narratore, -trice *mf*

narrow /ˈnærəʊ/ *a* stretto; (*fig: views*) ristretto; (*margin, majority*) scarso ● *vi* restringersi. **~ly** *adv* **~ly escape death** evitare la morte per un pelo. **~-ˈminded** *a* di idee ristrette

nasal /ˈneɪzl/ *a* nasale

nastily /ˈnɑːstɪlɪ/ *adv* (*spitefully*) con cattiveria

nasty /ˈnɑːstɪ/ *a* (**-ier, -iest**) (*smell, person, remark*) cattivo; (*injury, situation, weather*) brutto; **turn ~** (*person:*) diventare cattivo

nation /ˈneɪʃn/ *n* nazione *f*

national /ˈnæʃənl/ *a* nazionale ● *n* cittadino, -a *mf*

national: **~ ˈanthem** *n* inno *m* nazionale. **N~ ˈHealth Service** *n* servizio *m* sanitario britannico. **N~ Inˈsurance** *n* Previdenza *f* sociale

nationalism /ˈnæʃənəlɪzm/ *n* nazionalismo *m*

nationality /næʃəˈnælətɪ/ *n* nazionalità *f* inv

national|ization /næʃənəlarˈzeɪʃn/ *n* nazionalizzazione. **~ize** /ˈnæʃənəlaɪz/ *vt* nazionalizzare. **~ly** /ˈnæʃənəlɪ/ *adv* a livello nazionale

ˈnation-wide *a* su scala nazionale

native /ˈneɪtɪv/ *a* nativo; (*innate*) innato ● *n* nativo, -a *mf*; (*local inhabitant*) abitante *mf* del posto; (*outside Europe*) indigeno, -a *mf*; **she's a ~ of Venice** è originaria di Venezia

native: **~ ˈland** *n* paese *m* nativo. **~ language** *n* lingua *f* madre

Nativity /nəˈtɪvətɪ/ *n* **the ~** la Natività *f*. **~ play** *n* rappresentazione *f* sulla nascita di Gesù

natter /ˈnætə(r)/ *vi fam* chiacchierare

natural /ˈnætʃrəl/ *a* naturale

natural: **~ ˈgas** *n* metano *m*. **~ ˈhistory** *n* storia *f* naturale

naturalist /ˈnætʃ(ə)rəlɪst/ *n* naturalista *mf*

natural|ization /nætʃ(ə)rələrˈzeɪʃn/ *n* naturalizzazione *f*. **~ize** /ˈnætʃ(ə)rəlaɪz/ *vt* naturalizzare

naturally /ˈnætʃ(ə)rəlɪ/ *adv* (*of course*) naturalmente; (*by nature*) per natura

nature /'neɪtʃə(r)/ n natura f; **by ~** per natura. **~ reserve** n riserva f naturale

naughtily /'nɔːtɪlɪ/ adv male

naughty /'nɔːtɪ/ a (**-ier, -iest**) monello; (*slightly indecent*) spinto

nausea /'nɔːzɪə/ n nausea f

nause|ate /'nɔːzɪeɪt/ vt nauseare. **~ating** a nauseante. **~ous** /-ɪəs/ a **I feel ~ous** ho la nausea

nautical /'nɔːtɪkl/ a nautico. **~ mile** n miglio m marino

naval /'neɪvl/ a navale

nave /neɪv/ n navata f centrale

navel /'neɪvl/ n ombelico m

navigable /'nævɪgəbl/ a navigabile

navigat|e /'nævɪgeɪt/ vi navigare; *Auto* fare da navigatore ● vt navigare su (*river*). **~ion** /-'geɪʃn/ n navigazione f. **~or** n navigatore m

navy /'neɪvɪ/ n marina f ● **~ [blue]** a blu scuro m inv ● n blu m inv scuro

Neapolitan /nɪə'pɒlɪtən/ a & n napoletano, -a mf

near /nɪə(r)/ a vicino; (*future*) prossimo; **the ~est bank** la banca più vicina ● adv vicino; **draw ~** avvicinarsi; **~ at hand** a portata di mano ● prep vicino a; **he was ~ to tears** aveva le lacrime agli occhi ● vt avvicinarsi a

near: **~by** a & adv vicino. **~ly** adv quasi; **it's not ~ly enough** non è per niente sufficiente. **~ness** n vicinanza f. **~ side** a *Auto* (*wheel*) (*left*) sinistro; (*right*) destro. **~sighted** a *Am* miope

neat /niːt/ a (*tidy*) ordinato; (*clever*) efficace; (*undiluted*) liscio. **~ly** adv ordinatamente; (*cleverly*) efficacemente. **~ness** n (*tidiness*) ordine m

necessarily /nesə'serɪlɪ/ adv necessariamente

necessary /'nesəsərɪ/ a necessario

necessit|ate /nɪ'sesɪteɪt/ vt rendere necessario. **~y** n necessità f inv

neck /nek/ n collo m; (*of dress*) colletto m; **~ and ~** testa a testa

necklace /'neklɪs/ n collana f

neck: **~line** n scollatura f. **~tie** n cravatta f

neé /neɪ/ a **~ Brett** nata Brett

need /niːd/ n bisogno m; **be in ~ of** avere bisogno di; **if ~ be** se ce ne fosse bisogno; **there is a ~ for** c'è bisogno di; **there is no ~ for that** non ce n'è bisogno; **there is no ~ for you to go** non c'è bisogno che tu vada ● vt aver bisogno di; **I ~ to know** devo saperlo; **it ~s to be done** bisogna farlo ● v aux

you ~ not go non c'è bisogno che tu vada; **~ I come?** devo [proprio] venire?

needle /'niːdl/ n ago m; (*for knitting*) uncinetto m; (*of record player*) puntina f ● vt (*fam: annoy*) punzecchiare

needless /'niːdlɪs/ a inutile

'needlework n cucito m

needy /'niːdɪ/ a (**-ier, -iest**) bisognoso

negation /nɪ'geɪʃn/ n negazione f

negative /'negətɪv/ a negativo ● n negazione f; *Phot* negativo m; **in the ~** *Gram* alla forma negativa

neglect /nɪ'glekt/ n trascuratezza f; **state of ~** stato m di abbandono ● vt trascurare; **he ~ed to write** non si è curato di scrivere. **~ed** a trascurato. **~ful** a negligente; **be ~ful of** trascurare

négligée /'neglɪʒeɪ/ n négligé m inv

negligen|ce /'neglɪdʒəns/ n negligenza f. **~t** a negligente

negligible /'neglɪdʒəbl/ a trascurabile

negotiable /nɪ'gəʊʃəbl/ a (*road*) transitabile; *Comm* negoziabile; **not ~** (*cheque*) non trasferibile

negotiat|e /nɪ'gəʊʃɪeɪt/ vt negoziare; *Auto* prendere (*bend*) ● vi negoziare. **~ion** /-'eɪʃn/ n negoziato m. **~or** n negoziatore, -trice mf

Negro /'niːgrəʊ/ a & n (pl **-es**) negro, -a mf

neigh /neɪ/ vi nitrire

neighbour /'neɪbə(r)/ n vicino, -a mf. **~hood** n vicinato m; **in the ~hood of** nei dintorni di; *fig* circa. **~ing** a vicino. **~ly** a amichevole

neither /'naɪðə(r)/ a & pron nessuno dei due, né l'uno né l'altro ● adv **~... nor** né... né ● conj nemmeno, neanche; **~ do/did I** nemmeno io

neon /'niːɒn/ n neon m. **~ light** n luce f al neon

nephew /'nevjuː/ n nipote m

nerve /nɜːv/ n nervo m; (*fam: courage*) coraggio m; (*fam: impudence*) faccia f tosta; **lose one's ~** perdersi d'animo. **~-racking** a logorante

nervous /'nɜːvəs/ a nervoso; **he makes me ~** mi mette in agitazione; **be a ~ wreck** avere i nervi a pezzi. **~ 'breakdown** n esaurimento m nervoso. **~ly** adv nervosamente. **~ness** n nervosismo m; (*before important event*) tensione f

nervy /'nɜːvɪ/ a (**-ier, -iest**) nervoso; (*Am: impudent*) sfacciato

nest /nest/ n nido m ● vi fare il nido. **~-egg** n gruzzolo m

nestle /'nesl/ *vi* accoccolarsi

net¹ /net/ *n* rete *f* ● *vt* (*pt/pp* **netted**) (*catch*) prendere (*con la rete*)

net² *a* netto ● *vt* (*pt/pp* **netted**) incassare un utile netto di

'**netball** *n* sport *m inv* femminile, simile a pallacanestro

Netherlands /'neðələndz/ *npl* the ~ i Paesi Bassi

netting /'netɪŋ/ *n* [wire] ~ reticolato *m*

nettle /'netl/ *n* ortica *f*

'**network** *n* rete *f*

neuralgia /njʊə'rældʒə/ *n* nevralgia *f*

neurolog|ist /njʊə'rɒlədʒɪst/ *n* neurologo, -a *mf*

neur|osis /njʊə'rəʊsɪs/ *n* (*pl* -**oses** /-si:z/) nevrosi *f inv*. ~**otic** /-'rɒtɪk/ *a* nevrotico

neuter /'nju:tə(r)/ *a Gram* neutro ● *n Gram* neutro *m* ● *vt* sterilizzare

neutral /'nju:tral/ *a* neutro; (*country, person*) neutrale ● *n* in ~ *Auto* in folle. ~**ity** /-'trælətɪ/ *n* neutralità *f*. ~**ize** *vt* neutralizzare

never /'nevə(r)/ *adv* [non...] mai; (*fam: expressing disbelief*) ma va; ~ **again** mai più; **well** I ~! chi l'avrebbe detto!. ~-**ending** *a* interminabile

nevertheless /nevəðə'les/ *adv* tuttavia

new /nju:/ *a* nuovo

new: ~**born** *a* neonato. ~**comer** *n* nuovo, -a arrivato, a *mf*. ~**fangled** /-'fæŋgld/ *a pej* modernizzante. ~-**laid** *a* fresco

'**newly** *adv* (*recently*) di recente; ~-**built** costruito di recente. ~-**weds** *npl* sposini *mpl*

new: ~ '**moon** *n* luna *f* nuova. ~**ness** *n* novità *f*

news /nju:z/ *n* notizie *fpl*; *TV* telegiornale *m*; *Radio* giornale *m* radio; **piece of** ~ notizia *f*

news: ~**agent** *n* giornalaio, -a *mf*. ~**bulletin** *n* notiziario *m*. ~**caster** *n* giornalista *mf* televisivo, -a/radiofonico, -a ~**flash** *n* notizia *f* flash. ~**letter** *n* bollettino *n* d'informazione. ~**paper** *n* giornale *m*; (*material*) carta *f* di giornale. ~**reader** *n* giornalista *mf* televisivo, -a/radiofonico, -a

new: ~**year** *n* (*next year*) anno *m* nuovo; **N**~ **Year's Day** *n* Capodanno *m*. **N**~ **Year's 'Eve** *n* vigilia *f* di Capodanno. **N**~ **Zealand** /'zi:lənd/ *n* Nuova Zelanda *f*. **N**~ **Zealander** *n* neozelandese *mf*

next /nekst/ *a* prossimo; (*adjoining*) vicino; **who's** ~? a chi tocca?; ~ **door** accanto; ~ **to nothing** quasi niente; **the** ~ **day** il giorno dopo; ~ **week** la settimana prossima; **the week after** ~ fra due settimane ● *adv* dopo; **when will you see him** ~? quando lo rivedi la prossima volta?; ~ **to** accanto a a ● *n* seguente *mf*; ~ **of kin** parente *m* prossimo

NHS *n abbr* **National Health Service**

nib /nɪb/ *n* pennino *m*

nibble /'nɪbl/ *vt/i* mordicchiare

nice /naɪs/ *a* (*day, weather, holiday*) bello; (*person*) gentile, simpatico; (*food*) buono; **it was** ~ **meeting you** è stato un piacere conoscerla. ~**ly** *adv* gentilmente; (*well*) bene. ~**ties** /'naɪsətɪz/ *npl* finezze *fpl*

niche /ni:ʃ/ *n* nicchia *f*

nick /nɪk/ *n* tacca *f*; (*on chin etc*) taglietto *m*; (*fam: prison*) galera *f*; (*fam: police station*) centrale *f* [di polizia]; **in the** ~ **of time** *fam* appena in tempo ● *vt* intaccare; (*fam: steal*) fregare; (*fam: arrest*) beccare; ~ **one's chin** farsi un taglietto nel mento

nickel /'nɪkl/ *n* nichel *m*; *Am* moneta *f* da cinque centesimi

'**nickname** *n* soprannome *m* ● *vt* soprannominare

nicotine /'nɪkəti:n/ *n* nicotina *f*

niece /ni:s/ *n* nipote *f*

Nigeria /naɪ'dʒɪərɪə/ *n* Nigeria *f*. ~**n** *a* & *n* nigeriano, -a *mf*

niggling /'nɪglɪŋ/ *a* (*detail*) insignificante; (*pain*) fastidioso; (*doubt*) persistente

night /naɪt/ *n* notte *f*; (*evening*) sera *f*; **at** ~ la notte, di notte; (*in the evening*) la sera, di sera; **Monday** ~ lunedì notte/sera ● *a* di notte

night: ~**cap** *n* papalina *f*; (*drink*) bicchierino *m* bevuto prima di andare a letto. ~-**club** *n* locale *m* notturno, night[-club] *m inv*. ~-**dress** *n* camicia *f* da notte. ~-**fall** *n* crepuscolo *m*. ~-**gown**, *fam* ~**ie** /'naɪtɪ/ *n* camicia *f* da notte

nightingale /'naɪtɪŋgeɪl/ *n* usignolo *m*

night: ~-**life** *n* vita *f* notturna. ~-**ly** *a* di notte, di sera ● *adv* ogni notte, ogni sera. ~**mare** *n* incubo *m*. ~-**school** scuola *f* serale. ~-**time** *n* **at** ~-**time** di notte, la notte. ~-'**watchman** *n* guardiano *m* notturno

nil /nɪl/ *n* nulla *m*; *Sport* zero *m*

nimbl|e /'nɪmbl/ *a* agile. ~**y** *adv* agilmente

nine /naɪn/ a nove inv ●n nove m.
~'**teen** a diciannove inv ●n diciannove
m. ~'**teenth** a & n diciannovesimo, -a
mf

ninetieth /'naɪntɪɪθ/ a & n novantesi-
mo, -a mf

ninety /'naɪntɪ/ a novanta inv ●n novanta m

ninth /naɪnθ/ a & n nono, -a mf

nip /nɪp/ n pizzicotto m; (bite) morso m
●vt pizzicare; (bite) mordere; ~ **in the
bud** fig stroncare sul nascere ●vi (fam:
run) fare un salto

nipple /'nɪpl/ n capezzolo m; (Am: on
bottle) tettarella f

nippy /'nɪpɪ/ a (-ier, -iest) fam (cold)
pungente; (quick) svelto

nitrogen /'naɪtrədʒn/ n azoto m

nitwit /'nɪtwɪt/ n fam imbecille mf

no /nəʊ/ adv no ●n (pl **noes**) no m inv
●a nessuno; **I have no time** non ho
tempo; **in no time** in un baleno; '**no
parking**' 'sosta vietata'; '**no smoking**'
'vietato fumare'; **no one** = **nobody**

nobility /nə'bɪlətɪ/ n nobiltà f

noble /'nəʊbl/ a nobile. ~**man** n nobile m

nobody /'nəʊbədɪ/ pron nessuno; **he
knows** ~ non conosce nessuno ●n
he's a ~ non è nessuno

nocturnal /nɒk'tɜ:nl/ a notturno

nod /nɒd/ n cenno m del capo ●v (pt/pp
nodded) ●vi fare un cenno col capo; (in
agreement) fare di sì col capo ●vt ~
one's head fare di sì col capo. **nod off**
vi assopirsi

nodule /'nɒdju:l/ n nodulo m

noise /nɔɪz/ n rumore m; (loud) rumore
m, chiasso m. ~**less** a silenzioso.
~**lessly** adv silenziosamente

noisy /'nɔɪzɪ/ a (-ier, -iest) rumoroso

nomad /'nəʊmæd/ n nomade mf. ~**ic**
/-'mædɪk/ a nomade

nominal /'nɒmɪnl/ a nominale

nominate /'nɒmɪneɪt/ vt proporre
come candidato; (appoint) designare.
~**ion** /-'neɪʃn/ n nomina f; (person
nominated) candidato, -a mf

nominative /'nɒmɪnətɪv/ a & n Gram
~ [**case**] nominativo m

nominee /nɒmɪ'ni:/ n persona f nomi-
nata

nonchalant /'nɒnʃələnt/ a disinvolto

non-com'missioned /nɒn-/ a ~
officer sottufficiale m

non-com'mittal a che non si sbilan-
cia

nondescript /'nɒndɪskrɪpt/ a qualunque

none /nʌn/ pron (person) nessuno;
(thing) niente; ~ **of us** nessuno di noi;
~ **of this** niente di questo; **there's** ~
left non ce n'è più ●adv ~ **too
pleased** non è per niente soddisfatta;
I'm ~ **the wiser** non ne so più di prima

nonentity /nɒ'nentətɪ/ n nullità f inv

non-event n delusione f

non-ex'istent a inesistente

non-'fiction n saggistica f

non-'iron a che non si stira

nonplussed /nɒn'plʌst/ a perplesso

nonsens|e /'nɒnsəns/ n sciocchezze
fpl. ~**ical** /-'sensɪkl/ a assurdo

non-'smoker n non fumatore, -trice
mf; (compartment) scompartimento m
non fumatori

non-'stick a antiaderente

non-'stop a ~ '**flight** volo m diretto
●adv senza sosta; (fly) senza scalo

non-'violent a non violento

noodles /'nu:dlz/ npl taglierini mpl

nook /nʊk/ n cantuccio m

noon /nu:n/ n mezzogiorno m; **at** ~ a
mezzogiorno

noose /nu:s/ n nodo m scorsoio

nor /nɔ:(r)/ adv & conj nè; ~ **do I** neppure io

Nordic /'nɔ:dɪk/ a nordico

norm /nɔ:m/ n norma f

normal /'nɔ:ml/ a normale. ~**ity**
/-'mælətɪ/ n normalità f. ~**ly** adv
(usually) normalmente

north /nɔ:θ/ n nord m; **to the** ~ **of** a
nord di ●a del nord, settentrionale
●adv a nord

north: N~ America n America f del
Nord. ~**-bound** a Auto in direzione
nord. ~**-east** a di nord-est,
nordorientale ●n nord-est m ●adv a
nord-est; (travel) verso nord-est

norther|ly /'nɔ:ðəlɪ/ a (direction) nord;
(wind) del nord. ~**n** a del nord, settentrionale. **N~n Ireland** n Irlanda f del
Nord

north: N~ 'Pole n polo m nord. **N~
'Sea** n Mare m del Nord. ~**ward[s]**
/-wəd[z]/ adv verso nord. ~**-west** a di
nord-ovest, nordoccidentale ●n nord-
ovest m ●adv a nord-ovest; (travel) verso nord-ovest

Nor|way /'nɔ:weɪ/ n Norvegia f.
~**wegian** /-'wi:dʒn/ a & n norvegese mf

nose /nəʊz/ n naso m

nose: ~bleed n emorragia f nasale.
~**dive** n Aeron picchiata f

nostalg|ia /nɒ'stældʒɪə/ n nostalgia f.
~**ic** a nostalgico

nostril /'nɒstrəl/ n narice f

nosy /'nəʊzɪ/ a (-ier, -iest) fam ficcanaso inv

not /nɒt/ adv non; **he is ~ Italian** non è italiano; **I hope ~** spero di no; **~ all of us have been invited** non siamo stati tutti invitati; **if ~** se no; **~ at all** niente affatto; **~ a bit** per niente; **~ even** neanche; **~ yet** non ancora; **~ only... but also...** non solo... ma anche...

notabl|e /'nəʊtəbl/ a (remarkable) notevole. **~y** adv (in particular) in particolare

notary /'nəʊtərɪ/ n notaio m; **~ 'public** notaio m

notch /nɒtʃ/ n tacca f ● notch up vt (score) segnare

note /nəʊt/ n nota f; (short letter, banknote) biglietto m; (memo, written comment etc) appunto m; **of ~** (person) di spicco; (comments, event) degno di nota; **make a ~ of** prendere nota di; **take ~ of** (notice) prendere nota di ● vt (notice) notare; (write) annotare. note down vt annotare

'notebook n taccuino m; Comput notebook m inv

noted /'nəʊtɪd/ a noto, celebre (**for** per)

note: **~paper** n carta f da lettere. **~worthy** a degno di nota

nothing /'nʌθɪŋ/ pron niente, nulla ● adv niente affatto; **for ~** (free, in vain) per niente; (with no reason) senza motivo; **~ but** nient'altro che; **~ much** poco o nulla; **~ interesting** niente di interessante; **it's ~ to do with you** non ti riguarda

notice /'nəʊtɪs/ n (on board) avviso m; (review) recensione f; (termination of employment) licenziamento m; [advance] **~** preavviso m; **two months' ~** due mesi di preavviso; **at short ~** con breve preavviso; **until further ~** fino nuovo avviso; **give [in one's]** (employee) dare le dimissioni; **give an employee ~** dare il preavviso a un impiegato; **take no ~ of** non fare caso a; **take no ~!** non farci caso! ● vt notare. **~able** /-əbl/ a evidente. **~ably** adv sensibilmente. **~-board** n bacheca f

noti|fication /nəʊtɪfɪ'keɪʃn/ n notifica f. **~fy** /'nəʊtɪfaɪ/ vt (pt/pp -ied) notificare

notion /'nəʊʃn/ n idea f, nozione f; **~s** pl (Am: haberdashery) merceria f

notoriety /nəʊtə'raɪətɪ/ n notorietà f

notorious /nəʊ'tɔːrɪəs/ a famigerato; **be ~ for** essere tristemente famoso per

notwith'standing prep malgrado ● adv cionononstante

nougat /'nuːgɑː/ n torrone m

nought /nɔːt/ n zero m

noun /naʊn/ n nome m, sostantivo m

nourish /'nʌrɪʃ/ vt nutrire. **~ing** a nutriente. **~ment** n nutrimento m

novel /'nɒvl/ a insolito ● n romanzo m. **~ist** n romanziere, -a mf. **~ty** n novità f; **~ties** pl (objects) oggettini mpl

November /nəʊ'vembə(r)/ n novembre m

novice /'nɒvɪs/ n novizio, -a mf

now /naʊ/ adv ora, adesso; **by ~** ormai; **just ~** proprio ora; **right ~** subito; **~ and again, ~ and then** ogni tanto; **~, ~!** su! ● conj **~ [that]** ora che, adesso che

'nowadays adv oggigiorno

nowhere /'nəʊ-/ adv in nessun posto, da nessuna parte

noxious /'nɒkʃəs/ a nocivo

nozzle /'nɒzl/ n bocchetta f

nuance /'njuːɒs/ n sfumatura f

nuclear /'njuːklɪə(r)/ a nucleare

nucleus /'njuːklɪəs/ n (pl -lei /-lɪaɪ/) nucleo m

nude /njuːd/ a nudo ● n nudo m; **in the ~** nudo

nudge /nʌdʒ/ n colpetto m di gomito ● vt dare un colpetto col gomito a

nudism /'njuːdɪzm/ n nudismo m

nud|ist /'njuːdɪst/ n nudista mf. **~ity** n nudità f

nugget /'nʌgɪt/ n pepita f

nuisance /'njuːsns/ n seccatura f; (person) piaga f; **what a ~!** che seccatura!

null /nʌl/ a **~ and void** nullo

numb /nʌm/ a intorpidito; **~ with cold** intirizzito dal freddo

number /'nʌmbə(r)/ n numero m; **a ~ of people** un certo numero di persone ● vt numerare; (include) annoverare. **~-plate** n targa f

numeral /'njuːmərəl/ n numero m, cifra f

numerate /'njuːmərət/ a **be ~** saper fare i calcoli

numerical /nju:'merɪkl/ a numerico; **in ~ order** in ordine numerico

numerous /'njuːmərəs/ a numeroso

nun /nʌn/ n suora f

nurse /nɜːs/ n infermiere, -a mf; **children's ~** bambinaia f ● vt curare

nursery /'nɜːsərɪ/ n stanza f dei bambini; (for plants) vivaio m; [day] **~** asilo *m.* ~ **rhyme** *n* filastrocca *f.* ~ **school** *n* scuola *f* materna

nursing /'nɜ:sɪŋ/ *n* professione *f* d'infermiere. ~ **home** *n* casa *f* di cura per anziani

nurture /'nɜ:tʃə(r)/ *vt* allevare; *fig* coltivare

nut /nʌt/ *n* noce *f*; *Techn* dado *m*; (*fam: head*) zucca *f*; ~**s** *npl* frutta *f* secca; **be** ~**s** *fam* essere svitato. ~**crackers** *npl*

schiaccianoci *m inv.* ~**meg** *n* noce *f* moscata

nutrit|ion /nju:'trɪʃn/ *n* nutrizione *f.* ~**ious** /-ʃəs/ *a* nutriente

'**nutshell** *n* **in a** ~ *fig* in parole povere

nuzzle /'nʌzl/ *vt* ⟨*horse, dog:*⟩ strofinare il muso contro

nylon /'naɪlɒn/ *n* nailon *m*; ~**s** *pl* calze *fpl* di nailon ● *a* di nailon

O /əʊ/ *n Teleph* zero *m*

oaf /əʊf/ *n* (*pl* **oafs**) zoticone, -a *mf*

oak /əʊk/ *n* quercia *f* ● *attrib* di quercia

OAP *n abbr* (**old-age pensioner**) pensionato, -a *mf*

oar /ɔ:(r)/ *n* remo *m.* ~**sman** *n* vogatore *m*

oasis /əʊ'eɪsɪs/ *n* (*pl* **oases** /-si:z/) oasi *f inv*

oath /əʊθ/ *n* giuramento *m*; (*swearword*) bestemmia *f*

oatmeal /'əʊt-/ *n* farina *f* d'avena

oats /əʊts/ *npl* avena *fsg*; *Culin* [**rolled**] ~ fiocchi *mpl* di avena

obedien|ce /ə'bi:dɪəns/ *n* ubbidienza *f.* ~**t** *a* ubbidiente

obes|e /ə'bi:s/ *a* obeso. ~**ity** *n* obesità *f*

obey /ə'beɪ/ *vt* ubbidire a; osservare ⟨*instructions, rules*⟩ ● *vi* ubbidire

obituary /ə'bɪtjʊərɪ/ *n* necrologio *m*

object¹ /'ɒbdʒɪkt/ *n* oggetto *m*; *Gram* complemento *m* oggetto; **money is no** ~ i soldi non sono un problema

object² /əb'dʒekt/ *vi* (*be against*) opporsi (**to** a); ~ **that...** obiettare che...

objection /əb'dʒekʃn/ *n* obiezione *f*; **have no** ~ non avere niente in contrario. ~**able** /-əbl/ *a* discutibile; ⟨*person*⟩ sgradevole

objectiv|e /əb'dʒektɪv/ *a* oggettivo ● *n* obiettivo *m.* ~**ely** *adv* obiettivamente. ~**ity** /-'tɪvətɪ/ *n* oggettività *f*

obligation /ɒblɪ'geɪʃn/ *n* obbligo *m*; **be under an** ~ avere un obbligo; **without** ~ senza impegno

obligatory /ə'blɪgətrɪ/ *a* obbligatorio

oblig|e /ə'blaɪdʒ/ *vt* (*compel*) obbligare;

much ~**ed** grazie mille. ~**ing** *a* disponibile

oblique /ə'bli:k/ *a* obliquo; *fig* indiretto ● *n* ~ [**stroke**] barra *f*

obliterate /ə'blɪtəreɪt/ *vt* obliterare

oblivion /ə'blɪvɪən/ *n* oblio *m*

oblivious /ə'blɪvɪəs/ *a* **be** ~ essere dimentico (**of, to** di)

oblong /'ɒblɒŋ/ *a* oblungo ● *n* rettangolo *m*

obnoxious /əb'nɒkʃəs/ *a* detestabile

oboe /'əʊbəʊ/ *n* oboe *m inv*

obscen|e /əb'si:n/ *a* osceno; ⟨*profits, wealth*⟩ vergognoso. ~**ity** /-'senətɪ/ *n* oscenità *f inv*

obscur|e /əb'skjʊə(r)/ *a* oscuro ● *vt* oscurare; (*confuse*) mettere in ombra. ~**ity** *n* oscurità *f*

obsequious /əb'si:kwɪəs/ *a* ossequioso

observa|nce /əb'zɜ:vəns/ *n* (*of custom*) osservanza *f.* ~**nt** *a* attento. ~**tion** /ɒbzə'veɪʃn/ *n* osservazione *f*

observatory /əb'zɜ:vətrɪ/ *n* osservatorio *m*

observe /əb'zɜ:v/ *vt* osservare; (*notice*) notare; (*keep, celebrate*) celebrare. ~**r** *n* osservatore, -trice *mf*

obsess /əb'ses/ *vt* **be** ~**ed by** essere fissato con. ~**ion** /-eʃn/ *n* fissazione *f.* ~**ive** /-ɪv/ *a* ossessivo

obsolete /'ɒbsəli:t/ *a* obsoleto; ⟨*word*⟩ desueto

obstacle /'ɒbstəkl/ *n* ostacolo *m*

obstetrician /ɒbstə'trɪʃn/ *n* ostetrico, -a *mf.* **obstetrics** /əb'stetrɪks/ *n* ostetricia *f*

obstina|cy /ˈɒbstɪnəsɪ/ n ostinazione f. **~te** /-nət/ a ostinato

obstreperous /əbˈstrepərəs/ a turbolento

obstruct /əbˈstrʌkt/ vt ostruire; (hinder) ostacolare. **~ion** /-ʌkʃn/ n ostruzione f; (obstacle) ostacolo m. **~ive** /-ɪv/ a be **~ive** (person:) creare dei problemi

obtain /əbˈteɪn/ vt ottenere. **~able** /-əbl/ a ottenibile

obtrusive /əbˈtruːsɪv/ a (object) stonato

obtuse /əbˈtjuːs/ a ottuso

obvious /ˈɒbvɪəs/ a ovvio. **~ly** adv ovviamente

occasion /əˈkeɪʒn/ n occasione f; (event) evento m; **on ~** talvolta; **on the ~ of** in occasione di

occasional /əˈkeɪʒənl/ a saltuario; **he has the ~ glass of wine** ogni tanto beve un bicchiere di vino. **~ly** adv ogni tanto

occult /ɒˈkʌlt/ a occulto

occupant /ˈɒkjupənt/ n occupante mf; (of vehicle) persona f a bordo

occupation /ɒkjuˈpeɪʃn/ n occupazione f; (job) professione f **~al** a professionale

occupier /ˈɒkjupaɪə(r)/ n residente mf

occupy /ˈɒkjupaɪ/ vt (pt/pp occupied) occupare; (keep busy) tenere occupato

occur /əˈkɜː(r)/ vi (pt/pp occurred) accadere; (exist) trovarsi; **it ~red to me that** mi è venuto in mente che. **~rence** /əˈkʌrəns/ n (event) fatto m

ocean /ˈəʊʃn/ n oceano m

o'clock /əˈklɒk/ adv **it's 7 ~** sono le sette; **at 7 ~** alle sette:

octave /ˈɒktɪv/ n Mus ottava f

October /ɒkˈtəʊbə(r)/ n ottobre m

octopus /ˈɒktəpəs/ n (pl -puses) polpo m

odd /ɒd/ a (number) dispari; (not of set) scompagnato; (strange) strano; **forty ~** quaranta e rotti; **~ jobs** lavoretti mpl; **the ~ one out** l'eccezione f; **at ~ moments** a tempo perso; **have the ~ glass of wine** avere un bicchiere di vino ogni tanto

odd|ity /ˈɒdɪtɪ/ n stranezza f. **~ly** adv stranamente; **~ly enough** stranamente. **~ment** n (of fabric) scampolo m

odds /ɒdz/ npl (chances) probabilità fpl; **at ~** in disaccordo; **~ and ends** cianfrusaglie fpl; **it makes no ~** non fa alcuna differenza

ode /əʊd/ n ode f

odour /ˈəʊdə(r)/ n odore m. **~less** a inodore

of /ɒv/, /əv/ prep di; **a cup of tea/coffee** una tazza di tè/caffè; **the hem of my skirt** l'orlo della mia gonna; **the summer of 1989** l'estate del 1989; **the two of us** noi due; **made of** di; **that's very kind of you** è molto gentile da parte tua; **a friend of mine** un mio amico; **a child of three** un bambino di tre anni; **the fourth of January** il quattro gennaio; **within a year of their divorce** a circa un anno dal loro divorzio; **half of it** la metà; **the whole of the room** tutta la stanza

off /ɒf/ prep da; (distant from) lontano da; **take £10 ~ the price** ridurre il prezzo di 10 sterline; **~ the coast** presso la costa; **a street ~ the main road** una traversa della via principale; (near) una strada vicino alla via principale; **get ~ the ladder** scendere dalla scala; **get ~ the bus** uscire dall'autobus; **leave the lid ~ the saucepan** lasciare la pentola senza il coperchio ● adv (button, handle) staccato; (light, machine) spento; (brake) tolto; (tap) chiuso; **'off'** (on appliance) 'off'; **2 kilometres ~** a due chilometri di distanza; **a long way ~** molto distante; (time) lontano; **~ and on** di tanto in tanto; **with his hat/coat ~** senza il cappello/cappotto; **with the light ~** a luce spenta; **20% ~** 20% di sconto; **be ~** (leave) andar via; Sport essere partito; (food:) essere andato a male; (all gone) essere finito; (wedding, engagement:) essere cancellato; **I'm ~ alcohol** ho smesso di bere; **be ~ one's food** non avere appetito; **she's ~ today** (ill) è malata oggi; **I'm ~ home** vado a casa; **you'd be better ~ doing...** faresti meglio a fare...; **have a day ~** avere un giorno di vacanza; **drive/sail ~** andare via

offal /ˈɒfl/ n Culin frattaglie fpl

'off-beat a insolito

'off-chance n possibilità f remota

off-colour a (not well) giù di forma; (joke, story) sporco

offence /əˈfens/ n (illegal act) reato m; **give ~** offendere; **take ~** offendersi (at per)

offend /əˈfend/ vt offendere. **~er** n Jur colpevole mf

offensive /əˈfensɪv/ a offensivo ● n offensiva f

offer /ˈɒfə(r)/ n offerta f ● vt offrire; opporre ⟨resistance⟩; ~ **sb sth** offrire qcsa a qcno; ~ **to do sth** offrirsi di fare qcsa. ~**ing** n offerta f

off'hand a ⟨casual⟩ spiccio ●adv su due piedi

office /'ɒfɪs/ n ufficio m; ⟨post, job⟩ carica f. ~ **hours** pl orario m di ufficio

officer /'ɒfɪsə(r)/ n ufficiale m; ⟨police⟩ agente m [di polizia]

official /ə'fɪʃl/ a ufficiale ●n funzionario, -a mf; Sport dirigente m. ~**ly** adv ufficialmente

officiate /ə'fɪʃɪeɪt/ vi officiare

'offing n **in the** ~ in vista

'off-licence n negozio m per la vendita di alcolici

off-'load vt scaricare

off-'putting a fam scoraggiante

'offset vt ⟨pt/pp -**set**, pres p -**setting**⟩ controbilanciare

'offshoot n ramo m; fig diramazione f

'offshore a ⟨wind⟩ di terra; ⟨company, investment⟩ offshore inv. ~ **rig** n piattaforma f petrolifera. off-shore m inv

off'side a Sport [in] fuori gioco; ⟨wheel etc⟩ ⟨left⟩ sinistro; ⟨right⟩ destro

'offspring n prole m

off'stage adv dietro le quinte

off-'white a bianco sporco

often /'ɒfn/ adv spesso; **how** ~ ogni quanto; **every so** ~ una volta ogni tanto

ogle /'əʊgl/ vt mangiarsi con gli occhi

oh /əʊ/ int oh!; ~ **dear** oh Dio!

oil /ɔɪl/ n olio m; ⟨petroleum⟩ petrolio m; ⟨for heating⟩ nafta f ●vt oliare

oil: ~**field** n giacimento m di petrolio. ~-**painting** n pittura f a olio. ~-**refinery** n raffineria f di petrolio. ~ **rig** n piattaforma f petrolifera. ~-**skins** npl vestiti mpl di tela cerata. ~-**slick** n chiazza f di petrolio. ~-**tanker** n petroliera f. ~ **well** n pozzo m petrolifero

oily /'ɔɪlɪ/ a ⟨-ier, -iest⟩ unto; fig untuoso

ointment /'ɔɪntmənt/ n pomata f

OK /əʊ'keɪ/ int va bene, o.k. ●a **if that's OK with you** se ti va bene; **she's OK** ⟨well⟩ sta bene; **is the milk still OK?** il latte è ancora buono? ●adv ⟨well⟩ bene ●vt ⟨anche **okay**⟩ ⟨pt/pp **OK'd**, **okayed**⟩ dare l'o.k. a

old /əʊld/ a vecchio; ⟨girlfriend⟩ ex; **how** ~ **is she?** quanti anni ha?; **she is ten years** ~ ha dieci anni

old: ~ '**age** n vecchiaia f. ~-**age 'pensioner** n pensionato, -a mf. ~ **boy** n Sch ex-allievo m. ~-**fashioned** a anti-

quato. ~ **girl** n Sch ex-allieva f. ~ '**maid** n zitella f

olive /'ɒlɪv/ n ⟨fruit, colour⟩ oliva f; ⟨tree⟩ olivo m ●a d'oliva; ⟨colour⟩ oliva-stro. ~ **branch** n fig ramoscello m d'olivo. ~ '**oil** n olio m di oliva

Olympic /ə'lɪmpɪk/ a olimpico; ~**s,** ~ **Games** Olimpiadi fpl

omelette /'ɒmlɪt/ n omelette f inv

omen /'əʊmən/ n presagio m

ominous /'ɒmɪnəs/ a sinistro

omission /ə'mɪʃn/ n omissione f

omit /ə'mɪt/ vt ⟨pt/pp **omitted**⟩ omettere; ~ **to do sth** tralasciare di fare qcsa

omnipotent /ɒm'nɪpətənt/ a onnipotente

on /ɒn/ prep su; ⟨on horizontal surface⟩ su, sopra; **on Monday** lunedì; **on Mondays** di lunedì; **on the first of May** il primo di maggio; **on arriving** all'arrivo; **on one's finger** ⟨cut⟩ nel dito; ⟨ring⟩ al dito; **on foot** a piedi; **on the right/left** a destra/sinistra; **on the Rhine/Thames** sul Reno/Tamigi; **on the radio/television** alla radio/televisione; **on the bus/train** in autobus/treno; **go on the bus/train** andare in autobus/treno; **get on the bus/train** salire sull'autobus/sul treno; **on me** ⟨with me⟩ con me; **it's on me** fam tocca a me ●adv ⟨further on⟩ dopo; ⟨switched on⟩ acceso; ⟨brake⟩ inserito; ⟨in operation⟩ in funzione; **'on'** ⟨on machine⟩ 'on'; **he had his hat/coat on** portava il cappello/cappotto; **without his hat/coat on** senza cappello/cappotto; **with/without the lid on** senza coperchio; **be on** ⟨film, programme, event:⟩ esserci; **it's not on** fam non è giusto; **be on at** fam tormentare ⟨**to** per⟩; **on and on** senza sosta; **on and off** a intervalli; **and so on** e così via; **go on** continuare; **drive on** spostarsi ⟨con la macchina⟩; **stick on** attaccare; **sew on** cucire

once /wʌns/ adv una volta; ⟨formerly⟩ un tempo; ~ **upon a time there was** c'era una volta; **at** ~ subito; ⟨at the same time⟩ contemporaneamente; ~ **and for all** una volta per tutte ●conj [non] appena. ~-**over** n fam **give sb/sth the** ~-**over** ⟨look, check⟩ dare un'occhiata veloce a qcno/qcsa

'oncoming a che si avvicina dalla direzione opposta

one /wʌn/ a uno, una; **not** ~ **person** nemmeno una persona ●n uno m ●pron uno; ⟨impersonal⟩ si; ~ **another**

l'un l'altro; ~ **by** ~ [a] uno a uno; ~ **never knows** non si sa mai

one: ~-**eyed** a con un occhio solo. ~-**off** a unico. ~-**parent** 'family n famiglia f con un solo genitore. ~**self** pron (reflexive) si; (emphatic) sé, se stesso; **by** ~**self** da solo; **be proud of** ~**self** essere fieri di sé. ~-**sided** a unilaterale. ~-**way** a (street) a senso unico; (ticket) di sola andata

onion /'ʌnjən/ n cipolla f

'**onlooker** n spettatore, -trice mf

only /'əʊnlı/ a solo; ~ **child** figlio, -a mf unico, -a ● adv & conj solo, solamente; ~ **just** appena

on'/off switch n pulsante m di accensione

'**onset** n (beginning) inizio m

onslaught /'ɒnslɔːt/ n attacco m

onus /'əʊnəs/ n **the** ~ **is on me** spetta a me la responsabilità (**to** di)

onward[s] /'ɒnwəd[z]/ adv in avanti; **from then** ~ da allora [in poi]

ooze /uːz/ vi fluire

opal /'əʊpl/ n opale f

opaque /əʊ'peɪk/ a opaco

open /'əʊpən/ a aperto; (free to all) pubblico; (job) vacante; **in the** ~ **air** all'aperto ● n **in the** ~ all'aperto; fig alla luce del sole ● vt aprire ● vi aprirsi; (shop:) aprire; (flower:) sbocciare. **open up** vt aprire ● vi aprirsi

open: ~-**air 'swimming pool** n piscina f all'aperto. ~ **day** n giorno m di apertura al pubblico

opener /'əʊpənə(r)/ n (for tins) apriscatole m inv; (for bottles) apribottiglie m inv

opening /'əʊpənɪŋ/ n apertura f; (beginning) inizio m; (job) posto m libero; ~ **hours** npl orario m d'apertura

openly /'əʊpənlɪ/ adv apertamente

open: ~-'minded a aperto; (broad-minded) di vedute larghe. ~-**plan** a a pianta aperta. ~ 'sandwich n tartina f. ~ secret n segreto m di Pulcinella. O~ University corsi mpl universitari per corrispondenza

opera /'ɒprə/ n opera f

operable /'ɒpərəbl/ a operabile

opera: ~-**glasses** npl binocolo msg da teatro. ~-**house** n teatro m lirico. ~-**singer** n cantante mf lirico, -a

operate /'ɒpəreɪt/ vt far funzionare (machine, lift); azionare (lever, brake); mandare avanti (business) ● vi Techn funzionare; (be in action) essere in fun-

zione; Mil, fig operare; ~ **on** Med operare

operatic /ɒpə'rætɪk/ a lirico, operistico

operation /ɒpə'reɪʃn/ n operazione f; Tech funzionamento m; **in** ~ Techn in funzione; **come into** ~ fig entrare in funzione; (law:) entrare in vigore; **have an** ~ Med subire un'operazione. ~**al** a operativo; (law etc) in vigore

operative /'ɒpərətɪv/ a operativo

operator /'ɒpəreɪtə(r)/ n (user) operatore, -trice mf; Teleph centralinista mf

operetta /ɒpə'retə/ n operetta f

opinion /ə'pɪnjən/ n opinione f; **in my** ~ secondo me. ~**ated** a dogmatico

opponent /ə'pəʊnənt/ n avversario, -a mf

opportun|e /'ɒpətjuːn/ a opportuno. ~**ist** /-'tjuːnɪst/ n opportunista mf. ~**istic** a opportunistico

opportunity /ɒpə'tjuːnətɪ/ n opportunità f inv

oppos|e /ə'pəʊz/ vt opporsi a; **be** ~**ed to sth** esssere contrario a qcsa; **as** ~**ed to** al contrario di. ~**ing** a avversario; (opposite) opposto

opposite /'ɒpəzɪt/ a opposto; (house) di fronte; ~ **number** fig controparte f; **the** ~ **sex** l'altro sesso ● n contrario m ● adv di fronte ● prep di fronte a

opposition /ɒpə'zɪʃn/ n opposizione f

oppress /ə'pres/ vt opprimere. ~**ion** /-eʃn/ n oppressione f. ~**ive** /-ɪv/ a oppressivo; (heat) opprimente. ~**or** n oppressore m

opt /ɒpt/ vi ~ **for** optare per; ~ **out** dissociarsi (**of** da)

optical /'ɒptɪkl/ a ottico; ~ **illusion** illusione f ottica

optician /ɒp'tɪʃn/ n ottico, -a mf

optimis|m /'ɒptɪmɪzm/ n ottimismo m. ~**t** /-mɪst/ n ottimista mf. ~**tic** /-'mɪstɪk/ a ottimistico

optimum /'ɒptɪməm/ a ottimale ● n (pl -**ima**) optimum m

option /'ɒpʃn/ n scelta f; Comm opzione f. ~**al** a facoltativo; ~**al extras** optional m inv

opulen|ce /'ɒpjʊləns/ n opulenza f. ~**t** a opulento

or /ɔː(r)/ conj o, oppure; (after negative) né; **or [else]** se no; **in a year or two** fra un anno o due

oracle /'ɒrəkl/ n oracolo m

oral /'ɔːrəl/ a orale ● n fam esame m orale. ~**ly** adv oralmente

orange /'ɒrɪndʒ/ n arancia f; (colour)

arancione *m* ● *a* arancione. **~ade** /-ˈdʒeɪd/ *n* aranciata *f*. **~ juice** *n* succo *m* d'arancia

orator /ˈɒrətə(r)/ *n* oratore, -trice *mf*

oratorio /ɒrəˈtɔːrɪəʊ/ *n* oratorio *m*

oratory /ˈɒrətərɪ/ *n* oratorio *m*

orbit /ˈɔːbɪt/ *n* orbita *f* ● *vt* orbitare. **~al** *a* **~al road** tangenziale *f*

orchard /ˈɔːtʃəd/ *n* frutteto *m*

orches|tra /ˈɔːkɪstrə/ *n* orchestra *f*. **~tral** /-ˈkestrəl/ *a* orchestrale. **~trate** *vt* orchestrare

orchid /ˈɔːkɪd/ *n* orchidea *f*

ordain /ɔːˈdeɪn/ *vt* decretare; *Relig* ordinare

ordeal /ɔːˈdiːl/ *n fig* terribile esperienza *f*

order /ˈɔːdə(r)/ *n* ordine *m*; *Comm* ordinazione *f*; **out of ~** ⟨machine⟩ fuori servizio; **in ~ that** affinché; **in ~ to** per ● *vt* ordinare

orderly /ˈɔːdəlɪ/ *a* ordinato ● *n Mil* attendente *m*; *Med* inserviente *m*

ordinary /ˈɔːdɪnərɪ/ *a* ordinario

ordination /ɔːdɪˈneɪʃn/ *n Relig* ordinazione *f*

ore /ɔː(r)/ *n* minerale *m* grezzo

organ /ˈɔːgən/ *n Anat, Mus* organo *m*

organic /ɔːˈɡænɪk/ *a* organico; ⟨without chemicals⟩ biologico. **~ally** *adv* organicamente; **~ally grown** coltivato biologicamente

organism /ˈɔːgənɪzm/ *n* organismo *m*

organist /ˈɔːgənɪst/ *n* organista *mf*

organization /ɔːgənaɪˈzeɪʃn/ *n* organizzazione *f*

organize /ˈɔːgənaɪz/ *vt* organizzare. **~r** *n* organizzatore, -trice *mf*

orgasm /ˈɔːgæzm/ *n* orgasmo *m*

orgy /ˈɔːdʒɪ/ *n* orgia *f*

Orient /ˈɔːrɪənt/ *n* Oriente *m*. **o~al** /-ˈentl/ *a* orientale ● *n* orientale *mf*

orient|ate /ˈɔːrɪenteɪt/ *vt* **~ate oneself** orientarsi. **~ation** /-ˈteɪʃn/ *n* orientamento *m*

origin /ˈɒrɪdʒɪn/ *n* origine *f*

original /əˈrɪdʒɪnl/ *a* originario; ⟨not copied, new⟩ originale ● *n* originale *m*; **in the ~** in versione originale. **~ity** /-ˈnælətɪ/ *n* originalità *f*. **~ly** *adv* originariamente

originat|e /əˈrɪdʒɪneɪt/ *vi* **~e in** avere origine in. **~or** *n* ideatore, -trice *mf*

ornament /ˈɔːnəmənt/ *n* ornamento *m*; (on mantelpiece etc) soprammobile *m*. **~al** /-ˈmentl/ *a* ornamentale. **~ation** /-ˈteɪʃn/ *n* decorazione *f*

ornate /ɔːˈneɪt/ *a* ornato

orphan /ˈɔːfn/ *n* orfano, -a *mf* ● *vt* rendere orfano; **be ~ed** rimanere orfano. **~age** /-ɪdʒ/ *n* orfanotrofio *m*

orthodox /ˈɔːθədɒks/ *a* ortodosso

orthopaedic /ɔːθəˈpiːdɪk/ *a* ortopedico

oscillate /ˈɒsɪleɪt/ *vi* oscillare

ostensibl|e /ɒˈstensəbl/ *a* apparente. **~y** *adv* apparentemente

ostentat|ion /ɒstenˈteɪʃn/ *n* ostentazione *f*. **~ious** /-ʃəs/ *a* ostentato

osteopath /ˈɒstɪəpæθ/ *n* osteopata *mf*

ostracize /ˈɒstrəsaɪz/ *vt* bandire

ostrich /ˈɒstrɪtʃ/ *n* struzzo *m*

other /ˈʌðə(r)/ *a, pron & n* altro, -a *mf*; **the ~** [one] l'altro, -a *mf*; **the ~ two** gli altri due; **two ~s** altri due; **~ people** gli altri; **any ~ questions?** altre domande?; **every ~ day** ⟨alternate days⟩ a giorni alterni; **the ~ day** l'altro giorno; **the ~ evening** l'altra sera; **someone/something or ~** qualcuno/ qualcosa ● *adv* **~ than him** tranne lui; **somehow or ~** in qualche modo; **somewhere or ~** da qualche parte **'otherwise** *adv* altrimenti; ⟨differently⟩ diversamente

otter /ˈɒtə(r)/ *n* lontra *f*

ouch /aʊtʃ/ *int* ahi!

ought /ɔːt/ *v aux* **I/we ~ to stay** dovrei/dovremmo rimanere; **he ~ not to have done it** non avrebbe dovuto farlo; **that ~ to be enough** questo dovrebbe bastare

ounce /aʊns/ *n* oncia *f* (= 28, 35 g)

our /ˈaʊə/ *poss a* il nostro *m*, la nostra *f*, i nostri *mpl*, le nostre *fpl*; **~ mother/ father** nostra madre/nostro padre

ours /ˈaʊəz/ *poss pron* il nostro *m*, la nostra *f*, i nostri *mpl*, le nostre *fpl*; **a friend of ~** un nostro amico; **friends of ~** dei nostri amici; **that is ~** quello è nostro; (as opposed to yours) quello è il nostro

ourselves /aʊəˈselvz/ *pers pron* (reflexive) ci; (emphatic) noi, noi stessi; **we poured ~ a drink** ci siamo versati da bere; **we heard it ~** l'abbiamo sentito noi stessi; **we are proud of ~** siamo fieri di noi; **by ~** da soli

out /aʊt/ *adv* fuori; (not alight) spento; **be ~** ⟨flower:⟩ essere sbocciato; ⟨workers:⟩ essere in sciopero; ⟨calculation:⟩ essere sbagliato; *Sport* essere fuori; ⟨unconscious⟩ aver perso i sensi; ⟨fig: not feasible⟩ fuori questione; **the sun is ~** è uscito il sole; **~ and about in** piedi; **get ~!** *fam* fuori!; **you should get**

~ **more** dovresti uscire più spesso; ~
with it! *fam* sputa il rospo!; ● *prep* ~ **of**
fuori da; ~ **of date** non aggiornato;
⟨*passport*⟩ scaduto; ~ **of order** guasto;
~ **of print/stock** esaurito; **be** ~ **of**
bed/the room fuori dal letto/dalla stanza; ~ **of breath** senza fiato; ~ **of**
danger fuori pericolo; ~ **of work**
disoccupato; **nine** ~ **of ten** nove su dieci; **be** ~ **of sugar/bread** rimanere senza zucchero/pane; **go** ~ **of the room**
uscire dalla stanza

out'bid *vt* (*pt/pp* -**bid**, *pres p* -**bidding**)
~ **sb** rilanciare l'offerta di qcno
'outboard *a* ~ **motor** motore *m*
'outbreak *n* (*of war*) scoppio *m*; (*of*
disease) insorgenza *f*
'outbuilding *n* costruzione *f* annessa
'outburst *n* esplosione *f*
'outcome *n* risultato *m*
'outcry *n* protesta *f*
out'dated *a* sorpassato
out'do *vt* (*pt*-**did**, *pp*-**done**) superare
'outdoor *a* ⟨*life, sports*⟩ all'aperto; ~
clothes *pl* vestiti per uscire; ~
swimming pool piscina *f* scoperta
out'doors *adv* all'aria aperta; **go** ~
uscire [all'aria aperta]
'outer *a* esterno
'outfit *n* equipaggiamento *m*; (*clothes*)
completo *m*; (*fam: organization*) organizzazione *f*. ~**ter** *n* **men's** ~**ter's** negozio *m* di abbigliamento maschile
'outgoing *a* (*president*) uscente; ⟨*mail*⟩
in partenza; (*sociable*) estroverso ● *npl*
~**s** uscite *fpl*
out'grow *vi* (*pt*-**grew**, *pp*-**grown**) diventare troppo grande per
'outhouse *n* costruzione *f* annessa
'outing /'aυtıŋ/ *n* gita *f*
out'landish /aυt'lændıʃ/ *a* stravagante
'outlaw *n* fuorilegge *mf inv* ● *vt* dichiarare illegale
'outlay *n* spesa *f*
'outlet *n* sbocco *m*; *fig* sfogo *m*; *Comm*
punto *m* [di] vendita
'outline *n* contorno *m*; (*summary*) som-
mario *m* ● *vt* tracciare il contorno di;
(*describe*) descrivere
out'live *vt* sopravvivere a
'outlook *n* vista *f*; (*future prospect*)
prospettiva *f*; (*attitude*) visione *f*
'outlying *a* ~ **areas** zone *fpl* periferi-
che
out'number *vt* superare in numero
'out-patient *n* paziente *mf* esterno, -a;
~**s' department** ambulatorio *m*
'output *n* produzione *f*

'outrage *n* oltraggio *m* ● *vt* oltraggia-
re. ~**ous** /-'reıdʒəs/ *a* oltraggioso;
⟨*price*⟩ scandaloso
'outright¹ *a* completo; ⟨*refusal*⟩ netto
out'right² *adv* completamente; (*at*
once) immediatamente; (*frankly*) francamente
'outset *n* inizio *m*; **from the** ~ fin dal-
l'inizio
'outside¹ *a* esterno ● *n* esterno *m*;
from the ~ dall'esterno; **at the** ~ al
massimo
out'side² *adv* all'esterno, fuori; (*out of*
doors) fuori; **go** ~ andare fuori ● *prep*
fuori da; (*in front of*) davanti a
out'sider *n* estraneo, -a *mf*
'outskirts *npl* sobborghi *mpl*
out'spoken *a* franco
out'standing *a* eccezionale; ⟨*land-*
mark⟩ prominente; (*not settled*) in sospeso
out'stretched *a* allungato
out'strip *vt* (*pt/pp*-**stripped**) superare
out'vote *vt* mettere in minoranza
'outward /-wəd/ *a* esterno; ⟨*journey*⟩ di
andata ● *adv* verso l'esterno. ~**ly** *adv*
esternamente. ~**s** *adv* verso l'esterno
out'weigh *vt* aver maggior peso di
out'wit *vt* (*pt/pp* -**witted**) battere in
astuzia
oval /'əυvl/ *a* ovale ● *n* ovale *m*
ovary /'əυvərı/ *n Anat* ovaia *f*
ovation /əʊ'veıʃn/ *n* ovazione *f*
oven /'ʌvn/ *n* forno *m*. ~**-ready** *a* pronto da mettere in forno
over /'əυvə(r)/ *prep* sopra; (*across*) al di
là di; (*during*) durante; (*more than*) più
di; ~ **the phone** al telefono; ~ **the**
page alla pagina seguente; **all** ~ **Italy**
in tutta [l']Italia; ⟨*travel*⟩ per l'Italia
● *adv Math* col resto di; (*ended*) finito;
~ **again** un'altra volta; ~ **and** ~ più
volte; ~ **and above** oltre a; ~ **here/**
there qui/là; **all** ~ (*everywhere*) dappertutto; **it's all** ~ è tutto finito; **I ache**
all ~ ho male dappertutto; **come/**
bring ~ venire/portare; **turn** ~ girare
over- *pref* (*too*) troppo
overall¹ /'əυvərɔːl/ *n* grembiule *m*; ~**s**
pl tuta *fsg* [da lavoro]
overall² /əʊvər'ɔːl/ *a* complessivo;
(*general*) generale ● *adv* complessiva-
mente
over'balance *vi* perdere l'equilibrio
over'bearing *a* prepotente
'overboard *adv Naut* in mare
'overcast *a* coperto
over'charge *vt* ~ **sb** far pagare più

del dovuto a qcno ●*vi* far pagare più del dovuto

'overcoat *n* cappotto *m*

over'come *vt* (*pt* **-came**, *pp* **-come**) vincere; **be ~ by** essere sopraffatto da

over'crowded *a* sovraffollato

over'do *vt* (*pt* **-did**, *pp* **-done**) esagerare; *(cook too long)* stracuocere; **~ it** *(fam: do too much)* strafare

'overdose *n* overdose *f inv*

'overdraft *n* scoperto *m*; **have an ~** avere il conto scoperto

over'draw *vt* (*pt* **-drew**, *pp* **-drawn**) **~ one's account** andare allo scoperto; **be ~n by** *(account:)* essere [allo] scoperto di

over'due *a* in ritardo

over'estimate *vt* sopravvalutare

'overflow¹ *n* *(water)* acqua *f* che deborda; *(people)* pubblico *m* in eccesso; *(outlet)* scarico *m*

over'flow² *vi* debordare

over'grown *a* *(garden)* coperto di erbacce

'overhaul¹ *n* revisione *f*

over'haul² *vt* Techn revisionare

over'head¹ *adv* in alto

'overhead² *a* aereo; *(railway)* sopraelevato; *(lights)* da soffitto ●*npl* **~s** spese *fpl* generali

over'hear *vt* (*pt/pp* **-heard**) sentire per caso *(conversation)*

over'heat *vi* Auto surriscaldarsi ●*vt* surriscaldare

over'joyed *a* felicissimo

'overland *a & adv* via terra; **~ route** via *f* terrestre

over'lap *v* (*pt/pp* **-lapped**) ●*vi* sovrapporsi ●*vt* sovrapporre

over'leaf *adv* sul retro

over'load *vt* sovraccaricare

over'look *vt* dominare; *(fail to see, ignore)* lasciarsi sfuggire

overly /'əʊvlɪ/ *adv* eccessivamente

over'night¹ *adv* per la notte; **stay ~** fermarsi a dormire

'overnight² *a* notturno. **~ bag** piccola borsa *f* da viaggio; **~ stay** sosta *f* per la notte

'overpass *n* cavalcavia *m inv*

over'pay *vt* (*pt/pp* **-paid**) strapagare

over'populated *a* sovrappopolato

over'power *vt* sopraffare. **~ing** *a* insostenibile

over'priced *a* troppo caro

overpro'duce *vt* produrre in eccesso

over'rate *vt* sopravvalutare. **~d** *a* sopravvalutato

over'reach *vt* **~ oneself** puntare troppo in alto

overre'act *vi* avere una reazione eccessiva. **~ion** *n* reazione *f* eccessiva

over'rid|e *vt* (*pt* **-rode**, *pp* **-ridden**) passare sopra a. **~ing** *a* prevalente

over'rule *vt* annullare *(decision)*

over'run *vt* (*pt* **-ran**, *pp* **-run**, *pres p* **-running**) invadere; oltrepassare *(time)*; **be ~ with** essere invaso da

over'seas¹ *adv* oltremare

'overseas² *a* d'oltremare

over'see *vt* (*pt* **-saw**, *pp* **-seen**) sorvegliare

over'shadow *vt* adombrare

over'shoot *vt* (*pt/pp* **-shot**) oltrepassare

'oversight *n* disattenzione *f*; **an ~** una svista

over'sleep *vi* (*pt/pp* **-slept**) svegliarsi troppo tardi

over'step *vt* (*pt/pp* **-stepped**) **~ the mark** oltrepassare ogni limite

overt /əʊ'vɜ:t/ *a* palese

over'tak|e *vt/i* (*pt* **-took**, *pp* **-taken**) sorpassare. **~ing** *n* sorpasso *m*; **no ~ing** divieto di sorpasso

over'tax *vt fig* abusare di

'overthrow¹ *n* Pol rovesciamento *m*

over'throw² *vt* (*pt* **-threw**, *pp* **-thrown**) Pol rovesciare

'overtime *n* lavoro *m* straordinario ●*adv* **work ~** fare lo straordinario

over'tired *a* sovraffaticato

'overtone *n fig* sfumatura *f*

overture /'əʊvətjʊə(r)/ *n Mus* preludio *m*; **~s** *pl fig* approccio *msg*

over'turn *vt* ribaltare ●*vi* ribaltarsi

over'weight *a* sovrappeso

overwhelm /-'welm/ *vt* sommergere (**with** di); *(with emotion)* confondere. **~ing** *a* travolgente; *(victory, majority)* schiacciante

over'work *n* lavoro *m* eccessivo ●*vt* far lavorare eccessivamente ●*vi* lavorare eccessivamente

ow|e /əʊ/ *vt also fig* dovere ([**to**] **sb** a qcno); **~e sb sth** dovere qcsa a qcno. **~ing** *a* **be ~ing** *(money:)* essere da pagare ●*prep* **~ing to** a causa di

owl /aʊl/ *n* gufo *m*

own¹ /əʊn/ *a* proprio ●*pron* **a car of my ~** una macchina per conto mio; **on one's ~** da solo; **hold one's ~ with** tener testa a; **get one's ~ back** *fam* prendersi una rivincita

own² *vt* possedere; *(confess)* ammettere;

I don't ~ it non mi appartiene. **own up** *vi* confessare (**to sth** qcsa)

owner /'əʊnə(r)/ *n* proprietario, -a *mf*. **~ship** *n* proprietà *f*

ox /ɒks/ *n* (*pl* **oxen**) bue *m* (*pl* buoi)

oxide /'ɒksaɪd/ *n* ossido *m*

oxygen /'ɒksɪdʒən/ *n* ossigeno *m*. **~ mask** *n* maschera *f* a ossigeno

oyster /'ɔɪstə(r)/ *n* ostrica *f*

ozone /'əʊzəʊn/ *n* ozono *m*. **~-'friendly** *a* che non danneggia l'ozono. **~ layer** *n* fascia *f* d'ozono

Pp

PA *abbr* (**per annum**) all'anno

pace /peɪs/ *n* passo *m*; (*speed*) ritmo *m*; **keep ~ with** camminare di pari passo con ● *vi* **~ up and down** camminare avanti e indietro. **~-maker** *n Med* pacemaker *m*; (*runner*) battistrada *m*

Pacific /pə'sɪfɪk/ *a & n* **the ~ [Ocean]** l'oceano *m* Pacifico, il Pacifico

pacifier /'pæsɪfaɪə(r)/ *n Am* ciuccio *m*, succhiotto *m*

pacifist /'pæsɪfɪst/ *n* pacifista *mf*

pacify /'pæsɪfaɪ/ *vt* (*pt/pp* **-ied**) placare ⟨*person*⟩; pacificare ⟨*country*⟩

pack /pæk/ *n* (*of cards*) mazzo *m*; (*of hounds*) muta *f*; (*of wolves, thieves*) branco *m*; (*of cigarettes etc*) pacchetto *m*; **a ~ of lies** un mucchio di bugie ● *vt* impacchettare ⟨*article*⟩; fare ⟨*suitcase*⟩; mettere in valigia ⟨*swimsuit etc*⟩; (*press down*) comprimere; **~ed [out]** (*crowded*) pieno zeppo ● *vi* fare i bagagli; **send sb ~ing** *fam* mandare qcno a stendere. **pack up** *vt* impacchettare ● *vi fam* ⟨*machine:*⟩ piantare in asso

package /'pækɪdʒ/ *n* pacco *m* ● *vt* impacchettare. **~ deal** offerta *f* tutto compreso. **~ holiday** *n* vacanza *f* organizzata. **~ tour** viaggio *m* organizzato

packaging /'pækɪdʒɪŋ/ *n* confezione *f*

packed 'lunch *n* pranzo *m* al sacco

packet /'pækɪt/ *n* pacchetto *m*; **cost a ~** *fam* costare un sacco

packing /'pækɪŋ/ *n* imballaggio *m*

pact /pækt/ *n* patto *m*

pad¹ /pæd/ *n* imbottitura *f*; (*for writing*) bloc-notes *m inv*, taccuino *m*; (*fam: home*) [piccolo] appartamento *m* ● *vt* (*pt/pp* **padded**) imbottire. **pad out** *vt* gonfiare

pad² *vi* (*pt/pp* **padded**) camminare con passo felpato

padded /'pædɪd/ *a* **~ bra** reggiseno *m* imbottito

padding /'pædɪŋ/ *n* imbottitura *f*; (*in written work*) fronzoli *mpl*

paddle¹ /'pæd(ə)l/ *n* pagaia *f* ● *vt* (*row*) spingere remando

paddle² *vi* (*wade*) sguazzare

paddock /'pædək/ *n* recinto *m*

padlock /'pædlɒk/ *n* lucchetto *m* ● *vt* chiudere con lucchetto

paediatrician /pi:dɪə'trɪʃn/ *n* pediatra *mf*

paediatrics /pi:dɪ'ætrɪks/ *n* pediatria *f*

page¹ /peɪdʒ/ *n* pagina *f*

page² *n* (*boy*) paggetto *m*; (*in hotel*) fattorino *m* ● *vt* far chiamare ⟨*person*⟩

pageant /'pædʒənt/ *n* parata *f*. **~ry** *n* cerimoniale *m*

pager /'peɪdʒə(r)/ *n* cercapersone *m inv*

paid /peɪd/ *see* **pay** ● *a* **~ employment** lavoro *m* remunerato; **put ~ to** mettere un termine a

pail /peɪl/ *n* secchio *m*

pain /peɪn/ *n* dolore *m*; **be in ~** soffrire; **take ~s to** fare il possibile per; **~ in the neck** *fam* spina *f* nel fianco

pain: **~ful** *a* doloroso; (*laborious*) penoso. **~-killer** *n* calmante *m*. **~less** *a* indolore

painstaking /'peɪnzteɪkɪŋ/ *a* minuzioso

paint /peɪnt/ *n* pittura *f*; **~s** *pl* colori *mpl* ● *vt/i* pitturare; ⟨*artist:*⟩ dipingere. **~brush** *n* pennello *m*. **~er** *n* pittore, -trice *mf*; (*decorator*) imbianchino *m*. **~ing** *n* pittura *f*; (*picture*) dipinto *m*. **~work** *n* pittura *f*

pair /peə(r)/ *n* paio *m*; (*of people*) coppia *f*; **~ of trousers** paio *m* di pantaloni; **~ of scissors** paio *m* di forbici

pajamas /pə'dʒɑːməz/ *npl Am* pigiama *msg*

Pakistan /pɑːkɪˈstɑːn/ n Pakistan m. **~i** a pakistano ● n pakistano, -a mf

pal /pæl/ n fam amico, -a mf

palace /ˈpælɪs/ n palazzo m

palatable /ˈpælətəbl/ a gradevole (al gusto)

palate /ˈpælət/ n palato m

palatial /pəˈleɪʃl/ a sontuoso

palaver /pəˈlɑːvə(r)/ n (fam: fuss) storie fpl

pale /peɪl/ a pallido

Palestin|e /ˈpælɪstaɪn/ n Palestina f. **~ian** /-ˈstɪnɪən/ a palestinese ● n palestinese mf

palette /ˈpælɪt/ n tavolozza f

pall|id /ˈpælɪd/ a pallido. **~or** n pallore m

palm /pɑːm/ n palmo m; (tree) palma f; P~ **Sunday** n Domenica f delle Palme ● **palm off** vt ~ **sth off on sb** rifilare qcsa a qcno

palpable /ˈpælpəbl/ a palpabile; (perceptible) tangibile

palpitat|e /ˈpælpɪteɪt/ vi palpitare. **~ions** /-ˈteɪʃnz/ npl palpitazioni fpl

paltry /ˈpɔːltrɪ/ a (-ier, -iest) insignificante

pamper /ˈpæmpə(r)/ vt viziare

pamphlet /ˈpæmflɪt/ n opuscolo m

pan /pæn/ n tegame m, pentola f; (for frying) padella f; (of scales) piatto m ● vt (pt/pp panned) (fam: criticize) stroncare

panache /pəˈnæʃ/ n stile m

'pancake n crêpe f inv, frittella f

pancreas /ˈpæŋkrɪəs/ n pancreas m inv

panda /ˈpændə/ n panda m inv. **~ car** n macchina f della polizia

pandemonium /pændɪˈməʊnɪəm/ n pandemonio m

pander /ˈpændə(r)/ vi ~ **to sb** compiacere qcno

pane /peɪn/ n ~ [of glass] vetro m

panel /ˈpænl/ n pannello m; (group of people) giuria f; ~ **of experts** gruppo m di esperti. **~ling** n pannelli mpl

pang /pæŋ/ n ~s **of hunger** morsi mpl della fame; **~s of conscience** rimorsi mpl di coscienza

panic /ˈpænɪk/ n panico m ● vi (pt/pp panicked) lasciarsi prendere dal panico. **~-stricken** a in preda al panico

panoram|a /pænəˈrɑːmə/ n panorama m. **~ic** /-ˈræmɪk/ a panoramico

pansy /ˈpænzɪ/ n viola f del pensiero; (fam: effeminate man) finocchio m

pant /pænt/ vi ansimare

panther /ˈpænθə(r)/ n pantera f

panties /ˈpæntɪz/ npl mutandine fpl

pantomime /ˈpæntəmaɪm/ n pantomima f

pantry /ˈpæntrɪ/ n dispensa f

pants /pænts/ npl (underwear) mutande fpl; (woman's) mutandine fpl; (trousers) pantaloni mpl

'pantyhose n Am collant m inv

papal /ˈpeɪpl/ a papale

paper /ˈpeɪpə(r)/ n carta f; (wallpaper) carta f da parati; (newspaper) giornale m; (exam) esame m; (treatise) saggio m; **~s** pl (documents) documenti mpl; (for identification) documento m [d'identità]; **on ~** in teoria; **put down on ~** mettere per iscritto ● attrib di carta ● vt tappezzare

paper: ~back n edizione f economica. **~clip** n graffetta f. **~knife** n tagliacarte m inv. **~weight** n fermacarte m inv. **~work** n lavoro m d'ufficio

par /pɑː(r)/ n (in golf) par m inv; **on a ~ with** alla pari con; **feel below ~** essere un po' giù di tono

parable /ˈpærəbl/ n parabola f

parachut|e /ˈpærəʃuːt/ n paracadute m inv ● vi lanciarsi col paracadute. **~ist** n paracadutista f

parade /pəˈreɪd/ n (military) parata f militare ● vi sfilare ● vt (show off) far sfoggio di

paradise /ˈpærədaɪs/ n paradiso m

paradox /ˈpærədɒks/ n paradosso m. **~ical** /-ˈdɒksɪkl/ a paradossale. **~ically** adv paradossalmente

paraffin /ˈpærəfɪn/ n paraffina f

paragon /ˈpærəgən/ n ~ **of virtue** modello m di virtù

paragraph /ˈpærəgrɑːf/ n paragrafo m

parallel /ˈpærəlel/ a & adv parallelo. ~ **bars** npl parallele fpl. ~ **port** n Comput porta f parallela ● n Geog, fig parallelo m; (line) parallela f ● vt essere paragonabile a

paralyse /ˈpærəlaɪz/ vt also fig paralizzare

paralysis /pəˈrælɪsɪs/ n (pl -ses) /-siːz/ paralisi f inv

parameter /pəˈræmɪtə(r)/ n parametro m

paramount /ˈpærəmaʊnt/ a supremo; **be ~** essere essenziale

paranoia /pærəˈnɔɪə/ n paranoia f

paranoid /ˈpærənɔɪd/ a paranoico

paraphernalia /pærəfəˈneɪlɪə/ n armamentario m

paraphrase /ˈpærəfreɪz/ n parafrasi f inv ● vt parafrasare

paraplegic /pærə'pli:dʒɪk/ a paraplegico ● n paraplegico, -a mf

parasite /'pærəsaɪt/ n parassita mf

parasol /'pærəsɒl/ n parasole m

paratrooper /'pærətru:pə(r)/ n paracadutista m

parcel /'pɑ:sl/ n pacco m

parch /pɑ:tʃ/ vt disseccare; **be ~ed** ⟨person:⟩ morire dalla sete

pardon /'pɑ:dn/ n perdono m; Jur grazia f; **~?** prego?; **I beg your ~?** fml chiedo scusa?; **I do beg your ~** (sorry) chiedo scusa! ● vt perdonare; Jur graziare

pare /peə(r)/ vt (peel) pelare

parent /'peərənt/ n genitore, -trice mf; **~s** pl genitori mpl. **~al** /pə'rentl/ a dei genitori

parenthesis /pə'renθəsɪs/ n (pl **-ses** /-si:z/) parentesi m inv

Paris /'pærɪs/ n Parigi f

parish /'pærɪʃ/ n parrocchia f. **~ioner** /pə'rɪʃənə(r)/ n parrocchiano, -a mf

Parisian /pə'rɪzɪən/ a & n parigino, -a mf

parity /'pærətɪ/ n parità f

park /pɑ:k/ n parco m ● vt/i Auto posteggiare, parcheggiare; **~ oneself** fam installarsi

parka /'pɑ:kə/ n parka m inv

parking /'pɑ:kɪŋ/ n parcheggio m, posteggio m; **'no ~'** 'divieto di sosta'. **~-lot** n Am posteggio m, parcheggio m. **~-meter** n parchimetro m. **~ space** n posteggio m, parcheggio m

parliament /'pɑ:ləmənt/ n parlamento m. **~ary** /-'mentərɪ/ a parlamentare

parlour /'pɑ:lə(r)/ n salotto m

parochial /pə'rəʊkɪəl/ a parrocchiale; fig ristretto

parody /'pærədɪ/ n parodia f ● vt (pt/pp **-ied**) parodiare

parole /pə'rəʊl/ n **on ~** in libertà condizionale ● vt mettere in libertà condizionale

parquet /'pɑ:keɪ/ n **~ floor** parquet m inv

parrot /'pærət/ n pappagallo m

parry /'pærɪ/ vt (pt/pp **-ied**) parare ⟨blow⟩; (in fencing) eludere

parsimonious /pɑ:sɪ'məʊnɪəs/ a parsimonioso

parsley /'pɑ:slɪ/ n prezzemolo m

parsnip /'pɑ:snɪp/ n pastinaca f

parson /'pɑ:sn/ n pastore m

part /pɑ:t/ n parte f; (of machine) pezzo m; **for my ~** per quanto mi riguarda; **on the ~ of** da parte di; **take sb's ~**

prendere le parti di qcno; **take ~ in** prendere parte a ● adv in parte ● vt **~ one's hair** farsi la riga ● vi ⟨people:⟩ separare; **~ with** separarsi da

part-ex'change n take in **~** prendere indietro

partial /'pɑ:ʃl/ a parziale; **be ~ to** aver un debole per. **~ly** adv parzialmente

particip|ant /pɑ:'tɪsɪpənt/ n partecipante mf. **~ate** /-peɪt/ vi partecipare (**in** a). **~ation** /-'peɪʃn/ n partecipazione f

participle /'pɑ:tɪsɪpl/ n participio m; **present/past ~** participio m presente/ passato

particle /'pɑ:tɪkl/ n Phys, Gram particella f

particular /pə'tɪkjʊlə(r)/ a particolare; (precise) meticoloso; pej noioso; **in ~** in particolare. **~ly** adv particolarmente. **~s** npl particolari mpl

parting /'pɑ:tɪŋ/ n separazione f; (in hair) scriminatura f ● attrib di commiato

partisan /pɑ:tɪ'zæn/ n partigiano, -a mf

partition /pɑ:'tɪʃn/ n (wall) parete f divisoria; Pol divisione f ● vt dividere (in parti). **partition off** vt separare

partly /'pɑ:tlɪ/ adv in parte

partner /'pɑ:tnə(r)/ n Comm socio, -a mf; (sport, in relationship) compagno, -a mf. **~ship** n Comm società f inv

partridge /'pɑ:trɪdʒ/ n pernice f

part-'time a & adv part time; **be or work ~** lavorare part time

party /'pɑ:tɪ/ n ricevimento m, festa f; (group) gruppo m; Pol partito m; Jur parte f [in causa]; **be ~ to** essere parte attiva in

'party line[1] n Teleph duplex m inv

party 'line[2] n Pol linea f del partito

pass /pɑ:s/ n lasciapassare m inv; (in mountains) passo m; Sport passaggio m; Sch (mark) [voto m] sufficiente m; **make a ~ at** fam fare delle avances a ● vt passare; (overtake) sorpassare; (approve) far passare; fare ⟨remark⟩; Jur pronunciare ⟨sentence⟩; **~ the time** passare il tempo ● vi passare; (in exam) essere promosso. **pass away** vi mancare. **pass down** vt passare; fig trasmettere. **pass out** vi fam svenire. **pass round** vt passare. **pass through** vt attraversare. **pass up** vt passare; (fam: miss) lasciarsi scappare

passable /'pɑ:səbl/ a (road) praticabile; (satisfactory) passabile

passage /'pæsɪdʒ/ n passaggio m;

(corridor) corridoio *m*; *(voyage)* traversata *f*

passenger /'pæsɪndʒə(r)/ *n* passeggero, -a *mf*. **~ seat** *n* posto *m* accanto al guidatore

passer-by /pɑːsə'baɪ/ *n* *(pl* **~s-by)** passante *mf*

'passing place *n* piazzola *f* di sosta *per consentire il transito dei veicoli nei due sensi*

passion /'pæʃn/ *n* passione *f*. **~ate** /-ət/ *a* appassionato

passive /'pæsɪv/ *a* passivo ● *n* passivo *m*. **~ness** *n* passività *f*

'pass-mark *n Sch* [voto *m*] sufficiente *m*

Passover /'pɑːsəʊvə(r)/ *n* Pasqua *f* ebraica

pass: **~port** *n* passaporto *m*. **~word** *n* parola *f* d'ordine

past /pɑːst/ *a* passato; *(former)* ex; **in the ~ few days** nei giorni scorsi; **that's all ~** tutto questo è passato; **the ~ week** la settimana scorsa ● *n* passato *m* ● *prep* oltre; **at ten ~ two** alle due e dieci ● *adv* oltre; **go/come ~** passare

pasta /'pæstə/ *n* pasta[sciutta] *f*

paste /peɪst/ *n* pasta *f*; *(dough)* impasto *m*; *(adhesive)* colla *f* ● *vt* incollare

pastel /'pæstl/ *n* pastello *m* ● *attrib* pastello

pasteurize /'pɑːstʃəraɪz/ *vt* pastorizzare

pastille /'pæstl/ *n* pastiglia *f*

pastime /'pɑːstaɪm/ *n* passatempo *m*

pastoral /'pɑːstərəl/ *a* pastorale

pastrami /pæ'strɑːmɪ/ *n* carne *f* di *manzo affumicata*

pastr|y /'peɪstrɪ/ *n* pasta *f*; **~ies** *pl* pasticcini *mpl*

pasture /'pɑːstʃə(r)/ *n* pascolo *m*

pasty¹ /'pæstɪ/ *n* pasticcio *m*

pasty² /'peɪstɪ/ *a* smorto

pat /pæt/ *n* buffetto *m*; *(of butter)* pezzetto *m* ● *adv* **have sth off ~** conoscere qcsa a menadito ● *vt* *(pt/pp* **patted)** dare un buffetto a; **~ sb on the back** *fig* congratularsi con qcno

patch /pætʃ/ *n* toppa *f*; *(spot)* chiazza *f*; *(period)* periodo *m*; **not a ~ on** *fam* molto inferiore a ● *vt* mettere una toppa su. **patch up** *vt* riparare alla bell'e meglio; appianare *(quarrel)*

patchy /'pætʃɪ/ *a* incostante

pâté /'pæteɪ/ *n* pâté *m inv*

patent /'peɪtnt/ *a* palese ● *n* brevetto *m* ● *vt* brevettare. **~ leather shoes** *npl* scarpe *fpl* di vernice. **~ly** *adv* in modo palese

patern|al /pə'tɜːnl/ *a* paterno. **~ity** *n* paternità *f*

path /pɑːθ/ *n* *(pl* **~s** /pɑːðz/) sentiero *m*; *(orbit)* traiettoria *f*; *fig* strada *f*

pathetic /pə'θetɪk/ *a* patetico; *(fam: very bad)* penoso

patholog|ical /pæθə'lɒdʒɪkl/ *a* patologico. **~ist** /pə'θɒlədʒɪst/ *n* patologo, -a *mf*. **~y** patologia *f*

pathos /'peɪθɒs/ *n* pathos *m*

patience /'peɪʃns/ *n* pazienza *f*; *(game)* solitario *m*

patient /'peɪʃnt/ *a* paziente ● *n* paziente *mf*. **~ly** *adv* pazientemente

patio /'pætɪəʊ/ *n* terrazza *f*

patriot /'pætrɪət/ *n* patriota *mf*. **~ic** /-'ɒtɪk/ *a* patriottico. **~ism** *n* patriottismo *m*

patrol /pə'trəʊl/ *n* pattuglia *f* ● *vt/i* pattugliare. **~ car** *n* autopattuglia *f*

patron /'peɪtrən/ *n* patrono *m*; *(of charity)* benefattore, -trice *mf*; *(of the arts)* mecenate *mf*; *(customer)* cliente *mf*

patroniz|e /'pætrənaɪz/ *vt* frequentare abitualmente; *fig* trattare con condiscendenza. **~ing** *a* condiscendente. **~ingly** *adv* con condiscendenza

patter¹ /'pætə(r)/ *n* picchiettio *m* ● *vi* picchiettare

patter² *n* *(of salesman)* chiacchiere *fpl*

pattern /'pætn/ *n* disegno *m* *(stampato)*; *(for knitting, sewing)* modello *m*

paunch /pɔːntʃ/ *n* pancia *f*

pause /pɔːz/ *n* pausa *f* ● *vi* fare una pausa

pave /peɪv/ *vt* pavimentare; **~ the way** preparare la strada **(for** a). **~ment** *n* marciapiede *m*

pavilion /pə'vɪljən/ *n* padiglione *m*

paw /pɔː/ *n* zampa *f* ● *vt* *fam* mettere le zampe addosso a

pawn¹ /pɔːn/ *n* *(in chess)* pedone *m*; *fig* pedina *f*

pawn² *vt* impegnare ● *n* **in ~** in pegno. **~broker** *n* prestatore, -trice *mf* su pegno. **~shop** *n* monte *m* di pietà

pay /peɪ/ *n* paga *f*. **~ of** a soldo di ● *v* *(pt/pp* **paid)** ● *vt* pagare; prestare *(attention)*; fare *(compliment, visit)*; **~ cash** pagare in contanti ● *vi* pagare; *(be profitable)* rendere; **it doesn't ~ to...** *fig* è fatica sprecata...; **~ for sth** pagare per qcsa. **pay back** *vt* ripagare. **pay in** *vt* versare. **pay off** *vt* saldare *(debt)* ● *vi fig* dare dei frutti. **pay up** *vi* pagare

payable /'peɪəbl/ *a* pagabile; **make ~ to** intestare a

payee /peɪˈiː/ n beneficiario m (di una somma)

payment /ˈpeɪmənt/ n pagamento m

pay: ~ **packet** n busta f paga. ~ **phone** n telefono m pubblico

PC n abbr (**personal computer**) PC m inv

pea /piː/ n pisello m

peace /piːs/ n pace f; ~ **of mind** tranquillità f

peace|able /ˈpiːsəbl/ a pacifico. ~**ful** a calmo, sereno. ~**fully** adv in pace. ~**maker** n mediatore, -trice mf

peach /piːtʃ/ n pesca f; (tree) pesco m

peacock /ˈpiːkɒk/ n pavone m

peak /piːk/ n picco m; fig culmine m. ~**ed** ˈcap n berretto m a punta. ~ **hours** npl ore fpl di punta

peaky /ˈpiːkɪ/ a malaticcio

peal /piːl/ n (of bells) scampanio m; ~**s of laughter** pl fragore m di risate

'peanut n nocciolina f [americana]; ~**s** pl fam miseria f

pear /peə(r)/ n pera f; (tree) pero m

pearl /pɜːl/ n perla f

peasant /ˈpeznt/ n contadino, -a mf

pebble /ˈpebl/ n ciottolo m

peck /pek/ n beccata f; (kiss) bacetto m ● vt beccare; (kiss) dare un bacetto a. ~**ing order** n gerarchia f. **peck at** vt beccare

peckish /ˈpekɪʃ/ a **be** ~ fam avere un languorino [allo stomaco]

peculiar /prˈkjuːlɪə(r)/ a strano; (special) particolare; ~ **to** tipico di. ~**ity** /-ˈærətɪ/ n stranezza f; (feature) particolarità f inv

pedal /ˈpedl/ n pedale m ● vi pedalare. ~ **bin** n pattumiera f a pedale

pedantic /prˈdæntɪk/ a pedante

pedestal /ˈpedɪstl/ n piedistallo m

pedestrian /prˈdestrɪən/ n pedone m ● a fig scadente. ~ ˈcrossing n passaggio m pedonale. ~ ˈprecinct n zona f pedonale

pedicure /ˈpedɪkjʊə(r)/ n pedicure f inv

pedigree /ˈpedɪɡriː/ n pedigree m inv; (of person) lignaggio m ● attrib ⟨animal⟩ di razza, con pedigree

pee /piː/ vi (pt/pp **peed**) fam fare [la] pipì

peek /piːk/ vi fam sbirciare

peel /piːl/ n buccia f ● vt sbucciare ● vi (nose etc:) spellarsi; (paint:) staccarsi

peep /piːp/ n sbirciata f ● vi sbirciare

peer[1] /pɪə(r)/ vi ~ **at** scrutare

peer[2] n nobile m; **his** ~**s** pl (in rank) i suoi pari; (in age) i suoi coetanei. ~**age** n nobiltà f

peeved /piːvd/ a fam irritato

peg /peɡ/ n (hook) piolo m; (for tent) picchetto m; (for clothes) molletta f; **off the** ~ fam prêt-à-porter

pejorative /prˈdʒɒrətɪv/ a peggiorativo

pelican /ˈpelɪkən/ n pellicano m

pellet /ˈpelɪt/ n pallottola f

pelt /pelt/ vt bombardare ● vi (fam: run fast) catapultarsi; ~ [**down**] ⟨rain:⟩ venir giù a fiotti

pelvis /ˈpelvɪs/ n Anat bacino m

pen[1] /pen/ n (for animals) recinto m

pen[2] n penna f; (ball-point) penna f a sfera

penal /ˈpiːnl/ a penale. ~**ize** vt penalizzare

penalty /ˈpenltɪ/ n sanzione f; (fine) multa f; (in football) ~ [**kick**] [calcio m di] rigore m; ~ **area** or **box** area f di rigore

penance /ˈpenəns/ n penitenza f

pence /pens/ see **penny**

pencil /ˈpensl/ n matita f. ~-**sharpener** n temperamatite m inv

pendant /ˈpendənt/ n ciondolo m

pending /ˈpendɪŋ/ a in sospeso ● prep in attesa di

pendulum /ˈpendjʊləm/ n pendolo m

penetrat|e /ˈpenɪtreɪt/ vt/i penetrare. ~**ing** a acuto; (sound, stare) penetrante. ~**ion** /-ˈtreɪʃn/ n penetrazione f

'penfriend n amico, -a mf di penna

penguin /ˈpeŋgwɪn/ n pinguino m

penicillin /penɪˈsɪlɪn/ n penicillina f

peninsula /prˈnɪnsjʊlə/ n penisola f

penis /ˈpiːnɪs/ n pene m

peniten|ce /ˈpenɪtəns/ n penitenza f. ~**t** a penitente ● n penitente mf

penitentiary /penɪˈtenʃərɪ/ n Am penitenziario m

pen: ~**knife** n temperino m. ~-**name** n pseudonimo m

pennant /ˈpenənt/ n bandiera f

penniless /ˈpenɪlɪs/ a senza un soldo

penny /ˈpenɪ/ n (pl **pence**; single coins **pennies**) penny m; Am centesimo m; **spend a** ~ fam andare in bagno

pension /ˈpenʃn/ n pensione f. ~**er** n pensionato, -a mf

pensive /ˈpensɪv/ a pensoso

Pentecost /ˈpentɪkɒst/ n Pentecoste f

pent-up /ˈpentʌp/ a represso

penultimate /prˈnʌltɪmət/ a penultimo

people /ˈpiːpl/ npl persone fpl, gente

fsg; (*citizens*) popolo *msg*; **a lot of ~** una marea di gente; **the ~** la gente; **English ~** gli inglesi; **~ say** si dice; **for four ~** per quattro ● *vt* popolare

pepper /'pepə(r)/ *n* pepe *m*; (*vegetable*) peperone *m* ● *vt* (*season*) pepare

pepper: ~corn *n* grano *m* di pepe. **~ mill** macinapepe *m inv*. **~mint** *n* menta *f* peperita; (*sweet*) caramella *f* alla menta. **~pot** *n* pepiera *f*

per /pɜː(r)/ *prep* per; **~ annum** all'anno; **~ cent** percento

perceive /pə'siːv/ *vt* percepire; (*interpret*) interpretare

percentage /pə'sentɪdʒ/ *n* percentuale *f*

perceptible /pə'septəbl/ *a* percettibile; (*difference*) sensibile

perception /pə'sepʃn/ *n* percezione *f*. **~ive** /-tɪv/ *a* perspicace

perch /pɜːtʃ/ *n* pertica *f* ● *vi* (*bird:*) appollaiarsi

percolator /'pɜːkəleɪtə(r)/ *n* caffettiera *f* a filtro

percussion /pə'kʌʃn/ *n* percussione *f*. **~ instrument** *n* strumento *m* a percussione

peremptory /pə'remptəri/ *a* perentorio

perennial /pə'reniəl/ *a* perenne ● *n* pianta *f* perenne

perfect[1] /'pɜːfɪkt/ *a* perfetto ● *n Gram* passato *m* prossimo

perfect[2] /pə'fekt/ *vt* perfezionare. **~ion** /-ekʃn/ *n* perfezione *f*; **to ~ion** alla perfezione. **~ionist** *n* perfezionista *mf*

perfectly /'pɜːfɪktlɪ/ *adv* perfettamente

perforate /'pɜːfəreɪt/ *vt* perforare. **~ed** *a* perforato; (*ulcer*) perforante. **~ion** *n* perforazione *f*

perform /pə'fɔːm/ *vt* compiere, fare; eseguire (*operation, sonata*); recitare (*role*); mettere in scena (*play*) ● *vi Theat* recitare; *Techn* funzionare. **~ance** *n* esecuzione *f*; (*at theatre, cinema*) rappresentazione *f*; *Techn* rendimento *m*. **~er** *n* artista *mf*

perfume /'pɜːfjuːm/ *n* profumo *m*

perfunctory /pə'fʌŋktəri/ *a* superficiale

perhaps /pə'hæps/ *adv* forse

peril /'peril/ *n* pericolo *m*. **~ous** /-əs/ *a* pericoloso

perimeter /pə'rɪmɪtə(r)/ *n* perimetro *m*

period /'pɪərɪəd/ *n* periodo *m*; (*menstruation*) mestruazioni *fpl*; *Sch*

ora *f* di lezione; (*full stop*) punto *m* fermo ● *attrib* (*costume*) d'epoca; (*furniture*) in stile. **~ic** /-'ɒdɪk/ *a* periodico. **~ical** /-'ɒdɪkl/ *n* periodico *m*, rivista *f*

peripheral /pə'rɪfərəl/ *a* periferico. **~y** *n* periferia *f*

periscope /'perɪskəup/ *n* periscopio *m*

perish /'perɪʃ/ *vi* (*rot*) deteriorarsi; (*die*) perire. **~able** /-əbl/ *a* deteriorabile

perjure /'pɜːdʒə(r)/ *vt* **~ oneself** spergiurare. **~y** *n* spergiuro *m*

perk[1] /pɜːk/ *n fam* vantaggio *m*

perk up *vt* tirare su ● *vi* tirarsi su

perky /'pɜːkɪ/ *a* allegro

perm /pɜːm/ *n* permanente *f* ● *vt* **~ sb's hair** fare la permanente a qno

permanent /'pɜːmənənt/ *a* permanente; (*job, address*) stabile. **~ly** *adv* stabilmente

permeate /'pɜːmɪeɪt/ *vt* impregnare

permissible /pə'mɪsəbl/ *a* ammissibile

permission /pə'mɪʃn/ *n* permesso *m*

permissive /pə'mɪsɪv/ *a* permissivo

permit[1] /pə'mɪt/ *vt* (*pt/pp* **-mitted**) permettere; **~ sb to do sth** permettere a qcno di fare qcsa

permit[2] /'pɜːmɪt/ *n* autorizzazione *f*

perpendicular /pɜːpən'dɪkjulə(r)/ *a* perpendicolare ● *n* perpendicolare *f*

perpetual /pə'petjuəl/ *a* perenne. **~ly** *adv* perennemente

perpetuate /pə'petjueɪt/ *vt* perpetuare

perplex /pə'pleks/ *vt* lasciare perplesso. **~ed** *a* perplesso. **~ity** *n* perplessità *f inv*

persecute /'pɜːsɪkjuːt/ *vt* perseguitare. **~ion** /-'kjuːʃn/ *n* persecuzione *f*

perseverance /pɜːsɪ'vɪərəns/ *n* perseveranza *f*

persevere /pɜːsɪ'vɪə(r)/ *vi* perseverare. **~ing** *a* assiduo

Persian /'pɜːʃn/ *a* persiano

persist /pə'sɪst/ *vi* persistere; **~ in doing sth** persistere nel fare qcsa. **~ence** *n* persistenza *f*. **~ent** *a* persistente. **~ently** *adv* persistentemente

person /'pɜːsn/ *n* persona *f*; **in ~** di persona

personal /'pɜːsənl/ *a* personale. **~ 'hygiene** *n* igiene *f* personale. **~ly** *adv* personalmente. **~ organizer** *n Comput* agenda *f* elettronica

personality /pɜːsə'næləti/ *n* personalità *f inv*; (*on TV*) personaggio *m*

personnel /pɜːsəˈnel/ n personale m

perspective /pəˈspektɪv/ n prospettiva f

persp|iration /pɜːspɪˈreɪʃn/ n sudore m. ~**ire** /-ˈspaɪə(r)/ vi sudare

persua|de /pəˈsweɪd/ vt persuadere. ~**sion** /-eɪʒn/ n persuasione f; (belief) convinzione f

persuasive /pəˈsweɪsɪv/ a persuasivo. ~**ly** adv in modo persuasivo

pertinent /ˈpɜːtɪnənt/ a pertinente (**to** a)

perturb /pəˈtɜːb/ vt perturbare

peruse /pəˈruːz/ vt leggere

perva|de /pəˈveɪd/ vt pervadere. ~**sive** /-sɪv/ a pervasivo

pervers|e /pəˈvɜːs/ a irragionevole. ~**ion** /-ʒn/ n perversione f

pervert /ˈpɜːvɜːt/ n pervertito, -a mf

perverted /pəˈvɜːtɪd/ a perverso

pessimis|m /ˈpesɪmɪzm/ n pessimismo m. ~**t** /-mɪst/ n pessimista mf. ~**tic** /-ˈmɪstɪk/ a pessimistico. ~**tically** adv in modo pessimistico

pest /pest/ n piaga f; (fam: person) peste f

pester /ˈpestə(r)/ vt molestare

pesticide /ˈpestɪsaɪd/ n pesticida m

pet /pet/ n animale m domestico; (favourite) cocco, -a mf ● a prediletto ● v (pt/pp petted) ● vt coccolare ● vi (couple:) praticare il petting

petal /ˈpetl/ n petalo m

peter /ˈpiːtə(r)/ vi ~ **out** finire

petite /pəˈtiːt/ a minuto

petition /pəˈtɪʃn/ n petizione f

pet 'name n vezzeggiativo m

petrif|y /ˈpetrɪfaɪ/ vt (pt/pp -**ied**) pietrificare. ~**ied** a (frightened) pietrificato

petrol /ˈpetrəl/ n benzina f

petroleum /prɪˈtrəʊliəm/ n petrolio m

petrol: ~**-pump** n pompa f di benzina. ~ **station** n stazione f di servizio. ~ **tank** n serbatoio m della benzina

'pet shop n negozio m di animali [domestici]

petticoat /ˈpetɪkəʊt/ n sottoveste f

petty /ˈpetɪ/ a (-**ier**, -**iest**) insignificante; (mean) meschino. ~ '**cash** n cassa f per piccole spese

petulant /ˈpetjʊlənt/ a petulante

pew /pjuː/ n banco m (di chiesa)

pewter /ˈpjuːtə(r)/ n peltro m

phallic /ˈfælɪk/ a fallico

phantom /ˈfæntəm/ n fantasma m

pharmaceutical /fɑːməˈsjuːtɪkl/ a farmaceutico

pharmac|ist /ˈfɑːməsɪst/ n farmacista mf. ~**y** n farmacia f

phase /feɪz/ n fase f ● vt **phase in/out** introdurre/eliminare gradualmente

Ph.D. n abbr (**Doctor of Philosophy**) dottorato m di ricerca

pheasant /ˈfeznt/ n fagiano m

phenomen|al /fɪˈnɒmɪnl/ a fenomenale; (incredible) incredibile. ~**ally** adv incredibilmente. ~**on** n (pl -**na**) fenomeno m

philanderer /fɪˈlændərə(r)/ n donnaiolo m

philanthrop|ic /fɪlənˈθrɒpɪk/ a filantropico. ~**ist** /fɪˈlænθrəpɪst/ n filantropo, -a mf

philatel|y /fɪˈlætəlɪ/ n filatelia f. ~**ist** n filatelico, -a mf

philharmonic /fɪlhɑːˈmɒnɪk/ n (orchestra) orchestra f filarmonica ● a filarmonico

Philippines /ˈfɪlɪpiːnz/ npl Filippine fpl

philistine /ˈfɪlɪstaɪn/ n filisteo, -a mf

philosoph|er /fɪˈlɒsəfə(r)/ n filosofo, -a mf. ~**ical** /fɪləˈsɒfɪkl/ a filosofico. ~**ically** adv con filosofia. ~**y** n filosofia f

phlegm /flem/ n Med flemma f

phlegmatic /flegˈmætɪk/ a flemmatico

phobia /ˈfəʊbɪə/ n fobia f

phone /fəʊn/ n telefono m; **be on the** ~ avere il telefono; (be phoning) essere al telefono ● vt telefonare a ● vi telefonare. **phone back** vt/i richiamare. ~**book** n guida f del telefono. ~ **box** n cabina f telefonica. ~ **card** n scheda f telefonica. ~ **call** telefonata f. ~**-in** n trasmissione f con chiamate in diretta. ~ **number** n numero m telefonico

phonetic /fəˈnetɪk/ a fonetico. ~**s** n fonetica f

phoney /ˈfəʊnɪ/ a (-**ier**, -**iest**) fasullo

phosphorus /ˈfɒsfərəs/ n fosforo m

photo /ˈfəʊtəʊ/ n foto f; ~ **album** album m inv di fotografie. ~**copier** n fotocopiatrice f. ~**copy** n fotocopia f ● vt fotocopiare

photogenic /fəʊtəʊˈdʒenɪk/ a fotogenico

photograph /ˈfəʊtəgrɑːf/ n fotografia f ● vt fotografare

photograph|er /fəˈtɒgrəfə(r)/ n fotografo, -a mf. ~**ic** /fəʊtəˈgræfɪk/ a fotografico. ~**y** n fotografia f

phrase /freɪz/ n espressione f ● vt esprimere. ~**-book** n libro m di fraseologia

physical /'fɪzɪkl/ a fisico. ~ **edu'cation** n educazione f fisica. ~**ly** adv fisicamente

physician /fɪ'zɪʃn/ n medico m

physic|ist /'fɪzɪsɪst/ n fisico, -a mf. ~**s** n fisica f

physiology /fɪzɪ'ɒlədʒɪ/ n fisiologia f

physio'therap|ist /fɪzɪəʊ-/ n fisioterapista mf. ~**y** n fisioterapia f

physique /fɪ'ziːk/ n fisico m

pianist /'pɪənɪst/ n pianista mf

piano /pɪ'ænəʊ/ n piano m

pick¹ /pɪk/ n (tool) piccone m

pick² n scelta f; **take your ~** prendi quello che vuoi ● vt (select) scegliere; cogliere (flowers); scassinare (lock); borseggiare (pockets); ~ **and choose** fare il difficile; ~ **one's nose** mettersi le dita nel naso; ~ **a quarrel** attaccar briga; ~ **holes in** fam criticare; ~ **at one's food** spilluzzicare. **pick on** vt (fam: nag) assillare; **he always ~s on me** ce l'ha con me. **pick out** vt (identify) individuare. **pick up** vt sollevare; (off the ground, information) raccogliere; prendere in braccio (baby); (learn) imparare; prendersi (illness); (buy) comprare; captare (signal); (collect) andare/venire a prendere; prendere (passengers, habit); (police:) arrestare (criminal); fam rimorchiare (girl); ~ **oneself up** riprendersi ● vi (improve) recuperare; (weather:) rimettersi

'pickaxe n piccone m

picket /'pɪkɪt/ n picchettista mf ● vt picchettare. ~ **line** n picchetto m

pickle /'pɪkl/ n ~**s** pl sottaceti mpl; **in a** ~ fig nei pasticci ● vt mettere sottaceto

pick: ~**pocket** n borsaiolo m. ~**-up** n (truck) furgone m; (on record-player) pickup m inv

picnic /'pɪknɪk/ n picnic m ● vi (pt/pp -nicked) fare un picnic

picture /'pɪktʃə(r)/ n (painting) quadro m; (photo) fotografia f; (drawing) disegno m; (film) film m inv; **put sb in the** ~ fig mettere qcno al corrente; **the** ~**s** il cinema ● vt (imagine) immaginare

picturesque /pɪktʃə'resk/ a pittoresco

pie /paɪ/ n torta f

piece /piːs/ n pezzo m; (in game) pedina f; **a** ~ **of bread/paper** un pezzo di pane/carta; **a** ~ **of news/advice** una notizia/un consiglio; **take to** ~**s** smontare. ~**meal** adv un po' alla volta.

~**work** n lavoro m a cottimo ● **piece together** vt montare; fig ricostruire

pier /pɪə(r)/ n molo m; (pillar) pilastro m

pierc|e /pɪəs/ vt perforare; ~ **a hole in sth** fare un buco in qcsa. ~**ing** a penetrante

pig /pɪɡ/ n maiale m

pigeon /'pɪdʒɪn/ n piccione m. ~**-hole** n casella f

piggy /'pɪɡɪ/ ~**back** n **give sb a** ~**back** portare qcno sulle spalle. ~ **bank** n salvadanaio m

pig'headed a fam cocciuto

pig: ~**skin** n pelle f di cinghiale. ~**tail** n (plait) treccina f

pile /paɪl/ n (heap) pila f ● vt ~ **sth on to sth** appilare qcsa su qcsa. **pile up** vt accatastare ● vi ammucchiarsi

piles /paɪlz/ npl emorroidi fpl

'pile-up n tamponamento m a catena

pilfering /'pɪlfərɪŋ/ n piccoli furti mpl

pilgrim /'pɪlɡrɪm/ n pellegrino, -a mf. ~**age** /-ɪdʒ/ n pellegrinaggio m

pill /pɪl/ n pillola f

pillage /'pɪlɪdʒ/ vt saccheggiare

pillar /'pɪlə(r)/ n pilastro m. ~**-box** n buca f delle lettere

pillion /'pɪljən/ n sellino m posteriore; **ride** ~ viaggiare dietro

pillory /'pɪlərɪ/ vt (pt/pp -ied) fig mettere alla berlina

pillow /'pɪləʊ/ n guanciale m. ~**case** n federa f

pilot /'paɪlət/ n pilota mf ● vt pilotare. ~**-light** n fiamma f di sicurezza

pimp /pɪmp/ n protettore m

pimple /'pɪmpl/ n foruncolo m

pin /pɪn/ n spillo m; Electr spinotto m; Med chiodo m; **I have ~s and needles in my leg** fam mi formicola una gamba ● vt (pt/pp pinned) appuntare (to/on su); (sewing) fissare con gli spilli; (hold down) immobilizzare; ~ **sb down to a date** ottenere un appuntamento da qcno; ~ **sth on sb** fam addossare a qcno la colpa di qcsa. **pin up** vt appuntare; (on wall) affiggere

pinafore /'pɪnəfɔː(r)/ n grembiule m. ~ **dress** n scamiciato m

pincers /'pɪnsəz/ npl tenaglie fpl

pinch /pɪntʃ/ n pizzicotto m; (of salt) presa f; **at a** ~ fam in caso di bisogno ● vt pizzicare; (fam: steal) fregare ● vi (shoe:) stringere

'pincushion n puntaspilli m inv

pine¹ /paɪn/ n (tree) pino m

pine² vi **she is pining for you** le manchi molto. **pine away** vi deperire

pineapple /'pain-/ n ananas m inv
ping /pɪŋ/ n rumore m metallico
'ping-pong /ˈpɪŋpɒŋ/ n ping-pong m
pink /pɪŋk/ a rosa inv
pinnacle /'pɪnəkl/ n guglia f
PIN number n codice m segreto
pin: ~**point** vt definire con precisione.
~**stripe** a gessato
pint /paint/ n pinta f (= 0,571, Am: 0,47
l); **a** ~ fam una birra media
'pin-up n ragazza f da copertina,
pin-up f inv
pioneer /paɪəˈnɪə(r)/ n pioniere, -a mf
● vt essere un pioniere di
pious /'paɪəs/ a pio
pip /pɪp/ n (seed) seme m
pipe /paip/ n tubo m; (for smoking) pipa
f; the ~**s** Mus la cornamusa ● vt far arrivare con tubature (water, gas etc).
pipe down vi fam abbassare la voce
pipe: ~**-cleaner** n scovolino m.
~**-dream** n illusione f. ~**line** n
conduttura f; **in the** ~**line** fam in cantiere
piper /ˈpaɪpə(r)/ n suonatore m di cornamusa
piping /ˈpaɪpɪŋ/ a ~ **hot** bollente
pirate /ˈpaɪrət/ n pirata m
Pisces /ˈpaɪsiːz/ n Astr Pesci mpl
piss /pɪs/ vi sl pisciare
pistol /ˈpɪstl/ n pistola f
piston /ˈpɪstn/ n Techn pistone m
pit /pit/ n fossa f; (mine) miniera f; (for
orchestra) orchestra f ● vt (pt/pp
pitted) fig opporre (against a)
pitch¹ /pɪtʃ/ n (tone) tono m; (level) altezza f; (in sport) campo m; (fig: degree)
grado m ● vt montare (tent). **pitch in** vi
fam mettersi sotto
pitch² n ~-'**black** a nero come la pece.
~-'**dark** a buio pesto
'pitchfork n forca f
piteous /ˈpɪtɪəs/ a pietoso
'pitfall n fig trabocchetto m
pith /pɪθ/ n (of lemon, orange) interno
m della buccia
pithy /ˈpɪθɪ/ a (-ier, -iest) fig conciso
piti|ful /ˈpɪtɪfl/ a pietoso. ~**less** a spietato
pittance /ˈpɪtns/ n miseria f
pity /ˈpɪtɪ/ n pietà f; [**what a**] ~! che
peccato!; **take** ~ **on** avere compassione
di ● vt aver pietà di
pivot /ˈpɪvət/ n perno m; fig fulcro m
● vi imperniarsi (**on** su)
pizza /ˈpiːtsə/ n pizza f
placard /ˈplækɑːd/ n cartellone m
placate /pləˈkeɪt/ vt placare

place /pleis/ n posto m; (fam: house)
casa f; (in book) segno m; **feel out of** ~
sentirsi fuori posto; **take** ~ aver luogo;
all over the ~ dappertutto ● vt collocare; (remember) identificare; ~ **an
order** fare un'ordinazione; **be** ~**d** (in
race) piazzarsi. ~**-mat** n sottopiatto m
placid /ˈplæsɪd/ a placido
plagiar|ism /ˈpleɪdʒərɪzm/ n plagio m.
~**ize** vt plagiare
plague /pleɪg/ n peste f
plaice /pleis/ n inv platessa f
plain /plein/ a chiaro; (simple) semplice; (not pretty) scialbo; (not patterned)
normale; (chocolate) fondente; **in** ~
clothes in borghese ● adv (simply)
semplicemente ● n pianura f. ~**ly** adv
francamente; (simply) semplicemente;
(obviously) chiaramente
plaintiff /ˈpleɪntɪf/ n Jur parte f lesa
plaintive /ˈpleɪntɪv/ a lamentoso
plait /plæt/ n treccia f ● vt intrecciare
plan /plæn/ n progetto m, piano m ● vt
(pt/pp **planned**) progettare; (intend)
prevedere
plane¹ /plein/ n (tree) platano m
plane² n aeroplano m
plane³ n (tool) pialla f ● vt piallare
planet /ˈplænɪt/ n pianeta m
plank /plæŋk/ n asse f
planning /ˈplænɪŋ/ n pianificazione f.
~ **permission** n licenza f edilizia
plant /plɑːnt/ n pianta f; (machinery)
impianto m; (factory) stabilimento m
● vt piantare. ~**ation** /plɑːnˈteɪʃn/ n
piantagione f
plaque /plɑːk/ n placca f
plasma /ˈplæzmə/ n plasma m
plaster /ˈplɑːstə(r)/ n intonaco m; Med
gesso m; (sticking ~) cerotto m; ~ **of
Paris** gesso m ● vt intonacare (wall);
(cover) ricoprire. ~**ed** a sl sbronzo. ~**er**
n intonacatore m
plastic /ˈplæstɪk/ n plastica f ● a plastico
Plasticine® /ˈplæstɪsiːn/ n plastilina® f
plastic: ~ '**surgeon** n chirurgo m plastico. ~ **surgery** n chirurgia f plastica
plate /pleit/ n piatto m; (flat sheet) placca f; (gold and silverware) argenteria f;
(in book) tavola f [fuori testo] ● vt
(cover with metal) placcare
plateau /ˈplætəʊ/ n (pl ~**x** /-əʊz/)
altopiano m
platform /ˈplætfɔːm/ n (stage) palco m;
Rail marciapiede m; Pol piattaforma f;
~ **5** binario 5

platinum /'plætɪnəm/ n platino m ● a di platino

platitude /'plætɪtju:d/ n luogo m comune

platonic /plə'tɒnɪk/ a platonico

platoon /plə'tu:n/ n Mil plotone m

platter /'plætə(r)/ n piatto m da portata

plausible /'plɔ:zəbl/ a plausibile

play /pleɪ/ n gioco m; Theat, TV rappresentazione f; Radio sceneggiato m radiofonico; ~ **on words** gioco m di parole ● vt giocare a; (act) recitare; suonare (instrument); giocare (card) ● vi giocare; Mus suonare; ~ **safe** non prendere rischi. **play down** vt minimizzare. **play up** vi fam fare i capricci

play: ~**boy** n playboy m inv. ~**er** n giocatore, -trice mf. ~**ful** a scherzoso. ~**ground** n Sch cortile m (per la ricreazione). ~**group** n asilo m

playing: ~**card** n carta f da gioco. ~**-field** n campo m da gioco

play: ~**mate** n compagno, -a mf di gioco. ~**-pen** n box m inv. ~**thing** n giocattolo m. ~**wright** /-raɪt/ n drammaturgo, -a mf

plc n abbr (**public limited company**) s.r.l.

plea /pli:/ n richiesta f; **make a ~ for** fare un appello a

plead /pli:d/ vi fare appello (**for** a); ~ **guilty** dichiararsi colpevole; ~ **with sb** implorare qcno

pleasant /'plez(ə)nt/ a piacevole. ~**ly** adv piacevolmente; (say, smile) cordialmente

please /pli:z/ adv per favore; ~**e do** prego ● vt far contento; ~**e oneself** fare il proprio comodo; ~**e yourself!** come vuoi!; pej fai come ti pare!. ~**ed** a lieto; ~**ed with/about** contento di. ~**ing** a gradevole

pleasurable /'pleʒərəbl/ a gradevole

pleasure /'pleʒə(r)/ n piacere m; **with ~** con piacere, volentieri

pleat /pli:t/ n piega f ● vt pieghettare. ~**ed 'skirt** n gonna f a pieghe

pledge /pledʒ/ n pegno m; (promise) promessa f ● vt impegnarsi a; (pawn) impegnare

plentiful /'plentɪfl/ a abbondante

plenty /'plentɪ/ n abbondanza f; ~ **of money** molti soldi; ~ **of people** molta gente; **I've got ~** ne ho in abbondanza

pliable /'plaɪəbl/ a flessibile

pliers /'plaɪəz/ npl pinze fpl

plight /plaɪt/ n condizione f

plimsolls /'plɪmsɒlz/ npl scarpe fpl da ginnastica

plinth /plɪnθ/ n plinto m

plod /plɒd/ vi (pt/pp **plodded**) trascinarsi; (work hard) sgobbare

plonk /plɒŋk/ n fam vino m mediocre

plot /plɒt/ n complotto m; (of novel) trama f; ~ **of land** appezzamento m [di terreno] ● vt/i (pt/pp **plotted**) complottare

plough /plaʊ/ n aratro m ● vt/i arare. ~**man's [lunch]** piatto m di formaggi e sottaceti, servito con pane. **plough back** vt Comm reinvestire

ploy /plɔɪ/ n fam manovra f

pluck /plʌk/ n fegato m ● vt strappare; depilare (eyebrows); spennare (bird); cogliere (flower). **pluck up** vt ~ **up courage** farsi coraggio

plucky /'plʌkɪ/ a (-ier, -iest) coraggioso

plug /plʌg/ n tappo m; Electr spina f; Auto candela f; (fam: advertisement) pubblicità f inv ● vt (pt/pp **plugged**) tappare; (fam: advertise) pubblicizzare con insistenza. **plug in** vt Electr inserire la spina di

plum /plʌm/ n prugna f; (tree) prugno m

plumage /'plu:mɪdʒ/ n piumaggio m

plumb /plʌm/ a verticale ● adv esattamente ● **plumb in** vt collegare

plumb|er /'plʌmə(r)/ n idraulico m. ~**ing** n impianto m idraulico

'plumb-line n filo m a piombo

plume /plu:m/ n piuma f

plummet /'plʌmɪt/ vi precipitare

plump /plʌmp/ a paffuto ● **plump for** vt scegliere

plunge /plʌndʒ/ n tuffo m; **take the ~** fam buttarsi ● vt tuffare; fig sprofondare ● vi tuffarsi

plunging /'plʌndʒɪŋ/ a (neckline) profondo

plu'perfect /plu:-/ n trapassato m prossimo

plural /'plʊərəl/ a plurale ● n plurale m

plus /plʌs/ prep più ● a in più; **500 ~** più di 500 ● n più m; (advantage) extra m inv

plush /plʌʃ[ɪ]/ a lussuoso

plutonium /plu:'təʊnɪəm/ n plutonio m

ply /plaɪ/ vt (pt/pp **plied**) ~ **sb with drink** continuare a offrire da bere a qcno. ~**wood** n compensato m

p.m. abbr (**post meridiem**) del pomeriggio

PM n abbr **Prime Minister**

pneumatic /nju:'mætɪk/ a pneumatico. ~ '**drill** n martello m pneumatico

pneumonia /nju:'məʊnɪə/ n polmonite f

P.O. abbr Post Office

poach /pəʊtʃ/ vt Culin bollire; cacciare di frodo ⟨deer⟩; pescare di frodo ⟨salmon⟩; ~**ed egg** uovo m in camicia. ~**er** n bracconiere m

pocket /'pɒkɪt/ n tasca f; **be out of** ~ rimetterci ● vt intascare. ~-**book** n taccuino m; ⟨wallet⟩ portafoglio m. ~-**money** n denaro m per le piccole spese

pod /pɒd/ n baccello m

podgy /'pɒdʒɪ/ a (-ier, -iest) grassoccio

poem /'pəʊɪm/ n poesia f

poet /'pəʊɪt/ n poeta m. ~**ic** /-'etɪk/ a poetico

poetry /'pəʊɪtrɪ/ n poesia f

poignant /'pɔɪnjant/ a emozionante

point /pɔɪnt/ n punto m; ⟨sharp end⟩ punta f; ⟨meaning, purpose⟩ senso m; Electr presa f [di corrente]; ~**s** pl Rail scambio m; ~ **of view** punto m di vista; **good/bad** ~**s** aspetti mpl positivi/ negativi; **what is the** ~? a che scopo?; **the** ~ **is** il fatto è; **I don't see the** ~ non vedo il senso; **up to a** ~ fino a un certo punto; **be on the** ~ **of doing sth** essere sul punto di fare qcsa ● vt puntare (**at** verso) ● vi ⟨with finger⟩ puntare il dito; ~ **at/to** ⟨person:⟩ mostrare col dito; ⟨indicator:⟩ indicare. **point out** vt far notare ⟨fact⟩; ~ **sth out to sb** far notare qcsa a qcno

point-'blank a a bruciapelo

point|ed /'pɔɪntɪd/ a appuntito; ⟨question⟩ diretto. ~**ers** npl ⟨advice⟩ consigli mpl. ~**less** a inutile

poise /pɔɪz/ n padronanza f. ~**d** a in equilibrio; ~**d to** sul punto di

poison /'pɔɪzn/ n veleno m ● vt avvelenare. ~**ous** a velenoso

poke /pəʊk/ n [piccola] spinta f ● vt spingere; ⟨put⟩ attizzare; ⟨fire⟩ attizzare; ~ **fun at** prendere in giro. **poke about** vi frugare

poker[1] /'pəʊkə(r)/ n attizzatoio m

poker[2] n ⟨card game⟩ poker m

poky /'pəʊkɪ/ a (-ier, -iest) angusto

Poland /'pəʊlənd/ n Polonia f

polar /'pəʊlə(r)/ a polare. ~ '**bear** n orso m bianco. ~**ize** vt polarizzare

Pole /pəʊl/ n polacco m, -a mf

pole[1] n palo m

pole[2] n Geog, Electr polo m

'**pole-star** n stella f polare

'**pole-vault** n salto m con l'asta

police /pə'li:s/ npl polizia f ● vt pattugliare ⟨area⟩

police: ~**man** n poliziotto m. ~ **state** n stato m militarista. ~ **station** n commissariato m. ~**woman** n donna f poliziotto

policy[1] /'pɒlɪsɪ/ n politica f

policy[2] n ⟨insurance⟩ polizza f

polio /'pəʊlɪəʊ/ n polio f

Polish /'pəʊlɪʃ/ a polacco ● n ⟨language⟩ polacco m

polish /'pɒlɪʃ/ n ⟨shine⟩ lucentezza f; ⟨substance⟩ lucido m; ⟨for nails⟩ smalto m; fig raffinatezza f ● vt lucidare; fig smussare. **polish off** vt fam finire; far fuori ⟨food⟩

polished /'pɒlɪʃt/ a ⟨manner⟩ raffinato; ⟨performance⟩ senza sbavature

polite /pə'laɪt/ a cortese. ~**ly** adv cortesemente. ~**ness** n cortesia f

politic /'pɒlɪtɪk/ a prudente

politic|al /pə'lɪtɪkl/ a politico. ~**ally** adv dal punto di vista politico. ~**ian** /pɒlɪ'tɪʃn/ n politico m

politics /'pɒlɪtɪks/ n politica f

poll /pəʊl/ n votazione f; ⟨election⟩ elezioni fpl; [opinion] ~ sondaggio m d'opinione; **go to the** ~**s** andare alle urne ● vt ottenere ⟨votes⟩

pollen /'pɒlən/ n polline m

polling /'pəʊlɪŋ/: ~-**booth** n cabina f elettorale. ~-**station** n seggio m elettorale

'**poll tax** n imposta f locale sulle persone fisiche

pollutant /pə'lu:tənt/ n sostanza f inquinante

pollut|e /pə'lu:t/ vt inquinare. ~**ion** /-u:ʃn/ n inquinamento m

polo /'pəʊləʊ/ n polo m. ~-**neck** n collo m alto. ~-**shirt** n dolcevita f

polyester /pɒlɪ'estə(r)/ n poliestere m

polystyrene® /pɒlɪ'staɪri:n/ n polistirolo m

polytechnic /pɒlɪ'teknɪk/ n politecnico m

polythene /'pɒlɪθi:n/ n politene m. ~ **bag** n sacchetto m di plastica

polyun'saturated a polinsaturo

pomegranate /'pɒmɪgrænɪt/ n melagrana f

pomp /pɒmp/ n pompa f

pompon /'pɒmpɒn/ n pompon m

pompous /'pɒmpəs/ a pomposo

pond /pɒnd/ n stagno m

ponder /'pɒndə(r)/ vt/i ponderare

pong /pɒŋ/ *n fam* puzzo *m*

pontiff /'pɒntɪf/ *n* pontefice *m*

pony /'pəʊnɪ/ *n* pony *m inv*. **~-tail** *n* coda *f* di cavallo. **~-trekking** *n* escursioni *fpl* col pony

poodle /'puːdl/ *n* barboncino *m*

pool¹ /puːl/ *n* (*of water, blood*) pozza *f*; [**swimming**] ~ piscina *f*

pool² *n* (*common fund*) cassa *f* comune; (*in cards*) piatto *m*; (*game*) biliardo *m* a buca. ~s *npl* ≈ totocalcio *msg* ● *vt* mettere insieme

poor /pʊə(r)/ *a* povero; (*not good*) scadente; **in ~ health** in cattiva salute ● *npl* **the ~** i poveri. **~ly** *a* **be ~ly** non stare bene ● *adv* male

pop¹ /pɒp/ *n* botto *m*; (*drink*) bibita *f* gasata ● *v* (*pt/pp* **popped**) ● *vt* (*fam: put*) mettere; (*burst*) far scoppiare ● *vi* (*burst*) scoppiare. **pop in/out** *vi fam* fare un salto/un salto fuori

pop² *n fam* musica *f* pop ● *attrib* pop *inv*

popcorn *n* popcorn *m inv*

pope /pəʊp/ *n* papa *m*

poplar /'pɒplə(r)/ *n* pioppo *m*

poppy /'pɒpɪ/ *n* papavero *m*

popular /'pɒpjʊlə(r)/ *a* popolare; (*belief*) diffuso. **~ity** /-'lærətɪ/ *n* popolarità *f*

populat|e /'pɒpjʊleɪt/ *vt* popolare. **~ion** /-'leɪʃn/ *n* popolazione *f*

porcelain /'pɔːsəlɪn/ *n* porcellana *f*

porch /pɔːtʃ/ *n* portico *m*; *Am* veranda *f*

porcupine /'pɔːkjʊpaɪn/ *n* porcospino *m*

pore¹ /pɔː(r)/ *n* poro *m*

pore² *vi* **~ over** immergersi in

pork /pɔːk/ *n* carne *f* di maiale

porn /pɔːn/ *n fam* porno *m*. **~o** *a fam* porno *inv*

pornograph|ic /pɔːnə'græfɪk/ *a* pornografico. **~y** /-'nɒgrəfɪ/ *n* pornografia *f*

porous /'pɔːrəs/ *a* poroso

porpoise /'pɔːpəs/ *n* focena *f*

porridge /'pɒrɪdʒ/ *n* farinata *f* di fiocchi d'avena

port¹ /pɔːt/ *n* porto *m*

port² *n* (*Naut: side*) babordo *m*

port³ *n* (*wine*) porto *m*

portable /'pɔːtəbl/ *a* portatile

porter /'pɔːtə(r)/ *n* portiere *m*; (*for luggage*) facchino *m*

portfolio /pɔːt'fəʊlɪəʊ/ *n* cartella *f*; *Comm* portafoglio *m*

porthole *n* oblò *m inv*

portion /'pɔːʃn/ *n* parte *f*, (*of food*) porzione *f*

portly /'pɔːtlɪ/ *a* (**-ier, -iest**) corpulento

portrait /'pɔːtrɪt/ *n* ritratto *m*

portray /pɔː'treɪ/ *vt* ritrarre; (*represent*) descrivere; (*actor:*) impersonare. **~al** *n* ritratto *m*

Portug|al /'pɔːtjʊgl/ *n* Portogallo *m*. **~uese** /-'giːz/ *a* portoghese ● *n* portoghese *mf*; (*language*) portoghese *m*

pose /pəʊz/ *n* posa *f* ● *vt* porre (*problem, question*) ● *vi* (*for painter*) posare; **~ as** atteggiarsi a

posh /pɒʃ/ *a fam* lussuoso; (*people*) danaroso

position /pə'zɪʃn/ *n* posizione *f*; (*job*) posto *m*; (*status*) ceto *m* [sociale] ● *vt* posizionare

positive /'pɒzɪtɪv/ *a* positivo; (*certain*) sicuro; (*progress*) concreto ● *n* positivo *m*. **~ly** *adv* positivamente; (*decidedly*) decisamente

possess /pə'zes/ *vt* possedere. **~ion** /pə'zeʃn/ *n* possesso *m*; **~ions** *pl* beni *mpl*

possess|ive /pə'zesɪv/ *a* possessivo. **~iveness** *n* carattere *m* possessivo. **~or** *n* possessore, -ditrice *mf*

possibility /pɒsə'bɪlətɪ/ *n* possibilità *f inv*

possib|le /'pɒsɪbl/ *a* possibile. **~ly** *adv* possibilmente; **I couldn't ~ly accept** non mi è possibile accettare; **he can't ~ly be right** non è possibile che abbia ragione; **could you ~ly…?** potrebbe per favore…?

post¹ /pəʊst/ *n* (*pole*) palo *m* ● *vt* affiggere (*notice*)

post² *n* (*place of duty*) posto *m* ● *vt* appostare; (*transfer*) assegnare

post³ *n* (*mail*) posta *f*; **by ~** per posta ● *vt* spedire; (*put in letter-box*) imbucare; (*as opposed to fax*) mandare per posta; **keep sb ~ed** tenere qcno al corrente

post- *pref* dopo

postage /'pəʊstɪdʒ/ *n* affrancatura *f*. **~ stamp** *n* francobollo *m*

postal /'pəʊstl/ *a* postale. **~ order** *n* vaglia *m inv* postale

post: ~-box *n* cassetta *f* delle lettere. **~card** *n* cartolina *f*. **~code** *n* codice *m* postale. **~-date** *vt* postdatare

poster /'pəʊstə(r)/ *n* poster *m inv*; (*advertising, election*) cartellone *m*

posterior /pɒ'stɪərɪə(r)/ *n fam* posteriore *m*

posterity /pɒ'sterətɪ/ *n* posterità *f*

posthumous /'pɒstjʊməs/ *a* postumo. **~ly** *adv* dopo la morte

post: ~**man** *n* postino *m*. ~**mark** *n* timbro *m* postale

post-mortem /-'mɔːtəm/ *n* autopsia *f*

'post office *n* ufficio *m* postale

postpone /pəʊst'pəʊn/ *vt* rimandare. ~**ment** *n* rinvio *m*

posture /'pɒstʃə(r)/ *n* posizione *f*

post-'war *a* del dopoguerra

pot /pɒt/ *n* vaso *m*; (*for tea*) teiera *f*; (*for coffee*) caffettiera *f*; (*for cooking*) pentola *f*; ~**s of money** *fam* un sacco di soldi; **go to** ~ *fam* andare in malora

potassium /pə'tæsɪəm/ *n* potassio *m*

potato /pə'teɪtəʊ/ *n* (*pl* -**es**) patata *f*

poten|t /'pəʊtənt/ *a* potente. ~**tate** *n* potentato *m*

potential /pə'tenʃl/ *a* potenziale ● *n* potenziale *m*. ~**ly** *adv* potenzialmente

pot: ~**hole** *n* cavità *f inv*; (*in road*) buca *f*. ~**holer** *n* speleologo, -a *mf*. ~**luck** *n* **take** ~**luck** affidarsi alla sorte. ~ '**plant** *n* pianta *f* da appartamento. ~**-shot** *n* **take a** ~**-shot at** sparare a casaccio a

potted /'pɒtɪd/ *a* conservato; (*shortened*) condensato. ~ '**plant** *n* pianta *f* da appartamento

potter¹ /'pɒtə(r)/ *vi* ~ [**about**] gingillarsi

potter² *n* vasaio, -a *mf*. ~**y** *n* lavorazione *f* della ceramica; (*articles*) ceramiche *fpl*; (*place*) laboratorio *m* di ceramiche

potty /'pɒtɪ/ *a* (-**ier, -iest**) *fam* matto ● *n* vasino *m*

pouch /paʊtʃ/ *n* marsupio *m*

pouffe /puːf/ *n* pouf *m inv*

poultry /'pəʊltrɪ/ *n* pollame *m*

pounce /paʊns/ *vi* balzare; ~ **on** saltare su

pound¹ /paʊnd/ *n* libbra *f* (= *0,454 kg*); (*money*) sterlina *f*

pound² *vt* battere ● *vi* ⟨*heart:*⟩ battere forte; (*run heavily*) correre pesantemente

pour /pɔː(r)/ *vt* versare ● *vi* riversarsi; (*with rain*) piovere a dirotto. **pour out** *vi* riversarsi fuori ● *vt* versare ⟨*drink*⟩; sfogare ⟨*troubles*⟩

pout /paʊt/ *vi* fare il broncio ● *n* broncio *m*

poverty /'pɒvətɪ/ *n* povertà *f*

powder /'paʊdə(r)/ *n* polvere *f*; (*cosmetic*) cipria *f* ● *vt* polverizzare; (*face*) incipriare. ~**y** *a* polveroso

power /'paʊə(r)/ *n* potere *m*; *Electr* corrente *f* [elettrica]; *Math* potenza *f*. ~ **cut** *n* interruzione *f* di corrente. ~**ed a** ~**ed by electricity** dotato di corrente

[elettrica]. ~**ful** *a* potente. ~**less** *a* impotente. ~**-station** *n* centrale *f* elettrica

PR *n abbr* **public relations**

practicable /'præktɪkəbl/ *a* praticabile

practical /'præktɪkl/ *a* pratico. ~ '**joke** *n* burla *f*. ~**ly** *adv* praticamente

practice /'præktɪs/ *n* pratica *f*; (*custom*) usanza *f*; (*habit*) abitudine *f*; (*exercise*) esercizio *m*; *Sport* allenamento *m*; **in** ~ (*in reality*) in pratica; **out of** ~ fuori esercizio; **put into** ~ mettere in pratica

practise /'præktɪs/ *vt* fare pratica in; (*carry out*) mettere in pratica; esercitare ⟨*profession*⟩ ● *vi* esercitarsi; ⟨*doctor:*⟩ praticare. ~**d** *a* esperto

pragmatic /præg'mætɪk/ *a* pragmatico

praise /preɪz/ *n* lode *f* ● *vt* lodare. ~**worthy** *a* lodevole

pram /præm/ *n* carrozzella *f*

prance /prɑːns/ *vi* saltellare

prank /præŋk/ *n* tiro *m*

prattle /'prætl/ *vi* parlottare

prawn /prɔːn/ *n* gambero *m*. ~ '**cocktail** *n* cocktail *m inv* di gamberetti

pray /preɪ/ *vi* pregare. ~**er** /preə(r)/ *n* preghiera *f*

preach /priːtʃ/ *vt/i* predicare. ~**er** *n* predicatore, -trice *mf*

preamble /priː'æmbl/ *n* preambolo *m*

pre-ar'range /priː-/ *vt* predisporre

precarious /prɪ'keərɪəs/ *a* precario. ~**ly** *adv* in modo precario

precaution /prɪ'kɔːʃn/ *n* precauzione *f*; **as a** ~ per precauzione. ~**ary** *a* preventivo

precede /prɪ'siːd/ *vt* precedere

preceden|ce /'presɪdəns/ *n* precedenza *f*. ~**t** *n* precedente *m*

preceding /prɪ'siːdɪŋ/ *a* precedente

precinct /'priːsɪŋkt/ *n* (*traffic-free*) zona *f* pedonale; (*Am: district*) circoscrizione *f*

precious /'preʃəs/ *a* prezioso; ⟨*style*⟩ ricercato ● *adv fam* ~ **little** ben poco

precipice /'presɪpɪs/ *n* precipizio *m*

precipitate /prɪ'sɪpɪteɪt/ *vt* precipitare

précis /'preɪsiː/ *n* (*pl* **précis** /-siːz/) sunto *m*

precis|e /prɪ'saɪs/ *a* preciso. ~**ely** *adv* precisamente. ~**ion** /-'sɪʒn/ *n* precisione *f*

precursor /priː'kɜːsə(r)/ *n* precursore *m*

predator /'predətə(r)/ *n* predatore, -trice *mf*. ~**y** *a* rapace

predecessor /'pri:dɪsesə(r)/ n predecessore, -a mf

predicament /prɪ'dɪkəmənt/ n situazione f difficile

predicat|e /'predɪkət/ n Gram predicato m. ~**ive** /prɪ'dɪkətɪv/ a predicativo

predict /prɪ'dɪkt/ vt predire. ~**able** /-əbl/ a prevedibile. ~**ion** /-'dɪkʃn/ n previsione f

pre'domin|ant /prɪ-/ a predominante. ~**ate** vi predominare

pre-'eminent /prɪ-/ a preminente

preen /pri:n/ vt lisciarsi; ~ **oneself** fig farsi bello

pre|fab /'pri:fæb/ n fam casa f prefabbricata. ~**'fabricated** a prefabbricato

preface /'prefɪs/ n prefazione f

prefect /'pri:fekt/ n Sch studente, -tessa mf della scuola superiore con responsabilità disciplinari ecc

prefer /prɪ'fɜ:(r)/ vt (pt/pp **preferred**) preferire

prefera|ble /'prefərəbl/ a preferibile (**to** a). ~**bly** adv preferibilmente

preferen|ce /'prefərəns/ n preferenza f. ~**tial** /-'renʃl/ a preferenziale

prefix /'pri:fɪks/ n prefisso m

pregnan|cy /'pregnənsɪ/ n gravidanza f. ~**t** a incinta

prehi'storic /pri:-/ a preistorico

prejudice /'predʒʊdɪs/ n pregiudizio m ●vt influenzare (**against** contro); (harm) danneggiare. ~**d** a prevenuto

preliminary /prɪ'lɪmɪnərɪ/ a preliminare

prelude /'prelju:d/ n preludio m

pre-'marital a prematrimoniale

premature /'premətjʊə(r)/ a prematuro

pre'meditated /pri:-/ a premeditato

premier /'premɪə(r)/ a primario ●n Pol primo ministro m, premier m inv

première /'premɪeə(r)/ n prima f

premises /'premɪsɪz/ npl locali mpl; **on the** ~ sul posto

premium /'pri:mɪəm/ n premio m; **be at a** ~ essere una cosa rara

premonition /premə'nɪʃn/ n presentimento m

preoccupied /pri:-'ɒkjʊpaɪd/ a preoccupato

prep /prep/ n Sch compiti mpl

preparation /prepə'reɪʃn/ n preparazione f. ~**s** pl preparativi mpl

preparatory /prɪ'pærətrɪ/ a preparatorio ●adv ~ **to** per

prepare /prɪ'peə(r)/ vt preparare ●vi prepararsi (**for** per); ~**d to** disposto a

pre'pay /pri:-/ vt (pt/pp **-paid**) pagare in anticipo

preposition /prepə'zɪʃn/ n preposizione f

prepossessing /pri:pə'zesɪŋ/ a attraente

preposterous /prɪ'pɒstərəs/ a assurdo

prerequisite /pri:'rekwɪzɪt/ n condizione f sine qua non

prescribe /prɪ'skraɪb/ vt prescrivere

prescription /prɪ'skrɪpʃn/ n Med ricetta f

presence /'prezns/ n presenza f; ~ **of mind** presenza f di spirito

present[1] /'preznt/ a presente ●n presente m; **at** ~ attualmente

present[2] n (gift) regalo m; **give sb sth as a** ~ regalare qcsa a qcno

present[3] /prɪ'zent/ vt presentare; ~ **sb with an award** consegnare un premio a qcno. ~**able** /-əbl/ a **be** ~**able** essere presentabile

presentation /prezn'teɪʃn/ n presentazione f

presently /'prezntlɪ/ adv fra poco; (Am: now) attualmente

preservation /prezə'veɪʃn/ n conservazione f

preservative /prɪ'zɜ:vətɪv/ n conservante n

preserve /prɪ'zɜ:v/ vt preservare; (maintain, Culin) conservare ●n (in hunting & fig) riserva f; (jam) marmellata f

preside /prɪ'zaɪd/ vi presiedere (**over** a)

presidency /'prezɪdənsɪ/ n presidenza f

president /'prezɪdənt/ n presidente m. ~**ial** /-'denʃl/ a presidenziale

press /pres/ n (machine) pressa f; (newspapers) stampa f ●vt premere; pressare (flower); (iron) stirare; (squeeze) stringere ●vi (urge) incalzare.

press for vi fare pressione per; **be** ~**ed for** essere a corto di. **press on** vi andare avanti

press: ~ **conference** n conferenza f stampa. ~ **cutting** n ritaglio m di giornale. ~**ing** a urgente. ~**stud** n [bottone m] automatico m. ~-**up** n flessione f

pressure /'preʃə(r)/ n pressione f ●vt = **pressurize.** ~-**cooker** n pentola f a pressione. ~ **group** n gruppo m di pressione

pressurize /'preʃəraɪz/ vt far pressione su. ~**d** a pressurizzato

prestig|e /pre'sti:ʒ/ n prestigio m.
~ious /-'stɪdʒəs/ a prestigioso

presumably /prɪ'zju:məblɪ/ adv
presumibilmente

presume /prɪ'zju:m/ vt presumere; **~
to do sth** permettersi di fare qcsa

presumpt|ion /prɪ'zʌmpʃn/ n presunzione f; (boldness) impertinenza f.
~uous /-'zʌmptjʊəs/ a impertinente

presup'pose /pri:-/ vt presupporre

pretence /prɪ'tens/ n finzione f;
(pretext) pretesto m: **it's all ~** è tutta
una scena

pretend /prɪ'tend/ vt fingere; (claim)
pretendere • vi fare finta

pretentious /prɪ'tenʃas/ a pretenzioso

pretext /'pri:tekst/ n pretesto m

pretty /'prɪtɪ/ a (-ier, -iest) carino
• adv (fam: fairly) abbastanza

prevail /prɪ'veɪl/ vi prevalere; **~ on sb
to do sth** convincere qcno a fare qcsa.
~ing a prevalente

prevalen|ce /'prevələns/ n diffusione
f. **~t** a diffuso

prevent /prɪ'vent/ vt impedire; **~ sb
[from] doing sth** impedire a qcno di
fare qcsa. **~ion** /-enʃn/ n prevenzione f.
~ive /-ɪv/ a preventivo

preview /'pri:vju:/ n anteprima f

previous /'pri:vɪəs/ a precedente. **~ly**
adv precedentemente

pre-'war /pri:-/ a anteguerra

prey /preɪ/ n preda f; **bird of ~** uccello
m rapace • vi **~ on** far preda di; **~ on
sb's mind** attanagliare qcno

price /praɪs/ n prezzo m • vt Comm fissare il prezzo di. **~less** a inestimabile;
(fam:˙ amusing) spassosissimo. **~y** a
fam caro

prick /prɪk/ n puntura f • vt pungere.
prick up vt **~ up one's ears** rizzare le
orecchie

prickl|e /'prɪkl/ n spina f; (sensation)
formicolio m. **~y** a pungente; (person)
irritabile

pride /praɪd/ n orgoglio m • vt **~
oneself on** vantarsi di

priest /pri:st/ n prete m

prim /prɪm/ a (**primmer, primmest**)
perbenino

primarily /'praɪmərɪlɪ/ adv in primo
luogo

primary /'praɪmərɪ/ a primario; (chief)
principale. **~ school** n scuola f elementare

prime¹ /praɪm/ a principale, primo;
(first-rate) eccellente • n **be in one's ~**
essere nel fiore degli anni

prime² vt preparare (surface, person)

Prime Minister n Primo Ministro m

primeval /praɪ'mi:vl/ a primitivo

primitive /'prɪmɪtɪv/ a primitivo

primrose /'prɪmrəʊz/ n primula f

prince /prɪns/ n principe m

princess /prɪn'ses/ n principessa f

principal /'prɪnsəpl/ a principale • n
Sch preside m

principality /prɪnsɪ'pælətɪ/ n principato m

principally /'prɪnsəplɪ/ adv principalmente

principle /'prɪnsəpl/ n principio m; **in
~** in teoria; **on ~** per principio

print /prɪnt/ n (mark, trace) impronta f;
Phot copia f; (picture) stampa f; **in ~**
(printed out) stampato; (book) in commercio; **out of ~** esaurito • vt stampare; (write in capitals) scrivere in stampatello. **~ed matter** n stampe fpl

print|er /'prɪntə(r)/ n stampante f; Typ
tipografo. -a mf. **~er port** n Comput
porta f per la stampante. **~ing** n tipografia f

'printout n Comput stampa f

prior /'praɪə(r)/ a precedente. **~ to** prep
prima di

priority /praɪ'ɒrətɪ/ n precedenza f;
(matter) priorità f inv

prise /praɪz/ vt **~ open/up** forzare

prison /'prɪz(ə)n/ n prigione f. **~er** n
prigioniero, -a mf

privacy /'prɪvəsɪ/ n privacy f

private /'praɪvət/ a privato; (car,
secretary, letter) personale • n Mil soldato m semplice; **in ~** in privato. **~ly**
adv (funded, educated etc) privatamente; (in secret) in segreto; (confidentially)
in privato; (inwardly) interiormente

privation /praɪ'veɪʃn/ n privazione f;
~s pl stenti mpl

privatize /'praɪvətaɪz/ vt privatizzare

privilege /'prɪvəlɪdʒ/ n privilegio m.
~d a privilegiato

privy /'prɪvɪ/ a **be ~ to** essere al corrente di

prize /praɪz/ n premio m • a (idiot etc)
perfetto • vt apprezzare. **~-giving** n
premiazione f. **~-winner** n vincitore,
-trice mf. **~-winning** a vincente

pro /prəʊ/ n (fam: professional) professionista mf; **the ~s and cons** il pro e il
contro

probability /prɒbə'bɪlətɪ/ n probabilità f inv

probabl|e /'prɒbəbl/ a probabile. **~y** adv probabilmente

probation /prə'beɪʃn/ n prova f; Jur libertà f vigilata. **~ary** a in prova; **~ary period** periodo m di prova

probe /prəʊb/ n sonda f; (fig: investigate) indagine f ● vt sondare; (investigate) esaminare a fondo

problem /'prɒbləm/ n problema m ● a difficile. **~atic** /-'mætɪk/ a problematico

procedure /prə'siːdʒə(r)/ n procedimento m

proceed /prə'siːd/ vi procedere ● vt **~ to do sth** proseguire facendo qcsa

proceedings /prə'siːdɪŋz/ npl (report) atti mpl; Jur azione fsg legale

proceeds /'prəʊsiːdz/ npl ricavato msg

process /'prəʊses/ n processo m; (procedure) procedimento m; **in the ~** nel far ciò ● vt trattare; Admin occuparsi di; Phot sviluppare

procession /prə'seʃn/ n processione f

proclaim /prə'kleɪm/ vt proclamare

procure /prə'kjʊə(r)/ vt ottenere

prod /prɒd/ n colpetto m ● vt (pt/pp **prodded**) punzecchiare; fig incitare

prodigal /'prɒdɪgl/ a prodigo

prodigious /prə'dɪdʒəs/ a prodigioso

prodigy /'prɒdɪdʒi/ n [infant] **~** bambino m prodigio

produce¹ /'prɒdjuːs/ n prodotti mpl; **~ of Italy** prodotto in Italia

produce² /prə'djuːs/ vt produrre; (bring out) tirar fuori; (cause) causare; (fam: give birth to) fare. **~r** n produttore m

product /'prɒdʌkt/ n prodotto m. **~ion** /prə'dʌkʃn/ n produzione f; Theat spettacolo m

productiv|e /prə'dʌktɪv/ a produttivo. **~ity** /-'tɪvəti/ n produttività f

profan|e /prə'feɪn/ a profano; (blasphemous) blasfemo. **~ity** /-'fænəti/ n (oath) bestemmia f

profession /prə'feʃn/ n professione f. **~al** a professionale; (not amateur) professionista; (piece of work) da professionista; (man) di professione ● n professionista mf. **~ally** adv professionalmente

professor /prə'fesə(r)/ n professore m [universitario]

proficien|cy /prə'fɪʃnsi/ n competenza f. **~t** a **be ~t** in essere competente in

profile /'prəʊfaɪl/ n profilo m

profit /'prɒfɪt/ n profitto m ● vi **~ from** trarre profitto da. **~able** /-əbl/ a proficuo. **~ably** adv in modo proficuo

profound /prə'faʊnd/ a profondo. **~ly** adv profondamente

profus|e /prə'fjuːs/ a **~e apologies** una profusione di scuse. **~ion** /-'juːʒn/ n profusione f; **in ~ion** in abbondanza

progeny /'prɒdʒəni/ n progenie f inv

prognosis /prɒg'nəʊsɪs/ n (pl **-oses**) prognosi f inv

program /'prəʊgræm/ n programma m ● vt (pt/pp **programmed**) programmare

programme /'prəʊgræm/ n Br programma m. **~r** n Comput programmatore, -trice mf

progress¹ /'prəʊgres/ n progresso m; **in ~** in corso; **make ~** fig fare progressi

progress² /prə'gres/ vi progredire; fig fare progressi

progressive /prə'gresɪv/ a progressivo; (reforming) progressista. **~ly** adv progressivamente

prohibit /prə'hɪbɪt/ vt proibire. **~ive** /-ɪv/ a proibitivo

project¹ /'prɒdʒekt/ n progetto m; Sch ricerca f

project² /prə'dʒekt/ vt proiettare (film, image) ● vi (jut out) sporgere

projectile /prə'dʒektaɪl/ n proiettile m

projector /prə'dʒektə(r)/ n proiettore m

prolific /prə'lɪfɪk/ a prolifico

prologue /'prəʊlɒg/ n prologo m

prolong /prə'lɒŋ/ vt prolungare

promenade /prɒmə'nɑːd/ n lungomare m inv

prominent /'prɒmɪnənt/ a prominente; (conspicuous) di rilievo

promiscu|ity /prɒmɪ'skjuːəti/ n promiscuità f. **~ous** /prə'mɪskjʊəs/ a promiscuo

promis|e /'prɒmɪs/ n promessa f ● vt promettere; **~e sb sth** promettere a qcno che; **I ~ed to** l'ho promesso. **~ing** a promettente

promot|e /prə'məʊt/ vt promuovere; **be ~ed** Sport essere promosso. **~ion** /-əʊʃn/ n promozione f

prompt /prɒmpt/ a immediato; (punctual) puntuale ● adv in punto ● vt incitare (**to** a); Theat suggerire a ● vt suggerire. **~er** n suggeritore, -trice mf. **~ly** adv puntualmente

Proms /prɒmz/ npl rassegna f di concerti estivi di musica classica presso l'Albert Hall a Londra

prone /prəʊn/ *a* be ~ to do sth essere incline a fare qcsa

prong /prɒŋ/ *n* dente *m* (*di forchetta*)

pronoun /'prəʊnaʊn/ *n* pronome *m*

pronounce /prə'naʊns/ *vt* pronunciare; (*declare*) dichiarare. ~**d** *a* (*noticeable*) pronunciato

pronunciation /prənʌnsɪ'eɪʃn/ *n* pronuncia *f*

proof /pru:f/ *n* prova *f*, *Typ* bozza *f*, prova *f* ● *a* ~ **against** a prova di

prop¹ /prɒp/ *n* puntello *m* ● *vt* (*pt/pp* **propped**) ~ **open** tenere aperto; ~ **against** (*lean*) appoggiare a. **prop up** *vt* sostenere

prop² *n* *Theat, fam* accessorio *m* di scena

propaganda /prɒpə'gændə/ *n* propaganda *f*

propel /prə'pel/ *vt* (*pt/pp* **propelled**) spingere. ~**ler** *n* elica *f*

proper /'prɒpə(r)/ *a* corretto; (*suitable*) adatto; (*fam: real*) vero [e proprio]. ~**ly** *adv* correttamente. ~ '**name**, ~ '**noun** *n* nome *m* proprio

property /'prɒpətɪ/ *n* proprietà *f* *inv*. ~ **developer** *n* impresario *m* edile. ~ **market** *n* mercato *m* immobiliare

prophecy /'prɒfəsɪ/ *n* profezia *f*

prophesy /'prɒfɪsaɪ/ *vt* (*pt/pp* -**ied**) profetizzare

prophet /'prɒfɪt/ *n* profeta *m*. ~**ic** /prə'fetɪk/ *a* profetico

proportion /prə'pɔːʃn/ *n* proporzione *f*; (*share*) parte *f*; ~**s** *pl* (*dimensions*) proporzioni *fpl*. ~**al** *a* proporzionale. ~**ally** *adv* in proporzione

proposal /prə'pəʊzl/ *n* proposta *f*; (*of marriage*) proposta *f* di matrimonio

propose /prə'pəʊz/ *vt* proporre; (*intend*) proporsi ● *vi* fare una proposta di matrimonio

proposition /prɒpə'zɪʃn/ *n* proposta *f*; (*fam: task*) impresa *f*

proprietor /prə'praɪətə(r)/ *n* proprietario, -a *mf*

prosaic /prə'zeɪɪk/ *a* prosaico

prose /prəʊz/ *n* prosa *f*

prosecut|e /'prɒsɪkjuːt/ *vt* intentare azione contro. ~**ion** /-'kjuːʃn/ *n* azione *f* giudiziaria; **the ~ion** l'accusa *f*. ~**or** *n* [**Public**] **P~or** Pubblico Ministero *m*

prospect¹ /'prɒspekt/ *n* (*expectation*) prospettiva *f*

prospect² /prə'spekt/ *vi* ~ **for** cercare

prospective /prə'spektɪv/ *a* (*future*) futuro; (*possible*) potenziale. ~**or** *n* cercatore *m*

prospectus /prə'spektəs/ *n* prospetto *m*

prosper /'prɒspə(r)/ *vi* prosperare; (*person:*) stare bene finanziariamente. ~**ity** /-'sperətɪ/ *n* prosperità *f*

prosperous /'prɒspərəs/ *a* prospero

prostitut|e /'prɒstɪtjuːt/ *n* prostituta *f*. ~**ion** /-'tjuːʃn/ *n* prostituzione *f*

prostrate /'prɒstreɪt/ *a* prostrato; ~ **with grief** *fig* prostrato dal dolore

protagonist /prəʊ'tægənɪst/ *n* protagonista *mf*

protect /prə'tekt/ *vt* proteggere (**from** da). ~**ion** /-ekʃn/ *n* protezione *f*. ~**ive** /-ɪv/ *a* protettivo. ~**or** *n* protettore, -trice *mf*

protégé /'prɒtɪʒeɪ/ *n* protetto *m*

protein /'prəʊtiːn/ *n* proteina *f*

protest¹ /'prəʊtest/ *n* protesta *f*

protest² /prə'test/ *vt/i* protestare

Protestant /'prɒtɪstənt/ *a* protestante ● *n* protestante *mf*

protester /prə'testə(r)/ *n* contestatore, -trice *mf*

protocol /'prəʊtəkɒl/ *n* protocollo *m*

prototype /'prəʊtə-/ *n* prototipo *m*

protract /prə'trækt/ *vt* protrarre

protrude /prə'truːd/ *vi* sporgere

proud /praʊd/ *a* fiero (**of** di). ~**ly** *adv* fieramente

prove /pruːv/ *vt* provare ● *vi* ~ **to be a lie** rivelarsi una bugia. ~**n** *a* dimostrato

proverb /'prɒvɜːb/ *n* proverbio *m*. ~**ial** /prə'vɜːbɪəl/ *a* proverbiale

provide /prə'vaɪd/ *vt* fornire; ~ **sb with sth** fornire qcsa a qcno ● *vi* ~ **for** (*law:*) prevedere

provided /prə'vaɪdɪd/ *conj* ~ [**that**] purché

providen|ce /'prɒvɪdəns/ *n* provvidenza *f*. ~**tial** /-'denʃl/ *a* provvidenziale

providing /prə'vaɪdɪŋ/ *conj* = **provided**

provinc|e /'prɒvɪns/ *n* provincia *f*; *fig* campo *m*. ~**ial** /prə'vɪnʃl/ *a* provinciale

provision /prə'vɪʒn/ *n* (*of food, water*) approvvigionamento *m* (**of** di); (*of law*) disposizione *f*; ~**s** *pl* provviste *fpl*. ~**al** *a* provvisorio

proviso /prə'vaɪzəʊ/ *n* condizione *f*

provocat|ion /prɒvə'keɪʃn/ *n* provocazione *f*. ~**ive** /prə'vɒkətɪv/ *a* provocatorio; (*sexually*) provocante. ~**ively** *adv* in modo provocatorio

provoke /prə'vəʊk/ *vt* provocare

prow /praʊ/ *n* prua *f*

prowess /'praʊɪs/ *n* abilità *f* *inv*

prowl /praʊl/ *vi* aggirarsi ● *n* **on the ~** in cerca di preda. **~er** *n* tipo *m* sospetto

proximity /prɒk'sɪmətɪ/ *n* prossimità *f*

proxy /'prɒksɪ/ *n* procura *f*; (*person*) persona *f* che agisce per procura

prude /pruːd/ *n* **be a ~** essere eccessivamente pudico

pruden|ce /'pruːdəns/ *n* prudenza *f*. **~t** *a* prudente; (*wise*) oculatezza *f*

prudish /'pruːdɪʃ/ *a* eccessivamente pudico

prune¹ /pruːn/ *n* prugna *f* secca

prune² *vt* potare

pry /praɪ/ *vi* (*pt/pp* **pried**) ficcare il naso

psalm /sɑːm/ *n* salmo *m*

pseudonym /'sjuːdənɪm/ *n* pseudonimo *m*

psychiatric /saɪkɪ'ætrɪk/ *a* psichiatrico

psychiatr|ist /saɪ'kaɪətrɪst/ *n* psichiatra *mf*. **~y** *n* psichiatria *f*

psychic /'saɪkɪk/ *a* psichico; **I'm not ~** non sono un indovino

psycho|'analyse /saɪkəʊ-/ *vt* psicanalizzare. **~a'nalysis** *n* psicanalisi *f*. **~'analyst** *n* psicanalista *mf*

psychological /saɪkə'lɒdʒɪkl/ *a* psicologico

psycholog|ist /saɪ'kɒlədʒɪst/ *n* psicologo, -a *mf*. **~y** *n* psicologia *f*

psychopath /'saɪkəpæθ/ *n* psicopatico, -a *mf*

P.T.O. *abbr* (**please turn over**) vedi retro

pub /pʌb/ *n fam* pub *m inv*

puberty /'pjuːbətɪ/ *n* pubertà *f*

public /'pʌblɪk/ *a* pubblico ● *n* **the ~** il pubblico; **in ~** in pubblico

publican /'pʌblɪkən/ *n* gestore, -trice *mf*/proprietario, -a *mf* di un pub

publication /pʌblɪ'keɪʃn/ *n* pubblicazione *f*

public: ~ con'venience *n* gabinetti *mpl* pubblici. **~ 'holiday** *n* festa *f* nazionale. **~ 'house** *n* pub *m inv*

publicity /pʌb'lɪsɪtɪ/ *n* pubblicità *f*

publicize /'pʌblɪsaɪz/ *vt* pubblicizzare

public 'library *n* biblioteca *f* pubblica

publicly /'pʌblɪklɪ/ *adv* pubblicamente

public: ~ re'lations pubbliche relazioni *fpl*. **~ school** *n* scuola *f* privata; *Am* scuola *f* pubblica. **~-'spirited** *a* **be ~spirited** essere dotato di senso civico. **~ 'transport** *n* mezzi *mpl* pubblici

publish /'pʌblɪʃ/ *vt* pubblicare. **~er** *n* editore *m*; (*firm*) editore *m*, casa *f* editrice. **~ing** *n* editoria *f*

pudding /'pʊdɪŋ/ *n* dolce *m* cotto al vapore; (*course*) dolce *m*

puddle /'pʌdl/ *n* pozzanghera *f*

pudgy /'pʌdʒɪ/ *a* (**-ier, -iest**) grassoccio

puff /pʌf/ *n* (*of wind*) soffio *m*; (*of smoke*) tirata *f*; (*for powder*) piumino *m* ● *vt* sbuffare. **puff at** *vt* tirare boccate da ⟨*pipe*⟩. **puff out** *vt* lasciare senza fiato ⟨*person*⟩; spegnere ⟨*candle*⟩. **~ed** *a* (*out of breath*) senza fiato. **~ pastry** *n* pasta *f* sfoglia

puffy /'pʌfɪ/ *a* gonfio

pull /pʊl/ *n* trazione *f*; (*fig: attraction*) attrazione *f*; (*fam: influence*) influenza *f* ● *vt* tirare; estrarre ⟨*tooth*⟩; stirarsi ⟨*muscle*⟩; **~ faces** far boccace; **~ oneself together** cercare di controllarsi; **~ one's weight** mettercela tutta; **~ sb's leg** *fam* prendere in giro qcno. **pull down** *vt* (*demolish*) demolire. **pull in** *vi Auto* accostare. **pull off** *vt* togliere; *fam* azzeccare. **pull out** *vt* tirar fuori ● *vi Auto* spostarsi; (*of competition*) ritirarsi. **pull through** *vi* (*recover*) farcela. **pull up** *vt* sradicare ⟨*plant*⟩; (*reprimand*) rimproverare ● *vi Auto* fermarsi

pulley /'pʊlɪ/ *n Techn* puleggia *f*

pullover /'pʊləʊvə(r)/ *n* pullover *m inv*

pulp /pʌlp/ *n* poltiglia *f*; (*of fruit*) polpa *f*; (*for paper*) pasta *f*

pulpit /'pʊlpɪt/ *n* pulpito *m*

pulsate /pʌl'seɪt/ *vi* pulsare

pulse /pʌls/ *n* polso *m*

pulses /'pʌlsɪz/ *npl* legumi *mpl* secchi

pulverize /'pʌlvəraɪz/ *vt* polverizzare

pumice /'pʌmɪs/ *n* pomice *f*

pummel /'pʌml/ *vt* (*pt/pp* **pummelled**) prendere a pugni

pump /pʌmp/ *n* pompa *f* ● *vt* pompare; **~ sb for sth** *fam* cercare di estorcere qcsa da qcno. **pump up** *vt* (*inflate*) gonfiare

pumpkin /'pʌmpkɪn/ *n* zucca *f*

pun /pʌn/ *n* gioco *m* di parole

punch¹ /pʌntʃ/ *n* pugno *m*; (*device*) pinza *f* per forare ● *vt* dare un pugno a; forare ⟨*ticket*⟩; perforare ⟨*hole*⟩

punch² *n* (*drink*) ponce *m inv*

punch: ~ line *n* battuta *f* finale. **~-up** *n* rissa *f*

punctual /'pʌŋktjʊəl/ *a* puntuale. **~ity** /-'ælətɪ/ *n* puntualità *f*. **~ly** *adv* puntualmente

punctuat|e /'pʌŋktjʊeɪt/ *vt* punteggiare. **~ion** /-'eɪʃn/ *n* punteggiatura *f*. **~ion mark** *n* segno *m* di interpunzione

puncture /'pʌŋktʃə(r)/ *n* foro *m*; (*tyre*) foratura *f* ● *vt* forare

pungent /'pʌndʒənt/ a acre
punish /'pʌnɪʃ/ vt punire. **~able** /-əbl/ a punibile. **~ment** n punizione f
punitive /'pju:nɪtɪv/ a punitivo
punk /pʌŋk/ n punk m inv
punnet /'pʌnɪt/ n cestello m (per frutta)
punt /pʌnt/ n (boat) barchino m
punter /'pʌntə(r)/ n (gambler) scommettitore, -trice mf; (client) consumatore, -trice mf
puny /'pju:nɪ/ a (-ier, -iest) striminzito
pup /pʌp/ n = **puppy**
pupil /'pju:pl/ n alluno, -a mf; (of eye) pupilla f
puppet /'pʌpɪt/ n marionetta f; (glove ~, fig) burattino m
puppy /'pʌpɪ/ n cucciolo m
purchase /'pɜ:tʃəs/ n acquisto m; (leverage) presa f ● vt acquistare. **~r** n acquirente mf
pure /pjʊə(r)/ a puro
purée /'pjʊəreɪ/ n purè m inv
purely /'pjʊəlɪ/ adv puramente
purgatory /'pɜ:gətrɪ/ n purgatorio m
purge /pɜ:dʒ/ Pol n epurazione f ● vt epurare
puri|fication /pjʊərɪfɪ'keɪʃn/ n purificazione f. **~fy** /'pjʊərɪfaɪ/ vt (pt/pp **-ied**)
puritan /'pjʊərɪtən/ n puritano, -a mf. **~ical** a puritano
purity /'pjʊərɪtɪ/ n purità f
purple /'pɜ:pl/ a viola inv
purpose /'pɜ:pəs/ n scopo m; (determination) fermezza f; **on** ~ apposta. **~-built** a costruito ad hoc. **~ful** a deciso. **~fully** adv con decisione. **~ly** adv apposta
purr /pɜ:(r)/ vi (cat:) fare le fusa
purse /pɜ:s/ n borsellino m; (Am: handbag) borsa f ● vt increspare (lips)
pursue /pə'sju:/ vt inseguire; fig proseguire. **~r** /-ə(r)/ n inseguitore, -trice mf
pursuit /pə'sju:t/ n inseguimento m; (fig: of happiness) ricerca f; (pastime) attività f inv; **in** ~ all'inseguimento
pus /pʌs/ n pus m
push /pʊʃ/ n spinta f; (fig: effort) sforzo m; (drive) iniziativa f; **at a** ~ in caso di bisogno; **get the** ~ fam essere licenziato ● vt spingere; premere (button); (pressurize) far pressione su. **be ~ed for time** fam non avere tempo ● vi spingere. **push aside** vt scostare. **push back** vt respingere. **push off** vt togliere ● vi (fam: leave) levarsi dai

piedi. **push on** vi (continue) continuare.
push up vt alzare (price)
push: **~-button** n pulsante m. **~-chair** n passeggino m. **~-over** n fam bazzecola f. **~-up** n flessione f
pushy /'pʊʃɪ/ a fam troppo intraprendente
puss /pʊs/ n, **pussy** /'pʊsɪ/ n micio m
put /pʊt/ vt (pt/pp **put**, pres p **putting**) mettere; ~ **the cost at 5 million** valutare il costo a 5 milioni ● vi ~ **to sea** salpare. **put aside** vt mettere da parte. **put away** vt mettere via. **put back** vt rimettere; mettere indietro (clock). **put by** vt mettere da parte. **put down** vt mettere giù; (suppress) reprimere; (kill) sopprimere; (write) annotare; ~ **one's foot down** fam essere fermo; Auto dare un'accelerata; ~ **down to** (attribute) attribuire. **put forward** vt avanzare; mettere avanti (clock). **put in** vt (insert) introdurre; (submit) presentare ● vi ~ **in for** far domanda di. **put off** vt spegnere (light); (postpone) rimandare; ~ **sb off** tenere a bada qcno; (deter) smontare qcno; (disconcert) distrarre qcno; ~ **sb off sth** (disgust) disgustare qcno di qcsa. **put on** vt mettersi (clothes); mettere (brake); Culin mettere su; accendere (light); mettere in scena (play); prendere (accent); ~ **on weight** mettere su qualche chilo. **put out** vt spegnere (fire, light); tendere (hand); (inconvenience) creare degli inconvenienti a. **put through** vt far passare; Teleph **I'll** ~ **you through to him** glielo passo. **put up** vt alzare; erigere (building); montare (tent); aprire (umbrella); affiggere (notice); aumentare (price); ospitare (guest); ~ **sb up to sth** mettere qcsa in testa a qcno ● vi (at hotel) stare; ~ **up with** sopportare ● a **stay ~!** rimani lì!
putty /'pʌtɪ/ n mastice m
put-up /'pʊtʌp/ a ~ **job** truffa f
puzzl|e /'pʌzl/ n enigma m; (jigsaw) puzzle m inv ● vt lasciare perplesso ● vi **~e over** scervellarsi su. **~ing** a inspiegabile
pygmy /'pɪgmɪ/ n pigmeo, -a mf
pyjamas /pə'dʒɑ:məz/ npl pigiama msg
pylon /'paɪlən/ n pilone m
pyramid /'pɪrəmɪd/ n piramide f
python /'paɪθn/ n pitone m

Qq

quack¹ /kwæk/ n qua qua m inv ● vi fare qua qua

quack² n (doctor) ciarlatano m

quad /kwɒd/ n (fam: court) = **quadrangle**. **~s** pl = **quadruplets**

quadrangle /'kwɒdræŋgl/ n quadrangolo m; (court) cortile m quadrangolare

quadruped /'kwɒdrʊped/ n quadrupede m

quadruple /'kwɒdrʊpl/ a quadruplo ● vt quadruplicare ● vi quadruplicarsi. **~ts** /-plɪts/ npl quattro gemelli mpl

quagmire /'kwɒgmaɪə(r)/ n pantano m

quaint /kweɪnt/ a pittoresco; (odd) bizzarro

quake /kweɪk/ n fam terremoto m ● vi tremare

qualification /kwɒlɪfɪ'keɪʃn/ n qualifica f. **~ied** /-faɪd/ a qualificato; (limited) con riserva

qualify /'kwɒlɪfaɪ/ v (pt/pp -**ied**) ● vt ⟨course:⟩ dare la qualifica a (**as** di); (entitle) dare diritto a; (limit) precisare ● vi ottenere la qualifica; Sport qualificarsi

quality /'kwɒlətɪ/ n qualità f inv

qualm /kwɑːm/ n scrupolo m

quandary /'kwɒndərɪ/ n dilemma m

quantity /'kwɒntətɪ/ n quantità f inv; **in ~** in grande quantità

quarantine /'kwɒrəntiːn/ n quarantena f

quarrel /'kwɒrəl/ n lite f ● vi (pt/pp **quarrelled**) litigare. **~some** a litigioso

quarry¹ /'kwɒrɪ/ n (prey) preda f

quarry² n cava f

quart /kwɔːt/ n 1.14 litro

quarter /'kwɔːtə(r)/ n quarto m; (of year) trimestre m; Am 25 centesimi mpl; **~s** pl Mil quartiere msg; **at** [**a**] **~ to six** alle sei meno un quarto ● vt dividere in quattro. **~·'final** n quarto m di finale

quarterly /'kwɔːtəlɪ/ a trimestrale ● adv trimestralmente

quartet /kwɔː'tet/ n quartetto m

quartz /kwɔːts/ n quarzo m. **~ watch** n orologio m al quarzo

quash /kwɒʃ/ vt annullare; soffocare (rebellion)

quaver /'kweɪvə(r)/ vi tremolare

quay /kiː/ n banchina f

queasy /'kwiːzɪ/ a **I feel ~** ho la nausea

queen /kwiːn/ n regina f. **~ mother** n regina f madre

queer /kwɪə(r)/ a strano; (dubious) sospetto; (fam: homosexual) finocchio ● n fam finocchio m

quell /kwel/ vt reprimere

quench /kwentʃ/ vt **~ one's thirst** dissetarsi

query /'kwɪərɪ/ n domanda f; (question mark) punto m interrogativo ● vt (pt/pp -**ied**) interrogare; (doubt) mettere in dubbio

quest /kwest/ n ricerca f (**for** di)

question /'kwestʃn/ n domanda f; (for discussion) questione f; **out of the ~** fuori discussione; **without ~** senza dubbio; **in ~** in questione ● vt interrogare; (doubt) mettere in dubbio. **~able** /-əbl/ a discutibile. **~ mark** n punto m interrogativo

questionnaire /kwestʃə'neə(r)/ n questionario m

queue /kjuː/ n coda f, fila f ● vi **~** [**up**] mettersi in coda (**for** per)

quick /kwɪk/ a veloce; **be ~!** sbrigati!; **have a ~ meal** fare uno spuntino ● adv in fretta ● n **be cut to the ~** fig essere punto sul vivo. **~ly** adv in fretta. **~-tempered** a collerico

quid /kwɪd/ n inv fam sterlina f

quiet /'kwaɪət/ a (calm) tranquillo; (silent) silenzioso; (voice, music) basso; **keep ~ about** fam non raccontare a nessuno ● n quiete f; **on the ~** di nascosto. **~ly** adv (peacefully) tranquillamente; ⟨say⟩ a bassa voce

quiet|en /'kwaɪətn/ vt calmare. **quieten down** vi calmarsi. **~ness** n quiete f

quilt /kwɪlt/ n piumino m. **~ed** a trapuntato

quins /kwɪnz/ npl fam = **quintuplets**

quintet /kwɪn'tet/ n quintetto m

quintuplets /'kwɪntjʊplɪts/ npl cinque gemelli mpl

quip /kwɪp/ n battuta f

quirk /kwɜːk/ n stranezza f

quit /kwɪt/ v (pt/pp quitted, quit) ● vt lasciare; (give up) smettere (doing of fare) ● vi (fam: resign) andarsene; Comput uscire; **give sb notice to ~** ⟨landlord:⟩ dare a qcno il preavviso di sfratto

quite /kwaɪt/ adv (fairly) abbastanza; (completely) completamente; (really) veramente; **~ [so]!** proprio così!; **~ a few** parecchi

quits /kwɪts/ a pari

quiver /'kwɪvə(r)/ vi tremare

quiz /kwɪz/ n (game) quiz m inv ● vt (pt/pp quizzed) interrogare

quota /'kwəʊtə/ n quota f

quotation /kwəʊ'teɪʃn/ n citazione f; (price) preventivo m; (of shares) quota f. **~ marks** npl virgolette fpl

quote /kwəʊt/ n fam = quotation; **in ~s** tra virgolette ● vt citare; quotare (price)

Rr

---

rabbi /'ræbaɪ/ n rabbino m; (title) rabbi

rabbit /'ræbɪt/ n coniglio m

rabble /'ræbl/ n the ~ la plebaglia

rabies /'reɪbiːz/ n rabbia f

race¹ /reɪs/ n (people) razza f

race² n corsa f ● vi correre ● vt gareggiare con; fare correre (horse)

race: **~course** n ippodromo m. **~horse** n cavallo m da corsa. **~-track** n pista f

racial /'reɪʃl/ a razziale. **~ism** n razzismo m

racing /'reɪsɪŋ/ n corse fpl; (horse-) corse fpl dei cavalli. **~ car** n macchina f da corsa. **~ driver** n corridore m automobilistico

racis|m /'reɪsɪzm/ n razzismo m. **~t** /-ɪst/ a razzista ● n razzista mf

rack¹ /ræk/ n (for bikes) rastrelliera f; (for luggage) portabagagli m inv; (for plates) scolapiatti m inv ● vt **~ one's brains** scervellarsi

rack² n **go to ~ and ruin** andare in rovina

racket¹ /'rækɪt/ n Sport racchetta f

racket² n (din) chiasso m; (swindle) truffa f; (crime) racket m inv, giro m

radar /'reɪdɑː(r)/ n radar m

radian|ce /'reɪdɪəns/ n radiosità f. **~t** a raggiante

radiat|e /'reɪdɪeɪt/ vt irradiare ● vi ⟨heat:⟩ irradiarsi. **~ion** /-'eɪʃn/ n radiazione f

radiator /'reɪdɪeɪtə(r)/ n radiatore m

radical /'rædɪkl/ a radicale ● n radicale mf. **~ly** adv radicalmente

radio /'reɪdɪəʊ/ n radio f inv

radio|active a radioattivo. **~ac'tivity** n radioattività f

radiograph|er /reɪdɪ'ɒɡrəfə(r)/ n radiologo, -a mf. **~y** n radiografia f

radio'therapy n radioterapia f

radish /'rædɪʃ/ n ravanello m

radius /'reɪdɪəs/ n (pl -dii /-dɪaɪ/) raggio m

raffle /'ræfl/ n lotteria f

raft /rɑːft/ n zattera f

rafter /'rɑːftə(r)/ n trave f

rag /ræɡ/ n straccio m; (pej: newspaper) giornalaccio m; **in ~s** stracciato

rage /reɪdʒ/ n rabbia f; **all the ~** fam all'ultima moda ● vi infuriarsi; ⟨storm:⟩ infuriare; ⟨epidemic:⟩ imperversare

ragged /'ræɡɪd/ a logoro; ⟨edge⟩ frastagliato

raid /reɪd/ n (by thieves) rapina f; Mil incursione f, raid m inv; (police) irruzione f ● vt Mil fare un'incursione in; ⟨police, burglars:⟩ fare irruzione in. **~er** n (of bank) rapinatore, -trice mf

rail /reɪl/ n ringhiera f; (hand~) ringhiera f; Naut parapetto m; **by ~** per ferrovia

railroad n Am = railway

railway n ferrovia f. **~man** n ferroviere m. **~ station** n stazione f ferroviaria

rain /reɪn/ n pioggia f ● vi piovere

rain: **~bow** n arcobaleno m. **~coat** n impermeabile m. **~fall** n precipitazione f [atmosferica]

rainy /'reɪnɪ/ a (-ier, -iest) piovoso

raise /reɪz/ n Am aumento m ● vt alza

re; levarsi ⟨hat⟩; allevare ⟨children, animals⟩; sollevare ⟨question⟩; ottenere ⟨money⟩

raisin /'reɪzn/ n uva f passa

rake /reɪk/ n rastrello m ● vt rastrellare. **rake up** vt raccogliere col rastrello; fam rivangare

rally /'rælɪ/ n raduno m; Auto rally m inv; Tennis scambio m ● v (pt/pp -ied) ● vt radunare ● vi radunarsi; ⟨recover strength⟩ riprendersi

ram /ræm/ n montone m; Astr Ariete m ● vt (pt/pp **rammed**) cozzare contro

RAM /ræm/ n [memoria f] RAM f

ramble /'ræmbl/ n escursione f ● vi gironzolare; ⟨in speech⟩ divagare. **~er** n escursionista mf; ⟨rose⟩ rosa f rampicante. **~ing** a ⟨in speech⟩ sconnesso; ⟨club⟩ escursionistico

ramp /ræmp/ n rampa f; Aeron scaletta f mobile ⟨di aerei⟩

rampage /'ræmpeɪdʒ/ n **be/go on the ~** vi **~ through the streets** scatenarsi per le strade

rampant /'ræmpənt/ a dilagante

rampart /'ræmpɑːt/ n bastione f

ramshackle /'ræmʃækl/ a sgangherato

ran /ræn/ see **run**

ranch /rɑːntʃ/ n ranch m inv

rancid /'rænsɪd/ a rancido

rancour /'ræŋkə(r)/ n rancore m

random /'rændəm/ a casuale; **~ sample** campione m a caso ● n **at ~** a casaccio

randy /'rændɪ/ a (-ier, -iest) fam eccitato

rang /ræŋ/ see **ring²**

range /reɪndʒ/ n serie f; Comm, Mus gamma f; ⟨of mountains⟩ catena f; ⟨distance⟩ raggio m; ⟨for shooting⟩ portata f; ⟨stove⟩ cucina f economica; **at a ~ of** a una distanza di ● vi estendersi; **~ from... to...** andare da... a... **~r** n guardia f forestale

rank /ræŋk/ n ⟨row⟩ riga f; Mil grado m; ⟨social position⟩ rango m; **the ~ and file** la base; **the ~s** pl Mil i soldati semplici ● vt ⟨place⟩ annoverare (**among** tra) ● vi ⟨be placed⟩ collocarsi

rankle /'ræŋkl/ vi fig bruciare

ransack /'rænsæk/ vt rovistare; ⟨pillage⟩ saccheggiare

ransom /'rænsəm/ n riscatto m; **hold sb to ~** tenere qcno in ostaggio ⟨per il riscatto⟩

rant /rænt/ vi **~ [and rave]** inveire;

what's he ~ing on about? cosa sta blaterando?

rap /ræp/ n colpo m ⟨secco⟩; Mus rap m ● v (pt/pp **rapped**) ● vt dare colpetti a ● vi **~ at** bussare a

rape /reɪp/ n ⟨sexual⟩ stupro m ● vt violentare, stuprare

rapid /'ræpɪd/ a rapido. **~ity** /rə'pɪdətɪ/ n rapidità f. **~ly** adv rapidamente

rapids /'ræpɪdz/ npl rapida fsg

rapist /'reɪpɪst/ n violentatore m

rapport /ræ'pɔː(r)/ n rapporto m di intesa

rapture /'ræptʃə(r)/ n estasi f. **~ous** /-rəs/ a entusiastico

rare¹ /reə(r)/ a raro. **~ly** adv raramente

rare² a Culin al sangue

rarefied /'reərɪfaɪd/ a rarefatto

rarity /'reərətɪ/ n rarità f

rascal /'rɑːskl/ n mascalzone m

rash¹ /ræʃ/ n Med eruzione f

rash² a avventato. **~ly** adv avventatamente

rasher /'ræʃə(r)/ n fetta f di pancetta

rasp /rɑːsp/ n ⟨noise⟩ stridio m. **~ing** a stridente

raspberry /'rɑːzbərɪ/ n lampone m

rat /ræt/ n topo m; ⟨fam: person⟩ carogna f; **smell a ~** fam sentire puzzo di bruciato

rate /reɪt/ n ⟨speed⟩ velocità f inv; ⟨of payment⟩ tariffa f; ⟨of exchange⟩ tasso m; **~s** pl ⟨taxes⟩ imposte fpl comunali sui beni immobili; **at any ~** in ogni caso; **at this ~** di questo passo ● vt stimare; **~ among** annoverare tra ● vi **~ as** essere considerato

rather /'rɑːðə(r)/ adv piuttosto; **~!** eccomel; **~ too...** un po' troppo...

ratification /rætɪfɪ'keɪʃn/ n ratifica f. **~fy** /'rætɪfaɪ/ vt (pt/pp -**ied**) ratificare

rating /'reɪtɪŋ/ n **~s** pl Radio, TV indice m d'ascolto, audience f inv

ratio /'reɪʃɪəʊ/ n rapporto m

ration /'ræʃn/ n razione f ● vt razionare

rational /'ræʃənl/ a razionale. **~ize** vt/i razionalizzare

'rat race n fam corsa f al successo

rattle /'rætl/ n tintinnio m; ⟨toy⟩ sonaglio m ● vi tintinnare ● vt ⟨shake⟩ scuotere; fam innervosire. **rattle off** vt fam sciorinare

'rattlesnake n serpente m a sonagli

raucous /'rɔːkəs/ a rauco

rave /reɪv/ vi vaneggiare; **~ about** andare in estasi per

raven /'reɪvn/ n corvo m imperiale

ravenous /'rævənəs/ a ⟨person⟩ affamato

ravine /rə'vi:n/ n gola f

raving /'reɪvɪŋ/ a ~ **mad** fam matto da legare

ravishing /'rævɪʃɪŋ/ a incantevole

raw /rɔ:/ a crudo; (not processed) grezzo; ⟨weather⟩ gelido; (inexperienced) inesperto; **get a ~ deal** fam farsi fregare. ~ **ma'terials** npl materie fpl prime

ray /reɪ/ n raggio m; ~ **of hope** barlume m di speranza

raze /reɪz/ vt ~ **to the ground** radere al suolo

razor /'reɪzə(r)/ n rasoio m. ~ **blade** n lametta f da barba

re /ri:/ prep con riferimento a

reach /ri:tʃ/ n portata f; **within ~** a portata di mano; **out of ~ of** fuori dalla portata di; **within easy ~** facilmente raggiungibile ● vt arrivare a ⟨place, decision⟩; (contact) contattare; (pass) passare; **I can't ~ it** non ci arrivo ● vi arrivare (**to** a); ~ **for** allungare la mano per prendere

re'act /rɪ-/ vi reagire

re'action /rɪ-/ n reazione f. ~**ary** a & n reazionario, -a mf

reactor /rɪ'æktə(r)/ n reattore m

read /ri:d/ vt (pt/pp read /red/) leggere; Univ studiare ● vi leggere; ⟨instrument⟩ indicare. **read out** vt leggere ad alta voce

readable /'ri:dəbl/ a piacevole a leggersi; (legible) leggibile

reader /'ri:də(r)/ n lettore, -trice mf; (book) antologia f

readily /'redɪlɪ/ adv volentieri; (easily) facilmente. ~**ness** n disponibilità f; **in ~ness** pronto

reading /'ri:dɪŋ/ n lettura f

rea'djust /ri:-/ vt regolare di nuovo ● vi riabituarsi (**to** a)

ready /'redɪ/ a (-ier, -iest) pronto; (quick) veloce; **get ~** prepararsi

ready: ~-**'made** a confezionato. ~ **'money** n contanti mpl. ~-**to-'wear** a prêt-à-porter

real /ri:l/ a vero; (increase) reale ● adv Am fam veramente. ~ **estate** n beni mpl immobili

realis|m /'rɪəlɪzm/ n realismo m. ~**t** ·lɪst/ n realista mf. ~**tic** /-'lɪstɪk/ a realistico

reality /rɪ'ælətɪ/ n realtà f inv

realization /rɪələ'zeɪʃn/ n realizzazione f

realize /'rɪəlaɪz/ vt realizzare

really /'rɪəlɪ/ adv davvero

realm /relm/ n regno m

realtor /'rɪəltə(r)/ n Am agente mf immobiliare

reap /ri:p/ vt mietere

reap'pear /ri:-/ vi riapparire

rear[1] ·/rɪə(r)/ a posteriore; Auto di dietro; ~ **end** fam didietro m ● n **the** ~ (of building) il retro; (of bus, plane) la parte posteriore; **from the** ~ da dietro

rear[2] vt allevare ● vi ~ [**up**] ⟨horse:⟩ impennarsi

'rear-light n luce f posteriore

re'arm /ri:-/ vt riarmare ● vi riarmarsi

rear'range /ri:-/ vt cambiare la disposizione di

rear-view 'mirror n Auto specchietto m retrovisore

reason /'ri:zn/ n ragione f; **within ~** nei limiti del ragionevole ● vi ragionare; ~ **with** cercare di far ragionare. ~**able** /-əbl/ a ragionevole. ~**ably** /-əblɪ/ adv (in reasonable way, fairly) ragionevolmente

reas'sur|ance /ri:-/ n rassicurazione f. ~**e** vt rassicurare; ~**e sb of sth** rassicurare qcno su qcsa. ~**ing** a rassicurante

rebate /'ri:beɪt/ n rimborso m; (discount) deduzione f

rebel[1] /'rebl/ n ribelle mf

rebel[2] /rɪ'bel/ vi (pt/pp rebelled) ribellarsi. ~**lion** /-jən/ n ribellione f. ~**lious** /-jəs/ a ribelle

re'bound[1] /rɪ-/ vi rimbalzare; fig ricadere

'rebound[2] /ri:-/ n rimbalzo m

rebuff /rɪ'bʌf/ n rifiuto m

re'build /ri:-/ vt (pt/pp -**built**) ricostruire

rebuke /rɪ'bju:k/ vt rimproverare

rebuttal /rɪ'bʌtl/ n rifiuto m

re'call /rɪ-/ n richiamo m; **beyond ~** irrevocabile ● vt richiamare; riconvocare ⟨diplomat, parliament⟩; (remember) rievocare

recap /'ri:kæp/ vt/i fam = **recapitulate** ● n ricapitolazione f

recapitulate /ri:kə'pɪtjʊleɪt/ vt/i ricapitolare

re'capture /ri:-/ vt riconquistare; ricatturare ⟨person, animal⟩

reced|e /rɪ'si:d/ vi allontanarsi. ~**ing** a ⟨forehead, chin⟩ sfuggente; **have ~ing hair** essere stempiato

receipt /rɪ'si:t/ n ricevuta f; (receiving) ricezione f; ~**s** pl Comm entrate fpl

receive /rɪ'siːv/ vt ricevere. **~r** n Teleph ricevitore m; Radio, TV apparecchio m ricevente; (of stolen goods) ricettatore, -trice mf

recent /'riːsnt/ a recente. **~ly** adv recentemente

receptacle /rɪ'septəkl/ n recipiente m

reception /rɪ'sepʃn/ n ricevimento m; (welcome) accoglienza f; Radio ricezione f; ~ [**desk**] (in hotel) reception f inv. **~ist** n persona f alla reception

receptive /rɪ'septɪv/ a ricettivo

recess /rɪ'ses/ n rientranza f; (holiday) vacanza f; Am Sch intervallo m

recession /rɪ'seʃn/ n recessione f

re'charge /riː-/ vt ricaricare

recipe /'resəpɪ/ n ricetta f

recipient /rɪ'sɪpɪənt/ n (of letter) destinatario, -a mf; (of money) beneficiario, -a mf

recipro|cal /rɪ'sɪprəkl/ a reciproco. **~cate** /-keɪt/ vt ricambiare

recital /rɪ'saɪtl/ n recital m inv

recite /rɪ'saɪt/ vt recitare; (list) elencare

reckless /'reklɪs/ a (action, decision) sconsiderato; **be a ~ driver** guidare in modo spericolato. **~ly** adv in modo sconsiderato. **~ness** n sconsideratezza f

reckon /'rekən/ vt calcolare; (consider) pensare. **reckon on/with** vt fare i conti con

re'claim /rɪ-/ vt reclamare; bonificare (land)

reclin|e /rɪ'klaɪn/ vi sdraiarsi. **~ing** a (seat) reclinabile

recluse /rɪ'kluːs/ n recluso, -a mf

recognition /rekəg'nɪʃn/ n riconoscimento m; **beyond ~** irriconoscibile

recognize /'rekəgnaɪz/ vt riconoscere

re'coil /rɪ-/ vi (in fear) indietreggiare

recollect /rekə'lekt/ vt ricordare. **~ion** /-ekʃn/ n ricordo m

recommend /rekə'mend/ vt raccomandare. **~ation** /-'deɪʃn/ n raccomandazione f

recompense /'rekəmpens/ n ricompensa f

recon|cile /'rekənsaɪl/ vt riconciliare; conciliare (facts); **~cile oneself to** rassegnarsi a. **~ciliation** /-sɪlɪ'eɪʃn/ n riconciliazione f

recon'dition /riː-/ vt ripristinare. **~ed engine** n motore m che ha subito riparazioni

reconnaissance /rɪ'kɒnɪsns/ n Mil ricognizione f

reconnoitre /rekə'nɔɪtə(r)/ vi (pres p -tring) fare una recognizione

recon'sider /riː-/ vt riconsiderare

recon'struct /riː-/ vt ricostruire. **~ion** n ricostruzione f

record¹ /rɪ'kɔːd/ vt registrare; (make a note of) annotare

record² /'rekɔːd/ n (file) documentazione f; Mus disco m; Sport record m inv; **~s** pl (files) schedario msg; **keep a ~ of** tener nota di; **off the ~** in via ufficiosa; **have a [criminal] ~** avere la fedina penale sporca

recorder /rɪ'kɔːdə(r)/ n Mus flauto m dolce

recording /rɪ'kɔːdɪŋ/ n registrazione f

'record-player n giradischi m inv

recount /rɪ'kaʊnt/ vt raccontare

re-'count¹ /riː-/ vt ricontare (votes etc)

're-count² /'riː-/ n Pol nuovo conteggio m

recoup /rɪ'kuːp/ vt rifarsi di (losses)

recourse /rɪ'kɔːs/ n **have ~ to** ricorrere a

re-'cover /riː-/ vt rifoderare

recover /rɪ'kʌvə(r)/ vt/i recuperare. **~y** n recupero m; (of health) guarigione f

recreation /rekrɪ'eɪʃn/ n ricreazione f. **~al** a ricreativo

recrimination /rɪkrɪmɪ'neɪʃn/ n recriminazione f

recruit /rɪ'kruːt/ n Mil recluta f; **new ~** (member) nuovo, -a adepto, -a mf; (worker) neoassunto, -a mf ● vt assumere (staff). **~ment** n assunzione f

rectangle /'rektæŋgl/ n rettangolo m. **~ular** /-'tæŋgjʊlə(r)/ a rettangolare

rectify /'rektɪfaɪ/ vt (pt/pp -ied) rettificare

recuperate /rɪ'kuːpəreɪt/ vi ristabilirsi

recur /rɪ'kɜː(r)/ vi (pt/pp recurred) ricorrere; (illness:) ripresentarsi

recurren|ce /rɪ'kʌrəns/ n ricorrenza f; (of illness) ricomparsa f. **~t** a ricorrente

recycle /riː'saɪkl/ vt riciclare

red /red/ a (redder, reddest) rosso ● n rosso m; **in the ~** (account) scoperto. **R~ Cross** n Croce f rossa

redd|en /'redn/ vt arrossare ● vi arrossire. **~ish** a rossastro

re'decorate /riː-/ vt (paint) ridipingere; (wallpaper) ritappezzare

redeem /rɪ'diːm/ vt **~ing quality** unico aspetto m positivo

redemption /rɪ'dempʃn/ n riscatto m

rede'ploy /riː-/ vt ridistribuire

red: **~-haired** *a* con i capelli rossi. **~-'handed** *a* **catch sb ~-handed** cogliere qcno con le mani nel sacco. **~'herring** *n* diversione *f*. **~-hot** *a* rovente

red: **~ 'light** *n Auto* semaforo *m* rosso

re'double /ri:-/ *vt* raddoppiare

redress /rɪ'dres/ *n* riparazione *f* ● *vt* ristabilire *‹balance›*

red 'tape *n fam* burocrazia *f*

reduc|e /rɪ'dju:s/ *vt* ridurre; *(for)* consumare. **~tion** /-'dʌkʃn/ *n* riduzione *f*

redundan|cy /rɪ'dʌndənsɪ/ *n* licenziamento *m*; *(payment)* cassa *f* integrazione. **~t** superfluo; **make ~t** licenziare; **be made ~t** essere licenziato

reed /ri:d/ *n Bot* canna *f*

reef /ri:f/ *n* scogliera *f*

reek /ri:k/ *vi* puzzare **(of** di)

reel /ri:l/ *n* bobina *f* ● *vi (stagger)* vacillare. **reel off** *vt fig* snocciolare

refectory /rɪ'fektərɪ/ *n* refettorio *m*; *Univ* mensa *f* universitaria

refer /rɪ'fɜ:(r)/ *v (pt/pp referred)* ● *vt* rinviare *‹matter›* **(to** a); indirizzare *‹person›* ● *vi* **~ to** fare allusione a; *(consult)* rivolgersi a *‹book›*

referee /refə'ri:/ *n* arbitro *m*; *(for job)* garante *mf* ● *vt/i (pt/pp refereed)* arbitrare

reference /'refərəns/ *n* riferimento *m*; *(in book)* nota *f* bibliografica; *(for job)* referenza *f*; *Comm* **'your ~'** 'riferimento'; **with ~ to** con riferimento a; **make [a] ~ to** fare riferimento a. **~ book** *n* libro *m* di consultazione. **~ number** *n* numero *m* di riferimento

referendum /refə'rendəm/ *n* referendum *m inv*

re'fill¹ /ri:-/ *vt* riempire di nuovo; ricaricare *‹pen, lighter›*

'refill² /'ri:-/ *n (for pen)* ricambio *m*

refine /rɪ'faɪn/ *vt* raffinare. **~d** *a* raffinato. **~ment** *n* raffinatezza *f*; *Techn* raffinazione *f*. **~ry** /-ərɪ/ *n* raffineria *f*

reflect /rɪ'flekt/ *vt* riflettere; **be ~ed in** essere riflesso in ● *vi (think)* riflettere **(on** su); **~ badly on sb** *fig* mettere in cattiva luce qcno. **~ion** /-ekʃn/ *n* riflessione *f*; *(image)* immagine *m*; **on ~ion** dopo riflessione. **~ive** /-ɪv/ *a* riflessivo. **~or** *n* riflettore *m*

reflex /'ri:fleks/ *n* riflesso *m* ● *attrib* di riflesso

reflexive /rɪ'fleksɪv/ *a* riflessivo

reform /rɪ'fɔ:m/ *n* riforma *f* ● *vi* riformare ● *vi* correggersi. **R~ation** /refə'meɪʃn/ *n Relig* Riforma *f*. **~er** *n* riformatore, -trice *mf*

refrain¹ /rɪ'freɪn/ *n* ritornello *m*

refrain² *vi* astenersi **(from** da)

refresh /rɪ'freʃ/ *vt* rinfrescare. **~ing** *a* rinfrescante. **~ments** *npl* rinfreschi *mpl*

refrigerat|e /rɪ'frɪdʒəreɪt/ *vt* conservare in frigo. **~or** *n* frigorifero *m*

re'fuel /ri:-/ *v (pt/pp -fuelled)* ● *vt* rifornire *(di carburante)* ● *vi* fare rifornimento

refuge /'refju:dʒ/ *n* rifugio *m*; **take ~** rifugiarsi

refugee /refju'dʒi:/ *n* rifugiato, -a *mf*

'refund¹ /'ri:-/ *n* rimborso *m*

re'fund² /rɪ-/ *vt* rimborsare

refusal /rɪ'fju:zl/ *n* rifiuto *m*

refuse¹ /rɪ'fju:z/ *vt/i* rifiutare; **~ to do sth** rifiutare di fare qcsa

refuse² /'refju:s/ *n* rifiuti *mpl*. **~ collection** *n* raccolta *f* dei rifiuti

refute /rɪ'fju:t/ *vt* confutare

re'gain /rɪ-/ *vt* riconquistare

regal /'ri:gl/ *a* regale

regalia /rɪ'geɪlɪə/ *npl* insegne *fpl* reali

regard /rɪ'gɑ:d/ *n (heed)* riguardo *m*; *(respect)* considerazione *f*. **~s** *pl* saluti *mpl*; **send/give my ~s to your brother** salutami tuo fratello ● *vt (consider)* considerare **(as** come); **as ~s** riguardo a. **~ing** *prep* riguardo a. **~less** *adv* lo stesso; **~ of** senza badare a

regatta /rɪ'gætə/ *n* regata *f*

regenerate /rɪ'dʒenəreɪt/ *vt* rigenerare ● *vi* rigenerarsi

regime /reɪ'ʒi:m/ *n* regime *m*

regiment /'redʒɪmənt/ *n* reggimento *m*. **~al** /-'mentl/ *a* reggimentale. **~ation** /-mən'teɪʃn/ *n* irreggimentazione *f*

region /'ri:dʒən/ *n* regione *f*; **in the ~ of** *fig* approssimativamente. **~al** *a* regionale

register /'redʒɪstə(r)/ *n* registro *m* ● *vt* registrare; mandare per raccomandata *‹letter›*; assicurare *‹luggage›*; immatricolare *‹vehicle›*; mostrare *‹feeling›* ● *vi* *‹instrument:›* funzionare; *‹student:›* iscriversi **(for** a); **~ with** iscriversi nella lista di *‹doctor›*

registrar /redʒɪ'strɑ:(r)/ *n* ufficiale *m* di stato civile

registration /redʒɪ'streɪʃn/ *n (of vehicle)* immatricolazione *f*; *(of letter)* raccomandazione *f*; *(of luggage)* assicurazione *f*; *(for course)* iscrizione *f*. **~ number** *n Auto* [numero *m* di] targa *f*

registry office /'redʒɪstrɪ-/ n anagrafe f

regret /rɪ'gret/ n rammarico m ●vt (pt/pp **regretted**) rimpiangere; **I ~ that** mi rincresce che. **~fully** adv con rammarico

regrettab|le /rɪ'gretəbl/ a spiacevole. **~ly** adv spiacevolmente; (before adjective) deplorevolmente

regular /'regjʊlə(r)/ a regolare; (usual) abituale ●n cliente mf abituale. **~ity** /-'lærətɪ/ n regolarità f. **~ly** adv regolarmente

regulat|e /'regʊleɪt/ vt regolare. **~ion** /-'leɪʃn/ n (rule) regolamento m

rehabilitat|e /ri:hə'bɪlɪteɪt/ vt riabilitare. **~ion** /-'teɪʃn/ n riabilitazione f

rehears|al /rɪ'hɜ:sl/ n Theat prova f. **~e** vt/i provare

reign /reɪn/ n regno m ●vi regnare

reimburse /ri:ɪm'bɜ:s/ vt ~ **sb for sth** rimborsare qcsa a qcno

rein /reɪn/ n redine f

reincarnation /ri:ɪnkɑ:'neɪʃn/ n reincarnazione f

reinforce /ri:ɪn'fɔ:s/ vt rinforzare. **~d 'concrete** n cemento m armato. **~ment** n rinforzo m

reinstate /ri:ɪn'steɪt/ vt reintegrare

reiterate /ri:'ɪtəreɪt/ vt reiterare

reject /rɪ'dʒekt/ vt rifiutare. **~ion** /-ekʃn/ n rifiuto m; Med rigetto m

rejoic|e /rɪ'dʒɔɪs/ vi liter rallegrarsi. **~ing** n gioia f

rejuvenate /rɪ'dʒu:vəneɪt/ vt ringiovanire

relapse /rɪ'læps/ n ricaduta f ●vi ricadere

relate /rɪ'leɪt/ vt (tell) riportare; (connect) collegare ●vi ~ **to** riferirsi a; identificarsi con (person). **~d** a imparentato (**to** a); (ideas etc) affine

relation /rɪ'leɪʃn/ n rapporto m; (person) parente mf. **~ship** n rapporto m (blood tie) parentela f; (affair) relazione f

relative /'relətɪv/ n parente mf ●a relativo. **~ly** adv relativamente

relax /rɪ'læks/ vt rilassare; allentare (pace, grip) ●vi rilassarsi. **~ation** /ri:læk'seɪʃn/ n rilassamento m, relax m; (recreation) svago m. **~ing** a rilassante

relay[1] /ri:'leɪ/ vt (pt/pp **-layed**) ritrasmettere; Radio, TV trasmettere

relay[2] /'ri:leɪ/ n Electr relais m inv; **work in ~s** fare i turni. **~ [race]** n [corsa f a] staffetta f

release /rɪ'li:s/ n rilascio m; (of film) distribuzione f ●vt liberare; lasciare (hand); togliere (brake); distribuire (film); rilasciare (information etc)

relegate /'relɪgeɪt/ vt relegare; **be ~d** Sport essere retrocesso

relent /rɪ'lent/ vi cedere. **~less** a inflessibile; (unceasing) incessante. **~lessly** adv incessantemente

relevan|ce /'reləvəns/ n pertinenza f. **~t** a pertinente (**to** a)

reliab|ility /rɪlaɪə'bɪlətɪ/ n affidabilità f. **~le** /-'laɪəbl/ a affidabile. **~ly** adv in modo affidabile; **be ~ly informed** sapere da fonte certa

relian|ce /rɪ'laɪəns/ n fiducia f (**on** in). **~t** a fiducioso (**on** in)

relic /'relɪk/ n Relig reliquia f; **~s** pl resti mpl

relief /rɪ'li:f/ n sollievo m; (assistance) soccorso m; (distraction) diversivo m; (replacement) cambio m; (in art) rilievo m; **in ~** in rilievo. **~ map** n carta f in rilievo. **~ train** n treno m supplementare

relieve /rɪ'li:v/ vt alleviare; (take over from) dare il cambio a; ~ **of** liberare da (burden)

religion /rɪ'lɪdʒən/ n religione f

religious /rɪ'lɪdʒəs/ a religioso. **~ly** adv (conscientiously) scrupolosamente

relinquish /rɪ'lɪŋkwɪʃ/ vt abbandonare; ~ **sth to sb** rinunciare a qcsa in favore di qcno

relish /'relɪʃ/ n gusto m; Culin salsa f ●vt fig apprezzare

relo'cate /ri:-/ vt trasferire

reluctan|ce /rɪ'lʌktəns/ n riluttanza f. **~t** a riluttante. **~tly** adv a malincuore

rely /rɪ'laɪ/ vi (pt/pp **-ied**) ~ **on** dipendere da; (trust) contare su

remain /rɪ'meɪn/ vi restare. **~der** n resto m. **~ing** a restante. **~s** npl resti mpl; (dead body) spoglie fpl

remand /rɪ'mɑ:nd/ n **on ~** in custodia cautelare ●vt ~ **in custody** rinviare con detenzione provvisoria

remark /rɪ'mɑ:k/ n osservazione f ●vt osservare. **~able** /-əbl/ a notevole. **~ably** adv notevolmente

remarry /ri:-/ vi (pt/pp **-ied**) risposarsi

remedial /rɪ'mi:dɪəl/ a correttivo; Med curativo

remedy /'remədɪ/ n rimedio m (**for** contro) ●vt (pt/pp **-ied**) rimediare a

remember /rɪ'membə(r)/ vt ricordare,

ricordarsi; ~ **to do sth** ricordarsi di fare qcsa; ~ **me to him** salutamelo ● *vi* ricordarsi

remind /rɪˈmaɪnd/ *vt* ~ **sb of sth** ricordare qcsa a qcno. ~**er** *n* ricordo *m*; (*memo*) promemoria *m inv*; (*letter*) lettera *f* di sollecito

reminisce /remɪˈnɪs/ *vi* rievocare il passato. ~**nces** /-ənsɪz/ *npl* reminiscenze *fpl*. ~**nt** *a* **be** ~**nt of** richiamare alla memoria

remiss /rɪˈmɪs/ *a* negligente

remission /rɪˈmɪʃn/ *n* remissione *f*; (*of sentence*) condono *m*

remit /rɪˈmɪt/ *vt* (*pt/pp* **remitted**) rimettere ⟨*money*⟩. ~**tance** *n* rimessa *f*

remnant /ˈremnənt/ *n* resto *m*; (*of material*) scampolo *m*; (*trace*) traccia *f*

remonstrate /ˈremənstreɪt/ *vi* fare rimostranze ⟨**with sb** a qcno⟩

remorse /rɪˈmɔːs/ *n* rimorso *m*. ~**ful** *a* pieno di rimorso. ~**less** *a* spietato. ~**lessly** *adv* senza pietà

remote /rɪˈməʊt/ *a* remoto; (*slight*) minimo. ~ **access** *n Comput* accesso *m* remoto. ~ **con'trol** *n* telecomando *m*. ~-**con'trolled** *a* telecomandato. ~**ly** *adv* lontanamente; **be not** ~**ly**... non essere lontanamente...

re'movable /rɪ-/ *a* rimovibile

removal /rɪˈmuːvl/ *n* rimozione *f*; (*from house*) trasloco *m*. ~ **van** *n* camion *m inv* da trasloco

remove /rɪˈmuːv/ *vt* togliere; togliersi ⟨*clothes*⟩; eliminare ⟨*stain, doubts*⟩

remuneration /rɪmjuːnəˈreɪʃn/ *n* rimunerazione *f*. ~**ive** /-ˈmjuːnərətɪv/ *a* rimunerativo

render /ˈrendə(r)/ *vt* rendere ⟨*service*⟩

rendering /ˈrend(ə)rɪŋ/ *n Mus* interpretazione *f*

renegade /ˈrenɪgeɪd/ *n* rinnegato, -a *m*

renew /rɪˈnjuː/ *vt* rinnovare ⟨*contract*⟩. ~**al** *n* rinnovo *m*

renounce /rɪˈnaʊns/ *vt* rinunciare a

renovat|e /ˈrenəveɪt/ *vt* rinnovare. ~**ion** /-ˈveɪʃn/ *n* rinnovo *m*

renown /rɪˈnaʊn/ *n* fama *f*. ~**ed** *a* rinomato

rent /rent/ *n* affitto *m* ● *vt* affittare; ~ ⟨**out**⟩ dare in affitto. ~**al** *n* affitto *m*

renunciation /rɪnʌnsɪˈeɪʃn/ *n* rinuncia *f*

re'open /riː-/ *vt/i* riaprire

re'organize /riː-/ *vt* riorganizzare

rep /rep/ *n Comm* rappresentante *mf*; *Theat* ≈ teatro *m* stabile

repair /rɪˈpeə(r)/ *n* riparazione *f*; **in**

good/bad ~ in buone/cattive condizioni ● *vt* riparare

repatriat|e /riːˈpætrɪeɪt/ *vt* rimpatriare. ~**ion** /-ˈeɪʃn/ *n* rimpatrio *m*

re'pay /riː-/ *vt* (*pt/pp* **-paid**) ripagare. ~**ment** *n* rimborso *m*

repeal /rɪˈpiːl/ *n* abrogazione *f* ● *vt* abrogare

repeat /rɪˈpiːt/ *n TV* replica *f* ● *vt/i* ripetere; ~ **oneself** ripetersi. ~**ed** *a* ripetuto. ~**edly** *adv* ripetutamente

repel /rɪˈpel/ *vt* (*pt/pp* **repelled**) respingere; *fig* ripugnare. ~**lent** *a* ripulsivo

repent /rɪˈpent/ *vi* pentirsi. ~**ance** *n* pentimento *m*. ~**ant** *a* pentito

repercussions /riːpəˈkʌʃnz/ *npl* ripercussioni *fpl*

repertoire /ˈrepətwɑː(r)/ *n* repertorio *m*

repetit|ion /repɪˈtɪʃn/ *n* ripetizione *f*. ~**ive** /rɪˈpetɪtɪv/ *a* ripetitivo

re'place /rɪ-/ *vt* (*put back*) rimettere a posto; (*take the place of*) sostituire; ~ **sth with sth** sostituire qcsa con qcsa. ~**ment** *n* sostituzione *f*; (*person*) sostituto, -a *mf*. ~**ment part** *n* pezzo *m* di ricambio

'replay /ˈriː-/ *n Sport* partita *f* ripetuta; ⟨*action*⟩ ~ replay *m inv*

replenish /rɪˈplenɪʃ/ *vt* rifornire ⟨*stocks*⟩; (*refill*) riempire di nuovo

replica /ˈreplɪkə/ *n* copia *f*

reply /rɪˈplaɪ/ *n* risposta *f* ⟨**to** a⟩ ● *vt/i* (*pt/pp* **replied**) rispondere

report /rɪˈpɔːt/ *n* rapporto *m*; *TV, Radio* servizio *m*; *Journ* cronaca *f*; *Sch* pagella *f*; (*rumour*) diceria *f* ● *vt* riportare; ~ **sb to the police** denunciare qcno alla polizia ● *vi* riportare; (*present oneself*) presentarsi ⟨**to** a⟩. ~**edly** *adv* secondo quanto si dice. ~**er** *n* cronista *mf*, reporter *mf inv*

repose /rɪˈpəʊz/ *n* riposo *m*

repos'sess /riː-/ *vt* riprendere possesso di

reprehensible /reprɪˈhensəbl/ *a* riprovevole

represent /reprɪˈzent/ *vt* rappresentare

representative /reprɪˈzentətɪv/ *a* rappresentativo ● *n* rappresentante *mf*

repress /rɪˈpres/ *vt* reprimere. ~**ion** /-eʃn/ *n* repressione *f*. ~**ive** /-ɪv/ *a* repressivo

reprieve /rɪˈpriːv/ *n* commutazione *f* della pena capitale; (*postponement*) sospensione *f* della pena capitale; *fig* tre-

427

gua *f* ● *vt* sospendere la sentenza a; *fig* risparmiare

reprimand /'reprɪmɑːnd/ *n* rimprovero *m* ● *vt* rimproverare

'**reprint**[1] /'riː-/ *n* ristampa *f*

re'print[2] /riː-/ *vt* ristampare

reprisal /rɪ'praɪzl/ *n* rappresaglia *f*: **in ~** per rappresaglia contro

reproach /rɪ'prəʊtʃ/ *n* ammonimento *m* ● *vt* ammonire. **~ful** *a* riprovevole. **~fully** *adv* con aria di rimprovero

repro'duc|e /riː-/ *vt* riprodurre ● *vi* riprodursi. **~tion** /-'dʌkʃn/ *n* riproduzione *f*. **~tive** /-'dʌktɪv/ *a* riproduttivo

reprove /rɪ'pruːv/ *vt* rimproverare

reptile /'reptaɪl/ *n* rettile *m*

republic /rɪ'pʌblɪk/ *n* repubblica *f*. **~an** *a* repubblicano ● *n* repubblicano, -a *mf*

repudiate /rɪ'pjuːdɪeɪt/ *vt* ripudiare; respingere (*view, suggestion*)

repugnan|ce /rɪ'pʌgnəns/ *n* ripugnanza *f*. **~t** *a* ripugnante

repuls|ion /rɪ'pʌlʃn/ *n* repulsione *f*. **~ive** /-ɪv/ *a* ripugnante

roputable /'rɒpjʊtəbl/ *a* affidabile

reputation /repjʊ'teɪʃn/ *n* reputazione *f*

repute /rɪ'pjuːt/ *n* reputazione *f*. **~d** /-ɪd/ *a* presunto: **he is ~d to be** si presume che sia. **~dly** *adv* presumibilmente

request /rɪ'kwest/ *n* richiesta *f* ● *vt* richiedere. **~ stop** *n* fermata *f* a richiesta

require /rɪ'kwaɪə(r)/ *vt* (*need*) necessitare di; (*demand*) esigere. **~d** *a* richiesto: **I am ~d to do** si esige che io faccia. **~ment** *n* esigenza *f*; (*condition*) requisito *m*

requisite /'rekwɪzɪt/ *a* necessario ● *n* **toilet/travel ~s** *pl* articoli *mpl* da toilette/viaggio

re'sale /riː-/ *n* rivendita *f*

rescue /'reskjuː/ *n* salvataggio *m* ● *vt* salvare. **~r** *n* salvatore, -trice *mf*

research /rɪ'sɜːtʃ/ *n* ricerca *f* ● *vt* fare ricerche su: *Journ* fare un'inchiesta su ● *vi* **~ into** fare ricerche su. **~er** *n* ricercatore, -trice *mf*

resem|blance /rɪ'zembləns/ *n* rassomiglianza *f*. **~ble** /-bl/ *vt* rassomigliare a

resent /rɪ'zent/ *vt* risentirsi per. **~ful** *a* pieno di risentimento. **~fully** *adv* con risentimento. **~ment** *n* risentimento *m*

reservation /rezə'veɪʃn/ *n* (*booking*) prenotazione *f*; (*doubt, enclosure*) riserva *f*

reserve /rɪ'zɜːv/ *n* riserva *f*; (*shyness*) riserbo *m* ● *vt* riservare; riservarsi (*right*). **~d** *a* riservato

reservoir /'rezəvwɑː(r)/ *n* bacino *m* idrico

re'shape /riː-/ *vt* ristrutturare

re'shuffle /riː-/ *n Pol* rimpasto *m* ● *vt Pol* rimpastare

reside /rɪ'zaɪd/ *vi* risiedere

residence /'rezɪdəns/ *n* residenza *f*; (*stay*) soggiorno *m*. **~ permit** *n* permesso *m* di soggiorno

resident /'rezɪdənt/ *a* residente ● *n* residente *mf*. **~ial** /-'denʃl/ *a* residenziale

residue /'rezɪdjuː/ *n* residuo *m*

resign /rɪ'zaɪn/ *vt* dimettersi da; **~ oneself to** rassegnarsi a ● *vi* dare le dimissioni. **~ation** /rezɪg'neɪʃn/ *n* rassegnazione *f*; (*from job*) dimissioni *fpl*. **~ed** *a* rassegnato

resilient /rɪ'zɪlɪənt/ *a* elastico; *fig* con buone capacità di ripresa

resin /'rezɪn/ *n* resina *f*

resist /rɪ'zɪst/ *vt* resistere a ● *vi* resistere. **~ance** *n* resistenza *f*. **~ant** *a* resistente

resolut|e /'rezəluːt/ *a* risoluto. **~ely** *adv* con risolutezza. **~ion** /-'luːʃn/ *n* risolutezza *f*

resolve /rɪ'zɒlv/ *vt* **~ to do** decidere di fare

resonan|ce /'rezənəns/ *n* risonanza *f*. **~t** *a* risonante

resort /rɪ'zɔːt/ *n* (*place*) luogo *m* di villeggiatura: **as a last ~** come ultima risorsa ● *vi* **~ to** ricorrere a

resound /rɪ'zaʊnd/ *vi* risonare (**with** di). **~ing** *a* (*success*) risonante

resource /rɪ'sɔːs/ *n* **~s** *pl* risorse *fpl*. **~ful** *a* pieno di risorse; (*solution*) ingegnoso. **~fulness** *n* ingegnosità *f*

respect /rɪ'spekt/ *n* rispetto *m*; (*aspect*) aspetto *m*; **with ~ to** per quanto riguarda ● *vt* rispettare

respectability /rɪspektə'bɪlətɪ/ *n* rispettabilità *f*

respect|able /rɪ'spektəbl/ *a* rispettabile. **~ably** *adv* rispettabilmente. **~ful** *a* rispettoso

respective /rɪ'spektɪv/ *a* rispettivo. **~ly** *adv* rispettivamente

respiration /respɪ'reɪʃn/ *n* respirazione *f*

respite /'respaɪt/ *n* respiro *m*

respond /rɪ'spɒnd/ *vi* rispondere; (*react*) reagire (**to** a); (*patient:*) rispondere (**to** a)

response /rɪˈspɒns/ n risposta f; (reaction) reazione f

responsibility /rɪspɒnsɪˈbɪlətɪ/ n responsabilità f inv

responsib|le /rɪˈspɒnsəbl/ a responsabile; (job) impegnativo

responsive /rɪˈspɒnsɪv/ a be ~ (audience etc:) reagire; (brakes:) essere sensibile

rest[1] /rest/ n riposo m; Mus pausa f; have a ~ riposarsi ● vt (lean) appoggiare (on su); (place) appoggiare ● vi riposarsi; (elbows:) appoggiarsi; (hopes:) riposare; it ~s with you sta a te

rest[2] n the ~ il resto; (people) gli altri

restaurant /ˈrestərɒnt/ n ristorante m. ~ car n vagone m ristorante

restful /ˈrestfl/ a riposante

restive /ˈrestɪv/ a irrequieto

restless /ˈrestlɪs/ a nervoso

restoration /restəˈreɪʃn/ n (of building) restauro m

restore /rɪˈstɔː(r)/ vt ristabilire; restaurare (building); (give back) restituire

restrain /rɪˈstreɪn/ vt trattenere; ~ oneself controllarsi. ~ed a controllato. ~t n restrizione f; (moderation) ritegno m

restrict /rɪˈstrɪkt/ vt limitare; ~ oneself to limitarsi a. ~ion /-ɪkʃn/ n limite m; (restraint) restrizione f. ~ive /-ɪv/ a limitativo

'**rest room** n Am toilette f inv

result /rɪˈzʌlt/ n risultato m; as a ~ a causa (of di) ● vi ~ from risultare da; ~ in portare a

resume /rɪˈzjuːm/ vt/i riprendere

résumé /ˈrezjʊmeɪ/ n riassunto m; Am curriculum vitae m inv

resumption /rɪˈzʌmpʃn/ n ripresa f

resurgence /rɪˈsɜːdʒəns/ n rinascita f

resurrect /rezəˈrekt/ vt fig risuscitare. ~ion /-ekʃn/ n the R~ion Relig la Risurrezione

resuscitat|e /rɪˈsʌsɪteɪt/ vt rianimare. ~ion /-ˈteɪʃn/ n rianimazione f

retail /ˈriːteɪl/ n vendita f al minuto o al dettaglio ● a & adv al minuto ● vt vendere al minuto ● vi ~ at essere venduto al pubblico al prezzo di. ~er n dettagliante mf

retain /rɪˈteɪn/ vt conservare; (hold back) trattenere

retaliat|e /rɪˈtælɪeɪt/ vi vendicarsi. ~ion /-ˈeɪʃn/ n rappresaglia f; in ~ion for per rappresaglia contro

retarded /rɪˈtɑːdɪd/ a ritardato

retentive /rɪˈtentɪv/ a (memory) buono

rethink /riːˈθɪŋk/ vt (pt/pp rethought) ripensare

reticen|ce /ˈretɪsəns/ n reticenza f. ~t a reticente

retina /ˈretɪnə/ n retina f

retinue /ˈretɪnjuː/ n seguito m

retire /rɪˈtaɪə(r)/ vi andare in pensione; (withdraw) ritirarsi ● vt mandare in pensione (employee). ~d a in pensione. ~ment n pensione f; since my ~ment da quando sono andato in pensione

retiring /rɪˈtaɪərɪŋ/ a riservato

retort /rɪˈtɔːt/ n replica f ● vt ribattere

re'touch /riː-/ vt Phot ritoccare

re'trace /rɪ-/ vt ripercorrere; ~ one's steps ritornare sui propri passi

retract /rɪˈtrækt/ vt ritirare; ritrattare (statement, evidence) ● vi ritrarsi

re'train /riː-/ vt riqualificare ● vi riqualificarsi

retreat /rɪˈtriːt/ n ritirata f; (place) ritiro m ● vi ritirarsi; Mil battere in ritirata

re'trial /riː-/ n nuovo processo m

retribution /retrɪˈbjuːʃn/ n castigo m

retrieval /rɪˈtriːvl/ n recupero m

retrieve /rɪˈtriːv/ vt recuperare

retrograde /ˈretrəɡreɪd/ a retrogrado

retrospect /ˈretrəspekt/ n in ~ guardando indietro. ~ive /-ˈspektɪv/ a retrospettivo; (legislation) retroattivo ● n retrospettiva f

return /rɪˈtɜːn/ n ritorno m; (giving back) restituzione f; Comm profitto m; (ticket) biglietto m di andata e ritorno; by ~ [of post] a stretto giro di posta; in ~ in cambio (for di); many happy ~s! cento di questi giorni! ● vi ritornare ● vt (give back) restituire; ricambiare (affection, invitation); (put back) rimettere; (send back) mandare indietro; (elect) eleggere

return: ~ flight n volo m di andata e ritorno. ~ match n rivincita f. ~ ticket n biglietto m di andata e ritorno

reunion /riːˈjuːnjən/ n riunione f

reunite /riːjʊˈnaɪt/ vt riunire

re'us|able /riː-/ a riutilizzabile. ~e vt riutilizzare

rev /rev/ n Auto, fam giro m (di motore) ● v (pt/pp revved) ● vt ~ [up] far andare su di giri ● vi andare su di giri

reveal /rɪˈviːl/ vt rivelare; (dress:) scoprire. ~ing a rivelatore; (dress) osé inv

revel /ˈrevl/ vi (pt/pp revelled) ~ in sth godere di qcsa

revelation /revə'leɪʃn/ n rivelazione f

revelry /'revlrɪ/ n baldoria f

revenge /rɪ'vendʒ/ n vendetta f; Sport rivincita f; **take ~** vendicarsi ● vt vendicare

revenue /'revənju:/ n reddito m

reverberate /rɪ'vɜ:bəreɪt/ vi riverberare

revere /rɪ'vɪə(r)/ vt riverire. **~nce** /'revərəns/ n riverenza f

Reverend /'revərənd/ a reverendo

reverent /'revərənt/ a riverente

reverse /rɪ'vɜ:s/ a opposto; **in ~ order** in ordine inverso ● n contrario m; (back) rovescio m; Auto marcia m indietro ● vt invertire; **~ the car into the garage** entrare in garage a marcia indietro; **~ the charges** Teleph fare una telefonata a carico del destinatario ● vi Auto fare marcia indietro

revert /rɪ'vɜ:t/ vi **~ to** tornare a

review /rɪ'vju:/ n (survey) rassegna f; (re-examination) riconsiderazione f; Mil rivista f; (of book, play) recensione f ● vt riesaminare (situation); Mil passare in rivista; recensire (book, play). **~er** n critico, -a mf

revile /rɪ'vaɪl/ vt ingiuriare

revis|e /rɪ'vaɪz/ vt rivedere; (for exam) ripassare. **~ion** /-'vɪʒn/ n revisione f; (for exam) ripasso m

revival /rɪ'vaɪvl/ n ritorno m; (of patient) recupero m; (from coma) risveglio m

revive /rɪ'vaɪv/ vt resuscitare; rianimare (person) ● vi riprendersi; (person:) rianimarsi

revoke /rɪ'vəʊk/ vt revocare

revolt /rɪ'vəʊlt/ n rivolta f ● vi ribellarsi ● vt rivoltare. **~ing** a rivoltante

revolution /revə'lu:ʃn/ n rivoluzione f; Auto **~s per minute** giri mpl al minuto. **~ary** /-ərɪ/ a & n rivoluzionario, -a mf. **~ize** vt rivoluzionare

revolve /rɪ'vɒlv/ vi ruotare; **~ around** girare intorno a

revolv|er /rɪ'vɒlvə(r)/ n rivoltella f, revolver m inv. **~ing** a ruotante

revue /rɪ'vju:/ n rivista f

revulsion /rɪ'vʌlʃn/ n ripulsione f

reward /rɪ'wɔ:d/ n ricompensa f ● vt ricompensare. **~ing** a gratificante

re'write /ri:-/ vt (pt **rewrote**, pp **rewritten**) riscrivere

rhapsody /'ræpsədɪ/ n rapsodia f

rhetoric /'retərɪk/ n retorica f. **~al** /rɪ'tɒrɪkl/ a retorico

rheuma|tic /rʊ'mætɪk/ a reumatico. **~tism** /'ru:mətɪzm/ n reumatismo m

Rhine /raɪn/ n Reno m

rhinoceros /raɪ'nɒsərəs/ n rinoceronte m

rhubarb /'ru:bɑ:b/ n rabarbaro m

rhyme /raɪm/ n rima f; (poem) filastrocca f ● vi rimare

rhythm /'rɪðm/ n ritmo m. **~ic[al]** a ritmico. **~ically** adv con ritmo

rib /rɪb/ n costola f

ribald /'rɪbld/ a spinto

ribbon /'rɪbən/ n nastro m; **in ~s** a brandelli

rice /raɪs/ n riso m

rich /rɪtʃ/ a ricco; (food) pesante ● n **the ~** pl i ricchi; **~es** pl ricchezze fpl. **~ly** adv riccamente; (deserve) largamente

rickety /'rɪkɪtɪ/ a malfermo

ricochet /'rɪkəʃeɪ/ vi rimbalzare ● n rimbalzo m

rid /rɪd/ vt (pt/pp **rid**, pres p **ridding**) sbarazzare (**of** di); **get ~ of** sbarazzarsi di

riddance /'rɪdns/ n **good ~!** che liberazione!

ridden /'rɪdn/ see ride

riddle /'rɪdl/ n enigma m

riddled /'rɪdld/ a **~ with** crivellato di

ride /raɪd/ n (on horse) cavalcata f; (in vehicle) giro m; (journey) viaggio m; **take sb for a ~** fam prendere qcno in giro ● v (pt **rode**, pp **ridden**) ● vt montare (horse); andare su (bicycle) ● vi andare a cavallo; (jockey, showjumper:) cavalcare; (cyclist:) andare in bicicletta; (in vehicle) viaggiare. **~r** n cavallerizzo, -a mf; (in race) fantino m; (on bicycle) ciclista mf; (in document) postilla f

ridge /rɪdʒ/ n spigolo m; (on roof) punta f; (of mountain) cresta f

ridicule /'rɪdɪkju:l/ n ridicolo m ● vt mettere in ridicolo

ridiculous /rɪ'dɪkjʊləs/ a ridicolo

riding /'raɪdɪŋ/ n equitazione f ● attrib d'equitazione

rife /raɪf/ a **be ~** essere diffuso; **~ with** pieno di

riff-raff /'rɪfræf/ n marmaglia f

rifle /'raɪfl/ n fucile m. **~-range** n tiro m al bersaglio ● vt **~ [through]** mettere a soqquadro

rift /rɪft/ n fessura f; fig frattura f

rig[1] /rɪg/ n equipaggiamento m; (at sea) piattaforma f [per trivellazioni subacquee] ● vt **rig out** vt (pt/pp **rigged**) equipaggiare. **rig up** vt allestire

rig² *vt* (*pt/pp* **rigged**) manovrare ⟨*election*⟩

right /raɪt/ *a* giusto; (*not left*) destro; **be ~** ⟨*person:*⟩ aver ragione; ⟨*clock:*⟩ essere giusto; **put ~** mettere all'ora ⟨*clock*⟩; correggere ⟨*person*⟩; rimediare a ⟨*situation*⟩; **that's ~!** proprio così! ● *adv* (*correctly*) bene; (*not left*) a destra; (*directly*) proprio; (*completely*) completamente; **~ away** immediatamente ● *n* giusto *m*; (*not left*) destra *f*; (*what is due*) diritto *m*; **on/to the ~** a destra; **be in the ~** essere nel giusto; **know ~ from wrong** distinguere il bene dal male; **by ~s** secondo giustizia; **the R~** *Pol* la destra ● *vt* raddrizzare; **~ a wrong** *fig* riparare a un torto. **~ angle** *n* angolo *m* retto

rightful /'raɪtfl/ *a* legittimo

right: **~-'handed** *a* che usa la mano destra. **~-hand 'man** *fig* braccio *m* destro

rightly /'raɪtlɪ/ *adv* giustamente

right: **~ of way** *n* diritto *m* di transito; (*path*) passaggio *m*; *Auto* precedenza *f*. **~-'wing** *a* *Pol* di destra ● *n* *Sport* ala *f* destra

rigid /'rɪdʒɪd/ *a* rigido. **~ity** /-'dʒɪdatɪ/ *n* rigidità *f*

rigmarole /'rɪgmərəʊl/ *n* trafila *f*; (*story*) tiritera *f*

rigorous /'rɪgərəs/ *a* rigoroso

rile /raɪl/ *vt* *fam* irritare

rim /rɪm/ *n* bordo *m*; (*of wheel*) cerchione *m*

rind /raɪnd/ *n* (*on fruit*) scorza *f*; (*on cheese*) crosta *f*; (*on bacon*) cotenna *f*

ring¹ /rɪŋ/ *n* (*circle*) cerchio *m*; (*on finger*) anello *m*; (*boxing*) ring *m* *inv*; (*for circus*) pista *f*; **stand in a ~** essere in cerchio

ring² *n* suono *m*; **give sb a ~** *Teleph* dare un colpo di telefono a qcno ● *vt* (*pt* **rang**, *pp* **rung**) ● *vt* suonare; **~ [up]** *Teleph* telefonare a ● *vi* suonare; *Teleph* **~ [up]** telefonare. **ring back** *vt/i* *Teleph* richiamare. **ring off** *vi* *Teleph* riattaccare

ring: **~leader** *n* capobanda *m*. **~ road** *n* circonvallazione *f*

rink /rɪŋk/ *n* pista *f* di pattinaggio

rinse /rɪns/ *n* risciacquo *m*; (*hair colour*) cachet *m* *inv* ● *vt* sciacquare

riot /'raɪət/ *n* rissa *f*; (*of colour*) accozzaglia *f*; **~s** *pl* disordini *mpl*; **run ~** impazzare ● *vi* creare disordini. **~er** *n* dimostrante *mf*. **~ous** /-əs/ *a* sfrenato

rip /rɪp/ *n* strappo *m* ● *vt* (*pt/pp* **ripped**)

strappare; **~ open** aprire con uno strappo. **rip off** *vt* *fam* fregare

ripe /raɪp/ *a* maturo; ⟨*cheese*⟩ stagionato

ripen /'raɪpn/ *vi* maturare; ⟨*cheese:*⟩ stagionarsi ● *vt* far maturare; stagionare ⟨*cheese*⟩

ripeness /'raɪpnɪs/ *n* maturità *f*

'rip-off *n* *fam* frode *f*

ripple /'rɪpl/ *n* increspatura *f*; (*sound*) mormorio *m* ●

rise /raɪz/ *n* (*of sun*) levata *f*; (*fig: to fame, power*) ascesa *f*; (*increase*) aumento *m*; **give ~ to** dare adito a ● *vi* (*pt* **rose**, *pp* **risen**) alzarsi; ⟨*sun:*⟩ sorgere; ⟨*dough:*⟩ lievitare; ⟨*prices, water level:*⟩ aumentare; (*to power, position*) arrivare (**to** a). **~r** *n* **early ~r** persona *f* mattiniera

rising /'raɪzɪŋ/ *a* ⟨*sun*⟩ levante; **~ generation** nuova generazione *f* ● *n* (*revolt*) sollevazione *f*

risk /rɪsk/ *n* rischio *m*; **at one's own ~** a proprio rischio e pericolo ● *vt* rischiare

risky /'rɪskɪ/ *a* (**-ier, -iest**) rischioso

risqué /'rɪskeɪ/ *a* spinto

rite /raɪt/ *n* rito *m*; **last ~s** estrema unzione *f*

ritual /'rɪtjʊəl/ *a* rituale ● *n* rituale *m*

rival /'raɪvl/ *a* rivale ● *n* rivale *mf*; **~s** *pl* *Comm* concorrenti *mpl* ● *vt* (*pt/pp* **rivalled**) rivaleggiare con. **~ry** *n* rivalità *f* *inv*; *Comm* concorrenza *f*

river /'rɪvə(r)/ *n* fiume *m*. **~-bed** *n* letto *m* del fiume

rivet /'rɪvɪt/ *n* rivetto *m* ● *vt* rivettare; **~ed by** *fig* inchiodato da

Riviera /rɪvɪ'eərə/ *n* **the Italian ~** la riviera ligure

road /rəʊd/ *n* strada *f*, via *f*; **be on the ~** viaggiare

road: **~-block** *n* blocco *m* stradale. **~-hog** *n* *fam* pirata *m* della strada. **~-map** *n* carta *f* stradale. **~ safety** *n* sicurezza *f* sulle strade. **~ sense** *n* prudenza *f* (*per strada*). **~side** *n* bordo *m* della strada. **~-sign** *n* cartello *m* stradale. **~way** *n* carreggiata *f*, corsia *f*. **~-works** *npl* lavori *mpl* stradali. **~worthy** *a* sicuro

roam /rəʊm/ *vi* girovagare

roar /rɔː(r)/ *n* ruggito *m*; **~s of laughter** scroscio *msg* di risa ● *vi* ruggire; ⟨*lorry, thunder:*⟩ rombare; **~ with laughter** ridere fragorosamente. **~ing** *a* **do a ~ing trade** *fam* fare affari d'oro

roast /rəʊst/ *a* arrosto; **~ pork** arrosto

m di maiale ● *n* arrosto *m* ● *vt* arrostire ⟨*meat*⟩ ● *vi* arrostirsi

rob /rɒb/ *vt* (*pt/pp* **robbed**) derubare (**of** di); svaligiare ⟨*bank*⟩. **~ber** *n* rapinatore *m*. **~bery** *n* rapina *f*

robe /rəʊb/ *n* tunica *f*; (*Am: bathrobe*) accappatoio *m*

robin /ˈrɒbɪn/ *n* pettirosso *m*

robot /ˈrəʊbɒt/ *n* robot *m inv*

robust /rəʊˈbʌst/ *a* robusto

rock¹ /rɒk/ *n* roccia *f*; (*in sea*) scoglio *m*; (*sweet*) zucchero *m* candito. **on the ~s** ⟨*ship*⟩ incagliato; ⟨*marriage*⟩ finito; ⟨*drink*⟩ con ghiaccio

rock² *vt* cullare ⟨*baby*⟩; ⟨*shake*⟩ far traballare; ⟨*shock*⟩ scuotere ● *vi* dondolarsi

rock³ *n Mus* rock *m*

rock-'bottom *a* bassissimo ● *n* livello *m* più basso

rockery /ˈrɒkərɪ/ *n* giardino *m* roccioso

rocket /ˈrɒkɪt/ *n* razzo *m* ● *vi* salire alle stelle

rocking /ˈrɒkɪŋ/: **~-chair** *n* sedia *f* a dondolo. **~-horse** *n* cavallo *m* a dondolo

rocky /ˈrɒkɪ/ *a* (**-ier, -iest**) roccioso; *fig* traballante

rod /rɒd/ *n* bacchetta *f*; (*for fishing*) canna *f*

rode /rəʊd/ *see* **ride**

rodent /ˈrəʊdnt/ *n* roditore *m*

roe /rəʊ/ *n* (*pl* **roe** *or* **roes**) **~[-deer]** capriolo *m*

rogue /rəʊg/ *n* farabutto *m*

role /rəʊl/ *n* ruolo *m*

roll /rəʊl/ *n* rotolo *m*; (*bread*) panino *m*; (*list*) lista *f*; (*of ship, drum*) rullio *m* ● *vi* rotolare; **be ~ing in money** *fam* nuotare nell'oro ● *vt* spianare ⟨*lawn, pastry*⟩. **roll over** *vi* rigirarsi. **roll up** *vt* arrotolare; rimboccarsi ⟨*sleeves*⟩ ● *vi fam* arrivare

'roll-call *n* appello *m*

roller /ˈrəʊlə(r)/ *n* rullo *m*; (*for hair*) bigodino *m*. **~ blind** *n* tapparella *f*. **~-coaster** *n* montagne *fpl* russe. **~-skate** *n* pattino *m* a rotelle

'rolling-pin *n* mattarello *m*

Roman /ˈrəʊmən/ *a* romano ● *n* romano, -a *mf*. **~ Catholic** *a* cattolico ● *n* cattolico, -a *mf*

romance /rəʊˈmæns/ *n* (*love-affair*) storia *f* d'amore; (*book*) romanzo *m* rosa

Romania /rəʊˈmeɪnɪə/ *n* Romania *f*. **~n** *a* rumeno ● *n* rumeno, -a *mf*; (*language*) rumeno *m*

romantic /rəʊˈmæntɪk/ *a* romantico.

~ally *adv* romanticamente. **~ism** /-tɪsɪzm/ *n* romanticismo *m*

Rome /rəʊm/ *n* Roma *f*

romp /rɒmp/ *n* gioco *m* rumoroso ● *vi* giocare rumorosamente. **~ers** *npl* pagliaccetto *msg*

roof /ru:f/ *n* tetto *m*; (*of mouth*) palato *m* ● *vt* mettere un tetto su. **~-rack** *n* portabagagli *m inv*. **~-top** *n* tetto *m*

rook /rʊk/ *n* corvo *m*; (*in chess*) torre *f*

room /ru:m/ *n* stanza *f*; (*bedroom*) camera *f*; (*for functions*) sala *f*; (*space*) spazio *m*. **~y** *a* spazioso; ⟨*clothes*⟩ ampio

roost /ru:st/ *vi* appollaiarsi

root¹ /ru:t/ *n* radice *f*; **take ~** metter radici ● **root out** *vt fig* scovare

root² *vi* **~ about** grufolare; **~ for sb** *Am fam* fare il tifo per qcno

rope /rəʊp/ *n* corda *f*; **know the ~s** *fam* conoscere i trucchi del mestiere ● **rope in** *vt fam* coinvolgere

rosary /ˈrəʊzərɪ/ *n* rosario *m*

rose¹ /rəʊz/ *n* rosa *f*; (*of watering-can*) bocchetta *f*

rose² *see* **rise**

rosé /ˈrəʊzeɪ/ *n* [vino *m*] rosé *m inv*

rosemary /ˈrəʊzmərɪ/ *n* rosmarino *m*

rosette /rəʊˈzet/ *n* coccarda *f*

roster /ˈrɒstə(r)/ *n* tabella *f* dei turni

rostrum /ˈrɒstrəm/ *n* podio *m*

rosy /ˈrəʊzɪ/ *a* (**-ier, -iest**) roseo

rot /rɒt/ *n* marciume *m*; (*fam: nonsense*) sciocchezze *fpl* ● *vi* (*pt/pp* **rotted**) marcire

rota /ˈrəʊtə/ *n* tabella *f* dei turni

rotary /ˈrəʊtərɪ/ *a* rotante

rotat|e /rəʊˈteɪt/ *vt* far ruotare; avvicendare ⟨*crops*⟩ ● *vi* ruotare. **~ion** /-eɪʃn/ *n* rotazione *f*; **in ~ion** a turno

rote /rəʊt/ *n* **by ~** meccanicamente

rotten /ˈrɒtn/ *a* marcio; *fam* schifoso; ⟨*person*⟩ penoso

rotund /rəʊˈtʌnd/ *a* paffuto

rough /rʌf/ *a* (*not smooth*) ruvido; ⟨*ground*⟩ accidentato; ⟨*behaviour*⟩ rozzo; ⟨*sport*⟩ violento; ⟨*area*⟩ malfamato; ⟨*crossing, time*⟩ brutto; ⟨*estimate*⟩ approssimativo ● *adv* ⟨*play*⟩ grossolanamente; **sleep ~** dormire sotto i ponti ● *vt* **~ it** vivere senza confort. **rough out** *vt* abbozzare

roughage /ˈrʌfɪdʒ/ *n* fibre *fpl*

rough 'draft *n* abbozzo *m*

rough|ly /ˈrʌflɪ/ *adv* rozzamente; (*more or less*) pressappoco. **~ness** *n* ruvidità *f*; (*of behaviour*) rozzezza *f*

rough paper *n* carta *f* da brutta

roulette /ru:ˈlet/ *n* roulette *f*

round /raʊnd/ a rotondo ● n tondo m; (slice) fetta f; (of visits, drinks) giro m; (of competition) partita f; (boxing) ripresa f, round m inv; **do one's ~s** (doctor:) fare il giro delle visite ● prep intorno a; **open ~ the clock** aperto ventiquattr'ore ● adv **all ~** tutt'intorno; **ask sb ~** invitare qcno; **go/come ~ to** (a friend etc) andare da; **turn/look ~** girarsi; **~ about** (approximately) intorno a ● vt arrotondare; girare (corner). **round down** vt arrotondare (per difetto). **round off** vt (end) terminare. **round on** vt aggredire. **round up** vt radunare; arrotondare (prices)

roundabout /'raʊndəbaʊt/ a indiretto ● n giostra f; (for traffic) rotonda f

round: ~ 'trip n viaggio m di andata e ritorno

rous|e /raʊz/ vt svegliare; risvegliare (suspicion, interest). **~ing** a di incoraggiamento

route /ruːt/ n itinerario m; Naut, Aeron rotta f; (of bus) percorso m

routine /ruː'tiːn/ a di routine ● n routine f inv; Theat numero m

rov|e /rəʊv/ vi girovagare. **~ing** a (reporter, ambassador) itinerante

row¹ /rəʊ/ n (line) fila f; **three years in a ~** tre anni di fila

row² /rəʊ/ vi (in boat) remare

row³ /raʊ/ n fam (quarrel) litigata f; (noise) baccano m ● vi fam litigare

rowdy /'raʊdi/ a (-ier, -iest) chiassoso

rowing boat /'rəʊɪŋ-/ n barca f a remi

royal /'rɔɪəl/ a reale

royal|ty /'rɔɪəltɪ/ n appartenenza f alla famiglia reale; (persons) i membri della famiglia reale. **~ies** npl (payments) diritti mpl d'autore

rpm abbr **revolutions per minute**

rub /rʌb/ n **give sth a ~** dare una sfregata a qcsa ● vt (pt/pp rubbed) sfregare. **rub in** vt **don't ~ it in** fam non rigirare il coltello nella piaga. **rub off** vt mandar via sfregando (stain); (from blackboard) cancellare ● vi andar via; **~ off on** essere trasmesso a. **rub out** vt cancellare

rubber /'rʌbə(r)/ n gomma f; (eraser) gomma f [da cancellare]. **~ band** n elastico m. **~y** a gommoso

rubbish /'rʌbɪʃ/ n immondizie fpl; (fam: nonsense) idiozie fpl; (fam: junk) robaccia f ● vt fam fare a pezzi. **~ bin** n pattumiera f. **~ dump** n discarica f; (official) discarica f comunale

rubble /'rʌbl/ n macerie fpl

ruby /'ruːbɪ/ n rubino m ● attrib di rubini; (lips) scarlatta

rucksack /'rʌksæk/ n zaino m

rudder /'rʌdə(r)/ n timone m

ruddy /'rʌdɪ/ a (-ier, -iest) rubicondo; fam maledetto

rude /ruːd/ a scortese; (improper) spinto. **~ly** adv scortesemente. **~ness** n scortesia f

rudiment /'ruːdɪmənt/ n **~s** pl rudimenti mpl. **~ary** /-'mentərɪ/ a rudimentale

rueful /'ruːfl/ a rassegnato

ruffian /'rʌfɪən/ n farabutto m

ruffle /'rʌfl/ n gala f ● vt scompigliare (hair)

rug /rʌg/ n tappeto m; (blanket) coperta f

rugby /'rʌgbɪ/ n ~ [football] rugby m

rugged /'rʌgɪd/ a (coastline) roccioso

ruin /'ruːɪn/ n rovina f; **in ~s** in rovina ● vt rovinare. **~ous** /-əs/ a estremamente costoso

rule /ruːl/ n regola f; (control) ordinamento m; (for measuring) metro m; **~s** pl regolamento msg; **as a ~** generalmente ● vt governare; dominare (colony, behaviour); **~ that** stabilire che ● vi governare. **rule out** vt escludere

ruled /ruːld/ a (paper) a righe

ruler /'ruːlə(r)/ n capo m di Stato; (sovereign) sovrano, -a mf; (measure) righello m, regolo m

ruling /'ruːlɪŋ/ a (class) dirigente; (party) di governo ● n decisione f

rum /rʌm/ n rum m inv

rumble /'rʌmbl/ n rombo m; (of stomach) brontolio m ● vi rombare; (stomach:) brontolare

rummage /'rʌmɪdʒ/ vi rovistare (in/through in)

rummy /'rʌmɪ/ n ramino m

rumour /'ruːmə(r)/ n diceria f ● vt **it is ~ed that** si dice che

rump /rʌmp/ n natiche fpl. **~ steak** n bistecca f di girello

rumpus /'rʌmpəs/ n fam baccano m

run /rʌn/ n (on foot) corsa f; (distance to be covered) tragitto m; (outing) giro m; Theat rappresentazioni fpl; (in skiing) pista f; (Am: ladder) smagliatura f (in calze); **at a ~** di corsa; **~ of bad luck** periodo m sfortunato; **on the ~** in fuga; **have the ~ of** avere a disposizione; **in the long ~** a lungo termine ● v (pt ran, pp run, pres p running) ● vi correre; (river:) scorrere; (nose, makeup:) colare; (bus:) fare servizio; (play:) essere in cartellone; (colours:) sbiadire; (in

433

election) presentarsi [come candidato]
● vt (manage) dirigere; tenere (house);
(drive) dare un passaggio a; correre
(risk); Comput lanciare; Journ pubblicare (article); (pass) far scorrere (eyes,
hand); ~ **a bath** far scorrere l'acqua
per il bagno. **run across** vt (meet, find)
imbattersi in. **run away** vi scappare
[via]. **run down** vi scaricarsi; (clock:)
scaricarsi; (stocks:) esaurirsi ● vt Auto
investire; (reduce) esaurire; (fam:
criticize) denigrare. **run in** vi entrare di
corsa. **run into** vi (meet) imbattersi in;
(knock against) urtare. **run off** vi andare via di corsa ● vt stampare (copies).
run out vi uscire di corsa; (supplies,
money:) esaurirsi; **~ out of** rimanere
senza. **run over** vi correre; (overflow)
traboccare ● vt Auto investire. **run
through** vt scorrere. **run up** vi salire di
corsa; (towards) arrivare di corsa ● vt
accumulare (debts, bill); (sew) cucire
'**runaway** n fuggitivo, -a mf
run-'down a (area) in abbandono;
(person) esaurito ● n analisi f
rung[1] /rʌŋ/ n (of ladder) piolo m
rung[2] see **ring**[2]
runner /'rʌnə(r)/ n podista mf; (in race)
corridore, -trice mf; (on sledge) pattino
m. **~ bean** n fagiolino m. **~-up** n secondo, -a mf classificato, -a
running /'rʌnɪŋ/ a in corsa; (water)
corrente; **four times ~** quattro volte di

seguito ● n corsa f; (management) direzione f; **be in the ~** essere in lizza. ~
'**commentary** n cronaca f
runny /'rʌnɪ/ a semiliquido; **~ nose**
naso che cola
run: ~-of-the-'mill a ordinario. **~-up** n
Sport rincorsa f; **the ~-up to** il periodo
precedente. **~way** n pista f
rupture /'rʌptʃə(r)/ n rottura f; Med ernia f ● vt rompere; **~ oneself** farsi venire l'ernia ● vi rompersi
rural /'rʊərəl/ a rurale
ruse /ruːz/ n astuzia f
rush[1] /rʌʃ/ n Bot giunco m
rush[2] n fretta f; **in a ~** di fretta ● vi precipitarsi ● vt far premura a; **~ sb to
hospital** trasportare qcno di corsa al-
l'ospedale. **~-hour** n ora f di punta
rusk /rʌsk/ n biscotto m
Russia /'rʌʃə/ n Russia f. **~n** a & n russo, -a mf; (language) russo m
rust /rʌst/ n ruggine f ● vi arrugginirsi
rustic /'rʌstɪk/ a rustico
rustle /'rʌsl/ vi frusciare ● vt far
frusciare; Am rubare (cattle). **rustle up**
vt fam rimediare
'**rustproof** a a prova di ruggine
rusty /'rʌstɪ/ a (-ier, -iest) arrugginito
rut /rʌt/ n solco m; **in a ~** fam nella
routine
ruthless /'ruːθlɪs/ a spietato. **~ness** n
spietatezza f
rye /raɪ/ n segale f

Ss

sabbath /'sæbəθ/ n domenica f;
(Jewish) sabato m
sabbatical /sə'bætɪkl/ n Univ anno m
sabbatico
sabot|age /'sæbətɑːʒ/ n sabotaggio m
● vt sabotare. **~eur** /-'tɜː(r)/ n sabo-
tatore, -trice mf
saccharin /'sækərɪn/ n saccarina f
sachet /'sæʃeɪ/ n bustina f; (scented)
sacchetto m profumato
sack[1] /sæk/ vt (plunder) saccheggiare
sack[2] n sacco m; **get the ~** fam essere
licenziato ● vt fam licenziare. **~ing** n
tela f per sacchi; (fam: dismissal) licenziamento m

sacrament /'sækrəmənt/ n sacramen-
to m
sacred /'seɪkrɪd/ a sacro
sacrifice /'sækrɪfaɪs/ n sacrificio m
● vt sacrificare
sacrilege /'sækrɪlɪdʒ/ n sacrilegio m
sad /sæd/ a (sadder, saddest) triste.
~den vt rattristare
saddle /'sædl/ n sella f ● vt sellare;
I've been ~d with... fig mi hanno af-
fibbiato...
sadis|m /'seɪdɪzm/ n sadismo m. **~t**
/-dɪst/ n sadico, -a mf. **~tic** /sə'dɪstɪk/ a
sadico
sad|ly /'sædlɪ/ adv tristemente; (unfor-

tunately) sfortunatamente. **~ness** *n* tristezza *f*

safe /seif/ *a* sicuro; *(out of danger)* salvo; *(object)* al sicuro; **~ and sound** sano e salvo ● *n* cassaforte *f*. **~guard** *n* protezione *f* ● *vt* proteggere. **~ly** *adv* in modo sicuro; *(arrive)* senza incidenti; *(assume)* con certezza

safety /'seifti/ *n* sicurezza *f*. **~-belt** *n* cintura *f* di sicurezza. **~-deposit box** *n* cassetta *f* di sicurezza. **~-pin** *n* spilla *f* di sicurezza o da balia. **~-valve** *n* valvola *f* di sicurezza

sag /sæg/ *vi* (*pt/pp* sagged) abbassarsi

saga /'sɑ:gə/ *n* saga *f*

sage /seidʒ/ *n* (*herb*) salvia *f*

Sagittarius /sædʒɪ'teərɪəs/ *n* Sagittario *m*

said /sed/ *see* say

sail /seil/ *n* vela *f*; (*trip*) giro *m* in barca a vela ● *vi* navigare; *Sport* praticare la vela; (*leave*) salpare ● *vt* pilotare

'**sailboard** *n* tavola *f* del windsurf. **~ing** *n* windsurf *m inv*

sailing /'seilɪŋ/ *n* vela *f*. **~-boat** *n* barca *f* a vela. **~-ship** *n* veliero *m*

sailor /'seilə(r)/ *n* marinaio *m*

saint /seint/ *n* santo, -a *mf*. **~ly** *a* di santo

sake /seik/ *n* **for the ~ of** (*person*) per il bene di; (*peace*) per amor di; **for the ~ of it** per il gusto di farlo

salad /'sæləd/ *n* insalata *f*. **~ bowl** *n* insalatiera *f*. **~ cream** *n* salsa *f* per condire l'insalata. **~dressing** *n* condimento *m* per insalata

salary /'sælərɪ/ *n* stipendio *m*

sale /seil/ *n* vendita *f*; (*at reduced prices*) svendita *f*; **for/on ~** in vendita. '**for ~**' 'vendesi'

sales|man /'seilzmən/ *n* venditore *m*; (*traveller*) rappresentante *m*. **~woman** *n* venditrice *f*

salient /'seiliənt/ *a* saliente

saliva /sə'laivə/ *n* saliva *f*

sallow /'sæləʊ/ *a* giallastro

salmon /'sæmən/ *n* salmone *m*

saloon /sə'lu:n/ *n* *Auto* berlina *f*; (*Am: bar*) bar *m*

salt /sɔ:lt/ *n* sale *m* ● *a* salato; (*fish, meat*) sotto sale ● *vt* salare; (*cure*) mettere sotto sale. **~-cellar** *n* saliera *f*. '~ **water** *n* acqua *f* di mare. **~y** *a* salato

salutary /'sæljʊtərɪ/ *a* salutare

salute /sə'lu:t/ *Mil* *n* saluto *m* ● *vt* salutare ● *vi* fare il saluto

salvage /'sælvidʒ/ *n* *Naut* recupero *m* ● *vt* recuperare

salvation /sæl'veiʃn/ *n* salvezza *f*. **S~ Army** *n* Esercito *m* della Salvezza

salvo /'sælvəʊ/ *n* salva *f*

same /seim/ *a* stesso (**as** di) ● *pron* **the ~** lo stesso; **be all the ~** essere tutti uguali ● *adv* **the ~** nello stesso modo; **all the ~** (*however*) lo stesso; **the ~ to you** altrettanto

sample /'sɑ:mpl/ *n* campione *m* ● *vt* testare

sanatorium /sænə'tɔ:rɪəm/ *n* casa *f* di cura

sanctimonious /sæŋktɪ'məʊnɪəs/ *a* moraleggiante

sanction /'sæŋkʃn/ *n* (*approval*) autorizzazione *f*; (*penalty*) sanzione *f* ● *vt* autorizzare

sanctity /'sæŋktəti/ *n* santità *f*

sanctuary /'sæŋktjʊərɪ/ *n* *Relig* santuario *m*; (*refuge*) asilo *m*; (*for wildlife*) riserva *f*

sand /sænd/ *n* sabbia *f* ● *vt* **~** [**down**] carteggiare

sandal /'sændl/ *n* sandalo *m*

sand: ~bank *n* banco *m* di sabbia. **~paper** *n* carta *f* vetrata ● *vt* cartavetrare. **~pit** *n* recinto *m* contenente sabbia dove giocano i bambini

sandwich /'sænwidʒ/ *n* tramezzino *m* ● *vt* **~ed between** schiacciato tra

sandy /'sændi/ *a* (**-ier, -iest**) (*beach, soil*) sabbioso; (*hair*) biondiccio

sane /sein/ *a* (*not mad*) sano di mente; (*sensible*) sensato

sang /sæŋ/ *see* sing

sanitary /'sænitərɪ/ *a* igienico; (*system*) sanitario. **~ napkin** *n* *Am*, **~ towel** *n* assorbente *m* igienico

sanitation /sænɪ'teiʃn/ *n* impianti *mpl* igienici

sanity /'sænəti/ *n* sanità *f* di mente; (*common sense*) buon senso *m*

sank /sæŋk/ *see* sink

sapphire /'sæfaiə(r)/ *n* zaffiro *m* ● *a* blu zaffiro *inv*

sarcas|m /'sɑ:kæzm/ *n* sarcasmo *m*. **~tic** /-'kæstɪk/ *a* sarcastico

sardine /sɑ:'di:n/ *n* sardina *f*

Sardinia /sɑ:'dɪnɪə/ *n* Sardegna *f*. **~n** *a & n* sardo, -a *mf*

sardonic /sɑ:'dɒnɪk/ *a* sardonico

sash /sæʃ/ *n* fascia *f*; (*for dress*) fusciacca *f*

sat /sæt/ *see* sit

satanic /sə'tænɪk/ *a* satanico

satchel /'sætʃl/ *n* cartella *f*

satellite /'sætəlait/ *n* satellite *m*. **~**

dish n antenna f parabolica. **~ television** n televisione f via satellite

satin /'sætɪn/ n raso m ● attrib di raso

satire /'sætaɪə(r)/ n satira f

satirical /sə'tɪrɪkl/ a satirico

satir|ist /'sætɪrɪst/ n scrittore, -trice mf satirico, -a; (comedian) comico, -a mf satirico, -a. **~ize** vt satireggiare

satisfaction /sætɪs'fækʃn/ n soddisfazione f; **be to sb's ~** soddisfare qcno

satisfactor|y /sætɪs'fæktərɪ/ a soddisfacente. **~ily** adv in modo soddisfacente

satisf|y /'sætɪsfaɪ/ vt (pp/pp -ied) soddisfare; (convince) convincere; **be ~ied** essere soddisfatto. **~ying** a soddisfacente

saturat|e /'sætʃəreɪt/ vt inzuppare (**with** di); Chem, fig saturare (**with** di). **~ed** a saturo

Saturday /'sætədeɪ/ n sabato m

sauce /sɔːs/ n salsa f; (cheek) impertinenza f. **~pan** n pentola f

saucer /'sɔːsə(r)/ n piattino m

saucy /'sɔːsɪ/ a (-ier, -iest) impertinente

Saudi Arabia /saudɪə'reɪbɪə/ n Arabia f Saudita

sauna /'sɔːnə/ n sauna f

saunter /'sɔːntə(r)/ vi andare a spasso

sausage /'sɒsɪdʒ/ n salsiccia f; (dried) salame m

savage /'sævɪdʒ/ a feroce; (tribe, custom) selvaggio ● n selvaggio, -a mf ● vt fare a pezzi. **~ry** n ferocia f

save /seɪv/ n Sport parata f ● vt salvare (**from** da); (keep, collect) tenere; risparmiare (time, money); (avoid) evitare; Sport parare (goal); Comput salvare, memorizzare ● vi **~ [up]** risparmiare ● prep salvo

saver /'seɪvə(r)/ n risparmiatore, -trice mf

savings /'seɪvɪŋz/ npl (money) risparmi mpl. **~ account** n libretto m di risparmio. **~ bank** n cassa f di risparmio

saviour /'seɪvjə(r)/ n salvatore m

savour /'seɪvə(r)/ n sapore m ● vt assaporare. **~y** a salato; fig rispettabile

saw¹ /sɔː/ see **see¹**

saw² n sega f ● vt/i (pt **sawed**, pp **sawn** or **sawed**) segare. **~dust** n segatura f

saxophone /'sæksəfəʊn/ n sassofono m

say /seɪ/ n have one's **~** dire la propria; **have a ~** avere voce in capitolo ● vt/i (pt/pp **said**) dire; **that is to ~** cioè; **that goes without ~ing** questo è

ovvio; **when all is said and done** alla fine dei conti. **~ing** n proverbio m

scab /skæb/ n crosta f; pej crumiro m

scaffold /'skæfəld/ n patibolo m. **~ing** n impalcatura f

scald /skɔːld/ vt scottare; (milk) scaldare ● n scottatura f

scale¹ /skeɪl/ n (of fish) scaglia f

scale² n scala f; **on a grand ~** su vasta scale ● vt (climb) scalare. **scale down** vt diminuire

scales /skeɪlz/ npl (for weighing) bilancia fsg

scallop /'skɒləp/ n (shellfish) pettine m

scalp /skælp/ n cuoio m capelluto

scalpel /'skælpl/ n bisturi m inv

scam /skæm/ n fam fregatura f

scamper /'skæmpə(r)/ vi **~ away** sgattaiolare via

scampi /'skæmpɪ/ npl scampi mpl

scan /skæn/ n Med scanning m inv. scansioscintigrafia f ● vt (pt/pp **scanned**) scrutare; (quickly) dare una scorsa a; Med fare uno scanning di

scandal /'skændl/ n scandalo m; (gossip) pettegolezzi mpl. **~ize** /-d(ə)laɪz/ vt scandalizzare. **~ous** /-əs/ a scandaloso

Scandinavia /skændɪ'neɪvɪə/ n Scandinavia f. **~n** a & n scandinavo, -a mf

scanner /'skænə(r)/ n Comput scanner m inv

scant /skænt/ a scarso

scant|y /'skæntɪ/ a (-ier, -iest) scarso; (clothing) succinto. **~ily** adv scarsamente; (clothed) succintamente

scapegoat /'skeɪp-/ n capro m espiatorio

scar /skɑː(r)/ n cicatrice f ● vt (pt/pp **scarred**) lasciare una cicatrice a

scarc|e /skeəs/ a scarso; fig raro; **make oneself ~e** fam svignarsela. **~ely** adv appena; **~ely anything** quasi niente. **~ity** n scarsezza f

scare /skeə(r)/ n spavento m; (panic) panico m ● vt spaventare; **be ~d** aver paura (**of** di)

'scarecrow n spaventapasseri m inv

scarf /skɑːf/ n (pl **scarves**) sciarpa f; (square) foulard m inv

scarlet /'skɑːlət/ a scarlatto. **~ 'fever** n scarlattina f

scary /'skeərɪ/ a **be ~** far paura

scathing /'skeɪðɪŋ/ a mordace

scatter /'skætə(r)/ vt spargere; (disperse) disperdere ● vi disperdersi. **~-brained** a fam scervellato. **~ed** a sparso

scatty /'skætɪ/ a (-ier, -iest) fam svitato

scavenge /'skævɪndʒ/ vi frugare nella spazzatura. ~r n persona f che fruga nella spazzatura

scenario /sɪ'nɑːrɪəʊ/ n scenario m

scene /siːn/ n scena f; (quarrel) scenata f; behind the ~s dietro le quinte

scenery /'siːnərɪ/ n scenario m

scenic /'siːnɪk/ a panoramico

scent /sent/ n odore m; (trail) scia f; (perfume) profumo m. ~ed a profumato (with di)

sceptic|al /'skeptɪkl/ a scettico. ~ism /-tɪsɪzm/ n scetticismo m

schedule /'ʃedjuːl/ n piano m, programma m; (of work) programma m; (timetable) orario m; behind ~ in ritardo; on ~ nei tempi previsti; according to ~ secondo i tempi previsti ● vt prevedere. ~d flight n volo m di linea

scheme /skiːm/ n (plan) piano m; (plot) macchinazione f ● vi pej macchinare

schizophren|ia /skɪtsə'friːnɪə/ n schizofrenia f. ~ic /-'frenɪk/ a schizofrenico

scholar /'skɒlə(r)/ n studioso, -a mf. ~ly a erudito. ~ship n erudizione f; (grant) borsa f di studio

school /skuːl/ n scuola f; (in university) facoltà f; (of fish) branco m

school: ~boy n scolaro m. ~girl n scolara f. ~ing n istruzione f. ~teacher n insegnante mf

sciatica /saɪ'ætɪkə/ n sciatica f

scien|ce /'saɪəns/ n scienza f; ~ce fiction fantascienza f. ~tific /-'tɪfɪk/ a scientifico. ~tist n scienziato, -a mf

scintillating /'sɪntɪleɪtɪŋ/ a brillante

scissors /'sɪzəz/ npl forbici fpl

scoff¹ /skɒf/ vi ~ at schernire

scoff² vt fam divorare

scold /skəʊld/ vt sgridare. ~ing n sgridata f

scone /skɒn/ n pasticcino m da tè

scoop /skuːp/ n paletta f; Journ scoop m inv ● scoop out vt svuotare. scoop up vt tirar su

scoot /skuːt/ vi fam filare. ~er n motoretta f

scope /skəʊp/ n portata f; (opportunity) opportunità f inv

scorch /skɔːtʃ/ vt bruciare. ~er n fam giornata f torrida. ~ing a caldissimo

score /skɔː(r)/ n punteggio m; Mus partitura f; (for film, play) musica f; a ~ [of] (twenty) una ventina [di]; keep [the] ~ tenere il punteggio; on that ~

a questo proposito ● vt segnare (goal); (cut) incidere ● vi far punti; (in football etc) segnare; (keep score) tenere il punteggio. ~r n segnapunti m inv; (of goals) giocatore, -trice mf che segna

scorn /skɔːn/ n disprezzo m ● vt disprezzare. ~ful a sprezzante

Scorpio /'skɔːpɪəʊ/ n Astr Scorpione m

scorpion /'skɔːpɪən/ n scorpione m

Scot /skɒt/ n scozzese mf

Scotch /skɒtʃ/ a scozzese ● n (whisky) whisky m [scozzese]

scotch vt far cessare

scot-'free a get off ~ cavarsela impunemente

Scot|land /'skɒtlənd/ n Scozia f. ~s, ~tish a scozzese

scoundrel /'skaʊndrəl/ n mascalzone m

scour¹ /'skaʊə(r)/ vt (search) perlustrare

scour² vt (clean) strofinare

scourge /skɜːdʒ/ n flagello m

scout /skaʊt/ n Mil esploratore m ● vi ~ for andare in cerca di

Scout n [Boy] ~ [boy]scout m inv

scowl /skaʊl/ n sguardo m torvo ● vi guardare [di] storto

Scrabble® /'skræbl/ n Scarabeo® m

scraggy /'skrægɪ/ a (-ier, -iest) pej scarno

scram /skræm/ vi fam levarsi dai piedi

scramble /'skræmbl/ n (climb) arrampicata f ● vi (clamber) arrampicarsi; ~ for azzuffarsi per ● vt Teleph creare delle interferenze in; (eggs) strapazzare

scrap¹ /skræp/ n (fam: fight) litigio m

scrap² n pezzetto m; (metal) ferraglia f; ~s pl (of food) avanzi mpl ● vt (pt/pp scrapped) buttare via

'scrap-book n album m inv

scrape /skreɪp/ vt raschiare; (damage) graffiare. scrape through vi passare per un pelo. scrape together vt racimolare

scraper /'skreɪpə(r)/ n raschietto m

scrappy /'skræpɪ/ a frammentario

'scrap-yard n deposito m di ferraglia; (for cars) cimitero m delle macchine

scratch /skrætʃ/ n graffio m; (to relieve itch) grattata f; start from ~ partire da zero; up to ~ (work) all'altezza ● vt graffiare; (to relieve itch) grattare ● vi grattarsi

scrawl /skrɔːl/ n scarabocchio m ● vt/i scarabocchiare

scrawny /'skrɔːnɪ/ a (-ier, -iest) pej magro

scream /skri:m/ n strillo m ● vt/i strillare

screech /skri:tʃ/ n stridore m ● vi stridere ● vt strillare

screen /skri:n/ n paravento m; Cinema, TV schermo m ● vt proteggere; (conceal) riparare; proiettare (film); (candidates) passare al setaccio; Med sottoporre a visita medica. ~ing n Med visita f medica; (of film) proiezione f. ~play n sceneggiatura f

screw /skru:/ n vite f ● vt avvitare. **screw up** vt (crumple) accartocciare; strizzare (eyes); storcere (face); (sl: bungle) mandare all'aria

'screwdriver n cacciavite m inv

screwy /'skru:i/ a (-ier, -iest) fam svitato

scribble /'skrɪbl/ n scarabocchio m ● vt/i scarabocchiare

script /skrɪpt/ n scrittura f (a mano); (of film) sceneggiatura f

'script-writer n sceneggiatore, -trice m f

scroll /skrəʊl/ n rotolo m (di pergamena); (decoration) voluta f

scrounge /skraʊndʒ/ vt/i scroccare. ~r n scroccone, -a f

scrub¹ /skrʌb/ n (land) boscaglia f

scrub² vt/i (pt/pp **scrubbed**) strofinare; (fam: cancel) cancellare (plan)

scruff /skrʌf/ n **by the ~ of the neck** per la collottola

scruffy /'skrʌfi/ a (-ier, -iest) trasandato

scrum /skrʌm/ n (in rugby) mischia f

scruple /'skru:pl/ n scrupolo m

scrupulous /'skru:pjʊləs/ a scrupoloso

scrutin|ize /'skru:tɪnaɪz/ vt scrutinare. ~y n (look) esame m minuzioso

scuffle /'skʌfl/ n tafferuglio m

sculpt /skʌlpt/ vt/i scolpire. ~or /'skʌlptə(r)/ n scultore m. ~ure /-tʃə(r)/ n scultura f

scum /skʌm/ n schiuma f; (people) feccia f

scurrilous /'skʌrɪləs/ a scurrile

scurry /'skʌri/ vi (pt/pp -**ied**) affrettare il passo

scuttle /'skʌtl/ vi (hurry) ~ **away** correre via

sea /si:/ n mare m; **at** ~ in mare; fig confuso; **by** ~ via mare. ~**board** n costiera f. ~**food** n frutti mpl di mare. ~**gull** n gabbiano m

seal¹ /si:l/ n Zool foca f

seal² n sigillo m; Techn chiusura f er-

metica. ● vt sigillare; Techn chiudere ermeticamente. **seal off** vt bloccare (area)

'sea-level n livello m del mare

seam /si:m/ n cucitura f; (of coal) strato m

'seaman n marinaio m

seamless /'si:mlɪs/ a senza cucitura

seamy /'si:mɪ/ a sordido; (area) malfamato

seance /'seɪɑ:ns/ n seduta f spiritica

sea: ~**plane** n idrovolante m. ~**port** n porto m di mare

search /sɜ:tʃ/ n ricerca f; (official) perquisizione f; **in** ~ **of** alla ricerca di ● vt frugare (**for** alla ricerca di); perlustrare (area); (officially) perquisire ● vi ~ **for** cercare. ~**ing** a penetrante

search: ~**light** n riflettore m. ~-**party** n squadra f di ricerca

sea: ~**sick** a be/get ~ avere il mal di mare. ~**side** n at/to the ~**side** al mare. ~**side resort** n stazione f balneare. ~**side town** n città f di mare

season /'si:zn/ n stagione f ● vt (flavour) condire. ~**able** /-əbl/, ~**al** a stagionale. ~**ing** n condimento m

'season ticket n abbonamento m

seat /si:t/ n (chair) sedia f; (in car) sedile m; (place to sit) posto m [a sedere]; (bottom) didietro m; (of government) sede f; **take a** ~ sedersi ● vt mettere a sedere; (have seats for) aver posti [a sedere] per; **remain** ~**ed** mantenere il proprio posto. ~-**belt** n cintura f di sicurezza

sea: ~**weed** n alga f marina. ~**worthy** a in stato di navigare

secateurs /sekə'tɜ:z/ npl cesoie fpl

seclu|ded /sɪ'klu:dɪd/ a appartato. ~**sion** /-ʒn/ n isolamento m

second¹ /sɪ'kɒnd/ vt (transfer) distaccare

second² /'sekənd/ a secondo; **on** ~ **thoughts** ripensandoci meglio ● n secondo m; ~**s** pl (goods) merce fsg di seconda scelta; **have** ~**s** (at meal) fare il bis; **John the S**~ Giovanni Secondo ● adv (in race) al secondo posto ● vt assistere; appoggiare (proposal)

secondary /'sekəndri/ a secondario. ~ **school** n scuola f media (inferiore e superiore)

second: ~-**best** a secondo dopo il migliore; **be** ~-**best** pej essere un ripiego. ~ '**class** adv (travel, send) in seconda classe. ~-**class** a di seconda classe

'second hand n (on clock) lancetta f dei secondi

second-'hand *a & adv* di seconda mano

secondly /'sekəndlɪ/ *adv* in secondo luogo

second-'rate *a* di second'ordine

secrecy /'si:krəsɪ/ *n* segretezza *f*; **in ~** in segreto

secret /'si:krɪt/ *a* segreto ● *n* segreto *m*

secretarial /sekrə'teərɪəl/ *a* ‹work, staff› di segreteria

secretary /'sekrətərɪ/ *n* segretario, -a *mf*

secret|e /sɪ'kri:t/ *vt* secernere ‹poison›. **~ion** /-i:ʃn/ *n* secrezione *f*

secretive /'si:krətɪv/ *a* riservato. **~ness** *n* riserbo *m*

secretly /'si:krɪtlɪ/ *adv* segretamente

sect /sekt/ *n* setta *f*. **~arian** *a* settario

section /'sekʃn/ *n* sezione *f*

sector /'sektə(r)/ *n* settore *m*

secular /'sekjʊlə(r)/ *a* secolare; ‹education› laico

secure /sɪ'kjʊə(r)/ *a* sicuro ● *vt* proteggere; chiudere bene ‹door›; rendere stabile ‹ladder›; ‹obtain› assicurarsi. **~ly** *adv* saldamente

security /sɪ'kjʊərətɪ/ *n* sicurezza *f*; ‹for loan› garanzia *f*. **~ies** *npl* titoli *mpl*

sedate¹ /sɪ'deɪt/ *a* posato

sedate² *vt* somministrare sedativi a

sedation /sɪ'deɪʃn/ *n* somministrazione *f* di sedativi; **be under ~** essere sotto l'effetto di sedativi

sedative /'sedətɪv/ *a* sedativo ● *n* sedativo *m*

sedentary /'sedəntərɪ/ *a* sedentario

sediment /'sedɪmənt/ *n* sedimento *m*

seduce /sɪ'dju:s/ *vt* sedurre

seduct|ion /sɪ'dʌkʃn/ *n* seduzione *f*. **~ive** /-tɪv/ *a* seducente

see /si:/ *v* (*pt* **saw**, *pp* **seen**) ● *vt* vedere; ‹understand› capire; ‹escort› accompagnare; **go and ~** andare a vedere; ‹visit› andare a trovare; **~ you!** ci vediamo!; **~ you later!** a più tardi!; **~ing that** visto che ● *vi* vedere; ‹understand› capire; **~ that** ‹make sure› assicurarsi che; **~ about** occuparsi di. **see off** *vt* veder partire; ‹chase away› mandar via. **see through** *vi* vedere attraverso; *fig* non farsi ingannare da ● *vt* portare a buon fine. **see to** *vi* occuparsi di

seed /si:d/ *n* seme *m*; *Tennis* testa *f* di serie; **go to ~** fare seme; *fig* lasciarsi andare. **~ed player** *n* *Tennis* testa *f* di serie. **~ling** *n* pianticella *f*

seedy /'si:dɪ/ *a* (**-ier, -iest**) squallido

seek /si:k/ *vt* (*pt/pp* **sought**) cercare

seem /si:m/ *vi* sembrare. **~ingly** *adv* apparentemente

seen /si:n/ *see* **see¹**

seep /si:p/ *vi* filtrare

see-saw /'si:sɔ:/ *n* altalena *f*

seethe /si:ð/ *vi* **~ with anger** ribollire di rabbia

'see-through *a* trasparente

segment /'segmənt/ *n* segmento *m*; ‹of orange› spicchio *m*

segregat|e /'segrɪgeɪt/ *vt* segregare. **~ion** /-'geɪʃn/ *n* segregazione *f*

seize /si:z/ *vt* afferrare; *Jur* confiscare. **seize up** *vi* *Techn* bloccarsi

seizure /'si:ʒə(r)/ *n* *Jur* confisca *f*; *Med* colpo *m* [apoplettico]

seldom /'seldəm/ *adv* raramente

select /sɪ'lekt/ *a* scelto; ‹exclusive› esclusivo ● *vt* scegliere; selezionare ‹team›. **~ion** /-ekʃn/ *n* selezione *f*. **~ive** /-ɪv/ *a* selettivo. **~or** *n* *Sport* selezionatore, -trice *mf*

self /self/ *n* io *m*

self: **~-ad'dressed** *a* con il proprio indirizzo. **~-ad'hesive** *a* autoadesivo. **~-as'surance** *n* sicurezza *f* di sé. **~-as'sured** *a* sicuro di sé. **~-'catering** *a* in appartamento attrezzato di cucina. **~-'centred** *a* egocentrico. **~-'confidence** *n* fiducia *f* in se stesso. **~-'confident** *a* sicuro di sé. **~-'conscious** *a* impacciato. **~-con'tained** *a* ‹flat› con ingresso indipendente. **~-con'trol** *n* autocontrollo *m*. **~-de'fence** *n* autodifesa *f*; *Jur* legittima difesa *f*. **~-de'nial** *n* abnegazione *f*. **~-determi'nation** *n* autodeterminazione *f*. **~-em'ployed** *a* che lavora in proprio. **~-e'steem** *n* stima *f* di sé. **~-'evident** *a* ovvio. **~-'governing** *a* autonomo. **~-'help** *n* iniziativa *f* personale. **~-in'dulgent** *a* indulgente con se stesso. **~-'interest** *n* interesse *m* personale

self|ish /'selfɪʃ/ *a* egoista. **~ishness** *n* egoismo *m*. **~less** *a* disinteressato

self: **~-made** *a* che si è fatto da sé. **~-pity** *n* autocommiserazione *f*. **~-'portrait** *n* autoritratto *m*. **~-pos'sessed** *a* padrone di sé. **~-preser'vation** *n* istinto *m* di conservazione. **~-re'spect** *n* amor *m* proprio. **~-'righteous** *a* presuntuoso. **~-'sacrifice** *n* abnegazione *f*. **~-'satisfied** *a* compiaciuto di sé. **~-'service** *n* self-service *m* *inv* ● *attrib*

self-service. **~-suf'ficient** *a* autosuffi-
ciente. **~-'willed** *a* ostinato

sell /sel/ *v* (*pt/pp* **sold**) ● *vt* vendere; **be
sold out** essere esaurito ● *vi* vendersi.
sell off *vt* liquidare

seller /'selə(r)/ *n* venditore, -trice *mf*

Sellotape® /'seləʊ-/ *n* nastro *m* adesivo, scotch® *m*

'**sell-out** *n* (*fam: betrayal*) tradimento
m; **be a ~** (*concert:*) fare il tutto esaurito

selves /selvz/ *pl of* **self**

semblance /'sembləns/ *n* parvenza *f*

semen /'si:mən/ *n* Anat liquido *m* se-
minale

semester /sɪ'mestə(r)/ *n* Am semestre *m*

semi /'semɪ/. **~breve** /'semɪbri:v/ *n*
semibreve *f*. **~circle** /'semɪsɜ:k(ə)l/ *n*
semicerchio *m*. **~'circular** *a* semi-
circolare. **~'colon** *n* punto e virgola *m*.
~-de'tached *a* gemella ● *n* casa *f* gemella. **~-'final** *n* semifinale *f*

seminar /'semɪnɑ:(r)/ *n* seminario *m*.
~y /-nərɪ/ *n* seminario *m*

semolina /semə'li:nə/ *n* semolino *m*

senate /'senət/ *n* senato *m*. **~or** *n* se-
natore *m*

send /send/ *vt/i* (*pt/pp* **sent**) mandare;
~ for mandare a chiamare (*person*); far
venire (*thing*). **~er** *n* mittente *mf*.
~-off *n* commiato *m*

senile /'si:naɪl/ *a* arteriosclerotico; Med
senile. **~ity** /sɪ'nɪlətɪ/ *n* senilismo *m*

senior /'si:nɪə(r)/ *a* più vecchio; (*in
rank*) superiore ● *n* (*in rank*) superiore
mf; (*in sport*) senior *mf*; **she's two
years my ~** è più vecchia di me di due
anni. **~ citizen** *n* anziano, -a *mf*

seniority /si:nɪ'ɒrətɪ/ *n* anzianità *f* di
servizio

sensation /sen'seɪʃn/ *n* sensazione *f*.
~al *a* sensazionale. **~ally** *adv* in modo
sensazionale

sense /sens/ *n* senso *m*; (*common ~*)
buon senso *m*; **in a ~** in un certo senso;
make ~ aver senso ● *vt* sentire. **~less**
a insensato; (*unconscious*) privo di sensi

sensible /'sensəbl/ *a* sensato;
(*suitable*) appropriato. **~y** *adv* in modo
appropriato

sensitive /'sensətɪv/ *a* sensibile;
(*touchy*) suscettibile. **~ly** *adv* con sensibilità. **~ity** /-'tɪvɪtɪ/ *n* sensibilità *f inv*

sensory /'sensərɪ/ *a* sensoriale

sensual /'sensjʊəl/ *a* sensuale. **~ity**
/-'ælɪ/ *n* sensualità *f inv*

sensuous /'sensjʊəs/ *a* voluttuoso

sent /sent/ *see* **send**

sentence /'sentəns/ *n* frase *f*; Jur sentenza *f*; (*punishment*) condanna *f* ● *vt* **~
to** condannare a

sentiment /'sentɪmənt/ *n* sentimento
m; (*opinion*) opinione *f*; (*sentimentality*)
sentimentalismo *m*. **~al** /-'mentl/ *a* sen-
timentale; *pej* sentimentalista. **~ality**
/-'tælətɪ/ *n* sentimentalità *f inv*

sentry /'sentrɪ/ *n* sentinella *f*

separable /'sepərəbl/ *a* separabile

separate¹ /'sepərət/ *a* separato. **~ly**
adv separatamente

separate² /'sepəreɪt/ *vt* separare ● *vi*
separarsi. **~ion** /-'reɪʃn/ *n* separazione *f*

September /sep'tembə(r)/ *n* settem-
bre *m*

septic /'septɪk/ *a* settico; **go ~** infettarsi. **~ tank** *n* fossa *f* biologica

sequel /'si:kwəl/ *n* seguito *m*

sequence /'si:kwəns/ *n* sequenza *f*

sequin /'si:kwɪn/ *n* lustrino *m*,
paillette *f inv*

serenade /serə'neɪd/ *n* serenata *f* ● *vt*
fare una serenata a

serene /sɪ'ri:n/ *a* sereno. **~ity**
/-'renətɪ/ *n* serenità *f inv*

sergeant /'sɑ:dʒənt/ *n* sergente *m*

serial /'sɪərɪəl/ *n* racconto *m* a puntate;
TV sceneggiato *m* a puntate; *Radio* commedia *f* radiofonica a puntate. **~ize** *vt*
pubblicare a puntate; *Radio, TV* trasmettere a puntate. **~ killer** *n* serial killer *mf inv*. **~ number** *n* numero *m* di serie. **~ port** *n* Comput porta *f* seriale

series /'sɪəri:z/ *n* serie *f inv*

serious /'sɪərɪəs/ *a* serio; (*illness,
error*) grave. **~ly** *adv* seriamente; (*ill*)
gravemente; **take ~ly** prendere sul serio. **~ness** *n* serietà *f*; (*of situation*)
gravità *f*

sermon /'sɜ:mən/ *n* predica *f*

serpent /'sɜ:pənt/ *n* serpente *m*

serrated /se'reɪtd/ *a* dentellato

serum /'sɪərəm/ *n* siero *m*

servant /'sɜ:vənt/ *n* domestico, -a *mf*

serve /sɜ:v/ *n* Tennis servizio *m* ● *vt*
servire; scontare (*sentence*); **~ its
purpose** servire al proprio scopo; **it
~s you right!** ben ti sta!; **~s two** per
due persone ● *vi* prestare servizio; Ten-
nis servire; **~ as** servire da

server /'sɜ:və(r)/ *n* Comput server *m
inv*

service /'sɜ:vɪs/ *n* servizio *m*; Relig
funzione *f*; (*maintenance*) revisione *f*;
~s *pl* forze *fpl* armate; (*on motorway*)
area *f* di servizio. **in the ~s** sotto le
armi; **of ~ to** utile a; **out of ~**

⟨machine:⟩ guasto ● vt Techn revisionare. **~able** /-əbl/ a utilizzabile; ⟨hardwearing⟩ resistente; ⟨practical⟩ pratico **service:** **~ area** n area f di servizio. **~ charge** n servizio m. **~man** n militare m. **~ provider** n fornitore, -trice mf di servizi. **~ station** n stazione f di servizio

serviette /sɜːvɪ'et/ n tovagliolo m

servile /'sɜːvaɪl/ a servile

session /'seʃn/ n seduta f; Jur sessione f; Univ anno m accademico

set /set/ n serie f inv, set m inv; ⟨of crockery, cutlery⟩ servizio m; TV, Radio apparecchio m; Math insieme m; Theat scenario m; Cinema, Tennis set m inv; ⟨of people⟩ circolo m; ⟨of hair⟩ messa f in piega ● a ⟨ready⟩ pronto; ⟨rigid⟩ fisso; ⟨book⟩ in programma; **be ~ on doing sth** essere risoluto a fare qcsa; **be ~ in one's ways** essere abitudinario ● v (pt/pp **set**, pres p **setting**) ● vt mettere, porre; mettere ⟨alarm clock⟩; assegnare ⟨task, homework⟩; fissare ⟨date, limit⟩; chiedere ⟨questions⟩; montare ⟨gem⟩; assestare ⟨bone⟩; apparecchiare ⟨table⟩; **~ fire to** dare fuoco a; **~ free** liberare ● vi ⟨sun:⟩ tramontare; ⟨jelly, concrete:⟩ solidificare; **~ about doing sth** mettersi a fare qcsa. **set back** vt mettere indietro; ⟨hold up⟩ ritardare; ⟨fam: cost⟩ costare a. **set off** vi partire ● vt avviare; mettere ⟨alarm⟩; fare esplodere ⟨bomb⟩. **set out** vi partire; **~ out to do sth** proporsi di fare qcsa ● vt disporre; ⟨state⟩ esporre. **set to** vi mettersi all'opera. **set up** vt fondare ⟨company⟩; istituire ⟨committee⟩

'set-back n passo m indietro

set 'meal n menù m inv fisso

settee /se'tiː/ n divano m

setting /'setɪŋ/ n scenario m; ⟨position⟩ posizione f; ⟨of sun⟩ tramonto m; ⟨of jewel⟩ montatura f

settle /'setl/ vt ⟨decide⟩ definire; risolvere ⟨argument⟩; fissare ⟨date⟩; calmare ⟨nerves⟩; saldare ⟨bill⟩ ● vi ⟨to live⟩ stabilirsi; ⟨snow, dust, bird:⟩ posarsi; ⟨subside⟩ assestarsi; ⟨sediment:⟩ depositarsi. **settle down** vi sistemarsi; ⟨stop making noise⟩ calmarsi. **settle for** vt accontentarsi di. **settle up** vi regolare i conti

settlement /'setlmənt/ n ⟨agreement⟩ accordo m; ⟨of bill⟩ saldo m; ⟨colony⟩ insediamento m

settler /'setlə(r)/ n colonizzatore, -trice mf

'set-to n fam zuffa f; ⟨verbal⟩ battibecco m

'set-up n situazione f

seven /'sevn/ a & n sette m. **~teen** a & n diciassette m. **~'teenth** a & n diciassettesimo, -a mf

seventh /'sevnθ/ a & n settimo, -a mf

seventieth /'sevntɪɪθ/ a & n settantesimo, -a mf

seventy /'sevntɪ/ a & n settanta m

several /'sevrəl/ a & pron parecchi

sever|e /sɪ'vɪə(r)/ a severo; ⟨pain⟩ violento; ⟨illness⟩ grave; ⟨winter⟩ rigido. **~ely** adv severamente; ⟨ill⟩ gravemente. **~ity** /-'verətɪ/ n severità f; ⟨of pain⟩ violenza f; ⟨of illness⟩ gravità f; ⟨of winter⟩ rigore m

sew /səʊ/ vt/i (pt **sewed**, pp **sewn** or **sewed**) cucire. **sew up** vt ricucire

sewage /'suːɪdʒ/ n acque fpl di scolo

sewer /'suːə(r)/ n fogna f

sewing /'səʊɪŋ/ n cucito m; ⟨work⟩ lavoro m di cucito. **~ machine** n macchina f da cucire

sewn /səʊn/ see **sew**

sex /seks/ n sesso m; **have ~** avere rapporti sessuali. **~ist** a sessista. **~ offence** n delitto m a sfondo sessuale

sexual /'seksjʊəl/ a sessuale. **~ 'intercourse** n rapporti mpl sessuali. **~ity** /-'ælɪtɪ/ n sessualità f. **~ly** adv sessualmente

sexy /'seksɪ/ a (**-ier**, **-iest**) sexy inv

shabb|y /'ʃæbɪ/ a (**-ier**, **-iest**) sciabo; ⟨treatment⟩ meschino. **~iness** n trasandatezza f; ⟨of treatment⟩ meschinità f inv

shack /ʃæk/ n catapecchia f ● **shack up with** vt fam vivere con

shade /ʃeɪd/ n ombra f; ⟨of colour⟩ sfumatura f; ⟨for lamp⟩ paralume m; ⟨Am: for window⟩ tapparella f; **a ~ better** un tantino meglio ● vt riparare dalla luce; ⟨draw lines on⟩ ombreggiare. **~s** npl fam occhiali mpl da sole

shadow /'ʃædəʊ/ n ombra f; **S~ Cabinet** governo m ombra ● vt ⟨follow⟩ pedinare. **~y** a ombroso

shady /'ʃeɪdɪ/ a (**-ier**, **-iest**) ombroso; ⟨fam: disreputable⟩ losco

shaft /ʃɑːft/ n Techn albero m; ⟨of light⟩ raggio m; ⟨of lift, mine⟩ pozzo m

shaggy /'ʃægɪ/ a (**-ier**, **-iest**) irsuto; ⟨animal⟩ dal pelo arruffato

shake /ʃeɪk/ n scrollata f ● v (pt **shook**, pp **shaken**) ● vt scuotere; agitare ⟨bottle⟩; far tremare ⟨building⟩; **~ hands with** stringere la mano a ● vi tremare. **shake off** vt scrollarsi di dos-

441

so. **~-up** n Pol rimpasto m; Comm ristrutturazione f

shaky /'ʃeɪkɪ/ a (-ier, -iest) tremante; ⟨table etc⟩ traballante; ⟨unreliable⟩ vacillante

shall /ʃæl/ v aux I ~ go andrò; we ~ see vedremo; **what ~ I do?** cosa faccio?; **I'll come too, ~ I?** vengo anch'io, no?; **thou shalt not kill** liter non uccidere

shallow /'ʃæləʊ/ a basso, poco profondo; ⟨dish⟩ poco profondo; fig superficiale

sham /ʃæm/ a falso ●n finzione f; ⟨person⟩ spaccone, -a mf ●vt (pt/pp **shammed**) simulare

shambles /'ʃæmblz/ n baraonda fsg

shame /ʃeɪm/ n vergogna f; **it's a ~ that** è un peccato che; **what a ~!** che peccato! **~-faced** a vergognoso

shame|ful /'ʃeɪmfl/ a vergognoso. **~less** a spudorato

shampoo /ʃæm'puː/ n shampoo m inv ●vt fare uno shampoo a

shandy /'ʃændɪ/ n bevanda f a base di birra e gassosa

shan't /ʃɑːnt/ = **shall not**

shanty town /'ʃæntɪtaʊn/ n bidonville f inv, baraccopoli f inv

shape /ʃeɪp/ n forma f; ⟨figure⟩ ombra f; **take** ~ prendere forma; **get back in** ~ ritornare in forma ●vt dare forma a ⟨into di⟩ ●vi ~ [up] mettere la testa a posto; ~ **up nicely** mettersi bene. **~less** a informe

shapely /'ʃeɪplɪ/ a (-ier, -iest) ben fatto

share /ʃeə(r)/ n porzione f; Comm azione f ●vt dividere; condividere ⟨views⟩ ●vi dividere. **~holder** n azionista mf

shark /ʃɑːk/ n squalo m, pescecane m; fig truffatore, -trice mf

sharp /ʃɑːp/ a ⟨knife etc⟩ tagliente; ⟨pencil⟩ appuntito; ⟨drop⟩ a picco; ⟨reprimand⟩ severo; ⟨outline⟩ marcato; ⟨alert⟩ acuto; ⟨unscrupulous⟩ senza scrupoli; ~ **pain** fitta f ●adv in punto; Mus fuori tono; **look ~!** sbrigati! ●n Mus diesis m inv. **~en** vt affilare ⟨knife⟩; appuntire ⟨pencil⟩

shatter /'ʃætə(r)/ vt frantumare; fig mandare in frantumi; **~ed** ⟨fam: exhausted⟩ a pezzi ●vi frantumarsi

shav|e /ʃeɪv/ n rasatura f; **have a ~e** farsi la barba ●vt radere ●vi radersi. **~er** n rasoio m elettrico. **~ing-brush** n pennello m da barba. **~ing foam** n schiuma f da barba; **~ing soap** n sapone m da barba

shawl /ʃɔːl/ n scialle m

she /ʃiː/ pers pron lei

sheaf /ʃiːf/ n (pl **sheaves**) fascio m

shear /ʃɪə(r)/ vt (pt **sheared**, pp **shorn** or **sheared**) tosare

shears /ʃɪəz/ npl ⟨for hedge⟩ cesoie fpl

sheath /ʃiːθ/ n (pl ~s /ʃiːðz/) guaina f

shed¹ /ʃed/ n baracca f; ⟨for cattle⟩ stalla f

shed² vt (pt/pp **shed**, pres p **shedding**) perdere; versare ⟨blood, tears⟩; ~ **light on** far luce su

sheen /ʃiːn/ n lucentezza f

sheep /ʃiːp/ n inv pecora f. **~-dog** n cane m da pastore

sheepish /'ʃiːpɪʃ/ a imbarazzato. **~ly** adv con aria imbarazzata

'sheepskin n [pelle f di] montone m

sheer /ʃɪə(r)/ a puro; ⟨steep⟩ a picco; ⟨transparent⟩ trasparente ●adv a picco

sheet /ʃiːt/ n lenzuolo m; ⟨of paper⟩ foglio m; ⟨of glass, metal⟩ lastra f

shelf /ʃelf/ n (pl **shelves**) ripiano m; ⟨set of shelves⟩ scaffale m

shell /ʃel/ n conchiglia f; ⟨of egg, snail, tortoise⟩ guscio m; ⟨of crab⟩ corazza f; ⟨of unfinished building⟩ ossatura f; Mil granata f ●vt sgusciare ⟨peas⟩; Mil bombardare. **shell out** vi fam sborsare

'shellfish n inv mollusco m; Culin frutti mpl di mare

shelter /'ʃeltə(r)/ n rifugio m; ⟨air raid ~⟩ rifugio m antiaereo ●vt riparare ⟨from da⟩; fig mettere al riparo; ⟨give lodging to⟩ dare asilo a ●vi rifugiarsi. **~ed** a ⟨spot⟩ riparato; ⟨life⟩ ritirato

shelve /ʃelv/ vt accantonare ⟨project⟩

shelves /ʃelvz/ see **shelf**

shelving /'ʃelvɪŋ/ n ⟨shelves⟩ ripiani mpl

shepherd /'ʃepəd/ n pastore m ●vt guidare. **~'s pie** n pasticcio m di carne tritata e patate

sherry /'ʃerɪ/ n sherry m inv

shield /ʃiːld/ n scudo m; ⟨for eyes⟩ maschera f; Techn schermo m ●vt proteggere ⟨from da⟩

shift /ʃɪft/ n cambiamento m; ⟨in position⟩ spostamento m; ⟨at work⟩ turno m ●vt spostare; ⟨take away⟩ togliere; riversare ⟨blame⟩ ●vi spostarsi; ⟨wind:⟩ cambiare; ⟨fam: move quickly⟩ darsi una mossa

'shift work n turni mpl

shifty /'ʃɪftɪ/ a (-ier, -iest) pej losco; ⟨eyes⟩ sfuggente

shilly-shally /'ʃɪlɪʃælɪ/ vi titubare

shimmer /'ʃɪmə(r)/ n luccichio m • vi luccicare

shin /ʃɪn/ n stinco m

shine /ʃaɪn/ n lucentezza f; **give sth a ~** dare una lucidata a qcsa • v (pt/pp **shone**) • vi splendere; (reflect light) brillare; (hair, shoes:) essere lucido • vt **~ a light on** puntare una luce su

shingle /'ʃɪŋgl/ n (pebbles) ghiaia f

shingles /'ʃɪŋglz/ n Med fuochi mpl di Sant'Antonio

shiny /'ʃaɪnɪ/ a (-ier, -iest) lucido

ship /ʃɪp/ n nave f • vt (pt/pp **shipped**) spedire; (by sea) spedire via mare

ship: ~ment n spedizione f; (consignment) carico m. **~per** n spedizioniere m. **~ping** n trasporto m; (traffic) imbarcazioni fpl. **~shape** a & adv in perfetto ordine. **~wreck** n naufragio m. **~wrecked** a naufragato. **~yard** n cantiere m navale

shirk /ʃɜːk/ vt scansare. **~er** n scansafatiche mf inv

shirt /ʃɜːt/ n camicia f; **in ~-sleeves** in maniche di camicia

shit /ʃɪt/ vulg n & int merda f • vi (pt/pp **shit**) cagare

shiver /'ʃɪvə(r)/ n brivido m • vi rabbrividire

shoal /ʃəʊl/ n (of fish) banco m

shock /ʃɒk/ n (impact) urto m; Electr scossa f [elettrica]; fig colpo m, shock m inv; Med shock m inv; **get a ~** Electr prendere la scossa • vt scioccare. **~ing** a scioccante; (fam: weather, handwriting etc) tremendo

shod /ʃɒd/ see **shoe**

shoddy /'ʃɒdɪ/ a (-ier, -iest) scadente

shoe /ʃuː/ n scarpa f; (of horse) ferro m • vt (pt/pp **shod**, pres p **shoeing**) ferrare (horse)

shoe: ~horn n calzante m. **~-lace** n laccio m da scarpa. **~maker** n calzolaio m. **~-shop** n calzoleria f. **~-string** n on a **~-string** fam con una miseria

shone /ʃɒn/ see **shine**

shoo /ʃuː/ vt **~ away** cacciar via • int sciò

shook /ʃʊk/ see **shake**

shoot /ʃuːt/ n Bot germoglio m; (hunt) battuta f di caccia • v (pt/pp **shot**) • vt sparare; girare (film) • vi (hunt) andare a caccia. **shoot down** vt abbattere. **shoot out** vi (rush) precipitarsi fuori. **shoot up** vi (grow) crescere in fretta; (prices:) salire di colpo

'shooting-range n poligono m di tiro

shop /ʃɒp/ n negozio m; (workshop) of-

ficina f; **talk ~** fam parlare di lavoro • vi (pt/pp **shopped**) far compere; **go ~ping** andare a fare compere. **shop around** vi confrontare i prezzi

shop: ~ assistant n commesso, -a mf. **~keeper** n negoziante mf. **~-lifter** n taccheggiatore, -trice mf. **~-lifting** n taccheggio m; **~per** n compratore, -trice mf

shopping /'ʃɒpɪŋ/ n compere fpl; (articles) acquisti mpl; **do the ~** fare la spesa. **~ bag** n borsa f per la spesa. **~ centre** n centro m commerciale. **~ trolley** n carrello m

shop: ~-steward n rappresentante mf sindacale. **~-'window** n vetrina f

shore /ʃɔː(r)/ n riva f

shorn /ʃɔːn/ see **shear**

short /ʃɔːt/ a corto; (not lasting) breve; (person) basso; (curt) brusco; **a ~ time ago** poco tempo fa; **be ~ of** essere a corto di; **be in ~ supply** essere scarso; fig essere raro; **Mick is ~ for Michael** Mick è il diminutivo di Michael • adv bruscamente; **in ~** in breve; **~ of doing** a meno che di fare; **go ~** essere privato (of di); **stop ~ of doing sth** non arrivare fino a fare qcsa; **cut ~** interrompere (meeting, holiday); **to cut a long story ~** per farla breve

shortage /'ʃɔːtɪdʒ/ n scarsità f inv

short: ~bread n biscotto m di pasta frolla. **~ 'circuit** n corto m circuito. **~coming** n difetto m. **~ 'cut** n scorciatoia f

shorten /'ʃɔːtn/ vt abbreviare; accorciare (garment)

short: ~hand n stenografia f. **~-'handed** a a corto di personale. **~hand 'typist** n stenodattilografo, -a mf. **~ list** n lista f dei candidati selezionati per un lavoro. **~-lived** /-lɪvd/ a di breve durata

short|ly /'ʃɔːtlɪ/ adv presto; **~ly before/after** poco prima/dopo. **~ness** n brevità f inv; (of person) bassa statura f

short-range a di breve portata

shorts /ʃɔːts/ npl calzoncini mpl corti

short: ~-'sighted a miope. **~-'sleeved** a a maniche corte. **~-'staffed** a a corto di personale. **~ 'story** n racconto m, novella f. **~-'tempered** a irascibile. **~-'term** a a breve termine. **~ wave** n onde fpl corte

shot /ʃɒt/ see **shoot** • n colpo m; (person) tiratore m; Phot foto f inv; (injection) puntura f; (fam: attempt) pro-

443 | should | side

va *f*; **like a ~** *fam* come un razzo. **~gun** *n* fucile *m* da caccia

should /ʃʊd/ *v aux* **I → go** dovrei andare; **I ~ have seen him** avrei dovuto vederlo; **I ~ like** mi piacerebbe; **this ~ be enough** questo dovrebbe bastare; **if he ~ come** se dovesse venire

shoulder /ˈʃəʊldə(r)/ *n* spalla *f* ● *vt* mettersi in spalla; *fig* accollarsi. **~-bag** *n* borsa *f* a tracolla. **~-blade** *n* scapola *f*. **~-strap** *n* spallina *f*; *(of bag)* tracolla *f*

shout /ʃaʊt/ *n* grido *m* ● *vt/i* gridare. **shout at** *vi* alzar la voce con. **shout down** *vt* azzittire gridando

shouting /ˈʃaʊtɪŋ/ *n* grida *fpl*

shove /ʃʌv/ *n* spintone *m* ● *vt* spingere; *(fam: put)* ficcare ● *vi* spingere. **shove off** *vi fam* togliersi di torno

shovel /ˈʃʌvl/ *n* pala *f* ● *vt* *(pt/pp* **shovelled**) spalare

show /ʃəʊ/ *n* *(display)* manifestazione *f*; *(exhibition)* mostra *f*; *(ostentation)* ostentazione *f*; *Theat, TV* spettacolo *m*; *(programme)* programma *m*; **on ~** esposto ● *v* *(pt* **showed**, *pp* **shown**) ● *vt* mostrare; *(put on display)* esporre; proiettare *(film)* ● *vi* *(film:)* essere proiettato; **your slip is ~ing** ti si vede la sottoveste. **show in** *vt* fare accomodare. **show off** *vi fam* mettersi in mostra ● *vt* mettere in mostra. **show up** *vi* risaltare; *(fam: arrive)* farsi vedere ● *vt* *(fam: embarrass)* far fare una brutta figura *f*

'show-down *n* regolamento *m* dei conti

shower /ˈʃaʊə(r)/ *n* doccia *f*; *(of rain)* acquazzone *m*; **have a ~** fare la doccia ● *vt* **~ with** coprire di ● *vi* fare la doccia. **~proof** *a* impermeabile. **~y** *a* da acquazzoni

'show-jumping *n* concorso *m* ippico

shown /ʃəʊn/ *see* **show**

'show-off *n* esibizionista *mf*

showy /ˈʃəʊi/ *a* appariscente

shrank /ʃræŋk/ *see* **shrink**

shred /ʃred/ *n* brandello *m*; *fig* briciolo *m* ● *vt* *(pt/pp* **shredded**) fare a brandelli; *Culin* tagliuzzare. **~der** *n* distruttore *m* di documenti

shrewd /ʃruːd/ *a* accorto. **~ness** *n* accortezza *f*

shriek /ʃriːk/ *n* strillo *m* ● *vt/i* strillare

shrift /ʃrɪft/ *n* **give sb short ~** liquidare qcno rapidamente

shrill /ʃrɪl/ *a* penetrante

shrimp /ʃrɪmp/ *n* gamberetto *m*

shrine /ʃraɪn/ *n* *(place)* santuario *m*

shrink /ʃrɪŋk/ *vi* *(pt* **shrank**, *pp* **shrunk**) restringersi; *(draw back)* ritrarsi *(from* da)

shrivel /ˈʃrɪvl/ *vi* *(pt/pp* **shrivelled**) raggrinzare

shroud /ʃraʊd/ *n* sudario *m*; *fig* manto *m*

Shrove /ʃrəʊv/ *n* **~ 'Tuesday** martedì *m* grasso

shrub /ʃrʌb/ *n* arbusto *m*

shrug /ʃrʌɡ/ *n* scrollata *f* di spalle ● *vt/i* *(pt/pp* **shrugged**) **~ [one's shoulders]** scrollare le spalle

shrunk /ʃrʌŋk/ *see* **shrink**. **~en** *a* rimpicciolito

shudder /ˈʃʌdə(r)/ *n* fremito *m* ● *vi* fremere

shuffle /ˈʃʌfl/ *vi* strascicare i piedi ● *vt* mescolare *(cards)*

shun /ʃʌn/ *vt* *(pt/pp* **shunned**) rifuggire

shunt /ʃʌnt/ *vt* smistare

shush /ʃʊʃ/ *int* zitto!

shut /ʃʌt/ *v* *(pt/pp* **shut**, *pres p* **shutting**) ● *vt* chiudere ● *vi* chiudersi; *(shop:)* chiudere. **shut down** *vt/i* chiudere. **shut up** *vt* chiudere. *fam* far tacere ● *vi fam* stare zitto; **~ up!** stai zitto!

'shut-down *n* chiusura *f*

shutter /ˈʃʌtə(r)/ *n* serranda *f*; *Phot* otturatore *m*

shuttle /ˈʃʌtl/ *n* navetta *f* ● *vi* far la spola

shuttle: ~cock *n* volano *m*. **~ service** *n* servizio *m* pendolare

shy /ʃaɪ/ *a* *(timid)* timido. **~ness** *n* timidezza *f*

Siamese /saɪəˈmiːz/ *a* siamese

sibling /ˈsɪblɪŋz/ *n* *(brother)* fratello *m*; *(sister)* sorella *f*; **~s** *pl* fratelli *mpl*

Sicily /ˈsɪsɪli/ *n* Sicilia *f*. **~ian** *a* & *n* siciliano, -a *mf*

sick /sɪk/ *a* ammalato; *(humour)* macabro; **be ~** *(vomit)* vomitare; **be ~ of sth** *fam* essere stufo di qcsa; **feel ~** aver la nausea

sicken /ˈsɪkn/ *vt* disgustare ● *vi* **be ~ing for something** covare qualche malanno. **~ing** *a* disgustoso

sickly /ˈsɪkli/ *a* *(-ier, -iest)* malaticcio. **~ness** *n* malattia *f*; *(vomiting)* nausea *f*. **~ness benefit** *n* indennità *f* di malattia

side /saɪd/ *n* lato *m*; *(of person, mountain)* fianco *m*; *(of road)* bordo *m*; **on the ~** *(as sideline)* come attività secondaria; **~ by ~** fianco a fianco; **take ~s** immischiarsi; **take sb's ~** prende-

re le parti di qcno; **be on the safe ~**
andare sul sicuro ●*attrib* laterale ●*vi*
~ with parteggiare per

side: ~board *n* credenza *f*. **~burns** *npl*
basette *fpl*. **~-effect** *n* effetto *m*
collaterale. **~lights** *npl* luci *fpl* di posizione. **~line** *n* attività *f inv* complementare. **~-show** *n* attrazione *f*.
~-step *vt* schivare. **~-track** *vt* sviare.
~walk *n Am* marciapiede *m*. **~ways**
adv obliquamente

siding /'saɪdɪŋ/ *n* binario *m* di raccordo

sidle /'saɪdl/ *vi* camminare furtivamente (**up to** verso)

siege /siːdʒ/ *n* assedio *m*

sieve /sɪv/ *n* setaccio *m* ● *vt* setacciare

sift /sɪft/ *vt* setacciare; **~ [through]** *fig*
passare al setaccio

sigh /saɪ/ *n* sospiro *m* ● *vi* sospirare

sight /saɪt/ *n* vista *f*; (*on gun*) mirino *m*;
the ~s *pl* le cose da vedere; **at first ~** a
prima vista; **be within/out of ~**
essere/non essere in vista; **lose ~ of**
perdere di vista; **know by ~** conoscere
di vista. **have bad ~** vederci male ● *vt*
avvistare

'sightseeing *n* **go ~** andare a visitare
posti

sign /saɪn/ *n* segno *m*; (*notice*) insegna *f*
● *vt/i* firmare. **sign on** *vi* (*as
unemployed*) presentarsi all'ufficio di
collocamento; *Mil* arruolarsi

signal /'sɪgnl/ *n* segnale *m* ● *v* (*pt/pp*
signalled) ● *vt* segnalare ● *vi* fare se-
gnali; **~ to sb** far segno a qcno (**to** di).
~-box *n* cabina *f* di segnalazione

signature /'sɪgnətʃə(r)/ *n* firma *f*. **~
tune** *n* sigla *f* [musicale]

signet-ring /'sɪgnɪt-/ *n* anello *m* con sigillo

significan|ce /sɪg'nɪfɪkəns/ *n* significa-
cato *m*. **~t** *a* significativo

signify /'sɪgnɪfaɪ/ *vt* (*pt/pp* **-ied**) indicare

sign-language *n* linguaggio *m* dei se-
gni

signpost /'saɪn-/ *n* segnalazione *f* stradale

silence /'saɪləns/ *n* silenzio *m* ● *vt* far
tacere. **~r** *n* (*on gun*) silenziatore *m*;
Auto marmitta *f*

silent /'saɪlənt/ *a* silenzioso; (*film*)
muto; **remain ~** rimanere in silenzio.
~ly *adv* silenziosamente

silhouette /sɪlʊ'et/ *n* sagoma *f*, silhouette *f inv* ● *vt* **be ~d** profilarsi

silicon /'sɪlɪkən/ *n* silicio *m*. **~ chip**
piastrina *f* di silicio

silk /sɪlk/ *n* seta *f* ● *attrib* di seta.
~worm *n* baco *m* da seta

silky /'sɪlkɪ/ *a* (**-ier, -iest**) come la seta

sill /sɪl/ *n* davanzale *m*

silly /'sɪlɪ/ *a* (**-ier, -iest**) sciocco

silo /'saɪləʊ/ *n* silo *m*

silt /sɪlt/ *n* melma *f*

silver /'sɪlvə(r)/ *a* d'argento; (*paper*)
argentato ● *n* argento *m*; (*silverware*)
argenteria *f*

silver: ~-plated *a* placcato d'argento.
~ware *n* argenteria *f*. **~ 'wedding** *n*
nozze *fpl* d'argento

similar /'sɪmɪlə(r)/ *a* simile. **~ity**
/-'lærətɪ/ *n* somiglianza *f*. **~ly** *adv* in
modo simile

simile /'sɪmɪlɪ/ *n* similitudine *f*

simmer /'sɪmə(r)/ *vi* bollire lentamente ● *vt* far bollire lentamente. **simmer
down** *vi* calmarsi

simple /'sɪmpl/ *a* semplice; (*person*)
sempliciotto. **~-'minded** *a* sempliciotto

simplicity /sɪm'plɪsətɪ/ *n* semplicità *f*

simpli|fication /sɪmplɪfɪ'keɪʃn/ *n*
semplificazione *f*. **~fy** /'sɪmplɪfaɪ/ *vt*
(*pt/pp* **-ied**) semplificare

simply /'sɪmplɪ/ *adv* semplicemente

simulat|e /'sɪmjʊleɪt/ *vt* simulare.
~ion /-'leɪʃn/ *n* simulazione *f*

simultaneous /sɪml'teɪnɪəs/ *a* simul-
taneo

sin /sɪn/ *n* peccato *m* ● *vi* (*pt/pp*
sinned) peccare

since /sɪns/ *prep* da ● *adv* da allora
● *conj* da quando; (*because*) siccome

sincere /sɪn'sɪə(r)/ *a* sincero. **~ly** *adv*
sinceramente; **Yours ~ly** distinti saluti

sincerity /sɪn'serətɪ/ *n* sincerità *f*

sinful /'sɪnfl/ *a* peccaminoso

sing /sɪŋ/ *vt/i* (*pt* **sang**, *pp* **sung**) cantare

singe /sɪndʒ/ *vt* (*pres p* **singeing**) bru-
ciacchiare

singer /'sɪŋə(r)/ *n* cantante *mf*

single /'sɪŋgl/ *a* solo; (*not double*) semplice; (*unmarried*) celibe; (*woman*) nubile; (*room*) singolo; (*bed*) a una piazza
● *n* (*ticket*) biglietto *m* di sola andata;
(*record*) singolo *m*; **~s** *pl Tennis* singolo
m ● **single out** *vt* scegliere; (*distinguish*) distinguere

single: ~-breasted *a* a un petto.
~-handed *a & adv* da solo. **~-minded** *a*
risoluto. **~ 'parent** *n* genitore *m* che alleva il figlio da solo

singly /'sɪŋglɪ/ *adv* singolarmente

singular /'sɪŋgjʊlə(r)/ *a Gram* singolare •*n* singolare *m.* ~**ly** *adv* singolarmente

sinister/'sınıstə(r)/ *a* sinistro

sink/sıŋk/ *n* lavandino *m* •*v* (*pt* **sank**, *pp* **sunk**) •*vi* affondare •*vt* affondare ‹*ship*›; scavare ‹*shaft*›; investire ‹*money*›. **sink in**^{vi} penetrare; **it took a while to ~ in** (*fam: be understood*) c'è voluto un po' a capirlo

sinner/'sınə(r)/ *n* peccatore, -trice *mf*

sinus/'saınəs/ *n* seno *m* paranasale. ~**itis** *n* sinusite *f*

sip/sıp/ *n* sorso *m.* •*vt* (*pt/pp* **sipped**) sorseggiare

siphon/'saıfn/ *n* (*bottle*) sifone *m* • **siphon off** *vt* travasare (con sifone)

sir/sɜː(r)/ *n* signore *m*; **S~** (*title*) Sir *m*; **Dear S~s** Spettabile ditta

siren/'saırən/ *n* sirena *f*

sissy/'sısı/ *n* femminuccia *f*

sister/'sıstə(r)/ *n* sorella *f*; (*nurse*) [infermiera *f*] caposala *f.* ~**-in-law** *n* (*pl* ~**s-in-law**) cognata *f.* ~**ly** *a* da sorella

sit/sıt/ *v* (*pt/pp* **sat**,^{pres p} **sitting**) •*vi* essere seduto, (*sit down*) sedersi; (*committee:*) riunirsi •*vt* sostenere ‹*exam*›. **sit back** *vi fig* starsene con le mani in mano. **sit down**^{vi} mettersi a sedere. **sit up** *vi* mettersi seduto; (*not slouch*) star seduto diritto; (*stay up*) stare alzato

site/saıt/ *n* posto *m*; *Archaeol* sito *m*; (*building ~*) cantiere *m* •*vt* collocare

sit-in/'sıtın/ *n* occupazione *f* (*di fabbrica ecc*)

sitting/'sıtıŋ/ *n* seduta *f*; (*for meals*) turno *m.* ~**-room** *n* salotto *m*

situat|e/'sıtjʊeıt/ *vt* situare. ~**ed** *a* situato. ~**ion** /-'eıʃn/ *n* situazione *f*; (*location*) posizione *f*; (*job*) posto *m*

six/sıks/ *a & n* sei *m.* ~**teen** *a & n* sedici *m.* ~**teenth** *a & n* sedicesimo, -a *mf*

sixth/sıksθ/ *a & n* sesto, -a *mf*

sixtieth/'sıkstııθ/ *a & n* sessantesimo, -a *mf*

sixty/'sıkstı/ *a & n* sessanta *m*

size/saız/ *n* dimensioni *fpl*; (*of clothes*) taglia *f*, misura *f*; (*of shoes*) numero *m*; **what ~ is the room?** che dimensioni ha la stanza? • **size up** *vt fam* valutare

sizeable/'saızəbl/ *a* piuttosto grande

sizzle/'sızl/ *vi* sfrigolare

skate¹/skeıt/ *n inv* (*fish*) razza *f*

skate² *n* pattino *m* •*vi* pattinare

skateboard/'skeıtbɔːd/ *n* skate-board *m inv*

skater/'skeıtə(r)/ *n* pattinatore, -trice *mf*

skating/'skeıtıŋ/ *n* pattinaggio *m.* ~**-rink** *n* pista *f* di pattinaggio

skeleton/'skelıtn/ *n* scheletro *m.* ~ '**key** *n* passe-partout *m inv.* ~ '**staff** *n* personale *m* ridotto

sketch/sketʃ/ *n* schizzo *m*; *Theat* sketch *m inv* •*vt* fare uno schizzo di

sketch|y/'sketʃı/ *a* (**-ier, -iest**) abbozzato. ~**ily** *adv* in modo abbozzato

skewer/'skjʊə(r)/ *n* spiedo *m*

ski/skiː/ *n* sci *m inv* •*vi* (*pt/pp* **skied**, *pres p* **skiing**) sciare; **go ~ing** andare a sciare

skid/skıd/ *n* slittata *f* •*vi* (*pt/pp* **skidded**) slittare

skier/'skiːə(r)/ *n* sciatore, -trice *mf*

skiing/'skiːıŋ/ *n* sci *m*

skilful/'skılfl/ *a* abile

'**ski-lift** *n* impianto *m* di risalita

skill/skıl/ *n* abilità *f inv.* ~**ed** *a* dotato; ‹*worker*› specializzato

skim/skım/ *vt* (*pt/pp* **skimmed**) schiumare; scremare ‹*milk*›. **skim off** *vt* togliere. **skim through** *vt* scorrere

skimp/skımp/ *vi* ~ **on** lesinare su

skimpy/'skımpı/ *a* (**-ier, -iest**) succinto

skin/skın/ *n* pelle *f*; (*on fruit*) buccia *f* •*vt* (*pt/pp* **skinned**) spellare

skin: ~**-deep** *a* superficiale. ~**-diving** *n* nuoto *m* subacqueo

skinflint/'skınflınt/ *n* miserabile *mf*

skinny/'skını/ *a* (**-ier, -iest**) molto magro

skip¹/skıp/ *n* (*container*) benna *f*

skip² *n* salto *m* •*v* (*pt/pp* **skipped**) •*vi* saltellare; (*with rope*) saltare la corda •*vt* omettere

skipper/'skıpə(r)/ *n* skipper *m inv*

skipping-rope/'skıpıŋrəʊp/ *n* corda *f* per saltare

skirmish/'skɜːmıʃ/ *n* scaramuccia *f*

skirt/skɜːt/ *n* gonna *f* •*vt* costeggiare

skit/skıt/ *n* bozzetto *m* comico

skittle/'skıtl/ *n* birillo *m*

skive/skaıv/ *vi fam* fare lo scansafatiche

skulk/skʌlk/ *vi* aggirarsi furtivamente

skull/skʌl/ *n* cranio *m*

skunk/skʌŋk/ *n* moffetta *f*

sky/skaı/ *n* cielo *m.* ~**light** *n* lucernario *m.* ~**scraper** *n* grattacielo *m*

slab/slæb/ *n* lastra *f*; (*slice*) fetta *f*; (*of chocolate*) tavoletta *f*

slack/slæk/ *a* lento; ‹*person*› fiacco •*vi* fare lo scansafatiche. **slack off** *vi* rilassarsi

slacken/'slækn/ *vi* allentare; ~ [**off**]

⟨*trade:*⟩ rallentare; ⟨*speed, rain:*⟩ diminuire ●*vt* allentare; diminuire ⟨*speed*⟩

slacks /slæks/ *npl* pantaloni *mpl* sportivi

slag /slæg/ *n* scorie *fpl* ● **slag off** *vt* (*pt/pp* **slagged**) *Br fam* criticare

slain /sleɪn/ *see* slay

slam /slæm/ *v* (*pt/pp* **slammed**) ●*vt* sbattere; (*fam: criticize*) stroncare ●*vi* sbattere –

slander /'slɑːndə(r)/ *n* diffamazione *f* ●*vt* diffamare. **~ous** /-rəs/ *a* diffamatorio

slang /slæŋ/ *n* gergo *m*. **~y** *a* gergale

slant /slɑːnt/ *n* pendenza *f*; ⟨*point of view*⟩ angolazione *f*; **on the ~** in pendenza ●*vt* pendere; *fig* distorcere ⟨*report*⟩ ●*vi* pendere

slap /slæp/ *n* schiaffo *m* ●*vt* (*pt/pp* **slapped**) schiaffeggiare; (*put*) schiaffare ●*adv* in pieno

slap: ~dash *a fam* frettoloso. **~-up** *a fam* di prim'ordine

slash /slæʃ/ *n* taglio *m* ●*vt* tagliare; ridurre drasticamente ⟨*prices*⟩

slat /slæt/ *n* stecca *f*

slate /sleɪt/ *n* ardesia *f* ●*vt fam* fare a pezzi

slaughter /'slɔːtə(r)/ *n* macello *m*; (*of people*) massacro *m* ●*vt* macellare; massacrare ⟨*people*⟩. **~house** *n* macello *m*

Slav /slɑːv/ *a* slavo ●*n* slavo, -a *f*

slave /sleɪv/ *n* schiavo, -a *mf* ●*vi* **~ [away]** lavorare come un negro. **~-driver** *n* schiavista *mf*

slav|ery /'sleɪvərɪ/ *n* schiavitù *f*. **~ish** *a* servile

Slavonic /slə'vɒnɪk/ *a* slavo

slay /sleɪ/ *vt* (*pt* **slew**, *pp* **slain**) ammazzare

sleazy /'sliːzɪ/ *a* (**-ier, -iest**) sordido

sledge /sledʒ/ *n* slitta *f*. **~-hammer** *n* martello *m*

sleek /sliːk/ *a* liscio, lucente; (*well-fed*) pasciuto

sleep /sliːp/ *n* sonno *m*; **go to ~** addormentarsi; **put to ~** far addormentare ●*v* (*pt/pp* **slept**) ●*vi* dormire ●*vt* **~s six** ha sei posti letto. **~er** *n* Rail treno *m* con vagoni letto; (*compartment*) vagone *m* letto; **be a light/heavy ~er** avere il sonno leggero/pesante

sleeping: ~-bag *n* sacco *m* a pelo. **~-car** *n* vagone *m* letto. **~-pill** *n* sonnifero *m*

sleep: ~less *a* insonne. **~lessness** *n* insonnia *f*. **~-walker** *n* sonnambulo, -a *mf*. **~-walking** *n* sonnambulismo *m*

sleepy /'sliːpɪ/ *a* (**-ier, -iest**) assonnato; **be ~** aver sonno

sleet /sliːt/ *n* nevischio *m* ●*vi* **it is ~ing** nevischia

sleeve /sliːv/ *n* manica *f*; (*for record*) copertina *f*. **~less** *a* senza maniche

sleigh /sleɪ/ *n* slitta *f*

sleight /slaɪt/ *n* **~ of hand** gioco *m* di prestigio

slender /'slendə(r)/ *a* snello; ⟨*fingers, stem*⟩ affusolato; *fig* scarso; ⟨*chance*⟩ magro

slept /slept/ *see* sleep

sleuth /sluːθ/ *n* investigatore *m*, detective *m inv*

slew¹ /sluː/ *vi* girare

slew² *see* slay

slice /slaɪs/ *n* fetta *f* ●*vt* affettare; **~d bread** pane *m* a cassetta

slick /slɪk/ *a* liscio; (*cunning*) astuto ●*n* (*of oil*) chiazza *f* di petrolio

slid|e /slaɪd/ *n* scivolata *f*; (*in playground*) scivolo *m*; (*for hair*) fermaglio *m* (*per capelli*); *Phot* diapositiva *f* ●*v* (*pt/pp* **slid**) ●*vi* scivolare ●*vt* far scivolare. **~-rule** *n* regolo *m* calcolatore. **~ing** *a* ⟨*door, seat*⟩ scorrevole. **~ing scale** *n* scala *f* mobile

slight /slaɪt/ *a* leggero, ⟨*importance*⟩ poco; ⟨*slender*⟩ esile. **~est** minimo; **not in the ~est** niente affatto ●*vt* offendere ●*n* offesa *f*. **~ly** *adv* leggermente

slim /slɪm/ *a* (**slimmer, slimmest**) snello; *fig* scarso; ⟨*chance*⟩ magro ●*vi* dimagrire

slim|e /slaɪm/ *n* melma *f*. **~y** *a* melmoso; *fig* viscido

sling /slɪŋ/ *n* Med benda *f* al collo ●*vt* (*pt/pp* **slung**) *fam* lanciare

slip /slɪp/ *n* scivolata *f*; (*mistake*) lieve errore *m*; (*petticoat*) sottoveste *f*; (*for pillow*) federa *f*; (*paper*) scontrino *m*; **give sb the ~** sbarazzarsi di qcno; **~ of the tongue** lapsus *m inv* ●*v* (*pt/pp* **slipped**) ●*vi* scivolare; (*go quickly*) sgattaiolare; (*decline*) retrocedere ●*vt* **he ~ped it into his pocket** se l'è infilato in tasca; **~ sb's mind** sfuggire di mente a qcno. **slip away** *vi* sgusciar via; ⟨*time:*⟩ sfuggire. **slip into** *vi* infilarsi ⟨*clothes*⟩. **slip up** *vi fam* sbagliare

slipped 'disc *n* Med ernia *f* del disco

slipper /'slɪpə(r)/ *n* pantofola *f*

slippery /'slɪpərɪ/ *a* scivoloso

slip-road *n* bretella *f*

slipshod /'slɪpʃɒd/ *a* trascurato

'slip-up *n fam* sbaglio *m*

slit /slɪt/ n spacco m; (tear) strappo m; (hole) fessura f ● vt (pt/pp **slit**) tagliare

slither /'slɪðə(r)/ vi scivolare

sliver /'slɪvə(r)/ n scheggia f

slobber /'slɒbə(r)/ vi sbavare

slog /slɒg/ n (**hard**) ~ sgobbata f ● vi (pt/pp **slogged**) (work) sgobbare

slogan /'sləʊgən/ n slogan m inv

slop /slɒp/ v (pt/pp **slopped**) ● vt versare. **slop over** vi versarsi

slop|e /sləʊp/ n pendenza f; (ski ~) pista f ● vi essere inclinato, inclinarsi. **~ing** a in pendenza

sloppy /'slɒpɪ/ a (**-ier, -iest**) (work) trascurato; (worker) negligente; (in dress) sciatto; (sentimental) sdolcinato

slosh /slɒʃ/ vi fam (person, feet:) sguazzare; (water:) scrosciare ● vt (fam: hit) colpire

sloshed /slɒʃt/ a fam sbronzo

slot /slɒt/ n fessura f; (time-~) spazio m ● v (pt/pp **slotted**) ● vt infilare. **slot in** vi incastrarsi

'slot-machine n distributore m automatico; (for gambling) slot-machine f inv

slouch /slaʊtʃ/ vi (in chair) stare scomposto

slovenl|y /'slʌvnlɪ/ a sciatto. **~iness** n sciatteria f

slow /sləʊ/ a lento; **be** ~ (clock:) essere indietro; **in** ~ **motion** al rallentatore ● adv lentamente ● **slow down, up** vt/i rallentare

slow: **~coach** n fam tartaruga f. **~ly** adv lentamente. **~ness** n lentezza f

sludge /slʌdʒ/ n fanghiglia f

slug /slʌg/ n lumacone m; (fam: bullet) pallottola f

sluggish /'slʌgɪʃ/ a lento

sluice /slu:s/ n chiusa f

slum /slʌm/ n (house) tugurio m; **~s** pl bassifondi mpl

slumber /'slʌmbə(r)/ vi dormire

slump /slʌmp/ n crollo m; (economic) depressione f ● vi crollare

slung /slʌŋ/ see **sling**

slur /slɜ:(r)/ n (discredit) calunnia f ● vt (pt/pp **slurred**) biascicare

slurp /slɜ:p/ vt/i bere rumorosamente

slush /slʌʃ/ n pantano m nevoso; fig sdolcinatezza f. **~ fund** n fondi mpl neri

slushy /'slʌʃɪ/ a fangoso; (sentimental) sdolcinato

slut /slʌt/ n sgualdrina f

sly /slaɪ/ a (**-er, -est**) scaltro ● n **on the** ~ di nascosto

smack¹ /smæk/ n (on face) schiaffo m; (on bottom) sculaccione m ● vt (on face) schiaffeggiare; (on bottom) sculacciare; ~ **one's lips** far schioccare le labbra ● adv fam in pieno

smack² vi ~ **of** fig sapere di

small /smɔ:l/ a piccolo; **be out/work until the** ~ **hours** fare le ore piccole ● adv **chop up** ~ fare a pezzettini ● n **the** ~ **of the back** le reni

small: ~ **ads** n annunci mpl [commerciali]. **'change** n spiccioli mpl. **~-holding** n piccola tenuta f. **~pox** n vaiolo m. ~ **talk** n chiacchiere fpl

smarmy /'smɑ:mɪ/ a (**-ier, -iest**) fam untuoso

smart /smɑ:t/ a elegante; (clever) intelligente; (brisk) svelto; **be** ~ (fam: cheeky) fare il furbo ● vi (hurt) bruciare

smarten /'smɑ:tn/ vt ~ **oneself up** farsi bello

smash /smæʃ/ n fragore m; (collision) scontro m; Tennis schiacciata f ● vt spaccare; Tennis schiacciare ● vi spaccarsi; (crash) schiantarsi (into contro). ~ |**hit**| n successo m. **~ing** a fam fantastico

smattering /'smætərɪŋ/ n infarinatura f

smear /smɪə(r)/ n macchia f; Med striscio m ● vt imbrattare; (coat) spalmare (with di); fig calunniare

smell /smel/ n odore m; (sense) odorato m ● v (pt/pp **smelt** or **smelled**) ● vt odorare; (sniff) annusare ● vi odorare (of di)

smelly /'smelɪ/ a (**-ier, -iest**) puzzolente

smelt¹ /smelt/ see **smell**

smelt² vt fondere

smile /smaɪl/ n sorriso m ● vi sorridere; ~ **at** sorridere a (sb); sorridere di (sth)

smirk /smɜ:k/ n sorriso m compiaciuto

smithereens /smɪðə'ri:nz/ npl **to/in** ~ in mille pezzi

smitten /'smɪtn/ a ~ **with** tutto preso da

smock /smɒk/ n grembiule m

smog /smɒg/ n smog m inv

smoke /sməʊk/ n fumo m ● vt/i fumare. **~less** a senza fumo; (fuel) che non fa fumo

smoker /'sməʊkə(r)/ n fumatore, -trice mf; Rail vagone m fumatori

'smoke-screen n cortina f di fumo

smoking /'sməʊkɪŋ/ n fumo m; **'no ~'** 'vietato fumare'

448

smoky /'sməʊkɪ/ a (-ier, -iest) fumoso; ⟨taste⟩ di fumo

smooth /smu:ð/ a liscio; ⟨movement⟩ scorrevole; ⟨sea⟩ calmo; ⟨manners⟩ melifluo ● vt lisciare. **smooth out** vt lisciare. **~ly** adv in modo scorrevole

smother /'smʌðə(r)/ vt soffocare

smoulder /'sməʊldə(r)/ vi fumare; ⟨with rage⟩ consumarsi

smudge /smʌdʒ/ n macchia f ● vt/i imbrattare

smug /smʌg/ a (**smugger, smuggest**) compiaciuto. **~ly** adv con aria compiaciuta

smuggl|e /'smʌgl/ vt contrabbandare. **~er** n contrabbandiere, -a mf. **~ing** n contrabbando m

smut /smʌt/ n macchia f di fuliggine; fig sconcezza f

smutty /'smʌtɪ/ a (-ier, -iest) fuligginoso; fig sconcio

snack /snæk/ n spuntino m. **~-bar** n snack bar m inv

snag /snæg/ n ⟨problem⟩ intoppo m

snail /sneɪl/ n lumaca f; **at a ~'s pace** a passo di lumaca

snake /sneɪk/ n serpente m

snap /snæp/ n colpo m secco; ⟨photo⟩ istantanea f ● attrib ⟨decision⟩ istantaneo ● v (pt/pp **snapped**) ● vi ⟨break⟩ spezzarsi; **~ at** ⟨dog:⟩ cercare di azzannare; ⟨person:⟩ parlare seccamente a ● vt ⟨break⟩ spezzare; ⟨say⟩ dire seccamente; Phot fare un'istantanea di. **snap up** vt afferrare

snappy /'snæpɪ/ a (-ier, -iest) scorbutico; ⟨smart⟩ elegante; **make it ~!** sbrigati!

'**snapshot** n istantanea f

snare /sneə(r)/ n trappola f

snarl /snɑ:l/ n ringhio m ● vi ringhiare

snatch /snætʃ/ n strappo m; ⟨fragment⟩ brano m; ⟨theft⟩ scippo m; **make a ~ at sth** cercare di afferrare qcsa ● vt strappare [di mano] (**from** a); ⟨steal⟩ scippare; rapire ⟨child⟩

sneak /sni:k/ n fam spia f ● vi ⟨fam: tell tales⟩ fare la spia ● vt ⟨take⟩ rubare; **~ a look at** dare una sbirciata a. **sneak in/out** vi sgattaiolare dentro/ fuori

sneakers /'sni:kəz/ npl Am scarpe fpl da ginnastica

sneaking /'sni:kɪŋ/ a furtivo; ⟨suspicion⟩ vago

sneaky /'sni:kɪ/ a sornione

sneer /snɪə(r)/ n ghigno m ● vi sogghignare; ⟨mock⟩ ridere di

sneeze /sni:z/ n starnuto m ● vi starnutire

snide /snaɪd/ a fam insinuante

sniff /snɪf/ n ⟨of dog⟩ annusata f ● vi tirare su col naso ● vt odorare ⟨flower⟩; sniffare ⟨glue, cocaine⟩; ⟨dog:⟩ annusare

snigger /'snɪgə(r)/ n risatina f soffocata ● vi ridacchiare

snip /snɪp/ n taglio m; ⟨fam: bargain⟩ affare m ● vt/i (pt/pp **snipped**) **~** [**at**] tagliare

snipe /snaɪp/ vi **~ at** tirare su; fig sparare a zero su. **~r** n cecchino m

snippet /'snɪpɪt/ n **a ~ of information/news** una breve notizia/ informazione

snivel /'snɪvl/ vi (pt/pp **snivelled**) piagnucolare. **~ling** a piagnucoloso

snob /snɒb/ n snob mf inv. **~bery** n snobismo m. **~bish** a da snob

snooker /'snu:kə(r)/ n snooker m

snoop /snu:p/ n spia f ● vi fam curiosare

snooty /'snu:tɪ/ a fam sdegnoso

snooze /snu:z/ n sonnellino m ● vi fare un sonnellino

snore /snɔ:(r)/ vi russare

snorkel /'snɔ:kl/ n respiratore m

snort /snɔ:t/ n sbuffo m ● vi sbuffare

snout /snaʊt/ n grugno m

snow /snəʊ/ n neve f ● vi nevicare; **~ed under with** fig sommerso di

snow: ~ball n palla f di neve ● vi fare a palle di neve. **~-drift** n cumulo m di neve. **~-drop** n bucaneve m inv. **~fall** n nevicata f. **~flake** n fiocco m di neve. **~man** n pupazzo m di neve. **~-plough** n spazzaneve m inv. **~storm** n tormenta f. **~y** a nevoso

snub /snʌb/ n sgarbo m ● vt (pt/pp **snubbed**) snobbare

'**snub-nosed** a dal naso all'insù

snuff /snʌf/ n tabacco m da fiuto

snug /snʌg/ a (**snugger, snuggest**) comodo; ⟨tight⟩ aderente

snuggle /'snʌgl/ vi rannicchiarsi (**up to** accanto a)

so /səʊ/ adv così; **so far** finora; **so am I** anch'io; **so I see** così pare; **that is so** è così; **so much** così tanto; **so much the better** tanto meglio; **so it is** proprio così; **if so** se è così; **so as to** in modo da; **so long!** fam a presto! ● pron **I hope/think/am afraid so** spero/ penso/temo di sì; **I told you so** te l'ho detto; **because I say so** perché lo dico io; **I did so!** è vero!; **so saying/ doing,...** così dicendo/facendo,...; **or so**

circa; **very much so** sì, molto; **and so forth** *or* **on** e così via ●*conj* (*therefore*) perciò; (*in order that*) così; **so that** affinché; **so there!** ecco!; **so what?** e allora?; **so where have you been?** allora, dove sei stato?

soak /səʊk/ *vt* mettere a bagno ●*vi* stare a bagno; **~ into** (*liquid:*) penetrare. **soak up** *vt* assorbire

soaking /ˈsəʊkɪŋ/ *n* ammollo *m* ●*a & adv* ~ **[wet]** *fam* inzuppato

so-and-so /ˈsəʊənsəʊ/ *n* Tal dei Tali *mf*; (*euphemism*) specie *f* di imbecille

soap /səʊp/ *n* sapone *m*. ~ **opera** *n* telenovela *f*, soap opera *f inv*. ~ **powder** *n* detersivo *m* in polvere

soapy /ˈsəʊpɪ/ *a* (**-ier, -iest**) insaponato

soar /sɔː(r)/ *vi* elevarsi; (*prices:*) salire alle stelle

sob /sɒb/ *n* singhiozzo *m* ●*vi* (*pt/pp* **sobbed**) singhiozzare

sober /ˈsəʊbə(r)/ *a* sobrio; (*serious*) serio ● **sober up** *vi* ritornare sobrio

'so-called *a* cosiddetto

soccer /ˈsɒkə(r)/ *n* calcio *m*

sociable /ˈsəʊʃəbl/ *a* socievole

social /ˈsəʊʃl/ *a* sociale; (*sociable*) socievole

socialis|m /ˈsəʊʃəlɪzm/ *n* socialismo *m*. ~**t** /-ɪst/ *a* socialista ●*n* socialista *mf*

socialize /ˈsəʊʃəlaɪz/ *vi* socializzare

socially /ˈsəʊʃəlɪ/ *adv* socialmente; **know sb** ~ frequentare qcno

social: ~ **se'curity** *n* previdenza *f* sociale. ~ **work** *n* assistenza *f* sociale. ~ **worker** *n* assistente *mf* sociale

society /səˈsaɪətɪ/ *n* società *f inv*

sociolog|ist /səʊsɪˈɒlədʒɪst/ *n* sociologo, -a *mf*. ~**y** *n* sociologia *f*

sock[1] /sɒk/ *n* calzino *m*; (*kneelength*) calza *f*

sock[2] *fam* *n* pugno *m* ●*vt* dare un pugno a

socket /ˈsɒkɪt/ *n* (*wall plug*) presa *f* [di corrente]; (*for bulb*) portalampada *m inv*

soda /ˈsəʊdə/ *n* soda *f*; *Am* gazzosa *f*. ~ **water** *n* seltz *m inv*

sodden /ˈsɒdn/ *a* inzuppato

sodium /ˈsəʊdɪəm/ *n* sodio *m*

sofa /ˈsəʊfə/ *n* divano *m*. ~ **bed** *n* divano *m* letto

soft /sɒft/ *a* morbido, soffice; (*voice*) sommesso; (*light, colour*) tenue; (*not strict*) indulgente; (*fam: silly*) stupido; **have a** ~ **spot for sb** avere un debole per qcno. ~ **drink** *n* bibita *f* analcolica

soften /ˈsɒfn/ *vt* ammorbidire; *fig* attenuare ●*vi* ammorbidirsi

softly /ˈsɒftlɪ/ *adv* (*say*) sottovoce; (*treat*) con indulgenza; (*play music*) in sottofondo

soft: ~ **toy** *n* pupazzo *m* di peluche. ~**ware** *n* software *m*

soggy /ˈsɒgɪ/ *a* (**-ier, -iest**) zuppo

soil[1] /sɔɪl/ *n* suolo *m*

soil[2] *vt* sporcare

solar /ˈsəʊlə(r)/ *a* solare

sold /səʊld/ *see* **sell**

solder /ˈsəʊldə(r)/ *n* lega *f* da saldatura ●*vt* saldare

soldier /ˈsəʊldʒə(r)/ *n* soldato *m* ● **soldier on** *vi* perseverare

sole[1] /səʊl/ *n* (*of foot*) pianta *f*; (*of shoe*) suola *f*

sole[2] *n* (*fish*) sogliola *f*

sole[3] *a* unico, solo. ~**ly** *adv* unicamente

solemn /ˈsɒləm/ *a* solenne. ~**ity** /səˈlemnətɪ/ *n* solennità *f inv*

solicit /səˈlɪsɪt/ *vt* sollecitare ●*vi* (*prostitute:*) adescare

solicitor /səˈlɪsɪtə(r)/ *n* avvocato *m*

solid /ˈsɒlɪd/ *a* solido; (*oak, gold*) massiccio ●*n* (*figure*) solido *m*; ~**s** *pl* (*food*) cibi *mpl* solidi

solidarity /sɒlɪˈdærətɪ/ *n* solidarietà *f inv*

solidify /səˈlɪdɪfaɪ/ *vi* (*pt/pp* **-ied**) solidificarsi

soliloquy /səˈlɪləkwɪ/ *n* soliloquio *m*

solitaire /sɒlɪˈteə(r)/ *n* solitario *m*

solitary /ˈsɒlɪtərɪ/ *a* solitario; (*sole*) solo. ~ **con'finement** *n* cella *f* di isolamento

solitude /ˈsɒlɪtjuːd/ *n* solitudine *f*

solo /ˈsəʊləʊ/ *n* *Mus* assolo *m* ●*a* (*flight*) in solitario ●*adv* in solitario. ~**ist** *n* solista *mf*

solstice /ˈsɒlstɪs/ *n* solstizio *m*

soluble /ˈsɒljʊbl/ *a* solubile

solution /səˈluːʃn/ *n* soluzione *f*

solve /sɒlv/ *vt* risolvere

solvent /ˈsɒlvənt/ *a* solvente ●*n* solvente *m*

sombre /ˈsɒmbə(r)/ *a* tetro; (*clothes*) scuro

some /sʌm/ *a* (*a certain amount of*) del; (*a certain number of*) qualche, alcuni; ~ **day** un giorno o l'altro; **I need** ~ **money/books** ho bisogno di soldi/libri; **do** ~ **shopping** fare qualche acquisto ●*pron* (*a certain amount*) un po'; (*a certain number*) alcuni; **I want** ~ ne voglio

some: ~**body** /-bədɪ/ *pron & n* qualcuno *m.* ~**how** *adv* in qualche modo; ~**how or other** in un modo o nell'altro. ~**one** *pron & n* = **somebody**

somersault /'sʌməsɔːlt/ *n* capriola *f*; **turn a** ~ fare una capriola

something *pron* qualche cosa, qualcosa; ~ **different** qualcosa di diverso; ~ **like** un po' come; *(approximately)* qualcosa come; **see** ~ **of sb** vedere qcno un po'

some: ~**time** *adv* un giorno o l'altro; ~**time last summer** durante l'estate scorsa. ~**times** *adv* qualche volta. ~**what** *adv* piuttosto. ~**where** *adv* da qualche parte ● *pron* ~**where to eat** un posto in cui mangiare

son /sʌn/ *n* figlio *m*

sonata /sə'nɑːtə/ *n* sonata *f*

song /sɒŋ/ *n* canzone *f*

sonic /'sɒnɪk/ *a* sonico. ~ '**boom** *n* bang *m inv* sonico

son-in-law *n* (*pl* ~**s-in-law**) genero *m*

sonnet /'sɒnɪt/ *n* sonetto *m*

soon /suːn/ *adv* presto; *(in a short time)* tra poco; **as** ~ **as** [non] appena; **as** ~ **as possible** il più presto possibile; ~**er or later** prima o poi; **the** ~**er the better** prima è, meglio è; **no** ~**er had I arrived than...** ero appena arrivato quando...; **I would** ~**er go** preferirei andare; ~ **after** subito dopo

soot /sʊt/ *n* fuliggine *f*

soothe /suːð/ *vt* calmare

sooty /'sʊtɪ/ *a* fuligginoso

sophisticated /sə'fɪstɪkeɪtɪd/ *a* sofisticato

soporific /sɒpə'rɪfɪk/ *a* soporifero

sopping /'sɒpɪŋ/ *a & adv* **be** ~ [**wet**] essere bagnato fradicio

soppy /'sɒpɪ/ *a* (**-ier, -iest**) *fam* svenevole

soprano /sə'prɑːnəʊ/ *n* soprano *m*

sordid /'sɔːdɪd/ *a* sordido

sore /sɔː(r)/ *a* dolorante; *(Am: vexed)* arrabbiato; **it's** ~ fa male; **have a** ~ **throat** avere mal di gola ● *n* piaga *f*. ~**ly** *adv* *(tempted)* seriamente

sorrow /'sɒrəʊ/ *n* tristezza *f*. ~**ful** *a* triste

sorry /'sɒrɪ/ *a* (**-ier, -iest**) *(sad)* spiacente; *(wretched)* pietoso; **you'll be** ~! te ne pentirai!; **I am** ~ mi dispiace; **be or feel** ~ **for** provare compassione per; ~! scusa!; *(more polite)* scusi!

sort /sɔːt/ *n* specie *f*; *(fam: person)* tipo *m*; **it's a** ~ **of** fish è un tipo di pesce; **be out of** ~**s** *(fam: unwell)* stare poco bene ● *vt* classificare. **sort out** *vt* sele-

zionare *(papers)*; *fig* risolvere *(problem)*; occuparsi di *(person)*

'so-so *a & adv* così così

sought /sɔːt/ *see* **seek**

soul /səʊl/ *n* anima *f*

sound[1] /saʊnd/ *a* sano; *(sensible)* saggio; *(secure)* solido; *(thrashing)* clamoroso ● *adv* ~ **asleep** profondamente addormentato

sound[2] *n* suono *m*; *(noise)* rumore *m*; **I don't like the** ~ **of it** *fam* non mi suona bene ● *vi* suonare; *(seem)* aver l'aria ● *vt* *(pronounce)* pronunciare; *Med* auscultare *(chest)*. ~ **barrier** *n* muro *m* del suono. ~ **card** *n* *Comput* scheda *f* sonora. ~**less** *a* silenzioso. **sound out** *vt fig* sondare

soundly /'saʊndlɪ/ *adv* *(sleep)* profondamente; *(defeat)* clamorosamente

'sound: ~**proof** *a* impenetrabile al suono. ~**track** *n* colonna *f* sonora

soup /suːp/ *n* minestra *f*. ~**ed-up** *a* *fam* *(engine)* truccato

soup: ~**-plate** *n* piatto *m* fondo. ~**-spoon** *n* cucchiaio *m* da minestra

sour /'saʊə(r)/ *a* agro; *(not fresh & fig)* acido

source /sɔːs/ *n* fonte *f*

south /saʊθ/ *n* sud *m*; **to the** ~ **of** a sud di ● *a* del sud, meridionale ● *adv* verso il sud

south: **S**~ '**Africa** *n* Sudafrica *f*. **S**~ **A'merica** *n* America *f* del Sud. **S**~ **American** *a & n* sud-americano, -a *mf*. ~-'**east** *n* sud-est *m*

southerly /'sʌðəlɪ/ *a* del sud

southern /'sʌðən/ *a* del sud, meridionale; ~ **Italy** il Mezzogiorno. ~**er** *n* meridionale *mf*

South 'Pole *n* polo *m* Sud

'southward[s] /-wəd[z]/ *adv* verso sud

souvenir /suːvə'nɪə(r)/ *n* ricordo *m*, souvenir *m inv*

sovereign /'sɒvrɪn/ *a* sovrano ● *n* sovrano, -a *mf*. ~**ty** *n* sovranità *f inv*

Soviet /'səʊvɪət/ *a* sovietico; ~ **Union** Unione *f* Sovietica

sow[1] /saʊ/ *n* scrofa *f*

sow[2] /səʊ/ *vt* (*pt* **sowed**, *pp* **sown** *or* **sowed**) seminare

soya /'sɔɪə/ *n* ~ **bean** soia *f*

spa /spɑː/ *n* stazione *f* termale

space /speɪs/ *n* spazio *m* ● *a* *(research etc)* spaziale ● *vt* ~ [**out**] distanziare

space: ~**ship** *n* astronave *f*. ~ **shuttle** *n* navetta *f* spaziale

spacious /'speɪʃəs/ *a* spazioso

spade /speɪd/ *n* vanga *f*; *(for child)* pa-

letta *f.* **~s** *pl* (*in cards*) picche *fpl.*
~work *n* lavoro *m* preparatorio
Spain /speɪn/ *n* Spagna *f*
span¹ /spæn/ *n* spanna *f*; (*of arch*) luce
f; (*of time*) arco *m*; (*of wings*) apertura *f*
● *vt* (*pt/pp* **spanned**) estendersi su
span² *see* **spick**
Span|iard /'spænjəd/ *n* spagnolo, -a
mf. **~ish** *a* spagnolo ● *n* (*language*) spagnolo *m*; **the ~ish** *pl* gli spagnoli
spank /spæŋk/ *vt* sculacciare. **~ing** *n*
sculacciata *f*
spanner /'spænə(r)/ *n* chiave *f* inglese
spar /spɑː(r)/ *vi* (*pt/pp* **sparred**)
(*boxing*) allenarsi; (*argue*) litigare
spare /speə(r)/ *a* (*surplus*) in più;
(*additional*) di riserva ● *n* (*part*) ricambio *m* ● *vt* risparmiare; (*do without*)
fare a meno di; **can you ~ five**
minutes? avresti cinque minuti?; **to ~**
(*surplus*) in eccedenza. **~ part** pezzo
m di ricambio. **~ time** *n* tempo *m* libero. **~ wheel** *n* ruota *f* di scorta
sparing /'speərɪŋ/ *a* parco (**with** di).
~ly *adv* con parsimonia
spark /spɑːk/ *n* scintilla *f*. **~ing-plug** *n*
Auto candela *f*
sparkl|e /'spɑːkl/ *n* scintillio *m* ● *vi*
scintillare. **~ing** *a* frizzante; (*wine*)
spumante
sparrow /'spærəʊ/ *n* passero *m*
sparse /spɑːs/ *a* rado. **~ly** *adv* scarsamente; **~ly populated** a bassa densità
di popolazione
spartan /'spɑːtn/ *a* spartano
spasm /'spæzm/ *n* spasmo *m*. **~odic**
/-'mɒdɪk/ *a* spasmodico
spastic /'spæstɪk/ *a* spastico ● *n*
spastico, -a *mf*
spat /spæt/ *see* **spit¹**
spate /speɪt/ *n* (*series*) successione *f*;
be in full ~ essere in piena
spatial /'speɪʃl/ *a* spaziale
spatter /'spætə(r)/ *vt* schizzare
spatula /'spætjʊlə/ *n* spatola *f*
spawn /spɔːn/ *n* uova *fpl* (*di pesci, rane*
ecc) ● *vi* deporre le uova ● *vt fig* generare
spay /speɪ/ *vt* sterilizzare
speak /spiːk/ *v* (*pt* **spoke**, *pp* **spoken**)
● *vi* parlare (**to** a); **~ing!** *Teleph* sono
io! ● *vt* dire; **~ one's mind** dire quello
che si pensa. **speak up** *vi* parlare più forte;
~ up for oneself farsi valere
speaker /'spiːkə(r)/ *n* parlante *mf*; (*in*
public) oratore, -trice *mf*; (*of stereo*) cassa *f*

spear /spɪə(r)/ *n* lancia *f*
spec /spek/ *n* **on ~** *fam* senza certezza
special /'speʃl/ *a* speciale. **~ist** *n* specialista *mf*. **~ity** /-ʃɪ'ælətɪ/ *n* specialità
f inv
special|ize /'speʃəlaɪz/ *vi* specializ-
zarsi. **~ly** *adv* specialmente; (*particu-*
larly) particolarmente
species /'spiːʃiːz/ *n* specie *f inv*
specific /spə'sɪfɪk/ *a* specifico. **~ally**
adv in modo specifico
specifications /spesɪfɪ'keɪʃnz/ *npl*
descrizione *f*
specify /'spesɪfaɪ/ *vt* (*pt/pp* **-ied**) speci-
ficare
specimen /'spesɪmən/ *n* campione *m*
speck /spek/ *n* macchiolina *f*; (*parti-*
cle) granello *m*
speckled /'spekld/ *a* picchiettato
specs /speks/ *npl fam* occhiali *mpl*
spectacle /'spektəkl/ *n* (*show*) spettacolo *m*. **~s** *npl* occhiali *mpl*
spectacular /spek'tækjʊlə(r)/ *a*
spettacolare
spectator /spek'teɪtə(r)/ *n* spettatore,
-trice *mf*
spectre /'spektə(r)/ *n* spettro *m*
spectrum /'spektrəm/ *n* (*pl* **-tra**) spettro *m*; *fig* gamma *f*
speculat|e /'spekjʊleɪt/ *vi* speculare.
~ion /-'leɪʃn/ *n* speculazione *f*. **~ive**
/-ɪv/ *a* speculativo. **~or** *n* speculatore,
-trice *mf*
sped /sped/ *see* **speed**
speech /spiːtʃ/ *n* linguaggio *m*; (*ad-*
dress) discorso *m*. **~less** *a* senza parole
speed /spiːd/ *n* velocità *f inv*; (*gear*)
marcia *f*; **at ~** a tutta velocità ● *vi*
(*pt/pp* **sped**) andare veloce, (*pt/pp*
speeded) (*go too fast*) andare a velocità
eccessiva. **speed up** (*pt/pp* **speeded**
up) *vt/i* accelerare
speed: ~boat *n* motoscafo *m*. **~ing** *n*
eccesso *m* di velocità. **~ limit** *n* limite
m di velocità
speedometer /spiː'dɒmɪtə(r)/ *n* tachimetro *m*
speed|y /'spiːdɪ/ *a* (**-ier**, **-iest**) rapido.
~ily *adv* rapidamente
spell¹ /spel/ *n* (*turn*) turno *m*; (*of*
weather) periodo *m*
spell² *v* (*pt/pp* **spelled** *or* **spelt**) ● *vt*
how do you ~...? come si scrive...?;
could you ~ that for me? me lo può
compitare?; **~ disaster** essere disa-
stroso ● *vi* **he can't ~** fa molti errori
d'ortografia

spell³ n (magic) incantesimo m. **~bound** a affascinato

spelling /'spelɪŋ/ n ortografia f

spelt /spelt/ see **spell**²

spend /spend/ vt/i (pt/pp **spent**) spendere; passare ⟨time⟩

spent /spent/ see **spend**

sperm /spɜ:m/ n spermatozoo m; ⟨semen⟩ sperma m

spew /spju:/ vt/i vomitare

spher|e /sfɪə(r)/ n sfera f. **~ical** /'sferɪkl/ a sferico

spice /spaɪs/ n spezia f; fig pepe m

spick /spɪk/ a **~ and span** lindo

spicy /'spaɪsɪ/ a piccante

spider /'spaɪdə(r)/ n ragno m

spik|e /spaɪk/ n punta f; Bot, Zool spina f; ⟨on shoe⟩ chiodo m. **~y** a ⟨plant⟩ pungente

spill /spɪl/ v (pt/pp **spilt** or **spilled**) ● vt versare ⟨blood⟩ ● vi rovesciarsi

spin /spɪn/ v (pt/pp **spun**, pres p **spinning**) ● vt far girare; filare ⟨wool⟩; centrifugare ⟨washing⟩ ● vi girare; ⟨washing machine:⟩ centrifugare ● n rotazione f; ⟨short drive⟩ giretto m. **spin out** vt far durare

spinach /'spɪnɪdʒ/ n spinaci mpl

spinal /'spaɪnl/ a spinale. **~ 'cord** n midollo m spinale

spindl|e /'spɪndl/ n fuso m. **~y** a affusolato

spin-'drier n centrifuga f

spine /spaɪn/ n spina f dorsale; ⟨of book⟩ dorso m; Bot, Zool spina f. **~less** a fig smidollato

spinning /'spɪnɪŋ/ n filatura f. **~-wheel** n filatoio m

'spin-off n ricaduta f

spiral /'spaɪrəl/ a a spirale ● n spirale f ● vi (pt/pp **spiralled**) formare una spirale. **~ 'staircase** n scala f a chiocciola

spire /'spaɪə(r)/ n guglia f

spirit /'spɪrɪt/ n spirito m; ⟨courage⟩ ardore m; **~s** pl ⟨alcohol⟩ liquori mpl; **in good ~s** di buon umore; **in low ~s** abbattuto

spirited /'spɪrɪtɪd/ a vivace; ⟨courageous⟩ pieno d'ardore

spirit: ~-level n livella f a bolla d'aria. **~ stove** n fornellino m [da campeggio]

spiritual /'spɪrɪtjʊəl/ a spirituale ● n spiritual m. **~ism** /-ɪzm/ n spiritismo m. **~ist** /-ɪst/ n spiritista mf

spit¹ /spɪt/ n (for roasting) spiedo m

spit² n sputo m ● vt/i (pt/pp **spat**, pres p **spitting**) sputare; ⟨cat:⟩ soffiare; ⟨fat:⟩

sfrigolare; **it's ~ting [with rain]** pioviggina; **the ~ting image of** il ritratto spiccicato di

spite /spaɪt/ n dispetto m; **in ~ of** malgrado ● vt far dispetto a. **~ful** a indispettito

spittle /'spɪtl/ n saliva f

splash /splæʃ/ n schizzo m; ⟨of colour⟩ macchia f; ⟨fam: drop⟩ goccio m ● vt schizzare; **~ sb with sth** schizzare qcno di qcsa ● vi schizzare. **splash about** vi schizzarsi. **splash down** vi ⟨spacecraft:⟩ ammarare

spleen /spli:n/ n Anat milza f

splendid /'splendɪd/ a splendido

splendour /'splendə(r)/ n splendore m

splint /splɪnt/ n Med stecca f

splinter /'splɪntə(r)/ n scheggia f ● vi scheggiarsi

split /splɪt/ n fessura f; ⟨quarrel⟩ rottura f; ⟨division⟩ scissione f; ⟨tear⟩ strappo m ● v (pt/pp **split**, pres p **splitting**) ● vt spaccare; ⟨share, divide⟩ dividere; ⟨tear⟩ strappare ● vi spaccarsi; ⟨tear⟩ strapparsi; ⟨divide⟩ dividersi; **~ on sb** fam denunciare qcno ● a **a ~ second** una frazione di secondo. **split up** vt dividersi ● vi ⟨couple:⟩ separarsi

splutter /'splʌtə(r)/ n farfugliare

spoil /spɔɪl/ n **~s** pl bottino msg ● v (pt/pp **spoilt** or **spoiled**) ● vt rovinare; viziare ⟨person⟩ ● vi andare a male. **~sport** n guastafeste mf inv

spoke¹ /spəʊk/ n raggio m

spoke², **spoken** /'spəʊkn/ see **speak**

'spokesman n portavoce m inv

sponge /spʌndʒ/ n spugna f ● vt pulire ⟨con la spugna⟩ ● vi **~ on** fam scroccare da. **~-cake** n pan m di Spagna

spong|er /'spʌndʒə(r)/ n scroccone, -a mf. **~y** a spugnoso

sponsor /'spɒnsə(r)/ n garante mf; Radio, TV sponsor m inv; ⟨god-parent⟩ padrino m, madrina f; ⟨for membership⟩ socio, -a mf garante ● vt sponsorizzare. **~ship** n sponsorizzazione f

spontaneous /spɒn'teɪnɪəs/ a spontaneo

spoof /spu:f/ n fam parodia f

spooky /'spu:kɪ/ a (**-ier, -iest**) fam sinistro

spool /spu:l/ n bobina f

spoon /spu:n/ n cucchiaio m ● vt mettere col cucchiaio. **~-feed** vt (pt/pp **-fed**) fig imboccare. **~ful** n cucchiaiata f

sporadic /spə'rædɪk/ a sporadico

sport /spɔ:t/ n sport m inv ● vt sfoggiare. **~ing** a sportivo; **~ing chance** possibilità f inv

sports: **~car** n automobile f sportiva. **~ coat** n, **~ jacket** n giacca f sportiva. **~man** n sportivo m. **~woman** n sportiva f

sporty /'spɔːtɪ/ a (**-ier, -iest**) sportivo

spot /spɒt/ n macchia f; (*pimple*) brufolo m; (*place*) posto m; (*in pattern*) pois m inv; (*of rain*) goccia f; (*of water*) goccio m; **~s** pl (*rash*) sfogo msg; **a ~ of** fam un po' di; **a ~ of bother** qualche problema; **on the ~** sul luogo; (*immediately*) immediatamente; **in a [tight] ~** fam in difficoltà ●vt (pt/pp **spotted**) macchiare; (fam: *notice*) individuare

spot: **~ 'check** n (*without warning*) controllo m a sorpresa; **do a ~ check on sth** dare una controllata a qcsa. **~less** a immacolato. **~light** n riflettore m

spotted /'spɒtɪd/ a (*material*) a pois

spotty /'spɒtɪ/ a (**-ier, -iest**) (*pimply*) brufoloso

spouse /spaʊz/ n consorte mf

spout /spaʊt/ n becco m ●vi zampillare (**from** da)

sprain /spreɪn/ n slogatura f ●vt slogare

sprang /spræŋ/ see **spring²**

sprawl /sprɔːl/ vi (*in chair*) stravaccarsi; (*city etc.*) estendersi; **go ~ing** (*fall*) cadere disteso

spray /spreɪ/ n spruzzo m; (*preparation*) spray m inv; (*container*) spruzzatore m ●vt spruzzare. **~-gun** n pistola f a spruzzo

spread /spred/ n estensione f; (*of disease*) diffusione f; (*paste*) crema f; (fam: *feast*) banchetto m ●v (pt/pp **spread**) ●vt spargere; spalmare (*butter, jam*); stendere (*cloth, arms*); diffondere (*news, disease*); dilazionare (*payments*); **~ with** spalmare qcsa di ●vi spargersi; (*butter:*) spalmarsi; (*disease:*) diffondersi. **~sheet** n Comput foglio m elettronico. **spread out** vt sparpagliare ●vi sparpagliarsi

spree /spriː/ n fam **go on a ~** far baldoria; **go on a shopping ~** fare spese folli

sprig /sprɪɡ/ n rametto m

sprightly /'spraɪtlɪ/ a (**-ier, -iest**) vivace

spring¹ /sprɪŋ/ n primavera f ●attrib primaverile

spring² n (*jump*) balzo m; (*water*) sor-

gente f; (*device*) molla f; (*elasticity*) elasticità f ●v (pt **sprang**, pp **sprung**) ●vi balzare; (*arise*) provenire (**from** da) ●vt he just sprang it on me me l'ha detto a cose fatte compiuto. **spring up** balzare; fig spuntare

spring: **~board** n trampolino m. **~-'cleaning** n pulizie fpl di Pasqua. **~time** n primavera f

sprinkl|e /'sprɪŋkl/ vt (*scatter*) spruzzare (*liquid*); spargere (*flour, cocoa*); **~ sth with** spruzzare qcsa di (*liquid*); cospargere qcsa di (*flour, cocoa*). **~er** n sprinkler m inv; (*for lawn*) irrigatore m. **~ing** n (*of liquid*) spruzzatina f; (*of pepper, salt*) pizzico m; (*of flour, sugar*) spolverata f; (*of knowledge*) infarinatura f; (*of people*) pugno m

sprint /sprɪnt/ n sprint m inv ●vi fare uno sprint; Sport sprintare. **~er** n sprinter mf inv

sprout /spraʊt/ n germoglio m; [**Brussels**] **~s** pl cavolini mpl di Bruxelles ●vi germogliare

spruce /spruːs/ a elegante ●n abete m

sprung /sprʌŋ/ see **spring²** ●a molleggiato

spud /spʌd/ n fam patata f

spun /spʌn/ see **spin**

spur /spɜː(r)/ n sperone m; (*stimulus*) stimolo m; (*road*) svincolo m; **on the ~ of the moment** su due piedi ●vt (pt/pp **spurred**) **~ [on]** fig spronare [a]

spurious /'spjʊərɪəs/ a falso

spurn /spɜːn/ vt sdegnare

spurt /spɜːt/ n getto m; Sport scatto m; **put on a ~** fare uno scatto ●vi sprizzare; (*increase speed*) scattare

spy /spaɪ/ n spia f ●v (pt/pp **spied**) ●vi spiare ●vt (fam: *see*) spiare. **spy on** vi spiare

spying /'spaɪɪŋ/ n spionaggio m

squabble /'skwɒbl/ n bisticcio m ●vi bisticciare

squad /skwɒd/ n squadra f

squadron /'skwɒdrən/ n Mil squadrone m; Aeron, Naut squadriglia f

squalid /'skwɒlɪd/ a squallido

squalor /'skwɒlə(r)/ n squallore m

squander /'skwɒndə(r)/ vt sprecare

square /skweə(r)/ a quadrato; (*meal*) sostanzioso; (fam: *old-fashioned*) vecchio stampo; **all ~** fam pari ●n quadrato m; (*in city*) piazza f; (*on chessboard*) riquadro m ●vt (*settle*) far quadrare; Math elevare al quadrato ●vi (*agree*) armonizzare

squash /skwɒʃ/ n (*drink*) spremuta f;

(*sport*) squash *m*; (*vegetable*) zucca *f* ● *vt* schiacciare; soffocare ‹*rebellion*›

squat /skwɒt/ *a* tarchiato ● *n fam* edificio *m* occupato abusivamente ● *vi* (*pt/pp* **squatted**) accovacciarsi; ~ **in** occupare abusivamente. **~ter** *n* occupante *mf* abusivo, -a

squawk /skwɔːk/ *n* gracchio *m* ● *vi* gracchiare

squeak /skwiːk/ *n* squittio *m*; (*of hinge, brakes*) scricchiolio *m* ● *vi* squittire; ‹*hinge, brakes:*› scricchiolare

squeal /skwiːl/ *n* strillo *m*; (*of brakes*) cigolio *m* ● *vi* strillare; *sl* spifferare

squeamish /ˈskwiːmɪʃ/ *a* dallo stomaco delicato

squeeze /skwiːz/ *n* stretta *f*; (*crush*) pigia pigia *m inv* ● *vt* premere; (*to get juice*) spremere; stringere ‹*hand*›; (*force*) spingere a forza; (*fam: extort*) estorcere (**out of** da). **squeeze in/out** *vi* sgusciare dentro/fuori. **squeeze up** *vi* stringersi

squelch /skweltʃ/ *vi* sguazzare

squid /skwɪd/ *n* calamaro *m*

squiggle /ˈskwɪɡl/ *n* scarabocchio *m*

squint /skwɪnt/ *n* strabismo *m* ● *vi* essere strabico

squire /ˈskwaɪə(r)/ *n* signorotto *m* di campagna

squirm /skwɜːm/ *vi* contorcersi; (*feel embarrassed*) sentirsi imbarazzato

squirrel /ˈskwɪrəl/ *n* scoiattolo *m*

squirt /skwɜːt/ *n* spruzzo *m*; (*fam: person*) presuntuoso *m* ● *vt/i* spruzzare

St *abbr* (**Saint**) S; *abbr* **Street**

stab /stæb/ *n* pugnalata *f*, coltellata *f*; (*sensation*) fitta *f*; (*fam: attempt*) tentativo *m* ● *vt* (*pt/pp* **stabbed**) pugnalare, accoltellare

stability /stəˈbɪlətɪ/ *n* stabilità *f inv*

stabilize /ˈsteɪbɪlaɪz/ *vt* stabilizzare ● *vi* stabilizzarsi

stable[1] /ˈsteɪbl/ *a* stabile

stable[2] *n* stalla *f*; (*establishment*) scuderia *f*

stack /stæk/ *n* catasta *f*; (*of chimney*) comignolo *m*; (*chimney*) ciminiera *f*; (*fam: large quantity*) montagna *f* ● *vt* accatastare

stadium /ˈsteɪdɪəm/ *n* stadio *m*

staff /stɑːf/ *n* (*stick*) bastone *m*; (*employees*) personale *m*; (*teachers*) corpo *m* insegnante; *Mil* Stato *m* Maggiore ● *vt* fornire di personale. **~-room** *n Sch* sala *f* insegnanti

stag /stæɡ/ *n* cervo *m*

stage /steɪdʒ/ *n* palcoscenico *m*;

(*profession*) teatro *m*; (*in journey*) tappa *f*; (*in process*) stadio *m*; **go on the** ~ darsi al teatro; **by** *or* **in** ~**s** a tappe ● *vt* mettere in scena; (*arrange*) organizzare **stage:** ~ **door** *n* ingresso *m* degli artisti. ~ **fright** *n* panico *m* da scena. ~ **manager** *n* direttore, -trice *mf* di scena

stagger /ˈstæɡə(r)/ *vi* barcollare ● *vt* sbalordire; scaglionare ‹*holidays etc*›; **I was** ~**ed** sono rimasto sbalordito ● *n* vacillamento *m*. ~**ing** *a* sbalorditivo

stagnant /ˈstæɡnənt/ *a* stagnante

stagnat|e /stæɡˈneɪt/ *vi fig* [ri]stagnare. ~**ion** /-ˈneɪʃn/ *n fig* inattività *f*

'stag party *n* addio *m* al celibato

staid /steɪd/ *a* posato

stain /steɪn/ *n* macchia *f*; (*for wood*) mordente *m* ● *vt* macchiare; (*wood*) dare il mordente a; ~**ed glass** vetro *m* colorato; ~**ed-glass window** vetrata *f* colorata. ~**less** *a* senza macchia; (*steel*) inossidabile. ~ **remover** *n* smacchiatore *m*

stair /steə(r)/ *n* gradino *m*; ~**s** *pl* scale *fpl*. ~**case** *n* scale *fpl*

stake /steɪk/ *n* palo *m*; (*wager*) posta *f*; *Comm* partecipazione *f*; **at** ~ in gioco ● *vt* puntellare; (*wager*) scommettere

stale /steɪl/ *a* stantio; (*air*) viziato; (*uninteresting*) trito [e ritrito]. ~**mate** *n* (*in chess*) stallo *m*; (*deadlock*) situazione *f* di stallo

stalk[1] /stɔːk/ *n* gambo *m*

stalk[2] *vt* inseguire ● *vi* camminare impettito

stall /stɔːl/ *n* box *m inv*; ~**s** *pl Theat* platea *f*; (*in market*) bancarella *f* ● *vi* ‹*engine:*› spegnersi; *fig* temporeggiare ● *vt* far spegnere ‹*engine*›; tenere a bada ‹*person*›

stallion /ˈstæljən/ *n* stallone *m*

stalwart /ˈstɔːlwət/ *a* fedele

stamina /ˈstæmɪnə/ *n* [capacità *f inv* di] resistenza *f*

stammer /ˈstæmə(r)/ *n* balbettio *m* ● *vt/i* balbettare

stamp /stæmp/ *n* (*postage* ~) francobollo *m*; (*instrument*) timbro *m*; *fig* impronta *f* ● *vt* affrancare ‹*letter*›; timbrare ‹*bill*›; battere ‹*feet*›. **stamp out** *vt* spegnere; *fig* soffocare

stampede /stæmˈpiːd/ *n* fuga *f* precipitosa, fuggi-fuggi *m inv fam* ● *vi* fuggire precipitosamente

stance /stɑːns/ *n* posizione *f*

stand /stænd/ *n* (*for bikes*) rastrelliera *f*; (*at exhibition*) stand *m inv*; (*in market*)

bancarella *f*; (*in stadium*) gradinata *f*;
fig posizione *f* ● *v* (*pt/pp* **stood**) ● *vi*
stare in piedi; (*rise*) alzarsi [in piedi];
(*be*) trovarsi; (*be candidate*) essere candidato **for** a); (*stay valid*) rimanere valido; **~ still** non muoversi; **I don't
know where I ~** non so qual'è la mia
posizione; **~ firm** *fig* tener duro; **~
together** essere solidali; **~ to lose/
gain** rischiare di perdere/vincere; **~ to
reason** essere logico ● *vt* (*withstand*)
resistere a; (*endure*) sopportare; (*place*)
mettere; **~ a chance** avere una possibilità; **~ one's ground** tener duro; **~
the test of time** superare la prova del
tempo; **~ sb a beer** offrire una birra a
qcno. **stand by** *vi* stare a guardare; (*be
ready*) essere pronto ● *vt* (*support*) appoggiare. **stand down** *vi* (*retire*) ritirarsi. **stand for** *vt* (*mean*) significare;
(*tolerate*) tollerare. **stand in for** *vt* sostituire. **stand out** *vi* spiccare. **stand
up** *vi* alzarsi [in piedi]. **stand up for** *vt*
prendere le difese di; **~ up for oneself**
farsi valere. **stand up to** *vt* affrontare
standard /'stændəd/ *a* standard; **be ~
practice** essere pratica corrente ● *n*
standard *m inv*; *Techn* norma *f*; (*level*)
livello *m*; (*quality*) qualità *f inv*; (*flag*)
stendardo *m*; **~s** *pl* (*morals*) valori *mpl*;
~ of living tenore *m* di vita. **~ize** *vt*
standardizzare
'standard lamp *n* lampada *f* a stelo
'stand-by *n* riserva *f*; **on ~** (*at airport*)
in lista d'attesa
'stand-in *n* controfigura *f*
standing /'stændɪŋ/ *a* (*erect*) in piedi;
(*permanent*) permanente ● *n* posizione
f; (*duration*) durata *f*. **~ 'order** *n*
addebitamento *m* diretto. **~-room** *n* posti *mpl* in piedi
stand: **~-offish** /stænd'ɒfɪʃ/ *a* scostan-
te. **~point** *n* punto *m* di vista. **~still** *n*
come to a ~still fermarsi; **at a ~still**
in un periodo di stasi
stank /stæŋk/ *see* **stink**
staple¹ /'steɪpl/ *n* (*product*) prodotto *m*
principale
staple² *n* graffa *f* ● *vt* pinzare. **~r** *n*
pinzatrice *f*, cucitrice *f*
star /stɑː(r)/ *n* stella *f*; (*asterisk*) asterisco *m*; *Theat, Cinema, Sport* divo, -a *mf*,
stella *f* ● *vi* (*pt/pp* **starred**) essere l'interprete principale
starboard /'stɑːbəd/ *n* tribordo *m*
starch /stɑːtʃ/ *n* amido *m* ● *vt* inamida-
re. **~y** *a* ricco di amido; *fig* compito
stare /steə(r)/ *n* sguardo *m* fisso ● *vi*

it's rude to ~ è da maleducati fissare
la gente; **~ at** fissare; **~ into space**
guardare nel vuoto
'starfish *n* stella *f* di mare
stark /stɑːk/ *a* austero; (*contrast*) forte
● *adv* completamente; **~ naked** completamente nudo
starling /'stɑːlɪŋ/ *n* storno *m*
'starlit *a* stellato
starry /'stɑːrɪ/ *a* stellato
start /stɑːt/ *n* inizio *m*; (*departure*) partenza *f*; (*jump*) sobbalzo *m*; **from the ~**
[fin] dall'inizio; **for a ~** tanto per cominciare; **give sb a ~** *Sport* dare un
vantaggio a qcno ● *vi* [in]cominciare;
(*set out*) avviarsi; (*engine, car*) partire;
(*jump*) trasalire. **to ~ with,...** tanto per
cominciare,... ● *vt* [in]cominciare; (*cause*) dare inizio a; (*found*) mettere su;
mettere in moto (*car*); mettere in giro
(*rumour*). **~er** *n* *Culin* primo *m* [piatto
m]; (*in race: giving signal*) starter *m inv*;
(*participant*) concorrente *mf*; *Auto* motorino *m* d'avviamento. **~ing-point** *n*
punto *m* di partenza
startle /'stɑːtl/ *vt* far trasalire; (*news:*)
sconvolgere
starvation /stɑː'veɪʃn/ *n* fame *f*
starve /stɑːv/ *vi* morire di fame ● *vt* far
morire di fame
stash /stæʃ/ *vt* *fam* [**away**] nascondere
state /steɪt/ *n* stato *m*; (*grand style*)
pompa *f*; **~ of play** punteggio *m*; **be in
a ~** (*person:*) essere agitato; **lie in ~**
es-sere esposto ● *attrib* di Stato; *Sch* pubblico; (*with ceremony*) di gala ● *vt* dichiarare; (*specify*) precisare. **~less** *a*
apolide
stately /'steɪtlɪ/ *a* (**-ier, -iest**) maestoso. **~ 'home** *n* dimora *f* signorile
statement /'steɪtmənt/ *n* dichiarazione *f*; *Jur* deposizione *f*; (*in banking*)
estratto *m* conto; (*account*) rapporto *m*
'statesman *n* statista *m*
static /'stætɪk/ *a* statico
station /'steɪʃn/ *n* stazione *f*; (*police*)
commissariato *m* ● *vt* appostare
(*guard*); **be ~ed in Germany** essere di
stanza in Germania. **~ary** /-ərɪ/ *a* immobile
stationer /'steɪʃənə(r)/ *n* **~'s** [**shop**]
cartoleria *f*. **~y** *n* cartoleria *f*
'station-wagon *n* *Am* familiare *f*
statistic|al /stə'tɪstɪkl/ *a* statistico.
~s *n* & *pl* statistica *f*
statue /'stætjuː/ *n* statua *f*
stature /'stætʃə(r)/ *n* statura *f*

status /'stertəs/ n condizione f; (high rank) alto rango m. **~ symbol** n status symbol m inv

statut|e /'stætju:t/ n statuto m. **~ory** a statutario

staunch /stɔ:ntʃ/ a fedele. **~ly** adv fedelmente

stave /sterv/ vt **~ off** tenere lontano

stay /ster/ n soggiorno m ●vi restare, rimanere; (reside) alloggiare; **~ the night** passare la notte; **~ put** non muoversi ●vt **~ the course** resistere fino alla fine. **stay away** vi stare lontano. **stay behind** vi non andare con gli altri. **stay in** vi (at home) stare in casa; Sch restare a scuola dopo le lezioni. **stay up** vi stare su; (person:) stare alzato

stead /sted/ n **in his ~** in sua vece; **stand sb in good ~** tornare utile a qcno. **~fast** a fedele; (refusal) fermo

steadily /'stedɪlɪ/ adv (continually) continuamente

steady /'stedɪ/ a (-ier, -iest) saldo, fermo; (breathing) regolare; (job, boyfriend) fisso; (dependable) serio

steak /sterk/ n (for stew) spezzatino m; (for grilling, frying) bistecca f

steal /sti:l/ v (pt stole, pp stolen) ●vt rubare (from da). **steal in/out** vi entrare/uscire furtivamente

stealth /stelθ/ n **by ~** di nascosto. **~y** a furtivo

steam /sti:m/ n vapore m; **under one's own ~** fam da solo ●vt Culin cucinare a vapore ●vi fumare. **steam up** vi appannarsi

'steam-engine n locomotiva f

steamer /'sti:mə(r)/ n piroscafo m; (saucepan) pentola f a vapore

'steamroller n rullo m compressore

steamy /'sti:mɪ/ a appannato

steel /sti:l/ n acciaio m ●vt **~ oneself** temprarsi

steep¹ /sti:p/ vt (soak) lasciare a bagno

steep² a ripido; (fam: price) esorbitante. **~ly** adv ripidamente

steeple /'sti:pl/ n campanile m. **~chase** n corsa f ippica a ostacoli

steer /stɪə(r)/ vt/i guidare; **~ clear of** stare alla larga da. **~ing** n Auto sterzo m. **~ing-wheel** n volante m

stem¹ /stem/ n stelo m; (of glass) gambo m; (of word) radice f ●vi (pt/pp stemmed) **~ from** derivare da

stem² vt (pt/pp stemmed) contenere

stench /stentʃ/ n fetore m

step /step/ n passo m; (stair) gradino m; **~s** pl (ladder) scala f portatile; **in ~** al passo; **be out of ~** non stare al passo; **~ by ~** un passo alla volta ●vi (pt/pp stepped) **~** into entrare in; **~ out of** uscire da; **~ out of line** sgarrare. **step down** vi fig dimettersi. **step forward** vi farsi avanti. **step in** vi fig intervenire. **step up** vt (increase) aumentare

step: ~brother n fratellastro m. **~child** n figliastro, -a mf. **~daughter** n figliastra f. **~father** n patrigno m. **~ladder** n scala f portatile. **~mother** n matrigna f

'stepping-stone n pietra f per guadare; fig trampolino m

step: ~sister n sorellastra f. **~son** n figliastro m

stereo /'sterɪəʊ/ n stereo m; **in ~** in stereofonia. **~phonic** /-'fɒnɪk/ a stereofonico

stereotype /'sterɪətaɪp/ n stereotipo m. **~d** a stereotipato

steril|e /'steraɪl/ a sterile. **~ity** /stə'rɪlətɪ/ n sterilità f

steriliz|ation /sterəlaɪ'zeɪʃn/ n sterilizzazione f. **~e** /'ster-/ vt sterilizzare

sterling /'stɜ:lɪŋ/ a fig apprezzabile; **~ silver** argento m pregiato ●n sterlina f

stern¹ /stɜ:n/ a severo

stern² n (of boat) poppa f

stethoscope /'steθəskəʊp/ n stetoscopio m

stew /stju:/ n stufato m; **in a ~** fam agitato ●vt/i cuocere in umido; **~ed fruit** frutta f cotta

steward /'stju:əd/ n (at meeting) organizzatore, -trice mf; (on ship, aircraft) steward m inv. **~ess** n hostess f inv

stick¹ /stɪk/ n bastone m; (of celery, rhubarb) gambo m; Sport mazza f

stick² v (pt/pp stuck) ●vt (stab) [con]ficcare; (glue) attaccare; (fam: put) mettere; (fam: endure) sopportare ●vi (adhere) attaccarsi (to a); (jam) bloccarsi; **~ to** attenersi a (facts); mantenere (story); perseverare in (task); **~ at it** fam tener duro; **~ at nothing** fam non fermarsi di fronte a niente; **be stuck** (vehicle, person:) essere bloccato; (drawer:) essere incastrato; **be stuck with sth** fam farsi incastrare con qcsa.

stick out vi (project) sporgere; (fam: catch the eye) risaltare ●vt fam fare (tongue). **stick up for** vt fam difendere

sticker /'stɪkə(r)/ n autoadesivo m

'sticking plaster n cerotto m

stick-in-the-mud n retrogrado m

stickler /'stɪklə(r)/ n **be a ~ for** tenere molto a

sticky /'stɪkɪ/ a (**-ier, -iest**) appicciccoso; ⟨adhesive⟩ adesivo; ⟨fig: difficult⟩ difficile

stiff /stɪf/ a rigido; ⟨brush, task⟩ duro; ⟨person⟩ controllato; ⟨drink⟩ forte; ⟨penalty⟩ severo; ⟨price⟩ alto; **bored ~** fam annoiato a morte; **~ neck** torcicollo m. **~en** vt irrigidire ● vi irrigidirsi. **~ness** rigidità f

stifl|e /'staɪfl/ vt soffocare. **~ing** a soffocante

stigma /'stɪgmə/ n marchio m

stiletto /stɪ'letəʊ/ n stiletto m; **~ heels** tacchi mpl a spillo; **~s** ⟨pl: shoes⟩ scarpe fpl coi tacchi a spillo

still[1] /stɪl/ n distilleria f

still[2] a fermo; ⟨drink⟩ non gasato; **keep/stand ~** stare fermo ● n quiete f; ⟨photo⟩ posa f ● adv ancora; ⟨nevertheless⟩ nondimeno, comunque; **I'm ~ not sure** non sono ancora sicuro

'stillborn a nato morto

still 'life n natura f morta

stilted /'stɪltɪd/ a artificioso

stilts /stɪlts/ npl trampoli mpl

stimulant /'stɪmjʊlənt/ n eccitante m

stimulat|e /'stɪmjʊleɪt/ vt stimolare. **~ion** /-'leɪʃn/ n stimolo m

stimulus /'stɪmjʊləs/ n (pl **-li** /-laɪ/) stimolo m

sting /stɪŋ/ n puntura f; ⟨organ⟩ pungiglione m ● v (pt/pp stung) ● vt pungere; ⟨jellyfish:⟩ pizzicare ● vi ⟨insect:⟩ pungere. **~ing nettle** n ortica f

stingy /'stɪndʒɪ/ a (**-ier, -iest**) tirchio

stink /stɪŋk/ n puzza f ● vi (pt **stank**, pp **stunk**) puzzare

stint /stɪnt/ n lavoro m; **do one's ~** fare la propria parte ● vt **~ on** lesinare su

stipulat|e /'stɪpjʊleɪt/ vt porre come condizione. **~ion** /-'leɪʃn/ n condizione f

stir /stɜ:(r)/ n mescolata f; ⟨commotion⟩ trambusto m ● v (pt/pp **stirred**) ● vt muovere; ⟨mix⟩ mescolare ● vi muoversi

stirrup /'stɪrəp/ n staffa f

stitch /stɪtʃ/ n punto m; ⟨in knitting⟩ maglia f; ⟨pain⟩ fitta f; **have sb in ~s** fam far ridere qcno a crepapelle ● vt cucire

stock /stɒk/ n ⟨for use or selling⟩ scorta f, stock m inv; ⟨livestock⟩ bestiame m; ⟨lineage⟩ stirpe f; Fin titoli mpl, Culin brodo m; **in ~** disponibile; **out of ~** esaurito; **take ~** fig fare il punto ● a solito ● vt ⟨shop⟩ vendere; approvvigio-

nare ⟨shelves⟩. **stock up** vi far scorta (**with** di)

stock: ~broker n agente m di cambio. **~ cube** n dado m [da brodo]. **S~ Exchange** n Borsa f Valori

stocking /'stɒkɪŋ/ n calza f

stockist /'stɒkɪst/ n rivenditore m

stock: ~market n mercato m azionario. **~pile** vt fare scorta di ● n riserva f. **~'still** a immobile. **~-taking** n Comm inventario m

stocky /'stɒkɪ/ a (**-ier, -iest**) tarchiato

stodgy /'stɒdʒɪ/ a indigesto

stoic /'stəʊk/ n stoico, -a mf. **~al** a stoico. **~ism** /-sɪzm/ stoicismo m

stoke /stəʊk/ vt alimentare

stole[1] /stəʊl/ n stola f

stole[2], **stolen** /'stəʊln/ see **steal**

stolid /'stɒlɪd/ a apatico

stomach /'stʌmək/ n pancia f; Anat stomaco m ● vt fam reggere. **~-ache** n mal m di pancia

stone /stəʊn/ n pietra f; ⟨in fruit⟩ nocciolo m; Med calcolo m; ⟨weight⟩ 6,348 kg ● a di pietra; ⟨wall, Age⟩ della pietra ● vt snocciolare ⟨fruit⟩. **~-cold** a gelido. **~-'deaf** a fam sordo come una campana

stony /'stəʊnɪ/ a pietroso; ⟨glare⟩ glaciale

stood /stʊd/ see **stand**

stool /stu:l/ n sgabello m

stoop /stu:p/ n curvatura f ● vi stare curvo; ⟨bend down⟩ chinarsi; fig abbassarsi

stop /stɒp/ n ⟨break⟩ sosta f; ⟨for bus, train⟩ fermata f; Gram punto m; **come to a ~** fermarsi; **put a ~ to sth** mettere fine a qcsa ● v (pt/pp **stopped**) ● vt fermare; arrestare ⟨machine⟩; ⟨prevent⟩ impedire; **~ sb doing sth** impedire a qcno di fare qcsa; **~ doing sth** smettere di fare qcsa; **~ that!** smettila! ● vi fermarsi; ⟨rain:⟩ smettere ● int fermo!. **stop off** vi fare una sosta. **stop up** vt otturare ⟨sink⟩; tappare ⟨hole⟩. **stop with** vi ⟨fam: stay with⟩ fermarsi da

stop: ~gap n palliativo f; ⟨person⟩ tappabuchi m inv. **~-over** n sosta f; Aeron scalo m

stoppage /'stɒpɪdʒ/ n ostruzione f; ⟨strike⟩ interruzione f; ⟨deduction⟩ trattenute fpl

stopper /'stɒpə(r)/ n tappo m

stop: ~-press n ultimissime fpl. **~-watch** n cronometro m

storage /'stɔ:rɪdʒ/ n deposito m; ⟨in

warehouse) immagazzinaggio *m*; *Comput* memoria *f*

store /stɔː(r)/ *n* (*stock*) riserva *f*; (*shop*) grande magazzino *m*; (*depot*) deposito *m*;**in ~** in deposito;**what the future has in ~ for me** cosa mi riserva il futuro;**set great ~ by** tenere in gran conto ● *vt* tenere; (*in warehouse, Comput*) immagazzinare. **~-room** *n* magazzino *m*

storey /ˈstɔːrɪ/ *n* piano *m*

stork /stɔːk/ *n* cicogna *f*

storm /stɔːm/ *n* temporale *m*; (*with thunder*) tempesta *f* ● *vt* prendere d'assalto. **~y** *a* tempestoso

story /ˈstɔːrɪ/ *n* storia *f*; (*in newspaper*) articolo *m*

stout /staʊt/ *a* (*shoes*) resistente; (*fat*) robusto; (*defence*) strenuo

stove /staʊ/ *n* stufa *f*; (*for cooking*) cucina *f* [economica]

stow /staʊ/ *vt* metter via. **~away** *n* passeggero, -a *mf* clandestino, -a

straddle /ˈstrædl/ *vt* stare a cavalcioni su; (*standing*) essere a cavallo su

straggl|e /ˈstrægl/ *vi* crescere disordinatamente; (*dawdle*) rimanere indietro. **~er** *n* persona *f* che rimane indietro. **~y** *a* in disordine

straight /streɪt/ *a* diritto, dritto; (*answer, question, person*) diretto; (*tidy*) in ordine; (*drink, hair*) liscio ● *adv* diritto, dritto; (*directly*) direttamente; **~ away** immediatamente;**~ on** *or***ahead** diritto; **~ out** *fig* apertamente; **go ~** *fam* rigare diritto; **put sth ~** mettere qcsa in ordine;**sit**/**stand up ~** stare diritto

straighten /ˈstreɪtn/ *vt* raddrizzare ● *vi* raddrizzarsi; **~ [up]** (*person:*) mettersi diritto. **straighten out** *vt fig* chiarire (*situation*)

straight'**forward** *a* franco; (*simple*) semplice

strain[1] /streɪn/ *n* (*streak*) vena *f*; *Bot* varietà *f inv*; (*of virus*) forma *f*

strain[2] /streɪn/ *n* tensione *f*; (*injury*) stiramento *m*; **~s** *pl* (*of music*) note *fpl* ● *vt* tirare; sforzare (*eyes, voice*); stirarsi (*muscle*); *Culin* scolare ● *vi* sforzarsi. **~ed** *a* (*relations*) teso. **~er** *n* colino *m*

strait /streɪt/ *n* stretto *m*; **in dire ~s** in serie difficoltà. **~-jacket** *n* camicia *f* di forza. **~-laced** *a* puritano

strand[1] /strænd/ *n* (*of thread*) gugliata *f*; (*of beads*) filo *m*; (*of hair*) capello *m*

strand[2] *vt* **be ~ed** rimanere bloccato

strange /streɪndʒ/ *a* strano; (*not known*) sconosciuto; (*unaccustomed*) estraneo. **~ly** *adv* stranamente; **~ly enough** curiosamente. **~r** *n* estraneo, -a *mf*

strangle /ˈstræŋgl/ *vt* strangolare; *fig* reprimere

strangulation /stræŋgjʊˈleɪʃn/ *n* strangolamento *m*

strap /stræp/ *n* cinghia *f*; (*to grasp in vehicle*) maniglia *f*; (*of watch*) cinturino *m*; (*shoulder* ~) bretella *f*, spallina *f*● *vt* (*pt*/*pp***strapped**) legare;**~ in** *or***down** assicurare

strapping /ˈstræpɪŋ/ *a* robusto

strata /ˈstrɑːtə/ *npl see***stratum**

stratagem /ˈstrætədʒəm/ *n* stratagemma *m*

strategic /strəˈtiːdʒɪk/ *a* strategico

strategy /ˈstrætədʒɪ/ *n* strategia *f*

stratum /ˈstrɑːtəm/ *n* (*pl***strata**) strato *m*

straw /strɔː/ *n* paglia *f*; (*single piece*) fuscello *m*; (*for drinking*) cannuccia *f*; **the last ~** l'ultima goccia

strawberry /ˈstrɔːbərɪ/ *n* fragola *f*

stray /streɪ/ *a* (*animal*) randagio ● *n* randagio *m* ● *vi* andarsene per conto proprio; (*deviate*) deviare (**from** da)

streak /striːk/ *n* striatura *f*; (*fig: trait*) vena *f* ● *vi* sfrecciare. **~y** *a* striato; (*bacon*) grasso

stream /striːm/ *n* ruscello *m*; (*current*) corrente *f*; (*of blood, people*) flusso *m*; *Sch* classe *f* ● *vi* scorrere. **stream in**/**out** *vi* entrare/uscire a fiotti

streamer /ˈstriːmə(r)/ *n* (*paper*) stella *f* filante; (*flag*) pennone *m*

'**streamline** *vt* rendere aerodinamico; (*simplify*) snellire. **~d** *a* aerodinamico

street /striːt/ *n* strada *f*; **~car** *n* Am tram *m inv*. **~lamp** *n* lampione *m*

strength /streŋθ/ *n* forza *f*; (*of wall, bridge etc*) solidità *f*; **~s** *pl* punti *mpl* forti; **on the ~ of** grazie a. **~en** *vt* rinforzare

strenuous /ˈstrenjʊəs/ *a* faticoso; (*attempt, denial*) energico

stress /stres/ *n* (*emphasis*) insistenza *f*; *Gram* accento *m* tonico; (*mental*) stress *m inv*; *Mech* spinta *f* ● *vt* (*emphasize*) insistere su; *Gram* mettere l'accento [tonico] su. **~ed** *a* (*mentally*) stressato. **~ful** *a* stressante

stretch /stretʃ/ *n* stiramento *m*; (*period*) periodo *m* di tempo; (*of road*) tratto *m*; (*elasticity*) elasticità *f*; **at a ~** di fila; **have a ~** stirarsi ● *vt* tirare; allargare (*shoes, arms etc*); (*person:*) allungare ●vi (become wider) allargarsi; (extend) estendersi; (person:) stirarsi. ~er n barella f

strew /stru:/ vt (pp **strewn** or **strewed**) sparpagliare

stricken /'strɪkn/ a prostrato; ~ **with** affetto da (illness)

strict /strɪkt/ a severo; (precise) preciso. ~**ly** adv severamente; ~**ly speaking** in senso stretto

stride /straɪd/ n [lungo] passo m; **take sth in one's** ~ accettare qcsa con facilità ●vi (pt **strode**, pp **stridden**) andare a gran passi

strident /'straɪdənt/ a stridente; (colour) vistoso

strife /straɪf/ n conflitto m

strike /straɪk/ n sciopero m; Mil attacco m; **on** ~ in sciopero ●v (pt/pp **struck**) ●vt colpire; accendere (match); trovare (oil, gold); (delete) depennare; (occur to) venire in mente a; Mil attaccare ●vi (lightning:) cadere; (clock:) suonare; Mil attaccare; (workers:) scioperare; ~ **lucky** azzeccarla. **strike off**, **strike out** vt eliminare. **strike up** vt fare (friendship); attaccare (conversation). ~-**breaker** n persona f che non aderisce a uno sciopero

striker /'straɪkə(r)/ n scioperante mf

striking /'straɪkɪŋ/ a impressionante; (attractive) affascinante

string /strɪŋ/ n spago m; (of musical instrument, racket) corda f; (of pearls) filo m; (of lies) serie f; **the** ~**s** pl Mus gli archi; **pull** ~**s** fam usare le proprie conoscenze ●vt (pt/pp **strung**) (thread) infilare (beads). ~**ed** a (instrument) a corda

stringent /'strɪndʒnt/ a rigido

strip /strɪp/ n striscia f ●v (pt/pp **stripped**) ●vt spogliare; togliere le lenzuola da (bed); scrostare (wood, furniture); smontare (machine); (deprive) privare (of di) ●vi (undress) spogliarsi. ~ **cartoon** n striscia f. ~ **club** n locale m di strip-tease

stripe /straɪp/ n striscia f; Mil gallone m. ~**d** a a strisce

'**striplight** n tubo m al neon

stripper /'strɪpə(r)/ n spogliarellista mf; (solvent) sverniciatore m

strip-'tease n spogliarello m, strip-tease m inv

strive /straɪv/ vi (pt **strove**, pp **striven**) sforzarsi (**to** di); ~ **for** sforzarsi di ottenere

strode /strəʊd/ see **stride**

stroke[1] /strəʊk/ n colpo m; (of pen) tratto m; (in swimming) bracciata f; Med ictus m inv; ~ **of luck** colpo m di fortuna; **put sb off his** ~ far perdere il filo a qcno

stroke[2] vt accarezzare

stroll /strəʊl/ n passeggiata f ●vi passeggiare. ~**er** n (Am: push-chair) passeggino m

strong /strɒŋ/ a (-**er** /-gə(r)/, -**est** /-gɪst/) forte; (argument) valido

strong: ~-**box** n cassaforte f. ~-**hold** n roccaforte f. ~**ly** adv fortemente. ~-'**minded** a risoluto. ~-**room** n camera f blindata

stroppy /'strɒpɪ/ a scorbutico

strove /strəʊv/ see **strive**

struck /strʌk/ see **strike**

structural /'strʌktʃərəl/ a strutturale. ~**ly** adv strutturalmente

structure /'strʌktʃə(r)/ n struttura f

struggle /'strʌgl/ n lotta f; **with a** ~ con difficoltà ●vi lottare; ~ **for breath** respirare con fatica; ~ **to do sth** fare fatica a fare qcsa; ~ **to one's feet** alzarsi con fatica

strum /strʌm/ vt/i (pt/pp **strummed**) strimpellare

strung /strʌŋ/ see **string**

strut[1] /strʌt/ n (component) puntello m

strut[2] vi (pt/pp **strutted**) camminare impettito

stub /stʌb/ n mozzicone m; (counterfoil) matrice f ●vt (pt/pp **stubbed**) ~ **one's toe** sbattere il dito del piede (**on** contro). **stub out** vt spegnere (cigarette)

stubble /'stʌbl/ n barba f ispida. ~**ly** a ispido

stubborn /'stʌbən/ a testardo; (refusal) ostinato

stubby /'stʌbɪ/ a (-**ier**, -**iest**) tozzo

stucco /'stʌkəʊ/ n stucco m

stuck /stʌk/ see **stick**[2]. ~-'**up** a fam snob inv

stud[1] /stʌd/ n (on boot) tacchetto m; (on jacket) borchia f; (for ear) orecchino m [a bottone]

stud[2] n (of horses) scuderia f

student /'stju:dənt/ n studente m, studentessa f; (school child) scolaro, -a mf. ~ **nurse** n studente, studentessa infermiere, -a

studied /'stʌdɪd/ a intenzionale; (politeness) studiato

studio /'stju:dɪəʊ/ n studio m

studious /'stju:dɪəs/ a studioso; (attention) studiato

study /'stʌdɪ/ n studio m ●vt/i (pt/pp **studied**) studiare

stuff /stʌf/ n materiale m; (fam: things) roba f ●vt riempire; (with padding) imbottire; Culin farcire; ~ **sth into a drawer/one's pocket** ficcare qcsa alla rinfusa in un cassetto/in tasca. ~**ing** n (padding) imbottitura f; Culin ripieno m

stuffy /'stʌfɪ/ a (-ier, -iest) che sa di chiuso; (old-fashioned) antiquato

stumbl|e /'stʌmbl/ vi inciampare; ~**e across** or on imbattersi in. ~**ing-block** n ostacolo m

stump /stʌmp/ n ceppo m; (of limb) moncone m. ~**ed** a fam perplesso ●**stump up** vt/i fam sganciare

stun /stʌn/ vt (pt/pp **stunned**) stordire; (astonish) sbalordire

stung /stʌŋ/ see **sting**

stunk /stʌŋk/ see **stink**

stunning /'stʌnɪŋ/ a fam favoloso; (blow, victory) sbalorditivo

stunt¹ /stʌnt/ n fam trovata f pubblicitaria

stunt² vt arrestare lo sviluppo di. ~**ed** a stentato

stupendous /stju:'pendəs/ a stupendo. ~**ly** adv stupendamente

stupid /'stju:pɪd/ a stupido. ~**ity** /-'pɪdətɪ/ n stupidità f. ~**ly** adv stupidamente

stupor /'stju:pə(r)/ n torpore m

sturdy /'stɜ:dɪ/ a (-ier, -iest) robusto; (furniture) solido

stutter /'stʌtə(r)/ n balbuzie f ●vt/i balbettare

sty, stye /staɪ/ n (pl **styes**) Med orzaiolo m

style /staɪl/ n stile m; (fashion) moda f; (sort) tipo m; (hair~) pettinatura f; **in** ~ in grande stile

stylish /'staɪlɪʃ/ a elegante. ~**ly** adv con eleganza

stylist /'staɪlɪst/ n stilista mf; (hair-~) parrucchiere, -a mf. ~**ic** /-'lɪstɪk/ a stilistico

stylized /'staɪlaɪzd/ a stilizzato

stylus /'staɪləs/ n (on record player) puntina f

suave /swɑ:v/ a dai modi garbati

sub'conscious /sʌb-/ a subcosciente ●n subcosciente m. ~**ly** adv in modo inconscio

subcon'tract vt subappaltare (**to** a). ~**or** n subappaltatore m

'subdivi|de vt suddividere. ~**sion** n suddivisione f

subdue /səb'dju:/ vt sottomettere; (make quieter) attenuare. ~**d** a (light) attenuato; (person, voice) pacato

subhuman /sʌb'hju:mən/ a disumano

subject¹ /'sʌbdʒɪkt/ a ~ **to** soggetto a; (depending on) subordinato a; ~ **to availability** nei limiti della disponibilità ●n soggetto m; (of ruler) suddito, -a mf; Sch materia f

subject² /səb'dʒekt/ vt (to attack, abuse) sottoporre; assoggettare (country)

subjective /səb'dʒektɪv/ a soggettivo. ~**ly** adv soggettivamente

subjugate /'sʌbdʒʊgeɪt/ vt soggiogare

subjunctive /səb'dʒʌŋktɪv/ a & n congiuntivo m

sub'let vt (pt/pp -**let**, pres p -**letting**) subaffittare

sublime /sə'blaɪm/ a sublime. ~**ly** adv sublimamente

subliminal /sə'blɪmɪnl/ a subliminale

sub-ma'chine-gun n mitraglietta f

subma'rine n sommergibile m

submerge /səb'mɜ:dʒ/ vt immergere; **be** ~**d** essere sommerso ●vi immergersi

submiss|ion /səb'mɪʃn/ n sottomissione f. ~**ive** /-sɪv/ a sottomesso

submit /səb'mɪt/ v (pt/pp -**mitted**, pres p -**mitting**) ●vt sottoporre ●vi sottomettersi

subordinate /sə'bɔ:dɪneɪt/ vt subordinare (**to** a)

subscribe /səb'skraɪb/ vi contribuire; ~ **to** abbonarsi a (newspaper); sottoscrivere (fund); fig aderire a. ~**r** n abbonato, -a mf

subscription /səb'skrɪpʃn/ n (to club) sottoscrizione f; (to newspaper) abbonamento m

subsequent /'sʌbsɪkwənt/ a susseguente. ~**ly** adv in seguito

subservient /səb'sɜ:vɪənt/ a subordinato; (servile) servile. ~**ly** adv servilmente

subside /səb'saɪd/ vi sprofondare; (ground:) avvallarsi; (storm:) placarsi

subsidiary /səb'sɪdɪərɪ/ a secondario ●n ~ [company] filiale f

subsid|ize /'sʌbsɪdaɪz/ vt sovvenzionare. ~**y** n sovvenzione f

subsist /səb'sɪst/ vi vivere (**on** di). ~**ence** n sussistenza f

substance /'sʌbstəns/ n sostanza f

sub'standard a di qualità inferiore

substantial /səb'stænʃl/ a solido; (meal) sostanzioso; (considerable) notevole. **~ly** *adv* notevolmente; *(essentially)* sostanzialmente

substantiate /səb'stænʃɪeɪt/ *vt* comprovare

substitut|e /'sʌbstɪtjuːt/ *n* sostituto *m* ● *vt* **~e A for B** sostituire B con A ● *vi* **~e for sb** sostituire qcno. **~ion** /-'tjuːʃn/ *n* sostituzione *f*

subterranean /sʌbtə'reɪnɪən/ *a* sotterraneo

'subtitle *n* sottotitolo *m*

sub|tle /'sʌtl/ *a* sottile; *(taste, perfume)* delicato. **~tlety** *n* sottigliezza *f*. **~tly** *adv* sottilmente

subtract /səb'trækt/ *vt* sottrare. **~ion** /-ækʃn/ *n* sottrazione *f*

suburb /'sʌbɜːb/ *n* sobborgo *m*; **in the ~s** in periferia. **~an** /sə'bɜːbən/ *a* suburbano. **~ia** /sə'bɜːbɪə/ *n* sobborghi *mpl*

subversive /səb'vɜːsɪv/ *a* sovversivo

'subway *n* sottopassaggio *m*; *(Am: railway)* metropolitana *f*

succeed /sək'siːd/ *vi* riuscire; *(follow)* succedere a; **~ in doing** riuscire a fare ● *vt* succedere a *(king)*. **~ing** *a* successivo

success /sək'ses/ *n* successo *m*; **be a ~** *(in life)* aver successo. **~ful** *a* riuscito; *(businessman, artist etc)* di successo. **~fully** *adv* con successo

succession /sək'seʃn/ *n* successione *f*; **in ~** di seguito

successive /sək'sesɪv/ *a* successivo. **~ly** *adv* successivamente

successor /sək'sesə(r)/ *n* successore *m*

succinct /sək'sɪŋkt/ *a* succinto

succulent /'sʌkjʊlənt/ *a* succulento

succumb /sə'kʌm/ *vi* soccombere **(to** a)

such /sʌtʃ/ *a* tale; **~ a book** un libro di questo genere; **~ a thing** una cosa di questo genere; **~ a long time ago** talmente tanto tempo fa; **there is no ~ thing** non esiste una cosa così; **there is no ~ person** non esiste una persona così ● *pron* **as ~** come tale; **~ as** chi; **and ~** e simili; **~ as it is** così com'è. **~like** *pron fam* di tal genere

suck /sʌk/ *vt* succhiare. **suck up** *vt* assorbire. **suck up to** *vt fam* fare il lecchino con

sucker /'sʌkə(r)/ *n* Bot pollone *m*; *(fam: person)* credulone, -a *mf*

suction /'sʌkʃn/ *n* aspirazione *f*

sudden /'sʌdn/ *a* improvviso ● *n* **all of a ~** all'improvviso. **~ly** *adv* improvvisamente

sue /suː/ *v (pres p suing)* ● *vt* fare causa a **(for** per) ● *vi* fare causa

suede /sweɪd/ *n* pelle *f* scamosciata

suet /'suːɪt/ *n* grasso *m* di rognone

suffer /'sʌfə(r)/ *vi* soffrire **(from** per) ● *vt* soffrire; subire *(loss etc)*; *(tolerate)* subire. **~ing** *n* sofferenza *f*

suffice /sə'faɪs/ *vi* bastare

sufficient /sə'fɪʃənt/ *a* sufficiente. **~ly** *adv* sufficientemente

suffix /'sʌfɪks/ *n* suffisso *m*

suffocat|e /'sʌfəkeɪt/ *vt/i* soffocare. **~ion** /-'keɪʃn/ *n* soffocamento *m*

sugar /'ʃʊgə(r)/ *n* zucchero *m* ● *vt* zuccherare. **~ basin, ~-bowl** *n* zuccheriera *f*. **~y** *a* zuccheroso; *fig* sdolcinato

suggest /sə'dʒest/ *vt* suggerire; *(indicate, insinuate)* fare pensare a. **~ion** /-estʃən/ *n* suggerimento *m*; *(trace)* traccia *f*. **~ive** /-ɪv/ *a* allusivo. **~ively** *adv* in modo allusivo

suicidal /suːɪ'saɪdl/ *a* suicida

suicide /'suːɪsaɪd/ *n* suicidio *m*; *(person)* suicida *mf*; **commit ~** suicidarsi

suit /suːt/ *n* vestito *m*; *(woman's)* tailleur *m inv*; *(in cards)* seme *m*; *Jur* causa *f*; **follow ~** *fig* fare lo stesso ● *vt* andar bene a; *(adapt)* adattare **(to** a); *(be convenient for)* andare bene per; **be ~ed to** or **for** essere adatto a; **~ yourself!** fa' come vuoi!

suitab|le /'suːtəbl/ *a* adatto. **~y** *adv* convenientemente

'suitcase *n* valigia *f*

suite /swiːt/ *n* suite *f inv*; *(of furniture)* divano *m* e poltrone *fpl* assortiti

sulk /sʌlk/ *vi* fare il broncio. **~y** *a* imbronciato

sullen /'sʌlən/ *a* svogliato

sulphur /'sʌlfə(r)/ *n* zolfo *m*. **~ic** /-'fjuːrɪk/ **~ic acid** *n* acido *m* solforico

sultana /sʌl'tɑːnə/ *n* uva *f* sultanina

sultry /'sʌltrɪ/ *a* (**-ier, -iest**) *(weather)* afoso; *fig* sensuale

sum /sʌm/ *n* somma *f*; *Sch* addizione *f* ● **sum up** *v (pt/pp* **summed)** ● *vi* riassumere ● *vt* valutare

summar|ize /'sʌməraɪz/ *vt* riassumere. **~y** *n* sommario *m* ● *a* sommario; *(dismissal)* sbrigativo

summer /'sʌmə(r)/ *n* estate *f*. **~-house** *n* padiglione *m*. **~time** *n (season)* estate *f*

summery /'sʌmərɪ/ *a* estivo

summit /'sʌmɪt/ *n* cima *f*. **~ conference** *n* vertice *m*

summon /'sʌmən/ *vt* convocare; *Jur* citare. **summon up** *vt* raccogliere ⟨*strength*⟩; rievocare ⟨*memory*⟩

summons /'sʌmənz/ *n Jur* citazione *f* ●*vt* citare in giudizio

sump /sʌmp/ *n Auto* coppa *f* dell'olio

sumptuous /'sʌmptjʊəs/ *a* sontuoso. **~ly** *adv* sontuosamente

sun /sʌn/ *n* sole *m* ●*vt* (*pt/pp* **sunned**) **~ oneself** prendere il sole

sun: ~bathe *vi* prendere il sole. **~-bed** *n* lettino *m* solare. **~burn** *n* scottatura *f* ⟨*solare*⟩. **~burnt** *a* scottato ⟨*dal sole*⟩

sundae /'sʌndeɪ/ *n* gelato *m* guarnito

Sunday /'sʌndeɪ/ *n* domenica *f*

'sundial *n* meridiana *f*

sundry /'sʌndrɪ/ *a* svariati; **all and ~** tutti quanti

'sunflower *n* girasole *m*

sung /sʌŋ/ *see* **sing**

'sun-glasses *npl* occhiali *mpl* da sole

sunk /sʌŋk/ *see* **sink**

sunken /'sʌŋkn/ *a* incavato

'sunlight *n* [luce *f* del] sole *m*

sunny /'sʌnɪ/ *a* (**-ier, -iest**) assolato

sun: ~rise *n* alba *f*. **~-roof** *n Auto* tettuccio *m* apribile. **~set** *n* tramonto *m*. **~shade** *n* parasole *m*. **~shine** *n* [luce *f* del] sole *m*. **~stroke** *n* insolazione *f*. **~tan** *n* abbronzatura *f*. **~tanned** *a* abbronzato. **~tan oil** *n* olio *m* solare

super /'su:pə(r)/ *a fam* fantastico

superb /sʊ'pɜ:b/ *a* splendido

supercilious /su:pə'sɪlɪəs/ *a* altezzoso

superficial /su:pə'fɪʃl/ *a* superficiale. **~ly** *adv* superficialmente

superfluous /sʊ'pɜ:flʊəs/ *a* superfluo

super'human *a* sovrumano

superintendent /su:pərɪn'tendənt/ *n* ⟨*of police*⟩ commissario *m* di polizia

superior /su:'pɪərɪə(r)/ *a* superiore ●*n* superiore, -a *mf*. **~ity** /-'ɒrətɪ/ *n* superiorità *f*

superlative /su:'pɜ:lətɪv/ *a* eccellente ●*n* superlativo *m*

'superman *n* superuomo *m*

'supermarket *n* supermercato *m*

'supermodel *n* top model *f inv*

super'natural *a* soprannaturale

'superpower *n* superpotenza *f*

supersede /su:pə'si:d/ *vt* rimpiazzare

super'sonic *a* supersonico

superstiti|on /su:pə'stɪʃn/ *n* superstizione *f*. **~ous** /-'stɪʃəs/ *a* superstizioso

supervis|e /'su:pəvaɪz/ *vt* supervisionare. **~ion** /-'vɪʒn/ *n* supervisione *f*. **~or** *n* supervisore *m*

supper /'sʌpə(r)/ *n* cena *f*

supple /'sʌpl/ *a* slogato

supplement /'sʌplɪmənt/ *n* supplemento *m* ●*vt* integrare. **~ary** /-'mentərɪ/ *a* supplementare

supplier /sə'plaɪə(r)/ *n* fornitore, -trice *mf*

supply /sə'plaɪ/ *n* fornitura *f*; (*in economics*) offerta *f*; **supplies** *pl Mil* approvvigionamenti *mpl* ●*vt* (*pt/pp* **-ied**) fornire; **~ sb with sth** fornire qcsa a qcno

support /sə'pɔ:t/ *n* sostegno *m*; ⟨*base*⟩ supporto *m*; ⟨*keep*⟩ sostentamento *m* ●*vt* sostenere; mantenere ⟨*family*⟩; ⟨*give money to*⟩ mantenere finanziariamente; *Sport* fare il tifo per. **~er** *n* sostenitore, -trice *mf*; *Sport* tifoso, -a *mf*. **~ive** /-ɪv/ *a* incoraggiante

suppose /sə'pəʊz/ *vt* ⟨*presume*⟩ supporre; ⟨*imagine*⟩ pensare; **be ~d to do** dover fare; **not be ~d to/***fam* non avere il permesso di; **I ~ so** suppongo di sì. **~dly** /-ɪdlɪ/ *adv* presumibilmente

suppress /sə'pres/ *vt* sopprimere. **~ion** /-eʃn/ *n* oppressione *f*

supremacy /su:'preməsɪ/ *n* supremazia *f*

supreme /su:'pri:m/ *a* supremo

surcharge /'sɜ:tʃɑ:dʒ/ *n* supplemento *m*

sure /ʃʊə(r)/ *a* sicuro, certo; **make ~** accertarsi; **be ~ to do it** mi raccomando di farlo ●*adv Am fam* certamente; **~ enough** infatti. **~ly** *adv* certamente; (*Am: gladly*) volentieri

surety /'ʃʊərətɪ/ *n* garanzia *f*; **stand ~ for** garantire per

surf /sɜ:f/ *n* schiuma *f* ●*vt Comput* **~ the Net** surfare in Internet

surface /'sɜ:fɪs/ *n* superficie *f*; **on the ~** *fig* in apparenza ●*vi* ⟨*emerge*⟩ emergere. **~ mail** *n* **by ~ mail** per posta ordinaria

'surfboard *n* tavola *f* da surf

surfing /'sɜ:fɪŋ/ *n* surf *m inv*

surge /sɜ:dʒ/ *n* ⟨*of sea*⟩ ondata *f*; ⟨*of interest*⟩ aumento *m*; ⟨*in demand*⟩ impennata *f*; ⟨*of anger, pity*⟩ impeto *m* ●*vi* riversarsi; **~ forward** buttarsi in avanti

surgeon /'sɜ:dʒən/ *n* chirurgo *m*

surgery /'sɜ:dʒərɪ/ *n* chirurgia *f*; ⟨*place, consulting room*⟩ ambulatorio *m*; ⟨*hours*⟩ ore *fpl* di visita; **have ~** subire un'intervento [chirurgico]

surgical /'sɜ:dʒɪkl/ *a* chirurgico

surly /'sɜ:lɪ/ *a* (**-ier, -iest**) scontroso

surmise /sə'maɪz/ *vt* supporre

surmount /sə'maʊnt/ *vt* sormontare

surname /'sɜ:neɪm/ *n* cognome *m*

surpass /səˈpɑːs/ vt superare
surplus /ˈsɜːpləs/ a d'avanzo ● n sovrappiù m
surpris|e /səˈpraɪz/ n sorpresa f ● vt sorprendere; **be ~ed** essere sorpreso (**at** da). **~ing** a sorprendente. **~ingly** adv sorprendentemente
surrender /səˈrendə(r)/ n resa f ● vi arrendersi ● vt cedere
surreptitious /sʌrəpˈtɪʃəs/ a & adv di nascosto
surrogate /ˈsʌrəgət/ n surrogato m. **~ mother** n madre f surrogata
surround /səˈraʊnd/ vt circondare. **~ing** a circostante. **~ings** npl dintorni mpl
surveillance /səˈveɪləns/ n sorveglianza f
survey[1] /ˈsɜːveɪ/ n sguardo m; (poll) sondaggio m; (investigation) indagine f; (of land) rilevamento m; (of house) perizia f
survey[2] /səˈveɪ/ vt esaminare; fare un rilevamento di ⟨land⟩; fare una perizia di ⟨building⟩. **~or** n perito m; (of land) topografo, -a mf
survival /səˈvaɪvl/ n sopravvivenza f; (relic) resto m
surviv|e /səˈvaɪv/ vt sopravvivere a ● vi sopravvivere. **~or** n superstite mf; **be a ~or** fam riuscire sempre a cavarsela
susceptible /səˈseptəbl/ a influenzabile; **~ to** sensibile a
suspect[1] /səˈspekt/ vt sospettare; (assume) supporre
suspect[2] /ˈsʌspekt/ a & n sospetto, -a mf
suspend /səˈspend/ vt appendere; (stop, from duty) sospendere. **~er belt** n reggicalze m inv. **~ers** npl giarrettiere fpl; (Am: braces) bretelle fpl
suspense /səˈspens/ n tensione f; (in book etc) suspense f
suspension /səˈspenʃn/ n Auto sospensione f. **~ bridge** n ponte m sospeso
suspici|on /səˈspɪʃn/ n sospetto m; (trace) pizzico m; **under ~on** sospettato. **~ous** /-ɪʃəs/ a sospettoso; (arousing suspicion) sospetto. **~ously** adv sospettosamente; (arousing suspicion) in modo sospetto
sustain /səˈsteɪn/ vt sostenere; mantenere ⟨life⟩; subire ⟨injury⟩
sustenance /ˈsʌstɪnəns/ n nutrimento m
swab /swɒb/ n Med tampone m

swagger /ˈswægə(r)/ vi pavoneggiarsi
swallow[1] /ˈswɒləʊ/ vt/i inghiottire. **swallow up** vt divorare; ⟨earth, crowd:⟩ inghiottire
swallow[2] n (bird) rondine f
swam /swæm/ see **swim**
swamp /swɒmp/ n palude f ● vt fig sommergere. **~y** a paludoso
swan /swɒn/ n cigno m
swap /swɒp/ n fam scambio m ● vt (pt/pp **swapped**) fam scambiare (**for** con) ● vi fare cambio
swarm /swɔːm/ n sciame m ● vi sciamare; **be ~ing with** brulicare di
swarthy /ˈswɔːðɪ/ a (-ier, -iest) di carnagione scura
swastika /ˈswɒstɪkə/ n svastica f
swat /swɒt/ vt (pt/pp **swatted**) schiacciare
sway /sweɪ/ n fig influenza f ● vi oscillare; ⟨person:⟩ ondeggiare ● vt (influence) influenzare
swear /sweə(r)/ v (pt **swore**, pp **sworn**) ● vt giurare ● vi giurare; ⟨curse⟩ dire parolacce; **~ at sb** imprecare contro qcno; **~ by** fam credere ciecamente in. **~-word** n parolaccia f
sweat /swet/ n sudore m ● vi sudare
sweater /ˈswetə(r)/ n golf m inv
sweaty /ˈswetɪ/ a sudato
swede /swiːd/ n rapa f svedese
Swed|e n svedese mf. **~en** n Svezia f. **~ish** a svedese ● n (language) svedese m
sweep /swiːp/ n scopata f, spazzata f; (curve) curva f; (movement) movimento m ampio; **make a clean ~** fig fare piazza pulita ● v (pt/pp **swept**) ● vt scopare, spazzare ● vi (go swiftly) andare rapidamente; ⟨wind:⟩ soffiare. **sweep away** vt fig spazzare via. **sweep up** vt spazzare
sweeping /ˈswiːpɪŋ/ a (gesture) ampio; ⟨statement⟩ generico; ⟨changes⟩ radicale
sweet /swiːt/ a dolce; **have a ~ tooth** essere goloso ● n caramella f; (dessert) dolce m. **~ corn** n mais m
sweet-: ~heart n innamorato, -a mf; **hi, ~heart** ciao, tesoro. **~ness** n dolcezza f. **~ pea** n pisello m odoroso. **~-shop** n negozio m di dolciumi
swell /swel/ ● v (pt **swelled**, pp **swollen** or **swelled**) ● vi gonfiarsi; (increase) aumentare ● vt gonfiare; (increase) far salire. **~ing** n gonfiore m
swelter /ˈsweltə(r)/ vi soffocare [dal caldo]
swept /swept/ see **sweep**

swerve /swɜːv/ vi deviare bruscamente

swift /swɪft/ a rapido. **~ly** adv rapidamente

swig /swɪg/ n fam sorso m ● vt (pt/pp **swigged**) fam scolarsi

swill /swɪl/ n (for pigs) brodaglia f ● vt **~ [out]** risciacquare

swim /swɪm/ n **have a ~** fare una nuotata ● v (pt **swam**, pp **swum**) ● vi nuotare; ⟨room:⟩ girare; **my head is ~ming** mi gira la testa ● vt percorrere a nuoto. **~mer** n nuotatore, -trice mf

swimming /ˈswɪmɪŋ/ n nuoto m. **~-baths** npl piscina fsg. **~ costume** n costume m da bagno. **~-pool** n piscina f. **~ trunks** npl calzoncini mpl da bagno

'swim-suit n costume m da bagno

swindle /ˈswɪndl/ n truffa f ● vt truffare. **~r** n truffatore, -trice mf

swine /swaɪn/ n fam porco m

swing /swɪŋ/ n oscillazione f; ⟨shift⟩ cambiamento m; ⟨seat⟩ altalena f; Mus swing m; **in full ~** in piena attività ● v (pt/pp **swung**) ● vi oscillare; ⟨on swing, sway⟩ dondolare; ⟨dangle⟩ penzolare; ⟨turn⟩ girare ● vt oscillare; far deviare ⟨vote⟩. **~-'door** n porta f a vento

swingeing /ˈswɪndʒɪŋ/ a ⟨increase⟩ drastico

swipe /swaɪp/ n fam botta f ● vt fam colpire; ⟨steal⟩ rubare; far passare nella macchinetta ⟨credit card⟩

swirl /swɜːl/ n (of smoke, dust) turbine m ● vi ⟨water:⟩ fare mulinello

swish /swɪʃ/ a fam chic ● vi schioccare

Swiss /swɪs/ a & n svizzero, -a mf; **the ~** pl gli svizzeri. **~ 'roll** n rotolo m di pan di Spagna ripieno di marmellata

switch /swɪtʃ/ n interruttore m; ⟨change⟩ mutamento m ● vt cambiare; ⟨exchange⟩ scambiare ● vi cambiare; **~ to** passare a. **switch off** vt spegnere. **switch on** vt accendere

switch~: ~back n montagne fpl russe. **~board** n centralino m

Switzerland /ˈswɪtsələnd/ n Svizzera f

swivel /ˈswɪvl/ v (pt/pp **swivelled**) ● vt girare ● vi girarsi

swollen /ˈswəʊlən/ see swell ● a gonfio. **~-'headed** a presuntuoso

swoop /swuːp/ n (by police) incursione f ● vi **~ [down]** ⟨bird:⟩ piombare; fig fare un'incursione

sword /sɔːd/ n spada f

swore /swɔː(r)/ see swear

sworn /swɔːn/ see swear

swot /swɒt/ n fam sgobbone, -a mf ● vt (pt/pp **swotted**) fam sgobbare

swum /swʌm/ see swim

swung /swʌŋ/ see swing

syllable /ˈsɪləbl/ n sillaba f

syllabus /ˈsɪləbəs/ n programma m [dei corsi]

symbol /ˈsɪmbl/ n simbolo m (of di). **~ic** /-ˈbɒlɪk/ a simbolico. **~ism** /-ɪzm/ n simbolismo m. **~ize** vt simboleggiare

symmetr|ical /sɪˈmetrɪkl/ a simmetrico. **~y** /ˈsɪmɪtrɪ/ n simmetria f

sympathetic /sɪmpəˈθetɪk/ a ⟨understanding⟩ comprensivo; ⟨showing pity⟩ compassionevole. **~ally** adv con comprensione/compassione

sympathize /ˈsɪmpəθaɪz/ vi capire; ⟨in grief⟩ solidarizzare; **~ with sb** capire qcno/solidarizzare con qcno. **~r** n Pol simpatizzante mf

sympathy /ˈsɪmpəθɪ/ n comprensione f; ⟨pity⟩ compassione f; ⟨condolences⟩ condoglianze fpl; **in ~ with** ⟨strike⟩ per solidarietà con

symphony /ˈsɪmfənɪ/ n sinfonia f

symptom /ˈsɪmptəm/ n sintomo m. **~atic** /-ˈmætɪk/ a sintomatico (of di)

synagogue /ˈsɪnəgɒg/ n sinagoga f

synchronize /ˈsɪŋkrənaɪz/ vt sincronizzare

syndicate /ˈsɪndɪkət/ n gruppo m

syndrome /ˈsɪndrəʊm/ n sindrome f

synonym /ˈsɪnənɪm/ n sinonimo m. **~ous** /-ˈnɒnɪməs/ a sinonimo

synopsis /sɪˈnɒpsɪs/ n (pl **-opses** /-siːz/) (of opera, ballet) trama f; (of book) riassunto m

syntax /ˈsɪntæks/ n sintassi f inv

synthesize /ˈsɪnθəsaɪz/ vt sintetizzare. **~r** n Mus sintetizzatore m

synthetic /sɪnˈθetɪk/ a sintetico ● n fibra f sintetica

Syria /ˈsɪrɪə/ n Siria f. **~n** a & n siriano, -a mf

syringe /sɪˈrɪndʒ/ n siringa f

syrup /ˈsɪrəp/ n sciroppo m; Br tipo m di melassa

system /ˈsɪstəm/ n sistema m. **~atic** /-ˈmætɪk/ a sistematico

Tt

tab /tæb/ n linguetta f; (with name) etichetta f; **keep ~s on** fam sorvegliare; **pick up the ~** fam pagare il conto

tabby /'tæbɪ/ n gatto m tigrato

table /'teɪbl/ n tavolo m; (list) tavola f; **at [the] ~** a tavola; **~ of contents** tavola delle materie ● vt proporre. **~-cloth** n tovaglia f. **~spoon** n cucchiaio m da tavola. **~spoon[ful]** n cucchiaiata f

tablet /'tæblɪt/ n pastiglia f; (slab) lastra f; **~ of soap** saponetta f

'table tennis n tennis m da tavolo; (everyday level) ping pong m

tabloid /'tæblɔɪd/ n [giornale m formato] tabloid m inv; pej giornale m scandalistico

taboo /tə'buː/ a tabù inv ● n tabù m inv

tacit /'tæsɪt/ a tacito

taciturn /'tæsɪtɜːn/ a taciturno

tack /tæk/ n (nail) chiodino m; (stitch) imbastitura f; Naut virata f; fig linea f di condotta ● vt inchiodare; (sew) imbastire ● vi Naut virare

tackle /'tækl/ n (equipment) attrezzatura f; (football etc) contrasto m, tackle m inv ● vt affrontare

tacky /'tækɪ/ a (paint) non ancora asciutto; (glue) appiccicoso; fig pacchiano

tact /tækt/ n tatto m. **~ful** a pieno di tatto; (remark) delicato. **~fully** adv con tatto

tactic|al /'tæktɪkl/ a tattico. **~s** npl tattica fsg

tactless /'tæktlɪs/ a privo di tatto. **~ly** adv senza tatto. **~ness** n mancanza f di tatto; (of remark) indelicatezza f

tadpole /'tædpəʊl/ n girino m

tag[1] /tæg/ n (label) etichetta f ● vt (pt/pp tagged) attaccare l'etichetta a. **tag along** vi seguire passo passo

tag[2] n (game) acchiapparello m

tail /teɪl/ n coda f; **~s** pl (tailcoat) frac m inv ● vt (fam: follow) pedinare. **tail off** vi diminuire

tail: **~back** n coda f. **~-end** n parte f finale; (of train) coda f. **~ light** n fanalino m di coda

tailor /'teɪlə(r)/ n sarto m. **~-made** a fatto su misura

'tail wind n vento m di coda

taint /teɪnt/ vt contaminare

take /teɪk/ n Cinema ripresa f ● v (pt took, pp taken) ● vt prendere; (to a place) portare (person, object); (contain) contenere (passengers etc); (endure) sopportare; (require) occorrere; (teach) insegnare; (study) studiare (subject); fare (exam, holiday, photograph, walk, bath); sentire (pulse); misurare (sb's temperature); **take sb prisoner** fare prigioniero qcno; **be ~n ill** ammalarsi; **~ sth calmly** prendere con calma qcsa ● vi (plant:) attecchire. **take after** vt assomigliare a. **take away** vt (with one) portare via; (remove) togliere; (subtract) sottrarre; **'to ~ away'** 'da asporto'. **take back** vt riprendere; ritirare (statement); (return) riportare [indietro]. **take down** vt portare giù; (remove) tirare giù; (write down) prendere nota di. **take in** vt (bring indoors) portare dentro; (to one's home) ospitare; (understand) capire; (deceive) ingannare; riprendere (garment); (include) includere. **take off** vt togliersi (clothes); (deduct) togliere; (mimic) imitare; **~ time off** prendere delle vacanze; **~ oneself off** vi Aeron decollare. **take on** vt farsi carico di; assumere (employee); (as opponent) prendersela con. **take out** vt portare fuori; togliere (word, stain); (withdraw) ritirare (money, books); **~ out a subscription to sth** abbonarsi a qcsa; **~ it out on sb** fam prendersela con qcno. **take over** vt assumere il controllo di (firm) ● vi **~ over from sb** sostituire qcno; (permanently) succedere a qcno. **take to** vt (as a habit) darsi a; **I took to her** (liked) mi è piaciuta. **take up** vt portare su; accettare (offer); intraprendere (profession); dedicarsi a (hobby); prendere (time); occupare (space); tirare su (floor-boards); accorciare (dress); **~ sth up with sb** discutere qcsa con qcno ● vi **~ up with sb** legarsi a qcno

take: **~-away** n (meal) piatto m da asporto; (restaurant) ristorante m che prepara piatti da asporto. **~-off** n

Aeron decollo *m*. **~-over** *n* rilevamento *m*. **~-over bid** *n* offerta *f* di assorbimento

takings /'teɪkɪŋz/ *npl* incassi *mpl*

talcum /'tælkəm/ *n* **~ |powder|** talco *m*

tale /teɪl/ *n* storia *f*; *pej* fandonia *f*

talent /'tælənt/ *n* talento *m*. **~ed** *a* [ricco] di talento

talk /tɔːk/ *n* conversazione *f*; *(lecture)* conferenza *f*; *(gossip)* chiacchiere *fpl*: **make small ~** parlare del più e del meno ● *vi* parlare ● *vt* parlare di *(politics etc)*; **~ sb into sth** convincere qcno di qcsa. **talk over** *vt* discutere

talkative /'tɔːkətɪv/ *a* loquace

'talking-to *n* sgridata *f*

talk show *n* talk show *m inv*

tall /tɔːl/ *a* alto. **~boy** *n* cassettone *m*. **~ order** *n* impresa *f* difficile. **~ 'story** *n* frottola *f*

tally /'tælɪ/ *n* conteggio *m*; **keep a ~ of** tenere il conto di ● *vi* coincidere

tambourine /tæmbə'riːn/ *n* tamburello *m*

tame /teɪm/ *a* *(animal)* domestico; *(dull)* insulso ● *vt* domare. **~ly** *adv* docilmente. **~r** *n* domatore, -trice *mf*

tamper /'tæmpə(r)/ *vi* **~ with** manomettere

tampon /'tæmpɒn/ *n* tampone *m*

tan /tæn/ *a* marrone rossiccio ● *n* marrone *m* rossiccio; *(from sun)* abbronzatura *f* ● *v* *(pt/pp* **tanned**) ● *vt* conciare *(hide)* ● *vi* abbronzarsi

tang /tæŋ/ *n* sapore *m* forte; *(smell)* odore *m* penetrante

tangent /'tændʒənt/ *n* tangente *f*

tangible /'tændʒɪbl/ *a* tangibile

tangle /'tæŋgl/ *n* groviglio *m*; *(in hair)* nodo *m* ● *vt* **~ |up|** aggrovigliare ● *vi* aggrovigliarsi

tango /'tæŋgəʊ/ *n* tango *m inv*

tank /tæŋk/ *n* contenitore *m*; *(for petrol)* serbatoio *m*; *(fish ~)* acquario *m*; *Mil* carro *m* armato

tankard /'tæŋkəd/ *n* boccale *m*

tanker /'tæŋkə(r)/ *n* nave *f* cisterna; *(lorry)* autobotte *f*

tanned /tænd/ *a* abbronzato

tantalize /'tæntəlaɪz/ *vt* tormentare. **~ing** *a* allettante; *(smell)* stuzzicante

tantamount /'tæntəmaʊnt/ *a* **~ to** equivalente a

tantrum /'tæntrəm/ *n* scoppio *m* d'ira

tap /tæp/ *n* rubinetto *m*; *(knock)* colpo *m*; **on ~** *fig* a disposizione ● *v* *(pt/pp* **tapped**) ● *vt* dare un colpetto a; sfruttare *(resources)*; mettere sotto controllo

(telephone) ● *vi* picchiettare. **~-dance** *n* tip tap *m* ● *vi* ballare il tip tap

tape /teɪp/ *n* nastro *m*; *(recording)* cassetta *f* ● *vt* legare con nastro; *(record)* registrare

'tape: ~ backup drive *n* *Comput* unità *f* di backup a nastro. **~-deck** *n* piastra *f*. **~-measure** *n* metro *m* [a nastro]

taper /'teɪpə(r)/ *n* candela *f* sottile ● **taper off** *vi* assottigliarsi

'tape: ~ recorder *n* registratore *m*. **~ recording** *n* registrazione *f*

tapestry /'tæpɪstrɪ/ *n* arazzo *m*

'tap water *n* acqua *f* del rubinetto

tar /tɑː(r)/ *n* catrame *m* ● *vt* *(pt/pp* **tarred**) incatramare

tardy /'tɑːdɪ/ *a* (**-ier, -iest**) tardivo

target /'tɑːgɪt/ *n* bersaglio *m*; *fig* obiettivo *m*

tariff /'tærɪf/ *n* *(price)* tariffa *f*; *(duty)* dazio *m*

Tarmac® /'tɑːmæk/ *n* macadam *m* al catrame. **tarmac** *n* *Aeron* pista *f* di decollo

tarnish /'tɑːnɪʃ/ *vi* ossidarsi ● *vt* ossidare; *fig* macchiare

tarpaulin /tɑː'pɔːlɪn/ *n* telone *m* impermeabile

tart¹ /tɑːt/ *a* aspro; *fig* acido

tart² *n* crostata *f*; *(individual)* crostatina *f*; *(sl: prostitute)* donnaccia *f* ● **tart up** *vt fam* **~ oneself up** agghindarsi

tartan /'tɑːtn/ *n* tessuto *m* scozzese, tartan *m inv* ● *attrib* di tessuto scozzese

tartar /'tɑːtə(r)/ *n* *(on teeth)* tartaro *m*

tartar 'sauce /tɑːtə-/ *n* salsa *f* tartara

task /tɑːsk/ *n* compito *m*; **take sb to ~** riprendere qcno. **~ force** *n Pol* commissione *f*; *Mil* task-force *f inv*

tassel /'tæsl/ *n* nappa *f*

taste /teɪst/ *n* gusto *m*; *(sample)* assaggio *m*; **get a ~ of sth** *fig* assaporare il gusto di qcsa ● *vt* sentire il sapore di; *(sample)* assaggiare ● *vi* sapere **(of** di); **it ~s lovely** è ottimo. **~ful** *a* di [buon] gusto. **~fully** *adv* con gusto. **~less** *a* senza gusto. **~lessly** *adv* con cattivo gusto

tasty /'teɪstɪ/ *a* (**-ier, -iest**) saporito

tat /tæt/ *see* **tit²**

tatter|ed /'tætəd/ *a* cencioso; *(pages)* stracciato. **~s** *npl* **in ~s** a brandelli

tattoo¹ /tæ'tuː/ *n* tatuaggio *m* ● *vt* tatuare

tattoo² *n Mil* parata *f* militare

tatty /'tætɪ/ *a* (**-ier, -iest**) *(clothes, person)* trasandato; *(book)* malandato

taught /tɔːt/ *see* **teach**

taunt /tɔːnt/ *n* scherno *m* ● *vt* schernire

Taurus /'tɔːrəs/ n Astr Toro m

taut /tɔːt/ a teso

tawdry /'tɔːdrɪ/ a (**-ier, -iest**) pacchiano

tax /tæks/ n tassa f: (on income) imposte fpl: **before ~** (price) tasse escluse; (salary) lordo ● vt tassare; fig mettere alla prova; **~ with** accusare di. **~able** /-əbl/ a tassabile. **~ation** /-'seɪʃn/ n tasse fpl. **~ evasion** n evasione f fiscale. **~-free** a esentasse. **~ haven** n paradiso m fiscale

taxi /'tæksɪ/ n taxi m inv ● vi (pt/pp **taxied,** pres p **taxiing**) (aircraft:) rullare. **~ driver** n tassista mf. **~ rank** n posteggio m per taxi

'**taxpayer** n contribuente mf

tea /tiː/ n tè m inv. **~-bag** n bustina f di tè. **~-break** n intervallo m per il tè

teach /tiːtʃ/ vt/i (pt/pp **taught**) insegnare; **~ sb sth** insegnare qcsa a qcno. **~er** n insegnante mf; (primary) maestro, -a mf. **~ing** n insegnamento m

tea: ~-cloth n (for drying) asciugapiatti m. **~-cup** n tazza f da tè

teak /tiːk/ n tek m

'**tea-leaves** npl tè m inv sfuso, (when infused) fondi mpl di tè

team /tiːm/ n squadra f; fig équipe f inv ● **team up** vi unirsi

'**team-work** n lavoro m di squadra; fig lavoro m d'équipe

'**teapot** n teiera f

tear¹ /teə(r)/ n strappo m ● v (pt **tore,** pp **torn**) ● vt strappare ● vi strapparsi; (material:) strapparsi; (run) precipitarsi. **tear apart** vt (fig: criticize) fare a pezzi; (separate) dividere. **tear away** vt **~ oneself away** andare via; **~ oneself away from** staccarsi da (television). **tear open** vt aprire strappando. **tear up** vt strappare; rompere (agreement)

tear² /tɪə(r)/ n lacrima f. **~ful** a (person) in lacrime; (farewell) lacrimevole. **~fully** adv in lacrime. **~ gas** n gas m lacrimogeno

tease /tiːz/ vt prendere in giro (person); tormentare (animal)

tea: ~-set n servizio m da tè. **~ shop** n sala f da tè. **~spoon** n cucchiaino m [da tè]. **~spoon|ful** n cucchiaino m

teat /tiːt/ n capezzolo m; (on bottle) tettarella f

'**tea-towel** n strofinaccio m [per i piatti]

technical /'teknɪkl/ a tecnico. **~ity** /-'kælətɪ/ n tecnicismo m; Jur cavillo m giuridico. **~ly** adv tecnicamente; (strictly) strettamente

technician /tek'nɪʃn/ n tecnico, -a mf

technique /tek'niːk/ n tecnica f

technological /teknə'lɒdʒɪkl/ a tecnologico

technology /tek'nɒlədʒɪ/ n tecnologia f

teddy /'tedɪ/ n **~ [bear]** orsacchiotto m

tedious /'tiːdɪəs/ a noioso

tedium /'tiːdɪəm/ n tedio m

tee /tiː/ n (in golf) tee m inv

teem /tiːm/ vi (rain) piovere a dirotto; **be ~ing with** (full of) pullulare di

teenage /'tiːneɪdʒ/ a per ragazzi; **~ boy/girl** adolescente mf. **~r** n adolescente mf

teens /tiːnz/ npl the **~** l'adolescenza fsg; **be in one's ~** essere adolescente

teeny /'tiːnɪ/ a (**-ier, -iest**) piccolissimo

teeter /'tiːtə(r)/ vi barcollare

teeth /tiːθ/ see **tooth**

teeth|e /tiːð/ vi mettere i [primi] denti. **~ing troubles** npl fig difficoltà fpl iniziali

teetotal /tiː'təʊtl/ a astemio. **~ler** n astemio, -a mf

telecommunications /telɪkəm-juːnɪ'keɪʃnz/ npl telecomunicazioni fpl

telegram /'telɪgræm/ n telegramma m

telegraph /'telɪgrɑːf/ n telegrafo m. **~ic** /-'græfɪk/ a telegrafico. **~ pole** n palo m del telegrafo

telepathy /tɪ'lepəθɪ/ n telepatia f

telephone /'telɪfəʊn/ n telefono m; **be on the ~** avere il telefono; (be telephoning) essere al telefono ● vt telefonare a ● vi telefonare

telephone: ~ book n elenco m telefonico. **~ booth** n. **~ box** n cabina f telefonica. **~ directory** n elenco m telefonico. **~ number** n numero m di telefono

telephonist /tɪ'lefənɪst/ n telefonista mf

'**telephoto** /telɪ-/ a **~ lens** tele-obiettivo m

telescop|e /'telɪskəʊp/ n telescopio m. **~ic** /-'skɒpɪk/ a telescopico

televise /'telɪvaɪz/ vt trasmettere per televisione

television /'telɪvɪʒn/ n televisione f; **watch ~** guardare la televisione. **~ set** n televisore m

telex /'teleks/ n telex m inv

tell /tel/ vt (pt/pp **told**) dire; raccontare (story); (distinguish) distinguere (**from** da); **~ sb sth** dire qcsa a qcno; **~ the time** dire l'ora; **I couldn't ~ why...** non sapevo perché... ● vi (produce an effect) avere effetto; **time will ~** il tempo ce lo dirà; **his age is beginning to**

~ l'età comincia a farsi sentire [per lui];
you mustn't ~ non devi dire niente.
tell off *vt* sgridare

teller/'telə(r)/ *n* (*in bank*) cassiere, -a *mf*

telling /'telɪŋ/ *a* significativo; ⟨*argument*⟩ efficace

telly /'telɪ/ *n fam* tv *f inv*

temerity /tɪ'merətɪ/ *n* audacia *f*

temp /temp/ *n fam* impiegato, -a *mf* temporaneo, -a

temper /'tempə(r)/ *n* (*disposition*) carattere *m*; (*mood*) umore *m*; (*anger*) collera *f*; **lose one's** ~ arrabbiarsi; **be in a** ~ essere arrabbiato; **keep one's** ~ mantenere la calma

temperament /'temprəmənt/ *n* temperamento *m*. ~**al** /-'mentl/ *a* (*moody*) capriccioso

temperate /'tempərət/ *a* ⟨*climate*⟩ temperato

temperature /'temprətʃə(r)/ *n* temperatura *f*; **have a** ~ avere la febbre

tempest /'tempɪst/ *n* tempesta *f*. ~**uous** /-'pestjʊəs/ *a* tempestoso

temple[1] /'templ/ *n* tempio *m*

temple[2] *n Anat* tempia *f*

tempo /'tempəʊ/ *n* ritmo *m*; *Mus* tempo *m*

temporar|y /'tempərərɪ/ *a* temporaneo; ⟨*measure, building*⟩ provvisorio. ~**ily** *adv* temporaneamente; ⟨*introduced, erected*⟩ provvisoriamente

tempt /tempt/ *vt* tentare; sfidare ⟨*fate*⟩; ~ **sb to** indurre qcno a; **be** ~**ed** essere tentato (**to** di); **I am** ~**ed by the offer** l'offerta mi tenta. ~**ation** /-'teɪʃn/ *n* tentazione *f*. ~**ing** *a* allettante; ⟨*food, drink*⟩ invitante

ten /ten/ *a* & *n* dieci *m*

tenable /'tenəbl/ *a fig* sostenibile

tenaci|ous /tɪ'neɪʃəs/ *a* tenace. ~**ty** /-'næsətɪ/ *n* tenacia *f*

tenant /'tenənt/ *n* inquilino, -a *mf*; *Comm* locatario, -a *mf*

tend[1] /tend/ *vt* (*look after*) prendersi cura di

tend[2] *vi* ~ **to do sth** tendere a far qcsa

tendency /'tendənsɪ/ *n* tendenza *f*

tender[1] /'tendə(r)/ *n Comm* offerta *f*; **be legal** ~ avere corso legale ●*vt* offrire; presentare ⟨*resignation*⟩

tender[2] *a* tenero; (*painful*) dolorante. ~**ly** *adv* teneramente. ~**ness** *n* tenerezza *f*; (*painfulness*) dolore *m*

tendon /'tendən/ *n* tendine *m*

tenement /'tenəmənt/ *n* casamento *m*

tenner /'tenə(r)/ *n fam* biglietto *m* da dieci sterline

tennis /'tenɪs/ *n* tennis *m*. ~**-court** *n* campo *m* da tennis. ~ **player** *n* tennista *mf*

tenor /'tenə(r)/ *n* tenore *m*

tense[1] /tens/ *n Gram* tempo *m*

tense[2] *a* teso ●*vt* tendere ⟨*muscle*⟩. **tense up** *vi* tendersi

tension /'tenʃn/ *n* tensione *f*

tent /tent/ *n* tenda *f*

tentacle /'tentəkl/ *n* tentacolo *m*

tentative /'tentətɪv/ *a* provvisorio; ⟨*smile, gesture*⟩ esitante. ~**ly** *adv* timidamente; ⟨*accept*⟩ provvisoriamente

tenterhooks /'tentəhʊks/ *npl* **be on** ~ essere sulle spine

tenth /tenθ/ *a* decimo ●*n* decimo, -a *mf*

tenuous /'tenjʊəs/ *a fig* debole

tepid /'tepɪd/ *a* tiepido

term /tɜːm/ *n* periodo *m*; *Sch Univ* trimestre *m*; (*expression*) termine *m*; ~**s** *pl* (*conditions*) condizioni *fpl*; ~ **of office** carica *f*; **in the short/long** ~ a breve/lungo termine; **be on good/bad** ~**s** essere in buoni/cattivi rapporti; **come to** ~**s with** accettare ⟨*past, fact*⟩; **easy** ~**s** facilità *f* di pagamento

terminal /'tɜːmɪn(ə)l/ *a* finale; *Med* terminale ●*n Aeron* terminal *m inv*; *Rail* stazione *f* di testa; (*of bus*) capolinea *m*; (*on battery*) morsetto *m*; *Comput* terminale *m*. ~**ly** *adv* **be** ~**ly ill** essere in fase terminale

terminat|e /'tɜːmɪneɪt/ *vt* terminare; rescindere ⟨*contract*⟩; interrompere ⟨*pregnancy*⟩ ●*vi* terminare; ~**e in** finire in. ~**ion** /-'neɪʃn/ *n* termine *m*; *Med* interruzione *f* di gravidanza

terminology /tɜːmɪ'nɒlədʒɪ/ *n* terminologia *f*

terminus /'tɜːmɪnəs/ *n* (*pl* -**ni** /-naɪ/) (*for bus*) capolinea *m*; (*for train*) stazione *f* di testa

terrace /'terəs/ *n* terrazza *f*; (*houses*) fila *f* di case a schiera; **the** ~**s** *pl Sport* le gradinate. ~**d house** *n* casa *f* a schiera

terrain /te'reɪn/ *n* terreno *m*

terrib|le /'terəbl/ *a* terribile. ~**y** *adv* terribilmente

terrier /'terɪə(r)/ *n* terrier *m inv*

terrific /tə'rɪfɪk/ *a fam* (*excellent*) fantastico; (*huge*) enorme. ~**ally** *adv fam* terribilmente

terri|fy /'terɪfaɪ/ *vt* (*pt/pp* -**ied**) atterrire; **be** ~**fied** essere terrorizzato. ~**fying** *a* terrificante

territorial /terɪ'tɔːrɪəl/ *a* territoriale

territory /'terɪtərɪ/ *n* territorio *m*

terror /'terə(r)/ *n* terrore *m*. ~**ism**

/-ɪzm/ *n* terrorismo *m*. **~ist** /-ɪst/ *n* terrorista *mf*. **~ize** *vt* terrorizzare

terse /tɜːs/ *a* conciso

test /test/ *n* esame *m*; (*in laboratory*) esperimento *m*; (*of friendship, machine*) prova *f*; (*of intelligence, aptitude*) test *m inv*; **put to the ~** mettere alla prova ● *vt* esaminare; provare (*machine*)

testament /ˈtestəmənt/ *n* testamento *m*; **Old/New T~** Antico/Nuovo Testamento *m*

testicle /ˈtestɪkl/ *n* testicolo *m*

testify /ˈtestɪfaɪ/ *vt/i* (*pt/pp* **-ied**) testimoniare

testimonial /testɪˈməʊnɪəl/ *n* lettera *f* di referenze

testimony /ˈtestɪmənɪ/ *n* testimonianza *f*

'test: **~ match** *n* partita *f* internazionale. **~-tube** *n* provetta *f*. **~-tube baby** *n fam* bambino, -a *mf* in provetta

tetanus /ˈtetənəs/ *n* tetano *m*

tether /ˈteðə(r)/ *n* **be at the end of one's ~** non poterne più

text /tekst/ *n* testo *m*. **~book** *n* manuale *m*

textile /ˈtekstaɪl/ *a* tessile ● *n* stoffa *f*

texture /ˈtekstʃə(r)/ *n* (*of skin*) grana *f*; (*of food*) consistenza *f*; **of a smooth ~** (*to the touch*) soffice al tatto

Thai /taɪ/ *a & n* tailandese *mf*. **~land** *n* Tailandia *f*

Thames /temz/ *n* Tamigi *m*

than /ðən/, *accentato* /ðæn/ *conj* che; (*with numbers, names*) di; **older ~ me** più vecchio di me

thank /θæŋk/ *vt* ringraziare; **~ you [very much]** grazie [mille]. **~ful** *a* grato. **~fully** *adv* con gratitudine; (*happily*) fortunatamente. **~less** *a* ingrato

thanks /θæŋks/ *npl* ringraziamenti *mpl*; **~!** *fam* grazie!; **~ to** grazie a

that /ðæt/ *a & pron* (*pl* **those**) quel, quei *pl*; (*before s + consonant, gn, ps and z*) quello, quegli *pl*; (*before vowel*) quell' *mf*, quegli *mpl*, quelle *fpl*; **~ one** quello; **I don't like those** quelli non mi piacciono; **~ is** cioè; **is ~ you?** sei tu?; **who is ~?** chi è?; **what did you do after ~?** cosa hai fatto dopo?; **like ~** in questo modo, così; **a man like ~** un uomo così; **~ is why** ecco perché; **~'s it!** (*you've understood*) ecco!; (*I've finished*) ecco fatto!; (*I've had enough*) basta così!; (*there's nothing more*) tutto qui!; **~'s ~!** (*with job*) ecco fatto!; (*with relationship*) è tutto finito!; **and ~'s ~!** punto e basta! **all I know** tutto quello che so ● *adv* così; **it wasn't ~ good** non era poi così buono ● *rel pron* che; **the man ~ I spoke to**

l'uomo con cui ho parlato; **the day ~ I saw him** il giorno in cui l'ho visto; **all ~ I know** tutto quello che so ● *conj* che; **I think ~…** penso che…

thatch /θætʃ/ *n* tetto *m* di paglia. **~ed** *a* coperto di paglia

thaw /θɔː/ *n* disgelo *m* ● *vt* fare scongelare (*food*) ● *vi* (*food:*) scongelarsi; **it's ~ing** sta sgelando

the /ðə/, *di fronte a una vocale* /ðiː/ *def art* il, la *f*; i *mpl*, le *fpl*; (*before s + consonant, gn, ps and z*) lo, gli *mpl*; (*before vowel*) l' *mf*, gli *mpl*, le *fpl*; **at ~ cinema/station** al cinema/alla stazione; **from ~ cinema/station** dal cinema/dalla stazione ● *adv* **~ more ~ better** più ce n'è meglio è; (*with reference to pl*) più ce ne sono, meglio è; **all ~ better** tanto meglio

theatre /ˈθɪətə(r)/ *n* teatro *m*; *Med* sala *f* operatoria

theatrical /θɪˈætrɪkl/ *a* teatrale; (*showy*) melodrammatico

theft /θeft/ *n* furto *m*

their /ðeə(r)/ *poss a* il loro *m*, la loro *f*, i loro *mpl*, le loro *fpl*; **~ mother/father** la loro madre/il loro padre

theirs /ðeəz/ *poss pron* il loro *m*, la loro *f*, i loro *mpl*, le loro *fpl*; **a friend of ~** un loro amico; **friends of ~** dei loro amici; **those are ~** quelli sono loro; (*as opposed to ours*) sono loro

them /ðem/ *pron* (*direct object*) li *m*, le *f*; (*indirect object*) gli, loro *fml*; (*after prep: with people*) loro; (*after preposition: with things*) essi; **we haven't seen ~** non li/le abbiamo mai visti/viste; **give ~ the money** dai loro *or* dagli i soldi; **give it to ~** daglielo; **I've spoken to ~** ho parlato con loro; **it's ~** sono loro

theme /θiːm/ *n* tema *m*. **~ song** *n* motivo *m* conduttore

them'selves *pers pron* (*reflexive*) si; (*emphatic*) se stessi; **they poured ~ a drink** si sono versati da bere; **they said so ~** lo hanno detto loro stessi; **they kept it to ~** se lo sono tenuti per sé; **by ~** da soli

then /ðen/ *adv* allora; (*next*) poi; **by ~** (*in the past*) ormai; (*in the future*) per allora; **since ~** sin da allora; **before ~** prima di allora; **from ~ on** da allora in poi; **now and ~** ogni tanto; **there and ~** all'istante ● *a* di allora

theologian /θɪəˈləʊdʒɪən/ *n* teologo, -a *mf*. **~y** /-ˈɒlədʒɪ/ *n* teologia *f*

theorem /ˈθɪərəm/ *n* teorema *m*

theoretical /θɪəˈretɪkl/ *a* teorico

theory /'θɪərɪ/ n teoria f; **in ~** in teoria

therapeutic /θerə'pju:tɪk/ a terapeutico

therap|ist /'θerəpɪst/ n terapista mf. **~y** n terapia f

there /ðeə(r)/ adv là, lì; **down/up ~** laggiù/lassù; **~ is/are** c'è/ci sono; **~ he/she is** eccolo/eccola ● int **~, ~!** dai, su!

there: ~abouts adv [or] **~abouts** (roughly) all'incirca. **~'after** adv dopo di che. **~by** adv in tal modo. **~fore** /-fɔ:(r)/ adv perciò

thermal /'θɜ:m(ə)l/ a termale; **~ 'underwear** n biancheria f che mantiene la temperatura corporea

thermometer /θə'mɒmɪtə(r)/ n termometro m

Thermos® /'θɜ:məs/ n [flask] termos m inv

thermostat /'θɜ:məstæt/ n termostato m

thesaurus /θɪ'sɔ:rəs/ n dizionario m dei sinonimi

these /ði:z/ see **this**

thesis /'θi:sɪs/ n (pl **-ses** /-si:z/) tesi f inv

they /ðeɪ/ pron loro; **~ are tired** sono stanchi; **we're going, but ~ are not** noi andiamo, ma loro no; **~ say** (generalizing) si dice; **~ are building a new road** stanno costruendo una nuova strada

thick /θɪk/ a spesso; (forest) fitto; (liquid) denso; (hair) folto; (fam: stupid) ottuso; (fam: close) molto unito; **be 5 mm ~** essere 5 mm di spessore ● adv densamente ● n **in the ~** nel mezzo di. **~en** vt ispessire (sauce) ● vi ispessirsi; (fog:) infittirsi. **~ly** adv densamente; (cut) a fette spesse. **~ness** n spessore m

thick: ~set a tozzo. **~-'skinned** a fam insensibile

thief /θi:f/ n (pl **thieves**) ladro, -a mf

thieving /'θi:vɪŋ/ a ladro ● n furti mpl

thigh /θaɪ/ n coscia f

thimble /'θɪmbl/ n ditale m

thin /θɪn/ a (**thinner, thinnest**) sottile; (shoes, sweater) leggero; (liquid) liquido; (person) magro; (fig: excuse, plot) inconsistente ● adv = **thinly** ● v (pt/pp **thinned**) ● vt diluire (liquid) ● vi diradarsi. **thin out** vi diradarsi. **~ly** adv (populated) scarsamente; (disguised) leggermente; (cut) a fette sottili

thing /θɪŋ/ n cosa f; **~s** pl (belongings) roba fsg; **for one ~** in primo luogo; **the right ~** la cosa giusta; **just the ~!** pro-

prio quel che ci vuole!; **how are ~s?** come vanno le cose?; **the latest ~** fam l'ultima cosa; **the best ~ would be la** cosa migliore sarebbe; **poor ~!** poveretto!

think /θɪŋk/ vt/i (pt/pp **thought**) pensare; (believe) credere; **I ~ so** credo di sì; **what do you ~?** (what is your opinion?) cosa ne pensi?; **~ of/about** pensare a; **what do you ~ of it?** cosa ne pensi di questo?. **think over** vt riflettere su. **think up** vt escogitare

third /θɜ:d/ a e n terzo, -a mf. **~ly** adv terzo. **~-rate** a scadente

thirst /θɜ:st/ n sete f. **~ily** adv con sete. **~y** a assetato; **be ~y** aver sete

thirteen /θɜ:'ti:n/ a e n tredici m. **~th** a e n tredicesimo, -a mf

thirtieth /'θɜ:tɪɪθ/ a e n trentesimo, -a mf

thirty /'θɜ:tɪ/ a e n trenta m

this /ðɪs/ a (pl **these**) questo; **~ man/woman** quest'uomo/questa donna; **these men/women** questi uomini/queste donne; **~ one** questo; **~ morning/evening** stamattina/stasera ● pron (pl **these**) questo; **we talked about ~ and that** abbiamo parlato del più e del meno; **like ~** così; **~ is Peter** questo è Peter; Teleph sono Peter; **who is ~?** chi è?; Teleph chi parla? ● adv così; **~ big** così grande

thistle /'θɪsl/ n cardo m

thorn /θɔ:n/ n spina f. **~y** a spinoso

thorough /'θʌrə/ a completo; (knowledge) profondo; (clean, search, training) a fondo; (person) scrupoloso

thorough: ~bred n purosangue m inv. **~fare** n via f principale; **'no ~fare'** 'strada non transitabile'

thorough|ly /'θʌrəlɪ/ adv (clean, search, know sth) a fondo; (extremely) estremamente. **~ness** n completezza f

those /ðəʊz/ see **that**

though /ðəʊ/ conj sebbene; **as ~** come se ● adv fam tuttavia

thought /θɔ:t/ see **think** ● n pensiero m; (idea) idea f. **~ful** a pensieroso; (considerate) premuroso. **~fully** adv pensierosamente; (considerately) premurosamente. **~less** a (inconsiderate) sconsiderato. **~lessly** adv con noncuranza

thousand /'θaʊznd/ a **one/a ~** mille m inv ● n mille m inv; **~s of** migliaia fpl di. **~th** a millesimo ● n millesimo, -a mf

thrash /θræʃ/ vt picchiare; (defeat) sconfiggere. **thrash out** vt mettere a punto

thread /θred/ n filo m; (of screw) filetto

m ● *vt* infilare ⟨*beads*⟩; ~ **one's way through** farsi strada fra. ~**bare** *a* logoro

threat /θret/ *n* minaccia *f*

threaten /'θretn/ *vt* minacciare (**to do** di fare) ● *vi fig* incalzare. ~**ing** *a* minaccioso; ⟨*sky, atmosphere*⟩ sinistro

three /θri:/ *a & n* tre *m*. ~**fold** *a & adv* triplo. ~**some** -səm/ *n* trio *m*

thresh /θreʃ/ *vt* trebbiare

threshold /'θreʃəʊld/ *n* soglia *f*

threw /θru:/ *see* **throw**

thrift /θrɪft/ *n* economia *f*. ~**y** *a* parsimonioso

thrill /θrɪl/ *n* emozione *f*; ⟨*of fear*⟩ brivido *m* ● *vt* entusiasmare; **be ~ed with** essere entusiasta di. ~**er** *n* ⟨*book*⟩ [romanzo *m*] giallo *m*; ⟨*film*⟩ [film *m*] giallo *m*. ~**ing** *a* eccitante

thrive /θraɪv/ *vi* (*pt* **thrived** *or* **throve**, *pp* **thrived** *or* **thriven** /'θrɪvn/) ⟨*business:*⟩ prosperare; ⟨*child, plant:*⟩ crescere bene; **I ~ on pressure** mi piace essere sotto tensione

throat /θrəʊt/ *n* gola *f*. **sore ~** mal di gola

throb /θrɒb/ *n* pulsazione *f*; ⟨*of heart*⟩ battito *m* ● *vi* (*pt/pp* **throbbed**) ⟨*vibrate*⟩ pulsare; ⟨*heart:*⟩ battere

throes /θrəʊz/ *npl* **in the ~ of** *fig* alle prese con

thrombosis /θrɒm'bəʊsɪs/ *n* trombosi *f*

throne /θrəʊn/ *n* trono *m*

throng /θrɒŋ/ *n* calca *f*

throttle /'θrɒtl/ *n* ⟨*on motorbike*⟩ manopola *f* di accelerazione ● *vt* strozzare

through /θru:/ *prep* attraverso; ⟨*during*⟩ durante; ⟨*by means of*⟩ tramite; ⟨*thanks to*⟩ grazie a; **Saturday ~ Tuesday** *Am* da sabato a martedì incluso ● *adv* attraverso; **~ and ~** fino in fondo; **wet ~** completamente bagnato; **read sth ~** dare una lettura a qcsa; **let ~** lasciar passare ⟨*sb*⟩ ● *a* ⟨*train*⟩ diretto; **be ~** ⟨*finished*⟩ aver finito; *Teleph* avere la comunicazione

throughout /θru:'aʊt/ *prep* per tutto ● *adv* completamente; ⟨*time*⟩ per tutto il tempo

throw /θrəʊ/ *n* tiro *m* ● *vt* (*pt* **threw**, *pp* **thrown**) lanciare; ⟨*throw away*⟩ gettare; azionare ⟨*switch*⟩; disarcionare ⟨*rider*⟩; ⟨*fam: disconcert*⟩ disorientare; *fam* dare ⟨*party*⟩. **throw away** *vt* gettare via. **throw out** *vt* gettare via; rigettare ⟨*plan*⟩; buttare fuori ⟨*person*⟩. **throw up** *vt* alzare ● *vi* ⟨*vomit*⟩ vomitare.

throw-away *a* ⟨*remark*⟩ buttato lì; ⟨*paper cup*⟩ usa e getta *inv*

thrush /θrʌʃ/ *n* tordo *m*

thrust /θrʌst/ *n* spinta *f* ● *vt* (*pt/pp* **thrust**) ⟨*push*⟩ spingere; ⟨*insert*⟩ conficcare; **~ [up]on** imporre a

thud /θʌd/ *n* tonfo *m*

thug /θʌg/ *n* delinquente *m*

thumb /θʌm/ *n* pollice *m*; **as a rule of ~** come regola generale; **under sb's ~** succube di qcno ● *vt* **~ a lift** fare l'autostop. ~**index** *n* indice *m* a rubrica. ~**tack** *n Am* puntina *f* da disegno

thump /θʌmp/ *n* colpo *m*; ⟨*noise*⟩ tonfo *m* ● *vt* battere su ⟨*table, door*⟩; battere ⟨*fist*⟩; colpire ⟨*person*⟩ ● *vi* battere (**on** su); ⟨*heart:*⟩ battere forte. **thump about** *vi* camminare pesantemente

thunder /'θʌndə(r)/ *n* tuono *m*; ⟨*loud noise*⟩ rimbombo *m* ● *vi* tuonare; ⟨*make loud noise*⟩ rimbombare. ~**clap** *n* rombo *m* di tuono. ~**storm** *n* temporale *m*. ~**y** *a* temporalesco

Thursday /'θɜːzdeɪ/ *n* giovedì *m inv*

thus /ðʌs/ *adv* così

thwart /θwɔːt/ *vt* ostacolare

thyme /taɪm/ *n* timo *m*

Tiber /'taɪbə(r)/ *n* Tevere *m*

tick /tɪk/ *n* ⟨*sound*⟩ ticchettìo *m*; ⟨*mark*⟩ segno *m*; ⟨*fam: instant*⟩ attimo *m* ● *vi* ticchettare. **tick off** *vt* spuntare; *fam* sgridare. **tick over** *vi* ⟨*engine:*⟩ andare al minimo

ticket /'tɪkɪt/ *n* biglietto *m*; ⟨*for item deposited, library*⟩ tagliando *m*; ⟨*label*⟩ cartellino *m*; ⟨*fine*⟩ multa *f*. ~**-collector** *n* controllore *m*. ~**-office** *n* biglietteria *f*

tickle /'tɪkl/ *n* solletico *m* ● *vt* fare il solletico a; ⟨*amuse*⟩ divertire ● *vi* fare prurito. ~**lish** /'tɪklɪʃ/ *a* che soffre il solletico

tidal /'taɪdl/ *a* ⟨*river, harbour*⟩ di marea. ~ **wave** *n* onda *f* di marea

tiddly-winks /'tɪdlɪwɪŋks/ *n* gioco *m* delle pulci

tide /taɪd/ *n* marea *f*; ⟨*of events*⟩ corso *m*; **the ~ is in/out** c'è alta/bassa marea ● **tide over** *vt* **~ sb over** aiutare qcno a andare avanti

tidily /'taɪdɪlɪ/ *adv* in modo ordinato

tidiness /'taɪdɪnɪs/ *n* ordine *m*

tidy /'taɪdɪ/ *a* (**-ier, -iest**) ordinato; ⟨*fam: amount*⟩ bello ● *vt* (*pt/pp* **-ied**) ~ **[up]** ordinare; ~ **oneself up** mettersi in ordine

tie /taɪ/ *n* cravatta *f*; ⟨*cord*⟩ legaccio *m*; ⟨*fig: bond*⟩ legame *m*; ⟨*restriction*⟩ impedimento *m*; *Sport* pareggio *m* ● *v* (*pres p* **tying**) ● *vt* legare; fare ⟨*knot*⟩; **be ~d**

(in competition) essere in parità ● *vi* pareggiare. **tie in with** *vi* corrispondere a. **tie up** *vt* legare; vincolare ‹*capital*›; **be ~d up** *(busy)* essere occupato

tier /tɪə(r)/ *n* fila *f*; *(of cake)* piano *m*; *(in stadium)* gradinata *f*

tiff /tɪf/ *n* battibecco *m*

tiger /ˈtaɪgə(r)/ *n* tigre *f*

tight /taɪt/ *a* stretto; *(taut)* teso; *(fam: drunk)* sbronzo; *(fam: mean)* spilorcio; **~ corner** *fam* brutta situazione *f* ● *adv* strettamente; ‹*hold*› forte; ‹*closed*› bene

tighten /ˈtaɪtn/ *vt* stringere; avvitare ‹*screw*›; intensificare ‹*control*› ● *vi* stringersi

tight: ~-'fisted *a* tirchio. **~-fitting** *a* aderente. **~ly** *adv* strettamente; ‹*hold*› forte; ‹*closed*› bene. **~rope** *n* fune *f* (da funamboli)

tights /taɪts/ *npl* collant *m inv*

tile /taɪl/ *n* mattonella *f*; *(on roof)* tegola *f* ● *vt* rivestire di mattonelle ‹*wall*›

till[1] /tɪl/ *prep & conj* = **until**

till[2] *n* cassa *f*

tiller /ˈtɪlə(r)/ *n* barra *f* del timone

tilt /tɪlt/ *n* inclinazione *f*; **at full ~** a tutta velocità ● *vt* inclinare ● *vi* inclinarsi

timber /ˈtɪmbə(r)/ *n* legname *m*

time /taɪm/ *n* tempo *m*; *(occasion)* volta *f*; *(by clock)* ora *f*; **two ~s four** due volte quattro; **at any ~** in qualsiasi momento; **this ~** questa volta; **at ~s, from ~ to ~** ogni tanto; **~ and again** cento volte; **two at a ~** due alla volta; **on ~** in orario; **in ~** in tempo; *(eventually)* col tempo; **in no ~ at all** velocemente; **in a year's ~** fra un anno; **behind ~** in ritardo; **behind the ~s** antiquato; **for the ~ being** per il momento; **what is the ~?** che ora è?; **by the ~ we arrive** quando arriviamo; **did you have a nice ~?** ti sei divertito?; **have a good ~!** divertiti! ● *vt* scegliere il momento per; cronometrare ‹*race*›; **be well ~d** essere ben calcolato

time: ~ bomb *n* bomba *f* a orologeria. **~-lag** *n* intervallo *m* di tempo. **~less** *a* eterno. **~ly** *a* opportuno. **~-switch** *n* interruttore *m* a tempo. **~-table** *n* orario *m*

timid /ˈtɪmɪd/ *a* *(shy)* timido; *(fearful)* timoroso

timing /ˈtaɪmɪŋ/ *n* *Sport, Techn* cronometraggio *m*; **the ~ of the election** il momento scelto per le elezioni

tin /tɪn/ *n* stagno *m*; *(container)* barattolo *m* ● *vt* *(pt/pp* **tinned**) inscatolare. **~ foil** *n* [carta *f*] stagnola *f*

tinge /tɪndʒ/ *n* sfumatura *f* ● *vt* **~d with** *fig* misto a

tingle /ˈtɪŋgl/ *vi* pizzicare

tinker /ˈtɪŋkə(r)/ *vi* armeggiare

tinkle /ˈtɪŋkl/ *n* tintinnio *m*; *(fam: phone call)* colpo *m* di telefono ● *vi* tintinnare

tinned /tɪnd/ *a* in scatola

'tin opener *n* apriscatole *m inv*

tinsel /ˈtɪnsl/ *n* filo *m* d'argento

tint /tɪnt/ *n* tinta *f* ● *vt* tingersi ‹*hair*›

tiny /ˈtaɪnɪ/ *a* (**-ier, -iest**) minuscolo

tip[1] /tɪp/ *n* punta *f*

tip[2] *n* *(money)* mancia *f*; *(advice)* consiglio *m*; *(for rubbish)* discarica *f* ● *v* *(pt/pp* **tipped**) ● *vt* *(tilt)* inclinare; *(overturn)* capovolgere; *(pour)* versare; *(reward)* dare una mancia a ● *vi* inclinarsi; *(overturn)* capovolgersi. **tip off** *vt* **~ sb off** *(inform)* fare una soffiata a qcno. **tip out** *vt* rovesciare. **tip over** *vt* capovolgere ● *vi* capovolgersi

'tip-off *n* soffiata *f*

tipped /tɪpt/ *a* ‹*cigarette*› col filtro

tipsy /ˈtɪpsɪ/ *a fam* brillo

tiptoe /ˈtɪptəʊ/ **non ~** in punta di piedi

tiptop /tɪpˈtɒp/ *a fam* in condizioni perfette

tire /ˈtaɪə(r)/ *vt* stancare ● *vi* stancarsi. **~d** *a* stanco; **~d of** stanco di; **~d out** stanco morto. **~less** *a* instancabile. **~some** /-səm/ *a* fastidioso

tiring /ˈtaɪərɪŋ/ *a* stancante

tissue /ˈtɪʃuː/ *n* tessuto *m*; *(handkerchief)* fazzolettino *m* di carta. **~-paper** *n* carta *f* velina

tit[1] /tɪt/ *n* *(bird)* cincia *f*

tit[2] *n* **~ for tat** pan per focaccia

title /ˈtaɪtl/ *n* titolo *m*. **~-deed** *n* atto *m* di proprietà. **~-role** *n* ruolo *m* principale

tittle-tattle /ˈtɪtltætl/ *n* pettegolezzi *mpl*

to /tuː/, *atono* /tə/ *prep* a; *(to countries)* in; *(towards)* verso; *(up to, until)* fino a; **I'm going to John's/the butcher's** vado da John/dal macellaio; **come/go to sb** venire/andare da qcno; **to Italy/ Switzerland** in Italia/Svizzera; **I've never been to Rome** non sono mai stato a Roma; **go to the market** andare al mercato; **to the toilet/my room** in bagno/camera mia; **to an exhibition** a una mostra; **to university** all'università; **twenty/quarter to eight** le otto meno venti/un quarto; **5 to 6 kilos** da 5 a 6 chili; **to the end** alla fine; **to this day** fino a oggi; **to the best of my recollection** per quanto mi possa ricordare; **give/say sth to sb** dare/dire qcsa a qcno; **give it to me** dammelo; **there's nothing to it** è una cosa da niente ● *verbal constructions*

to go andare; **learn to swim** imparare a nuotare; **I want to/have to go** voglio/devo andare; **it's easy to forget** è facile da dimenticare; **too ill/tired to go** troppo malato/stanco per andare; **you have to** devi; **I don't want to** non voglio; **live to be 90** vivere fino a 90 anni; **he was the last to arrive** è stato l'ultimo ad arrivare; **to be honest,...** per essere sincero,... ● *adv* **pull to** chiudere; **to and fro** avanti e indietro

toad /təud/ *n* rospo *m*. **~stool** *n* fungo *m* velenoso

toast /təust/ *n* pane *m* tostato; (*drink*) brindisi *m inv* ● *vt* tostare (*bread*); (*drink a ~ to*) brindare a. **~er** *n* tostapane *m inv*

tobacco /tə'bækəu/ *n* tabacco *m*. **~nist's [shop]** *n* tabaccheria *f*

toboggan /tə'bɒgən/ *n* toboga *m inv* ● *vi* andare in toboga

today /tə'deɪ/ *a & adv* oggi *m*; **a week ~** una settimana a oggi; **~'s paper** il giornale di oggi

toddler /'tɒdlə(r)/ *n* bambino, -a *mf* ai primi passi

to-do /tə'du:/ *n fam* baccano *m*

toe /təu/ *n* dito *m* del piede; (*of footwear*) punta *f*; **big ~** alluce *m* ● *vt* **~ the line** rigar diritto. **~nail** *n* unghia *f* del piede

toffee /'tɒfɪ/ *n* caramella *f* al mou

together /tə'geðə(r)/ *adv* insieme; (*at the same time*) allo stesso tempo; **~ with** insieme a

toilet /'tɔɪlɪt/ *n* (*lavatory*) gabinetto *m*. **~ paper** *n* carta *f* igienica

toiletries /'tɔɪlɪtrɪz/ *npl* articoli *mpl* da toilette

toilet: ~ roll *n* rotolo *m* di carta igienica. **~ water** *n* acqua *f* di colonia

token /'təukən/ *n* segno *m*; (*counter*) gettone *m*; (*voucher*) buono *m* ● *attrib* simbolico

told /təuld/ *see* **tell** ● *a* **all ~** in tutto

tolerab|le /'tɒl(ə)rəbl/ *a* tollerabile; (*not bad*) discreto. **~y** *adv* discretamente

toleran|ce /'tɒl(ə)r(ə)ns/ *n* tolleranza *f*. **~t** *a* tollerante. **~tly** *adv* con tolleranza

tolerate /'tɒlərɛɪt/ *vt* tollerare

toll¹ /təul/ *n* pedaggio *m*; **death ~** numero *m* di morti

toll² *vi* suonare a morto

tom /tɒm/ *n* (*cat*) gatto *m* maschio

tomato /tə'mɑːtəu/ *n* (*pl* -**es**) pomodoro *m*. **~ ketchup** *n* ketchup *m*. **~ purée** *n* concentrato *m* di pomodoro

tomb /tu:m/ *n* tomba *f*

tomboy *n* maschiaccio *m*

tombstone *n* pietra *f* tombale

tom-cat *n* gatto *m* maschio

tomfoolery /tɒm'fu:lərɪ/ *n* stupidaggini *fpl*

tomorrow /tə'mɒrəu/ *a & adv* domani; **~ morning** domani mattina; **the day after ~** dopodomani; **see you ~!** a domani!

ton /tʌn/ *n* tonnellata *f* (= *1,016 kg.*); **~s** *of fam* un sacco di

tone /təun/ *n* tono *m*; (*colour*) tonalità *f inv* ● **tone down** *vt* attenuare. **tone up** *vt* tonificare (*muscles*)

toner /'təunə(r)/ *n* toner *m*

tongs /tɒnz/ *npl* pinze *fpl*

tongue /tʌn/ *n* lingua *f*; **~ in cheek** (*fam: say*) ironicamente. **~-twister** *n* scioglilingua *m inv*

tonic /'tɒnɪk/ *n* tonico *m*; (*for hair*) lozione *f* per i capelli; *fig* toccasana *m inv*; **~ [water]** acqua *f* tonica

tonight /tə'naɪt/ *adv* stanotte; (*evening*) stasera ● *n* questa notte *f*; (*evening*) questa sera *f*

tonne /tʌn/ *n* tonnellata *f* metrica

tonsil /'tɒnsl/ *n* Anat tonsilla *f*. **~litis** /-sə'laɪtɪs/ *n* tonsillite *f*

too /tu:/ *adv* troppo; (*also*) anche; **~ many** troppi; **~ much** troppo; **~ little** troppo poco

took /tuk/ *see* **take**

tool /tu:l/ *n* attrezzo *m*

toot /tu:t/ *n* suono *m* di clacson ● *vi* Auto clacsonare

tooth /tu:θ/ *n* (*pl* teeth) dente *m*

tooth: ~ache *n* mal *m* di denti. **~brush** *n* spazzolino *m* da denti. **~less** *a* sdentato. **~paste** *n* dentifricio *m*. **~pick** *n* stuzzicadenti *m inv*

top¹ /tɒp/ *n* (*toy*) trottola *f*

top² /tɒp/ *n* Sch primo, -a *mf*; (*upper part or half*) parte *f* superiore; (*of page, list, street*) inizio *m*; (*upper surface*) superficie *f*; (*lid*) coperchio *m*; (*of bottle*) tappo *m*; (*garment*) maglia *f*; (*blouse*) camicia *f*; Auto marcia *f* più alta; **at the ~** *fig* al vertice; **at the ~ of one's voice** a squarciagola; **on ~/on ~ of** sopra; **on ~ of that** (*besides*) per di più; **from ~ to bottom** da cima a fondo ● *a* in alto; (*official, floor of building*) superiore; (*pupil, musician etc*) migliore; (*speed*) massimo ● *vt* (*pt/pp* **topped**) essere in testa a (*list*); (*exceed*) sorpassare; **~ped with ice-cream** ricoperto di gelato. **top up** *vt* riempire

top: ~ 'floor *n* ultimo piano *m*. **~ hat** *n*

cilindro *m*. **~-heavy** *a* con la parte superiore sovraccarica

topic /'tɒpɪk/ *n* soggetto *m*; *(of conversation)* argomento *m*. **~al** *a* d'attualità

top: **~less** *a* & *adv* topless. **~most** *a* più alto

topple /'tɒpl/ *vt* rovesciare ●*vi* rovesciarsi. **topple off** *vi* cadere

top-'secret *a* segretissimo, top secret *inv*

topsy-turvy /tɒpsɪ'tɜ:vɪ/ *a* & *adv* sottosopra

torch /tɔ:tʃ/ *n* torcia *f* [elettrica]; *(flaming)* fiaccola *f*

tore /tɔ:(r)/ *see* **tear**[1]

torment[1] /'tɔ:ment/ *n* tormento *m*

torment[2] /tɔ:'ment/ *vt* tormentare

torn /tɔ:n/ *see* **tear**[1] ●*a* bucato

tornado /tɔ:'neɪdəʊ/ *n* *(pl* **-es)** tornado *m inv*

torpedo /tɔ:'pi:dəʊ/ *n* *(pl* **-es)** siluro *m* ●*vt* silurare

torrent /'tɒrənt/ *n* torrente *m*. **~ial** /təˈrenʃl/ *a* *(rain)* torrenziale

torso /'tɔ:səʊ/ *n* torso *m*; *(in art)* busto *m*

tortoise /'tɔ:təs/ *n* tartaruga *f*

tortuous /'tɔ:tʃʊəs/ *a* tortuoso

torture /'tɔ:tʃə(r)/ *n* tortura *f*. ●*vt* torturare

Tory /'tɔ:rɪ/ *a* & *n* *fam* conservatore, -trice *mf*

toss /tɒs/ *vt* gettare; *(into the air)* lanciare in aria; *(shake)* scrollare; *(horse:)* disarcionare; mescolare *(salad)*: rivoltare facendo saltare in aria *(pancake)*: **~ a coin** fare testa o croce ●*vi* **~ and turn** *(in bed)* rigirarsi; **let's ~ for it** facciamo testa o croce

tot[1] /tɒt/ *n* bimbetto, -a *mf*; *(fam: of liquor)* goccio *m*

tot[2] *vt* *(pt/pp* **totted)** **~ up** *fam* fare la somma di

total /'təʊtl/ *a* totale ●*n* totale *m* ●*vt* *(pt/pp* **totalled)** ammontare a; *(add up)* sommare

totalitarian /təʊtælɪ'teərɪən/ *a* totalitario

totally /'təʊtəlɪ/ *adv* totalmente

totter /'tɒtə(r)/ *vi* barcollare; *(government:)* vacillare

touch /tʌtʃ/ *n* tocco *m*; *(sense)* tatto *m*; *(contact)* contatto *m*; *(trace)* traccia *f*; *(of irony, humour)* tocco *m*; **get/be in ~** mettersi/essere in contatto ●*vt* toccare; *(lightly)* sfiorare; *(equal)* eguagliare; *(fig: move)* commuovere ●*vi* toccarsi. **touch down** *vi* Aeron

atterrare. **touch on** *vt fig* accennare a. **touch up** *vt* ritoccare *(painting)*

touch|ing /'tʌtʃɪŋ/ *a* commovente. **~y** *a* permaloso; *(subject)* delicato

tough /tʌf/ *a* duro; *(severe, harsh)* severo; *(durable)* resistente; *(resilient)* forte

toughen /'tʌfn/ *vt* rinforzare. **toughen up** *vt* rendere più forte *(person)*

tour /tʊə(r)/ *n* giro *m*; *(of building, town)* visita *f*; *Theat, Sport* tournée *f*; *(of duty)* servizio *m* ●*vt* visitare ●*vi* fare un giro turistico; *Theat* essere in tournée

touris|m /'tʊərɪzm/ *n* turismo *m*. **~t** /-rɪst/ *n* turista *mf* ●*attrib* turistico. **~t office** *n* ufficio *m* turistico

tournament /'tʊənəmənt/ *n* torneo *m*

'tour operator *n* tour operator *mf inv*, operatore, -trice *mf* turistico, -a

tousle /'taʊzl/ *vt* spettinare

tout /taʊt/ *n* *(ticket* ~) bagarino *m*; *(horse-racing)* informatore *m* ●*vi* **~ for** sollecitare

tow /təʊ/ *n* rimorchio *m*; **'on ~'**'a rimorchio'; **in ~** *fam* al seguito ●*vt* rimorchiare. **tow away** *vt* portare via col carro attrezzi

toward[s] /tə'wɔ:d(z)/ *prep* verso *(with respect to)* nei riguardi di

towel /'taʊəl/ *n* asciugamano *m*. **~ling** *n* spugna *f*

tower /'taʊə(r)/ *n* torre *f* ●*vi* **~ above** dominare. **~ block** *n* palazzone *m*. **~ing** *a* torreggiante; *(rage)* violento

town /taʊn/ *n* città *f inv*. **~ 'hall** *n* municipio *m*

tow: **~-path** *n* strada *f* alzaia. **~-rope** *n* cavo *m* da rimorchio

toxic /'tɒksɪk/ *a* tossico

toxin /'tɒksɪn/ *n* tossina *f*

toy /tɔɪ/ *n* giocattolo *m*. **~shop** *n* negozio *m* di giocattoli. **toy with** *vt* giocherellare con

trace /treɪs/ *n* traccia *f* ●*vt* seguire le tracce di; *(find)* rintracciare; *(draw)* tracciare; *(with tracing-paper)* ricalcare

track /træk/ *n* traccia *f*; *(path, Sport)* pista *f*; *Rail* binario *m*; **keep ~ of** tenere d'occhio ●*vt* seguire le tracce di. **track down** *vt* scovare

'track: ~ball *n* Comput trackball *f inv*. **~suit** *n* tuta *f* da ginnastica

tractor /'træktə(r)/ *n* trattore *m*

trade /treɪd/ *n* commercio *m*; *(line of business)* settore *m*; *(craft)* mestiere *m*; **by ~** di mestiere ●*vt* commerciare; **~ sth for sth** scambiare qcsa per qcsa ●*vi* commerciare. **trade in** *vt* *(give in* *part exchange)* dare in pagamento parziale

'**trade mark** *n* marchio *m* di fabbrica

trader /'treɪdə(r)/ *n* commerciante *mf*

trade: ~sman *n (joiner etc)* operaio *m*. **~ 'union** *n* sindacato *m*. **~ 'unionist** *n* sindacalista *mf*

trading /'treɪdɪŋ/ *n* commercio *m*. **~ estate** *n* zona *f* industriale

tradition /trə'dɪʃn/ *n* tradizione *f*. **~al** *a* tradizionale. **~ally** *adv* tradizionalmente

traffic /'træfɪk/ *n* traffico *m* ● *vi (pt/pp* **trafficked)** trafficare

traffic: ~ circle *n Am* isola *f* rotatoria. **~ jam** *n* ingorgo *m*. **~ lights** *npl* semaforo *msg*. **~ warden** *n* vigile *m* [urbano]; *(woman)* vigilessa *f*

tragedy /'trædʒədɪ/ *n* tragedia *f*

tragic /'trædʒɪk/ *a* tragico. **~ally** *adv* tragicamente

trail /treɪl/ *n* traccia *f*; *(path)* sentiero *m* ● *vi* strisciare; *(plant:)* arrampicarsi; **~ [behind]** rimanere indietro; *(in competition)* essere in svantaggio ● *vt* trascinare

trailer /'treɪlə(r)/ *n Auto* rimorchio *m*; *(Am: caravan)* roulotte *f inv; (film)* presentazione *f (di un film)*

train /treɪn/ *n* treno *m*; **~ of thought** filo *m* dei pensieri ● *vt* formare professionalmente; *Sport* allenare; *(aim)* puntare; educare *(child)*; addestrare *(animal, soldier)* ● *vi* fare il tirocinio; *Sport* allenarsi. **~ed** *a (animal)* addestrato **(to do** a fare)

trainee /treɪ'niː/ *n* apprendista *mf*

train|er /'treɪnə(r)/ *n Sport* allenatore. -trice *mf; (in circus)* domatore. -trice *mf; (of dog, race-horse)* addestratore, -trice *mf*; **~ers** *pl* scarpe *fpl* da ginnastica. **~ing** *n* tirocinio *m; Sport* allenamento *m; (of animal, soldier)* addestramento *m*

traipse /treɪps/ *vi* **~ around** *fam* andare in giro

trait /treɪt/ *n* caratteristica *f*

traitor /'treɪtə(r)/ *n* traditore, -trice *mf*

tram /træm/ *n* tram *m inv*. **~-lines** *npl* rotaie *fpl* del tram

tramp /træmp/ *n (hike)* camminata *f; (vagrant)* barbone. -a *mf; (of feet)* calpestio *m* ● *vi* camminare con passo pesante; *(hike)* percorrere a piedi

trample /'træmpl/ *vt/i* **~ [on]** calpestare

trampoline /'træmpəlɪn/ *n* trampolino *m*

trance /trɑːns/ *n* trance *f inv*

tranquil /'træŋkwɪl/ *a* tranquillo. **~lity** /-'kwɪlətɪ/ *n* tranquillità *f*

tranquillizer /'træŋkwɪlaɪzə(r)/ *n* tranquillante *m*

transact /træn'zækt/ *vt* trattare. **~ion** /-ækʃn/ *n* transazione *f*

transatlantic /trænzət'læntɪk/ *a* transatlantico

transcend /træn'send/ *vt* trascendere

transfer¹ /'trænsfɜː(r)/ *n* trasferimento *m; Sport* cessione *f; (design)* decalcomania *f*

transfer² /træns'fɜː(r)/ *v (pt/pp* **transferred)** ● *vt* trasferire; *Sport* cedere ● *vi* trasferirsi; *(when travelling)* cambiare. **~able** /-əbl/ *a* trasferibile

transform /træns'fɔːm/ *vt* trasformare. **~ation** /-fə'meɪʃn/ *n* trasformazione *f*. **~er** *n* trasformatore *m*

transfusion /træns'fjuːʒn/ *n* trasfusione *f*

transient /'trænzɪənt/ *a* passeggero

transistor /træn'zɪstə(r)/ *n* transistor *m inv; (radio)* radiolina *f* a transistor

transit /'trænzɪt/ *n* transito *m*; **in ~** *(goods)* in transito

transition /træn'zɪʃn/ *n* transizione *f*. **~al** *a* di transizione

transitive /'trænzɪtɪv/ *a* transitivo

transitory /'trænzɪtərɪ/ *a* transitorio

translat|e /trænz'leɪt/ *vt* tradurre. **~ion** /-'leɪʃn/ *n* traduzione *f*. **~or** *n* traduttore, -trice *mf*

transmission /trænz'mɪʃn/ *n* trasmissione *f*

transmit /trænz'mɪt/ *vt (pt/pp* **transmitted)** trasmettere. **~ter** *n* trasmettitore *m*

transparen|cy /træn'spærənsɪ/ *n Phot* diapositiva *f*. **~t** *a* trasparente

transpire /træn'spaɪə(r)/ *vi* emergere; *(fam: happen)* accadere

transplant¹ /'trænsplɑːnt/ *n* trapianto *m*

transplant² /træns'plɑːnt/ *vt* trapiantare

transport¹ /'trænspɔːt/ *n* trasporto *m*

transport² /træn'spɔːt/ *vt* trasportare. **~ation** /-'teɪʃn/ *n* trasporto *m*

transvestite /trænz'vestaɪt/ *n* travestito, -a *mf*

trap /træp/ *n* trappola *f; (fam: mouth)* boccaccia *f* ● *vt (pt/pp* **trapped)** intrappolare; schiacciare *(finger in door)*. **~'door** *n* botola *f*

trapeze /trə'piːz/ *n* trapezio *m*

trash /træʃ/ *n* robaccia *f; (rubbish)* spazzatura *f; (nonsense)* schiocchezze *fpl*. **~can** *n Am* secchio *m* della spazzatura. **~y** *a* scadente

trauma /'trɔːmə/ *n* trauma *m*. **~tic**

/-'mætik/ a traumatico. **~tize** /-taiz/ traumatizzare

travel /'trævl/ n viaggi mpl ● v (pt/pp **travelled**) ● vi viaggiare; (to work) andare ● vt percorrere ⟨distance⟩. **~ agency** n agenzia f di viaggi. **~ agent** n agente mf di viaggio

traveller /'trævlə(r)/ n viaggiatore, -trice mf; Comm commesso m viaggiatore; **~s** pl ⟨gypsies⟩ zingari mpl. **~'s cheque** n traveller's cheque m inv

trawler /'trɔ:lə(r)/ n peschereccio m

tray /trei/ n vassoio m; (for baking) teglia f; (for documents) vaschetta f sparticarta; (of printer, photocopier) vassoio m

treacher|ous /'tretʃərəs/ a traditore; ⟨weather, currents⟩ pericoloso. **~y** n tradimento m

treacle /'tri:kl/ n melassa f

tread /tred/ n andatura f; (step) gradino m; (of tyre) battistrada m inv ● v (pt trod, pp trodden) ● vi ⟨walk⟩ camminare. **tread on** vt calpestare ⟨grass⟩; pestare ⟨foot⟩

treason /'tri:zn/ n tradimento m

treasure /'treʒə(r)/ n tesoro m ● vt tenere in gran conto. **~r** n tesoriere, -a mf

treasury /'treʒəri/ n **the T~** il Ministero del Tesoro

treat /tri:t/ n piacere m; (present) regalo m; **give sb a ~** fare una sorpresa a qcno ● vt trattare; Med curare; **~ sb to sth** offrire qcsa a qcno

treatise /'tri:tiz/ n trattato m

treatment /'tri:tmənt/ n trattamento m; Med cura f

treaty /'tri:ti/ n trattato m

treble /'trebl/ a triplo ● n Mus ⟨voice⟩ voce f bianca ● vt triplicare ● vi triplicarsi. **~ clef** n chiave f di violino

tree /tri:/ n albero m

trek /trek/ n scarpinata f; (as holiday) trekking m inv ● vi (pt/pp **trekked**) farsi una scarpinata; (on holiday) fare trekking

tremble /'trembl/ vi tremare

tremendous /tri'mendəs/ a (huge) enorme; (fam: excellent) formidabile. **~ly** adv (very) straordinariamente; (a lot) enormemente

tremor /'tremə(r)/ n tremito m; [earth] **~** scossa f [sismica]

trench /trentʃ/ n fosso m; Mil trincea f. **~ coat** n trench m inv

trend /trend/ n tendenza f; (fashion) moda f. **~y** a (-ier, -iest) fam di or alla moda

trepidation /trepi'deiʃn/ n trepidazione f

trespass /'trespas/ vi **~ on** introdursi abusivamente in; fig abusare di. **~er** n intruso, -a mf

trial /'traiəl/ n Jur processo m; (test, ordeal) prova f; **on ~** in prova; Jur in giudizio; **by ~ and error** per tentativi

triang|le /'traiæŋgl/ n triangolo m. **~ular** /-'æŋgjʊlə(r)/ a triangolare

tribe /traib/ n tribù f inv

tribulation /tribjʊ'leiʃn/ n tribolazione f

tribunal /trai'bju:nl/ n tribunale m

tributary /'tribjʊtəri/ n affluente m

tribute /'tribju:t/ n tributo m; **pay ~** rendere omaggio

trice /trais/ n **in a ~** in un attimo

trick /trik/ n trucco m; (joke) scherzo m; (in cards) presa f; **do the ~** fam funzionare; **play a ~ on** fare uno scherzo a ● vt imbrogliare

trickle /'trikl/ vi colare

trick|ster /'trikstə(r)/ n imbroglione, -a mf. **~y** a (-ier, -iest) a ⟨operation⟩ complesso; ⟨situation⟩ delicato

tricycle /'traisikl/ n triciclo m

tried /traid/ see try

trifl|e /'traifl/ n inezia f; Culin zuppa f inglese. **~ing** a insignificante

trigger /'trigə(r)/ n grilletto m ● vt **~ [off]** scatenare

trigonometry /trigə'nɒmitri/ n trigonometria f

trim /trim/ a (**trimmer, trimmest**) curato; ⟨figure⟩ snello ● n (of hair, hedge) spuntata f; (decoration) rifinitura f; **in good ~** in buono stato; ⟨person⟩ in forma ● vt (pt/pp **trimmed**) spuntare ⟨hair etc⟩; (decorate) ornare; Naut orientare. **~ming** n bordo m; **~mings** pl (decorations) guarnizioni fpl; **with all the ~mings** Culin guarnito

trinket /'triŋkit/ n ninnolo m

trio /'tri:əʊ/ n trio m

trip /trip/ n (excursion) gita f; (journey) viaggio m; (stumble) passo m falso ● v (pt/pp **tripped**) ● vt far inciampare ● vi inciampare (**on/over** in). **trip up** vt far inciampare

tripe /traip/ n trippa f; (sl: nonsense) fesserie fpl

triple /'tripl/ a triplo ● vt triplicare ● vi triplicarsi

triplets /'triplits/ npl tre gemelli mpl

triplicate /'triplikət/ n **in ~** in triplice copia

tripod /'traipɒd/ n treppiede m inv

tripper /'tripə(r)/ n gitante mf

trite /traɪt/ a banale

triumph /'traɪʌmf/ n trionfo m ● vi trionfare (**over** su). **~ant** /-'ʌmf(ə)nt/ a trionfante. **~antly** adv ⟨exclaim⟩ con tono trionfante

trivial /'trɪvɪəl/ a insignificante. **~ity** /-'ælətɪ/ n banalità f inv

trod, trodden /trɒd, 'trɒdn/ see tread

trolley /'trɒlɪ/ n carrello m; ⟨Am: tram⟩ tram m inv. **~ bus** n filobus m inv

trombone /trɒm'bəʊn/ n trombone m

troop /tru:p/ n gruppo m; **~s** pl truppe fpl ● vi **~ in/out** entrare/uscire in gruppo

trophy /'trəʊfɪ/ n trofeo m

tropic /'trɒpɪk/ n tropico m; **~s** pl tropici mpl. **~al** a tropicale

trot /trɒt/ n trotto m ● vi (pt/pp **trotted**) trottare

trouble /'trʌbl/ n guaio m; ⟨difficulties⟩ problemi mpl; ⟨inconvenience, Med⟩ disturbo m; ⟨conflict⟩ conflitto m; **be in ~** essere nei guai; ⟨swimmer, climber:⟩ essere in difficoltà; **get into ~** finire nei guai; **get sb into ~** mettere qcno nei guai; **take the ~ to do sth** darsi la pena di far qcsa ● vt ⟨worry⟩ preoccupare; ⟨inconvenience⟩ disturbare; ⟨conscience, old wound:⟩ tormentare ● vi **don't ~!** non ti disturbare!. **~-maker** n be a **~-maker** seminare zizzania. **~some** /-səm/ a fastidioso

trough /trɒf/ n trogolo m; ⟨atmospheric⟩ depressione f

trounce /traʊns/ vt ⟨in competition⟩ schiacciare

troupe /tru:p/ n troupe f inv

trousers /'traʊzəz/ npl pantaloni mpl

trout /traʊt/ n inv trota f

trowel /'traʊəl/ n ⟨for gardening⟩ paletta f; ⟨for builder⟩ cazzuola f

truant /'tru:ənt/ n **play ~** marinare la scuola

truce /tru:s/ n tregua f

truck /trʌk/ n ⟨lorry⟩ camion m inv

trudge /trʌdʒ/ n camminata f faticosa ● vi arrancare

true /tru:/ a vero; **come ~** avverarsi

truffle /'trʌfl/ n tartufo m

truism /'tru:ɪzm/ n truismo m

truly /'tru:lɪ/ adv veramente; **Yours ~** distinti saluti

trump /trʌmp/ n ⟨in cards⟩ atout m inv

trumpet /'trʌmpɪt/ n tromba f. **~er** n trombettista mf

truncheon /'trʌntʃn/ n manganello m

trunk /trʌŋk/ n ⟨of tree, body⟩ tronco m; ⟨of elephant⟩ proboscide f; ⟨for travelling, storage⟩ baule m; ⟨Am: of car⟩ bagagliaio m; **~s** pl calzoncini mpl da bagno

truss /trʌs/ n Med cinto m erniario

trust /trʌst/ n fiducia f; ⟨group of companies⟩ trust m inv; ⟨organization⟩ associazione f; **on ~** sulla parola ● vt fidarsi di; ⟨hope⟩ augurarsi ● vi **~ in** credere in; **~ to** affidarsi a. **~ed** a fidato

trustee /trʌs'ti:/ n amministratore, -trice mf fiduciario, -a

'trust|ful /'trʌstfl/ a fiducioso. **~ing** a fiducioso. **~worthy** a fidato

truth /tru:θ/ n (pl -s /tru:ðz/) verità f inv. **~ful** a veritiero. **~fully** adv sinceramente

try /traɪ/ n tentativo m, prova f; ⟨in rugby⟩ meta f ● v (pt/pp **tried**) ● vt provare; ⟨be a strain on⟩ mettere a dura prova; Jur processare ⟨person⟩; discutere ⟨case⟩; **~ to do sth** provare a fare qcsa ● vi provare. **try on** vt provarsi ⟨garment⟩. **try out** vt provare

trying /'traɪɪŋ/ a duro; ⟨person⟩ irritante

T-shirt /'ti:-/ n maglietta f

tub /tʌb/ n tinozza f; ⟨carton⟩ vaschetta f; ⟨bath⟩ vasca f da bagno

tuba /'tju:bə/ n Mus tuba f

tubby /'tʌbɪ/ a (-ier, -iest) tozzo

tube /tju:b/ n tubo m; ⟨of toothpaste⟩ tubetto m; Rail metro f

tuber /'tju:bə(r)/ n tubero m

tuberculosis /tju:bɜ:kjʊ'ləʊsɪs/ n tubercolosi f

tubular /'tju:bjʊlə(r)/ a tubolare

tuck /tʌk/ n piega f ● vt ⟨put⟩ infilare. **tuck in** vt rimboccare; **~ sb in** rimboccare le coperte a qcno ● vi ⟨fam: eat⟩ mangiare con appetito. **tuck up** vt rimboccarsi ⟨sleeves⟩; ⟨in bed⟩ rimboccare le coperte a

Tuesday /'tju:zdeɪ/ n martedì m inv

tuft /tʌft/ n ciuffo m

tug /tʌg/ n strattone m; Naut rimorchiatore m ● v (pt/pp **tugged**) ● vt tirare ● vi dare uno strattone. **~ of war** n tiro m alla fune

tuition /tju:'ɪʃn/ n lezioni fpl

tulip /'tju:lɪp/ n tulipano m

tumble /'tʌmbl/ n ruzzolone m ● vi ruzzolare. **~-down** a cadente. **~-drier** n asciugabiancheria f

tumbler /'tʌmblə(r)/ n bicchiere m (senza stelo)

tummy /'tʌmɪ/ n fam pancia f

tumour /'tju:mə(r)/ n tumore m

tumult /'tju:mʌlt/ n tumulto m. **~uous** /-'mʌltjʊəs/ a tumultuoso

tuna /'tju:nə/ n tonno m

tune /tjuːn/ n motivo m; **out of/in ~** ⟨instrument⟩ scordato/accordato; ⟨person⟩ stonato/intonato; **to the ~ of** fam per la modesta somma di ● vt accordare ⟨instrument⟩; sintonizzare ⟨radio, TV⟩; mettere a punto ⟨engine⟩. **tune in** vt sintonizzare ● vi sintonizzarsi (**to** su).
tune up vi Mus accordare gli strumenti

tuneful /ˈtjuːnfl/ a melodioso

tuner /ˈtjuːnə(r)/ n accordatore, -trice mf; Radio, TV sintonizzatore m

tunic /ˈtjuːnɪk/ n tunica f; Mil giacca f; Sch grembiule m

Tunisia /tjuːˈnɪzɪə/ n Tunisia f. **~n** a & n tunisino, -a mf

tunnel /ˈtʌnl/ n tunnel m, inv ● vi (pt/pp **tunnelled**) scavare un tunnel

turban /ˈtɜːbən/ n turbante m

turbine /ˈtɜːbaɪn/ n turbina f

turbulen|ce /ˈtɜːbjʊləns/ n turbolenza f. **~t** a turbolento

turf /tɜːf/ n erba f; ⟨segment⟩ zolla f erbosa ● **turf out** vt fam buttar fuori

Turin /tjuːˈrɪn/ n Torino f

Turk /tɜːk/ n turco, -a mf

turkey /ˈtɜːki/ n tacchino m

Turk|ey n Turchia f. **~ish** a turco

turmoil /ˈtɜːmɔɪl/ n tumulto m

turn /tɜːn/ n (rotation, short walk) giro m; (in road) svolta f, curva f; (development) svolta f; Theat numero m; (fam: attack) crisi f inv; **a ~ for the better/worse** un miglioramento/peggioramento; **do sb a good ~** rendere un servizio a qcno; **take ~s** fare a turno; **in ~** a turno; **out of ~** (speak) a sproposito; **it's your ~** tocca a te ● vt girare; voltare ⟨back, eyes⟩; dirigere ⟨gun, attention⟩ ● vi girare; ⟨person:⟩ girarsi; ⟨leaves:⟩ ingiallire; (become) diventare; **~ right/left** girare a destra/sinistra; **~ sour** inacidirsi; **~ to sb** girarsi verso qcno; fig rivolgersi a qcno. **turn against** vi diventare ostile a ● vt mettere contro. **turn away** vt mandare via ⟨people⟩; girare dall'altra parte ⟨head⟩ ● vi girarsi dall'altra parte. **turn down** vt piegare ⟨collar⟩; abbassare ⟨heat, gas, sound⟩; respingere ⟨person, proposal⟩. **turn in** vt ripiegare in dentro ⟨edges⟩; consegnare ⟨lost object⟩ ● vi (fam: go to bed) andare a letto; **~ into the drive** entrare nel viale. **turn off** vt spegnere; chiudere ⟨tap, water⟩ ● vi ⟨car:⟩ girare. **turn on** vt accendere; aprire ⟨tap, water⟩; (fam: attract) eccitare ● vi (attack) attaccare. **turn out** vt (expel) mandar via; spegnere ⟨light,

gas⟩; (produce) produrre; (empty) svuotare ⟨room, cupboard⟩ ● vi (transpire) risultare; **~ out well/badly** ⟨cake, dress:⟩ riuscire bene/male; ⟨situation:⟩ andare bene/male. **turn over** vt girare ● vi girarsi; **please ~ over** vedi retro. **turn round** vi girarsi; ⟨car:⟩ girare. **turn up** vt tirare su ⟨collar⟩; alzare ⟨heat, gas, sound, radio⟩ ● vi farsi vedere

turning /ˈtɜːnɪŋ/ n svolta f. **~-point** n svolta f decisiva

turnip /ˈtɜːnɪp/ n rapa f

turn: **~-out** n (of people) affluenza f. **~over** n Comm giro m d'affari; (of staff) ricambio m. **~pike** n Am autostrada f. **~stile** n cancelletto m girevole. **~table** n piattaforma f girevole; (on record-player) piatto m (di giradischi). **~-up** n (of trousers) risvolto m

turpentine /ˈtɜːpəntaɪn/ n trementina f

turquoise /ˈtɜːkwɔɪz/ a (colour) turchese ● n turchese m

turret /ˈtʌrɪt/ n torretta f

turtle /ˈtɜːtl/ n tartaruga f acquatica

tusk /tʌsk/ n zanna f

tussle /ˈtʌsl/ n zuffa f ● vi azzuffarsi

tutor /ˈtjuːtə(r)/ n insegnante mf privato, -a; Univ insegnante mf universitario, -a che segue individualmente un ristretto numero di studenti. **~ial** /-ˈtɔːrɪəl/ n discussione f col tutor

tuxedo /tʌkˈsiːdəʊ/ n Am smoking m inv

TV n abbr (**television**) tv f inv, tivù f inv

twaddle /ˈtwɒdl/ n scemenze fpl

twang /twæŋ/ n (in voice) suono m nasale ● vt far vibrare

tweed /twiːd/ n tweed m inv

tweezers /ˈtwiːzəz/ npl pinzette fpl

twelfth /twelfθ/ a & n dodicesimo, -a mf

twelve /twelv/ a & n dodici m

twentieth /ˈtwentɪθ/ a & n ventesimo, -a mf

twenty /ˈtwenti/ a & n venti m

twerp /twɜːp/ n fam stupido, -a mf

twice /twaɪs/ adv due volte

twiddle /ˈtwɪdl/ vt giocherellare con; **~ one's thumbs** fig girarsi i pollici

twig¹ /twɪg/ n ramoscello m

twig² vt/i (pt/pp **twigged**) fam intuire

twilight /ˈtwaɪ-/ n crepuscolo m

twin /twɪn/ n gemello, -a mf ● attrib gemello. **~ beds** npl letti mpl gemelli

twine /twaɪn/ n spago m ● vi intrecciarsi; ⟨plant:⟩ attorcigliarsi ● vt intrecciare

twinge /twɪndʒ/ n fitta f; **~ of conscience** rimorso m di coscienza

twinkle /'twɪŋkl/ n scintillio m ● vi scintillare

twin '**town** n città f inv gemellata

twirl /twɜ:l/ vt far roteare ● vi volteggiare ● n piroetta f

twist /twɪst/ n torsione f; (curve) curva f; (in rope) attorcigliata f; (in book, plot) colpo m di scena ● vt attorcigliare (rope); torcere (metal); girare (knob, cap); (distort) distorcere; ~ **one's ankle** storcersi la caviglia ● vi attorcigliarsi; (road:) essere pieno di curve

twit /twɪt/ n fam cretino, -a mf

twitch /twɪtʃ/ n tic m inv; (jerk) strattone m ● vi contrarsi

twitter /'twɪtə(r)/ n cinguettio m ● vi cinguettare; (person:) cianciare

two /tu:/ a & n due m

two: ~-**faced** a falso. ~-**piece** a (swimsuit) due pezzi m inv; (suit) comple-

to m. ~**some** /-səm/ n coppia f. ~-**way** a (traffic) a doppio senso di marcia

tycoon /taɪ'ku:n/ n magnate m

tying /'taɪɪŋ/ see **tie**

type /taɪp/ n tipo m; (printing) carattere m [tipografico] ● vt/i scrivere a macchina. ~**writer** n macchina f da scrivere. ~**written** a dattiloscritto

typhoid /'taɪfɔɪd/ n febbre f tifoidea

typical /'tɪpɪkl/ a tipico. ~**ly** adv tipicamente; (as usual) come al solito

typify /'tɪpɪfaɪ/ vt (pt/pp -**ied**) essere tipico di

typing /'taɪpɪŋ/ n dattilografia f

typist /'taɪpɪst/ n dattilografo, -a mf

typography /taɪ'pɒgrəfi/ n tipografia f

tyrannical /tɪ'rænɪkl/ a tirannico

tyranny /'tɪrəni/ n tirannia f

tyrant /'taɪrənt/ n tiranno, -a mf

tyre /'taɪə(r)/ n gomma f, pneumatico m

Uu

ubiquitous /ju:'bɪkwɪtəs/ a onnipresente

udder /'ʌdə(r)/ n mammella f (di vacca, capra etc)

ugl|iness /'ʌglɪnɪs/ n bruttezza f. ~**y** a (-**ier**, -**iest**) brutto

UK n abbr **United Kingdom**

ulcer /'ʌlsə(r)/ n ulcera f

ulterior /ʌl'tɪərɪə(r)/ a ~ **motive** secondo fine m

ultimate /'ʌltɪmət/ a definitivo; (final) finale; (fundamental) fondamentale. ~**ly** adv alla fine

ultimatum /ʌltɪ'meɪtəm/ n ultimatum m inv

ultrasound /'ʌltrə-/ n Med ecografia f

ultra'**violet** a ultravioletto

umbilical /ʌm'bɪlɪkl/ a ~ **cord** cordone m ombelicale

umbrella /ʌm'brelə/ n ombrello m

umpire /'ʌmpaɪə(r)/ n arbitro m ● vt/i arbitrare

umpteen /ʌmp'ti:n/ a fam innumerevole. ~**th** a fam ennesimo; **for the** ~**th time** per l'ennesima volta

UN n abbr (**United Nations**) ONU f

un'**able** /ʌn-/ a **be** ~ **to do sth** non po-

tere fare qcsa; (not know how) non sapere fare qcsa

una'**bridged** a integrale

unac'**companied** a non accompagnato; (luggage) incustodito

unac'**countabl|e** a inspiegabile. ~**y** adv inspiegabilmente

unac'**customed** a insolito; **be** ~ **to** non essere abituato a

una'**dulterated** a (water) puro; (wine) non sofisticato; fig assoluto

un'**aided** a senza aiuto

unanimity /ju:nə'nɪmətɪ/ n unanimità f

unanimous /ju:'nænɪməs/ a unanime. ~**ly** adv all'unanimità

un'**armed** a disarmato. ~ **combat** n lotta f senza armi

unas'**suming** a senza pretese

unat'**tached** a staccato; (person) senza legami

unat'**tended** a incustodito

un'**authorized** a non autorizzato

una'**voidable** a inevitabile

una'**ware** a **be** ~ **of sth** non rendersi conto di qcsa. ~**s** /-eəz/ adv **catch sb** ~**s** prendere qcno alla sprovvista

un'**balanced** a non equilibrato; (mentally) squilibrato un'bearabl|e *a* insopportabile. ~y *adv* insopportabilmente

unbeat|able /ʌn'biːtəbl/ *a* imbattibile. ~en *a* imbattuto

unbeknown /ʌnbɪ'nəʊn/ *a fam* ~ to me a mia insaputa

unbe'lievable *a* incredibile

un'bend *vi* (*pt/pp* -bent) (*relax*) distendersi

un'biased *a* obiettivo

un'block *vt* sbloccare

un'bolt *vt* togliere il chiavistello di

un'breakable *a* infrangibile

unbridled /ʌn'braɪdld/ *a* sfrenato

un'burden *vt* ~ oneself *fig* sfogarsi (to con)

un'button *vt* sbottonare

uncalled-for /ʌn'kɔːldfɔː(r)/ *a* fuori luogo

un'canny *a* sorprendente; (*silence, feeling*) inquietante

un'ceasing *a* incessante

uncere'monious *a* (*abrupt*) brusco. ~ly *adv* senza tante cerimonie

un'certain *a* incerto; (*weather*) instabile; in no ~ terms senza mezzi termini. ~ty *n* incertezza *f*

un'changed *a* invariato

un'charitable *a* duro

uncle /'ʌŋkl/ *n* zio *m*

un'comfortabl|e *a* scomodo; imbarazzante (*silence, situation*); feel ~e *fig* sentirsi a disagio. ~y *adv* (*sit*) scomodamente; (*causing alarm etc*) spaventosamente

un'common *a* insolito

un'compromising *a* intransigente

uncon'ditional *a* incondizionato. ~ly *adv* incondizionatamente

un'conscious *a* privo di sensi; (*unaware*) inconsapevole; be ~ of sth non rendersi conto di qcsa. ~ly *adv* inconsapevolmente

uncon'ventional *a* poco convenzionale

unco'operative *a* poco cooperativo

un'cork *vt* sturare

uncouth /ʌn'kuːθ/ *a* zotico

un'cover *vt* scoprire; portare alla luce (*buried object*)

unde'cided *a* indeciso; (*not settled*) incerto

undeniabl|e /ʌndɪ'naɪəbl/ *a* innegabile. ~y *adv* innegabilmente

under /'ʌndə(r)/ *prep* sotto; (*less than*) al di sotto di; ~ there lì sotto; ~ repair/construction in riparazione/costruzione; ~ way *fig* in corso ●*adv*

(~ *water*) sott'acqua; (*unconscious*) sotto anestesia

'undercarriage *n* Aeron carrello *m*

'underclothes *npl* biancheria *fsg* intima

under'cover *a* clandestino

'undercurrent *n* corrente *f* sottomarina; *fig* sottofondo *m*

under'cut *vt* (*pt/pp* -cut) Comm vendere a minor prezzo di

'underdog *n* perdente *m*

under'done *a* (*meat*) al sangue

under'estimate *vt* sottovalutare

under'fed *a* denutrito

under'foot *adv* sotto i piedi; trample ~ calpestare

under'go *vt* (*pt* -went, *pp* -gone) subire (*operation, treatment*); ~ repair essere in riparazione

under'graduate *n* studente, -tessa *mf* universitario, -a

'underground[1] *adv* sottoterra

'underground[2] *a* sotterraneo; (*secret*) clandestino ●*n* (*railway*) metropolitana *f*. ~ car park *n* parcheggio *m* sotterraneo

'undergrowth *n* sottobosco *m*

'underhand *a* subdolo

'underlay *n* strato *m* di gomma o feltro posto sotto la moquette

under'lie *vt* (*pt* -lay, *pp* -lain, *pres p* -lying) *fig* essere alla base di

under'line *vt* sottolineare

underling /'ʌndəlɪŋ/ *n pej* subalterno, -a *mf*

under'lying *a fig* fondamentale

under'mine *vt fig* minare

underneath /ʌndə'niːθ/ *prep* sotto; ~ it sotto ●*adv* sotto

under'paid *a* mal pagato

'underpants *npl* mutande *fpl*

'underpass *n* sottopassaggio *m*

under'privileged *a* non abbiente

under'rate *vt* sottovalutare

'underseal *n* Auto antiruggine *m inv*

'undershirt *n* Am maglia *f* della pelle

understaffed /-'stɑːft/ *a* a corto di personale

under'stand *vt* (*pt/pp* -stood) capire; I ~ that... (*have heard*) mi risulta che... ●*vi* capire. ~able *a* comprensibile. ~ably /-əblɪ/ *adv* comprensibilmente

under'standing *a* comprensivo ●*n* comprensione *f*; (*agreement*) accordo *m*; on the ~ that a condizione che

'understatement *n* understatement *m inv*

'understudy *n* Theat sostituto, -a *mf*

under'take *vt* (*pt* -took, *pp* -taken)

intraprendere; ~ **to do sth** impegnarsi a fare qcsa

'under'taker *n* impresario *m* di pompe funebri; [**firm of**] ~**s** *n* impresa *f* di pompe funebri

under'taking *n* impresa *f*; (*promise*) promessa *f*

'undertone *n fig* sottofondo *m*; **in an** ~ sottovoce

under'value *vt* sottovalutare

'underwater¹ *a* subacqueo

under'water² *adv* sott'acqua

'underwear *n* biancheria *f* intima

'underweight *a* sotto peso

'underworld *n* (*criminals*) malavita *f*

'underwriter *n* assicuratore *m*

unde'sirable *a* indesiderato; (*person*) poco raccomandabile

undies /'ʌndɪz/ *npl fam* biancheria *fsg* intima (*da donna*)

un'dignified *a* non dignitoso

un'do *vt* (*pt* -**did**, *pp* -**done**) disfare; slacciare (*dress, shoes*); sbottonare (*shirt*); *fig, Comput* annullare

un'done *a* (*shirt, button*) sbottonato; (*shoes, dress*) slacciato; (*not accomplished*) non fatto; **leave** ~ (*job*) tralasciare

un'doubted *a* indubbio. ~**ly** *adv* senza dubbio

un'dress *vt* spogliare; **get** ~**ed** spogliarsi ● *vi* spogliarsi

un'due *a* eccessivo

undulating /'ʌndjʊleɪtɪŋ/ *a* ondulato; (*country*) collinoso

un'duly *adv* eccessivamente

un'dying *a* eterno

un'earth *vt* dissotterrare; *fig* scovare; scoprire (*secret*). ~**ly** *a* soprannaturale; **at an** ~**ly hour** *fam* a un'ora impossibile

un'easle *n* disagio *m*. ~**y** *a* a disagio; (*person*) inquieto; (*feeling*) inquietante; (*truce*) precario

un'eatable *a* immangiabile

uneco'nomic *a* poco remunerativo

uneco'nomical *a* poco economico

unem'ployed *a* disoccupato ● *npl* **the** ~ i disoccupati

unem'ployment *n* disoccupazione *f*. ~ **benefit** *n* sussidio *m* di disoccupazione

un'ending *a* senza fine

un'equal *a* disuguale; (*struggle*) impari; **be** ~ **to a task** non essere all'altezza di un compito

unequivocal /ʌnɪ'kwɪvəkl/ *a* inequivocabile; (*person*) esplicito

unerring /ʌn'ɜːrɪŋ/ *a* infallibile

un'ethical *a* immorale

un'even *a* irregolare; (*distribution*) ineguale; (*number*) dispari

unex'pected *a* inaspettato. ~**ly** *adv* inaspettatamente

un'failing *a* infallibile

un'fair *a* ingiusto. ~**ly** *adv* ingiustamente. ~**ness** *n* ingiustizia *f*

un'faithful *a* infedele

unfa'miliar *a* sconosciuto; **be** ~ **with** non conoscere

un'fasten *vt* slacciare; (*detach*) staccare

un'favourable *a* sfavorevole; (*impression*) negativo

un'feeling *a* insensibile

un'finished *a* da finire; (*business*) in sospeso

un'fit *a* inadatto; (*morally*) indegno; *Sport* fuori forma; ~ **for work** non in grado di lavorare

un'flinching *a* risoluto

un'fold *vt* spiegare; (*spread out*) aprire; *fig* rivelare ● *vi* (*view:*) spiegarsi

unfore'seen *a* imprevisto

unforgettable /ʌnfə'getəbl/ *a* indimenticabile

unforgivable /ʌnfə'gɪvəbl/ *a* imperdonabile

un'fortunate *a* sfortunato; (*regrettable*) spiacevole; (*remark, choice*) infelice. ~**ly** *adv* purtroppo

un'founded *a* infondato

unfurl /ʌn'fɜːl/ *vt* spiegare

un'furnished *a* non ammobiliato

ungainly /ʌn'geɪnlɪ/ *a* sgraziato

ungodly /ʌn'gɒdlɪ/ *a* empio; ~ **hour** *fam* ora *f* impossibile

un'grateful *a* ingrato. ~**ly** *adv* senza riconoscenza

un'happily *adv* infelicemente; (*unfortunately*) purtroppo. ~**ness** *n* infelicità *f*

un'happy *a* infelice; (*not content*) insoddisfatto (**with** di)

un'harmed *a* incolume

un'healthy *a* poco sano; (*insanitary*) malsano

un'hook *vt* sganciare

un'hurt *a* illeso

unhy'gienic *a* non igienico

unification /juːnɪfɪ'keɪʃn/ *n* unificazione *f*

uniform /'juːnɪfɔːm/ *a* uniforme ● *n* uniforme *f*. ~**ly** *adv* uniformemente

unify /'juːnɪfaɪ/ *vt* (*pt/pp*-**ied**) unificare

uni'lateral /juːnɪ/ *a* unilaterale

uni'maginable *a* inimmaginabile

unim'portant *a* irrilevante

unin'habited *a* disabitato

unin'tentional a involontario. ~**ly** adv involontariamente

union /'ju:nɪən/ n unione f; (trade ~) sindacato m. **U~ Jack** n bandiera f del Regno Unito

unique /ju:'ni:k/ a unico. ~**ly** adv unicamente

unison /'ju:nɪsn/ n **in** ~ all'unisono

unit /'ju:nɪt/ n unità f inv; (department) reparto m; (of furniture) elemento m

unite /ju:'naɪt/ vt unire ● vi unirsi

united /ju:'naɪtɪd/ a unito. **U~ 'Kingdom** n Regno m Unito. **U~ 'Nations** n [Organizzazione f delle] Nazioni Unite fpl. **U~ States [of America]** n Stati mpl Uniti [d'America]

unity /'ju:nətɪ/ n unità f; (agreement) accordo m

universal /ju:nɪ'vɜ:sl/ a universale. ~**ly** adv universalmente

universe /'ju:nɪvɜ:s/ n universo m

university /ju:nɪ'vɜ:sətɪ/ n università f inv ● attrib universitario

un'just a ingiusto

unkempt /ʌn'kempt/ a trasandato; (hair) arruffato

un'kind a scortese. ~**ly** adv in modo scortese. ~**ness** n mancanza f di gentilezza

un'known a sconosciuto

un'lawful a illecito, illegale

unleaded /ʌn'ledɪd/ a senza piombo

un'leash vt fig scatenare

unless /ən'les/ conj a meno che; ~ **I am mistaken** se non mi sbaglio

un'like a (not the same) diversi ● prep diverso da; **that's** ~ **him** non è da lui; ~ **me, he...** diversamente da me, lui...

un'likely a improbabile

un'limited a illimitato

un'load vt scaricare

un'lock vt aprire (con chiave)

un'lucky a sfortunato; **it's** ~ **to...** porta sfortuna...

un'manned a senza equipaggio

un'married a non sposato. ~ **'mother** n ragazza f madre

un'mask vt fig smascherare

unmistakabl|e /ʌnmɪ'steɪkəbl/ a inconfondibile. ~**y** adv chiaramente

un'mitigated a assoluto

un'natural a innaturale; pej anormale. ~**ly** adv in modo innaturale; pej in modo anormale

unneces'sarily adv inutilmente

un'necessary a inutile

un'noticed a inosservato

unob'tainable a (products etc) intro-

vabile; (telephone number) non ottenibile

unob'trusive a discreto. ~**ly** adv in modo discreto

unof'ficial a non ufficiale. ~**ly** adv ufficiosamente

un'pack vi disfare le valigie ● vt svuotare (parcel); spacchettare (books); ~ **one's case** disfare la valigia

un'paid a da pagare; (work) non retribuito

un'palatable a sgradevole

un'paralleled a senza pari

un'pick vt disfare

un'pleasant a sgradevole; (person) maleducato. ~**ly** adv sgradevolmente; (behave) maleducatamente. ~**ness** n (bad feeling) tensioni fpl

un'plug vt (pt/pp -**plugged**) staccare

un'popular a impopolare

un'precedented a senza precedenti

unpre'dictable a imprevedibile

unpre'meditated a involontario

unpre'pared a impreparato

unpre'tentious a senza pretese

un'principled a senza principi; (behaviour) scorretto

unpro'fessional a non professionale; **it's** ~ è una mancanza di professionalità

un'profitable a non redditizio

un'qualified a non qualificato; (fig: absolute) assoluto

un'questionable a incontestabile

un'quote vi chiudere le virgolette

unravel /ʌn'rævl/ vt (pt/pp -**ravelled**) districare; (in knitting) disfare

un'real a irreale; fam inverosimile

un'reasonable a irragionevole

unre'lated a (fact) senza rapporto (**to** con); (person) non imparentato (**to** con)

unre'liable a inattendibile; (person) inaffidabile, che non dà affidamento

unrequited /ʌnrɪ'kwaɪtɪd/ a non corrisposto

unreservedly /ʌnrɪ'zɜ:vɪdlɪ/ adv senza riserve; (frankly) francamente

un'rest n fermenti mpl

un'rivalled a ineguagliato

un'roll vt srotolare ● vi srotolarsi

un'ruly /ʌn'ru:lɪ/ a indisciplinato

un'safe a pericoloso

un'said a inespresso

un'salted a non salato

unsatis'factory a poco soddisfacente

un'savoury a equivoco

unscathed /ʌn'skeɪðd/ a illeso

un'screw vt svitare

un'scrupulous a senza scrupoli

un'seemly a indecoroso
un'selfish a disinteressato
un'settled a in agitazione; ⟨weather⟩ variabile; ⟨bill⟩ non saldato
unshakeable /ʌn'ʃeɪkəbl/ a categorico
unshaven /ʌn'ʃeɪvn/ a non rasato
unsightly /ʌn'saɪtlɪ/ a brutto
un'skilled a non specializzato. ~ worker n manovale m
un'sociable a scontroso
unso'phisticated a semplice
un'sound a ⟨building, reasoning⟩ poco solido; ⟨advice⟩ poco sensato; of ~ mind malato di mente
unspeakable /ʌn'spiːkəbl/ a indicibile
un'stable a instabile; ⟨mentally⟩ squilibrato
un'steady a malsicuro
un'stuck a come ~ staccarsi; ⟨fam: project⟩ andare a monte
unsuc'cessful a fallimentare; be ~ ⟨in attempt⟩ non aver successo. ~ly adv senza successo
un'suitable a ⟨inappropriate⟩ inadatto; ⟨inconvenient⟩ inopportuno
unsu'specting a fiducioso
unthinkable /ʌn'θɪŋkəbl/ a impensabile
un'tidiness n disordine m
un'tidy a disordinato
un'tie vt slegare
until /ən'tɪl/ prep fino a; not ~ non prima di; ~ the evening fino alla sera; ~ his arrival fino al suo arrivo ● conj finché, fino a quando; not ~ you've seen it non prima che tu l'abbia visto
untimely /ʌn'taɪmlɪ/ a inopportuno; ⟨premature⟩ prematuro
un'tiring a instancabile
un'told a ⟨wealth⟩ incalcolabile; ⟨suffering⟩ indescrivibile; ⟨story⟩ inedito
unto'ward a if nothing ~ happens se non capita un imprevisto
un'true a falso; that's ~ non è vero
unused¹ /ʌn'juːzd/ a non [ancora] usato
unused² /ʌn'juːst/ a be ~ to non essere abituato a
un'usual a insolito. ~ly adv insolitamente
un'veil vt scoprire
un'wanted a indesiderato
un'warranted a ingiustificato
un'welcome a sgradito
un'well a indisposto
unwieldy /ʌn'wiːldɪ/ a ingombrante
un'willing a riluttante. ~ly adv malvolentieri
un'wind v ⟨pt/pp unwound⟩ ● vt svolgere, srotolare ● vi svolgersi, srotolarsi; ⟨fam: relax⟩ rilassarsi
un'wise a imprudente
unwitting /ʌn'wɪtɪŋ/ a involontario; ⟨victim⟩ inconsapevole. ~ly adv involontariamente
un'worthy a non degno
un'wrap vt ⟨pt/pp -wrapped⟩ scartare ⟨present, parcel⟩
un'written a tacito
up /ʌp/ adv su; ⟨not in bed⟩ alzato; ⟨road⟩ smantellato; ⟨theatre curtain, blinds⟩ alzato; ⟨shelves, tent⟩ montato; ⟨notice⟩ affisso; ⟨building⟩ costruito; prices are up i prezzi sono aumentati; be up for sale essere in vendita; up here/there quassù/lassù; time's up tempo scaduto; what's up? fam cosa è successo?; up to ⟨as far as⟩ fino a; be up to essere all'altezza di ⟨task⟩; what's he up to? fam cosa sta facendo?; ⟨plotting⟩ cosa sta combinando?; I'm up to page 100 sono arrivato a pagina 100; feel up to it sentirsela; be one up on sb fam essere in vantaggio su qcno; go up salire; lift up alzare; up against fig alle prese con ● prep su; the cat ran/is up the tree il gatto è salito di corsa/è sull'albero; further up this road più avanti su questa strada; row up the river risalire il fiume; go up the stairs salire su per le scale; be up the pub fam essere al pub; be up on or in sth essere bene informato su qcsa ● n ups and downs npl alti mpl e bassi
'upbringing n educazione f
up'date¹ vt aggiornare
'update² n aggiornamento m
up'grade vt promuovere ⟨person⟩; modernizzare ⟨equipment⟩
upgradeable /ʌp'greɪdəbl/ a Comput upgradabile
upheaval /ʌp'hiːvl/ n scompiglio m
up'hill a in salita; fig arduo ● adv in salita
up'hold vt ⟨pt/pp upheld⟩ sostenere ⟨principle⟩; confermare ⟨verdict⟩
upholster /ʌp'həʊlstə(r)/ vt tappezzare. ~er n tappezziere, -a mf. ~y n tappezzeria f
'upkeep n mantenimento m
up-'market a di qualità
upon /ə'pɒn/ prep su; ~ arriving home una volta arrivato a casa
upper /'ʌpə(r)/ a superiore ● n ⟨of shoe⟩ tomaia f
upper: ~ circle n seconda galleria f. ~ class n alta borghesia f. ~ hand n have the ~ hand avere il sopravvento.

~**most** *a* più alto; **that's ~most in my mind** è la mia preoccupazione principale

upright *a* dritto; ⟨*piano*⟩ verticale; ⟨*honest*⟩ retto ● *n* montante *m*

uprising *n* rivolta *f*

uproar *n* tumulto *m*; **be in an ~** essere in trambusto

up'root *vt* sradicare

up'set[1] *vt* (*pt*/*pp* **upset**, *pres p* **upsetting**) rovesciare; sconvolgere ⟨*plan*⟩; ⟨*distress*⟩ turbare; **get ~ about sth** prendersela per qcsa; **be very ~** essere sconvolto; **have an ~ stomach** avere l'intestino disturbato

'upset[2] *n* scombussolamento *m*

'upshot *n* risultato *m*

upside 'down *adv* sottosopra; **turn ~ ~** capovolgere

up'stairs[1] *adv* [al piano] di sopra

'upstairs[2] *a* del piano superiore

'upstart *n* arrivato, -a *mf*

up'stream *adv* controcorrente

'upsurge *n* (*in sales*) aumento *m* improvviso; ⟨*of enthusiasm, crime*⟩ ondata *f*

'uptake *n* **be slow on the ~** essere lento nel capire; **be quick on the ~** capire le cose al volo

up'tight *a* teso

up-to-'date *a* moderno; ⟨*news*⟩ ultimo; ⟨*records*⟩ aggiornato

'upturn *n* ripresa *f*

upward /'ʌpwəd/ *a* verso l'alto, in su; ~ **slope** salita *f* ● *adv* ~[**s**] verso l'alto; ~**s** oltre

uranium /jʊ'reɪnɪəm/ *n* uranio *m*

urban /'ɜːbən/ *a* urbano

urge /ɜːdʒ/ *n* forte desiderio *m* ● *vt* esortare (**to** a). **urge on** *vt* spronare

urgen|cy /'ɜːdʒənsɪ/ *n* urgenza *f*. ~**t** *a* urgente

urinate /'jʊərɪneɪt/ *vi* urinare

urine /'jʊərɪn/ *n* urina *f*

urn /ɜːn/ *n* urna *f*; ⟨*for tea*⟩ contenitore *m* munito di cannella che si trova nei self-service, mense ecc

us /ʌs/ *pers pron* ci; ⟨*after prep*⟩ noi; **they know us** ci conoscono; **give us**

the money dateci i soldi; **give it to us** datecelo; **they showed it to us** ce l'hanno fatto vedere; **they meant us, not you** intendevano noi, non voi; **it's us** siamo noi; **she hates us** ci odia

US[A] *n[pl] abbr* (**United States [of America]**) U.S.A. *mpl*

usable /'juːzəbl/ *a* usabile

usage /'juːsɪdʒ/ *n* uso *m*

use[1] /juːs/ *n* uso *m*; **be of ~** essere utile; **be of no ~** essere inutile; **make ~ of** usare; ⟨*exploit*⟩ sfruttare; **it is no ~** è inutile; **what's the ~?** a che scopo?

use[2] /juːz/ *vt* usare. **use up** *vt* consumare

used[1] /juːzd/ *a* usato

used[2] /juːst/ *pt* **be ~ to sth** essere abituato a qcsa; **get ~ to** abituarsi a; **he ~ to live here** viveva qui

useful /'juːsfl/ *a* utile. ~**ness** *n* utilità *f*

useless /'juːslɪs/ *a* inutile; ⟨*fam: person*⟩ incapace

user /'juːzə(r)/ *n* utente *mf*. ~-**'friendly** *a* facile da usare

usher /'ʌʃə(r)/ *n Theat* maschera *f*; *Jur* usciere *m*; ⟨*at wedding*⟩ persona *f* che accompagna gli invitati a un matrimonio ai loro posti in chiesa ● **usher in** *vt* fare entrare

usherette /ʌʃə'ret/ *n* maschera *f*

usual /'juːʒʊəl/ *a* usuale; **as ~** come al solito. ~**ly** *adv* di solito

usurp /jʊ'zɜːp/ *vt* usurpare

utensil /jʊ'tensl/ *n* utensile *m*

uterus /'juːtərəs/ *n* utero *m*

utilitarian /jʊtɪlɪ'teərɪən/ *a* funzionale

utility /jʊ'tɪlətɪ/ *n* servizio *m*. ~ **room** *n* stanza *f* in casa privata per il lavaggio, la stiratura dei panni ecc

utilize /'juːtɪlaɪz/ *vt* utilizzare

utmost /'ʌtməʊst/ *a* estremo ● *n* **one's ~** tutto il possibile

utter[1] /'ʌtə(r)/ *a* totale. ~**ly** *adv* completamente

utter[2] *vt* emettere ⟨*sigh, sound*⟩; proferire ⟨*word*⟩. ~**ance** /-əns/ *n* dichiarazione *f*

U-turn /'juː-/ *n Auto* inversione *f* a U; *fig* marcia *f* in dietro

Vv

vacan|cy /'veɪk(ə)nsɪ/ n ⟨job⟩ posto m vacante; ⟨room⟩ stanza f disponibile. **~t** a libero; ⟨position⟩ vacante; ⟨look⟩ assente
vacate /və'keɪt/ vt lasciare libero
vacation /və'keɪʃn/ n Univ & Am vacanza f
vaccinat|e /'væksɪneɪt/ vt vaccinare. **~ion** /-'neɪʃn/ n vaccinazione f
vaccine /'væksiːn/ n vaccino m
vacuum /'vækjʊəm/ n vuoto m ● vt passare l'aspirapolvere in/su. **~ cleaner** n aspirapolvere m inv. **~ flask** n thermos® m inv. **~-packed** a confezionato sottovuoto
vagabond /'vægəbɒnd/ n vagabondo, -a mf
vagina /və'dʒaɪnə/ n Anat vagina f
vagrant /'veɪgrənt/ n vagabondo, -a mf
vague /veɪg/ a vago; ⟨outline⟩ impreciso; ⟨absent-minded⟩ distratto; **I'm still ~ about it** non ho ancora le idee chiare in proposito. **~ly** adv vagamente
vain /veɪn/ a vanitoso; ⟨hope, attempt⟩ vano; **in ~** invano. **~ly** adv vanamente
valentine /'væləntaɪn/ n ⟨card⟩ biglietto m di San Valentino
valiant /'væliənt/ a valoroso
valid /'vælɪd/ a valido. **~ate** vt ⟨confirm⟩ convalidare. **~ity** /və'lɪdətɪ/ n validità f
valley /'vælɪ/ n valle f
valour /'vælə(r)/ n valore m
valuable /'væljʊəbl/ a di valore; fig prezioso. **~s** npl oggetti mpl di valore
valuation /væljʊ'eɪʃn/ n valutazione f
value /'væljuː/ n valore m; ⟨usefulness⟩ utilità f ● vt valutare; ⟨cherish⟩ apprezzare. **~ added tax** n imposta f sul valore aggiunto
valve /vælv/ n valvola f
vampire /'væmpaɪə(r)/ n vampiro m
van /væn/ n furgone m
vandal /'vændl/ n vandalo, -a mf. **~ism** /ɪzm/ n vandalismo m. **~ize** vt vandalizzare
vanilla /və'nɪlə/ n vaniglia f
vanish /'vænɪʃ/ vi svanire
vanity /'vænətɪ/ n vanità f. **~ bag** or **case** n beauty-case m inv

vantage-point /'vɑːntɪdʒ-/ n punto m d'osservazione; fig punto m di vista
vapour /'veɪpə(r)/ n vapore m
variable /'veərɪəbl/ a variabile; ⟨adjustable⟩ regolabile
variance /'veərɪəns/ n **be at ~** essere in disaccordo
variant /'veərɪənt/ n variante f
variation /veərɪ'eɪʃn/ n variazione f
varicose /'værɪkəʊs/ a **~ veins** vene fpl varicose
varied /'veərɪd/ a vario; ⟨diet⟩ diversificato; ⟨life⟩ movimentato
variety /və'raɪətɪ/ n varietà f inv
various /'veərɪəs/ a vario
varnish /'vɑːnɪʃ/ n vernice f; ⟨for nails⟩ smalto m ● vt verniciare; **~ one's nails** mettersi lo smalto
vary /'veərɪ/ vt/i ⟨pt/pp -ied⟩ variare. **~ing** a variabile; ⟨different⟩ diverso
vase /vɑːz/ n vaso m
vast /vɑːst/ a vasto; ⟨difference, amusement⟩ enorme. **~ly** adv ⟨superior⟩ di gran lunga; ⟨different, amused⟩ enormemente
vat /væt/ n tino m
VAT /viː'eɪtiː, væt/ n abbr ⟨**value added tax**⟩ I.V.A. f
vault¹ /vɔːlt/ n ⟨roof⟩ volta f; ⟨in bank⟩ caveau m inv; ⟨tomb⟩ cripta f
vault² n salto m ● vt/i **~** ⟨**over**⟩ saltare
VDU n abbr ⟨**visual display unit**⟩ VDU m
veal /viːl/ n carne f di vitello ● attrib di vitello
veer /vɪə(r)/ vi cambiare direzione; Naut, Auto virare
vegetable /'vedʒtəbl/ n ⟨food⟩ verdura f; ⟨when growing⟩ ortaggio m ● attrib ⟨oil, fat⟩ vegetale
vegetarian /vedʒɪ'teərɪən/ a & n vegetariano, -a mf
vegetat|e /'vedʒɪteɪt/ vi vegetare. **~ion** /-'teɪʃn/ n vegetazione f
vehemen|ce /'viːəmæns/ n veemenza f. **~t** a veemente. **~tly** adv con veemenza
vehicle /'viːɪkl/ n veicolo m; ⟨fig: medium⟩ mezzo m
veil /veɪl/ n velo m ● vt velare

vein /veɪn/ n vena f; (*mood*) umore m; (*manner*) tenore m. **~ed** a venato

Velcro® /'velkrəʊ/ n **~ fastening** chiusura f con velcro*

velocity /vɪ'lɒsətɪ/ n velocità f

velvet /'velvɪt/ n velluto m. **~y** a vellutato

vendetta /ven'detə/ n vendetta f

vending-machine /'vendɪŋ-/ n distributore m automatico

veneer /və'nɪə(r)/ n impiallacciatura f; fig vernice f. **~ed** a impiallacciato

venereal /vɪ'nɪərɪəl/ a **~ disease** malattia f venerea

Venetian /və'niːʃn/ a & n veneziano, -a mf. **v~ blind** n persiana f alla veneziana

vengeance /'vendʒəns/ n vendetta f; **with a ~** fam a più non posso

Venice /'venɪs/ n Venezia f

venison /'venɪsn/ n Culin carne f di cervo

venom /'venəm/ n veleno m. **~ous** /-əs/ a velenoso

vent¹ /vent/ n presa f d'aria; **give ~ to** fig dar libero sfogo a ● vt fig sfogare 〈anger〉

vent² n (*in jacket*) spacco m

ventilat|e /'ventɪleɪt/ vt ventilare. **~ion** /-'leɪʃn/ n ventilazione f; (*installation*) sistema m di ventilazione. **~or** n ventilatore m

ventriloquist /ven'trɪləkwɪst/ n ventriloquo, -a mf

venture /'ventʃə(r)/ n impresa f ● vt azzardare ● vi avventurarsi

venue /'venjuː/ n luogo m (*di convegno, concerto, ecc.*)

veranda /və'rændə/ n veranda f

verb /vɜːb/ n verbo m. **~al** a verbale

verbatim /vɜː'beɪtɪm/ a letterale ● adv parola per parola

verbose /vɜː'bəʊs/ a prolisso

verdict /'vɜːdɪkt/ n verdetto m; (*opinion*) parere m

verge /vɜːdʒ/ n orlo m; **be on the ~ of doing sth** essere sul punto di fare qcsa ● **verge on** vt fig rasentare

verger /'vɜːdʒə(r)/ n sagrestano m

verify /'verɪfaɪ/ vt (pt/pp **-ied**) verificare; (*confirm*) confermare

vermin /'vɜːmɪn/ n animali mpl nocivi

vermouth /'vɜːməθ/ n vermut m inv

vernacular /və'nækjʊlə(r)/ n vernacolo m

versatil|e /'vɜːsətaɪl/ a versatile. **~ity** /-'tɪlətɪ/ n versatilità f

verse /vɜːs/ n verso m; (*of Bible*) versetto m; (*poetry*) versi mpl

versed /vɜːst/ a **~ in** versato in

version /'vɜːʃn/ n versione f

versus /'vɜːsəs/ prep contro

vertebra /'vɜːtɪbrə/ n (pl **-brae** /-briː/) Anat vertebra f

vertical /'vɜːtɪkl/ a & n verticale m

vertigo /'vɜːtɪgəʊ/ n Med vertigine f

verve /vɜːv/ n verve f

very /'verɪ/ adv molto; **~ much** molto; **~ little** pochissimo; **~ many** moltissimi; **~ few** pochissimi; **~ probably** molto probabilmente; **~ well** benissimo; **at the ~ most** tutt'al più; **at the ~ latest** al più tardi ● a **the ~ first** il primissimo; **the ~ thing** proprio ciò che ci vuole; **at the ~ end/beginning** proprio alla fine/all'inizio; **that ~ day** proprio quel giorno; **the ~ thought** la sola idea; **only a ~ little** solo un pochino

vessel /'vesl/ n nave f

vest /vest/ n maglia f della pelle; (*Am: waistcoat*) gilè m inv. **~ed interest** n interesse m personale

vestige /'vestɪdʒ/ n (*of past*) vestigio m

vestment /'vestmənt/ n Relig paramento m

vestry /'vestrɪ/ n sagrestia f

vet /vet/ n veterinario, -a mf ● vt (pt/pp **vetted**) controllare minuziosamente

veteran /'vetərən/ n veterano, -a mf

veterinary /'vetərɪnərɪ/ a veterinario. **~ surgeon** n medico m veterinario

veto /'viːtəʊ/ n (pl **-es**) veto m ● vt proibire

vex /veks/ vt irritare. **~ation** /-'seɪʃn/ n irritazione f. **~ed** a irritato; **~ed question** questione f controversa

VHF n abbr (**very high frequency**) VHF

via /'vaɪə/ prep via; (*by means of*) attraverso

viable /'vaɪəbl/ a 〈*life form, relationship, company*〉 in grado di sopravvivere; 〈*proposition*〉 attuabile

viaduct /'vaɪədʌkt/ n viadotto m

vibrat|e /vaɪ'breɪt/ vi vibrare. **~ion** /-'breɪʃn/ n vibrazione f

vicar /'vɪkə(r)/ n parroco m (*protestante*). **~age** /-rɪdʒ/ n casa f parrocchiale

vicarious /vɪ'keərɪəs/ a indiretto

vice¹ /vaɪs/ n vizio m

vice² n Techn morsa f

vice 'chairman n vicepresidente mf

vice 'president n vicepresidente mf

vice versa /vaɪsɪ'vɜːsə/ adv viceversa

vicinity /vɪ'sɪnətɪ/ n vicinanza f; **in the ~ of** nelle vicinanze di

vicious /'vɪʃəs/ a cattivo; 〈*attack*〉 brutale; ⟨animal⟩ pericoloso. ~ 'circle n circolo m vizioso. ~ly adv ⟨attack⟩ brutalmente

victim /'vɪktɪm/ n vittima f. ~ize vt fare delle rappresaglie contro

victor /'vɪktə(r)/ n vincitore m

victor|ious /vɪk'tɔːrɪəs/ a vittorioso. ~y /'vɪktərɪ/ n vittoria f

video /'vɪdɪəʊ/ n video m; ⟨cassette⟩ videocassetta f; ⟨recorder⟩ videoregistratore m ● attrib video ● vt registrare

video: ~ card n Comput scheda f video. ~ cas'sette n videocassetta f. ~confer-ence n videoconferenza f. ~ game n videogioco m. ~ recorder n videoregistratore m. ~-tape n videocassetta f

vie /vaɪ/ vi ⟨pres p vying⟩ rivaleggiare

view /vjuː/ n vista f; ⟨photographed, painted⟩ veduta f; ⟨opinion⟩ visione f; **look at the ~** guardare il panorama; **in my ~** secondo me; **in ~ of** in considerazione di; **on ~** esposto; **with a ~ to** con l'intenzione di ● vt visitare ⟨house⟩; ⟨consider⟩ considerare ● vi TV guardare. ~er n TV telespettatore, -trice mf; Phot visore m

view: ~finder n Phot mirino m. ~point n punto m di vista

vigil /'vɪdʒɪl/ n veglia f

vigilan|ce /'vɪdʒɪləns/ n vigilanza f. ~t a vigile

vigorous /'vɪgərəs/ a vigoroso

vigour /'vɪgə(r)/ n vigore m

vile /vaɪl/ a disgustoso; ⟨weather⟩ orribile; ⟨temper, mood⟩ pessimo

villa /'vɪlə/ n ⟨for holidays⟩ casa f di villeggiatura

village /'vɪlɪdʒ/ n paese m. ~r n paesano, -a mf

villain /'vɪlən/ n furfante m; ⟨in story⟩ cattivo m

vindicate /'vɪndɪkeɪt/ vt ⟨from guilt⟩ discolpare; **you are ~d** ti sei dimostrato nel giusto

vindictive /vɪn'dɪktɪv/ a vendicativo

vine /vaɪn/ n vite f

vinegar /'vɪnɪgə(r)/ n aceto m

vineyard /'vɪnjɑːd/ n vigneto m

vintage /'vɪntɪdʒ/ a ⟨wine⟩ d'annata ● n ⟨year⟩ annata f

viola /vɪ'əʊlə/ n Mus viola f

violat|e /'vaɪəleɪt/ vt violare. ~ion /-'leɪʃn/ n violazione f

violen|ce /'vaɪələns/ n violenza f. ~t a violento

violet /'vaɪələt/ a violetto ● n ⟨flower⟩ violetta f; ⟨colour⟩ violetto m

violin /vaɪə'lɪn/ n violino m. ~ist n violinista mf

VIP n abbr (very important person) vip mf

virgin /'vɜːdʒɪn/ a vergine ● n vergine f. ~ity /-'dʒɪnətɪ/ n verginità f

Virgo /'vɜːgəʊ/ n Astr Vergine f

viril|e /'vɪraɪl/ a virile. ~ity /-'rɪlətɪ/ n virilità f

virtual /'vɜːtjʊəl/ a effettivo. ~ reality n realtà f virtuale. ~ly adv praticamente

virtue /'vɜːtjuː/ n virtù f inv; ⟨advantage⟩ vantaggio m; **by** or **in ~ of** a causa di

virtuoso /vɜːtʊ'əʊzəʊ/ n ⟨pl -si '-zɪː⟩ virtuoso m

virtuous /'vɜːtjʊəs/ a virtuoso

virulent /'vɪrʊlənt/ a virulento

virus /'vaɪərəs/ n virus m inv

visa /'viːzə/ n visto m

vis-à-vis /viːzɑː'viː/ prep rispetto a

viscount /'vaɪkaʊnt/ n visconte m

viscous /'vɪskəs/ a vischioso

visibility /vɪzə'bɪlətɪ/ n visibilità f

visibl|e /'vɪzəbl/ a visibile. ~y adv visibilmente

vision /'vɪʒn/ n visione f; ⟨sight⟩ vista f

visit /'vɪzɪt/ n visita f ● vt andare a trovare ⟨person⟩; andare da ⟨doctor etc⟩; visitare ⟨town, building⟩. ~ing hours npl orario m delle visite. ~or n ospite mf; ⟨of town, museum⟩ visitatore, -trice mf; ⟨in hotel⟩ cliente mf

visor /'vaɪzə(r)/ n visiera f; Auto parasole m

vista /'vɪstə/ n ⟨view⟩ panorama m

visual /'vɪzjʊəl/ a visivo. ~ aids npl supporto m visivo. ~ 'display unit n visualizzatore m ~ly adv visualmente; ~ly handicapped non vedente

visualize /'vɪzjʊəlaɪz/ vt visualizzare

vital /'vaɪtl/ a vitale. ~ity /vaɪ'tælətɪ/ n vitalità f. ~ly /'vaɪtlɪ/ adv estremamente

vitamin /'vɪtəmɪn/ n vitamina f

vivaci|ous /vɪ'veɪʃəs/ a vivace. ~ty /-'væsətɪ/ n vivacità f

vivid /'vɪvɪd/ a vivido. ~ly adv in modo vivido

vocabulary /və'kæbjʊlərɪ/ n vocabolario m; ⟨list⟩ glossario m

vocal /'vəʊkl/ a vocale; ⟨vociferous⟩ eloquente ~ cords npl corde fpl vocali

vocalist /'vəʊkəlɪst/ n vocalista mf

vocation /və'keɪʃn/ n vocazione f. ~al a di orientamento professionale

vociferous /və'sɪfərəs/ a vociante

vodka /'vɒdkə/ n vodka f inv

vogue /vəʊg/ n moda f; **in ~** in voga

voice /vɔɪs/ n voce f ● vt esprimere.
~**mail** n posta f elettronica vocale

void /vɔɪd/ a (not valid) nullo; ~ **of** privo di ● n vuoto m

volatile /'vɒlətaɪl/ a volatile; (person) volubile

volcanic /vɒl'kænɪk/ a vulcanico

volcano /vɒl'keɪnəʊ/ n vulcano m

volition /və'lɪʃn/ n **of his own** ~ di sua spontanea volontà

volley /'vɒlɪ/ n (of gunfire) raffica f; Tennis volée f inv

volt /vəʊlt/ n volt m inv. ~**age** /-ɪdʒ/ n Electr voltaggio m

voluble /'vɒljʊbl/ a loquace

volume /'vɒljuːm/ n volume m; (of work, traffic) quantità f inv. ~ **control** n volume m

voluntar|y /'vɒləntərɪ/ a volontario. ~**y work** n volontariato m. ~**ily** adv volontariamente

volunteer /vɒlən'tɪə(r)/ n volontario, -a mf ● vt offrire volontariamente (information) ● vi offrirsi volontario; Mil arruolarsi come volontario

voluptuous /və'lʌptjʊəs/ a voluttuoso

vomit /'vɒmɪt/ n vomito m ● vt/i vomitare

voracious /və'reɪʃəs/ a vorace

vot|e /vəʊt/ n voto m; (ballot) votazione f; (right) diritto m di voto; **take a ~e on** votare su ● vi votare ● vt ~**e sb president** eleggere qcno presidente. ~**er** n elettore, -trice mf. ~**ing** n votazione f

vouch /vaʊtʃ/ vi ~ **for** garantire per. ~**er** n buono m

vow /vaʊ/ n voto m ● vt giurare

vowel /'vaʊəl/ n vocale f

voyage /'vɔɪdʒ/ n viaggio m [marittimo]; (in space) viaggio m [nello spazio]

vulgar /'vʌlgə(r)/ a volgare. ~**ity** /-'gærətɪ/ n volgarità f inv

vulnerable /'vʌlnərəbl/ a vulnerabile

vulture /'vʌltʃə(r)/ n avvoltoio m

vying /'vaɪɪŋ/ see **vie**

Ww

wad /wɒd/ n batuffolo m; (bundle) rotolo m. ~**ding** n ovatta f

waddle /'wɒdl/ vi camminare ondeggiando

wade /weɪd/ vi guadare; ~ **through** fam procedere faticosamente in (book)

wafer /'weɪfə(r)/ n cialda f, wafer m inv; Relig ostia f

waffle[1] /'wɒfl/ vi fam blaterare

waffle[2] n Culin cialda f

waft /wɒft/ vt trasportare ● vi diffondersi

wag /wæg/ v (pt/pp **wagged**) ● vt agitare ● vi agitarsi

wage[1] /weɪdʒ/ vt dichiarare (war); lanciare (campaign)

wage[2] n, & ~**s** pl salario msg. ~ **packet** n busta f paga

waggle /'wægl/ vt dimenare ● vi dimenarsi

wagon /'wægən/ n carro m; Rail vagone m merci

wail /weɪl/ n piagnucolio m; (of wind) lamento m; (of baby) vagito m ● vi piagnucolare; (wind:) lamentarsi; (baby:) vagire

waist /weɪst/ n vita f. ~**coat** /'weɪskəʊt/ n gilè m inv; (of man's suit) panciotto m. ~**line** n vita f

wait /weɪt/ n attesa f; **lie in** ~ **for** appostarsi per sorprendere ● vi aspettare; ~ **for** aspettare ● vt ~ **one's turn** aspettare il proprio turno. **wait on** vt servire

waiter /'weɪtə(r)/ n cameriere m

waiting /'weɪtɪŋ/ n ~-**list** n lista f d'attesa. ~-**room** n sala f d'aspetto

waitress /'weɪtrɪs/ n cameriera f

waive /weɪv/ vt rinunciare a (claim); non tener conto di (rule)

wake[1] /weɪk/ n veglia f funebre ● v (pt **woke**, pp **woken**) ~ **[up]** ● vt svegliare ● vi svegliarsi

wake[2] n Naut scia f; **in the** ~ **of** fig nella scia di

waken /'weɪkn/ vt svegliare ● vi svegliarsi

Wales /weɪlz/ n Galles m

walk /wɔːk/ n passeggiata f; (gait) andatura f; (path) sentiero m; **go for a** ~ andare a fare una passeggiata ● vi camminare; (as opposed to drive etc) andare a piedi; (*ramble*) passeggiare ● *vt* portare a spasso (*dog*); percorrere (*streets*). **walk out** *vi* (*husband, employee:*) andarsene; (*workers:*) scioperare. **walk out on** *vt* lasciare

walker /'wɔːkə(r)/ *n* camminatore, -trice *mf*; (*rambler*) escursionista *mf*

walking /'wɔːkɪŋ/ *n* camminare *m*; (*rambling*) fare *m* delle escursioni. **~-stick** *n* bastone *m* da passeggio

'Walkman® *n* Walkman *m inv*

walk: **~-out** *n* sciopero *m*. **~-over** *n fig* vittoria *f* facile

wall /wɔːl/ *n* muro *m*; **go to the ~** *fam* andare a rotoli; **drive sb up the ~** *fam* far diventare matto qcno ● **wall up** *vt* murare

wallet /'wɒlɪt/ *n* portafoglio *m*

wallop /'wɒləp/ *n fam* colpo *m* ● *vt* (*pt/pp* **walloped**) *fam* colpire

wallow /'wɒləʊ/ *vi* sguazzare; (*in self-pity, grief*) crogiolarsi

'wallpaper *n* tappezzeria *f* ● *vt* tappezzare

walnut /'wɔːlnʌt/ *n* noce *f*

waltz /wɔːlts/ *n* valzer *m inv* ● *vi* ballare il valzer

wan /wɒn/ *a* esangue

wand /wɒnd/ *n* (*magic ~*) bacchetta *f* [magica]

wander /'wɒndə(r)/ *vi* girovagare; (*fig: digress*) divagare. **wander about** *vi* andare a spasso

wane /weɪn/ *n* **be on the ~** essere in fase calante ● *vi* calare

wangle /'wæŋgl/ *vt fam* rimediare (*invitation, holiday*)

want /wɒnt/ *n* (*hardship*) bisogno *m*; (*lack*) mancanza *f* ● *vt* volere; (*need*) aver bisogno di; **~ [to have]** sth volere qcsa; **~ to do** sth voler fare qcsa; **we ~ to stay** vogliamo rimanere; **I ~ you to go** voglio che tu vada; **it ~s painting** ha bisogno d'essere dipinto; **you ~ to learn to swim** bisogna che impari a nuotare ● *vi* **~ for** mancare di. **~ed** *a* ricercato. **~ing** *a* **be ~ing** mancare; **be ~ing in** mancare di

wanton /'wɒntən/ *a* (*cruelty, neglect*) gratuito; (*morally*) debosciato

war /wɔː(r)/ *n* guerra *f*; *fig* lotta *f* (*on* contro); **at ~** in guerra

ward /wɔːd/ *n* (*in hospital*) reparto *m*; (*child*) minore *m* sotto tutela ● **ward off** *vt* evitare; parare (*blow*)

warden /'wɔːdn/ *n* guardiano, -a *mf*

warder /'wɔːdə(r)/ *n* guardia *f* carceraria

wardrobe /'wɔːdrəʊb/ *n* guardaroba *m*

warehouse /'weəhaʊs/ *n* magazzino *m*

war: **~fare** *n* guerra *f*. **~head** *n* testata *f*

warily /'weərɪlɪ/ *adv* cautamente

warlike /'wɔːlaɪk/ *a* bellicoso

warm /wɔːm/ *a* caldo; (*welcome*) caloroso; **be ~** (*person:*) aver caldo; **it is ~** (*weather*) fa caldo ● *vt* scaldare. **warm up** *vt* scaldare ● *vi* scaldarsi; *fig* animarsi. **~-hearted** *a* espansivo. **~ly** *adv* (*greet*) calorosamente; (*dress*) in modo pesante

warmth /wɔːmθ/ *n* calore *m*

warn /wɔːn/ *vt* avvertire. **~ing** *n* avvertimento *m*; (*advance notice*) preavviso *m*

warp /wɔːp/ *vt* deformare; *fig* distorcere ● *vi* deformarsi

war-path *n* **on the ~** sul sentiero di guerra

warped /wɔːpt/ *a fig* contorto; (*sexuality*) deviato; (*view*) distorto

warrant /'wɒrənt/ *n* (*for arrest, search*) mandato *m* ● *vt* (*justify*) giustificare; (*guarantee*) garantire

warranty /'wɒrəntɪ/ *n* garanzia *f*

warring /'wɔːrɪŋ/ *a* in guerra

warrior /'wɒrɪə(r)/ *n* guerriero, -a *mf*

'warship *n* nave *f* da guerra

wart /wɔːt/ *n* porro *m*

'wartime *n* tempo *m* di guerra

wary /'weərɪ/ *a* (**-ier, -iest**) (*careful*) cauto; (*suspicious*) diffidente

was /wɒz/ *see* **be**

wash /wɒʃ/ *n* lavata *f*; (*clothes*) bucato *m*; (*in washing machine*) lavaggio *m*; **have a ~** darsi una lavata ● *vt* lavare; (*sea:*) bagnare; **~ one's hands** lavarsi le mani ● *vi* lavarsi. **wash out** *vt* sciacquare (*soap*); sciacquarsi (*mouth*). **wash up** *vt* lavare ● *vi* lavare i piatti; *Am* lavarsi

washable /'wɒʃəbl/ *a* lavabile

wash: **~-basin** *n* lavandino *m*. **~ cloth** *n Am* guanto *m* da bagno

washed 'out *a* (*faded*) scolorito; (*tired*) spossato

washer /'wɒʃə(r)/ *n* Techn guarnizione *f*; (*machine*) lavatrice *f*

washing /'wɒʃɪŋ/ *n* bucato *m*. **~-machine** *n* lavatrice *f*. **~-powder** *n* detersivo *m*. **~-'up** *n* **do the ~-up** lavare i piatti. **~-'up liquid** *n* detersivo *m* per i piatti

wash: **~-out** *n* disastro *m*. **~-room** *n* bagno *m*

wasp /wɒsp/ *n* vespa *f*

wastage /'weɪstɪdʒ/ *n* perdita *f*

waste /weɪst/ *n* spreco *m*; (*rubbish*) ri-

fiuto *m*; ~ **of time** perdita *f* di tempo
● *a* (*product*) di scarto; (*land*) desolato;
lay ~ devastare ● *vt* sprecare. **waste
away** *vi* deperire

waste: **~-di'sposal unit** *n* eliminatore
m di rifiuti. **~-ful** *a* dispendioso. ~ '**paper**
n carta *f* straccia. **~-'paper basket** *n* cestino *m* per la carta [straccia]

watch /wɒtʃ/ *n* guardia *f*; (*period of
duty*) turno *m* di guardia; (*timepiece*)
orologio *m*; **be on the** ~ stare all'erta
● *vt* guardare (*film, match, television*);
(*be careful of, look after*) stare attento a
● *vi* guardare. **watch out** *vi* (*be careful*)
stare attento (**for** a). **watch out for** *vt*
(*look for*) fare attenzione all'arrivo di
(*person*)

watch: **~-dog** *n* cane *m* da guardia.
~-ful *a* attento. **~-maker** *n* orologiaio, -a
mf. **~-man** *n* guardiano *m*. **~-strap** *n*
cinturino *m* dell'orologio. **~-word** *n*
motto *m*

water /'wɔ:tə(r)/ *n* acqua *f* ● *vt* annaf-
fiare (*garden, plant*); (*dilute*) annacqua-
re ● *vi* (*eyes:*) lacrimare; **my mouth
was ~ing** avevo l'acquolina in bocca.
water down *vt* diluire; *fig* attenuare

water: **~-colour** *n* acquerello *m*.
~cress *n* crescione *m*. **~fall** *n* cascata *f*

'**watering-can** *n* annaffiatoio *m*

water: **~-lily** *n* ninfea *f*. **~-logged** *a* inzuppato. **~-main** *n* conduttura *f* dell'acqua. ~ **polo** *n* pallanuoto *f*. **~-power** *n*
energia *f* idraulica. **~-proof** *a* impermeabile. **~-shed** *n* spartiacque *m* *inv*; *fig*
svolta *f*. **~-skiing** *n* sci *m* nautico.
~-tight *a* stagno; *fig* irrefutabile. **~-way**
n canale *m* navigabile

watery /'wɔ:tərɪ/ *a* acquoso; (*eyes*) la-
crimoso

watt /wɒt/ *n* watt *m* *inv*

wave /weɪv/ *n* onda *f*; (*gesture*) cenno
m; *fig* ondata *f* ● *vt* agitare; ~ **one's
hand** agitare la mano ● *vi* far segno;
(*flag:*) sventolare. **~-length** *n* lunghezza
f d'onda

waver /'weɪvə(r)/ *vi* vacillare; (*hesitate*)
esitare

wavy /'weɪvɪ/ *a* ondulato

wax¹ /wæks/ *vi* (*moon:*) crescere; (*fig:
become*) diventare

wax² *n* cera *f*; (*in ear*) cerume *m* ● *vt*
dare la cera a. **~-works** *n* museo *m* delle
cere

way /weɪ/ *n* percorso *m*; (*direction*) direzione *f*; (*manner, method*) modo *m*; **~s** *pl*
(*customs*) abitudini *fpl*; **be in the** ~ essere in mezzo; **on the** ~ **to Rome** an-

dando a Roma; **I'll do it on the** ~ lo
faccio mentre vado; **it's on my** ~ è sul
mio percorso; **a long** ~ **off** lontano;
this ~ da questa parte; (*like this*) così;
by the ~ a proposito; **by** ~ **of** come;
(*via*) via; **either** ~ (*whatever we do*) in
un modo o nell'altro; **in some** ~s sotto
certi aspetti; **in a** ~ in un certo senso;
in a bad ~ (*person*) molto grave; **out of
the** ~ fuori mano; **under** ~ in corso;
lead the ~ far strada; *fig* aprire la strada; **make** ~ far posto (**for** a); **give** ~
Auto dare la precedenza; **go out of
one's** *fig* scomodarsi (**to** per); **get
one's** [**own**] ~ averla vinta ● *adv* ~
behind molto indietro. ~ '**in** *n* entrata *f*

way-lay *vt* (*pt/pp* **-laid**) aspettare al
varco (*person*)

way '**out** *n* uscita *f*; *fig* via *f* d'uscita

way-'out *a fam* eccentrico

wayward /'weɪwəd/ *a* capriccioso

WC *n abbr* WC; **the WC** il gabinetto

we /wi:/ *pers pron* noi; **we're the last**
siamo gli ultimi; **they're going, but
we're not** loro vanno, ma noi no

weak /wi:k/ *a* debole; (*liquid*) leggero.
~en *vt* indebolire ● *vi* indebolirsi.
~ling *n* smidollato, -a *mf*. **~ness** *n* debolezza *f*; (*liking*) debole *m*

wealth /welθ/ *n* ricchezza *f*; *fig* gran
quantità *f*. **~-y** *a* (**-ier, -iest**) ricco

wean /wi:n/ *vt* svezzare

weapon /'wepən/ *n* arma *f*

wear /weə(r)/ *n* (*clothing*) abbigliamento *m*; **for everyday** ~ da portare tutti i
giorni; ~ [**and tear**] usura *f* ● *v* (*pt
wore, pp worn*) ● *vt* portare; (*damage*)
consumare; ~ **a hole in sth** bucare
qcsa fino a fare un buco; **what shall I
~?** cosa mi metto? ● *vi* consumarsi;
(*last*) durare. **wear off** *vi* scomparire;
(*effect:*) finire. **wear out** *vt* consumare
[fino in fondo]; (*exhaust*) estenuare ● *vi*
estenuarsi

wearable /'weərəbl/ *a* portabile

wear-y /'wɪərɪ/ *a* (**-ier, -iest**) sfinito ● *v*
(*pt/pp* **wearied**) ● *vt* sfinire ● *vi* ~ **y of**
stancarsi di. **~-ily** *adv* stancamente

weasel /'wi:zl/ *n* donnola *f*

weather /'weðə(r)/ *n* tempo *m*; **in this**
~ con questo tempo; **under the** ~ *fam*
giù di corda ● *vt* sopravvivere a (*storm*)

weather: **~-beaten** (*face*) segnato
dalle intemperie. **~-cock** *n* gallo *m*
segnavento. ~ **forecast** *n* previsioni
fpl del tempo

weave¹ /wi:v/ *vi* (*pt/pp* **weav**
(*move*) zigzagare

weave² n tessuto m ● vt (pt **wove**, pp **woven**) tessere; intrecciare (flowers etc); intrecciare la fila di (story etc). **~r** n tessitore, -trice mf

web /web/ n rete f; (of spider) ragnatela f. **~bed feet** npl piedi mpl palmati. **~ page** n Comput pagina f web; **~ site** n Comput sito m web

wed /wed/ vt (pt/pp **wedded**) sposare ● vi sposarsi. **~ding** n matrimonio m

wedding: ~ cake n torta f nuziale. **~ day** n giorno m del matrimonio. **~ dress** n vestito m da sposa. **~ring** n fede f

wedge /wedʒ/ n zeppa f; (for splitting wood) cuneo m; (of cheese) fetta f ● vt (fix) fissare

wedlock /'wedlɒk/ n **born out of ~** nato fuori dal matrimonio

Wednesday /'wenzdeɪ/ n mercoledì m inv

wee¹ /wi:/ a fam piccolo

wee² vi fam fare la pipi

weed /wi:d/ n erbaccia f; (fam: person) mollusco m ● vt estirpare le erbacce da ● vi estirpare le erbacce. **weed out** vt fig eliminare

'**weed-killer** n erbicida m

weedy /'wi:dɪ/ a fam mingherlino

week /wi:k/ n settimana f. **~day** n giorno m feriale. **~end** n fine m settimana

weekly /'wi:klɪ/ a settimanale ● n settimanale m ● adv settimanalmente

weep /wi:p/ vi (pt/pp **wept**) piangere

weigh /weɪ/ vt/i pesare; **~ anchor** levare l'ancora. **weigh down** vt fig piegare. **weigh up** vt fig soppesare; valutare (person)

weight /weɪt/ n peso m; **put on/lose ~** ingrassare/dimagrire.   **~ing** n (allowance) indennità f inv

weight: ~lessness n assenza f di gravità. **~-lifting** n sollevamento m pesi

weighty /'weɪtɪ/ a (-ier, -iest) pesante; (important) di un certo peso

weir /wɪə(r)/ n chiusa f

weird /wɪəd/ a misterioso; (bizarre) bizzarro

welcome /'welkəm/ a benvenuto; **you're ~!** prego!; **you're ~ to have it/to come** prendilo/vieni pure ● n accoglienza f ● vt accogliere; (appreciate) gradire

weld /weld/ vt saldare. **~er** n saldatore m

welfare /'welfeə(r)/ n benessere m; (aid) assistenza f. **W~ State** n Stato m assistenziale

well¹ /wel/ n pozzo m; (of staircase) tromba f

well² adv (**better, best**) bene; **as ~** anche; **as ~ as** (in addition) oltre a; **~ done!** bravo!; **very ~** benissimo ● a he **is not ~** non sta bene; **get ~ soon!** guarisci presto! ● int beh!; **~ I never!** ma va!

well: ~-behaved a educato. **~-being** n benessere m. **~-bred** a beneducato. **~-heeled** a fam danaroso

wellingtons /'welɪŋtənz/ npl stivali mpl di gomma

well: ~-known a famoso. **~-meaning** a con buone intenzioni. **~-meant** a con le migliori intenzioni. **~-off** a benestante. **~-read** a colto. **~-to-do** a ricco

Welsh /welʃ/ a & n gallese; (language) gallese m; **the ~** pl i galesi. **~man** n gallese m. **~ rabbit** n toast m inv al formaggio

went /went/ see **go**

wept /wept/ see **weep**

were /wɜ:(r)/ see **be**

west /west/ n ovest m; **to the ~ of** a ovest di; **the W~** l'Occidente m ● a occidentale ● adv verso occidente; **go ~** fam andare in malora. **~erly** a verso ovest; occidentale (wind). **~ern** a occidentale ● n western m inv

West: ~ 'Germany n Germania f Occidentale. **~ 'Indian** a & n antillese mf. **~ 'Indies** /'ɪndɪz/ npl Antille fpl

'**westward[s]** /-wəd[z]/ adv verso ovest

wet /wet/ a (**wetter, wettest**) bagnato; fresco (paint); (rainy) piovoso; (fam: person) smidollato; **get ~** bagnarsi ● vt (pt/pp **wet, wetted**) bagnare. **~ blanket** n guastafeste mf inv

whack /wæk/ n fam colpo m ● vt fam dare un colpo a. **~ed** a fam stanco morto. **~ing** a (fam: huge) enorme

whale /weɪl/ n balena f; **have a ~ of a time** fam divertirsi un sacco

wham /wæm/ int bum

wharf /wɔ:f/ n banchina f

what /wɒt/ pron che, [che] cosa; **~ for?** perché?; **~ is that for?** a che cosa serve?; **~ is it?** (what do you want) cosa c'è?; **~ is it like?** com'è?; **~ is your name?** come ti chiami?; **~ is the weather like?** com'è il tempo?; **~ is he talking about?** di cosa parla il film?; **~ is he talking about?** di cosa sta parlando?; **he asked me ~ she had said** mi ha chiesto cosa ha detto; **~ about going to the cinema?** e se andassimo al cinema?; ~ **about the children?** (*what will they do*) e i bambini?; ~ **if it rains?** e se piove? ●*a* quale, che; **take ~ books you want** prendi tutti i libri che vuoi; ~ **kind of a** che tipo di; **at ~ time?** a che ora? ●*adv* che; ~ **a lovely day!** che bella giornata! ●*int* ~! [che] cosa!; ~**?** [che] cosa?

what'ever *a* qualunque ●*pron* qualsiasi cosa; ~ **is it?** cos'è?; ~ **he does** qualsiasi cosa faccia; ~ **happens** qualunque cosa succeda; **nothing ~** proprio niente

whatso'ever *a & pron* = **whatever**

wheat /wi:t/ *n* grano *m*, frumento *m*

wheedle /'wi:d(ə)l/ *vt* ~ **sth out of sb** ottenere qcsa da qualcuno con le lusinghe

wheel /wi:l/ *n* ruota *f*; (*steering* ~) volante *m*; **at the** ~ al volante ●*vt* (*push*) spingere ●*vi* (*circle*) ruotare; ~ **[round]** ruotare

wheel: ~**barrow** *n* carriola *f*. ~**chair** *n* sedia *f* a rotelle. ~**-clamp** *n* ceppo *m* bloccaruote

wheeze /wi:z/ *vi* ansimare

when /wen/ *adv & conj* quando; **the day** ~ il giorno in cui; ~ **swimming/ reading** nuotando/leggendo

when'ever *adv & conj* in qualsiasi momento; (*every time that*) ogni volta che; ~ **did it happen?** quando è successo?

where /weə(r)/ *adv & conj* dove; **the street** ~ **I live** la via in cui abito; ~ **do you come from?** da dove vieni?

whereabouts¹ /weərə'baʊts/ *adv* dove

'whereabouts² *n* **nobody knows his** ~ nessuno sa dove si trova

where'as *conj* dal momento che; (*in contrast*) mentre

where'by *adv* attraverso il quale

whereu'pon *adv* dopo di che

wher'ever *adv & conj* dovunque; ~ **is he?** dov'è mai?; ~ **possible** dovunque sia possibile

whet /wet/ *vt* (*pt/pp* **whetted**) aguzzare ⟨*appetite*⟩

whether /'weðə(r)/ *conj* se; ~ **you like it or not** che ti piaccia o no

which /wɪtʃ/ *a & pron* quale; ~ **one?** quale?; ~ **one of you?** chi di voi?; ~ **way?** (*direction*) in che direzione? ●*rel pron* (*object*) che; ~ **he does frequently** cosa che fa spesso; **after** ~ dopo di che; **in** ~ su/in cui

which'ever *a & pron* qualunque; ~ **it is** qualunque sia; ~ **one of you** chiunque tra voi

whiff /wɪf/ *n* zaffata *f*; **have a** ~ **of sth** odorare qcsa

while /waɪl/ *n* **a long** ~ un bel po'; **a little** ~ un po' ●*conj* mentre; (*as long as*) finché; (*although*) sebbene ● **while away** *vt* passare ⟨*time*⟩

whilst /waɪlst/ *conj see* **while**

whim /wɪm/ *n* capriccio *m*

whimper /'wɪmpə(r)/ *vi* piagnucolare; ⟨*dog:*⟩ mugolare

whimsical /'wɪmzɪkl/ *a* capriccioso; ⟨*story*⟩ fantasioso

whine /waɪn/ *n* lamento *m*; (*of dog*) guaito *m* ●*vi* lamentarsi; ⟨*dog:*⟩ guaire

whip /wɪp/ *n* frusta *f*; (*Pol: person*) parlamentare *mf* incaricato, -a di assicurarsi della presenza dei membri del suo partito alle votazioni ●*vt* (*pt/pp* **whipped**) frustare; *Culin* sbattere; (*snatch*) afferrare; (*fam: steal*) fregare. **whip up** *vt* (*incite*) stimolare; *fam* improvvisare ⟨*meal*⟩. ~**ped 'cream** *n* panna *f* montata

whirl /wɜ:l/ *n* (*movement*) rotazione *f*; **my mind's in a** ~ ho le idee confuse ●*vi* girare rapidamente ●*vt* far girare rapidamente. ~ **pool** *n* vortice *m*. ~ **wind** *n* turbine *m*

whirr /wɜ:(r)/ *vi* ronzare

whisk /wɪsk/ *n Culin* frullino *m* ●*vt Culin* frullare. **whisk away** *vt* portare via

whisker /'wɪskə(r)/ *n* ~**s** baffi *mpl*; (*on man's face*) basette *fpl*; **by a** ~ per un pelo

whisky /'wɪski/ *n* whisky *m inv*

whisper /'wɪspə(r)/ *n* sussurro *m*; (*rumour*) diceria *f* ●*vt/i* sussurrare

whistle /'wɪsl/ *n* fischio *m*; (*instrument*) fischietto *m* ●*vt* fischiare ●*vi* fischiettare; ⟨*referee*⟩ fischiare

white /waɪt/ *a* bianco; **go** ~ (*pale*) sbiancare ●*n* bianco *m*; (*of egg*) albume *m*; (*person*) bianco, -a *mf*

white: ~**'coffee** *n* caffè *m inv* macchiato. ~**-'collar worker** *n* colletto *m* bianco

'Whitehall *n* strada *f* di Londra, sede degli uffici del governo britannico; *fig* amministrazione *f* britannica

white 'lie *n* bugia *f* pietosa

whiten /'waɪtn/ *vt* imbiancare ●*vi* sbiancare

whiteness /'waɪtnɪs/ *n* bianchezza *f*

'whitewash *n* intonaco *m*; *fig* copertura *f* ●*vt* dare una mano d'intonaco a; *fig* coprire

Whitsun /'wɪtsn/ *n* Pentecoste *f*

whittle /'wɪtl/ *vt* ~ **down** ridurre

whiz[z] /wɪz/ vi (pt/pp **whizzed**) sibilare. **~-kid** n fam giovane m prodigio

who /hu:/ inter pron chi ● rel pron che; **the children, ~ were all tired,...** i bambini, che erano tutti stanchi,...

who'ever pron chiunque; **~ he is** chiunque sia; **~ can that be?** chi può mai essere?

whole /həʊl/ a tutto; (not broken) intatto; **the ~ truth** tutta la verità; **the ~ world** il mondo intero; **the ~ lot** (everything) tutto; (pl) tutti; **the ~ lot of you** tutti voi ● n tutto m; **as a ~** nell'insieme; **on the ~** tutto considerato; **the ~ of Italy** tutta l'Italia

whole: ~food n cibo m macrobiotico. **~-'hearted** a di tutto cuore. **~meal** a integrale

'wholesale a & adv all'ingrosso; fig in massa. **~r** n grossista mf

wholesome /'həʊlsəm/ a sano

wholly /'həʊlɪ/ adv completamente

whom /hu:m/ rel pron che; **the man ~ I saw** l'uomo che ho visto; **to/with ~** a/con cui ● inter pron chi; **to ~ did you speak?** con chi hai parlato?

whooping cough /'hu:pɪŋ/ n pertosse f

whopping /'wɒpɪŋ/ a fam enorme

whore /hɔ:(r)/ n puttana f vulg

whose /hu:z/ rel pron il cui; **people ~ name begins with D** le persone i cui nomi cominciano con la D ● inter pron di chi; **~ is that?** di chi è quello? ● a **~ car did you use?** di chi è la macchina che hai usato?

why /waɪ/ adv (inter) perché; **the reason ~** la ragione per cui; **that's ~** per questo ● int diamine

wick /wɪk/ n stoppino m

wicked /'wɪkɪd/ a cattivo; (mischievous) malizioso

wicker /'wɪkə(r)/ n vimini mpl ● attrib di vimini

wide /waɪd/ a largo; (experience, knowledge) vasto; (difference) profondo; (far from target) lontano; **10 cm ~** largo 10 cm; **how ~ is it?** quanto è largo? ● adv (off target) lontano dal bersaglio; **~ awake** del tutto sveglio; **~ open** spalancato; **far and ~** in lungo e in largo. **~ly** adv largamente; (known, accepted) generalmente; (different) profondamente

widen /'waɪdn/ vt allargare ● vi allargarsi

'widespread a diffuso

widow /'wɪdəʊ/ n vedova f. **~ed** a vedovo. **~er** n vedovo m

width /wɪdθ/ n larghezza f; (of material) altezza f

wield /wi:ld/ vt maneggiare; esercitare (power)

wife /waɪf/ n (pl **wives**) moglie f

wig /wɪg/ n parrucca f

wiggle /'wɪgl/ vi dimenarsi ● vt dimenare

wild /waɪld/ a selvaggio; (animal, flower) selvatico; (furious) furibondo; (applause) fragoroso; (idea) folle; (with joy) pazzo; (guess) azzardato; **be ~ about** (keen on) andare pazzo per ● adv **run ~** crescere senza controllo ● n **in the ~** allo stato naturale; **the ~s** pl le zone sperdute

wilderness /'wɪldənɪs/ n deserto m; (fig: garden) giungla f

'wildfire n **spread like ~** allargarsi a macchia d'olio

wild: ~'goose chase n ricerca f inutile. **~life** n animali mpl selvatici

wilful /'wɪlfl/ a intenzionale; (person, refusal) ostinato. **~ly** adv intenzionalmente; (refuse) ostinatamente

will¹ /wɪl/ v aux **he ~ arrive tomorrow** arriverà domani; **I won't tell him** non glielo dirò; **you ~ be back soon, won't you?** tornerai presto, no?; **he ~ be there, won't he?** sarà là, no?; **she ~ be there by now** sarà là ormai; **~ you go?** (do you intend to go) pensi di andare?; **~ you go to the baker's and buy...?** puoi andare dal panettiere a comprare...?; **~ you be quiet!** vuoi stare calmo!; **~ you have some wine?** vuoi del vino?; **the engine won't start** la macchina non parte

will² n volontà f inv; (document) testamento m

willing /'wɪlɪŋ/ a disposto; (eager) volonteroso. **~ly** adv volentieri. **~ness** n buona volontà f

willow /'wɪləʊ/ n salice m

'will-power n forza f di volontà

willy-'nilly adv (at random) a casaccio; (wanting to or not) volente o nolente

wilt /wɪlt/ vi appassire

wily /'waɪlɪ/ a (-ier, -iest) astuto

wimp /wɪmp/ n rammollito, -a mf

win /wɪn/ n vittoria f; **have a ~** riportare una vittoria ● v (pt/pp **won**; pres p **winning**) ● vt vincere; conquistare (fame) ● vi vincere. **win over** vt convincere

wince /wɪns/ *vi* contrarre il viso

winch /wɪntʃ/ *n* argano *m*

wind¹ /wɪnd/ *n* vento *m*; *(breath)* fiato *m*; *(fam: flatulence)* aria *f*; **get/have the ~ up** *fam* aver fifa; **get ~ of** aver sentore di; **in the ~** nell'aria ● *vt* ~ **sb** lasciare qcno senza fiato

wind² /waɪnd/ *v* (*pt/pp* **wound**) ● *vt* *(wrap)* avvolgere; *(move by turning)* far girare; caricare *(clock)* ● *vi* *(road:)* serpeggiare. **wind up** *vt* caricare *(clock)*; concludere *(proceedings)*; *fam* prendere in giro *(sb)*

wind /wɪnd/: **~fall** *n fig* fortuna *f* inaspettata

winding /'waɪndɪŋ/ *a* tortuoso

wind: ~ **instrument** *n* strumento *m* a fiato. **~mill** *n* mulino *m* a vento

window /'wɪndəʊ/ *n* finestra *f*; *(of car)* finestrino *m*; *(of shop)* vetrina *f*

window: **~-box** *n* cassetta *f* per i fiori. **~-cleaner** *n* *(person)* lavavetri *mf inv*. **~-dresser** *n* vetrinista *mf*. **~-dressing** *n* vetrinistica *f*; *fig* fumo *m* negli occhi. **~-pane** *n* vetro *m*. **~-shopping** *n*: **go ~-shopping** andare in giro a vedere le vetrine. **~-sill** *n* davanzale *m*

'windscreen *n*, *Am* **'windshield** *n* parabrezza *m inv*. **~ washer** *n* getto *m* d'acqua. **~-wiper** *n* tergicristallo *m*

wind: ~ **surfing** *n* windsurf *m inv*. **~swept** *a* esposto al vento; *(person)* scompigliato

windy /'wɪndɪ/ *a* (**-ier, -iest**) ventoso

wine /waɪn/ *n* vino *m*

wine: **~-bar** *n* ≈ enoteca *f*. **~glass** *n* bicchiere *m* da vino. **~-list** *n* carta *f* dei vini

winery /'waɪnərɪ/ *n Am* vigneto *m*

'wine-tasting *n* degustazione *f* di vini

wing /wɪŋ/ *n* ala *f*; *Auto* parafango *m*; **~s** *pl Theat* quinte *fpl*. **~er** *n Sport* ala *f*

wink /wɪŋk/ *n* strizzata *f* d'occhio; **not sleep a ~** non chiudere occhio ● *vi* strizzare l'occhio; *(light:)* lampeggiare

winner /'wɪnə(r)/ *n* vincitore, -trice *mf*

winning /'wɪnɪŋ/ *a* vincente; *(smile)* accattivante. **~-post** *n* linea *f* d'arrivo. **~s** *npl* vincite *fpl*

wint|er /'wɪntə(r)/ *n* inverno *m*. **~ry** *a* invernale

wipe /waɪp/ *n* passata *f*; *(to dry)* asciugata *f* ● *vt* strofinare; *(dry)* asciugare. **wipe off** *vt* asciugare; *(erase)* cancellare. **wipe out** *vt* annientare; eliminare *(village)*; estinguere *(debt)*. **wipe up** *vt* asciugare *(dishes)*

wire /'waɪə(r)/ *n* fil *m* di ferro; *(electrical)* filo *m* elettrico

wireless /'waɪəlɪs/ *n* radio *f inv*

wire 'netting *n* rete *f* metallica

wiring /'waɪərɪŋ/ *n* impianto *m* elettrico

wiry /'waɪərɪ/ *a* (**-ier, -iest**) *(person)* dal fisico asciutto; *(hair)* ispido

wisdom /'wɪzdəm/ *n* saggezza *f*; *(of action)* sensatezza *f*. **~ tooth** *n* dente *m* del giudizio

wise /waɪz/ *a* saggio; *(prudent)* sensato. **~ly** *adv* saggiamente; *(act)* sensatamente

wish /wɪʃ/ *n* desiderio *m*; **make a ~** esprimere un desiderio; **with best ~es** con i migliori auguri ● *vt* desiderare; ~ **sb well** fare tanti auguri a qcno; **I ~ you every success** ti auguro buona fortuna; **I ~ you could stay** vorrei che tu potessi rimanere ● *vi* ~ **for sth** desiderare qcsa. **~ful** *a* **~ful thinking** illusione *f*

wishy-washy /'wɪʃɪwɒʃɪ/ *a* *(colour)* spento; *(personality)* insignificante

wisp /wɪsp/ *n* *(of hair)* ciocca *f*; *(of smoke)* filo *m*; *(of grass)* ciuffo *m*

wistful /'wɪstfl/ *a* malinconico

wit /wɪt/ *n* spirito *m*; *(person)* persona *f* di spirito; **be at one's ~s' end** non saper che pesci pigliare

witch /wɪtʃ/ *n* strega *f*. **~-craft** *n* magia *f*. **~-hunt** *n* caccia *f* alle streghe

with /wɪð/ *prep* con; *(fear, cold, jealousy etc)* di; **I'm not ~ you** *fam* non ti seguo; **can I leave it ~ you?** *(task)* puoi occupartene tu?; **~ no regrets/money** senza rimpianti/soldi; **be ~ it** *fam* essere al passo coi tempi; *(alert)* essere concentrato

with'draw *v* (*pt* **-drew**, *pp* **-drawn**) ● *vt* ritirare; prelevare *(money)* ● *vi* ritirarsi. **~al** *n* ritiro *m*; *(of money)* prelevamento *m*; *(from drugs)* crisi *f inv* di astinenza; *Psych* chiusura *f* in se stessi. **~al symptoms** *npl* sintomi *mpl* da crisi di astinenza

with'drawn *see* **withdraw** ● *a* *(person)* chiuso in se stesso

wither /'wɪðə(r)/ *vi* *(flower:)* appassire

with'hold *vt* (*pt/pp* **-held**) rifiutare *(consent)* **(from** a); nascondere *(information)* **(from** a); trattenere *(smile)*

with'in *prep* in; *(before the end of)* entro; ~ **the law** legale ● *adv* all'interno

with'out *prep* senza; ~ **stopping** senza fermarsi

with'stand *vt* (*pt/pp* **-stood**) resistere a

witness /'wɪtnɪs/ *n* testimone *mf* ● *vt* autenticare *(signature)*; essere testimo-

ne di ⟨accident⟩. **~-box**, Am **~-stand** n
banco m dei testimoni

witticism /'wıtısızm/ n spiritosaggine f

wittingly /'wıtıŋlı/ adv consapevolmente

witty /'wıtı/ a (**-ier**, **-iest**) spiritoso

wives /waıvz/ see **wife**

wizard /'wızəd/ n mago m. **~ry** n stre-
goneria f

wobb|le /'wɒbl/ vi traballare. **~ly** a
traballante

wodge /wɒdʒ/ n fam mucchio m

woe /wəʊ/ n afflizione f

woke, woken /wəʊk, 'wəʊkn/ see
wake¹

wolf /wʊlf/ n (pl **wolves** /wʊlvz/) lupo
m; (fam: womanizer) donnaiolo m ● vt
~ ⟨**down**⟩ divorare. **~ whistle** n fischio m ● vi **~-whistle at sb** fischiare
dietro a qcno

woman /'wʊmən/ n (pl **women**) donna
f. **~izer** n donnaiolo m. **~ly** a femmineo

womb /wu:m/ n utero m

women /'wımın/ see **woman**. **W~'s
Libber** /'lıbə(r)/ n femminista f. **W~'s
Liberation** n movimento m femminista

won /wʌn/ see **win**

wonder /'wʌndə(r)/ n meraviglia f;
(surprise) stupore m; **no ~!** non c'è da
stupirsi!; **it's a ~ that...** è incredibile
che... ● vi restare in ammirazione; (be
surprised) essere sorpreso; **I ~** è quello
che mi chiedo; **I ~ whether she is ill**
mi chiedo se è malata?. **~ful** a meraviglioso. **~fully** adv meravigliosamente

won't /wəʊnt/ = **will not**

woo /wu:/ vt corteggiare; fig cercare di
accattivarsi ⟨voters⟩

wood /wʊd/ n legno m; (for burning) legna f; (forest) bosco m; **out of the ~** fig
fuori pericolo; **touch ~!** tocca ferro!

wood: **~ed** /-ıd/ a boscoso. **~en** a di legno; fig legnoso. **~ wind** n strumenti mpl
a fiato. **~work** n (wooden parts) parti fpl
in legno; (craft) falegnameria f. **~worm** n
tarlo m. **~y** a legnoso; ⟨hill⟩ boscoso

wool /wʊl/ n lana f ● attrib di lana. **~len**
a di lana. **~lens** npl capi mpl di lana.

woolly /'wʊlı/ a (**-ier**, **-iest**) ⟨sweater⟩
di lana; fig confuso

word /wɜ:d/ n parola f; (news) notizia f;
by ~ of mouth a viva voce; **have a ~
with** dire due parole a; **have ~s** bisticciare; **in other ~s** in altre parole. **~ing**
n parole fpl. **~ processor** n programma m di videoscrittura, word processor
m inv

wore /wɔ:(r)/ see **wear**

work /wɜ:k/ n lavoro m; (of art) opera f;
~s pl (factory) fabbrica fsg;
(mechanism) meccanismo msg; **at ~** al
lavoro; **out of ~** disoccupato ● vi lavorare; ⟨machine, ruse:⟩ funzionare; ⟨
study⟩ studiare ● vt far funzionare
⟨machine⟩; far lavorare ⟨employee⟩; far
studiare ⟨student⟩. **work off** vt sfogare
⟨anger⟩; lavorare per estinguere ⟨debt⟩;
fare sport per smaltire ⟨weight⟩. **work
out** vt elaborare ⟨plan⟩; calcolare
⟨problem⟩; calcolare ⟨bill⟩; **I ~ed out
how he did it** ho capito come l'ha fatto
● vi evolvere. **work up** vt **I've ~ed up
an appetite** mi è venuto appetito;
don't get ~ed up (anxious) non farti
prendere dal panico; (angry) non arrab-
biarti

workable /'wɜ:kəbl/ a (feasible) fatti-
bile

workaholic /wɜ:kə'hɒlık/ n stacca-
novista mf

worker /'wɜ:kə(r)/ n lavoratore, -trice
mf; (manual) operaio, -a mf

working /'wɜ:kıŋ/ a ⟨clothes etc⟩ da lavoro; ⟨day⟩ feriale; **in ~ order** funzio-
nante. **~ class** n classe f operaia.
~-class a operaio

work: **~man** n operaio m. **~manship**
n lavorazione f. **~-out** n allenamento m.
~shop n officina f; (discussion) dibattito m

world /wɜ:ld/ n mondo m; **a ~ of
difference** una differenza abissale; **out
of this ~** favoloso; **think the ~ of sb**
andare matto per qcno. **~ly** a materiale; ⟨person⟩ materialista. **~-wide** a
mondiale ● adv mondialmente

worm /wɜ:m/ n verme m ● vt **~ one's
way into sb's confidence** conquistar
si la fiducia di qcno in modo subdolo.
~-eaten a tarlato

worn /wɔ:n/ see **wear** ● a sciupato.
~-out a consumato; ⟨person⟩ sfinito

worried /'wʌrıd/ a preoccupato

worr|y /'wʌrı/ n preoccupazione f ● v
(pt/pp **worried**) ● vt preoccupare;
(bother) disturbare ● vi preoccuparsi.
~ing a preoccupante

worse /wɜ:s/ a peggiore ● adv peggio
● n peggio m

worsen /'wɜ:sn/ vt/i peggiorare

worship /'wɜ:ʃıp/ n culto m; (service)
funzione f; **Your/His W~** (to judge) signor giudice/il giudice ● v (pt/pp
-shipped) ● vt venerare ● vi andare a
messa

worst /wɜ:st/ a peggiore ● adv peggio

[di tutti] ● *n* the ~ il peggio; **get the ~ of it** avere la peggio; **if the ~ comes to the ~** nella peggiore delle ipotesi
worth /wɜːθ/ *n* valore *m*; **£10 ~ of petrol** 10 sterline di benzina ●*a* **be ~** valere; **be ~ it** *fig* valerne la pena; **it's ~ trying** vale la pena di provare; **it's ~ my while** mi conviene. **~less** *a* senza valore. **~while** *a* che vale la pena; ⟨cause⟩ lodevole
worthy /'wɜːðɪ/ *a* degno; ⟨cause, motive⟩ lodevole
would /wʊd/ *v aux* **I ~ do it** lo farei; **~ you go?** andresti?; **~ you mind if I opened the window?** ti dispiace se apro la finestra?; **he ~ come if he could** verrebbe se potesse; **he said he ~n't** ha detto di no; **~ you like a drink?** vuoi qualcosa da bere?; **what ~ you like to drink?** cosa prendi da bere?; **you ~n't, ~ you?** non lo faresti, vero?
wound[1] /wuːnd/ *n* ferita *f* ●*vt* ferire
wound[2] /waʊnd/ *see* **wind**[2]
wove, woven /wəʊv, 'wəʊvn/ *see* **weave**[2]
wrangle /'ræŋgl/ *n* litigio *m* ●*vi* litigare
wrap /ræp/ *n* ⟨shawl⟩ scialle *m* ●*vt* (*pt/pp* **wrapped**) **~ [up]** avvolgere; incartare ⟨present⟩; **be ~ped up in** *fig* essere completamente preso da ●*vi* **~ up warmly** coprirsi bene. **~per** *n* ⟨for sweet⟩ carta *f* [di caramella]. **~ping** *n* materiale *m* da imballaggio. **~ping paper** *n* carta *f* da pacchi; ⟨for gift⟩ carta *f* da regalo
wrath /rɒθ/ *n* ira *f*
wreak /riːk/ *vt* **~ havoc with sth** scombussolare qcsa
wreath /riːθ/ *n* (*pl* **~s** /-ðz/) corona *f*
wreck /rek/ *n* ⟨of ship⟩ relitto *m*; ⟨of car⟩ carcassa *f*; ⟨person⟩ rottame *m* ●*vt* far naufragare; demolire ⟨car⟩. **~age** /-ɪdʒ/ *n* rottami *mpl*; *fig* brandelli *mpl*
wrench /rentʃ/ *n* ⟨injury⟩ slogatura *f*; ⟨tool⟩ chiave *f* inglese; ⟨pull⟩ strattone *m* ●*vt* ⟨pull⟩ strappare; slogarsi ⟨wrist, ankle etc⟩
wrest /rest/ *vt* strappare (**from** a)
wrestl|e /'resl/ *vi* lottare corpo a cor-

po; *fig* lottare. **~er** *n* lottatore, -trice *mf*. **~ing** *n* lotta *f* libera; ⟨all-in⟩ catch *m*
wretch /retʃ/ *n* disgraziato, -a *mf*. **~ed** /-ɪd/ *a* odioso; ⟨weather⟩ orribile; **feel ~ed** ⟨unhappy⟩ essere triste; ⟨ill⟩ sentirsi malissimo
wriggle /'rɪgl/ *n* contorsione *f* ●*vi* contorcersi; ⟨move forward⟩ strisciare; **~ out of sth** *fam* sottrarsi a qcsa
wring /rɪŋ/ *vt* (*pt/pp* **wrung**) torcere ⟨sb's neck⟩; strizzare ⟨clothes⟩; **~ one's hands** torcersi le mani; **~ing wet** inzuppato
wrinkle /'rɪŋkl/ *n* grinza *f*; ⟨on skin⟩ ruga *f* ●*vt/i* raggrinzire. **~d** *a* ⟨skin, face⟩ rugoso; ⟨clothes⟩ raggrinzito
wrist /rɪst/ *n* polso *m*. **~-watch** *n* orologio *m* da polso
writ /rɪt/ *n* *Jur* mandato *m*
write /raɪt/ *vt/i* (*pt* **wrote**, *pp* **written**, *pres p* **writing**) scrivere. **write down** *vt* annotare. **write off** *vt* cancellare ⟨debt⟩; distruggere ⟨car⟩
'write-off *n* ⟨car⟩ rottame *m*
writer /'raɪtə(r)/ *n* autore, -trice *mf*; **she's a ~** è una scrittrice
'write-up *n* ⟨review⟩ recensione *f*
writhe /raɪð/ *vi* contorcersi
writing /'raɪtɪŋ/ *n* ⟨occupation⟩ scrivere *m*; ⟨words⟩ scritte *fpl*; ⟨handwriting⟩ scrittura *f*; **in ~** per iscritto. **~-paper** *n* carta *f* da lettera
written /'rɪtn/ *see* **write**
wrong /rɒŋ/ *a* sbagliato; **be ~** ⟨person:⟩ sbagliare; **what's ~?** cosa c'è che non va? ●*adv* sbagliare in modo sbagliato; **go ~** ⟨person:⟩ sbagliare; ⟨machine:⟩ funzionare male; ⟨plan:⟩ andar male ●*n* ingiustizia *f*; **in the ~** dalla parte del torto; **know right from ~** distinguere il bene dal male ●*vt* fare torto a. **~ful** *a* ingiusto. **~ly** *adv* in modo sbagliato; ⟨accuse, imagine⟩ a torto; ⟨informed⟩ male
wrote /rəʊt/ *see* **write**
wrought'iron /rɔːt-/ *n* ferro *m* battuto ● *attrib* di ferro battuto
wrung /rʌŋ/ *see* **wring**
wry /raɪ/ *a* (**-er, -est**) ⟨humour, smile⟩ beffardo

Xx

Xmas /'krɪsməs/ *n fam* Natale *m*
'X-ray *n* (*picture*) radiografia *f*; **have** an ~ farsi fare una radiografia ● *vt* passare ai raggi X

Yy

yacht /jɒt/ *n* yacht *m inv*; (*for racing*) barca *f* a vela. **~ing** *n* vela *f*

Yank /jæŋk/ *n fam* americano, -a *mf*

yank *vt fam* tirare

yap /jæp/ *vi* (*pt/pp* **yapped**) ⟨*dog:*⟩ guaire

yard¹ /jɑːd/ *n* cortile *m*; (*for storage*) deposito *m*

yard² *n* iarda *f* (= 91,44 cm). **~stick** *n* fig pietra *f* di paragone

yarn /jɑːn/ *n* filo *m*; (*fam: tale*) storia *f*

yawn /jɔːn/ *n* sbadiglio *m* ● *vi* sbadigliare. **~ing** *a* **~ing gap** sbadiglio *m*

year /jɪə(r)/ *n* anno *m*; (*of wine*) annata *f*; **for ~s** *fam* da secoli. **~-book** *n* annuario *m*. **~ly** *a* annuale ● *adv* annualmente

yearn /jɜːn/ *vi* struggersi. **~ing** *n* desiderio *m* struggente

yeast /jiːst/ *n* lievito *m*

yell /jel/ *n* urlo *m* ● *vi* urlare

yellow /'jeləʊ/ *a & n* giallo *m*

yelp /jelp/ *n* (*of dog*) guaito *m* ● *vi* ⟨*dog:*⟩ guaire

yen /jen/ *n* forte desiderio *m* (**for** di)

yes /jes/ *adv* sì ● *n* sì *m inv*

yesterday /'jestədeɪ/ *n & adv* ieri *m inv*; **~'s paper** il giornale di ieri; **the day before ~** l'altroieri

yet /jet/ *adv* ancora; **as ~** fino ad ora; **not ~** non ancora; **the best ~** il migliore finora ● *conj* eppure

yew /juː/ *n* tasso *m* (*albero*)

yield /jiːld/ *n* produzione *f*; (*profit*) reddito *m* ● *vt* produrre; fruttare ⟨*profit*⟩ ● *vi* cedere, *Am Auto* dare la precedenza

yodel /'jəʊdl/ *vi* (*pt/pp* **yodelled**) cantare jodel

yoga /'jəʊgə/ *n* yoga *m*

yoghurt /'jɒgət/ *n* yogurt *m inv*

yoke /jəʊk/ *n* giogo *m*; (*of garment*) carré *m inv*

yokel /'jəʊkl/ *n* zotico, -a *mf*

yolk /jəʊk/ *n* tuorlo *m*

you /juː/ *pers pron* (*subject*) tu, voi *pl*; (*formal*) lei, voi *pl*; (*direct/indirect object*) ti, vi *pl*; (*formal: direct object*) la; (*formal: indirect object*) le; (*after prep*) te, voi *pl*; (*formal: after prep*) lei; **~ are very kind** (*sg*) sei molto gentile; (*formal*) è molto gentile; (*pl & formal pl*) siete molto gentili; **~ can stay, but he has to go** (*sg*) tu puoi rimanere, ma lui deve andarsene; (*pl*) voi potete rimanere, ma lui deve andarsene; **all of ~** tutti voi; **I'll give ~ the money** (*sg*) ti darò i soldi; (*pl*) vi darò i soldi; **I'll give it to ~** (*sg*) te/(*pl*) ve lo darò; **it was ~!** (*sg*) eri tu!; (*pl*) eravate voi!; **~ have to be careful** (*one*) si deve fare attenzione

young /jʌŋ/ *a* giovane ● *npl* (*animals*) piccoli *mpl*; **the ~** (*people*) i giovani. **~ lady** *n* signorina *f*. **~ man** *n* giovanotto *m*. **~ster** *n* ragazzo, -a *mf*; (*child*) bambino, -a *mf*

your /jɔː(r)/ *poss a* il tuo *m*, la tua *f*, i tuoi *mpl*, le tue *fpl*; (*formal*) il suo *m*, la sua *f*, i suoi *mpl*, le sue *fpl*; (*pl & formal pl*) il vostro *m*, la vostra *f*, i vostri *mpl*, le vostre *fpl*; **~ mother/father** tua madre/tuo padre; (*formal*) sua madre/suo padre; (*pl & formal pl*) vostra madre/vostro padre

yours /jɔːz/ *poss pron* il tuo *m*, la tua *f*, i tuoi *mpl*, le tue *fpl*; (*formal*) il suo *m*, la sua *f*, i suoi *mpl*, le sue *fpl*; (*pl & formal pl*) il vostro *m*, la vostra *f*, i vostri *mpl*, le vostre *fpl*; **a friend of** ~ un tuo/suo/vostro amico; **friends of** ~ dei tuoi/vostri/suoi amici; **that is** ~ quello è tuo/suo/vostro; (*as opposed to mine*) quello è il tuo/il vostro/il suo

your'self *pers pron* (*reflexive*) ti; (*formal*) si; (*emphatic*) te stesso; (*formal*) sé, se stesso; **do pour** ~ **a drink** versati da bere; (*formal*) si versi da bere; **you said so** ~ lo hai detto tu stesso; (*formal*) lo ha detto lei stesso; **you can**

be proud of ~ puoi essere fiero di te/di sé; **by** ~ da solo

your'selves *pers pron* (*reflexive*) vi; (*emphatic*) voi stessi; **do pour** ~ **a drink** versatevi da bere; **you said so** ~ lo avete detto voi stessi; **you can be proud of** ~ potete essere fieri di voi; **by** ~ da soli

youth /juːθ/ *n* (*pl* **youths** /-ðːz/) gioventù *f inv*; (*boy*) giovanetto *m*; **the** ~ (*young people*) i giovani. ~**ful** *a* giovanile. ~ **hostel** *n* ostello *m* [della gioventù]

Yugoslav /'juːgəslɑːv/ *a & n* jugoslavo, -a *mf*

Yugoslavia /-'slɑːvɪə/ *n* Jugoslavia *f*

Zz

zany /'zeɪnɪ/ *a* (**-ier, -iest**) demenziale

zeal /ziːl/ *n* zelo *m*

zealous /'zeləs/ *a* zelante. ~**ly** *adv* con zelo

zebra /'zebrə/ *n* zebra *f*. ~**-'crossing** *n* passaggio *m* pedonale. zebre *fpl*

zero /'zɪərəʊ/ *n* zero *m*

zest /zest/ *n* gusto *m*

zigzag /'zɪgzæg/ *n* zigzag *m inv* ● *vi* (*pt/pp* **-zagged**) zigzagare

zilch /zɪltʃ/ *n fam* zero *m* assoluto

zinc /zɪŋk/ *n* zinco *m*

zip /zɪp/ *n* ~ [**fastener**] cerniera *f* [lampo] ● *vt* (*pt/pp* **zipped**) ~ [**up**] chiudere con la cerniera [lampo]

'Zip code *n Am* codice *m* postale

zipper /'zɪpə(r)/ *n Am* cerniera *f* [lampo]

zodiac /'zəʊdɪæk/ *n* zodiaco *m*

zombie /'zɒmbɪ/ *n fam* zombi *mf inv*

zone /zəʊn/ *n* zona *f*

zoo /zuː/ *n* zoo *m inv*

zoolog|ist /zəʊ'ɒlədʒɪst/ *n* zoologo, -a *mf*. ~**y** zoologia *f*

zoom /zuːm/ *vi* sfrecciare. ~ **lens** *n* zoom *m inv*

ITALIAN VERB TABLES

REGULAR VERBS:

1. in **-are** (*eg* compr|**are**)

   Present ~o, ~i, ~a, ~iamo, ~ate, ~ano
   Imperfect ~avo, ~avi, ~ava, ~avamo, ~avate, ~avano
   Past historic ~ai, ~asti, ~ò, ~ammo, ~aste, ~arono
   Future ~erò, ~erai, ~erà, ~eremo, ~erete, ~eranno
   Present subjunctive ~i, ~i, ~i, ~iamo, ~iate, ~ino
   Past subjunctive ~assi, ~assi, ~asse, ~assimo, ~aste, ~assero
   Present participle ~ando
   Past participle ~ato
   Imperative ~a (*fml* ~i), ~iamo, ~ate
   Conditional ~erei, ~eresti, ~erebbe, ~eremmo, ~ereste, ~erebbero

2. in **-ere** (*eg* vend|**ere**)

   Pres ~o, ~i, ~e, ~iamo, ~ete, ~ono
   Impf ~evo, ~evi, ~eva, ~evamo, ~evate, ~evano
   Past hist ~ei *or* ~etti, ~esti, ~è *or* ~ette, ~emmo, ~este, ~erono *or* ~ettero
   Fut ~erò, ~erai, ~erà, ~eremo, ~erete, ~eranno
   Pres sub ~a, ~a, ~a, ~iamo, ~iate, ~ano
   Past sub ~essi, ~essi, ~esse, ~essimo, ~este, ~essero
   Pres part ~endo
   Past part ~uto
   Imp ~i (*fml* ~a), ~iamo, ~ete
   Cond ~erei, ~eresti, ~erebbe, ~eremmo, ~ereste, ~erebbero

3. in **-ire** (*eg* dorm|**ire**)

   Pres ~o, ~i, ~e, ~iamo, ~ite, ~ono
   Impf ~ivo, ~ivi, ~iva, ~ivamo, ~ivate, ~ivano
   Past hist ~ii, ~isti, ~ì, ~immo, ~iste, ~irono
   Fut ~irò, ~irai, ~irà, ~iremo, ~irete, ~iranno
   Pres sub ~a, ~a, ~a, ~iamo, ~iate, ~ano
   Past sub ~issi, ~issi, ~isse, ~issimo, ~iste, ~issero
   Pres part ~endo
   Past part ~ito
   Imp ~i (*fml* ~a), ~iamo, ~ite
   Cond ~irei, ~iresti, ~irebbe, ~iremmo, ~ireste, ~irebbero

Notes

- Many verbs in the third conjugation take *isc* between the stem and the ending in the first, second, and third person singular and in the third person plural of the present, the present subjunctive, and the imperative: fin|ire **Pres** ~isco, ~isci, ~isce, ~iscono. **Pres sub** ~isca, ~iscano **Imp** ~isci.

- The three forms of the imperative are the same as the corresponding forms of the present for the second and third conjugation. In the first conjugation the forms are also the same except for the second person singular: present *compri*, imperative *compra*. The negative form of the second person singular is formed by putting *non* before the infinitive for all conjugations: *non comprare*. In polite forms the third person of the present subjunctive is used instead for all conjugations: *compri*.

IRREGULAR VERBS:

Certain forms of all irregular verbs are regular (except for *essere*). These are: the second person plural of the present, the past subjunctive, and the present participle. All forms not listed below are regular and can be derived from the parts given. Only those irregular verbs considered to be the most useful are shown in the tables.

accadere   *as* **cadere**

accendere   • **Past hist** accesi, accendesti • **Past part** acceso

affliggere   • **Past hist** afflissi, affliggesti • **Past part** afflitto

ammettere   *as* **mettere**

andare   • **Pres** vado, vai, va, andiamo, andate, vanno • **Fut** andrò *etc* • **Pres sub** vada, vadano • **Imp** va', vada, vadano

apparire   • **Pres** appaio *or* apparisco, appari *or* apparisci, appare *or* apparisce, appaiono *or* appariscono • **Past hist** apparvi *or* apparsi, apparisti, apparve *or* appari *or* apparse, apparvero *or* apparirono *or* apparsero • **Pres sub** appaia *or* apparisca

aprire   • **Pres** apro • **Past hist** aprii, apristi • **Pres sub** apra • **Past part** aperto

avere   • **Pres** ho, hai, ha, abbiamo, hanno • **Past hist** ebbi, avesti, ebbe, avemmo, aveste, ebbero • **Fut** avrò *etc* • **Pres sub** abbia *etc* • **Imp** abbi, abbia, abbiate, abbiano

bere   • **Pres** bevo *etc* • **Impf** bevevo *etc* • **Past hist** bevvi *or* bevetti, bevesti • **Fut** berrò *etc* • **Pres sub** beva *etc* • **Past sub** bevessi *etc* • **Pres part** bevendo • **Cond** berrei *etc*

cadere   • **Past hist** caddi, cadesti • **Fut** cadrò *etc*

chiedere   • **Past hist** chiesi, chiedesti • **Pres sub** chieda *etc* • **Past part** chiesto *etc*

chiudere   • **Past hist** chiusi, chiudesti • **Past part** chiuso

cogliere   • **Pres** colgo, colgono • **Past hist** colsi, cogliesti • **Pres sub** colga • **Past part** colto

correre   • **Past hist** corsi, corresti • **Past part** corso

crescere   • **Past hist** crebbi • **Past part** cresciuto

cuocere   • **Pres** cuocio, cuociamo, cuociono • **Past hist** cossi, cocesti • **Past part** cotto

dare   • **Pres** do, dai, dà, diamo, danno • **Past hist** diedi *or* detti, desti • **Fut** darò *etc* • **Pres sub** dia *etc* • **Past sub** dessi *etc* • **Imp** da' (*fml* dia)

dire
• **Pres** dico, dici, dice, diciamo, dicono • **Impf** dicevo *etc* • **Past hist** dissi, dicesti • **Fut** dirò *etc* • **Pres sub** dica, diciamo, diciate, dicano • **Past sub** dicessi *etc* • **Pres part** dicendo • **Past part** detto • **Imp** di' (*fml* dica)

dovere
• **Pres** devo *or* debbo, devi, deve, dobbiamo, devono *or* debbono • **Fut** dovrò *etc* • **Pres sub** deva *or* debba, dobbiamo, dobbiate, devano *or* debbano • **Cond** dovrei *etc*

essere
• **Pres** sono, sei, è, siamo, siete, sono • **Impf** ero, eri, era, eravamo, eravate, erano • **Past hist** fui, fosti, fu, fummo, foste, furono • **Fut** sarò *etc* • **Pres sub** sia *etc* • **Past sub** fossi, fossi, fosse, fossimo, foste, fossero • **Past part** stato • **Imp** sii (*fml* sia), siate • **Cond** sarei *etc*

fare
• **Pres** faccio, fai, fa, facciamo, fanno • **Impf** facevo *etc* • **Past hist** feci, facesti • **Fut** farò *etc* • **Pres sub** faccia *etc* • **Past sub** facessi *etc* • **Pres part** facendo • **Past part** fatto • **Imp** fa' (*fml* faccia) • **Cond** farei *etc*

fingere
• **Past hist** finsi, fingesti, finsero • **Past part** finto

giungere
• **Past hist** giunsi, giungesti, giunsero • **Past part** giunto

leggere
• **Past hist** lessi, leggesti • **Past part** letto

mettere
• **Past hist** misi, mettesti • **Past part** messo

morire
• **Pres** muoio, muori, muore, muoiono • **Fut** morirò *or* morrò *etc* • **Pres sub** muoia • **Past part** morto

muovere
• **Past hist** mossi, movesti • **Past part** mosso

nascere
• **Past hist** nacqui, nascesti • **Past part** nato

offrire
• **Past hist** offersi *or* offrii, offristi • **Pres sub** offra • **Past part** offerto

parere
• **Pres** paio, pari, pare, pariamo, paiono • **Past hist** parvi *or* parsi, paresti • **Fut** parrò *etc* • **Pres sub** paia, paiamo *or* pariamo, pariate, paiano • **Past part** parso

piacere
• **Pres** piaccio, piaci, piace, piacciamo, piacciono • **Past hist** piacqui, piacesti, piacque, piacemmo, piaceste, piacquero • **Pres sub** piaccia *etc* • **Past part** piaciuto

porre
• **Pres** pongo, poni, pone, poniamo, ponete, pongono • **Impf** ponevo *etc* • **Past hist** posi, ponesti • **Fut** porrò *etc* • **Pres sub** ponga, poniamo, poniate, pongano • **Past sub** ponessi *etc*

potere
• **Pres** posso, puoi, può, possiamo, possono • **Fut** potrò *etc* • **Pres sub** possa, possiamo, possiate, possano • **Cond** potrei *etc*

prendere
• **Past hist** presi, prendesti • **Past part** preso

ridere
• **Past hist** risi, ridesti • **Past part** riso

rimanere	• **Pres** rimango, rimani, rimane, rimaniamo, rimangono • **Past hist** rimasi, rimanesti • **Fut** rimarrò *etc* • **Pres sub** rimanga • **Past part** rimasto • **Cond** rimarrei
salire	• **Pres** salgo, sali, sale, saliamo, salgono • **Pres sub** salga, saliate, salgano
sapere	• **Pres** so, sai, sa, sappiamo, sanno • **Past hist** seppi, sapesti • **Fut** saprò *etc* • **Pres sub** sappia *etc* • **Imp** sappi (*fml* sappia), sappiate • **Cond** saprei *etc*
scegliere	• **Pres** scelgo, scegli, sceglie, scegliamo, scelgono • **Past hist** scelsi, scegliesti *etc* • **Past part** scelto
scrivere	• **Past hist** scrissi, scrivesti *etc* • **Past part** scritto
sedere	• **Pres** siedo *or* seggo, siedi, siede, siedono • **Pres sub** sieda *or* segga
spegnere	• **Pres** spengo, spengono • **Past hist** spensi, spegnesti • **Past part** spento
stare	• **Pres** sto, stai, sta, stiamo, stanno • **Past hist** stetti, stesti • **Fut** starò *etc* • **Pres sub** stia *etc* • **Past sub** stessi *etc* • **Past part** stato • **Imp** sta' (*fml* stia)
tacere	• **Pres** taccio, tacciono • **Past hist** tacqui, tacque, tacquero • **Pres sub** taccia
tendere	• **Past hist** tesi • **Past part** teso
tenere	• **Pres** tengo, tieni, tiene, tengono • **Past hist** tenni, tenesti • **Fut** terrò *etc* • **Pres sub** tenga
togliere	• **Pres** tolgo, tolgono • **Past hist** tolsi, tolse, tolsero • **Pres sub** tolga, tolgano • **Past part** tolto • **Imp** *fml* tolga
trarre	• **Pres** traggo, trai, trae, traiamo, traete, traggono • **Past hist** trassi, traesti • **Fut** trarrò *etc* • **Pres sub** tragga • **Past sub** traessi *etc* • **Past part** tratto
uscire	• **Pres** esco, esci, esce, escono • **Pres sub** esca • **Imp** esci (*fml* esca)
valere	• **Pres** valgo, valgono • **Past hist** valsi, valesti • **Fut** varrò *etc* • **Pres sub** valga, valgano • **Past part** valso • **Cond** varrei *etc*
vedere	• **Past hist** vidi, vedesti • **Fut** vedrò *etc* • **Past part** visto *or* veduto • **Cond** vedrei *etc*
venire	• **Pres** vengo, vieni, viene, vengono • **Past hist** venni, venisti • **Fut** verrò *etc*
vivere	• **Past hist** vissi, vivesti • **Fut** vivrò *etc* • **Past part** vissuto • **Cond** vivrei *etc*
volere	• **Pres** voglio, vuoi, vuole, vogliamo, volete, vogliono • **Past hist** volli, volesti • **Fut** vorrò *etc* • **Pres sub** voglia *etc* • **Imp** vogliate • **Cond** vorrei *etc*

English irregular verbs

Infinitive	Past Tense	Past Participle	Infinitive	Past Tense	Past Participle
Infinito	*Passato*	*Participio passato*	*Infinito*	*Passato*	*Participio passato*
arise	arose	arisen	feed	fed	fed
awake	awoke	awoken	feel	felt	felt
be	was	been	fight	fought	fought
bear	bore	borne	find	found	found
beat	beat	beaten	flee	fled	fled
become	became	become	fling	flung	flung
begin	began	begun	fly	flew	flown
behold	beheld	beheld	forbid	forbade	forbidden
bend	bent	bent	forget	forgot	forgotten
beseech	beseeched besought	beseeched besought	forgive forsake	forgave forsook	forgiven forsaken
bet	bet, betted	bet, betted	freeze get	froze got	frozen got, gotten *Am*
bid	bade, bid	bidden, bid	give	gave	given
bind	bound	bound	go	went	gone
bite	bit	bitten	grind	ground	ground
bleed	bled	bled	grow	grew	grown
blow	blew	blown	hang	hung, hanged (*vt*)	hung, hanged
break	broke	broken			
breed	bred	bred	have	had	had
bring	brought	brought	hear	heard	heard
build	built	built	hew	hewed	hewed, hewn
burn	burnt, burned	burnt, burned			
burst	burst	burst	hide	hid	hidden
bust	busted, bust	busted, bust	hit	hit	hit
			hold	held	held
buy	bought	bought	hurt	hurt	hurt
cast	cast	cast	keep	kept	kept
catch	caught	caught	kneel	knelt	knelt
choose	chose	chosen	know	knew	known
cling	clung	clung	lay	laid	laid
come	came	come	lead	led	led
cost	cost, costed (*vt*)	cost, costed	lean	leaned, leant	leaned, leant
creep	crept	crept	leap	leapt, leaped	leapt, leaped
cut	cut	cut	learn	learnt, learned	learnt, learned
deal	dealt	dealt			
dig	dug	dug	leave	left	left
do	did	done	lend	lent	lent
draw	drew	drawn	let	let	let
dream	dreamt, dreamed	dreamt, dreamed	lie	lay	lain
			light	lit, lighted	lit, lighted
drink	drank	drunk			
drive	drove	driven	lose	lost	lost
dwell	dwelt	dwelt	make	made	made
eat	ate	eaten	mean	meant	meant
fall	fell	fallen	meet	met	met